THE LAW OF THE EUROPEAN UNION

This textbook offers a comprehensive account of European Union law, written in a single analytical voice. It covers the EU's constitutional foundations, institutional framework and substantive policies, treating the economic dimensions of integration, including the regulation of the digital market, alongside its constitutional architecture.

Written by an author who works as both a scholar and a practising lawyer, the book uses a doctrinal approach to European Union law within the practical context in which it operates. It is designed to be accessible without sacrificing analytical depth, and is particularly suited to courses taught in the continental tradition.

The Law of the European Union

Daniel Sarmiento

•HART•
OXFORD • LONDON • NEW YORK • NEW DELHI • SYDNEY

HART PUBLISHING
Bloomsbury Publishing Plc
Kemp House, Chawley Park, Cumnor Hill, Oxford, OX2 9PH, UK
1385 Broadway, New York, NY 10018, USA
Bloomsbury Publishing Ireland Limited, 29 Earlsfort Terrace, Dublin 2, D02 AY28, Ireland

HART PUBLISHING, the Hart/Stag logo, BLOOMSBURY and the Diana logo are trademarks of Bloomsbury Publishing Plc

First published in Great Britain 2026

1

A catalogue record for this book is available from the British Library.

A catalogue record for this book is available from the Library of Congress.

ISBN: HB: 978-1-50999-695-7
PB: 978-1-50999-691-9
ePDF: 978-1-50999-693-3
ePub: 978-1-50999-692-6

Typeset by Amnet
Printed and bound in Great Britain

For product safety related questions contact productsafety@bloomsbury.com

To find out more about our authors and books visit www.hartpublishing.co.uk. Here you will find extracts, author information, details of forthcoming events and the option to sign up for our newsletters.

A Belén

El alma luminosa

La luz que ve

Introduction

THIS BOOK IS the result of more than 25 years devoted to the study, teaching and practice of European Union law. It does not intend to be an exhaustive and descriptive survey of the law. The book aims to provide a holistic view of the law of the European Union as it stands today, but from a personal perspective, a snapshot of a legal system through the eyes of an author who has opinions (many of them contestable or flawed, no dobut) on many of the issues covered in its pages.

European Union law is an open-ended legal system, much like the European Union itself. It evolves, mutates and adapts to reality in ways that traditional states and national legal systems are unable to. This fluidity coexists with a core content, a set of rigid principles that act as the pillars of the edifice. This book attempts to describe and explain those pillars, while also portraying the European project's flexible and constantly evolving features and its rules of law.

I am indebted to many. The list of colleagues and dear friends who have contributed to my education and development as a scholar and practitioner is very long. This education is ongoing, and recognition is not only retrospective but also prospective. They all know who they are.

Finally, a word on the background story of this book is due. In 2016, I published a textbook in Spanish (*El Derecho de la Unión Europea*, Marcial Pons), which grew into a voluminous treatise after several editions. That longer version was translated, expanded and developed into a quite different creature that the reader now holds. Overall, it has been close to 15 years of work since I started writing the first Spanish edition, until this English version has finally seen the light of day.

During this long period, I had the unwavering support of my wife, Belén. For that reason, and many more that need no explanation here, this book is for her.

Daniel Sarmiento
Madrid, May 2026

Brief Contents

Contents

Table of Cases

Cases presented in chronological order by case reference or date within each institution, with the exception of the European Court of Human Rights, presented in alphabetical order.

European Union Institutions

Court of Justice

Commission Decisions

International Jurisdictions

European Court of Human Rights

PCIJ

National Courts

Czech Republic

Constitutional Court

Denmark

France

Conseil Constitutionnel

Table of Legislation

Instruments are presented in alphabetical order, except for EU secondary legislation, where categories are laid out alphabetically, but within categories individual instruments are ordered chronologically.

Treaties, Agreements, Conventions, Protocols and Related Instruments

EU Secondary Legislation

National Legislation

1

Theories and Evolution of European Integration

I. THEORIES OF EUROPEAN INTEGRATION

THE EUROPEAN UNION is the most ambitious political and economic project to emerge on the continent since the fall of the Roman Empire. For nearly two millennia, Europe was unable to establish a representative, effective, and authoritative political system over its territory, a failure most evident in the trail of wars that the last centuries of Europe's eventful and deadly history have left behind. The consequences of this evolution are difficult to quantify in human and economic terms. The only certainty is that Europe had the sad honour of becoming the bloodiest and most bellicose continent on the planet. This trait was subsequently exported to the rest of the world as Europeans expanded their dominions globally from the fifteenth century onwards.

To better understand why Europeans decided to end this appalling record and opted for the political and economic integration of the continent, it is necessary to examine two decisive historical events. The first took place in the first half of the twentieth century and is none other than the two World Wars. Although they are generally referred to as 'world' wars, they were, in fact, eminently 'European' wars. The First World War was undoubtedly so. The Second World War had its origins in the political, social, and economic turmoil that took place in Europe during the late 1920s and the 1930s.

The desolation that befell the European continent for half a century, reflected in the almost 70 million human lives sacrificed, was at the very root of a profound reflection at the political and social level on how to avoid such developments from happening ever again. The two world wars showed that the destructive capacity of armed confrontation had now become an existential concern, particularly after the advent of nuclear warfare. Europe's history of war and destruction needed to come to an end.

The second event at the heart of the European integration process emerged in the second half of the twentieth century: globalisation. The two world wars, in addition to their human and economic impact, also entailed the political decadence of the former European global powers. After the Second World War, the United Kingdom, France and to a lesser extent Italy, Belgium and Spain, became victims of a slow but unstoppable process of decolonisation that would eventually deprive them of their former global dominions. European states shrank as the world became increasingly interconnected and interdependent. Just as the world was becoming a unified space due to modern transportation and telecommunications, the countries of Europe emerged as modest players on the international stage. With the rise of new global poles of power, primarily the United States and China, the countries of Europe have lost their ability to influence the international scene individually. This decline included the defensive and military weakening of formerly colossal empires but now modest countries, such as France, the United Kingdom and Spain. This shrinkage also brought significant risks to the territorial integrity of individual European countries. The two world wars had reduced Europe's states politically, territorially and defensively, while globalisation further diminished them by facilitating the emergence of geopolitical giants in every continent, except in Europe.

From the outset, the European integration project had the objective of avoiding war in Europe at all costs, but it later also took on the mission of providing the states of Europe with a single, strong, and influential voice on the global stage. These are two objectives that can be described as *existential* for European states. The first guarantees the physical existence of the states and their citizens, since any armed conflict would assuredly bring about the destruction of all the participants involved. The second gives those same states the capacity to influence, shape, and decide on the international scene, thus preventing the great power blocs from rendering the sovereignty of Europe's modest states a nullity. These are the objectives pursued by European countries when they chose the path of integration. This project is today represented by an organisation under the name of the European Union.

The European Union is an international organisation, established by several states to which they assign legal personality, allowing it to act within the international community. However, the European Union is much more than that, as it would be impossible to achieve its ambitious objectives through the means of a conventional international organisation. The European Union has been described as a complex political entity that is difficult to classify, existing somewhere between an international organisation and a federal state, yet without fitting into any of the traditional categories. For this reason, it seems more useful to identify the European Union, which will be referred to from now on as 'the Union', by examining the various theories of integration developed over time to explain the underlying reasons supporting the Union's existence. These theories can be grouped into three different theories of integration. In fact, the history of the Union reveals that its Member States have put into practice all three theories, placing a greater emphasis on one at the expense of the others in each stage of the Union's evolution.

1. Functionalism

Functionalism was the foundational theory that inspired the project of European integration from its very beginnings. The core principles of functionalism are evident in the political declarations that led to the creation of the European Coal and Steel Community in 1951, the initial step in the integration process, as well as in the works of those who designed the structure and competences of the first European institutions.[1] Jean Monnet, a senior French official and the intellectual father of the European project, explained in his memoirs the theoretical basis on which he and his colleagues worked in the early 1950s:

> The Community we have created is not an end in itself. It is a process of change, in continuity with the processes which in earlier periods gave rise to our national systems. The sovereign nations of the past can no longer solve the problems of the present: they can neither ensure their progress nor control their own future. And the Community is only one step on the road to the organised world of tomorrow.[2]

[1] The founding work on functionalism is generally attributed to D Mitrany, *A Working Peace System: An Argument for the Functional Development of International Organization* (Royal Institute of International Affairs, 1943).

[2] J Monnet, *Memoirs* (Doubleday, 1978) 524.

For functionalist theorists, integration is a *process* aimed at achieving specific objectives through strategic means. Political integration is not necessarily the primary aim of functionalists. It might be for some advocates of functionalism, but it is not inherently the ultimate purpose of functionalism. Ultimately, the long-term aim of functionalism is to promote close cooperation among states that prevents the escalation of armed conflict between them. To reach this overarching aim, functionalism supports particular objectives in strategic areas, especially those closely related to economic activity.

For example, establishing a common energy market, a highly strategic sector for all participating states, would force these states to cooperate closely, fostering political, economic, and social bonds that would eventually make armed conflict unimaginable. As the well-known saying goes, functionalism aims to create '*de facto* solidarities': states end up sharing their resources not out of generosity but out of necessity. Simultaneously, this process fosters other shared benefits, such as the long-term maintenance of peace. In the case of energy, the outcomes of a functionalist approach are evident: by sharing coal, steel, or atomic energy, each state, along with its businesses and citizens, gains access to the resources of other participating states; energy companies expand their markets, and consumers enjoy lower prices. A functionalist approach to policy would not only end war in Europe but also promote wealth and well-being for businesses and citizens across all the participating states.[3]

Functionalism is also characterised by its belief in the spill-over effect of *de facto* solidarities.[4] That is, the creation of cooperation in one area will inevitably lead to further cooperation in other areas. The creation of a market for energy resources will spontaneously encourage the development of a market for distributing those resources, followed by a market for transport, as well as a labour market in that sector, and then additional cooperation in taxation, and so on.

Another example makes the point: the liberalisation of the telecoms sector helps harmonise the conditions under which telecoms operators operate in the Member States, encouraging them to establish themselves in other states and create large European telecoms groups. As a result, consumers will demand equal rights in all states. At the end of the process, telecom companies will demand the removal of barriers in national telecoms markets that restrict their ability to compete, thereby creating a European telecoms market and establishing a common European telecoms regulatory authority. Over time, what started as a modest liberalisation effort will, almost spontaneously and after years or even decades, culminate in the creation of a supranational telecommunications market characterised by a common authority, shared rights and obligations for companies and consumers. This sector, of great strategic importance for the economic and defence interests of the Member States, is surrounded by a complex web of agreements, commitments, interests and loyalties that make an armed conflict between the participating states inconceivable.

Functionalism has faced significant criticism in recent years. It might seem paradoxical, but this criticism stems from the success of policies rooted in functionalist theories. It can be argued that functionalism has become a victim of its own success, as the growth of European policies has prompted criticism from those who perceive a disturbing lack of popular will in this approach towards integration. The fact that functionalism depends on the spontaneous and almost automatic expansion of integration policies challenges the democratic principles

[3] W Sandholtz and A Stone Sweet, 'Neo-Functionalism and Supranational Governance' in E Jones, A Menon and S Weatherill (eds), *The Oxford Handbook of the European Union* (Oxford University Press, 2012) 19–22.

[4] See EB Haas, *The Uniting of Europe: Political, Social, and Economic Forces, 1950–1957* (Stanford University Press, 1958).

upon which European liberal democracies are founded.[5] Functionalism may have made the mistake of treating citizens and their governments as pawns in a chess game, where the outcome is already predetermined.

The criticism is not only theoretical but also practical and empirical. When citizens have participated in the process of European integration, their reactions have not always aligned with what a functionalist theorist might expect.[6] We need only recall the French and Dutch 'no' to the European Constitution, as well as the repeated refusals of several states to join the euro or to ratify some of the reform treaties (the Danish referendum on the Maastricht Treaty, or the Irish referendum over the Lisbon Treaty). The strong social protests against the austerity measures imposed by the Union in 2010 showed that what might seem to serve a functionalist project does not necessarily align with the interests of a social majority. The emergence of citizens' representative institutions such as the European Parliament, the increasing role of national parliaments in European decision-making, the creation of Union citizenship, and the growing role played by national heads of state and government in the European Council are proof that functionalism cannot be the sole integration theory underpinning the European project.

2. Intergovernmentalism

Behind this unattractive neologism lies a *realist* approach to European integration. The supporters of intergovernmentalism see it as an empirically grounded theory to explain and steer the integration process, emphasising the importance of national governments and the defence of national interests.[7] According to this theory of integration, the aggregate of all national interests translates into a European interest, rather than the other way around. Furthermore, European policies should not arise spontaneously from a spill-over effect, as functionalists argue, but should be the result of deliberate decisions made by each state based on the realisation of their national interests. The term 'intergovernmental' originates from the central role played by national governments in the integration process, rather than European institutions or citizens. The vital role of governments also strengthens the democratic nature of the process, as no European policy can succeed without taking into account the interests of all governments, which are themselves democratically elected within their domestic national polities.

Intergovernmentalism emerged as a theoretical alternative to functionalism in the 1960s and 1970s, a period marked by political stagnation in European integration, partly due to the rise of General de Gaulle on the French and European political scene. The first stage of the transitional period that had allowed governments to make unanimous decisions in the Council of Ministers ended in 1962. From then onwards, governments were subject to a system of qualified majority voting in the Council in several areas. As a result, one or several countries could be legally bound by a Community decision despite their opposition. For the Gaullist Government, this outcome was unacceptable and resulted in the temporary withdrawal of French representation from the Council, a decision that caused an unprecedented paralysis

[5] A Follesdal and S Hix, 'Why There is a Democratic Deficit in the EU: A Response to Majone and Moravcsik' (2006) 44 *Journal of Common Market Studies* 533.

[6] L Hooghe and G Marks, 'A Postfunctionalist Theory of European Integration: From Permissive Consensus to Constraining Dissensus' (2009) 39 *British Journal of Political Science* 1.

[7] A Moravcsik, *The Choice for Europe: Social Purpose and State Power from Messina to Maastricht* (Cornell University Press, 1998).

of the European Communities at the time. The crisis was resolved with the 'Luxembourg compromise', an informal agreement whereby any state could request that the Council of Ministers agree unanimously on matters of particular interest to that state, even if they were subject to qualified majority voting. The 'Luxembourg compromise' indirectly created a veto right in favour of the Member States across all areas of action of the European Communities, thus prioritising the individual interests of each Member State over the common European interest.[8]

Although the impact of the 'Luxembourg compromise' was more symbolic than practical, the notion that functionalism was not an ideal theoretical foundation was reinforced in 1973 with the informal creation of the European Council, a gathering of heads of state and government, together with the president of the European Commission. Its purpose was (and still is) to advance the agenda of integration with a broad and long-term vision. National governments took control of the Community's agenda, to ensure their national interests were protected by a set of European institutions that were increasingly seen as too independent and disconnected from the specific interests of the Member States.

Intergovernmentalism, like functionalism, is not a perfect descriptive theory of European integration either. This theory makes it difficult to explain the strategic role historically played by the European Commission, which will be discussed in chapter three, as well as the European Parliament, whose track record shows that its decisions have not always aligned with the aggregate individual interests of national governments. Nor is intergovernmentalism helpful in explaining the importance of citizens, including in the judicial sphere, where national courts can, at the request of any individual, set aside national laws contrary to Union law, regardless of the government's views on the matter. The European project is too complex to be reduced to a simple sum of individual governmental interests. However, it must be recognised that intergovernmentalism offers a reliable account of some major developments in the history of integration, while also contributing to a better understanding of the role of certain European institutions, most notably the European Council. As mentioned above, integration theories are not mutually exclusive; rather, they coexist and hold varying degrees of prominence during different periods of the European project's evolution.

Beyond its flaws, the *normative* aspect of intergovernmentalism has also faced criticism. While functionalism has been criticised for its lack of democratic sensitivity, intergovernmentalism has been criticised for relying too heavily on the democratic legitimacy of national governments. This belief leads to an integration process that is continually at risk of stalling, as the normative intergovernmental rationale allows any state to veto decisions that harm its national interests. Additionally, this approach creates a democratic paradox, as prioritising the interests of each government can undermine the democratic principle at the European level. If democracy involves prioritising the will of the majority over that of the minority, a system that grants one state the right to veto majoritarian decisions is hardly consistent with democratic ideals.[9] These shortcomings of intergovernmentalism, observed in European integration practices, have been addressed in recent years. For example, the Union's Treaties have been amended to include simplified procedures for their reform. Meanwhile, 'enhanced cooperation' has been introduced since 2001, enabling a reduced group of Member States to develop Union policies among themselves, excluding others. Like functionalism, intergovernmentalism has adapted to a changing landscape.

[8] AL Teasdale, 'The Life and Death of the Luxembourg Compromise' (1993) 31 *Journal of Common Market Studies* 567.

[9] FW Scharpf, *Governing in Europe: Effective and Democratic?* (Oxford University Press, 1999).

3. Federalism

Federalism is arguably the most common and effective theory of political integration among states. Unlike functionalism and intergovernmentalism, federalism has a long history of both theoretical and practical contributions. It serves as a model of integration on which countries such as the United States of America, the Federal Republic of Germany, and the Federative Republic of Brazil, among others, have been built. Although federalism was present in the early works that led to the European Communities, it did not find its full expression for the European project until the 1980s and 1990s. During this period, the Communities transformed into a Union, where the 'single market' became an 'internal market' and where the concept of Union citizenship, with associated political and social rights, was introduced. Until then, federalism had mostly been an aspiration of some European intellectuals and politicians, who had to accept (and live with) the limitations of a functionalist and intergovernmental approach to European integration.[10]

Federalism, both as a descriptive and normative theory of integration, involves a union of states established by a political decision of constitutional relevance.[11] In this process, sovereign competences are transferred to a newly created entity, the Union, which possesses its own international legal personality.[12] The transfer of competences requires an unambiguous division of tasks between the states and the Union. At the institutional level, bodies representing governments and citizens are formed, alongside independent institutions entrusted with promoting the general interests of the Union. Agreements made at the Union level take precedence over all national laws and can be invoked directly and immediately by citizens in national courts.[13] Union citizenship is created, granting citizens two simultaneous and compatible loyalties: one to their national community and another to the Union. Both loyalties derive their legitimacy from distinct sources, as citizens enjoy political rights to participate at both the Union and state levels.

The European Union is currently close to the federal ideal, yet far enough from claiming to be a fully federal political organisation. The founding treaties are indeed international agreements with constitutional significance in all Member States, as national constitutions generally include specific ratification procedures solely for these treaties, thereby shaping the transfer of sovereign powers through constitutional channels. In theory, the Union's institutional structure resembles that of a federal organisation, with a European Parliament representing citizens' interests, a Council representing national governments, and a European Commission, a Court of Justice, and a European Central Bank (ECB) operating independently in pursuit of the general European interest. The status of Union citizenship is declared in the Treaties and it encompasses political rights and freedom of movement for nationals of the Member States, while a Charter of Fundamental Rights safeguards individuals' fundamental rights. The allocation and types of competences support a clear division of responsibilities between the Union and the Member States, a hallmark of any federal system. Union law prevails over national law. All signs point to the Union being a federation, or at least a project, involving all the necessary features to be considered one.

[10] See, for example, the contribution of A Spinelli, E Colorni and E Rossi, *The Ventotene Manifesto* (The Altiero Spinelli Institute for Federalist Studies, 1941).

[11] See M Forsyth, *Unions of States: The Theory and Practice of Confederation* (Leicester University Press, 1981) and O Beaud, *Théorie de la Fédération* (PUF, 2007).

[12] JHH Weiler, 'The Transformation of Europe' (1991) 100 *Yale Law Journal* 2403.

[13] D Kelemen,*The Rules of Federalism: Institutions and Regulatory Politics in the EU and Beyond* (Harvard University Press, 2004).

However, the simple fact remains that the Union is far from being a federation. Federalism is a useful but also risky tool for explaining the European project. The aim of any federation is to create a new state, which is not among the current aims of the European Union. Political integration is indeed real, but there is still a long way to go from the existing political union to the creation of a fully fledged European state. Furthermore, the Union still lacks many features of a federal organisation, such as a foreign or defence policy, which are still tightly held by the Member States. The institutional design still reflects the workings of a functionalist organisation rather than those of a federal state. For instance, the European Parliament has no power of legislative initiative of its own, something unthinkable in modern parliamentary practice, while the European Commission is an indirectly elected executive body answerable only to the European Parliament, whose powers, as we have noted, are still limited.

However, if one must choose the narrative that best fits the spirit and *telos* that have characterised the past seven decades of European integration, federalism certainly emerges as the most fitting theory.[14] Functionalism revealed its limitations when it clashed with the democratic principle. Intergovernmentalism explained European *realpolitik* when it entered the scene, but it cannot fully account for the fact that states are subject to qualified majorities and they exercise their veto powers only sparingly, aware of the negative implications of conflated national interests. Ultimately, the story that best describes the history of European integration is that of a federation in progress, with its virtues and flaws, but making increasingly significant steps towards a federal organisation. This is why federalism is only partially reflected in the Union, but a reflection that, as will now be explained, is becoming more discernible over time.

II. A BRIEF HISTORY OF THE UNION

The three theories of European integration have appeared throughout the history of the Union, but with varying degrees of prominence. While the early years were characterised by orthodox functionalism, the 1960s and 1970s witnessed the rise of intergovernmentalism. The 1980s and 1990s were marked by a strong influence of federalism, especially after the signing of the Single European Act in 1986 and, above all, the Maastricht Treaty in 1992. In the following years, the three theories have coexisted in a stable balance. However, following the financial crisis that began in 2008, there has been a slight decline in functionalism, replaced by the growing influence of federalism and intergovernmentalism. Let us now examine this evolution in more detail.

1. The Early Years: Jean Monnet, the European Communities and the Rise of Functionalism

The Union is the direct successor of the European Communities, three international organisations established to create a common market for goods, services, labour, and capital, as well as a shared market for coal, steel, and a framework of cooperation and regulation in the field of atomic energy. To understand how today's Union works and is organised, it is essential first to examine the origins and development of the European Communities, three organisations with a remarkable and successful history, whose beginnings trace back to the early 1950s, shortly after the end of the Second World War.

[14] D Sidjanski, *L'avenir fédéraliste de l'Europe: La Communauté européenne, des origines au traité de Maastricht* (Presses universitaires de France, 1992).

Although the idea of a European federation or confederation was not new at the end of the Second World War, the success of the European Communities mainly stems from a functionalist approach to integration, endorsed by the governments of several European countries at the time. Jean Monnet, a senior French official who had spent much of the Second World War in exile in London, recognised the challenges in any effort to promote political integration among European states. At the same time, well aware that the continent's future depended on some form of union that would definitively end armed conflict, Monnet focused on creating an organisation with a very specific purpose: pooling energy resources and establishing an energy market regulated and managed by independent European institutions. The idea was as simple as it was revolutionary, but it proved useful for the Western European states of the post-war period. With enthusiastic backing from the US administration, which viewed European integration as a means to contain the Soviet Union's westward expansion, the six participating states – France, Germany, Luxembourg, Belgium, the Netherlands, and Italy – found compelling (albeit sometimes divergent) reasons to pursue the initiative. Consequently, the European Coal and Steel Community (ECSC) was established by the Treaty of Paris of 1951, including an independent High Authority responsible for overseeing the coal and steel market in the six Member States, a Council of Ministers representing their governments, a Common Assembly composed of delegates from national parliaments, and a Court of Justice.

Almost immediately and with hardly any time to assess the impact of the ECSC's policies, the Member States, again supported by the United States, launched in 1952 an even more ambitious project: the creation of a European Defence Community, followed in 1953 by a draft Treaty establishing a European Political Community. However, by that time the political landscape had started to sour, particularly in France, where the Mendès-France Government faced the rejection of the Treaty establishing the European Defence Community by the French National Assembly on 30 August 1954. In response to this failure, both initiatives were swiftly removed from the political agenda. Europe's integration would not happen all at once, as Robert Schuman had correctly predicted in his famous declaration of 9 May 1950, but gradually, step by step. Therefore, the governments of the six ECSC Member States shifted their approach, focusing on a 'step-by-step' method and choosing to establish a dedicated organisation for cooperation in the nuclear field, and a broader one aimed at the gradual creation of a common market: the European Atomic Energy Community and the European Economic Community, respectively.

The Treaties of the two new international organisations were signed in Rome on 25 March 1957 by representatives of the Governments of France, Germany, Luxembourg, Belgium, the Netherlands, and Italy, and they entered into force on 1 January 1958.[15] The three organisations that would form the basis of the so-called 'European Communities', a term that encompassed the ECSC, the European Atomic Energy Community (EURATOM), and the European Economic Community (EEC), began to coexist and interact as a cohesive trio with shared objectives. Although each organisation operated independently with its own institutional framework, their founding Treaties displayed obvious similarities: they were structured as a *traité-cadre*, a comprehensive legal document that provided all necessary elements to ensure the functioning of each Community. The institutional structures and sources of law were substantially alike. From a policy perspective, the three Communities were dedicated to creating a market, ensuring free movement, establishing minimum conditions for free competition among companies

[15] On 25 March 1957, in Rome, the heads of state and government signed a document with a proper cover but a bundle of blank documents attached, because the local printer missed the deadlines and the copies of the text of the Treaties never arrived at Capitoline Hill on time. This was a prescient sign of the open-ended process into the unknown that the founding Member States were embarking on.

across Europe, and allowing for the adoption of uniform or harmonised rules within each respective market, albeit with differing sectoral scopes and degrees of integration.

Like the ECSC Treaty, the most innovative aspect of the two new Communities was their institutional and decision-making system. The Council of Ministers enacted the EURATOM and EEC rules, with the Common Assembly at that time exercising primarily consultative and supervisory functions, upon the proposal of an independent body outside the control of national governments: the European Commission. This body not only held a monopoly on legislative proposals but also possessed executive exclusive powers in areas such as competition and state aid. Member States were legally obliged to comply with the Commission's decisions when acting within its competences, together with their right to appeal to a Court of Justice established for this purpose. Furthermore, the 1960s marked the close of the transitional period that Member States had set until then, now empowering the Council of Ministers to make decisions by qualified majority rather than unanimously. This change raised the possibility that Member States could be left in a minority yet still required to comply with agreements made by the majority, something close to inconceivable in international practice. The adoption of majoritarian decision-making within the Council of Ministers reflected the genuine intention of the Member States to strengthen the effectiveness of the newly created Communities.

Of the three Communities, the most prominent was the EEC, both in scope and future potential. Seen through the lens of functionalism, the EEC was a highly effective policy-making machine, capable of generating spillovers into all areas of economic activity within the Member States. Its provisions guaranteed the free movement of all factors of production and the creation of a common customs tariff for all Member States, facilitating the removal of internal trade barriers. The Commission had the authority to propose measures in sectors as diverse and relevant as agriculture, transport, energy, and many others. Meanwhile, qualified majority voting exerted sufficient pressure on all Member States to compel them to reach agreements by consensus, thereby strengthening the system's legitimacy and efficiency.

The three Communities began their work under a complex system of seat allocation. While the Member States chose to locate the ECSC institutions in the Grand Duchy of Luxembourg, the EURATOM and EEC Treaties established a provisional system of seat allocation among Luxembourg, Brussels, and Strasbourg, which will be discussed later.

2. The 1960s and 1970s: the Emergence of European Intergovernmental Politics

European enthusiasm soon ran into trouble. The end of the transitional period was to arrive in 1970, marking a new stage in the development of the Communities, with a Council of Ministers authorised to make decisions by qualified majority in several policy areas. At the same time, several countries, including the United Kingdom, Ireland, Norway, and Denmark, were knocking on the Communities' door with applications for membership, clearly indicating that functionalism was attracting the interest of other nations, and that a 'step-by-step' approach to integration was the right approach to deepen and expand the project. These circumstances were seen with optimism in some quarters, but met with hostility from General de Gaulle, who had just become President of the newly established French Fifth Republic in 1958.

The end of the transitional period was regarded with hostility by General de Gaulle, especially in 1965 during the negotiations over the reform of the Communities' budget. Anticipating that France would be repeatedly outvoted in a Council moving towards qualified majority voting and rejecting the Commission's package on own resources and parliamentary powers, General de Gaulle withdrew French representation from the Council of Ministers, sparking the 'empty chair crisis'. The resolution to this dispute would come a few months later, in January 1966, when the Member States agreed on the 'Luxembourg compromise', which states as follows:

> Where, in the case of decisions which may be taken by majority vote on a proposal of the Commission, very important interests of one or more partners are at stake, the Members of the Council will endeavour, within a reasonable time, to reach solutions which can be adopted by all the Members of the Council while respecting their mutual interests and those of the Community.

Despite its apparent simplicity, the agreement reflected a significant change in the Communities' functionalist approach. In areas subject to qualified majority voting, if a Member State felt at risk of being in the minority in a matter of particular sensitivity to its national interests, it could invoke the Luxembourg compromise to establish *de facto* unanimity in the Council.

An intergovernmental Europe was emerging at the expense of functionalism, a phenomenon that would recur throughout the 1960s and 1970s, as later confirmed by the launch in 1970 of the European Political Cooperation, a forum for discussion and informal decision-making among Member States in the field of foreign policy, followed by the first meeting of the European Council in 1975, after its political creation at the Paris Summit of 1974. This new body, like the European Political Cooperation, was established outside the formal institutional framework of the European Communities, but its purpose was clearly linked to them. The European Council was created to provide political impetus to the activities of the three Communities through three annual meetings of the heads of state and government of the Member States and the President of the European Commission. Member States were beginning to take control of the European political initiative, a common practice in international forums, but this was unusual because the Communities' logic was conceived as an alternative to traditional international decision-making.

The arrival of General de Gaulle also influenced the pace of expansion of the Communities. In 1961, Ireland, Denmark, and the United Kingdom applied for membership, only to be met with a French rejection that immediately blocked the opening of accession negotiations. De Gaulle viewed the expansion towards Anglo-Saxon and Scandinavian countries as a serious threat to France's interests, fearing marginalisation within a Community dominated by the Nordics, Germans, and a United Kingdom whose interests were allegedly closer to the United States than those of continental Europe. The worsening bilateral relations between de Gaulle and the United States administration contributed to the French refusal, leading to a period of cooling relations between the Member States that lasted until 1969, when de Gaulle stepped down from the French presidency and was succeeded by Georges Pompidou, a politician more supportive of the enlargement of the Communities. The accession of the United Kingdom, Ireland, and Denmark became effective on 1 January 1973, despite some setbacks, including Norway's refusal to join after a negative referendum in 1972.

However, the 1960s and 1970s were not characterised solely by setbacks. Functionalist dynamics persisted, exemplified by the merger of the institutions of the three Communities in 1967. The fragmented institutional framework that had arisen in 1958 was consolidated into a single one, although each Community maintained its own legal personality. Additionally, in 1970, the first agreement on the Communities' budget was reached, granting each Community the authority to gather its own resources, mostly from revenue generated by the customs union and a common value-added tax. From that point, the Communities were no longer entirely reliant on budgetary transfers from Member States, indicating financial independence and granting enhanced autonomy to the European institutions' operations. In 1979, the first elections to the European Parliament (still formally designated as the 'Assembly' in the Treaties until the Single European Act) were held by universal and direct suffrage, significantly reinforcing the democratic legitimacy of the European project and distancing it further from the customary practices of international organisations. In legal terms, integration was well underway: in 1963, the Court of Justice issued a landmark judgment in the case of *Van Gend en Loos*, followed by the 1964 judgment in the *Costa/Enel* case. These rulings established the direct effect and the primacy of Community law, enabling individuals to invoke Community rules before national courts and, where incompatible, to set aside national law. The functionalist approach continued to operate, although it now had to coexist with the increasing influence of Member State governments. The period of cohabitation between functionalism and intergovernmentalism had begun.

3. The 1980s and 1990s: from the Communities to the Union

A significant breakthrough took place in 1986, and more specifically in 1992. Throughout most of the 1980s, the prospect of profound institutional reform of the Communities was consistently on the agenda of the Member States. Various initiatives, including a draft European Constitution drafted by the European Parliament under the guidance of Altiero Spinelli, was good proof of a certain degree of fatigue with the original Community model. The functionalist approach, begun in the 1950s, needed to evolve with the times, especially after Greece's accession in 1981 and Spain and Portugal's in 1986, which confirmed the extensive territorial ambitions of the Communities, now fully realised in southern Europe. This led to the convening of an intergovernmental conference at the European Council in Milan, which resulted in the Single European Act of 1986, a targeted yet symbolic reform of the founding treaties that enhanced the powers of the European Parliament and broadened the scope of decisions on which the Council could decide by qualified majority.

However, the event that was to radically transform the political landscape arrived in 1989. In an unexpected turn of events, on 9 November, the Berlin Wall fell, and so did the Soviet Union in December 1991, bringing the Cold War to a close and triggering the most significant period of reform in European politics since the end of World War II. The geopolitical importance of these events is clear in the collapse of the Soviet Union and in the rise of new liberal democracies in Eastern Europe, now free from Soviet control and eager to join the European Communities. The most notable event was not the emergence of a *new* state but the *reunification* of the two German republics. The spectre of a large, reunified, and potentially hegemonic Germany – a ghost that had haunted European history for decades – was about to reemerge.

From 1989 onwards, a crucial period in European history began, during which not only the future of the Communities but also that of the entire continent was reshaped. It was evident from the start that the continent's destiny would need to be guided by the Communities. Consequently, just three years after the fall of the Berlin Wall, the Member States undertook another significant reform, embodied in the Treaty signed in Maastricht on 7 February 1992.

The reforms introduced by the Maastricht Treaty can be briefly summarised by dividing them into two. On the *geostrategic level*, the Member States agreed on the reunification of the two German republics, considering it technically as an 'internal enlargement'. However, it was clear that the change was much more than that, as one Member State, the Federal Republic of Germany, would now gain approximately 16 million more inhabitants and significantly increase the size of its territory. This decision was the most delicate of all, as it confirmed the emergence within the Communities of a new and preeminent Member State in demographic terms, but also in economic and, as would be revealed later, political terms. The reluctance of the United Kingdom and France towards German reunification was resolved through an agreement that would influence the continent's immediate future: the creation of the euro. In exchange for the acceptance of reunification by its European allies, Germany relinquished its powerful currency, the Deutsche Mark, extending to the other Member States the stability of a common currency backed by the German economy, which would enable the new European currency to compete with the dollar and the yen, and ensure price stability within the internal market. The fact that the euro's design and rulebook closely resembled the main features that had governed the Deutsche Mark underscored the strong German influence on the newly established common currency.

At the *institutional level*, the Maastricht Treaty triggered a profound reform of the European project's internal architecture, primarily through the creation of the European Union, an entity built on the so-called 'three pillars': one dedicated to the common foreign and security policy; another to justice and home affairs; and a third, the Community pillar, where the three European Communities were located. Although the European Union lacked legal personality, the Member States acted (particularly within the first two pillars) as constituent states of the Union. It was a sophisticated design that aimed not to make too explicit what was already apparent: the transition from the Communities to a Union endowed not only with economic policies but also with policies closely linked to national sovereignty, such as monetary policy, foreign policy, defence, and home affairs. This was accompanied by the establishment of the ECB, the creation of a new status of Union citizenship including political rights, and a significant expansion of the European Community's competences, which shed its 'Economic' label to emphasise that its objectives were no longer limited to the market. The Member States had taken a significant step towards a more federal vision of Europe.

The significance of the Maastricht Treaty was clear throughout its turbulent ratification process in the Member States, marked by plenty of drama. Denmark rejected ratification in a first popular referendum, while France ratified the text with a narrow 51.05 per cent of the popular vote, also through a referendum. Spain, like Germany and France, had to amend its constitution. In some cases, consultation was required with constitutional courts that proved to be highly critical of the direction of European integration, a direction that, unsurprisingly, challenged traditional notions of the nation-state. However, the growing concerns and the signs of euroscepticism in some Member States were unable to stop the process that had just begun, and on 1 November 1993, the Maastricht Treaty came into force.

The events that began with the symbolic and physical fall of the Berlin Wall took several years to redraw the new map of Europe. During this period, the newly formed Union underwent multiple reforms, including the signing of the Treaty of Amsterdam in 1997, the Treaty of Nice in 2001, and the Treaty of Lisbon in 2007. The 1990s witnessed the accession of Sweden, Finland, and Austria, while accession negotiations began with several states, including some of the newly independent republics that emerged following the fall of the Soviet Union. Poland, the Czech Republic, Slovakia, Slovenia, Hungary, Latvia, Lithuania, Estonia, Malta, and Cyprus joined in 2004, followed by Bulgaria and Romania in 2007 and Croatia in 2013. The European Union was adapting to the new geopolitical map of Europe, while the countries of Europe adapted to a Union that could finally call itself truly European.

4. The Twenty-first Century: an Enlarged European Union in Times of 'Polycrisis'

With the arrival of the twenty-first century, changes in Europe and its Union continued. The great enlargement of the Union was accompanied by an ambitious project of institutional and political reform that aimed to go beyond the Maastricht process. The goal was to adapt the Union to many new Member States and to focus more on the effectiveness of Union action rather than the prevention of war, which was considered by some as an outdated aim due to 'the end of history' and the spread of democracy across the European continent. An era of liberal-democratic optimism began, in which discussions about the European project focused on improving policies rather than preventing conflicts. It was in this context that the work of the Convention on the Future of Europe began in 2002, primarily resulting in the drafting of the Treaty establishing a Constitution for Europe. However, the project failed after being rejected in the referenda held in France and the Netherlands. Following the rejection by two founding countries, it became apparent that the draft Constitutional Treaty had no future, prompting Member States to reconsider their approach to reform.

After two years of reflection and discreet behind-the-scenes negotiations, the Treaty of Lisbon was signed on 13 December 2007, a diluted version of the failed Constitutional Treaty. However, it incorporated many of the Convention's contributions. Following a long and complex ratification process, the Lisbon Treaty took effect on 1 December 2009. Among its main new features was the disappearance of the European Community (the ECSC had already expired in 2002), replaced by the European Union, which assumed a single legal personality. The Union ceased to be a mere framework for a complex system of international organisations. The Union was now granted an ambitious Charter of Fundamental Rights of the European Union, as well as the power to accede to the European Convention on Human Rights. The Treaty of Lisbon included and clarified for the first time the distribution of competences between the Union and the Member States, and strengthened the democratic principle by reinforcing the role of national parliaments in the European legislative process. The system of sources of law was refined by introducing new legal instruments for delegated and implementing acts, to enhance the Union's effectiveness in its actions. The old 'pillars' disappeared entirely and were integrated into the traditional method of Community action, albeit with special features in the case of the common foreign and security policy. In short, the Treaty of Lisbon took important steps towards simplifying the institutional framework and the Union's instruments, although it fell short of the most symbolic constitutional reforms envisioned by the Convention.

The most ambitious leap forward did not come with the Lisbon Treaty or the failed Constitutional Treaty, but with a financial crisis that started in 2008 and shook markets and economies worldwide, especially in Europe. What began as a financial crisis eventually spread to many Member States, forcing them to inject billions of euros into the banking sector to prevent its collapse. The cost of the bailouts raised doubts about the solvency of several Member States, notably Greece, Italy, Spain, Portugal, Ireland, and Cyprus, whose economies were heavily exposed to the financial sector and real estate markets. Investors lost confidence in these countries overnight, preventing them from accessing the bond market. This sequence of events prompted the financial rescue of several Member States, an operation jointly coordinated by the Commission, the Eurogroup and the International Monetary Fund.

At that point, a period of intense political and economic upheaval followed, under the threat of the euro's collapse. Some leaders considered temporarily ejecting the most vulnerable Member States from the common currency, an action that risked being seen by markets as a failure of the euro as a shared currency. The euro had been central to the Maastricht negotiations, and without it, maintaining the geostrategic balance that led Member States to ratify the Maastricht Treaty would be difficult. The fall of the euro would also have meant the fall of the Union, or at least of a Union with the federal features that had emerged in 1992.

After three years of negotiations, reforms and intense political drama, the euro was preserved, and no Member State was compelled to leave the common currency. The cost was a complex mixture of federalism and intergovernmentalism that left a lasting impact on the European project. The crisis revealed the euro's structural weaknesses. It affirmed the concerns of economists who had warned about the dubious sustainability of a common European currency lacking a unified economic and fiscal policy. Despite the euro's creation, economic and fiscal policies remained under the control of Member States, a domain of national competence that kept revenue and expenditure of the national budget in the hands of each Member State. This two-tiered structure and distribution of tasks are enshrined in the Treaties, which prohibit any financial assistance from the Union or other Member States. However, the severity of the economic crisis proved that this arrangement was impractical. A strict interpretation of the Treaties would have resulted in several Member States withdrawing from the Eurozone, likely leading to fragmentation and the collapse of the common currency.

In barely four years, the Member States, particularly the Eurozone countries, made significant progress and further developed a European economic policy. This period confirmed that European integration was not only the sum of individual national interests; otherwise, some countries would have had no hesitation in leaving or pushing others to leave the euro. The crisis also demonstrated the existence of a core group of countries leading integration – namely, the Member States whose currency is the euro – whose commitment to a more political Union became clear. This series of events compelled some Member States, especially those whose scepticism towards European integration had grown over time, such as the United Kingdom, to confront their European dilemmas. After decades of hesitations regarding its participation in the Union, the United Kingdom decided, following a referendum on 23 June 2016, to withdraw from the project.

The economic crisis left deep social and political scars in several Member States. Shortly after the euro crisis was finally stabilised, a new crisis emerged, this time with more political features. A different type of crisis developed in some Member States with the rise of local authoritarianism, a mix of nativist nationalism, appeals to citizens' fears, and a search for diffuse 'enemies of the people' abroad and within. The emergence of strong, authoritarian leaders willing to challenge the liberal values established during the post-war period led to the rise of new political movements that questioned everything that the Union represents: multilateralism, globalisation, multiculturalism, free trade, and human rights protection. These movements reached the highest levels of government in several Member States, including Hungary, Poland, Austria, Slovenia, Slovakia, and Italy, as well as in one of the Union's most prominent allies: the United States of America.

To complicate matters further, in March 2020, the Union faced the most severe health, economic, and social crisis in its history. The COVID-19 virus, with a high mortality rate and rapid transmission among asymptomatic individuals, led to strict lockdowns across most Member States, the closing of borders and the suspension of economic activity throughout the continent. Within weeks, the Union experienced its worst recession since the Second World War, coupled with a challenging health crisis, an area of policy in which Member States hold most of the competences. At first, the Union tolerated disorderly border closures and a *de facto* suspension of the Schengen area, with limited room for manoeuvre. Once the initial shock subsided, the Union and its Member States began to regain control of the situation. In just a few months, an unprecedented commitment was made to support the Union's economy, including the development of the first stages of a fiscal union. The Commission issued mutualised debt in the financial markets to fund a monumental rescue package for Member States. An extraordinary external shock demonstrated to the world that the Union was prepared to take a Hamiltonian leap forward and harness genuine financial firepower, an initiative finally agreed upon at a historic European Council of 17 to 21 July 2020. The launch of a massive stimulus programme, under the name of NextGeneration EU, alongside record purchases of vaccines to protect citizens and the decisive intervention by the ECB in public and private debt markets, proved that the Union possessed the firepower to stabilise one of the worst economic, political, and social crises faced by Member States in recent history.

If COVID-19 was an external economic and health shock, the invasion of Ukraine by Russian forces on 24 February 2022 represented an external *security* and *defence* shock. The Russian offensive rattled the world with its brutality and the precedent it set, reminiscent of German expansionist drives prior to the outbreak of the Second World War. For the Union, the invasion was a warning sign of the challenges facing its fragmented security and defence policy. Following the invasion, the Union saw its geopolitical strategy shift significantly and approved the largest arsenal of economic sanctions ever imposed, targeting Russia and the network of interests within Vladimir Putin's inner circle. The Union also began the difficult process of reducing its reliance on Russian oil and gas, while organising political, economic, and military support for Ukraine, an unprecedented level of involvement in a foreign armed conflict. The Union took the first steps to establish the core pillars of a genuine security and defence architecture, while fundamentally reshaping its enlargement strategy, granting Ukraine candidate status in June 2022 and devising a plan to support Ukraine's reconstruction, which is likely to require the development of new and innovative financial instruments.

The EU's response to a scenario of 'polycrises' has demonstrated that the pillars of the European project are much more resilient than the doomsayers assume. Once again, recent years have shown that it is precisely during the most severe crises that the Union makes significant advances. Paradoxically, the United Kingdom's formal withdrawal from the Union on 31 January 2020 (an event initially seen as a sign of the European project's decline) enabled Member States to build consensus more rapidly during crises, free from the traditional British reluctance to deepen integration. The COVID-19 pandemic prompted the Union to undertake an unprecedented effort to provide financial resources to facilitate a swift economic recovery through joint financial instruments. The Russian invasion of Ukraine triggered an intense pooling of energy resources and integration in a key sector that had traditionally been guarded by national interests.

However, despite the Union's resilience in withstanding crises and its ability to adapt to new and challenging environments, the global landscape is evolving and will likely present even more difficult tests in the years to come. The growing emergence of authoritarian global powers is transforming the international scene into a battleground where only the rule of the jungle applies. The rising influence of an undemocratic China, combined with the autocratic tendencies of Russia, India and the United States under the second presidency of Donald Trump, is prompting the Union to reassess its role on the international stage. An organisation once created to replace power politics with rule-based rational decision-making is now confronted with a world in which rules matter very little. The *herbivore* Union, with its functionalist spirit and liberal values, must now reflect on how to survive as a *carnivore* in a ruthless global environment. The powers conferred upon the Union may not be sufficient to meet this challenge, but it is also unclear whether Member States are willing or able to take further steps in integration. A misstep in the coming years could strike a lethal blow to the European project, but a clever reaction could set it on a path towards another long period of integration. Once again, the changing nature of the Union will be revealed and will be put to the test in the years ahead.

GENERAL BIBLIOGRAPHY

Davies, G, and Rasmussen, M (eds), *The History of European Union Law. Constitutional Practice, 1950 to 1993* (Cambridge University Press, 2026).

Gilbert, M, *European Integration. A Concise History* (Rowman & Littlefield, 2012).

Judt, T, *Postwar. A History of Europe since 1945* (Penguin, 2006).

Krastev, I, *After Europe* (University of Pennsylvania Press, 2017).
Lieshout, R, *The Struggle for the Organization of Europe* (Edward Elgar, 1999).
Lipgens, W, *A History of European Integration* (Clarendon Press, 1982).
Marsh, D, *The Euro. The Battle for the New Global Currency* (Yale University Press, 2011).
Moravcsik, A, *The Choice for Europe: Social Purpose and State Power from Messina to Maastricht* (Cornell University Press, 1998).
Pavone, T, *The Ghostwriters. Lawyers and the Politics behind the Judicial Construction of Europe* (Cambridge University Press, 2022).
Pisani-Ferry, J, *The Euro Crisis and Its Aftermath* (Oxford University Press, 2014).
Scharpf, FW, *Governing in Europe: Effective and Democratic?* (Oxford University Press, 1999).
Schütze, R, '"Integration-through-Law": grand theory, revisionist history' (2025) 4 *European Law Open* 162.
Sidjanski, D, *L'avenir fédéraliste de l'Europe: La Communauté européenne, des origines au traité de Maastricht* (Presses universitaires de France, 1992).
Weiler, JHH, 'The Transformation of Europe' (1991) 100 *Yale Law Journal* 2403.

FURTHER READING

Theories of Integration

Bellamy, RA, *Republican Europe of States: Cosmopolitanism, Intergovernmentalism and Democracy in the EU* (Cambridge University Press, 2019).
Börzel, A (ed), *The Disparities of European Integration: Revisiting Neofunctionalism in Honour of Ernst B. Haas* (Routledge, 2006).
Burgess, M, *Federalism and European Union. Political Ideas, Influences and Strategies in the European Community 1972–1987* (Routledge, 1989).
Eleftheriadis, P, *A Union of Peoples* (Oxford University Press, 2020).
Haas, EB, *The Uniting of Europe: Political, Social and Economic Forces, 1950–1957* (Stanford University Press, 1958).
Hooghe L and Marks, G, 'Grand Theories of European Integration in the Twenty-First Century' (2019) 26 *Journal of European Public Policy* 1128.
Kelemen, D, *The Rules of Federalism: Institutions and Regulatory Politics in the EU and Beyond* (Harvard University Press, 2004).
Larsen, S, *The Constitutional Theory of the Federation and the European Union* (Oxford University Press, 2020).
Mitrany, D, *A Working Peace System: An Argument for the Functional Development of International Organization* (Royal Institute of International Affairs, 1943).
Pollack, M, *The Engines of European Integration* (Oxford University Press, 2003).
Rosamond, B, *Theories of European Integration* (Palgrave, 2000).
Stone Sweet, A, Sandholtz, W and Fligstein, N (eds), *The Institutionalization of Europe* (Oxford University Press, 2001).
Tsebelis, G and Garrett, G, 'The Institutional Foundations of Intergovernmentalism and Supranationalism in the European Union' (2001) 55 *International Organization* 357.
Waltz, K, *Theory of International Politics* (McGraw-Hill, 1979).
Wiener, A and Díez, T, *European Integration Theory*, 2nd edn (Oxford University Press, 2009).

The Protagonists of Integration

Delors, J, *Mémoires* (Plon, 2004).
Duchêne, F, *Jean Monnet, The First Statesman of Interdependence* (Norton, 1994).
Grant, C, *Delors: The House that Jacques Built* (Brealey, 1994).
Griffiths, RT, 'The Founding Fathers' in E Jones, A Menon and S Weatherill (eds), The Oxford Handbook of the European Union (Oxford University Press, 2012).
Ludlow, P, 'Problematic Partners: de Gaulle, Thatcher, and their Impact' in E Jones, A Menon and S Weatherill (eds), *The Oxford Handbook of the European Union* (Oxford University Press, 2012).

Marjolin, R, *Architect of European Unity. Memoirs 1911–1986* (Weidenfeld and Nicholson, 1989).
Monnet, J, *Mémoires* (Le Livre de Poche, 2007).

From the ECSC to the Treaty of Rome

Dumoulin, M, *The European Commission, 1958–1972, History and Memories* (Publications Office, 2007).
Gilbert, M, 'The Treaties of Rome' in E Jones, A Menon and S Weatherill (eds), *The Oxford Handbook of the European Union* (Oxford University Press, 2012).
Kaiser, W, Leucht, B and Rasmussen, M, *The History of the European Union: Origins of a Trans- and Supranational Polity, 1950–1972* (Routledge, 2009).
Ludlow, P, *The European Community and the Crises of the 1960s: Negotiating the Gaullist Challenge* (Routledge, 2006).
Mattera, A, 'De la deuxième guerre mondiale au projet européen de Jean Monnet' (2002) 2 Revue de Droit de l'Union Européenne 217.
Rittberger, B, 'The Treaties of Paris' in E Jones, A Menon and S Weatherill (eds), *The Oxford Handbook of the European Union* (Oxford University Press, 2012).
Trachtenberg, M, *A Constructed Peace: The Making of the European Settlement 1945–1963* (Palgrave, 1997).
Winand, P, *Eisenhower, Kennedy and the United States of Europe* (St. Martin's Press, 1993).

From the Community to the Union

Baun, M, *An Imperfect Union: The Maastricht Treaty and the New Politics of European Integration* (Westview Press, 1996).
Connolly, B, *The Rotten Heart of Europe* (Faber and Faber, 1995).
Corbett, R, *The Treaty of Maastricht: From Conception to Ratification* (Longman, 1993).
Devuyst, Y, 'The Constitutional and Lisbon Treaties' in E Jones, A Menon and S Weatherill (eds), *The Oxford Handbook of the European Union* (Oxford University Press, 2012).
Dyson, K and Featherstone, K, *The Road to Maastricht: Negotiating Economic and Monetary Union* (Oxford University Press, 1999).
Green Cowles, M, 'The Single European Act' in E Jones, A Menon and S Weatherill (eds), *The Oxford Handbook of the European Union* (Oxford University Press, 2012).
Keohane, R and Hoffmann, S, *The New European Community* (Boulder Westview Press, 1993).
Laursen, F, 'The Treaty of Maastricht' in E Jones, A Menon and S Weatherill (eds), *The Oxford Handbook of the European Union* (Oxford University Press, 2012).
Padoa-Schioppa, T, *The Road to Monetary Union in Europe* (Clarendon Press, 1994).
Ross, G, *Jacques Delors and European Integration* (Oxford University Press, 1995).
Thomas, D, The Helsinki Effect: International Norms, Human Rights and the Demise of Communism (Princeton University Press, 2001).

The Post-Maastricht European Union

Amtenbrink, F, 'The Metamorphosis of European Economic and Monetary Union' in A Arnull and D Chalmers (eds), *The Oxford Handbook of European Union Law* (Oxford University Press, 2015).
Armstrong, K, *Brexit Time. Leaving the EU: Why, How and When?* (Cambridge University Press, 2017).
Barnier, M, *My Secret Brexit Diary: A Glorious Illusion* (Polity, 2021).
Bradford, A, *The Brussels Effect. How the European Union Rules the World* (Oxford University Press, 2020).
Krastev, I, *After Europe*, 2nd edn (University of Pennsylvania Press, 2020).
Norman, P, *The Accidental Constitution. The Making of Europe's Constitutional Treaty*, 2nd edn (Eurocomment, 2005).
Piris, J-C, *The Constitutional Treaty for Europe. A Legal Analysis* (Cambridge University Press, 2006).
— *The Future of Europe. Towards a Two-Speed Europe* (Cambridge University Press, 2011).
Van Middelaar, L, *Pandemonium. Saving Europe* (Agenda Publishing, 2021).

2

Definition, Values and Reform of the Union

I. WHAT IS THE UNION?

THE THEORIES OF integration that underpin the European integration process, along with the project's historical development, explain the context, origins, and circumstances of the current European Union. However, an important question remains unanswered: what *is* the European Union and what are its *main features*?

In short, the European Union is a supranational organisation, probably the most sophisticated in the current global landscape, whose Member States have decided to share sovereign powers, to preserve peace and promote the values of democracy, freedom, equality, solidarity and the rule of law. But the Union is also an organisation in constant motion, a political and rule-making structure that mutates regularly and never remains unaltered. For this reason, to properly understand the Union and its defining features, we must also take a closer look at how it changes and the procedures through which it undertakes its reform.

1. The Union as a Supranational Organisation

The Union is a supranational organisation, a designation that confirms its status as an international legal subject while also setting it apart from other international organisations. It is an *organisation* because it is built through the establishment of institutions equipped with material and human resources, acquiring legal personality through explicit recognition in Article 47 of the Treaty on European Union (TEU). It is *supranational* because Member States have entrusted it with sovereign powers. Nations receive a mandate from the sovereign (the people), including a monopoly on the legitimate use of force and other responsibilities aimed at ensuring citizens' well-being and security. Some of these powers have been transferred from the Member States to the Union, with the consent of their citizens, as expressed through internal constitutional procedures. Consequently, the Union functions as an organisation whose powers resemble those of a nation-state more than those of an international organisation, yet without adopting the form of a state. The outcome is a supranational organisation, an entity with the external characteristics of an international organisation, but with an internal structure and powers closer to those of a state.

2. The Union's Core Constitutional Features

The supranational character of the Union is reflected in its foundational acts, which the Court of Justice initially called the Union's 'constitutional charter'[1] and more recently the Union's 'constitutional framework'.[2] Unlike an international organisation, the Union's foundational act consists of international treaties with unique features, both in form and content.

The TEU and the Treaty on the Functioning of the European Union (TFEU) are the two founding Treaties of the Union.[3] The TEU establishes the general institutional framework of the Union, whilst the TFEU further details the Union's competences, policies and institutions. Both Treaties have the same legal value (Article 1, third paragraph TEU). They are *sui generis* treaties because their negotiation, conclusion and ratification have taken place under special procedures.

The negotiations of these Treaties took place within an intergovernmental conference, with the peculiarity that the decision to convene it was made by a majority vote in the European Council.[4] This practice is now reflected in the Treaties and marks a significant departure from traditional international practice.[5] The ratification process also has specific features in the Member States, as national constitutions require special procedures to ratify an agreement that transfers sovereign powers to the Union. These procedures may involve qualified majorities or referenda, reflecting the importance of the decision and its impact on the internal distribution of powers.[6] For example, in the German *Grundgesetz*, Article 23 states that Germany may transfer sovereign powers by law with the consent of the Bundesrat, but such transfers must follow the rules governing constitutional amendments. Article 93 of the Spanish Constitution states that only an organic law requiring an absolute majority in Congress can authorise the conclusion of treaties conferring on an international organisation or institution the exercise of competences derived from the Constitution. These provisions, with their specificities, can be found in most Member States' constitutions.

The constitutional features of the Union are also reflected in its institutional structure and decision-making processes.

- *The institutional framework.* As outlined in the Treaties, the Council and the European Parliament pass legislative acts, while the European Commission holds an executive role, and the Court of Justice carries out judicial functions. The Treaties also establish a European Central Bank responsible for monetary policy and banking supervision, as well as a Court of Auditors that oversees the implementation and discharge of the Union's finances. As the body setting the overall political direction and priorities of the Union, the European Council brings together, in a single institution, the heads of state or government of the Member States, its President and the President of the Commission. The High Representative of the Union for Foreign Affairs and Security Policy participates in the work of the European Council. This institutional framework reflects the traditional organisation

[1] Case 294/83 *Parti Écologiste 'Les Verts' v European Parliament* EU:C:1986:166, para 23.

[2] Opinion 1/17 (CETA) EU:C:2019:341, para 110; Case C-234/17 *XC and Others v Generalprokuratur* EU:C:2018:853, para 45, and Case C-741/19 *Republic of Moldova v Komstroy* LLC EU:C:2021:655, para 44.

[3] It should be noted that the Euratom Treaty is still in force and, as a result, the European Atomic Energy Community, as an independent supranational organisation, is in operation to date, although nuclear energy today operates alongside, and in coordination with, the Union's energy policy. See S Wolf, 'Euratom, the European Court of Justice, and the Limits of Nuclear Integration in Europe' (2011) 12 *German Law Journal* 1637, and A Popov, 'La Communauté Euratom: de la personnalité juridique distincte à la consécration d'un ordre juridique propre?' (2018) 54 *Cahiers de droit européen* 363.

[4] L Van Middelaar, *The Passage to Europe. How a Continent Became a Union* (Yale University Press, 2014) 100.

[5] Art 48(3) TEU.

[6] M Claes, 'Constitutionalizing Europe at Its Source: The "European Clauses" in the National Constitutions: Evolution and Typology' (2005) 24 *Yearbook of European Law* 81.

of a state with a clear separation of powers, combined with intergovernmental features reminiscent of the Union's international origins.

- *The decision-making process*. The Union's decision-making process is characterised by the widespread use of majority voting procedures, rather than unanimous votes and individual vetoes. Although some policies still require unanimity in the Council, the decision-making process, aligned with democratic principles, operates predominantly on a majority basis. Additionally, the will of the people is recognised within the Union, either through the European Parliament's participation in the legislative process or through national parliaments, which have a specific role in the Union's legislative procedures. Since the entry into force of the Treaty of Lisbon, and operational since 2012, citizens have the power to submit legislative initiatives to the Commission, a mechanism of citizen participation inspired by the constitutional traditions of the Member States.
- *An autonomous legal order*. Due to the nature of the powers transferred to the Union, the decisions made by the Union's institutions originate from and become part of an *autonomous* legal order. This new legal order, the law of the Union, is then integrated into the legal systems of each Member State while maintaining its autonomy. This feature prevents Union law from being subordinate to the law of the Member States. Whenever a conflict arises between the two legal systems, Union law takes precedence over national law. As a result, national authorities are obliged to set aside conflicting national rules and, subsequently, to remove the incompatibility from the national legal system.

3. The Values of the Union

Article 2 TEU enumerates the values on which the Union is founded. These values are fundamental features of a liberal democracy, rooted in respect for fundamental rights and the rule of law. The Union's values reflect the political and social progress achieved through the liberal revolutions of the eighteenth and nineteenth centuries, as well as the advancements made by the welfare state in the twentieth century. It is no coincidence that these values are enshrined in the opening provisions of the Treaties, in Article 2 TEU, a provision that reaffirms the Union's resolute commitment to supporting and promoting these values:

> The Union is founded on the values of respect for human dignity, freedom, democracy, equality, the rule of law and respect for human rights, including the rights of persons belonging to minorities. These values are common to the Member States in a society in which pluralism, non-discrimination, tolerance, justice, solidarity and equality between women and men prevail.

The Court of Justice emphasises that the values referred to in Article 2 TEU 'define the very identity of the European Union as a common legal order'.[7] Consequently, the Union must not only respect these values, but it must also actively promote and defend them. The fact that the values are part of the Union's 'identity' has important symbolic and practical implications, particularly in shaping the Union's constitutional identity.

The Union's values are not only policy goals; they have legal effects, and those effects materialise in certain procedures, such as Article 7 TEU, which authorises the Union to act against any Member State that undermines the values (see section II.4 of this chapter). The values also serve as limits that prevent Member States from backsliding after joining the Union. In

[7] Case C-156/21 *Hungary v European Parliament and Council of the European Union* EU:C:2022:97, para 127; and Case C-157/21 *Republic of Poland v European Parliament and Council of the European Union* EU:C:2022:98, para 145.

Repubblika,[8] the Court of Justice introduced the principle of 'non-regression', which requires Member States to avoid reverting in the protection of the Union's values following their accession. When referring to the value of the rule of law and judicial independence, the Court of Justice defined the principle of 'non-regression' as follows:

> [C]ompliance by a Member State with the values enshrined in Article 2 TEU is a condition for the enjoyment of all of the rights deriving from the application of the Treaties to that Member State. A Member State cannot therefore amend its legislation in such a way as to bring about a reduction in the protection of the value of the rule of law, a value which is given concrete expression by, inter alia, Article 19 TEU . . .
>
> . . .
>
> The Member States are thus required to ensure that, in the light of that value, any regression of their laws on the organisation of justice is prevented, by refraining from adopting rules which would undermine the independence of the judiciary. . . .[9]

While some values, such as the value of equality, are given concrete expression in provisions of primary and secondary legislation, others, like democracy and the rule of law, are mainly based on Article 2 TEU and are developed through the case law of the Court of Justice, which will be referenced in the following sections.

In the seminal case of *Commission v Hungary*,[10] the Court of Justice stated that Article 2 TEU is a legally binding provision that produces effects and can be autonomously breached by a Member State. The Court of Justice rejected the view that Article 2 TEU is merely a programmatic rule. To justify this finding, the judgment situates the provision within the Union's unique constitutional framework, in which the values of human dignity, democracy, the rule of law and fundamental rights form part of the very identity of the EU legal order.[11] These values are not aspirational, but the foundational premise of mutual trust between Member States and a continuing condition for the enjoyment of Treaty rights. Accordingly, compliance with Article 2 TEU is not limited to the accession phase under Article 49 TEU but constitutes an ongoing obligation, coupled with a prohibition of regression in the level of protection of those values.[12]

Building on this premise, the Court of Justice emphasises that Article 2 TEU is legally binding *per se*.[13] While those values are given concrete expression in more specific Treaty provisions, general principles, and the Charter, this does not diminish their autonomous normative force. On the contrary, the wording, context, and *travaux préparatoires* of Article 2 TEU confirm that it establishes binding commitments on Member States to respect, maintain, and promote those values.[14] The Court thus conceptualises Article 2 TEU as a constitutional provision delimiting the core commitments underpinning the Union's legal order, rather than a mere interpretative aid or political declaration.

The Court of Justice has also confirmed the justiciability of those obligations. In the aforementioned judgment, it rejected Hungary's argument that enforcement of Article 2 TEU is confined to the political mechanism of Article 7 TEU, holding instead that infringement proceedings under Article 258 TFEU remain available to the Commission and the Member States. Given the Court of Justice's jurisdiction under Article 19 TEU to ensure observance of

[8] Case C-896/19 *Repubblika v Il-Prim Ministru* EU:C:2021:311.

[9] ibid, paras 63–64. See also *Hungary v European Parliament and Council* (n 7) para 126; *Poland v European Parliament and Council* (n 7) para 144.

[10] Case C-769/22 *Commission v Hungary* EU:C:2026:326.

[11] ibid, paras 521-523.

[12] ibid, para 523.

[13] ibid, paras 525 and 536.

[14] ibid, paras 529-536.

the law, it may review compliance with Article 2 TEU in the context of such actions, provided the Union acts within its competences.[15] Article 7 TEU is therefore not an exclusive and monopolising political remedy, but part of a broader enforcement architecture in which judicial mechanisms complement political safeguards to ensure effective protection of the Union's foundational values.[16]

The practical implementation of this approach is subject to some constraints. First, the Court of Justice has made it clear that every breach of EU law, or every breach of a Charter right, does not automatically become a breach of Article 2 TEU. The contrary would exceed the limits of Union competence and undermine Article 51(1) of the Charter, which binds Member States only when they are implementing Union law. The case law is therefore careful in preserving the limits of Union competence and the scope of application of EU law.[17]

Instead, Article 2 TEU is engaged only where the breach is "manifest and particularly serious", affecting one or more of the Union's foundational values in a way incompatible with the very identity of the Union as a common legal order.[18] Therefore, the violation must be of a significant gravity, similar to the type of breach of the "essence" of a fundamental right, which requires a degree of severity that goes beyond a standard violation.

It should also be noted that a violation of Article 2 cannot be justified on the grounds of the protection of a Member State's national identity under Article 4(2) TEU.[19] While Member States retain a margin of assessment in giving effect to common values, national identity cannot be used to escape Article 2 TEU. Article 4(2) must itself be read consistently with Article 2, in a way that protects national identity only when it is compatible with the Union's foundational values.

Therefore, Article 4(2) TEU must be interpreted consistently with Article 2 TEU, protecting national identity only insofar as it is compatible with the Union's foundational values. This role of Article 2 TEU confirms the existence of an indirect hierarchy of rules within the Treaties, in which their core content, reflected in the provisions that materialise the "very identity of the Union", holds a preeminent interpretative role over the rest of the provisions in the Treaties.

A self-standing violation of Article 2 TEU will coexist with the violation of other Union rules. The limits of Union competence and the Member State conduct involved in such a violation will inevitably lead to a breach not only of Article 2 TEU, but of other Union rules of primary and/or secondary law. Doubts can therefore arise as to the practical use of Article 2 TEU in such cases, but the implications of a violation of this nature can be significant: in the context of enforcement proceedings pursuant to Article 260(2) TFEU, a violation of Article 2 TEU will justify the adoption of more severe lump sums and penalty payments. Furthermore, a violation of the said provision will always entail a "manifest breach" for the purposes of bringing damages claims against Member States for the breach of Union law. Also, a declaration by the Court of Justice confirming a violation of Article 2 TEU facilitates and indirectly confirms the fulfilment of the substantive requirements for initiating proceedings under Article 7 TEU.

3.1. *Democracy*

The powers transferred to the Union by the Member States are subject to the principle of conferral. Under this principle, the Union shall act only within the limits of the competences

[15] ibid, para 550.
[16] ibid, para 542.
[17] ibid, para 550.
[18] ibid, para 551.
[19] ibid, paras 557-562.

conferred upon it by the Member States in the Treaties to achieve the objectives set out therein.[20] However, the practical implementation of this principle differs from the practice of ordinary international organisations: the Union must exercise its competence in accordance with the value of democracy and the principles underpinning a representative democracy.

Article 10(1) TEU states that 'the functioning of the Union shall be founded on representative democracy'. This provision later translates into multiple ways for individuals to participate in the Union's decision-making processes at the legislative, administrative, and judicial levels. Such participation also depends on having proper information and understanding of the activities and policies developed by Union institutions. Only well-informed citizens, aware of the issues addressed by the Union through its policies, can actively participate and exert their influence. For these reasons, the Treaties and secondary legislation guarantee public access to documents from Union institutions.[21] Furthermore, representative democracy within the Union is bolstered by granting political fundamental rights to European citizens. The Charter of Fundamental Rights of the European Union recognises, among other rights, the fundamental right to vote and stand as a candidate in municipal and European Parliament elections,[22] the right to petition,[23] the right of access to documents, and the right to good administration.[24] Additionally, representative democracy is reinforced by the introduction of citizen legislative initiatives, which seek to encourage citizens' participation in the democratic process.[25]

The principle of representative democracy is a specific expression of the value of democracy recognised in Article 2 TEU.[26] As the Court of Justice has stated, as 'a principle common to the Member States, it must be taken into account when interpreting [the] Directives and, in particular, their disputed provisions'.[27] Therefore, all of the Union's actions, as well as those of the Member States when implementing Union law, must take into account the principle of representative democracy and must avoid interpretations that compromise its full effectiveness.[28]

The Union must promote and enforce respect for the democratic principle not only within its institutions but also in the Member States. According to Article 7 TEU, the Union can determine that there is a clear risk of a serious breach by a Member State of the values referred to in Article 2 TEU, including the democratic principle.[29] The importance of strong and well-functioning democracies in the Member States is reflected in the fact that national parliaments are involved in the Union's legislative process. Article 12 TEU entrusts the parliaments of the Member States with the implementation of the subsidiarity early warning mechanism, through which national parliaments can express their opposition to legislative proposals put

[20] Art 5(1)–(2) TEU.

[21] ibid, Art 15(3) TFEU, as well as Art 42 of the Charter and Regulation (EC) No 1049/2001 of the European Parliament and of the Council of 30 May 2001 regarding public access to European Parliament, Council and Commission documents.

[22] Arts 39–40 of the Charter.

[23] ibid, Art 44.

[24] ibid, Art 41.

[25] Case C-418/18 P *Patrick Grégor Puppinck and Others v European Commission* EU:C:2019:1113, para 65.

[26] Case C-502/19 *Junqueras Vies* EU:C:2019:1115, para 63.

[27] Case C-718/18 *Commission v Germany* EU:C:2021:662, para 125.

[28] For example, the Court of Justice has examined whether the establishment of independent authorities outside the hierarchy of administration in the Member States infringes the principle of representative democracy. The answer to this question was in the negative, but it reflects how Union law, as well as national law, can be conditioned by the value of democracy provided for in Art 2 TEU (see Case C-518/07 *Commission v Germany* EU:C:2010:125, paras 42, 43 and 46 and *Commission v Germany* (n 27) paras 126–127. Similarly, the Court of Justice has examined whether the exclusion of abstentions in the counting of votes in the context of a vote of the European Parliament under Art 354(4) TFEU infringes the principle of representative democracy, to which it also answered in the negative (Case C-650/18 *Hungary v European Parliament* EU:C:2021:426, paras 94–96) K. Lenaerts, «Democracy as an EU Value», Trier Lecture on the Future of Europe, *Verein für Recht und Digitalisierung e.V.,* 2025.

[29] See section II.4 of this chapter.

forward by the Commission on the grounds that the proposal does not comply with the principle of subsidiarity. If one third of the national parliaments oppose a legislative initiative, the Commission reviews it and may decide to maintain, amend or withdraw the proposal, giving reasons for its decision. National parliaments are also granted a veto over legislative initiatives in the field of family law with cross-border implications[30] and in the use of the *passerelle* clauses provided in Article 48(7) TEU, which will be explained in more detail in section II.1.3 of this chapter.[31]

The promotion of the democratic principle influences the Union's external relations. Article 21 TEU states that 'the Union's action on the international scene shall be guided by the principles which have inspired its own creation, development and enlargement, and which it seeks to advance in the wider world', the first of which is democracy. The Union has made a substantial contribution, through both financial and human resources, to strengthening democracy in third countries, especially those with historical or strategic links to the Union or its Member States.

3.2. Freedom

The Treaties also recognise the importance of individuals' fundamental freedoms. While in the early years of the European project the goal of the Communities was to establish a common market, a project closely associated with a liberal conception of the economy, the development of a European *political* project strengthened the value of freedom to the extent of creating a framework for protecting individual freedom in all activities, not just economic ones. As with the democratic principle, the value of freedom influences and shapes all actions of the Union, as well as those of Member States when they implement Union law.

The importance of freedom is closely linked to that of democracy, as only free citizens can participate in a genuinely representative democracy. However, the value of freedom is not solely a foundation of democracy. The role of individual freedom is deeply embedded in the history of liberal democracies and in the struggle of individuals against the arbitrary or abusive use of power. Europe's history shows the disastrous consequences of the absence of individual freedoms. Therefore, it is no coincidence that Member States, in their efforts to establish the Union as a legitimate public authority, have placed fundamental rights at the centre of European integration.

The Union's commitment to fundamental rights is reflected in Article 6(1) TEU, which states that '[the] Union recognises the rights, freedoms and principles set out in the Charter of Fundamental Rights of the European Union . . . , which shall have the same legal value as the Treaties'. The Union's attachment to a legally binding Charter marks a significant development, as it means that all Union institutions, as well as Member States when implementing Union law, are bound by a comprehensive catalogue of fundamental rights. Until 1 December 2009, the date of the Charter's entry into force, fundamental rights were recognised in Union law through the case law of the Court of Justice as general principles of Union law; however, they had never been formally enshrined in a comprehensive, legally binding written document. The introduction of the Charter has brought about both symbolic and practical change, facilitating the power of European citizens to rely on an extensive array of fundamental rights protected and promoted by the Union.

To maximise the effectiveness of the value of freedom and the rights enshrined in the Charter, the Court of Justice has developed a body of case law that empowers national courts

[30] Art 81(3), third subparagraph TFEU.
[31] Art 48(7), third subparagraph TEU.

to enforce the Charter and, where appropriate, to disapply rules or acts of Member States that come into conflict with it.[32]

3.3. *Equality and Solidarity*

The value of equality is explicitly enshrined in Article 2 TEU, in terms that reflect the relationship between the individual and the state, as well as the relations between the Member States.

The Union guarantees equal treatment for all individuals, especially those from vulnerable groups that have traditionally faced discrimination. Therefore, the principle of non-discrimination on the grounds of sex is a particularly important mandate, enshrined in both the Treaties and secondary legislation.[33] The protection provided by the principle of non-discrimination has been extended to other vulnerable groups, with the Union having a specific legal basis (Article 19 TFEU) to legislate on the matter.[34] The value of equality in EU law has a *horizontal* dimension, producing effects in relations between individuals, but it also has a *vertical* dimension, applying to the relations between individuals and all public authorities, including the Union and its Member States.

The value of equality holds specific significance in the relations between Member States, a dimension that the Treaty guarantees under Article 4(2) TEU. Nonetheless, the value of equality also embodies a guarantee of solidarity among Member States. As stated in the Preamble of the TEU, the founding members of the Union aimed to 'deepen the solidarity between their peoples' through the creation of the Union. Furthermore, Article 3(3) TEU articulates that the Union shall promote 'economic, social and territorial cohesion, and solidarity among Member States'. Additionally, Article 122(1) TFEU refers to 'a spirit of solidarity between Member States' in cases of emergency in the context of economic policy.

The value of solidarity, in connection with the value of equality, holds particular significance in the realm of fundamental rights. Chapter IV of the Charter of Fundamental Rights of the European Union is specifically dedicated to 'Solidarity', encompassing rights of a socio-economic nature based on the pursuit of redistributive justice. The Union can only partially achieve this goal, as many of the competences with a socio-economic impact remain within the authority of the Member States. However, the Union has competence in some particularly sensitive areas, such as the coordination of social security systems, the harmonisation of legislation in the field of social policy, and economic, social, and territorial cohesion policy.

The Court of Justice has emphasised the 'social purpose' of the Union and takes it into account when interpreting the Treaties:

> [S]ince the [Union] has thus not only an economic but also a social purpose, the rights under the provisions of the [TFEU] on the free movement of goods, persons, services and capital must be balanced against the objectives pursued by social policy, which include, as is clear from the first paragraph of Article [151 TFEU], inter alia, improved living and working conditions, so as to make possible their harmonisation while improvement is being maintained, proper social protection and dialogue between management and labour.[35]

[32] See the extensive work by S Peers *et al* (eds), *The Charter of Fundamental Rights. A Commentary* (Hart, 2014) and S Iglesias Sánchez, 'The Court and the Charter: The Impact of the Entry into Force of the Lisbon Treaty on the ECJ's Approach to Fundamental Rights' (2012) 49 *Common Market Law Review* 1565.

[33] See, in particular, Art 3(3)(1) TEU and Arts 8–10 and 157 TFEU.

[34] See Art 19 TFEU and legislation adopted in support of this legal basis: Council Directive 2000/43/EC implementing the principle of equal treatment between persons irrespective of racial or ethnic origin and Council Directive 2000/78/EC establishing a general framework for equal treatment in employment and occupation.

[35] Case C-341/05 *Laval un Partneri* EU:C:2007:809, para 105; and Case C-438/05 *International Transport Workers' Federation and Finnish Seamen's Union* EU:C:2007:772, para 79.

The value of solidarity carries both financial and redistributive implications, as is evident in the Union's budget and in the mutual trust that the Member States maintain with each other. It is in this context that the Court of Justice has described solidarity not only as a value, but also as a 'fundamental principle',[36] which is fully justiciable and can be used as a benchmark for assessing Union and Member State actions.[37] As stated by the Court of Justice:

> The principle of solidarity underpins the entire legal system of the European Union . . . and it is closely linked to the principle of sincere cooperation, laid down in Article 4(3) TEU, pursuant to which the European Union and the Member States are, in full mutual respect, to assist each other in carrying out tasks which flow from the Treaties. [This] principle not only obliges the Member States to take all the measures necessary to guarantee the application and effectiveness of EU law but also imposes on the EU institutions mutual duties to cooperate in good faith with the Member States . . . .[38]

This dimension of the value of solidarity has important practical implications, for instance, in the energy sector, where energy solidarity among Member States is particularly significant.[39] Likewise, the adoption of a system of financial conditionality, which is subject to compliance with the Union's values, has been deemed compatible with the Treaties because, among other reasons, it enhances trust between Member States and bolsters the mechanisms of redistributive solidarity within the Union.[40] The Court of Justice has also highlighted the value of solidarity in defining the statute of European citizenship, which is characterised by a bond of solidarity and good faith, based on a reciprocity of rights and duties between an individual and the Union.[41]

3.4. Rule of Law

The value of the rule of law is deeply rooted in the constitutional traditions of the Member States, and it has taken its current form primarily from the constitutional practices in Europe during the nineteenth and twentieth centuries. As stated by Advocate General Cruz Villalón:

> The idea of a Union based on the rule of law, hereinafter the value of the rule of law, requires not only respect for fundamental rights and that the institutions be subject to judicial review of the compatibility of their acts with the constitutional charter, the Treaties, and general principles of law, but also that secondary legislation adopted by the European Union be created democratically, which implies equal participation of all the Member States, be it directly, through Members of the European Parliament or through the representatives of the Member States at the European Council or Council, or indirectly in the context of a delegation of Council powers or, now, of Parliament and Council powers.[42]

The value of the rule of law has a relevant impact on the functioning of all public institutions and the stability of liberal democracies. It acts as a structural safeguard to prevent the arbitrary exercise of power, especially when such abuse results in systemic malfunctioning of the institutions.

The Court of Justice has repeatedly referred to the rule of law as a 'constitutional guarantee'[43] that embodies the value of a 'Union based on the rule of law'.[44] As the Court of Justice has consistently stated:

[36] Case C-848/19 P *Germany v Poland* EU:C:2021:598, para 38.
[37] ibid, paras 42–43.
[38] ibid, para 41.
[39] ibid.
[40] Case C-156/21 *Hungary v European Parliament and Council* EU:C:2022:97, para 129, and Case C-157/21 *Poland v European Parliament and Council* EU:C:2022:98, para 147.
[41] Case C-181/23 *Commission v Malta* EU:C:2025:283, para 97.
[42] Case C-336/09 P *Poland v Commission* EU:C:2011:860, Opinion of AG Cruz Villalón, para 30.
[43] Joined Cases C-584/10 P and C-595/10 P *Commission and Others v Kadi (II)* EU:C:2013:518, para 66.
[44] ibid.

> [T]he [Union] is based on the rule of law, inasmuch as neither its Member States nor its institutions can avoid review of the conformity of their acts with the basic constitutional charter, the [Treaties], which established a complete system of legal remedies and procedures designed to enable the Court of Justice to review the legality of acts of the institutions.[45]

Consequently, the rule of law requires judicial review, ensuring that the Union's institutions, bodies, offices and agencies are accountable for the conformity of their acts, especially with the Treaties.[46] The rule of law mandates a *complete* system of judicial review, encompassing all areas of public power and leaving no room for immunity.[47]

The value of the rule of law is a binding norm that produces its legal effects throughout the Union and its Member States, regardless of the policy area.[48] For example, if a Member State undermines the value of the rule of law by interfering with judicial independence, this course of action can breach Articles 2 and 19 TEU. This was the outcome in cases concerning, for example, the temporary reduction of salaries for national judges,[49] a Member State's failure to comply with the judgments of the Court of Justice,[50] or national legislation imposing severe disciplinary measures on judges that indermined their independence.[51] In such cases, the Court of Justice declared itself competent to review the legality of Member State actions that posed a threat to the Union's value of the rule of law.[52]

The value of the rule of law also has a financial dimension in the Union and its Member States. The Union budget acts as a redistributive instrument, promoting financial solidarity among Member States. Nevertheless, the distribution of Union funds must be accompanied by guarantees of sound financial management, including robust mechanisms to fight corruption and to protect the Union's budget. Without these measures, the redistributive function of the EU budget and the mutual trust among Member States would be seriously undermined. As a result, the EU legislature introduced Regulation 2020/2092,[53] also known as the financial conditionality Regulation, which enables the Council, upon a proposal from the Commission, to suspend or reduce the disbursement of EU funds to a Member State in case of a violation of the rule of law that affects or seriously risks affecting the sound financial management of the Union budget or the protection of the financial interests of the Union. The Court of Justice has upheld the legality of this Regulation, emphasising that its primary objective is to safeguard the Union's financial interests.[54]

[45] Joined Cases C-402/05 P and C-415/05 *P Kadi and Al Barakaat International Foundation v Council and Commission* EU:C:2008:461, para 281; *Kadi (II)* (n 43) para 66; Case C-550/09 *E and F*, EU:C:2010:382, para 44; *Poland v Commission* (n 42) para 30; and Case C-335/09 P *Poland v Commission* EU:C:2012:385, para 42.

[46] Case C-533/10 *Civad* EU:C:2012:347, para 30.

[47] Joined Cases C-399/06 P and C-403/06 P *Hassan and Ayadi v Council and Commission* EU:C:2009:748, paras 69–75, and, more recently, Case C-548/09 P *Bank Melli Iran v Council* EU:C:2011:735.

[48] See, for example, in the field of restrictive measures adopted by the EU legislature, Case T-290/17 *Edward Stavystskyi v Council* EU:T:2019:37, paras 67–69.

[49] Case C-64/16 *Associação Sindical dos Juízes Portugueses* EU:C:2018:117, paras 30–34 and 42.

[50] Case C-441/17 R *Commission v Poland* EU:C:2018:877, para 102.

[51] See, inter alia, the judgments handed down in connection with the changes to the Polish judicial statute, including those in Case C-192/18 *Commission v Poland* EU:C:2019:924; Case C-558/18 *Miasto Łowicz* EU:C:2020:234; Case C-585/18 *AK* EU:C:2019:982; and Case C-619/18 *Commission v Poland* EU:C:2019:531.

[52] Case C-216/18 *PPU Minister for Justice and Equality v LM* EU:C:2018:586, para 72.

[53] Regulation (EU, Euratom) 2020/2092 of the European Parliament and of the Council of 16 December 2020 on a general regime of conditionality for the protection of the Union budget [2020] OJ L433I/1.

[54] Case C-156/21 *Hungary v European Parliament and Council* EU:C:2022:97, paras 129ff; and Case C-157/21 *Poland v European Parliament and Council* EU:C:2022:98, paras 147ff.

II. A UNION ON THE MOVE: REFORM, ACCESSION AND WITHDRAWAL

Unlike a state, the Union has a remarkable capacity to adapt its constitutional features to evolving socio-political and economic circumstances. The rules governing the revision of the Treaties, despite their apparent rigidity, are more flexible than they appear. The Union's ongoing process of enlargement to new Member States is a strong indication of its ability to adapt to emerging geopolitical realities. Additionally, the Treaties include a procedure for voluntary withdrawal from the Union. The Union's ability to reform, expand, and contract is central to the success of the project. This section will outline the legal foundations and procedures through which the Union adapts to a changing environment.

1. Treaty Reform

Article 48 TEU sets out the general framework governing the reform of the Treaties, broadly referred to as the 'review' procedures. This provision includes three procedures through which the Treaties can be amended: the ordinary revision procedure; the simplified revision procedure; and the *passerelle* clauses. In addition, the Treaties include other means of reform, which will be discussed below.

1.1. *The Ordinary Revision Procedure*

Article 48(1)–(5) TEU outlines the rules for the standard review procedure, known as the 'ordinary revision procedure'. These provisions are inspired by the previous Treaties[55] and organise the process into three stages:

(1) The right of initiative for an ordinary revision procedure rests with any Member State, the European Parliament, or the Commission, which submits a proposal to the Council. The Council then forwards the proposal to the European Council, where a decision by a simple majority determines whether the proposal will be 'examined'. The European Council also decides whether to convene a Convention or a conference of representatives, depending on the ambition and scope of the proposal. The fact that this decision is made by a simple majority originates from the European Council of Milan in 1985, where the proposal that led to the Single European Act was referred to an intergovernmental conference following a majority vote, rather than a unanimous one.[56]

(2) If a Convention is convened, it examines the proposals for amendments and adopts by consensus a recommendation to a conference of representatives of the Governments of the Member States, convened by the President of the Council, for the purpose of determining by common accord the amendments to be made to the Treaties.

(3) Following the signing and ratification in all Member States, the amendments enter into force. However, if, two years after the signing of the amendments, four-fifths of the Member States have ratified it and one or more Member States have encountered difficulties in proceeding with ratification, Article 48(5) TEU provides that 'the matter shall be referred to the European Council'. In other words, the onus is placed on the European Council to reach a consensus among the Member States, with the aim of facilitating ratification in the Member State/s concerned.

[55] M Böttner, 'The Treaty Amendment Procedures and the Relationship between Article 31(3) TEU and the General Bridging Clause of Article 48(7) TEU' (2015) 11 *European Constitutional Law Review* 499.

[56] Van Middelaar (n 4) 100.

1.2. *The Simplified Revision Procedure*

To avoid the risks associated with a ratification process across all 27 Member States, Article 48(6) TEU introduces a fast-track procedure that does not require the convening of a Convention or an intergovernmental conference. The simplified procedure is solely limited to the revision of provisions of Part Three of the TFEU, which governs the Union's internal policies and actions. This procedure cannot be used to increase the competences conferred on the Union in the Treaties,[57] nor to 'encroach on the Union's exclusive competences'.[58]

The simplified revision process consists of three stages.

(1) A Member State, the European Parliament or the Commission has the authority to submit to the European Council a proposal for revising all or part of the provisions of Part Three of the TFEU.
(2) The European Council adopts a decision by unanimity after consulting the European Parliament, the Commission, and, where appropriate, the European Central Bank. It should be noted that the European Council enacts a *decision*, an act of the Union, and not a draft international treaty subject to signature and ratification.
(3) Following the unanimous vote in the European Council, the Member States 'approve' the decision 'in accordance with their respective constitutional requirements', after which the reform enters into force. It should be noted that Article 48(6) TEU does not refer the matter to the Member States for ratification, but for 'approval'. The Member States can therefore decide, depending on their internal constitutional arrangements, the appropriate course of action to give their consent to the amendment of the Treaties.

The simplified revision procedure was used for the first time in 2011 to introduce an additional paragraph to Article 136 TFEU. The amendment was adopted by Decision 2011/199, which has been in force since 1 May 2013, establishing a legal basis for the introduction of the European Stability Mechanism. The Decision was challenged before the Court of Justice in the case of *Pringle*,[59] where the Court stated that a Decision of the European Council amending the Treaties by way of the simplified revision procedure is subject to judicial review by the Court of Justice.

1.3. Passerelle *Clauses*

Article 48(7) TEU introduces a separate procedure for amending the voting rules in the Council and the type of legislative procedure set out in the Treaties. For voting rules in the Council, the purpose of the *passerelle* is to change the rule requiring unanimity to one allowing a qualified majority. In relation to legislative procedures, the *passerelle* provides for the permanent transformation of a special legislative procedure into an ordinary legislative procedure. The *passerelle* offers a way to amend a specific aspect of the Treaties (namely, voting rules and legislative procedures) without undertaking an ordinary or simplified revision procedure.[60]

The use of *passerelles* requires three conditions to be met: unanimous approval in the European Council; consent of the European Parliament; and no objection from a national parliament of a Member state within six months of notification.

In the specific case of *passerelles* affecting voting rules in the Council, Article 48(7)(1) TEU states that the procedure does not apply to decisions with military implications or those in the

[57] Art 48(6), third subpara TEU.
[58] Case C-370/12 *Pringle* EU:C:2012:756, para 52.
[59] ibid.
[60] It should be noted that the German Federal Constitutional Court has ruled that the use of *passerelles* is tantamount to a reform of the Treaty, thus imposing specific constitutional constraints on the German Government before it votes in the Council in favour of the use of these clauses.

area of defence. In addition, the Treaties provide for specific *passerelles* in some policy areas, which will be referenced in section1.4.2 of this chapter.

To date, the general *passerelles* under Article 48(7) TEU have not been put into practice. However, in 2019, the Commission made two proposals pursuant to Article 48(7) TEU in the fields of taxation[61] and energy.[62] In 2024, the debate on the use of *passerelles* was reactivated within the institutions, with the aim of making use of this procedure in the Common Foreign and Security Policy (CFSP).[63]

1.4. *Other Procedures for the Revision or Supplementing of the Treaties*

Besides the standard procedures outlined in Article 48 TEU, the Treaties encompass other mechanisms that introduce specific *passerelles* or additional requirements beyond the standard legislative processes, aiming to strengthen the legitimacy of Union actions. These procedures can be divided into two categories, depending on whether they require the approval of all Member States in accordance with their respective constitutional requirements.

1.4.1. Procedures Requiring Approval by all Member States in Accordance with their Respective Constitutional Requirements

Citizenship of the Union. The Council, acting unanimously in accordance with a special legislative procedure and after obtaining the consent of the European Parliament, may adopt provisions to strengthen or to add to the rights listed in Article 20(2) TFEU. These provisions shall enter into force once approved by the Member States in accordance with their respective constitutional requirements.[64]

Accession to the European Convention on Human Rights. The Council must act unanimously to approve the Union's accession to the European Convention for the Protection of Human Rights and Fundamental Freedoms. The decision concluding such an agreement will enter into force once it has been approved by the Member States in accordance with their respective constitutional requirements.[65]

Electoral arrangements for the European Parliament. The Council, acting unanimously on a proposal from the European Parliament and after obtaining its consent, shall lay down the necessary provisions for the election of Members of the European Parliament by direct universal suffrage in accordance with 'a uniform procedure in all Member States' or in accordance with principles common to all Member States.[66] These provisions shall enter into force after they have been approved by the Member States in accordance with their respective constitutional requirements.

Jurisdiction of the Court of Justice in matters of intellectual or industrial property. The Council, acting unanimously, in accordance with a special legislative procedure and after consulting the European Parliament, may adopt provisions conferring jurisdiction on the Court of Justice of the European Union in disputes concerning the application of acts adopted on the basis of the Treaties establishing European intellectual property rights. These provisions

[61] Commission, 'Toward a more efficient and democratic decision making in EU tax policy' (Communication) COM(2019) 8 final.

[62] Commission, 'A more efficient and democratic decision making in EU energy and climate policy' (Communication) COM(2019) 177 final.

[63] See European Parliamentary Research Service, 'Qualified majority voting in EU common foreign and security policy' report (2023).

[64] Art 25(2) TFEU.

[65] ibid, Art 218(8).

[66] ibid, Art 223(1).

come into force following approval by the Member States in accordance with their respective constitutional requirements.[67]

The Union's own resources. The Council, acting unanimously and in accordance with a special legislative procedure after consulting the European Parliament, shall adopt a decision laying down the provisions relating to the system of own resources of the Union. Within this framework, it is possible to establish new categories of own resources or abolish an existing category. Such a decision will only come into force once the Member States have approved it in accordance with their respective constitutional requirements.[68]

1.4.2. Procedures not Requiring Approval by all the Member States in Accordance with their Respective Constitutional Requirements

Common Foreign and Security Policy. In addition to the general rules on *passerelles* described above, Article 31(3) TEU contains a specific *passerelle* applicable only to the CFSP. This *passerelle* is less cumbersome than the general one outlined in Article 48(7) TEU, as it does not require the approval of all Member States in accordance with their respective constitutional requirements. For foreign and security policy, the European Council may adopt a decision by unanimity, allowing the Council to act by qualified majority in cases where unanimity is needed, provided that the decision does not have military or defence implications.[69]

Other Specific Passerelles. The Treaties include specific *passerelles* in certain policy areas that, unlike Article 48(7) TEU, do not require notification to national parliaments with a right of objection. This applies in the following policy areas:

- Social policy: certain matters listed in Article 153.1(d), (f) and (g) *(health and safety, working conditions, social security, information and consultation of workers, etc)* can be subject to a *passerelle* to amend the special legislative procedure into an ordinary legislative procedure.[70]
- Environment: certain matters listed in Article 192.1(a)–(c) *(environmental taxes, rules on planning, management of water resources, and land use)* include a *passerelle* in the third subparagraph allowing the Council, acting unanimously on a proposal from the Commission and after consulting the European Parliament, the Economic and Social Committee and the Committee of the Regions, to make the ordinary legislative procedure applicable.[71]
- Enhanced cooperation: where a provision of the Treaties that may be applied in the context of enhanced cooperation states that the Council, acting unanimously in accordance with the arrangements laid down in Article 330 TFEU, may adopt a decision providing that it shall act by qualified majority. Where the Treaties provide that the Council shall adopt acts under a special legislative procedure, the Council, acting unanimously, may adopt a decision allowing it to act under the ordinary legislative procedure.[72]

Family law with cross-border implications. The Council, acting unanimously after consulting the European Parliament and on a proposal from the Commission, may adopt a decision determining those aspects of family law with cross-border implications that may be the subject of

[67] ibid, Art 262.

[68] ibid, Art 311, third para.

[69] See Commission, 'A stronger actor on the global stage: more efficient decision-making in the Common Foreign and Security Policy' (Communication) COM(2018) 647 final.

[70] Art 153(2), fourth subpara TFEU. See Commission, 'Making social policy more efficient in lawmaking: identifying areas where more use should be made of qualified majority voting' (Communication) COM(2019) 186 final.

[71] Art 192(2) TFEU. In this regard, see Commission, 'A more efficient and democratic decision making in EU energy and climate policy.' (Communication) COM(2019) 177 final.

[72] Art 333 TFEU.

acts adopted under the ordinary legislative procedure rather than the special legislative procedure, which is the general rule in this area. However, although this *passerelle* does not require approval by all Member States, the measure can be vetoed by a national parliament if it objects within six months of being notified.[73]

Judicial cooperation in criminal matters. In this policy area, the following measures allow for the extension of provisions in the Treaties:

- The Council may identify other specific aspects of criminal procedure subject to the establishment of minimum rules, beyond those listed in Article 82(2) TFEU, acting unanimously and after obtaining the consent of the European Parliament.[74]
- The Council, acting unanimously and after obtaining the consent of the European Parliament, may identify other areas of particularly serious crime with a cross-border dimension that may be subject to the establishment of minimum rules concerning the definition of criminal offences and sanctions, as provided for in Article 83(1) TFEU, third subparagraph.[75]
- The European Council may broaden the powers of the European Public Prosecutor's Office to combat serious crime with a cross-border dimension, acting unanimously after obtaining the consent of the European Parliament and after consulting the Commission.[76]

Economic and monetary policy. The Council, or the Council and the European Parliament acting jointly in accordance with the ordinary legislative procedure, may of provisions to the Statute of the ESCB and of the ECB (Protocol No 4), specifically those listed in Article 129(3) TFEU.[77]

Court of Justice of the European Union. The European Parliament and the Council, acting in accordance with the ordinary legislative procedure, may amend the provisions of the Statute, with the exception of Title I and Article 64. The European Parliament and the Council shall act either at the request of the Court of Justice and after consultation with the Commission, or based on a proposal from the Commission and following consultation with the Court of Justice.[78]

European Investment Bank. The Council, acting unanimously in accordance with a special legislative procedure, may amend the Statute of the European Investment Bank either at the request of the European Investment Bank and after consulting the European Parliament and the Commission, or on a proposal from the Commission following consultation with the European Parliament and the European Investment Bank.[79]

1.5. *Limits to the Reform of the Treaties*

In contrast to the practice of international law, Union law allows the reform of the Treaties only through the procedures specified in Article 48 TEU and other specific provisions cited above. In international law, parties to a treaty can amend it by mutual agreement among all signatories, a pragmatic approach that allows them to bypass the reform procedures outlined in the treaty itself, if any. Academic debates have arisen over whether the Union's Treaties can be amended outside the rules and procedures outlined in Article 48 TEU.[80] This course of action, which

[73] ibid, Art 81(3).
[74] ibid, Art 82(2)(d).
[75] ibid, Art 83(1), third subpara.
[76] ibid, Art 86(4).
[77] ibid, Arts 126(14), second subpara, 127(6) and 129(3).
[78] ibid, Art 281, second subpara.
[79] ibid, Art 308, third subpara.
[80] See, for example, the debate between M Deliège-Sequaris, 'Révision des traités européens en dehors des procédures prévues' (1980) 1 *Cahiers de droit européen* 539, and J-V Louis, 'Quelques considérations sur la révision des traités instituant les Communautés' (1980) 1 *Cahiers de droit européen* 553, and the bibliography cited therein.

found support in the Treaty establishing the European Coal and Steel Community (ECSC), was twice put into practice in the past to reform the Treaties without following the outlined revision procedure.[81] However, the Court of Justice has consistently rejected this interpretation in a consistent line of case law, declaring the unlawfulness of any reform outside the procedures specified in Article 48 TEU, whether through Article 352 TFEU[82] or by common agreement among Member States.[83] In *United Kingdom v Council*, the Court of Justice stated that 'the rules regarding the manner in which the [Union] institutions arrive at their decisions are laid down in the Treaty and are not at the disposal of the Member States or of the institutions themselves'.[84] Consequently, 'the Treaty can only be modified by means of the amendment procedure carried out in accordance with Article [48 TEU]'.[85]

A different matter is whether the Treaties contain any substantive limits, any areas excluded from amendment. This issue has been the subject of prolonged debate, especially following case law from the Court of Justice that prevented the Union from concluding or giving effect to international agreements that posed a serious risk to its core values. According to some authors, this restriction on the Union's powers in its external relations also applies to the revision procedures of Article 48 TEU.[86] In rulings such as *Kadi I*, the Court of Justice introduced substantive limits on the enforcement of international law within the Union, particularly in the protection of fundamental rights.[87] In another line of case law starting with *Ruiz Zambrano*, the Court of Justice referred to the 'genuine enjoyment of the substance of the rights attached to the status of citizen of the Union'[88] as a limit on Member State action even within the scope of their own exclusive competences, such as in cases of immigration policy affecting nationals of third countries.

More recently, the Court of Justice has openly endorsed the notion of a constitutional core of the Union, protected from international and national interference, and has identified this core with the values outlined in Article 2 TEU. After a series of events in which several Member States openly questioned the Union's core values, particularly the rule of law, the case law described these values as 'the very identity of the European Union as a common legal order'.[89] This description indicates the presence of a constitutional core within the Union's legal framework. This core can be identified as the areas that are immune to any amendments, including through the review procedures under Article 48 TEU.

The existence of substantive limits to Treaty reform resembles the position taken by the constitutional courts of several Member States. According to a well-established practice in some national constitutional courts, which will be discussed in more detail in chapter ten, there are immutable or unamendable provisions in the Constitution that are excluded from the reform process. While nothing prevents a sovereign nation from amending its Constitution, if the amendment concerns one of the immutable provisions, it would amount to regime change

[81] Amendments made by a Treaty amending the ECSC Treaty of 27 October 1956 and the Convention of 25 March 1957. It should be noted that both amendments were agreed during a transitional period which prevented the use of Art 96 of the ECSC Treaty.

[82] Opinion of the Court 2/94, EU:C:1996:140, para 30.

[83] Case 59/75 *Manghera* EU:C:1976:14, paras 19–21; and Case 43/75 *Defrenne II* EU:C:1976:56, paras 57–58.

[84] Case C-68/86 *United Kingdom v Council* EU:C:1988:85, para 38.

[85] *Defrenne II* (n 83) para 58.

[86] See JL Da Cruz Vilaça and N Piçarra, 'Y a-t-il des limites matérielles à la révision des traités instituant les Communautés européennes?' (1993) 29 *Cahiers de droit européen* 3; S Adam and F Mena Parra, 'The European Stability Mechanism Through the Legal Meanderings of the Union's Constitutionalism: A Comment on Pringle' (2013) 38 *European Law Review* 848, and D Sarmiento, 'The EU's Constitutional Core' in A Sáiz Arnáiz and C Alcoberro Llivina (eds), *National Constitutional Identity and European Integration* (Intersentia, 2013).

[87] Case C-402/05 P *Kadi and Al Barakaat International Foundation v Council and Commission* EU:C:2008:461.

[88] Case C-34/09 *Ruiz Zambrano* EU:C:2011:124.

[89] Case C-156/21 *Hungary v European Parliament and Council* EU:C:2022:97, para 127; Case C-157/21 *Poland v European Parliament and Council* EU:C:2022:98, para 145, and Case C-769/22 *Commission v Hungary* EU:C:2026:326, para 499.

rather than a constitutional amendment. The Union remains in its early stages of development, and it is uncertain whether such 'unamendable' content of the Treaties actually exists. For now, it can be stated that a constitutional core has been established, and it is described as the Union's 'very identity'. In this author's view, any amendment to this 'very identity' would involve a broader transformation of the Union, rather than a revision of the Treaties.

2. Accession of New Member States

The European Union is an organisation open to any 'European State', as established in Article 49 TEU. The notion of a 'European State' must be understood, as the Commission has argued,[90] in both geographical and historical terms. This means that, in addition to a territorial connection to the continent, the country must have been considered 'European' at some point in time. This approach explains the opening of accession negotiations with Turkey in 2005, a country that has been considered, despite its geographical proximity to the Middle East, to be part of the European nations. The same criterion led to the Council's rejection of Morocco's application for membership in 1987.[91]

Besides being 'European', the applicant state must respect the values outlined in Article 2 TEU: democracy, freedom, equality, solidarity, the rule of law, and respect for human rights. The Court of Justice has reaffirmed these conditions of access in the case of *Wightman*, emphasising that

> the [Union] is composed of States which have freely and voluntarily committed themselves to those values, and EU law is thus based on the fundamental premise that each Member State shares with all the other Member States, and recognises that those Member States share with it, those same values.[92]

This requirement is mandatory both *before* and *after* accession, preventing a new Member State from backsliding in the future.[93]

The requirements for accession were codified in the 'Copenhagen criteria', adopted at the European Council held in Copenhagen on 21 and 22 June 1993.[94] Article 49 TEU implicitly references these criteria when it states that 'the conditions of eligibility agreed by the European Council shall be taken into account'.

The Copenhagen criteria extend beyond the values listed in Article 2 TEU, as they require candidate states to meet specific institutional and economic conditions. The requirements can be summarised as follows:

- The political criterion: stability of institutions guaranteeing democracy, the rule of law, human rights and respect for and protection of minorities.
- The economic criterion: a functioning market economy, and the capacity to cope with competition pressures and market forces within the Union.

[90] K Lenaerts and P Van Nuffel, *EU Constitutional Law (*Oxford University Press, 2021) 62ff.

[91] [1987] OJ C 9, pt 2.2.19.

[92] Case C-621/18 *Wightman* EU:C:2018:999, para 63, as well as Case C-216/18 *PPU Minister for Justice and Equality* EU:C:2018:586, para 35.

[93] Case C-896/19 *Repubblika* EU:C:2021:311, paras 63–64, and Case C-769/22 *Commission v Hungary* EU:C:2026:326, para 521.

[94] On the Copenhagen criteria, see M Cremona, 'EU Enlargement: Solidarity and Conditionality' (2005) 30 *European Law Review* 3; D Kochenov, *EU Enlargement and the Failure of Conditionality: Pre-Accession Conditionality in the Fields of Democracy and the Rule of Law* (Kluwer Law, 2008) 358ff; AF Tatham, *Enlargement of the European Union* (Kluwer Law International 2009) ch 8; and A Williams, 'Enlargement of the Union and Human Rights Conditionality: A Policy of Distinction?' (2000) 25 *European Law Review* 601.

- The *acquis communautaire* criterion: administrative and institutional capacity to effectively assume the *acquis* and to take on the obligations of membership.

The Union's own ability to integrate new members while maintaining the momentum of European integration is also a key consideration ('absorption capacity' or 'integration capacity'). In any event, the Union retains the right to determine when a candidate country has fulfilled the Copenhagen criteria and the appropriate time to agree on the accession of the candidate state.

According to Article 49 TEU, the accession process starts with a formal request from the applicant state addressed to the Council. The application is then forwarded to the European Parliament and the national parliaments. In the following stage, the European Parliament gives its consent by a majority of its members, and the Commission is consulted. Ultimately, the Council makes a unanimous decision after assessing whether the Copenhagen criteria are satisfied. In practice, the Council adopts a preliminary decision, before the final approval, to begin the negotiation process. Once the negotiations are concluded, an agreement on the conditions of admission and adjustments to the Treaties is reached between the Member States and the applicant State. The agreement is submitted for ratification by all contracting states in accordance with their respective constitutional requirements.

The conditions of accession, along with any necessary adjustments to the Treaties, are set out in an Act annexed to the Accession Treaty. It is important to note that any adjustments to the Treaties must be strictly limited to what is essential for achieving the aims of the accession of the new Member State(s).[95] The accession process will also result in the amendment of secondary legislation, which may be introduced *explicitly* through an authorisation in the Accession Treaty, or *tacitly*[96] if there is any incompatibility between earlier secondary legislation and the Accession Treaty. In this regard, the Court of Justice has clarified the definition of 'necessary amendments' to secondary legislation via the Act of Accession, stating that they will be strictly confined to the 'amendments necessary to ensure the full applicability of acts of the institutions to the new Member States and which are intended, with that in mind, to complement those acts in the long term'.[97]

3. Withdrawal from the Union

Until the entry into force of the Lisbon Treaty in 2009, the Treaties did not provide for a procedure by which a Member State could withdraw from the Union. Due to the supranational nature of the Union, which prevents a state from withdrawing through the usual routes of unilateral denunciation of an international treaty, a Member State's withdrawal could only occur through the revision procedures specified in the Treaties. This framework changed with the introduction of Article 50 TEU, which sets out a specific procedure for a Member State's voluntary withdrawal from the Union.

[95] According to the Court of Justice, 'provisions in an Act of Accession which permit exceptions to or derogations from rules laid down by the EC Treaty must be interpreted restrictively with reference to the Treaty provisions in question and *must be limited to what is absolutely necessary in order to attain its objective*' (emphasis added). See, to that effect, Case C-420/07 *Apostolides* EU:C:2009:271, para 35; Case C-539/13 *Merck Canada* EU:C:2015:87, para 25; and Case C-681/16 *Pfizer Ireland Pharmaceuticals, Operations Support Group* EU:C:2018:484, para 41. However, in some cases the strict interpretation must be projected on rules of secondary law and not on the Act of Accession. This, for example, was the case regarding the derogation of free movement of goods in the territory of Gibraltar, the interpretation of which required a restrictive reading of the applicability of a directive in order to maintain the integrity of the derogation provided for in the Act concerning the conditions of accession of the Kingdom of Denmark, Ireland and the United Kingdom of Great Britain and Northern Ireland. In that regard, see Case C-267/16 *Albert Buhagiar and Others* EU:C:2018:26, para 65.

[96] Case C-413/04 Parliament *v Council* EU:C:2006:741, paras 31–38; Case C-414/04 *Parliament v Council* EU:C:2006:742, paras 29–36; Case C-273/04 *Poland v Council EU:C:2007:622*, paras 45–51.

[97] Case C-413/04 *Parliament v Council* EU:C:2006:741, para 32.

The withdrawal process is outlined in Article 50 TEU and comprises four stages:

(1) The withdrawing Member State, after an internal decision in line with its constitutional requirements, notifies the European Council of its intention.
(2) Following the notification, negotiations for withdrawal take place between the withdrawing Member State and the Union. These negotiations, insofar as they seek to conclude an international agreement between the Union and the withdrawing Member State, are conducted in accordance with Article 218(3) TFEU. During these negotiations, the representative of the withdrawing Member State does not participate in discussions or decisions of the Council or the European Council concerning the withdrawal.
(3) Once negotiations are completed, the Council concludes the agreement on behalf of the Union, acting by qualified majority, after obtaining the consent of the European Parliament. It should be noted that, unlike an Accession Treaty, the withdrawal agreement is a bilateral agreement concluded between the withdrawing state *and the Union*, not between the withdrawing state and the individual Member States. As a result, the withdrawal agreement cannot introduce any amendments to the Treaties, and the negotiations must always respect the Union's constitutional framework enshrined in the Treaties.
(4) The Treaties cease to apply to the withdrawing state from the date of entry into force of the withdrawal agreement or, failing that, two years after the notification of withdrawal, unless the European Council, in agreement with the state concerned, unanimously decides to extend that period. In the *Wightman* case, the Court of Justice was asked to interpret Article 50 TEU to determine whether a notification of withdrawal request is revocable. In its judgment, the Court of Justice stated that the withdrawing state may unilaterally revoke its notification of withdrawal request, provided that the revocation is formulated in 'clear and unconditional terms' and is made within the aforementioned two-year period (or its extension).[98]

As long as the withdrawal has not taken effect,

> notification [of withdrawal] does not have the effect of suspending the application of EU law in the Member State that has given notice of its intention to withdraw from the European Union and, consequently, EU law . . . continues in full force and effect in that State until the time of its actual withdrawal from the European Union.[99]

Withdrawal from the Union means that any future attempt to rejoin the Union must follow the ordinary accession process outlined in Article 49 TEU. No special arrangements can be included in the withdrawal agreement for a hypothetical future re-entry scenario. This is clearly set out in Article 50(5) TEU, which states that 'if a State which has withdrawn from the Union asks to rejoin, its request shall be subject to the procedure referred to in Article 49'.

The withdrawal procedure was implemented for the first time in 2017, following a referendum in the United Kingdom held on 23 June 2016. Nearly a year later, on 29 March 2017, the United Kingdom officially notified the European Council of its intention to withdraw from the Union. From that point on, the United Kingdom and the Union negotiated a withdrawal agreement under Article 50 TEU. The agreement was signed, ratified, and came into force on 31 January 2020 (midnight Brussels time), the date on which the United Kingdom effectively withdrew from the Union.

The EU–UK withdrawal agreement covers various matters, including the rights of British and European citizens who exercised free movement before the withdrawal from the Union, the settlement of the United Kingdom's outstanding financial obligations, and a transitional period allowing for the applicability of the Treaties in the United Kingdom (the 'transition

[98] Case C-621/18 *Wightman* EU:C:2018:999, para 71.
[99] Case C-327/18 *PPU RO* EU:C:2018:733, para 45; and Case C-661/17 *MA and Others* EU:C:2019:53, para 54.

period') until 31 December 2020. It also includes, among other provisions, a Protocol on Ireland/Northern Ireland, which was at the centre of rising tensions between the United Kingdom and the European Union due to commitments made between the United Kingdom and the Republic of Ireland under the Good Friday Agreement in 1998 to maintain peace in the region. Both parties agreed to keep an open, borderless area between Northern Ireland and the Republic of Ireland. However, the Good Friday Agreement was severely affected by the reintroduction of controls on goods and persons following the United Kingdom's withdrawal from the internal market, a situation that led to the adoption of the Windsor Framework, an arrangement reached in 2023 to facilitate trade between Britain and Northern Ireland and, consequently, safeguard the Good Friday Agreement.

Before the expiry of the transition period, the United Kingdom and the Union negotiated an agreement on their future trade relationship, now formalised in the EU–UK Trade and Cooperation Agreement,[100] which became effective on 1 January 2021.[101] This bilateral framework creates a comprehensive partnership in areas including trade in goods and services, covering digital trade, intellectual property, public procurement, aviation and road transport, energy, and fisheries. The agreement also establishes coordination mechanisms in areas such as social security, police and judicial cooperation in criminal matters, and participation in EU programmes. In 2025, a 'political reset' in EU–UK relations was agreed following the arrival of a new government in Britain, leading to significant agreements on security and defence, access to UK fishing waters and youth mobility, and in December 2025 both parties agreed the UK's return to Erasmus+ from 2027.

4. Suspension of Treaty Rights: the Procedure of Article 7 TEU and Financial Conditionality

A Member State's obligations towards the Union cannot be terminated or suspended unilaterally by the Member State concerned, or through a collective decision of the other Member States acting outside the Treaty framework. Similarly, Member States cannot rely on the failure of other Member States to meet their obligations as a justification for violating Union law. As early as 1964, the Court of Justice ruled that the *exceptio non adimpleti contractus* maxim did not apply in Union law,[102] despite its long-standing tradition in international law.[103]

The Treaties outline two routes through which Member States' rights and obligations under Union law may be terminated or suspended: voluntary withdrawal from the Union in accordance with Article 50 TEU (see section II.3 of this chapter) and temporary suspension for breach of the Union's values, as specified in Article 7 TEU.

A temporary suspension of rights is a coercive measure that does not involve a formal expulsion of a Member State from the Union. If the European Council establishes the existence of a serious and persistent breach of the values referred to in Article 2 TEU, the Council

[100] Trade and cooperation agreement between the European Union and the European Atomic Energy Community, of the one part, and the United Kingdom of Great Britain and Northern Ireland, of the other part [2020] OJ L444/14.

[101] The Agreement was provisionally applied from 1 January 2021 and formally entered into force on 1 May 2021.

[102] Joined Cases 90/63 and 91/63 *Commission v Luxembourg and Belgium* EU:C:1964:80): 'the Treaty is not limited to creating reciprocal obligations between the different natural and legal persons to whom it is applicable, but establishes a new legal order which governs the powers, rights and obligations of the said persons, as well as the necessary procedures for taking cognizance of and penalizing any breach of it. Therefore, except where otherwise expressly provided, the basic concept of the Treaty requires that the Member States not take the law into their own hands. Therefore the fact that the Council failed to carry out its obligations cannot relieve the defendants from carrying out theirs'.

[103] F Fontanelli, 'The Invocation of the Exception of Non-Performance: A Case-Study on the Role and Application of General Principles of International Law of Contractual Origin' (2012) 1 *Cambridge Journal of International and Comparative Law* 119.

may suspend 'certain of the rights deriving from the application of the Treaties to the Member State in question'. This measure aims to address the root cause of the breach by modifying the conduct of the Member States.

The procedure in Article 7 TEU is divided into two stages: first, the Council, acting by a majority of four fifths of its members on a reasoned proposal from one third of the Member States, the European Parliament, or the Commission, may determine that there is a 'clear risk of a serious breach' by a Member State of the values set out in Article 2 TEU.[104] This finding requires a certain level of imminence and seriousness in the acts of the Member State concerned, and the burden of proof rests with the proponent of the measure. Before making this determination, the Council must hear the Member State concerned and may address recommendations to it. The Council's determination under Article 7(1) TEU is not subject to judicial review under Article 269 TFEU, which limits the Court of Justice's jurisdiction to reviewing the procedural stipulations of Article 7 TEU, at the request of the Member State concerned. This first stage does not entail the suspension of the Member State's rights.

The second stage requires the intervention of the European Council, as the only institution authorised to establish the 'existence of a serious and persistent breach' of the values referred to in Article 2 TEU by the Member State concerned. It should be emphasised that the European Council's determination does not pertain to a risk, but to the *existence of* a breach. Additionally, the violation must be *serious* and *persistent*, thereby ruling out occasional or sporadic conduct by the Member State involved. The European Council adopts its determination by unanimity, after inviting the Member State concerned to submit its observations, in a vote which must exclude the Member State concerned[105] and after securing the consent of the European Parliament. Only after this determination has been made may the Council, acting by qualified majority, decide to suspend certain Treaty rights of the Member State concerned.

The first attempt to trigger the procedure in Article 7 TEU took place in 2000, following the Freedom Party of Austria (FPÖ)'s entry into a coalition government in Austria, making it the first political party with historical connections to far-right ideology to join a Member State's government since the Second World War. Before the reforms introduced by the Nice Treaty in 2001, the procedure outlined in Article 7 TEU did not allow for the adoption of measures in the event of a *risk* of breach. Due to the absence of a serious and persistent breach of the values of Article 2 TEU, the European Council quietly closed the case only a few months later.[106] The limited outcome of this initial attempt to invoke Article 7 TEU led to the amendment of the provision and the introduction of the preliminary phase now found in Article 7(1) TEU, aimed at conduct which may *anticipate* a subsequent serious and persistent breach.

In the aftermath of the 2008 financial crisis, some Member States faced a serious institutional deterioration, particularly in Hungary and Poland. This development raised concerns over these countries' alignment with the Union's values in Article 2 TEU. Given the high thresholds set by Article 7 TEU, the Commission established a more pragmatic and cooperative mechanism to support and supplement the procedure outlined in Article 7 TEU. The Rule of Law Framework was introduced by a Commission Communication of 11 March 2014, a preventive tool to identify systemic threats to the rule of law in any of the Member States at an

[104] On the initiation of the first stage at the initiative of the European Parliament and the conditions for a parliamentary vote to agree to initiate the procedure, see Case C-650/18 *Hungary v European Parliament* EU:C:2021:426.

[105] Art 354(1) TFEU.

[106] On the Austrian precedent of 2000, see R Burchill, 'The Promotion and Protection of Democracy by Regional Organisations in Europe: The Case of Austria' (2001) 7 *European Public Law* 79.

early stage, fostering a dialogue that could eventually lead to the triggering of the procedure in Article 7 TEU.[107]

The Rule of Law Framework consists of three stages. In its first stage, the Commission gathers and examines information from the Member State concerned and conducts a case-by-case assessment, which may lead to the adoption of a 'rule of law opinion' to the Member State concerned. In the second stage, if the issue remains unresolved, the Commission issues a 'rule of law recommendation' to the Member State concerned. The recommendation explains the grounds for the Commission's concerns and proposes specific measures within a set timeframe. In the third stage, the Commission monitors the follow-up actions taken by the Member State in response to the recommendation. Only when there is no satisfactory follow-up within the designated time limit does the Commission evaluate the possibility of activating one of the mechanisms outlined in Article 7 TEU.

The Rule of Law Framework was first applied to Poland in January 2016 as a result of measures taken by the Polish Government and Parliament, aimed at limiting the powers of the Polish Constitutional Court and other judicial bodies. After several rounds of dialogue and the issuance of four successive rule of law recommendations, on 20 December 2017 the European Commission submitted a reasoned proposal to the Council under Article 7(1) TEU.[108]

Other initiatives have followed the Rule of Law Framework, emphasising dialogue and the use of *soft law*, such as the annual Rule of Law Review Cycle (commonly referred to as the 'Rule of Law Mechanism') launched in 2020. This tool establishes a procedure for an annual dialogue between the Commission, the Council, the European Parliament, Member States, their national parliaments, civil society, and other stakeholders. Central to the Rule of Law Mechanism are the annual Rule of Law Reports, which assess significant developments, both positive and negative, concerning the rule of law in each Member State. The Report addresses four pillars: the justice system; the anti-corruption framework; media freedom and pluralism; and other institutional issues related to checks and balances. Since 2022, the Reports include country-specific recommendations. The Mechanism is supported by the creation of a network of national contact points on the rule of law and by country visits and stakeholder consultations in each Member State.

Simultaneously, the Commission publishes the EU Justice Scoreboard annually, providing an overview of indicators on the efficiency, quality, and independence of the justice systems across Member States. The Scoreboard includes individual assessments of each Member State, aiming to support the improvement of national justice systems by offering objective, reliable, and comparable data. Additionally, the European Semester, an annual cycle of economic governance that includes country-specific assessments incorporates specific references and recommendations to Member States concerning the protection of the rule of law.

The procedure outlined in Article 7 TEU has proven to be politically burdensome and difficult to implement in practice. Member States are hesitant to suspend the rights of another country, while the procedure is structurally defective when an alleged breach occurs in two or more Member States, which can use mutual vetoes to block the activation of Article 7 TEU procedures. For nearly a decade, Hungary and Poland have experienced a significant erosion of the independence

[107] Commission, '*A new EU Framework to strengthen the Rule of Law*' *(Communication)* COM/2014/0158 final. In this respect, see C Closa, D Kochenov and JHH Weiler, 'Reinforcing Rule of Law Oversight in the European Union', EUI Working Papers RSCAS 2014/25; and L Pech, 'The Rule of Law as a Constitutional Principle of the European Union', Jean Monnet Working Paper No 04/09.

[108] On 12 September 2018 the European Parliament voted in favour of triggering an Art 7(1) TEU procedure against Hungary. See the Resolution of 12 September 2018 on a proposal calling on the Council to establish, pursuant to Article 7(1) of the Treaty on European Union, that there is a risk of a serious breach by Hungary of the values on which the Union is founded [2017/2131/(INL)].

of their judiciaries, with no measures taken by the Council or the European Council under Article 7 TEU, highlighting the limitations of this tool in the face of political pressures.

Following the introduction of a massive stimulus plan to address the economic consequences of the COVID-19 pandemic, the Union decided to establish yet another mechanism, this time to safeguard the Union's financial interests in Member States that do not adhere to specific rule-of-law standards. As an alternative to Article 7 TEU, a mechanism was designed to condition access to Union funds on proper compliance with the principles of the rule of law. This new approach led to the adoption of Regulation 2020/2092, which introduces a general regime of conditionality to protect the Union budget, also known as 'the financial conditionality Regulation'.[109]

The Regulation provides a broad definition of the rule of law in Article 2(a), which refers to 'the Union value enshrined in Article 2 TEU' and encompasses the principles of legality, legal certainty, prohibition of arbitrariness, effective judicial protection, separation of powers, non-discrimination, and equality before the law,[110] but it also introduces an 'indicative list' of breaches of the principles of the rule of law, which comprises three situations:

- endangering the independence of the judiciary;
- failing to prevent, correct or sanction arbitrary or unlawful decisions by public authorities, including by law-enforcement authorities, withholding financial and human resources affecting their proper functioning or failing to ensure the absence of conflicts of interest;
- limiting the availability and effectiveness of legal remedies, including through restrictive procedural rules and a lack of implementation of judgments, or limiting the effective investigation, prosecution or sanctioning of breaches of law.

The procedure under the financial conditionality Regulation begins with a written notification from the Commission addressed to the Member State concerned. This notification outlines the factual elements and specific grounds upon which the Commission bases its findings.[111] If the Commission is not satisfied with the Member State's response, it submits a proposal for an implementing decision on appropriate measures to the Council,[112] which must make a decision within one month, extendable by a further two months in exceptional circumstances, acting by qualified majority.[113]

The 'appropriate measures' proposed by the Commission and approved by the Council will differ depending on whether the Union budget is implemented through direct, indirect, or shared management with the Member States.[114] The 'appropriate measures' may include, among others, the suspension of payments, the prohibition to enter into new legal commitments, the suspension or reduction of disbursements, the reduction of pre-financing, or the suspension or early repayment of loans guaranteed by the Union budget.[115]

[109] Regulation 2020/2092 of the European Parliament and of the Council of 16 December 2020 on a general regime of conditionality for the protection of the Union budget [2020] OJ L433I/1. Unsurprisingly, the two Member States most affected by the Regulation immediately brought an action against it in the Court of Justice, which was eventually dismissed. See Case C-156/21 *Hungary v European Parliament and Council* EU:C:2022:97; and Case C-157/21 *Poland v European Parliament and Council* EU:C:2022:98.

[110] Article 2(a) Reg 2020/2092 defines the rule of law as 'the value of the Union as enshrined in Article 2 TEU. It comprises the principles of legality, which implies a transparent, democratic, pluralist and accountable legislative process; legal certainty; prohibition of arbitrariness of the executive; effective judicial protection, which includes access to justice, including in respect of fundamental rights, by independent and impartial courts; separation of powers; and non-discrimination and equality before the law. The rule of law shall be understood in the light of the other values and principles of the Union as enshrined in Article 2 TEU'.

[111] Art 6(1) Regulation 2020/2092.

[112] ibid, Art 6(7)–(9).

[113] ibid, Art 6(11).

[114] ibid, Art 5(1).

[115] ibid, Art 5(1).

The financial conditionality Regulation was challenged by Hungary and Poland in the Court of Justice.[116] In its judgment and in the Opinion of the Advocate General in this case, it was emphasised that the mechanism does not primarily aim to protect the rule of law as such, but rather to safeguard the Union budget by establishing a sufficient connection between breaches of the principles of the rule of law and the sound financial management of the Union budget or the protection of the Union's financial interests. This requirement is of practical importance, since the adoption of any 'appropriate measure', besides being proportionate, must demonstrate a genuine link or a serious risk of such a link between the rule of law breach and the impact on the Union budget. The financial conditionality Regulation cannot be used to address a regression of rule-of-law standards in a Member State in the abstract, but only to address the impact of such regression on the protection of the Union's financial interests.

In 2026, the Court of Justice stated that the values of Article 2 TEU are binding obligations on the Member State, which can justify initiating an infringement procedure against a Member State.[117] A self-standing violation of Article 2 TEU is compatible with the use of Article 7 TEU, a procedure that serves different aims and operates mostly at a political level. This avenue is nevertheless subject to various constraints: not every breach of Union law or of a Charter right amounts to a violation of Article 2 TEU, since such an expansion would exceed the Union's competence and come into conflict with Article 51(1) of the Charter.[118] An autonomous violation of Article 2 TEU is engaged only where the breach is "manifest and particularly serious," affecting one of the Union's foundational values in a manner incompatible with its identity as a common legal order, a threshold comparable to a violation of the "essence" of a fundamental right.[119] Nor may a Member State invoke national identity under Article 4(2) TEU to evade this obligation.[120]

III. THE TERRITORIAL AND TEMPORAL SCOPE OF THE UNION'S ACTIONS

1. Territorial Scope

Article 52(1) TEU states that the Treaties apply to the Member States listed therein. Therefore, the territorial scope of the Union's actions and its legal order extends throughout the physical space over which the Member States exercise their sovereign rights in accordance with international law. The Union has no territory of its own; it is the territory of the Member States, as defined by international law, that sets the territorial perimeter of legitimate Union action.

As a consequence of Article 52(1) TEU, Union law extends to the land, maritime zones, and airspace of the Member States. Concerning maritime areas, the Union has been a party to the 1982 United Nations Convention on the Law of the Sea since 1 April 1998. Accordingly, it exercises its competences in the maritime domain in accordance with the delimitation rules specified therein.[121]

[116] See Case C-156/21 *Hungary v European Parliament and Council* EU:C:2022:97; and Case C-157/21 *Poland v European Parliament and Council* EU:C:2022:98.

[117] Case C-769/22 *Commission v Hungary* EU:C:2026:326.

[118] Ibid, para 550

[119] Ibid, para 551

[120] Ibid, paras 557-562

[121] Council Decision 98/392/EC of 23 March 1998 concerning the conclusion by the European Community of the United Nations Convention on the Law of the Sea of 10 December 1982 and the Agreement of 28 July 1994 relating to the implementation of Part XI of that Convention. The Court of Justice has held that the Convention does not have direct effect (Case C-308/06 Intertanko and Others EU:C:2008:312). However, it is a valuable source of interpretation

Although Article 52(1) TEU is formulated in general terms, the Treaties include several special regimes applicable to particular territories, as detailed in Article 355 TFEU and further specified in the Accession Treaties of various Member States. For instance, the following territories merit specific mention:

- Overseas Countries and Territories (OCTs): Part Four TFEU sets out a special association regime for the OCTs, notable for their historic and political ties to certain Member States, principally France, the Netherlands and Denmark. The OCTs are territories connected to a Member State but not forming part of the Union's territory for the purposes of the Treaty. Union law does not directly apply in the OCTs, only the provisions of Part Four TFEU and the implementing decisions adopted thereunder govern their relationship with the Union. The Court of Justice recognises the unique status of these territories and has even acknowledged that a court of an OCT is a 'court or tribunal of a Member State' with the authority to refer questions for a preliminary ruling.[122]
- Outermost regions: Article 355(1) TFEU, read in conjunction with Article 349 TFEU, identifies the outermost regions as territories where Union law applies in full, subject to specific measures taking account of their structural social and economic situation, which is compounded by their remoteness, insularity, small size, difficult topography and climate, and economic dependence on a few products. The outermost regions currently comprise Guadeloupe, French Guiana, Martinique, Mayotte, Réunion, Saint Martin, the Azores, Madeira, and the Canary Islands as territories where Union law applies. These territories benefit from 'specific measures' aimed, in particular, 'at laying down the conditions of application of the Treaties to those regions'. These measures concern areas such as customs and trade policies, fiscal policy, free zones, agriculture and fisheries policies, conditions for the supply of raw materials and essential consumer goods, state aids, and the conditions of access to structural funds and to horizontal Union programmes as enumerated in Article 349 TFEU. The said measures are adopted by the Council, on a proposal from the Commission, and after consulting the European Parliament.[123] In some cases, special arrangements are introduced through an Accession Treaty, as with the Spanish autonomous cities of Ceuta and Melilla, covered in Article 25 of the Act of Accession of Spain and Portugal, which are formally not overseas territories but have a status with coincident features. As of 2014, the archipelago of Mayotte changed its status from OCT to an outermost region subject to the provisions of Article 355(1) TFEU.[124]
- European territories for whose external relations a Member State is responsible: Before the United Kingdom's departure from the Union, Gibraltar was included among these territories, subject to a special regime under Article 355(3) TFEU. The details of this regime were

for the resolution of cases where doubts arise as to the powers of the Union and the Member States in maritime space. In this respect, see eg Case C-347/10 *Salemink* EU:C:2012:17, para 33.

[122] Joined Cases C-100/89 and C-101/89 *Kaefer and Procacci* EU:C:1990:456, and Case C-260/90 *Leplat* EU:C:1992:66. On the OCTs and their special status, see L Tesoka and J Ziller (eds), *Union Européenne et outre-mers. Unis dans leur diversité* (Presses Universitaires d'Aix-Marseille, 2008), and D Kochenov (ed), *EU Law of the Overseas: Outermost Regions, Associated Overseas Countries and Territories, Territories Sui Generis* (Kluwer Law International 2011).

[123] Art 349 TFEU, first para.

[124] On the change of status of Mayotte, see the judgment in Joined Cases C-132/14 to C-136/14 *Parliament and Commission v Council* EU:C:2015:813 and European Council Decision 2012/419/EU, of 11 July 2012 amending the status of Mayotte with regard to the European Union [2012] OJ L204/131.It should be noted that Saint-Barthélemy was originally listed in Article 355(1) as an outermost region but opted for a change of status to OCT in 2012 pursuant to European Council Decision 2010/718/EU, of 29 October 2010 amending the status with regard to the European Union of the island of Saint-Barthélemy [2010] OJ L325/4–5.

outlined in the Accession Treaty of Denmark, Ireland, and the United Kingdom, which excluded Gibraltar from the Customs Union.

- Excluded territories: Article 355(5) TFEU enumerates the European territories excluded from the Treaties' territorial scope, which currently includes the Faroe Islands. The other references to excluded territories concern territories of the United Kingdom, such as the Sovereign Base Areas of Akrotiri and Dhekelia, or the Channel Islands and the Isle of Man. Following the United Kingdom's withdrawal from the Union, these references, with the exception of the Sovereign Base Areas of Akrotiri and Dhekelia, are devoid of purpose.

In addition to Articles 52 TEU and 355 TFEU, the Union can enact provisions extending the territorial scope of the Treaties beyond the territory of the Member States. For example, if a Member State has entered into an agreement with a third country concerning matters within the Union's competence, the Union may adopt acts that have effects in that third country. This is the case of the EU customs territory, which encompasses Monaco as a result of the Franco-Monegasque Customs Convention of 1963. Under this Convention, French authorities are responsible for customs inspection, clearance, and the levying of customs duty on behalf of Monaco.[125] Another example is the euro, which is legal tender in Monaco, San Marino, Andorra, and the Vatican City State due to several acts of Union law applicable in these third countries. The applicability of these Union acts is facilitated by pre-existing international agreements between the third countries and Member States (Monaco with France; San Marino and the Vatican City State with Italy) on monetary policy.[126]

It should also be acknowledged that Union law can have extraterritorial effects in certain circumstances. This is the case, for example, of decisions of the Commission in the field of competition when they address the conduct of an undertaking in a third country that has effects within the Union's internal market.[127] Such situations also arise when Union law imposes obligations on undertakings operating both inside and outside the Union, such as rules on data protection,[128] environmental standards, corporate sustainability, or highly mobile activities, like maritime or air transport.[129] In these cases, the Court of Justice has held that as long as there is a connecting link with the Union's territory, the extraterritorial effects of Union acts are lawful.[130]

[125] Art 4(2)(a) Reg(EU) No 952/2013 of the European Parliament and of the Council of 9 October 2013 laying down the Union Customs Code. See in this respect the judgment in Case C-291/09 *Guarneri* EU:C:2011:217, para 14.

[126] See Declaration No 6 annexed to the Maastricht Treaty concerning monetary relations with San Marino, the Holy See and Monaco. The monetary agreements between the so-called 'microstates' and the Union include an obligation to transpose numerous Union acts, such as Directive 2014/62/EU of the European Parliament and of the Council of 15 May 2014 on the protection of the euro and other currencies against counterfeiting by criminal law, and Council Regulation (EC) No 1339/2001 of 28 June 2001 extending the effects of Regulation (EC) No 1338/2001 laying down measures necessary for the protection of the euro against counterfeiting to those Member States which have not adopted the euro as their single currency.

[127] The *leading* judgment on this issue was delivered in the 'wood pulp' case, in the field of competition (Joined Cases C-89/85, C-104/85, C-116/85, C-117/85 and C-125/85 to C-129/85 *A Ahlström Osakeyhti and Others v Commission* EU:C:1988:447). In its judgment, the Court of Justice confirmed the powers of the Commission to impose measures targeting agreements made by the undertakings concerned in third countries, but implemented in the territory of the Member States. See Case C-89/85 A *Ahlström Osakeyhtiö and Others v Commission of the European Communities* EU:C:1988:447, paras 12–14.

[128] Case C-131/12 *Google Spain and Google* EU:C:2014:317, paras 55–56; and Case C-362/14 *Schrems* EU:C:2015:650.

[129] See, inter alia, Case C-381/98 *Ingmar* EU:C:2000:605, para 25; Case C-188/07 *Commune de Mesquer* EU:C:2008:359, paras 60–63; and Case C-366/10 *Air Transport Association of America and Others* EU:C:2011:864, para 125.

[130] In other instances, the Court has taken a more cautious approach, as in the case of the so-called 'humanitarian visa', which raised the question of the extraterritorial application of fundamental rights of the Union. This question was addressed in detail by Advocate General Mengozzi, who concluded that the applicability of the Charter extended to the case of a visa application at diplomatic and/or consular representations of Member States in third states, but the Court of Justice disagreed. On this point, see Case C-638/16 *PPU X and X* EU:C:2017:93, pts 49–70.

2. Temporal Scope

The Treaties were concluded for an unlimited period.[131] The Union, therefore, has no expiry date, unlike the ECSC, whose Treaty expired on 23 July 2002.

The temporal scope of application of Union law raises frequent questions in the case of the accession of a new Member State. In such cases, doubts emerge over the applicability of Union law during the transition from pre-accession to full membership. These issues are typically addressed through transitional provisions in the Accession Treaties, but unforeseen situations can occur, requiring a case-by-case approach that is frequently guided by the Court of Justice's case law.

As a starting point, the case law has refrained from applying Union law to facts that occurred *before* a Member State's accession.[132] However, when previously established legal situations prior to accession fall within the scope of Union law, those situations must adapt to the new legal framework. This is the standard position in the case law, as evidenced in cases involving facts that predated accession but where judicial disputes arise *after* the accession.[133] The same applies where a contract was concluded in a Member State before its accession, and the contract and its performance continue to have effects after the accession.[134] To ensure observance of the principles of legal certainty and the protection of legitimate expectations, the substantive rules of Union law should only be regarded as applying to situations existing prior to their entry into force if it is clearly evident from the terms, objectives, or overall scheme of the contract that such effects are intended.[135]

IV. UNION ACTION BEYOND UNION LAW

The Union must act within the boundaries of Union law, otherwise its actions will be in breach of the principle of conferral. However, there are specific instances in which the Union's institutions are used in intergovernmental arrangements to involve the Union in decisions and actions outside the scope of the Treaties, but in matters with close connections to policy areas within the Union's competence.

This situation arose following the 2008 financial and economic crisis. As the economic and political turmoil increased and the Eurozone's economic conditions deteriorated, the Member States needed to act swiftly, despite the Union's limited competence in the field of economic policy. Eventually, intergovernmental measures were taken among Member States, including arrangements limited to euro area Member States often with the close involvement of Union institutions, such as the Commission or the European Central Bank, or other entities such as the Eurogroup. As a result, several Union institutions assumed specific tasks under international agreements concluded among a group of Member States, even in areas beyond the Union's direct scope of competence. Although there were precedents for similar practices in the

[131] Arts 53 TEU, 356 TFEU and 208 EAEC Treaty.

[132] Case C-321/97 *Andersson and Guaneras-Andersson* EU:C:1999:307, para 31; and Case C-302/04 *Ynos* EU:C:2006:9, paras 36–37.

[133] Case C-96/08 *CIBA* EU:C:2010:185, paras 13–14; Case C-64/06 *Telefonica O2* EU:C:2007:348, paras 22–23; and Case C-283/10 *Circul Globus Bucureşti* EU:C:2011:772, para 28.

[134] Case C-256/15 *Nemec* EU:C:2016:954, paras 22–23; and Joined Cases C-52/16 and C-113/16 *Segro and Horváth* EU:C:2018:157, paras 38 and 40. On the tax consequences of this line of case law, see Case C-242/18 *UniCredit Leasing EAD* EU:C:2019:558, paras 32–34.

[135] Case C-162/00 *Pokrzeptowicz-Meyer* EU:C:2002:57, para 49; Case C-441/08 *Elektrownia Pątnów II* EU:C:2009:698, para 33; and Case T-348/04 *SIDE v Commission* EU:T:2008:109, paras 50–56.

past, particularly in the field of external relations,[136] the financial crisis highlighted the most prominent examples of Union institutions operating outside the bounds of the Treaties. The most notable examples are found in the Treaty on Stability, Coordination and Governance in the Economic and Monetary Union and the Treaty establishing the European Stability Mechanism. Both agreements confer tasks on the Commission, the European Central Bank, and the Court of Justice.[137]

In the case of *Pringle*, the Court of Justice ruled on the legality of this practice and upheld the conferral of the said tasks, 'provided that [they] do not alter the essential character of the powers conferred on those institutions by the EU and FEU Treaties'.[138] It follows from the judgment in *Pringle* that the tasks must be conferred in areas in which the Union does not hold exclusive competence, or has not yet exercised shared competence.

Consequently, in matters that do not fall within the exclusive competence of the Union, the Member States are entitled to entrust tasks to institutions outside the Union framework, such as coordinating joint actions undertaken by the Member States or managing financial assistance, as long as these functions do not affect the powers conferred on those institutions by the founding Treaties.[139]

When performing the tasks outlined above, Union institutions are subject to Union law at all times, including the Charter of Fundamental Rights. For instance, this was the case of the Commission's actions within the framework of the *troika*, an informal arrangement comprising the Commission, the European Central Bank, and the International Monetary Fund, entrusted with overseeing the enforcement of the conditionality measures imposed by the financial assistance programmes during the economic and financial crisis of 2008–2013. In the case of *Ledra Advertising*, the Court of Justice confirmed that, while the Commission had the discretionary power to sign a Memorandum of Understanding with a beneficiary Member State, it also had the authority to refuse to sign if it considered that the provisions of the Memorandum of Understanding breached the Charter of Fundamental Rights.[140] The tasks assigned to the Commission in the international agreement entered into by the euro-area Member States require it to ensure that the actions taken during the implementation of the agreement are consistent with Union law.[141] Therefore, to the extent that the Commission, within its discretion, decides to sign the Memorandum of Understanding, it is liable in tort for any damages it may cause as a result of a decision made in breach of Union law in that specific context.[142]

A specific variant of actions related to the Union but decided outside the standard arrangements are the decisions made by the governments of Member States in areas of Union competence, where they act through their representatives rather than in Council meetings.

[136] Joined Cases C-181/91 and C-248/91 *Parliament v Council and Commission* EU:C:1993:271, paras 16, 20 and 22; Case C-316/91 *Parliament v Council* EU:C:1994:76, paras 26, 34 and 41.

[137] See Arts 5, 7 and 12 of the Treaty on Stability, Coordination and Governance in the Economic and Monetary Union, and Arts 4.4, 5, 6.2, 13, 14.6, 15.5, 16.5 and 17.5 of the Treaty establishing the European Stability Mechanism.

[138] Case C-370/12 *Pringle* EU:C:2012:756, para 158.

[139] Opinion of the Court 1/92 EU:C:1992:189, paras 32 and 41; Opinion of the Court 1/00 EU:C:2002:231, para 20; Opinion of the Court 1/09 EU:C:2011:123, para 75; and *Pringle* (n 138) para 158.

[140] Case C-8/15 P *Ledra Advertising v Commission and ECB* EU:C:2016:701, para 59.

[141] *Ledra* (n 140) para 58.

[142] This approach also extends to the implementation of a Memorandum of Understanding, in the framework of a financial assistance programme, by the authorities of the Member States. See the judgments in Case C-258/14 *Florescu* EU:C:2017:448; and Case C-64/16 *Associação Sindical dos Juízes Portugueses* EU:C:2018:117. However, the case law provides for exceptions, as in the case of the EU–Turkey Agreement, the legal nature of which gives rise to doubts and, in the view of the General Court, is not an act of the Union and therefore not open to judicial review (see the Orders in Case T-192/16 *NF v European Council* EU:T:2017:128; Case T-193/16 *NG v European Council* EU:T:2017:129; and Case T-257/16 *NM v European Council* EU:T:2017:130).

These are actions in which the governments of the Member States take control of the decision-making process to the detriment of the Union's institutions, in areas that, a priori, fall within the Union's competence. An example is found in Article 19(2) TEU, Article 253(1) TFEU and Article 254(1) TFEU, where the power to appoint judges and Advocates General of the Court of Justice and judges of the General Court is granted to 'the governments of the Member States' rather than to the Council. Another example is in Article 341 TFEU, which states that 'the seat of the institutions of the Union shall be determined by common accord of the governments of the Member States'. This peculiarity raises doubts about the nature of the governments' actions, as it is unclear whether it is a decision 'of the Union' or 'of the Member States'.[143] For the time being, the Court of Justice tends to categorise these decisions as international in nature, rather than as part of the Union's decision-making process. Consequently, they can be exempt from judicial review unless procedural issues related to the decision are disputed.[144]

GENERAL BIBLIOGRAPHY

Bakardjieva Engelbrekt, A and Groussot, X (eds), *The Future of Europe, Political and Legal Integration Beyond Brexit* (Hart, 2019).

Blockmans, S and Russack, S (eds), Representative Democracy in the EU: Recovering Legitimacy (CEPS, 2019).

de Witte, B, 'The European Union as an International Legal Experiment' in G de Búrca and JHH Weiler (eds), The Worlds of European Constitutionalism (Oxford University Press, 2011).

Hoeksma, J, 'The Nature of the European Union in the 21st Century' (2024) 177 *EU Law Live Weekend Edition* 3.

Ioannidis, M, 'Europe's new transformations: how the EU economic constitution changed during the Eurozone Crisis' (2016) 53 *Common Market Law Review* 1237.

Magnette, P, What is the European Union? The Nature of the European Union (Macmillan, 2005).

Pitruzzella, G, 'Identity of the European Union and Identities of the Member States: Which Relationship?' (2024) 182 *EU Law Live Weekend Edition* 3.

Scholtes, J, 'Constitutionalising the end of history? Pitfalls of a non-regression principle for Article 2 TEU' (2023) 19 *European Constitutional Law Review* 59.

Schütze, R, *From Dual to Cooperative Federalism. The Changing Structure of European Law* (Oxford University Press, 2009).

Spieker, L, *EU Values before the Court of Justice: Foundations, Potential, Risks* (Oxford University Press, 2023).

Weatherill, S, *Law and Values in the European Union* (Oxford University Press, 2016).

Weiler, JHH, *The Constitution of Europe. 'Do the New Clothes have an Emperor?' and Other Essays on European Integration* (Cambridge University Press, 1999).

Williams, A, *The Ethos of Europe: Values, Law and Justice in the EU* (Cambridge University Press, 2010).

[143] See Joined Cases C-59/18 and C-182/18 *Italian Republic and Comune di Milano v Council* EU:C:2021:567 and Case C-743/19 *European Parliament v Council* EU:C:2021:534, Opinion of AG Bobek, para 176: 'After all, the agency to be established is an agency of the Union, not of the Member States'.

[144] The Court of Justice dismissed the actions brought by former Advocate General Sharpston against the decision of the governments of the Member States to dismiss her and to appoint her successor immediately after the withdrawal of the United Kingdom. Since those decisions were taken by the governments of the Member States and not by the Council, the Court held that it had no jurisdiction to rule on the lawfulness of those acts. See Case C-684/20 P *Sharpston v Council and Representatives of the Governments of the Member States* EU:C:2021:486; and Case C-685/20 P *Sharpston v Council and Representatives of the Governments of the Member States* EU:C:2021:485. See D Kochenov and G Butler, 'The Independence and Lawful Composition of the Court of Justice of the European Union: Replacement of Advocate General Sharpston and the Battle for the Integrity of the Institution', Jean Monnet Working Paper No 2/2020. However, in the cases concerning the reallocation of the seat of the European Medicines Agency, cited in the previous footnote, where the challenged decision was once again made by the representatives of the governments, the Court found a way to review the merits of the decision.

FURTHER READING

The Revision of the Treaties

Baquero Cruz, J, 'Between Unanimity and Utopia: Constitutional Change in the Union' in J Baquero and C Closa, *European Integration from Rome to Berlin: 1957–2007, History, Law and Politics* (Peter Lang, 2009).
Bast, J and von Bogdandy, A, 'The constitutional core of the Union: On the CJEU's new, principled constitutionalism' (2024) 61(6) *Common Market Law Review* 1471.
Bieber, R, 'Les limites matérielles et formelles à la révision des traités établissant la Communauté européenne' (1993) *Revue du Marché Commun*, 443.
Cruz Mantilla de los Ríos, P, 'European Constitutional Identity as the Unamendable Core of the EU Treaties' (2024) 20 *European Constitutional Law Review* 545.
Cruz Vilaça, JL and Piçarra, N, 'Y a-t-il des limites matérielles à la révision des traités instituant les Communautés européennes?' (1993) 1–2 *Cahiers de Droit Européen* 3.
Debard, T, and Philip, Chr (eds), *Les procédures de révision des traités communautaires, du droit international au droit constitutionnel* (Bruylant, 2001).
Dehousse, F and Coussens, W, 'Rethinking the revision and entry into force clauses of the European Constitution' (2003) 56 *Studia diplomatica* 35.
De Witte, B, 'Treaty Revision Procedures After Lisbon' in A Biondi, P Eeckhout and S Ripley (eds), *EU Law after Lisbon* (Oxford University Press, 2012).
Jacqué, J-P, 'Les dispositions générales et finales du traité établissant une Constitution pour l'Europe' (2005) 4 *Revue Trimestrielle de Droit Européen.*
Louis, J-V, 'Quelques considérations sur la révision des traités instituant la Communauté' (1980) 16 *Cahiers de Droit Européen* 121.

The Accession of New Member States

Becker, U, 'EU-enlargements and Limits to Amendments of the EC Treaty' (2001) 15 Jean Monnet Working Paper.
Cremona, M, 'Accession to the European Union: Membership Conditionality and Accession Criteria' (2001) 25 *Polish Yearbook of International Law* 119.
— 'EU Enlargement: Solidarity and Conditionality' (2005) 30 *European Law Review* 574.
Fromage, D (ed), *Redefining EU Membership: Differentiation In and Outside the European Union* (Oxford University Press, 2024).
Hillion, C, 'The European Union is Dead. Long Live the European Union' (2004) 29 *European Law Review* 595.
— *EU Enlargement* (Hart, 2004).
— 'EU Enlargement' in P Craig and G De Búrca, *The Evolution of EU Law*, 3rd edn (Oxford University Press, 2021).
Kochenov, D, *EU Enlargement and the Failure of Conditionality: Pre-Accession Conditionality in the Fields of Democracy and the Rule of Law* (Kluwer Law, 2008).
Petrov, R, 'All's well that ends well: short story of Ukraine's road towards European Union membership' (2024) 43 *Yearbook of European Law* 3.
Tatham, A, *Enlargement of the European Union* (Kluwer Law, 2009).

Voluntary Withdrawal from the Union

Craig, P, 'Brexit a Drama, The Endgame – Part II: Trade, Sovereignty and Control' (2021) 46 *European Law Review* 135.
Dougan, M, *The UK's Withdrawal from the EU: A Legal Analysis* (Oxford University Press, 2021).
Eeckhout, P and Frantziou, E, 'Brexit and Article 50 TEU: A Constitutionalist Reading' (2017) 54 *Common Market Law Review* 695.
Fabbrini, F (ed), *The Law and Politics of Brexit* (Oxford University Press, 2017).
— *The Withdrawal Agreement* (Oxford University Press, 2020).
Friel, RJ, 'Providing a Constitutional Framework for Withdrawal from the EU: Article 59 of the Draft European Constitution' (2004) 53 *International and Comparative Law Quarterly* 407.

Garner, O, 'Seven Reforms to Article 50 TEU' (2021) 46 *European Law Review* 767.
Gatti, M, 'Article 50 TEU: A Well-Designed Secession Clause?' (2017) 2 *European Papers* 159.
Grosclaude, L, 'La clause de retrait du Traité établissant une Constitution pour l'Europe: réflexions sur un possible marché de dupes' (2005) 41 *Revue Trimestrielle de Droit Européen.*
Harbo, F, 'Secession Right – An Anti-Federal Principle? Comparative Study of Federal States and the EU' (2008) 1 *Journal of Politics and Law* 132.
Herbst, J, 'Observations on the Right to Withdraw from the European Union: Who are the "Masters of the Treaties"?' (2005) 6 *German Law Journal* 1755.
Hillion, C, 'Withdrawal under Article 50 TEU: An Integration-friendly Process' (2018) 55 *Common Market Law Review* 29.
Hofmeister, H, '"Should I Stay or Should I Go?" – A Critical Analysis of the Right to Withdraw From the EU' (2010) 16 *European Law Journal* 589.
Kellerbauer, M, Dumitriu-Segnana, E and Liefländer, T, *The UK–EU Withdrawal Agreement. A Commentary* (Oxford University Press, 2021).
Lazowski, A, 'Withdrawals from the European Union and Alternatives to Membership' (2012) 37 *European Law Review* 523.
Louis, J-V, 'Le droit de retrait de l'Union Européenne' (2006) *Cahiers de Droit Européen.*
Nicolaides, P, 'Withdrawal from the European Union: A Typology of Effects' (2013) 20 *Maastricht Journal of European and Comparative Law* 209.
Vahlas, A, 'Souveraineté et droit de retrait au sein de l'Union européenne' (2005) 6 *Revue de Droit Public.*

The Mechanisms for Guaranteeing the Rule of Law in the Union

Burchill, R, 'The Promotion and Protection of Democracy by Regional Organisations in Europe: The Case of Austria' (2001) 7 *European Public Law* 363.
Closa, C, and Kochenov, D (eds), Reinforcing Rule of Law Oversight in the European Union (Cambridge University Press, 2016).
Closa, C, Kochenov, D and Weiler, JHH, 'Reinforcing Rule of Law Oversight in the European Union' (2014) 25 EUI Working Papers RSCAS.
Jakab, A and Kochenov, D, *The Enforcement of EU Law and Values: Ensuring Member States' Compliance* (Oxford University Press, 2017).
Jakab A and Kirchmair L, Saving the European Union from its Illiberal Member States' (Oxford University Press, 2025).
Kirst, N, 'The Conditionality Regulation in Action. The Case of Hungary' (2023) 146 *EU Law Live Weekend Edition* 3.
Kochenov, D and Pech, L, 'Monitoring and Enforcement of the Rule of Law in the EU: Rhetoric and Reality' (2015) 11 *European Constitutional Law Review* 512.
Konstantinides, T, *The Rule of Law in the European Union: The Internal Dimension* (Oxford University Press, 2017).
Lenaerts, K, 'On Checks and Balances: The Rule of Law within the EU' (2023) 29 *Columbia Journal of European Law* 25.
Luque Lora, J, 'Beyond Dialogue. The Case for More European Parliament Involvement in Conditionality' (2025) 234 *EU Law Live Weekend Edition* 3.
Pech, L, 'The Rule of Law as a Constitutional Principle of the European Union' (2009) 4 Jean Monnet Working Paper.
— 'The Rule of Law as a Well-Established and Well-Defined Principle of EU Law' (2022) 14 *Hague Journal on the Rule of Law* 25.
Pohjankoski, P and Kirst, N (eds.) 'The Court of Justice's Judgments on the Rule-of-Law Financial Conditionality Regulation' (2022) 91 *EU Law Live Weekend Edition* 3.
Rosas, A, Raitio, J and Pohjankoski, P (eds), *The Rule of Law's Anatomy in the EU: Foundations and Protections* (Hart, 2023).
Von Bogdandy, A, 'Principles of a Systemic Deficiencies Doctrine: How to Protect Checks and Balances in the Member States' (2020) 57 *Common Market Law Review* 705.
Von Bogdandy, A and Spieker, L, 'Transformative Constitutionalism in Luxembourg: How the Court Can Support Democratic Transitions' (2023) 29 *Columbia Journal of European Law* 65.
Waelbroeck, M and Oliver, P, 'La crise de l'État de droit dans l'Union européenne: que faire?' (2017) 53 *Cahiers de Droit Européen* 327.

Union Action outside the Union

Buchta T, 'Judgments on the Selection of the Seats of EU Agencies: Challenges and What Will Change' (2022) 29 *Maastricht Journal of European and Comparative Law* 786.

Craig, P, 'Pringle and Use of EU Institutions outside the EU Legal Framework: Foundations, Procedure and Substance' (2013) 9 *European Constitutional Law Review* 263.

de Witte, B, 'Using International Law in the Euro Crisis: Causes and Consequences' (ARENA Working Paper 04/2013).

Kochenov DV and Butler G, 'Independence of the Court of Justice of the European Union: Unchecked Member States' Power after the Sharpston Affair' (2021) 27 *European Law Journal* 262.

Peers, S, 'Towards a New Form of EU Law?: The Use of EU Institutions outside the EU Legal Framework' (2013) 9 *European Constitutional Law Review* 37.

Puetter, U, *The European Council and the Council: New Intergovernmentalism and Institutional Change* (Oxford University Press, 2014).

Spaventa E, 'Constitutional Creativity or Constitutional Deception? Acts of the Member States Acting Collectively and Jurisdiction of the Court of Justice' (2021) 58 *Common Market Law Review* 1697.

3

The Institutions, Bodies, Offices, and Agencies of the Union

I. THE INSTITUTIONAL FRAMEWORK OF THE UNION

THE MEMBER STATES have entrusted the Union with the human and material resources necessary to attain the objectives laid down in the Treaties. These resources are distributed among the institutions, bodies, offices, and agencies that together constitute a single institutional framework. Through this framework, the Union's policies are translated into concrete action. Its design reflects the democratic principle, ensuring that Union entities operate in a transparent and representative manner, while respecting both the separation of powers and the principle of sincere cooperation. This constitutional objective is expressly articulated in Article 13(1) Treaty on European Union (TEU), which provides that the Union is to have an institutional framework 'which shall aim to promote its values, advance its objectives, serve its interests, those of its citizens and those of the Member States, and ensure the consistency, effectiveness, and continuity of its policies and actions'.

Consistent with the blend of functionalism and federalism that characterised the early European Communities, the Union's institutional architecture today encompasses bodies of differing nature and function. On the one hand, it includes institutions of a predominantly *political* character, notably the European Parliament, the European Council, the Council of the European Union, and the European Commission, which together exercise the core legislative and executive functions of the Union. On the other hand, the institutional framework also comprises entities that are *independent*, judicial, supervisory, or technical in nature, including the Court of Justice of the European Union, the European Central Bank (ECB), and the European Court of Auditors. This latter category also encompasses a wide range of agencies, bodies, and offices endowed with specialised technical expertise in specific fields of Union policy.

From a formal perspective, the Treaties structure the Union's institutional framework into four distinct categories: the institutions enumerated in Article 13 TEU; the agencies; the bodies; and the offices. This classification recurs throughout the Treaties and is consistently reflected in secondary legislation, serving as an organising principle for the allocation of competences, responsibilities, and resources within the Union's administrative and constitutional system.[1]

[1] See Arts 9, 24, 40 and 42 TEU and Arts 15, 16(2), 24, 71, 123(1), 124, 125(1), 127(4), 130, 226, 228(1), 263, 265, 267, 282(3), 287, 298 and 325 TFEU.

II. THE INSTITUTIONS OF THE UNION

Article 13 TEU provides an exhaustive enumeration of the institutions of the Union, which are the following:

- the European Parliament;
- the European Council;
- the Council;
- the European Commission;
- the Court of Justice of the European Union;
- the European Central Bank;
- the Court of Auditors.

The enumeration not only recognises the importance of the institutions within the Union's framework, but it also reflects the protection they enjoy through their specific recognition in the Treaties. Unlike agencies, bodies, or offices, the Union's institutions are governed in their fundamental features directly by the Treaties, and therefore any amendment to their core powers or organisation will require a Treaty reform in accordance with the procedures outlined in Article 48 TEU. Furthermore, the Treaties confer on all or some of these institutions, to varying degrees, specific rights and privileges, such as privileged standing to bring direct actions in the Union courts.[2]

According to Article 47 TEU, the Union has legal personality.[3] Consequently, it is the responsibility of the institutions to act as *agents* of the Union. In contrast, and with the sole exception of the ECB as outlined in Article 282(3) TFEU, these institutions do not have independent legal personality.[4]

As a general rule, the Commission represents the Union in every Member State (Article 335 TFEU).[5] However, the Union is represented by each of the institutions, by virtue of their administrative autonomy, in matters relating to their respective operations.

1. The European Parliament

The European Parliament is the Union's only institution with *direct* democratic legitimacy, acting through a mandate from the peoples of Europe, renewed every five years through an electoral process based on direct universal suffrage. In its early years, the European Parliament was established as a 'Common Assembly' of the ECSC, and as the 'Assembly' of the EEC and Euratom. These three assemblies were unified by the Convention on Certain Common Institutions, which entered into force on 1 January 1958, as the 'European Parliamentary Assembly', which renamed itself 'European Parliament' by resolution of 30 March 1962. This name was incorporated into the Treaties only with the Single European Act of 1986. The first

[2] Art 263, second paragraph TFEU.

[3] The European Atomic Energy Community, still operational, exists independently of the Union with its own legal personality.

[4] There are further exceptions to this rule that apply to agencies and bodies, as in the case of the European Investment Bank provided for in Art 308 TFEU, the Single Resolution Board (see Art 42 of Regulation (EU) No 806/2014 of the European Parliament and of the Council of 15 July 2014 establishing uniform rules and a uniform procedure for the resolution of credit institutions and certain investment firms in the framework of a Single Resolution Mechanism and a Single Resolution Fund [2014] *OJ* L225/1 and the European Data Protection Board (see Art 68 GDPR)).

[5] On the scope of the Commission's power of representation, see Case C-137/10 *Région Bruxelles-Capitale* EU:C:2011:280, paras 17–20; and Case C-199/11 *Otis and Others* EU:C:2012:684, paras 27–36.

election by universal direct suffrage took place in 1979. This institution plays a crucial role in the Union's institutional framework, embodying the democratic representation of the peoples of Europe, expressed through the vote of its citizens.

1.1. *Legal statute*

The European Parliament is the first of the seven institutions listed in Article 13 TEU, recognising its significance and the unique legitimacy it holds. The basic features of the institution are outlined in Article 14 TEU, while Articles 223–234 TFEU specify additional rules governing its powers and composition. The European Parliament has its own rules of procedure, established through a specific legal basis in Article 232 TFEU, which requires a 'majority of its Members' for approval.

Article 223 TFEU states that the European Parliament shall draw up a proposal to lay down provisions on the election of its members by direct universal suffrage in accordance with a uniform procedure in all Member States, or consistent with principles common to the Member States. Although the 'uniform procedure' previously mentioned has not yet been adopted, the Electoral Act[6] was introduced on 20 September 1976 (substantially amended in 2002 and 2018, the latter still pending ratification). This act defines the main aspects of the electoral process, particularly the election system based on proportional representation under the list system or the single transferable vote (see section 1.4.1, below). This framework is complemented by Directive 93/109/EC, which harmonises the rules on the right to vote and to stand as a candidate in European Parliament elections for citizens of the Union residing in a Member State of which they are not nationals.[7]

1.2. *Seat*

According to Protocol No. 6 on the location of the seats of the institutions, the European Parliament has its seat in Strasbourg, where the 12 periods of monthly plenary sessions, including the budget session, take place. Additional plenary sessions, as well as the European Parliament's committees, are held in Brussels. The General Secretariat of the European Parliament, together with its various departments, is located in Luxembourg.

This 'three-headed' arrangement results from the intergovernmental agreement reached in the Edinburgh European Council of 11-12 December 1992, which codified the previous practice of holding monthly plenary meetings in Strasbourg. Since 1999 (Treaty of Amsterdam), these agreements have been elevated to the status of primary law. They are legally binding on the institutions, and their interpretation has been the subject of various disputes before the Court of Justice (eg, regarding the obligation to hold strictly 12 sessions in Strasbourg).[8]

1.3. *Powers*

1.3.1. Legislative Power

The European Parliament, together with the Council, is the Union's co-legislator. This division of legislative tasks is in line with standard parliamentary practice, similar to that in bicameral systems in Member States such as Germany, France, Italy, Spain, or Poland. In such systems, two

[6] Decision 76/787/ECSC, EEC, EURATOM.

[7] Council Directive 93/109/EC of 6 December 1993 laying down detailed arrangements for the exercise of the right to vote and stand as a candidate in elections to the European Parliament for citizens of the Union residing in a Member State of which they are not nationals [1993] OJ L329/34.

[8] See Case C-345/95 *France v European Parliament* EU:C:1997:450; Case C-237/11 *France v European Parliament* EU:C:2012:796; Case C-73/17 *France v European Parliament* EU:C:2018:787; and Case C-92/18 *France v European Parliament* EU:C:2020:506.

chambers cooperate in the legislative process, each representing different sources of legitimacy and interests. One chamber often represents the interests of citizens, while the other chamber represents, for example, the interests of territories or regions. This is the model followed by the Union, in which the European Parliament represents the interests of the citizens and the Council embodies the interests of the Member States.

The Lisbon Treaty, in force since 2009, established the 'ordinary legislative procedure' as well as several 'special legislative procedures', reflecting the different means of interaction between the European Parliament and the Council in the course of the legislative process. However, and in contrast to traditional parliamentary practice in Member States, the European Parliament does not have the right of legislative initiative. This power has been granted exclusively to the Commission with very few exceptions. At most, the European Parliament can, under Article 225 TFEU, 'request the Commission to submit any appropriate proposal on matters on which it considers that a Union act is required for the purpose of implementing the Treaties'. The Commission must consider the request and, if it does not submit a proposal, it must inform the requesting institution of the reasons.

1.3.2. Supervision of other Institutions, Agencies, Offices and Bodies

The European Parliament exercises political oversight over the actions of the Union's executive branch, the Commission. This power is implemented through the following three channels:

- Election of the President of the Commission and a vote on the College of Commissioners. Articles 14(1) and 17(7) TEU grant the European Parliament the power to elect, by a majority of its members, the President of the Commission proposed by the European Council following the European Parliament elections. The President of the Commission, the High Representative of the Union for Foreign Affairs and Security Policy, and the other members of the Commission are subject 'as a body' to a vote of consent by the European Parliament.
- Ordinary political control. Article 14(1) TEU states that the European Parliament conducts functions of political control and consultation. This role is reflected in the obligation for the Commission, as specified in Article 230 TFEU, to respond either orally or in writing to questions raised by the European Parliament.
- Motion of censure. The Treaties empower the European Parliament to adopt a motion of censure on the activities of the Commission. Article 234 TFEU requires a two-thirds majority of the votes cast, representing a majority of the members of the European Parliament. In such an event, the members of the Commission will resign 'as a body', and the High Representative will also resign from their duties within the Commission. To date, ten motions of censure have been put to the vote without ever securing the necessary majority. The motion of censure tabled in 1999 against the Commission led by Jacques Santer, although it did not gather enough votes, prompted the collective resignation of the Commission.[9]

Although the European Parliament's political oversight primarily focuses on the Commission's activities, this responsibility extends to other institutions, agencies, bodies, and offices. For instance, Article 36(2) TEU authorises the European Parliament to address questions or issue recommendations to the Council or the High Representative in matters of foreign affairs and security policy. In addition, Article 15(6)(d) TEU requires the President of the European Council to present a report to the European Parliament after each meeting of the European Council.

[9] A MacMullen, 'Political Responsibility for the Administration of Europe: The Commission's Resignation March 1999' (1999) 52 *Parliamentary Affairs* 703, and A Topan, 'The Resignation of the Santer-Commission: The Impact of "Trust" and "Reputation"' (2002) 6 *European Integration Online Papers* 14.

1.3.3. Budgetary Powers

The European Parliament and the Council act jointly as the Union's budgetary authority. The Parliament's budgetary powers operate at two levels. First, under Article 312 TFEU, the Parliament gives its consent to the multiannual financial framework (MFF), the regulation that sets expenditure ceilings for a period of at least five years.[10] Although the MFF is adopted by the Council acting unanimously, Parliament's consent gives it an effective veto over the framework within which annual budgets are set. Second, the Parliament co-adopts the annual budget alongside the Council under the procedure laid down in Article 314 TFEU. In addition, under Article 319 TFEU, the Parliament grants discharge to the Commission on the implementation of the budget, a power that serves as a key instrument of budgetary oversight.[11] Through these budgetary powers, including in the area of the Common Foreign and Security Policy (CFSP), the European Parliament exercises political oversight in this otherwise intergovernmental field of Union activities, where the Treaties limit its decision-making powers.

1.3.4. Other Powers

Alongside its core legislative and budgetary functions, the European Parliament holds a set of additional institutional powers. These powers concern the approval of certain international agreements, the establishment of committees of inquiry, and the reception of petitions from Union citizens. They strengthen the Parliament's oversight role and its connection with the Union's citizens.

- *International agreements.* Pursuant to Article 218(6) TFEU, the European Parliament grants its consent prior to the Council concluding an international agreement in the following cases:
  - association agreements;
  - agreement on Union accession to the European Convention on Human Rights;
  - agreements establishing a specific institutional framework by organising cooperation procedures;
  - agreements with important budgetary implications for the Union;
  - agreements covering fields to which either the ordinary legislative procedure applies, or the special legislative procedure where consent by the European Parliament is required.
- *Inquiries.* In line with national parliamentary practice, the European Parliament may establish temporary Committees of Inquiry to investigate alleged contraventions or maladministration in the implementation of Union law, except when a court is examining the alleged facts and the case is still subject to legal proceedings.[12] The work of these committees has a broad scope, encompassing inquiries into the activities of Union institutions, bodies, offices, or agencies, as well as those of Member States in cases involving the implementation of Union law. Following its review, the Committee of Inquiry submits a report, and immediately after this, it ceases to exist.[13]
- *Right to petition.* European citizens and any natural or legal person residing or having its registered office in a Member State, shall have the right to petition, enshrined in Articles

[10] Art 312 TFEU.
[11] ibid, Art 319.
[12] ibid, Art 226 and Decision 95/167/EC, Euratom, ECSC of the European Parliament, the Council and the Commission of 19 April 1995 on the detailed provisions governing the exercise of the European Parliament's right of enquiry.
[13] Art 226 TFEU and Articles 226-229 of the Rules of Procedure of the European Parliament.

20 and 24 TFEU and Article 44 of the Charter of Fundamental Rights of the European Union ('the Charter'). Article 227 TFEU emphasises that European citizens have the right to exercise this right, either individually or in association with other citizens or persons, 'on a matter which comes within the Union's fields of activity and which affects him, her or it directly'. The right to petition is further elaborated in the European Parliament's Rules of Procedure, particularly in Articles 226–229.[14]

1.4. *Composition and Functioning*

Article 14(2) TEU states that the European Parliament shall be composed of 'representatives of the Union's citizens', a new wording introduced in the Lisbon Treaty that amends the previous reference to the 'representatives of the peoples of the States brought together in the Community'.[15] The current provision reflects the direct and individual link created between the European citizen and its representative institution at Union level, rather than a collective regrouping of representatives from different constituent states.

Article 14(2) TEU also establishes the maximum number of members of the European Parliament, which must not exceed a total of 750, plus the President. The representation of citizens is degressively proportional, with a minimum threshold of six members per Member State and a maximum of 96 seats per Member State.

The Treaties specify that the European Parliament draws up a proposal to establish the rules for the election of its members by direct universal suffrage in accordance with a uniform procedure across all Member States or in accordance with principles common to all Member States (Article 223(1) TFEU). Although the uniform procedure has not been adopted, the second alternative is reflected in the 1976 Electoral Act (as amended in 2002), which lays down common principles applicable across Member States. A further amendment was adopted in 2018 (Council Decision (EU, Euratom) 2018/994), but has not yet entered into force pending completion of the national approval procedures required in all Member States. Article 1(1) of the Act states that in each Member State, 'members of the European Parliament shall be elected based on proportional representation, using the list system or the single transferable vote'. Although Member States may establish a minimum threshold for the allocation of seats, it must not exceed five per cent of the votes cast.[16]

Members are elected for a five-year term of office, which coincides with the term of each legislature.[17] The nomination of the Commission President is linked to the European Parliament elections under Article 17(7) TEU, although in practice the new Commission typically takes office several months after the newly elected Parliament. The term of office begins at the opening of the first session of the European Parliament following each election.[18]

The European Parliament elects its President and Vice-Presidents for a term of two-and-a-half years.[19] Meetings are held in plenary sessions or in committees, and their activities are supported by a Bureau responsible, inter alia, for financial, organisational, and administrative

[14] N Vogiatzis, 'The Past and Future of the Right to Petition the European Parliament' (2021) 40 *Yearbook of European Law* 195, and A Alemanno, 'Strengthening the Role and Impact of Petitions as an Instrument of Participatory Democracy' (European Parliament, 2021) PE 694.837.

[15] See former Art 189 Treaty Establishing the European Community (TEC), prior to the introduction of Article 14(2) TEU.

[16] Art 3 Electoral Act. It should be noted that the 2018 reform of the 1976 Electoral Act, adopted by Council Decision 2018/994 pursuant to Art 223(1) TFEU, requires Member States with more than 35 seats to introduce a minimum threshold between 2% and 5% of valid votes, thereby transforming what had previously been a purely optional ceiling of 5% into a binding obligation for larger constituencies. In 2026, this reform was pending approval in all the Member States.

[17] Art 14(3) TEU.

[18] Art 5 Electoral Act.

[19] Art 14(4) TEU and r 17 of the Rules of Procedure of the European Parliament.

decisions regarding the internal organisation of Parliament, its Secretariat, and its bodies.[20] The organisational arrangements also include the Secretariat.[21] Members of the European Parliament are organised into parliamentary groups according to their political affiliation, rather than their nationality. Under the Parliament's Rules of Procedure, a political group must comprise a minimum of 23 members elected in at least one quarter of the Member States.

The European Parliament holds an annual session and meets, without having to be convened, on the second Tuesday in March.[22] It can also convene in extraordinary part-sessions at the request of a majority of its component Members or at the request of the Council, or the Commission.[23]

As previously mentioned, the European Parliament is organised into parliamentary groups based on ideological affiliation. However, national party politics still play a significant role, particularly in the electoral process. To avoid national fragmentation in debates and in the functioning of the European Parliament, proposals have been made to introduce European electoral lists and a European common constituency. These proposals gained considerable political momentum, particularly in 2017, and in 2022 the European Parliament adopted a legislative initiative proposing a reform of the EU electoral law, with a view to replacing the 1976 Electoral Act, including, among other innovations, the introduction of a Union-wide constituency with transnational lists. However, support for these reforms remains far from reaching a consensus among the Member States.

In any event, efforts to 'Europeanise' the process continue, most notably through the *Spitzenkandidaten* (lead candidate) system. Under Article 17(7) TEU, the European Council proposes a candidate for Commission President 'taking into account the elections to the European Parliament and after having held the appropriate consultations', a formulation that neither requires nor prohibits the lead candidate system, which accordingly operates on an informal basis. This dynamic materialised for the first time during the 2014 elections, when Jean-Claude Juncker, the lead candidate of the largest group, the European People's Party (EPP), was elected Commission President. However, the method was bypassed in 2019 when the European Council selected Ursula von der Leyen, who had not campaigned as a lead candidate. This decision cast doubt on the system's viability until the 2024 elections, when Ursula von der Leyen ran as the official EPP *Spitzenkandidat* and secured a second term, thereby partially restoring the link between the electoral outcome and the executive presidency.[24]

1.4.1. Voting Rights

Article 22(2) TFEU and Article 39(1) of the Charter guarantee every Union citizen residing in a Member State of which they are not a national the right to vote and stand as a candidate in European Parliament elections in that Member State under the same conditions as nationals of that state. The conditions for exercising this right are harmonised by Directive 93/109/EC,[25] which affirms that Union citizens who are not nationals of the Member State of residence have the right to vote and stand for election, provided they meet the same conditions imposed by the

[20] ibid, r 25.

[21] ibid, rr 28 and 234.

[22] Art 229(1) TFEU.

[23] ibid, Art 229(2).

[24] M Goldoni, 'Politicising EU Law: The Case of the *Spitzenkandidaten*' (2016) 22 *European Law Journal* 279, and SB Hobolt, 'A Vote for the President? The Role of *Spitzenkandidaten* in the 2014 European Parliament Elections' (2014) 21 *Journal of European Public Policy* 1528.

[25] Council Directive 93/109/EC of 6 December 1993 laying down detailed arrangements for the exercise of the right to vote and stand as a candidate in elections to the European Parliament for citizens of the Union residing in a Member State of which they are not nationals [1993] OJ L329/34.

law of the Member State of residence on its own nationals.[26] Directive 93/109/EC, as amended by Directive 2013/1/EU, prevents any person from voting more than once in the same election, and prohibits standing as a candidate in more than one Member State during the same election.[27] If a Union citizen has been deprived of their right to vote or to stand as a candidate by an individual civil law or criminal law decision in either their Member State of origin or of residence, they are likewise disqualified from exercising that right in the Member State of residence.[28]

The Court of Justice has confirmed that Member States retain broad discretion in defining the electorate for European Parliament elections. In its judgment in *Spain v United Kingdom*, the Court upheld the legality of a British measure that extended voting rights to Commonwealth citizens residing in Gibraltar who were not Union citizens but had close historical ties to the United Kingdom.[29] In *Eman and Sevinger*, the Court found that the Netherlands had breached the principle of equal treatment by excluding Dutch nationals residing in Aruba — a separate country within the Kingdom of the Netherlands listed as an Overseas Country and Territory (OCT) — from voting in European Parliament elections, while allowing Dutch nationals residing in third countries to vote.[30] According to the Court of Justice:

> [I]n the current state of [Union] law, the definition of the persons entitled to vote and to stand as a candidate in elections to the European Parliament falls within the competence of each Member State in compliance with [Union] law, and that Articles [223, 20 and 22 TFEU] do not preclude the Member States from granting that right to vote and to stand as a candidate to certain persons who have close links to them, other than their own nationals or citizens of the Union resident in their territory.[31]

1.4.2. The Right to Stand as a Candidate

Regarding the right to stand as a candidate in elections to the European Parliament, the Electoral Act of 1976 sets out several requirements for eligible citizens, including rules on incompatibilities,[32] vacancies,[33] and privileges and immunities of MEPs.[34] Article 6 of the Electoral Act establishes the principle of the free mandate, providing that members of the European Parliament vote on an individual and personal basis, and 'shall not be bound by any instructions and shall not receive a binding mandate'.

These rights and duties have the duration of the five-year term of the legislature, which begins at the opening of the first session following each election.[35] However, regarding the privileges and immunities of Members of the European Parliament, the Court of Justice has clarified that the protection provided by Protocol No 7 begins at the time of the official proclamation of the results during the national electoral process, not from the opening of the first session following the elections.[36]

[26] ibid, Art 3.

[27] ibid, Art 4.

[28] ibid, Arts 6–7. However, the power of Member States to deprive a Union citizen of the right to vote and to stand as a candidate is not absolute, as confirmed by the European Court of Human Rights (*Hirst v United Kingdom (No 2)* [GC] App no 74026/01, 2005-IX; *Frodl v Austria, App* no 20201/04; *Scoppola v Italy (No 3)* [GC] App no 126/05; *Greens and MT v United Kingdom, App* nos 60041/08 and 60054/08) and the Court of Justice, Case C-650/13 *Delvigne* EU:C:2015:648).

[29] Case C-145/04 *Spain v United Kingdom* EU:C:2006:543.

[30] Case C-300/04 *Eman and Sevinger* EU:C:2006:545.

[31] *Spain v United Kingdom* (n 29) para 78.

[32] Art 7 of the Electoral Act.

[33] ibid, Art 13.

[34] ibid, Art 6(2), with reference to the Protocol of Privileges.

[35] ibid, Art 5.

[36] Case C-502/19 *Junqueras Vies* EU:C:2019:1115, para 87, and C-600/22 P *Puigdemont i Casamajó* EU:C:2024:803, paras 65–71.

2. The European Council

The Lisbon Treaty introduced the European Council as one of the seven institutions enumerated in the Treaties. Until then, the European Council had remained in an institutional *terra incognita*, officially recognised in the Treaties but lacking the status of a formal institution. Following its inclusion in Article 13 TEU, the European Council appears and operates within the Union's formal institutional framework. It has been part of the EU institutions since 2009, serving as a meeting of the heads of state and government of the Member States, the President of the European Council and the President of the Commission. Due to its high-profile composition, the decisions made by this institution risk destabilising the delicate balance of power that exists among the Commission, the Council, and the European Parliament. Concerns over the proper functioning of this balance explain why the Treaties prevent the European Council from exercising any legislative power.[37]

The European Council exemplifies the Union's intergovernmental nature. Established in the 1970s as a response to what some Member States perceived as an excessively independent drift of the Communities of the time, the European Council reflects the will of the Member States by setting the Union's long-term strategic objectives. As outlined in Article 15(1) TEU, the role of the European Council is to provide the Union 'with the necessary impetus for its development and shall define the general political directions and priorities thereof'. Article 15(1) TEU also specifies that the European Council 'shall not exercise legislative functions', a constitutional limitation that distinguishes it from the Council and the European Parliament.

Despite their terminological similarities, the European Council is a distinct institution from the Council. While the former oversees the political impetus and overall political direction of the Union, the latter acts as the Union's co-legislator, responsible for decision-making in areas of policy outlined in the Treaties. This important distinction is not made easier to grasp by the fact that both institutions share common services, including premises and the General Secretariat of the Council, which supports the European Council and its President.[38]

2.1. Composition and Legal Framework

Article 15 TEU and Articles 235–236 TFEU set out the fundamental rules on the composition and operation of the European Council, supplemented by the institution's Rules of Procedure, approved on 1 December 2009. The European Council is composed of the Heads of State or Government of the Member States, together with its President and the President of the Commission. The High Representative of the Union for Foreign Affairs and Security Policy takes part in its work (Article 15(2) TEU). The Treaties include additional specific provisions relating to the European Council, to which reference will be made below.

2.2. Seat

The European Council meets in Brussels, although the institution's Rules of Procedure allow, on an extraordinary basis, for meetings to be held in other locations.[39] This exception is a remnant of the practice that characterised the European Council from its inception until 2004, when meetings were held in the Member State holding the rotating presidency of the Council at the time.

[37] Art 15(1) TEU.

[38] Art 13 of the Rules of Procedure of the European Council of 1 December 2009 [2009] *OJ* L315/51.

[39] Art 1(2) of the Rules of Procedure of the European Council (n 38).

2.3. *Powers*

Although the European Council's primary role is to set the general political orientation and priorities of the Union, the Treaties also grant it individual decision-making powers in areas such as the CFSP, the area of freedom, security and justice, and social security, as well as constitutional functions in procedures for revising the Treaties or during the voluntary withdrawal of a Member State from the Union. The European Council generally acts by consensus (Article 15(4) TEU), except where the Treaties provide otherwise.

2.3.1. General Political Direction

According to Article 15(1) TEU, the European Council 'shall provide the Union with the necessary impetus for its development and shall define the general political directions and priorities thereof'. In addition, the Treaties include additional powers of orientation in other provisions:

- *Common foreign and security policy*: the European Council identifies the Union's strategic interests and objectives, establishes the objectives of and defines the general guidelines for the CFSP, and regularly evaluates the threats facing the Union to enable the Union and its Member States to take effective action.[40]
- *Area of freedom, security and justice*: the European Council sets out 'the strategic guidelines for legislative and operational planning within the area of freedom, security and justice'.[41]
- *Economic policy*: on the basis of a report from the Council, the European Council can discuss a conclusion regarding the broad guidelines of the economic policies of the Member States and of the Union.[42]
- *Employment*: each year, the European Council examines the employment situation in the Union and adopts conclusions based on a joint annual report by the Council and the Commission.[43]

2.3.2. Conciliation

In addition to the powers of general political direction, the European Council plays an important role of conciliation between the EU institutions and between Member States. This is not a general power, but a specifically attributed power by the Treaties in each policy area.

- *Common foreign and security policy*: on a proposal from the Council, and following a declaration by a Member State indicating its intention to oppose the adoption of a decision of vital interest, the matter may be referred to the European Council for a decision by unanimity.[44]
- *Social security*: if a draft legislative act significantly impacts its social security system, any Member State may refer the matter to the European Council, which can either send the draft back to the Council or ask the Commission to submit a new proposal.[45]
- *Area of freedom, security and justice*: when a draft directive provided for in Articles 82(3) and 83(3) (harmonisation in the field of judicial procedural cooperation and cross-border

[40] Arts 22(1) and 26(1) TEU and Art 222(4) TFEU.
[41] Art 68 TFEU.
[42] ibid, Art 121(2).
[43] ibid, Art 148(1).
[44] Art 31(2) TEU.
[45] Art 48 TFEU.

crimes) affects fundamental aspects of a Member State's criminal justice system, it may refer the matter to the European Council so that, if necessary, it can refer the draft back to the Council.[46] A similar power is attributed to the European Council in negotiations on a draft regulation establishing the European Public Prosecutor's Office[47] and regarding measures on operational cooperation between police, customs, and other specialised law enforcement services in relation to the prevention, detection, and investigation of criminal offences.[48]

2.3.3. Specific Powers

The Treaties grant powers to the European Council in specific policy areas. These decisions, which have legal effects and can be judicially reviewed by the Court of Justice as outlined in Article 263(1) TFEU,[49] are available in the following areas:

- determination of the existence of a serious and persistent breach by a Member State of the values referred to in Article 2 TEU;[50]
- election of the President of the European Council;[51]
- establishment of the system of strict equal rotation between the Member States in the appointment of members of the Commission;[52]
- appointment of the High Representative of the Union for Foreign Affairs and Security Policy;[53]
- appointment of the President, the Vice-President and the other members of the Executive Board of the ECB;[54]
- amendment of the status of a Danish, French or Netherlands country or territory referred to in Article 355(1)–(2) TFEU.[55]

2.3.4. Constituent Powers

The European Council also exercises powers of a constitutional nature, insofar as they affect the basic organisation of the Union. They can be summarised as follows:

- *Revision of the Treaties*: the European Council decides whether to proceed with an amendment of the Treaties under the ordinary procedure[56] or through a simplified review process.[57]
- *Voluntary withdrawal from the Union*: the European Council sets the 'guidelines' under which the Union negotiates and concludes an agreement with a withdrawing state.[58]

[46] ibid, Arts 82(3) and 83(3).
[47] ibid, Art 86(1).
[48] ibid, Art 87(3).
[49] Art 263(1) TFEU confers on the Court of Justice of the European Union jurisdiction to review 'the legality . . . of acts . . . of the European Council intended to produce legal effects vis-à-vis third parties'.
[50] Art 7(2) TEU.
[51] ibid, Art 15(5).
[52] ibid, Art 17(5) and Art 244 TFEU.
[53] Art 18(1) TEU.
[54] Art 283(2) TFEU.
[55] ibid, Art 355(6).
[56] Art 48(2)–(3) TEU.
[57] ibid, Art 48(6).
[58] ibid, Art 50(2).

- *Passerelle clauses*: it is for the European Council to decide on the activation of the *passerelle* clauses regarding the voting system and the legislative procedure,[59] as well as on the CFSP[60] and the adoption of the multiannual financial framework.[61]
- *EPPO's powers*: the European Council may extend the powers of the European Public Prosecutor's Office as outlined in Article 86(4) TFEU.[62]

2.4. *Composition and Functioning*

The European Council is composed of the heads of state or government of the Member States, along with its President and the President of the Commission. Each member of the European Council may be assisted by a minister and, in the case of the Commission, by a member of the Commission.[63] The High Representative of the Union for Foreign Affairs and Security Policy also participates in the work of the European Council.[64]

Since 2009, the European Council has had a permanent President, elected by the institution by qualified majority for a term of two-and-a-half years, renewable once. According to Article 15(6) TEU, the President of the European Council chairs and leads the work of the institution, ensures its preparation and continuity, and strives to foster cohesion and consensus among the members. After each European Council meeting, the President reports to the European Parliament. The President also ensures the external representation of the Union on issues concerning its common foreign and security policy, without prejudice to the powers of the High Representative of the Union for Foreign Affairs and Security Policy (Article 15(6) TEU). The President of the European Council shall not hold a national office (Article 15(6) TEU).

The European Council meets at least four times a year, convened by its President. The President can also call special meetings when the situation so requires.[65] In practice, the frequency of meetings has regularly exceeded this Treaty minimum, particularly during periods of crisis.

The decisions of the European Council are taken by consensus, unless the Treaties specify otherwise. This applies to cases in which the Treaties allow the European Council to decide by simple majority,[66] qualified majority,[67] or unanimity.[68] When deciding by qualified majority, the European Council follows the voting requirements set out in Article 16(4) TEU and Article 238(2) TFEU for the definition of a qualified majority. The President of the European Council and the President of the Commission do not take part in votes (Article 235(1) TFEU).[69]

3. The Council

The Council, jointly with the European Parliament, acts as a co-legislator for the Union. As an institution representing the interests of the Member States, the Council plays a role similar

[59] ibid, Art 48(7).
[60] ibid, Art 31(3).
[61] ibid, Art 312(2).
[62] ibid, Art 86(4).
[63] Art 15(3) TEU.
[64] ibid, Art 15(2).
[65] Arts 15(3) and 1(3) of the Rules of Procedure of the European Council.
[66] Art 48(3) TEU and Art 235(3) TFEU.
[67] Arts 15(5), 17(7) and 18(1) TEU, and Arts 236 and 283(2) TFEU.
[68] Arts 7(2), 14(2), second subparagraph, 17(5), 22, 24, 31, 42(2) and 48 TEU, and Arts 86(4), 244, 312 and 355(6) TFEU.
[69] Art 235(1) subpara 2 TFEU.

to the parliamentary chambers of territorial representation found in decentralised and bicameral political systems, such as the *Senado* in Spain, the *Sénat* in Belgium, or the *Bundesrat* in Austria and Germany. In addition to its role as a co-legislator, the Council holds other powers, including budgetary, executive and constitutional powers, making it a mixed institution that combines legislative, budgetary, constituent, and executive functions. This unique role of the Council stems from the original institutional design of the European Communities, in which the Council held a wide range of powers. The gradual consolidation of the Commission as the Union's executive, the establishment of specialised agencies, and the rise of the European Council have gradually circumscribed the Council's powers primarily to the legislative domain. Nevertheless, there remain areas where the institution does not act as a legislative chamber and continues to perform additional functions, as will now be explained.

3.1. *Legal Statute*

Article 16 TEU and Articles 237–243 TFEU provide the basic legal statute of the Council, to which the Rules of Procedure of the institution, adopted on 1 December 2009, should be added.[70]

3.2. *Seat*

Protocol No 6 on the location of the institutions' seats states that the Council has its seat in Brussels. As an exception to this rule, the Protocol specifies that the Council's meetings are held in Luxembourg during April, June, and October.[71]

3.3. *Powers*

Article 16(1) TEU enumerates the powers of the Council, which include the legislative and budgetary powers, as well as policy-defining and coordinating functions as laid down in the Treaties. Additionally, the Council has other powers specifically assigned by the Treaties, such as concluding international agreements, or the enactment of executive measures through implementing acts, as outlined below.

3.3.1. Legislative Powers

When Article 16(1) TEU states that the Council exercises a 'legislative function', the provision does not fully capture the complexity of this task. The Council's margin of manoeuvre when performing legislative tasks is very broad, ranging from powers to establish general criteria and guidelines of a more political nature to the enactment of detailed legislative instruments. In summary, the Council's legislative and decision-making functions can be outlined as follows:

- *Co-legislator of the Union*: the Council acts as a co-legislator, sharing responsibility for the adoption of legislative acts together with the European Parliament under the ordinary legislative procedure, and acting alone with the Parliament's consent or after consulting it under the special legislative procedures.[72] Although it has no power of legislative initiative,

[70] Council Decision 2009/937/EU of 1 December 2009.

[71] Sole Article, point (b) of Protocol No 6 on the location of the seats of the institutions and of certain bodies, offices, agencies and departments of the European Union.

[72] Art 294 TFEU.

the Council may request the Commission to undertake any studies it considers necessary for the attainment of the common objectives, and submit to it any appropriate proposals.[73]

- *Co-responsibility for the common foreign and security policy*: although the Treaties prohibit the adoption of legislative acts in this policy area, the Council and the European Council, acting together and generally unanimously, define and implement the CFSP.[74] It is also the responsibility of the Council, together with the Commission and the High Representative, to ensure the coherence of the Union's external action.[75]
- *Decisions on international agreements*: the Council authorises the opening of negotiations, adopts negotiating directives, authorises the signing of agreements, and concludes them.[76]
- *Individual decisions*: the Council has the power to decide on issues of significant importance and of a hybrid nature, blending legislative and executive features, as in the case of, inter alia, the authorisation of aid for the protection of enterprises handicapped by structural or natural conditions,[77] the decision on whether restrictive tax measures of a Member State are compatible with free movement of capital,[78] or the enactment of safeguard measures regarding third countries in exceptional circumstances that may threaten or cause serious difficulties for the operation of economic and monetary union.[79]

3.3.2. Budgetary Powers

The Council plays a key role in the adoption of the Union's budget, a task that it shares with the European Parliament. On the one hand, the Council is responsible for approving, after consulting the European Parliament, the decision that lays down the provisions relating to the Union's system of own resources.[80] This power includes the ability to introduce new categories of resources or abolish existing categories. All decisions regarding the Union's own resources depend on the 'approval' of Member States in line with their respective constitutional requirements. On the other hand, the Council and the European Parliament co-adopt the Union's annual budget under the procedure laid down in Article 314 TFEU. As regards the multiannual financial framework, the Council adopts it unanimously, with the consent of the European Parliament (Article 312 TFEU).[81]

3.3.3. Policy-making and Coordinating Powers

Article 16(1) TEU states that the Council carries out policy-making and coordinating functions as laid down in the Treaties. These powers are further detailed in the provisions governing the Union's economic policy and the CFSP.

- *Economic policy:* the Council adopts broad guidelines for the economic policies of the Member States and the Union, on a recommendation from the Commission and following a report to the European Council.[82] It is for the Council to address recommendations and,

[73] ibid, Art 241.
[74] Art 24(1) subpara 2 TEU.
[75] Arts 21(3) and 26(2) subpara 2 TEU.
[76] ibid, Art 218(2), (5) and (6) TFEU.
[77] ibid, Art 42(2).
[78] ibid, Art 65(4).
[79] ibid, Art 66.
[80] ibid, Art 311.
[81] ibid, Arts 312 and 314.
[82] ibid, Art 121(1)–(2).

where appropriate, to give notice to a Member State incurring an excessive deficit and for proposing measures to reduce the deficit and address the situation.[83]

- *Common foreign and security policy*: Member States shall consult one another within the European Council and the Council on any matter of foreign and security policy of general interest in order to determine a common approach.[84]

3.3.4. Executive Powers

The executive function is primarily vested in the Commission. However, the Lisbon Treaty, which has been in force since 1 December 2009, established a new regime of delegated and implementing acts, granting the Council the power to adopt implementing acts.[85] This authority is limited to 'duly justified specific cases' only.[86] Additionally, the Council may adopt decisions in the field of the CFSP, which, while not legislative in nature, constitute the primary means through which the policy is implemented, as outlined in Articles 24 and 26 TEU.

3.3.5. Constitutional and Appointment Powers

The Treaties entrust the Council with powers of a constitutional nature, mostly linked to the appointment of authorities of the Union's institutions. It is for the Council to determine:

- the salaries, allowances, and pensions of the President of the European Council, the President of the Commission, the High Representative of the Union for Foreign Affairs and Security Policy, the Members of the Commission, the Presidents, Members, and Registrars of the Court of Justice of the European Union, and the Secretary-General of the Council;[87]
- the list of persons proposed for appointment as members of the Commission, by common accord with the President-elect of the Commission;
- the appointment of members of the Court of Auditors;[88]
- the composition of the Economic and Social Committee and the Committee of the Regions.[89]

3.4. *Composition and Operations*

According to Article 16(2) TEU, the Council comprises a representative of each Member State at ministerial level, who may commit the government of the respective Member State and cast its vote.[90]

The Council does not have a uniform composition but acts through 'configurations' divided into sectoral areas. This is confirmed by Article 16(6) TEU, which states that the Council meets 'in different configurations'. The complete list of Council configurations is

[83] ibid, Arts 126(9) and (11).

[84] Art 32 TEU.

[85] Art 291(2) TFEU.

[86] See Case T-395/22 *Hypo Vorarlberg Bank AG v SRB* EU:T:2024:333, paras 32–41; and Case T-406/22 *Volkskreditbank v SRB* EU:T:2024:439, paras 32–41.

[87] Art 243 TFEU.

[88] ibid, Art 286(2).

[89] ibid, Arts 301(2) and 305(2).

[90] On the internal functioning of the Council, see the official publication 'Observations on the Council's Rules of Procedure' (Luxembourg, 2016), prepared by the General Secretariat of the Institution and available *at* www.consilium.europa.eu/media/29808/qc0415692esn.pdf.

adopted by the European Council by a qualified majority. However, two configurations are explicitly identified in Articles 16(6) and 236(a) TFEU: the General Affairs Council, responsible for ensuring consistency across the different Council configurations and for preparing the meetings of the European Council;[91] and the Foreign Affairs Council, responsible for shaping the Union's external action according to strategic guidelines set by the European Council, and for ensuring that the Union's actions are consistent.[92] Aside from these two configurations explicitly mentioned in the Treaties, the European Council has established a list of 10 Council configurations.[93] In addition to these 10 configurations, reference should also be made to the Eurogroup, an informal body established under Article 137 TFEU and Protocol No 14, in which the ministers of the Member States whose currency is the euro meet to discuss matters related to the single currency. The Eurogroup is not a Council configuration and has no formal decision-making powers under the Treaties, but it plays a significant role in the coordination of euro area economic policies.[94]

The Presidency of the Council's configurations is based on an equal rotation among Member States, except for the Foreign Affairs Council, whose presidency is held by the High Representative for Foreign Affairs and Security Policy. The Presidency of the Council's configurations rotates every six months, in an order pre-established by the European Council by a qualified majority[95] and implemented by the Council.[96] Currently, the order of rotation among the Member States has been agreed until December 2030.[97]

The Council is assisted by the General Secretariat, under the responsibility of a Secretary-General, who is appointed by the Council (Article 240(2) TFEU). The General Secretariat is responsible for managing the institution's services, including the Legal Service and the Directorates-General.[98] It should be noted that the General Secretariat also provides secretarial assistance to the European Council.[99]

The Council makes decisions through the individual votes of each representative, using one of the three voting systems outlined in the Treaties: simple majority, qualified majority, and unanimity. Article 16(3) TEU states that, as a general rule, the Council acts by qualified majority unless the Treaties specify otherwise.

The rule establishing a qualified majority is enshrined in Article 16(4) TEU. After several decades during which qualified majority voting was calculated using a system of weighted voting, which the Nice Treaty supplemented with additional thresholds based on the number of Member States and, optionally, on population, the Treaty establishing a Constitution for Europe introduced the current double-majority criterion, which was retained by the Treaty of

[91] Art 16(6) subpara 3 TEU.

[92] ibid, Art 16(2), subpara 3.

[93] See Annex I of the Council's Rules of Procedure, which lists the 10 Council configurations currently in force: General affairs; Foreign affairs; Economic and financial affairs; Justice and home affairs; Employment, social policy, health and consumer affairs; Competitiveness (internal market, industry, research and space); Transport, telecommunications and energy; Agriculture and fisheries; Environment; and Education, youth, culture and sport.

[94] The status of the Eurogroup is laid down in Art 137 TFEU and, in more detail, in Protocol No 14 on the Eurogroup. On the legal nature of the Eurogroup, see Joined Cases C-597/18 P, C-598/18 P, C-603/18 P and C-604/18 P *Council v K Chrysostomides & Co and Others* EU:C:2020:1028, and Case C-105/15 P *Mallis and Malli v Commission and ECB* EU:C:2016:702, paras 52–53.

[95] Art 236(b) TFEU and European Council Decision of 1 December 2009 on the exercise of the Presidency of the Council [2009] OJ L315/50.

[96] Council Decision of 1 December 2009 laying down measures for the implementation of the European Council Decision on the exercise of the Presidency of the Council, and on the chairmanship of preparatory bodies of the Council [2009] OJ L322/28, amended in 2016 and 2021.

[97] See Annex I of the Council Decision of 1 December 2009.

[98] Art 240(2) TFEU.

[99] ibid, Art 235(4).

Lisbon. Under transitional arrangements set out in Protocol No 36, the new rules became fully applicable on 1 April 2017, and are now reflected in Article 16(4) TEU.

A qualified majority is defined as at least 55 per cent of the members of the Council, comprising at least 15 of them and representing Member States that account for at least 65 per cent of the Union's population. A blocking minority must consist of at least four Council members; otherwise, the qualified majority will be considered achieved.

This seemingly simple rule is, in reality, rather complex. First, because it has two important exceptions and a related mechanism:

- When the Council makes a decision in which not all Member States participate in voting, the qualified majority will be defined as at least 55 per cent of the members of the Council representing the participating Member States, comprising at least 65 per cent of the population of these states. A blocking minority must include at least the minimum number of Council members representing more than 35 per cent of the population of the participating Member States, plus one member, failing which the qualified majority will be deemed attained.[100]
- Where the Council does not act on a proposal from the Commission or the High Representative of the Union for Foreign Affairs and Security Policy, a qualified majority will be defined as at least 72 per cent of the members of the Council representing the participating Member States comprising at least 65 per cent of the population of these states.[101]
- In addition, the so-called Ioannina mechanism, reflected in Declaration No 7 annexed to the Lisbon Treaty and implemented in Council practice, provides that where members of the Council representing a significant proportion of the population or of the number of Member States necessary to constitute a blocking minority indicate their opposition to a proposed act, the Council must do everything within its power, within a reasonable period of time, to reach a satisfactory solution. This mechanism does not prevent the Council from ultimately proceeding to a vote.

Secondly, and despite the practical and symbolic significance of qualified majority voting, the Council's decision-making process primarily relies on consensus.[102] When a policy area requires a qualified majority, all Member States face pressure to avoid being in the minority. This risk encourages all Member States to reach a consensus rather than leave the final decision to a vote, where some might lose and others win. As a result, the practice of decision-making through consensus is generally the norm in the Council. However, the Presidency is not precluded from calling a vote, particularly in policy areas that require a qualified majority.

The Committee of Permanent Representatives of the Governments of the Member States (COREPER) is responsible for preparing the work of the Council, as outlined in Article 16(7) TEU and Article 240 TFEU. COREPER brings together the Permanent Representatives of the governments to the Union, who serve as the 'ambassadors' of the Member States. All initiatives submitted to the Council for decision-making are first discussed in COREPER, unless the Council's Rules of Procedure provide otherwise. COREPER operates in two configurations: COREPER I includes the Deputy Permanent Representatives and covers the internal market and other technical issues; COREPER II comprises the Permanent Representatives and focuses on general issues and foreign policy. Based on COREPER's outcomes, the Council's agendas

[100] ibid, Art 238(3)(a).

[101] ibid, Art 238(3)(b).

[102] F Hayes-Renshaw, W van Aken and H Wallace, 'When and Why the EU Council of Ministers Votes Explicitly' (2006) 44 *Journal of Common Market Studies* 161.

are divided into two sections: 'A' items addressing issues negotiated and agreed upon within COREPER or at working group level, which only requires formal approval without debate in the Council; and 'B' items covering unresolved issues within COREPER that need discussion and a decision in the relevant Council configuration.[103]

The Council delegates much of its preparatory works to 'committees' and 'working groups', most of which are temporary bodies formed specifically to study, propose or coordinate particular issues. However, in some instances, their establishment is intended to be permanent, as in the case of the Financial Services Committee[104] or the Economic and Financial Committee.[105] A specific type of Committee is provided for in Regulation 182/2011, pursuant to Article 291 TFEU regarding implementing acts, a subject covered in chapters five and eight of this book.

The Council meets publicly when it deliberates and votes on a draft legislative act.[106] To achieve this, each Council meeting is divided into two parts: one dedicated to deliberations on legislative acts; and another on non-legislative activities. Although the Treaties do not require it, when a non-legislative proposal is tabled in the Council relating to the adoption of rules that are legally binding for the Member States through regulations, directives, or decisions, the Council's first deliberation on important new proposals is open to the public.[107] This rule is subject to derogation in the case of internal measures, administrative or budgetary acts, acts concerning interinstitutional or international relations, or non-binding acts such as conclusions, recommendations, or resolutions.

4. The European Commission

While the European Parliament represents the interests of citizens and the Council embodies the interests of the Member States, the Commission is responsible for defending the interests of the Union. The Commission is the institution that best embodies the Union's objectives, and it dedicates itself solely to their promotion and defence. For this reason, the Commission is not only the executive authority of the Union but also the 'guardian of the Treaties', assigned the responsibility of ensuring compliance with Union law throughout the Member States. This explains why the members of the Commission, although nominated by the Member States, are under a legal duty to act independently and subject to no external mandate. As a result, the Commission operates independently, being answerable to the broader European interest and, more specifically, to the European Parliament through parliamentary oversight and the power to table a motion of censure against the Commission.

The Commission is a unique organisation on the international scene, as it has a significant level of independence and strong enforcement powers binding on Member States and individuals. In some areas, such as competition policy or state aid, the Commission holds exclusive powers. Furthermore, the Commission is the only institution with the power of legislative initiative, a feature that confers a highly strategic position within the Union's legislative process.

[103] Art 3(6) of the Rules of Procedure of the Council. In any event, the fact that an item is categorised as an A item does not exclude the possibility of any member of the Council or of the Commission expressing an opinion at the time of the approval of these items and having statements included in the minutes.

[104] Council Decision 2003/165/EC of 18 February 2003 setting up the Financial Services Committee [2003] *OJ* L 67/17.

[105] Art 134(2) TFEU.

[106] Art 16(8) TEU.

[107] Art 8(1) of the Council's Rules of Procedure.

The Commission is the institution with the highest number of staff – close to 33,000 – including permanent and contractual personnel, a figure that reflects the quantitative and qualitative importance of its powers.[108]

4.1. *Legal Statute*

Article 17 TEU and Articles 244–250 TFEU establish the basic rules regarding the composition, powers, and organisation of the Commission. The Commission has also adopted its own Rules of Procedure through the Decision of 4 December 2024.[109]

4.2. *Seat*

The main seat of the Commission is in Brussels, but Protocol No 6 on the location of the seats of the institutions and of certain bodies, offices, agencies and departments of the European Union clarifies that certain Commission departments referred to in Articles 7–9 of the Decision of 8 April 1965 are based in Luxembourg. The services involved include the Publications Office and Eurostat.[110]

4.3. *Powers*

The Commission is primarily entrusted with the powers necessary to ensure that the Treaties are applied in all the Member States. In this regard, it acts as 'guardian of the Treaties'. Additionally, it plays a significant role in the Union's rule-making activities in two main ways: firstly, in the legislative process, where it holds a monopoly on the initiative to propose legislative acts, save where the Treaties provide otherwise; and secondly, in the exercise of executive tasks, which include the adoption of non-legislative acts. The Commission also exercises budgetary functions: it submits the draft annual budget to the European Parliament and the Council (Article 314 TFEU) and implements the budget on its own responsibility (Article 317 TFEU). The Commission also holds relevant powers in the field of external relations, as it assumes external representation of the Union.

4.4. *The Commission as 'Guardian of the Treaties'*

The Treaties entrust the Commission with the necessary powers to supervise and ensure that Union law is applied in all the Member States, but also within the Union itself. In this regard, the Commission acts as a powerful overseer of the proper implementation of Union law, often called the 'guardian of the Treaties', exercising its powers over Member States, Union institutions, offices, agencies, as well as private individuals, including companies and natural persons. To this end, Article 337 TFEU empowers the Commission to 'collect any information and carry out any checks required for the performance of the tasks entrusted to it'. Besides the gathering of information, the Commission also produces statistics where necessary for the performance of its tasks.[111] Any citizen or undertaking has the right to submit a complaint to

[108] Source: European Commission.

[109] Rules of Procedure of the Commission [C/2024/10000 [2024] OJ L2024/3080].

[110] It should be noted that Luxembourg is the historical seat of the European Atomic Energy Community (Euratom). Consequently, the specific directorates within DG Energy that deal with nuclear safeguards and radiation protection are located in Luxembourg. The rest of the DG (renewables, gas, electricity markets) is in Brussels.

[111] Art 338(1) TFEU and Regulation (EC) No 223/2009 of the European Parliament and of the Council of 11 March 2009 on European statistics and repealing Regulation (EC, Euratom) No 1101/2008 of the European Parliament and of the Council on the transmission of data subject to statistical confidentiality to the Statistical Office of the European Communities, Council Regulation (EC) No 322/97 on Community Statistics, and Council Decision 89/382/EEC, Euratom establishing a Committee on the Statistical Programmes of the European Communities [2009] OJ L87/164.

the Commission regarding a breach of Union law.[112] Although the Commission is not required to pursue every complaint, it must register and examine them in line with principles of good administration, and it typically informs complainants of the outcome and reasons. Individual complaints have proven to be a highly valuable source of information for the Commission to perform its role as 'guardian of the Treaties'.

The remedies available to the Commission to challenge a breach of Union law are mostly of a judicial nature. When the breach involves an institution, agency, body, or office, the Commission can bring an action for annulment or for failure to act before the Court of Justice or the General Court, as specified in Articles 263 and 265 TFEU, respectively. If the alleged infringement results from the actions of one or more Member States, the Commission can initiate an infringement procedure, a remedy that requires the Commission to first address the issue in a pre-litigation phase, and if unresolved, the case can be brought before the Court of Justice pursuant to Article 258 TFEU. Should the Court of Justice find that a Member State or States have breached Union law, the Commission will oversee the enforcement of the judgment in the relevant Member State(s). In cases of non-compliance, further remedies are available, including the right to request that the Court of Justice impose a lump sum and/or penalty payments on the Member State(s) involved.[113]

In the field of competition and State Aid, the Commission holds significant enforcement powers, including the power to impose financial penalties on undertakings that breach Articles 101–102 TFEU,[114] as well as the power to order Member States to recover from their beneficiaries the full amount of unlawful or incompatible State Aid.[115] These decisions are subject to judicial review before the Union courts.

4.5. *Executive Powers*

A substantial part of the Commission's operations entails the enactment and/or implementation of executive acts. To this end, the Commission implements legislative acts through delegated or implementing acts, but it also launches projects and programmes, manages Union funds, and implements the budget. These activities consume a considerable portion of the Commission's human and financial resources and require close collaboration with other agencies, bodies, offices, and the authorities of the Member States.

4.5.1. Delegated and Implementing Acts

The adoption of delegated and implementing acts has been a longstanding activity of the Commission, primarily aimed at developing the legal framework introduced by a Union legislative act. Following the entry into force of the Lisbon Treaty in 2009, this power has been codified in the Treaties in Articles 290–291 TFEU. As elaborated further in chapters five and eight, the Treaties confer on the Commission the power to adopt 'delegated acts' and 'implementing acts'. The main purpose of these acts is to support Union legislation by providing detailed and more specific rules in areas requiring technical expertise or swift normative action (including the amendment of non-essential parts of legislative acts in the case of delegated acts).

[112] On the functioning of the system of complaints to the Commission, see Commission, 'Updating the handling of relations with the complainant in respect of the application of Union law (Communication)' COM(2012) 0154 final.

[113] Art 260 TFEU.

[114] ibid, Art 105. However, it should be noted that this competence in the field of competition is currently exercised in practice together with national competition authorities, as a result of the decentralisation measures introduced by Regulation 1/2003.

[115] ibid, Art 108.

4.5.2. Administrative Implementation

The Commission is responsible for implementing a broad range of programmes and managing Union funds. This task demands significant human and material resources, as well as close collaboration with various agencies, bodies, offices, and authorities of the Member States. It is common for the Commission to implement a programme through shared management, an arrangement in which the Commission establishes the framework of the programme, and the Member States undertake its implementation at the closest level to the citizen or the undertakings concerned, managing the funds, issuing calls for grants or public tenders, and providing remedies for interested parties, among other activities. Under the Financial Regulation, the Commission may also implement the budget through direct management or indirect management, the latter entailing the delegation of implementation tasks to third countries, international organisations, or other entities.

When carrying out these tasks, the Commission can adopt acts, primarily through decisions. These acts can produce legal effects on their addressees or third parties and are therefore subject to judicial review in Union courts.

4.5.3. Budgetary Implementation

Article 317 TFEU assigns the Commission the responsibility to implement the Union budget in cooperation with the Member States. This duty falls upon the Commission 'on its own responsibility' and in accordance with the 'principles of sound financial management'. To fulfil its accountability obligations, the Commission submits annually to the European Parliament and the Council the accounts of the previous financial year concerning the implementation of the Union budget. The Commission also presents an evaluation report on the Union's finances based on the results achieved (Article 318 TFEU). This report includes the financial statements of the Union's assets and liabilities.[116] These duties related to the implementation of the budget are carried out alongside the Commission's tasks regarding the discharge of the budget, which the European Parliament, acting upon a recommendation from the Council, grants to the Commission.[117] The discharge procedure involves an assessment of the Commission's management of the budget based, inter alia, on the annual report of the Court of Auditors (Article 319 TFEU).

4.5.4. External Representation of the Union

According to Article 17(1) TEU, the Commission ensures 'the Union's external representation', with the exception of the CFSP and other cases provided for in the Treaties.[118] Despite the derogations, the Commission's power of external representation is highly significant, as the institution plays a vital role in designing and implementing the common commercial policy, including negotiations within multilateral international organisations such as the World Trade

[116] ibid, Arts 317–18.

[117] ibid, Art 319.

[118] Art 335 TFEU refers to the legal capacity of the Union in the Member States, for which it attributes a power of representation to the Commission. This provision, although it refers to representation in the *Member States*, has been interpreted as supporting the attribution of external representation powers to the Commission on behalf of the Union. See, for example, the judgment in Case C-73/14 *Council v Commission* (submission of observations to the International Tribunal for the Sea) EU:C:2015:663, paras 56–59. This line of reasoning was later confirmed in Case C-551/21 *Commission v High Representative and Council* EU:C:2024:281, para 73: 'The wording of the sixth sentence of Article 17(1) TEU, according to which the Commission is to 'ensure the Union's external representation', thus tends to establish that that provision confers on the Commission the power to take, outside of the CFSP and unless the Treaties provide for a different allocation of powers on that point, any action that, following a decision of the Council authorising the signing of an international agreement on behalf of the European Union, ensures that that signature is given.'

Organization, as well as representing the Union in international judicial disputes where the Union participates as a party or an intervener. Furthermore, Article 218 TFEU entrusts the Commission with the role of presenting recommendations to the Council for the opening of negotiations of international agreements (except in the field of CFSP, where this role falls to the High Representative) and conducting negotiations on behalf of the Union in accordance with the Council's negotiating directives.

4.5.5. Legislative Initiative

The Commission plays a vital role in the Union's legislative process, as it holds the general right to submit legislative proposals to the European Parliament and the Council.[119] This power gives the Commission substantial political influence, as any legislative measures can only be proposed and approved with the Commission's agreement to introduce the proposal, except where the Treaties provide otherwise (Article 17(2) TEU). The European Parliament and the Council can invite the Commission to submit proposals in specific policy areas, but the Commission is free to choose whether to respond to the invitation.[120] Article 17(2) TEU acknowledges that this power may be subject to exceptions; however, the Treaties provide only a few derogations, mainly confined to the area of freedom, security, and justice. Further exceptions exist for proposals by the European Central Bank in specific monetary matters (e.g. Article 129(4) TFEU), by the Court of Justice regarding the Statute of the Court (Article 281 TFEU), and by the European Investment Bank regarding its own Statute (Article 308 TFEU).

The Commission's role in the legislative process extends beyond merely submitting a proposal; it also involves participating in all Council meetings where the initiative is discussed and in sessions of the European Parliament. Additionally, the Commission maintains significant negotiating power throughout the process (particularly at first reading), as it must approve any modifications the Council makes to its proposal. According to Article 293(1) TFEU, the Council can only deviate unilaterally from the Commission's original proposal by a unanimous vote.[121] For its part, the Commission can amend or even withdraw its proposal, provided it justifies its decision.[122] In any case, the power of the Commission to unilaterally withdraw its proposals does not amount to a veto right, as the Court of Justice has confirmed.[123]

4.6. *Composition and Functioning*

The Commission is a collegiate body consisting of 27 members, including its President and the High Representative of the Union for Foreign Affairs and Security Policy. Regarding the number of members, Article 17(5) TEU states that, from 1 November 2014, the Commission should comprise a number of members amounting to two thirds of the number of Member States, unless the European Council, acting unanimously, decides to change this number. Following the rejection of the Lisbon Treaty in the first Irish referendum of June 2008, where the loss of a Commissioner became a contentious political issue, the European Council committed in December 2008 to maintain one Commissioner per Member State, a commitment subsequently implemented through European Council Decision 2013/272/EU, which remains in force to this day.[124]

[119] Art 17(2) TEU.

[120] ibid, Art 17(1).

[121] Except in the cases referred to in Arts 294(10) and (13) TFEU, in Arts 310, 312 and 314 TFEU, and in the second para of Art 315 TFEU.

[122] Art 293(2) TFEU.

[123] Case C-409/13 *Council v Commission* EU:C:2015:217, para 74. On the limitations of the power to withdraw an initiative, see ch 5, section III.1.

[124] European Council Decision 2013/272/EU of 22 May 2013 concerning the number of members of the European Commission [2013] OJ L165/98.

The members of the Commission are selected based on their general competence and European commitment, from individuals whose independence is beyond doubt.[125] Except for its President, who is proposed to the European Parliament by the European Council acting by qualified majority,[126] the members of the Commission are appointed by the European Council, after the European Parliament's vote of consent on the Commission as a body, following the adoption of the list of Commissioners by common accord by the Council with the President-elect. The European Parliament plays a vital role in the appointment process, holding a veto over both the appointment of the President and the election of the College of Commissioners.

The Commission's term of office lasts five years and is linked to the electoral cycle of the European Parliament's term of office. In addition, when proposing the candidate for President of the Commission, the European Council must take into account the outcome of the elections to the European Parliament.[127] Therefore, the Treaty stipulates that the composition of the Commission must reflect the outcome of the European elections.

The President defines the Commission's guidelines and decides on its internal organisation (Article 17(6) TEU). The President has the authority to appoint the Vice-Presidents of the Commission, except for the High Representative, whose Vice-Presidency is established directly by the Treaty.[128] The President also has the authority to allocate and reshuffle responsibilities among the Commissioners during the term of office.

As a collegiate body, the internal functioning and accountability of the Commission are also collegial. The institution makes decisions and is collectively accountable for them, rather than individually.[129] However, under the Framework Agreement on relations between the European Parliament and the Commission, each Member of the Commission assumes political responsibility for his or her area of competence and is individually accountable to the European Parliament, without prejudice to the principle of collegiality.[130] Following the Nice Treaty, a member of the Commission shall resign if the President so requests.[131] However, the High Representative is subject to a distinct procedure: the European Council, acting by qualified majority and with the agreement of the President, may end the High Representative's term of office (Article 18(1) TEU).

The Commission organises its internal services through Directorates-General, each typically headed by a Director-General and further subdivided into Directorates. The Secretariat-General, the Legal Service and Eurostat are among the services that support the work of the College of Commissioners.[132]

4.7. *Internal and Interinstitutional 'Services' Linked to the European Commission*

'Services' are administrative units established by one or more institutions to carry out specific tasks. Unlike agencies which will be examined in section III.5 of this chapter, the 'services' rely on the institution they serve ('internal services') or are designed to deliver services to multiple

[125] Art 17(3) subpara 2 TEU.
[126] ibid, Art 17(7).
[127] ibid, Art 17(7).
[128] ibid, Art 17(6).
[129] Art 250(1) TFEU.
[130] Parliament–Commission Framework Agreement of 20 October 2010, as well as Art 17(8) TEU, which proclaims the collegial nature of the Commission's accountability to the European Parliament.
[131] Art 17(6) TEU. See J Cotter and G Butler, 'The president of the European Commission and the power to request a Commissioner's resignation' (2024) 61 *Common Market Law Review* 593.
[132] See the full organisation chart of the Commission at https://commission.europa.eu/about/departments-and-executive-agencies_en.

institutions ('interinstitutional services'). Examples of the former include the European Anti-Fraud Office (OLAF), the Foreign Policy Instruments (FPI), and the Health and Food Audits and Analysis service. Examples of the latter include the European Personnel Selection Office (EPSO) and the Publications Office of the European Union.

5. The Court of Justice of the European Union

The Union's judiciary consists of the Court of Justice of the European Union and the courts of the Member States. The Court of Justice of the European Union is an institution entrusted with jurisdiction to judicially review Union acts. It is also the highest judicial instance tasked with the authoritative interpretation of Union law. The courts of the Member States are tasked with resolving disputes between individuals and between individuals and the Member States when the dispute concerns Union law. Together, the Court of Justice of the European Union and the national courts form the Union's complete system of legal remedies and procedures. The division of tasks between Union and national courts is explained in detail in chapters eleven and twelve.

The institution referred to in the Treaties comprises two independent jurisdictions: the Court of Justice and the General Court. The Treaties also provide for the possibility of establishing specialised courts attached to the General Court (Article 257 TFEU). The Civil Service Tribunal, established in 2004, was the only such court, but it was dissolved in 2016 when its jurisdiction was transferred to the General Court as part of the reform that doubled the latter's number of judges.

It should be noted that when the Treaty refers to the *Court of Justice of the European Union*, it relates to the *Institution of* the Union. The two courts mentioned above are the *courts or jurisdictions* within this Institution. The Institution has its own President, Vice-President and Registrar, who also serve as the President, Vice-President and Registrar of the Court of Justice. It is supported by the services common to both jurisdictions, including the Directorate-General for Multilingualism, the Directorate-General for Information, and the Directorate-General for Administration.

The Court of Justice of the European Union has its seat in Luxembourg.

5.1. *The Court of Justice*

5.1.1. Composition

The Court of Justice is composed of one judge from each Member State and 11 Advocates General, selected among individuals whose independence is beyond doubt and 'who possess the qualifications required for appointment to the highest judicial offices in their respective countries or who are jurisconsults of recognised competence'.[133] In most Member States, the process of selecting candidates, before they are formally put forward to the Council's Secretariat, is conducted through an open and competitive procedure, which may involve additional specific requirements beyond those outlined in the Treaties.[134]

The members of the Court of Justice are not appointed by the Council, but 'by common accord of the governments of the Member States'.[135] Before their appointment, candidates

[133] Art 19(2) subpara 3 TEU and Art 253(1) TFEU.

[134] On the selection procedures introduced by the Member States and the requirements imposed on them by Union law, see Case C-119/23 *Virgilijus Valančius* EU:C:2024:653.

[135] Art 19(2) subpara 2 TEU.

must be assessed by a panel, expressly provided for in Article 255 TFEU, which will give an opinion on the candidate's suitability.[136] The committee's opinion is not binding, but it has consistently had a significant influence on the final decisions made by the governments of the Member States. In practice, no candidate who has received a negative opinion from the panel has subsequently been appointed. Once appointed, the term of office of a member of the Court of Justice is six years, and it is renewable with no limitations.[137] To guarantee their independence, the members of the Court of Justice may be removed from office only by a unanimous decision of the judges and Advocates General of the Court of Justice if they 'no longer fulfil[s] the requisite conditions or meets the obligations arising from his [or her] office'.[138]

The Advocate General is a figure unfamiliar in most legal traditions of the Member States. Its origins can be traced to the French judicial tradition, particularly in the Council of State and French administrative justice, and it derives from the *commissaire du gouvernement*, now known as the *rapporteur public*. Like its French precursor, the Advocate General delivers his or her Opinion at the final stage of the oral procedure. The Advocate General's Opinion is not binding on the Court of Justice, but their proposals are followed in most cases. Advocates General are independent members of the Court of Justice, subject to the same rules on privileges and immunities that apply to the judges.

The President and Vice-President of the Court of Justice are elected from among the judges for a three-year term, renewable without limit. The Court of Justice is supported by a Registrar, who is responsible for the management of the Registry. The judges and Advocates General lead their individual cabinets, which include legal secretaries (*référendaires*) in charge of the examination of cases and the drafting of decisions.

5.1.2. Organisation

The Court deliberates and decides cases in collegiate formations called chambers, which can be composed of three or five judges. The Grand Chamber sits with 15 judges, including the President, the Vice-President, three Presidents of Chambers of five judges, and 10 judges who rotate in every case. The Full Court comprises all the judges of the Court of Justice.

The criterion for allocating cases among the different formations is based on the relevance of the case. The Full Court hears cases involving major constitutional points of law. The Grand Chamber deals with cases involving new points of law or constitutional principle, or when requested by a Member State or institution that is party to the proceedings. Five- and three-judge chambers resolve cases that do not require a ruling on a point of principle and which can be resolved based on previous case law. The assignment of cases to formations is decided by the Court on a proposal from the Judge-Rapporteur after hearing the Advocate General.

The deliberations of the Court of Justice are conducted in French, without interpreters, in camera and in the sole presence of the judges of the formation. Decisions are taken by majority vote, although in practice consensus is frequently reached. The decisions are generally made by consensus, and judges are not allowed to issue dissenting opinions.

[136] On the work of this committee, see M Bobek (ed), *Selecting Europe's Judges: A Critical Review of the Appointment Procedures to the European Courts* (Oxford University Press, 2015), and EU Law Live, *The Selection of EU Judges and the 255 Committee* (Symposium, November 2024).

[137] ibid.

[138] Art 6 of the Statute of the Court of Justice of the European Union.

5.2. *The General Court*

5.2.1. Composition

The General Court consists of two judges from each Member State, totalling 54 judges. This structure results from the reform of the General Court adopted in 2015, which doubled the number of judges and incorporated the judges of the now-abolished Civil Service Tribunal.[139]

The judges of the General Court are subject to the same system of appointment and removal from office as the judges and Advocates General of the Court of Justice. There are no permanent Advocates General at the General Court, but the Treaties allow for the appointment of a Judge of the General Court to perform the task of an Advocate General in cases of particular complexity or importance, as well as in cases where the General Court hears a preliminary reference.[140]

5.2.2. Organisation

The General Court deliberates and adjudicates in chambers that range from a single judge to a Full Court. In the first case, a single judge may sit in cases showing a 'lack of difficulty of the questions of law or fact raised . . . or the absence of other special circumstances'.[141] Chambers are composed of three or five judges, depending on the importance of the case, with the possibility of ruling in an 'intermediate chamber' of up to nine judges in preliminary ruling proceedings. The Grand Chamber of the General Court, composed of 15 judges and presided over by the President, is available for cases raising questions of particular importance or constitutional principle and those of significant relevance for the consistency or development of the case law.

Deliberations at the General Court are conducted in French, behind closed doors and without interpreters. However, English is gradually being introduced into the Court's daily work. The judges are the heads of their individual chambers, which include legal secretaries (*référendaires*) responsible for research, analysis of cases and the drafting of documents.

5.3. *Specialised Courts*

The Treaty of Nice introduced the possibility for the Council, on a proposal from the Court of Justice, to establish specialised courts to relieve the General Court of certain cases. This possibility remains in force today in Article 257 TFEU and was implemented in 2004 with the creation of the Civil Service Tribunal, the first and only specialised court established under that provision. The Civil Service Tribunal was abolished following the reform of 2015, with the incorporation of some of its members into the General Court. The option of functional decentralisation of Union courts, as set out in the Nice Treaty, has been discarded in favour of further specialisation of the General Court. This approach was reaffirmed in the 2024 reform of the Statute, which introduced a partial transfer of the preliminary reference jurisdiction, granting jurisdiction to the General Court to hear preliminary references in 'specific areas', which are dealt with in specialised chambers.

[139] Regulation (EU, Euratom) 2015/2422 of the European Parliament and of the Council of 16 December 2015 amending Protocol No. 3 on the Statute of the Court of Justice of the European Union.

[140] Art 49 of the Statute of the Court of Justice of the European Union.

[141] ibid, Art 50(2) and Art 29(1) of the Rules of Procedure of the General Court.

6. The European Central Bank

The ECB is the institution holding exclusive competence to conduct the monetary policy of the Union. Together with the national central banks of the Member States, it forms the European System of Central Banks (ESCB). The central banks of Member States whose currency is the euro are integrated alongside the ECB in the Eurosystem, which is the subsystem responsible for conducting the monetary policy of the euro area (Article 282(1) TFEU).[142]

The ECB is the only institution with its own legal personality.[143] This feature gives it the capacity to act in its own name in legal and financial matters, including the authority to decide on the issuance of the euro and to conduct its monetary policy operations in the markets, while also ensuring its functional independence. The ECB enjoys robust independence, and the Treaties provide for specific guarantees to protect this status, to avoid any external interference when conducting the Union's monetary policy.[144]

The ECB's competences, as well as those of the European System of Central Banks, are subject to the fulfilment of two objectives: to maintain price stability; and, without prejudice to this objective, to support the general economic policies of the Union, in line with the principle of an open market economy with free competition.[145] All actions taken by the ECB and the European System of Central Banks aim to achieve these objectives. This also applies to actions that may affect the Member States' access to financial markets, provided their ultimate aim is either to ensure price stability or to support the general economic policies of the Union.[146]

The ECB comprises two decision-making bodies: the Governing Council and the Executive Board. The Governing Council includes the members of the Executive Board and the governors of the national central banks of the Member States whose currency is the euro.[147] The Executive Board is composed of the President, the Vice-President, and four other members.[148] The members of the Executive Board are appointed by the European Council, acting by qualified majority, based on a recommendation from the Council and after consulting the European Parliament and the Governing Council of the ECB.[149] The members of the Executive Board must be individuals of recognised standing and professional experience in monetary or banking matters. They serve a non-renewable eight-year term of office and must be nationals of a Member State.[150] A third body, the General Council, exists as a transitional arrangement for as long as there are Member States whose currency is not the euro (Article 141(1) TFEU and Article 44 of the Statute of the ESCB). The General Council comprises the President and Vice-President of the ECB and the governors of the national central banks of all Member States.

The ECB carries out additional tasks conferred by legislative acts, such as the supervision of significant credit institutions established in the euro area[151] and supporting the activities of

[142] Art 282(1) TFEU.

[143] ibid, Art 282(3).

[144] ibid, Arts 130 and 282(3), as well as Art 7 of the Statute of the ESCB and the ECB.

[145] According to Art 119(2) TFEU, the adoption of an economic policy 'shall include a single currency, the euro, and the definition and conduct of a single monetary policy and exchange-rate policy *the primary objective of both of which shall be to maintain price stability* and, without prejudice to this objective, to support the general economic policies in the Union' (emphasis added).

[146] Case C-62/14 *Gauweiler* EU:C:2015:400, paras 47–56; and Case C-493/17 *Weiss* EU:C:2018:1000.

[147] Art 283(1) TFEU.

[148] ibid, Art 283(2).

[149] ibid, Art 283(2) subpara 1.

[150] ibid, Art 283(2) subparas 2–4.

[151] Council Regulation (EU) No 1024/2013 of 15 October 2013 entrusting the European Central Bank with specific tasks concerning policies relating to the prudential supervision of credit institutions [2013] OJ L287/63.

the European Systemic Risk Board.[152] Furthermore, within the scope of the European Stability Mechanism's powers, the ECB participates in overseeing the implementation of financial assistance programmes to the Member States and credit institutions in the euro area.[153] In addition, the ECB holds a consultative role: the ECB must be consulted on any proposed Union act or draft national legislation in its fields of competence (Article 127(4) TFEU and Council Decision 98/415/EC). The ECB also has the right to submit opinions and, in specific cases provided for in the Treaties, the right of legislative initiative (e.g. Article 129(4) TFEU).

The ECB is based in the city of Frankfurt am Main, in the Federal Republic of Germany.

7. The Court of Auditors

The Court of Auditors is the institution responsible for the external audit of the Union's finances. It examines the accounts of all revenue and expenditure of the Union's institutions, as well as of the bodies, offices, and agencies, except where the constituent instruments of such a body preclude this (Article 287(1) TFEU).[154] It performs this task through its annual reports, which are presented to the European Parliament and the Council and published in the *Official Journal of the European Union*.[155] In addition, the Court of Auditors issues a Statement of Assurance on the reliability of the Union's accounts and the legality and regularity of the underlying transactions.[156] Pursuant to Article 287(1) TFEU, the Statement of Assurance is the mandatory annual audit opinion issued by the Court of Auditors, attesting to the reliability of the consolidated accounts and the legality and regularity of the underlying transactions based on a materiality threshold of two per cent. This declaration serves as a key evidentiary basis for the European Parliament's exercise of the discharge procedure under Article 319 TFEU, determining whether the Commission's financial management satisfies the requirements of accountability and legal compliance.

Beyond its annual reporting, the Court of Auditors may also submit observations, particularly in the form of special reports, on specific questions, and may deliver opinions at the request of one of the other institutions of the Union (Article 287(4) TFEU). The Court's special reports have become an increasingly important tool for assessing the performance and value for money of Union spending, going beyond mere compliance auditing to encompass performance auditing.

To prepare its annual reports and any special reports which it deems necessary,[157] the Court of Auditors has powers of audit, including the authority to request information from Union institutions, bodies, offices, agencies, Member States, or any natural or legal persons in receipt of payments from the Union budget.[158] Audits in Member States are carried out in liaison with the national audit bodies or, if these do not have the necessary powers, with the competent

[152] Council Regulation (EU) No 1096/2010 of 18 November 2010 entrusting the European Central Bank with specific tasks concerning the functioning of the European Systemic Risk Board [2010] OJ L331/162.

[153] See, for example, the general terms and conditions of the financial assistance arrangements, approved by the ESM Board of Directors on 22 November 2012 (available at www.esm.europa.eu), confirming the role of the ECB in the monitoring of the financial assistance programmes (in particular, see Arts 3.3.2, 3.4.2, 5.3.4, 5.12.1, 6.2.6, 9.6, 9.8.2 and 12.2).

[154] Art 287(1) TFEU.

[155] ibid, Art 287(1) subpara 2.

[156] ibid, Arts 287(1) subpara 2, and 319.

[157] ibid, Art 287(4) subpara 2.

[158] ibid, Art 287(3). On the powers of the Court of Auditors, see Case C-315/99 *Ismeri Europa v European Court of Auditors* EU:C:2001:391; and Case C-539/09 *Commission v Germany* EU:C:2011:733, paras 58–62.

national departments (Article 287(3) TFEU). The Court of Auditors and the national audit institutions cooperate in a spirit of trust while maintaining their independence.

The Court of Auditors is composed of one national of each Member State (Article 285 TFEU). The members are chosen from among persons who have belonged to or are currently part of external audit bodies in their respective states, or who are particularly qualified for this office.[159] The independence of the members of the Court of Auditors must be beyond question, being appointed for a renewable term of six years.

The Court of Auditors acts as a collegiate body. It adopts its annual reports, special reports, and opinions by a majority of its members (Article 287(4) TFEU). For the purposes of adopting certain categories of reports and opinions, the Court may establish internal chambers (Article 287(4) TFEU). The Court does not have judicial powers: it cannot impose sanctions or legally compel the institutions or Member States to act on its findings. Its influence derives from the authority of its reports and the political consequences that flow from the discharge procedure.

The Court of Auditors has its seat in Luxembourg.

III. BODIES, OFFICES AND AGENCIES

1. Advisory Bodies

The Treaties establish two advisory bodies of the Union which must be consulted in the cases provided for by the Treaties, thereby providing additional democratic legitimacy to the decision-making process: the European Economic and Social Committee and the Committee of the Regions. Both bodies represent the socio-economic and territorial interests of the Union and serve an advisory, non-binding role in the legislative procedure. The Treaties specify the circumstances in which these bodies are consulted. Their mandatory consultation where required by the Treaties is a procedural requirement which, if omitted, can lead to the annulment of the act concerned.[160]

1.1. The European Economic and Social Committee

The European Economic and Social Committee (EESC) is an advisory body representing the interests of employers, workers, and other civil society groups, particularly in socio-economic, civic, professional, and cultural fields.[161] Its members are appointed by a decision of the Council, based on a proposal from the Member States and after consulting the Commission, for a term of five years.[162] The Treaties set a maximum limit of 350 members of the Committee.[163]

The Committee appoints a president every two and a half years, along with the two vice-presidents and the Bureau, from among its members.[164] The Bureau reflects the composition of the Committee and ensures a balanced representation of all its members. The Committee organises its work through plenary sessions and subject-specific commissions.

[159] Art 286(1) TFEU. On the appointment and removal of office of members of the Court of Auditors, see Case C-130/19 *Court of Auditors v Pinxten* EU:C:2021:782.

[160] Case 138/79 *Roquette Frères v Council* EU:C:1980:249 and the consistent line of case law thereafter; on EESC/CoR consultation specifically, see Case C-378/00 *Commission v European Parliament and Council* EU:C:2003:42.

[161] Art 300(1) TFEU.

[162] ibid, Art 301.

[163] ibid, Art 301(1). See also Council Decision 2019/853 of 21 May 2019 determining the composition of the European Economic and Social Committee [2019] OJ L139/15.

[164] Rules of procedure and code of conduct for members of the European Economic and Social Committee [2022] OJ L149/1.

1.2. *The Committee of the Regions*

The Committee of the Regions (CoR) is a consultative body representing the interests of the regions and other local and regional authorities of the Member States.[165] Its members, which must not exceed 350, are representatives of regional and local bodies who either hold a regional or local authority electoral mandate or are politically accountable to an elected assembly.[166] Each Member State is allocated several representatives on the Committee of the Regions, and it is up to each Member State to propose to the Council the designation of the members assigned to that state.[167] The term of office for the members is five years, renewable without limitation.[168]

The Committee of the Regions appoints its President and Bureau every two and a half years.[169] Similar to the Economic and Social Committee, the work of the Committee of the Regions is carried out in plenary sessions and specialised commissions. Members are organised based on nationality and political affiliation.

The Lisbon Treaty granted the Committee of the Regions standing to bring actions before the Court of Justice of the European Union 'for the purpose of protecting [its] prerogatives'.[170] To date, the Committee has not exercised this power.

1.3. *Other Advisory Bodies*

Article 242 TFEU empowers the Council to lay down, after consulting the Commission, 'the rules governing the committees provided for in the Treaties'. The provision relates to certain specialised consultative bodies listed from time to time and assigned to specific EU policies, such as the Advisory Committee on Transport (Article 99 TFEU), the European Social Fund Committee (Article 163 TFEU), the Social Protection Committee (Article 160 TFEU), and the Economic and Financial Committee (Article 134 TFEU). These committees typically comprise members appointed by Member States and the Commission and serve to provide technical expertise and facilitate coordination in their respective policy fields. The Employment Committee (Article 150 TFEU) should also be noted among the Treaty-based advisory committees, given its significant role in the coordination of employment policies under the European Semester.

2. The European Investment Bank

Articles 308–309 TFEU introduce the basic rules of the European Investment Bank, a body of the Union with its own legal personality composed of representatives from the Member States,[171] headquartered in Luxembourg.[172] The Bank's mission is to contribute, through access to capital markets and the use of its own resources, to the balanced and steady development of the internal market in the interest of the Union.[173] Such projects are specifically targeted at the

[165] Art 300(3) TFEU.
[166] ibid.
[167] ibid, Art 305(3).
[168] ibid.
[169] ibid, Art 306.
[170] ibid, Art 263(3) and Art 8 of Protocol (No 2), annexed to the TEU and TFEU, on the application of the principles of subsidiarity and proportionality [2008] OJ C115/206. See C Panara, 'The "Europe with the Regions" before the Court of Justice (2019) 26 *Maastricht Journal of European and Comparative Law* 157.
[171] Art 308(1)–(2) TFEU.
[172] See also Protocol No 5 on the Statute of the European Investment Bank [2016] OJ C202/251.
[173] Art 309 TFEU.

development of less-developed regions,[174] the modernisation or conversion of undertakings,[175] or projects of common interest to several Member States.[176] Additionally, the Bank may finance investment in third countries in support of the Union's external action objectives, including development cooperation policy. The EIB has become one of the world's largest multilateral lending institutions, and its role has expanded significantly over time, notably through the European Fund for Strategic Investments (EFSI) launched in 2015 and its successor, the InvestEU programme, which leverage EIB financing to mobilise private investment across the Union.

The Bank's organisation is primarily divided into the Board of Governors, the Board of Directors, and the Management Committee, as specified in its Statute.[177] The Board of Governors consists of ministers from the Member States, most of whom hold economic portfolios, and it defines the Bank's credit policy. The Board of Directors, whose meetings are presided over by the President of the Bank (or, in his or her absence, by a Vice-President) without voting rights, comprises directors appointed by the Member States and the Commission, and approves lending and borrowing operations.[178] The Management Committee is the Bank's executive body, responsible for handling the day-to-day operations, comprising the President and eight Vice-Presidents, who are appointed for a six-year term by the Board of Governors based on a proposal from the Board of Directors.[179]

The EIB's lending activities are distinct from Union budgetary expenditure: the Bank raises funds on the capital markets by issuing bonds and lends on favourable terms, rather than distributing grants from the Union budget. However, the EIB may also manage Union budgetary resources on behalf of the Commission under mandate, as occurs under certain financial instruments and guarantee programmes.

3. The European Ombudsman

According to Article 228 TFEU, the European Parliament elects the European Ombudsman, a body responsible for receiving and investigating complaints of maladministration by the institutions, bodies, offices, and agencies of the Union. The European Ombudsman can receive complaints from any citizen of the Union or any natural or legal person residing in, or having its registered office in, a Member State; however, the Ombudsman's findings and recommendations are not legally binding.[180] The Ombudsman's inquiries are confined to the activities of the Union's institutions, bodies, offices, and agencies, thus excluding the activities of the Member States, even when they are implementing Union law. Furthermore, Article 228(1) TFEU excludes from the European Ombudsman's remit any actions taken by the Court of Justice of the European Union in the exercise of its judicial duties.[181]

The Ombudsman is elected following each European Parliament election for the duration of the Parliament's term of office. This term lasts five years and can be renewed indefinitely.[182] The Ombudsman carries out its duties independently and on an exclusive basis, being

[174] ibid, Art 309(a).
[175] ibid, Art 309(b).
[176] ibid, Art 309(c).
[177] Protocol (No 5) on the Statute of the European Investment Bank, Art 6ff.
[178] Art 9 of the Statute of the European Investment Bank.
[179] ibid, Art 11.
[180] Art 228(1) TFEU.
[181] ibid, Art 228(1).
[182] ibid, Art 228(2).

precluded from engaging in any other occupation during its tenure, whether gainful or not.[183] The Ombudsman can only be dismissed by the Court of Justice, upon request of the European Parliament, if he or she 'no longer fulfils the conditions required for the performance of his [or her] duties or if he [or she] is guilty of serious misconduct'.[184]

The Ombudsman's primary role is to conduct inquiries, either on its own initiative or based on a complaint. As mentioned above, these inquiries involve allegations of maladministration by an institution, body, office, or agency of the Union (excluding the Court of Justice of the European Union when acting in its judicial capacity). If the Ombudsman determines that maladministration has occurred, it refers the matter to the relevant institution, body, office, or agency, which has three months to make a statement of its position.[185] The Ombudsman will subsequently forward a report to the European Parliament and to the institution, body, office, or agency concerned, and will also inform the person who initially raised the inquiry. Additionally,[186] the Ombudsman submits an annual report to the European Parliament detailing the outcomes of these inquiries.[187]

As the Court of Justice has stated, any wrongful conduct resulting from the abnormal functioning of the European Ombudsman's office may give rise to non-contractual liability of the Union under Article 340 TFEU.[188]

4. The European External Action Service

The European External Action Service (EEAS) is a functionally autonomous body of the Union entrusted with supporting the High Representative of the Union for Foreign Affairs and Security Policy in fulfilling his or her mandate, as set out in Article 27(3) TEU. It operates as a functionally autonomous service while maintaining close institutional links with the Council and the Commission, and operates under the authority of the High Representative.[189] It is comprised of officials from the General Secretariat of the Council and from the Commission, as well as staff seconded from the diplomatic services of the Member States who are appointed as temporary agents.[190] While the High Representative directs the Service, it is managed on a day-to-day basis by an Executive Secretary-General, assisted by Deputy Secretaries-General.[191] The Service includes a central administration in Brussels, organised into geographical and thematic managing directorates and crisis management structures, alongside delegations in third countries and at international organisations, which represent the Union and operate under the authority of the High Representative.[192]

The Service lacks its own legal personality, but Decision 2010/427 grants it the legal capacity necessary to carry out its tasks and accomplish its objectives.[193]

[183] ibid, Art 228(3).
[184] ibid, Art 228(2) subpara 2.
[185] ibid, Art 228(1) subpara 2.
[186] ibid.
[187] ibid, Art 228(1) subpara 3.
[188] See judgments in Case C-234/02 P *Ombudsman v Lamberts* EU:C:2004:174, para 49; and Case C-337/15 P *Ombudsman v Staelen* EU:C:2017:256, para 31.
[189] Art 27(3) TEU.
[190] Art 6 of Council Decision of 26 July 2010 establishing the organisation and functioning of the European External Action Service [2010] OJ L201/30.
[191] ibid, Art 4(1)–(2).
[192] ibid, Art 5.
[193] ibid, Art 1(2).

5. Agencies

The agencies of the Union stem from the need for specialised, autonomous, and operational administrative structures across Europe in specific policy areas. These agencies are legally distinct from the institutions listed in Article 13 TEU; they are established by legislative acts, but they currently lack a common legal framework. Since the 1970s, various agencies have been created, and by early 2026 there were over 40 operating agencies (the most recently created agency, the Anti-Money Laundering Authority, started operation on 1 July 2025).

Agencies can be categorised into the following main three types:

- *Decentralised agencies*: autonomous entities with legal personality, located in a Member State, responsible for contributing to the development or implementation of a Union policy in a specific sector. Examples of decentralised agencies include the European Fisheries Control Agency (Vigo, Spain), the European Union Agency for Fundamental Rights (Vienna, Austria), the European Medicines Agency (Amsterdam, the Netherlands) or the European Union Intellectual Property Office (Alicante, Spain).
- *Executive agencies*: Unlike decentralised agencies, executive agencies are governed by a common legal framework established by Council Regulation (EC) No 58/2003. They do not exercise regulatory or policy-making powers, but are entrusted with programme implementation tasks, including budget execution, grant management and project monitoring. The Commission retains ultimate responsibility for the programmes managed by executive agencies and exercises close supervision over their activities. In practice, executive agencies are located at the Commission's main sites in Brussels and Luxembourg. Examples include the European Climate, Infrastructure and Environment Executive Agency, the European Health and Digital Executive Agency, the European Research Executive Agency, the European Innovation Council and SMEs Executive Agency, the European Research Council Executive Agency, or the European Education and Culture Executive Agency.[194]
- *Independent bodies*: entities endowed with a special degree of autonomy due to their subject matter, such as the European Data Protection Supervisor, the European Data Protection Board, the Authority for European Political Parties and European Political Foundations, or the European Institute of Innovation and Technology.

6. Bodies Linked to the CFSP and the Area of Freedom, Security and Justice

In the area of the CFSP, the Treaties and CFSP decisions allow the Union to establish specialised agencies and bodies, such as the European Union Institute for Security Studies, the European Union Satellite Centre, and the European Defence Agency.[195] In the area of freedom, security

[194] Commission Implementing Decision (EU) 2021/173 of 12 February 2021 establishing the European Climate, Infrastructure and Environment Executive Agency, the European Health and Digital Executive Agency, the European Research Executive Agency, the European Innovation Council and SMEs Executive Agency, the European Research Council Executive Agency, and the European Education and Culture Executive Agency and repealing Implementing Decisions 2013/801/EU, 2013/771/EU, 2013/778/EU, 2013/779/EU, 2013/776/EU and 2013/770/EU [2021] OJ L50/9.

[195] This is the case of Arts 42(3) and 45 TEU, regarding the European Defence Agency, or the European Union Institute for Security Studies and the European Union Satellite Centre, established by CFSP Council Joint Actions / Decisions on the grounds of Articles 42 to 46 TEU. See Council Decision 2014/75/CFSP of 10 February 2014 on the European Union Institute for Security Studies [2014] OJ L41/13, and Council Decision 2014/401/CFSP of 20 June 2014 on the EU Satellite Centre [2014] OJ L221/42.

and justice, Articles 85 and 88 TFEU expressly regulate Eurojust and Europol as Union bodies for judicial and police cooperation in criminal matters.

Likewise, in 2017, the European Public Prosecutor's Office was established through enhanced cooperation and under the provisions of Article 86 TFEU, creating a body based on a system of shared competences between the European Public Prosecutor's Office and the national authorities responsible for combating offences affecting the Union's financial interests.[196]

GENERAL BIBLIOGRAPHY

Bradley, K. 'Institutional Design in the Treaty of Nice' (2001) 38 *Common Market Law Review* 1095.

Craig, P, 'Institutions, Power and Institutional Balance' in P Craig and G De Búrca, *The Evolution of EU Law*, 2nd edn (Oxford University Press, 2011).

Curtin, D and Dekker, IF, 'The European Union from Maastricht to Lisbon: Institutional and Legal Unity out of the Shadows' in P Craig and G De Búrca, *The Evolution of EU Law*, 2nd edn (Oxford University Press, 2011).

Hodson, D, Puetter U, Saurugger, S and Peterson, J, (eds), *The Institutions of the European Union* (Oxford University Press, 2021).

Lenaerts, K, 'Constitutionalism and the Many Faces of Federalism' (1991) 38 *American Journal of Comparative Law* 205.

Nugent, N, *The Government and Politics of the European Union* 8th edn (Macmillan, 2017).

Schütze, R, 'On "Federal" Ground: The European Union as an (Inter)national Phenomenon' (2009) 46 *Common Market Law Review* 1069.

FURTHER READING

The Institutional Architecture of the Union

Blumann, C, 'Les institutions de l'Union dans le cadre du traité établissant une Constitution pour l'Europe' (2005) 2 *Revue Trimestrielle de Droit Européen* 295.

Curtin, D, 'The Constitutional Structure of the Union: A Europe of Bits and Pieces' (1993) 30 *Common Market Law Review* 17.

Dehousse, R, 'European Institutional Architecture after Amsterdam: Parliamentary System or Regulatory Structure?' (1998) 35 *Common Market Law Review* 595.

Driessen, B, 'Interinstitutional Conventions and Institutional Balance' (2008) 33 *European Law Review* 550.

Dougan, M, 'The Treaty of Lisbon 2007: Winning Minds, Not Hearts' (2008) 45 *Common Market Law Review* 617.

Lenaerts, K, and Desomer, M, 'La recherche d'un équilibre pour l'Union – répartition des compétences et équilibre institutionnel dans le projet de Constitution' in O De Schutter and P Nihoul (eds), *Une Constitution pour l'Europe – Réflexions sur la transformation du droit de l'Union Européenne* (Larcier, 2004).

The European Parliament

Blumann, C, *La fonction législative communautaire* (LGDJ, 1995).

Bressanelli, E and Chelotti, N (eds.), *The European Parliament in the Contested Union. Power and Influence Post-Lisbon* (Routledge, 2020).

Corbett, R, Jacobs, F and Shackleton, M, *The European Parliament*, 8th edn (Macmillan, 2011).

Costa, O, *The European Parliament in Times of EU Crisis. Dynamics and Transformations* (Palgrave Macmillan, 2019).

[196] Council Regulation (EU) 2017/1939 of 12 October 2017 establishing enhanced cooperation for the establishment of the European Public Prosecutor's Office [2017] *OJ* L283/1.

Judge, D and Earnshaw, D, *The European Parliament*, 2nd edn (Palgrave Macmillan, 2008).
Raunio, T, 'The European Parliament' in E Jones, A Menon and S Weatherill (eds), *The Oxford Handbook of the European Union* (Oxford University Press, 2012).

The European Council

Bulmer, S and Wessels, W, *The European Council. Decision-Making in European Politics* (Macmillan, 1987).
Capotorti, F, 'Le statut juridique du Conseil européen à la lumière de l'Acte unique' in *Du Droit International au Droit de l'Integration. Liber Amicorum Pierre Pescatore* (Nomos, 1987).
Lewis, J, 'Council of Ministers and European Council' in E Jones, A Menon and S Weatherill (eds), *The Oxford Handbook of the European Union* (Oxford University Press, 2012).
Picod F, 'Le rôle du Conseil européen dans le processus de decisión' (2002) *Revue de Droit Public.*
Taulegne, B, *Le Conseil européen* (Presses Universitaires de France, 1993).
Van de Steeg, M, 'The European Council's Evolving Political Accountability' in M Bovens, D Curtin and P Hart (eds), *The Real World of EU Accountability: What Deficit?* (Oxford University Press, 2010).
Werts, J, *The European Council* (Harper Publishing, 2008).
Wessels, W, 'The European Council: Beyond the Traditional View Towards a Fusion', *Chemins d'Europe: Mélanges en l'honneur de Jean Paul Jacqué* (Dalloz, 2010).

The Council

Constantinesco, V and Simon, D (eds), *Le COREPER dans tous ses états* (Presses universitaires, 2000).
Hayes-Renshaw, F and Wallace, H, *The Council of Ministers*, 2nd edn, (Macmillan, 2006).
Jacqué, J-P, 'Le Conseil européen et le Conseil de l'Union européenne' in *Traité de droit administratif européen* (Bruylant, 2014).
Lewis, J, 'Council of Ministers and European Council' in E Jones, A Menon and S Weatherill (eds), *The Oxford Handbook of the European Union* (Oxford University Press, 2012).
Louis, J-V, 'L'évolution du Conseil européen à la lumière de la réalisation de l'Union économique et monétaire' in *Studi in onore di Francesco Capotorti* (Giuffrè, 1999).
Puetter U, *The European Council and the Council: New Intergovernmentalism and Institutional Change* (Oxford University Press 2014).
Westlake, M and Galloway, D, *The Council of the European Union*, 3rd edn, (Harper Publishing, 2004).

The European Commission

Cini, M, *The European Commission: Leadership, Organisation and Culture in the EU Administration* (Manchester University Press, 1996).
Cotter, J, and Butler, G, 'The president of the European Commission and the power to request a Commissioner's resignation' (2024) 61 *Common Market Law Review* 593.
Craig, P, 'The Fall and Renewal of the Commission: Accountability, Contract and Administrative Organizations' (2000) 6 *European Law Journal* 98.
Louis, J-V and Waelbroeck, D (eds), *La Commission au coeur du système institutionnel des Communautés européennes* (Éd de l'Université, 1989).
Magnette, P, 'Appointing and Censuring the European Commission: The Adaptation of Parliamentary Institutions to the Community Context' (2001) 7 *European Law Journal* 292.
Muller, H, *Political Leadership and the European Commission Presidency* (Oxford University Press, 2020).
Noel, E, 'The Commission's Power of Initiative' (1973) 10 *Common Market Law Review* 197.
Nugent, N, *The European Commission* (Palgrave Macmillan, 2001).
Patrin, M, Collegiality in the European Commission: Legal Substance and Institutional Practice (Oxford University Press, 2023).

Schmidt, SK and Wonka, A, 'European Commission' in E Jones, A Menon and S Weatherill (eds), *The Oxford Handbook of the European Union* (Oxford University Press, 2012).
Spence, D, and Edwards, G (eds), *The European Commission* (Harper Publishing, 2006).

The Court of Justice

Alonso García, R, 'The Persian Jurist in Luxembourg. On the Decentralisation of the Preliminary Ruling Procedure' (2024) 195 *EU Law Live Weekend Edition* 3.
Alter, K, *The European Court's Political Power* (Oxford University Press, 2009).
Arnull, A, *The European Union and Its Court of Justice*, 2nd edn (Oxford University Press, 2006).
Azoulai, L and Dehousse, R, 'The European Court of Justice and the Legal Dynamics of Integration' in E Jones, A Menon and S Weatherill (eds), *The Oxford Handbook of the European Union* (Oxford University Press, 2012).
Bobek, M, 'The Court of Justice of the European Union' in A Arnull and D Chalmers, *The Oxford Handbook of European Union Law* (Oxford University Press, 2015).
Bobek, M (ed), *Selecting Europe's Judges: A Critical Appraisal of the Judicial Appointments Process* (Oxford University Press 2020).
— 'The Past and the Future of the 255 Panel' (2025) 236 *EU Law Live Weekend Edition* 3.
Burrows, N, and Greaves, R, *The Advocate General and EC Law* (Oxford University Press, 2007).
Clément-Wilz, L, Le rôle politique de la cour de justice de l'Union européenne (Bruylant, 2019).
De Búrca, G, and Weiler, JHH (eds), *The European Court of Justice* (Oxford University Press, 2001).
Dehousse, R, *The European Court of Justice* (Macmillan, 1998).
Lecourt, R, *L'Europe des juges* (Bruylant, 1993).
Lenaerts, K, 'The Rule of Law and the Coherence of the Judicial System of the European Union' (2007) 44 *Common Market Law Review* 1625.
Vogiatzis, N, 'The Administrative Functions of the Court of Justice of the European Union' (2022) 2 *European Law Review* 175.
VVAA, 'The Court of Justice of the European Union as a Relational Actor' 2023) 2 European Law Open 233.

The European Central Bank

Dyson, K, 'Economic and Monetary Union' in E Jones, A Menon and S Weatherill (eds), *The Oxford Handbook of the European Union* (Oxford University Press, 2012).
Krauskopf, B and Steven, C, 'The Institutional Framework of the European System of Central Banks: Legal Issues in the Practice of the First Ten Years of Existence' (2009) 46 *Common Market Law Review* 115.
Smits, R, *The European Central Bank. Institutional Aspects* (Kluwer Law, 1997).
— 'The European Constitution and EMU: An Appraisal' (2005) 42 *Common Market Law Review* 425.
Zilioli, C and Selmayr, M, 'The European Central Bank: An Independent Specialised Organisation of Community Law' (2000) 37 *Common Market Law Review* 591.
— *The Law of the European Central Bank* (Hart, 2001).

Bodies and Agencies of the Union

Cananea, G della (ed), *European Regulatory Agencies* (ISUPE, 2005).
Chamon, M, EU Agencies. Legal and Political Limits to the Transformation of the EU Administration (Oxford University Press, 2016).
Chamon, M, Volpato, A, and Eliantonio, M, *Boards of Appeal of EU Agencies. Towards Judicialization of Administrative Review?* (Oxford University Press, 2022).
Chiti, E, 'An Important Part of the EU's Institutional Machinery: Features, Problems and Perspectives of European Agencies (2009) 46 *Common Market Law Review* 1395.
Comte, F, 'Agences européennes: relance d'une réflexion interinstitutionelle' (2008) 3 *Revue du Droit de l'Union Européenne* 595.

Dehousse, R, 'Regulation by Networks in the EC: The Role of European Agencies' (1997) 4 *Journal of European Public Policy* 246.

Hofmann, HCH, Vos, E and Chamon, M (eds), *The External Dimension of EU Agencies and Bodies: Law and Policy* (Edward Elgar, 2019).

Keleman, D, 'European Union Agencies' in E Jones, A Menon and S Weatherill (eds), *The Oxford Handbook of the European Union* (Oxford University Press, 2012).

Vogiatzis, N, *The European Ombudsman and Good Administration in the European Union* (Palgrave, 2018).

4

The Vertical Distribution of Powers: Competence of the Union

I. COMPETENCE OF THE UNION AND THE PRINCIPLE OF CONFERRAL

EVERY ACTION OF the Union must be founded on competence. The Union can only adopt and implement policies within the competences granted by the Member States through the Treaties. As a result, the Treaties include a comprehensive typology of competences that define *how the* Union operates in each policy field. To understand how the Union acts and the limits of its actions, it is essential to determine not only whether the Union *has* competence, but also *what type* of competence.

Before delving into the typology of Union competences and the distribution of power between the Union and its Member States, it is worth recalling the nature of the powers conferred on the Union, as well as the legal basis under which such conferral occurs under national law. Due to the specific type of transfer that characterises the conferral of powers to the Union, the division of powers between the Union and the Member States differs from the standard practice of other international organisations. The transfer of powers to the Union shares significant features with the creation of a federal state. However, the Union is not a state, nor are there any prospects that it will become one soon. This does not preclude the Union from sharing features with a federal organisation, particularly in the manner in which the Member States transfer sovereign powers to the Union.

1. The Principle of Conferral and the Transfer of Sovereign Powers to the Union

The principle of conferral, as outlined in Article 5(2) Treaty on European Union (TEU), states that 'the Union shall act only within the limits of the competences conferred upon it by the Member States in the Treaties to attain the objectives set out therein'. This principle requires the Union to rely on a competence established in the Treaties to undertake any action, regardless of its scale, nature, or scope. If the Union does not have an attributed competence, it cannot act, as that competence remains with the Member States. As the final sentence of Article 5(2) TEU states, 'competences not conferred upon the Union in the Treaties remain with the Member States'. An act of the Union lacking competence can be challenged and annulled by the Court of Justice.[1]

[1] See, inter alia, Opinion 2/94 EU:C:1996:140; and Case C-376/98 *Germany v Parliament and Council* EU:C:2000:544. See also A Türk, *Judicial Review in EU Law* (Edward Elgar, 2009) 106–13.

The principle of conferral is fundamental to a system of power-sharing between the Member States and the Union, in which the Member States confer a limited set of competences on the Union. This distribution of powers between the Member States and the Union has been defined as a *vertical* division of powers.[2]

The Court of Justice has repeatedly stated, most notably in the early cases of *Van Gend en Loos* and *Costa/Enel*, that the competences conferred on the Union have a special significance. Both judgments emphasise that the Union has led to the creation of 'institutions endowed with sovereign rights',[3] as well as the emergence of 'a new legal order of international law for the benefit of which the states have limited their sovereign rights, albeit within limited fields'.[4] The competences of the Union are therefore based on a limited transfer of sovereign powers by the Member States, whereby they limit and pool their sovereignty collectively under the framework of the Treaties.

As will be explained below, the transfer involves particularly significant powers that enable the Union to enact and enforce legally binding decisions vis-a-vis the Member States and individuals. These powers can be described as 'sovereign', as they include part of the Member State's monopoly on the use of force. Recent declarations referring to a 'European sovereignty' highlight that the powers conferred on the Union include those of a sovereign nature.[5]

2. The Attribution of Sovereign Competences in the Member States: a Comparative Analysis

The Member States have transferred some of their sovereign powers to the Union through specific procedures outlined in their respective Constitutions. These channels establish both procedural requirements and substantive constraints. The existence of these requirements highlights the significance of every transfer of power to the Union, including its expansion to new Member States. This approach differs from the traditional procedures and substantive criteria used for ratifying other international treaties. A brief review of some of the constitutional requirements in several Member States reveals common features among these procedures.[6]

In Germany, Article 23(1) of the Basic Law states that the Federation 'may transfer sovereign powers by a law with the consent of the Bundesrat'. Such a transfer can occur through the creation of a treaty, comparable rules, or their amendment, with approval only possible through the procedures outlined in Article 79(2)–(3), which refers to the amendment of the Basic Law. Consequently, transferring sovereign powers to the Union requires a two-thirds majority in the Bundestag and in the Bundesrat. Additionally, the German Constitutional Court has established several substantive limitations on Germany's participation in the European Union, predominantly aimed at protecting German competences and its constitutional identity.

[2] K Lenaerts, *Le juge et la constitution aux États-Unis d'Amérique et dans l'ordre juridique européen* (Bruylant, 1988).

[3] Case C-26/62 *Van Gend en Loos* EU:C:1963:1, p. 593: 'this view is confirmed by the Preamble to the Treaty which refers not only to governments but to peoples. It is also confirmed more specifically by the establishment of institutions endowed with sovereign rights, the exercise of which affects Member States and also their citizens'. In Case C-6/64 *Costa/Enel* EU:C:1964:66, para 593, the Court developed the same idea in the following terms: 'By creating a Community of unlimited duration, having its own institutions, its own personality, its own legal capacity and capacity of representation on the international plane and, more particularly, real powers stemming from a limitation of sovereignty or a transfer of powers from the States to the Community, the Member States have limited their sovereign rights, albeit within limited fields, and have thus created a body of law which binds both their nationals and themselves'.

[4] *Van Gend en Loos* (n 3) 12.

[5] See the Versailles Declaration of 10–11 March 2022, where the European Council called 'to take greater responsibility for our security and take further decisive steps towards building our European sovereignty'. Along the same lines, the Granada Declaration of the European Council of 6 October 2023 highlights that 'we will reinforce our position as a geostrategic, sovereign power . . . giving us the necessary tools to protect our citizens'.

[6] For an overview of the 'Europe clauses' in national Constitutions, see 'National Constitutional Avenues for Further EU Integration', Study of the European Parliament (DG for Internal Policies, PE 493.046).

In the Czech Republic, Article 10a(2) of the Constitution states that ratifying a treaty that transfers 'certain powers of Czech Republic authorities' requires a three-fifths majority in both the Chamber of Deputies and the Senate, unless a constitutional act requires a referendum. This was the case with the Accession Treaty, which the Czech Parliament considered necessary for the country's accession to the Union in 2004.[7] The Constitutional Court of the Czech Republic has also imposed several substantive limitations on the country's participation in the Union.[8]

In Italy, participation in the Union is governed by Article 11 of the Constitution, which permits Italy to agree 'to the limitations of sovereignty that may be necessary to a world order ensuring peace and justice among Nations'. According to the Italian Constitutional Court, this provision applies to the process of European integration, viewing it as the foundation of Italy's accession to the Union.[9] Furthermore, Article 117 of the Constitution introduces restrictions on the legislative powers of the state and the regions, recognising the constitutional importance of Union law and its primacy over domestic legislation.

In the case of Spain, the attribution of sovereign powers to the Union is based on Article 93 of the Constitution, which states that the *Cortes* may authorise, through an organic law, 'the conclusion of treaties conferring on an international organisation or institution the exercise of competences derived from the Constitution'. When referring to competences derived from the Constitution, the fundamental norm highlights the special importance of the process of European integration, which it does not explicitly mention but implies tacitly. The 'competences deriving from the Constitution' are, as is clear, the same 'sovereign powers' referred to by the Court of Justice in the judgments in *Van Gend en Loos* and *Costa/Enel*.[10]

In other Member States, such as Finland, instead of a broad enabling clause in the Constitution, an amendment was introduced with every relevant reform undertaken in the Union during its initial decades of participation. Following accession in 1995, several constitutional and legislative amendments were introduced to facilitate Finland's ratification of the Treaties of Amsterdam, Nice, and Lisbon. Finally, in 2011, a general provision was added to the Constitution (Article 94) requiring at least two-thirds of the votes cast in Parliament for any 'transfer of authority to the European Union . . . that is of significance with regard to Finland's sovereignty'.

II. THE DIVISION OF COMPETENCES BETWEEN THE UNION AND ITS MEMBER STATES

The Lisbon Treaty introduced in 2009 a typology of the Union's competences, establishing a clear division of tasks between the Union and the Member States. Title I of Part One of the TFEU, in Articles 2–6, provides an exhaustive list of the policy areas conferred on the Union

[7] Constitutional Act of Law No 515/2002 Coll of 14 November 2002, on the referendum on accession of the Czech Republic to the European Union.

[8] See the judgment of 26 November 2008 on the compatibility of the Lisbon Treaty with the Czech Constitution (Pl ÚS 19/08).

[9] See Judgment 14/1964 of 24 February 1964.

[10] In Declaration 1/2004, the Spanish Constitutional Court emphasised that the attribution of sovereign powers provided for in Art 93 of the Constitution also contains material limits. The state cannot use Art 93 of the Constitution to transfer powers the exercise of which would allow the European Union to issue acts contrary to the Constitution. This is logical, as otherwise Art 93 of the Constitution would be used as an indirect means of reforming the Constitution, avoiding the procedures expressly envisaged for its reform. However, the Constitutional Court restricted the scope of this limitation, circumscribing it only to particularly serious violations of the Constitution that affect the indispensable core of the constitutional text.

by the Member States, as well as a typology of competences based on their features. The Union can exercise exclusive competences (Article 3 TFEU), shared competences (Article 4 TFEU), and competences to support, coordinate, or supplement the actions of the Member States (Article 6 TFEU). Due to its specific characteristics, Union competence in the area of economic policy, employment policy, and the coordination of Member States' economic and social policies is categorised separately as a different type of competence (Article 5 TFEU). The Union's powers to define and implement a common foreign and security policy, including the framing of a common defence policy, also merit a separate competence, halfway between a functional and an intergovernmental conception of integration (Articles 21–46 TEU).

The exercise of the competences listed in the Treaties is subject to the principle of conferral (Article 5(2) TEU), as well as to the principles of subsidiarity and proportionality (Article 5(3)–(4) TEU), to which reference will be made later in this chapter.

The introduction of a typology of Union competences serves a twofold purpose. Firstly, it aims to bring transparency to the division of powers between the Union and the Member States. Secondly, it clarifies the scope of each type of competence, thereby facilitating judicial and political oversight of the Union's actions.[11]

Furthermore, by introducing an exhaustive set of competences, the Union assumes a common feature of federal systems, where the constituent states assign to the federal level a defined range of competences, reserving all other competences not explicitly transferred to the Federation for themselves. The residual competence of the Member States, consistent with federal practice, is reflected in Article 4(1) TEU, which states that 'competences not conferred upon the Union in the Treaties remain with the Member States'.

1. Exclusive Competences

The exclusive competences of the Union are enumerated in Article 3 TFEU, and their definition is provided in Article 2(1) TFEU as follows:

> When the Treaties confer on the Union exclusive competence in a specific area, only the Union may legislate and adopt legally binding acts, the Member States being able to do so themselves only if so empowered by the Union or for the implementation of Union acts.

The areas in which the Union has exclusive competence under Article 3(1) TFEU are listed as follows:

- the customs union;
- the establishment of competition rules necessary for the functioning of the internal market;
- monetary policy for the Member States whose currency is the euro;
- the conservation of marine biological resources under the common fisheries policy;
- common commercial policy.

The Union held these exclusive competences before the Lisbon Treaty, but their conferral was spread across various Treaty provisions and instruments. While the exclusive competences related to the internal market (competition), the customs union, the common commercial policy, and monetary policy were already included in the Treaties, the conservation of marine biological resources as an exclusive competence was reflected in the case law of the Court of

[11] A Dashwood, 'The Limits of European Community Powers' (1996) 21 *European Law Review* 113.

Justice.[12] Article 3(1) TFEU now codifies in a single provision all the exclusive competences that existed before the Lisbon Treaty's reforms.

In addition to the policy areas enumerated in Article 3(1) TFEU, there are also *inherent* exclusive competences of the Union, resulting from the powers of self-organisation derived from the ordinary functioning of the Union's institutions. This is the case, for example, of the Union's competence to establish rules introducing rights and obligations applicable to its own staff.[13]

When the Union exercises an exclusive competence, Member States are barred from unilaterally intervening in that policy field. Consequently, the existence of exclusive competence *precludes* in principle any action by Member States, a restriction that can only be waived through explicit authorisation from the Union empowering the Member State(s) to act, or when Member State action is essential to implement the Union's policies in that area. In any case, the Union cannot delegate exclusive competences to Member States, or it would distort the balance of powers established in the Treaties. Therefore, the Court of Justice authorises the Union to issue only 'specific authorisations' in favour of Member States in areas covered by exclusive competence.[14] These 'specific authorisations' are exceptional, narrowly construed and require close supervision by the Union.[15]

In summary, when exclusive competence is conferred on the Union, the Member States immediately lose that competence. Unlike in the case of Union shared competence, it is irrelevant whether the Union has actually exercised its exclusive competence or not. When Member States confer an exclusive competence on the Union, they automatically lose their competence in that field of policy.[16]

The exclusive competences enumerated in Article 3(1) TFEU also have an *external* dimension, closely linked to the Union's international relations. According to Article 3(2) TFEU:

> The Union shall also have exclusive competence for the conclusion of an international agreement when its conclusion is provided for in a legislative act of the Union or is necessary to enable the Union to exercise its internal competence, or in so far as its conclusion may affect common rules or alter their scope.

This provision codifies, in a single passage, a long-standing line of case law of the Court of Justice. The wording of the provision outlines three distinct scenarios of Union action in the realm of external relations,[17] which are elaborated in detail in chapter sixteen of this book. The provision also affirms that the Union holds exclusive competence to conclude international

[12] As regards the conservation of marine biological resources within the common fisheries policy, see Joined Cases C-3/76, 4/76 and 6/76 *Cornelis Kramer and others* EU:C:1977:114, paras 39–41; and Case C-804/79 *Commission v United Kingdom* EU:C:1981:93, paras 17–18. In the 1970s, the Court of Justice confirmed the Union's exclusive competence in the common commercial policy in Opinion 1/75 EU:C:1975:145. See also Case C-41/76 *Donckerwolcke* EU:C:1976:182, para 32; and Case C-347/03 *Regione autonoma Friuli-Venezia Giulia*, EU:C:2005:285, paras 71–83.

[13] Case C-690/15 *Wenceslas de Lobkowicz* EU:C:2017:355, para 46: 'National legislation, such as that at issue in the main proceedings, which subjects the income of an EU official to contributions and social levies specifically allocated for the funding of the social security schemes of the Member State concerned, therefore infringes the *exclusive* competence of the European Union under Article 14 of the Protocol and the relevant provisions of the Staff Regulations, in particular those which prescribe mandatory contributions to the funding of a social security scheme by EU officials' (emphasis added).

[14] *Donckerwolcke* (n 12), para 32: 'As full responsibility in the matter of commercial policy was transferred to the [Union] by means of [Article 207 TFEU] measures of commercial policy of a national character are only permissible after the end of the transitional period by virtue of specific authorization by the [Union]'.

[15] *Commission v United Kingdom* (n 12) para 30; and Case C-174/84 *Bulk Oil* EU:C:1986:60, para 33.

[16] *Commission v United Kingdom* (n 12) para 20; and Case C-422/19 *Hessischer Rundfunk* EU:C:2021:63, para 54.

[17] The first situation was confirmed in Opinion 1/94 EU:C:1994:384, the second is reflected in Opinion 1/76 EU:C:1977:63, and the third appears in Case C-22/70 *Commission v Council* EU:C:1971:32, also known as ERTA. See also the 'Open Skies' cases (Case C-466/98 *Commission v United Kingdom* EU:C:2002:624; Case C-467/98 *Commission v Denmark* EU:C:2002:625; Case C-468/98 *Commission v Sweden* EU:C:2002:626; Case C-469/98 *Commission v Finland* EU:C:2002:627; Case C-470/98 *Commission v Greece* EU:C:2002:326; Case C-471/98 *Commission v Belgium* EU:C:2002:628; and Case C-472/98 *Commission v Luxembourg* EU:C:2002:629).

agreements in policy areas where it has internal shared competence. Therefore, Article 3(2) TFEU enables the Union to exercise external exclusive competence through the conclusion of international agreements with third parties, including states and international organisations, even in areas of internal shared competence that involve an external dimension, where the conditions of that provision are satisfied.[18]

There is no strict or automatic parallelism between the Union's internal and external exclusive competences. For instance, if the Union has a shared competence in the field of environmental protection, exercising this competence *internally* can transform it into an exclusive external competence, provided it is established in a legislative act or if its external competence may affect common rules or alter their scope. Furthermore, in some cases the determination of an external exclusive competence may occur independently of whether the Union has exercised its internal shared competence.[19] While a parallel exists between the Union's internal and external competences, it is an imperfect one, dependent on the development of each policy area, as explained in chapter sixteen.

Finally, it should also be noted that Article 20(1) TEU precludes Member States from establishing enhanced cooperation in the 'fields of exclusive competence' of the Union.[20] Therefore, in areas of Union exclusive competence, it is for *all* Member States to participate uniformly in the development of such policy fields under Union-level governance. This prohibition is subject to a notable exception in the field of the Union's monetary policy, which is an exclusive competence yet is nonetheless divided at present between Member States whose currency is the euro and those subject to a derogation and whose currency is not the euro at the present time.[21]

2. Shared Competences

When the actions of the Union are based on a shared competence, it will do so in close cooperation with the Member States in a specific policy area. This outcome is outlined in Article 2(2) TFEU, which describes the Union's shared competences in the following terms:

> When the Treaties confer on the Union a competence shared with the Member States in a specific area, the Union and the Member States may legislate and adopt legally binding acts in that area. The Member States shall exercise their competence to the extent that the Union has not exercised its competence. The Member States shall again exercise their competence to the extent that the Union has decided to cease exercising its competence.

The policy areas in which the Union acts under shared competences are listed in Article 4(2) TFEU. They are the following:

- the internal market;
- social policy, for the aspects defined in the Treaty;
- economic, social and territorial cohesion;
- agriculture and fisheries, excluding the conservation of marine biological resources;

[18] See the judgments in the 'Open Skies' cases, cited ibid, as well as Opinion 1/03 (EU:C:2006:81). See also I MacLeod, I Hendry and S Hyett, *The External Relations of the European Communities* (Oxford University Press, 1996) 47–55, and P Eeckhout, *EU External Relations Law, 2nd edn* (Oxford University Press, 2011) ch 3.

[19] See, inter alia, Case C-600/14 *Germany v Council* EU:C:2017:935, paras 61–71.

[20] In this respect, see Case C-146 /13 *Spain v Council* EU:C:2015:298 and the arguments put forward by the Kingdom of Spain, albeit without a reply from the Court of Justice (paras 91–103).

[21] See Arts 136–138 TFEU and Protocol No 16 on certain provisions relating to Denmark.

- environment;
- consumer protection;
- transport;
- trans-European networks;
- energy;
- the area of freedom, security and justice;
- common safety concerns in public health matters, for the aspects defined in the Treaty;
- research, technological development and space;
- development cooperation and humanitarian aid.

Shared competences are a default category in the typology of competences established by the TFEU. In cases of doubt regarding the determination of a competence in a policy area, Article 4(2) TFEU establishes a presumption in favour of the shared nature of the competence. The presumption operates by turning the list of policy areas into an open-ended enumeration, in contrast to the lists provided for areas of exclusive competence and support, coordination, or supplement competences. The default role of shared competence appears in Article 4(2) TFEU, which describes the enumeration of policy areas subject to a shared competence as 'the following *principal* areas' (emphasis added), and not 'the *following* areas' (emphasis added), as provided in Articles 3(1) and 6 TFEU.

Despite the literal terms of the definition contained in Article 2(2) TFEU, shared competences do not empower the Member States to act simultaneously or concurrently with the Union. Instead, shared competences allow Member States to act within a specific policy area *until the Union decides to exercise its competence*. Once the Union exercises its competence, the Member States lose theirs, and any national measures enacted until then will become devoid of any effect if incompatible with Union measures. Therefore, shared competences relate to a *sequential* exercise of authority over time, rather than to concurrent action within the same policy area at the same time. Depending on how extensively the Union exercises a shared competence, it may act in 'exclusive' terms, without this implying that the competence has thereby become exclusive in nature under the meaning of Article 3 TFEU.

It should be noted that in two policy areas, Article 4 TFEU exceptionally allows for the exercise of a genuinely shared and concurrent competence. This applies to research, technological development, and space, as well as development cooperation and humanitarian aid. In both policy areas, the Union has competence to carry out activities, 'but the exercise of that competence shall not result in Member States being prevented from exercising theirs' (Article 4(3)–(4) TFEU). These two categories therefore represent a structural departure from the general pre-emption logic that otherwise governs shared competences, and more closely resemble the parallel competences associated with the support, coordination, and supplementary competences listed in Article 6 TFEU, though they remain formally categorised as shared competences under Article 4 TFEU.

Apart from these two policy areas where concurrent shared competence is allowed, the effects of shared competences will materialise through one of the following four scenarios.

2.1. *Shared Competence not yet Exercised by the Union*

If the Union has shared competence in an area where it has not yet adopted any measures, Member States are free to adopt any measures they deem necessary, in accordance with the terms that they themselves determine.[22] Member States are only bound by the prohibitions explicitly laid out in Union law. For instance, in the internal market, particularly in the area of free movement, Member States are precluded from adopting acts that breach free movement rules, even in policy areas where the Union has not yet exercised shared competence. Therefore, if the Union has not exercised shared competence in social policy (an area that falls under a shared competence, pursuant to Article 4(2)(b) TFEU), a Member State operating within that area is nevertheless liable for breaches of, for example, Article 45 TFEU on free movement of workers.[23]

2.2. *Shared Competence Exercised by the Union*

When the Union exercises a shared competence, the resulting Union acts will supersede any previous measures taken by the Member States and replace them with the newly introduced Union measures. This outcome is often referred to as *field preemption*, an effect in which the adoption of Union acts comprehensively covers a policy area and, from that point forward, prevents the Member States from acting unless the Union act expressly or impliedly allows them to do so. The exercise of a shared competence by the Union therefore has two consequences: first, it prevents the Member States from legislating or otherwise acting in the policy area covered by the Union's act, and second, it displaces and renders inapplicable any acts previously adopted by the Member States on that matter.

The Court of Justice held, as early as 1971 in the *AETR* case, that 'to the extent to which [Union] rules are promulgated for the attainment of the objectives of the Treaty, the Member States cannot, outside the framework of the [Union] Institutions, assume obligations which might affect those rules or alter their scope'.[24] This statement, delivered in the context of the Union's external relations, is also applicable to the exercise of internal shared competences.[25]

The scope of a *field preemption* does not encompass the entire policy area of shared competence, but only those aspects explicitly regulated by the Union act. Therefore, Member States remain prima facie competent to act on all aspects where the Union acts remain silent on that policy area. According to the Court of Justice,

> under the shared competence enjoyed by the European Union and the Member States . . . , where a criterion necessary for the implementation of a directive . . . has not been defined in the directive, such a definition falls within the competence of the Member States and they have broad discretion, in compliance with the Treaty rules, when establishing national rules. . .[26]

[22] See, inter alia, Case C-431/05 *Merck Genericos* EU:C:2007:496, para 34: 'when the field is one in which the Community has not yet legislated and which consequently falls within the competence of the Member States, the protection of intellectual property rights and measures taken for that purpose by the judicial authorities do not fall within the scope of [Union] law, so that the latter neither requires nor forbids the legal order of a Member State to accord to individuals the right to rely directly on a rule laid down in the TRIPs Agreement or to oblige the courts to apply that rule of their own motion'. In the same terms, see Case C-373/11 *Panellinios Syndesmos Viomichanion Metapoiisis Kapnou* EU:C:2013:567, para 26; and Case C-2/18 *Lietuvos Respublikos Seimo narių grupė* EU:C:2019:962, para 28.

[23] See, inter alia, Case C-438/05 *Viking Line* EU:C:2007:772; and Case C-341/05 *Laval un Partneri* EU:C:2007:809.

[24] See Case C-22/70 *Commission v Council* (AETR) EU:C:1971:32, para 22. See also Opinion 2/91 EU:C:1993:106, para 9; Opinion 1/94 (n 17) paras 72–105; Opinion 2/92 EU:C:1995:83, paras 31–36 and Opinion 1/03 (n 18) paras 115–32.

[25] Opinion 2/91 (n 24) para 10: 'the authority of the decision in that case [AETR] cannot be restricted to instances where the [Union] has adopted [Union] rules within the framework of a common policy. In all the areas corresponding to the objectives of the Treaty, Article 5 requires Member States to facilitate the achievement of the Community's tasks and to abstain from any measure which could jeopardise the attainment of the objectives of the Treaty'.

[26] Case C-254/08 *Futura Immobiliare and Others* EU:C:2009:479, paras 48, 52 and 55; and Case C-378/08 *ERG* EU:C:2010:126, para 55.

This principle has been expressly codified in primary law by Protocol No 25 on the exercise of shared competence, annexed to the TEU and TFEU, which states that 'when the Union has taken action in a certain area, the scope of this exercise of competence only covers those elements governed by the Union act in question and therefore does not cover the whole area'.

2.3. *Shared Competence Exercised by the Union, but Delegated to the Member States*

Just as the Union can grant 'specific authorisations' to Member States in areas of exclusive Union competence, this option is also frequently used in cases of shared competence. This involvement is in part the result of the principle of subsidiarity, which requires that Union actions in areas of shared competence will only be introduced when the objectives of the proposed action 'cannot be sufficiently achieved by the Member States' (Article 5(3) TEU). There is also a practical reason supporting the involvement of the Member States: shared competences cover many policy areas, whose full regulation and implementation require extensive bureaucratic infrastructure and resources that the Union does not always possess. It is therefore frequent for the Union to set the basic rules in a shared competence policy area, leaving Member States to supplement these rules and provide the resources needed for effective implementation and enforcement by companies and individuals. To achieve this, Union measures will involve Member States very closely, and as a result, the exercise of a Union shared competence is generally carried out with significant institutional and administrative involvement of the Member States.

2.4. *Shared Competence no longer Exercised by the Union*

Article 2(2) TFEU states that the 'Member States shall again exercise their competence to the extent that the Union has decided to cease exercising its competence'. This repatriation of competence from the Union by the Member States pertains only to areas of Union *shared* competence. Although this scenario is not common in practice, the Treaties nonetheless expressly account for it. This rule can be deduced *a contrario* from the wording of the first two sentences of Article 2(2). In a system of conferred powers, where the powers transferred to the Union only affect the exercise of a competence, the Union's decision to cease exercising a competence results in the *repatriation of that* competence to the Member States.

This scenario is the subject of an interpretative clarification contained in Declaration No 18, which states that:

> When the Treaties confer on the Union a competence shared with the Member States in a specific area, the Member States shall exercise their competence to the extent that the Union has not exercised, or has decided to cease exercising, its competence. The latter situation arises when the relevant EU institutions decide to repeal a legislative act, in particular better to ensure constant respect for the principles of subsidiarity and proportionality.

3. Competence to Support, Coordinate or Supplement the Actions of the Member States

The third type of competence included in the Treaties authorises the Union to support, coordinate, or supplement the actions of the Member States, as defined in Article 2(5) TFEU:

> In certain areas and under the conditions laid down in the Treaties, the Union shall have competence to carry out actions to support, coordinate or supplement the actions of the Member States, without thereby superseding their competence in these areas.

The policy areas where the Union may exercise competence to support, coordinate, or supplement the actions of Member States are listed in Article 6 TFEU as follows:

- protection and improvement of human health;
- industry;
- culture;
- tourism;
- education, vocational training, youth and sport;
- civil protection;
- administrative cooperation.

It should be noted that this list is expressed as exhaustive, unlike the open-ended enumeration of shared competences under Article 4(2) TFEU, and refers only to the areas mentioned above 'at European level', thereby excluding Union action when these policy areas have a strictly domestic scope. For example, the Union may not support or coordinate national education policy if its aims have no cross-border effects. Any Union measure to support, coordinate or supplement Member State actions must serve the Union's interests and must reflect, directly or indirectly, the achievement of the Union's objectives.[27]

Competences to support, coordinate, or supplement the actions of Member States expressly preclude the Union from harmonising the laws or regulations of the Member States. This limitation is outlined in Article 2(5) TFEU, which states that 'legally binding acts of the Union adopted on the basis of the provisions of the Treaties relating to these areas shall not entail harmonisation of Member States' laws or regulations'. This provision introduces a significant restriction on the Union's powers in these policy areas, as it prevents the adoption of Union measures that introduce general regulatory frameworks. To support, coordinate, or supplement action in one of the policy areas listed in Article 6 TFEU, the Union will be limited to adopting programmes, disbursing funds, enacting soft law acts, etc, for the purpose of incentivising specific aims in these policy areas, but without introducing general harmonisation measures.

These competences also confer on the Union the power to pursue not a 'policy', as provided for by other provisions of the TFEU, but an 'action' in a number of specific areas, including sport. Their insertion in Part Three of the TFEU, devoted to 'Union policies and internal actions', has been held by the Court of Justice to entail their exclusion from Part One of the TFEU, which contains provisions of principle, including, under Title II, 'provisions having general application', relating, inter alia, to the promotion of a high level of employment, the guarantee of adequate social protection, the fight against any discrimination, environmental protection and consumer protection. The consequence of this exclusion is that the objectives and principles set out in Part One of the TFEU do not operate as autonomous legal bases or mandatory integration requirements in the context of Union action under Article 6 TFEU. However, they may nonetheless inform the interpretation and exercise of those competences as general principles of the Union legal order. As a result, when referring to the supporting competence of the Union in the field of sport, the Court has stated that

> although the competent Union institutions must take account of the different elements and objectives listed in Article 165 TFEU when they adopt, on the basis of that article and in accordance with the

[27] On the competences to support, coordinate or supplement the actions of the Member States, see the Opinion of Advocate General Mengozzi, in particular in the field of education, in Case C-20/12 *Giersch* EU:C:2013:70, paras 45–46. See also the material limits to these powers, as defined by the General Court in Case T-529/13 *Balázs-Árpád Izsák* EU:T:2016:282, paras 100–03.

> conditions fixed therein, incentive measures or recommendations in the area of sport, those different elements and objectives, as well as those incentive measures and recommendations need not be integrated or taken into account in a binding manner in the application of the rules on the interpretation of which the referring court is seeking guidance from the Court, irrespective of whether they concern the freedom of movement of persons, services and capital (Articles 45, 49, 56 and 63 TFEU) or the competition rules (Articles 101 and 102 TFEU). More broadly, nor must Article 165 TFEU be regarded as being a special rule exempting sport from all or some of the other provisions of primary EU law liable to be applied to it or requiring special treatment for sport in the context of that application.[28]

4. Specific Competences: the Case of Economic and Employment Policies, and the Common Foreign and Security Policy

The TFEU identifies two areas in which the Union exercises a *specific* competence, positioned between shared competence and competence to support, coordinate, or supplement the actions of the Member States. These include economic policy, employment policy and social policy coordination (Articles 2(3) and 5 TFEU), and the Common Foreign and Security Policy (CFSP) (Article 2(4) TFEU and Title V TEU). It should be noted at the outset that these two categories are not homogeneous: they differ significantly in their institutional architecture, legal instruments, and degree of supranational integration, and their common classification as 'specific competences' reflects their hybrid character rather than any substantive similarity between them.

In the case of economic and employment policies, the Union exercises its competence through the coordination of Member States' policies, primarily through 'broad guidelines', but not exclusively. Regarding economic policy, Article 5(1) TFEU states that the Member States 'shall coordinate their economic policies within the Union [and,] to this end, the Council shall adopt measures, in particular broad guidelines for these policies'. This is a policy area with significant intergovernmental features, where the roles of the Commission and the European Parliament are partly sidelined in favour of the Council.

The case of the CFSP shows even stronger intergovernmental features, as its main provisions are not located in the TFEU, but in Title V of the TEU, specifically Articles 21 to 46 TEU. In this policy area, decision-making primarily falls within the European Council and the Council, through procedures requiring either a unanimous vote or consensus. Under Title V TEU, CFSP acts adopted by the Council are binding on Member States, but they lack direct effect and the Court of Justice's jurisdiction to review them is significantly restricted under Article 275 TFEU. In the CFSP, the Commission and the European Parliament play a secondary role,[29] underscoring the predominantly intergovernmental nature of this policy area.[30]

Both policy areas raise questions about their delimitation with other policies falling within the spheres of exclusive or shared competence of the Union. For instance, the areas of the internal market and economic policy are closely linked through their subject matter. For example, a Union measure on the capital requirements applied to banks serves the purpose of guaranteeing the smooth functioning of the Union's financial markets (internal market policy), but it also supports the Union's economic policy, as significant credit institutions are vital

[28] Case C-333/21 *European Superleague Company* EU:C:2023:1011, para 101; and Case C-680/21 *Royal Antwerp Football Club* EU:C:2023:1010, para 69.

[29] Good proof of the sidelining of the Commission and the European Parliament in the CFSP is Declaration No 14, annexed to the Treaties, the second paragraph of which states that 'the provisions covering the Common Foreign and Security Policy do not give new powers to the Commission to initiate decisions nor do they increase the role of the European Parliament'.

[30] On the intergovernmental traits and operations of the CFSP, see ch 16.

for the growth and stability of Member States' economies. The same applies to the common commercial policy and the CFSP: adopting trade coercion measures against a third country can be categorised as a purely commercial policy decision (since it affects the import and export of goods and services between the Union and a third country), or as a measure within the Union's foreign policy framework if it pursues broader geopolitical aims. These tensions between policy areas are especially relevant when choosing the legal basis to act, a topic that will be discussed in detail in chapter five.

5. General Competences

Apart from the competences outlined above, the Treaties include two additional powers that allow the Union to act in a broad range of situations. These are often described as 'flexibility clauses', which enable the Union to address policy areas not explicitly covered by other types of competence or whose scope does not strictly fall within a single policy area. These serve as *general* competences acting as a fallback option for Union action.

5.1. *Article 352 TFEU*

Article 352 TFEU is a provision with strong ties to the history and evolution of European integration. Its predecessors (Article 235 of the Treaty establishing the European Economic Community and, following the entry into force of the Treaty of Amsterdam, Article 308 of the Treaty Establishing the European Community) served as the legal bases for multiple Union acts in policy areas where competence had not yet been explicitly attributed in the Treaties. The provision has now lost some of its practical relevance, as the Treaties already cover a broad range of policy areas following successive rounds of Treaty reform. Additionally, Article 352 TFEU introduces a cumbersome procedure with high procedural thresholds, requiring the unanimous approval of all Member States in the Council, as well as the consent of the European Parliament. The terms under which this provision can be used are as follows:

> If action by the Union should prove necessary, within the framework of the policies defined in the Treaties, to attain one of the objectives set out in the Treaties, and the Treaties have not provided the necessary powers, the Council, acting unanimously on a proposal from the Commission and after obtaining the consent of the European Parliament, shall adopt the appropriate measures. Where the measures in question are adopted by the Council in accordance with a special legislative procedure, it shall also act unanimously on a proposal from the Commission and after obtaining the consent of the European Parliament.

Article 352 TFEU is based on a factual premise and two substantive requirements. The factual premise is the demonstrated *need for* Union action. The two substantive requirements are first, the connection of Union action with the specific *policies* outlined in the Treaties and, second, its relation to at least one of the *objectives* specified by the Treaties. When these three conditions are met, the Union may adopt 'appropriate measures'. Article 352 TFEU thereby grants the Union authority to act in areas not explicitly covered by the Treaties but that are closely connected to the existing policies and objectives set out therein. As a result, Article 352 TFEU cannot be used to adopt measures that are clearly unrelated to the Union's policies and objectives.

The Court of Justice has emphasised that measures enacted under Article 352 TFEU must be confined to areas closely linked to the policies and objectives outlined in the Treaties; otherwise, the provision could be used as a means of de facto indirect revision of the Treaties. In

Opinion 2/94, on the accession of the European Communities to the European Convention on Human Rights, the Court of Justice outlined the boundaries of Article 352 TFEU as follows:

> [Article 352 TFEU], being an integral part of an institutional system based on the principle of conferred powers, cannot serve as a basis for widening the scope of [Union] powers beyond the general framework created by the provisions of the Treaty as a whole and, in particular, by those that define the tasks and the activities of the [Union]. On any view, Article [352] cannot be used as a basis for the adoption of provisions whose effect would, in substance, be to amend the Treaty without following the procedure which it provides for that purpose.[31]

The literal wording of Opinion 2/94 is now included in Declaration No 42, which emphasises that any measure taken under Article 352 TFEU must be closely linked to one of the policies and objectives outlined in the Treaties.[32]

Article 352(3)–(4) TFEU introduces two additional explicit requirements and one explicit exclusion applicable to this general competence. On the one hand, Article 352(3) prevents the use of the powers under this provision as a means to harmonise the laws and regulations of the Member States 'in cases where the Treaties exclude such harmonisation'. As a result, this paragraph precludes the use of Article 352 TFEU in all policy areas subject to a Union competence to support, coordinate, or supplement the actions of the Member States, which exclude any harmonisation measures (Article 2(5) TFEU). On the other hand, Article 352(4) excludes the use of Article 352 TFEU in the CFSP.[33]

The use of Article 352 TFEU requires the Commission's prior legislative initiative, a unanimous vote in the Council, and the consent of the European Parliament. Article 352(2) TFEU additionally mandates that the Commission refer any proposals made under this provision to national parliaments, following the procedure for monitoring the principle of subsidiarity outlined in Article 5(3) TEU and Protocol No 2. As Article 352 TFEU does not specify the type of legal act to be used, it must be understood that the Union can act through a regulation, a directive, or a decision as appropriate, having regard to the nature and objectives of the measure in question and the general principles governing the choice of legal instrument under Article 296 TFEU.

5.2. *Article 114 TFEU*

The Union can adopt a wide range of measures under Article 114 TFEU, which allows for the adoption of measures 'which have as their object the establishment and functioning of the internal market'. Although Article 114 TFEU falls under the policy area of the internal market, its scope is wide and it has frequently been categorised as a quasi-general competence

[31] Opinion 2/94 (n 1) para 30.

[32] 'The Conference underlines that, in accordance with the settled case law of the Court of Justice of the European Union, Article 352 of the Treaty on the Functioning of the European Union, being an integral part of an institutional system based on the principle of conferred powers, cannot serve as a basis for widening the scope of Union powers beyond the general framework created by the provisions of the Treaties as a whole and, in particular, by those that define the tasks and the activities of the Union. In any event, this Article cannot be used as a basis for the adoption of provisions whose effect would, in substance, be to amend the Treaties without following the procedure which they provide for that purpose.'

[33] Declaration 41 on Article 352 of the Treaty on the Functioning of the European Union states as follows: 'The Conference declares that the reference in Article 352(1) of the Treaty on the Functioning of the European Union to objectives of the Union refers to the objectives as set out in Article 3(2) and (3) of the Treaty on European Union and to the objectives of Article 3(5) of the said Treaty with respect to external action under Part Five of the Treaty on the Functioning of the European Union. It is therefore excluded that an action based on Article 352 of the Treaty on the Functioning of the European Union would only pursue objectives set out in Article 3(1) of the Treaty on European Union. In this connection, the Conference notes that in accordance with Article 31(1) of the Treaty on European Union, legislative acts may not be adopted in the area of the Common Foreign and Security Policy.'

of the Union. This provision is often compared to the US commerce clause of Article I, Section 8, Clause 3 of the US Constitution, which authorises the US Congress 'to regulate Commerce with foreign Nations, and among the several States, and with the Indian Tribes'.[34] In this comparative context, Article 114 TFEU serves a similar function to its US counterpart, both in terms of the measures undertaken and in its relevance to the Union's broader legislative agenda.[35] The analogy has merit insofar as both provisions have served as elastic constitutional bases for broad legislative intervention, and both have generated significant judicial controversy regarding their outer limits.

In an extensive body of case law, the Court of Justice has emphasised that

> recourse to Article [114 TFEU] as a legal basis is possible if the aim is to prevent the emergence of future obstacles to trade resulting from multifarious development of national laws. However, the emergence of such obstacles must be likely and the measure in question must be designed to prevent them.[36] In other words, any Union action based on Article 114 TFEU must demonstrate a real impact on the internal market, as well as the need to combat a situation of national regulatory disparity affecting trade or competition.[37]

In some cases, the need for Union action under Article 114 TFEU will be so evident that it will not require detailed evidence. However, in other instances, the links with the internal market may not be so obvious. For example, in the judgment in the first Directive on tobacco advertising, the Court of Justice stated that the public health objectives of the measure were compatible with the objectives of the internal market, but it also noted that the Directive's provisions did not guarantee the free movement of the goods it regulated, nor did they prevent distortions of competition within the internal market.[38] By contrast, in the case of *Vodafone*, where a telecoms operator challenged a Union legislative measure introducing a uniform pricing scale for roaming services under Article 114 TFEU, the connection to the internal market and the previous failure of Member State action to properly address the matter were deemed sufficient to justify the measure.

The Court of Justice has confirmed that Article 114 TFEU allows the Union legislator to adopt uniform legislative measures, such as regulations, when the subject matter so requires.[39] The measures enacted pursuant to Article 114 TFEU can include requiring all Member States to authorise the marketing of a good or service, introducing specific requirements for obtaining such authorisation, or even temporarily or permanently banning the marketing of a good or service.[40] This legal basis also allows the Union legislature to delegate discretional powers to Union agencies, provided that this is justified by the technical complexity of the topic and that the regulatory framework adequately constrains the agency's discretion to allow for

[34] R Bork and DE Troy, 'Locating the Boundaries: The Scope of Congress's Power to Regulate Commerce' (2002) 25 *Harvard Journal of Law and Public Policy* 849.

[35] On the parallelisms between Art 114 TFEU and the US commerce clause, see K Lenaerts, 'Constitutionalism and the Many Faces of Federalism' (1990) 38 *American Journal of Comparative Law* 205, and R Schütze, *From Dual to Cooperative Federalism: The Changing Structure of European Law* (Oxford University Press, 2009).

[36] Case C-376/98 *Germany v Parliament and Council* EU:C:2000:544, para 86. See also Case C-350/92 *Spain v Council* EU:C:1995:237, para 35; Case C-377/98 *Netherlands v Parliament and Council* EU:C:2001:523, para 15; Case C-491/01 *British American Tobacco* EU:C:2002:741, para 61.

[37] Case C-217/04 *United Kingdom v Parliament and Council* EU:C:2006:279, para 42; Case C-380/03 *Germany v Parliament and Council* EU:C:2006:772, para 37; Case C-376/98 *Germany v Parliament and Council* (n 36) paras 84 and 106.

[38] Case C-376/98 *Germany v Parliament and Council* (n 36) para 96ff.

[39] Case C-58/08 *Vodafone and others* EU:C:2010:321, para 47.

[40] Case C-547/14 *Philip Morris Brands and Others* EU:C:2016:325, para 64; and Case C-151/17 *Swedish Match AB* EU:C:2018:938, para 72.

judicial review.[41] Likewise, Article 114 TFEU allows the creation of legal regimes for groups of Member States, in ways that are reminiscent of enhanced cooperation.[42] The Court of Justice has further affirmed that Article 114 TFEU is a dynamic legal basis, permitting the repeal or amendment of previous acts enacted under other legal bases, so that the Union legislature

> cannot be denied the possibility of adapting, on the basis of Article 114 TFEU, an act . . . to any change in circumstances or development of knowledge having regard to its task of safeguarding the general interests recognised by the Treaties, including the maintenance of public security.[43]

Despite the general terms of the wording of Article 114 TFEU, paragraphs 2–10 introduce several restrictions on the exercise of this competence:

- Article 114 TFEU cannot be used to adopt fiscal provisions, measures relating to the free movement of persons, or those related to the rights and interests of employed persons (Article 114(2)).
- In the areas of health, safety, environmental protection, and consumer protection, the Commission must submit its proposals based on a high level of protection, taking into account, in particular, any new developments based on scientific facts (Article 114(3)).
- The Member States will retain the power to maintain pre-existing national measures, provided they are based on one or more of the grounds referred to in Article 36 TFEU and are notified to the Commission (Article 114(4)). The same power exists in respect of subsequent national measures in the field of the protection of the environment or the work environment, provided that they are supported by new scientific evidence (Article 114(5)). The Commission has six months to assess the compliance of the Member State's proposal; if no decision is made within that period, the measures will be considered approved.

Measures adopted under Article 114 TFEU may include provisions permitting other mechanisms for unilateral action by Member States, in addition to those set out in Article 114(4)–(5) TFEU, provided that they are based on overriding non-economic reasons listed in Article 36 TFEU.

Furthermore, the TFEU introduces several derogations that prevent the use of Article 114 TFEU as a legal basis in connection with other policy areas, where the Treaties have provided specific legal bases that expressly exclude harmonisation. These include incentive measures in the field of equality (Article 19(2) TFEU), public health (Article 168(5) TFEU), industry (Article 173(3) TFEU), culture (Article 167(5) TFEU) and employment (Article 149 TFEU).

It should also be noted that Article 115 TFEU contains a different legal basis from Article 114 TFEU, under which the Union may adopt directives for the approximation of national provisions that 'directly affect the establishment or functioning of the internal market'. Unlike Article 114 TFEU, which concerns national rules relating to the market, Article 115 TFEU authorises the Union to harmonise national rules that are *not* aimed at regulating the market but which nevertheless have a direct effect on it.[44] This applies, for example, to areas such as direct taxation, certain aspects of social policy, or culture, which can have a material impact on the functioning of the market. The requirement that the national provisions in question 'directly' affect the internal market has been interpreted as imposing a stricter nexus than that

[41] Case C-217/04 *United Kingdom v Parliament and Council* (n 37) paras 102–16.

[42] This is the case of the Single Resolution Mechanism created by Regulation 806/2014, applicable, in principle, to the Member States in which the institutions subject to the European resolution system are established, although with the possibility of other Member States joining it.

[43] Case C-482/17 *Czech Republic v Parliament and Council* EU:C:2019:1035, para 56.

[44] Opinion of Advocate General Kokott in Case C-524/23 *Commission/Belgium* EU:C:2025:381, paras 26–31.

required under Article 114 TFEU, thereby limiting the scope of Article 115 TFEU to those national measures whose market effects are immediate and substantial rather than merely incidental or indirect. When the Union seeks to harmonise these areas of national regulation, it must do so under Article 115 TFEU which requires a unanimous vote in the Council. This legal basis also limits the European Parliament's role to a mere consultation procedure, and it allows for only the adoption of directives as the available legal instrument, thereby precluding the use of regulations or decisions on this legal basis.

In contrast, the adoption of measures based on Article 114 TFEU is characterised by simplified decision-making requirements within the Council (a qualified majority) and the full involvement of the European Parliament through an ordinary legislative procedure.

5.3. *The Doctrine of Implied Powers*

The Union may exercise powers not explicitly provided for in the Treaties, provided they are 'indispensable' for carrying out a specific task entrusted to a Union institution by the Treaties.[45] Due to its exceptional nature, this power must be interpreted narrowly.[46]

Where the Union relies on the doctrine of implied powers, it must pursue a goal that directly aligns with and is inseparable from a competence expressly conferred by the Treaties. For example, if a Union measure aims to achieve an environmental protection objective and the legislator properly justifies the link between the measure's objectives and the Union's environmental competence, the legal basis will be Article 192 TFEU.[47] If the measure seeks to harmonise, for instance, the residence requirements for students exercising free movement, a matter directly connected to the free movement of persons, the legal basis will be Article 21(2) TFEU.[48] The same applies to the EU institutions' 'powers of internal organisation', which authorise them to take appropriate measures in order to ensure their internal operation in conformity with the interests of good administration'.[49]

The doctrine of implied powers entails the recognition of the existence of certain *inherent* competences of the Union. This approach enables the Union to take certain decisions, provided they are functionally essential and logically inseparable from other policies over which it holds an express competence outlined in the Treaties. It is not so much a question of justifying an inherent competence in areas outside the Union's remit, but about exercising an instrumental and indispensable competence close to the areas within its remit, the adoption of which is vital for the proper realisation of the objectives of the Treaties. Although the Court of Justice has not explicitly acknowledged the existence of inherent competences of the Union in categorical terms, its case law provides evidence of their existence.[50]

[45] See the judgments in Case C-8/55 *Fédération charbonnière de Belgique* (*Fédéchar*) EU:C:1956:11; Case C-25/59 *The Netherlands v High Authority* EU:C:1960:34; Case C-22/70 *Commission v Council* EU:C:1971:32, para 28; Opinion 1/76 EU:C:1977:63, 754; and Joined Cases C-281, 283-285 and 287/85 *Germany, France, the Netherlands, Denmark and the United Kingdom v Commission* EU:C:1987:351, para 36.

[46] According to the General Court in Case T-496/11 *United Kingdom v ECB* EU:T:2015:133, 'when an article of the Treaty confers a specific task on an institution, it must be accepted, if that provision is not to be rendered wholly ineffective, that it confers on that institution necessarily and per se the powers which are indispensable in order to carry out that task'. On this point, see Joined Cases C-281, 283-285 and 287/85 *Germany, France, Netherlands, Denmark, United Kingdom v Commission* (n 45) para 28; Case T-240/04 *France v Commission* EU:T:2007:290, para 36; Case T-143/06 *MTZ Polyfilms v Council* EU:T:2009:441, para 47; and Case T-320/09 *Planet v Commission* EU:T:2015:223, para 60; and Case T-245/17 *ViaSat Inc* EU:T:2021:128, para 203.

[47] Case C-176/03 *Commission v Council* EU:C:2005:542, para 48.

[48] Case C-295/90 *Parliament v Council* EU:C:1992:294, para 19.

[49] Case C-230/81 *Luxembourg v European Parliament* EU:C:1983:32, paras 37–38; and Case C-58/94 *Netherlands v Council* EU:C:1996:171, para 37.

[50] See, inter alia, Case C-521/15 *Spain v Council* EU:C:2017:982, paras 48–49, where the Court of Justice recognised the existence of implementing acts of the Union other than those provided for in Article 291 TFEU. Interpreted *a contrario, the* existence of Union implementing acts without Member State intervention or in the absence of a

6. Principles Governing the Exercise of the Union's Competences: Subsidiarity and Proportionality

The Treaties introduce a set of tools to monitor the exercise of the Union's competence. These tools mainly rely on the principles of subsidiarity and proportionality, along with specific procedures involving national parliaments. The principles of subsidiarity and proportionality were introduced with a view to preventing excessive Union intervention in the exercise of its competences. The main beneficiaries of these principles are the Member States, whose competences are compromised if an action by the Union exceeds its authorised powers. Private individuals can also invoke these principles, which are often cited when the Union's acts are challenged in court.

6.1. *The Principle of Subsidiarity*

Article 5(3) TEU enshrines the principle of subsidiarity in Union law. This principle was introduced into Union law by the Maastricht Treaty in 1992 (then Article 3b of the EC Treaty) and further developed through the conclusions of the Edinburgh European Council of 11–12 December 1992. The Amsterdam Treaty subsequently codified these arrangements in Protocol No 30. The principle is now enshrined in the aforementioned Article 5(3) TEU, along with Protocol No 2 on the application of the principles of subsidiarity and proportionality. Article 5(3) defines the principle as follows:

> Under the principle of subsidiarity, in areas which do not fall within its exclusive competence, the Union shall act only if and in so far as the objectives of the proposed action cannot be sufficiently achieved by the Member States, either at central level or at regional and local level, but can rather, by reason of the scale or effects of the proposed action, be better achieved at Union level.

It is clear from Article 5(3) TEU that the principle of subsidiarity applies only to the *exercise* of competences, not to their conferral by the Member States. The principle does not monitor the terms on which the Member States have conferred powers to the Union; it only governs the terms under which the Union exercises its competences in a specific policy area. Therefore, the principle of subsidiarity does not alter the vertical distribution of powers outlined in the Treaties, but operates as a procedural and justificatory constraint that simply ensures that the Union's competences are exercised in a way that respects the scope of action of the Member States and their respective territorial distribution of domestic political decision-making.

When examining the impact of a Union measure in accordance with the principle of subsidiarity, the assessment considers the position of all Member States as a whole, not that of one or several individual Member States. As the Court of Justice has emphasised:

> The subsidiarity principle is not intended to limit the EU's competence on the basis of the situation of any particular Member State taken individually, but requires only that the proposed action can, by reason of its scale or effects, be better achieved at EU level, given its objectives listed in Article 3 TEU and provisions specific to various areas, including to the various freedoms, such as the freedom of establishment, laid down in the Treaties.[51]

The principle of subsidiarity applies only to the exercise of shared competences and competences to support, coordinate or supplement the actions of the Member States, as well as to the specific competences in the areas of economic policy, employment policy and the CFSP. Therefore, the principle does not apply to the policy areas listed in Article 3 TFEU, which are within the exclusive competence of the Union.

committee is recognition of an inherent competence of the Union to adopt implementing acts in cases other than those provided in Art 291 TFEU.

[51] Case C-508/13 *Estonia v European Parliament and Council* EU:C:2015:403, para 53.

The principle focuses on two cumulative features: the inability of Member States to take *comprehensive* action and the *effectiveness* of such intervention. Although the two issues are connected, Article 5(3) TEU addresses them separately.

To justify Union action under Article 5(3) TEU, the Union institutions must demonstrate, first, that the objectives of the proposed action cannot be sufficiently achieved by the Member States (at central, regional, or local level), and second, that by reason of the scale or effects of the proposed action, they can be better achieved at Union level. The first requirement calls for the necessary capacity of the states to address a policy area comprehensively, while the second focuses on whether the proposed action can be better achieved at Union level.

The principle of subsidiarity does not govern the allocation of powers between the Union and its Member States; rather, it sets limits to the exercise of the exercise of Union powers in each specific case. The principle can therefore be used to challenge a particular aspect of a measure adopted by the Union, rather than its entire scope, and it may also be used to contest the means by which the Union adopts measures (for instance, a regulation rather than a directive).

So far, the Court of Justice's interpretation of the principle of subsidiarity has been characterised by granting the Union legislature a very broad scope of manoeuvre.[52] To date, no Union legislative act has been annulled for breaching the principle of subsidiarity.

6.2. *The Principle of Proportionality*

Article 5(4) TEU refers to the principle of proportionality, according to which 'the content and form of Union action shall not exceed what is necessary to achieve the objectives of the Treaties'. The principle of proportionality is also subject to the provisions of Protocol No 2 on the principles of subsidiarity and proportionality. Furthermore, the principle of proportionality is a relevant ground for review in other areas of Union law. For example, Article 52(1) of the Charter of Fundamental Rights of the European Union introduces the principle as a basis for reviewing restrictions on fundamental rights by both the Union and the Member States. The principle of proportionality also plays a vital role in the internal market, particularly in the rules governing free movement that apply to the Member States.

Unlike the principle of subsidiarity, which is confined to the review of the Union's exercise of shared competence, the principle of proportionality applies to the exercise of *all* types of competences, including exclusive competences. The principle of proportionality can be invoked to review an entire Union measure altogether, as well as specific provisions of a Union act.[53]

The Court of Justice has interpreted the principle of proportionality as a teleological, goal-oriented review tool. In essence, the principle assesses the *means* used by the Union in relation to the *aims* being pursued.[54] Once the objectives of the reviewed act are established, the principle of proportionality first examines whether the means are objectively suitable to achieve those ends.[55] The next step is to assess whether the means are strictly necessary to attain

[52] See Case C-377/98 *Netherlands v Parliament and Council* EU:C:2001:523, paras 30–33; Joined Cases C-154 and 155/03 *Alliance for Natural Health* EU:C:2005:449, paras 99–108; Case C-518/07 *Commission v Germany* EU:C:2010:125, paras 52–55; Case C-58/08 *Vodafone and Others* EU:C:2010:321, paras 72–80; Case C-176/09 *Luxembourg v Parliament and Council* EU:C:2010:32, paras 72–80; Case C-276/14 *Gmina Wroclaw* EU:C:2015:635, para 41; Case C-547/14 *Philip Morris Brands and Others* EU:C:2016:325; Case C-151/17 *Swedish Match* EU:C:2018:938, paras 65–76, and Case C-264/18 *PM* EU:C:2019:472, paras 19–22.

[53] K Lenaerts, 'Proportionality as a Matrix Principle Promoting the Effectiveness of EU Law and the Legitimacy of EU Action', *Continuity and Change. How the Challenges of Today Prepare the Ground for Tomorrow*, ECB Legal Conference (Frankfurt, ECB, 2021) 29–35.

[54] Joined Cases C-286/87, C-340/95, C-401/95 and C-47/96 *Garage Molenheide* EU:C:1997:623, paras 46–49.

[55] Case C-40/72 *Schröder* EU:C:1973:14, para 14; Case C-265/87 *Schräder* EU:C:1989:303, para 22; Joined Cases C-133/93, C-300/93 and C-362/93 *Crispoltoni* EU:C:1994:364, paras 43–48; Case C-84/94 *United Kingdom v Council*

the pursued aims.[56] The first is an 'adequacy' test, while the second is a 'necessity' test. When applying both tests, the Union is granted a broad margin of appreciation, especially when the act under review involves an analysis of a technical nature requiring specialised expertise in non-legal matters.[57]

In the field of competence review, the Court of Justice's case law is characterised by having set a low standard of scrutiny, thus leaving a broad margin of action to the political and/or technical decision-making process. According to the case law:

> [T]he European Union legislature must be allowed a broad discretion in an area which entails political, economic and social choices on its part, and in which it is called upon to undertake complex assessments. The legality of a measure adopted in that sphere can be affected only if the measure is manifestly inappropriate having regard to the objective which the competent institutions are seeking to pursue.[58]

The reference to a 'manifestly inappropriate' measure highlights the difficulty of undertaking proportionality control within the scope of Union competence. This low standard of review has prompted some national constitutional courts, such as the German Federal Constitutional Court, to question the effectiveness of this principle when examining the exercise of Union powers. In its judgment in the *Weiss* case, after referring a question for a preliminary ruling to the Court of Justice, the German Constitutional Court openly questioned the intensity of the review conducted by the Court of Justice when undertaking a proportionality review, and it declared the judgment of the Court of Justice ultra vires in Germany.[59]

6.3. *Mechanisms for the Application of the Principles of Subsidiarity and Proportionality*

In 1997, as part of the amendments introduced by the Amsterdam Treaty, a Protocol on the application of the principles of subsidiarity and proportionality was added and annexed to the Treaties. This Protocol was significantly reformed in 2009 in the Lisbon Treaty, with the introduction of a procedure involving national parliaments in the application of both principles. The procedure is now included in Protocol No 2 on the application of the principles of subsidiarity and proportionality, which can be divided into three main parts.

Firstly, Protocol No 2 establishes a system of *consultation* aimed at ensuring the enforcement of both principles at the earliest stage of a legislative process, even before the legislative initiative is formally submitted to the Council and the European Parliament. The Commission, as the main holder of the legislative initiative, has an obligation to 'consult widely' before proposing a legislative act. Such consultations must, where appropriate, take into account the regional and local dimension of the proposed action.[60] This obligation is waived only in duly justified cases of 'exceptional urgency'. The results of these consultations must be reflected in

EU:C:1996:431, para 58; Case C-233/94 *Germany v Parliament and Council* EU:C:1997:231, paras 55–56; Case C-157/96 *National Farmers' Union* EU:C:1998:191, para 61; and Case C-210/03 *Swedish Match* EU:C:2004:802, para 48.

[56] Joined Cases C-453/03, C-11/04, C-12/04 and C-194/04 *ABNA and Others* EU:C:2005:741, paras 76–88; Case C-189/01 *Jippes and Others* EU:C:2001:420, paras 80–100; and Case C-562/08 *Müller Fleisch* EU:C:2010:93, paras 43–47.

[57] See, among many others, Case C-343/09 *Afton Chemical* EU:C:2010:419, para 46; Case C-203/12 *Billerud Karlsborg and Billerud Skärblacka* EU:C:2013:664, para 35; and Case C-62/14 *Gauweiler and Others* EU:C:2015:400, para 68.

[58] See, among many others, *Afton Chemical* (n 57) para 28; *Billerud Karlsborg and Billerud Skärblacka* (n 57), para 35; *Gauweiler and Others* (n 57) para 68; Case C-358/14 *Poland v Parliament and Council* EU:C:2016:323, para 79; and Case C-643/15 *Slovakia and Hungary v Council* EU:C:2017:631, para 207.

[59] Judgment of 5 May 2020 of the German Constitutional Court, in response to the judgment of the Court of Justice delivered in the preliminary ruling on validity in Case C-493/17 *Weiss* EU:C:2018:1000.

[60] Art 2 Protocol No 2.

an impact statement accompanying the Commission's proposal, assessing compliance with the principles of subsidiarity and proportionality.[61]

Secondly, Protocol No 2 establishes a framework for the *participation of national parliaments in the legislative process*, although confined to the principle of subsidiarity. This framework applies to all draft legislative acts, regardless of their origin (the Commission, and in exceptional cases, Member States, the European Parliament, the Court of Justice, or the European Central Bank), and must be transmitted to national parliaments at the same time as to the Union legislature.[62] Within eight weeks of transmission, any national parliament or any chamber thereof may send to the Presidents of the European Parliament, the Council, and the Commission a reasoned opinion explaining why it considers that the draft does not adhere to the principle of subsidiarity. Each national parliament has two votes, allocated according to its parliamentary system. In a bicameral system, each chamber holds one vote. If reasoned opinions on a draft legislative act's non-compliance with the principle of subsidiarity amount to at least one third of all votes allocated to national parliaments, the draft must be reviewed.[63] After re-examination, the institution can decide to keep, amend, or withdraw the draft.[64] Under the ordinary legislative procedure, if reasoned opinions indicating the draft's non-compliance with subsidiarity reach at least a simple majority of the votes allocated to national parliaments, the proposal will be reviewed. The Commission can then choose to maintain, amend, or withdraw the proposal.[65]

Thirdly, Article 8 of Protocol No 2 introduces a remedy 'in actions on grounds of infringement of the principle of subsidiarity by a legislative act' before the Court of Justice. This remedy can only be triggered by the Member States, but 'on behalf of their national Parliament or a chamber thereof'. The remedy is extended to the Committee of the Regions, which 'may also bring such actions against legislative acts for the adoption of which the [TFEU] provides that it be consulted'.[66] It should be noted that this remedy can only be brought to review the compliance of a legislative act with the principle of subsidiarity. To date, this remedy has been used by national parliaments only once.[67]

III. THE PARTICIPATION OF THE MEMBER STATES IN THE UNION'S DECISION-MAKING PROCESS

The way Member States participate and become involved in the Union's tasks is based on the principle of institutional autonomy. According to this well-established principle, Member States have the authority, in line with their procedural and institutional autonomy, to set the conditions under which their public authorities and bodies may participate in the enactment and implementation of Union law.[68] Therefore, it is for each Member State to choose the means

[61] ibid, Art 5.

[62] ibid, Art 4.

[63] It should be noted that this threshold must be a quarter in the case of a draft legislative act submitted on the basis of Art 76 TFEU on the Area of Freedom, Security and Justice.

[64] Art 7(2) Protocol No 2.

[65] ibid, Art 7(3).

[66] ibid, Art 8(2).

[67] Case C-553/24 *Assemblée nationale v Parliament and Council*, pending, in which the French National Assembly challenged the validity of Regulation (EU) 2024/1351 of the European Parliament and of the Council of 14 May 2024 on asylum and migration management.

[68] Case C-82/07 *Comisión del Mercado de las Telecomunicaciones* EU:C:2008:143, para 24; Case C-389/08 *Base and Others* EU:C:2010:584, para 26; Case C-85/14 *KPN* EU:C:2015:610, para 53; Case C-424/15 *Ormaetxea Garai and Lorenzo Almendros* EU:C:2016:780, para 30; and Case C-772/21 *Brink's Lithuania* EU:C:2022:1005, Opinion of AG Medina, point 71.

that best articulate its actions within the Council and other Union institutions, agencies, or bodies, as well as the arrangements designed to implement Union law most effectively. In highly decentralised Member States, such as Austria, Belgium, Germany or Spain, the principle of institutional autonomy safeguards the Member State's composite structure from any centralising effect produced by Union law.

When it comes to participating in the Union's decision-making process, Member States must provide for adequate internal procedures to determine their official positions. This is typically the case during the Council's meetings, where decisions are made either by unanimity or by a qualified majority, calculated by the sum of votes cast by the representatives of the governments of each Member State. At the time of implementing Union law, Member States must set out the means to ensure the smooth and effective achievement of the Union's objectives. This task generally falls to the legislative and executive branches of the Member States, which are responsible for enacting national law to complement the obligations under Union law, and for providing the administrative resources necessary for the proper implementation of Union policies at the national level.

The first scenario is known as the 'upstream phase', where the Member State acts and determines its position in the Union's decision-making process. The second scenario, which involves the means of implementing Union law at the national level, is referred to as the 'downstream phase'.

1. The Member States and 'Upstream' Participation in the Union's Decision-making Process

As a general rule, Union law does not assign specific powers to the internal branches or institutions of a Member State. Instead, the Union recognises that, when participating in the Union's institutions, the constitutional framework of each Member State is solely responsible for allocating tasks and responsibilities between the two main political branches: the legislature and the executive. As stated in Article 4(2) TEU, the Union must respect the national identities of the Member States, which are 'inherent in their fundamental political and constitutional structures', including their local and regional dimension. This provision also emphasises that the Union 'shall respect the essential functions of the State'. Therefore, there is a principle of non-interference by the Union in the basic constitutional arrangements of each Member State, which includes a duty to respect the means of representation of each Member State within the Union.

The participation of Member States in the Union's decision-making bodies is generally assigned to the executive branch. This is the result of constitutional provisions that confer on the government the power of external representation of the state. As a result, the representation of the Member States in the Union's decision-making bodies will generally be assigned to members of the executive branch, unless the Constitution provides otherwise. Union law can introduce specific derogations to this rule, but mostly focused on the level of representation of the Member States in Union institutions. For instance, Member States can participate in the European Council only through their head of state or government, depending on which authority holds the power of external representation under national law.[69] In the case of the Council, Article 16(2) TEU states that it must comprise a representative of each Member State 'at ministerial level'. In other cases, the Treaties directly call on the legislative branch of

[69] Art 15(2) TEU.

Member States to participate in Union affairs, as exemplified by Protocol 2 on the principles of subsidiarity and proportionality, which establishes a procedure for national parliaments to participate in the Union's legislative process.

This framework becomes more complex in the case of highly decentralised Member States, with legislative and executive powers distributed across different territorial levels of governance. These arrangements are usually embedded in the national constitutional framework, and regional and local powers are granted constitutional protection. The need to ensure effective participation in Union affairs does not justify overriding these constitutional arrangements. Therefore, a decentralised Member State must find suitable methods to ensure that its position reflects the interests of the majority across all territorial levels of governance. This is particularly challenging when the Union adopts policies that fall within the exclusive competence of a Member State's regions. As a result, decentralised Member States require intense coordination between the central authorities and the regions, so that the competences of all territorial levels are properly respected when establishing a common position in the Union's decision-making process.

2. The Member States and 'Downstream' Participation in the Implementation of the Union's Policies

Once a legally binding Union act enters into force, Member States must ensure its effective implementation within their territory. Unless the Union identifies a specific addressee, legal acts bind the Member States as subjects of law that represent all the public authorities of the state. Consequently, failure by any of the decentralised public authorities of the Member States (such as regions, municipalities, island territories, etc) to comply with Union law will be attributed exclusively to the Member State. It is therefore important that, when fulfilling their obligations under Union law, Member States rely on effective cooperation mechanisms among all national public authorities at every territorial level.

The Union does not determine the Member State's branches, bodies, or agencies responsible for implementing Union law. Under the principle of institutional autonomy, Member States have the power to adapt the implementation of their Union obligations to their constitutional structures, including their decentralised authorities. If the Union were to impose an obligation that would jeopardise or undermine the internal allocation of territorial powers between central and regional authorities of the Member States, such a measure would breach Article 4(2) TEU, which safeguards the 'constitutional structures' of the Member States from Union intervention.

The need to ensure uniform and effective implementation of Union law can create tensions within the internal distribution of territorial powers. However, such tensions cannot result in a permanent or structural alteration of the distribution of powers as provided in the national Constitution. This is a principled stance that has been reaffirmed in the case law of the constitutional courts of decentralised Member States. For example, the Spanish Constitutional Court has addressed the issue in the following terms:

> [B]oth the need to provide the Government with the indispensable instruments to perform the function attributed to it by Article 93 [of the Constitution] . . . and, on the other hand, the fact that it is the Central Administration . . . [that] is competent to carry out actions which, when this connection with the outside world is not present, correspond to the Administration of the Autonomous [regional] Communities, make it necessary to articulate the exercise of the competences of the State and the Autonomous Community in such a way that one and the other, without invading another's sphere of

competence, do not hinder the performance of the functions attributed to it by the Constitution and the Statutes, nor place unnecessary burdens on citizens.[70]

Therefore, the duty of a decentralised Member State to comply with Union law does not alter the internal distribution of powers between the central authorities and the regions; however, it requires coordinated action across all territorial levels to ensure proper and consistent implementation. This is why most decentralised Member States introduce measures to coordinate the implementation of Union law across all territorial levels, even though such measures may restrict the decision-making power of the regions.

Insofar as the Member States are solely responsible for the infringements of Union law when obligations are addressed to them, the liability for a violation of Union law falls on the Member State as a legal subject of international law, not on the branch of government or region that committed the breach. Consequently, the Member State as a whole is accountable to the Union for the damages caused by a region or local authority. This does not prevent national law from introducing internal rules that reallocate the final liability to the authority that caused the breach.

For instance, Article 104a of the German Basic Law states that '[the] Federation and the Länder shall bear separately the expenses arising from the performance of their tasks', a liability of the Länder that extends to the violation of Union obligations, pursuant to the Act on the Sharing of Burdens between the Federal Government and the States in the Event of Violations of Supranational or International Law Obligations.[71]

The Spanish Organic Law 2/2012 on Budgetary Stability and Financial Sustainability establishes a similar rule in Article 8(1), in the following terms:

> Public administrations that fail to comply with the obligations contained in this Law, as well as those that provoke or contribute to the failure to comply with the commitments assumed by Spain in accordance with European regulations or the provisions contained in international treaties or conventions to which Spain is a party, shall assume, in the part attributable to them, the responsibilities derived from such non-compliance.[72]

2.1. *Legislative Implementation of Union Law*

Union law can be implemented in the Member States through parliamentary statutes, either because the Constitution requires Parliament to regulate certain subjects, or because the national legislator chooses to do so voluntarily. Union law does not require the use of a specific type of national act, provided the legal instrument used is sufficiently clear, precise, and unambiguous. For example, the Court of Justice has rejected the use of internal administrative guidelines or instructions as a means to implement Union law, arguing that 'mere administrative practices, which by their nature are alterable at will by the authorities and are not given the appropriate publicity, cannot be regarded as constituting the proper fulfilment of a Member State's obligations under the Treaty'.[73] With this caveat in mind, the Member States are free

[70] STC 252/88, FJ 2. See also SSTC 64/1991, FJ 4 and 76/1991, FJ 3.

[71] *Lastentragungsgesetz* of 5 September 2006 (BGBl. I S. 2098, 2105). According to § 1(1), 'Obligations of the Federal Republic of Germany to make financial payments due to the violation of supranational or international law obligations in the areas of legislation, administration, or jurisdiction shall be borne by the federal and state governments in proportion to the extent to which the breach of duty giving rise to the burden occurred within their domestic areas of responsibility and competence.'

[72] This provision is implemented in further detail in the Royal Decree 515/2013 of 5 July, introducing the criteria and procedure for determining and passing on liability for non-compliance with Union law.

[73] See Case C-80/92 *Commission v Belgium* EU:C:1994:2, para 20; Case C-151/94 *Commission v Luxembourg* EU:C:1995:357, para 18; Case C-415/01 *Commission v Belgium* EU:C:2003:118, para 21; and Case C-296/01 *Commission*

to select the necessary legal act, whether a parliamentary statute, an administrative decree, or even a rule of a *sui generis* nature, such as a collective agreement.

2.2. *Administrative Implementation of Union Law*

The implementation of Union law is a competence that Article 291(1) TFEU generally assigns to the Member States, which 'shall adopt all measures of national law necessary to implement legally binding Union acts'. This task primarily falls on the administrative authorities of the Member States. When referring to the 'implementation' of Union law, reference is made mainly to the activity undertaken by government authorities at the central, regional, or local levels, in accordance with the constitutional rules on the division of powers between the legislative and executive branches.

As an exception to the rule, the Union is entitled to assume implementing powers, a task that Article 291(2) TFEU allocates to the Commission, subject to the oversight of the Council and the European Parliament through committees. In 'duly justified cases', this task may also be undertaken by the Council.[74]

National governmental authorities, including administrative bodies, serve as the agents of *indirect* public administration, dedicating their material and human resources to the achievement of the objectives of Union law and policy. To this end, national administrative authorities must comply with the obligations arising from Union law in accordance with the principle of sincere cooperation (Article 4(3) TEU) and possess specific powers to ensure the proper implementation of Union law, including the power to set aside national law, including parliamentary statutes.[75]

2.3. *Judicial Enforcement of Union Law*

Article 19(1), second paragraph TEU states that the Member States 'shall provide remedies sufficient to ensure effective legal protection in the fields covered by Union law'. This provision reflects a widespread and well-known reality in the Union's judicial practice: the role of national judges as 'European judges of common law'. As a result of the direct effect of Union law, individuals can invoke Union law directly in national courts, both in disputes between individuals and in disputes against public authorities. National courts thus become the standard *fora* to resolve judicial disputes involving Union law, mainly those brought by natural or legal persons. As detailed in chapters eleven and twelve of this book, national courts act as Union courts, without prejudice to the jurisdiction of the Court of Justice of the European Union.

Member States have the obligation to ensure the proper enforcement of judgments issued by national courts, as well as rulings delivered by the Court of Justice of the European Union. According to Article 280 TFEU, read together with Article 299 TFEU, judgments of the Union's courts 'shall be enforceable' in all Member States 'with enforcement governed by the rules of civil procedure in force in the State of execution.'[76]

v France EU:C:2003:626, para 54.

[74] See Case T-395/22 *Hypo Vorarlberg Bank AG v SRB* EU:T:2024:333, paras 32–41; and Case T-406/22 *Volkskreditbank v SRB* EU:T:2024:439, paras 32–41.

[75] Case C-103/88 *Costanzo* EU:C:1989:256, para 31. See M Bobek, 'Thou Shalt Have Two Masters: The Application of European Law by Administrative Authorities in the New Member States' (2008) 1 *Review of European Administrative Law* 51, 62–63.

[76] Art 299, second paragraph TFEU.

GENERAL BIBLIOGRAPHY

Bermann, GA, 'Competences of the Union' in T Tridimas and P Nebbia (eds), *European Union Law for the Twenty-First Century* (Hart, 2004).
Craig, P, *The Lisbon Treaty: Law, Politics and Treaty Reform* (Oxford University Press, 2010).
Eeckhout, P, *EU External Relations Law*, 2nd edn (Oxford University Press, 2011).
Michel, V, *Recherches sur les compétences de la Communauté* (L'Harmattan, 2003).
Neframi, E, *L'action extérieure de l'Union européenne: Fondements, moyens, principes* (LGDJ, 2010).
Velyvyte, V, *Judicial Authority in EU Internal Market Law: Implications for the Balance of Competences and Powers* (Hart, 2022).
Weatherill, S, 'Competence' in B de Witte (ed), *Ten Reflections on the Constitutional Treaty for Europe* (EUI, 2003).
de Witte, B, and de Búrca, G, 'The Delimitation of Powers Between the EU and Its Member States' in A Arnull and D Wincott (eds), *Accountability and Legitimacy in the European Union* (Oxford University Press, 2002).

FURTHER READING

The Principles of Conferral of Powers and Loyal Cooperation

Dashwood, A, 'The Limits of European Community Powers' (1996) 21 *European Law Review* 113.
Dougan, M, 'EU Competences In An Age of Complexity And Crisis: Challenges And Tensions In the System of Attributed Powers' (2024) 61 *Common Market Law Review* 93.
Gautron, J-C, 'Article I-11' in L Burgorgue-Larsen, A Levade and F Picod (eds), *Traité établissant une Constitution pour l'Europe: Commentaire article par article* (Bruylant, 2007).
Kirchhof, P, 'The Balance of Powers Between National and European Institutions' (1999) 5 *European Law Journal* 225.
Neframi, E, 'The Duty of Loyalty: Rethinking Its Scope Through Its Application in the Field of EU External Relations' (2010) 47 *Common Market Law Review* 323.
—— 'Le principe de coopération loyale comme fondement identitaire de l'Union européenne' (2012) 556 *Revue du Marché Commun et de l'Union Européenne* 135.
Weatherill, S, 'Competence Creep and Competence Control' (2004) 23 *Yearbook of European Law* 1.

The Union's Categories of Competence

von Bogdandy, A and Bast, J, 'The European Union's Vertical Order of Competences: The Current Law and Proposals for Its Reform' (2002) 39 *Common Market Law Review* 227.
Burgorgue-Larsen, L, 'À propos de la notion de compétence partagée: du particularisme de l'analyse en droit communautaire' (2006) 2 *Revue Générale de Droit International Public* 373.
Craig, P, 'Competence, Clarity, Conferral, Containment and Consideration' (2004) 29 *European Law Review* 323.
Garben, S and Govaere, I (eds), *The Division of Competences between the EU and the Member States* (Hart, 2017).
Schütze, R, 'EU Competences: Existence and Exercise' in A Arnull and D Chalmers (eds), *The Oxford Handbook of European Union Law* (Oxford University Press, 2015).

The Union's External Competences

Butler, G, *Constitutional Law of the EU's Common Foreign and Security Policy* (Hart, 2019).
Chamon, M, 'Implied Exclusive Powers in the ECJ's Post-Lisbon Jurisprudence: The Continued Development of the ERTA Doctrine' (2018) 55 *Common Market Law Review* 1101.
Cremona, M, 'External Relations and External Competence of the European Union: The Emergence of an Integrated Policy' in P Craig and G de Búrca (eds), *The Evolution of EU Law*, 3rd edn (Oxford University Press, 2021).

Koutrakos, P, 'External Action: Common Commercial Policy, Common Foreign and Security Policy, Common Security and Defence Policy' in A Arnull and D Chalmers (eds), *The Oxford Handbook of European Union Law* (Oxford University Press, 2015).

Weatherill, S, 'Beyond Pre-emption? Shared Competence and Constitutional Change in the European Community' in D O'Keeffe and P Twomey (eds), *Legal Issues of the Maastricht Treaty* (Chancery Lane Publishing, 1994).

The Principles of Subsidiarity and Proportionality

Biondi, A, 'Subsidiarity in the Courtroom' in A Biondi, P Eeckhout and S Ripley (eds), *EU Law After Lisbon* (Oxford University Press, 2012).

Cooper, I, 'The Watchdogs of Subsidiarity: National Parliaments and the Logic of Arguing in the EU' (2006) 44 *Journal of Common Market Studies 281.*

D'Atena, A, 'Subsidiarity and Division of Competences Between European Union, Its Member States and Their Regions' in I Pernice and R Miccù (eds), *The European Constitution in the Making* (Nomos, 2005).

Estella de Noriega, A, *The EU Principle of Subsidiarity and Its Critique* (Oxford University Press, 2002).

Fromage, D, *Les Parlements dans l'Union Européenne après le Traité de Lisbonne* (L'Harmattan, 2015).

Kiiver, P, *The Early Warning System for the Principle of Subsidiarity: Constitutional Theory and Empirical Reality* (Routledge, 2012).

Lenaerts, K and van Ypersele, P, 'Le principe de subsidiarité et son contexte: étude de l'article 3B du Traité CE' (1994) 30 *Cahiers de Droit Européen 3.*

Schütze, R, 'Subsidiarity After Lisbon: Reinforcing the Safeguards of Federalism?' (2009) 68 *Cambridge Law Journal 525.*

5

The Horizontal Distribution of Powers: Legal Basis, Delegation and Differentiation

I. THE HORIZONTAL DISTRIBUTION OF POWERS IN THE UNION: THE 'UNION METHOD', INSTITUTIONAL BALANCE AND DEMOCRACY

THE UNION'S DECISION-MAKING process involves three institutions with legislative (the European Parliament and the Council) and executive powers (the Commission). Each institution acts within the powers conferred on it by the Treaties, with the aim of maintaining a high level of democratic representation throughout the legislative and executive procedures. The Treaties create a framework where the three institutions remain in constant balance, ensuring stable and structured representation of all the interests at stake: the interests of the peoples of Europe (the European Parliament), of the Member States (the Council), and of the Union as a whole (the Commission). This balance is maintained through a clear division of responsibilities among the three institutions, a model inspired by the separation of powers envisioned by Montesquieu in *De l'esprit des lois,* now tailored to the Union's specific features.

1. The Union Method

The distribution of power among the Union's institutions results from what has traditionally been called the 'Community method', a term that, following the entry into force of the Lisbon Treaty, was updated to the 'Union method'. This term describes the decision-making process of the Union and its predecessor, the Communities, whereby an independent Commission holds a monopoly on the power to introduce legislative initiatives, while the Council, representing the Member States, approves these proposals jointly with the European Parliament, which represents the citizens of the Union. The Union method reflects the Union's unique decision-making working ethos, which differs considerably from the standard practice in international organisations, where the individual interests of states often override the collective good, and decisions are usually made through unanimity to protect sovereign interests. Conversely, the Union's decision-making process relies on a complex balancing of interests represented by three different institutions, with a notable predominance of qualified majority voting in the Council. Furthermore, the Union method serves as a means for adopting policy measures in areas within the Union's competence, most of which are directly related to developing the internal market and have considerable economic implications. It can be argued that the Union method is the most faithful representation of functionalism in action.

The Union method differs from the Union's approach in the Common Foreign and Security Policy (CFSP), where the organisation operates according to intergovernmental standards: the sovereign will of the Member States (materialised through the actions of the European Council and the Council) takes precedence, legislative acts are expressly excluded (Article 24(1) TEU and Article 31(1) TEU), and the roles of the Commission and the European Parliament are significantly reduced. The jurisdiction of the Court of Justice is also largely excluded in this area, except as provided in Article 275 TFEU. While the intergovernmental method prioritises the role of the Member States through the strengthened role of the European Council and the Council, the Union method carefully avoids giving any single institution a dominant position over the others. Instead, the aim of the Union method is to ensure that no one institution holds a predominant role, so that all interests – those of the Union, the Member States, and the citizens – are equally reflected in the final decision.

With the exception of the CFSP referred to above, the Union's policies follow the Union method. However, some Union policies exhibit specific features with occasional deviations from the Union method. This applies to the Union's economic policy, where the Council plays a prominent role at the expense of the Commission and the European Parliament. The same is true in certain aspects of the Area of Freedom, Security and Justice, where the Council holds exceptional powers not found in other policy areas,[1] and national parliaments have a veto power over initiatives of judicial cooperation that touch on family law.[2]

2. Institutional Balance

Article 13(2) of the Treaty on European Union (TEU) contains a mandate addressed to the institutions of the Union, according to which each institution shall act 'within the limits of the powers conferred on it in the Treaties, and in conformity with the procedures, conditions and objectives set out in them'. This provision reflects in legal terms the essential balance that must exist in the relations among the Union's three political institutions, which is a consequence of the Union method. It should be noted that the principle of institutional balance is not confined to the three 'political' institutions (Parliament, Council, Commission) but extends to all seven institutions listed in Article 13(1) TEU, as well as to the relations between institutions and other bodies, offices, and agencies. The principle of institutional balance has been described by the Court of Justice's case law as follows:

> Under Article 13(2) TEU, each EU institution is to act within the limits of the powers conferred on it in the Treaties, and in conformity with the procedures, conditions and objectives set out in them. That provision reflects the principle of institutional balance, characteristic of the institutional structure of the European Union, a principle which requires that each of the institutions must exercise its powers with due regard for the powers of the other institutions.[3]

The principle of institutional balance is a legally binding provision, the basis of which is found in Article 13(2) TEU. The scope of application of the principle is primarily concerned with the relations between the institutions, bodies, offices and agencies of the Union, so that individuals cannot invoke it.[4] However, the principle can be relevant to Member States in their actions before the Union institutions, as in the case of their standing to bring an action before the

[1] Arts 82(3), 83(3) and 89 TFEU.

[2] ibid, Art 81(3).

[3] See, inter alia, Case C-611/22 P *Illumina v Grail* EU:C:2024:677, para 215; Case C-551/21 *Commission v Council* EU:C:2024:281, para 62; Case C-275/20 *Commission v Council* EU:C:2022:142, para 32; Case C-409/13 *Council v Commission* EU:C:2015:217, para 64; Case C-425/13 *Commission v Council* EU:C:2015:483, para 69; and Case C-73/14 *Council v Commission* EU:C:2015:663, para 61.

[4] See Case C-70/88 *Parliament v Council* EU:C:1991:373, paras 21–23; Case C-301/02 *Tralli v ECB* EU:C:2005:306, para 46.

Court of Justice. When considering whether the regions of the Member States have privileged standing under Article 263(2) of the Treaty on the Functioning of the European Union (TFEU), the Court of Justice answered in the negative, stating that the opposite result would be incompatible with the principle of institutional balance.[5]

The principle of institutional balance also applies to the CFSP. According to the Court of Justice, Articles 5(1)–(2) TEU, in conjunction with Article 13(2) TEU, encompass all areas of Union policy action, including intergovernmental areas, such as the CFSP.[6]

The purpose of the principle of institutional balance is to protect the prerogatives granted to each institution by the Treaties, precluding any actions or measures that could jeopardise them. For example, the principle precludes the Commission from exercising an unlimited power to withdraw its legislative initiatives during the legislative procedure; otherwise, an unfettered right of withdrawal would amount to a veto power that the Treaty has not granted to the Commission.[7] However, the Commission's power of initiative cannot be undermined by the Council or the European Parliament either, or else the principle of institutional balance would be undermined.[8] The same logic applies to the prerogatives of the European Parliament, which the Council and the Commission must respect. Any action by the Council intended to or effectively limit the European Parliament's participation during the legislative process will breach the principle of institutional balance.[9] Likewise, the European Parliament must respect the prerogatives of the other institutions, including the Council's right to act unanimously to amend a Commission proposal (Article 293(1) TFEU) and the Commission's exclusive right of initiative where the Treaty so provides.

3. The Democratic Principle

The Union's decision-making process aims to maximise the representation of all the stakeholders involved. A long-standing debate about the Union's perceived democratic deficit has been addressed through a series of measures designed to ensure the representation of Member States, citizens, regions, and social and economic actors throughout the decision-making process. The democratic principle is thus reflected not only in the composition of the European Parliament

[5] According to the Court of Justice, 'the term Member State, for the purposes of the institutional provisions and, in particular, those relating to proceedings before the courts, refers only to government authorities of the Member States of the European [Union] and cannot include the governments of regions or of autonomous communities, irrespective of the powers they may have. If the contrary were true, it would undermine the institutional balance provided for by the Treaties, which determine the conditions under which the Member States, that is to say the States party to the Treaties establishing the [Union] and the Accession Treaties, participate in the functioning of the [Union] institutions'. (Order in Case C-180/97 *Regione Toscana v Commission* EU:C:1997:451, paras 6 and 8; Case C-95/97 *Région Wallonne v Commission* EU:C:1997:184; and the judgments in Case C-452/98 *Nederlandse Antillen v Council* EU:C:2001:623, para 50; and in Case C-417/04 *Regione Siciliana* EU:C:2006:282, para 21).

[6] Case C-29/22 P *KS and KD* EU:C:2024:725, para 72.

[7] Case C-409/13 *Council v Commission* EU:C:2015:217, para 75: 'The power of withdrawal which the Commission derives from the provisions mentioned in the preceding paragraph of the present judgment cannot, however, confer upon that institution a right of veto in the conduct of the legislative process, a right which would be contrary to the principles of conferral of powers and institutional balance'.

[8] In this respect, see Case C-40/10 *Commission v Council* EU:C:2010:713, paras 78–80.

[9] See Case C-408/95 *Eurotunnel and Others* EU:C:1997:532, para 45: 'It is to be remembered that due consultation of the Parliament in the cases provided for by the Treaty constitutes an essential formal requirement, breach of which renders the measure concerned void. Effective participation of the Parliament in the [Union's] legislative process, in accordance with the procedures laid down by the Treaty, represents an essential factor in the institutional balance intended by the Treaty. This function reflects the fundamental democratic principle that the people should take part in the exercise of power through the intermediary of a representative assembly'. See also Case C-392/95 *Parliament v Council* EU:C:1997:289, para 14 and, in the field of the CFSP, Case C-263/14 *Parliament v Council* EU:C:2015:729 and the Opinion of Advocate General Kokott delivered in that case, at points 76–82.

and its powers in the legislative process but also in the participation of national parliaments, citizens, political parties with a European dimension, and regions and municipalities.

Title II of the TEU is dedicated to 'provisions on democratic principles'. Article 10(1) TEU declares that 'the functioning of the Union shall be founded on representative democracy'. Citizens are directly represented at Union level through the European Parliament, while Member States are represented in the European Council and the Council. Article 10(2) TEU further provides that Member States' governments are themselves 'democratically accountable either to their national Parliaments, or to their citizens', thereby establishing a chain of democratic legitimacy running from the citizen through to the Union level. Consequently, the dual legitimacy of the legislative process, reflecting both the will of citizens and Member States, is explicitly confirmed in Article 10(2) TEU when referring to the representation of citizens and Member States in the Union's political institutions.

This understanding has also been emphasised by the Court of Justice, which has repeatedly stated:

> Under Article 10(1) TEU, the functioning of the European Union is to be founded on representative democracy, which gives concrete expression to democracy as a value. Democracy is, under Article 2 TEU, one of the values on which the European Union is founded.[10]

Articles 11–12 TEU also refer to citizens and representative associations, which must be provided with appropriate channels to express and publicly share their views.[11] Article 11 TEU establishes several dimensions of participatory democracy: the institutions shall give citizens and representative associations the opportunity to make known and publicly exchange their views (Article 11(1) TEU); the institutions shall maintain an open, transparent and regular dialogue with representative associations and civil society (Article 11(2) TEU); and the Commission shall carry out broad consultations with parties concerned in order to ensure that the Union's actions are coherent and transparent (Article 11(3) TEU). In the case of citizen participation, Article 11(4) TEU states that at least one million Union citizens may invite the Commission to submit a legislative initiative.[12] National parliaments also hold several prerogatives aimed at increasing their involvement in the Union's legislative procedures.[13] Article 12 TEU sets out the role of national parliaments, which hold several prerogatives aimed at strengthening their involvement in the Union's decision-making. These include, inter alia, receiving information and draft legislative acts from the Union institutions (Article 12(a) TEU); ensuring that the principle of subsidiarity is respected, in accordance with the procedures provided for in Protocol No 2 on the application of the principles of subsidiarity and proportionality (Article 12(b) TEU), and participating in the evaluation mechanisms for the implementation of Union policies in the Area of Freedom, Security and Justice (Article 12(c) TEU).

The principle of transparency, proclaimed in Article 15 TFEU, also serves to uphold and promote the democratic principle within the Union. Citizens and their representatives must be well informed before exercising their rights, including their participation in the Union's

[10] Case C-418/18 P *Puppinck and Others v Commission* EU:C:2019:1113, para 64; Case C-502/19 *Junqueras Vies* EU:C:2019:1115, para 63; Case C-808/21 *Commission v Czech* Republic EU:C:2024:962, para 114; and Case C-814/21 *Commission v Poland* EU:C:2024:963, para 112.

[11] Art 11(1)–(2) TEU.

[12] In this regard, see Regulation (EU) 2019/788 of the European Parliament and of the Council of 17 April 2019 on the European citizens' initiative [2019] OJ L130/55, as well as the case law of the Court of Justice and the General Court to date: Case C-589/15 P *Anagnostakis v Commission* EU:C:2017:663; Case T-754/14 *Efler v Commission*, EU:T:2017:323; Case T-561/14 *One of Us and Others v Commission* EU:T:2018:210; Case T-44/14 *Constantini v Commission* EU:T:2016:223; Case T-646/13 *Bürgerausschuss für die Bürgerinitiative Minority SafePack - one million signatures for diversity in Europe* EU:T:2017:59; Case T-529/13 *Balázs-Árpád Izsák* EU:T:2016:282.

[13] Art 12 TEU.

decision-making process. Therefore, it is vital that the Union's institutions adhere to the principle of transparency, which allows every citizen to access the information needed to articulate an informed opinion on the matter. The link between the democratic principle and the principle of transparency has been emphasised by the Court of Justice and the General Court, particularly in the context of legislative procedures, where the principle of transparency plays a particularly important role.[14]

In sum, while the principle of institutional balance aims to achieve a harmonious equilibrium in the interactions among the Union's institutions, the democratic principle emphasises the necessity for the Union's political institutions to represent the interests of their respective constituents. Consequently, the Union's legislative process results in a balance of all the interests involved, particularly those of citizens and of the Member States, including their national parliaments. This is why the Court of Justice has described the democratic principle as a 'fundamental principle', a core pillar guiding the functioning of the Union's institutional framework.[15]

II. THE CHOICE OF LEGAL BASIS

Every action of the Union must be based on a legal basis provided by the Treaties. While the competence grants the Union authority to act in a specific policy area (eg, environment, internal market, transport), the legal basis is the specific provision in the Treaty that authorises the Union to act and defines the *scope* of that competence in the given area. The legal basis will specify key features of the Union's competence, such as the subject matter and substantive scope (excluding certain matters, like fiscal provisions such as Article 114(2) TFEU), the type of act that may be adopted (regulation, directive, etc), the legislative procedure (the ordinary or special legislative procedure), the voting rule in the Council (qualified majority or unanimity), the involvement of other institutions or bodies (such as the European Central Bank (ECB), the European Economic and Social Committee, the Committee of the Regions, etc), or even national parliaments (eg, in Articles 70, 81(3), and 82(3) TFEU).

The sum of all these elements will determine the balance sought by the Treaties in each area of Union policy, as well as define the scope of the Union's competence in that field. If the legal basis requires the act to be adopted through a regulation, using the ordinary legislative procedure with a qualified majority in the Council and involving both Union advisory bodies, we are dealing with a competence where the Union method is applied with full vigour. However, if the legal basis requires the use of a directive, a special legislative procedure involving only the consultation of the European Parliament, a unanimous vote in the Council, and no participation from any advisory body, the Union's competence will reflect the predominance of the Member States and of the intergovernmental method. Between these two poles, many legal bases combine elements in different configurations. For example, the ordinary legislative procedure with unanimity in the Council, or special legislative procedures requiring the European Parliament's consent rather than mere consultation, thus creating a spectrum of institutional arrangements rather than a binary choice.

[14] See, inter alia, Case C-280/11 P *Access Info Europe v Council* EU:C:2013:671, paras 32 and 33; Case T-540/15 *De Capitani v European Parliament* EU:T:2018:167, paras 80 and 98, and Case C-408/21 P *Pech v Council* EU:C:2023:461, para 41.

[15] Case C-138/79 *Roquette v Council* EU:C:1980:249, para 33; Case C-155/07 *Parliament v Council* EU:C:2008:605, para 78; Case C-130/10 *Parliament v Council* EU:C:2012:472, para 81; and Case C-658/11 *Parliament v Council* EU:C:2014:2025, para 81.

1. Criteria for the Choice of Legal Basis

The choice of legal basis is not a discretional political decision immune to judicial review. In a well-established case law, the Court of Justice has defined the criteria on which the political institutions must rely to select a legal basis for each policy decision. These criteria are based on 'objective factors' and are not solely subjective convictions of the institution. As the Court of Justice states:

> [I]n the context of the organisation of the powers of the [Union] the choice of the legal basis for a measure may not depend simply on an institution's conviction as to the objective pursued but must be based on objective factors which are amenable to judicial review.[16]

The 'objective factors' referred to by the Court of Justice are, in particular, the *purpose* and *content* of the act.[17] Both elements act as the guiding criteria for reviewing the choice of legal basis. Regarding the purpose of the act, the Court of Justice avoids conducting a strict review of legality. The purpose is indeed open to judicial review, but it will be carried out only to scrutinise manifest errors of assessment by the institution or institutions that adopted the act.[18]

Although the criteria for choosing a legal basis are objective, it is not always easy to determine whether a measure should be adopted under one legal basis or another. For instance, rules on the advertising of tobacco products can be approached as a matter affecting the internal market or as part of the Union's public health policy. Similarly, a tax on carbon dioxide emissions might fall under fiscal measures or, alternatively, be considered part of the Union's environmental policy. The choice between these options can have significant practical implications in the decision-making process. Therefore, the act must define its aims as clearly as possible.

When a measure serves multiple aims and potentially engages various legal bases, the institutions must apply a 'centre of gravity' test, whereby the legal basis is determined by the 'principal or predominant' aim. If the act appears to pursue several aims but one is clearly predominant, the act must be based on a single legal basis, namely the one aligned with the predominant aim.[19]

This methodology applies to the choice of the legal basis provided for the policies in Part Three TFEU, but the Court of Justice has confirmed that the same approach extends to legal bases related to the CFSP, found in Title V TEU and characterised by their strong intergovernmental features. In such cases, the Court of Justice has confirmed the use of the same criteria outlined above, which require identifying the 'centre of gravity' of the measure, from which the predominant aim will guide the correct choice of legal basis.[20]

In some cases, the Court of Justice has used a different criterion from the 'centre of gravity', opting for a test based on the lex specialis principle. As Engel has explained, this second criterion operates as follows:

[16] Case C-45/86 *Commission v Council* EU:C:1987:163, para 11.

[17] Case C-300/89 *Commission v Council* EU:C:1991:244 ('titanium dioxide'), para 10; Case C-176/03 *Commission v Council* EU:C:2005:542, para 45; Case C-440/05 *Commission v Council* EU:C:2007:625, para 61; Case C-267/16 *Buhagiar and Others* EU:C:2018:26, para 41; Case C-626/15 *Commission v Council* EU:C:2018:925, paras 76–78; Case C-482/17 *Czech Republic v European Parliament and Council* EU:C:2019:1035, paras 36–38; Case C-620/18 *Hungary v European Parliament and Council* EU:C:2020:1001, paras 40–41; and Case C-626/18 *Poland v European Parliament and Council* EU:C:2020:1000, paras 45–46.

[18] Case C-331/88 *Fedesa* EU:C:1990:391, para 8.

[19] Case C-36/98 *Spain v Council* EU:C:2001:64, para 59; Case C-211/01 *Commission v Council* EU:C:2003:452, para 39; Case C-338/01 *Commission v Council* EU:C:2004:253, para 55, and Case C-180/20 *Commission v Council* (agreement with Armenia) EU:C:2021:658, para 15.

[20] Case C-244/17 *Commission v Council* EU:C:2018:662 (partnership agreement with Kazakhstan), para 38; and Case C-180/20 *Commission v Council* EU:C:2021:658 (agreement with Armenia), para 35.

> [W]hile under the 'centre of gravity' theory two different provisions with two different aims are at stake; the lex specialis derogat legi generali principle concerns two different provisions, both of which have the same aim, but one being more specific than the other.[21]

In the first case, the Union legislature aims to introduce a legal framework that addresses both environmental protection and energy policies. In the second case, the new legal framework focuses solely on environmental protection, but it may also fall under a different legal basis within the same policy field. In the first scenario the 'centre of gravity' test would apply, whilst the lex specialis principle applies to the second.[22]

2. Joint Legal Bases

In exceptional circumstances, a measure pursues several aims that are inextricably linked, all of which are equally relevant or predominant. In such cases, the resulting act may be founded on the various legal bases involved, provided their procedural requirements are compatible.[23] For example, it is possible to use two legal bases where both require a qualified majority vote in the Council and an ordinary legislative procedure.[24] However, a joint legal basis is excluded when one legal basis requires a unanimous vote in the Council and the other demands a qualified majority. The same incompatibility applies where one legal basis prescribes an ordinary legislative procedure and the other requires a special legislative procedure with limited participation rights of the European Parliament.[25]

Consequently, the use of a joint legal basis cannot lead to conflicting voting rules[26] or divergent legislative procedures[27] within the same decision-making process. In such cases, where the procedures are incompatible but the objectives of the act are genuinely inseparable, the only solution available to the legislature is to split the measure into two separate acts, each governed by its own legal basis. This is the only way to guarantee that the Union's competences are exercised in accordance with the scope and procedures required by the Treaties in each policy area.

The use of joint legal bases is also excluded when a measure engages both a competence under the TFEU and the provisions of the TEU on the CFSP. Article 40(1) TEU states that the implementation of the CFSP 'shall not affect the application of the procedures and the extent of the powers of the institutions laid down … in Articles 3 to 6 [TFEU]'. The Court of Justice, referring to the equivalent provision prior to the TFEU, stated that

> since Article [40 TEU] precludes the Union from adopting, on the basis of the [TEU], a measure which could properly be adopted on the basis of the [TFEU], the Union cannot have recourse to a legal basis falling within the CFSP in order to adopt provisions which also fall within a competence conferred by the [TFEU].[28]

[21] A Engel, *The Choice of Legal Basis for Acts of the European Union* (Springer, 2018) 19.

[22] See, for example, Case C-48/14 *European Parliament v Council* EU:C:2015:91.

[23] Case C-165/87 *Commission v Council* EU:C:1988:458, para 11; Case C-178/03 *Commission v Parliament and Council* EU:C:2006:4, para 59; Case C-336/00 *Huber* EU:C:2002:509, para 31; Case C-281/01 *Commission v Council* EU:C:2002:761, para 35; Case C-377/12 *Commission v Council* EU:C:2014:1903, para 34; Case C-263/14 *Parliament v Council* EU:C:2016:435, para 44; and Case C-244/17 *Commission v Council* EU:C:2018:662, para 37.

[24] Case C-491/01 *British American Tobacco* EU:C:2002:741, paras 102–11, more specifically, a co-decision procedure, a direct predecessor of the current ordinary legislative procedure.

[25] Case C-300/89 *Commission v Council* EU:C:1991:244, paras 17–25; and Case C-178/03 *Commission v Parliament and Council* EU:C:2006:4, para 57.

[26] Case C-338/01 *Commission v Council* EU:C:2004:253, para 58.

[27] ibid.

[28] Case C-91/05 *Commission v Council* EU:C:2008:288, para 77.

III. LEGISLATIVE POWERS

Using the organisation of a liberal democracy as a template, the Treaties allocate powers among the legislative, executive, and judicial branches of the Union. The legislative power is held by both the Council and the European Parliament. In 2009, the Treaty of Lisbon introduced for the first time the formal categories of 'legislative procedures', through which 'legislative acts' of the Union are adopted. These procedures are divided into two categories: the ordinary legislative procedure and the special legislative procedure. The Treaties also establish other decision-making procedures involving the Council, the European Parliament, and the Commission, but these are not classified as 'legislative'.[29] In such cases, the resulting measures cannot be regarded as a 'legislative act' inasmuch as the procedure for their adoption is not a 'legislative procedure'. This distinction, introduced by the Lisbon Treaty, has significant legal consequences: it determines the applicable rules on transparency (the Council must deliberate publicly on legislative acts under Article 16(8) TEU), the standing of private applicants to challenge acts before the Union courts (Article 263, fourth paragraph TFEU), the scope of national parliaments' subsidiarity review (Protocol No 2), and the classification of acts for the purposes of delegated and implementing powers (Articles 290 and 291 TFEU).

The difference between the ordinary legislative procedure and the special legislative procedure lies in the institutional balance struck between the Council and the European Parliament. In the ordinary legislative procedure, both institutions share equal influence in negotiating the measure, as they both act as co-legislators with veto power. However, in the special legislative procedure, the powers of the European Parliament vary significantly. In some cases, the Parliament's consent is required, giving it an effective veto, as with the adoption of the multiannual financial framework (Article 312(2) TFEU) or measures combating discrimination (Article 19(1) TFEU). In other cases, its role is only consultative, leaving the substantive decision-making and policy design in the hands of the Council.

Despite the differences between the two types of legislative procedure, they also share common features. National parliaments may intervene in all legislative procedures under Protocol No 2 on the application of the principles of subsidiarity and proportionality. Furthermore, all legislative acts, regardless of the type of legislative procedure through which they are adopted, are subject to certain specific rules of judicial review, particularly regarding the standing of private applicants who challenge legislative acts in actions for annulment, as described in chapter eleven. Both types of legislative procedure also share the Commission's right of legislative initiative, a prerogative held as a general rule by the guardian of the Treaties, as will be explained in the following section.

1. The Commission's General Power of Legislative Initiative

Article 17(2) TEU states that 'Union legislative acts may only be adopted on the basis of a Commission proposal, except where the Treaties provide otherwise'. This provision affirms that, as a general rule, the Commission holds the right to table legislation, meaning that the Council and the European Parliament can exercise their legislative powers only if the Commission has previously submitted a legislative initiative. This right of initiative gives the Commission a significant role in the legislative process. Since the Council can only amend the Commission's proposal by unanimity (Article 293(1) TFEU), and the Commission may

[29] Arts 74 and 103 TFEU.

withdraw its proposal at any stage (subject to the limits established by the Court of Justice), the Commission's influence extends well beyond the initial proposal.

The exceptions referred to in Article 17(2) TEU can be categorised into three types, as set out below:

(1) *Initiative of other institutions*: the Treaties specify certain cases where the European Parliament (Articles 223(1) and 226 TFEU), the ECB (Articles 129(3)–(4) and 219(1) TFEU), the Court of Justice of the European Union (Articles 252(1), 257, and 281 TFEU), or the European Investment Bank (Article 308(3) TFEU) can also take the initiative, particularly in areas generally confined to the governance of the institution itself or in areas where the institution holds a specific competence or expertise.
(2) *Initiative by a group of Member States*: in the Area of Freedom, Security and Justice, Article 76(*b*) TFEU confers the power of legislative initiative on a quarter of the Member States, as well as on the Commission. This shared power of initiative is confined to Chapters 4–5 of Title V TFEU (judicial cooperation in criminal matters and police cooperation), as well as to measures on administrative cooperation outlined in Article 74 TFEU.
(3) *European Citizens' Initiative*: Article 11(4) TEU grants at least one million citizens of the Union, from a representative number of Member States, the right to invite the European Commission to submit a proposal for a Union legislative act. This right of initiative has been developed by Regulation 2019/788 on the European Citizens' Initiative,[30] but it is important to note that the formal power of initiative remains with the Commission under Article 17(2) TEU. Therefore, it is an *indirect* form of initiative, as it is the Commission that decides to formally present a legislative proposal at the citizens' initiative.[31]

Subject to these exceptions, the Commission has a discretional and broad power to decide, in light of its own legislative agenda and the interests of the Union, whether to propose legislation. However, pursuant to Article 225 TFEU, the European Parliament has the authority to request the Commission to 'submit any appropriate proposal on matters on which it [the European Parliament] considers that a Union act is required for the purpose of implementing the Treaties'. This requirement does not legally compel the Commission to act, but it must give reasons if it ultimately chooses not to exercise its power of initiative. The Council has an equivalent power set out in Article 241 TFEU. In any event, the Treaties do not make the Commission's right of initiative conditional upon receiving prior guidance or instructions from other institutions, including the European Council.[32] In practice, the European Council has increasingly shaped the Commission's legislative agenda through its strategic guidelines and conclusions, as provided in Article 15(1) TEU.

As the Court of Justice has held, 'in view of [its] power [of initiative], the Commission is a *key player* in the legislative process'.[33]

The Commission publishes its legislative agenda, known as the Commission Work Programme, on an annual basis and presents it to the Council and the European Parliament

[30] Regulation (EU) 2019/788 of the European Parliament and of the Council of 17 April 2019 on the European citizens' initiative [2019] OJ L130/55, and Commission Implementing Regulation (EU) No 1179/2011 of 17 November laying down technical specifications for collection systems via websites pursuant to Regulation (EU) No 211/2011 [2011] *OJ* L301/3.

[31] On the powers of the Commission when dealing with a citizen's legislative initiative, see Case C-589/15 P *Anagnostakis* EU:C:2017:663; Case C-420/16 P *Balázs-Árpád Izsák* EU:C:2019:177; and Case C-418/18 P *Puppinck and Others* EU:C:2019:1113.

[32] See the judgment in Joined Cases C-643/15 and C-647/15 *Slovak Republic and Hungary v Council* EU:C:2017:631, paras 146–147.

[33] Case C-57/16 P *ClientEarth* EU:C:2018:660, para 88 (italics added).

for debate.[34] This practice is based on Article 11(3) TEU, which states that the Commission 'shall carry out broad consultations with parties concerned in order to ensure that the Union's actions are coherent and transparent'. The Work Programme outlines the Commission's priorities, the general content and strategy of the initiatives it intends to propose, and a timetable. The final version of the Work Programme results from close cooperation and interinstitutional discussions between the Commission, the Council, and the European Parliament.

The Commission's legislative proposals, designated as 'COM documents', can be published in the *Official Journal of the European Union* C Series under the heading 'Information and Notices.' Legislative initiatives are also forwarded to national parliaments in accordance with Protocol No 1, so they can put into practice the procedures on the principles of subsidiarity and proportionality. All legislative initiatives and their preparatory documents are available on the *Eur-Lex website*.[35]

As a result of its right of legislative initiative, the Commission has the power of amendment during the legislative procedure, as provided for in Article 293 TFEU. The Commission 'may alter its proposal at any time during the procedures leading to the adoption of a Union act', as long as the Council has not yet acted (Article 293(2) TFEU). Furthermore, Article 293(1) TFEU states that when the Council acts upon a legislative proposal from the Commission, it may amend that proposal only by acting unanimously.[36] In practice, the Commission holds significant influence throughout the legislative procedure, particularly when the legal basis requires a qualified majority vote in the Council. If the Council acts unanimously, the Commission's influence is reduced, since once unanimity is reached among the Member States, the Commission's proposal can be amended without its consent. However, the Council's power to amend is not unlimited; it can only introduce amendments that remain within the scope of the initiative, 'as defined in the original proposals from the Commission'.[37]

Article 293 TFEU also encompasses, as confirmed by the case law of the Court of Justice, the power of the Commission to withdraw its legislative proposals.[38] However, the Court of Justice has emphasised that this power 'cannot . . . confer upon that institution a right of veto in the conduct of the legislative process, a right which would be contrary to the principles of conferral of powers and institutional balance'.[39] The Commission must give reasons for its decision to withdraw the initiative, and it must justify the withdrawal on the grounds of objective criteria. For example, a justified reason to withdraw an initiative could emerge if the amendments planned by the Parliament and the Council risked distorting the proposal 'to the point of depriving it of its *raison d'être*, in a manner contrary to the various objectives pursued by the proposal'.[40] The Commission's decision to withdraw its initiative is subject to judicial review before the Court of Justice through an action for annulment under Article 263 TFEU.

[34] See Annex IV of the Rules of Procedure of the European Parliament on the Framework Agreement on relations between the European Parliament and the European Commission, in particular paras 33–36.

[35] See the section 'preparatory documents' of Eur-Lex, available at *https://eur-lex.europa.eu/collection/eu-law/pre-acts.html*.

[36] However, this rule is subject to the exceptions provided for in Arts 294(10) and (13), 310, 312, 314 and 315(2) TFEU.

[37] Case C-408/95 *Eurotunnel and others* EU:C:1997:532, para 39, following the precedent set in Case C-355/87 *Commission v Council* EU:C:1989:220, paras 42–44.

[38] Case C-409/13 *Council v Commission* EU:C:2015:217, para 74. On the Commission's right of withdrawal of legislative proposals, see M Chamon, 'Upholding the "Community Method": Limits to the Commission's Power to Withdraw Legislative Proposals: Council v Commission (C-409/13)' (2015) 40 *European Law Review* 895, and N Lupo, 'The Commission's Power to Withdraw Legislative Proposals and its "Parliamentarisation", Between Technical and Political Grounds' (2018) 14 *European Constitutional Law Review* 311.

[39] ibid, para 75.

[40] ibid, para 80.

The Commission has no legal obligation to propose legislation unless the Treaties specify otherwise. One such case is Article 215 TFEU, which pertains to the interruption or reduction of economic and financial relations with a third country. In this context, the Council and the Commission 'shall adopt the necessary measures' after a decision is made under Chapter 2 of Title V TEU. As a general rule, the Commission has broad discretion that makes it difficult for other institutions or individuals to successfully bring an action for failure to act under Article 265 TFEU if the Commission fails to submit a legislative proposal at their request. A limit to this broad discretional power of the Commission is found in the principle of sincere cooperation, which requires the Commission not to obstruct the ordinary functioning of the legislative procedures.[41] An unjustified or arbitrary obstruction of the normal legislative process would amount to a breach of the principle of sincere cooperation, although such a scenario has not been confirmed to date.

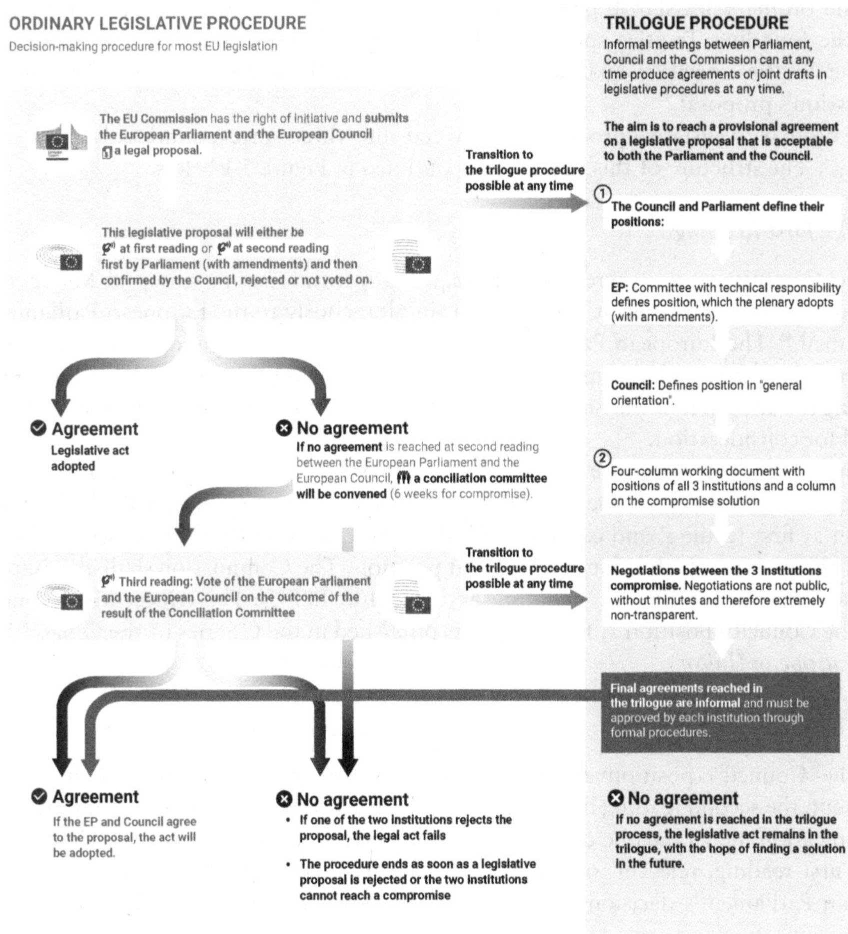

Figure 5.1 Ordinary legislative procedure: decision-making procedure for most EU legislation (source: European Parliament)

[41] ibid, paras 98–109.

2. The Ordinary Legislative Procedure

Article 294 TFEU describes the main features and steps of the ordinary legislative procedure, which builds upon the former co-decision procedure. The ordinary legislative procedure involves active participation from the three political institutions – the Commission, the Council, and the European Parliament – and the joint adoption of legislative acts by the Council and the European Parliament, signed by the presidents of both institutions.[42] Unlike special legislative procedures, the ordinary legislative procedure is characterised by the equal powers of the European Parliament and the Council, with both institutions holding veto rights that can put an end to the proposal tabled by the Commission. The ordinary legislative procedure applies wherever the Treaties specifically designate it as the applicable procedure for the adoption of a particular measure. It is excluded in the area of the CFSP, as explicitly stated in Articles 24(1) and 31(1) TEU.

In the ordinary legislative procedure, the Council decides by qualified majority, except where the founding Treaties specify otherwise.[43] The Council must also act unanimously when the Treaties specify a qualified majority vote and the institution decides to amend the Commission's proposal.[44]

The ordinary legislative procedure is divided into three stages, commonly referred to as 'readings'. The structure of this procedure is outlined in Figure 5.1 below.

2.1. *The First Reading*

Once the Commission or, where appropriate, other institutions or a group of Member States submit a legislative initiative, it is forwarded simultaneously to the European Parliament and the Council.[45] The European Parliament is the first institution to adopt its position on the initiative, which may include amendments, on which the Commission can adopt a position.[46] Following the adoption of the European Parliament's position, the initiative is forwarded to the Council for consideration.

If the Council approves the European Parliament's position, the act is adopted.[47] If, on the other hand, the Council does not approve the Parliament's position, it shall adopt its own 'position at first reading' and communicate it to the European Parliament, with a full statement of the reasons which led it to adopt that position. The Commission shall also inform the European Parliament fully of its position (Article 294(6) TFEU). This triggers the second reading.[48] The Council's position at first reading is published in the C Series of the *Official Journal of the European Union*.

2.2. *The Second Reading*

Once the Council's position at first reading has been communicated to the European Parliament, the second reading begins. The European Parliament, within three months of such communication, may take one of three courses of action: it may approve the Council's position at first reading, reject it, or propose amendments to it.[49] In the event of rejection, the European Parliament's decision will put an end to the procedure, and the act can only be

[42] Art 297(1) TFEU.
[43] Art 16(3) TEU.
[44] Art 293(1) TFEU.
[45] ibid, Art 294(2).
[46] ibid, Art 294(3).
[47] ibid, Art 294(4).
[48] ibid, Art 294(5).
[49] ibid, Art 294(7).

reconsidered by reconvening the procedure.[50] If the European Parliament approves the initiative, the act is adopted.[51] However, if the European Parliament proposes amendments, the initiative is forwarded to the Council, following the Commission's opinion, which takes a position on the amendments proposed by the European Parliament.[52] From this point onwards, the Commission loses its right to amend the proposal, although the Court of Justice has confirmed that it retains a power to withdraw the initiative in exceptional circumstances, specifically if the amendments distort the proposal's essential objectives.

From the receipt of the initiative, the Council has three months to approve the European Parliament's amendments or to reject them partially or entirely. In the latter case, a Conciliation Committee is convened, in agreement with the President of the European Parliament.[53] The Conciliation Committee is composed of members of the Council or their representatives and an equal number of representatives of the European Parliament,[54] and the Commission may participate in its meetings and take all necessary initiatives with a view to reconciling the positions of the European Parliament and the Council,[55] but it can no longer withdraw its legislative proposal. The Committee must approve a joint text within six weeks of being convened; if it fails to do so, the proposed act shall be deemed not to have been adopted.[56] If, however, the Committee approves a joint text, the matter is referred to the European Parliament and the Council for the third reading.

2.3. *The Third Reading*

The European Parliament and the Council must decide on the joint text within six weeks of the approval by the Conciliation Committee, without being able to propose any additional amendments at this stage. If both institutions approve the joint text, the Council, acting by a qualified majority, and the European Parliament, acting by a majority of the votes cast, the act shall be deemed to have been adopted.[57] If, however, either institution rejects the joint text, the act is considered not to have been adopted.[58]

2.4. *The Trilogues and their Impact on the Ordinary Legislative Procedure*

The ordinary legislative procedure is not characterised by simplicity or flexibility, at least as it is portrayed in Article 294 TFEU. This may explain why, in practice, there are significant deviations from what is reflected in the Treaties, mainly as a result of the widespread use of trilogues, informal interinstitutional meetings between the Commission, the Council, and the European Parliament, in which the positions of the three institutions are brought closer together until an agreement is reached between the three institutions. Trilogues operate at all stages of the ordinary legislative procedure and have a relevant impact: during the 2019–24 parliamentary term, 86 per cent of legislative proposals were adopted at the first reading, with 973 trilogue meetings held during that period.[59] Trilogues typically involve the European Parliament's rapporteur and shadow rapporteurs (representing the political groups), the presidency of the Council (representing the Member States), and representatives of the Commission. The Parliament's

[50] ibid, Art 294(7)(*b*).
[51] ibid, Art 294(7)(*a*).
[52] ibid, Art 294(7)(*c*).
[53] ibid, Art 294(8)(*b*).
[54] ibid, Art 294(10)–(11).
[55] ibid, Art 294(11).
[56] ibid, Art 294(12).
[57] ibid, Art 294(13).
[58] ibid.
[59] Activity Report: Developments and trend of the ordinary legislative procedure 2019–24, ninth parliamentary term. Directorate-General for internal Policies. European Parliament.

negotiating mandate is established through a vote in the competent parliamentary committee, and in some cases confirmed by the plenary. The Council's mandate is established through a 'general approach' adopted by the relevant Council configuration, or through a position agreed within COREPER.

2.5. *Special Features of the Ordinary Legislative Procedure*

The Treaties include some variations and derogations from the standard rules of the ordinary legislative procedure, of which the following should be noted:

- If the legislative proposal does not originate from the Commission, Article 294(15) TFEU still guarantees the Commission's right to give its opinion on the initiative throughout the procedure and to participate in the Conciliation Committee. However, the specific rule in Article 293(1) TFEU requiring the Council to act unanimously to amend the Commission's proposal does not apply where the proposal does not originate from the Commission, since the rationale for that rule (protecting the Commission's initiative) is devoid of purpose.
- Article 48 TFEU, which applies to the area of coordination of social security systems, allows for the possibility of suspending the ordinary legislative procedure 'Where a member of the Council declares that a draft legislative act [in this field] would affect important aspects of its social security system, including its scope, cost or financial structure, or would affect the financial balance of that system'. In this case, the issue can be referred to the European Council, which, within four months, will either refer the draft back to the Council or request the Commission to submit a new proposal, with the initially proposed act considered not to have been adopted.
- In the area of judicial cooperation in criminal matters, Articles 82(3) and 83(3) TFEU empower any Member State to refer a draft directive to the European Council when it concerns 'fundamental aspects of its criminal justice system', in which case the ordinary legislative procedure is suspended. In this case, the draft will be referred back to the Council only when an agreement has been reached within the European Council. Otherwise, the act is deemed not to have been adopted, or the Member States concerned will be called upon to proceed with enhanced cooperation.

3. Special Legislative Procedures

In contrast to the ordinary legislative procedure, special legislative procedures are characterised by an increased role for the Council at the expense of the European Parliament. The reduced role of the European Parliament is reflected in two ways: through a right of consultation or a right of consent. In the first case, the European Parliament must be consulted by the Council, and its opinion is not binding; in the second case, the European Parliament gives its consent to the proposal but without the power to introduce amendments, before its adoption by the Council. Special legislative procedures with a right of consultation for the European Parliament are significantly more numerous than those involving a right of consent.[60]

[60] The special legislative procedures with a right of consultation of the European Parliament are provided in the following articles of the TFEU: Art 21(3) (social security); Art 22(1) (municipal elections and elections to the European Parliament); Art 23 (directives on diplomatic and consular protection); Art 77(3) (passports, identity cards and residence permits); Art 81(3) (family law in cross-border situations); Art 89 (operations of police authorities in other Member States); Art 113 (harmonisation of legislation on indirect taxation); Art 115 (harmonisation of legislation affecting the internal market); Art 118 (European intellectual or industrial property rights); Art 126(14) (excessive

In exceptional cases which may have an impact on the prerogatives of the European Parliament, the special legislative procedure is reversed, and it falls primarily on the European Parliament to adopt an initiative, while the Council retains a right of consent.[61] This applies to matters concerning the general conditions governing the performance of the duties of Members of the European Parliament (Article 223(2) TFEU), the exercise of the right of inquiry (Article 226 TFEU), and the Statute of the European Ombudsman (Article 228(4) TFEU). In these cases, the European Parliament holds not only the principal decision-making powers but may also hold the right of initiative.

3.1. *Special Legislative Procedures with Consultation of the European Parliament*

Where the Treaties specify that a special legislative procedure requires 'prior consultation of the European Parliament', the latter's role is limited to providing a non-binding opinion to the Council.[62] Although this involvement will not condition the approval of the proposal, as it deprives the European Parliament of its veto rights, the case law of the Court of Justice emphasises the 'essential' nature of the consultation procedure.[63] Consequently, if the Council adopts the measure without seeking or awaiting the European Parliament's opinion,[64] the act may be annulled for infringement of an essential procedural requirement.

In the specific case of initiatives already consulted by the European Parliament and subsequently amended in the Council, the Court of Justice emphasises the obligation to re-consult the European Parliament, unless the amendment concerns specific technical details[65] or reflects a position previously expressed by the European Parliament in its opinion.[66] Failure to re-consult the European Parliament after the adoption of substantial amendments by the Council will result in the legislative act being declared null and void.[67]

deficits); Art 127(6) (specific tasks for the ECB in the field of prudential supervision); Art 153(2) second subparagraph (social policy measures); Art 182(4) (specific research and technological development programmes); Art 192(2) (environmental policy measures); Art 194(3) (energy taxation); Art 203 (association with overseas countries and territories); Art 262 (jurisdiction over European intellectual or industrial property rights); Art 308 third subparagraph (amendments to the Statute of the EIB) and Art 311(3) (own resources of the Union). On the other hand, special legislative procedures with the right of consent of the European Parliament are provided for in Arts 19(1) (anti-discrimination); Art 25, second subparagraph (Union citizenship status rights); Art 82(2)(d) (criminal proceedings); Art 86(1) (establishment of the European Public Prosecutor's Office), and Art 311(4) (measures implementing the Union's own resources system) and Art 352 (flexibility clause).

[61] The Council intervenes in the consent procedure in the cases referred to in Art 223(2) TFEU (duties of Members of the European Parliament); Art 228(4) TFEU (duties of the Ombudsman), and Art 226(3) TFEU (right of inquiry of the European Parliament).

[62] See n 60.

[63] Case C-138/79 *Roquette v Council* EU:C:1980:249, paras 33–37; and Case C-139/79 *Maizena v Council* EU:C:1980:250, paras 34–38.

[64] Case C-417/93 *Parliament v Council* EU:C:1995:127, para 10. However, the Council may adopt the measure without awaiting the opinion of the European Parliament if the latter does not act in accordance with the principle of sincere cooperation and, for example, if there are unnecessary delays in an urgent procedure. On this point, see Case C-65/93 *Parliament v Council* EU:C:1995:91, paras 24–28.

[65] Case C-41/69 *Chemiefarma* EU:C:1970:71, paras 68–70; Case C-817/79 *Buyl and Others v Commission* EU:C:1982:36, paras 23–24; Case C-828/79 *Adam v Commission* EU:C:1982:37, paras 24–25; Case C-280/93 *Germany v Council* EU:C:1994:367, paras 38–42; Case C-417/93 *Parliament v Council* EU:C:1995:127, paras 16–26; and Case C-58/01 *Océ van der Grinten* EU:C:2003:495, paras 101–102.

[66] Joined Cases C-13/92 and 16/92 *Driessen and others* EU:C:1993:828, paras 23–25; and Case C-408/95 *Eurotunnel and others* EU:C:1997:532, paras 46–63.

[67] Case C-65/90 *Parliament v Council* EU:C:1992:325, paras 20–21; Case C-388/92 *Parliament v Council* EU:C:1994:213, para 19; and Case C-21/94 *Parliament v Council* EU:C:1995:220, paras 17–28.

3.2. *Special Legislative Procedures, Subject to the Consent of the European Parliament*

The founding Treaties refer at times to special legislative procedures that are adopted 'after obtaining the consent of the European Parliament'. In such cases, the European Parliament's opinion is essential and binding on the Council, but unlike the ordinary legislative procedure, it does not allow for the introduction of amendments. The European Parliament will give its consent to the initiative after it has been discussed in the Council. However, if the Council introduces amendments following the vote of the European Parliament, the initiative must be submitted again to the chamber to secure its consent.

4. European Citizens' Initiative

The Treaty of Lisbon introduced the possibility for at least one million citizens of the Union from at least seven Member States to invite the Commission to submit a legislative proposal on matters falling within the Union's competence. The scope of a European citizens' initiative covers 'matters where citizens consider that a legal act of the Union is required for the purpose of implementing the Treaties'. Article 11(4) TEU and Article 24(1) TFEU specify the basic conditions under which the citizens' initiative is organised, a framework currently elaborated in Regulation 2019/788 on the European citizens' initiative.[68]

A European citizens' initiative must be supported by at least one million citizens who are nationals of a Member State and of voting age for elections to the European Parliament. Article 3 of Regulation 2019/788 introduces two criteria to ensure broad territorial representativeness of the initiative: first, the initiative must receive support from at least one million citizens across the Union, from at least one quarter of the Member States; and second, in at least one quarter of the Member States, the number of signatories must be at least equal to the minimum number specified in Annex I of the Regulation. This number corresponds to the number of Members of the European Parliament elected in each Member State, multiplied by the total number of Members of the European Parliament, at the time of registration of the initiative. By way of example, in Germany, a minimum of 67,680 signatories is required, while in Ireland, 9,165 are needed, and 41,595 in Spain.

Each initiative must be prepared and managed by a group of at least seven natural persons (the 'group organisers', according to the Regulation), responsible for the organisation of the initiative and its representation vis-a-vis the Union institutions. Before collecting statements of support, the initiative is submitted for registration to the Commission, having fulfilled all the formal requirements set out in Regulation 2019/788. At the initial stage of registration, the Commission conducts an admissibility check, which includes a review of the Union's competence to decide on the matter. The Commission's decision of inadmissibility must be justified, and it is subject to judicial review before the Court of Justice.[69]

Following the gathering of support, the organisers submit the initiative to the Commission. Within six months, the Commission must present its legal and political conclusions on the

[68] Regulation (EU) 2019/788 of the European Parliament and of the Council of 17 April 2019 on the European citizens' initiative [2019] OJ L130/55 and its corresponding implementing act provided for in Commission Implementing Regulation (EU) 2019/1799 of 22 October 2019 laying down technical specifications for individual online collection systems in accordance with Regulation (EU) 2019/788 of the European Parliament and of the Council on the European citizens' initiative [2019] OJ L274/3.

[69] Case C-589/15 P *Anagnostakis* EU:C:2017:663; Case C-420/16 P *Balázs-Árpád Izsák v Commission* EU:C:2019:177; Case C-418/18 P *Puppinck* EU:C:2019:1113; Case C-899/19 P *Romania v Commission* EU:C:2022:41; and Case C-54/22 P *Romania v Commission* EU:C:2024:164.

initiative in a communication. Article 15 of Regulation 2019/788 confirms the non-binding nature of the initiative, leaving it to the Commission's discretion whether to act on it by submitting a formal legislative proposal. The Commission is under no legal obligation to submit a proposal, but it is obliged to provide a reasoned explanation of its decision. The European Parliament may also hold a debate on a successful initiative and adopt a resolution expressing its position. To date, a total of 10 initiatives have been answered by the Commission, including initiatives on the right to water quality, the limitation of animal testing, the protection of national and linguistic minorities, the ban on glyphosate, and the ban on the use of individual cages for farmed animals.[70]

5. Non-legislative Procedures with Legislative Relevance

The TFEU empowers the Council and the European Parliament to adopt acts of material legislative relevance without following a formal legislative procedure as defined in Article 289(3) TFEU. These acts are not 'legislative acts' in the strict sense because they are not enacted through an ordinary or special legislative procedure, but they can still be regarded as of 'legislative relevance' due to their content and impact. As a result, there is no hierarchical relation between the two types of acts. This is the case of Article 74 TFEU, which provides a legal basis in the field of administrative cooperation measures in the Area of Freedom, Security and Justice. Similarly, Article 103 TFEU authorises the Council to adopt regulations or directives to give effect to the principles laid down in Articles 101–102 TFEU, a legal basis that has enabled the adoption of the current framework of the Union's competition policy.[71] Furthermore, Article 122(1) confers on the Council the power to introduce 'measures' to address 'severe difficulties [that] arise in the supply of certain products, notably in the area of energy', including broad normative measures of general scope and impact comparable to those of a legislative act.[72]

IV. EXECUTIVE POWERS

1. The Executive Regulatory Powers of Articles 290–291 TFEU

Like any political organisation with the power to adopt legislation, the Union grants its executive authorities the authority to establish provisions that develop or supplement the Union's legislative acts. This task primarily falls to the Commission and is set out in Articles 290–291 TFEU, introduced by the Treaty of Lisbon. These provisions result from a long evolution in the relations between the Commission and the co-legislators, which began in the 1960s with the development of what became known as 'comitology'. In earlier years of European integration, it was clear that, due to the technical complexity of many policy areas, the Commission

[70] On the European legislative initiative and its legal implications, see A Karatzia, 'The European Citizens' Initiative and the EU Institutional Balance: On Realism and the Possibilities of Affecting EU Lawmaking' (2017) 54 *Common Market Law Review* 117.

[71] Council Regulation (EC) No 1/2003 of 16 December 2002 on the implementation of the rules on competition laid down in Articles 101 and 102 of the Treaty [2003] OJ L 1/1.

[72] Article 122(1) has been frequently used in recent times, for example in Council Regulation (EU) 2022/1854 of 6 October 2022 on an emergency intervention to address high energy prices [2022] OJ LI 261/1. See M Chamon *The use of Article 122 TFEU – Institutional implications and impact on democratic accountability*, DG for Internal Policies, European Parliament (2023).

needed to assume the task of developing or supplementing acts adopted by the Council and the Parliamentary Assembly. As a result of the hesitations from the Member States, this task was to be assigned to the Commission under close scrutiny by the Member States through 'committees' composed of national representatives operating within the Council framework. The Court of Justice upheld the legality of this practice,[73] but tensions soon emerged between the three political institutions. Although the practice of 'comitology' was eventually recognised through a provision in the Treaties[74] and a decision governing its formation and day-to-day operations, tensions among the three institutions continued.

Articles 290–291 TFEU sought to resolve the tensions from the pre-Lisbon era by distinguishing between two types of non-legislative regulatory measures: firstly, rules that supplement or amend certain non-essential elements of a legislative act (Article 290 TFEU); secondly, rules to introduce uniform conditions for implementing legally binding Union acts (Article 291 TFEU). For the first type, only the Commission is empowered to adopt *delegated acts* without prior approval in a committee. For the second, the Commission or the Council, in duly justified cases, may adopt *implementing acts following* the procedures outlined in Regulation 182/2011.[75] These procedures include mechanisms for Member States to oversee the Commission's exercise of implementing powers, which are left in the hands of committees.

The purpose of this distinction is clear: to support the Commission's executive tasks, especially when it comes to the enactment of acts supplementing or amending legislative acts. In these cases, where the Commission has received a delegation to introduce additional rules of an executive nature, its scope for action is broad, but subject to mechanisms of political supervision by the Council and the European Parliament. When introducing a regulatory act aimed at specifying the content of a legislative act to ensure uniform conditions for implementation, the Commission adopts an implementing act within a committee, thereby losing the broad margin of action it enjoys under Article 290 TFEU. In duly justified cases only, implementing acts can be adopted by the Council, provided that sufficient reasons are given in the legislative act itself for conferring implementing powers on the Council rather than the Commission (Article 291(2) TFEU).[76]

The fact that Articles 290–291 TFEU provide for a system of delegated and implementing acts does not prevent the legislature from using other routes to make delegations or request implementing acts from the Commission or the Council. In *United Kingdom v Council and Parliament*, the Court of Justice confirmed the possibility for the Union legislature to make delegations to specialised agencies without resorting to the procedure under Article 290 TFEU.[77] In *Spain v Council*, the Court of Justice held that the Union institutions can exercise implementing powers through instruments other than those outlined in Article 291 TFEU, as is the case of a Council implementing decision imposing a fine on a Member State in the context of the economic and budgetary surveillance framework applicable to the euro area.[78]

[73] Case C-25/70 *Einfuhr- und Vorratsstelle für Getreide und Futtermittel* EU:C:1970:115.

[74] Art 202 Treaty Establishing the European Community.

[75] Regulation (EU) No 182/2011 of the European Parliament and of the Council of 16 February 2011 laying down the rules and general principles concerning mechanisms for control by Member States of the Commission's exercise of implementing powers [2011] OJ L55/13.

[76] Case T-395/22 *Hypo Vorarlberg Bank AG v SRB* EU:T:2024:333, paras 34–42.

[77] Case C-270/12 *United Kingdom v European Parliament and Council of the European Union* EU:C:2014:18, paras 78–80.

[78] Case C-521/15 *Spain v Council* EU:C:2017:982, paras 46–51.

2. The Distinction between Delegated and Implementing Powers

Articles 290 and 291 TFEU leave several unresolved issues, starting with the distinction between acts 'supplementing or amending' non-essential elements of a legislative act, and acts intended to ensure 'uniform conditions for implementation'. The difference is not trivial, as the Commission's powers and the applicable control mechanisms will vary significantly depending on the type of act it is empowered to adopt.

The Court of Justice has offered some useful interpretative guidance on this distinction, which can be summarised as follows:

- The function of delegated acts mainly aims to supplement a legislative act, whereas implementing acts are intended to 'provide further detail in relation to the content of a legislative act' in order to ensure that it is applied under uniform conditions in all Member States.[79] The distinction between 'supplementing' and 'further detail' seems to depend on *the degree of normative development needed by the legislative act*. To 'supplement' an act, there must be an area not covered by the basic legislative act, an intentionally created gap by the legislator, that requires additional rules. Conversely, providing 'detail' on a legislative act indicates that the normative framework is complete, but specific aspects need further specification through additional rules to ensure uniform application across the Member States.
- In the case of delegated acts 'amending' legislative acts, the scope of the amendment or the need to adopt other non-legislative acts is irrelevant in determining the scope of the Commission's powers. The only relevant criterion is the existence of an amendment to a legislative act.[80]
- Since Articles 290–291 TFEU serve different purposes and have different scopes of application, the legislator cannot use them interchangeably.[81] However, the Court of Justice grants the Union legislator a wide margin of discretion when choosing between a delegated or an implementing act. Therefore, although it is possible to judicially review the legislature's choice, the decision will breach the Treaties only in the case of a manifest error of assessment.[82]
- In the same way that the case law gives the legislator a broad margin of discretion to decide between conferring delegated or implementing powers on the Commission, the Commission also enjoys a wide margin of manoeuvre when it comes to performing the delegation or implementation. The Court of Justice has held that implementing acts are not constrained by the specifics previously determined by the legislator. Instead, when providing 'further detail' to a legislative act through an implementing act, the Commission may introduce certain measures that were not included in the legislative act, as long as they align with the

[79] Case C-427/12 *Commission v Parliament and Council* EU:C:2014:170, paras 39 and 52.

[80] Case C-88/14 *Commission v Parliament and Council* EU:C:2015:499, paras 42–44 and 46.

[81] Case C-65/13 *Parliament v Commission* EU:C:2014:2289, para 45: 'it follows from Article 290(1) TFEU in conjunction with Article 291(2) TFEU that in exercising an implementing power, the Commission may neither amend nor supplement the legislative act, even as to its non-essential elements'.

[82] Case C-427/12 *Commission v Parliament and Council* (n 79) para 40: 'It must be noted that the EU legislature has discretion when it decides to confer a delegated power on the Commission pursuant to Article 290(1) TFEU or an implementing power pursuant to Article 291(2) TFEU. Consequently, judicial review is limited to manifest errors of assessment as to whether the EU legislature could reasonably have taken the view, first, that, in order to be implemented, the legal framework which it laid down regarding the system of fees referred to in Article 80(1) of Regulation No 528/2012 needs only the addition of further detail, without its non-essential elements having to be amended or supplemented and, secondly, that the provisions of Regulation No 528/2012 relating to that system require uniform conditions for implementation.'

'essential general aims pursued by the legislative act' and are necessary or appropriate for its implementation without supplementing or amending it.[83]

- An element adopted by the Commission in the exercise of its power to 'supplement' a legislative act, but which is an integral part of that act, cannot, therefore, be replaced or deleted under the same power that led to its adoption, since such actions require a power to 'amend' that act. It is therefore for the legislature to intervene when it becomes necessary to replace or delete the added element, either by establishing a legislative act itself or by granting a delegated power to the Commission to 'amend' the act in question. Accordingly, in the context of the exercise of a power to supplement a legislative act, to include an element in the text of that act would undermine the effective application of such a power.[84] By contrast, when the Commission 'supplements' a legislative act by adopting a separate act, it may, insofar as necessary, amend that separate act without needing to amend the original legislative act itself. As a result, the exercise of a delegated power to 'supplement' a legislative act within the meaning of Article 290 TFEU requires the Commission to adopt a separate act.[85]

Regarding the content, limits, and procedures for adopting delegated and implementing acts, further details are provided in chapter eight.

3. Other Executive Powers

The Union holds significant powers across many policy areas, which require an administrative infrastructure to implement them effectively. To achieve this, aside from the non-legislative powers conferred on the Commission under Articles 290–291 TFEU, the Treaties and various legislative acts also confer powers on other institutions, bodies, offices, and agencies. When these executive powers are outlined in the Treaties, the relevant provision defines the terms and conditions under which the executive power is exercised. When it comes to delegations in legislative acts, the Court of Justice has established limits on the legislature's power of delegation, as outlined in the *Meroni* case law described below.

3.1. Executive Powers Provided for in the Treaties

The ECB holds executive powers under Article 132 TFEU and Article 34 of the Protocol on the Statute of the European System of Central Banks and of the ECB, a provision of primary law annexed to the Treaties. However, this power is limited, as the ECB only adopts regulations when essential for the exercise of its tasks relating to monetary policy, foreign exchange operations, the holding and management of official foreign reserves of the Member States, the promotion of the smooth operation of the payment systems, minimum reserves, external financial operations, and prudential supervision. The ECB's regulatory powers in the field of prudential supervision derive not from the Statute directly but from Council Regulation (EU) No 1024/2013 (the SSM Regulation), which confers specific supervisory tasks on the ECB under Article 127(6) TFEU. In addition, the ECB holds the power to impose sanctions on undertakings for failure to comply with its regulations and decisions (Article 132(3) TFEU).

[83] Case C-65/13 *Parliament v Commission* (n 81) para 46. See also Case C-696/15 P *Czech Republic v Commission* EU:C:2017:595, paras 50–53.

[84] Case C-65/13 *Parliament v Commission* (n 81).

[85] ibid, paras 56–57.

Similarly, the Treaties confer specific functions on the European Investment Bank, an independent body with its own legal personality, whose powers are outlined in Articles 308–309 TFEU, as well as in its Statute. However, unlike the ECB, the European Investment Bank has no executive regulatory powers beyond the authority to adopt its own rules of procedure.

The Treaties also grant powers to Eurojust and Europol, bodies linked to the Area of Freedom, Security and Justice. However, these powers are not defined in detail in the Treaties and are subject to further development through legislative acts.[86]

The question arises as to whether the Union legislature can create secondary legal bases that establish specific procedures and voting rules for the adoption of executive regulatory acts. In its case law, the Court of Justice rejected such practice, arguing that 'the manner in which the [Union] institutions arrive at their decisions are laid down in the Treaty and are not at the disposal of the Member States or of the institutions themselves'.[87] While the Treaties may empower an institution to amend a decision-making procedure established by the Treaty, to acknowledge that an institution can introduce secondary legal bases, whether to strengthen or ease the rules for the adoption of an act, 'is tantamount to according that institution a legislative power which exceeds that provided by the Treaty'.[88]

3.2. *Executive Powers Provided for in Legislation*

Executive powers can be delegated to bodies or agencies by the Union legislature. This delegation is not carried out directly by the Commission but through a legislative act adopted by the Council and the European Parliament. In most cases, the delegation is defined in the legislative act establishing the agency or body. This practice is compatible with the Treaties, including Articles 290–291 TFEU, as confirmed by the Court of Justice.[89]

The executive powers delegated to a body or agency may include regulatory or advisory powers in technical fields requiring specialised expertise. However, to prevent a body or agency from developing a policy of its own with the risk of departing from the mandate conferred by the Union legislature, delegations are subject to limitations. In *Meroni*, the Court of Justice stated that delegations of executive powers, including executive regulatory powers, can only involve 'clearly defined executive powers, the use of which must be entirely subject to the supervision of [the delegating institution]'.[90] This case law precludes the conferral of 'a discretionary power, implying a wide margin of discretion which may, according to the use which is made of it, make possible the execution of actual economic policy'.[91] For this reason, agencies rarely exercise genuine regulatory powers with binding effects on third parties. These powers generally remain within the remit of the Commission. However, the expansion of agencies and bodies in recent years has led institutions to increasingly rely on their specialised expertise in technical matters.

[86] Regulation (EU) 2018/1727 of the European Parliament and of the Council of 14 November 2018 on the European Union Agency for Criminal Justice Cooperation (Eurojust) and replacing and repealing Council Decision 2002/187/JHA [2018] OJ L295/138; Regulation (EU) 2016/794 of the European Parliament and of the Council of 11 May 2016 on the European Union Agency for Law Enforcement Cooperation (Europol) and replacing and repealing Council Decisions 2009/371/JHA and others [2016] OJ L135/53, as amended by Regulation (EU) 2022/991 of the European Parliament and of the Council of 8 June 2022 [2022] OJ L169/1.

[87] Case 68/86 *United Kingdom v Council* EU:C:1988:85, para 38; and Case C-133/06 *Parliament v Council* EU:C:2008:257, para 54.

[88] Case C-133/06 *Parliament v Council* (n 87) para 56.

[89] Case C-270/12 *United Kingdom v Parliament and Council* (n 77) paras 85–86.

[90] Case C-9/56 *Meroni v High Authority* EU:C:1958:7, 149. See also Case C-98/80 *Romano* EU:C:1981:104, para 20; Case C-270/12 *United Kingdom v Parliament and Council* (n 77) paras 41 and 42; and Case C-551/22 P *Commission v SRB* EU:C:2023:846, paras 70–81.

[91] *Meroni* (n 90) 149.

The conferral of executive powers on an agency or body must fall within the scope of the delegating authority. Consequently, an agency can only be granted powers that the Union legislature is itself competent to confer. The principle *nemo plus iuris transferre potest quam ipse habet* applies: the legislature cannot confer on an agency powers that exceed those which the Treaties confer on the Union itself, or powers that the Treaties reserve to a specific institution. As explained above, a delegated power cannot be subject to further delegations, particularly when the delegation is provided in the Treaties. In other words, secondary legal bases are precluded from the practice of EU institutions, since to

> acknowledge that an institution can establish secondary legal bases, whether for the purpose of strengthening or easing the detailed rules for the adoption of an act, is tantamount to according that institution a legislative power which exceeds that provided for by the Treaty.[92]

Furthermore, the case law underscores that an agency's actions within its delegated powers are subject to judicial review. This requirement is outlined in Article 263(1) TFEU, with the final paragraph stating that the Court of Justice of the European Union reviews 'the legality of acts of bodies, offices or agencies of the Union intended to produce legal effects *vis-à-vis* third parties'.

3.3. *Implied Executive Powers*

In addition to the executive powers granted in the Treaties and secondary law, the Court of Justice has recognised the existence of implied executive powers, derived from explicit powers in the Treaties but necessary for their effective implementation.[93] For example, if the Union has exclusive competence to regulate the working conditions of its staff, and this implies a prohibition on Member States taxing the income of civil servants, the Union, even if not explicitly stated in the Treaties, has the power to regulate the conditions under which its staff are taxed on their income.[94]

V. DIFFERENTIATION: TWO-SPEED EUROPE

Some Union policies operate through the Union method, but without involving all the Member States. This applies to areas such as the Union's monetary policy or the Area of Freedom, Security and Justice, where the Union's powers do not involve all 27 Member States. The reluctance of certain Member States to participate in these policy areas has led to a complex system of opt-ins and opt-outs with varying degrees of involvement from other Member States. Additionally, the Treaties of Amsterdam and Nice introduced the possibility for a smaller group of Member States to advance on certain matters, creating enhanced cooperation within a sector of Union policy. The outcome of such cooperation is a binding Union act that applies solely to the participating Member States and excludes the rest, thus creating an asymmetrical and fragmented legal regime targeting a selective group of Member States.

[92] Case C-133/06 *Parliament v Council* EU:C:2008:257, para 56; Joined Cases C-14/15 and C-116/15 *Parliament v Council* EU:C:2016:715, para 47, and Case C-275/20 *Commission v Council* EU:C:2022:142, para 32.

[93] On the doctrine of implied powers of the Union, see ch 4, section II.5.3.

[94] See, inter alia, Case C-230/81 *Luxembourg v European Parliament* EU:C:1983:32, paras 37–38; and Case C-58/94 *Netherlands v Council* EU:C:1996:171, para 37, and, *a contrario,* Case C-521/15 *Spain v Council* EU:C:2017:982, para 48.

1. Monetary Policy and Member States whose Currency is not the Euro

The most prominent example of a Union policy operating at different speeds is monetary policy. The Union's common currency was established in 1992, but it was strongly opposed by the United Kingdom and Denmark at the time. Both countries failed to veto the introduction of the euro, but they managed to secure their exclusion from the process, although in different terms. Furthermore, the technical challenges and the specific economic requirements for a country to join the euro forced the introduction of individual transitional periods for each Member State. Consequently, there are currently two arrangements in place for Member States whose currency is not the euro: the general transitional regime; and the regime applicable to Denmark.

1.1. Member States whose Currency is not the Euro, Subject to a Derogation

Member States whose currency is not the euro, defined in the Treaties as 'Member States with a derogation', are, as a rule, subject to the transitional regime set out in Articles 139–144 TFEU. Therefore, Member States with a derogation do not participate in the euro and are not bound by the economic policy guidelines that apply to the euro area, nor by the rules on addressing excessive deficits or by acts of the ECB. They also do not participate in the governing bodies of the ECB nor in the formations of the Council of the Member States whose currency is the euro (the Eurogroup).

However, at least every two years, the Commission and the ECB must report to the Council on the progress made by Member States with a derogation towards fulfilling their obligations regarding the achievement of economic and monetary union (EMU). These 'convergence reports' assess compliance with four convergence criteria: a high degree of price stability; the sustainability of the government's financial position; observance of the normal fluctuation margins of the ERM II exchange-rate mechanism for at least two years without severe tensions; and the durability of convergence as reflected in long-term interest rate levels (Article 140(1) TFEU, read in conjunction with Protocol No 13 on the convergence criteria). If the Council considers that the Member State concerned meets the conditions enumerated in Article 140(1) TFEU, it will decide on the Member State's accession to the common currency after consulting the European Parliament, based on a proposal from the Commission and after discussion in the European Council. The Council will act after receiving a recommendation supported by a qualified majority of its members representing Member States whose currency is the euro.

Currently, the Member States whose currency is not the euro and that are subject to the transitional regime are the Czech Republic, Hungary, Poland, Romania and Sweden.

1.2. The Case of Denmark, as a Member State whose Currency is not the Euro and Subject to an Exemption

In the case of Denmark, Protocol 16 ensures that Denmark's move to the third stage of EMU will only begin when Denmark requests it, not automatically. This discretion allows Denmark to link its entry into the common currency to internal procedures, including holding a referendum. This approach was already put into practice in 2000, when the matter was put to a referendum and the Danish people rejected joining the euro by 53.2 per cent of the votes.[95]

[95] M Qvortrup, 'The Danish referendum on Euro entry, September 2000' (2002) 21 *Electoral Studies* 493.

2. The Area of Freedom, Security and Justice

Union acts adopted under Title V of Part Three of the TFEU, concerning the Area of Freedom, Security, and Justice, apply to all the Member States, except Ireland and Denmark. Neither of these Member States is subject to this policy area nor to the international agreements concluded in this field.

Despite the derogation, Protocol No 21 grants Ireland the right to opt in to certain acts in the Area of Freedom, Security, and Justice. Within three months, Ireland may notify the Council 'that it wishes to take part in the adoption and application of any such proposed measures', a decision to be made by the Council unanimously.[96] Ireland may also, after a measure has been adopted without its participation, notify the Council and the Commission that it wishes to accept that measure (Article 4 of Protocol No 21). In such cases, the procedure under Article 331(1) TFEU on enhanced cooperation applies mutatis mutandis. Declaration No 56, annexed to the Treaties, records Ireland's intention 'to exercise its right under Article 3 of Protocol No 21 to take part in the adoption of measures pursuant to Title V of Part Three of the TFEU to the maximum possible extent'. In practice, Ireland has opted into a significant proportion of AFSJ measures, particularly in the field of police cooperation and judicial cooperation in criminal matters.

In the case of Denmark, Protocol No 22 shares similar features with the Irish case. However, it excludes certain matters from the *opt-out*, such as measures determining the third countries whose nationals must hold a visa when crossing the external borders of the Member States, or measures relating to a uniform format for visas.[97]

In any event, both Denmark and Ireland may at any time notify their decision not to use these special regimes, in whole or in part.[98] Denmark held a referendum in 2015 to decide on converting its *opt-out* system from the Area of Freedom, Security and Justice into a selective *opt-in* regime, like Ireland's, but it was rejected by a majority of 53.1 per cent of the vote.

A special *opt-out* regime applies to the Schengen *acquis*, a body of Union law aimed at the gradual abolition of checks at internal borders between Member States. The Schengen acquis was originally developed outside the EU framework through the 1985 Schengen Agreement and the 1990 Schengen Convention, before being integrated into the EU legal framework by the Treaty of Amsterdam through a Protocol. It is now governed by Protocol No 19 on the Schengen acquis integrated into the framework of the European Union. Ireland and Denmark have an *opt-out*, currently contained in Protocols 19 and 22, which allow both countries to remain outside the *acquis* under different constitutional arrangements: Ireland may request to participate in certain provisions subject to Council approval, whereas Denmark is subject to a general opt-out from Title V TFEU and participates in post-Lisbon Schengen developments on an intergovernmental basis, but with the right to join under terms similar to those set out for the Area of Freedom, Security and Justice. As a result, Denmark joined the Schengen area in 2001, having signed the original Schengen Agreement in 1996, prior to the integration of the Schengen *acquis* into the EU framework by the Treaty of Amsterdam in 1999. Protocol 19 also provides for the possibility of associating third states, such as Iceland, Norway, Liechtenstein, and Switzerland, with the Schengen area, their participation being based on specific agreements concluded with the Union. This association has materialised in the case of all four countries, which have joined the Schengen *acquis* and enjoy borderless access to the Union,

[96] Art 3 of Protocol No 21 on the position of Ireland in respect of the Area of Freedom, Security and Justice.
[97] Art 6 of Protocol No 22 on the position of Denmark.
[98] Art 8 of Protocol No 21 and Art 3 of Protocol No 22.

that is, within the Schengen area, though not in respect of Member States that are not yet fully part of Schengen. As in the case of the euro, several Member States were subject to a transitional regime and joined the Schengen area at different speeds. Currently, the only Member State that has not yet fully joined the Schengen area is Cyprus, whose accession remains pending, partly due to the unresolved division of the island and the related challenges of applying the Schengen *acquis* to the territory not under the effective control of the Government of the Republic of Cyprus.

3. The Common Security and Defence Policy

Denmark had an *opt-out* from the Common Security and Defence Policy, as specified in Article 5 of Protocol No 22. This provision states that measures adopted by the Council under Articles 26(1), 42–43 and 46 TEU will not apply to Denmark if they involve defence implications. However, Denmark is committed not to prevent other Member States from further developing cooperation in this area. Following the invasion of Ukraine by Russian forces, the Danish Government held a referendum on 1 June 2022 to ask the public whether the defence *opt-out* should continue. A broad majority of 66.9 per cent voted to put an end to Denmark's *opt-out*.[99]

4. Enhanced Cooperation

Member States can promote Union policies with the involvement of only a small group of Member States. When it is not possible to reach a sufficient majority or a unanimous vote in the Council, the Treaties provide the option for a significant number of Member States to initiate enhanced cooperation. This procedure will allow a group of Member States to launch the initiative through the Union's decision-making procedures and adopt it as a Union act, but only applicable to the Member States participating in the enhanced cooperation.

Enhanced cooperation allows for the development of Union policies at different speeds, involving various Member States that participate in deeper integration within a specific policy area, while leaving the rest behind. For example, enhanced cooperation on a European unitary patent was adopted with the support of all Member States except Spain and Italy, which had vetoed the initiative in the Council (although in 2015 Italy joined the project, leaving Spain as the only dissenting Member State).[100] Enhanced cooperation was also used to introduce a regulation on the law applicable to divorce and legal separation, this time involving Spain and Italy, but excluding countries such as the Netherlands, Poland, Slovakia, and Cyprus.[101] Additionally, enhanced cooperation was employed to launch significant initiatives touching on sensitive matters in the fields of criminal and civil law, such as the European Public Prosecutor's Office[102] and the regulation on jurisdiction, applicable law, and recognition of

[99] See Council Decision (CFSP) 2023/994 of 22 May 2023 on the consequences of Denmark informing the other Member States that it no longer wishes to avail itself of Article 5 of Protocol No 22 on the position of Denmark, and amending Decision (CFSP) 2021/509 establishing a European Peace Facility and Decision 2014/401/CFSP on the European Union Satellite Centre [2023] OJ L135/120.

[100] Council Regulation (EU) No 1260/2012 of 17 December 2012 implementing enhanced cooperation in the area of the creation of unitary patent protection with regard to the applicable translation arrangements [2012] OJ L361/89.

[101] Council Regulation 1259/2010 of 20 December 2010 implementing enhanced cooperation in the area of the law applicable to divorce and legal separation [2010] OJ L343/10.

[102] Council Regulation 2017/1939 of 12 October 2017 implementing enhanced cooperation for the establishment of the European Public Prosecutor's Office [2017] OJ L283/1.

the property consequences of registered partnerships.[103] Enhanced cooperation has also been triggered to establish a EUR 90 billion financial support mechanism for Ukraine for the period 2026–27, thereby overcoming the opposition of the Czech Republic, Hungary and Slovakia.[104] This measure empowers the Commission to issue Union bonds backed exclusively by the national guarantees and budget headroom of the participating states, while legally insulating the non-participating Member States from financial liability in accordance with Article 332 TFEU.

Enhanced cooperation has proven to be a valuable tool for facilitating measures necessary to improve the internal market, but it can also cause distortions within the internal market and create legal uncertainty. The Treaties, therefore, allow for the enactment of enhanced cooperation, but strict conditions are attached to ensure that its use does not undermine the unity and coherence of the Union's policies and legal system.[105]

4.1. *Scope of Application, Exclusions and Requirements*

The Treaties establish a general framework for enhanced cooperation under Title IV of the TEU and Title III of Part Six of the TFEU. Three additional types of enhanced cooperation can be classified as such, but holding singular features:

- enhanced cooperation in the area of the CFSP (Articles 328(2), 329(2) and 331(2) TFEU);
- permanent structured cooperation in the field of the Common Security and Defence Policy (Article 46 TEU and Protocol No 10 on permanent structured cooperation established by Article 42 of the Treaty on European Union);
- enhanced cooperation in the Schengen area (Article 1 of Protocol No 19 on the Schengen *acquis* integrated into the framework of the European Union).

The general system of enhanced cooperation enables the Council to use this procedure across all fields of Union policy, with the exception of those subject to exclusive competence (Article 20 TEU and Article 329(1) TFEU). Consequently, the policy areas listed in Article 3 TFEU remain outside the remit of enhanced cooperation, including crucial sectors such as the customs union, competition, and the Common Commercial Policy.

Furthermore, the Treaties impose strict substantive requirements, aimed at ensuring that enhanced cooperation is employed only as a last resort in the decision-making

[103] Council Regulation 2016/1104 of 24 June 2016 implementing enhanced cooperation in the field of jurisdiction, applicable law, recognition and enforcement of decisions in matters relating to the property consequences of registered partnerships [2016] OJ L183/30.

[104] Council Decision (EU) 2026/258 of 29 January 2026 authorising enhanced cooperation on the establishment of a Loan for Ukraine [2026] OJ L2026/258. See also European Commission, 'Proposal for a Regulation implementing enhanced cooperation on the establishment of the Ukraine Support Loan for 2026 and 2027' COM(2026) 20 final, 14 January 2026 (CELEX: 52026PC0020).

[105] As of early 2026, there are six instances of enhanced cooperation that have been fully adopted and put into practice: (1) the law applicable to divorce and legal separation ('Rome III', Council Regulation (EU) No 1259/2010); (2) the creation of unitary patent protection (Regulation (EU) No 1257/2012 and Council Regulation (EU) No 1260/2012 on translation arrangements); (3) jurisdiction, applicable law, recognition and enforcement of decisions in matters of matrimonial property regimes (Council Regulation (EU) 2016/1103); (4) jurisdiction, applicable law, recognition and enforcement of decisions in matters of the property consequences of registered partnerships (Council Regulation (EU) 2016/1104); (5) the European Public Prosecutor's Office (Council Regulation (EU) 2017/1939); and (6) the Ukraine Support Loan (Council Decision (EU) 2026/258 authorising enhanced cooperation, and accompanying implementing regulation). The matrimonial property regimes and registered partnerships regulations, while authorised by the same Council Decision (Council Decision (EU) 2016/954 of 9 June 2016), constitute two distinct instruments of enhanced cooperation. Additionally, a further initiative has been tabled under Art 20 TEU but remains stalled in a political impasse (financial transaction tax).

process. The participating Member States, particularly the Council, must meet the following requirements:

- the aim of the enhanced cooperation should be to further the Union's objectives, protect its interests and reinforce the integration process;[106]
- the authorisation of the enhanced cooperation by the Council is to be adopted as a last resort 'when it has established that the objectives of such cooperation cannot be attained within a reasonable period by the Union as a whole';[107]
- the enhanced cooperation must not undermine the internal market or economic, social and territorial cohesion;[108]
- the enhanced cooperation must not constitute a barrier to or discrimination in trade between Member States, nor may it lead to distortions of competition between them;[109]
- the enhanced cooperation must respect the competences, rights and obligations of non-participating Member States.[110]

Although enhanced cooperation will always involve a smaller number of Member States, Article 328 TFEU states that once established, 'it shall be open to all Member States'. Participating Member States cannot veto the participation of a non-participating Member State that voluntarily decides to join the enhanced cooperation.

4.2. *Procedure for Adopting Enhanced Cooperation*

The enactment of enhanced cooperation requires the participation of at least nine Member States and authorisation by the Council. The procedure for establishing enhanced cooperation starts with a request from the Member States concerned, addressed to the Commission and specifying the scope and objectives of the enhanced cooperation envisaged.[111] The Commission has an exclusive right of legislative initiative, enabling it to approve or reject the request made by the group of Member States. In the event of rejection, the Commission must inform the Member States of the reasons underlying its decision.[112]

Authorisation to proceed with enhanced cooperation is granted by the Council, acting on a proposal from the Commission and after obtaining the consent of the European Parliament. The Council acts by qualified majority, but it acts unanimously when the enhanced cooperation is established within the framework of the CFSP.[113]

If a non-participating Member State subsequently chooses to join an existing enhanced cooperation, it must notify its intention to the Council and the Commission. The Commission is required to decide on the request within four months, considering whether the conditions for participation have been met and, where appropriate, implementing transitional measures to facilitate the application of the acts already adopted within the framework of the enhanced cooperation.[114] The Council will decide on the request in accordance with Article 330 TFEU, which requires a vote involving the Member States participating in the enhanced cooperation only.

[106] Art 20(1)second subparagraph TEU.
[107] ibid, Art 20(2).
[108] Art 326(2) TFEU.
[109] ibid, Art 326(2).
[110] ibid, Art 327.
[111] ibid, Art 329(1).
[112] ibid, Art 329(1).
[113] ibid, Art 329(2)(2).
[114] ibid, Art 331(1).

4.3. *Adoption of Acts and their Effects*

Article 20(4) TEU states that acts adopted within the framework of enhanced cooperation bind only the participating Member States. They will not be considered part of the *acquis*, which must be accepted by candidate states seeking accession to the Union. From a procedural standpoint, this provision implies that only the Member States involved in the enhanced cooperation have voting rights in the Council.[115] However, Article 330 TFEU guarantees non-participating Member States the right to take part in the Council's deliberations, as a means to balance the political impact of their lack of voting rights.

Acts adopted through enhanced cooperation will only apply to the participating Member States. This feature introduces a degree of fragmentation into the Union's legal system, but the Court of Justice has confirmed that such an effect is inherent to enhanced cooperation, and the Treaties have enabled such a procedure to exist:

> The fact that the establishment of limited forms of cooperation may lead to fragmentation of the rules applicable in that area, assuming that to be the case, cannot call that conclusion into question, as the implementation of enhanced cooperation inevitably leads to a certain fragmentation of the rules applicable to the Member States in the area concerned.[116]

Acts adopted through enhanced cooperation are subject to judicial review by the Court of Justice. This includes decisions to authorise enhanced cooperation[117] and the acts resulting from it.[118] However, this rule does not apply to acts adopted through enhanced cooperation in the CFSP, where the Court of Justice's jurisdiction is limited.[119] Nonetheless, the Court of Justice has jurisdiction to monitor compliance with Article 40 TEU, in order to ensure compliance with the procedures and competence used in the CFSP.

Enhanced cooperation offers the participating Member States access to the human and material resources of the Union's institutions, bodies, offices, and agencies. Administrative costs incurred by these institutions will be charged to the Union's common budget. However, expenses other than administrative costs, in accordance with Article 332 TFEU, will be borne solely by the participating Member States unless the Council, acting unanimously and after consulting the European Parliament, decides otherwise.

GENERAL BIBLIOGRAPHY

Auby, J-B and Dutheil de la Rochère, J, (eds.) *Traité de droit administratif européen*, 2nd edn (Bruylant, 2014).

Bradley, K, 'Institutional Design in the Treaty of Nice' (2001) 38 *Common Market Law Review 1095*.

Craig, P, 'Institutions, Power and Institutional Balance' in P Craig and G de Búrca (eds), *The Evolution of EU Law*, 3rd edn (Oxford University Press, 2021).

— *EU Administrative Law*, 3rd edn (Oxford University Press, 2019).

Curtin, D, *Executive Power of the European Union: Law, Practices and the Living Constitution* (Oxford University Press, 2009).

[115] According to Art 330 TFEU, unanimity is constituted only by the votes of the representatives of the participating Member States, whilst a qualified majority is defined in accordance with Art 238(3) TFEU.

[116] Case C-44/14 *Spain v Parliament and Council* EU:C:2015:554, para 55.

[117] As the Court recalled in Case C-209/13 *United Kingdom v Council* EU:C:2014:283, paras 33–34: 'in the context of an action for the annulment of a Council decision which, like the contested decision, has as its subject-matter the authorisation of enhanced cooperation on the basis of Article 329 TFEU, the Court's review is related to the issue of whether that decision is valid as such in the light of, inter alia, the provisions, contained in Article 20 TEU and in Articles 326 TFEU to 334 TFEU, which define the substantive and procedural conditions relating to the granting of such authorisation. … That review should not be confused with the review which may be undertaken, in the context of a subsequent action for annulment, of a measure adopted for the purposes of the implementation of the authorised enhanced cooperation.'

[118] *Spain v Parliament and Council* (n 116).

[119] Art 275 TFEU.

Curtin, D and Dekker, IF, 'The European Union from Maastricht to Lisbon: Institutional and Legal Unity out of the Shadows' in P Craig and G de Búrca (eds), *The Evolution of EU Law*, 2nd edn (Oxford University Press, 2011).
Harlow, C, *Accountability in the European Union* (Oxford University Press, 2002).
Hofmann, H, Rowe, G and Türk, A, *Administrative Law and Policy of the European Union* (Oxford University Press, 2011).
Jacqué, J-P, 'The Principle of Institutional Balance' (2004) 41 *Common Market Law Review 383.*
Lenaerts, K, 'Constitutionalism and the Many Faces of Federalism' (1990) 38 *The American Journal of Comparative Law 205.*
— 'Some Reflexions on the Separation of Powers in the European Community' (1991) 28 *Common Market Law Review 11.*
Lenaerts, K and Verhoeven, A, 'Institutional Balance as a Guarantee for Democracy in EU Governance' in C Joerges and R Dehousse (eds), *Good Governance in Europe's Integrated Market*, Studies No 36 (2002).
Majone, G, 'Delegation of Regulatory Powers in a Mixed Polity' (2002) 8 *European Law Journal 319.*
Mendes, J, *Participation in EU Rule-making. A Rights-Based Approach* (Oxford University Press, 2011).
Nicolaïdis, K and Howse, R (eds), *The Federal Vision: Legitimacy and Levels of Governance in the United States and the European Union* (Oxford University Press, 2000).
Pollack, M, *The Engines of European Integration: Delegation, Agency and Agenda-Setting in the EU* (Oxford University Press, 2003).
Smismans, S, *Law, Legitimacy and European Governance: Functional Participation in Social Regulation* (Oxford University Press, 2004).
Smulders, B and Eisele, K, 'Reflections on the Institutional Balance, the Community Method and the Interplay Between Jurisdictions After Lisbon' (2012) 31 *Yearbook of European Law* 112.

FURTHER READING

Choice of Legal Bases

Bradley, K, 'Powers and Procedures in the EU Constitution: Legal Bases and the Court' in P Craig and G de Búrca (eds), *The Evolution of EU Law*, 2nd edn (Oxford University Press, 2011).
Caziero, M, 'What legal basis for an EU tax?' (2024) 61 *Common Market Law Review* 1527.
Engel, A, *The Choice of Legal Basis for Acts of the European Union* (Springer, 2018).

Legislative Procedures

Chalmers, D, 'The Democratic Ambiguity of EU Law-Making and Its Enemies' in A Arnull and D Chalmers (eds), *The Oxford Handbook of European Union Law* (Oxford University Press, 2015).
Chamon, M, *The European Parliament and Delegated Legislation* (Hart, 2022).
Craig, P and Harlow, C, *Lawmaking in the European Union* (Kluwer, 1998).
Karatzia, A, 'The European Citizens' Initiative and the EU Institutional Balance: On Realism and the Possibilities of Affecting EU Law-Making' (2017) 54 *Common Market Law Review* 177.
Raworth, P, *The Legislative Process in the EC* (Kluwer, 1993).
Rugge, G, *Trilogues. The Democratic Secret of European Legislation* (Cambridge University Press, 2025).
Türk, A, *The Concept of Legislation in European Community Law* (Kluwer, 2006).
Westlake, M, *The Commission and the Parliament: Partners and Rivals in the European Policy-Making Process* (Butterworths, 1994).

Delegated, Implementing and other Non-legislative Acts

Andenas, M and Türk, A (eds), *Delegated Legislation and the Role of Committees in the EC* (Kluwer, 2000).
Bergström, CF, *Comitology: Delegation of Powers in the European Union and the Committee System* (Oxford University Press, 2005).
Bergström, CF and Ritleng, D (eds), *Rulemaking by the Commission: The New System* (Oxford University Press, 2015).

Bermann, GA, 'Executive Power in the New European Constitution' (2005) 3 *International Journal of Constitutional Law* 440.
Bignami, F, 'The Democratic Deficit in European Community Rule-Making: A Call for Notice and Comment in Comitology' (1999) 40 *Harvard International Law Journal* 451.
Blom-Hansen, J, *The EU Comitology System in Theory and Practice: Keeping an Eye on the Commission?* (Palgrave, 2011).
Bradley, K, 'Comitology and the Courts: Tales of the Unexpected' in H Hofmann and A Türk (eds), *EU Administrative Governance* (Edward Elgar, 2006).
Brandsma, GJ and Blom-Hansen, J, *Controlling the EU Executive? The Politics of Delegation in the European Union* (Oxford University Press, 2018).
Chiti, E, 'The Emergence of a Community Administration: The Case of European Agencies' (2000) 37 *Common Market Law Review* 309.
Christiansen, T and Dobbels, M, 'Non-Legislative Rule-Making After the Lisbon Treaty: Implementing the New System of Comitology and Delegated Acts' (2013) 19 *European Law Journal* 42.
Curtin, D, *Executive Power of the European Union. Law, Practices, and the Living Constitution* (Oxford University Press, 2009).
Dehousse, R, 'Comitology: Who Watches the Watchmen?' (2003) 10 *Journal of European Public Policy* 152.
Fromage, D and Herranz-Surrallés, A (eds), *Executive-Legislative (Im)balance in the European Union* (Hart, 2021).
Hofmann, H, 'Legislation, Delegation and Implementation Under the Treaty of Lisbon' (2009) 15 *European Law Journal* 482.
Joerges, C and Vos, E (eds), *EU Committees: Social Regulation, Law and Politics* (Oxford University Press, 1999).
Lenaerts, K, 'Regulating the Regulatory Process: Delegation of Powers in the European Community' (1993) 18 *European Law Review* 23.
Ponzano, P, 'Executive and Delegated Acts: The Situation After the Lisbon Treaty' in S Griller and J Ziller (eds), *The Lisbon Treaty: EU Constitutionalism Without a Constitutional Treaty?* (Springer, 2008).
Tauschinsky, E, *A Fiduciary Approach to Delegated and Implementing Rule-Making in the EU* (Springer, 2020).
Türk, A, 'Comitology' in A Arnull and D Chalmers (eds), *The Oxford Handbook of European Union Law* (Oxford University Press, 2015).

Enhanced Cooperation and Variable Speed Policies

Böttner, R, *The Constitutional Framework for Enhanced Cooperation in EU Law* (Brill Nijhoff, 2021).
De Areilza Carvajal, JM, 'Enhanced Cooperation in the Treaty of Amsterdam: Some Critical Remarks' (1998) *Harvard Jean Monnet Working Paper*.
De Witte, B, Ott, A and Vos, E (eds), *Between Flexibility and Disintegration. The Trajectory of Differentiation in EU Law* (Edward Elgar, 2017).
Cremona, M, 'Enhanced Cooperation and the Common Foreign and Security and Defence Policies of the EU' (2009) EUI Working Papers (Law).
Curtin, D, 'From a Europe of Bits and Pieces to a Union of Variegated Differentiation', in Craig, P, and De Búrca, G (eds), *The Evolution of EU Law* (Oxford University Press, 2021).
Heber, C, *Enhanced Cooperation and European Tax Law* (Oxford University Press, 2021).
Leruth, B, Gänzle, S and Trondal, J (eds), *The Routledge Handbook of Differentiation in the European Union* (Routledge, 2024).
Miglio, A, 'Differentiated integration and the principle of loyalty' (2018) 14 *European Constitutional Law Review* 475.
Pistoia, E, 'Enhanced cooperation as a tool to… enhance integration? Spain and Italy v. Council' (2014) 51 *Common Market Law Review* 247.
Schimmelfennig, F, and Winzen, T (eds), *Ever Looser Union? Differentiated European Integration* (Oxford University Press, 2020).
Tuytschaever, F, *Differentiation in European Union Law* (Hart, 1999).

6

Citizenship and Fundamental Rights

I. THE INDIVIDUAL AND EUROPEAN INTEGRATION

INDIVIDUALS PLAY A prominent role in European integration. The importance of the individual has grown over time, playing both a symbolic and pragmatic role in the Union's daily affairs. Citizens have their own representative institution, the European Parliament, which embodies the citizens' interests in the legislative process. Democracy and citizen participation are core values of the Union, explicitly acknowledged in the Treaties. Nationals of the Member States also have a specific and complementary status alongside their nationality: Union citizenship. This status grants rights and obligations that are fully enforceable against both the Union and the Member States. To safeguard the position of individuals, the Union guarantees a wide range of fundamental rights enshrined in a Charter that holds the same legal value as the Treaties. The development and protection of Union citizenship and the fundamental rights granted to individuals through Union law are the subject matter of this chapter.

The individual is a source of legitimacy for the Union. The Union's actions are strengthened and gain more authority when they have the consent of its addressees. Therefore, the Treaties ensure the involvement of the European Parliament in the Union's decision-making, particularly in major policy decisions such as the enactment of legislative acts. Citizens can also use the legislative initiative, allowing at least one million citizens to call on the Commission to introduce legislative measures. The Union's institutions are bound by rules on transparency that give the public access to information held by the Union's authorities, with the aim of increasing scrutiny and accountability of the Union. The closer and more accessible the European decision-making process is to its citizens, the more legitimate the Union's acts will be.

The role of the individual in the Union has grown in importance over the years, regardless of whether the individual is economically active or not. The early European Communities, which aimed to create a common market, saw the individual as part of the process of establishing this market. The main beneficiaries of integration were workers, employers, and workers' families living in other Member States, but not students, voters, retirees, or any groups outside the direct functioning of a common market. This approach underwent a significant shift during the 1980s and 1990s, ultimately recognising the individual – in their economic, political, social, or cultural roles – as a recipient of rights and obligations directly granted by the Union.[1]

Since the Maastricht Treaty of 1992, individuals are holders of the status of European citizenship, directly conferred by the Treaties and dependent on the holding of the nationality of a Member State. As explained in chapter nine, Union law has direct effect. It can be invoked before all public authorities, whether of the Union or of the Member States, because

[1] N Nic Shuibhne, 'The Resilience of EU Market Citizenship' (2010) 47 *Common Market Law Review* 1597; and C O'Brien, 'I Trade, Therefore I Am: Legal Personhood in the European Union' (2013) 50 *Common Market Law Review 1643.*

the individual is both a source of legitimacy and an addressee of Union rules. This feature stems from the landmark ruling in *Van Gend en Loos*, where the Court of Justice emphasised that European integration is not only aimed at establishing a Union of states but also of citizens. These citizens, who comprise the 'peoples of Europe', are at the very heart of the Union's legal order and its practical application, as the direct addressees of its rules.[2]

The most relevant body of rights granted by the Union to individuals, particularly to European citizens, is contained in the status of European citizenship and the fundamental rights and freedoms proclaimed in the Charter of Fundamental Rights of the European Union ('the Charter'). On the one hand, European citizenship creates an autonomous and complementary status to that of national citizenship held by nationals of the Member States. On the other hand, the fundamental rights contained in the Charter grant individuals, including third country nationals, inalienable rights founded on human dignity. Both sets of rights – those forming part of Union citizenship and those proclaimed by the Charter – constitute the essential legal patrimony of the individual in relation to the Union and to the Member States when implementing Union law.

II. CITIZENSHIP OF THE UNION

In 1992, the Maastricht Treaty established Union citizenship as an independent and individual status, aiming to strengthen the bond between nationals of Member States and the European project. At the request of the Spanish delegation during the negotiations of the Inter-Governmental Conference that led to the Maastricht Treaty,[3] Union citizenship was introduced into the Treaties for the first time, and it is currently enshrined in Articles 9 TEU and 20(1) TFEU.

All nationals of the Member States are citizens of the Union. The status of Union citizenship is overlaid upon, or added to, the status of nationality. Article 9 TEU recalls that Union citizenship 'is additional to national citizenship without replacing it'. Union citizenship is consequently established simultaneously with the bond of nationality between an individual and a Member State. The trigger that confers Union citizenship on the individual is a prior act: the acquisition of the nationality of a Member State.[4]

However, as will be explained below, Member States do not have unfettered discretion to grant or revoke nationality, as such decisions directly affect the status of Union citizenship.[5] National decisions on the acquisition and loss of nationality, although falling within the competence of the Member States, also serve as a gateway to Union citizenship. In these instances, Member States must have due regard to Union law when exercising their powers in matters of nationality and, consequently, their decisions are subject not only to national law, but also to Union law.[6]

[2] W Maas, 'The Origins, Evolution, and Political Objectives of EU Citizenship' (2014) 15 *German Law Journal* 283.

[3] S O'Leary, *The Evolving Concept of Community Citizenship: From the Free Movement of Persons to Union Citizenship* (Kluwer, 1996); and C Closa, 'The Concept of Citizenship in the Treaty on European Union' (1992) 29 *Common Market Law Review* 1137.

[4] D Kochenov, 'Rounding Up the Circle. The Mutation of Member States Nationalities under Pressure from EU citizenship' EUI RSCAS Working Paper 2010/23.

[5] Case C-369/90 *Micheletti* EU:C:1992:295, para 10; Case C-179/98 *Mesbah* EU:C:1999:549, para 29; Case C-192/99 *Kaur* EU:C:2001:106, para 19; and Case C-200/02 *Chen* EU:C:2004:639, para 39.

[6] Case C-135/08 *Rottmann* EU:C:2010:104; Case C-34/09 *Ruiz Zambrano* EU:C:2011:124; and Case C-181/23 *Commission v. Malta* EU:C:2025:283.

The evolution of Union citizenship illustrates how this status has gradually transformed into a fundamental status for nationals of the Member States. In its early case law, the Court of Justice referred to Union citizenship as 'destined to become the fundamental status of nationals of the Member States'.[7] Over time, the initial aspirational and forward-looking case law has evolved, and by 2025, the Court of Justice explicitly referred to Union citizenship as '*the* fundamental status of nationals of the Member States'.[8] It remains unclear what constitutional developments have occurred within the Union to substantiate the view that Union citizenship is currently *the* primary point of reference for nationals of the Member States, particularly given that the Treaty provisions on Union citizenship have remained unaltered since their introduction in 1992.

Although the Treaties have remained substantially unchanged regarding Union citizenship, the Court of Justice's case law has evolved significantly, adopting a more principled and values-oriented perspective. This evolution has resulted in an interpretation of the Treaties that has progressively strengthened and constitutionalised the concept of Union citizenship. In this regard, the Court of Justice explicitly asserts that 'the bedrock of the bond of nationality of a Member State is formed by the special relationship of solidarity and good faith between that State and its nationals and the reciprocity of rights and duties'. This bond is now articulated as a mandate stemming from Union law and directly binding the Member States, thereby creating obligations to ensure that the status of Union citizenship is conferred, withdrawn, and exercised in accordance with core values and principles of the Union's legal system.

1. The Status of Union Citizenship

The rights that comprise the status of Union citizenship are enumerated in Article 9 Treaty on European Union (TEU), Articles 18–24 Treaty on the Functioning of the European Union (TFEU), and Articles 39–46 of the Charter. Some rights are subject to subsequent legislative measures, such as the right to freedom of movement,[9] the right to vote and to stand as a candidate in municipal elections[10] and elections to the European Parliament,[11] or the European citizens' initiative.[12]

1.1. Non-discrimination on Grounds of Nationality

The status of Union citizenship encompasses a right that acts as the foundation for other citizenship rights: the prohibition of discrimination on the grounds of nationality. Article 18 TFEU states that 'any discrimination on grounds of nationality shall be prohibited', a mandate that appears again in Article 21(2) of the Charter. This right acts as a *genus* for the other rights

[7] Case C-184/99 *Grzelczyk* EU:C:2001:458, para 31.

[8] Case C-689/21 *Udlændinge- og Integrationsministeriet* EU:C:2023:626, paras 29 and 38; and Case C-181/23 *Commission v Malta* EU:C:2025:283, para 92.

[9] Directive 2004/38/EC of the European Parliament and of the Council of 29 April 2004 on the right of citizens of the Union and their family members to move and reside freely within the territory of the Member States [2004] OJ L158/77.

[10] Council Directive 94/80/EC laying down detailed arrangements for the exercise of the right to vote and to stand as a candidate in municipal elections by citizens of the Union residing in a Member State of which they are not nationals [1994] OJ L368/38.

[11] Council Directive 93/109/EC laying down detailed arrangements for the exercise of the right to vote and to stand as a candidate in elections to the European Parliament for citizens of the Union residing in a Member State of which they are not nationals [1993] OJ L329/34.

[12] Regulation (EU) 2019/788 of the European Parliament and of the Council of 17 April 2019 on the European citizens' initiative [2019] OJ L130/55.

that comprise the status of Union citizenship: political rights ensure equal treatment between the nationals of a Member State and those of other Member States residing there; the right to free movement and residence in other Member States includes equal treatment between nationals and incoming residents from other Member States.

Evidence of the strong links between the prohibition of discrimination on the grounds of nationality and the status of Union citizenship is found in the case law of the Court of Justice, according to which:

> Union citizenship is destined to be the fundamental status of nationals of the Member States, enabling those who find themselves in the same situation to enjoy the same treatment in law irrespective of their nationality, subject to such exceptions as are expressly provided for.[13]

The right enshrined in Article 18 TFEU forms part of the status of Union citizenship and applies to both natural and legal persons, irrespective of whether they engage in economic activities. The prohibition of discrimination based on nationality operates alongside other provisions of Union law, allowing Article 18 TFEU to be invoked together with other provisions of Union law, as confirmed in Austria/Germany[14] and TÜV Rheinland.[15] The practical consequence of this approach is to provide European citizens with additional grounds for review that offer as many remedial courses of action as possible.

However, it is important to note that Article 18 TFEU operates as a subsidiary rule that is applicable only when no other, more specific provisions of the Treaty apply. If a case falls within the scope of Union law but is not covered by other provisions of primary or secondary law, an individual holding the nationality of a Member State can always rely on Article 18 TFEU.[16] For example, if an individual has exercised free movement rights for non-economic reasons, he or she may not be entitled to rely on the freedom of movement for workers or the self-employed. However, he or she can invoke the right not to be discriminated against on the grounds of nationality, in accordance with Article 18 TFEU.[17]

[13] *Grzelczyk* (n 7) para 31.

[14] Case C-591/17 *Austria v Germany* EU:C:2019:504, para 39.

[15] Case C-581/18 *TÜV Rheinland* EU:C:2020:453, paras 31–33.

[16] See Case C-382/08 *Neukirchinger* EU:C:2011:27 concerning discrimination suffered by an undertaking in the air transport sector, providing hot-air balloon services. According to Art 58(1) TFEU, freedom to provide services in the field of transport is governed by the provisions of the Title relating to transport. However, Union legislation on transport omits any references to the commercial activity of hot-air balloons. Considering this gap, the question raised was whether Art 18 TFEU was applicable to the case, to which the Court of Justice answered in the affirmative in the following terms: 'Thus, while the exclusion provided for under Article 1(2) of Regulation No 2407/92 can obviously be accounted for by the fact that the specific nature of the air transport sector did not justify carriage by air of passengers in a hot-air balloon for commercial purposes being made subject to the rules provided for under that regulation, it does not, however, follow that, by that exclusion, the Community legislature had intended to remove such a mode of transport completely from the scope of application of the Treaty. It follows from all of the foregoing that carriage by air of passengers in a hot-air balloon for commercial purposes, such as that at issue in the main proceedings, falls within the scope of the ... Treaty and that it is therefore subject to a general rule of the Treaty, such as Article [18 TFEU].' See Case C-628/11 *International Jet Management* EU:C:2014:171. This line of case law appears to have been more strictly circumscribed, particularly following Case C-581/18 *TÜV Rheinland* EU:C:2020:453. This more restrictive approach can be inferred from the Opinion of AG Bobek in *TÜV Rheinland*, very critical of the potential of Art 18 TFEU to distort the allocation of powers between the Union and the Member States. See also Case C-535/19 *Latvijas Republikas Veselības ministrija* EU:C:2021:595, para 40.

[17] Case C-182/15 *Petruhhin* EU:C:2016:630; Case C-191/16 *Pisciotti* EU:C: 2018:222; Case C-247/17 *Raugevicius* EU:C:2018:898; and Case C-237/21 *SM and Generalstaatsanwaltschaft München* EU:C:2022:1017. In *Petruhhin* and *Pisciotti*, the Court of Justice ruled that there was no breach of Art 18 TFEU, but confirmed the applicability of the provision to cases where there is not only movement within the Union, but also an external movement to a third country, under discriminatory conditions.

The rule enshrined in Article 18 TFEU aims to combat measures adopted by any Member State that directly or indirectly discriminate against Union citizens on grounds of their nationality. Therefore, a measure can discriminate in the following two ways:

- Direct discrimination on grounds of nationality: measures with effects on all nationals of all the Member States, but with discriminatory consequences with a more restrictive impact on nationals of other Member States;
- Indirect discrimination on grounds of nationality: measures that, although neutrally formulated and applicable to all nationals, in practice have a more restrictive impact on nationals of other Member States than on nationals of the host Member State (for example, residence requirements, language requirements, or qualifications obtained in the host state).

In the latter case, if the measure proves to affect nationals of other Member States more severely, it will amount to an *indirect* discrimination on the grounds of nationality, precluded by Article 18 TFEU.[18]

Article 18 TFEU is addressed to both the Member States and to individuals. It is, therefore, a fundamental right with a horizontal scope of application, allowing it to be invoked between private parties. The case law of the Court of Justice has been cautious in this respect, but over time it has gradually confirmed the expansive nature of the provision, which now applies to cases with vertical (against Member States) and horizontal (against private parties) effects.[19]

A discriminatory measure on the grounds of nationality is unlawful, unless it is justified on the basis of objective and reasonable grounds.[20] As a result, the contested measure is subject to a proportionality test, in which the defendant must prove that the measure pursues a legitimate aim of general interest by employing means that are adequate and strictly necessary to achieve those aims.

1.2. *Free Movement and Residence of Citizens of the Union*

Every Union citizen has the right to reside and move freely within the territory of the Union, as stated in Article 21(1) TFEU. This right is also set out in Article 45 of the Charter:

(1) Every citizen of the Union has the right to move and reside freely within the territory of the Member States.
(2) Freedom of movement and residence may be granted, in accordance with the provisions of the Treaties, to nationals of third countries who are legally resident in the territory of a Member State.

The right to free movement and residence has a broad scope of application. Union citizens who can benefit from this right include those who undertake an economic activity, as well as those who are non-economically active. Consequently, the right encompasses a wide range of profiles, from students and jobseekers to tourists or amateur sportspersons.[21] These are just a

[18] Case C-274/96 *Bickel Franz* EU:C:1998:563; Case C-322/13 *Rüffer* EU:C:2014:189; Case C-520/04 *Turpeinen* EU:C:2006:703; Case C-224/02 *Pusa* EU:C:2004:273; Case C-470/04 N EU:C:2006:525; Case C-76/05 *Schwarz* EU:C:2007:492; Case C-56/09 *Zanotti* EU:C:2010:288; and Case C-192/05 *Tas-Hagen* EU:C:2006:676.

[19] This is, in fact, the same approach that applies to all fundamental freedoms, as seen in the development of the case law from Case C-36/74 *Walrave and Koch* EU:C:1974:140 and Case C-415/93 *Bosman* EU:C:1995:463 to Case C-281/98 *Angonese* EU:C:2000:296, and, more recently, in the field of fundamental rights, starting in Case C-144/04 *Mangold* EU:C:2005:709 and followed, inter alia, in Case C-176/12 *Association de Médiation Sociale* EU:C:2014:2; Case C-193/17 *Cresco Investigation* EU:C:2018:614; and Case C-569/16 *Bauer* EU:C:2018:871. In *TÜV Rheinland* (n 15), the Court of Justice was specifically asked on the matter, but it declined to respond.

[20] Case C-73/08 *Bressol and Others* EU:C:2010:181, paras 71ff; and *Rottmann* (n 6) paras 55–59.

[21] Case C-403/03 *Schempp* EU:C:2005:446; and Case C-22/18 *TopFit eV* EU:C:2019:497.

few examples of individuals who are not directly engaged in economic activity but may face discriminatory treatment that breaches free movement rules. The impact of a discriminatory national measure ultimately deters Union citizens from exercising their free movement rights conferred by Union law, thus having a chilling effect that undermines the objectives of the Treaties.

The addressees of the rule enshrined in Article 21(1) TFEU are the Member States that host Union citizens from other Member States. However, the Court of Justice has determined that Article 21(1) TFEU also applies to returning citizens who have previously enjoyed free movement rights.[22] For instance, a German student studying in Belgium can invoke Article 21(1) TFEU against the German authorities if they create unjustifiably difficult circumstances for her after a period of study in Belgium when seeking to have her studies recognised in Germany.

The beneficiaries of Article 21(1) TFEU are Union citizens who exercise the right to move or reside in another Member State. In addition, both secondary legislation and the case law of the Court of Justice recognise the importance of family members of a Union citizen exercising free movement rights, even when those family members hold the nationality of a third country. If a Member State restricts the right to move or reside for the family members of a Union citizen, regardless of their nationality, such measures breach Article 21(1) and, where applicable, the provisions of secondary law relevant to this situation. As explained below, Article 21(1) has direct beneficiaries (Union citizens) and indirect beneficiaries (holders of a derivative right to free movement, such as family members of a Union citizen).[23]

Article 21(1) TFEU protects the right to move and reside in a Member State other than the one of the citizen's nationality. Consequently, to invoke Article 21(1) TFEU, it is necessary to establish the existence of a cross-border link, or otherwise the case will be deemed purely internal, and the provision cannot be relied on.[24] The Court of Justice has interpreted this requirement broadly, to the extent that physical movement between Member States is not always essential. The link may stem from a legal connection with another Member State (for instance, by holding dual nationality of two Member States), or it may represent a prospective link (the measure restricts the citizen's future ability to move), as long as it significantly undermines or deters the citizen's ability to move to or reside in another Member State.

For example, in *García Avello*,[25] the Belgian rules regarding the registration of names were challenged because they prevented the children of a Spanish national and a Belgian national residing in Belgium from registering both the children's paternal and maternal surnames, as permitted by Spanish law (applicable to the personal status of the children, who held both Belgian and Spanish nationality). The Court of Justice ruled that this restriction discouraged the exercise of free movement for persons, as it required citizens of the Union born in a Member State different from their Member State of nationality to register and record a name other than that required by the law of their nationality.[26]

A similar issue arose in *Chen*,[27] a case involving an infant child born in Belfast, the daughter of Chinese nationals residing in the UK, who acquired Irish nationality as a result of Ireland's

[22] Case C-115/78 *Knoors* EU:C:1979:31, para 24; Case C-61/89 *Bouchoucha* EU:C:1990:343, para 13; Case C-19/92 *Kraus* EU:C:1993:125, paras 15–16; and Case C-673/16 *Coman and Others* EU:C:2018:385, para 40.

[23] Case C-488/21 *GV v Chief Appeals Officer* EU:C:2023:1013, paras 46–50. On the definition of family members with a 'relationship of dependence', see Case C-22/21 *SRS, AA v Minister for Justice and Equality* EU:C:2022:683.

[24] Case C-40/11 *Iida* EU:C:2012:691; Case C-434/09 *McCarthy* EU:C:2011:277; and Case C-456/12 *O and B* EU:C:2014:135.

[25] Case C-148/02 *García Avello* EU:C:2003:539.

[26] Case C-353/06 *Grunkin Paul* EU:C:2008:559); Case C-208/09 *Sayn-Wittgenstein* EU:C:2010:806; Case C-391/09 *Runevič-Vardyn and Wardyn* EU:C:2011:291; and Case C-438/14 *Bogendorff von Wolffersdorff* EU:C:2016:401.

[27] Case C-200/02 *Chen* (n 5).

extraterritorial nationality rules at that time, which conferred citizenship on persons born on the island of Ireland. Although neither the child nor the mother moved within the Union before or after the child's birth (at a time when the UK was still part of the Union), the fact that the child held the nationality of another Member State (Ireland) was sufficient to establish a cross-border element and trigger the protection of Article 21(1) TFEU.

In *Coman*, a Romanian national returned to his Member State of nationality after a prolonged period of residence in Belgium. Mr Coman had married his same-sex partner, an American national, in Belgium, where same-sex marriage was legally recognised. Upon their decision to reside in Romania, the local authorities denied Mr Coman's spouse the right of residence as a family member. Despite the fact that Mr Coman was a Romanian national invoking Union law against the Romanian authorities, the Court of Justice confirmed that the measure restricted Mr Coman's ability to exercise free movement. The policy argument underlying this ruling indicates that such measures discourage nationals of the Member State from leaving the territory, as they will later face restrictive measures upon their return.[28]

In *Pancharevo*, the Court of Justice faced a case involving a child born in Spain to a Bulgarian national and her same-sex spouse, a Gibraltarian national, whose marriage had been concluded in Spain. The Bulgarian authorities refused to issue a birth certificate for the child, on the ground that Bulgarian law did not permit the recording of two female parents on a birth certificate and required identification of the child's biological mother. The absence of a Bulgarian birth certificate prevented the child from obtaining Bulgarian identity documents, necessary for the exercise of free movement rights and registration procedures in Spain, where the family resided. Given these circumstances, the Court of Justice determined that, according to Bulgarian law, the child was a national of that country and thus also a citizen of the Union, entitled to free movement rights, including in relation to her Member State of origin.[29]

If a Union citizen exercises free movement rights and, after a period of residence in the host Member State, acquires the nationality of that country, the Court of Justice has ruled that the citizen no longer holds the right of residence under Article 21(1) TFEU and Union secondary legislation. However, the Member State of the newly acquired nationality cannot impose more restrictive conditions of movement or residence on the Union citizen than those stipulated in Union law. Otherwise, the measures would act as a disincentive to the acquisition of nationality of another Member State, a matter not covered by Union law, but which creates a chilling effect on the Union citizen intending to make use of free movement.[30]

Article 21(1) TFEU has direct effect and may be invoked by any natural person within the personal scope of free movement and residence rules.[31] The Union legislature is bound by Article 21(1) TFEU and its interpretation by the Court of Justice. Consequently, secondary legislation on the right to freedom of movement and residence must be interpreted in light of primary law and the relevant case law.[32] When secondary law does not apply to a case with a

[28] Case C-673/16 *Coman* (n 22).

[29] Case C-490/20 *VMA and Stolichna obshtina, rayon 'Pancharevo'* EU:C:2021:1008, paras 42–44.

[30] Case C-165/16 *Lounes* EU:C:2017:862, paras 56 and 57: 'the rights conferred on a Union citizen by Article 21(1) TFEU, including the derived rights enjoyed by his family members, are intended, amongst other things, to promote the gradual integration of the Union citizen concerned in the society of the host Member State. Union citizens . . . who, after moving, in the exercise of their freedom of movement, to the host Member State and residing there for a number of years pursuant to and in accordance with Article 7(1) or Article 16(1) of Directive 2004/38, acquire the nationality of that Member State, intend to become permanently integrated in that State.'

[31] Case C-413/99 *Baumbast and R* EU:C:2002:493, para 84.

[32] However, see Case C-456/12 *O and B* EU:C:2014:135, para 61, interpreting the Treaty *in light of a directive*, following the precedent of Case C-297/05 *Eind* EU:C:2007:771, operative part. This approach was strongly criticised by AG Szpunar in his Opinion in Case C-202/13 *McCarthy* EU:C:2014:345, para 82.

trans-frontier link, Article 21(1) TFEU may be directly relied upon by the Union citizen and/or the citizen's family members.

The main instrument of secondary law implementing the rights enshrined in Article 21(1) TFEU is Directive 2004/38, on the right of Union citizens and their family members to move and reside freely within the territory of the Member States. Directive 2004/38 establishes the conditions under which the rights to free movement and residence in the Union are exercised, defining the addressees (the Member States) and the beneficiaries (Union citizens and their family members), while providing for three distinct situations with their respective legal frameworks:

- *Free residence:* Article 6 of Directive 2004/38 states that Union citizens have the right to reside in the territory of another Member State for a period of up to three months without any conditions or formalities, apart from the requirement to hold a valid identity card or passport.
- *Non-permanent residence*: Article 7 of Directive 2004/38 states that all Union citizens have the right to reside in the territory of another Member State for over three months if they are workers, self-employed individuals, or if they possess sufficient resources, along with their family members.[33] In such cases, Union citizens and their families may be required by the host Member State to register and apply for a residence card.[34]
- *Permanent residence*: Article 16 of the Directive states that Union citizens who have legally resided for a continuous duration of five years in the host Member State possess the right to permanent residence there, as well as their family members.[35]

Article 24 of the Directive establishes a principle of equal treatment applicable to Union citizens, prohibiting any difference in treatment compared to the nationals of the host Member State. According to the first paragraph of this provision, this principle protects all Union citizens 'residing . . . in the territory of the host Member State' as well as 'family members who are not nationals of a Member State and who have the right of residence or permanent residence'. Family members include the spouse or partner in an equivalent relationship, direct descendants who are under the age of 21 or dependent, and dependent direct relatives in an ascending line.[36] Although the Court of Justice has interpreted the concept of family membership broadly, it has also set certain limits, particularly when the legal bond does not meet the criteria under the applicable national law. This applies, for instance, to a child placed in the permanent legal guardianship of a Union citizen under the Algerian *kafala* system, which does not establish any parent–child relationship under the laws of a Member State. Nevertheless, the Court of Justice determined that, in such a scenario, nothing prevents the national authorities from

[33] On the notion of 'sufficient resources', the Court of Justice has provided a broad interpretation with the aim of facilitating free movement. Therefore, 'resources' are not required to be generated by the Union citizen; they may originate from a third party with whom there is genuine dependence (ie, the third-country national parents). See, in this regard, the judgment in *Chen* (n 5) para 30; Case C-93/18 *Bajratari* EU:C:2019:809, paras 47–48; and Case C-836/18 *Subdelegación del Gobierno en Ciudad Real* EU:C:2020:119, para 31.

[34] A residence card is merely a *declarative* document that confirms the pre-existence of a residence right; it is not a requirement that triggers the creation of a residence right. Therefore, failure to apply for a residence card cannot deprive a Union citizen of his or her right to free movement. See Case C-48/75 *Royer* EU:C:1976:57, para 23; and Case C-408/03 *Commission v Belgium* EU:C:2005:638, paras 62–63.

[35] On the criteria to calculate the five-year residence period, see Case C-162/09 *Lassal* EU:C:2010:592; Case C-424/10 *Ziolkowski and Szeja* EU:C:2011:866; Case C-325/09 *Dias* EU:C:2011:498; and Case C-378/12 *Onuekwere* EU:C:2014:13.

[36] See the definition of family members set out in Art 2 of Directive 2004/38. On the definition of 'dependency' in Art 2 of Directive 2004/38, see Case C-165/16 *Lounes* EU:C:2017:862; and Case C-607/21 *XXX and État belge* EU:C:2025:264.

conducting an individualised assessment of all relevant circumstances and confirming the existence of 'genuine family life' and, consequently, providing protection under Union law.[37]

The second paragraph of Article 24 of the Directive introduces derogations regarding social assistance. This provision states that a host Member State is not obliged to grant such entitlements in three circumstances:

- Union citizens exercising free residence (residence for a period of less than three months, in accordance with Article 6 of Directive 2004/38);
- Union citizens entering the host state for the purpose of seeking employment, for as long as they can provide evidence that they are continuing to seek employment and have a genuine chance of being engaged;
- the granting of maintenance aid for studies, including vocational training, to individuals other than workers, self-employed persons, and those who maintain such status, along with their family members.

The first derogation aims to address situations of abuse in which a Union citizen travels to another Member State without engaging in economic activity or holding sufficient resources. However, the Court of Justice has required this exception to be interpreted restrictively, allowing discriminatory measures only when the Union citizen has engaged in the practice of 'welfare tourism' and holds no connection with the host Member State.[38] Furthermore, if the Union citizen can demonstrate a prior connection to the host Member State, or if a jobseeker is applying for a grant designed to facilitate their access to the labour market, the host Member State must not discriminate and must provide the aid under the same conditions applicable to its own nationals.[39] In any event, the case law insists on the need for Union citizens requesting access to social benefits to hold legal residence in the host Member State, in accordance with the terms provided in Directive 2004/38. The earlier approach in the case law, which admitted the applicability of equal treatment rights to Union citizens holding residence rights under conditions different from those enumerated in Directive 2004/38, was overruled in 2014 by the Court of Justice.[40]

Some years later, the case law introduced an additional nuance, broadening the scope of application to cases beyond the strict conditions of Directive 2004/38. In the judgment in *Department for Communities in Northern Ireland*,[41] the Court of Justice addressed the case of a Union citizen holding legal residence in a host Member State (but not under Directive 2004/38), in a situation of serious economic vulnerability affecting her dependent children. In this case, the Court of Justice relied on the right of Union citizens to live with their children in

[37] Case C-129/18 *SM and Entry Clearance Officer, UK Visa Section* EU:C:2019:248.

[38] Case C-22/08 *Vatsouras and Others* EU:C:2009:344.

[39] Case C-224/98 *D'Hoop* EU:C:2002:432; C-138/02 *Collins* EU:C:2004:172; Case C-258/04 *Ioannidis* EU:C:2005:559; *Vatsouras* (n 36); and Case C-67/14 *Alimanovic* EU:C:2015:597.

[40] At first, in Case C-456/02 *Trojani* EU:C:2004:488, the Court of Justice ruled that Art 18 TFEU precludes any discriminatory treatment where a residence permit is held in accordance with national law, albeit under more favourable conditions than those required by Directive 2004/38. According to the Court of Justice, 'a citizen of the Union who is not economically active may rely on Article [18 TFEU] EC where he has been lawfully resident in the host Member State for a certain time *or possesses a residence permit*' (para 43, emphasis added). Some years later, in Case C-333/13 *Dano* EU:C:2014:2358, the Court of Justice reversed this approach and came to a stricter conclusion: 'so far as concerns access to social benefits, such as those at issue in the main proceedings, a Union citizen can claim equal treatment with nationals of the host Member State only *if his residence in the territory of the host Member State complies with the conditions of Directive 2004/38*' (para 69, emphasis added). This solution was further qualified, albeit in the opposite sense, in 2021 in Case C-709/20 *CG v Department for Communities in Northern Ireland* EU:C:2021:602.

[41] *CG v Department for Communities in Northern Ireland* (n 40).

dignified conditions (Article 1 of the Charter). In such instances, the host Member State cannot discriminate between Union citizens; therefore, access to social assistance benefits cannot be denied for failing to meet the legal residence requirements set forth in Directive 2004/38.[42]

The second derogation concerns students exercising free movement rights, as their eligibility to access student grants or loans is significantly limited. According to Article 24(2) of Directive 2004/38, a student exercising free movement rights cannot apply for student grants in the host Member State until she obtains the right to permanent residence, which requires a prior five-year period of legal residence. This lengthy duration can lead to disproportionate restrictions; however, the validity of this provision was confirmed by the Court of Justice in *Förster*.[43]

Furthermore, Article 24(2) of Directive 2004/38 applies only where there are no more specific secondary law rules applicable to the case. For instance, when a Union citizen exercises the right to free movement of workers alongside his or her family, Article 10 of Regulation 492/11 applies,[44] superseding the provisions and exceptions of Article 24(2) of Directive 2004/38.[45]

Directive 2004/38 establishes the conditions for the expulsion of Union citizens residing in another Member State, as well as other forms of restrictions on free movement, such as prohibitions on entry and/or exit (as enacted during the COVID-19 pandemic in most Member States and reviewed in *Nordic Info*).[46] Articles 28–33 of the Directive codify the Court of Justice's case law on this issue, imposing on Member States the duty to carry out an individualised assessment of each expulsion case. This assessment must take into account the length of residence in the territory, the individual's age, state of health, family and economic circumstances, social and cultural integration into the host Member State, as well as the extent of their connections with their country of origin. In cases involving Union citizens with permanent rights of residence, expulsion is only allowed on serious grounds of public policy or public security.[47] In the case of Union citizens who have resided in the host Member State for at least 10 years, or for minors, expulsion is permitted solely on imperative grounds of public security.[48]

1.3. *Political Rights*

The political participation of Union citizens is significant for ensuring their direct involvement in the Union's decision-making processes and in their closest political community. The

[42] Member States are also precluded from discriminating on the grounds of nationality when the benefit extends to third parties, such as the children of the direct beneficiary. See Case C-397/23 *Jobcenter Arbeitplus Bielefeld* EU:C:2025:602, para 44.

[43] It should be noted that, at first, the case law developed a flexible approach to the specific circumstances of the student (see the judgment in Case C-209/03 *Bidar* EU:C:2005:169), an approach subsequently reconsidered in Case C-158/07 *Förster* EU:C:2008:630. However, in cases involving grants *for studies abroad*, the case law used a more flexible approach, as can be seen in Case C-11/06 *Morgan* EU:C:2007:626; Case C-523/11 *Prinz and Seeberger* EU:C:2013:524; Case C-272/12 *Elrick* EU:C:2013:684; Case C-220/12 *Meneses* EU:C:2013:683; and Case C-359/13 *Martens* EU:C:2015:118.

[44] Regulation No 492/2011 of the European Parliament and of the Council of 5 April 2011 on freedom of movement for workers within the Union [2011] OJ L141/1.

[45] Case C-181/19 *Jobcenter Krefeld* EU:C:2020:794, paras 60–65.

[46] Case C-128/22 *Nordic Info* BV EU:C:2023:951.

[47] Arts 27ff of Directive 2004/38.

[48] See Case C-430/10 *Gaydarov* EU:C:2011:749; Case C-249/11 *Byankov* EU:C:2012:608; Case C-145/09 *Tsakouridis* EU:C:2010:708; Joined Cases C-316/16 and C-424/16 *B and Vomero v Land Baden-Württemberg* EU:C:2018:256, and Case C-62/23 *Pedro Francisco* EU:C:2024:502. Similarly, prohibitions on the *exit* from a Member State were subject to review in Case C-434/10 *Aladzhov* EU:C:2011:750. Regarding the relationship between the conditions for expulsion provided for in Directive 2004/38 and prior refugee status, see Joined Cases C-331/16 and C-366/16 *K and HF* EU:C:2018:296.

following section covers two specific political dimensions governed by the Treaties: first, the right to vote and stand as a candidate in elections to the European Parliament and in the local elections of the host Member State; second, the right to petition the European Parliament.

1.3.1. The Right to Vote and to Stand as a Candidate in Elections to the European Parliament and Municipal Elections

Article 22 TFEU enshrines the right of 'every citizen of the Union residing in a Member State of which he is not a national' to vote and to stand as a candidate in elections to the European Parliament and in municipal elections in their Member State of residence. Articles 39–40 of the Charter proclaim the same right, which is further developed in Directives 93/109 and 94/80, which lay down detailed arrangements for exercising the right to vote and to stand as a candidate in elections to the European Parliament and in municipal elections, respectively.[49]

Although Article 22 TFEU refers to 'every citizen of the Union', the Court of Justice has interpreted the provision as allowing Member States to extend the right to vote and stand as a candidate to nationals of third countries, provided they have a close link with the Member State of residence.[50]

Member States have a wide margin of discretion in defining the conditions of the exercise of the right to vote and stand as a candidate, particularly in municipal elections. However, Member States cannot impose disproportionate restrictions that would prevent or obstruct citizens from effectively exercising this fundamental right. For instance, Member States can deny individuals convicted by a final judgment their right to vote, provided that the restriction is proportionate to the seriousness of the offence committed. In *Delvigne*, the Court of Justice upheld a French rule that deprived individuals sentenced to more than five years of imprisonment of their right to vote, including the right to vote in elections to the European Parliament.[51] Insofar as the rule did not disenfranchise offenders of minor crimes, specifically those sentenced to less than five years' imprisonment, the Court considered it a proportionate measure in conformity with the Charter.[52] The same applies to the conditions for accessing the office of member of the European Parliament, particularly those relating to the act of acceding to the member's seat, which should not constitute an effective impediment to the exercise of the office.[53] This also applies to national rules that restrict the right to become a member of a political party to nationals of the Member State only.[54] The Court of Justice stated that membership in a political party or political movement contributes significantly to the effective exercise of the right to stand for election, as conferred by Article 22 TFEU.[55] A national rule that restricts membership in a political party or movement to nationals of the Member State,

[49] Council Directive 93/109/EC of 6 December 1993 laying down detailed arrangements for the exercise of the right to vote and stand as a candidate in elections to the European Parliament for citizens of the Union residing in a Member State of which they are not nationals [1993] OJ L329/34; and Council Directive 94/80/EC of 19 December 1994 laying down detailed arrangements for the exercise of the right to vote and to stand as a candidate in municipal elections by citizens of the Union residing in a Member State of which they are not nationals [1994] OJ L368/38.

[50] Case C-145/04 *Spain v United Kingdom* EU:C:2006:543; and Case C-300/04 *Eman and Sevinger* EU:C: 2006:545.

[51] Case C-650/13 *Delvigne* EU:C:2015:648.

[52] It should be noted that the European Court of Human Rights, prior to *Delvigne*, ruled out a British blanket prohibition that automatically disenfranchised any person convicted of a criminal offence (*Hirst v United Kingdom (No 2)* [GC] No 74026/01, 2005-IX, para 82; *Frodl v Austria*, No 20201/04, para 25; *Scoppola v Italy*, No 126/05, para 96).

[53] Case C-502/19 *Junqueras Vies* EU:C:2019:1115, paras 86–87; and Case C-600/22 P *Puigdemont i Casamajó and Comín i Oliveres* EU:C:2024:803, paras 81–84.

[54] Case C-808/21 *Commission v Czech Republic* EU:C:2024:962; and Case C-814/21 *Commission v Poland* EU:C:2024:963.

[55] *Commission v Czech Republic* (n 54) para 122; and *Commission v Poland* (n 54) para 120.

thereby excluding Union citizens residing in that Member State, constitutes a restriction on Article 22 TFEU that must be justified and proportionate.[56]

1.3.2. Petitions to the European Parliament, Appeals to the European Ombudsman and Rights of Consultation

In addition to the rights of political participation, the Treaties also provide citizens with the right to engage directly with the Union's institutions and, in particular, to petition the European Parliament and to lodge complaints before the European Ombudsman. These rights are part of the range of powers available to Union citizens in their relations with these institutions, aiming to strengthen the link between citizens and the Union.[57] Article 20(2)(d) TFEU provides for the right of every citizen to 'petition the European Parliament, to apply to the European Ombudsman, and to address the institutions and advisory bodies of the Union in any of the Treaty languages and to obtain a reply in the same language'.

The right of access to documents, enshrined in Article 42 of the Charter, and the right to good administration, provided in Article 41 of the Charter, also deserve mention. Both rights are addressed to the Union (not to the Member States), which is subject to obligations of transparency and efficiency that empower Union citizens to exercise their citizenship rights more effectively.

1.4. *Diplomatic and Consular Protection*

Article 23 TFEU and Article 46 of the Charter grant Union citizens the right to protection by the diplomatic or consular authorities of any Member State in the territory of a third country where the Member State of which they are nationals is not represented, under the same conditions as the nationals of that Member State.[58] Article 23 TFEU specifies that this right extends to situations where the citizen's own Member State has no 'accessible' diplomatic or consular representation, a concept that encompasses not only the complete absence of an embassy or consulate but also situations where, although a representation exists, it is effectively unable to provide protection in a given case. This right has been further developed by the Council, specifically in Directive 2015/637 and Directive 2019/997.[59] The Lisbon Treaty introduced the current wording of Article 23(2) TFEU, which allows the Council to adopt directives, following a special legislative procedure, to establish the measures necessary for coordinating and cooperating in the diplomatic and consular protection of citizens of the Union by a Member State other than their country of nationality. This serves as the legal basis for both Directives, mentioned earlier. The right to diplomatic and consular protection is one of the least developed citizenship rights in practice, but it has gained increased significance in the context of crises

[56] *Commission v Czech Republic* (n 54) paras 146–52; and *Commission v Poland* (n 54) paras 144–50.

[57] The response of the European Parliament to a petition is not subject to judicial review, but a breach of its formal or procedural requirements can be challenged in court, as confirmed in Case C-261/13 *Schönberger* EU:C:2014:2423, paras 21–24. In the case of the Ombudsman, although its decisions are subject to judicial review, the negligent handling of a case can give rise to the non-contractual liability of the Ombudsman (Case C-337/15 *Ombudsman v Claire Staelen* EU:C:2017:256).

[58] P Vigni, 'The Right of EU Citizens to Diplomatic and Consular Protection: A Step Towards Recognition of EU Citizenship in Third Countries?' in D Kochenov (ed), *EU Citizenship and Federalism: The Role of Rights* (Cambridge University Press, 2017).

[59] Council Directive (EU) 2015/637 of 20 April 2015 on the coordination and cooperation measures to facilitate consular protection for unrepresented citizens of the Union in third countries and repealing Decision 95/553/EC [2015] OJ L106/1; and Council Directive (EU) 2019/997 of 18 June 2019 establishing an EU Emergency Travel Document and repealing Decision 96/409/CFSP [2019] OJ L163/1.

affecting Union citizens abroad, such as natural disasters, armed conflicts, and the COVID-19 pandemic, which required coordinated action by the Member States and the EEAS.

2. Article 20 TFEU and Protection of the Status of Union Citizenship

As mentioned above, although the Treaty provisions on citizenship have remained unchanged since their introduction in 1992, the case law of the Court of Justice has certainly evolved, to the point of transforming the status of Union citizenship into a federal tool of integration. The Court of Justice appears satisfied with its contribution, as it now refers to Union citizenship not as an aspiration, but as '*the* fundamental status of the nationals of the Member States'.[60] This evolution implies that the status of Union citizenship has close connections with the founding provisions of the Treaties, including the values enshrined in Article 2 TEU. This approach to Union citizenship has changed how the Court of Justice approaches citizenship cases, which were once closer to the logic of free movement and the internal market, but are now more aligned with the development of a European polity based on the values of a constitutional liberal democracy.

This values-based approach to Union citizenship has materialised in two strands of case law that deserve specific attention. Firstly, the case law has developed a criterion that defines the bond between the individual and the status of Union citizenship (and of nationality of a Member State). This bond has a normative content directly derived from Article 20 TFEU and creates rights and obligations, particularly at the time of acquisition of the status. Secondly, the case law has also determined the 'substance of the rights' that form the status of Union citizenship. This core also derives from Article 20 TFEU and precludes Member States from acting in any way that may undermine it, even in cases without any cross-border connection.

2.1. *Protecting the Bond of Solidarity and Good Faith*

In *Commission v Malta*, the Court of Justice outlined the connecting features between the status of Union citizenship and the values that underpin the Union's identity. In this regard, the Court stated:

> Union citizenship is based on the common values contained in Article 2 TEU and on the mutual trust between the Member States as regards the fact that none of them is to exercise that power in a way that is manifestly incompatible with the very nature of Union citizenship.[61]

In its case law, the Court of Justice had previously referred to the bond of nationality of Member States, defining it as the 'special relationship of solidarity and good faith between that State and its nationals and the reciprocity of rights and duties'. In *Commission v Malta,* the Court of Justice took a further step and concluded that such a bond is extendable to Union citizenship, thus deriving specific obligations from Article 20 TFEU. As a result,

> the special relationship of solidarity and good faith between each Member State and its nationals also forms the basis of the rights and obligations reserved to Union citizens by the Treaties.[62]

In the case at hand, the Court of Justice was called upon to rule on the compatibility with Union law of Malta's framework on citizenship by investment, a legal route that granted

[60] *Commission v Malta* (n 6) para 92.
[61] ibid, para 95.
[62] ibid, para 96.

access to Maltese nationality through substantial investments. The Court of Justice stated that a means of commercialisation of access to nationality is incompatible with the notion of a special relationship of solidarity and good faith between the Member State and the individual. Therefore, it ruled that such a framework breached Article 20 TFEU, together with the principle of sincere cooperation.

Following this judgment, it is clear that the Member States are now bound by Article 20 TFEU when defining the terms of access to nationality, regardless of the requirements or scope of the national rules. Since the acquisition of nationality also serves as the gateway to the bond of solidarity and good faith between the individual and the Union, nationality law now falls under the purview of Article 20 TFEU and the jurisdiction of the Court of Justice. This outcome is even more striking when attention is drawn to Declaration No 2 on nationality of a Member State, annexed by the Member States to the final act of the Treaty on European Union,[63] which states:

> [W]herever in the Treaty establishing the European Community reference is made to nationals of the Member States, the question whether an individual possesses the nationality of a Member State shall be settled solely by reference to the national law of the Member State concerned.

Despite the categorical terms of the Declaration, Article 20 TFEU has now become a central feature of the Member States' naturalisation policies. The precise scope of this provision remains open to question. While the Court of Justice has rejected a transactional framework that facilitates access to nationality through predetermined payments, questions arise regarding the discretionary powers of Member States to grant nationality through executive prerogative, typically under strict confidentiality conditions. Furthermore, the generous rules on naturalisation for large groups based on vague historical or distant family connections to a Member State will also fall under the purview of Article 20 TFEU.

By opening the door to reviewing the Member States' nationality policies, the Court of Justice has transformed Union citizenship into the primary status of the individual, marginalising the role of national nationality and reducing it to an accessory that facilitates access to Union citizenship. It is too early to determine whether the Member States will be satisfied with this approach, or whether it represents a further step toward federalising a legal status to reinforce further the Union and the effectiveness of integration through law.

2.2. *Protecting the Genuine Enjoyment of the Substance of the Rights Attached to the Status of Union Citizenship*

The status of Union citizenship can be affected by national measures that undermine the overall bundle of rights that comprise this status. A decision by a Member State may be so restrictive that it ultimately impacts not only the right to free movement of a Union citizen, but also his or her rights to political participation, as well as the very essence of the citizen's rights as a whole. In such cases, the national measure affects not only a specific right linked to the status, but also the status of Union citizenship as a whole.

The Court of Justice developed this approach in two seminal judgments delivered in *Rottmann* and *Ruiz Zambrano*.[64] Both cases concerned the conformity with Union law of national measures that severely restricted Union citizenship rights. The Court of Justice held that, in such circumstances, which will be explained in detail in the following sections, there is a breach of the status of Union citizenship, understood as a set of rights for individual

[63] Treaty on European Union [1992] OJ C191/1.

[64] See *Rottmann* (n 6) and *Ruiz Zambrano* (n 6).

enjoyment by citizens. It is, in the words of the Court of Justice, a 'deprivation of the genuine enjoyment of the substance of the rights attaching to the status of Union citizen'. In such cases, the Member State violates Article 20(1) TFEU, the provision that establishes the status of Union citizenship and confers it on the nationals of the Member States.[65]

Moreover, Member States can breach Article 20(1) TFEU in situations where there is no cross-border link with another Member State. Therefore, it is not necessary to exercise free movement rights beforehand; it is enough that the contested national measure compromises the genuine enjoyment of the substance of the rights attached to the status of Union citizenship, including the rights of nationals of the same Member State enacting the measure.

The case law has established two situations in which a breach of the bundle of rights attached to the status of Union citizenship can take place: first, in cases involving a de jure loss of the status of Union citizenship, and second, in cases involving a de facto loss of that status. These situations have been addressed respectively in *Rottmann* and *Ruiz Zambrano*, cited above.

2.3. *Measures Involving the De Jure Loss of Status of Union Citizenship*

Measures that result in the loss of Union citizenship can breach Article 20(1) TFEU if they impose an unjustified restriction on the status. Such instances primarily arise when a Member State decides to withdraw the nationality of one of its nationals. Although these measures are outlined in national legislation, they remain exceptional and require careful, individualised assessment.

In the case of *Rottmann*, the Court of Justice ruled on whether a decision by the German authorities to deprive a Union citizen of German nationality, due to the provision of false information at the time of application, constituted a breach of Union law. In its judgment, the Court made three relevant findings.

First, cases in which a Member State deprives its own nationals of nationality fall within the scope of Union law, as they affect the status of Union citizenship. Therefore, it is unnecessary for the applicant to prove the existence of a trans-frontier link.[66]

Second, these cases do not constitute a violation of the free movement of persons, but rather a breach of the fundamental status of Union citizenship. Consequently, the relevant applicable provision is Article 20(1) TFEU, and not Article 21 TFEU.[67]

Third, Article 20(1) TFEU requires an individualised assessment subject to a case-by-case analysis in accordance with the principle of proportionality.[68] Therefore, even if the measure restricts the rights attached to the status of citizenship, there will be circumstances in which the restriction can be justified, provided that the Member State pursues an objective of general interest and the measure complies with the principle of proportionality. For instance, in *Rottmann*, the Court of Justice found that the withdrawal of nationality by the German authorities was justified, as the applicant's German nationality had been granted based on false information supplied by the applicant in bad faith. Applications involving fraud are among the limited cases under international law that entitle states to revoke a person's nationality, a factor that the Court of Justice closely examined when assessing the proportionality of the German decision to withdraw Mr. Rottmann's German nationality. Likewise, in *Tjebbes*, the Court of Justice ruled that an automatic deprivation of nationality can be in line with Article 20(1)

[65] See K Hailbronner and D Thym (2011) 48 *Common Market Law Review* 1253.

[66] The absence of a cross border link was explicitly confirmed by the Court of Justice in Case C-221/17 *Tjebbes* EU:C:2019:189, para 32.

[67] *Rottmann* (n 6) para 42.

[68] ibid, para 58.

TFEU, provided it is proportionate given the facts leading to the loss of status, allows for an individual assessment of the case, and offers sufficient procedural safeguards for the individual to assert her rights.[69] In *Wiener Landesregierung*, the Court of Justice reiterated the criteria to follow when applying the principle of proportionality in cases concerning the loss of Union citizenship. It concluded that denying the granting of nationality based on a traffic fine, which risks rendering the Union citizen stateless, constituted a disproportionate measure and, therefore, violated Article 20(1) TFEU.[70]

2.4. *Measures Involving the De Facto Loss of Status of Union Citizenship*

There are instances where the loss of Union citizenship occurs through indirect, or even unintended, actions taken by a Member State. In these cases, there is a de facto loss of status: the citizen still retains the status, but with little to no practical effect or purpose. This was evident in *Ruiz Zambrano*, which involved a decision by the Belgian authorities to expel a Colombian national from Belgium, the father of two minor children holding Belgian nationality. The Court determined that, under these circumstances, the father's expulsion would lead to a de facto expulsion of the family unit, including the Union citizens. For the children, the expulsion would result in a de facto loss of the bundle of rights associated with Union citizenship status: being compelled to leave the territory of the Union, and exercising the rights linked to this status, would hold little to no practical effect or purpose.

The judgment in *Ruiz Zambrano* complements the case law delivered in *Rottmann*. It also provides an explicit definition of the test applicable to these situations of loss: 'deprivation of the genuine enjoyment of the substance of the rights attaching to the status of European Union citizen', an outcome that breaches Article 20(1) TFEU. In subsequent case law, the Court of Justice has emphasised that the test applies in exceptional situations only. However, the reality is that Member States must develop their migration policies in accordance with the standards introduced by this case law. On the one hand, the *Rottmann* doctrine imposes an additional level of scrutiny on measures depriving a Union citizen of their nationality. On the other hand, the *Ruiz Zambrano* doctrine calls for special attention to national measures that may lead to a de facto loss of Union citizenship. This outcome can materialise in cases of expulsion of a parent, a dependant, or a vulnerable Union citizen.[71]

The Court of Justice has further developed the ruling in *Ruiz Zambrano* in recent years. It is now well established that the protection conferred by Article 20 TFEU also extends to situations that restrict fundamental rights affecting family life, as confirmed in the cases of *Rendón Marin* and *CS*,[72] but particularly in *Chávez-Vilchez*[73] and *Subdelegación del Gobierno en Toledo*.[74] Likewise, in *KA*[75] and, more recently, in *X v Staatssecretaris van Justitie en Veiligheid*,[76] the Court of Justice applied the *Ruiz Zambrano* doctrine to situations affecting the *entry* of third-country nationals who are parents of infant minors holding Union citizenship into the Union's territory.[77]

[69] *Tjebbes* (n 66) paras 41ff.

[70] Case C-118/20 *Wiener Landesregierung* EU:C:2022:34, para 73. See also Case C-689/21 *Udlændinge og Integrationsministeriet* EU:C:2023:626.

[71] Case C-165/14 *Rendón Marín* EU:C:2016:675; and Case C-304/14 *CS* EU:C:2016:674.

[72] ibid.

[73] Case C-133/15 *Chávez-Vilchez* EU:C:2017:354, para 70.

[74] Joined Cases C-451/19 and C-532/19 *Subdelegación del Gobierno en Toledo and XU* and *QP* EU:C:2022:24.

[75] Case C-82/16 *KA and Others* EU:C:2018:308.

[76] Case C-459/20 *X v Staatssecretaris van Justitite en Veiligheid* EU:C:2023:499.

[77] D Sarmiento, 'The "Substance of the Rights" Test: Moving a Values-Based Union Forward' in C Barnard, A Lazowski and D Sarmiento (eds), *Pursuit of Legal Harmony in a Turbulent Europe. Essays in Honour of Eleanor Sharpston* (Hart, 2024).

The development of a standard of review in Union law to scrutinise the loss of Union citizenship confirms the autonomy of this status over the nationality laws of the Member States. While it is true that Union citizenship is an *addition* to the status of nationality of a Member State, this does not imply that Union citizenship is *subordinated* to the status of nationality of a Member State. On the contrary, the acquisition of a Member State's nationality triggers the attribution of the fundamental status of the individual: Union citizenship. Once the status has been established, the Member State does not possess unfettered discretion to dispose of it. Otherwise, Member States would be free to render meaningless none other than the fundamental status of Union citizenship, an outcome that runs counter to the objectives of the Treaties.

III. FUNDAMENTAL RIGHTS

Following the Second World War, various European countries embraced liberal democracy and turned the protection of fundamental rights into a central objective, enshrined in their constitutions and supported by effective legal remedies. Fundamental rights are grounded in the protection of human dignity, which confers upon them a unique role and significance within the legal systems of the Member States. For the Union – an organisation founded on the same values as its Member States – the Treaties make it clear that it must respect the fundamental rights of Union citizens and all individuals, irrespective of their nationality.

In its early years, the European Communities lacked any reference to the protection of fundamental rights in the founding Treaties. The European Communities were organisations primarily focused on establishing a common market. Fundamental rights were applicable in the administrative relations between the Community institutions and the undertakings and other economic operators that engaged with them. It was not until 1969 that the Court of Justice ruled that fundamental rights formed part of Community law, recognised as general principles of law.[78] The enactment of a legal instrument that enumerates and enshrines fundamental rights in Union law did not take place until 2000, when the Union's political institutions solemnly proclaimed the Charter of Fundamental Rights of the European Union.[79] Full recognition of the Charter as an instrument of primary law would not occur until 1 December 2009, when the Lisbon Treaty entered into force. From that date onward, the Charter has been a binding instrument to the Union's institutions, bodies, offices, and agencies, as well as to the Member States only when they are implementing Union law.

The legal framework governing the protection of fundamental rights in Union law is not only confined to the Charter. The European Convention on Human Rights, an international treaty to which the Union is not yet a party and which was established within the Council of Europe, also plays a significant role in Union law. Public international law, including principles that reflect the protection of certain fundamental rights, is binding on the Union. Furthermore, the Charter coexists with unwritten rules of law, developed by the case law of the Court of Justice through general principles based on the constitutional traditions common to the Member States. The manner in which these instruments interact to elaborate the content of the Charter is the subject of the following section.

[78] See, inter alia, P Pescatore, 'Les droits de l'homme et l'intégration européenne' (1968) 4 *Cahiers de droit européen;* and A Rosas, 'The European Court of Justice and Fundamental Rights: Yet Another Case of Judicial Activism?' in C Baudenbacher and H Bull (eds), *European Integration Through Interaction of Legal Regimes* (Universitetsforlaget, 2007).

[79] On the genesis of the Charter, see G De Búrca, 'The Drafting of the European Union Charter of Fundamental Rights' (2001) 26 *European Law Review 126, and G De Búrca,* 'The Drafting of a Constitution for the European Union: Europe's Madisonian Moment or a Moment of Madness?' (2004) 61 *Washington & Lee Law Review* 555.

1. Fundamental Rights as General Principles of Union Law

In the 1960s, when the Communities still lacked a written catalogue of fundamental rights, German courts explored the possibility of reviewing Community acts in light of the fundamental rights provided in the German Basic Law. If the Communities adopted measures that breached fundamental rights, the only way to protect those rights, in the absence of fundamental rights in Union law, would be to review such measures by invoking the Constitution of the Member State.[80] Faced with this risk, which could have led to a fragmentation of Union law throughout the Member States, the Court of Justice reacted in the strongest terms in the cases of *Stauder*[81] and *Internationale Handelsgesellschaft*[82] to proclaim the existence of fundamental rights within the Union's legal system, in the form of general principles of law. Once it was confirmed that the Communities possessed their own set of fundamental rights, it became the responsibility of the Court of Justice (and the Union's legal system) to review the conformity of Union acts with fundamental rights.

Since 1970, the Union's fundamental rights have been central to the Union's legal system as general principles of law, articulated on a case-by-case basis through the case law of the Court of Justice. An enumeration of the fundamental rights recognised as general principles of law can be found in chapter seven, section II.2.3.1.

In determining the existence and scope of a fundamental right as a general principle of law, the Court of Justice draws inspiration from the constitutional traditions common to the Member States, as well as from international instruments for the protection of human rights. Both sources provide interpretative guidance but do not serve as binding sources of law. The Court of Justice analyses the fundamental right, its development in the Member States and in international law, and selects the content best suited to the Union's objectives. As explained in chapter seven, section II.2.1, the methodology employed by the Court of Justice to declare the existence of a general principle of Union law is primarily pragmatic and conducted on a case-by-case basis.

When the Charter entered into force on 1 December 2009, questions arose regarding the existence of fundamental rights as general principles of Union law. Once the Union's fundamental rights were incorporated into a written text with the status of primary law, some authors questioned the consequences of maintaining the coexistence of two sources of law for the same rights.[83] The Court of Justice addressed this matter and confirmed that, despite the entry into force of the Charter, general principles of Union law remain a relevant instrument for the protection of fundamental rights. This is especially true when the Charter contains a fundamental right with a limited scope. For instance, the fundamental right to be heard in an administrative procedure, enshrined in Article 41 of the Charter, applies only to the institutions, agencies, bodies, and offices of the Union, not to the Member States. Consequently, when a Member State implements Union law, the right to be heard may be invoked as a general

[80] On the tensions between the German courts and the Court of Justice during the 1960s and 1970s, see the account by K Alter, *Establishing the Supremacy of European Law. The Making of an International Rule of Law in Europe* (Oxford University Press, 2001).

[81] Case C-29/69 *Stauder* EU:C:1969:57.

[82] Case C-11/70 *Internationale Handelsgesellschaft* EU:C:1970:114.

[83] E Muir, 'The Court of Justice in the Novel system for the Protection of Fundamental Rights in the EU' (2012) 5 *Maastricht Working Paper*. In fact, the Charter has served as a source of inspiration when developing general principles of Union law, as explained by K Lenaerts and JA Gutiérrez-Fons, 'The Charter in the EU Constitutional Edifice' in S Peers, T Hervey, J Kenner and A Ward, *The EU Charter of Fundamental Rights. A Commentary* (Beck-Hart-Nomos, 2014). Such was the case of the principle of non-discrimination on the grounds of age in Case C-144/04 *Mangold* EU:C:2005:709; and Case C-555/07 *Kücükdeveci* EU:C:2010:21.

principle of Union law, but not as a fundamental right enshrined in the Charter.[84] Also, general principles may protect rights that are not expressly codified in the Charter at all. While the Charter is comprehensive, it does not purport to be exhaustive, and the Court has on occasion relied on general principles to recognise protections that go beyond the Charter's express provisions.

2. Fundamental Rights in International Law

2.1. *Council of Europe: the European Convention on Human Rights and the European Social Charter*

Among the instruments of international law on fundamental rights, those enacted within the framework of the Council of Europe play a particularly significant role, most notably the Convention for the Protection of Human Rights and Fundamental Freedoms of 1950 and the European Social Charter of 1961. These instruments produce effects in the Union's legal system, as demonstrated by the numerous references in the Treaties and the frequent use made of them by the Court of Justice in the interpretation of Union law.

The European Convention on Human Rights (ECHR) is particularly important because, in addition to being an international treaty explicitly mentioned in Article 6(3) TEU and Article 52(3) of the Charter, the Union is legally obliged to accede to it, as mandated by Article 6(2) TEU. The Union's accession to the ECHR will transform this instrument into a legally binding text for both the Union and the Member States when they implement Union law. Moreover, rulings of the Court of Justice will be subject to external judicial review by the European Court of Human Rights.[85]

At present, accession to the ECHR has not taken place, but this does not mean that the Union has sidelined or minimised the importance of the case law developed by the European Court of Human Rights. On the contrary, since the 1970s, the Court of Justice has used the ECHR as a key reference point in cases concerning the protection of fundamental rights,[86] to the extent of adopting the level of protection of fundamental rights as a minimum standard for the Union's fundamental rights.[87] This practice is now codified in Article 6(3) TEU, according to which the rights guaranteed by the ECHR 'shall constitute general principles of the Union's law'. Likewise, Article 52(3) of the Charter states that in so far as it contains rights that correspond to rights guaranteed by the ECHR, 'the meaning and scope of those rights shall be the same as those laid down by the [ECHR]'.

Although the ECHR is not formally incorporated as a binding instrument of Union law, it has acquired 'special significance', distinct from that of any other international treaty. This

[84] Case C-161/15 *Bensada Benallal* EU:C:2016:3, Opinion of AG Mengozzi, pts 28–33, summarising the position of the case law thus far.

[85] See, inter alia, C Eckes, 'EU Accession to the ECHR: Between Autonomy and Adaptation' (2013) 76 *Modern Law Review*; P Gragl, *The Accession of the European Union to the European Convention on Human Rights* (Hart, 2013); J-P Jacqué, 'The Accession of the European Union to the European Convention on Human Rights and Fundamental Freedoms' (2011) 48 *Common Market Law Review 995;* and T Lock, 'End of an Epic? The Draft Agreement on the EU's Accession to the ECHR' (2012) 31 *Yearbook of European Law* 162.

[86] A practice that began in Case C-36/75 *Rutili* EU:C:1975:137 and continued in Case C-222/84 *Johnston* EU:C:1986:206; Case C-579/13 *P and S* EU:C:2015:369; and Case C-465/00 *Österreichischer Rundfunk* EU:C:2003:294, among others.

[87] See, inter alia, Case C-94/00 *Roquette Frères* EU:C:2002:603; Case C-117/01 *KB* EU:C:2004:7; and Case C-411/10 *NS* EU:C:2011:865.

status of the ECHR is articulated in a formulation frequently used in the case law, stating as follows:

> [T]he Court draws inspiration from the constitutional traditions common to the Member States and from the guidelines supplied by international treaties for the protection of human rights on which the Member States have collaborated or of which they are signatories . . . The European Convention on Human Rights has special significance in that respect . . . It follows that the [Union] cannot accept measures which are incompatible with observance of the human rights thus recognized and guaranteed.[88]

Shortly after the Charter came into force, the ECHR appeared to lose some of its prominence in the case law of the Court of Justice.[89] Initially, the case law seemed to prioritise the Charter, resorting to the ECHR only in instances that required a particular interpretative effort,[90] or when the level of protection provided by the European Court of Human Rights was higher than that afforded by Union law.[91]

Furthermore, the Court of Justice emphasised that the entry into force of the Charter has not altered the formal status of the ECHR within Union law. The Court of Justice made it clear that individuals cannot rely on the ECHR as such under the same conditions as they can rely on the Charter or other rules of Union law:

> [W]hilst, as Article 6(3) TEU confirms, fundamental rights recognised by the ECHR constitute general principles of the European Union's law and whilst Article 52(3) of the Charter requires rights contained in the Charter which correspond to rights guaranteed by the ECHR to be given the same meaning and scope as those laid down by the ECHR, the latter does not constitute, as long as the European Union has not acceded to it, a legal instrument which has been formally incorporated into European Union law. Consequently, European Union law does not govern the relations between the ECHR and the legal systems of the Member States, nor does it determine the conclusions to be drawn by a national court in the event of conflict between the rights guaranteed by that convention and a rule of national law.[92]

This development in the case law confirmed an inclination to strengthen the 'autonomy of the Charter' at the expense of the ECHR's gradual marginalisation as a key reference in the interpretation of fundamental rights. The objective of the Court of Justice appeared to be the consolidation of the Charter as the principal normative text of Union law on fundamental rights,[93] thereby avoiding the risk that the ECHR would interfere with or compromise the effectiveness and autonomy of Union law.[94] However, this apparent trend to sideline the ECHR as a secondary reference has not materialised. In recent years, the role and influence of the

[88] Case C-260/89 *ERT* EU:C:1991:254, para 41.

[89] Some of the landmark rulings on the interpretation of the Charter, such as Case C-650/13 *Delvigne* EU:C:2015:648; Case C-362/14 *Schrems* EU:C:2015:650; Case C-293/12 *Digital Rights Ireland* EU:C:2014:238; or Case C-617/10 *Akerberg Fransson* EU:C:2013:105, reveal a surprising lack of engagement with the case law of the European Court of Human Rights.

[90] See, inter alia, Case C-279/09 *DEB* EU:C:2010:811, exploring the issue that legal persons are holders of fundamental rights. In Case C-601/15 PPU *JN* EU:C:2016:84, paras 78–82, the validity of a directive was reviewed in light of a fundamental right on which the European Court of Human Rights had developed an abundant case law. When reviewing the validity of the Directive, the reasoning of the Court of Justice was directly conditioned by the case law of the European Court of Human Rights on Art 5 ECHR.

[91] Case C-411/10 *NS and Others* EU:C:2011:865.

[92] Case C-617/10 *Akerberg Fransson* (n 89) para 44; and Case C-571/10 *Kamberaj* EU:C:2012:233, para 62.

[93] See V Skouris, 'Recent Developments in the Protection of Fundamental Rights in the European Union: The "Melloni" and "Åkerberg Fransson" judgments' (2013) 18 *Il Diritto dell'Unione Europea*.

[94] The explanations refer to Art 52(3) of the Charter and confirm that the aim of the provision is to ensure consistency between the Charter and the ECHR, 'without thereby adversely affecting the autonomy of Union law and that of the Court of Justice of the European Union'. See Case C-601/15 PPU N EU:C:2016:84, para 47.

case law of the European Court of Human Rights has grown and intensified, particularly in areas such as the protection of privacy and private life, effective judicial protection (especially in cases affecting the rule of law and the independence of the judiciary), and in the field of immigration and asylum. While the Charter remains the Union's primary reference and legal instrument for the protection of fundamental rights, the ECHR is currently a deeply embedded instrument that guides the case law of the Court of Justice and, at times, interacts dynamically with the cross-influences that have contributed to building Europe's framework on fundamental rights protection.[95]

The current situation will change even further when the Union accedes to the ECHR, as mandated by Article 6(2) TEU. In Opinion 2/13, the Court of Justice raised several objections to the first draft accession agreement of the Union to the ECHR. These objections made it difficult to conceive a model of accession that would satisfy the Court of Justice's demands. The situation was particularly challenging, given that the first draft accession agreement incorporated suggestions from the Court of Justice itself during negotiations between the Member States and the Council of Europe. [96] The efforts persisted and, following a new round of negotiations with the Council of Europe, a revised draft agreement emerged in March 2023, addressing the objections of the Court of Justice in Opinion 2/13, now awaiting the blessing of the Court of Justice in an advisory opinion procedure.[97] The new draft agreement provides a reasonable response to the objections raised by the Court of Justice in Opinion 2/13, and it is expected that the accession procedure will materialise sooner rather than later.[98]

Another significant instrument, also adopted within the framework of the Council of Europe, is the European Social Charter, signed in Turin on 18 October 1961 and revised in 1996.[99] The Court of Justice has drawn upon it as a source of inspiration when interpreting the fundamental rights of the Charter, particularly those in the realms of social and labour law.[100] The Explanations to the Charter emphasise that a primary point of reference for interpreting Chapter IV of the Charter is the European Social Charter, a fact confirmed by the Court of Justice when interpreting fundamental rights of a social nature.[101]

However, the role of the European Social Charter in Union law is not comparable to that of the ECHR. The Court of Justice does not rely on the European Social Charter as frequently as it does on the ECHR, and it also refrains from citing the decisions of the body responsible for its interpretation: the European Committee of Social Rights. This body hears individual complaints under the Additional Protocol to the European Social Charter providing for a system of collective complaints (1995), but does not have the status of an international court. To date, the Court of Justice has not expressly relied on the decisions of the European

[95] See, for example, the evolution of the Court of Justice's case law on *ne bis in idem* in administrative and criminal proceedings, interacting closely with the case law of the European Court of Human Rights (contrast *A and B v Norway* with Case C-524/15 *Menci* EU:C:2018:197 and later with Case C-117/20 *bpost* EU:C:2022:202).

[96] Reflection Paper of the Court of Justice of the European Union on certain aspects of the accession of the European Union to the European Convention for the Protection of Human Rights and Fundamental Freedoms, 5 May 2010, available at *http://curia.europa.eu/jcms/upload/docs/application/pdf/2010-05/convention_es_2010-05-21_12-10-16_194.pdf*.

[97] Opinion 1/25 (pending).

[98] F Ronkes Agerbeek, 'EU Accession to the European Convention on Human Rights: A New Hope' (2024) 9 *European Papers* 695.

[99] European Social Charter, signed in Turin on 18 October 1961 and revised in Strasbourg on 3 May 1996.

[100] See, inter alia, Case C-438/05 *Viking Line* EU:C:2007:772, para 43; Case C-341/05 *Laval un Partneri* EU:C:2007:809, para 90; and Case C-268/06 *Impact* EU:C:2008:223, para 113.

[101] See, inter alia, Case C-173/99 *BECTU* EU:C:2001:356, para 43; and Case C-579/12 RX-II *Commission v Strack* EU:C:2013:570, para 26.

Committee of Social Rights, at least not explicitly and in the same terms as it has interacted with the European Court of Human Rights.[102]

2.2. *Other Instruments of International Law*

With the exception of the ECHR and the European Social Charter, the role of international law in shaping the Union's fundamental rights has been inconsistent over time. As early as 1974, in the judgment in *Nold*, the Court of Justice stated that 'international treaties for the protection of human rights of which the Member States have collaborated or of which they are signatories, can supply guidelines which should be followed within the framework of [Union] law',[103] but the fact remains that international agreements on human rights do not always play an equally prominent role in the case law of the Court of Justice.

First, there are international agreements on fundamental rights, or those that directly impact fundamental rights, to which the Union is a party, and produce their effects in the Union legal system. For example, the Union acceded to the United Nations Convention on the Rights of Persons with Disabilities. Following its ratification in 2009, in the case of *HK Danmark*, the Court of Justice adapted its interpretation of secondary law to align it with the Convention's binding terms.[104]

Second, international agreements to which the Member States (but not the Union) are parties, can be particularly relevant, although not at the same level as a binding instrument of international law to which the Union is a party. For example, the case law of the Court of Justice has frequently referred to and relied on international agreements such as the International Covenant on Civil and Political Rights,[105] or the Convention relating to the Status of Stateless Persons,[106] but on other occasions, it has declined to consider other potentially relevant international instruments that were relevant for the resolution of a case.[107]

Third, there are instances where Union secondary law explicitly refers to an instrument of international law, even though the Union is not a party to it. In those cases, the Court of Justice interprets the Union act in light of the provisions of the international instrument, in a manner similar to the role played by the ECHR. This is evident, for instance, in international agreements on asylum and international protection, which are repeatedly referenced in Directive 2013/32, Directive 2013/33, and Directive 2011/95, as well as in Regulation 604/13.[108] Article

[102] O De Schutter, 'Le statut de la Charte sociale européenne dans le droit de l'Union' in *Chemins de l'Europe: Mélanges en l'Honneur de Jean-Paul Jacqué* (Dalloz, 2010).

[103] Case C-4/73 *Nold KG v Commission* EU:C:1974:51, para 13.

[104] Case C-335/11 *HK Danmark* EU:C:2013:222, paras 36–38.

[105] See, inter alia, the judgments in Case C-374/87 *Orkem v Commission* EU:C:1989:387, para 31; Joined Cases C-297/88 and C-197/89 *Dzodzi* EU:C:1990:360, para 68; Case C-249/96 *Grant* EU:C:1998:63, para 44; and Case C-540/03 *European Parliament v Council* EU:C:2006:429, para 37.

[106] *Rottmann* (n 6) para 52.

[107] See, for example, the case of the Oviedo Convention on Human Rights and Biomedicine in Case C-237/09 *Belgica/De Fruytier* EU:C:2010:316, where the Court of Justice, in para 27, refused to rely on it on the following grounds: 'even though it is clear from the order for reference that in Belgium human organs and samples cannot be traded, and even though Article 21 of the Convention for the protection of human rights and dignity of the human being with regard to the application of biology and medicine: Convention on Human Rights and Biomedicine, concluded at Oviedo on 4 April 1997, provides, under the heading "Prohibition of financial gain", that the human body and its parts are not, as such, to give rise to financial gain, those factors in themselves cannot be regarded as wholly depriving Article 13(A)(1)(d) of the Sixth Directive of its effectiveness. That convention, open for signature in particular by the member States of the Council of Europe, on the one hand, and by the European Union, on the other hand, under Article 33(1) of the convention, has not been signed by the European Union. Moreover, of the Member States, only a small majority of them have actually ratified the convention.'

[108] Directive 2013/32/EU on common procedures for granting and withdrawing international protection; Directive 2013/33/EU laying down standards for the reception of applicants for international protection; Directive 2011/95/EU on standards for the qualification of third-country nationals or stateless persons as beneficiaries of international

78(1) TFEU provides that the Union's common policy on asylum must be 'in accordance with the Geneva Convention of 28 July 1951 and the Protocol of 31 January 1967', thereby elevating the Convention's requirements to a Treaty obligation. Throughout a wealth of case law on asylum, the Court of Justice has made numerous references to the Convention relating to the Status of Refugees (the Geneva Convention), in line with the relevance that the applicable Treaties, directives and regulations confer on the said instrument.[109]

Following the entry into force of the Charter in 2009, some commentators have identified a trend towards the marginalisation of the role of international fundamental rights law in Union law. This perception has been reinforced by the Court of Justice's tendency to rely on the autonomy of Union law to address situations involving standards of protection between Union and international law.[110] This development can be understood as a natural evolution of the Union's legal system, now that it has a Charter of Fundamental Rights. However, this tendency also risks isolating the Union at the international level. For the time being, the autonomy of Union law has served to overrule UN Security Council resolutions, obstruct the Union's accession to the ECHR, and preclude Member States from entering into bilateral agreements that include investor claims in international arbitration tribunals. While these decisions have reinforced the authority of Union law internally, they have also raised questions about the Union's commitment to international law, in an international environment in which the Union seeks to act as a leading example in the protection of human rights and the rule of law, particularly at a time when global trends increasingly appear to marginalise or openly question the role of international law.

3. The Constitutional Traditions Common to the Member States

Article 52(4) of the Charter states that 'in so far as this Charter recognises fundamental rights as they result from the constitutional traditions common to the Member States, those rights shall be interpreted in harmony with those traditions'. This 'harmonious interpretation' has been the trend since the judgment in *Nold* of 1974,[111] as the Court of Justice has continuously drawn inspiration from the constitutional traditions common to the Member States when developing the content and scope of fundamental rights in Union law.[112] This methodology was necessary because, at that time, the Communities' fundamental rights lacked a written legal basis. This

protection, for a uniform status for refugees or for persons eligible for subsidiary protection and for the content of the protection granted; and Regulation (EU) No 604/2013 establishing the criteria and mechanisms for determining the Member State responsible for examining an application for international protection lodged in one of the Member States by a third-country national or a stateless person. These instruments will be repealed and replaced by the new framework introduced in 2024, which also refer to the Geneva Convention.

[109] Joined Cases C-175-179/08 *Salahadin Abdulla and Others* EU:C:2010:105, paras 57 and 65; Case C-31/09 *Bolbol* EU:C:2010:351, paras 48ff; Joined Cases C-331/16 and C-366/16 *K and HF* EU:C:2018:296, paras 46–47; and Case C-349/20 NB and AB EU:C:2022:151, paras 45–52.

[110] Case C-402/05 P *Kadi and Al Barakaat International Foundation v Council and Commission* EU:C:2008:461, paras 281–94. G De Búrca, 'The European Court of Justice and the International Legal Order After Kadi' (2010) 51 *Harvard Journal of International Law* 1.

[111] Case C-4/73 *Nold*, EU:C:1974:51, para 13: 'in safeguarding these rights, the Court is bound to draw inspiration from constitutional traditions common to the Member States, and it cannot therefore uphold measures which are incompatible with fundamental rights recognized and protected by the Constitutions of those States'.

[112] In the wake of *Nold*, see Case C-44/79 *Hauer* EU:C:1979:290, where the Court of Justice, at para 15, developed the idea further by stating that 'fundamental rights form an integral part of the general principles of the law, the observance of which it ensures; that in safeguarding those rights, the Court is bound to draw inspiration from constitutional traditions common to the Member States, so that measures which are incompatible with the fundamental rights recognized by the constitutions of those States are unacceptable in the [Union]; and that, similarly, international treaties for the protection of human rights on which the Member States have collaborated or of which they are signatories, can supply guidelines which should be followed within the framework of [Union] law'.

situation led the Court of Justice to seek inspiration in the practices and constitutional sources of the Member States.

The constitutional traditions common to the Member States do not impose on the Court of Justice a minimum common denominator of protection. On the contrary, the case law shows that the constitutional traditions serve as a useful reference, an *à la carte* offer of sorts, from which the Court of Justice derives the necessary indications before determining its own criteria. This is why it is not uncommon for a judgment to regard the protection afforded to a right in some Member States as more relevant than that afforded in others.[113] The Court of Justice oversees the common constitutional traditions to find the most appropriate references that best suit the objectives of the Union, but does not treat them as a safety net providing a minimum level of protection of fundamental rights.[114]

The entry into force of the Charter has somewhat diminished the inspirational role of the constitutional traditions shared by Member States. However, this does not mean that national legal sources are irrelevant to the development of fundamental rights within Union law. Although not explicitly reflected in its decisions, the Court of Justice relies heavily on comparative law research conducted by the institution's Research and Documentation Directorate.[115] New general principles continue to emerge from the case law, such as the principle of legality of taxation, which is not provided for in the Charter but was confirmed as part of Union law in *Fiat Chrysler* in 2022.[116] Furthermore, Article 4(2) TEU imposes a duty on the Union to respect the national identity of the Member States. This duty can include the protection of rights of cultural, historical, or social significance to one or more Member States. The constitutional courts of the Member States are not inclined to relinquish their role as guarantors of fundamental rights. This reality compels the Court of Justice to develop constructive interpretations that must find an alignment between the objectives of Union law and the constitutional traditions of the Member States. Although the role of the constitutional traditions has evolved, they continue to hold a prominent position in the interpretation of the Union's fundamental rights.

4. The Charter of Fundamental Rights of the European Union

On 1 December 2009, the Charter of Fundamental Rights of the European Union entered into force. Although the Charter is formally detached from the Treaties, Article 6(1) TEU states that the Union recognises the rights, freedoms, and principles set out in the Charter, 'which shall have the same legal value as the Treaties'.

The Charter was originally drafted and adopted by a Convention and solemnly proclaimed by the European Parliament, the Council, and the Commission on 7 December 2000. In that

[113] See, inter alia, Case C-550/07 *Akzo Nobel Chemicals and Akcros Chemicals v Commission* EU:C:2010:229 (professional secrecy of *in-house lawyers*); Case C-112/00 *Schmidberger* EU:C:2003:333 (fundamental rights to freedom of expression and freedom of peaceful assembly); and Joined Cases C-120/06 P and C-121/06 P *FIAMM* EU:C:2008:476, paras 172–73 (right to property and non-contractual liability of the Union for lawful acts); Case C-42/17 *MAS* EU:C:2017:936, para 57 (principle of legality of criminal offences and penalties); Case C-64/16 *Associação Sindical dos Juízes Portugueses* EU:C:2018:117, para 35 (effective judicial protection); and Case C-505/19 *WS and Bundesrepublik Deutschland* EU:C:2021:376, para 70 (*ne bis in idem*).

[114] S Prechal and S Peers, 'Article 52: Scope of Guaranteed Rights' in S Peers, T Hervey, J Kenner and A Ward, *The EU Charter of Fundamental Rights. A Commentary* (Beck-Hart-Nomos, 2014) 1490–91.

[115] The reports available from 2019 onwards are available on the website of the Court of Justice: *https://curia.europa.eu/jcms/jcms/p1_2170124/en*.

[116] Joined Cases C-885/19 P and C-898/19 P *Fiat Chrysler Finance Europe and Ireland v Commission* EU:C:2022:859, para 97.

same year, during the negotiations that led to the Treaty of Nice, the Member States failed to reach agreement on the Charter's binding nature, but later decided to include it as Part II of the Treaty establishing a Constitution for Europe. This failed initiative was later incorporated into the Lisbon Treaty, which adopted the current wording of Article 6(1) TEU, a provision that came into force on 1 December 2009.

The Charter was published in the C Series of the *Official Journal of the European Union*, separate from the Treaties.[117] In addition, Protocol No 30 contains specific provisions regarding the applicability of the Charter in Poland, to which reference will be made below.

4.1. Content

4.1.1. Structure

The Charter comprises a Preamble, seven Titles, and 54 Articles. Titles I and II, referring respectively to 'Dignity' and 'Freedoms', align with what are sometimes described as the first generation of fundamental rights, which are found in most of the constitutions of the Member States, as well as in the ECHR. Titles III and IV, focusing respectively on 'Equality' and 'Solidarity', address the new generation of fundamental rights, such as the fundamental right to the environment, as well as socioeconomic rights included in the European Social Charter. Title V, concerning 'Citizenship', reiterates the rights already established in the TFEU that comprise the status of Union citizenship. Title VI is dedicated to 'Justice', providing a range of procedural guarantees, primarily (but not exclusively) in criminal proceedings.

Finally, Title VII of the Charter refers to the 'General provisions governing the interpretation and application of the Charter'. Articles 51–54 contain the provisions that outline the terms under which the Charter is to be applied by the Union and the Member States, as well as the conditions to be fulfilled by right-holders when invoking the Charter. Given the significance of Title VII, the following sections will focus on its content and the interpretation provided thus far by the Court of Justice.

4.1.2. 'Rights' and 'Principles'

Article 52(5) of the Charter introduces a distinction between fundamental rights, separating them into 'rights' and 'principles' and conferring a specific role on the latter:

> The provisions of this Charter which contain principles may be implemented by legislative and executive acts taken by institutions, bodies, offices and agencies of the Union, and by acts of Member States when they are implementing Union law, in the exercise of their respective powers. They shall be judicially cognisable only in the interpretation of such acts and in the ruling on their legality.

The rationale for this distinction lies in the concern of some Member States that certain socioeconomic rights outlined in Titles III and IV could impose a significant financial burden on national treasuries.[118] The risk that a broad interpretation of, for example, the fundamental right to the environment (Article 37 of the Charter), or to social security and social assistance (Article 34 of the Charter), would ultimately condition the policies of the Member States in these areas, or result in exorbitant fiscal obligations, led to the creation of a separate category of fundamental rights, labelled as 'principles'.

Unfortunately, the drafters of the Charter did not specify which provisions contain rights and which contain principles. Only the Explanations to the Charter identify some provisions

[117] Charter of Fundamental Rights of the European Union [2012] *OJ* C326/391.

[118] G Braibant, *La Charte des droits fondamentaux de l'Union européenne* (Seuil, 2001) 252.

as containing principles, but such references are not exhaustive, and the categorisation of many fundamental rights remains unresolved to this day. According to the Explanations, the following provisions serve as examples of principles:

- the right to the integrity of the person, including the right to free and informed consent and the prohibition of eugenic practices (Article 3(2) of the Charter);
- the rights of the elderly (Article 25 of the Charter);
- the integration of persons with disabilities (Article 26 of the Charter);
- health care (Article 35 of the Charter);
- environmental protection (Article 37 of the Charter).

The Explanations also indicate that, in certain instances, a provision of the Charter may encompass elements that derive from both a right and a principle. In this regard, the Explanations provide three examples:

- *Equality between women and men*. In Article 23 of the Charter, the first paragraph contains a right (equality between men and women), while the second paragraph sets out a principle (the maintenance or adoption of measures entailing specific advantages in favour of the under-represented sex).
- *Family life and professional life*. Article 33 of the Charter states that the first paragraph contains a principle (legal, economic and social protection of the family), while the second paragraph enumerates several rights (protection against dismissal on grounds of maternity, the right to paid maternity leave, or parental leave upon the birth or adoption of a child).
- *Social security and social assistance*. In Article 34 of the Charter, the first and second paragraphs establish a right (access to social security benefits and social services, and the right to non-discrimination in cases of free movement), while the third paragraph contains a principle (guaranteeing a dignified existence to all those who do not have sufficient resources).

The Court of Justice has thus far refrained from providing comprehensive criteria to distinguish between rights and principles. To date, only the judgments in *AMS*, *Plamaro*, and *Glatzel* provide some indications in this regard, confirming that a 'principle', in order to be fully effective, requires further normative development by Union or national law.[119] In *Glätzel*, when interpreting the scope of Article 26 of the Charter (which was already characterised as a principle in the Explanations), the Court of Justice added the following reasoning:

> In order for that article to be fully effective, it must be given more specific expression in European Union or national law. Accordingly, that article cannot by itself confer on individuals a subjective right which they may invoke as such.[120]

Article 51(1) of the Charter provides that, on the one hand, rights must be 'respected' by the Union and by the Member States. On the other hand, the principles must be 'observed' by the Union and by the Member States, which must also 'promote [their] application . . . in accordance with their respective powers and respecting the limits of the powers conferred on it in the Treaties'.

[119] *Association de Médiation Sociale* (n 19) para 45: 'It is therefore clear from the wording of Article 27 of the Charter that, for this article to be fully effective, it must be given more specific expression in European or national law'. In the same vein, see Case C-196/23 *Plamaro* EU:C:2024:596, paras 49–51.

[120] Case C-356/12 *Glatzel* EU:C:2014:350, para 78.

Further clarity is provided in Article 52(5) of the Charter, which specifies the legal effects of principles. Under this provision, principles play two roles:

- *They support the interpretation of Union law and national law that implements Union law.* Consequently, there is an obligation to interpret Union and national law (where Union law applies) in conformity with the principles enshrined in the Charter.
- *They serve as a parameter for reviewing the validity of Union law and national law that implements Union law.* Article 52(5) of the Charter emphasises that principles may also be invoked in a court or tribunal 'in the ruling on their legality.' In *Glätzel*, the Court of Justice appeared to limit this second role of principles by indicating that, in order to function as a parameter of validity for Union acts, the principles must be sufficiently specific not to require additional normative development. This requirement eliminates any useful role of principles as parameters of validity for Union acts, as it imposes the need for additional rules that will ultimately act as the parameters of validity, not the principle.[121]

In contrast to principles, Charter rights can be directly invoked by their holders against the Union and the Member States, without the need for any additional normative development and without limiting their role to the interpretation or review of the validity of Union acts, or Member State acts that implement Union law. Rights can be invoked to compel the Union or a Member State to provide certain services or to refrain from engaging in specific conduct. However, the full direct invocability of rights is available only in cases where Union law is applicable, as will be explained below in section. 4.2.2. This requirement is particularly important for Member States, which are bound by the Charter only when they are implementing Union law.

4.1.3. The Interpretative Value of the Explanations of the Charter

Article 6(1), third paragraph TEU states that the rights, freedoms and principles in the Charter are to be interpreted 'with due regard to the explanations referred to in the Charter, that set out the sources of those provisions'. The explanations are also mentioned in the Charter itself, in Article 52(7), which provides that the 'explanations drawn up as a way of providing guidance in the interpretation of this Charter shall be given due regard by the courts of the Union and of the Member States'.

The Explanations were originally drafted by the Praesidium of the first Convention that elaborated the Charter in 1999-2000 and were subsequently updated by the Praesidium of the Convention on the Future of Europe, clarifying the sources of inspiration for each fundamental right. To limit the courts' discretion when interpreting the Charter, the Explanations were assigned a subtle yet significant legal value as a tool solely for interpretative purposes. However, the influence of the Explanations has proved rather limited, as their content does not offer much clarity on the scope and substance of individual Charter provisions, often limited to referencing the corresponding provisions of the European Convention on Human Rights or the European Social Charter upon which the provisions are based.[122]

[121] N Lazzerini, '(Some of) the Fundamental Rights Granted by the Charter May Be a Source of Obligations for Private Parties: *AMS*' (2014) 51 *Common Market Law Review* 907.

[122] On the origin and role of the Explanations, see J-P Jacqué, 'The Explanations Relating to the Charter of Fundamental Rights of the European Union' in S Peers, T Hervey, J Kenner and A Ward, *The EU Charter of Fundamental Rights. A Commentary* (Beck-Hart-Nomos, 2014); and J Ziller, 'Le fabuleux destin des explications relative à la Charte des droits fondamentaux' in *A Collection in Honour of Jean-Paul Jacqué* (Dalloz, 2010).

The Court of Justice tends to make limited use of the Explanations. Since the entry into force of the Charter, it has been relatively uncommon to find substantial references to the Explanations in the case law on fundamental rights.[123] Furthermore, the Court of Justice has on occasion departed from the content of the Explanations: in the case of *Spasic*, it rejected a limitation on the fundamental right of ne bis in idem (Article 50 of the Charter), despite the explanations openly recognising such a restriction. Nothing stopped the Court of Justice from reviewing the legality of the restriction and ultimately contradicting the terms of the Explanations, a result that has inevitably diminished their interpretative value.[124]

4.1.4. Protocol No 30 on Poland

In the negotiations leading to the Lisbon Treaty, two Member States – the United Kingdom and Poland – secured an opt-out from the Charter, now reflected in Protocol No 30. Following the United Kingdom's withdrawal from the Union on 31 January 2020, the Protocol applies only to Poland. Despite the original intentions of the two Member States, Protocol No 30 does not introduce a *lex specialis* but merely reaffirms some safeguards already present in the wording of the Charter. For example, the Protocol emphasises that the Charter does not extend the competences of the Union, a concern already expressed in Article 51(2) of the Charter.[125] While Protocol No 30 insists that the principles of the Charter set out in Title IV, on 'Solidarity', can only be invoked before national courts to the extent that there is national implementing legislation, this requirement is already encompassed in Article 52(5) of the Charter.

The case law of the Court of Justice has confirmed the limited practical value of Protocol No 30. In *NS*, the Court of Justice stated that the Protocol 'does not intend to exempt the Republic of Poland . . . from the obligation to comply with the provisions of the Charter or to prevent a court of one of those Member States from ensuring compliance with those provisions'.[126] Referring to the case of Poland, the Court of Justice has stated that the Protocol 'does not call into question the applicability of the Charter in Poland, nor is it intended to exempt the Republic of Poland from the obligation to comply with the provisions of the Charter'.[127]

4.2. *Subjects*

4.2.1. Holders of Fundamental Rights

The Charter grants fundamental rights to a wide variety of persons and entities, but their effects depend on the content of each fundamental right. In line with other human rights instruments, the Charter includes a group of universal, inalienable, and non-renounceable fundamental rights that any individual can invoke before any public authority, irrespective of

[123] However, it is not an entirely exceptional practice, as can be seen, inter alia, in Case C-617/10 *Akerberg Fransson* EU:C:2013:105, para 20; *Association de Médiation Sociale* (n 19) para 46; Case C-334/12 RX-II *Arango Jaramillo* EU:C:2013:134, para 42; Case C-601/15 PPU *JN* EU:C:2016:84, para 47; Case C-294/16 PPU *JZ* EU:C:2016:610, para 50; and Case C-490/20 *VMA and Stolichna obshtina, rayon 'Pancharevo'* EU:C:2021:1008, para 63.

[124] Case C-129/14 PPU *Spasic* EU:C:2014:586, paras 54–55.

[125] See A Arnull, 'Protocol (No 30) on the Application of the Charter of Fundamental Rights of the European Union to Poland and the United Kingdom' in S Peers, T Hervey, J Kenner and A Ward, *The EU Charter of Fundamental Rights. A Commentary* (Beck-Hart-Nomos, 2014); C Barnard, 'The "Opt-Out" for the UK and Poland from the Charter of Fundamental Rights: Triumph of Rhetoric Over Reality?' in S Griller and J Ziller (eds), *The Lisbon Treaty* (Springer, 2008); G Guliyeva and M Wyrzykowski, 'Protocol (No 30) on the Application of the Charter of Fundamental Rights of the European Union to Poland and to the United Kingdom' in H-J Blanke and S Mangiameli (eds), *The Treaty on European Union (TEU): A Commentary* (Springer, 2013).

[126] *NS and Others* (n 91).

[127] Case C-619/18 *Commission v Poland* EU:C:2019:531, para 53.

nationality, residence, or age. This applies to the fundamental right to life and the fundamental right to integrity of the person, the beneficiaries of which are *all* natural persons.

However, there is a significant number of fundamental rights whose holders are confined to specific groups, including the following:

- *Citizens of the Union*: with the exception of the fundamental right to good administration (Article 41), all rights under Title V ('Citizenship') are held exclusively by Union citizens who possess the nationality of a Member State. In exceptional circumstances, the case law of the Court of Justice has allowed for the extension of these rights, such as the fundamental right to vote and to stand as a candidate, to nationals of third countries with close historical or cultural links to a Member State.[128]
- *Workers*: The Charter grants fundamental rights to 'workers', although without defining the concept, in Articles 27–28 and 30–31.
- *Minors:* the Charter provides for a set of fundamental rights addressed exclusively to 'children' (Articles 24 and 32) but also to 'young persons' (Article 32).
- *The elderly*: the fundamental right of the elderly to lead a dignified and independent life, as well as to participate in social and cultural life, is recognised in Article 25.
- *Persons with disabilities*: the Charter recognises and respects the rights of persons with disabilities to benefit from measures designed to ensure their independence and social and occupational integration (Article 26).

Although the Charter refers to legal persons in only a few provisions, in practice they are holders of the majority of fundamental rights contained in the Charter.[129] To date, legal persons have been recognised as holders of fundamental rights, such as privacy,[130] property,[131] freedom of enterprise,[132] freedom of information,[133] freedom of collective action,[134] and good administration,[135] as well as procedural fundamental rights, such as the right to a fair trial.[136] However, the Court of Justice has also stated that the scope of fundamental rights, when applied to legal persons, may be limited depending on the content and purpose of the fundamental right in question.[137]

The Charter also encompasses fundamental rights that Member States are entitled to invoke and rely on, particularly concerning procedural matters. In the case of Spain v Council, the Court of Justice ruled that a Member State is entitled to rely on Article 41 of the Charter, which provides for the fundamental right to good administration before the institutions, bodies, agencies, and offices of the Union.[138]

[128] *Spain v UK* (n 50) and *Eman Sevinger* (n 50).

[129] See P Oliver, 'Companies and their Fundamental Rights: A Comparative Perspective' (2015) 64 *International and Comparative Law Quarterly* 661.

[130] Case C-92/09 *Schecke* EU:C:2010:662.

[131] Case C-275/06 *Promusicae* EU:C:2008:54, para 61ff.

[132] Case C-426/11 *Alemo-Herron* EU:C:2013:521, paras 31–35.

[133] Case C-260/89 *ERT* EU:C:1991:254, para 44.

[134] *Viking* (n 100) and *Laval* (n 100).

[135] Case C-213/13 *Impresa Pizzarotti* EU:C:2014:2067.

[136] Case C-41/90 *Höfner* EU:C:1991:161, para 21; and Case C-279/09 *DEB* EU:C:2010:811, para 29.

[137] *Schecke* (n 130) paras 45–53.

[138] Case C-521/15 *Spain v Council* EU:C:2017:982, para 89: 'Without adopting a position as to whether a Member State may be regarded as or equated with a "person" within the meaning of that provision, and can on that basis rely on the right that it lays down, which the Council and the Commission dispute, it should be pointed out that that right reflects a general principle of EU law . . . which may be relied upon by the Member States and in the light of which the contested decision should therefore be assessed.'

4.2.2. Addressees

Article 51(1) of the Charter, in its first sentence, enumerates the addressees of the Charter's fundamental rights and states that 'the provisions of this Charter are addressed to the institutions, bodies, offices and agencies of the Union with due regard for the principle of subsidiarity and to the Member States only when they are implementing Union law'. Despite its apparent simplicity, this provision remains one of the most complex and contested provisions of the Charter. Although it refers to two categories of addressees (the Union and the Member States), it does not clarify whether this is a closed enumeration of addressees, nor does it specify the precise connection with Union law necessary to invoke the Charter, particularly as regards the Member States.

4.2.2.1. Institutions, Bodies, Offices and Agencies of the Union

The Union is the first addressee of the fundamental rights guaranteed in the Charter. Article 51(1) does not refer to the Union in general terms, but specifically to the 'institutions, bodies, offices and agencies' of the Union, opening the door to two conflicting interpretations: the provision suggests that the Charter applies to a smaller number of right holders than the Union itself, tacitly recognising the existence of areas of Union action in which the Charter does not apply; or it establishes the opposite, an exhaustive enumeration of Union components intended to extend the Charter to *all* Union action, whether conducted by an institution, a body, or any other administrative structure through which the Union typically operates. The Court of Justice has not directly addressed this issue to date, but some indications suggest a preference for the first option.

On one hand, there are areas of Union action that fall outside the scope of the Charter, as confirmed in the case of *Pringle*.[139] The decision of the Member States to establish the European Stability Mechanism through an international treaty outside the framework of the Union placed this newly created entity beyond the scope of Union law, including the Union institutions operating under that agreement. It follows from the judgment in *Pringle* that, to the extent that an 'institution, body, office or agency' of the Union acts at the request of the Member States in an area not governed by Union law, those actions are not subject to the Charter.[140] This outcome is questionable because the Union institutions may take decisions that directly affect individuals, including their fundamental rights, yet remain beyond scrutiny under the Charter. The experience of the financial assistance programmes during the 2008–2015 financial crisis demonstrates that the Union's involvement in the negotiation and implementation of such programmes can significantly impact the fundamental rights of individuals.[141]

In response to these criticisms, the Court of Justice recalibrated its position and confirmed the applicability of the Charter to the Union's institutions even when acting in the context of instruments adopted outside the Union framework. For instance, in *Ledra Advertising*, the Court of Justice ruled that the Charter applies to the actions of the Commission linked to the

[139] As confirmed by the Court of Justice in Case C-370/12 *Pringle* EU:C:2012:756, para 180, referring to the decision of several Member States to conclude an international treaty *inter se*: 'It must be observed that the Member States are not implementing Union law, within the meaning of Article 51(1) of the Charter, when they establish a stability mechanism such as the ESM where . . . the EU and FEU Treaties do not confer any specific competence on the Union to establish such a mechanism'.

[140] ibid.

[141] See, inter alia, Case C-128/12 *Sindicato dos Bancários* EU:C:2013:149; Case C-665/13 *Sindicato Nacional dos Profissionais de Seguros e Afins* EU:C:2014:2327); and Case C-8/15 P *Ledra Advertising* EU:C:2016:290, Opinion of AG Wahl; C Kilpatrick and B De Witte (eds), 'Social Rights in Times of Crisis in the Eurozone: The Role of Fundamental Rights' Challenges' EUI WP, Department of Law, 2014/05.

implementation of a financial assistance programme for a Member State. The Court held that, insofar as the Commission remains the guardian of the Treaties when agreeing to and signing the terms of a Memorandum of Understanding that outlines the conditions attached to the programme, it retains that same role when deciding to *refuse* agreement to it. Consequently, the Commission's decision to sign and implement the Memorandum of Understanding is subject to the fundamental rights outlined in the Charter.[142]

On the other hand, the case law has held that the Charter does not apply where an act has not been adopted by an institution, body, office, or agency of the Union, nor by a Member State implementing Union law. This was the case in *Livimaa Lihaveis*, where the Court of Justice was called to review a manual implementing the Estonia–Latvia cross-border operational programme, drawn up jointly by the Estonian and Latvian authorities, based, inter alia, on Regulation No 1083/2006 and Regulation No 1080/2006. Although the manual was not formally enacted by the Commission but by the programme's 'monitoring committee', comprised of the Estonian and Latvian authorities, it was an act based on Union rules. Despite the fact that its author was not a Member State but an ad hoc entity created by two Member States implementing Union law, the Court of Justice determined that it was not an act adopted by an institution, body, office, or agency of the Union.[143]

This restrictive reading of the first indent of Article 51(1) is countered by a considerably more expansive interpretation of its second indent, which concerns the applicability of the Charter in the Member States. The fact that the Charter does not apply to certain spheres of Union activity may be justified if, at some point, the harmful conduct can be finally attributed to a public authority of a Member State. The key objective is to avoid any situation of immunity in the protection of fundamental rights. Viewed from the individual's perspective, the question is not so much whether the respondent is the Union or a Member State, but whether there is effective legal protection in both substantive and procedural terms when addressing alleged violations of fundamental rights. As explained in the following section, the case law of the Court of Justice has offered a broad interpretation of the second indent of Article 51(1) of the Charter, to ensure that no area of public action remains immune to the protection of fundamental rights.

Despite the efforts of the case law to achieve this goal, the reality is that no perfect solution is in sight, as there remain areas where the full and effective protection of fundamental rights is too disconnected from the practical reality faced by individuals. Consider, for example, the case of the Unified Patent Court, a body that cannot be held liable for a breach of the Charter, deferring any remedial actions to a rather implausible scenario in which all signatory Member States are held jointly liable.[144] For someone seeking redress, this is an unrealistic scenario, far removed from the practical reality of everyday justice.

4.2.2.2. Member States Implementing Union Law

In addition to the 'institutions, bodies, offices and agencies of the Union', the second category of addressees of the Charter are the Member States, but 'only when they are implementing Union law'. The second indent of Article 51(1) of the Charter codifies well-established case

[142] Case C-8/15 P *Ledra Advertising* EU:C:2016:701, para 59: 'Consequently, the Commission, as it itself acknowledged in reply to a question asked at the hearing, retains, within the framework of the ESM Treaty, its role of guardian of the Treaties as resulting from Article 17(1) TEU, so that it should refrain from signing a memorandum of understanding whose consistency with EU law it doubts.'

[143] Case C-562/12 *Liivimaa Lihaveis* EU:C:2014:2229, para 58.

[144] See Art 22 of the Unified Patent Court Agreement, following the requirements set out in Opinion 1/09 EU:C:2011:123, para 88. See also S Peers, 'The Constitutional Implications of the EU Patent' (2011) 7 *European Constitutional Law Review* 229.

law of the Court of Justice dating back to the 1980s and early 1990s, which confirmed that the Member States are bound to the Union's fundamental rights while implementing Union law.[145] Whenever Member States find themselves in this situation, ie complying with the obligations set forth in the rules of Union law, not only do those rules apply to the case, but so do the fundamental rights enshrined in Union law. This scenario, which some authors have described as the 'agency situation',[146] is referred to in the second indent of Article 51(1) which states that Member States are subject to the Charter 'only when they are implementing Union law'.

The inclusion of the adverb 'only' was a novelty introduced by the Charter, which was not reflected in the prior case law of the Court of Justice. This textual innovation gave rise to a scholarly movement advocating for a narrow interpretation of the second indent of Article 51(1) and the applicability of the Charter in the Member States. Some Advocates General also supported this strict interpretation, although the Court of Justice was not inclined to follow it. In *Akerberg Fransson*, the *leading case* on the matter, the Court of Justice stated as follows:

> Since the fundamental rights guaranteed by the Charter must therefore be complied with where national legislation falls within the scope of European Union law, situations cannot exist which are covered in that way by European Union law without those fundamental rights being applicable. The applicability of European Union law entails applicability of the fundamental rights guaranteed by the Charter.[147]

By emphasising that 'situations cannot exist' in which Union law is applicable in the absence of the Charter, the Court of Justice adopted a broad interpretation of the scope of application of the Charter in the Member States.[148] This approach guarantees an extensive outreach of the Union's fundamental rights, but it also presents several practical challenges.

If a Member State transposes a Union directive through a parliamentary statute, followed by administrative implementing measures adopted by regional or local national authorities, does the Charter apply to the latter? On a strict reading, one might argue that the implementation of Union law pertains solely to the transposition of the Union directive through the parliamentary statute. A strict interpretation would conclude that the only authority in the Member State implementing Union law is Parliament. However, the Court of Justice has taken a broader approach, ruling that administrative implementing acts enforcing a statute transposing a Union directive also constitute an implementation of Union law under the second indent of Article 51(1) of the Charter.[149]

The fact that national legislation applicable to a case was not adopted specifically to transpose a directive or to implement a decision of a Union institution does not prevent an individual from relying on the Charter.[150] As long as the national legislation plays a role in the implementation or enforcement of Union obligations, it is regarded as a case of implementation of Union law pursuant to Article 51(1) of the Charter.

If a Union regulation or directive grants Member States discretion to choose between different measures, or confers the power to introduce more protective measures than those required by Union law, does the exercise of those powers constitute an implementation of Union law, to which the Charter applies? According to the Court of Justice, the answer is in the affirmative,

[145] See, inter alia, Case C-36/75 *Rutili* EU:C:1975:137; Case C-118/75 *Watson* EU:C:1976:106; Case C-222/84 *Johnston* EU:C:1986:206; Case C-5/88 *Wachauf* EU:C:1989:321; and Case C-20/00 *Booker Aquaculture* EU:C:2003:397.

[146] JHH Weiler, *The Constitution of Europe* (Cambridge University Press, 1999) 120ff.

[147] *Akerberg Fransson* (n 89) para 21.

[148] See K Lenaerts and JA Gutiérrez-Fons, 'The Charter in the EU Constitutional Edifice' in S Peers, T Hervey, J Kenner and A Ward, *The EU Charter of Fundamental Rights. A Commentary* (Beck-Hart-Nomos, 2014) 1567–68.

[149] *Booker Aquaculture* (n 145) para 88.

[150] Case C-185/23 *protectus s. r. o.* EU:C:2024:657, para 65.

insofar as the exercise of such power is the necessary consequence of the obligation to implement an obligation of Union law.[151]

If a Union regulation or directive imposes a broad and unclear obligation affecting a subject matter governed only in ambiguous terms, the question arises as to whether a Member State, when complying with these provisions, is implementing Union law. For example, if a Union directive harmonising a tax introduces a duty on Member States to 'impose other obligations which they deem necessary for the correct collection of the tax and for the prevention of evasion', are those additional obligations an implementation of Union law? The case law of the Court of Justice responds to this question affirmatively.[152]

The notion of implementation also applies when Member States perform obligations arising from an international agreement concluded by the Union, which forms an integral part of Union law from its entry into force. In such cases, the Member States must be considered to be implementing Union law, within the meaning of Article 51(1) of the Charter.[153]

As can be seen, the Member States will find it challenging to identify areas of action that are entirely outside the scope of the Charter. Therefore, it is unsurprising to hear criticism of the expansive approach adopted by the Court of Justice's case law. Notably, the German Federal Constitutional Court has expressed serious concerns about the correctness of the broad interpretation of the second indent of Article 51(1) as applied by the Court of Justice in cases such as *Akerberg Fransson*.[154]

These criticisms seem to have been acknowledged to some extent by the Court of Justice. In the years following *Akerberg Fransson*, the Court of Justice appeared to recalibrate its stance on the second indent of Article 51(1) of the Charter. In a series of judgments and orders issued shortly after the judgment in *Akerberg Fransson*, the case law reiterated the existence of limitations on the applicability of the Charter in the Member States, reflecting a subtle retreat towards a stricter approach on the matter.

For example, if a Union directive is only applicable ratione materiae to workers with fixed-term contracts, a worker with an indefinite contract cannot invoke the directive and, as a result, is not entitled to invoke the Charter.[155] The same applies to situations with a diffuse or distant link to the relevant rules of Union law, as was the case in *Torralbo Marcos*: the connection to Union law was too indirect to trigger the protection of the Charter, as the applicant sought to justify a link with a fund governed by Union law in a case where the duty under national law to pay court fees was contested.[156] The Court of Justice ruled that the connection with Union law was excessively vague and too distant to justify the applicability of the

[151] See, inter alia, *NS and Others* (n 91) para 68, as well as Case C-105/03 *Pupino* EU:C:2005:386, paras 55–56; and Case C-426/11 *Alemo-Herron and Others* EU:C:2013:521, paras 23 and 36.

[152] See, inter alia, Case C-105/14 *Taricco* EU:C:2015:555, where the Court of Justice recognised the *obligation* derived from Union law for Member States to adopt national measures of criminal law to ensure the proper enforcement of Union law, at para 39: 'Although the Member States have freedom to choose the applicable penalties — which may take the form of administrative penalties, criminal penalties or a combination of the two — in order to ensure that all VAT revenue is collected and, in so doing, that the financial interests of the European Union are protected in accordance with the provisions of Directive 2006/112 and Article 325 TFEU . . . , criminal penalties may nevertheless be essential to combat certain serious cases of VAT evasion in an effective and dissuasive manner.'

[153] Case C-66/18 *Commission v Hungary* (Higher education) EU:C:2020:792, paras 69 and 213; and Case C-655/21 *G. ST.T.* EU:C:2023:791, paras 40–46.

[154] Judgment of 24 April 2013 (1 BvR 1215/07). See F Fontanelli, 'Hic Sunt Nationes: The Elusive Limits of the EU Charter and the German Constitutional Watchdog: Court of Justice of the European Union: Judgment of 26 February 2013, Case C-617/10 Åklagaren v Hans Åkerberg Fransson' (2013) 9 *European Constitutional Law Review*.

[155] Case C-117/14 *Nisttahuz Poclava* EU:C:2015:60. See further references cited in D Sarmiento, 'Who's Afraid of the Charter? The Court of Justice, National Courts and the New Framework of Fundamental Rights Protection in Europe' (2013) 50 *Common Market Law Review* 1267, 1286–87.

[156] Case C-265/13 *Torralbo Marcos* EU:C:2014:187, paras 32–40.

Charter.[157] Similarly, in *TSN*, the Court of Justice ruled that the Charter does not apply to national rules that unilaterally extend the protection granted by a Union directive in the field of labour law.[158] In the same vein, the Charter is not applicable to a case intending to review the penalties imposed in the implementation of a direct tax, such as corporate tax, which is currently not subject to harmonisation under Union law, nor does its collection contribute to the Union's own resources.[159]

Despite these nuances, the current reality is that the scope of application of the Charter in the Member States is very broad and tends to expand over time. For example, the Court of Justice adopted an expansive approach in *Ledra Advertising* to confirm the applicability of the Charter when Member States are implementing financial assistance programmes, as was the case in *Florescu*[160] and *Associação Sindical dos Juízes Portugueses*.[161] The Charter also applies to criminal proceedings when the facts are connected to behaviours that are relevant for administrative penalties provided in a harmonised area of Union law.[162] Similarly, the existence of Union law instruments governing administrative cooperation among Member States in the field of taxation triggers the applicability of the Charter when a tax authority acts in response to a request for cooperation from another Member State.[163] In sum, the range of situations in which the Charter applies in the Member States is very broad, rejecting its application only in cases where there is an unequivocal lack of connection with Union law.

4.2.2.3. Individuals: the Horizontal Effect of the Charter

Article 51(1), when enumerating the addressees of the Charter, mentions the Union and the Member States. This approach reflects a traditional understanding of fundamental rights, viewed as prerogatives of the individual vis-a-vis public authorities alone. This position contrasts with the evolution of modern society, which has seen a transformation in the roles played by certain private actors, particularly by multinational corporations and technological giants, to the extent that some wield economic power or influence that may rival that of certain states or international organisations. Companies and organisations such as Google, FIFA or Amazon, or influential personalities such as Bill Gates or Elon Musk, can sway public opinion or influence policy decisions to an extent comparable to that of a sovereign state. Consequently, situations may arise in which fundamental rights are at stake in relationships between individuals, potentially leading to violations of fundamental rights by non-state actors. Most legal systems in European countries recognise this reality and confer a horizontal effect to fundamental rights in relations *inter privatos*, albeit with varying degrees and scope.

The wording of Article 51(1) raises the question of whether the Charter admits or excludes the horizontal effect of fundamental rights. Several Advocates General examined the matter and proposed conflicting interpretations,[164] until the Court of Justice took a position on the

[157] See Case C-498/12 *Pedone* EU:C:2013:76, paras 14–15; Case C-499/12 *Gentile* EU:C:2013:77, paras 14–15; Case C-555/12 *Loreti ea* EU:C:2013:174, paras 17–18; Case C-73/13 *T* EU:C:2013:299, paras 13–14; Joined Cases C-488/12, C-491/12 and C-526/12 EU:C:2013:703, paras 16–18; Case C-224/13 *Lorrai* EU:C:2013:750, paras 13–14; and Joined Cases C-614/12 and C-10/13 *Dutka et Sajtos* EU:C:2014:30, paras 14–16.

[158] Joined Case C-609 and 610/17 *TSN* EU:C:2019:981, para 53. See also Case C-257/21 *Coca-Cola European Partners Deutschland GmbH* EU:C:2022:529, paras 42–52.

[159] Case C-363/20 *CTMs* EU:C:2022:21, para 38.

[160] Case C-258/14 *Florescu and Others* EU:C:2017:448, para 48.

[161] Case C-64/16 *Associação Sindical dos Juízes Portugueses* EU:C:2018:117, para 40.

[162] Case C-524/15 *Menci* EU:C:2018:197; Joined Cases C-596 and 597/16 EU:C:2018:192 and Case C-537/17 *Garlsson* EU:C:2018:193.

[163] Case C-682/15 *Berlioz Investment Fund* EU:C:2017:373, paras 33–42; and Case C-437/19 *État luxembourgeois* EU:C:2021:953, paras 88–92.

[164] D Leczykiewicz, 'Horizontal Application of the Charter of Fundamental Rights' (2013) 38 *European Law Review*.

matter. In *AMS*, the Court of Justice confirmed the applicability of Articles 21 and 27 of the Charter in disputes between private parties, although it did not do so in explicit and clear terms.[165]

The case law of the Court of Justice acknowledges that certain fundamental rights can have effects between individuals, depending on the nature and objectives of those rights. For the time being, it appears that social labour rights fall into this category,[166] as does the prohibition of discrimination concerning particularly vulnerable groups.[167] Similarly, the fact that one individual wields power over another can be a decisive feature: if an individual holds a position of power equivalent to that of a public authority, fundamental rights can be invoked. This applies to private entities such as trade unions, sports federations, and public service concessionaires.[168] The Court of Justice had ruled that such private entities are bound by the Union's rules on free movement and the principle of non-discrimination. Following the entry into force of the Charter, this trend was extended to fundamental rights in relations among private parties.[169] In *Egenberger*, the Court of Justice, ruling on the effects of Article 21 of the Charter (non-discrimination), stated as follows:

> The prohibition of all discrimination on grounds of religion or belief is mandatory as a general principle of EU law. That prohibition, which is laid down in Article 21(1) of the Charter, is sufficient in itself to confer on individuals a right which they may rely on as such in disputes between them in a field covered by EU law . . .
>
> As regards its mandatory effect, Article 21 of the Charter is no different, in principle, from the various provisions of the founding Treaties prohibiting discrimination on various grounds, even where the discrimination derives from contracts between individuals.[170]

Reference should be made to situations in which conflicts arise between different fundamental rights held by private individuals. These cases differ from the standard situation of horizontal effect, where one individual holds a position of power equivalent to that of a public authority. In conflicts between fundamental rights held by private parties, the Court of Justice employs a balancing test to ensure that all rights and interests are considered. Various examples of this practice are found in conflicts between the fundamental right to property and intellectual property rights,[171] between the fundamental right to freedom of the media and the fundamental right to privacy,[172] or between the fundamental right to an effective remedy and the fundamental right to religious freedom,[173] to name only a few examples.

Finally, it should be noted that Article 47 of the Charter, which enshrines the fundamental right to an effective legal remedy, can be invoked in disputes between private parties, particularly

[165] Case C-176/12 *Association de Médiation Sociale* EU:C:2013:491. The Court of Justice ruled on whether Art 27 of the Charter was applicable, but not the basis of the addressee of the provision (the employer of the appellant worker), but on the degree of clarity and precision of the wording of the provision. It can be argued that the judgment in *Association de Médiation Sociale* implicitly confirms the ability of the Charter to deploy horizontal effects between private parties. See more recently, in the same sense, Case C-196/23 *Plamaro* EU:C:2024:596, paras 49–51.

[166] See, for example, the right to collective action, as discussed in the cases of *Viking* (n 100) and *Laval* (n 100).

[167] Situations of discrimination on the grounds of sex in the field of employment, as was the case, inter alia, in Case C-43/75 *Defrenne* EU:C:1976:56.

[168] See, inter alia, Case C-36/74 *Walrave and Koch* EU:C:1974:140, para 17; Case C-13/76 *Donà* EU:C:1976:115, para 17; Case C-415/93 *Bosman* EU:C:1995:463:463, para 82; Joined Cases C-51/96 and C-191/97 *Deliège* EU:C:2000:199, para 47; Case C-281/98 *Angonese* EU:C:2000:296, para 31; and Case C-309/99 *Wouters and others* EU:C:2002:98.

[169] Case C-414/16 *Egenberger* EU:C:2018:257.

[170] *Egenberger* (n 169) paras 76–77. See also Case C-569 and 570/16 *Bauer* EU:C:2018:871, para 89; Case C-684/16 *Max-Planck-Gesellschaft zur Förderung der Wissenschaften eV* EU:C:2018:874, para 78; Case C-193/17 *Cresco Investigation* EU:C:2019:43, paras 77–78; and Case C-68/17 *IR* EU:C:2018:696, para 69.

[171] Case C-275/06 *Promusicae* EU:C:2008:54, para 64.

[172] Case C-633/22 *Real Madrid Club de Fútbol* EU:C:2024:843.

[173] *Egenberger* (n 169) para 78; and *IR* (n 170) para 69.

when the behaviour of one party makes it difficult or impossible for the other party to obtain legal redress in court. In *KL*,[174] the Court of Justice reviewed national legislation stipulating that an employer was not required to provide written reasons for the termination of a fixed-term employment contract with a notice period, although it was bound by such an obligation in the event of termination of an indefinite employment contract. The Court of Justice ruled that, in such instances, the national court hearing a dispute between individuals is required to ensure the judicial protection that individuals derive from Article 47 of the Charter, to the extent of setting aside the national rule to resolve the dispute.[175]

4.3. *Limitations and Justifications: the Principle of Proportionality*

In line with other instruments regarding the protection of fundamental rights, Article 52(1) allows for the possibility of limiting the exercise of the rights and freedoms recognised by the Charter in the following terms:

> Any limitation on the exercise of the rights and freedoms recognised by this Charter must be provided for by law and respect the essence of those rights and freedoms. Subject to the principle of proportionality, limitations may be made only if they are necessary and genuinely meet objectives of general interest recognised by the Union or the need to protect the rights and freedoms of others.

Limitations to fundamental rights of the Charter are lawful, provided that three requirements are met:

- They must be 'provided by law', a reference that primarily pertains to the Union's legislative acts and not to regulatory acts, unless the regulatory act adheres to the standards required by the case law of the European Court of Human Rights concerning rank and legality certainty.[176]
- The limitation must respect 'the essence' of the right or freedom concerned, the core content of the fundamental right which, if affected, would deprive the right of its substance to such an extent that it would be rendered meaningless. For example, if an authority were entitled to expropriate property without compensation in all circumstances, the right to property would lose its economic purpose and transform into a different, ineffective right that offers no protection for an individual's assets.[177] In such a case, the 'essence' of the fundamental right is undermined, making it unnecessary to verify whether the public authority has any justification to undertake such action.[178]

[174] Case C-715/20 *KL* EU:C:2024:139.

[175] ibid, paras 77–81.

[176] Case C-407/08 *Knauf Gips* EU:C:2010:389, para 91; Case C-274/99 P *Connolly* EU:C:2001:127, para 51; Case T-187/11 *Trabelsi* EU:T:2013:273, paras 84–117; and Case T-132/07 *Fuji* EU:T:2011:344, para 159. In this respect, see Case C-70/10 *Scarlett Extended* EU:C:2011:771, Opinion of AG Cruz Villalón, point 58. K Lenaerts, 'Exploring the Limits of the EU Charter of Fundamental Rights' (2012) 8 *European Constitutional Law Review* 389–91.

[177] On this matter, see Cases C-165/14 and C-304/14 *Rendón Marín and CS* EU:C:2016:75, Opinion of AG Szpunar, pts 128–32.

[178] Case C-362/14 *Schrems* EU:C:2015:650, paras 94–95; and Case C-311/18 *Schrems II* EU:C:2020:559, para 187. Another example of a restriction on the 'essence' of a fundamental right can be found in Case C-437/19 *État luxembourgeois* EU:C:2021:953, para 94, referring to the fundamental right to effective judicial protection of Art 47 of the Charter. According to the Court of Justice, this fundamental right includes among its 'essence' the right of its holder 'of accessing a court or tribunal with the power to ensure respect for the rights guaranteed to that person by EU law and, to that end, to consider all the issues of fact and of law that are relevant for resolving the case before it, without being compelled to infringe a legal rule or obligation or be subject to the penalty attached to that offence'. On the 'essence' of the Charter's fundamental rights, see M Brkan, 'The Essence of the Fundamental Rights to Privacy and Data Protection: Finding the Way Through the Maze of the CJEU's Constitutional Reasoning' (2019) 20 *German Law Journal 864*, and D Sarmiento, 'The Essential Content of EU Fundamental Rights' (2020) 4 *Quaderni costituzionali* 851.

- The limitation must pursue a legitimate objective and comply with the principle of proportionality, ensuring it meets the criteria of adequacy and necessity: the measure must be suitable to achieve its aims and be strictly necessary only to the extent that there are no alternatives available to accomplish the same aims with an equivalent degree of effectiveness.[179]

4.4. *Level of Protection*

In a legal system with multiple instruments and levels of protection for fundamental rights, it is crucial to clarify the rules governing the applicable level of protection in the resolution of individual cases, as well as the interaction among various legal instruments on fundamental rights protection in play. In Europe 29 systems of fundamental rights protection coexist within the same legal space and time: the Charter, the ECHR, and 27 national legal systems, each with its own constitutional protection of fundamental rights. When a court of law is called to resolve a case involving a fundamental right, three distinct sets of fundamental rights instruments must be considered: the Charter, the ECHR, and the national constitution. In such a complex setting, the '*crowded house*' to which Cruz Villalón has referred[180], Articles 52(3) and 53 of the Charter, along with the case law of the Court of Justice, aim to clarify the coordinated use of all instruments in resolving an individual case.

As a starting point, it should be emphasised that the Court of Justice has not adopted a simple binary criterion to resolve conflicts between fundamental rights instruments. In other words, Union law and the case law of the Court of Justice reject a conception of fundamental rights whereby each instrument operates separately within watertight compartments. Such clear-cut distribution in which only one instrument of fundamental rights applies to resolve a case was advocated by some national constitutional courts, and it has its advantages, providing clarity regarding the applicable standard in solving a case. However, the Court of Justice has rejected this approach and embraced what Daniel Thym describes as the 'fusion thesis', whereby, once a link with Union law is established, all three instruments of fundamental rights interact with each other simultaneously.[181] The first step in determining the role of each fundamental rights instrument is therefore not to identify which one alone is applicable, but rather which level of protection is relevant to the case. The instrument that provides the appropriate level of protection will be the fundamental right that resolves the case. Consequently, in applying the complex network of fundamental rights instruments currently in force in Europe, it is essential to focus on the rules that determine the level of protection applicable to a case. These criteria are enshrined in Article 52(3) and 53 of the Charter, as well as in the case law of the Court of Justice.

4.4.1. The Charter versus the ECHR

Article 52(3) of the Charter establishes the role of the ECHR as a standard of protection, establishing a common minimum level of fundamental rights protection within the Union. Where fundamental rights recognised by the Charter correspond to those guaranteed by the ECHR, the meaning and scope of the Charter rights must be at least equivalent to those laid down by the ECHR. However, is nothing to prevent the Charter from providing a higher level

[179] *Schecke* (114) paras 72–86; Case C-70/10 *Scarlet Extended* EU:C:2011:771, paras 44–52; Case C-468/10 and C-469/10 *ASNEF* EU:C:2011:777, paras 42–49; Case C-584/10 P *Commission and Others v Kadi* EU:C:2013:518, paras 101ff; Case C-300/11 *ZZ* EU:C:2013:363, paras 52ff; and Case C-283/11 *Sky Österreich* EU:C:2013:28, paras 45–66.

[180] P Cruz Villalón, 'Rights in Europe: The Crowded House', *Working Papers in European Law 01/2012*, King's College, London.

[181] D Thym, 'Separation versus Fusion – or: How to Accommodate National Autonomy and the Charter? Diverging Visions of the German Constitutional Court and the European Court of Justice' (2013) 9 *European Constitutional Law Review* 391.

of protection than that provided by the ECHR. The wording of Article 52(3) of the Charter is clear in this regard:

> In so far as this Charter contains rights which correspond to rights guaranteed by the European Convention for the Protection of Human Rights and Fundamental Freedoms, the meaning and scope of those rights shall be the same as those laid down by the said Convention. This provision shall not prevent Union law from providing more extensive protection.

This provision codifies the position of the Court of Justice prior to the Charter, which closely followed the development of each right in the ECHR and, most notably, the interpretation provided by the European Court of Human Rights. Whenever the Strasbourg Court raised the level of protection of a fundamental right under the ECHR, the Court of Justice would adjust its own interpretation of the equivalent fundamental right in Union law. Numerous examples exist of this reaction by the Court of Justice both prior to and after the entry into force of the Charter in cases concerning the protection of privacy and family life,[182] the prohibition of discrimination on the grounds of sexual identity,[183] or the prohibition of inhuman or degrading treatment in the context of asylum procedures.[184]

Despite the apparent clarity of Article 52(3), the Court of Justice has on occasion been reluctant to fully align its standards with the minimum set by the ECHR. For instance, it took considerable time for the Court of Justice to bring its case law on the prohibition of *bis in idem* concerning the sanctioning procedures of the Commission in the field of competition into conformity with the Strasbourg Court's interpretation. The minimum standard of the ECHR is fully integrated into Union law regarding the Member States that implement Union law,[185] but the Commission is not bound to adhere to the minimum standard of protection, which requires more flexible conditions to prevent it from imposing an administrative penalty on an undertaking that violates Union competition rules.[186] The same holds true for the right against self-incrimination and the right to remain silent, which the Court of Justice has applied to administrative penalty procedures involving natural persons (in line with the Strasbourg case law) but was more reluctant to extend it fully to legal persons.[187]

Another area of potential friction between the Charter and the Union arises when Member States implement Union law, and their actions are eventually reviewed by the European Court of Human Rights. Although the Union is currently not subject to the jurisdiction of the Strasbourg Court, the actions of Member States certainly are, leading to an indirect recognition of the Strasbourg Court as an external reviewer of Union action. This risk was mitigated in the judgment of the European Court of Human Rights in *Bosphorus Airways v Ireland*.[188] This ruling introduced the notion of 'equivalent protection' of fundamental rights within both the Union legal system and the ECHR, meaning the European Court of Human Rights will refrain from reviewing measures of the Union's Member States that implement non-discretional Union acts. To some extent, the European Court of Human Rights is opting not to review Union action and is deferring the matter to the Court of Justice and the Charter. This approach of the Strasbourg case law has been questioned by various authors, and the

[182] Case C-94/00 *Roquette Frères* EU:C:2002:603.
[183] Case C-117/01 *KB* EU:C:2004:7.
[184] *NS* et al (n 77).
[185] See the judgment of the European Court of Human Rights in *A and B v Norway* App no 24130/11 (15 November 2016).
[186] Case C-17/10 *Toshiba Corporation ea* EU:C:2012:72, para 97.
[187] Case C-481/19 *Consob* EU:C:2021:84.
[188] *Bosphorus Airways v Ireland* App no 45036/98 (ECtHR, 30 June 2005).

European Court of Human Rights has had the opportunity to reassess its stance, although it has remained essentially unchanged to this date.[189]

Article 52(3) of the Charter will probably become a redundant provision once the Union accedes to the ECHR, as required by Article 6(2) TEU. At that point, the Court of Justice and the courts of the Member States will be bound by the ECHR and the case law of the European Court of Human Rights when implementing Union law, stemming from a duty derived from Union law itself. The mandate provided in Article 52(3) will then arise from the Union's obligation to comply with the international agreements it enters into, as well as the jurisdiction of the European Court of Human Rights, which will hear individual complaints against judgments delivered by the Court of Justice. Despite the setbacks that the accession process has witnessed in the past, mostly as a result of Opinion 2/13, recent efforts made by the Commission, the Member States, and the Council of Europe, along with certain developments in the case law of the Court of Justice,[190] have paved the way for the Union's accession to the ECHR in the coming years.[191]

4.4.2. The Charter Versus National Constitutions

An even more delicate and complex situation arises when a conflict occurs between the fundamental rights of the Charter and the equivalent rights provided in the constitution of a Member State. This conflict poses difficult questions, as most Member States have not accepted the unconditional primacy of Union law, in particular the ability of Union law to supersede national constitutions (see chapter 10). Although this immunity of the national constitution is typically limited to specific provisions only (what is commonly referred to as the 'constitutional core', 'constitutional identity' or 'national identity'), it remains true that fundamental rights frequently lie at the very heart of national constitutions. To overcome this tension and produce a functional solution to constitutional conflicts in the field of fundamental rights, the Court of Justice has provided a creative interpretation of Article 53 of the Charter. This case law is first reflected in the cases of *Melloni* and *Akerberg Fransson* (both decided on the same day, on 26 February 2013), followed later by a growing body of case law delivered in recent years.

In the event of a conflict between different levels of protection of fundamental rights in the Charter and a national constitution, Article 53 of the Charter, as interpreted by the Court of Justice, provides a criterion for resolving the conflict. This criterion is based on the existence of two distinct scenarios, depending on the degree of discretion granted by Union law to the Member States.

4.4.2.1. Situations not Entirely Determined by Union Law

The first scenario arises when Union law imposes an obligation on Member States but allows a margin of discretion, allowing them to choose among different policy options. Such cases are common, particularly in the transposition of directives, where Member States have an obligation regarding the outcome while retaining the freedom to select the means. These situations, defined by the case law as 'situations where action of the Member States is not entirely determined by Union law', lead the Court of Justice to provide the following rule:

[189] *Michaud v France* App no 12323/11 (ECtHR 6 December 2012) and, subsequent to Opinion 2/13 *Avotiņš v Latvia* App no 17502/07 (ECtHR 23 May 2016).

[190] Joined Cases C-29/22 P and C-44/22 P *KS and KD* EU:C:2024:725. See S Iglesias Sánchez, 'The Jurisdiction of European Courts in the CFSP. Between Exceptionalism and Consistency of Legal Remedies in a Union Based on the Rule of Law' (2025) 229 *EU Law Live Weekend Edition*.

[191] Opinion 2/13 EU:C:2014:2454.

> [W]here a court of a Member State is called upon to review whether fundamental rights are complied with by a national provision or measure which, in a situation where action of the Member States is not entirely determined by European Union law, implements the latter for the purposes of Article 51(1) of the Charter, national authorities and courts remain free to apply national standards of protection of fundamental rights, provided that the level of protection provided for by the Charter, as interpreted by the Court, and the primacy, unity and effectiveness of European Union law are not thereby compromised.[192]

This *dictum* sets out the steps a national court must take when faced with a conflict between the level of protection of fundamental rights in the Charter and that in the national constitution. If the situation is 'not entirely determined by Union law', thus granting the Member State some discretion in making policy choices, the national court will have the authority to choose between the level of protection provided by the Charter and that of the national constitution.[193] However, this authority is subject to two exceptions in which the Charter will take precedence over the constitution: first, when the Charter offers a higher level of protection than that provided by the constitution; and second, when the standard of protection enshrined in the constitution compromises the primacy, unity and effectiveness of Union law.[194]

The first exception seeks to ensure the predominance of the highest level of protection of the fundamental right at issue. Where the Charter, as interpreted by the Court of Justice, provides a higher standard of protection than the national constitution, the national court must apply the standard provided in the Charter. The national constitution cannot be used to lower the level of protection below the Charter's floor. This determination may require interpretative assistance from the Court of Justice through a preliminary reference.

The second exception is articulated in broader terms, making it more difficult to apply in specific cases. The national constitution can take precedence over the Charter only if it provides a higher level of protection and if this does not compromise 'the primacy, unity and effectiveness of Union law'. The precise scope and meaning of this proviso are not entirely clear, but it appears to refer to situations where a Member State relies on national fundamental rights to evade or sidestep its obligations under Union law.[195] This approach appears to be at work in Euro Box,[196] where the absence of judicial review could have posed a systemic risk of fraud and corruption, breaching the Union's rules on financial supervision. In this context, the Court found that a standard of protection in national law that posed a risk to the implementation of Union obligations in the field of financial supervision would compromise the 'primacy, unity and effectiveness of Union law'.[197]

In the case of *B*, the Court of Justice found an impairment of the 'primacy, unity and effectiveness of Union law' when a national constitutional court limited the temporal effects of its judgments in cases where Union law was at stake. The Court of Justice ruled that such a practice alters the uniform enforcement of Union law among the Member States, an outcome that seriously compromises the effectiveness of the Union's legal system.[198] A similar result emerged in *Lin*, where the Court of Justice stated that national courts cannot, in the context of judicial

[192] *Akerberg Fransson* (n 75) para 29; and Case C-399/11 *Melloni* EU:C:2012:600, para 60.

[193] Case C-42/17 *MAS and MB* EU:C:2017:936, para 47; Joined Cases C-357/19, C-379/19, C-547/19, C-811/19 and C-840/19 *Euro Box Promotion and Others* EU:C:2021:1034, para 211; and Case C-107/23 PPU *Lin* EU:C:2023:606, para 110.

[194] See, inter alia, Case C-469/17 *Funke Medien NRW GmbH* EU:C:2019:623, para 32; Case C-516/17 *Spiegel Online GmbH* EU:C:2019:625, para 21; Case C-476/17 *Pelham and Others* EU:C:2019:624, para 80; and Case C-507/17 *Google LLC* EU:C:2019:772, para 72.

[195] D Sarmiento, 'Who's Afraid of the Charter? The European Court of Justice, National Courts and the New Framework of Fundamental Rights Protection in Europe' (2013) 50 *Common Market Law Review* 1267.

[196] Joined Cases C-357, 379, 547, 811 and 840/19 *Euro Box and Others* EU:C:2021:1034.

[197] ibid, paras 211–212.

[198] Case C-439/19 *B* EU:C:2021:504, para 135.

proceedings seeking to impose criminal penalties for serious fraud offences affecting the financial interests of the Union, apply a national standard of protection relating to the principle of the retroactive application of the more lenient criminal law (*lex mitior*) to call into question the interruption of the limitation period for criminal liability by procedural acts which took place before a judgment of the national Constitutional Court.[199]

However, there are instances where the protection of fundamental rights in a Member State's constitution conflicts with Union law for duly justified reasons and can even prevail over the standards provided in the Charter. In such situations, the Court of Justice appears to carefully consider the circumstances of each case to accommodate both the interests of the national constitution and the 'primacy, unity and effectiveness' of Union law. This was evidenced in the case of *MAS*, a judgment of the Court of Justice that followed a request for a preliminary ruling from the Italian Constitutional Court, which prompted the Luxembourg court to reassess a previous ruling that conflicted with a fundamental right established in the Italian Constitution. To prevent an open conflict, the Court of Justice revisited its earlier case law to align with the protection standards provided by Italian law.[200] This outcome was later reiterated in the case of *Consob*, once again at the request of the Italian Constitutional Court, in which the Court of Justice clarified and partly rectified the scope of the Union's fundamental right not to incriminate oneself and to remain silent in administrative penalty proceedings, as applied to natural persons by the Member States when implementing Union law.[201]

4.4.2.2. Situations Entirely Determined by Union Law

When the Member State has no margin of manoeuvre and Union law imposes fully harmonised, non-discretionary obligations, the binding level of protection of fundamental rights is that provided by the Charter. If the national constitution offers a level of protection equivalent to that provided by the Charter, the national court is entitled to choose between either of the two instruments, as it is not the instrument that matters, but the level of protection afforded in resolving the case. If there is no such equivalence and the Member State has no discretion to make use of its own policy choices, the level of protection provided by Charter takes precedence over the national constitution, even if the former contains a lower level of protection. This rule of conflict was confirmed by the Court of Justice in its judgment in *Melloni*.

Regardless of how controversial this solution may appear, it is consistent with the constitutional character of the Union's legal system, where two autonomous legal systems coexist and overlap in common policy areas. If the Member States were permitted to impose their own fundamental rights standards unilaterally, even in areas where they have no discretion, such an outcome would effectively allow them to challenge the validity of Union law and review it in light of the national constitution. This outcome would undermine the uniformity of Union law and ultimately call into question its effectiveness among the Member States.

For instance, if a directive gives Member States the option to select one of three derogations to a general rule set out in the directive, a national court cannot introduce a fourth derogation based on the protection of a fundamental right guaranteed by the national constitution. Likewise, if a Member State enforces the non-discretional obligations outlined in a regulation, any assessment of the Member State's implementation concerning the fundamental rights enshrined in the constitution would amount to an indirect review of the regulation.

[199] *Lin* (n 193) para 124.

[200] Case C-42/17 *MAS* EU:C:2017:936, para 47. On the *MAS* judgment, see D Sarmiento, 'Adults in the (Deliberation) Room. A Comment on MAS' (2018) 38 *Quaderni costituzionali* 228.

[201] Case C-481/19 *Consob* EU:C:2021:84, paras 45–46.

Such a result would allow each Member State to unilaterally review and declare the invalidity of Union acts, thereby fragmenting the enforcement of Union law and undermining its unity and effectiveness.[202] The review of Union acts in light of fundamental rights is both possible and desirable; however, it must be undertaken by the Court of Justice in accordance with the Charter (against the backdrop of the ECHR as a minimum standard of protection).

To date, it remains debatable whether all the constitutional courts of the Member States have fully accepted this solution or whether they will do so unconditionally. One of the first opportunities to assess the degree of acceptance of the Court of Justice's stance arose in the case of *Melloni*, when the Spanish Constitutional Court had to deliver its final ruling following the preliminary ruling of the Court of Justice. Although the Spanish Constitutional Court agreed to review and overrule its previous case law to align it with the lower standard of protection granted by the Charter in that specific case, it also emphasised that this reversal of its prior case law was not due to Union law, but rather a decision made on its own authority interpreting the Spanish Constitution exclusively. The judgment of the Spanish Constitutional Court indicated that the ruling of the Court of Justice in *Melloni* was a 'very useful' reference only, suggesting that it did not feel bound by the Luxembourg judgment, but only by the constitution.[203]

Recent developments indicate that national constitutional courts are beginning to engage in a more constructive interaction with Union law concerning the protection of fundamental rights, particularly in cases where Union law allows no discretion to the Member States. In such circumstances, national jurisdictions, including the German Federal Constitutional Court, are opting to incorporate the Charter as a parameter for constitutional interpretation and review, giving it an equivalent status to the national constitution. This approach was adopted by the German court in two judgments regarding the right to be forgotten on the internet, where the Union's legal framework on data protection afforded no discretion to Member States. Instead of automatically assuming the standard of protection provided in the Charter, the German Federal Constitutional Court opted to interpret the Charter, adapting this instrument to turn it into a tool of domestic constitutional law.[204] Other national courts, such as the Italian Constitutional Court have also embraced a policy of direct interaction with the Court of Justice to seek the appropriate level of protection for fundamental rights in the Charter. This approach was implemented in the cases of *MAS* and *Consob*, yielding positive results for both courts, which avoid constitutional conflict and enhance cooperation with the Court of Justice.[205]

5. An EU Fundamental Rights Policy?

The Treaties do not explicitly establish a comprehensive and self-standing Union fundamental rights policy. However, the protection of fundamental rights permeates all areas of Union policy, acting as overarching rights that apply across all sectors of Union activity. Since the early 1970s, fundamental rights have become an integral part of the Union's legal order, acting as constraints that define the boundaries which Union institutions, agencies, bodies, offices, and Member States, when implementing Union law, cannot transgress. In these circumstances,

[202] See Joined Cases C-404/15 and 659/15 PPU *Aranyosi and Căldăraru* EU:C:2016:140, Opinion of AG Bot, pts 116–23.

[203] STC 26/2014, FJ 2°.

[204] M Wendel, 'The Two-faced Guardian: Or How One Half of the German Federal Constitutional Court Became a European Fundamental Rights Court' (2020) 57 *Common Market Law Review 1383*.

[205] D Tega, 'The Italian Constitutional Court in Its Context: A Narrative' (2021) 17 *European Constitutional Law Review* 369.

it is pertinent to ask if the Union has a fundamental rights policy of its own and how it is articulated.

The answer to this question is not straightforward. The Union does not have a legal basis to legislate in general terms on fundamental rights, nor is it a human rights organisation, in the manner of the Council of Europe. However, the protection of fundamental rights is one of the values enshrined in Article 2 TEU, and Article 6 TEU incorporates the Charter as a binding instrument of primary law, with the same legal value as the Treaties. Additionally, the Treaties include several sector-specific legal bases that relate closely to the protection of fundamental rights, such as Article 16 TFEU concerning the right to the protection of personal data, or Article 19 TFEU on measures to combat discrimination based on sex, racial or ethnic origin, religion or belief, disability, age, or sexual orientation. It should also be noted that the promotion of human rights is one of the objectives of the Union's external action, as outlined in Article 21 TEU.

The existence of various Union policy fields closely connected to the promotion and protection of fundamental rights, together with concerns about risks of democratic and rule of law backsliding in some Member States, justified the creation of the European Union Agency for Fundamental Rights (FRA), entrusted with the mission of assisting in the protection of fundamental rights to both the Union and its Member States.[206] The FRA commenced operations in 2007, and since its entry into operation, it has developed its consultative powers through various means, including the collection and analysis of law and data, independent advice on fundamental rights, and support for rights-compliant policy responses. The FRA's headquarters are located in Vienna.

The protection of fundamental rights has become even more challenging in recent years as a result of the expansion of digital technologies, the rise of new means of communication, growing polarisation, and fast-evolving rule of law backsliding in several Member States. Consequently, the Union has pursued an ambitious legislative agenda to address these developments, many of which focus on the specific protection of fundamental rights. A notable example is the protection of journalistic activity, which has come under pressure in several Member States, where attacks on journalists or independent media have prompted the adoption of various EU legislative measures, such as the Media Freedom Act or the SLAPP Directive.[207] The complexity of the current situation is exacerbated primarily by the impact of the digital sphere on individuals and companies, and, consequently, on the economic, social, and political environment.

GENERAL BIBLIOGRAPHY

Alston, P, Heenan, J and Bustelo, M (eds), *The EU and Human Rights* (Oxford University Press, 1999).

Arden, M, *Human Rights and European Law: Building New Legal Orders* (Oxford University Press, 2015).

Barnard, C, and Leinarte, E, 'The Creation of European Citizenship: Constitutional Miracle or Myopia?' (2022) 24 *Cambridge Yearbook of European Legal Studies* 24.

De Búrca, G, 'After the EU Charter of Fundamental Rights: The Court of Justice as a Human Rights Adjudicator?' (2013) 20 *Maastricht Journal of European and Comparative Law* 168.

Dawson, M, *The Governance of EU Fundamental Rights* (Cambridge University Press, 2017).

Douglas-Scott, S and Hatzis, N (eds), *Research Handbook on EU Law and Human Rights* (Edward Elgar, 2017).

[206] Council Regulation (EC) No 168/2007 of 15 February 2007 establishing a European Union Agency for Fundamental Rights [2007] OJ L53/1) and J Morijn and G Toggenburg, 'The EU's Agency for Fundamental Rights: The Past, the Present and the Future of an Atypical "Agency"' (2024) *EU Law Live Weekend Edition*.

[207] Regulation (EU) 2024/1083 of the European Parliament and of the Council of 11 April 2024 establishing a common framework for media services in the internal market and amending Directive 2010/13/EU [2024] OJ L 2024/1083, and Directive (EU) 2024/1069 of the European Parliament and of the Council of 11 April 2024 on protecting persons who engage in public participation from manifestly unfounded claims or abusive court proceedings [2024] OJ L 2024/1069.

Fabbrini, F, *Fundamental Rights in Europe: Challenges and Transformations in Comparative Perspective* (Oxford University Press, 2014).
Goudappel, F, *The Effects of EU Citizenship* (TMC Asser Press, 2010).
Guild, E, *Legal Elements of European Identity: EU Citizenship and Migration Law* (Kluwer Law, 2005).
Guild, E, Peers, S and Tomkin, J, *The Citizens' Rights Directive* (Oxford University Press, 2019).
Kochenov, D (ed), *EU Citizenship and Federalism: The Role of Rights* (Cambridge University Press, 2017).
Morano-Foadi, S and Vickers, L (eds), *Fundamental Rights in the EU* (Hart Publishing, 2015).
Morijn, J, and Toggenburg, G, 'The EU's Agency for Fundamental Rights. The Past, the Present and the Future of an Atypical "Agency"' (2024) 170 *EU Law Live Weekend Edition* 3.
Nic Shuibhne, N, *EU Citizenship Law* (Oxford University Press, 2024).
O'Leary, S, *The Evolving Concept of Community Citizenship: From the Free Movement of Persons to Union Citizenship* (Kluwer Law, 1996).
Peers, S, Hervey, T, Kenner, J and Ward, A (eds), *The Charter of Fundamental Rights: A Commentary*, 2nd edn (Hart, 2019).
Rizcallah, C, *The European Union and Human Rights. Understanding a Singular Regional Player* (Hart, 2025).
Shaw, J, *The Transformation of Citizenship in the European Union* (Cambridge University Press, 2007).
Spaventa, E, 'Seeing the Wood Despite the Trees? On the Scope of Union Citizenship and Its Constitutional Effects' (2008) 45 *Common Market Law Review* 13.
Thym, D (ed), *Questioning EU Citizenship: Judges and the Limits of Free Movement and Solidarity in the EU* (Hart, 2017).
Van Eijken, H, *EU Citizenship and the Constitutionalization of the European Union* (Europa Law Publishing, 2015).
Varju, M, *European Union Human Rights Law: The Dynamics of Interpretation and Context* (Edward Elgar, 2014).
Von Bogdandy, A, 'The European Union as a Human Rights Organization: Human Rights and the Core of the European Union' (2000) 37 *Common Market Law Review* 1307.
De Vries, S, Bernitz, U and Weatherill, S (eds), *The EU Charter of Fundamental Rights as a Binding Instrument: Five Years Old and Growing* (Hart, 2015).
Williams, A, *EU Human Rights Policies: A Study in Irony* (Oxford University Press, 2004).

FURTHER READING

The Statutes of Union Citizenship

Azoulai, L, 'La citoyenneté européenne, un statut d'intégration sociale' in *Chemins d'Europe. Mélanges en l'honneur de Jean Paul Jacqué* (Dalloz, 2010).
Closa, C, 'The Concept of Citizenship in the Treaty on European Union' (1992) 29 *Common Market Law Review* 1137.
de Groot, G-R and Chun Luk, N, 'Twenty Years of CJEU Jurisprudence on Citizenship' (2014) 15 *German Law Journal* 821.
Guild, E, Peers, S and Tomkin, J, *The EU Citizenship Directive: A Commentary* (Oxford University Press, 2014).
Kochenov, D and Plender, R, 'EU Citizenship: From an Incipient Form to an Incipient Substance? The Discovery of the Treaty Text' (2012) 37 *European Law Review* 369.
Kostakopoulou, D, *EU Citizenship Law and Policy: Beyond Brexit* (Edward Elgar, 2020).
Kostakopoulou, D, and Thym, D (eds), *Research Handbook on European Union Citizenship Law and Policy: Navigating Challenges and Crises* (Edward Elgar, 2022).
Nic Shuibhne, N, 'The Developing Legal Dimension of Union Citizenship' in A Arnull and D Chalmers (eds), *The Oxford Handbook of European Union Law* (Oxford University Press, 2015).
d'Oliveira, HUJJ, 'European Citizenship: Its Meaning, Its Potential' in R Dehousse (ed), *Europe after Maastricht: An Ever Closer Union?* (Law Books in Europe, 1994).
Sarmiento, D and Sharpston, E, 'European Citizenship and Its New Union: Time to Move On?' in D Kochenov (ed), *EU Citizenship and Federalism: The Role of Rights* (Cambridge University Press, 2017).
Shaw, J, *The Transformation of Citizenship in the European Union: Electoral Rights and the Restructuring of Political Space* (Cambridge University Press, 2007).

Thym, D, '"Public Policy" as a Chameleonlike Concept: The Quest for Coherence in the CJEU Case Law on Migration and Union Citizenship' (2024) 9 *European Papers* 1366.

Protecting the Substance of Union Citizenship Status Rights

Iglesias Sánchez, S, 'Fundamental Rights and Citizenship of the Union at a Crossroads' (2014) 20 *European Law Journal* 464.

Lenaerts, K, '"Civis Europaeus Sum": From the Cross-border Link to the Status of Citizen of the Union' in P Cardonnel, A Rosas and N Wahl (eds), *Constitutionalising the EU Judicial System: Essays in Honour of Pernilla Lindh* (Hart, 2012).

Mengozzi, P, 'Zambrano: An Unexpected Ruling' in P Cardonnel, A Rosas and N Wahl (eds), *Constitutionalising the EU Judicial System: Essays in Honour of Pernilla Lindh* (Hart, 2012).

Fundamental Rights as General Principles

Amalfitano, C, *General Principles of EU Law and the Protection of Fundamental Rights* (Edward Elgar, 2018).

Lock, T, 'Rights and Principles in the EU Charter of Fundamental Rights' (2019) 56 *Common Market Law Review* 1201.

Tridimas, T, *The General Principles of EU Law*, 2nd edn (Oxford University Press, 2006).

Williams, A, 'Human Rights in the EU' in A Arnull and D Chalmers (eds), *The Oxford Handbook of European Union Law* (Oxford University Press, 2015).

Genesis and Entry into Force of the Charter

Betten, L, 'The EU Charter of Fundamental Rights: A Trojan Horse or a Mouse?' (2001) 17 *International Journal of Comparative Labour Law and Industrial Relations 151.*

Bobek, M and Adams-Prassl, J, *The EU Charter of Fundamental Rights in the Member States* (Hart, 2021).

de Búrca, G, 'The Drafting of the European Union Charter of Fundamental Rights' (2001) 26 *European Law Review 214.*

Douglas-Scott, S, 'The European Union and Human Rights after the Treaty of Lisbon' (2011) 11 *Human Rights Law Review 645.*

Eriksen, E, Fossum, J and Menéndez, A (eds), *The Chartering of Europe* (Arena Report no 8/2001).

Feus, K (ed), *An EU Charter of Fundamental Rights: Text and Commentaries* (The Federal Trust, 2000).

Lenaerts, K and Gutiérrez-Fons, JA, 'The Place of the Charter in the EU Constitutional Edifice' in S Peers, T Hervey, J Kenner and A Ward (eds), *The Charter of Fundamental Rights: A Commentary* (Hart, 2014).

Muir, E, and Lorans, Y (eds), 'EU Fundamental Rights. Law and Policy in the Shadow of the Charter' (2021) 78 *EU Law Live Weekend Edition* 3.

de Witte, B, 'The Legal Status of the Charter: Vital Question or Non-Issue?' (2001) 8 *Maastricht Journal of European and Comparative Law 81.*

The Union and the European Convention of Human Rights

Gragl, P, *The Accession of the European Union to the European Convention on Human Rights* (Hart, 2013).

Kosta, V, Skoutaris, N and Tzevelekos, V (eds), *The EU Accession to the ECHR* (Hart, 2017).

Lenaerts, K, 'La vie après l'avis: Exploring the Principle of Mutual (Yet Not Blind) Trust' (2017) 54 *Common Market Law Review 805.*

Lock, T, 'The Influence of EU Law on Strasbourg Doctrines' (2016) 41 *European Law Review 804.*

Ronkes Agerbeek, F, 'EU Accession to the European Convention of Human Rights: An EU Negotiator's Perspective' (2024) 192 *EU Law Live Weekend Edition* 3.

Spaventa, E, 'A Very Fearful Court? The Protection of Fundamental Rights in the European Union after Opinion 2/13' (2015) 22 *Maastricht Journal of European and Comparative Law*.

Scope of the Charter

Frantziou, E, *The Horizontal Effect of Fundamental Rights in the European Union: A Constitutional Analysis* (Oxford University Press, 2019).

Lazzerini, N, '(Some of) the Fundamental Rights Granted by the Charter May Be a Source of Obligations for Private Parties: AMS' (2014) 51 *Common Market Law Review 907*.

Leczykiewicz, D, 'Horizontal Application of the Charter of Fundamental Rights' (2013) 38 *European Law Review 479*.

Murphy, C, 'Using the EU Charter of Fundamental Rights Against Private Parties after AMS' (2014) *European Human Rights Law Review 170*.

von Papp, K, 'A Federal Question Doctrine for EU Fundamental Rights Law: Making Sense of Articles 51 and 53 of the Charter of Fundamental Rights' (2018) 43 *European Law Review 511*.

Walkila, S, *Horizontal Effect of Fundamental Rights in EU Law* (Europa Law Publishing, 2016).

Ward, A, 'Field of Application' in S Peers, T Hervey, J Kenner and A Ward (eds), *The Charter of Fundamental Rights: A Commentary* (Hart, 2014).

Level of Protection of the Charter

Alonso García, R, 'The General Provisions of the Charter of Fundamental Rights of the European Union' (2002) 8 *European Law Journal 492*.

Besselink, L, 'Entrapped by the Maximum Standard: On Fundamental Rights, Pluralism and Subsidiarity in the European Union' (1998) 35 *Common Market Law Review 629*.

——, 'The Parameters of Constitutional Conflict after Melloni' (2014) 39 *European Law Review 531*.

De Boer, N, 'Addressing Rights Divergences Under the Charter: Melloni' (2013) 50 *Common Market Law Review 1083*.

Brkan, M, 'The Essence of the Fundamental Rights to Privacy and Data Protection: Finding the Way Through the Maze of the CJEU's Constitutional Reasoning' (2019) 20 *German Law Journal 864*.

De Cecco, F, 'The trouble with trumps: On how (and why) not to define the core of fundamental rights' (2023) 60 *Common Market Law Review* 1551.

Colella, S, *La restriction des droits fondamentaux dans l'Union européenne* (Bruylant, 2019).

Liisberg, J, 'Does the EU Charter of Fundamental Rights Threaten the Supremacy of Community Law?' (2001) 38 *Common Market Law Review 1171*.

Pliakos, A and Anagnostaras, G, 'Who is the Ultimate Arbiter? The Battle over Judicial Supremacy in the EU' (2011) 36 *European Law Review 109*.

Ritleng, D, 'De l'articulation des systèmes de protection des droits fondamentaux dans l'Union' (2013) 49 *Revue Trimestrielle de Droit Européen 267*.

Sarmiento, D, 'Who's Afraid of the Charter? The Court of Justice, National Courts and the New Framework of Fundamental Rights Protection in Europe' (2013) 50 *Common Market Law Review 1267*.

Spaventa, E, 'Should We "Harmonize" Fundamental Rights in the EU? Some Reflections About Minimum Standards and Fundamental Rights Protection in the EU Composite Constitutional System' (2018) 55 *Common Market Law Review 997* 35.

de Visser, M, 'Dealing with Divergences in Fundamental Rights Standards' (2013) 20 *Maastricht Journal of European and Comparative Law 576*.

Weiler, JHH, 'Fundamental Rights and Fundamental Boundaries' in JHH Weiler (ed), *The Constitution of Europe* (Cambridge University Press, 1999).

de Witte, B, 'Level of Protection' in S Peers, T Hervey, J Kenner and A Ward (eds), *The Charter of Fundamental Rights: A Commentary* (Hart Publishing, 2014).

7

The Sources of Union Law (I)

I. THE UNION'S LEGAL SYSTEM AND ITS AUTONOMY

THE UNION'S LEGAL system comprises a structured network of principles, rules and mutually interdependent legal relations, most of which are adopted by the Union's institutions following procedures laid down in the Treaties. It is also a legal system whose principles and rules are binding on all public authorities and individuals, including courts called upon to resolve disputes. Union law is a fully developed legal system with features comparable to those of the Member States' legal systems: binding authority; adoption through established procedures; effectiveness through enforcement mechanisms; and dispute-resolution mechanisms through courts of law.

Despite sharing features with national legal systems, Union law possesses qualities that highlight its distinct and unique nature. The fundamental norm of the Union legal system is not a constitution in the traditional sense or any other instrument approved by a constituent authority, but a set of international Treaties signed and ratified by the Member States. Despite this strong connection with international law at its foundation, Union law is not characterised as a creature of international law, but as an autonomous legal system. Its autonomy from international law was asserted from the very early stages of European integration, when the Court of Justice stated in the case of *Van Gend en Loos* that the Treaties are 'more than an agreement which merely creates mutual obligations between the contracting states'.[1] The fact that the Union legal order is 'more than an [international] agreement' is also reflected in the point, also highlighted in *Van Gend en Loos*, that it constitutes 'a new legal order of international law for the benefit of which the States have limited their sovereign rights, albeit in limited fields and the subjects of which comprise not only Member States but also their nationals'.[2]

Union law is integrated into each Member State's legal system while maintaining its autonomy. Union law becomes part of German, Danish, Czech, or Finnish law, for example, but with a status of autonomy that keeps the rules and principles of Union law separate from national law. The principle that establishes the autonomy of Union law vis-a-vis national law is rooted in the foundational norms of each legal system. In national systems, the foundational norm is typically enshrined in the constitution, whereas in the Union legal system, it is established in the Treaties. Likewise, the highest court of each Member State acts as the ultimate interpreter of national law, while the Court of Justice of the European Union is responsible for providing the authoritative interpretation of Union law. The Court of Justice defined the autonomy of Union law in 1964 in the judgment in *Costa/Enel*, stating that 'by contrast with ordinary international treaties, the [Union's Treaties have] created [their] own legal system which, on the

[1] Case C-26/62 *Van Gend & Loos* EU:C:1963:1.
[2] ibid.

entry into force of the [Treaties], became an integral part of the legal systems of the Member States and which their courts are bound to apply'.[3]

The autonomy of Union law produces its effects both internally and externally, vis-a-vis the Member States and the international legal order. As the Court of Justice has expressed it recently, the Union legal system

> has its own constitutional framework and founding principles, a particularly sophisticated institutional structure and a complete set of legal rules which ensure its functioning, and enjoys autonomy from the law of the Member States and from international law.[4]

Besides being incorporated autonomously into national law, Union law requires the cooperation of national laws and institutions to give effect to its rules and principles. For example, Union directives are specifically designed to be transposed into the legal systems of all Member States through acts of national law. Most Union rules and principles are implemented on a daily basis through national administrative bodies in the Member States. Likewise, national courts are heavily involved in settling disputes that depend on Union law for their resolution. The autonomy of the Union legal system thus coexists with a deep level of interaction with the legal systems of all the Member States.

The Union's legal system comprises a structured network of principles, rules and mutually interdependent legal relations organised in a hierarchical structure. Although the Treaties do not explicitly refer to this hierarchical arrangement within Union law, it has been a settled feature since the origins of the integration process. Primary law sits at the top of the legal system, including the Treaties, the general principles of law, and constituent acts. Primary law is immediately followed by international agreements to which the Union is a party. Secondary law is posited at the next level of the hierarchy (see chapter eight), comprising binding acts (such as regulations, directives, and decisions) and non-binding acts (such as recommendations, guidelines, and communications). Rules and principles of secondary law can also be organised within a hierarchy, as is the case between legislative acts and non-legislative acts (mostly delegated and implementing acts).

The hierarchical structure of the sources of Union law is confirmed in Article 263 TFEU, a provision that confers jurisdiction on the Court of Justice of the European Union to rule on the validity of Union acts that infringe 'the Treaties or any rule of law relating to their application or misuse of power'. By conferring the power to judicially review Union acts of secondary law that breach primary law, or any other rule related to their implementation, the Treaties have established a legal system based on a hierarchical criterion.[5] The Lisbon Treaty further reinforced this structure by introducing a formal distinction between legislative and non-legislative

[3] Case C-6/64 *Flaminio Costa v ENEL* EU:C:1964:66. The concept of 'autonomy' derives from the reference to the Union's 'own legal system' as 'an integral part of the legal systems of the Member States'. The Court of Justice adds immediately afterwards that the Union legal system stems from 'an independent source of law' (*une source autonome* in the French version) which 'because of its special and original nature, [cannot] be overridden by domestic legal provisions, however framed, without being deprived of its character as [Union] law and without the legal basis of the [Union] itself being called into question'. On the autonomy of Union law, see the seminal contribution of P Pescatore, *L'ordre juridique des Communautés Européennes. Étude des sources du droit Communautaire* (Bruylant, 2006) (reprint of the 1975 work) 163ff; and JHH Weiler and U Haltern, 'The Autonomy of the Community Legal Order: Through the Looking Glass' (1996) 37 *Harvard International Law Journal* 411.

[4] Opinion 2/13 (Accession of the European Union to the ECHR) EU:C:2014:2454, paras 158 and 170; Case C-157/21 *Poland v Parliament and Council* EU:C:2022:98, para 14, and Case C-448/23 *Commission v Poland*, EU:C:2025:975, para 166.

[5] On the criterion of hierarchy in the Union's sources of law, see H Hofmann, 'Legislation, Delegation and Implementation Under the Treaty of Lisbon: Typology Meets Reality' (2009) 15 *European Law Journal* 482, 483–86, and K Lenaerts and M Desomer, 'Towards a Hierarchy of Legal Acts in the European Union? Simplification of Legal Instruments and Procedures' (2005) 11 *European Law Journal* 744.

acts, with the latter being subordinate and subject to review in the event of conflict with the legislative act from which they originate.

II. PRIMARY LAW

The rules and principles referred to as primary law stand at the apex of the Union legal system and determine the validity of every other provision of Union law. This body of rules and principles includes the founding Treaties and their amendments, the Charter of Fundamental Rights, the Protocols and Annexes to the Treaties, the Acts of Accession of the Member States, general principles of law and constituent acts. While the Treaties, the Charter, the Protocols and Annexes to the Treaties, the Acts of Accession of the Member States and constituent acts are formal sources of written law enacted through specific instruments (such as an international treaty or a decision), general principles of law are developed through judicial precedent, gradually evolving in the Court of Justice's case law. In some legal traditions, this distinction is referred to as sources of *written* and *unwritten* law.

1. Formalised Sources of Primary Law

1.1. The Treaties

The main sources of formalised primary law are found in two international treaties: the Treaty on European Union (TEU) and the Treaty on the Functioning of the European Union (TFEU). Both treaties have the same legal value (Article 1, third paragraph TEU) and entered into force on 1 December 2009. Despite their foundational status and the novelty of their structure, they are a recast version of previous treaties, particularly the Treaty on European Union and the Treaty establishing the European Community. As explained in chapter one of this book, the current Treaties are the result of a decades-long process of reform and amendments, including the failed attempt to enact a Constitutional Treaty, aiming to reconcile provisions of the previous Treaties with new features introduced in 2009, such as the abolition of 'pillar structures' and the 'communities', or the attribution of international legal personality to the Union.[6] Due to their foundational role in the development of European integration, Article 1(3) TEU states that 'the Union *shall be founded* on the present Treaty and on the Treaty on the Functioning of the European Union' (emphasis added).

Although both instruments are formally international treaties, they possess a completely different status that contrasts with the typical features of ordinary treaties. Firstly, the Treaties have undergone specific and distinct ratification procedures in most Member States, in terms that are not applied to ordinary international treaties.[7] Secondly, the Treaties have their own provisions for their amendment, governed by Article 48 TEU, which differ from the general rules of international law regarding treaty reform. Article 48 TEU establishes an ordinary

[6] Although the TEU proclaims the legal personality of the Union, the Treaty of Lisbon did not repeal or supersede the Euratom Treaty. As a result, the Treaty establishing the European Atomic Energy Community currently coexists alongside the Treaties, on the basis of common institutions, but in terms that replicate the former structure of the Treaties prior to the reforms introduced in 2009. According to Art 106a(3) of the Euratom Treaty, 'The provisions of the Treaty on European Union and of the Treaty on the Functioning of the European Union shall not derogate from the provisions of this Treaty'.

[7] M Claes 'Constitutionalizing Europe at Its Source: The "European Clauses" in the National Constitutions: Evolution and Typology' (2005) 24 *Yearbook of European Law* 81.

review procedure that requires ratification by all Member States, alongside a simplified review procedure requiring unanimous agreement in the European Council. The Treaties can only be amended through these procedures, precluding any subsequent international agreements entered into by the Member States from altering the content of the Treaties.[8]

Third, the Treaties provide for the right of every Member State to voluntarily withdraw from the Union through a special procedure that involves a decision by the European Council, followed by negotiations and the conclusion of a withdrawal agreement between the withdrawing Member State and the Union (Article 50 TEU).

These features emphasise the specific legal nature of the Treaties and their similarities to certain characteristics of national constitutions. The procedures for ratifying the Treaties are closer to the process of enacting or amending a constitution than to that of ratifying an ordinary international treaty. The legal effects of the Treaties, not only within Union law but also in relation to national law, including their self-proclaimed primacy and direct effect, are more akin to those of a constitution than of an international treaty.

As a result of the above, the Court of Justice has characterised the Treaties as *constitutional* in nature, referring to them as the 'basic constitutional charter' of the Union.[9] This definition underlines the supreme role of the Treaties within the Union's legal system, as well as its autonomy vis-a-vis international and national law.[10] By highlighting the constitutional role played by the Treaties, Union law affirms the existence of an autonomous and independent source of legitimacy, a source that strongly relies on basic values, including the rule of law, democracy, and the protection of fundamental rights, as enshrined in Article 2 TEU. Consequently, the case law has repeatedly referred to the Union as a 'Community of law' initially, and now as a 'Union of law'.[11] The constitutional values at the core of the Union's legal system, particularly democracy, freedom, solidarity and the rule of law, are reflected in the Treaties themselves through rules on legislative procedures, where the European Parliament[12] and national parliaments[13] have distinctive roles. These values also appear in Treaty rules laying down the conditions for the right to vote and to stand as a candidate in elections to the European Parliament,[14] or by conferring on the Charter of Fundamental Rights of the European Union the same legal value as the Treaties.[15]

In its recent case law, the Court of Justice has stated that the values of the Union, as enshrined in Article 2 TEU, are legally binding provisions that produce effects and can be autonomously breached by a Member State.[16] In that context, the Court of Justice added that other provisions of the Treaty, including Article 4(2) TEU, which refers to the protection of the national identity of the Member States, must be interpreted consistently with Article 2 TEU, protecting national

[8] On the exclusive nature of Art 48 TEU as the only available procedure to amend the Treaties, see ch 2 of this book.

[9] Case C-294/83 *Les Verts v Parliament* EU:C:1986:166, para 23. In later developments, the Court of Justice dropped the reference to the 'basic' features and simply refers to the treaties as the 'constitutional charter'. See, for example, to cite a recent precedent Case C-448/23 *Commission v Poland* EU:C:2025:975, para 164.

[10] As early as 1956, in Case C-8/55 *Fédération Charbonnière de Belgique* EU:C:1956:11, Advocate General Lagrange referred to the founding Treaties as, 'from a material point of view, the charter of the Community' although it was not until the judgment in *Les Verts* (Case C-294/83, EU:C:1986:166) that the Court of Justice defined the Treaties as constitutional in nature, an understanding of the Treaties that was later reiterated, inter alia, in Case C-15/00 *Commission v EIB* EU:C:2003:396, para 75; and Joined Cases C-402/05 P and C-415/05 P *Kadi and Al Barakaat International Foundation v Council and Commission* EU:C:2008:461, para 281.

[11] Case C-550/09 *E and F* EU:C:2010:382, para 44; Case C-64/16 *Associação Sindical dos Juízes Portugueses* EU:C:2018:117, para 31; and Case C-426/16 *Liga van Moskeeën en Islamitische Organisaties Provincie Antwerpen VZW and Others* EU:C:2018:335, para 38.

[12] Art 14 TEU.

[13] ibid, Art 12.

[14] ibid, Art 14.

[15] ibid, Art 6.

[16] Case C-769/22 *Commission v Hungary* EU:C:2026:326, paras 521–523

identity only insofar as it is compatible with the Union's foundational values[17]. Therefore, the case law confirms the existence of an indirect hierarchy of rules within the Treaties, in which their core content, reflected in the provisions that materialise the "very identity of the Union", holds a preeminent interpretative role over the rest of the provisions in the Treaties.

The TEU outlines the basic structural features of the Union, as well as the values and objectives that define the European project.[18] Its provisions specify and describe the Union's institutions and powers,[19] highlight the key features of its competences,[20] and set the territorial, material, and temporal scope of its framework.[21] In essence, the TEU serves as a framework Treaty, a *traité cadre*, establishing the Union's core features, structure, and identity.

The TEU is complemented by the Treaty on the Functioning of the European Union (TFEU), which further develops the Union's policies and institutional structure. As stated in Article 1(3) TEU, the 'two Treaties shall have the same legal value', and no hierarchy exists between them.

This division of the Union's constitutional charter into two Treaties has not been immune to criticism. The current structure is indeed simpler than the one that preceded it under the Maastricht Treaty of 1992, in which three European Communities operated under a Union governed by four treaties and a pillar-based system with autonomous intergovernmental policy areas. However, the current arrangement, comprising two treaties and various Union policies with differing approaches to decision-making, subtly reproduces many features inherited from the Maastricht framework, which could benefit from further simplification.[22]

1.2. *Protocols*

The Protocols annexed to the Treaties by common accord of the Member States also constitute a source of primary law. Article 51 TEU states that 'the Protocols and Annexes to the Treaties shall form an integral part thereof'. The TEU and TFEU currently include a total of 37 Protocols, with a legal value equivalent to that of the Treaties.

The role of the Protocols is diverse. In some cases, they provide a comprehensive and detailed overview of a sector of Union law, such as the Statute of the Court of Justice, the Statute of the European System of Central Banks and of the European Central Bank, and the Statute of the European Investment Bank, found in Protocols Nos 3, 4, and 5, respectively. In other instances, they contain special arrangements for one or several Member States, such as Protocol No 30 on the application of the Charter of Fundamental Rights of the European Union to Poland, or Protocol No 35 on Article 40(3)(3) of the Constitution of Ireland, concerning the prohibition of abortion.

In any case, Protocols cannot override a 'basic provision' of the Treaties to which they are annexed[23] and must always be interpreted in conformity with them.[24] This subtle dependence of the Protocols on the content of the Treaties has resulted in a certain hierarchy between the two sources of primary law, leaving the Protocols in a position of relative subordination to the Treaties.

Although the Protocols are in principle subject to the same revision procedure as the Treaties, some of their provisions can be amended through specific (and simplified) procedures

[17] ibid, paras 557–562
[18] ibid, Arts 2–3.
[19] ibid, Arts 13–19.
[20] ibid, Arts 4–5ff.
[21] ibid, Arts 5 and 52–53.
[22] J-P Jacqué, 'La complexité d'un traité simplifié. Le Traité de Lisbonne et la coexistence de trois traités' (2007–2008) 2 *Revue des Affaires Européennes / Law & European Affairs* 177, 178.
[23] Case C-280/93 *Germany v Council* EU:C:1994:367, para 117.
[24] Case C-445/00 *Austria v Council* EU:C:2003:445, para 73.

that differ from the ordinary and simplified review mechanisms outlined in Article 48 TEU,[25] as explained in chapter two of this book.

1.3. *Amending Treaties*

From the 1950s, the Treaties that preceded the current TEU and TFEU underwent multiple amendments. Such changes could take effect only through the adoption of a new amending Treaty, using the same procedures as those for the amended Treaty. In some cases, the Amending Treaties not only modified the content of the previous Treaties but also introduced entirely new substantive provisions that added content or established new policy areas. This was the case of Titles V and VI of the earlier version of the TEU, which contained provisions on the Union's Common Foreign and Security Policy (CFSP), as well as on Judicial and Police Cooperation in Civil and Criminal Matters. These provisions were introduced through Amending Treaties, although it is clear that their purpose was not simply to amend the previous Treaty, but to introduce an entirely new policy field for the Union with its own set of newly created Treaty rules.

The TEU and TFEU currently in force result from an amendment of the previous TEU and Treaty Establishing the European Community (TEC), carried out by the Lisbon Treaty. Although the main objective of the Lisbon Treaty was to amend both the TEU and the TEC, it also introduced new rules that added entirely new content to the Treaties. Furthermore, the Lisbon Treaty includes provisions not reflected in the TEU or the TFEU, which hold autonomous status and are only found in the Lisbon Treaty itself. This is the case of Article 5 of the Lisbon Treaty, which introduces a system of references and cross-references between the TEU, the TFEU, and the previous TEC; or Article 6(2), which establishes the entry into force of the Treaty and, indirectly, that of the TEU and TFEU.

1.4. *Accession Treaties*

The accession of a new Member State to the Union is formalised through a Treaty, to which both the acceding state and the Member States are parties. Given the importance and complexity of every new accession, which often involves the negotiation of transitional periods to facilitate the transition to full membership, the Accession Treaty is a key instrument of both political and legal significance. Consequently, Accession Treaties have the status of primary law, including the Act of Accession and the Protocols, Declarations and other provisions that form an integral part thereof.[26]

An Accession Treaty can introduce derogations from the rules of the original Treaties, but, in any event, they must be interpreted restrictively and in conformity with the latter. As the Court of Justice has repeatedly stated, 'the provisions of the Act of Accession must be

[25] See Art 126(14)(2) TFEU (amendment of Protocol No 12 on the excessive deficit procedure); Art 281(2) TFEU (amendment of the Statute of the Court of Justice as set out in Protocol No 3); Art 40 of Protocol No 4 (amendment of the Statute of the European System of Central Banks and of the European Central Bank); as well as Art 308(3) TFEU (amendment of the Statute of the European Investment Bank, as set out in Protocol No 5).

[26] Treaty of Accession of Denmark, Ireland and the United Kingdom of Great Britain and Northern Ireland and the Act concerning the conditions of accession of these three states of 22 January 1972; Treaty of Accession and Act concerning the conditions of accession of Greece of 28 May 1979; Treaty amending the Treaties establishing the European Communities with regard to Greenland of 13 March 1984; Treaty of Accession and Act concerning the conditions of accession of Spain and Portugal of 12 June 1985; Treaty of Accession and Act concerning the conditions of accession of Austria, Finland and Sweden of 24 June 1994; Treaty of Accession and Act concerning the conditions of accession of the Czech Republic, Estonia, Cyprus, Latvia, Lithuania, Hungary, Malta, Poland, Slovenia and Slovakia of 16 April 2003; Treaty of Accession and Act concerning the conditions of accession of Bulgaria and Romania of 25 April 2005; and Treaty of Accession and Act concerning the conditions of accession of the Republic of Croatia of 9 December 2011.

interpreted having regard to the foundations and the system of the [Union], as established by the Treaty'.[27]

Furthermore, an Accession Treaty can introduce amendments to the original Treaties and secondary legislation. In this regard, Article 49 TEU refers to the 'adjustments' that an Accession Treaty can make, although limited to the rules 'which such admission entails'. In other words, an Accession Treaty can amend the original Treaties or secondary legislation, provided that the amendment is directly connected to the necessary adjustments required by the accession process.[28]

1.5. *Withdrawal Agreement*

Article 50 TEU provides the procedure for a Member State to withdraw from the Union, which can result in two different scenarios: an agreed withdrawal, or a unilateral withdrawal.[29] In the first scenario, Article 50 TEU provides for the negotiation and conclusion of a specific type of bilateral agreement between the withdrawing Member State and the Union, which includes the terms of exit and the basic features of the future relationship. This agreement has the status of an international treaty, but its position within Union law has raised some questions. Firstly, the legal basis for the withdrawal agreement does not fall within any specific policy area, but under Article 50 TEU.[30] Secondly, since the withdrawal agreement sets out the fundamental aspects of the future relationship, it can predetermine or condition the content of future agreements between the Union and the former Member State. These unique features suggest that the withdrawal agreement is a *sui generis* international agreement with a hybrid status within the Union's legal system.

The Union concluded a withdrawal agreement with the United Kingdom of Great Britain and Northern Ireland, which came into force on 31 January 2020.[31] Evidence of the complexity and significance of this instrument is reflected in the several Protocols annexed to it, including the Protocol on Ireland and Northern Ireland, as well as the Political Declaration outlining the future relations between the United Kingdom and the Union. This document conditions the prospective relationship and legal instruments between the two parties. Currently, the withdrawal agreement retains some features that appear more consistent with the role of primary law, which confirms the *sui generis* nature of this source of Union law.

1.6. *Declarations*

When negotiating the content of the Treaties, Member States generally act within the framework of an Intergovernmental Conference. During the Conference, Member States may agree on the interpretation of certain Treaty provisions or acknowledge declarations made by other

[27] Case C-231/78 *Commission v United Kingdom* EU:C:1979:101, para 12; Joined Cases C-194/85 and C-241/85 *Commission v Greece* EU:C:1988:95, para 20; Case C-233/97 *KappAhl* EU:C:1998:585, para 15; Case C-420/07 *Apostolides* EU:C:2009:271, para 33; and Case C-408/16 *Compania Națională de Administrare a Infrastructurii Rutiere SA* EU:C:2017:940, para 37.

[28] ibid.

[29] Case C-327/18 PPU *RO* EU:C:2018:733; and Case C-621/18 *Wightman* EU:C:2018:999.

[30] Case C-479/21 PPU *SN, SD, Governor of Cloverhill Prison* EU:C:2021:929, para 54: 'Since the withdrawal agreement is intended to cover all of the fields and issues referred to in paragraph 50 above, and since it is not possible to add to Article 50(2) TEU legal bases laying down procedures which are incompatible with the procedure laid down in paragraphs 2 and 4 of that article . . . , it must be concluded that only Article 50 TEU, as an autonomous legal basis independent of any other legal basis set out in the treaties, can ensure that all of the fields falling within the scope of those treaties are treated consistently in the Withdrawal Agreement, thus enabling the withdrawal to take place in an orderly manner.'

[31] Agreement on the withdrawal of the United Kingdom of Great Britain and Northern Ireland from the European Union and the European Atomic Energy Community, published on 12 November 2019 (2019/C 384/I/01).

Member States. In both cases, these declarations are not legally binding and do not constitute a formal part of primary law, but they serve as a source of interpretation of the Treaties.[32] This interpretative role of declarations is not unique to Union law but is a common practice in international law.[33]

The Intergovernmental Conference that negotiated the Treaty of Lisbon introduced 43 declarations relating to provisions of the Treaties[34] and seven declarations relating to the Protocols[35], and took note of 15 unilateral declarations,[36] all of which are annexed to the Final Act of the Conference.

1.7. *The Charter of Fundamental Rights of the European Union*

According to Article 6(1), first paragraph TEU, the Union recognises the rights, freedoms, and principles outlined in the Charter of Fundamental Rights of the European Union of 7 December 2000, as amended on 12 December 2007 in Strasbourg. It also states that the Charter 'shall have the same legal value as the Treaties'.

The Charter has a troubled history.[37] Initially, the Cologne European Council of June 1999 entrusted the drafting of the Charter to a Convention, with the aim of drawing up a declaration of rights to be included in the Treaties. Resistance from some Member States derailed the original plan, but the European Parliament, the Commission, and the Council solemnly proclaimed the Charter in an interinstitutional agreement, committing to implement and uphold the rights set out therein.[38] Subsequently, and following the introduction of certain amendments during the Convention on the Future of Europe, the Charter was included as Part II of the failed Constitutional Treaty. When the time came to negotiate the Lisbon Treaty, the Member States agreed to keep the Charter, although it was not explicitly included in the Treaties due to its politically sensitive nature. This explains why the Charter is not currently included in the text of the original Treaties but is considered part of primary law through a cross-reference in Article 6(1), first paragraph TEU. This clause, as noted earlier, states that the Charter 'shall have the same legal value as the Treaties'.

The Charter, as an instrument of binding primary law, was published in the *Official Journal of the European Union* together with the Explanations relating to the Charter drawn up by the Praesidium of the Convention. The Explanations serve as a guide to interpreting the Charter, indicating the main sources of inspiration for each fundamental right, as well as certain features regarding the scope or level of protection of some fundamental rights. The significance of the Explanations is reflected in Article 52(7) of the Charter, which states that the Explanations 'shall be given due regard by the courts of the Union and of the Member States'.

Although the Charter is a formalised source of primary law, the Union's fundamental rights and their individual recognition have not become petrified due to the enactment of the Charter. As explained in section II.2.3.1 of this chapter, fundamental rights are also recognised as general principles of Union law, established through the case law of the Court of Justice. The fact that many of the fundamental rights now enshrined in the Charter were previously

[32] *KappAhl* (n 27) paras 22–23.

[33] See Art 31(2)(b) of the Vienna Convention on the Law of Treaties.

[34] Declarations 1–43.

[35] Declarations 44–50.

[36] Declarations 51–65.

[37] On the historical development of fundamental rights and the Charter in Union law, see G Braibant, *La Charte des droits fondamentaux de l'Union* européenne (Seuil, 2001) and G de Búrca, 'The Drafting of the European Union Charter of Fundamental Rights' (2001) 26 *European Law Review* 214.

[38] Interinstitutional Agreement of 7 December 2000 by which the European Parliament, the Council and the Commission solemnly proclaim the Charter of Fundamental Rights of the European Union [2000] *OJ* C364/01.

recognised as general principles does not prevent the Court of Justice from recognising new fundamental rights as general principles of law or from developing some fundamental rights in directions not explicitly provided for in the Charter.[39]

Since the entry into force of the Charter, the Court of Justice has interpreted its content, including the general provisions of Title VII, as explained in chapter six of this book.[40] Before it entered into force, the Charter had only an interpretative role,[41] as the Court of Justice confirmed.[42] After the Charter entered into force, the Court of Justice applied its provisions retroactively in cases involving facts that predated 1 December 2009.[43]

1.8. Constituent Acts

The Union can enact measures that follow equivalent procedures to those followed by formalised primary law. An example is the Decision of 20 September 1976, which introduces an Act concerning the election of members of the European Parliament by direct universal suffrage. This Act contains provisions on the electoral process for elections to the European Parliament, which need the prior approval of all the Member States in accordance with their respective constitutional requirements.[44]

Following the same pattern, Article 311 TFEU entrusts the Council with the adoption of 'a decision laying down the provisions relating to the system of own resources of the Union'. Given the importance of this decision, which involves introducing new means of financial resources or abolishing preexisting ones, Article 311 TFEU also specifies that this decision 'shall not enter into force until it is approved by the Member States in accordance with their respective constitutional requirements'.

The fact that these acts are adopted through procedures similar to those used for formalised instruments of primary law could raise doubts about their hierarchical rank and reviewability in Union courts.[45] However, the Court of Justice has confirmed that, regardless of their

[39] For example, Art 41 of the Charter enshrines, inter alia, the right to be heard in administrative proceedings, but only with regard to the institutions, bodies, offices and agencies of the Union, thus excluding Member States when they implement Union law. The Court of Justice has held that although Art 41 of the Charter does not apply to Member States, national proceedings are governed by the general principle of the right to be heard. In this regard, see Case C-349/07 *Sopropé* EU:C:2008:746, para 36; Case C-277/11 *M* EU:C:2012:744, paras 81–82; and Case C-249/13 *Boudjlida* EU:C:2014:2431, para 30. More recently, the Court has confirmed that the principle of tax legality, which is recognised as a fundamental right in the traditions of several Member States, is a general principle of EU law, despite the lack of explicit reference to it in the Charter: 'This finding is an expression of the principle of legality of taxation, which forms part of the legal order of the European Union as a general principle of law, requiring that any obligation to pay a tax and all the essential elements defining the substantive features thereof must be provided for by law, the taxable person having to be in a position to foresee and calculate the amount of tax due and determine the point at which it becomes payable' (see Case C-566/17 *Związek Gmin Zagłębia Miedziowego* EU:C:2019:390, para 39; Joined Cases C-885/19 P and C-898/19 P *Fiat Chrysler Finance Europe and Ireland v Commission* EU:C:2022:859, para 97; and Joined Cases C-451/21 P and C-454/21 P *Luxembourg and Engie v Commission* EU:C:2023:948, para 119).

[40] See, inter alia, Case C-555/07 *Kücükdeveci* EU:C:2010:21; Case C-400/10 PPU *McB* EU:C:2010:582; and Case C-92/09 *Volker und Markus Schecke* EU:C:2010:662.

[41] Since Case C-540/03 *Parliament v Council* EU:C:2006:429, delivered before the entry into force of the Charter, the Court of Justice has made reference to the text on several occasions as a source of interpretation. See, inter alia, Case C-432/05 *Unibet* EU:C:2007:163, para 37; Case C-303/05 *Advocaten voor de Wereld* EU:C:2007:261, para 46; and Case C-275/06 *Promusicae* EU:C:2007:454, para 64.

[42] Case C-540/03 *Parliament v Council* EU:C:2006:429, para 38.

[43] *Kücükdeveci* (n 40) para 22.

[44] Decision 76/787/ECSC, EEC, Euratom [1976] OJ L278/1 and 278/5, amended by Council Decision of 1 February 1993 OJ L33/15 and Council Decision of 25 June 2002 and 23 September 2002, concerning the election of the members of the European Parliament by direct universal suffrage.

[45] Irrespective of the lack of jurisdiction of Union courts to review constituent acts, nothing stops other jurisdictions from undertaking a direct or indirect review of these measures, as seen in the case of *Matthews v United Kingdom* of 18 February 1999, in which the European Court of Human Rights ruled that the United Kingdom breached Art 3 of

singular procedure of approval, constituent acts must be interpreted in accordance with the provisions of the Treaties.[46]

2. Sources of Primary Law Created or Developed by Case Law: General Principles of Law

2.1. *Origin and Role of General Principles*

The case law of courts can introduce new rules of law into a legal system, either by developing binding precedents over time or by crystallising legal concepts that consolidate through dispute-settlement practices. This is the case of general principles of Union law, which have developed through judicial decisions in Union courts or are subject to development in the case law following their generic recognition in the Treaties or other instruments of primary law.

Since its early years, the Court of Justice has relied on general principles to fill the gaps left by the Treaties. This task found its legal basis in the Treaties themselves, which confer on the Court of Justice the mission of ensuring that 'in the interpretation and application of the Treaties the law is observed' (Article 19(1) TEU). This reference to 'the law', as a legal concept that includes not only the Treaties but also other sources of Union law, was enough to empower the Court of Justice to develop a set of binding general principles of Union law.[47]

General principles are not created in a vacuum. They are shaped by the judicial practices of other national and international courts, by the understanding of the law in each historical period as reflected in government and court practices, or by the interpretations provided by legal scholarship. In the case of general principles of Union law, the main source of inspiration originates from the legal traditions of the Member States. This source finds its legal basis in Article 340 TFEU, which governs the law applicable to the non-contractual liability of the Union and states that such actions are held 'in accordance with the general principles common to the laws of the Member States'. A similar provision appears in Article 6(3) TEU, which provides that the Union's fundamental rights 'result from the constitutional traditions common to the Member States [and] shall constitute general principles of the Union's law'. These provisions draw inspiration from other instruments of international law which have been vital in shaping the development of general principles in the international legal order.[48]

In 1957, in *Algera v Common Assembly*, the Court of Justice stated that 'unless the Court is to deny justice it is therefore obliged to solve the problem by reference to the rules acknowledged by the legislation, the learned writing and the case-law of the member countries'.[49] This

---

the First Protocol to the European Convention on Human Rights by excluding British nationals resident in Gibraltar from the European Parliamentary electoral process, in accordance with Decision 76/787. As a follow-up to this ruling, see Case C-145/04 *Spain v United Kingdom* EU:C:2006:543.

[46] In Joined Cases C-393/07 and C-9/08 *Italy and Donnici v European Parliament* EU:C:2009:275, the Court of Justice confirmed that the Act was subject to the original Treaties, stating that 'an interpretation of Article 12 of the 1976 Act which would establish for the benefit of the Parliament a general power to review the official declaration made by the Member States' authorities would not only be contrary to the wording of that article, but would also be incompatible with the principle embodied in Articles 5 EC and 7 EC that the powers of the [Union] and its institutions are limited to those specifically conferred on it'. The same rationale, applied to the Union's own resources decision, is found in Case C-284/90 *Council v European Parliament* EU:C:1992:154, para 31.

[47] On the creation and development of the general principles of Union law, see X Groussot, *General Principles of Community Law* (Europa Law Publishing, 2006).

[48] See, for example, Art 38 of the Statute of the International Court of Justice, which allows recourse to 'the general principles of law recognised by civilised nations'. In the same sense, see Art 7 of the European Convention on Human Rights and Art 15 of the International Covenant on Civil and Political Rights.

[49] Joined Cases C-7/56, C-3/57 and C-7/57 *Algera v Joint Assembly* EU:C:1957:7.

statement illustrates the motivations behind the Court's decision to entrust general principles with a gap-filling role in the Union's legal system. Subsequent developments in the case law show that the role of general principles has expanded. For example, substantive Union law is often implemented by national authorities using national procedural law. When it comes to enforcing Union law, national procedural rules can be ineffective or overly burdensome, ultimately hindering the proper implementation of Union law. In such cases, general principles of Union law, such as the principles of effectiveness, equivalence or state liability, are binding on Member States and help ensure that national authorities apply Union law in ways that guarantee its proper enforcement.

The methodology used by the Court of Justice when establishing or developing a general principle is case-oriented, making it difficult to identify a consistent pattern or methodology. In some cases, the Court relies on a written rule in primary law as a starting point, then develops it further through a series of judicial rulings. For example, the principle of equality appears in the Treaties in various concrete forms, such as the prohibition of discrimination on the grounds of nationality (Article 18 TFEU) or sex (Article 157 TFEU). The fact that the Treaties specify particular grounds of discrimination does not mean these are the only types of discrimination prohibited in Union law. The Court has interpreted the general principle of equality broadly, preventing any measure that, within the scope of the Treaties, results in unjustified differential treatment of comparable situations.

Some general principles are not explicitly recognised in the Treaties but have nevertheless been developed and confirmed as part of the Union's legal system. For example, the general principles of proportionality and legitimate expectations were well established in the practice of German administrative law when the Court of Justice recognised them as binding general principles of Union law in the cases of *Internationale Handelsgesellschaft* and *Racke*.[50] This does not imply that some national legal traditions play a more prominent role than others, as both principles were recognised in several legal systems of the Member States at the time they were incorporated into Union law. The principle of proportionality has equivalent rules in other national legal orders, such as the principles of reasonableness (the Netherlands) or the *bilan Ville Nouvelle-Est* (France). Regarding the general principle of legitimate expectations, a comparable rule of law was acknowledged in the Member States through principles of legal certainty, good faith, and the doctrine of binding administrative precedent. The choice of the name of the general principle is explained by multiple factors, including the Member State from which the case originates, the wording used by the parties in their submissions, or the legal tradition of the Advocate General or judges hearing the case.

In sum, there is no rigid methodological rule explaining why a legal tradition might exert more influence on the development of a general principle in Union law. The process is case-specific, but also heavily influenced by the goals pursued by the Union in each policy area, as reflected in the Treaties. There is no quantitative or majoritarian logic whereby the legal tradition with the largest presence among Member States prevails. Advocate General Poiares Maduro emphasised this in *FIAMM* in the following terms:

> Although the Court of Justice must certainly be guided by the most characteristic provisions of the systems of domestic law, it must above all ensure that it adopts a solution appropriate to the needs and specific features of the [Union] legal system. In other words, the Court has the task of drawing on the legal traditions of the Member States in order to find an answer to similar legal questions arising under [Union] law that both respects those traditions and is appropriate to the context of the [Union]

[50] Case C-11/70 *Internationale Handelsgesellschaft* EU:C:1970:114; and Case C-98/78 *Racke* EU:C:1979:14.

> legal order. From that point of view, even a solution adopted by a minority may be preferred if it best meets the requirements of the [Union] system.[51]

2.2. *Effects*

The Court of Justice has reiterated that the general principles of Union law hold the status of primary law. Over time, these principles have been used as a benchmark to scrutinise the validity of secondary law, as well as the Union's decision to enter into international agreements.[52] Additionally, general principles of Union law are also the parameter of validity of Member State actions when implementing Union law. Consequently, general principles of Union law can be directly invoked in national courts and have primacy over national law.[53]

Apart from their role as standards of review for the validity of Union and Member State action, general principles of Union law also play an interpretative role. They guide the interpretation of formalised instruments of primary and secondary law, thereby promoting the uniform interpretation and application of Union law.[54] This hermeneutical role of the general principles extends to the law of the Member States, which must be interpreted and implemented in accordance with the general principles of Union law, as long as the Member States are implementing Union law.[55]

2.3. *Typology of General Principles*

The Treaties do not provide a systematic categorisation of the general principles of Union law, and to a large extent the same can be said of the Court of Justice's case law. The existing typologies of general principles are drawn from scholarly works, attempting to rationalise the diversity in the case law and to facilitate the understanding and implementation of these sources of law.[56] Among the many scholarly proposals that classify the general principles, the following three categories may be distinguished.

2.3.1. Constitutional Principles

Some general principles have a particularly broad scope and serve as structural features of the Union's legal system. The Court of Justice has described such general principles as 'constitutional'.[57] Their scope is all-encompassing, thus covering all areas of Union policy. Given their systemic importance for the Union as a whole, some constitutional principles are explicitly

[51] Joined Cases C-120/06 P and 121/06 P *FIAMM* EU:C:2008:98, Opinion of AG Poiares Maduro, pt 55.

[52] Case C-112/77 *Töpfer v Commission* EU:C:1978:94.

[53] Case C-230/78 *Eridiana* EU:C:1979:216, and Case C-205/20 *NE v Bezirkshauptmannschaft Hartberg-Fürstenfeld* EU:C:2022:168, para 37.

[54] See, for example, Case C-327/91 *France v Commission* EU:C:1994:305 as well as Opinion 1/91 EU:C:1991:490.

[55] Case C-294/83 *Les Verts v Parliament* EU:C:1986:166, para 36.

[56] See, for example, Groussot's typology (n 47) which classifies principles as complementary (or subsidiary), regulatory and operational. The first category fills gaps in Union law, the second has a regulatory role (free movement, subsidiarity or sincere cooperation) and the third serves as a parameter for the review of individual acts (proportionality, equality, legal certainty, etc).

[57] In Case C-101/08 *Audiolux* EU:C:2009:626, para 63, the Court held that the general principles of Union law have *constitutional* status. This is the first time that the Court referred to the general principles in such terms, but it did so to reinforce the *scope* of general principles as opposed to the more specific and instrumental features that characterise other principles enunciated by the Union legislature. This characterisation has been met with scholarly criticism (see, for example, J Bengoetxea, 'Audiolux' (2010) 47 *Common Market Law Review* 1173), while the Court has insisted on it on other occasions, such as in Case C-174/08 *NCC Construction Danmark A/S* EU:C:2009:669, para 42 and, implicitly, in Case C-251/16 *Cussens* EU:C:2017:881, para 31.

enshrined in the Treaties, while others are found solely in the case law of the Court of Justice. A non-exhaustive, but representative, enumeration of constitutional general principles of Union law can be inferred as follows.

The principles of *subsidiarity and proportionality* are enshrined in Article 5 TEU and Protocol No 2. As stated in Article 5(3) TEU:

> Under the principle of subsidiarity, in areas which do not fall within its exclusive competence, the Union shall act only if and in so far as the objectives of the proposed action cannot be sufficiently achieved by the Member States, either at central level or at regional and local level, but can rather, by reason of the scale or effects of the proposed action, be better achieved at Union level.[58]

Furthermore, Article 5(4) TEU states that 'under the principle of proportionality, the content and form of Union action shall not exceed what is necessary to achieve the objectives of the Treaties'. Both principles can be implemented through a procedure outlined in Protocol No 2, aimed at ensuring their safeguarding through the involvement of national parliaments in the Union's legislative procedure. The details of this procedure are explained in chapter four of this book.

The principle of *conferral* requires the Union to act only within the competences attributed by the Treaties. This principle is enshrined in Article 5(1) and (2) TEU and reiterated in Article 4(1) TEU, which states that 'competences not conferred upon the Union in the Treaties remain with the Member States'. Article 5(2) TEU further clarifies the principle by adding that 'the Union shall act only within the limits of the competences conferred upon it by the Member States in the Treaties to attain the objectives set out therein'.[59]

The principle of *sincere cooperation requires* the Union and its Member States to mutually assist each other in fulfilling obligations that arise under Union law.[60] In relations between the Union and its Member States, this principle operates in both directions, imposing duties on Member States as requested by the Union,[61] and vice versa. It also applies to interactions between Member States or between Union institutions, bodies, offices, and agencies. Article 4(3) TEU refers to this principle, stating that 'the Union and the Member States shall, in full mutual respect, assist each other in carrying out tasks which flow from the Treaties'.

The principle of *respect for the national identity of the Member States*, introduced in the Treaties in 1992, sets a limit on Union action that could undermine policies or features closely attached to a Member State's identity, especially if it might interfere with its core cultural or political characteristics. Article 4(2) TEU describes the national identity of Member States as 'inherent in their fundamental structures, political and constitutional, inclusive of regional and local self-government'. The provision goes on to enumerate some examples of features that form part of the Member States' national identity: 'the territorial integrity of the State, maintaining law and order and safeguarding national security'. The Court of Justice's case law so far seems cautious about defining the scope of 'national identity' as an autonomous concept of Union law. This minimalist stance has encouraged other courts, particularly national constitutional courts, to provide their own versions of what constitutes the national identity of each

[58] On the principle of subsidiarity, see A Estella de Noriega, *The EU Principle of Subsidiarity and Its Critique* (Oxford University Press, 2002).

[59] On the principle of conferral of competences and its role in the Union attribution of competences, see ch 4.

[60] See, inter alia, Case C-219/17 *Berlusconi and Fininvest* EU:C:2018:1023, para 47; Joined Cases C-200/07 and 201/07 *Marra* EU:C:2008:579, para 41; and Case C-502/19 *Junqueras Vies* EU:C:2019:1115, para 93.

[61] See, inter alia, Case C-263/98 *Belgium v Commission* EU:C:2001:455, paras 94–96; and Joined Cases C-622/16 P to C-624/16 P *Scuola Elementare Maria Montessori v Commission* EU:C:2018:873, para 84.

Member State.[62] The Court of Justice has begun to set limits to these tendencies stemming from the practice of national constitutional courts.[63]

The principle of *non-discrimination* is also a principle inherent in the integration process and applies across all areas of Union activity. As a starting point, Article 2 TEU identifies equality as one of the Union's values, alongside respect for human dignity, freedom, democracy, the rule of law, and human rights. As a tangible expression of a value that the Union is responsible for safeguarding, the principle of non-discrimination is enshrined to combat particularly heinous forms of treatment based on criteria such as nationality,[64] sex,[65] ethnicity,[66] disability,[67] or sexual orientation.[68] The freedoms of movement are also set out as non-discrimination mandates which prevent Member States from treating goods,[69] services,[70] workers[71], and capital[72] originating from other Member States differently. To address the forms of discrimination referred to in the Treaty, regulatory powers are granted to Union institutions to adopt positive measures to help eradicate unjustified differences of treatment.[73]

Before the Lisbon Treaty came into force, the Union's *fundamental rights* were part of Union law as general principles. The recognition of these rights as general principles was first established in the case of *Stauder*,[74] following which a long and comprehensive line of fundamental rights was developed on a case-by-case basis: dignity,[75] equality,[76] freedom of expression,[77] political participation,[78] freedom of religion,[79] effective judicial protection,[80] *nullum crimen*

[62] F-X Millet, *L'Union européenne et l'identité constitutionnelle des États membres* (LGDJ, 2013) and A Sáiz Arnáiz and C Alcoberro, *National Constitutional Identity and European Integration* (Intersentia, 2013). See, for example, the case of France, whose *Conseil Constitutionnel* has used the principle of national identity to define the limits of Union law when it comes into conflict with the French Constitution. In Case No 2006-540, the *Conseil Constitutionnel* uses the category of 'principles inherent to the French constitutional identity' as a limit to Union law vis-à-vis the French Constitution. See D Simon, 'L'obscure clarté de la jurisprudence du Conseil constitutionnel relative à la transposition des directives communautaires' (2006) 10 *Europe* 2. On the role of national identity as a limit to the primacy of Union law, see ch 10 of this book.

[63] Case C-448/23 *Commission v Poland* EU:C:2025:975, paras 224–36.

[64] Art 18 TFEU.

[65] Arts 2 and 10 TEU.

[66] ibid, Art 10.

[67] ibid.

[68] ibid.

[69] Arts 34–35 TFEU.

[70] ibid, Art 56.

[71] ibid, Art 45.

[72] ibid, Art 63.

[73] ibid, Arts 18(2), 19, 51(2) and 157(3) TFEU.

[74] Case C-29/69 *Stauder* EU:C:1969:57.

[75] Case C-377/98 *Netherlands v Parliament and Council* EU:C:2001:523, paras 70–77; and Case C-36/02 *Omega* EU:C:2004:614, paras 34–36. In this respect, see Art 1 of the Charter.

[76] Equality in the application of the law by Union institutions (Joined Cases C-124/76 and C-20/77 *Moulins et Huilieries de Pont-à-Mousson and Providence agricole de la Champagne judgments* EU:C:1977:161); equality between men and women (Case C-149/77 *Defrenne* EU:C:1978:130, paras 24–32); or more recent prohibitions of discrimination, such as those relating to age (Case C-144/04 *Mangold* EU:C:2005:709, para 75 and *Kücükdeveci*, (n 40) paras 20–21); or disability (Case C-13/05 *Chacón Navas* EU:C:2006:456, para 46; and Case C-303/06 *Coleman* EU:C:2008:415, paras 50–51). See Arts 20–26 of the Charter.

[77] Joined Cases C-43/82 and C-63/82 *VBVB and VBBB v Commission* EU:C:1984:9, para 34; Joined Cases C-60/84 and 61/84 *Cinéthèque* EU:C:1985:329; Case C-159/90 *Society for the Protection of Unborn Children Ireland* EU:C:1991:378, paras 30–31; Case C-260/89 *ERT* EU:C:1991:254, para 44; Case C-112/00 *Schmidberger* EU:C:2003:333, paras 79–80; and Case C-274/99 P *Connolly v Commission* EU:C:2001:127, paras 37–56. See Art 11 of the Charter.

[78] Case C-145/04 *Spain v United Kingdom* EU:C:2006:543, paras 94–96. See Arts 39 and 49 of the Charter.

[79] Case C-130/75 *Prais v Council* EU:C:1976:142, paras 6–19. See Art 10 of the Charter.

[80] Case C-222/84 *Johnston* EU:C:1986:206, para 18; Case C-222/86 *Heylens and Others* EU:C:1987:442, para 14; Case C-97/91 *Oleificio Borelli v Commission* EU:C:1992:491, paras 13–14; Case C-269/99 *Carl Kühne and Others* EU:C:2001:659, paras 57–58; and *Kadi* (n 10) paras 335–336. See Arts 47–48 of the Charter.

sine lege,[81] collective action,[82] property[83], and the freedom to conduct a business,[84] among others. Since the Charter came into force, the Union's fundamental rights have been codified in a binding source of primary law, but this development does not prevent the Court of Justice from recognising new fundamental rights beyond those included in the Charter. The Charter does not carve in stone a fixed number of fundamental rights in Union law; it merely formalises and updates existing rights for the purpose of transparency and a more accessible understanding by citizens of their rights under Union law. Evidence of the ongoing and dynamic nature of this process of recognition of fundamental rights is found in Article 6(3) TEU, which states that 'fundamental rights . . . as they result from the constitutional traditions common to the Member States, constitute general principles of the Union's law'.

2.3.2. Principles of Administrative Law

In contrast to constitutional principles, other general principles operate primarily within specific areas of practice. This is especially true of the Union's administrative practice in implementing Union policies, which is governed by several standards of conduct now codified as general principles. Since these principles are closely linked to the Union's practice in the handling of administrative procedures and decision-making, they are categorised as general principles of administrative law, including the principles of legitimate expectations, proportionality, transparency, and good administration.

The principle of *legitimate expectations* embodies the principle of legal certainty as applied to the Union's administrative practice. The principle of legitimate expectations requires the Union's institutions, offices, bodies, and agencies to act in a predictable manner, avoiding actions that frustrate the expectations created by previous Union action. This principle is vital in restricting the Union's ability to revoke a previously settled position that grants individual rights, thus protecting those legitimate expectations. According to the case law of the Court of Justice, the principle of legitimate expectations precludes the Union from revoking lawful acts that confer individual rights[85] or from enacting retroactive measures that restrict those rights.[86] Additionally, it offers guarantees when the Union revokes unlawful acts, together with requirements on time limitations and standards of good faith on the part of the individuals concerned.[87] The principle also safeguards expectations created by the Union when its institutions, bodies, offices, or agencies make statements or declarations that serve as a roadmap for individual conduct.[88] While the Union is not precluded from departing from its previously

[81] Joined Cases C-74/95 and C-129/95 *X* EU:C:1996:491, para 25; Joined Cases C-189/02 P, C-202/02 P, C-205-208/02 *Dansk Rørindustri and Others v Commission* EU:C:2005:408, paras 215–19; and Case C-303/05 *Advocaten voor de Wereld* EU:C:2007:261, paras 49–50. See Art 49 of the Charter.

[82] Case C-341/05 *Laval un Partneri* EU:C:2007:341, para 90; and Case C-438/05 *International Transport Workers' Federation and Finnish Seamen's Union, known as 'Viking Line'* EU:C:2007:772, para 43.

[83] Case C-4/73 *Nold v Commission* EU:C:1974:51, para 14; Case C-44/79 *Hauer* EU:C:1979:290, paras 17–30; Case C-59/83 *Biovilac v EEC* EU:C:1984:380, paras 21–23; Case C-5/88 *Wachauf* EU:C:1989:321, paras 17–23; Joined Cases C-20/00 and C-64/00 *Booker Aquaculture and Hydro Seafood* EU:C:2003:397, paras 67–68; and Case C-275/06 *Promusicae* EU:C:2008:54, para 62. In this respect, see Art 17 of the Charter.

[84] Case C-230/78 *Eridiana* EU:C:1979:216, paras 20–22; Case C-240/83 *ADBHU* EU:C:1985:59, paras 9–13; and Case C-200/96 *Metronome Musik* EU:C:1998:172, para 21. See Art 16 of the Charter.

[85] As stated in Joined Cases C-7/56, C-3/57 and C-7/57 *Algera v Joint Assembly* EU:C:1957:7, but using an expression different from 'legitimate expectations'.

[86] It is precisely in its case law on the retroactivity of restrictive measures that the term 'legitimate expectations' first appeared in the case law. See Case C-98/78 *Racke* EU:C:1979:14, para 20.

[87] *Algera and Others* (n 83) 115; Case C-14/81 *Alpha Steel v Commission* EU:C:1982:76, para 10; and Case C-15/85 *Consorzio Cooperative d'Abruzzo v Commission* EU:C:1987:111, para 12.

[88] Case C-144/82 *Detti v Court of Justice* EU:C:1983:211; Case C-265/85 *Van den Bergh en Jurgens and Van Dijk Food Products Lopik v Commission* EU:C:1987:121; and Case C-313/90 *CIRFS and Others v Commission* EU:C:1993:111.

stated positions, the principle of legitimate expectations requires it to adhere to certain standards of conduct and to recognise the right of individuals to seek damages if it fails to provide consistent and stable guidance.[89]

The principle of *proportionality* plays a role in determining the scope of the Union's competence, as discussed above. Additionally, this principle is a crucial tool guiding the Union's administrative actions, requiring institutions, bodies, offices, and agencies to ensure that any interference in the legal sphere of individuals is adequate and strictly necessary to achieve the ends it pursues. The principle of proportionality is applied through three successive *tests*. The *adequacy* test requires the measure to be objectively suitable to achieve its objectives.[90] For example, a tax that charges for the use of telecommunications infrastructure does not serve any environmental purpose, and therefore it is not a suitable measure to achieve environmental goals. The test of *necessity* requires the Union's measures not to go beyond what is strictly necessary to attain their aims, using the least restrictive means among all viable and equally effective measures available.[91] For example, a prohibition on the marketing of a product is disproportionate if the same objective can be achieved, with equivalent degrees of effectiveness, through the use of inspection procedures rather than an outright prohibition. In some cases, case law applies the principle of proportionality adding a third test called the principle of proportionality *stricto sensu*. In this third test, the benefits of the measure must outweigh the harm it causes in the individual sphere. This test undertakes a balancing exercise in which the costs and benefits of the Union's measure are judicially scrutinised.[92]

The principle of *transparency* is enshrined in Article 10(3) TEU, which states that 'decisions shall be taken as openly and as closely as possible to the citizen'.[93] This provision reflects the growing concern about the Union's visibility towards its citizens and the need to make its decision-making procedures accessible and open to ensure the democratic quality of its activities. As early as 1993, the Council and the Commission introduced a Code of Conduct on public access to documents, which was later interpreted by the Court of Justice, paving the way for subsequent and more ambitious legal reforms in this area.[94] The principle of transparency also covers access to other sources of information beyond written documents: transcripts, digitalised information, audio, and audiovisual recordings fall within its scope. This broad scope aims to promote citizens' involvement in the Union's decision-making procedures. According to the Court of Justice, the principle of transparency makes it possible

> to enable citizens to participate more closely in the decision-making process [of the Union], to guarantee that the administration enjoys greater legitimacy and is more effective and more accountable to the citizen in a democratic system and to contribute to strengthening the principles of democracy and respect for fundamental rights.[95]

[89] Case C-112/77 *Töpfer* EU:C:1979:94, paras 18–20; and Case C-120/86 *Mulder* EU:C:1988:213.

[90] Case C-491/01 *British American Tobacco (Investments) and Imperial Tobacco* EU:C:2002:741, para 123; and Case C-210/03 *Swedish Match* EU:C:2004:802, para 48.

[91] Case C-8/89 *Zardi* EU:C:1990:260, para 10; Joined Cases C-133/93, C-300/93 and C-362/93 *Crispoltoni and Others* EU:C:1994:364, para 40; and Case C-41/03 P *Rica Foods (Free Zone) NV v Commission* EU:C:2005:456, paras 85–86.

[92] Case C-331/88 *Fedesa and others* EU:C:1990:391, para 13; and Case C-426/93 *Germany v Council* EU:C:1995:367, paras 49–50.

[93] This provision is partly reproduced in Art 298(1) TFEU, which states that 'In carrying out their missions, the institutions, bodies, offices and agencies of the Union shall have the support of an open, efficient and independent European administration.'

[94] Code of Conduct on public access to Council and Commission documents [1993] *OJ* L340/41. On the implementation of the Code, see inter alia, Case T-194/94 *Carvel and Guardian Newspapers v Council* EU:T:1995:183; Case T-105/95 *WWF UK v Commission* EU:C:1997:189; and Case C-353/99 P *Council v Hautala* EU:C:2001:661.

[95] See, inter alia, Case C-41/00 *Interporc v Commission* EU:C:2003:125, para 39; and Case C-28/08 P *Commission v Bavarian Lager* EU:C:2010:378, para 54.

The principle of transparency is reaffirmed in Article 15 TFEU, a provision that requires the Union to provide a policy of openness applicable to all policies and institutions, bodies, offices, and agencies.

The principle of transparency has undergone specific developments in the field of access to documents. While Article 15(3) TFEU and Article 42 of the Charter enshrine the right of access to documents, the practical means to implement this right are provided by a legislative instrument. Regulation 1049/2001 introduces a common framework applicable to the Union's institutions, bodies, offices and agencies, with some exceptions outlined in Article 15(3) TFEU. Despite the broad scope of application of Regulation 1049/2001, the principle of transparency remains a general principle of Union law and, consequently, Regulation 1049/2001 does not exhaust the entire scope of the principle.[96] Also, it is possible for other legislative acts to introduce specific rules on access to documents and transparency more generally, as a means to refine its applicability in certain policy areas.[97]

The principle of *good administration* sets standards of procedural fairness in the decision-making process of administrative authorities. These standards reflect, to a certain extent, the same rules of procedural fairness applicable to court proceedings, but are tailored to the realities and peculiarities of administrative procedures. The case law of the Court of Justice has elaborated on the principle of good administration so that it now includes a variety of procedural rights: the right to be heard, especially during proceedings leading to the imposition of sanctions;[98] the obligation to provide notification of the start and end of a procedure, as well as of any relevant procedural actions, within a reasonable time frame;[99] the duty to state reasons;[100] and the right of interested parties to be assisted by a lawyer, or the secrecy of lawyer–client communications.[101] In the course of administrative procedures leading to sanctions, such measures must not punish the same conduct twice, in accordance with the principle of *ne bis in idem*, which applies within the context of administrative sanctions as part of the general principle of good administration.[102]

2.3.3. Principles Governing the Relationship between EU and National Law

Union law is incorporated into the law of the Member States. Despite the autonomous nature of Union law vis-a-vis national law, both legal systems are closely interconnected. This reality becomes a practical necessity when it comes to implementing Union law in the Member States, a practice that will frequently require national rules to enforce rights and obligations derived

[96] Case C-213/15 P *Commission v Breyer* EU:C:2017:563, paras 49–52; and Case C-92/09 and 93/09 *Volker und Markus Schecke* EU:C:2010:662, para 68.

[97] See, for example, Articles 27(2), 28 and 30 of Council Regulation (EC) No 1/2003 of 16 December 2002 on the implementation of the rules on competition laid down in Articles 81 and 82 of the Treaty [2003] OJ L1/1), and Articles 88, 90–92 and 96(6) of Regulation (EU) No 806/2014 of the European Parliament and of the Council of 15 July 2014 establishing uniform rules and a uniform procedure for the resolution of credit institutions and certain investment firms in the framework of a Single Resolution Mechanism and a Single Resolution Fund and amending Regulation (EU) No 1093/2010 [2014] OJ L 225/1).

[98] Case C-85/76 *Hoffmann-La Roche v Commission* EU:C:1979:36, para 9; and Case C-135/92 *Fiskano v Commission* EU:C:1994:267, para 39.

[99] Case C-17/74 *Transocean Marine Paint v Commission* EU:C:1974:106, para 15.

[100] Case C-46/16 *Valsts ieņēmumu dienests* EU:C:2017:839, para 39; and Case C-564/16 P *EUIPO v Puma SE* EU:C:2018:509, para 80.

[101] Case C-155/79 *AM & S v Commission* EU:C:1982:157, paras 18–22; and Case C-550/07 P *Akzo Nobel Chemicals v Commission* EU:C:2010:512.

[102] Joined Cases C-18/65 and 35/65 *Gutmann v Commission* EU:C:1967:6; and Joined Cases C-238/99 P, C-244/99 P, C-245/99 P, C-247/99 P, C-250/99 P and C-252/99 P *Wacker-Chemie and Hoechst v Commission* EU:C:2002:582.

from Union law. In the daily operations of a Member State's public administration or courts, officials will apply both Union and national law in a manner that guarantees the proper implementation of rights and obligations stemming from Union law.

To ensure the smooth and effective interaction between Union law and the laws of the Member States, several principles articulate the relationship between the two legal systems. These principles aim to establish conditions for directly invoking Union law within the Member States, as well as conflict rules to resolve contradictions between Union law and national law. The principles of direct effect and primacy serve this purpose and are explained in detail in chapters nine and ten of this book.

There are differing views on the legal nature of these principles, as they are not standards of conduct that safeguard an individual's or an institution's legal sphere. The principles of direct effect and primacy do not directly confer individual rights; their aim is to articulate the proper relationship between two autonomous legal systems. It is no coincidence that the case law of the Court of Justice has refrained from using the term 'principle' when referring to direct effect, and it has done so only recently regarding primacy.[103] When referring to both principles jointly, the Court of Justice depicts them as the result of the autonomous nature of the Union's legal system, qualifying them as 'essential characteristics' that contribute to defining the features of Union law:

> Added to [the autonomous nature of Union law] are the essential characteristics of the EU legal order arising from that autonomous nature, such as its primacy over the laws of the Member States and the direct effect of a whole series of provisions which are applicable to their nationals and to the Member States themselves. Those essential characteristics of EU law have given rise to a structured network of principles, rules and mutually interdependent legal relations binding the European Union and its Member States reciprocally and binding its Member States to each other.[104]

III. INTERNATIONAL AGREEMENTS

According to Article 47 TEU, 'the Union shall have legal personality', a feature attributed initially to the European Communities that is now conferred on the Union.[105] One of the consequences of the Union's legal personality is outlined in Article 216(1) TFEU, which grants the Union the authority to enter into international agreements with third states and international organisations, thereby affirming the Union's status as a subject of rights and obligations under international law. The main sources of international rights and obligations for the Union are international treaties, but they are not the only sources: the Union can also be bound by decisions of international organisations of which it is a member or by obligations under general international law. This section provides an overview of the various instruments of international law by which the Union is bound, starting with some considerations on the position of international law in the Union's legal system.

[103] Case C-314/08 *Filipiak* EU:C:2009:719, para 44; *Kücükdeveci* (n 40) para 54; and Case C-409/06 *Winner Wetten* EU:C:2010:503, para 60.

[104] Case C-448/23 *Commission v Poland* EU:C:2025:975, para 167.

[105] However, the Euratom still remains in existence and it holds legal personality as a distinct supranational organisation, closely connected to the Union.

1. International Agreements in the Union Legal System

1.1. *Effectiveness of International Agreements Concluded by the Union*

Article 216(2) TFEU states that agreements concluded by the Union 'shall be binding upon the institutions of the Union and on its Member States' and consequently they form an integral part of Union law.[106] Just as Union law becomes an autonomous legal system within national law, international law undergoes a similar process when incorporated into Union law. Article 216(2) TFEU reflects a *monist* approach towards the incorporation of international agreements, meaning it is unnecessary to enact legislative measures to introduce obligations of international law into Union law. International agreements thus become part of Union law from the moment the Union gives its consent to be bound, the agreement is published, and it enters into force.[107]

As an integral part of the Union's legal system, the provisions of international agreements can in principle be directly effective and be relied upon by individuals in both Union and national courts. However, the case law of the Court of Justice has introduced significant nuances to its general doctrine on direct effect when applied to international agreements, which will be examined and discussed in chapter nine of this book.

1.2. *The Autonomy of Union law vis-a-vis International Law*

While international law that binds the Union forms part of Union law, its incorporation does not compromise the autonomy of Union law. Rules of international law cannot alter the essential characteristics of Union law, nor the way in which the latter interacts with national law. Therefore, international law and, in particular, international agreements concluded by the Union, cannot intrude on the institutional structure of the Union, on its sources of law, nor on the legal remedies available to ensure the uniform interpretation of Union law. Moreover, the Treaties attach particular importance to the role played by the Union's judiciary as a safeguard of the autonomy of Union law, as confirmed by Article 344 TFEU. According to this provision, 'Member States undertake not to submit a dispute concerning the interpretation or application of the Treaties to any method of settlement other than those provided for therein'.[108]

The Court of Justice has consistently affirmed that the autonomy of Union law acts as a limit to international law, including international agreements. In Opinion 1/76, the proposal to establish an international fund with a jurisdictional body that included judges of the Court of Justice sitting alongside a judge nominated by Switzerland was incompatible with the Treaty.[109] Such a design compromised the independence of the Court of Justice and negatively affected the consistency of the legal remedies guaranteeing the uniformity of Union law.

[106] Case C-181/73 *Haegeman* EU:C:1974:41, para 5; Case C-104/81 *Kupferberg* EU:C:1982:362, paras 11–13; and Case C-431/05 *Merck Genéricos – Produtos Farmacêuticos* EU:C:2007:496, para 31; as well as Opinion 1/91 (n 52) para 37.

[107] On the effects of agreements only subject to signature, see Case T-115/94 *Opel Austria v Council* EU:T:1997:3, paras 90–94, referring to Art 18 of the Vienna Convention on the Law of Treaties.

[108] The Court of Justice has repeatedly stated that Art 344 TFEU reinforces the autonomy of the Union's legal system: '[that] clause is, therefore, incompatible with the principle of sincere cooperation set out in the first subparagraph of Article 4(3) TEU and has an adverse effect on the autonomy of EU law enshrined, inter alia, in Article 344 TFEU'. See Case C-459/03 *Commission v Ireland* EU:C:2006:345, paras 123–124; Case C-284/16 *Achmea* EU:C:2018:158, paras 58–59; and Case C-109/20 *PL Holdings* EU:C:2021:875, para 46.

[109] Opinion 1/76 of 26 April 1977 EU:C:1977:63.

A similar outcome is found in Opinion 1/91,[110] where the Court of Justice rejected the establishment of a mixed court responsible for interpreting European Economic Area (EEA) law. The composition of such a court, coupled with the fact that EEA rules replicate the content of Union law, posed a risk of divergent interpretations that could undermine the autonomy of Union law. As a result, the Court of Justice declared that the agreement in question was incompatible with the Treaty 'and, more generally, [with] the very foundations of the [Union]'.[111]

This approach found its most notable expression in Opinion 2/13, on the draft agreement on the accession of the European Union to the European Convention on Human Rights. The Court of Justice considered that this agreement, which articulated the complex mechanisms governing the relationship between Union law, the Convention, and the jurisdictions of both the Court of Justice and the European Court of Human Rights, was liable to undermine the unity and coherence of Union law and, consequently, breached the autonomy of Union law. Despite the ambiguities in the reasoning of the Court of Justice, Opinion 2/13 confirms the importance of the notion of 'autonomy' as a limit to international law having any impact on the ordinary functions of the Union's institutional system.[112] This broad conception of the autonomy of Union law that appears in the case law has led some commentators to describe it as a 'super-principle' of Union law, an all-encompassing criterion that, nevertheless, remains ambiguous and subject to interpretation.[113]

2. International Agreements and their Interaction with other Sources of Union Law

2.1. *Relationship with Union Primary Law*

Once incorporated into Union law, international agreements hold a specific position within the Union's hierarchy of sources of law. As a starting point, international agreements are subject to the provisions of Union primary law, which include formalised primary law and general principles of Union law. This is implicitly reflected in Article 218(11) TFEU, which recognises the right of a Member State, the European Parliament, the Council or the Commission to request an opinion from the Court of Justice as to whether an agreement envisaged is compatible with the Treaties. The provision also adds that if the opinion of the Court is adverse, 'the agreement envisaged may not enter into force unless it is amended or the Treaties are revised'.

The primacy of primary law over international agreements is confirmed by the fact that the Court of Justice can review, through an action for annulment or actions for damages, the conformity of international agreements with formalised primary law or general principles of Union law, as well as the Charter of Fundamental Rights.[114] The scope of judicial review can

[110] Opinion 1/91 (n 52).

[111] ibid, para 3. See Opinion 1/00 EU:C:2002:231 and Opinion 1/09 EU:C:2011:123.

[112] Following Opinion 2/13, the Court of Justice once again emphasised the relevance of the autonomy of Union law when interacting with international law. This is the case of trade agreements (Opinion 2/15, EU:C:2017:376, paras 301–304) and bilateral investment protection agreements concluded between the Member States (Case C-284/16 *Achmea* EU:C:2018:158, paras 55–59).

[113] P Eeckhout, 'Opinion 2/13 on EU Accession to the ECHR and Judicial Dialogue: Autonomy or Autarky?' (2015) 38 *Fordham International Law Journal* 955; A Łazowski, 'When Caveats Turn into Locks: Opinion 2/13 on Accession of the European Union to the ECHR' (2015) 16 *German Law Journal* 179, and T Lock, 'The Future of the European Union's Accession to the European Convention on Human Rights after Opinion 2/13: Is it Still Possible and Is it Still Desirable?' (2015) 11 *European Constitutional Law Review* 239.

[114] Opinion 1/15 EU:C:2017:592, paras 119ff, on the EU–Canada air passenger data transfer agreement, in which the Court of Justice, for the first time, declared the incompatibility of certain provisions of an international agreement concluded by the Union with the Charter, in particular with the fundamental right to privacy and private life in Arts 7–8.

include procedural steps before the conclusion of the agreement, as well as the Union's competence,[115] or even the substantive content of the agreement.[116] When it comes to the substantive content of an international agreement, the Court of Justice will refrain from reviewing the agreement itself, focusing instead on the Council decision authorising its conclusion.

The case law provides several examples of how the rules of Union primary law hold a hierarchically supreme position over international agreements and international law generally. In *Kadi*, the Court of Justice stated that the Charter of the United Nations 'would have primacy over acts of secondary [Union] law', but 'that primacy at the level of [Union] law would not, however, extend to primary law, in particular to the general principles of which fundamental rights form part'.[117]

2.2. *Relationship with Union Secondary Law*

Since its judgment in *International Fruit Company* in 1972, the Court of Justice has confirmed its jurisdiction to review the conformity of Union secondary law with international agreements concluded by the Union.[118] Ever since, the case law has consistently emphasised that Union institutions are bound by these agreements, which take precedence over the provisions of secondary legislation.[119] Furthermore, secondary law must be interpreted, in so far as possible, in conformity with the international agreements concluded by the Union.[120]

If private parties intend to rely on international agreements to challenge Union secondary law, it is imperative that the international agreement meet the conditions for direct effect in accordance with the case law.[121] In *Intertanko*, the Court of Justice ruled out the review of the validity of a directive in light of the United Nations Convention on the Law of the Sea of 1982, on the grounds that the nature and broad logic of the Convention precluded such review. To perform the judicial review of the validity of Union secondary law in light of an international agreement, the Court of Justice requires three conditions to be satisfied: first, the Union must be bound by the international agreement; second, the 'nature and the broad logic' of the agreement must not preclude such a review; and third, the provisions of the agreement relied upon must be unconditional and sufficiently precise.[122]

This approach subtly diverges from the standard conditions for the direct effect of provisions of Union law, and it is confirmed in reiterated case law of the Court of Justice, including case law on the direct effect of decisions by international organisations to which the Union

[115] Case C-327/91 *France v Commission* EU:C:1994:305; and Case C-360/93 *Parliament v Council* EU:C:1996:84. A similar line of argument, albeit as an obiter dicta, can be found in Opinion 3/94 EU:C:1995:436, para 22.

[116] The Court of Justice has reviewed the substance of an international agreement, but with an invalidating effect on the ratification act, in, inter alia, Case C-122/95 *Germany v Council* EU:C:1998:94, paras 41–46, for the breach of the principle of equality.

[117] *Kadi* (n 10) paras 307–308; and Case C-308/06 *Intertanko and Others* EU:C:2008:312, para 42.

[118] Joined Cases C-21/72 and 24/72 *International Fruit Company and Others* EU:C:1972:115, para 6. See also Case C-181/73 *Haegeman* EU:C:1974:41; Case C-286/90 *Poulsen and Diva Navigation* EU:C:1992:453, para 9; *Kadi* (n 10) para 291; Case C-366/10 *Air Transport Association of America and Others* EU:C:2011:864, paras 101 and 102; Case C-266/16 *Western Sahara Campaign UK* EU:C:2018:118, para 47; Case C-654/18 *Interseroh Dienstleistungs GmbH* EU:C:2020:398, para 44; and Case C-352/19 P *Région de Bruxelles-Capitale* EU:C:2020:978, para 25.

[119] See, inter alia, Case C-61/94 *Commission v Germany* EU:C:1996:313, para 52; and Case C-311/04 *Algemene Scheeps Agentuur Dordrecht* EU:C:2006:23, para 25.

[120] Case C-382/21 P *EUIPO v The Kaikai Company* EU:C:2024:172, para 70: 'since the TRIPs Agreement is binding on the European Union and, accordingly, takes precedence over EU secondary legislation, the latter must be interpreted, as far as is possible, in accordance with the provisions of that agreement'. See also the Opinion of Advocate General Biondi in Case C-413/24 *Vlaams Gewest* EU:C:2025:490, pt 58, and Case C-188/23 *Conti 11* EU:C:2025:26, para 44.

[121] See ch 9.

[122] *Intertanko* (n 117) paras 43 and 45; and Case C-15/17 *Bosphorus Queen Shipping Ltd Corp* EU:C:2018:557, para 44.

is a party.[123] The divergence introduces an additional requirement ('the nature and the broad logic of the agreement') that is not present in the standard case law on direct effect, thus making it more difficult to successfully challenge Union secondary law in light of international agreements.

Overall, the case law shows a certain degree of deference towards Union rules of secondary law when they come under the scrutiny of international agreements. However, this approach contrasts with the standard of review applied when the target is the law of the Member States. In *Nederlandse Spoorwegen*,[124] the Court of Justice held that the Member States are also bound by the international agreements entered into by the Union. However, the case law indicates that the standard of review becomes significantly stricter when it comes to reviewing the conformity of national law with international agreements concluded by the Union.[125]

3. A Categorisation of International Agreements

When the Union concludes an international agreement, it must act within the competences conferred by the Member States. As explained in chapter four, the Union has exclusive, shared, and support competences, as well as specific competences in the field of economic policy and the CFSP. When the Union concludes an international agreement, it must exercise due care regarding the relevant field of competence to which the agreement pertains. Depending on the competence concerned, international agreements can be categorised as exclusive, mixed, or CFSP agreements.

3.1. *Exclusive agreements*

The Union is empowered to conclude international agreements in areas of its competence, regardless of whether such competence has been attributed explicitly or implicitly.

The TFEU refers to five cases of *explicit* areas for the Union to conclude international agreements:

- commercial policy (Article 207 TFEU);
- cooperation with third countries and humanitarian aid (Articles 208–214 TFEU);
- restrictive measures (Article 215 TFEU);
- relations with international organisations (Article 220 TFEU), with specific reference to the United Nations, the Council of Europe, the Organisation for Security and Cooperation in Europe and the Organisation for Economic Cooperation and Development;
- association of the overseas countries and territories (Article 198 TFEU).

[123] Case C-70/87 *Fediol v Commission* EU:C:1989:254, paras 19–22; and Case C-69/89 *Nakajima v Council* EU:C:1991:186, para 31. As regards WTO Agreements, see Case C-149/96 *Portugal v Council* EU:C:1999:574, para 49; Case C-93/02 P *Biret International v Council* EU:C:2003:517, para 40; and Case C-120/06 P and C-121/06 P *FIAMM and FIAMM Technologies v Council and Commission* EU:C:2008:476, para 112.

[124] Case C-38/75 *Douaneagent der NV Nederlandse Spoorwegen v Inspecteur der invoerrechten en accijnzen* EU:C:1975:154, para 16; Case C-104/81 *Kupferberg* EU:C:1982:362, para 14; and Case C-53/96 *Hermès* EU:C:1998:292, para 28.

[125] Compare Joined Cases C-194/85 and C-241/85 *Commission v Greece* EU:C:1988:95; Case C-469/93 *Chiquita Italy* EU:C:1995:435; Case C-61/94 *Commission v Germany* EU:C:1996:313; Case C-13/00 *Commission v Ireland* EU:C:2002:184, and Case C-66/18 *Commission v Hungary* EU:C:2020:792, with the standard of review in *Opel Austria v Council* (n 107); and Case C-76/00 P *Petrotub and Republic v Council* EU:C:2003:4.

Besides the fields of competence listed above, the Union can also enter into international agreements based on *implicit* competences. This is the case where the conclusion of an agreement is necessary to achieve, within the framework of the Union's policies, one of the objectives referred to in the Treaties, or is provided for in a legally binding Union act, or is likely to affect common rules or alter their scope. Articles 3(2) and 216 TFEU refer to the implied competences that the Union can enjoy, codifying the case law on this issue up to 2009, when the Treaty of Lisbon entered into force.[126]

International agreements concluded on the basis of an explicit or implied competence are negotiated, signed, and concluded by the Union alone.[127] As a rule, the Commission or the High Representative submits recommendations to the Council.[128] The Council agrees on the negotiating mandate,[129] the Commission or the High Representative conducts the negotiation[130] and the Council adopts a decision concluding the agreement,[131] with the prior consent of or after consultation of the European Parliament.[132]

In terms of their legal effects, exclusive agreements hold a higher rank vis-a-vis Union secondary law and national law. In respect of the latter, it should be noted that once the Union has exercised its competence, the Member States are pre-empted from taking any measures in the policy field covered by the Union's competence, including the conclusion of international treaties. The only exception to this pre-emptive effect appears when the Union authorises the Member States to act.[133]

3.2. *Mixed Agreements*

When the subject matter of an international agreement covers areas of competence belonging to both the Union and the Member States, the agreement takes the form of a mixed agreement, to which both the Union and the Member States are parties.[134] Mixed agreements are also used when Member States provide financing, and that financing is an essential component of the agreement.[135] A mixed agreement may also be required when the agreement concerns a territory associated with a Member State, but outside the territorial scope of Union law.[136]

Mixed agreements have proliferated in recent years, even in areas where their use is not legally required.[137] This is due to the political sensitivities of the Union's external action, which encourages institutions to exercise their external powers jointly with the Member States. These

[126] Case C-22/70 *Commission v Council (AETR)* EU:C:1971:32. On the AETR doctrine and its introduction in the Treaties, see ch 4.

[127] Art 218 TFEU.

[128] ibid, Art 218(3).

[129] ibid, Art 218(2).

[130] Art 218(4) TFEU does not explicitly refer to the Commission, thus paving the way to negotiations conducted by another institution.

[131] Art 218(5)–(6) TFEU.

[132] ibid, Art 218(6).

[133] Case C-41/76 *Donckerwolcke and others* EU:C:1976:182, para 32; and Case C-174/84 *Bulk Oil v Sun International* EU:C:1986:60, paras 31–33.

[134] Exceptionally, it may be possible for an agreement to be signed only by the Member States where the agreement does not provide for the participation of international organisations. See Opinion 2/91 EU:C:1993:106, para 5, where the Court of Justice stated that, even though 'under the ILO Constitution, the [Union] cannot itself conclude Convention No 170, its external competence may, if necessary, be exercised through the medium of the Member States acting jointly in the [Union's] interest'.

[135] Opinion 1/78 EU:C:1979:224, para 60. The limits of this case law were set out in Opinion 1/94 EU:C:1994:384, para 21.

[136] ibid, para 62, where the issue arose as to the representation of the Faroe Islands, which are part of the Kingdom of Denmark but outside the scope of the Treaties as an overseas territory.

[137] G De Baere, *Constitutional Principles of EU External Relations* (Oxford University Press, 2008) 232ff.

practices have led the Court of Justice to adopt a pragmatic approach, permitting the use of mixed agreements even in areas that may fall within the Union's exclusive competence.[138] The fact that a mixed agreement requires ratification by all signatory Member States exerts significant pressure on the Union's external policy, given the difficulty of securing 27 ratification decisions, especially when the agreement involves sensitive policy areas. While the Court of Justice has generally been pragmatic and flexible when reviewing the use of mixed agreements, it has also adopted a broad interpretation of the Union's exclusive external competences, probably with the aim of avoiding the logistical and political challenges associated with such agreements.[139]

In policy areas of shared competence, Member States retain the ability to act externally, but they must also refrain from taking measures that make it difficult or impossible to comply with the obligations stemming from the Union's exercise of its shared competence.[140] As a result, the Court of Justice has repeatedly held that the authorisation of the Commission to negotiate a mixed agreement marks the start of a concerted action at the international level.[141] Member States are therefore obliged to abstain from taking any measure that may undermine the Union's negotiating position, thereby ensuring the unity and coherence of the Union's international representation. This obligation stems from the principle of sincere cooperation, as provided in Article 4(3) TEU.

3.3. *CFSP Agreements*

Article 37 TEU provides that the Union can conclude agreements with one or more third States or international organisations in areas covered by the CFSP. Prior to the entry into force of the Lisbon Treaty, agreements in this field were concluded by a Union lacking international legal personality, subject to a unanimous vote of the Member States and following specific procedural rules. The Lisbon Treaty put an end to the previous framework by granting legal personality to the Union and avoiding in Article 37 TEU any references to specific rules on the negotiation, signature, or ratification of CFSP agreements.

Despite the uniform framework now governing the Union's international agreements, some relevant differences remain between the agreements concluded under the CFSP and those in other areas of Union policy. The fundamental difference lies in the uncertain role played by the principles of direct effect and primacy in the case of CFSP agreements. The Lisbon Treaty introduced a common procedural framework for the conclusion of international agreements. Moreover, Article 216(2) TFEU is applicable to CFSP agreements, so that their content is 'binding upon the institutions of the Union and on its Member States'. However, Article 24(1), second subparagraph, TEU and Article 275 TFEU state that the Court of Justice does not have jurisdiction to rule on provisions relating to the CFSP, nor on acts adopted on that legal basis. The only exception to this rule is found in Article 275, second paragraph TFEU, which derogates from the above and confers jurisdiction on the Court of Justice when it comes to monitoring compliance with Article 40 TEU and the legality of decisions on restrictive measures against natural or legal persons adopted by the Council.

As discussed in chapters nine and ten of this book, Article 24(1) TEU and Article 275 TFEU raise doubts about the primacy and direct effect of CFSP acts. These doubts extend to the

[138] See, inter alia, Case C-476/98 *Commission v Germany* EU:C:2002:631, paras 80–88.

[139] A paradigmatic example of this balance is reflected in Opinion 2/15 EU:C:2017:376 on the Free Trade Agreement between the European Union and the Republic of Singapore.

[140] Case C-266/03 *Commission v Luxembourg* EU:C:2005:341, paras 58 and 60; and Case C-433/03 *Commission v Germany* EU:C:2005:462, para 64.

[141] Ruling 1/78 of 14 November 1978 EU:C:1978:202, paras 34–36 (by analogy with the EAEC Treaty); Opinion 2/91 (n 134) para 36; Opinion 1/94 (n 135) para 108; and Case C-25/94 *Commission v Council* EU:C:1996:114, para 48.

effects of CFSP agreements and their ability to serve as a standard of review for Union secondary legislation and national law. Given the limited jurisdiction of the Court of Justice in CFSP matters, it can be argued that CFSP agreements have direct effect and primacy only when they cover areas that remain within the jurisdiction of the Court of Justice. In CFSP areas excluded from the jurisdiction of Union courts, CFSP agreements will only have direct effect in national courts in accordance with the constitutional arrangements of each Member State. For the time being, the legal effects of CFSP agreements appear significantly diminished compared with those of other international agreements entered into by the Union.

4. Decisions of Bodies Created in International Agreements

In the 1980s, the Court of Justice ruled that decisions adopted within the framework of an association agreement were part of the Union's legal order and had direct effect and primacy.[142] In Opinion 1/91,[143] the Court of Justice extended this line of reasoning to any organisation created by an international agreement to which the Union is a party, including the decisions of the organisation's dispute settlement mechanisms:

> Where, however, an international agreement provides for its own system of courts, including a court with jurisdiction to settle disputes between the Contracting Parties to the agreement, and, as a result, to interpret its provisions, the decisions of that court will be binding on the Community institutions, including the Court of Justice, inter alia where the Court of Justice is called upon to rule on the interpretation of the international agreement, in so far as that agreement is an integral part of the Community legal order.[144]

Accordingly, both the acts of bodies and the rulings of dispute-settlement mechanisms established by international agreements to which the Union is a party can have direct effect and primacy over Union secondary law and national law.[145] This outcome applies to decision-making bodies enshrined in both exclusive and mixed agreements. It should be noted that the ability of these acts to have direct effect depends on the specific conditions developed in the case law on international agreements, which, as previously explained, are stricter than those generally applied to Union primary and secondary law.[146]

5. Other Rules of International Law

Article 3(5) TEU states that the Union contributes to 'the strict observance and development of international law, including respect for the principles of the United Nations Charter'. Article 21(1) TEU adds that the Union's actions on the international scene 'shall be guided by . . . respect for the principles of the United Nations Charter and international law'. In

[142] Case C-204/86 *Greece v Council* EU:C:1988:450, para 20; Case C-30/88 *Greece v Commission* EU:C:1989:422, para 13; and Case C-192/89 *Sevince* EU:C:1990:322, para 9.

[143] Opinion 1/91 (n 52).

[144] ibid, *para 3. In* Opinion 1/91, the Court of Justice ruled that the judicial system of the first EEA Treaty breached Union law, due to the impact of such a structure on the autonomy of the Union's legal order. However, the Court of Justice agreed, on a point of principle, on the possibility for an organisation to set up, under an international agreement, its own judicial system with the power to deliver rulings with binding effects on the Union (para 40).

[145] Case C-237/91 *Kus* EU:C:1992:527, paras 27–36; Case C-255/93 *Eroglu* EU:C:1994:369, para 11; and Case C-171/01 *Wählergruppe Gemeinsam* EU:C:2003:260, paras 54–67.

[146] The Court of Justice has held that the said agreements did not have direct effect in *Kus* (n 145) paras 23–38; and Case C-262/96 *Sürül* EU:C:1999:228, para 60. Covering the case of the direct effect of WTO Agreements, formerly GATT, see ch 9.

a specific policy area, Article 214(2) TFEU, on humanitarian aid policy, reiterates that the Union's actions in this field 'shall be conducted in compliance with the principles of international law'.

According to the wording of the Treaties, international law is called on to play a prominent role in the Union's legal order. However, even before these references were incorporated into formalised rules of primary Union law, the case law of the Court of Justice had already relied on international law as a source of customary obligations binding on the Communities, and later on the Union. In *Poulsen*, the Court of Justice stated that 'the European [Union] must respect international law in the exercise of its powers',[147] while also complying with its obligation to interpret Union secondary legislation in accordance with international law.[148] The case law also emphasised the importance of general principles of international law, such as the principles of liability,[149] territoriality,[150] the prohibition of expulsion or restriction of entry of its own nationals,[151] as well as the rules laid down in the Vienna Convention on the Law of Treaties.[152] The customary rules on the law of the treaties were applied by the Court of Justice even before their codification in the Vienna Convention of 1969.[153]

However, the Court of Justice has also ruled that international law, despite its binding effects on the Union,

> cannot affect the allocation of powers fixed by the Treaties or, consequently, the autonomy of the [Union's] legal system, observance of which is ensured by the Court by virtue of the exclusive jurisdiction . . . , jurisdiction that the Court has, moreover, already held to form part of the very foundations of the [Union].[154]

This stance confirms that the autonomy of Union law contributes to the development of the Union's 'constitutional core', insulated from international law, including customary international law and the law of the United Nations. This core does not allow for derogations, although the case law has left the door open to future developments, particularly in the event of the creation of an equivalent system of judicial remedies at the international level.[155]

[147] Case C-286/90 *Poulsen and Diva Navigation* EU:C:1992:453, para 9.

[148] *Intertanko* (n 117) para 52.

[149] Case C-221/89 *R v Secretary of State for Transport, ex parte Factortame and Others* EU:C:1991:320, paras 15–16.

[150] Joined Cases C-89/85, C-104/85, C-114/85, C-116/85, C-117/85 and C-125/85 *Ahlström Osakeyhtiö and Others v Commission* EU:C:1993:120, para 18.

[151] Case C-41/74 *Van Duyn* EU:C:1974:133, para 22.

[152] Case C-432/92 *Anastasiou and Others* EU:C:1994:277, paras 43 and 50; *Racke* (n 86) para 46; Case C-466/98 *Commission v United Kingdom* EU:C:2002:624, para 24; Case C-268/94 *Portugal v Council* EU:C:1996:461, paras 19 and 27; Case C-386/08 *Brita* EU:C:2010:91, para 44; Case C-104/16 P *Council v Front Polisario* EU:C:2016:973, para 86; Case C-532/18 *GN* EU:C:2019:1127, para 31; Case C-627/22 *AB v Finanzamt Köln-Süd* EU:C:2024:431, para 47; and Case C-188/23 *Land Niedersachsen* EU:C:2025:26, para 47. In *Wightman*, the Court of Justice made use of the rules of the Vienna Convention to interpret Treaties, although it was careful to emphasise that the interpreted rule, Art 50 TEU, was originally drafted in the Convention on the Future of Europe, where the Vienna Convention was 'taken into consideration' as part of the *travaux préparatoires* (Case C-621/18 *Wightman* EU:C:2018:999, para 70). It can be argued that, in the case of the Treaties, the Vienna Convention plays an interpretative role, constrained to a criterion of historical interpretation that inspired the preparatory works which resulted in the Treaties.

[153] Case C-10/61 *Commission v Italy* EU:C:1962:2, para 10.

[154] *Kadi* (n 10) para 282.

[155] On the existence of a 'constitutional core' in Union law with effects vis-à-vis international law, see G de Búrca, 'The EU, the European Court of Justice and the International Legal Order after Kadi' *Jean Monnet Working Paper* 1/09; D Halberstam and E Stein, 'The United Nations, the European Union and the King of Sweden: Economic Sanctions and Individual Rights in a Plural World Order' (2009) 46 *Common Market Law Review 13,* and T Tridimas and JA Gutiérrez-Fons, 'EU Law, International Law and Economic Sanctions Against Terrorism: The Judiciary in Distress?' (2009) 32 *Fordham International Law Journal* 660.

GENERAL BIBLIOGRAPHY

Craig, P, *EU Administrative Law* 3rd ed (Oxford University Press, 2018).
Cremona, M and Kilpatrick, C (eds), EU Legal Acts: Challenges and Transformations (Oxford University Press, 2018).
Louis, J-V, *The Community Legal Order* (Publications Office, 1995).
Pescatore, P, *L'ordre juridique des Communautés Européennes. Étude des sources du droit Communautaire* (reprint, Bruylant, 2006).
Simon, D, *Le système juridique communautaire* (PUF, 1998).
Schwarze, J, *European Administrative Law* (Sweet & Maxwell, 2006).

FURTHER READING

The Union's Legal System

Barents, R, *The Autonomy of Community Law* (Kluwer Law, 2004).
Craig, P, 'The Hierarchy of Norms' in T Tridimas and P Nebbia (eds), *European Law for the Twenty-First Century: Rethinking the New Legal Order*, vol I (Hart, 2004).
Halberstam, D and Stein, E, 'The United Nations, the European Union and the King of Sweden: Economic Sanctions and Individual Rights in a Plural World Order' (2009) 46 *Common Market Law Review* 13.
Klamert, M, 'The autonomy of the EU (and of EU Law): Through the Kaleidoscope' (2017) 42 European Law Review 327.
Kukovec, D, 'Autonomy: The Central Idea of the Reasoning of the Court of Justice' (2023) 8 *European Papers* 1403.
Verhoeven, A, *The European Union in Search of a Democratic and Constitutional Theory* (Kluwer Law, 2002).
Weiler, JHH and Haltern, U, 'The Autonomy of the Community Legal Order: Through the Looking Glass' (1996) 37 *Harvard International Law Journal* 411.

Primary Law

Constantinesco, V, 'Les Protocoles et déclarations annexées au projet de traité instituant une Constitution pour l'Europe' in V Constantinesco, Y Gautier and V Michel (eds), *Le Traité établissant une Constitution pour l'Europe. Analyses & Commentaires* (PUS, 2005).
Jacqué, J-P, 'Le traité de Lisbonne: Une vue cavalière' (2008) 44 *Revue Trimestrielle de Droit Européen* 439.
Sowery, K, 'The Nature and Scope of the Primary Law-making Powers of the European Union: The Member States as the "Masters of the Treaties"' (2018) 43 *European Law Review* 157.

General Principles of Union Law

Groussot, X, *General Principles of Community Law* (Europa Law Publishing, 2006).
Leczykiewicz, D, 'Prohibition of abusive practices as a general principle of EU law' (2019) 56 *Common Market Law Review* 703.
Mendes, J, 'Taking on the structural weakness of EU Law's general principles' (2023) 2 *European Law Open* 693.
Tridimas, T, *The General Principles of EC Law*, 2nd edn (Oxford University Press, 2006).
Vogenauer, S and Weatherill, S (eds), *General Principles of Law: European and Comparative Perspectives* (Hart, 2017).

International Agreements

De Baere, G, *Constitutional Principles of EU External Relations* (Oxford University Press, 2008).
Butler, G, *Constitutional Law of the EU's Common Foreign and Security Policy* (Hart, 2021).

Cremona, M and de Witte, B (eds), *EU Foreign Relations Law: Constitutional Fundamentals* (Hart, 2008).
Eeckhout, P, *External Relations of the European Union: Legal and Constitutional Foundations* (Oxford University Press, 2004).
Hillion, C and Dashwood, A (eds), *The General Law of EC External Relations* (Sweet & Maxwell, 2000).

8

The Sources of Union Law (II)

THE UNION HAS been granted powers to enact rules of law with binding effect across the territory of the Member States. The Union's normative powers are one of the features underpinning the autonomous nature of the European legal order, enabling it to unilaterally adopt rules that are binding on institutions, Member States, and individuals alike. As early as 1963, in its judgment in *Van Gend en Loos*, the Court of Justice referred to the distinctive nature of the law of the Communities of the time, when pointing out 'the establishment of institutions endowed with sovereign rights, the exercise of which affects Member States and also their citizens'.[1]

The development of the Union's institutional system, as well as the competences it holds, has contributed to a broad and diverse body of rules. The result of this body of Union rules has traditionally been referred to as 'secondary law'. Hidden behind this term is a complex typology of acts, in which a distinction must be drawn between binding and non-binding secondary law. A second distinction was introduced by the Lisbon Treaty in 2009, aiming to simplify the typology of binding secondary legislation. This was partly successful, introducing a distinction between legislative and non-legislative acts, but still maintaining separate sources for certain policy areas, such as the Common Foreign and Security Policy (CFSP), or monetary policy. The Lisbon Treaty did not prevent the proliferation of non-binding acts, known as 'soft law', whose presence in the practice of the Union's institutions has become widespread.

Union secondary legislation is comprised of *acts*. The Union legal order does not make a distinction, as in the law of many Member States, between general rules (laws, regulations, decrees, etc) and individual administrative acts (decisions, orders, resolutions, etc). On the contrary, both general, abstract rules and individual decisions adopted by the institutions, offices, bodies, and agencies of the Union are generally referred to as *acts*. This chapter outlines the typology of Union acts, aiming to provide a comprehensive overview of the current framework of Union secondary law.

I. BINDING SECONDARY LAW

The Treaties distinguish between binding and non-binding Union acts. This distinction stems from Article 288, fifth paragraph, of the Treaty on the Functioning of the European Union (TFEU), which states that recommendations and opinions 'shall have no binding force'. As a result, the other acts listed in Article 288 TFEU are binding on their addressees. These binding acts can be categorised as follows.

[1] Case C-26/62 *Van Gend en Loos* EU:C:1963:1.

1. Typology

The first paragraph of Article 288 TFEU states that: 'To exercise the Union's competences, the institutions shall adopt regulations, directives, decisions, recommendations and opinions'. Article 289(3) TFEU adds that 'legal acts adopted by legislative procedure shall constitute legislative acts'. Consequently, secondary law comprises a body of binding acts that can be distinguished by two criteria: their *content* and the *procedure for their adoption*.

Depending on their *content*, the institutions can adopt binding general acts, binding individual acts, and binding results-based acts, for which regulations, decisions and directives, respectively, are envisaged.

Table 8.1

Regulations	→	General content
Decisions	→	Individual content
Directives	→	Results-based content

Depending on the *adoption procedure*, acts are the result of a legislative or non-legislative procedure and, in the case of the latter, are mainly delegated or implementing acts.

Table 8.2

Legislative acts	→	Legislative procedures
Delegated acts/implementing acts	→	Non-legislative procedures

The criterion based on the adoption procedure overlaps with the criterion based on the *content* of the act. Legislative acts are therefore classified as regulations, directives, and decisions, while all three types of acts can be used when adopting non-legislative acts.

The resulting scheme is as follows.

Table 8.3

	Legislative acts	**Non-legislative acts Delegated acts**	**Non-legislative acts Implementing acts**
Regulation	Legislative regulation	Delegated regulation	Implementing regulation
Directive	Legislative directive	Delegated directive	Implementing directive
Decision	Legislative decision	Delegated decision	Implementing decision

1.1. *Types of Binding Acts based on their Content*

1.1.1. Regulations

The second paragraph of Article 288 TFEU defines a regulation as an act of 'general application . . . binding in its entirety and directly applicable in all Member States'. To use a familiar reference, regulations are legal instruments akin to what is termed *statutory or parliamentary law* in the legal systems of the Member States. It is no coincidence that in the draft Constitutional Treaty, this type of act, while retaining the same definition found today in Article 288, second paragraph TFEU, was referred to as a 'European law'.

1.1.1.1. General Scope

Due to its general scope, a regulation is an instrument that governs a subject matter in an abstract, non-individualised manner, within the Union's sphere of competence. This definition, as held by the Court of Justice in *Confédération Nationale de fruits et légumes*, means that the key criterion for distinguishing between a regulation and a decision is the general scope of addressees that characterises a regulation. While 'the essential characteristics of a decision arise from the limitation of the persons to whom it is addressed', the characteristics of a regulation, as an instrument 'essentially of a legislative nature', focus not on 'a limited number of persons, defined or identifiable, but [on] categories of persons viewed abstractly and in their entirety'.[2]

Over time, the case law has taken a pragmatic approach to the general nature of regulations, recognising that such acts can include categories of individualised persons among their addressees. This approach is evident in *Zuckerfabrik Watenstedt*, dating back to 1968, where the Court of Justice ruled that:

> [A regulation] does not lose its character as a regulation simply because it may be possible to ascertain with a greater or lesser degree of accuracy the number or even the identity of the persons to which it applies at any given time as long as there is no doubt that the measure is applicable as a result of an objective situation of law or of fact which it specifies and which is in harmony with its ultimate objective.[3]

The result of this approach is that regulations can introduce measures of a materially individual content, imposing rights and duties on categories or on a grouped set of individual legal or natural persons.

Despite the wide range of situations in which a regulation can be used, there are limits that the institutions must respect, to the extent that a genuinely individual measure can be considered as such, even if it has been adopted in the form of a regulation. In such cases, the Court of Justice will examine the content and objectives of the act in detail, and if it concludes that the regulation is in substance a decision, it will grant the affected person the status of an individualised target of the act.[4]

The flexible approach to defining the general scope of regulations is now subject to further questions, particularly after the entry into force of the Lisbon Treaty. According to Article 290(1) TFEU, delegated acts must be of 'general application'. It is unclear whether the scope of this requirement matches the reference in Article 288, second paragraph TFEU, or if it has a different meaning in the specific context of delegated acts.

[2] Joined Cases C-16/62 and 17/62 *Confédération nationale des producteurs de fruits et légumes and Others v Council* EU:C:1962:47. See also, inter alia, Case C-6/68 *Zuckerfabrik Watenstedt v Council* EU:C:1968:43; Joined Cases C-789 and C-790/79 *Calpak Spa v Commission* EU:C:1980:159, para 8, and Case C-242/81 *Roquette Frères* EU:C:1982:325, para 8.

[3] *Zuckerfabrik Watenstedt* (n 2).

[4] Case C-64/69 *Compagnie française commerciale et financière v Commission* EU:C:1970:28, para 11; Case C-64/80 *Giuffrida and Campogrande v Council* EU:C:1981:58, para 7; Case C-45/81 *Alexander Moksel Import-Export v Commission* EU:C:1982:110, para 17; Case C-242/81 *Roquette Frères v Council* EU:C:1982:325, paras 5–7; and Joined Cases C-789/79 and C-790/79 *Calpak and Società Emiliana Lavorazione Frutta v Commission* EU:C:1980:159, para 9.

1.1.1.2. 'Binding in its Entirety'

While 'general application' is the key criterion for distinguishing between a regulation and a decision, being binding 'in its entirety' is what differentiates a regulation from a directive. According to Article 288 TFEU, a directive is only binding as to 'the results to be achieved', whereas a regulation is 'binding in its entirety'. In other words, a directive is binding only with respect to the objectives of the measure, leaving to the national authorities the choice of form and methods, whereas a regulation is binding with respect to both the objectives and the means. The result of this feature is that no additional measures, either by the Union or the Member States, are in principle required to comply with the provisions of a regulation.

The Court of Justice first referred to the comprehensive scope of regulations in *Commission v Italy*.[5] When faced with national measures which *partially* reproduced the obligations set out in a regulation, the Court of Justice stated that

> it cannot be accepted that a Member State should apply in an incomplete or selective manner provisions of a [Union] regulation so as to render abortive certain aspects of [Union] legislation which it has opposed or which it considers contrary to its national interests.[6]

The same conclusion was reached in *Granaria*, referring to the selective enforcement of a regulation, a practice that must be deemed to breach the Treaties, since otherwise Member States would be allowed to alter the scope of application of a regulation.[7]

1.1.1.3. 'Directly Applicable'

The final words of the second paragraph of Article 288 TFEU state that regulations are 'directly applicable in all Member States'. Consequently, Member States are not under the obligation to transpose the content of a regulation into national law. In so far as a regulation establishes rights and obligations that individuals can rely on, the need for further implementing rules is, in principle, unnecessary and in some cases the adoption of national transposing measures can be deemed to be unlawful.

If the regulation is 'directly applicable', it might be assumed that it will also have 'direct effect', a feature that is further developed in chapter nine of this book. However, this is an erroneous assumption that should be avoided, as a regulation can be unclear and imprecise, or it can introduce an incomplete framework that must be supplemented by other provisions.[8] In such cases, the relevant provisions of the regulation may not be 'directly applicable', but they will still have interpretative effects, and can guide the interpretation and implementation of other rules of law.[9]

To ensure the integrity and direct applicability of a regulation, Member States are, as a general rule, precluded from introducing measures to transpose it, whether to supplement or reproduce its content. The Court of Justice rejected such practices in *Commission v Italy*, cited above, stating that reproducing a regulation's rules in Italian law creates 'an ambiguity as to both the legal nature of the provisions applicable and the time of their entry into force'. According to the Court of Justice, this practice 'has the effect of creating an obstacle to the

[5] Case C-39/72 *Commission v Italy* EU:C:1973:13.

[6] ibid, para 20.

[7] Case C-18/72 *Granaria* EU:C:1972:108, paras 16–17.

[8] Case C-253/00 *Muñoz and Superior Fruiticola* EU:C:2002:497, para 27; and Joined Cases C-4/10 and C-27/10 *Bureau national interprofessionnel du Cognac* EU:C:2011:484, para 40.

[9] Case C-606/10 *Association nationale d'assistance aux frontières pour les étrangers* EU:C:2012:348, para 72; Case C-394/12 *Abdullahi* EU:C:2013:813, para 48; and Case C-283/16 *MS v PS* EU:C:2017:104, para 48.

direct effect of [Union] regulations and of jeopardising their simultaneous and uniform application in the whole of the [Union]'.[10]

The reasons behind this prohibition are connected to the principle of legal certainty. A redundant reproduction or development of a regulation in national law will raise doubts, for example, about the time of entry into force of the rule applicable to the case. Such a practice will also introduce uncertainty regarding the correct interpretation of the regulation and may encourage national courts to view the case as purely internal and outside the scope of Union law. If national courts perceive that the matter falls solely under national jurisdiction, they may avoid referring questions for a preliminary ruling to the Court of Justice, thereby undermining the uniform interpretation of Union law. As was held in the case of *Variola*:

> Member States are under an obligation not to introduce any measure which might affect the jurisdiction of the Court to pronounce on any question involving the interpretation of [Union] law or the validity of an act of the institutions of the [Union], which means that no procedure is permissible whereby the [Union] nature of a legal rule is concealed from those subject to it.[11]

The prohibition of the national reproduction of regulations is not absolute.[12] The case law allows it in specific circumstances, such as when Member States with multi-level governance structures (federal or regional) need to ensure coherent implementation of Union law across different territorial authorities.[13] The national reproduction of regulations has also been accepted if it helps raise awareness or publicise the content of a regulation within a Member State.[14]

In recent years, an increasing number of regulations include provisions that rely on national measures for their implementation. These regulations refer to provisions of national law or give Member States a degree of discretion to implement the regulation or to opt between several policy options. This practice assigns a role to the regulation similar to that of a directive, blurring the dividing line between these types of acts.[15] Examples include Regulation 2016/679 on data protection, or Regulation 575/2013 on prudential requirements for credit institutions and investment firms. These are relevant legal instruments which, due to their sensitive nature, have limited their direct applicability to accommodate Member State discretion. It is still too early to fully assess the impact of such a practice, but the case law appears inclined to maximise the effectiveness of these regulations, dismissing the need to enact national law as a prerequisite for implementation.[16]

[10] Case C-34/73 *Variola* EU:C:1973:101, para 11; and Case C-50/76 *Amsterdam Bulb* EU:C:1977:13, paras 4 and 7.

[11] *Variola* (n 10) para 11.

[12] Case C-316/10 *Danske Svineproducenter* EU:C:2011:863, paras 39–40; and Case C-372/20 *QY* EU:C:2021:962, paras 47–50.

[13] Case C-272/83 *Commission v Italy* EU:C:1985:147, para 27.

[14] Case C-20/72 *Cobelex* EU:C:1972:94, para 20: 'the authorities . . . may usefully draw the attention of those concerned to the existence and the possible consequences of [a regulation] by means of additional information'.

[15] According to Advocate General de la Tour, referring to an 'opening' provision of Regulation 2016/679 (GDPR): 'That provision is one of the numerous "opening clauses" in that regulation, which give it its distinctiveness by comparison with a traditional regulation and cause it to resemble a directive. The references to national law in those clauses may be binding, but most frequently constitute an option left to the Member States. It has been observed that these numerous references to national laws entail the risk of a new fragmentation of the arrangements for the protection of personal data within the European Union, running counter to the EU legislature's expressed desire to achieve greater uniformity in those arrangements and being capable of having negative effects on the effectiveness of that protection, and likewise on the ease with which controllers and processors are able to understand their obligations. The scope of the harmonisation brought about by Regulation 2016/679 is thus limited by the many "opening clauses" in that regulation' (Case C-319/20 *Meta Platforms Ireland Limited* EU:C:2021:979, Opinion of AG de la Tour, pt 55).

[16] See, for example, Case C-319/20 *Meta Platforms Ireland Limited* EU:C:2022:322, paras 58–60.

1.1.2. Directives

The third paragraph of Article 288 TFEU states that a directive 'shall be binding, as to the result to be achieved, upon each Member State to which it is addressed, but shall leave to the national authorities the choice of form and methods'. In contrast with regulations, the directive is an instrument of cooperation between two legal systems, insofar as it requires the active participation of national law for its provisions to be effective. In the words of Pierre Pescatore, unlike a regulation, 'a directive is a technique of indirect intervention: it does not in itself create legal rules, its effect being to assign to the Member States objectives which they must translate into national legislative, regulatory or administrative measures'.[17] Pescatore added that while the directive fulfils its mission mainly in areas where the Member States have reserved their legislative sovereignty, 'the regulation, on the contrary, enshrines a transfer of legislative power to the [Union]'.[18] The directive is therefore an incomplete instrument or, put differently, a *cooperative* instrument, the effects of which are only fully deployed once the Member States intervene through the enactment of transposition measures.

1.1.2.1. Member States as Sole Addressees

The directive is addressed only to the Member States. Unlike a regulation or a decision, individuals are not the immediate holders of the rights and obligations outlined in a directive: it is exclusively for the Member States to give effect to those rights and obligations contained therein, which is achieved through national law.

A directive can be addressed to one, several, or all Member States. Depending on the number of addressees, the rules governing the publication of a directive vary, as Article 297(2), second and third paragraphs TFEU specify that directives addressed to *all* Member States are published in the *Official Journal of the European Union*. On the other hand, directives that specify *one* or *more* addressees are only subject to notification 'to whom they are addressed and shall take effect upon such notification'.[19]

1.1.2.2. Obligation as to the Result

The directive is binding on its addressees, the Member States, only 'as to the result to be achieved' (Article 288, third paragraph TFEU). This obligation is evidenced by two relevant features: the deadline for transposition; and the substantive content of the transposition measures.

All directives specify the deadline by which the addressee Member State(s) must adopt all the appropriate measures to transpose a directive. The expiry of this period appears in the final provisions of the directive, under the heading 'Transposition'. These provisions also state that Member States 'shall communicate to the Commission the text of the main measures of national law which they adopt in the field covered' by the directive. If the Member States do not adopt the measures required by the directive within the specified period, or if they fail to communicate them to the Commission, such failure will amount to a breach of the directive.

Member States cannot breach the substantive content of a directive before the expiry of the transposition deadline. However, in its judgment in *Inter-Environnement Wallonie*, the Court of Justice held that during that period, Member States 'must refrain from taking any measures

[17] P Pescatore, *L'ordre juridique des Communautés Européennes: Étude des sources du droit communautaire* (Bruylant, 2006) 113.

[18] ibid, 114.

[19] Art 297(2), third para TFEU.

liable seriously to compromise the result prescribed'.[20] This duty does not derive directly from the directive but from the general principle of sincere cooperation enshrined in Article 4(3) TEU, as well as Article 288, third paragraph TFEU.

The 'results' mentioned in Article 288, third paragraph TFEU are *legal* outcomes, not factual ones. Member States have the obligation to adopt appropriate measures aimed at achieving the objectives of the directive. These measures must take the form of general and abstract binding rules (legislative acts, decrees, etc) or individual binding decisions (administrative acts, orders, instructions, etc). Therefore, Member States will not be liable if the directive's overall goals are not achieved in the long term, but will be liable if the means employed by the Member State are insufficient or inappropriate to attain the results specified in the directive.

1.1.2.3. Freedom of Choice of Form and Methods

The third paragraph of Article 288 TFEU emphasises that the directive 'shall leave to the national authorities the choice of form and methods'. As previously explained, giving Member States a margin of discretion does not amount to a blank cheque, but rather the opposite: both the Commission and the Court of Justice carry out intensive monitoring of the transposition process in the Member States, which is reflected in the following requirements.

1.1.2.4. Type of Transposition Measure

Regarding the choice of 'form', it is for the Member States to decide, in accordance with their constitutional provisions, the most suitable legal instrument to transpose a directive. As discussed in chapter five of this book, having the right to choose the 'form' of the transposition measure enables directives to be accommodated in different ways across the Member States, especially when there are constitutional requirements that impact the choices ultimately made. For instance, if a directive relates to an area where the national constitution requires a statutory act of a specific rank, and subject to qualified majorities in Parliament, the transposition of the directive must adhere to those requirements in that Member State. In another Member State, these requirements might not be necessary, and a different legal act can be used to transpose the directive. Union law does not interfere in this decision, leaving each Member State to adopt the measures needed to ensure the directive is transposed in accordance with their constitutional arrangements.

However, Member States do not enjoy unfettered freedom of choice and are subject to several requirements. First, many directives require Member States to include in the national transposition measures either a reference to the directive or a reference to it in the official publication. Second, Member States must avoid transposing a directive through a succession of individual national acts that create a fragmented legal framework, which can make it difficult to identify, understand, or properly comply with the directive.[21] This requirement of uniformity can be waived when the Member State is subject to internal rules of competence that require the involvement of different levels of government or various territories within

[20] Case C-129/96 *Inter-Environnement Wallonie* EU:C:1997:628, para 45, subsequently reiterated in Case C-212/04 *Adeneler and Others* EU:C:2006:443, para 117; Case C-138/05 *Stichting Zuid-Hollandse Milieufederatie* EU:C:2006:577, para 42; Case C-422/05 *Commission v Belgium* EU:C:2007:342 para 62; Case C-43/10 *Nomarchiaki Aftodioikisi Aitoloakarnanias* EU:C:2012:560, para 57; and Case C-104/14 *Federconsorzi* EU:C:2015:125, para 32.

[21] Case C-69/77 *Commission v Italy* EU:C:1978:167; Case C-102/79 *Commission v Belgium* EU:C:1980:120; Case C-116/86 *Commission v Italy* EU:C:1988:111; Case C-29/84 *Commission v Germany* EU:C:1985:229; Case C-131/88 *Commission v Germany* EU:C:1991:87; Cases C-361/88 and C-59/89 *Commission v Germany* EU:C:1991:224; and Case C-95/92 *Commission v Italy* EU:C:1993:231.

the Member State.[22] Third, the case law rejects the use of national rules that lack sufficient binding authority or status in the national legal order, as this fails to satisfy the requirements of legal certainty.[23] Referring to internal administrative practices, the Court of Justice justified this position as follows:

> The provisions of directives must be implemented with unquestionable binding force, and with the necessary specificity, precision and clarity, in order to satisfy the requirements of legal certainty. Mere administrative practices, which by their nature are alterable at will by the authorities and are not given appropriate publicity, cannot be regarded as constituting the proper fulfilment of a Member State's obligations flowing from [Union] law since they maintain, for the persons concerned, a state of uncertainty as regards the extent of their rights and obligations in a field governed by that law.[24]

In some cases, a directive can be transposed by relying on pre-existing national rules of law. This occurs when a directive introduces content that is already reflected in the national legal system, allowing the Member State to refrain from adopting new measures. The Court of Justice has accepted this approach

> provided that it does indeed guarantee the full application of the directive in a sufficiently clear and precise manner so that, where the directive is intended to create rights for individuals, the persons concerned can ascertain the full extent of their rights and, where appropriate, rely on them before the national courts.[25]

1.1.2.5. Transposition Methods

While the previous section focused on the 'form' of the national legal instruments of transposition, due attention must now be given to the methods used by the Member States to carry out the transposition of a directive.

Member States can involve different authorities in the transposition process, provided the process is carried out in a coordinated manner and does not compromise the uniform implementation of the directive within the Member State. If transposition occurs in a federal Member State, the domestic constitutional arrangements may require the involvement of both federal and sub-federal authorities, but must also establish specific coordination mechanisms between the two levels of government. These mechanisms can include general principles of constitutional law, and their implementation will be sufficient to ensure proper transposition of a directive, as long as those principles are 'sufficiently precise and clear and that the persons concerned are put in a position to know the full extent of their rights and, where appropriate, to be able to rely on them before national courts'.[26]

Member States may also be permitted to provide a higher level of protection than that required by the directive in specific areas, such as health, environment, or consumer protection. In such cases, transposition measures might include provisions that extend beyond the directive's objectives. This often occurs when transposing directives that establish a 'minimum harmonisation' of a policy area. This practice explicitly authorises Member States to introduce

[22] Joined Cases C-185/78 to C-204/78 *Van Dam and Others* EU:C:1979:177, para 10; Case C-177/94 *Perfili* EU:C:1996:24, para 17; Case C-403/03 *Schempp* EU:C:2005:446, para 34, and Case C-428/07 *Horvath* EU:C:2009:458, para 55.

[23] Case C-80/92 *Commission v Belgium* EU:C:1994:118, para 20; Case C-151/94 *Commission v Luxembourg* EU:C:1995:357, para 18; and Case C-415/01 *Commission v Belgium* EU:C:2003:118, para 21.

[24] Case C-296/01 *Commission v France* EU:C:2003:626, para 54.

[25] Case C-131/88 *Commission v Germany* EU:C:1991:87, para 6.

[26] Case C-32/05 *Commission v Luxembourg* EU:C:2006:749, para 34; and Case C-151/12 *Commission v Spain* EU:C:2013:690, paras 25–30.

or maintain additional measures that go beyond the standard of protection set out in the directive.[27] Minimum harmonisation can result from an explicit decision by the Union legislature when enacting a directive, from a choice inferred from the wording and history of the directive,[28] or from a Treaty mandate, as in the case of environmental policy and social policy.[29]

1.1.2.6. Limited Effects of Directives

The directive is binding only on the Member States, and its legal effects are in principle deployed on them alone. Even if the provisions of the directive confer rights to individuals, the legal obligation created by the directive is only incumbent on the Member States. Consequently, only Member States, as the sole addressees of the directive, can fail to comply with its provisions.

Despite the above, there are circumstances in which individuals can nevertheless rely on it to invoke rights derived from its provisions. This option is available to individuals in particular when the Member State to which the directive is addressed has failed to transpose it within the prescribed deadline, or has transposed it incorrectly. In such circumstances, a directive may have direct effect, an outcome that is explained in detail in chapter nine of this book.

1.1.3. Decisions

The fourth paragraph of Article 288 TFEU states that a decision 'shall be binding in its entirety', except when it 'specifies those to whom it is addressed', in which case it 'shall be binding only on them'. The main feature of a decision is its individual character, as opposed to the general and abstract nature of a regulation. A decision is the most suitable instrument for implementing regulations or directives in cases involving an individual or a group of individuals. A notable example of the use of a decision is the Commission's adoption of pecuniary fines addressed to undertakings that breach Union law.

Although decisions have traditionally been characterised by their individual scope, Article 288, fourth paragraph TFEU, in its post-Lisbon formulation, allows for the option of 'general decisions'.[30] This is the case of a decision that does not designate an individual addressee, thus lacking its individual nature. The concept of a 'general decision' arises from the practice of employing decisions to introduce self-binding obligations on Union institutions.[31] They are also frequently used when a legal basis in the TFEU requires the adoption of 'measures', without further specifying which particular form these measures should take. Such cases include decisions adopting an action programme under Article 352 TFEU,[32] or decisions authorising

[27] See, for example, Council Directive 85/577/EEC of 20 December 1985 to protect consumers in respect of contracts negotiated away from business premises [1985] OJ L372/31, Art 8; Council Directive 90/314/EEC of 13 June 1990 on package travel, package holidays and package tours [1990] OJ L158/59, Art 8; Council Directive 93/13/EEC of 5 April 1993 on unfair terms in consumer contracts [1993] OJ L 95/29, Art 8; and Directive 97/7/EC of the European Parliament and of the Council of 20 May 1997 on the protection of consumers in respect of distance contracts [1997] OJ L144/19, Art 14.

[28] Case C-11/92 *Gallagher* EU:C:1993:262, para 15.

[29] Arts 193 and 153(2)(b) TFEU. See, for an example in secondary law, Art 1(3) of Council Directive 89/391/EEC of 12 June 1989 on the introduction of measures to encourage improvements in the safety and health of workers at work [1989] OJ L183/1.

[30] A von Bogdandy, F Arndt and J Bast, 'Legal Instruments in European Union Law and their Reform: A Systematic Approach on an Empirical Basis' (2004) 23 *Yearbook of European Law* 97.

[31] See, for example, the provisions of the TFEU empowering the Commission to adopt *sui generis* decisions in sectors such as transport (Arts 95(4) and 96(2) paragraph 2) and competition (Arts 105(2) and 106(3)); or in favour of the Council in the field of monetary policy (Art 143(2)).

[32] Decision 87/327/EEC of 15 June 1987 adopting the Community action programme for student mobility (ERASMUS) [1987] OJ L166/20; and Decision 94/819/EC of 6 December 1994 establishing the 'Leonardo da Vinci' action programme for the implementation of a European Community vocational training policy [1994] OJ L340/8.

the signature or conclusion of an international agreement pursuant to Article 218(5)–(6). In these instances, the decision does not identify a specific individual addressee, although it can be inferred that the mandate is addressed to the Union as a whole. In German legal terminology, a distinction is drawn between *Beschluss* (decision without specified addressees) and *Entscheidung* (decision addressed to specified persons), although this terminological distinction is not reflected in the English language version of the Treaties, which uses 'decision' for both. The Lisbon Treaty confirmed the existence of both categories by stating that a decision is only binding on its addressees if they are 'specified' therein. In contrast, if the decision does not refer to any addressee, it must be regarded as a *sui generis* decision, a *Beschluss*, and is therefore binding only on the Union.[33]

The legal effects of a *sui generis* decision differ from those of an ordinary decision. While the latter has full legal effects vis-a-vis its addressee, a *sui generis* decision is binding only on the institution, body, office, or agency that has adopted it. Therefore, a *sui generis* decision is a self-binding instrument for its creator only, which can be invoked by third parties to compel the enacting institution, body, office, or agency to comply with it. As a result, a *sui generis* decision cannot produce legal effects vis-a-vis third parties. This outcome is the logical consequence of the need to respect the Union's system of sources of law, or otherwise a *sui generis* decision would transform into a covert regulation, thus violating the definitions and scheme of Union acts provided for in Article 288 TFEU. To maintain the integrity of the Union's system of secondary law, it is essential that *sui generis* decisions produce their effects only on the institution, body, office, or agency that adopted them.

The distinction between ordinary and *sui generis* decisions is again reflected in Article 297(2) TFEU, which refers to non-legislative acts adopted in the form of regulations, directives or decisions, 'when the latter do not specify to whom they are addressed'. This final indent clearly alludes to *sui generis* decisions, which are signed by the president of the institution that adopted them and published in the *Official Journal of the European Union*. Decisions that specify their addressees are notified to those addressees and take effect upon such notification (Article 297(2), second subparagraph, TFEU).

1.2. *Types of Binding Acts based on the Procedure for Adoption*

The Lisbon Treaty introduced significant changes to the Union's sources of law, including the introduction of a typology that distinguishes between 'legislative acts' and 'non-legislative acts'. The latter are further divided into 'delegated acts' and 'implementing acts'. This typology overlaps with the one explained above, which is based on the content of the acts. As a result, legislative acts can be adopted in the form of regulations, directives, and decisions, just as all three types of acts can be used for non-legislative acts (see Table 8.3 above).

The distinction between legislative and non-legislative acts stems from the draft Constitutional Treaty. One of the mandates given to the Convention on the Future of Europe focused on the 'simplification' of the Union's legal instruments.[34] In response, the

[33] On the distinction between *sui generis* decisions and ordinary decisions, see the Opinion of Advocate General Kokott in Case C-370/07 *Commission v Council* EU:C:2009:249, pts 44–58.

[34] The Laeken Declaration, adopted at the European Council meeting on 14–15 December 2001, recognised, in a paragraph under the heading 'Simplification of the Union's instruments', the need to reconsider the system of Union acts existing to date, placing particular emphasis on the differentiation between legislative and non-legislative acts: 'Who does what is not the only important question; the nature of the Union's action and what instruments it should use are equally important. Successive amendments to the Treaty have on each occasion resulted in a proliferation of instruments, and directives have gradually evolved towards more and more detailed legislation. The key question is therefore whether the Union's various instruments should not be better defined and whether their number should not be reduced. In other words, should a distinction be introduced between legislative and executive measures? Should

Convention established a working group dedicated to this issue, whose final report proposed introducing two categories of acts – legislative and non-legislative – based on the adoption procedure as the key distinguishing criterion.[35] In the draft Constitutional Treaty, legislative acts were referred to as 'European laws' and 'European framework laws'. Non-legislative acts were 'European regulations' and 'European decisions'. The purpose of this nomenclature, as explicitly acknowledged by the working group, was to establish a hierarchical relationship between legislative and non-legislative acts.[36]

The Lisbon Treaty recovered and incorporated most of the contributions of the draft Constitutional Treaty on 'simplification'. The main difference lies in the *nomenclature* of the acts, which dropped any reference to 'law', while retaining the substance of the proposals and their underlying aim.[37] It should be recalled that one of the objectives of simplification was to streamline the decision-making procedures in the Union, particularly its executive procedures. The absence of detailed rules governing the executive powers entrusted to the Commission or the Council led to a complex framework, conditioned by the presence of 'committees', which at times made it difficult to hold the institutions accountable. The reforms of the Lisbon Treaty, drawing on the contributions of the draft Constitutional Treaty, aim to clarify the allocation of tasks and introduce transparency into the Union's system of sources.

1.2.1. Legislative Acts

Article 289(3) TFEU states that 'legal acts adopted by legislative procedure shall constitute legislative acts'. According to the first two paragraphs of the same provision, the legislative procedure comprises both the ordinary legislative procedure and special legislative procedures. The act resulting from these procedures will, depending on its content, take the form of a legislative regulation, a legislative directive, or a legislative decision.

Two features characterise legislative acts. First, a legislative act is adopted following a legislative procedure, whether it is an ordinary or a special legislative procedure. Second, Article 296(3) TFEU provides that, when considering draft legislative acts, the European Parliament and the Council 'shall refrain from adopting acts not provided for by the relevant legislative procedure in the area in question'.

1.2.1.1. Formal and Substantive Legislative Acts

The wording of Article 289(3) TFEU is clear: only acts adopted through a legislative procedure are legislative acts. However, there are relevant policy areas where the Treaties omit all reference to a legislative procedure, despite the fact that the Union can adopt general measures in

the number of legislative instruments be reduced: directly applicable rules, framework legislation and non-enforceable instruments (opinions, recommendations, open coordination)? Is it or is it not desirable to have more frequent recourse to framework legislation, which affords the Member States more room for manoeuvre in achieving policy objectives? For which areas of competence are open coordination and mutual recognition the most appropriate instruments? Is the principle of proportionality to remain the point of departure?'

[35] Final Report of Working Group IX 'Simplification' of 29 November 2002 (CONV 424/02).

[36] On the typology of acts introduced in the Constitutional Treaty, see K Lenaerts and M Desomer, 'Towards a Hierarchy of Legal Acts in the European Union? Simplification of Legal Instruments and Procedures' (2005) 11 *European Law Journal* 744.

[37] Despite their similarities, there are also differences between the system of acts in the failed draft Constitutional Treaty and the Treaties now in force. In the Constitutional Treaty, the directive was repealed and adapted into 'European framework laws' (Art I-36 of the draft Constitutional Treaty). The Treaty of Lisbon, on the other hand, allows for the possibility of adopting directives and delegated decisions (the latter provided they are of a 'general nature').

those fields.[38] This is the case of competition,[39] state aid,[40] transport,[41] or economic policy,[42] where the Treaty grants the Council and the Commission significant regulatory powers, but not through legislative procedures. Consequently, the core framework governing competition policy, outlined in Regulation 1/2003, is not a legislative act because Article 103(1) TFEU empowers the Council, after consulting the European Parliament, to introduce 'the appropriate regulations or directives to give effect to the principles set out in Articles 101 and 102'.[43] This provision omits any reference to a legislative procedure, yet there is little doubt about the relevance of Regulation 1/2003. Therefore, such acts can also be termed 'material legislative acts', as they do not have the formal feature of being enacted through a legislative procedure but share, both in substance and in their approval procedure, characteristics of a legislative act.

By introducing material legislative acts, the Treaties leave unresolved the issue of whether such acts can serve as the basis for delegated acts. As will be explained below, delegated acts under Article 290 TFEU require a prior legislative act adopted through a legislative procedure. It can therefore be argued that material legislative acts, such as Regulation 1/2003, cannot authorise the Commission to adopt delegated acts pursuant to Article 290 TFEU. However, the practical implementation of such instruments shows that they contain delegations that allow the Commission to adopt measures that are functionally equivalent to delegated acts. Furthermore, regulations adopted under the legal basis of Article 122 TFEU also confer on the Commission powers to adopt implementing acts, but without any reference to Article 291 TFEU.[44] This gap in the system reinforces the view that the delegated and implementing acts provided for in Articles 290–291 TFEU are not the only executive normative measures available to Union institutions.[45]

1.2.1.2. The General and Individual Scope of Legislative Acts

The Treaties do not expressly define the general or individual scope of legislative acts. Article 290(1) TFEU states that delegated acts are adopted by the Commission and are described as 'non-legislative acts of general application'. This wording suggests that since delegated acts have a general scope, the same should apply to the legislative acts on which they are based. This result is consistent with the objectives and raison d'être of a normative delegation, which aim to specify and further develop the terms of a legislative act of general scope.

However, this interpretation is too formalistic. No provision in the Treaties precludes the adoption of legislative directives or decisions, which can be addressed to individual addressees. As previously mentioned, Article 289(1) TFEU states that regulations, directives, or decisions may be adopted under the ordinary legislative procedure. Furthermore, the requirement that delegated acts be of 'general application' is not intended to distinguish between legislative and delegated acts, but rather to distinguish between delegated and implementing acts. As will be explained in section 1.2.2.2 of this chapter, one of the distinguishing features of implementing acts provided for in Article 291 TFEU is their ability to have either a general or an individual

[38] P Craig, *The Lisbon Treaty: Law, Politics and Treaty Reform* (Oxford University Press, 2010) 258–60.

[39] Art 103(1) TFEU.

[40] ibid, Art 109.

[41] ibid, Art 95(3).

[42] ibid, Art 122(2).

[43] On the enactment of materially legislative acts, see ch 5 of this book.

[44] Article 14(2) of Council Regulation (EU) 2020/672 of 19 May 2020 on the establishment of a European instrument for temporary support to mitigate unemployment risks in an emergency (SURE) following the COVID-19 outbreak [2020] OJ L159/1.

[45] Craig *(n 38)* 259.

scope. This is a key distinguishing criterion between implementing and delegated acts: the latter must be of general application, while the former may be either general or individual in scope.

1.2.1.3. The Minimum Content of Legislative Acts

The Treaties do not require legislative acts to have a compulsory minimum content, except in two cases: first, if the Union legislature chooses to grant delegated or implementing powers to the Commission or Council, it must specifically refer to it in the legislative act; second, Article 290(1), second paragraph TFEU states that 'the essential elements of an area shall be reserved for the legislative act'. Consequently, the essential elements of the regulated area cannot be delegated and must be clearly defined within the legislative act itself. In the case of Article 291 TFEU, although it does not explicitly mention 'essential elements', it can be argued that an equivalent compulsory minimum content requirement applies to legislative acts that confer implementing powers.[46]

The definition and characterisation of an 'essential element of an area' are tasks assigned to the Court of Justice, which has developed its approach drawing on its earlier case law on the practice of comitology that preceded the Lisbon Treaty.[47] The Treaties provide limited guidance on this matter, as seen in Article 290(2) TFEU, which mandates that legislative acts containing a delegation must explicitly specify 'the objectives, content, scope and duration' of the delegation. These formal requirements should be distinguished from the essential elements of a legislative act, which rely on vague criteria. The recent case law refers to the same criteria developed in the 1990s, stemming from the practice of comitology. According to this line of case law, the 'essential elements' of a legislative act are those that require:

> [P]olitical choices falling within the responsibilities of the EU legislature, in that it requires the conflicting interests at issue to be weighed up on the basis of a number of assessments, or if it means that the fundamental rights of the persons concerned may be interfered with to such an extent that the involvement of the EU legislature is required.[48]

To identify the 'essential elements' of a legislative act, the assessment must 'rely on objective elements which may be subject to judicial review'. The case law emphasises that consideration must be given to 'the characteristics and particular features of the field concerned'.[49] There is no fixed and immutable essential content of legislative acts, but rather a context-dependent content that depends on the aims of each policy measure and the terms used to define the means of achieving the objectives in the legislative act.

1.2.2. Non-legislative Acts

Any act adopted through a procedure other than a legislative procedure is regarded as a non-legislative act. The Treaties refer to 'non-legislative acts' in Articles 290 and 297 TFEU. The distinction between legislative and non-legislative acts becomes blurred as a result of Article 263, fourth paragraph TFEU, which refers to 'regulatory acts'. The case law of the Court of Justice has confirmed that 'non-legislative acts' and 'regulatory acts' refer to the same

[46] H Hofmann, 'Legislation, Delegation and Implementation under the Treaty of Lisbon: Typology Meets Reality' (2009) 15 *European Law Journal* 482.

[47] Case C-355/10 *Parliament v Council* EU:C:2012:516, para 65.

[48] Case C-696/15 P *Czech Republic v Commission* EU:C:2017:595, paras 76 and 78; and Case C-759/23 *PJ Carroll & Company Ltd* EU:C:2025:477, para 27, expressly referring to case law prior to the entry into force of Article 290 TFEU, in particular Case C-355/10 *Parliament v Council* EU:C:2012:516, paras 65 and 76–77.

[49] Case C-540/14 P *DK Recycling und Roheisen v Commission* EU:C:2016:469, para 48; and Case C-44/16 P *Dyson v Commission* EU:C:2017:357, para 62.

category of acts, characterised by their adoption through procedures different from legislative procedures.[50]

Non-legislative acts are sometimes referred to as 'executive acts', in reference to the decision-making powers of executive authorities such as the Commission, bodies, offices, or agencies of the Union when they exercise executive or administrative powers of a non-legislative nature. Therefore, references to 'non-legislative acts', 'regulatory acts', and 'executive acts' point to the same types of Union acts: those adopted through non-legislative powers and with features that are typical of executive/administrative action.

The Lisbon Treaty established two specific types of non-legislative acts to enhance transparency in the Union's executive/administrative rule-making process. Article 290 TFEU introduces the category of 'delegated acts', while Article 291 TFEU refers to 'implementing acts'. These are not the only non-legislative acts available to the Union's executive/administrative authorities, but their inclusion in the Treaties makes them the standard instruments within the broader category of non-legislative acts.

1.2.2.1 Delegated Acts

The Lisbon Treaty, inspired by the work undertaken in the Convention that drafted the failed Constitutional Treaty, aimed to introduce greater clarity in the Union's executive powers and decision-making procedures. As explained in chapter five, the task of 'simplification' resulted in a significant attribution of executive power to the Commission, as well as a clearer division of legislative and non-legislative responsibilities between the Union institutions. Delegations contribute to achieving this result by reinforcing the separation of legislative and non-legislative acts, while granting the Commission an executive role alongside the Member States.[51]

In contrast with the case of legislative acts, delegated acts are not limited to the use of regulations, directives, and decisions. This results from an *a contrario* interpretation of Article 296, third paragraph TFEU, which excludes the use of 'acts not provided for by the relevant legislative procedure in the area in question', a tacit reference to regulations, directives, and decisions. While the Union legislature is bound to use the typology of acts provided in Article 288 TFEU, the Commission is not similarly constrained when making use of a delegation, unless the Union legislature has specified in the delegated rule the type of act the Commission must employ.

1.2.2.1.1. Content of the Delegation Article 290(1) TFEU empowers the Union legislature to delegate to the Commission the power to adopt non-legislative acts of general application to supplement or amend certain non-essential elements of the legislative act. The wording of the provision introduces two requirements that the Commission must respect at all times: the delegated act must be 'of general application'; and it must respect 'certain non-essential elements' of the legislative act.

Delegated acts under Article 290(1) TFEU must be of *general scope*. As a result, regulations are the most commonly used acts to undertake a delegation. Directives can also be used for adopting delegated acts, although this is less common in practice. In the case of decisions, a delegation under Article 290(1) TFEU can only involve such acts if it entails a *sui generis* decision with no identified addressees. This requirement must be interpreted in close connection

[50] Case C-583/11 P *Inuit Tapiriit Kanatami and Others v Commission* EU:C:2013:625, paras 58–60.

[51] See the Commission's document 'Implementation of the Treaty of Lisbon — Delegated Acts — Guidelines for the services of the Commission ('Guidelines on delegated acts')', annexed to document SEC(2011) 855 of 24 June 2011. The Court of Justice has referred on several occasions to these Guidelines (see, for example, Case C-696/15 P *Czech Republic v Commission* EU:C:2017:595, para 53) when interpreting Art 290 TFEU.

with the case law on the general application of regulations. It must be recalled that since the judgment in *Zuckerfabrik Watenstedt*, a Union act does not lose its general scope 'simply because it may be possible to ascertain with a greater or lesser degree of accuracy the number or even the identity of the persons to which it applies at any given time'.[52]

The delegation is made to *'supplement'* or *'amend'* certain non-essential elements of a legislative act. The delegation may entrust the Commission to accomplish one or both objectives within the same legislative act. To 'supplement' a legislative act, the Commission is empowered to cover a gap intentionally left by the legislature, generally in a technical area requiring further development.[53] The purpose of supplementary content is to add substantive details that make the legislative act fully applicable and of effective practical use by its addressees. As the Court of Justice states, 'the purpose of granting a delegated power is to achieve the adoption of rules coming within the regulatory framework as defined by the basic legislative act'. Before the enactment of the Lisbon Treaty, the practice of delegations proved that some areas of significant importance could be left as supplementary matters to be subsequently developed by the Commission.

The reference in Article 290(1) TFEU to the power to 'amend' a legislative act addresses a practical necessity that often arises in the practice of rulemaking. In highly technical areas subject to rapid change, it may be necessary to introduce amendments to a legislative act at a pace that does not align with the rhythm of standard legislative procedures. By giving the Commission such power, the drafters of the Lisbon Treaty

> wanted to cover hypothetical cases in which the Commission is empowered formally to amend a basic instrument. Such a formal amendment might relate to the text of one or more articles in the enacting terms or to the text of an annex that legally forms part of the legislative instrument.[54]

If the legislative act requires the Commission to adopt a delegated act to supplement specific contents, such contents cannot be enacted through other types of acts, such as an implementing act. In the case of *Meta Platforms v Commission*, the General Court annulled an implementing act that introduced a common methodology for calculating an annual fee, whereas the legislative act establishing the fee specified that the common methodology should be enacted through a delegated act.[55]

Article 290(3) TFEU requires the adjective 'delegated' to be inserted in the title of all delegated acts to distinguish them from implementing acts and legislative acts.

1.2.2.1.2. Limits to Delegation All delegated acts are subject to limits defined by the objectives, content, scope, and duration of the delegation, all of which must be explicitly specified in the basic legislative act conferring the delegation.[56]

[52] *Zuckerfabrik Watenstedt* (n 2) as well as the other case law cited in the same footnote.

[53] According to the case law, the aim of delegated acts is primarily to supplement or cover a gap in a legislative act, whereas implementing acts are intended 'to provide further detail in relation to the content of a legislative act, in order to ensure that it is implemented under uniform conditions in all Member States' (Case C-427/12 *Commission v Parliament and Council* EU:C:2014:170, para 39). The distinction between 'supplementing' and providing 'further detail' seems to rely on the degree of normative development required by the legislative act. In order to 'supplement', there must be an area not covered by the legislative act, a vacuum voluntarily created by the Union legislator requiring additional rules. On the other hand, providing 'further detail' to a legislative act implies that there are no gaps, but only predetermined aspects needing additional rules to ensure uniform application (*Commission v Parliament and Council*, ibid, paras 39 and 52).

[54] Communication from the Commission to the European Parliament and the Council of 9 December 2009 'on the implementation of Article 290 of the Treaty on the Functioning of the European Union' COM 2009 673 final, 4.

[55] Case T-55/24 *Meta Platforms Ireland Ltd v Commission* EU:T:2025:842, paras 35–40.

[56] Article 290(1) second para TFEU.

The Lisbon Treaty introduced substantive limits to the Union legislature's powers of delegation in primary law. As noted earlier, a legislative act can only delegate 'non-essential elements', while the 'essential elements' remain under the exclusive remit of the Union legislator. The definition of 'essential elements' has been developed by the case law of the Court of Justice, as discussed above. Initially, the case law showed considerable deference to the Union legislature, focusing its review mainly on the procedural aspects of the requirement.[57] When the analysis shifted towards the substantive aspects of the 'essential elements' of a legislative act, the case law traditionally applied a deferential approach toward the Union legislator and its executive/administrative authorities.[58] However, as of 2017, in *Dyson v Commission*, the Court of Justice adopted a more rigorous standard of scrutiny regarding the 'essential elements' of a legislative act.[59] This approach was subsequently reaffirmed in *Czech Republic v Commission*.[60]

In addition to substantive limits, Article 290(1) TFEU also sets temporal limits on a delegation. The delegating legislative act must explicitly lay down the conditions to which the delegation is subject, which under Article 290(2) TFEU include either a time limit on the delegation or a right of revocation by the European Parliament or the Council, as well as a right of objection. In practice, the legislator can introduce a delegation with a fixed or renewable expiry date, or even with an indefinite duration, and a right of revocation.[61]

1.2.2.1.3. Scrutiny of Delegated Acts Article 290(2) TFEU provides for two control mechanisms, allowing the Council and/or the European Parliament, as co-authors or author of the legislative act, to exercise control over the delegation conferred on the Commission: the 'revocation' of the delegation and the 'objection' to the delegated act. The two mechanisms are conceived as alternative mechanisms, not cumulative, although nothing prevents the basic legislative act from including both. The control mechanism must be explicitly incorporated into the basic legislative act, and it cannot be inferred or implied from the aims and/or wording of the basic legislative act.

Right of Revocation

According to Article 290(2)(a) TFEU, 'the European Parliament or the Council may decide to revoke the delegation', a power that must be outlined in the basic legislative act. The revocation of a delegation is an ex post decision that can be taken independently, by the European Parliament or the Council, in their capacity as co-authors of the legislative act. If the legislative act is solely the product of the Council, the authority to revoke the delegation resides exclusively with the Council. The right to revoke a delegation can be exercised at any time, as opposed to the right of 'objection', which is subject to specific time constraints.

Although the Council and the European Parliament have broad discretion in exercising the right of revocation, their decision must be properly reasoned. The Commission has stated

[57] Case C-84/94 *United Kingdom v Council* EU:C:1996:431, para 37; Case C-377/98 *Netherlands v Parliament and Council* EU:C:2001:523, paras 32–33; Case C-103/01 *Commission v Germany* EU:C:2003:301, para 47; Case C-257/01 *Commission v Council*, EU:C:2005:25, para 53; and Case C-143/04 *Alliance for Natural Health and Others* EU:C:2004:741, paras 101–06. In this sense, see A Bouveresse, *Le pouvoir discrétionnaire dans l'ordre juridique communautaire* (Bruylant, 2010) 184ff.

[58] Case C-25/70 *Köster* EU:C:1970:115; Case C-46/86 *Romkes* EU:C:1987:287, para 16; Case C-417/93 *Parliament v Council* EU:C:1995:127, para 30; and Case C-103/01 *Commission v Germany* EU:C:2003:301, paras 18–25.

[59] *Dyson v Commission* (n 49) paras 61–68.

[60] Case C-696/15 P *Czech Republic v Commission* EU:C:2017:595, para 83: 'the General Court disregarded the second sentence of the second subparagraph of Article 290(1) TFEU. Contrary to what that provision requires, the General Court did not make sure that, in the present case, the adoption of rules relating to the essential elements of the area in question remained reserved to the EU legislature and was not the subject of a delegation of power'.

[61] Commission Communication on Article 290 TFEU (n 54) 5–6.

that the statement of reasons is not a mere formality, but an essential feature with significant practical and institutional implications, as it enables the institution that has not exercised the right of revocation to understand the reasons behind the other institution's decision.[62] Furthermore, the duty to state reasons has a preventive effect on future delegations, as it guides the Commission in developing patterns of conduct when exercising future delegated powers.[63]

For the sake of legal certainty, legislative acts should specify the consequences of a revocation. For example, it should be stated that the revocation decision must explicitly target the delegated powers revoked, without affecting the delegated acts already in force.[64]

Right of Objection

Besides the right of revocation, Article 290(2)(b) TFEU states that 'the delegated act may enter into force only if no objection has been expressed by the European Parliament or the Council within a period set by the legislative act'. The right of opposition is included in the Treaty as a preventive measure enabling the legislative institutions to intervene *ex ante to* avert the entry into force of a delegated act which they consider incompatible with the legislative act.

In contrast to the right of revocation, an objection to a delegated act can only be exercised within the time limit set out in the legislative act. This period may vary from case to case, but it usually falls within a range of two to three months. The period begins from the date of notification by the Commission of the adopted delegated act in all official languages. Once this period has expired, the legislative institution retains only the right of revocation. The legislative institutions have broad discretion in deciding whether to exercise their right of opposition, but they remain under a duty to state reasons.

The effects of an opposition by the Council or the European Parliament are that the delegated act does not enter into force. The Commission must take into account the reasons provided by the objecting institution and may submit a new proposal for a delegated act.

1.2.2.1.4. Judicial Review Nothing prevents individuals, institutions, or Member States from challenging a delegated act in Union courts if they believe that the Commission has exceeded its delegated powers. This right of access to justice was clarified and reinforced following the reforms introduced by the Lisbon Treaty, which amended the provisions on the action for annulment to ease the conditions of access to Union courts to challenge non-legislative acts.[65] Article 263, fourth paragraph TFEU, as amended by the Lisbon Treaty, states that any natural or legal person may bring an action 'against a *regulatory act* which is of direct concern [to any natural or legal person] and which does not entail implementing measures' (emphasis added).

As discussed in chapter eleven of this book, the reference in Article 263(4) TFEU to 'regulatory acts' is a concept that originated in the draft Constitutional Treaty. A historical and systematic interpretation of this provision led the Court of Justice to conclude that the term 'regulatory acts' encompasses all 'non-legislative acts', including delegated acts.[66]

[62] ibid, 8.

[63] ibid, 9.

[64] According to the Interinstitutional Agreement between the European Parliament, the Council of the European Union and the European Commission on Better Law-Making [2016] OJ L123/1, a decision to revoke a delegation 'shall not affect the validity of any delegated acts already in force' and such assertion should be included in the delegating power.

[65] Proof of this is the existence of various judgments reviewing the validity of delegated acts as a result of actions brought by private parties. See, for example, *Dyson v Commission* (n 49).

[66] *Inuit Tapiriit Kanatami and Others* (n 50) paras 58–60.

1.2.2.2. Implementing Acts

Implementing acts form the second category of non-legislative acts included in the Treaties, as specified in Article 291 TFEU. The raison d'être of these acts is closely connected to the way in which executive powers are conceived in the Union. As outlined in chapter four, the Union's executive powers are mostly vested in the Member States and the Commission. Typically, Member States are responsible for implementing Union law, with the Commission only assuming such tasks where uniform conditions for implementation are needed. In duly justified circumstances, implementation powers can also be conferred on the Council.

Using this scheme as a basic premise, Article 291(1) TFEU states that 'Member States shall adopt all measures of national law necessary to implement legally binding Union acts'. The general rule, which states that it is for the Member States to implement Union law, is now explicitly enshrined in the Treaties. Immediately after, Article 291(2) TFEU adds that 'where uniform conditions for implementing legally binding Union acts are needed, those acts shall confer implementing powers on the Commission or, in duly justified specific cases . . . , on the Council'.

First, it should be emphasised that the adoption of implementing acts by the Commission or the Council should be viewed as the exception, the general rule being that it is for the Member States to adopt the implementing measures of Union acts. The Commission or the Council can only intervene and enact implementing acts when 'uniform conditions for implementing legally binding Union acts are needed'; otherwise, implementation is a matter for each Member State and must be carried out in accordance with its own national legal system.

Secondly, implementing acts must be preceded by a 'legally binding Union act', but the Treaty uses terms different from those set out for delegations in Article 290 TFEU. Unlike Article 290, which requires a prior 'legislative act', Article 291(2) TFEU refers to 'legally binding Union acts', a broader formulation that encompasses not only legislative acts but also delegated acts and other binding Union acts, including materially legislative acts (as is the case with the regulatory powers provided for in the Treaty under procedures other than ordinary and special legislative procedures). The act conferring implementing powers must specify the grounds on which it is based, and must explain the reasons justifying the conferral of implementing powers on the Commission or the Council.

Third, implementing acts can take the form of a regulation, a directive, or a decision, and unlike delegated acts, they are not required to be of 'general application', as implementing acts may have either general or individual scope. Also, Article 291(4) TFEU requires the word 'implementing' to be inserted in the title of all implementing acts.

1.2.2.2.1. Content of the Implementing Act The primary goal of an implementing act is to establish 'uniform conditions for implementing legally binding Union acts'. As a result, implementing acts do not 'supplement' or 'amend' a legislative act, but are solely intended to guarantee consistent application of the legislative act across the Union. Further details on the setting of 'uniform conditions' and the implementing function of these acts can be found in section IV of chapter five of this book.

1.2.2.2.2. Scrutiny of Implementing Acts: Committee Procedures Article 291(3) TFEU sets out the rules governing the oversight of implementing powers exercised by the Commission. The following features characterise these rules.

Article 291(3) TFEU does not specify the types of mechanisms available to the European Parliament and Council (in contrast with Article 290(2) TFEU). It leaves it to the legislator to develop the most suitable tools. These tools have materialised in Regulation 182/2011, which sets out the rules and general principles governing mechanisms for Member States to scrutinise the Commission's exercise of implementing powers.[67] Regulation 182/2011 replaced the preceding 'comitology decision' of 1999 and simplifies the committee structure that oversaw the Commission's implementation of regulatory measures. Under Regulation 182/2011 and in the interest of simplification, the number of committee procedures has been reduced to two: the advisory procedure and the examination procedure.

In addition to the committee procedures, Article 11 of Regulation 182/2011 provides a 'right of scrutiny' for the European Parliament and the Council when a basic act is adopted under the ordinary legislative procedure, according to which:

> [E]ither the European Parliament or the Council may at any time indicate to the Commission that, in its view, a draft implementing act exceeds the implementing powers provided for in the basic act. In such a case, the Commission shall review the draft implementing act, taking account of the positions expressed, and shall inform the European Parliament and the Council whether it intends to maintain, amend or withdraw the draft implementing act.

The examination procedure applies, in particular, for the adoption of implementing acts of general scope, and also to implementing acts relating to programmes with substantial implications; the common agricultural and common fisheries policies; the environment, security and safety, or protection of the health or safety, of humans, animals or plants; the common commercial policy, and taxation. The advisory procedure applies, as a general rule, for the adoption of implementing acts not falling within the categories subject to the examination procedure. However, the examination procedure can also be applied for the adoption of acts that would normally fall under the advisory procedure in duly justified cases.[68]

The powers of scrutiny under Article 291(3) TFEU refer solely to the exercise of implementing powers by the Commission, excluding from the scope of the provision the exercise of such powers by the Council.

Article 291(3) TFEU provides that mechanisms for the control by Member States of the Commission's exercise of implementing powers must be laid down in advance by the European Parliament and the Council. This provision forms the constitutional basis of the comitology system, under which committees composed of representatives of the Member States, and chaired by a non-voting representative of the Commission, oversee the adoption of implementing acts.

2. CFSP Acts

The simplification of the sources of Union law, which started during the Convention on the Future of Europe, stopped short when it reached the CFSP. As explained in chapters one and two, the Lisbon Treaty maintained the specificity and intergovernmental nature of the CFSP, including its own set of acts, as outlined in Article 25 TEU. In this policy area, the Union does not adopt 'legislative' and 'non-legislative' acts, as the procedures for enactment are specific to the CFSP. Moreover, CFSP acts have their own legal effects, which differ from the standard rules of direct effect and primacy that apply to other Union acts. This issue is further explored in chapters nine and ten of this book.

[67] Regulation (EU) 182/2011 of the European Parliament and of the Council of 16 February 2011 laying down the rules and general principles concerning mechanisms for control by Member States of the Commission's exercise of implementing powers [2011] OJ L55/13. This Regulation was adopted under the ordinary legislative procedure (Article 291(3) TFEU) and constitutes a legislative regulation, as confirmed in Case C-183/16 P Tilly-Sabco SAS v Commission EU:C:2017:704, para 91.

[68] Art 2(2)–(3) Regulation (EU) 182/2011.

According to Article 25 TEU, CFSP acts consist of two different instruments: general guidelines and decisions. A general guideline aims to define the basic strategic features of the CFSP. The authority to define general guidelines is entrusted to the European Council, and, due to their generic and programmatic nature, they do not have direct effect. The decision, unlike those outlined in Article 288, fourth paragraph TFEU, is approved by the European Council or Council and covers one or more of the following contents: actions to be undertaken by the Union; positions to be taken by the Union; or arrangements for the implementation of the other CFSP decisions. In contrast with general guidelines, the decisions under Article 25 TEU are binding on the Member States.

The acts enumerated in Article 25 TEU are not exhaustive and do not preclude the Council or the European Council from adopting other types of acts. Just as Union institutions can adopt atypical acts in areas not covered by a legislative procedure, the same applies to the Council and the European Council when acting within the framework of the CFSP.

3. Other Union Acts

The TEU and the TFEU refer to other Union acts besides those enumerated in Article 25 TEU and Article 288 TFEU. These are particular types of acts with their own procedural requirements, which can be summarised as follows.

3.1. *Inter-institutional Agreements*

Article 295 TFEU grants the European Parliament, the Council, and the Commission the authority to consult each other and by common agreement make arrangements for their cooperation. This provision allows the three institutions to enter into interinstitutional agreements that 'may be of a binding nature.' Specific references to interinstitutional arrangements are found in Article 287(3), third paragraph TFEU, and Article 17 TEU.

Interinstitutional agreements have long been a part of the Union's institutional practice, dating back to the early days of the European Communities.[69] However, it was only following the entry into force of the Lisbon Treaty that the institutions could rely on an explicit legal basis in the Treaties to adopt such agreements.[70]

[69] The first interinstitutional agreements were entered into by the Council and the European Parliament and date back to 1964 and 1973, when both institutions adopted the Luns and Westerterp procedures, respectively, on association and trade agreements. In 2002, both institutions signed an agreement on the European Parliament's access to sensitive Council information in the field of foreign, security and defence policy. Agreements have also been concluded between the Commission and the European Parliament, such as the Codes of Conduct of 1990, 1995, and 2000. Interinstitutional agreements between the Council, the European Parliament, and the Commission are also frequent. In procedural matters affecting the legislative procedure, the agreements of 4 March 1975, on the conciliation procedure, and those of 30 June 1982, 29 June 1988, 29 October 1993, 6 May 1999 and 7 November 2002, on the budgetary procedure, are worth highlighting. On matters other than procedural matters, see the agreements of 5 April 1977 on fundamental rights, 25 October 1993 on democracy, transparency and subsidiarity, and 28 February 2002 on the financing of the Convention on the Future of Europe.

[70] The most explicit legal basis is first to be found in Declaration No 3 to the Final Act of the Conference that negotiated the Treaty of Nice, which stated as follows: 'The Conference recalls that the duty of sincere cooperation which derives from Article 10 of the Treaty establishing the European Community and governs relations between the Member States and the Community institutions also governs relations between the Community institutions themselves. In relations between those institutions, when it proves necessary, in the context of that duty of sincere cooperation, to facilitate the application of the provisions of the Treaty establishing the European Community, the European Parliament, the Council and the Commission may conclude interinstitutional agreements. Such agreements may not amend or supplement the provisions of the Treaty and may be concluded only with the agreement of these three institutions'.

Article 295 TFEU reflects established case law of the Court of Justice, which states that interinstitutional agreements can produce legal effects.[71] The Treaty indicates that agreements 'may' have binding effects, thus confirming that the effects of an interinstitutional agreement must be reviewed on a case-by-case basis, taking into account the following features.[72]

First, the content of the agreement must be considered, as the provisions themselves may explicitly confirm the intention of the signatory institutions to give it binding effect. Second, the title of the agreement can be indicative of its binding nature: even if the formal title of the act is that of an interinstitutional agreement, the text might adopt a different designation that reflects its true character. For example, a 'code of conduct' may demonstrate the intention of the institutions to be bound by it, whereas a 'declaration' is less likely to do so. Third, the wording of the agreement will indicate the legal effects it aims to produce. Agreements that are purely political or declaratory, including general provisions and declarations of intent with rhetorical language, will have no binding legal effects between the parties.

Regardless of the agreement's binding effects, these instruments can play a significant role in interpreting Union law, including both primary[73] and secondary law.[74] The institutions' intentions as expressed in an inter-institutional agreement may have an interpretative effect that can provide valuable references when implementing Union law.

3.2. *Acts of the European Central Bank*

Article 132(1) TFEU empowers the European Central Bank (ECB) to adopt regulations, decisions, recommendations, and opinions. Furthermore, Article 12.1 of the Statute of the European System of Central Banks (ESCB) states that the Governing Council may adopt 'guidelines' and 'decisions', and the Executive Board is authorised to issue 'instructions' to national central banks. These instruments under Article 12 are binding, as confirmed by Article 14(3) of the Statute, which states that the actions of national central banks 'shall be in accordance with the guidelines and instructions issued by the ECB'.

Although the acts adopted by the ECB are typical acts following the enumeration of Article 288 TFEU (excluding directives, with the additional category of 'instructions' provided in Article 12 of the ESCB Statute), they are not classified as either 'legislative acts' or 'non-legislative acts' within the meaning of Article 289(3) TFEU. However, they remain subject to the general framework for Union acts, except in areas where the Treaty provides specific provisions, such as their publication requirements.[75]

3.3. *Acts of Union Bodies, Offices, and Agencies*

Chapter three of this book outlined the increasing importance of the Union's bodies, offices, and agencies. Among their various functions, the Union has established agencies with executive decision-making powers, such as the Community Plant Variety Office, the European Union Aviation Safety Agency, and the Single Resolution Board. These agencies make decisions that

[71] J Monar, 'Interinstitutional Agreements: The Phenomenon and Its New Dynamics after Maastricht' (1994) 31 *Common Market Law Review* 693, and A-M Tournepiche, 'La clarification du statut juridique des accords interinstitutionnels' (2002) 2 *Revue Trimestrielle de Droit Européen* 209.

[72] Case C-58/94 *Netherlands v Council* EU:C:1996:171, paras 23–27; and Case T-105/95 *WWF UK v Commission* EU:T:1997:26, paras 53–55.

[73] Case C-44/79 *Hauer* EU:C:1979:290, para 15; Case C-353/99 P *Council v Hautala* EU:C:2001:661; and Case T-194/94 *Carvel and Guardian Newspapers v Council* EU:T:1995:183.

[74] Case C-211/80 *Advernier and Others v Commission* EU:C:1984:15, para 22; and Case C-34/86 *Council v Parliament* EU:C:1986:291, para 50.

[75] Art 132(2) TFEU.

have legal effects on third parties, which can be appealed before a Board of Appeal and, ultimately, before the General Court.[76] The rules governing these agencies do not always include a uniform typology of acts they can adopt, referring to them as 'decisions', 'measures', or 'resolutions', among other titles.[77]

It is common for Union bodies, offices, and agencies to act in an advisory or coordinating capacity. In such instances, the acts adopted by these bodies and agencies are not directly binding unless the European Commission explicitly endorses them. When this occurs, the decision is deemed to be formally adopted by the Commission, not the agency. In such cases, if a direct action is brought against the act in Union courts, it must be directed against the Commission.[78]

4. Legal Regime

4.1. *Duty to State Reasons*

Union acts must state the reasons justifying their adoption. This requirement is outlined in Article 296, second paragraph TFEU, which states that 'legal acts shall state the reasons on which they are based and shall refer to any proposals, initiatives, recommendations, requests or opinions required by the Treaties'. The scope of the Union's duty to state reasons is broader than in many national legal systems, which generally exempt the legislature from being legally bound to justify its decisions. In contrast, the Union imposes this duty on both legislative and non-legislative acts, and it also applies to CFSP acts when they involve restrictive measures against natural or legal persons, as well as to acts of the ECB and acts of bodies, offices, and agencies. The same duty applies to legally binding atypical acts, such as interinstitutional agreements.

The rationale for this obligation is twofold: it ensures transparency in the functioning of the institutions, and it facilitates judicial review of Union acts. The Court of Justice has consistently referred to both objectives, stating that Article 296(2) TFEU

> is not taking mere formal considerations into account but seeks to give an opportunity to the parties of defending their rights, to the Court of exercising its supervisory functions and to Member States and to all interested nationals of ascertaining the circumstances in which the Commission has applied the Treaty.[79]

The content of the statement of reasons must refer to the legal basis and the mandatory formalities required by the Treaty,[80] as well as to the factual background[81] and the considerations which justify the act.[82] The absence of any of these features amounts to an infringement of an essential procedural requirement within the meaning of Article 263 TFEU, rendering the act liable to annulment, and may be raised by the Union courts of their own motion.[83] Exceptionally, the

[76] See, for example, Arts 35 and 45 of Council Regulation No 2100/94 of 27 July 1994 on Community plant variety rights [1994] OJ L227/1.

[77] P Craig, *EU Administrative Law*, 3rd edn (Oxford University Press, 2018) 157ff.

[78] See, for example, the case of the acts adopted by the European Anti-Fraud Office (OLAF), described in detail by X Groussot and Z Popov, 'What's Wrong with Olaf? Accountability, Due Process and Criminal Justice in European Anti-Fraud Policy' (2010) 47 *Common Market Law Review* 605. See Case C-551/22 P *Commission v SRB* EU:C:2024:520, para 96.

[79] Case C-24/62 *Germany v Commission* EU:C:1963:14, para 69; Case C-164/98 P *DIR International Film and Others v Commission* EU:C:2000:48, para 33; Case T-7/92 *Asia Motor France and Others v Commission* EU:T:1993:52, para 30; and Case T-241/00 *Le Canne v Commission* EU:T:2002:57, para 54.

[80] Case C-45/86 *Commission v Council* EU:C:1987:163, paras 8–10.

[81] Case C-73/74 *Groupement des fabricants de papiers peints de Belgique and Others v Commission* EU:C:1975:160, paras 29–31.

[82] ibid.

[83] Case C-18/57 *Nold v Haute Autorité* EU:C:1959:6, paras 51–52.

Court of Justice allows an act to refer to the statement of reasons set out in another act. This practice is justified, for example, where an institution adopts several acts with identical content.[84]

Although the obligation to state reasons applies to all Union authorities and acts, the intensity and scope of this requirement vary depending on several factors. The Court of Justice has ruled that the obligation outlined in the second paragraph of Article 296 TFEU must be assessed in the light of the circumstances of each case, particularly the content of the act, the nature of the grounds relied upon, and the interests of the addressees or other persons directly and individually concerned by the act in receiving explanations. This means that the statement of reasons does not necessarily have to specify all relevant matters of fact and law, insofar as the question of whether the statement of reasons meets the requirements of Article 296(2) TFEU must be assessed in relation not only to its wording but also to its context and the legal rules governing the matter.[85] The case law also highlights the importance of protecting confidential information that may be contained in the files related to the act. In such cases, the duty to state reasons must be balanced with the requirements of professional secrecy or applicable confidentiality rules, such as business secrecy, which is explicitly protected in various secondary legal instruments.[86]

4.2. *Signature, Publication and Notification*

All Union acts must be authenticated by the institution that adopts them to ensure that the final document accurately reflects the decision made by that institution.[87] Authentication through signature is also a prerequisite for the enforceability and validity of the act under Union law. Failure to authenticate an act constitutes an infringement of an essential procedural requirement, rendering the act liable to annulment.[88] Article 297 TFEU stipulates that legislative acts, as well as non-legislative acts adopted in the form of regulations, directives addressed to all Member States, or decisions which do not specify to whom they are addressed, must be signed by the presidents of the European Parliament and of the Council (in the case of legislative acts adopted under the ordinary legislative procedure) or by the president of the adopting institution in other cases. Non-legislative acts addressed to specified persons are authenticated in accordance with the internal procedures of the respective institution.[89]

Once signed, all legislative acts must be published in the *Official Journal of the European Union*, a rule that also applies to non-legislative acts of a general nature. However, while publication is an essential requirement, failure to publish does not necessarily invalidate the act.

[84] Case C-16/65 *Schwarze* EU:C:1965:117.

[85] Case C-367/95 P *Commission v Sytraval and Brink's France* EU:C:1998:154, para 63; Case C-5/67 *Beus* EU:C:1968:13, Joined Cases C-296/82 and C-318/82 *Netherlands and Leeuwarder Papierwarenfabriek v Commission* EU:C:1985:113, para 143; Case C-205/94 *Binder* EU:C:1996:234, paras 25–26; Case C-316/97 P *Parliament v Gaspari* EU:C:1998:558, para 26; Case C-301/96 *Germany v Commission* EU:C:2003:509, para 87; Case C-76/00 P *Petrotub and Republica v Council* EU:C:2003:4, para 81; Joined Cases C-341/06 P and C-342/06 P *Chronopost and La Poste/UFEX and Others* EU:C:2008:375, paras 108–11; Case C-629/11 P *Evropaïki Dynamiki v Commission* EU:C:2012:617, paras 21–22; and Joined Cases C-584/20 P and C-621/20 P *Commission v Landesbank Baden-Württemberg* EU:C:2021:601, paras 108–13.

[86] Joined Cases C-341/06 P and C-342/06 P *Chronopost and La Poste/UFEX and Others* EU:C:2008:375, paras 108–11; Case C-629/11 P *Evropaïki Dynamiki v Commission* EU:C:2012:617, paras 21–22; and Joined Cases C-584/20 P and C-621/20 P *Commission v Landesbank Baden-Württemberg* EU:C:2021:601, paras 108–13.

[87] Case C-286/95 P *Commission v ICC* EU:C:2000:188, para 62.

[88] Case C-137/92 P *Commission v BASF and Others* EU:C:1994:247, paras 75–78, where the Court of Justice rejected the position of the General Court, according to which the absence of a signature is a ground for the non-existence of the act. The judgment on appeal did not share this view and held that such a defect amounts to nullity.

[89] Art 15 of the Council's Rules of Procedure, authorising the signature of the Secretary-General and the Deputy Secretary-General, as well as delegation to Directors-General. See also Art 18 of the Commission's Rules of Procedure, limiting the power of signature to the President and the Secretary-General.

Following the judgment in *Racke*,[90] the Court of Justice held that an act is presumed to be known across the Union upon its publication, even if it is not simultaneously available in all the Member States. In *Skoma-Lux*,[91] the Court of Justice clarified this principle, ruling that failure to publish an act in an official Union language prevents the imposition of legal obligations on individuals in Member States where that language is an official language. As a result, the primary consequence of non-publication is that the provisions of the act are not enforceable against individuals, although Member States will remain bound by it. A similar conclusion was reached in *Heinrich*,[92] which involved a confidential annex to a regulation on aviation security that had not been published in the Official Journal. More recently, the Court applied the same reasoning to unpublished ISO technical standards incorporated by reference into Union legislation, holding that such standards cannot impose obligations on individuals if they have not been published in a manner that makes them accessible.[93]

Non-legislative acts with a specified addressee do not require publication in the Official Journal, but must be notified to the relevant party. In the case of the Council, unless decided otherwise, its rules of procedure require the publication of such acts in the *Official Journal of the European Union*.[94]

4.3. *Entry into Force and Implementation*

Legislative acts, as well as non-legislative acts of a general nature, come into force on the date specified in them or, in the absence of such a date, on the twentieth day after publication.[95] In contrast, non-legislative acts that specify an addressee take effect upon notification. Retroactive Union acts are only permitted insofar as they comply with the principles of legal certainty and legitimate expectations.

Regulations sometimes distinguish between 'entry into force' and 'date of application.' This distinction allows delegated and implementing acts envisaged by the regulation to be prepared and adopted while the regulation has entered into force but is not yet 'applicable'. The date on which the regulation becomes 'applicable' will generally coincide with the deadline for the Commission to adopt the regulation's delegated or implementing acts.

If an act imposes pecuniary obligations on persons other than Member States, it is enforceable in accordance with the rules of civil procedure in force in the Member State in the territory of which enforcement is carried out. Article 299 TFEU confirms that 'acts of the Council, the Commission or the European Central Bank which impose a pecuniary obligation on persons other than States, shall be enforceable'. Enforcement requires only that the national authority designated by the government of each Member State append the formula of enforcement, after verifying the authenticity of the act (Article 299, first paragraph, TFEU). Article 299, second paragraph, TFEU further emphasises that the role of the national authority is limited to verifying the authenticity of the act, without reviewing its substance. Enforcement may be suspended only by a decision of the Court of Justice (Article 299, fourth paragraph, TFEU).

[90] Case C-98/78 *Racke* EU:C:1979:14, paras 3–4.

[91] Case C-161/06 *Skoma-Lux* EU:C:2007:773, paras 58–60.

[92] Case C-345/06 *Heinrich* EU:C:2009:140, paras 42–47, contrary to the opinion of the Advocate General, who proposed that the Court should declare the contested regulation as non-existent.

[93] Case C-160/20 *Stichting Rookpreventie Jeugd and Others* EU:C:2022:101, paras 44–47 and Case C-588/21 P, Public.Resource.Org and Right to Know v Commission EU:C:2024:201, para 81.

[94] Art 17(2)(*b*) of the Rules of Procedure of the Council.

[95] Art 297(1), third para and (2), second para TFEU.

II. NON-BINDING SECONDARY LAW

The Treaties allow for the adoption of non-binding acts. Article 288, fifth paragraph, TFEU explicitly states that recommendations and opinions 'shall not be binding'. These acts form part of secondary legislation and are not limited to those listed in the said provision, as institutions can adopt non-binding instruments under various designations not specified in the Treaties. The Court of Justice has confirmed that non-binding Union acts are not devoid of all legal effects, meaning that their lack of binding force does not imply a complete absence of legal effects. Due to their unique and sometimes ambiguous legal nature, these non-binding acts are often referred to as *soft law*.

1. Typology

1.1. *Typical Soft Law*

As previously mentioned, Article 288, fifth paragraph, TFEU stipulates that recommendations and opinions are not binding, yet it also lists them among the Union's legal acts. As instruments explicitly included in the Treaty, they are considered *typical* forms of soft law, yet they are not the only ones present in primary law. Articles 26(3), 121(1), 171(1), and 219(2) TFEU empower the Council, based on a proposal from the Commission, to establish 'guidelines', while Article 68 TFEU assigns the same task to the European Council. Similarly, Article 287 TFEU empowers the Court of Auditors to issue a 'statement of assurance' on the reliability of the Union's accounts and the regularity of its underlying transactions. In the same vein, Articles 207(3) and 218(2) TFEU refer to the 'negotiating directive' that the Council issues to the Commission when the latter is tasked with negotiating an international agreement, which are of a different nature to the 'directives' of Article 288, third paragraph TFEU. Additionally, Article 148(1) TFEU provides that the European Council must annually examine the employment situation in the Union and adopt 'conclusions' on the matter.

1.2. *Atypical Soft Law*

In addition to the typical soft law acts mentioned above, the Union's institutional practice involves a wide range of non-binding instruments not explicitly provided for in the Treaties. These include, among others, 'codes of conduct', 'codes of good practice', 'communications', 'resolutions', as well as 'guidelines' or 'orientations' in areas beyond those specifically addressed in the Treaties.

2. Legal Status

Recommendations and opinions, as typical acts, may be adopted where the Treaty legal basis for a given policy area does not preclude them and where the relevant provision is not reserved for a binding typical act. Furthermore, in some cases, the Treaties will only allow for the adoption of a 'recommendation' or an 'opinion'. Both acts must comply with the general requirements regarding the statement of reasons, authentication, and publication, as outlined in section I.4 of this chapter.

In the case of recommendations, Article 292 TFEU grants the Council, the Commission and the ECB the power to adopt them subject to the following qualifications:

- where the Treaties provide for the Council to adopt acts on a proposal from the Commission, this rule applies to the adoption of recommendations;
- where unanimity is required for the adoption of a Union act, the same voting rule applies to recommendations.

On the other hand, atypical soft law acts are not subject to the same formal restrictions on their adoption, except as specified in Article 296, third paragraph TFEU, which prevents the European Parliament and the Council from adopting 'acts not provided for by the relevant applicable legislative procedure in the area in question' when a draft legislative act is submitted to them. Due to their heterogeneous nature, there is no general Treaty obligation to provide reasons or to publish atypical soft law, although the lack of such features may limit their interpretative effects.

As emphasised by the Court of Justice, the aim of typical soft law acts is to facilitate the promotion and/or understanding of policies developed by the Union's institutions, bodies, offices, and agencies. According to the case law, Article 288 TFEU is intended 'to confer on the institutions which may adopt recommendations a power to exhort and to persuade, distinct from the power to adopt acts having binding force'.[96] The challenge lies in determining where persuasion ends and regulation begins, a matter that will be explored in the following section.

3. Legal Effects

While Article 288, fifth paragraph TFEU states that recommendations and opinions 'shall have no binding force', this is complemented by Article 263, first paragraph TFEU, which lists the acts subject to judicial review without including recommendations and opinions. This limitation aligns with the fact that recommendations and opinions have no binding effect, a feature that, in principle, makes it unnecessary to challenge these acts in court.

However, the non-binding nature of soft law acts does not mean they are devoid of all legal effects. The Court of Justice has consistently stressed that non-binding acts can assist in interpreting binding rules of Union law,[97] provided they do not distort the content of those rules.[98] The leading case on the legal effects of Union soft law acts is found in *Grimaldi*, where the Court stated that:

> [N]ational courts are bound to take recommendations into consideration in order to decide disputes submitted to them, in particular where they cast light on the interpretation of national measures adopted in order to implement them or where they are designed to supplement binding Community provisions.[99]

Thus, although Union soft law does not impose obligations or grant rights, it binds national courts as an instrument 'to be taken into consideration'. This is not an obligation to 'apply', but rather to consider Union soft law during the decision-making process, without necessarily reaching a solution that aligns with its provisions. The judgment in *Grimaldi* effectively imposes on national courts a duty to take into account existing Union soft law instruments when interpreting related binding measures.

[96] Case C-16/16 P *Belgium v Commission* EU:C:2018:79, para 26. See also the Opinion of Advocate General Ćapeta in Case C-530/23 *Barało* EU:C:2024:955, pts 51–54.

[97] Case C-293/83 *Gravier* EU:C:1985:69, para 22; and Joined Cases C-281/85, C-283 to C-285/85 and C-287/85 *Germany and Others v Commission* EU:C:1987:351, para 17.

[98] Case C-59/75 *Manghera and Others* EU:C:1976:14, para 21; and *Belgium v Commission* (n 96) para 29.

[99] Case C-322/88 *Grimaldi* EU:C:1989:646, para 18. Similarly, see Case C-501/18 *Balgarska Narodna Banka* EU:C:2021:249, para 80; and Case C-911/19 *FBF* EU:C:2021:599, para 71.

Union soft law also plays a relevant role in guiding the institutions' future decisions and determining the Union's non-contractual liability. Statements made by the institutions may influence the behaviour of individuals or Member States, as seen in the case of recommendations under Article 288, fifth paragraph, TFEU or other soft law instruments provided in Union legislation. When such statements are made through soft law instruments, they can limit the institutions' ability to adopt later decisions that contradict them. For example, if the Commission issues a Communication encouraging Member States to support the textile sector, particularly by providing financial aid to companies with fewer than 15 workers, and later declares these subsidies as incompatible with State Aid rules, the initial Communication can have a self-binding effect on the Commission when developing its future policy. In such a case, affected parties could claim compensation for damages based on the principle of legitimate expectations, having relied on clear and unequivocal previous statements made by the Commission through soft law acts.

Advocate General Wahl has clearly explained this function of Union soft law by referring to the Commission's Communications:

> [F]or reasons of transparency, and in order to ensure equal treatment and legal certainty, the Commission may publish acts of 'soft law' (such as guidelines, notices or communications) with a view to announcing how it intends to make use, in certain situations, of . . . discretion. Although the Court has held that the provisions of such acts of 'soft law' are, by virtue of the duty of sincere cooperation enshrined in Article 4(3) TEU, to be taken into due account by the Member States' authorities, that duty cannot be understood as making those rules binding — not even de facto — on pain of eluding the legislative procedure set out in the FEU Treaty.

Therefore, those principles and rules are not binding upon Member States. The only effect those rules may directly produce is vis-a-vis the Commission, and even then merely as a limit on the exercise of its discretion: that institution is bound to accept measures which comply with those rules and it may not depart from them, unless it provides a valid reason for doing so. Failing a valid reason, a departure from those self-imposed rules may result in a breach of general principles of law, such as equal treatment or the protection of legitimate expectations. The Commission is thus bound by those rules, provided – however – that they are not contrary to the Treaties or other applicable legislation.[100]

Finally, the Court of Justice has recognised the possibility that a soft law act may in substance constitute a binding act. When such measures produce binding legal effects on private parties, Member States, or other Union institutions, they may be challenged regardless of their formal designation. In such cases, the Court of Justice has consistently held that if a non-binding act contains material obligations expressed in normative language, those provisions can be challenged in court (Union courts or national courts through preliminary references of validity) and will be regarded as a reviewable act.[101] Based on this premise, the case law has confirmed that actions of annulment can be brought against various types of soft law, including codes of conduct,[102] communications,[103] and internal guidelines of institutions,[104] qualifying them as reviewable acts for the purposes of an action of annulment pursuant to Article 263 TFEU.[105]

[100] Case C-526/14 *Kotnik* EU:C:2016:102, Opinion AG Wahl, pts 38–39.

[101] Case C-303/90 *France v Commission* EU:C:1991:424, paras 24–25; and *Belgium v Commission* (n 96) para 29.

[102] *Belgium v Commission (n 96);* Case C-501/18 *Balgarska Narodna Banka* EU:C:2021:249, para 83; and Case C-911/19 *FBF v ACPR* EU:C:2021:599, paras 53–57.

[103] Case C-325/91 *France v Commission* EU:C:1993:245, paras 6–10 and 24–26.

[104] Case C-366/88 *France v Commission* EU:C:1990:348, para 8.

[105] R Mastroianni, 'What's in a Recommendation?' (2020) MPILux Research Paper Series No 2.

GENERAL BIBLIOGRAPHY

Auby, J-B and Dutheil de la Rochère, J, *Traité de droit administratif européen*, 2nd edn (Bruylant, 2014).

Bast, J, 'Legal Instruments and Judicial Protection' in von Bogdandy, A and Bast, J (eds), *Principles of European Constitutional Law*, 2nd edn (Hart, 2010).

Craig, P, *The Treaty of Lisbon: Law, Politics and Treaty Reform* 3rd ed (Oxford University Press, 2010).

Louis, J-V, *The Community Legal Order* (Publications Office, 1995).

Pescatore, P, *L'ordre juridique des Communautés européennes: Étude des sources du droit communautaire* (Bruylant, 2006).

Prechal, S, *Directives in EC Law*, 2nd edn (Oxford University Press, 2005).

Senden, L, *Soft Law in European Community Law* (Hart, 2004).

Simon, D, *Le système juridique communautaire*, 3rd edn (PUF, 2001).

FURTHER READING

Union Binding Acts

Bast, J, 'New Categories of Acts after the Lisbon Reform: Dynamics of Parliamentarization in EU Law' (2012) 49 *Common Market Law Review* 885.

Lenaerts, K and Desomer, M, 'Towards a Hierarchy of Legal Acts in the European Union? Simplification of Legal Instruments and Procedures' (2005) 11 *European Law Journal* 744.

Liisberg, J, 'The EU Constitutional Treaty and Its Distinction between Legislative and Non-Legislative Acts' (2006) 1 *Jean Monnet Working Papers*.

Winter, G (ed), *Sources and Categories of European Union Law: A Comparative and Reform Perspective* (Nomos, 1996).

de Witte, B, 'Legal Instruments and Law-Making in the Lisbon Treaty' in S Griller and J Ziller (eds), *The Lisbon Treaty: EU Constitutionalism without a Constitutional Treaty* (Springer, 2008).

Delegated and Implementing Acts

Andenas, M and Türk, A (eds), *Delegated Legislation and the Role of Committees in the EC* (Kluwer Law, 2000).

Bergström, C F, *Comitology: Delegation of Powers in the European Union and the Committee System* (Oxford University Press, 2005).

Bradley, K, 'Comitology and the Law: Through a Glass Darkly' (1992) 29 *Common Market Law Review 693.*

Chamon, M, 'Institutional Balance and the Community Method in the Implementation of EU Legislation Following the Lisbon Treaty' (2016) 53 *Common Market Law Review* 1501.

Christiansen, T, and Dobbels, M, 'Non-Legislative Rule Making after the Lisbon Treaty: Implementing the New System of Comitology and Delegated Acts' (2013) 19 *European Law Journal* 42.

Craig, P, 'The Hierarchy of Norms' in Tridimas, T and Nebbia, P (eds), *European Law for the Twenty-First Century: Rethinking the New Legal Order*, vol I (Hart, 2004).

Driessen, B, 'Delegated Legislation after the Treaty of Lisbon: An Analysis of Article 290 TFEU (2010) 35 *European Law Review* 837.

Hofmann, H, 'Legislation, Delegation and Implementation under the Treaty of Lisbon' (2009) 15 *European Law Review* 482.

Lefevre, S, *Les actes communautaires atypiques* (Bruylant, 2006).

Mendes, J, 'Delegated and Implementing Rule Making: Proceduralisation and Constitutional Design' (2013) 19 *European Law Journal* 22.

Monar, J, 'Interinstitutional Agreements: The Phenomenon and its New Dynamics after Maastricht' (1994) 31 *Common Market Law Review* 693.

Ponzano, P, 'Executive and Delegated Acts: The Situation after the Lisbon Treaty' in S Griller and J Ziller (eds), *The Lisbon Treaty: EU Constitutionalism without a Constitutional Treaty* (Springer, 2008).

Tauschinsky, E, and Weiss, W (eds), The Legislative Choice Between Delegated and Implementing Acts in EU Law (Edward Elgar, 2018).

Thiery, S, *Les actes délégués en droit de l'Union européenne* (Bruylant, 2020).

Tournepiche, A-M, 'La clarification du statut juridique des accords interinstitutionnels' (2002) 38 *Revue Trimestrielle de Droit Européen* 73.
Vos, E, *Institutional Framework of Community Health and Safety Legislation: Committees, Agencies and Private Bodies* (Hart, 1999).

Union Non-binding Acts and Soft Law

Bobek, M, 'Legal Protection Against EU Soft Law. The Contribution of National Courts' (2025) 244 *EU Law Live Weekend Edition* 3.
Bracker, J, 'L'intensité normative de la soft law en matière de compatibilité des aides d'État' (2017) 53 *Cahiers de Droit Européen* 173.
Cini, M, 'The Soft Law Approach: Commission Rule-Making in the EU's State Aid Regime' (2001) 8 *Journal of European Public Policy* 192.
Cosma, H and Whish, R, 'Soft Law in the Field of EU Competition Policy' (2003) 14 *European Business Law Review* 25.
Klabbers, J, 'Informal Instruments before the Court of Justice' (1994) 31 *Common Market Law Review* 997.
Láncos, PL, Xanthoulis, N, and Arroyo Jiménez, L (eds), *The Legal Effects of EU Soft Law. Theory, Language and Sectoral Insights* (Edward Elgar, 2023).
Mastroianni, R, 'What's in a Recommendation?' (2020) 2 *MPILux Research Paper Series*.
Snyder, F, 'The Effectiveness of European Community Law: Institutions, Processes, Tools and Techniques' (1993) 56 *Modern Law Review* 19.
Trubek, D M, Cottrell, P and Nance, M, 'Soft Law, Hard Law and EU Integration' in G de Búrca and J Scott (eds), *Law and New Governance in the EU and the US* (Oxford University Press, 2006).
Vander Maelen, C, 'Hardly Law or Hard Law?: investigating the dimensions of functionality and legalisation of codes of conduct in recent EU legislation and the normative repercussions thereof' (2022) 47 *European Law Review* 752.
Wellens, KC and Borchardt, GM, 'Soft Law in EC Law' (1989) 14 *European Law Review* 267.

9

Union Law in National Legal Systems (I): Applicability and Direct Effect

ONE OF THE defining features of Union law is its autonomy. As a consequence, Union law is capable of producing legal effects by virtue of its own authority, without requiring the adoption of additional measures by the Member States to incorporate Union rules into their domestic legal systems. This feature entails that Union law may be relied upon by any legal subject, applied by all relevant institutions, and enforced, where necessary, by the national authorities responsible for the implementation of Union rules and principles.

To fully appreciate the scope of the applicability of Union law, it is useful to compare it with the manner in which international law takes effect within national legal systems. Under well-established practice, national constitutions determine the conditions under which international treaties are incorporated into domestic law.[1] States typically adopt one of two traditional approaches to the incorporation of international law: *monism* or *dualism*. In a monist system, an international treaty becomes part of domestic law upon ratification by the state and takes effect from the moment of its publication in the domestic official journal, provided that all internal formal requirements have been duly fulfilled.[2] By contrast, a dualist system requires the adoption of national legislative measures to incorporate an international treaty, typically through an intermediary domestic norm, with varying degrees of normative detail.[3] In either case, the decisive factor is the state's sovereign authority to choose between monism and dualism, a choice that is often enshrined in a constitutional provision.[4]

By contrast with international law, Union law removes from the Member States the power to unilaterally choose between the method of incorporation. Departing from the theory and practice of international law, Union law is distinctive in that, by virtue of its autonomy, it determines the manner in which it is to be integrated into the legal systems of the Member States. This feature, which the Member States have accepted through successive Treaty reforms,[5] was confirmed by the Court of Justice in its landmark judgment in *Van Gend en Loos* in 1963.[6]

[1] F Morgenstern, 'Judicial Practice and the Supremacy of International Law' (1950) 27 *British Yearbook of International Law* 42.

[2] This is the approach to the incorporation of international law used in France, Belgium, Cyprus, Greece, Luxembourg, the Netherlands, Portugal and Spain. Other jurisdictions use a mixed system combining features of monism and dualism, such as Hungary, Latvia, Lithuania, Poland and Slovenia.

[3] Examples of a strict dualist system are Denmark, Finland, Ireland, Malta and Sweden. Other jurisdictions use variants derived from the dualist system, such as Austria, Germany and Italy.

[4] J Crawford, *Brownlie's Principles of Public International Law*, 9th edn (Oxford University Press, 2019).

[5] However, the Amsterdam Treaty introduced a limit to the direct effect of Union law in the former 'third pillar', which corresponded with today's Area of Freedom, Security and Justice. Former Art 34(2)(b) TEU provided that Framework Decisions and Decisions 'shall not have direct effect'. This limitation, as well as Framework Decisions, was repealed in the Lisbon Treaty.

[6] Case C-26/62 *Van Gend en Loos v Administratie der Belastingen* EU:C:1963:1.

In that judgment, the Court held that the relationship between Union law and national legal systems follows a monist criterion, as implicitly established by the Treaties themselves.[7] The Court justified this conclusion by emphasising the need to ensure the uniform interpretation and application of Union law, together with its direct applicability. As discussed in section II.1 of this chapter, the reasoning in *Van Gend en Loos* is grounded in a systematic and teleological interpretation of the Treaties, which, both at the time of the judgment and today, do not expressly regulate the relationship between Union and national legal systems.

The applicability of Union law produces its most significant effects in the context of judicial disputes, in which courts, particularly national courts, are called upon to resolve cases governed by provisions of Union law.[8] As a consequence of that applicability, individuals are entitled to rely on Union law not only before the Union courts, but also (and, in quantitative terms, far more frequently) before national courts. Accordingly, the responsibility for ensuring compliance with Union law and securing its uniform interpretation is shared not only by the Court of Justice of the European Union, but also by national judiciaries.

Whereas international organisations typically entrust the resolution of disputes and the supervision of compliance with their rules to international tribunals, Union law assigns this task jointly to the Court of Justice of the European Union and to national courts. The Court of Justice acts as the authoritative and final interpreter of Union law, while national courts are responsible for adjudicating the vast majority of disputes brought by individuals in which Union law is invoked. The applicability of Union law therefore also entails the need to guarantee effective access to justice before both Union and national courts.

I. THE APPLICABILITY OF UNION LAW IN THE MEMBER STATES

By virtue of its autonomy, Union law independently and exclusively determines the legal effects of its provisions, irrespective of their rank, form or substantive content. As a general principle, provisions of Union law are characterised by their *applicability*, in the sense that any rule of Union law – whether deriving from primary law, secondary legislation or even soft law – may be invoked in the context of a legal dispute. That applicability extends equally to public authorities and to private parties, all of whom are bound by Union law. Consequently, once a provision of Union law enters into force, it forms part of the *law of the land* applicable throughout the territory of all Member States.

Although applicability constitutes the general rule, Union law employs a variety of techniques to modulate the scope and effects of its norms. Drawing on the legal traditions of the Member States, Union law differentiates the manner in which individual rules produce legal effects. Accordingly, while all Union rules are applicable, they are not all applied in the same way.

The main criterion for determining the effects of a rule of Union law is whether it has direct effect, a category examined in detail in section II of this chapter. Where a rule has direct effect, its applicability unfolds sequentially as follows. First, the authority entrusted with its application must attempt to interpret the national legal system in accordance with the rule of Union law (see section I.1.1). If that is not possible, the next step is to set aside the conflicting

[7] P Craig, 'Once Upon a Time in the West: Direct Effect and the Federalization of EEC Law' (1992) 12 *Oxford Journal of Legal Studies* 453; Wyatt D, 'New Legal Order or Old' (1982) 7 *European Law Review* 147, and B de Witte, 'Direct Effect, Primacy and the Nature of the Legal Order' in P Craig and G de Búrca (eds), *The Evolution of EU Law*, 3rd edn (Oxford University Press, 2021).

[8] M Waelbroeck, *Traités internationaux et juridictions internes dans les pays du Marché commun* (Pédone, 1969).

national rule (see sections I.1.2 and I.1.3) in order to ensure the effective implementation of the Union rule. If this cannot be done for the reasons explained below, the right-holders under the Union rule may bring a damages claim against the Member State to obtain financial compensation for the harm caused by the breach of Union law (see section I.1.4).

Where the rule of Union law has no direct effect, its application is also sequential but limited to two steps. First, national law must be interpreted in conformity with the Union rule (see section I.2.1). Secondly, as a remedy of last resort where a conform interpretation is not possible, damages actions seeking compensation for the harm caused by the breach of Union law must be made available (see section I.2.2).

1. Rules of Union Law with Direct Effect

1.1. Interpretation of National Law in Conformity with Union Rules having Direct Effect

Where a rule of Union law has direct effect, the first step in determining the manner of its applicability is to interpret national law in conformity with Union law. Once a rule of Union law forms part of the national legal order, all national provisions – including constitutional norms at the apex of the legal system – must, so far as possible, be interpreted in a way that avoids coming into conflict with Union law. The duty of conform interpretation is not a unique feature of the Union legal order; it reflects techniques familiar to the legal traditions of the Member States, which commonly recognise a general obligation to interpret statutory law in accordance with the constitution. In that sense, conform interpretation protects the hierarchical coherence of the legal system and promotes consistency and legal certainty.

The Court of Justice has repeatedly held that the duty of conform interpretation is not a discretionary option, but a binding obligation imposed on national authorities responsible for applying Union law. This obligation is 'inherent in the system of the Treaty', as it guarantees the full effectiveness of Union law whenever a national authority is tasked with resolving a dispute or implementing the law in an individual case.[9] The duty of conform interpretation also serves a systemic function by preserving the internal coherence of the national legal order. By avoiding direct clashes between national and Union law, it facilitates a harmonious coexistence between the two legal systems. Interpreting national law in conformity with Union law is therefore a more effective and less confrontational means of ensuring the applicability of Union law than resorting immediately to the setting aside of national provisions.

The duty of conform interpretation has a broad and general scope and is not confined to national provisions specifically intended to implement rules of Union law. It also extends to rules of secondary Union law when implementing international agreements concluded by the Union,[10] and, more generally, to all rules within the national legal system, irrespective of their connection with Union law or the date on which they were adopted.[11] That wide scope has important practical consequences. First, the national authority responsible for applying a rule of Union law may draw on the national legal system as a whole in its efforts to identify an interpretation consistent with Union law. Secondly, that authority may employ all interpretative methods available under national law, including techniques such as analogy, reliance on

[9] Joined Cases C-397/01 to C-403/01 *Pfeiffer and others* EU:C:2004:584, para 114; Case C-160/01 *Mau* EU:C:2003:280, para 34; and Case C-282/10 *Dominguez* EU:C:2012:33, para 24.

[10] Case C-382/21 P *EUIPO v The KaiKai Company Jaeger Wichmann* EU:C:2024:172, para 70.

[11] Case C-106/89 *Marleasing* EU:C:1990:395, para 8; Case C-131/97 *Carbonari and others* EU:C:1999:98, paras 49–50; *Pfeiffer* (n 9) para 115; and *Dominguez* (n 9) para 27.

general principles of law or established interpretative criteria, provided that those methods are capable of yielding an interpretation of national law compatible with Union law.[12]

The duty of conform interpretation further requires national courts to revisit their existing case law where it is founded on an interpretation of national law that conflicts with Union law. As the Court of Justice has made clear, a national court

> cannot validly claim in the main proceedings that it is impossible for it to interpret the national provision at issue in a manner that is consistent with EU law by the mere fact that it has consistently interpreted that provision in a manner incompatible with EU law.[13]

At the same time, the duty of conform interpretation is not without limits. Where the application of all interpretative tools available to the national authority is no longer capable of aligning national law with the relevant rule of Union law, a conforming interpretation becomes impossible. In that regard, the Court of Justice has clarified that the obligation of conform interpretation 'cannot serve as the basis for an interpretation of national law *contra legem*'.[14]

1.2. *Review of the Conformity of National Law in Light of Union Law having Direct Effect*

Where a national authority is unable to interpret national law in conformity with a rule of Union law that has direct effect, it is required to set aside the conflicting national provision and apply the Union rule directly. The setting aside of national law in such circumstances is a consequence of the principle of primacy, which is examined in detail in chapter ten of this book.

A rule of Union law with direct effect need not confer individual rights in order for an individual to rely on it and seek the setting aside of a national provision. It is sufficient that there exists an objective incompatibility between a rule of Union law and a rule of national law for the latter to be disapplied by the national authority when resolving a dispute. This mechanism has been described by some Advocates General and legal scholars as one of 'exclusionary invocability' (*invocabilité d'exclusion*), inasmuch as the rule of Union law is relied upon to exclude the application of the incompatible national provision in the case at hand. Other authors refer to this type of applicability as 'reactive direct effect', since it involves an individual invoking a directly effective rule of Union law in order to prevent the application of a national rule or act, rather than to claim the benefit of an individual right. By way of example, where a financial penalty is imposed by a national authority in breach of a directly effective rule of Union law, the addressee of that penalty may invoke the Union rule in order to prevent its enforcement and therefore avoid the imposition of the penalty.

In summary, where a rule of Union law has direct effect and a conforming interpretation of national law proves impossible, Union law empowers national authorities to rely on that rule in order to assess the compatibility of national law and, where appropriate, to set aside the incompatible national provision. Where the national authority is vested with the power to annul or repeal the conflicting rule of national law, it will proceed to do so in order to safeguard legal certainty. The hierarchical rank or legal status of the national provision is irrelevant for the purposes of ensuring the effectiveness of Union law, as will be explained in chapter ten, in particular in situations where national constitutional provisions come into conflict with rules of Union law.

[12] *Marleasing* (n 11) para 8 and *Pfeiffer* (n 9) para 116.

[13] Case C-441/14 *DI* EU:C:2016:278, paras 33–34; and Case C-414/16 *Egenberger* EU:C:2018:257, paras 72–73.

[14] Case C-105/03 *Pupino* EU:C:2005:386, paras 44 and 47; Case C-212/04 *Adeneler and others* EU:C:2006:443, para 110; Case C-268/06 *Impact* EU:C:2008:223, para 100; and *Dominguez* (n 9) para 25.

1.3. *Direct Invocability of Union Law in the Absence of National Law*

Where national law contains no domestic provisions implementing Union law, individuals must rely exclusively on Union law as the sole normative framework for resolving a dispute. This situation may arise in two different scenarios.

First, where a Member State has failed to transpose a Union directive within the prescribed time limit, individuals may directly invoke the provisions of that directive, provided that they are sufficiently clear, precise and unconditional. This is a frequent situation in practice, given the delays that often occur in the transposition of directives by Member States.

Secondly, Union acts such as regulations are, pursuant to Article 288, second paragraph Treaty on the Functioning of the European Union (TFEU), 'directly applicable in all Member States'. In such cases, where a provision of a regulation has direct effect, it may be invoked by individuals without the need for any national transposition or implementing measures.

The distinction between these two scenarios is significant. In the first, the individual seeks to enforce a right that the Member State was required to establish through a transposition measure. In the second, the individual relies on a self-executing Union rule that operates independently of any national act of incorporation.

In the first scenario, where a Member State has failed to adopt the mandatory transposition measures, the national court may be required to give effect to rights that the legislature was supposed to have established through transposition. This is particularly the case where the directive affords Member States a broad margin of discretion in defining individual rights, a situation commonly described in legal doctrine as 'substitutionary effect' or 'invocability of substitution'.[15] Such an outcome may raise questions about the internal balance of powers within the Member State, by requiring the judiciary to apply provisions that would ordinarily have been given concrete form by the legislature. For that reason, the case law of the Court of Justice requires that the Union rule governing the dispute be sufficiently clear and precise to define the rights conferred on individuals and thereby produce direct effect.[16]

In the second scenario, where the Union rule does not require any form of national regulatory mediation, the Court of Justice's case law adopts a more flexible approach to recognising the direct effect of Union provisions, even where the rule does not exhaustively define individual rights. The requirements governing direct effect are examined in detail in section II.2 of this chapter.

1.4. *Member State Liability for Breach of Union Law*

The final step that can result from the direct effect of Union law is the liability of the Member States for the breach of Union law. Individuals have the right to claim financial compensation in national courts for any harm caused by a Member State's breach of Union law. This remedy, which is grounded in the general principle of sincere cooperation,[17] allows individuals to seek financial compensation resulting from the Member State's non-compliance, provided that three conditions are satisfied:

- a sufficiently serious breach of a provision of Union law intended to confer rights on individuals;
- the existence of actual damage;
- a direct causal link between the breach and the damage suffered by the individual.[18]

[15] D Simon, *La directive européenne* (Dalloz, 1997).

[16] See, for example, Case C-14/83 *Von Colson and Kamann* EU:C:1984:153; and Case C-71/85 *Federatie Nederlandse Vakbeweging* EU:C:1986:465.

[17] See, inter alia, Joined Cases C-6/90 and C-9/90 *Francovich and others* EU:C:1991:428, para 36; Joined Cases C-46/93 and C-48/93 *Brasserie du pêcheur and Factortame* EU:C:1996:79, para 39; and Case C-445/06 *Danske Slagterier* EU:C:2009:178, para 19.

[18] See the case law in the previous footnote.

Union law also recognises the right to claim damages caused by the conduct of a private party in breach of Union law. This principle was established in the case of *Courage*, in which a party to an anti-competitive agreement sought damages from the other party for breach of Article 101 TFEU. This approach has since been expanded into other fields of policy, and Union legislation has introduced rules through directives and regulations to guarantee individuals' right to bring civil claims against other private parties for breaches of Union law.[19]

2. Rules of Union Law Lacking Direct Effect

Where a rule of Union law lacks direct effect, individuals cannot rely on it to disapply a national provision or to secure compliance in the absence of implementing national rules. Although that limitation may call into question the practical effectiveness of the Union provision, it does not render it irrelevant for the resolution of disputes. As noted above, applicability is a defining characteristic of all rules of Union law. While the absence of direct effect may diminish a rule's capacity to produce immediate legal consequences, it does not deprive it of all legal relevance. In such cases, a Union rule remains relevant for two principal purposes: the duty of conform interpretation; and actions for damages against the Member State for breach of Union law.

2.1. *Interpretation of National Law in Conformity with Union Rules Lacking Direct Effect*

As explained in section I.1.1, the obligation to interpret national law in conformity with Union law applies to all Union rules, but it assumes particular importance where those rules lack direct effect, since it becomes the primary means of ensuring their effectiveness. In the absence of the possibility of setting aside national law or relying directly on the Union provision, a rule of Union law lacking direct effect is therefore characterised predominantly by its interpretative effects.

Special attention must be paid to the case of Union soft law, namely non-binding instruments adopted, whether formally or informally, in order to assist or guide stakeholders in the interpretation and application of Union law. As discussed in chapter eight, Union soft law lacks direct effect by reason of its non-binding nature, but it nonetheless produces specific interpretative effects that differ from the duty of conform interpretation applicable to binding Union law. In particular, Member States are required to 'take into consideration' the provisions of Union soft law, in particular where they cast light on the interpretation of national measures adopted in order to implement them or where they are designed to supplement binding Union provisions.[20] That distinction is significant, since Member States are under a general obligation to interpret national law in conformity with binding Union law, whereas soft law imposes a more limited obligation requiring national authorities to take it into consideration.

[19] Directive 2014/104/EU of the European Parliament and of the Council of 26 November 2014 on certain rules governing actions for damages under national law for infringements of the competition law provisions of the Member States and of the European Union [2014] OJ L349/1. See also, for example, Art 82 of Regulation (EU) 2016/679 of the European Parliament and of the Council of 27 April 2016 on the protection of natural persons with regard to the processing of personal data and on the free movement of such data, and repealing Directive 95/46/EC [2016] OJ L119/1.

[20] Case C-322/88 *Grimaldi* EU:C:1989:646.

2.2. *Member State Liability for Breach of Union Law*

Where national law cannot be interpreted in conformity with a rule of Union law that lacks direct effect, the remedy available to the individual is an action for damages against the Member State. That remedy operates as a subsidiary safety net, applicable both to rules of Union law that lack direct effect and to situations in which conform interpretation proves impossible. In order to mitigate the risk of unenforceability, the case law of the Court of Justice has developed this form of liability, enabling individuals to seek financial compensation before national courts for harm caused by a Member State's breach of Union law, irrespective of whether the breached rule has direct effect. The conditions and procedural requirements governing such actions are examined in chapter twelve of this book.

II. THE DIRECT EFFECT OF RULES OF UNION LAW

Having outlined the foundations and context in which direct effect operates, it is time to examine its origins, requirements and derogations. In brief, the notion of direct effect should not be equated with the *applicability* of Union rules.[21] While Union law is fully applicable as a matter of principle, only rules with direct effect allow individuals to fully exercise their rights granted by Union law, including the ability to invoke the primacy of Union law and request the setting aside of national law that breaches Union law. To accurately determine if a rule of Union law has direct effect, due attention must be paid to the extensive and sometimes complex case law of the Court of Justice developed over the course of time.

1. Meaning

Since the early days of European integration, direct effect has played a key role in shaping the relationship between Union law and national law. As is known, the Court of Justice departed from traditional international law and asserted the authority of Union law, as 'a new legal order', to determine its own relationship with national law. This decision, which materialised in the landmark judgment in *Van Gend en Loos*, included an important caveat: although the relationship between the Union's and national legal systems is defined as monist, the full enforceability of Union law by individuals applies only where its provisions have direct effect. In this way, the Court of Justice sought to balance the autonomy of Union law with the notion that only provisions meeting specific criteria would have direct effect.[22]

The concept of direct effect, as introduced by the Court of Justice in 1963, was not entirely without precedent in public international law. The judgment in *Van Gend en Loos* drew some inspiration from the Advisory Opinion of the Permanent Court of International Justice on the

[21] The distinction between applicability and direct effect has no official recognition in the Treaties or in the case law, but is frequently found in scholarly writings, although not always with the same approach. See, inter alia, J Winter, 'Direct Applicability and Direct Effect: Two Distinct and Different Concepts in Community Law' (1972) 9 *Common Market Law Review* 425; A Bleckmann, 'L'applicabilité directe du droit communautaire' in A Bleckmann and others (eds), *Les recours des individus devant les instances nationales en cas de violation du droit européen* (Larcier, 1978); P Eleftheriadis, 'The Direct Effect of Community Law: Conceptual Issues' (1996) 16 *Yearbook of European Law* 205; and A Rosas and L Armati, *EU Constitutional Law: An Introduction* (Hart, 2018) 63–65.

[22] See the classic work of E Stein, 'Lawyers, Judges and the Making of a Transnational Constitution' (1981) 75 *American Journal of International Law* 1. A historical analysis of the judgment in *Van Gend en Loos* is available in A Vauchez, 'The Transnational Politics of Judicialization: *Van Gend en Loos* and the Making of EU Polity' (2010) 16 *European Law Journal* 1.

jurisdiction of the courts of Danzig in 1928.[23] In this opinion, the Permanent Court noted that while international treaties do not usually create individual rights and obligations, treaties may include rules intended to do so, which national courts can apply. This approach is restrictive, as it requires both the intent of the signatory states and the presence of clear elements in the rule to allow for its judicial invocability and enforcement. As stated in the Advisory Opinion:

> It may be readily admitted that, according to a well-established principle of international law, the *Beamtenabkommen*, being an international agreement, cannot, as such, create direct rights and obligations for private individuals. But it cannot be disputed that the very object of an international agreement, according to the intention of the contracting Parties, may be the adoption by the Parties of some definite rules creating individual rights and obligations and enforceable by the national courts.[24]

Another source of inspiration for the judgment in *Van Gend en Loos* came from the American legal tradition and the notion of self-executing treaties, which asserts that an international treaty has direct effect as long as it does not require further legislative action.[25] This more expansive doctrine allows for invoking international norms without necessarily determining the specific intent of the signatory states, provided that the states' internal separation of powers is respected.

The Court of Justice combined elements from both approaches when defining the direct effect of Union rules. In *Van Gend en Loos*, the Court of Justice examined whether the provisions of the Treaty could be directly enforceable based on the spirit, structure, general scheme, and wording of the Treaty. Union law, being autonomous from national law, creates obligations and rights that form part of the individual's legal heritage. In this regard, the Court relied on the US doctrine's emphasis on textual clarity, while also considering the Danzig Advisory Opinion's approach towards individual rights and obligations enforceable by national courts.

The rationale for Union rules having direct effect is clearly articulated in the judgment in *Van Gend en Loos* and rests on three arguments.

First, the Court of Justice introduced a constitutional argument: the founding Treaties established an organisation based on the transfer of sovereign powers from the Member States. These treaties created 'institutions endowed with sovereign rights', which characterise the Union as a supranational integration project rather than a traditional international organisation. As a result, rules created by its institutions must have unquestionable legal authority, in particular when granting rights or imposing obligations on individuals.

Second, the Court highlighted the role of the individual in the European integration project. The Union represents not only a union of states but also a union of citizens. The Treaty establishing the European Economic Community (TEEC), like the current Treaties, explicitly referred to the 'peoples' of Europe, who participate in the Union through political and institutional channels such as the European Parliament. Recognising this dual source of legitimacy, the Court concluded that both states and citizens are subjects of Union law.

Finally, the Court pointed to the existence of the preliminary ruling procedure, now enshrined in Article 267 TFEU. This procedure allows national courts to refer questions of interpretation or validity of Union law to the Court of Justice for the resolution of judicial disputes in those national courts, thereby confirming the expectation that rules of Union law

[23] PCIJ, Advisory Opinion No 15, Jurisdiction of the Courts of Danzig (1928).

[24] ibid, 17–18.

[25] A Riesenfeld, 'The Doctrine of Self-executing Treaties and *US v Postal*: Win at Any Price?' (1980) 74 *American Journal of International Law* 892; JJ Paust, 'Self-executing Treaties' (1988) 82 *American Journal of International Law* 760, and C Vázquez, 'Treaties as Law of the Land: The Supremacy Clause and the Judicial Enforcement of Treaties' (2008) 122 *Harvard Law Review* 599.

must be actionable before courts. Without direct effect, the preliminary reference procedure would be significantly diminished in its practical utility, since national courts would have no incentive to make use of this cooperation mechanism.

Over time, the doctrine of direct effect has evolved. At first, the case law required that a Union rule confer a 'right'; however, this requirement has gradually faded, and the Court of Justice now only occasionally relies on it. This shift has brought the concept closer to the US doctrine of 'self-executing' rules, while moving away from the more formalistic approach of the Permanent Court of International Justice.[26] In addition, the case law has confirmed that a Union rule lacking direct effect can still be relevant to the resolution of a dispute, as explained in section I.2 of this chapter. It is therefore important to distinguish between the applicability of Union law, which applies to *all* rules of Union law, and direct effect, which is a feature of *certain rules* and produces specific legal consequences. Despite the criticism from some commentators, determining when a rule of Union law has direct effect remains an essential step in shaping the practical interaction between Union and national law.

2. Requirements

The requirements for direct effect were first outlined in the judgment in *Van Gend en Loos*, where the Court of Justice stated that direct effect applies to provisions that are clear and unconditional, 'not qualified by any reservation on the part of the Member States which would make their implementation conditional upon a positive legislative measure enacted under national law'. This statement in *Van Gend en Loos* implies two requirements, which the Court of Justice assesses on a case-by-case basis: clarity and unconditionality.[27]

First, the rule must be 'clear', a term that the Court of Justice sometimes uses interchangeably or cumulatively with 'precision'. Ambiguous rules, whose wording does not plainly define rights or obligations, or which lack specific addressees, do not have direct effect.[28] For example, in *Zaera*,[29] the Court of Justice found that a provision in the former Article 2 TEEC, which stated a generic objective to 'promote throughout the Community a harmonious, balanced and sustainable development of economic activities [and] the raising of the standard of living and quality of life', lacked direct effect, as it was a broad objective rather than a specific legal obligation for Member States or an individual right for a particular addressee.[30] In contrast, in *Sambre & Biesme*, the Court of Justice ruled that a provision of a directive that codifies the

[26] P Pescatore, *L'ordre juridique des Communautés Européennes* (Bruylant, 2006) 202; and PJG Kapteyn, 'Application and Enforcement of Community Law' in PJG Kapteyn and P VerLoren van Themaat, *The Law of the European Union and the European Communities* (Kluwer Law, 2008) 514.

[27] In some cases, the Court of Justice will focus on whether the rule is 'precise' and 'unconditional' in some detail, whilst in other cases it simply asserts the fulfilment of both requirements without further reasoning. See Case C-301/82 *Clin-Midy and others* EU:C:1984:30; Case C-96/84 *Vereniging Slachtpluimvee-Export* EU:C:1985:154; and Case C-103/88 *Costanzo* EU:C:1989:256. In other cases, the terminology used changes, as can be seen in Case C-50/88 *Kühne* EU:C:1989:262, para 26, where the Court of Justice refers to a provision 'complete, legally perfect and consequently capable of producing direct effects in the legal relations between Member States and persons within their jurisdiction'. On other occasions, the Court of Justice has corrected its own understanding of whether or not a rule of Union law complies with the requirements of direct effect. See Case C-384/17 *Link Logistik N&N* EU:C:2018:810, where it was held that the principle of proportionality, as provided in a rule of secondary law, lacked direct effect, only to be shortly afterwards corrected in Case C-205/20 *NE and Bezirkshauptmannschaft Hartberg-Fürstenfeld* EU:C:2022:168, para 29.

[28] Case C-131/79 *Santillo* EU:C:1980:131; Joined Cases C-372/85, C-373/85 and C-374/85 *Traen and others* EU:C:1987:222; and Case C-31/87 *Beentjes* EU:C:1988:422.

[29] Case C-126/86 *Giménez Zaera* EU:C:1987:395.

[30] ibid, para 11.

case law on the requirements for implementing direct awards in public procurement procedures is enough to consider it 'sufficiently precise' to have direct effect.[31]

Second, the rule must be unconditional, meaning it should contain obligations that are not subject to conditions or reservations by the Member States or other authorities.[32] Direct effect is only established when a Union rule can be applied independently in resolving a dispute, without further legislative or regulatory action by Union or national authorities. This is typically the case of negative obligations or prohibitions, as happened in *Van Gend en Loos*, which involved an unconditional prohibition on Member States against introducing new customs duties in intra-community trade.[33] When a rule contains a transitional period that limits its temporal scope, the Court of Justice has held that it will not have direct effect until the end of that period.[34] The same applies when the discretion granted by the Union rule to the institutions or Member States is so wide that it affects the definition of the essential elements of the rule. This was the case in *Salgoil*, where the Court of Justice found that two provisions of the TEEC, former Articles 32 and 33, did not contain sufficient criteria to determine the scope of the prohibition as set out in their wording.[35]

The Court of Justice has rarely found Union rules to be conditional and therefore lacking in direct effect. The case law adopts a pragmatic approach and seeks to maximise the likelihood that a Union rule will be deemed unconditional. For example, a positive obligation, such as the one imposed by the former Article 95(3) TEEC, which required Member States to repeal any provisions in breach of the rules on free movement of goods and taxation, was considered unconditional.[36] Similarly, in *Becker*,[37] the Court of Justice ruled that unconditionality must be assessed in light of the specific provision applicable to the case, rather than the broader legislative context in which the provision is found. The Court of Justice held that:

> [T]he general nature of the directive in question or the discretion which, in other areas, it leaves to the Member States may not be relied upon in order to deny any effect to those provisions which in view of their subject-matter may be relied upon to good purpose before a court even though the directive as a whole has not been implemented.[38]

Similarly, the fact that a rule allows for derogations or justifications, as in the case of free movement provisions, which the Treaty allows to derogate from under specific conditions, does not deprive the rule of its direct effect, since:

> [T]he application of these limitations is, however, subject to judicial control, so that a Member State's right to invoke the limitations does not prevent the provisions of Article 48 . . . from conferring on individuals rights which are enforceable by them and which the national courts must protect.[39]

Although the judgment in *Van Gend en Loos* emphasised that Union rules not only impose obligations on individuals but also 'confer upon them rights which become part of their legal heritage', the criterion of the 'individual right' as a requirement for direct effect has diminished

[31] Joined Cases C-383/21 and C-384/21 *Sambre & Biesme SCRL* EU:C:2022:1022, para 50.

[32] Case C-194/08 *Gassmayr* EU:C:2010:386, para 45, Case C-387/19 *RTS infra and Aannemingsbedrijf Norré-Behaegel* EU:C:2021:13, para 46; and *Sambre & Biesme* (n 31) para 41.

[33] Case C-57/65 *Lütticke* EU:C:1966:34; Case C-28/67 *Molkerei-Zentrale Westfalen* EU:C:1968:17; and Case C-2/74 *Reyners* EU:C:1974:68.

[34] Case C-33/70 *SACE v Ministry of Finance of the Italian Republic* EU:C:1970:118; *Reyners* (n 33); and Case C-50/88 *Kühne* EU:C:1989:262.

[35] Case C-13/68 *Salgoil* EU:C:1968:54.

[36] *Lütticke* (n 33).

[37] Case C-8/81 *Becker* EU:C:1982:7.

[38] ibid, para 30.

[39] Case C-41/74 *Van Duyn* EU:C:1974:133, para 7. See also Case C-51/76 *Nederlandse Ondernemingen* EU:C:1977:12, para 24; Case C-184/83 *Hofmann* EU:C:1984:273, para 27. and Joined Cases C-19/90 and C-20/90 *Karella and Karellas* EU:C:1991:229, para 22.

in importance over time. In the 1970s, the case law frequently referred to the conferral of rights as an additional feature alongside the requirements of clarity and unconditionality,[40] but this approach gradually faded thereafter.[41]

In some Member States, the existence of a subjective right is a prerequisite for access to legal proceedings, as seen in the case of German administrative courts. In others, such as Spain or France, it is enough to demonstrate an 'individual interest' in challenging the legality of an act or provision. This diversity in the legal traditions of the Member States requires the Court of Justice to interpret the term 'right' broadly when determining whether a Union rule has direct effect. Therefore, the reference in *Van Gend en Loos* to 'rights which become part of [the] legal heritage' of the individual must be understood as including a wider scope than that of a 'subjective right',[42] covering any provision that allows an individual to make a claim based on their legal position.[43]

Nor can it be said that a rule lacks direct effect because it is open to interpretation. While it is true that ambiguous wording of a provision can lead to different interpretations, which will eventually need clarification by a court of law, it could be argued that such a rule is not precise and therefore does not have direct effect. However, the Court of Justice rejected this reasoning in the 1970s, in the case of *Van Duyn*, confirming that Union rules with direct effect may sometimes require further interpretation in court.[44] In this regard, Advocate General Jacobs stated as follows:

> Indeed, it would be a strange approach to the administration of justice in general to hold that a legislative provision could not be applied simply because it required interpretation by the courts. What is meant is rather that the content of the provision must be capable of clear and precise interpretation and of direct application by the national courts.[45]

The doctrine of direct effect is not confined to situations in which Union law is invoked against Member States. It also, in certain circumstances, allows relying on Union rules against individuals in disputes *inter privatos*. This leads to an important distinction in the case law on direct effect, which becomes especially significant when analysing the role of direct effect in the case of directives. Reliance on a rule of Union law by an individual against a Member State that is the addressee of the Union rule is known as '*vertical* direct effect'. In contrast, reliance on a rule of Union law in disputes between individuals is referred to as '*horizontal* direct effect'. In *Walrave*, the Court of Justice held that the Treaty provisions on freedom of movement for workers and freedom to provide services were applicable to rules adopted not by a Member State but by a private international sporting association.[46] The horizontal effect of Union rules was further affirmed in *Defrenne II*, where the Court of Justice stated that Article 157(1) TFEU, which introduces the principle of equal pay for women and men, has direct effect in national courts when the discrimination stems directly from legislative provisions or

[40] As early as the 1970s, the change was already in the making, as explained by C Timmermans, 'Directives: Their Effect Within the National Legal System' (1979) 16 *Common Market Law Review* 533. In the case law, see Case C-431/92 *Commission v Germany* EU:C:1995:260, para 26; Case C-96/95 *Commission v Germany* EU:C:1997:165, para 37; Case C-76/97 *Tögel* EU:C:1998:432, para 26; and Case C-162/00 *Pokrzeptowicz-Meyer* EU:C:2002:57, para 30, referring to a 'right to rely' on the rule, but not that the rule 'confers a right'.

[41] S Prechal, *Directives in EC Law*, 2nd edn (Oxford University Press, 2005) 99ff.

[42] ibid, 105–06.

[43] Seen in this light, the existence of a 'right' must be understood as a feature linked to the very nature of direct effect, which is linked to the effectiveness of Union law, and not as a requirement to be determined on a case-by-case basis. It could well be that Union law introduces a requirement in secondary law based on the existence of an individual right. See, inter alia, Case C-72/12 *Gemeinde Altrip and others* EU:C:2013:712; and Case C-137/14 *Commission v Germany* EU:C:2015:683.

[44] *Van Duyn* (n 39) para 14.

[45] Case C-150/99 *Stockholm Lindöpark* EU:C:2001:34, para 44.

[46] Case 36/74 *Walrave and Koch* EU:C:1974:140, paras 17–19.

collective labour agreements, as well as in cases where men and women receive unequal pay for equal work which is carried out in the same establishment or service, whether private or public.[47]

Following these rulings, the case law has confirmed the horizontal direct effect of various provisions in the Treaties, such as the principle of non-discrimination on grounds of age,[48] the free movement of workers,[49] the freedom to provide services,[50] and the freedom of establishment,[51] as well as the prohibition of anti-competitive agreements between undertakings.[52]

Finally, it should be noted that determining the direct effect of a provision of Union law is an exercise that must be carried out on a case-by-case basis. Currently, the case law provides a wealth of precedents, confirming both the existence and absence of the direct effect of various rules of Union law contained in the Treaties, international agreements, and secondary law. Moreover, the case law has introduced some refinements to its general doctrine on direct effect, tailoring it to the specific characteristics of different types of acts, such as directives, decisions, or international agreements. The development of these nuances will be discussed in the following sections of this chapter.

3. Direct Effect of Primary Law

The first provisions confirmed by the Court of Justice to have direct effect were rules in the Treaties. In the judgment in *Van Gend en Loos*, the direct effect of Article 12 TEEC (now Article 30 TFEU) was confirmed; in *Lütticke II*, the same result applied to Article 95 TEEC (now Article 110 TFEU), whilst the ruling in *Van Duyn* focused on Article 48 TEEC (now Article 45 TFEU), among others. In 2001, Schermers and Waelbroeck identified as many as 41 provisions of the TEEC (now TFEU) that the Court of Justice had confirmed as having direct effect.[53] In addition, they also noted fourteen provisions of the TEEC (now TFEU) that the Court found not to have direct effect.[54]

[47] Case C-43/75 *Defrenne II* EU:C:1976:56, para 40.

[48] Case C-144/04 *Mangold* EU:C:2005:709; and Case C-555/07 *Kücükdeveci* EU:C:2010:21.

[49] Case C-281/98 *Angonese* EU:C:2000:296, paras 32–36.

[50] Case C-13/76 *Donà* EU:C:1976:115, para 17; and Case C-415/93 *Bosman* EU:C:1995:463, paras 82–83.

[51] Case C-341/05 *Laval un Partneri* EU:C:2007:809, paras 98–99; and Case C-438/05 *International Transport Workers' Federation and The Finnish Seamen's Union, known as 'Viking Line'* EU:C:2007:772, paras 33–37.

[52] Case C-453/99 *Courage and Crehan* EU:C:2001:465.

[53] The case law has confirmed the direct effect of the following Treaty provisions: Art 18 TFEU (Case C-22/80 *Boussac Saint-Frères* EU:C:1980:251); Art 28 TFEU (Joined Cases C-2/69 and C-3/69 *Social Fonds voor de Diamantarbeiders* EU:C:1969:30); Art 30 TFEU (*Van Gend en Loos* (n 6)); Art 34 TFEU (Case C-74/76 *Iannelli & Volpi* EU:C:1977:51); Art 35 TFEU (Case C-83/78 *Redmond* EU:C:1978:214); Art 36 TFEU (Case C-78/70 *Deutsche Grammophon* EU:C:1971:59); Art 37 TFEU (Case C-59/75 *Manghera and others* EU:C:1976:14); Art 45 TFEU (*Van Duyn* (n 39)); Arts 45–48 TFEU (Case C-118/75 *Watson and Belmann* EU:C:1976:106, referring, in general, not to a specific rule but to Chs 1–2 of Title III TFEU); Art 56 TFEU (Case C-33/74 *van Binsbergen* EU:C:1974:131); Art 101 TFEU (Case C-127/73 *RT and Société belge des auteurs, compositeurs et éditeurs* EU:C:1974:25); Art 102 TFEU (Case C-155/73 *Sacchi* EU:C:1974:40); Art 106(1) TFEU (*Redmond*, cited above in this footnote); Art 108(3) TFEU (Case 120/73 *Lorenz* EU:C:1973:117); Art 110.2 TFEU (*Lütticke* (n 33)); and Art 157 TFEU (*Defrenne II* (n 47)). The Court of Justice also favoured the direct effect of Arts 11, 13(2), 16, 31, 32(1), 43 and 53 TEEC, which have now been repealed. Art 20 (Case C-135/08 *Rottmann* EU:C:2010:104) and Art 21 TFEU (Case C-413/99 *Baumbast and R* EU:C:2002:493) must be added to the list in Schermers and Waelbroeck.

[54] Article 1 TEU (Case T-191/99 *Petrie and others v Commission* EU:T:2001:284); Art 3 TEU (*Giménez Zaera* (n 29)); Art 4(3) TEU (Case C-9/73 *Carl Schlüter* EU:C:1973:110); Art 106(2) TFEU (Case C-10/71 *Ministère public luxembourgeois v Madeleine Muller, widow of JP Hein and others* EU:C:1971:85); Art 107 TFEU (Case C-77/72 *Carmine Capolongo* EU:C:1973:65); Art 117 TFEU; Art 130 TFEU (*Carl Schlüter*, cited above in this footnote); Art 51 TFEU (Joined Cases C-72/91 and C-73/91 *Sloman Neptun Schiffahrts AG v Bodo Ziesemer* EU:C:1993:97). Furthermore, Arts 32(2), 33, 67, 71, 91(1) and 97(1) TEEC, now repealed, were declared to be lacking direct effect.

Provisions of the Charter of Fundamental Rights of the European Union ('the Charter') can have direct effect if their wording is sufficiently clear, precise, and unconditional, thereby entitling individuals to invoke them before national courts.[55] However, Articles 51–52 of the Charter introduce a distinction by differentiating between two types of provisions: those containing 'rights' and those set forth as 'principles'. According to the Court of Justice's case law, provisions containing 'principles' within the meaning of Article 52(5) of the Charter are judicially cognisable only in the interpretation of implementing acts and in the ruling on their legality; they cannot by themselves confer on individuals a subjective right which they may invoke as such.[56] Consequently, it can be deduced that fundamental rights expressed as 'principles' in the Charter do not have direct effect.

General principles of Union law can have direct effect. As explained in chapter six, general principles bind Member States whenever they act within the scope of application of Union law.[57] This also includes horizontal direct effect, as may be inferred from principles that, by their very nature, can be invoked against individuals, such as the principle of non-discrimination on the grounds of sex or age.[58]

4. Direct Effect of International Agreements

International agreements to which the Union is a party produce legal effects, as Article 216(2) TFEU provides that such agreements are 'binding upon the institutions of the Union and on its Member States.' However, as with other provisions of Union law, it is essential to determine whether the provisions of an international agreement have direct effect before its legal effects can be fully realised. The Court of Justice applies a notion of direct effect to international agreements concluded by the Union that shares similarities with the criteria outlined above, while incorporating additional requirements. While these approaches differ only in degree and do not change the overall understanding of the notion of direct effect, some commentators have advised the Court of Justice to avoid using the term 'direct effect' when addressing the invocability of international agreements in order to avoid confusion with the direct effect of rules of Union primary and secondary law.[59]

According to settled case law, a provision of an international agreement concluded by the Union must be regarded as having direct effect

> when, regard being had to its wording and the purpose and the nature of the agreement itself, the provision contains a clear and precise obligation which is not subject, in its implementation or effects, to the adoption of any subsequent measure.[60]

This standard closely resembles the requirements introduced in *Van Gend en Loos*, with the addition of a criterion related to the 'purpose and nature of the agreement'.[61] Based on this approach, the Court of Justice carefully examines not only the specific wording of the provision

[55] Joined Cases C-92/09 and C-93/09 *Volker und Markus Schecke* EU:C:2010:662, paras 58 and 60; and Case C-279/09 *DEB* EU:C:2010:811, para 40.

[56] Case C-176/12 *Association de Médiation Sociale* EU:C:2014:2; and Case C-196/23 *Plamaro* EU:C:2024:596.

[57] Case C-205/20 *NE and Bezirkshauptmannschaft Hartberg-Fürstenfeld* EU:C:2022:168, para 29.

[58] *Mangold* (n 48) para 75; *Kücükdeveci* (n 48) para 21; and Case C-441/14 *Dansk Industri (DI)* EU:C:2016:278.

[59] See, inter alia, Joined Cases C-120/06 P and C-121/06 P *FIAMM* EU:C:2008:98, Opinion of AG Poiares Maduro, para 31.

[60] Case C-12/86 *Demirel* EU:C:1987:400, para 14.

[61] At times, the case law refers not to the nature, but to 'the spirit' or 'the general scheme' (*'l'économie'* in French) of the Treaties, albeit in synonymous terms. See, inter alia, Joined Cases C-21/72 to C-24/72 *International Fruit Company and others* EU:C:1972:115, para 20; and Case C-87/75 *Conceria Bresciani* EU:C:1976:18, para 16.

in question but also the entire international agreement, considering factors such as the reciprocity of obligations, the institutional framework of the agreement, and the inclusion in the text of derogation clauses. Although this analysis is stricter than the conventional criterion of direct effect, the Court of Justice has recognised the direct effect of multiple provisions in association agreements,[62] trade agreements[63] and cooperation agreements,[64] including in cases in which the signatory third state denies the direct effect of the agreement in its domestic legal system,[65] or when the agreement includes flexible dispute resolution mechanisms based on consultations and negotiation rather than judicial adjudication.[66] However, when an international agreement explicitly defines the effects of its provisions, it is not necessary to evaluate their direct effect; the interpreter must adhere to the terms of the agreement itself.[67]

This approach also applies to acts adopted by bodies or institutions created by an international agreement. The Court of Justice confirmed this approach in the 1980s and reiterated it in Opinion 1/91, noting that international agreements bind the institutions of the Union and its Member States, and that the acts adopted by bodies created by such agreement 'form an integral part, as from their entry into force, of the Union legal system'.[68] To determine whether such acts have direct effect, the Court of Justice examines the wording, subject matter, the nature of the underlying agreement, as well as their clarity and unconditionality. The same principle applies to decisions rendered by judicial bodies established under these agreements, with the Court of Justice noting that the decisions of such courts 'will be binding on the [Union] institutions, including the Court of Justice'.[69]

The case law has developed a particularly restrictive approach to the direct effect of provisions originating from the World Trade Organization (WTO) agreements and acts adopted within its institutional environment. This stance is rooted in the judgment delivered in 1972 in *International Fruit Company*, in which the Court of Justice addressed the direct effect of the General Agreement on Tariffs and Trade (GATT), the WTO's predecessor. The Court determined that the flexibility of GATT provisions, combined with the principle of negotiations based on reciprocity and mutual benefit, precluded the direct effect of GATT rules. This line of case law has been reaffirmed over time, despite scholarly criticism[70] and the sceptical views of several Advocates General.[71]

The Court of Justice's strict stance on WTO rules also applies to the review of the validity of Union secondary legislation, an area where the case law has consistently rejected the

[62] See, inter alia, *Conceria Bresciani* (n 61) paras 16–25 (Art 2.1 of the Yaoundé Convention); Case C-17/81 *Pabst & Richard* EU:C:1982:129, paras 25–27; Case C-432/92 *Anastasiou and others* EU:C:1994:277, paras 23–27 (Cyprus Association); Case C-469/93 *Chiquita Italia* EU:C:1995:435, paras 30–36 (Fourth ACP Convention); Case C-438/00 *Deutscher Handballbund* EU:C:2003:255, paras 24–30 (Association Poland, Bulgaria, Czech Republic and Slovakia).

[63] Case C-104/81 *Kupferberg* EU:C:1982:362, para 26 (Art 21 of the EEC–Portugal Free Trade Agreement).

[64] Case C-18/90 *Kziber* EU:C:1991:36, paras 15–23 (Art 41(1) Morocco Agreement); Case C-103/94 *Krid* EU:C:1995:97, paras 21–24 (Art 39(1) Algeria Agreement); and Case C-37/98 *Savas* EU:C:2000:224, paras 46–55 (Art 41(1) Additional Protocol to the Agreement with Turkey).

[65] *Kupferberg* (n 63) para 18.

[66] ibid, paras 20–21.

[67] ibid, para 17.

[68] Case C-30/88 *Greece v Commission* EU:C:1989:422, para 13; Case C-192/89 *Sevince* EU:C:1990:205, para 9; Opinion 1/91 EU:C:1991:490, para 3; Case C-260/20 *Commission v Hansol Paper* EU:C:2022:370, para 82; and Case C-891/19 *Commission v Hubei Xinyegang Special Tube Co Ltd* EU:C:2022:38, para 31.

[69] Opinion 1/91 (n 68) para 39.

[70] P Eeckhout, 'The Domestic Legal Status of the WTO Agreement: Interconnecting Legal Systems' (1997) *Common Market Law Review* 11; PJ Kuijper and M Bronckers, 'WTO Law in the European Court of Justice' (2005) *Common Market Law Review* 1313; S Peers, 'Fundamental Right or Political Whim? WTO Law and the European Court of Justice' in G de Búrca and J Scott (eds), *The EU and WTO* (Oxford University Press, 2001) 111.

[71] See Case C-149/96 *Portugal v Council* EU:C:1999:92, Opinion of AG Saggio; and Case C-53/96 *Hermès* EU:C:1997:539, Opinion of AG Tesauro, paras 28–37.

direct effect of WTO agreements. The Court of Justice has taken a different view only in the following cases: when the Union intends to comply with a specific WTO obligation; or when a Union act explicitly refers to a specific provision in a WTO agreement.[72] An additional way of providing further flexibility to ensure the effectiveness of WTO rules can be seen in recent case law that extends the duty of conform interpretation of Union secondary law in light of the international agreements concluded by the Union. In the case of *KaiKai*, the Court of Justice ruled that the TRIPs Agreement, as it is binding on the EU, must take precedence over Union secondary legislation and, consequently, it 'must be interpreted, as far as is possible, in accordance with the provisions of that agreement'.[73]

The enforcement of WTO rules has gained further momentum following the judgment in *Commission v Hungary* (higher education), in which the Court of Justice asserted its jurisdiction to adjudicate in actions against Member States for breach of WTO rules.[74] The existence of a dispute resolution mechanism at the WTO level does not exempt the Union – and particularly the Court of Justice – from reviewing Member States' actions in accordance with WTO law. In such a case, because of the procedural strictures of the infringement procedure, only the Commission and the Member States can initiate proceedings. In the context of an infringement action, the Court of Justice appears less inclined to focus on the direct effect of the provisions in a WTO agreement, as it conducts an objective rule-based review in which considerations of precision, unconditionality, or the nature of the agreement appear to play a secondary role.[75]

5. Direct Effect of Secondary Law

5.1. *Regulations*

According to Article 288, second paragraph, TFEU, a regulation 'shall be binding in its entirety and directly applicable in all Member States'. This provision confirms that regulations produce their effects through a specific means, which is an explicit provision of the Treaty rather than an individualised, case-by-case analysis based on the wording of each provision. The distinctive nature of regulations has led some authors to suggest that the effects produced by these acts differ from those of other Union acts.[76] Article 288, second paragraph, TFEU has even been cited to call into question the doctrine of direct effect, arguing that the Treaties only confer this feature on regulations, and, by *a contrario* interpretation, deny it to directives and decisions.

It is now clear that Article 288, second paragraph, TFEU does not call into question or derogate from the general notion of direct effect as developed in the case law. By declaring regulations to be 'directly applicable', the Treaty simply emphasises the effects of a particular type of act that holds a specific role in Union law, namely a general and abstract act that resembles the role of a 'law' or a parliamentary statute in the practice of the Member States.[77]

[72] Case C-93/02 P *Biret International v Council* EU:C:2003:517, para 53; and Case C-377/02 *Van Parys*, EU:C:2005:121, para 40.

[73] Case C-382/21 P *EUIPO v. The KaiKai Company Jaeger Wichmann* EU:C:2024:172, para 70. Outside the remit of WTO law, but following the same line of reasoning, see Case C-188/23 *Conti 11* EU:C:2025:26, para 44.

[74] Case C-66/18 *Commission v Hungary* EU:C:2020:792, paras 110–14.

[75] ibid, paras 128–34.

[76] See G Bebr, 'Directly Applicable Provisions of Community Law: The Development of a Community Concept' (1970) 19 *International and Comparative Law Quarterly* 257; and JA Winter, 'Direct Applicability and Direct Effect: Two Distinct and Different Concepts in Community Law' (1972) 9 *Common Market Law Review* 425.

[77] This was also the view of Advocate General Geelhoed in Case C-253/00 *Munoz and Superior Frutícola* EU:C:2002:698, Opinion of AG Geelhoed, pt 47: 'It must be examined on a case-by-case basis whether a provision of a regulation confers rights on individuals. In that connection it is immaterial whether the person concerned is relying

The practical implications of the Treaty's recognition of the direct effect of regulations are the following.

First, by declaring regulations to be 'directly applicable', the Treaty grants them a *presumption* of direct effect. This does not mean that the *criteria* of precision, clarity, and unconditionality, which characterise direct effect, can be ignored, and the Court of Justice has long held this to be the case. For example, in the judgment in *Schlüter*, delivered in 1973, the Court of Justice found that a provision in a customs regulation had direct effect, not on the basis of Article 288, second paragraph, TFEU, but on the general criteria of clarity, precision, and unconditionality set out in *Van Gend en Loos*.[78] Therefore, the recognition in the TFEU of the direct applicability of regulations generally presupposes that regulations include sufficiently clear, precise, and unconditional rules. However, nothing prevents the Union legislature or the executive from adopting regulations that are conditional upon the enactment of further implementing measures or contain provisions that are insufficiently precise to have direct effect. Where such limitations exist, they must be explicitly and clearly derived from the wording and objectives of the regulation.

Second, the applicability of regulations imposes specific constraints on Member States,[79] which must refrain from adopting detailed rules for the implementation of the regulation unless authorised by the regulation or where such measures are indispensable to ensure its effectiveness.[80] Member States are also precluded from reproducing the content of a regulation, in whole or in part, in a national legal act, as this practice can undermine the principle of legal certainty and jeopardise the uniform application of the regulation.[81] Similarly, Member States may not invoke national provisions or practices to justify their failure to comply with obligations set out in a regulation,[82] nor can they make the effects of the regulation conditional upon the entry into force of a national rule.[83]

5.2. *Decisions*

Decisions play various roles and take different forms, a feature that has an impact on how they produce legal effects. As explained in chapter eight, there are different types of decisions, displaying at times different features that contrast with the standard definition in Article 288, fourth paragraph TFEU. Furthermore, some decisions have no specified addressees, while others target multiple addressees in a single decision. To determine whether a decision has direct effect, it is essential to consider the standpoint of the parties invoking the direct effect of the decision.

on that right in proceedings against the authorities or against another person. Regard must always be had to whether the provision by its content and purport affords protection to the interests which he is invoking in law. There must be a link between the interest on which the person concerned is relying and the protection afforded by a provision of a regulation. In that connection I take the view that the requirements to be satisfied substantively by that link do not need to be too stringent. First, a provision of a regulation often protects several interests. That is true, for example, of Art 3(1) of Regulation No 2200/96 which extends protection to both fair trading and the consumer. Secondly, too strict a test would be detrimental to the direct effect of regulations.'

[78] Case C-9/73 *Carl Schlüter v Hauptzollamt Lörrach* EU:C:1973:110, para 32. See also Case C-43/71 *Politi* EU:C:1971:122, para 9; Case C-84/71 *Marimex* EU:C:1972:14, para 5; Case C-93/71 *Leonesio* EU:C:1972:39, para 5; and Case C-34/73 *Variola* EU:C:1973:101, para 8.

[79] See, in more detail, ch 8.

[80] *Variola* (n 78).

[81] ibid.

[82] Case C-30/72 *Commission v Italy* EU:C:1973:16.

[83] *Variola* (n 78) para 10; Case C-94/77 *Zerbone* EU:C:1978:17, para 23; Case C-31/78 *Bussone* EU:C:1978:217, para 30, as well as the case law cited in ch 5.

For the *addressee(s)* of a decision, if the decision is 'binding in its entirety' and is explicitly addressed to them, it has direct effect unless it clearly and unconditionally provides otherwise.

The invocability of a decision by those who *are not its addressees* is a different matter. In this case, it can be argued that the decision lacks direct effect, since, as it will be addressed to an individualised addressee or addressees, only they are the true beneficiaries of the rights contained therein. However, the case law of the Court of Justice has taken a different approach aimed at maximising the effectiveness of decisions. In 1970, in the case of *Grad*,[84] the Court of Justice stated as follows:

> It would be incompatible with the binding effect attributed to decisions by Article [288 TFEU] to exclude in principle the possibility that persons affected may invoke the obligation imposed by a decision. Particularly in cases where, for example, the [Union] authorities by means of a decision have imposed an obligation on a Member State or all the Member States to act in a certain way, the effectiveness (*'l'effet utile'*) of such a measure would be weakened if the nationals of that state could not invoke it in the courts and the national courts could not take it into consideration as part of [Union] law. Although the effects of a decision may not be identical with those of a provision contained in a regulation, this difference does not exclude the possibility that the end result, namely the right of the individual to invoke the measure before the courts, may be the same as that of a directly applicable provision of a regulation.[85]

It should be noted that *Grad* concerned the direct effect of a decision addressed to all Member States. In such a case, the Court of Justice stated that individuals could rely on the decision against any Member State to ensure compliance, provided it could be established that the decision would affect the legal position of the party invoking it.[86] As a result, *Grad* enshrines the *vertical* direct effect of decisions but leaves unresolved whether this solution also applies to horizontal relations, ie, whether a private individual can invoke a decision against another private individual.

On this point, a further distinction should be made depending on the addressees of the decision invoked. If the addressee is a private individual, there is nothing to prevent another private individual from invoking the decision against the addressee, provided that the provisions of the decision will affect the applicant's legal position, as inferred from clear, precise, and unconditional provisions in the decision. Furthermore, if the addressee of the decision is a Member State, the decision cannot be invoked by a private individual against another private party, but only against the Member State to which the decision is addressed.[87] Insofar as the addressee is a Member State and not a private individual, the rights deriving from the decision cannot be invoked against a private individual on whom the rule has not imposed an obligation. The obligation falls on the Member State, and it is for the Member State to respond in court when the decision is invoked against it by a private individual. As will be explained below, this outcome is consistent with the doctrine of direct effect applicable to directives. However, the latest trends in case law show an increasing inclination to extend the direct effect of directives to horizontal relations, a development that raises the question as to whether such an approach should also extend to decisions.

[84] Case C-9/70 *Franz Grad* EU:C:1970:78.

[85] ibid, para 5.

[86] ibid, para 9; Case C-104/81 *Kupferberg* EU:C:1982:362, paras 22–23; and Case C-280/93 *Germany v Council* EU:C:1994:367, para 110.

[87] Case C-80/06 *Carp* EU:C:2007:327, para 21: 'In accordance with Article [288 TFEU], Decision 1999/93 is binding only upon the Member States, which, under Article 4 of that decision, are the sole addressees. Accordingly, the considerations underpinning the case law referred to in the preceding paragraph with regard to directives apply *mutatis mutandis* to the question whether Decision 1999/93 may be relied upon as against an individual'. See also, to the same effect, Case C-584/18 *DZ and Blue Air* EU:C:2020:324, para 73.

Finally, reference must be made to the specific regime of decisions within the framework of the Common Foreign and Security Policy (CFSP). As explained in chapter eight, the CFSP has been assigned its own system of acts, as well as special provisions limiting the jurisdiction of Union courts. So far, the Court of Justice has not ruled on the direct effect of CFSP decisions, but it has assessed their reviewability before Union courts. In light of the case law delivered thus far, there are arguments in support of the direct effect of CFSP decisions. Some commentators highlight the importance of Article 275, second paragraph, TFEU, the wording of which recognises, albeit exceptionally, the competence of the Court of Justice to review the legality of CFSP decisions 'providing for restrictive measures against natural or legal persons'. Since these decisions are subject to judicial review in Union courts, it can be argued that individuals must be in a position to invoke the said measures if they are clear, precise, and unconditional.[88] This matter was addressed in the case of *Neves 77 Solutions*,[89] in which the Court of Justice stated that CFSP decisions introducing restrictive measures of a general scope do not have direct effect, but can nevertheless have interpretative effects, including the power of national courts to refer preliminary references of interpretation to the Court of Justice on matters pertaining to the interpretation of a CFSP decision. *A contrario*, it can be deduced that CFSP decisions adopting restrictive measures of an individual scope and targeting individualised addressees are subject to judicial review, and may produce direct effect and have primacy over national law.[90]

Following the ruling in *KS and KD*, the Court of Justice has confirmed its jurisdiction to review CFSP acts that do not involve 'political or strategic choices' reflecting core policy decisions. If such acts include provisions that are sufficiently clear, precise and unconditional, it can be argued that such provisions produce direct effect.[91]

5.3. *Directives*

The case of directives raises the thorniest questions regarding the doctrine of direct effect. As described in chapter eight, a directive is an act characterised by specific features, notably its binding nature only regarding the results to be achieved (not the means), the sole profile of its addressees (the Member States), and the introduction of deadlines for its transposition. As a result, Member States can have discretion and broad margins of appreciation when transposing a directive into national law. The fact that a directive is addressed solely to Member States means that individuals are not the direct addressees of the rights and obligations set out in the directive. The existence of a transposition period confirms the conditional, deferred, and interposed nature of the directive, as its provisions only become fully effective once they are incorporated into rules of national law.

The specific features of a directive explain why the Court of Justice has repeatedly stated, as a matter of principle, that directives do not have direct effect. This is only a principled starting point, subject to numerous qualifications and sub-exceptions that will now be outlined in the following sections. As the reader will observe, the qualifications to the general rule are so numerous that it could be argued that directives *have* direct effect, except in some specific cases. While this characterisation is deliberately provocative, it is a telling reflection of the current state of the case law regarding the direct effect of directives.

[88] Case C-455/14 P *H v Council and Commission* EU:C:2016:569, paras 40–59; and Case C-72/15 *Rosneft* EU:C:2017:236, paras 50–56.

[89] Case C-351/22 *Neves 77 Solutions* EU:C:2024:723.

[90] ibid., paras 37 and 44.

[91] Joined Cases C-29/22 P and C-44/22 P *KS and KD v Council and others* EU:C:2023:901, paras 116–20.

5.3.1. General Rule: Directives have no Direct Effect

From the moment the doctrine of direct effect emerged in the practice of Union law, it became apparent that directives could not easily satisfy the requirements of precision, clarity, and unconditionality laid down in the case law of the Court of Justice. Directives serve as harmonising tools, comprising rules that must necessarily be transposed into national law by Member States through means of national law, making them conditional upon the introduction of such national measures. Additionally, directives do not directly confer rights or obligations on individuals, since the only addressees of a directive are the Member States. This result seemed so evident that the Court of Justice did not have the opportunity to express its view on the matter until more than a decade had elapsed since the ruling in *Van Gend en Loos*.

5.3.2. Exception to the General Rule: Member States' Non-compliance with a Directive

By the end of the 1970s, the European Communities had achieved a high degree of development, marked by a robust regulatory agenda and the consolidation of its institutions. As a result of its success, the rules of Community law, as it was then, were frequently applied in the courts of the Member States, thereby confirming the importance of direct effect as a valuable tool for ensuring the enforcement of Community law through national courts.

This gradual 'normalisation' of European integration through law had two consequences that ultimately influenced the doctrine of direct effect as applied to directives.[92] First, directives proposed by the Commission and then adopted by the Council began to lose their initial vagueness and increasingly resembled regulations. The rules contained in directives became more detailed and, as a result, their content was no longer generic and became clearer and more precise. Second, Member States showed growing signs of reluctance to transpose certain directives. In some cases, this resistance was reflected in the absence of national transposition measures, but in others, it took a more problematic turn: defective transpositions increased at an alarming rate. By transposing directives through national provisions that did not always comply with the directive, Member States could argue that they had formally transposed in time, even though the actual content of the national rules distorted the aims pursued by the directive.

At a time when directives appeared to be victims of their own success, the Court of Justice handed down in 1974 its judgment in *Van Duyn*.[93] The case involved a Dutch national, employed as a secretary by the Church of Scientology in the United Kingdom, who was denied entry to the United Kingdom due, in the view of the British authorities, to the allegedly suspicious activities of her employer. Although Directive 64/221, concerning special measures on the residence of foreign nationals, allowed Member States to restrict the free movement of nationals of other Member States of the Union, it did so on the condition that any such decision took account of the individual circumstances of the person concerned, in particular the person's prior conduct. In Ms Van Duyn's case, the United Kingdom authorities failed to assess her prior individual conduct, relying instead on the nature of her employer's activities to refuse her entry. The High Court referred a question to the Court of Justice for a preliminary ruling on the invocability of that directive, which had clearly been infringed by the national authorities.

In its response to the High Court, the Court of Justice stated for the first time that a directive can have direct effect. In somewhat cryptic reasoning, the Court of Justice observed as follows:

[92] P Craig, 'The Legal Effect of Directives: Policy, Rules and Exceptions' (2009) 34 *European Law Review* 349.
[93] *Van Duyn* (n 39).

> In particular, where the [Union] authorities have, by directives, imposed on Member States the obligation to pursue a particular course of conduct, the useful effect of such an act would be weakened if individuals were prevented from relying on it before their national courts and if the latter were prevented from taking it into consideration as an element of [Union] law. Article [267 TFEU], which empowers national courts to refer to the Court questions concerning the validity and interpretation of all acts of the [Union] institutions, without distinction, implies furthermore that these acts may be invoked by individuals in the national courts.[94]

Accordingly, the Court of Justice concluded that directives 'are capable of having direct effect on the relations between Member States and individuals'.[95] However, this conclusion was limited to situations where a Member State fails to fulfil its obligation to transpose the directive. It is only when such a breach is established that the individual can invoke the directive before national courts, provided, of course, that the relevant provision of the directive is sufficiently clear, precise and unconditional. For this reason, the direct effect of directives has been described as a coercive tool, aimed at ensuring that a Member State in breach of its obligations under the directive is compelled to comply by allowing individuals to obtain through national courts what their Member State has failed to grant them through legislation.

The Court of Justice justifies this coercive variant of direct effect on three grounds. First, the *effet utile* of Union law: if the Member States were free to transpose a directive under any conditions that they saw fit, subject only to judicial review through an infringement procedure initiated by the Commission before the Court of Justice, the directive's effectiveness would be seriously undermined. Allowing individuals to directly invoke directives in national courts thus enhances the effectiveness of Union law. Second, the fact that the preliminary ruling procedure enables a national court to refer a question to the Court of Justice on the interpretation of any act of Union law, including directives, corroborates their invocability in national courts. The third argument relies on the doctrine of estoppel and was further developed in *Ratti*:[96] Member States cannot rely on their own failure to transpose to gain an advantage, a principle reflecting the Latin maxim *nemo auditur turpitudinem allegans propriam*, which states that no one should profit from their own misconduct. When it comes to directives, Union law prevents Member States from relying on their unlawful conduct to deny individuals the rights provided by a directive.[97]

Due to its coercive objective to deter Member State misconduct, the direct effect of directives can only arise in situations in which Member States have failed to comply with their obligations under Union law. This means that directives cannot have direct effect during their transposition period, as the obligation to transpose has not yet been breached at that time. Once the deadline has expired, the directive will be capable of producing direct effect vis-a-vis the Member State if it has not transposed the directive, or if the transposition is not in conformity with the directive. The latter scenario is often the most problematic in practice, as it requires an assessment of the provisions of national law and their conformity with the directive. This analysis is frequently preceded by the referral of a question for a preliminary ruling to the Court of Justice, providing the national court with the necessary guidance before confirming the breach and granting direct effect to the relevant provision of the directive.

[94] ibid, para 12.

[95] ibid.

[96] Case C-148/78 *Ratti* EU:C:1979:110.

[97] The appearance of this third ground is connected to the reactions stemming from some national jurisdictions following the judgment in *Van Duyn*. Both the French *Conseil d'État* and the German *Bundesfinanzhof* were openly hostile to the idea of directives having direct effect, nudging the Court of Justice into refining its arguments. On the interaction between the case law of the Court of Justice and the reactions from national courts, see P Pescatore, 'The Doctrine of Direct Effect: An Infant Disease of Community Law' (1983) 8 *European Law Review* 170.

Furthermore, a directive will only have direct effect if, in addition, the relevant provision is also sufficiently clear, precise, and unconditional. It was previously argued that directives have become detailed texts, sometimes so detailed that they meet the first requirement of direct effect: clarity and precision. The second requirement, unconditionality, is more problematic, as the directive is, by its very nature, followed by national transposition measures. The Court of Justice has taken a pragmatic approach to interpreting this requirement, focusing not so much on the existence of discretion at the time of transposition, but rather on the *degree* of discretion that the directive grants to Member States on a case-by-case basis. As a result, when a provision of a directive leaves no margin of discretion to the Member State, that provision ceases to be conditional and can be invoked by individuals in national courts.[98] The case law has also indicated that the requirement of unconditionality must be assessed in relation to the relevant provision being invoked, rather than in relation to the directive as a whole.[99]

5.3.3. Limits to the Direct Effect of Directives

Although the direct effect of directives is aimed at ensuring their effectiveness, there are several constraints that limit its scope. The main practical consequence of these limits is that an individual cannot rely on a directive directly in certain situations, even if a Member State has breached Union law by not transposing the directive correctly. For this reason, the case law tends to interpret these limitations strictly.

5.3.3.1. No Horizontal Direct Effect

The first limitation on the direct effect of directives already appeared in the judgment in *Van Duyn*, when the Court of Justice stated that directives 'are capable of having direct effect on the relations between Member States and individuals'.[100] In other words, directives only produce effects in disputes between a private individual and the Member State that has failed to comply with the directive, a 'vertical situation' involving an individual against a public authority of a Member State. This conclusion can be inferred from the judgment in *Van Duyn*, but it was explicitly confirmed in 1986 in the case of *Marshall*,[101] when the Court of Justice stated that 'the binding nature of a directive, which constitutes the basis for the possibility of relying on the directive before a national court, exists only in relation to 'each Member State to which it is addressed'.[102] The Court of Justice therefore concludes that 'a directive may not of itself impose obligations on an individual and that a provision of a directive may not be relied upon as such against such a person'.[103]

The arguments supporting the denial of horizontal direct effect of directives can be summarised as follows. First, Article 288, third paragraph TFEU clearly states that directives are only addressed to Member States and not to individuals. Because of the coercive aims of the direct

[98] Case C-441/99 *Gharehveran* EU:C:2001:551, paras 39–40: 'It must, however, be pointed out in this regard that, unlike the situations described in paragraphs 37 and 38 above, in which the [Member State] has still not used the discretion it enjoys or has made only partial use of that discretion, the main proceedings concern a situation in which the Member State concerned has designated itself the person liable to meet claims of pay guaranteed under the Directive. . . . In such circumstances, it must be accepted that the Member State has made full use of the discretion which it enjoys under Articles 3(1) and 5 of the Directive in the implementation of the Directive.'

[99] *Gharehveran* (n 98); Case C-346/97 *Braathens* EU:C:1999:291; and Joined Cases C-465/00, C-138/01 and C-139/01 *Österreichischer Rundfunk and others* EU:C:2003:294.

[100] *Van Duyn (n 39) para 12.*

[101] Case C-152/84 *Marshall* EU:C:1986:84.

[102] ibid, para 48.

[103] See, by way of example, Case C-232/20 *NP and Daimler AG* EU:C:2022:196, para 81; and Case C-261/20 *Thelen Technopark Berlin GmbH* EU:C:2022:33, para 32.

effect of directives, which serves as a mechanism to address a Member State's failure to comply with a directive, extending the doctrine to horizontal situations would be inconsistent with the rationale of the case law.[104] Second, extending direct effect to relations between private individuals would risk blurring the distinction between regulations and directives, since the Treaty confers on the former the power to directly create rights and obligations for individuals, a quality that directives do not possess.[105] Third, considerations of legal certainty must also be taken into account: a directive is intended to play a harmonising role, followed by transposition into national law. This outcome would be undermined if directives assumed a different role and acted as directly binding rules invokable against anyone, even those who are not formally bound by their provisions.

The case law has been consistent in maintaining the lack of horizontal direct effect of directives since *Van Duyn*,[106] despite the criticisms levelled at the reasoning by both academic commentators and several Advocates General.[107] The argument based on the addressee of a directive, which is a textual argument rooted in the wording of Article 288, third paragraph TFEU, is difficult to reconcile with other rulings where the Court of Justice has recognised the horizontal direct effect of a Union rule, even when it is clearly addressed to the Member States only. The most prominent example is Article 157 TFEU, which states that 'each Member State shall ensure that the principle of equal pay for male and female workers for equal work or work of equal value is applied'. In the judgment in *Defrenne II*, the Court of Justice ruled that, although this provision is explicitly addressed to the Member States, it has direct effect in relations between private individuals. This outcome sits uncomfortably with the case law on directives as developed in the judgments in *Van Duyn* and *Marshall.*

The argument based on the blurring of the distinction between regulations and directives is also not entirely conclusive, as the distinction depends not so much on the addressees but on the margin of discretion that the directive grants to the Member States compared to the directly applicable provisions of a regulation. Extending the direct effect of directives to disputes between private individuals would only serve to address the anomalous situation in which a Member State fails to properly transpose a directive. However, it does not mean that the Member State would be deprived of its transposition period or of the discretion to choose how to undertake the transposition of a clear, precise, and unconditional provision of a directive.[108]

The critique based on legal certainty also reveals some weaknesses, as it comes at the price of perpetuating a discriminatory outcome. The protection of legal certainty stands in contrast

[104] See the case law in the previous footnote.

[105] The argument was set out in Case C-91/92 *Faccini Dori* EU:C:1994:292, para 24, where the Court of Justice held that 'the effect of extending that case law to the sphere of relations between individuals would be to recognize a power in the [Union] to enact obligations for individuals with immediate effect, whereas it has competence to do so only where it is empowered to adopt regulations'. See, *a contrario*, the reasoning in Case C-108/01 *Consorzio del Prosciutto di Parma and Salumificio S Rita* EU:C:2003:296.

[106] For a recent example of this strict approach, see Case C-122/17 *Smith and others* EU:C:2018:631, paras 42–49.

[107] By way of illustration, see the works of W van Gerven, 'The Horizontal Direct Effect of Directive Provisions Revisited: The Reality of Catch-words' in T Heukels and D Curtin (eds), *Institutional Dynamics of European Integration* (Martinus Nijhoff Publishers, 1994); J Coppel, 'Horizontal Direct Effect of Directives' (1997) 26 *Industrial Law Journal* 69; M Dougan, 'The "Disguised" Vertical Direct Effect of Directives' (2000) 59 *Cambridge Law Journal* 586; and T Tridimas, 'Black, White, and Shades of Grey: Horizontality of Directives Revisited' (2002) 21 *Yearbook of European Law* 327. Among the Advocates General, see the Opinions of Advocate General Mancini in Joined Cases C-372/85, C-373/85 and C-374/85 *Traen* EU:C:1987:69 and Case C-14/86 *Pretore di Salò* EU:C:1987:136; Advocate General Van Gerven in Case C-271/91 *Marshall II* EU:C:1993:30; Advocate General Jacobs in Case C-316/93 *Vaneetveld* EU:C:1994:32; Advocate General Bot in Case C-122/17 *Smith* EU:C:2018:223; and Advocate General Szpunar in Case C-261/20 *Thelen Technopark Berlin GmbH* EU:C:2021:620.

[108] See the Opinion of Advocate General Jacobs in *Vaneetveld* (n 107) pt 25.

to the fact that some individuals can invoke the rights established by a directive against the authorities of the Member State, but not against private individuals, even when there is hardly any difference in the situations involved. For example, a fixed-term worker employed by a municipality-controlled corporation can invoke the direct effect of Directive 1999/70,[109] but a worker employed by a privately owned company in the same sector cannot, as the relationship takes place between two private individuals.[110]

To address some of the negative side effects of the *Marshall* doctrine, the case law has developed an autonomous and broad definition of the notion of 'Member State', aiming to expand the scope of vertical direct effect to as many public authorities as possible. The *leading case* on the matter is *Foster*,[111] where the Court of Justice ruled that a public undertaking, British Gas, although operating through a commercial entity in the form of a private corporation, was considered to be an emanation of the State as it was owned and controlled by a public authority and possessed special powers. According to the Court of Justice, a directive not transposed into national law can be invoked against 'organisations or bodies which were subject to the authority or control of the State or had special powers beyond those which result from the normal rules applicable to relations between individuals'.[112] The Court of Justice further clarified and defined the 'state' for the purpose of invoking direct effect in vertical relations as follows:

> [A] body, whatever its legal form, which has been made responsible, pursuant to a measure adopted by the State, for providing a public service under the control of the State and has for that purpose special powers beyond those which result from the normal rules applicable in relations between individuals is included in any event among the bodies against which the provisions of a directive capable of having direct effect may be relied upon.[113]

Although the judgment in *Foster* appeared to set out two cumulative requirements (control of the state and the existence of special powers), the Court of Justice has subsequently clarified that these are alternative requirements. It is therefore sufficient to prove either the existence of control of the state or of special powers to enable a private individual to rely on the direct effect of a defectively transposed directive.[114]

Case law has confirmed that directives can be invoked against the state in situations involving tax authorities,[115] local and regional authorities,[116] constitutional bodies,[117] health authorities[118], or publicly controlled corporations.[119] As Advocate General Sharpston pointed out in her Opinion in *Farrell*,[120] although in all these cases the state was found to be involved, the activities in dispute were sometimes far removed from the typical activities of a public

[109] Council Directive 1999/70/EC of 28 June 1999 concerning the framework agreement on fixed-term work concluded by ETUC, UNICE and CEEP [1999] OJ L175/43.

[110] See the criticism to the same effect in the Opinion of Advocate General van Gerven in *Marshall II* (n 107) pt 12.

[111] Case C-188/89 *Foster and others* EU:C:1990:259.

[112] ibid, para 18.

[113] ibid, para 20.

[114] Case C-413/15 *Farrell* EU:C:2017:745, para 34: 'Such organisations or bodies can be distinguished from individuals and must be treated as comparable to the State, *either because they are* legal persons governed by public law that are part of the State in the broad sense, or because they are subject to the authority or control of a public body, *or because they have been required*, by such a body, to perform a task in the public interest and have been given, for that purpose, such special powers' (emphasis added).

[115] *Becker* (n 37); and Case C-221/88 *Busseni* EU:C:1990:84.

[116] Case C-103/88 *Costanzo* EU:C:1989:256.

[117] Case C-222/84 *Johnston* EU:C:1986:206.

[118] *Marshall II* (n 107).

[119] Case C-157/02 *Rieser Internationale Transport* EU:C:2004:76.

[120] Case C-413/15 *Farrell* EU:C:2017:492, Opinion of AG Sharpston, pt 38ff.

authority. This flexible and pragmatic understanding of the concept of 'state' clearly aims to maximise the effectiveness of directives and ensure uniform implementation across all Member States. However, it can also be subject to some limitations, as in the case of private parties that claim the repayment of unlawful taxes charged in situations *inter privatos*.[121]

This effort has led the case law to recognise that directives can be relied upon in disputes between public authorities. In *Portgás*,[122] the Court of Justice ruled as follows:

> It would be contradictory to rule that State authorities and bodies satisfying the conditions set out [in the case law] are required to apply Directive 93/38, while denying those authorities the possibility to ensure compliance, if necessary before national courts, with the provisions of that directive by a body satisfying those conditions when that body must itself also comply with Directive 93/38.[123]

Despite the commendable efforts of the case law to maximise the number of cases in which a directive can have direct effect in vertical relations, the *Foster* ruling and its subsequent developments only partially address the shortcomings highlighted above.[124] The weaknesses in the case law may explain why the Court of Justice has continued to explore other avenues in an attempt to reduce as far as possible the situations in which individuals cannot rely on defectively transposed directives.

5.3.3.2. Protection of Legal Certainty and Reverse Direct Effect

The second limitation that applies to the direct effect of directives is linked to the principle of legal certainty. According to the Court of Justice, a directive

> cannot, of itself and independently of a national law adopted by a Member State for its implementation, have the effect of determining or aggravating the liability in criminal law of persons who act in contravention of the provisions of that directive.[125]

The rationale behind this limitation is as follows: a Member State that fails to comply with the directive cannot, at the same time, rely on the untransposed directive to impose burdens on individuals. For example, a directive harmonising a tax that a Member State has not transposed cannot be relied upon by the State to claim that tax from taxpayers solely on the basis of the directive. The same applies to punitive measures, whether criminal or administrative: a directive harmonising criminal offences, which a state has not transposed, cannot be used as the basis to establish the criminal or administrative liability of an individual or to aggravate it.[126] As can be seen, this approach resonates with the judgment in *Marshall*: the case law holds that it is unfair for a private individual to bear the legal burden that arises from the Member State's own failure to transpose. This approach, which aims to preclude the Member State

[121] Case C-316/22 *Gabel Industria Tessile* EU:C:2024:301, para 25: 'notwithstanding the absence of horizontal effect of a directive, a national court may allow a private party to rely on the unlawfulness of a tax which has been wrongly passed on to it by a supplier, in accordance with an option conferred on the latter by national legislation, in order to neutralise the additional economic burden which the private party has ultimately had to bear, if such a possibility is provided for by national legislation, which, in the case at issue in the main proceedings, it is for the referring court to determine'.

[122] Case C-425/12 *Portgás* EU:C:2013:829. See also Joined Cases C-383/21 and C-384/21, *Sambre & Biesme* SCRL EU:C:2022:1022, para 39.

[123] ibid, para 35.

[124] D Curtin, 'The Province of Government: Delimiting the Direct Effect of Directives in the Common Law Context' (1990) 15 *European Law Review* 195.

[125] Case C-14/86 *Pretore di Salò* EU:C:1987:136, para 20; Case C-80/86 *Kolpinghuis Nijmegen* EU:C:1987:431, para 13; Joined Cases C-74/95 and C-129/95 *X* EU:C:1996:491, para 25; and Case C-555/23 *Makeleio EPE* EU:C:2025:484, para 89.

[126] Case C-7/11 *Caronna* EU:C:2012:396, para 52; and Joined Cases C-508/21 P and C-509/21 P *Commission and IGG v Dansk Erhverv* EU:C:2023:669, para 86.

from invoking a defectively transposed directive to the detriment of an individual, is commonly known as 'reverse direct effect'.[127]

The prohibition of reverse direct effect applies principally to situations involving criminal or administrative sanctions or tax liability. This limited scope aims to balance the need for legal certainty with the goal of maximising the effectiveness of directives. This issue will be examined in section II.5.3.4.1 of this chapter, when analysing the relationship between legal certainty and the duty of conform interpretation.

The prohibition has also been qualified in cases where a directive is invoked to give effect to a general principle of Union law. In the so-called Danish judgments, the issue examined was whether a private individual can rely on a tax deduction provided in a directive but which was not transposed into national law. The Court of Justice ruled that it is possible to deny the right to a deduction based on a non-transposed directive if fraudulent or abusive practices are apparent from the facts of the case. In the words of the Court of Justice:

> Accordingly, since . . . abusive or fraudulent acts cannot found a right provided for by EU law, the refusal of an advantage under a directive, in this instance Directive 2003/49, does not amount to imposing an obligation on the individual concerned under that directive, but is merely the consequence of the finding that the objective conditions required for obtaining the advantage sought, prescribed by the directive as regards that right, are met only formally.[128]

This outcome is not entirely consistent with the prohibition of reverse direct effect, as it permits a Member State to rely on the content of a non-transposed directive to the detriment of a private individual, a result comparable to what the Court of Justice barred in *Pretore di Salò* and *Kolpinghuis Nijmegen*. It appears that the subject matter of the Danish judgments, tax law and the fight against tax fraud and abusive practices in aggressive tax planning, was regarded as particularly sensitive. Furthermore, the resolution of these cases could have been construed differently, by relying on the anti-abuse rules provided in national tax law, rather than creating an exception to an exception within the general doctrine on the direct effect of directives.

5.3.3.3. Time Limit to Transpose a Directive

In section II.5.3.2, reference was made to the transposition period as a limit to the direct effect of directives. Given that Member States are granted time to transpose a directive into their domestic law, the infringement will not occur until this period has elapsed, or if, having transposed the directive in advance of the deadline, the transposition is not in conformity with the directive. In its judgment in *Ratti*, the Court of Justice held that 'since a directive by its nature imposes obligations only on Member States, it is not possible for an individual to plead the principle of "legitimate expectations" before the expiry of the period prescribed for its implementation'.[129]

This temporal limitation to the direct effect of directives was qualified in the case of *Inter-Environnement Wallonie*,[130] according to which Member States, during the transposition period, 'must refrain from taking any measures liable seriously to compromise the result

[127] Joined Cases C-74/95 and C-129/95 X EU:C:1996:491, para 23; Joined Cases C-87/02, C-391/02 and C-403/02 *Berlusconi and others* EU:C:2004:363, para 74; Case C-384/02 *Grøngaard and Bang* EU:C:2005:708, para 30; and Case C-321/05 *Kofoed* EU:C:2007:408, para 45.

[128] Joined Cases C-115/16, C-118/16, C-119/16 and C-299/16 *N Luxembourg 1 and others* EU:C:2019:134, para 119.

[129] *Ratti* (n 96) para 8.

[130] Case C-129/96 *Inter-Environnement Wallonie* EU:C:1997:628, para 45.

prescribed'. This duty stems directly from Article 4(3) TEU read in conjunction with Article 288, third paragraph TFEU.[131]

The case law that emerges from the judgment in *Inter-Environnement Wallonie* precludes individuals from invoking the direct effect of a directive during its transposition period, but it allows them to challenge national measures that seriously undermine the goals of the directive. This represents a subtle variation of the doctrine of direct effect, which aims to prevent Member States from pursuing policies of *fait accompli* that jeopardise the effectiveness of a directive. It is for national courts to evaluate whether such national measures have been adopted, particularly to determine if the contested measures amount to a transposition of the directive and to assess the practical effects of the implementation of the national provisions that do not comply with the directive, and their duration. In the judgment in *Inter-Environnement Wallonie*, the Court of Justice provided two examples to assist national courts in conducting this analysis.

For example, if the provisions at issue are intended to constitute the full and definitive transposition of the directive, their incompatibility with the directive might give rise to the presumption that the result prescribed by the directive will not be achieved within the period prescribed if it is impossible to amend them in time.

Conversely, the national court could take into account the right of a Member State to adopt transitional measures or to implement the directive in stages. In such cases, the incompatibility of the transitional national measures with the directive, or the non-transposition of certain of its provisions, would not necessarily compromise the result prescribed.[132]

It is true that the judgment in *Inter-Environnement Wallonie* refers to 'provisions', a term that can be understood as limiting this doctrine to general rules of law only, thus excluding individual acts as well as administrative practices. The case law that followed rejected this strict interpretation. In the judgments in *Portgás*, *Aitoloakarnanias*, and *Sambre & Biesme SCRL*, the wording refers to a broader concept, such as 'any measure', thus allowing this case law to apply to all forms of Member State action.[133] Furthermore, the case law has also confirmed that it is irrelevant whether the national measure in question is specifically aimed at transposing the directive at issue.[134] However, the fact that a Member State transposes a directive partially and in several stages does not, in itself, constitute a measure that seriously compromises the aims pursued by the directive. As stated by the Court of Justice:

> [W]here the purpose of the adoption by a Member State of a measure is to transpose, even if only partially, a directive of the Union, and where that transposition is correct, the adoption of such a partial transposition measure cannot be regarded as likely to produce such an adverse effect, since it necessarily approximates national legislation to the directive which that legislation transposes, and thus contributes to the attainment of the objectives of that directive.[135]

[131] Case C-66/96 *Høj Pedersen and others* EU:C:1998:549, para 30; Case C-14/02 *ATRAL* EU:C:2003:265, para 58; Case C-157/02 *Rieser Internationale Transport* EU:C:2004:76, para 66; *Pfeiffer* (n 9) para 110; Case C-36/04 *Stichting Zuid-Hollandse Milieufederatie* EU:C:2006:209, para 42; Joined Cases C-261/07 and C-299/07 *VTB-VAB and Galatea* EU:C:2009:484, para 38; Case C-2/18 *Lietuvos Respublikos Seimo narių grupė* EU:C:2019:962, para 55; and Case C-181/20 *VYSOČINA WIND* a.s. EU:C:2022:51, para 75.

[132] *Inter-Environnement Wallonie* (n 130) paras 48–49.

[133] Case C-425/12 *Portgás* EU:C:2013:829, para 34. In Case C-43/10 *Nomarchiaki Aftodioikisi Aitoloakarnanias* EU:C:2012:560, para 57: 'it must be recalled that, in accordance with the Court's settled case law, during the period prescribed for transposition of a directive, the Member States to which it is addressed must refrain from taking any measures liable seriously to compromise the attainment of the result prescribed by that directive. Such an obligation to refrain owed by all the national authorities must be understood as referring to the adoption of any measure, general or specific, liable to produce such a compromising effect.' In Joined Cases C-383/21 and C-384/21 *Sambre & Biesme* SCRL EU:C:2022:1022, para 49.

[134] Case C-212/04 *Adeneler and others* EU:C:2006:443, paras 122–123; and Case C-439/16 PPU *Milev* EU:C:2016:818, para 32.

[135] Case C-83/20 *BPC Lux 2 Sàrl and others* EU:C:2022:346, para 72.

The consequences of *Inter-Environnement Wallonie* are different from those of the doctrine of direct effect. The former allows individuals to challenge national legislation or individual acts enacted during the transposition period of the directive, but not to directly invoke the rights that the directive may grant them. In other words, the *Inter-Environnement Wallonie* doctrine allows an individual to request the setting aside of a national measure, but they cannot subsequently rely on or enforce the provisions of the directive itself. This outcome is consistent with the coercive nature of the doctrine of the direct effect of directives, which aims to compel Member States to fulfil their obligations under a directive. If the transposition deadline has not yet expired, the Member State must be allowed to repeal the unlawful measures and comply with the law.[136] The case law in *Inter-Environnement Wallonie* helps to eliminate recalcitrant national laws or practices during the transposition period of a directive, but nothing more.[137]

5.3.4. The Applicability of Directives Lacking Direct Effect

As explained earlier in this chapter, all rules of Union law are *applicable*. However, it is the *means of application* that can differ depending on whether or not the rule has direct effect. In the case of directives, two approaches become particularly relevant once it is confirmed that their provisions do not have direct effect: the duty of conform interpretation; and the case of directives giving expression to general principles of Union law.

5.3.4.1. The Duty of Conform Interpretation

If a directive or some of its provisions lack direct effect, they cannot be invoked in national proceedings to directly enforce their content, but they will always have interpretative effects. The Court of Justice has established the duty to interpret all national law in conformity with the directive (see sections I.1.1 and I.2.1 of this chapter), a duty that is especially important as it compensates for some of the shortcomings caused by the absence of a directive's direct effect.

5.3.4.1.1. Horizontal Relations In disputes between private individuals, an applicant cannot invoke a directive against another individual. Instead, the national court resolving the case must apply national law, particularly the provisions of national law specifically adopted to transpose the directive, 'in the light of the wording and the purpose of the directive in order to achieve the result referred to in the third paragraph of Article [288 TFEU]'.[138] The duty of conform interpretation first emerged in the case law as a technique to ensure the applicability of directives in horizontal relations,[139] placing a significant burden on the national judge who must find an interpretation within national law that produces a result aligned with the terms of a directive that lacks direct effect.[140] Due to the incomplete effectiveness of the duty of conform interpretation, some scholars have defined it as the 'indirect effect' of directives.[141]

[136] M Klamert, 'Judicial Implementation of Directives and Anticipatory Indirect Effect: Connecting the Dots' (2006) 43 *Common Market Law Review* 1251.

[137] See Case C-422/05 *Commission v Belgium* EU:C:2007:342, where the Commission brought infringement proceedings against Belgium on the alleged violation of a directive during the transposition period. It should be noted that the Court of Justice confirmed the violation not only on the grounds of the directive itself, but also of Art 4(3) TEU and Art 288, third paragraph TFEU.

[138] Case C-14/83 *Von Colson and Kamann* EU:C:1984:153.

[139] ibid, para 26.

[140] ibid, paras 26–28.

[141] See, inter alia, G Betlem, 'The Principle of Indirect Effect of Community Law' (1995) 3 *European Review of Private Law* 1; P Craig, 'Directives: Direct Effect, Indirect Effect and the Construction of National Legislation' (1997) 22 *European Law Review* 519, and M Ruffert, 'Rights and Remedies in European Community Law: A Comparative View' (1997) 34 *Common Market Law Review* 307.

The earlier case law demanded a conforming interpretation of the national rules that specifically transposed the directive, but this duty later expanded to encompass the entire national legal system.[142] Each provision of national law can serve the aim of achieving an interpretation that is compliant with the directive. The only limitation to this duty is a *contra legem* interpretation of national law. In other words, the duty of conform interpretation cannot produce a result that contradicts the wording of the relevant national rule.[143] With this proviso, the national court must employ all available methods of interpretation within the national legal system to ensure effective compliance with the directive in relations between private individuals.

For example, in a national legal system neither the Companies Act nor the Commercial Code of a Member State enumerate the grounds for the nullity of a contract establishing a corporation, but the Civil Code does, which applies through a cross-reference in the Commercial Code. Among the grounds of nullity specified by the Civil Code, the absence of cause in the contract is included. However, a directive that harmonises certain aspects of national company law rejects the absence of cause as a ground for nullity. If a dispute arises between two parties over the nullity of a contract establishing a corporation due to its lack of cause, the national court faces a dilemma: the directive does not have direct effect because it is relied upon in a dispute between private parties, yet the use of a cross-reference in national law will lead to an outcome that breaches the directive. However, if national law provides for an interpretative criterion that gives preference to the *lex specialis*, according to which the rules in a specific area of law are not subject to the provisions of other fields of law, this interpretation will prevent the cross-reference to the Civil Code and ultimately lead to a decision compliant with the directive. As seen, this outcome results from a national court applying only national interpretative criteria, a method that allows the court to reach a decision in line with the directive without setting aside any rules of national law.[144]

In some cases, the duty of conform interpretation has gone so far that it comes close to producing effects equivalent to the direct effect of a directive. For example, in *Océano Grupo*,[145] the Court of Justice found that Spanish law conflicted with the obligation to carry out an *ex officio* review of unfair terms in consumer contracts. The Court of Justice ruled that Directive 93/13 requires national courts to review unfair terms on their own motion, including in disputes between private parties. This approach was not available in Spanish law, and the Court of Justice stated that

> the requirement for an interpretation in conformity with the Directive requires the national court, in particular, to favour the interpretation that would allow it to decline of its own motion the jurisdiction conferred on it by virtue of an unfair term.[146]

This ruling led the national court to set aside the traditional approach of the national courts, not because of the direct effect and primacy of the directive, but as a consequence of the methods of interpretation provided by Spanish law.[147]

[142] *Marleasing* (n 11) para 8.

[143] Although this limitation was tacitly present in the case law, it did not appear in explicit and clear terms until the judgment in Case C-105/03 *Pupino* EU:C:2005:386, para 47, a case concerning the direct effect of a Framework Decision. The terminology was later applied to directives in the case of *Pfeiffer* (n 9), only to become a standard reference in subsequent case law.

[144] This example is inspired by the facts of the case in *Marleasing* (n 11).

[145] Joined Cases C-240/98 to C-244/98 *Océano Grupo Editorial and Salvat Editores* EU:C:2000:346.

[146] ibid, para 32.

[147] See, to the same effect, *Faccini Dori* (n 105) para 27; Case C-334/92 *Miret* EU:C:1993:945, para 22; Case C-192/94 *El Corte Inglés* EU:C:1996:88, para 22; Case C-111/97 *EvoBus Austria* EU:C:1998:434, paras 18–21; Case C-131/97 *Carbonari and others* EU:C:1999:98, paras 48–50; Case C-185/97 *Coote* EU:C:1998:424, para 27; Case C-81/98 *Alcatel Austria and others* EU:C:1999:534, para 28; Case C-365/98 *Brinkmann Tabakfabriken* EU:C:2000:323, paras 38–40; Case C-465/98 *Darbo* EU:C:2000:184, para 19; and *Pfeiffer* (n 9) para 118.

The case law has never explicitly stated that the duty of conform interpretation is a variant derived from the doctrine of direct effect, or that the outcome of a conforming interpretation must involve the setting aside of a national rule. On the contrary, the Court of Justice has stated that the duty of conform interpretation is a requirement on national courts to explore all available interpretative avenues. If the final outcome involves the annulment or setting aside of a national rule, this outcome stems not from the directive's direct effect, but from the methods of interpretation in national law that produce such an effect.[148]

5.3.4.1.2. Time Limit to Transpose a Directive The direct effect of a directive does not materialise until the transposition period has expired. However, as previously explained, during this period Member States must refrain from adopting measures that could seriously compromise the directive's *effet utile*.

Following the judgment in *Inter-Environnement Wallonie*, another question arose: if a Member State is under a duty not to obstruct the *effet utile* of a directive during the transposition period, is there also a duty of conform interpretation during that time? This question was addressed in *Adeneler*,[149] to which the Court of Justice replied that

> from the date upon which a directive has entered into force, the courts of the Member States must refrain as far as possible from interpreting domestic law in a manner which might seriously compromise, after the period for transposition has expired, the attainment of the objective pursued by that directive.[150]

5.3.4.1.3. Legal Certainty The duty of conform interpretation finds yet another limitation in the principle of legal certainty. In sections I.1.1 and I.2.1 of this chapter, reference was made to the prohibition of *contra legem* interpretations of national law. In addition, Union law precludes interpretations of national law that aggravate the legal situation of the individual, in line with the prohibition of reverse direct effect described in section II.5.3.3.2 of this chapter. It should be noted that the case law does not restrict the position of the individual where the rule of the directive encroaches on the individual's *civil* status.

The principle of legal certainty is not compromised when the reliance on a directive in a vertical relation has, as a side effect, an impact on a private third party. Such situations often occur in areas such as public procurement or environmental protection, where a complaint by a private party vis-a-vis a public authority can have detrimental effects on the legal position of another private third party.[151] For instance, if a tenderer who was not awarded a contract in a public procurement procedure challenges the award made by the contracting authority, the dispute initially involves only a private individual and the Member State. However, the successful challenge can result in the annulment of an award granted to another private

[148] There are cases in which the distinction between horizontal and vertical direct effect became blurred or minimised to the extreme. This can be seen in Case C-194/94 *CIA Security International* EU:C:1996:172 and Case C-443/98 *Unilever* EU:C:2000:496, two cases involving a dispute between private parties, where one of the parties claimed the setting aside of a national rule for breach of a directive on a notification procedure in the field of technical standards and regulations. Some scholars have drawn general conclusions from these rulings, pointing to the weakening of the distinction between the horizontal and vertical direct effect of directives. However, this line of case law should be approached with caution, considering the specific circumstances and legal framework, which involves the procedural requirement of notification of technical rules, as a mechanism that plays an important role in the internal market. To extrapolate the findings in these rulings to any other directive is an exercise that should be handled with care. See M Dougan, 'When Worlds Collide: Competing Visions of the Relationship Between Direct Effect and Supremacy' (2007) 44 *Common Market Law Review* 931.

[149] Case C-212/04 *Adeneler and others* EU:C:2006:443.

[150] ibid, para 123.

[151] See, inter alia, Case C-201/02 *Wells* EU:C:2004:12; and Joined Cases C-152/07, C-153/07 and C-154/07 *Arcor and others* EU:C:2008:426.

individual, who will subsequently face the collateral consequences of the applicant's successful action. A similar scenario occurs when a private individual challenges a favourable environmental impact assessment for a public work. If the court rules in favour of the action, the outcome will have a detrimental effect on the legal situation of the private party contractually engaged in the public work.

These situations are referred to as a 'triangular direct effect', since they involve three different parties: two private individuals and a Member State. In these circumstances, the case law states that 'mere adverse repercussions on the rights of third parties, even if the repercussions are certain, do not justify preventing an individual from invoking the provisions of a directive against the Member State concerned'.[152]

5.3.4.2. Directives that Give Specific Expression to General Principles of Union Law

In addition to the duty of conform interpretation, a directive can have direct effect if its provisions give specific expression to a general principle of Union law, including in relations between private individuals. This outcome was first established in the seminal case of *Mangold*,[153] followed by other significant rulings in *Kücükdeveci*,[154] *Dansk Industri (DI)*,[155] *Max-Planck-Gesellschaft*,[156] *Bauer*,[157] and *Cresco Investigation*.[158]

In *Mangold*, the Court of Justice faced a dispute between two private individuals concerning age discrimination in the field of employment. Directive 2000/78/EC on equal treatment in employment and occupation prohibits, inter alia, discriminatory treatment on the grounds of age, a rule that was invoked in Germany to challenge the legality of a national statutory labour reform. In the main proceedings, a German court was asked to set aside the German provision in a dispute between a worker and his employer. Following a reference for a preliminary ruling, the Court of Justice stated that Directive 2000/78 was not the only relevant provision of Union law applicable to the case. Alongside the directive, the general principle of non-discrimination on the grounds of age was also applicable. The Court of Justice ruled that the matter must be resolved in accordance with the general principle of Union law prohibiting age discrimination, in conjunction with Directive 2000/78.[159] As a result of this combination, the judgment ruled as follows:

> [I]t is the responsibility of the national court, hearing a dispute involving the principle of non-discrimination in respect of age, to provide, in a case within its jurisdiction, the legal protection which individuals derive from the rules of [Union] law and to ensure that those rules are fully effective, setting aside any provision of national law which may conflict with that law.[160]

Following the judgment in *Mangold*, the ruling in *Kücükdeveci* marks a significant step forward, as it openly allows individuals to invoke rights granted by a directive in disputes between private parties, provided that the relevant provision of the directive *gives specific expression* to a general principle of Union law.[161] Such a development has had a significant impact on areas such as the protection of fundamental rights, which are recognised as general principles of Union law. As Advocate General Bot stated in his Opinion in *Kücükdeveci*:

[152] *Wells* (n 151) para 57.
[153] *Mangold* (n 48) para 76.
[154] *Kücükdeveci* (n 48).
[155] Case C-441/14 *Dansk Industri* EU:C:2016:278.
[156] Case C-684/16 *Max-Planck-Gesellschaft zur Förderung der Wissenschaften* EU:C:2018:874.
[157] Case C-569/16 *Bauer* EU:C:2018:871.
[158] Case C-193/17 *Cresco Investigation GmbH* EU:C:2019:43.
[159] *Mangold* (n 48).
[160] *Mangold* (n 48).
[161] K Lenaerts and J Gutiérrez-Fons, 'The Constitutional Allocation of Powers and General Principles of EU Law' (2010) 47 *Common Market Law Review* 1629.

> [G]iven the ever increasing intervention of [Union] law in relations between private persons, the Court will, in my view, be inevitably confronted with other situations which raise the question of the right to rely, in proceedings between private persons, on directives which contribute to ensuring observance of fundamental rights. Those situations will probably increase in number if the Charter of Fundamental Rights of the European Union becomes legally binding in the future, since among the fundamental rights contained in that charter are a number which are already part of the existing body of [Union] law in the form of directives. In that perspective, the Court must, in my view, think now about whether the designation of rights guaranteed by directives as fundamental rights does or does not strengthen the right to rely on them in proceedings between private parties.[162]

Despite the expansive scope of this case law, the Court of Justice has been careful to impose limitations on the ability of directives to produce horizontal direct effect. The argument developed in cases such as *Mangold* and *Kücükdeveci* only applies to general principles that do not require further normative development. For example, this includes the general principles of non-discrimination on grounds of sex or age, which are 'sufficient in [themselves] to confer on individuals an individual right which they may invoke as such'.[163] However, other general principles may need further development by the Union legislature, particularly the fundamental rights of the Charter categorised as 'principles' under Articles 51(1) and 52(5) of the Charter. In *AMS*, the Court of Justice rejected extending the *Mangold* case law to the fundamental right to information and consultation in the field of employment, as provided in Article 27 of the Charter. In the Court's view:

> It is therefore clear from the wording of Article 27 of the Charter that, for this article to be fully effective, it must be given more specific expression in European Union or national law.

A prohibition, as provided for in Article 3(1) of Directive 2002/14 and addressed to the Member States, on excluding from the calculation of the staff numbers in an undertaking a particular category of employees initially included in the group of persons to be taken into account in that calculation, cannot be inferred as a directly applicable rule of law either from the wording of Article 27 of the Charter or from the explanatory notes to that article.

> In this connection, the facts of the case may be distinguished from those which gave rise to Kücükdeveci in so far as the principle of non-discrimination on grounds of age at issue in that case, laid down in Article 21(1) of the Charter, is sufficient in itself to confer on individuals an individual right which they may invoke as such.
>
> Accordingly, Article 27 of the Charter cannot, as such, be invoked in a dispute, such as that in the main proceedings, in order to conclude that the national provision which is not in conformity with Directive 2002/14 should not be applied.[164]

The case law has become more pragmatic over time. In 2019, horizontal direct effect was extended to other grounds of discrimination beyond those based on sex or age, such as religion, and later, in 2025, to discrimination based on disability.[165] In 2018, in the cases of *Max-Planck-Gesellschaft* and *Bauer*, the Court of Justice held that the fundamental right to paid annual

[162] Opinion of Advocate General Bot in *Kücükdeveci* (n 48) pt 90.

[163] Case C-176/12 *Association de Médiation Sociale* EU:C:2014:2, para 47.

[164] ibid, paras 45–48. Confirming this line of case law, see also Case C-196/23 *Plamaro* EU:C:2024:596, paras 49–55, extending the analysis not only to Art 27 of the Charter, but also to Art 30. See M Steiert, 'The Landmark Case that Went Missing: Collective Redundancies, Unjustified Dismissal and the Denied Horizontality of the EU Charter of Fundamental Rights in C-196/23 Plamaro' (2025) 16 *European Labour Law Journal*.

[165] On discrimination based on religion, see *Cresco Investigation* (n 158). On discrimination based on disability, see Case C-631/22, *Ca Na Negreta* EU:C:2025:53, para 40; Case C-38/24 *G.L.* EU:C:2025:690, para 45; and Case C-5/24 *P.M.* EU:C:2025:689, para 32.

leave, enshrined in Article 31(2) of the Charter, had been given specific expression in Directive 2003/88/EC on the organisation of working time. This outcome confirmed that Article 7 of the Working Time Directive has direct effect between individuals, similar to the effects deployed by Directive 2000/78 following the rulings in *Mangold* and *Kücükdeveci*.[166]

6. Recap on Direct Effect

Following this overview of the doctrine of direct effect and its development in the Court of Justice's case law, it is time to draw some conclusions.

First, the chapter has shown that the practical consequences of direct effect are in many respects similar to those resulting from the general applicability of Union law. Both categories result in very similar outcomes. Although not all rules of Union law have direct effect, the reality is that the case law has expanded this concept to its fullest extent. Even in the case of directives, where significant restrictions on their direct effect still exist, the case law has paved the way for multiple techniques that enable directives to produce consequences that come close to a full direct effect. The doctrine of direct effect served a useful purpose in the early days of European integration, helping to ensure the effectiveness of Union law and distinguish it from the ordinary practice of international law. Seven decades later, with Union law fully incorporated into the national legal systems of the Member States, some scholars argue that the doctrine of direct effect appears more like a relic of the past, rather than an effective tool of a sophisticated and fully integrated legal order, such as Union law.

Second, there is a growing and justified criticism of the excessive complexity of the case law on direct effect, with its numerous variants, types and subtypes. In the previous sections, several references were made to 'indirect effect' (the duty of conform interpretation), 'reverse direct effect' (the prohibition of invoking non-transposed directives to aggravate the legal situation), or 'triangular direct effect' (the extension of direct effect to private third parties). If there is one term that best describes the doctrine of direct effect, it is certainly not 'simplicity'. The high level of sophistication in the case law has raised doubts about the purpose of a doctrine that aims to maximise the effectiveness of Union law, but does so in such complex terms that it hardly facilitates its practical application in the resolution of disputes.

Thus, if it appears that there is little difference between the applicability and the direct effect of Union rules, and if the complexity of the latter has reached its very limits, it is reasonable to conclude that the doctrine of direct effect merits thorough reconsideration both conceptually and practically.[167] In a well-known article whose title speaks for itself, Sacha Prechal raises this question and rightly concludes that the time has come to move away from conceptions more suitable to a European Economic Community than to the present Union.[168]

[166] However, in both cases (*Bauer* (n 157) paras 59 and 84, and *Max-Planck-Gesellschaft* (n 156) paras 54 and 73) the Court of Justice was careful to limit the result to cases affecting the 'essential content' of the fundamental right. The implications of this reference to the 'essential content' of the fundamental right to paid annual leave remain to be seen.

[167] Tridimas (n 107); K Lenaerts and T Corthaut, 'Of Birds and Hedges: The Role of Primacy in Invoking Norms of EU Law' (2006) 31 *European Law Review* 287; and S Prechal, 'Direct Effect, Indirect Effect, Supremacy and the Evolving Constitution of the European Union' *Jean Monnet Working Paper* 2/02; C Barnard, *The Fundamentals of EU Law Revisited: Assessing the Impact of the Constitutional Debate* (Oxford University Press, 2007).

[168] S Prechal, 'Does Direct Effect Still Matter?' (2000) 37 *Common Market Law Review* 1067.

GENERAL BIBLIOGRAPHY

Court of Justice of the European Union, *50th Anniversary of the Judgment in Van Gend en Loos 1963–2013: Conference Proceedings* (Publications Office, 2013).
Gallo, D, *Direct Effect in EU Law* (Oxford University Press, 2025).
Lenaerts, K and Corthaut, T, 'Of Birds and Hedges: The Role of Primacy in Invoking Norms of EU Law' (2006) 31 *European Law Review* 287.
Prechal, S, *Directives in EC Law*, 2nd edn (Oxford University Press, 2005).
Prinssen, J and Schrauwen, A (eds), *Direct Effect: Rethinking a Classic of EC Legal Doctrine* (Europa Law Publishing, 2003).
Simon, D, *La directive européenne* (Dalloz, 1997).

FURTHER READING

Direct Effect as a Principle

Craig, P, 'Once Upon a Time in the West: Direct Effect and the Federalisation of EEC Law' (1992) 12 *Oxford Journal of Legal Studies* 453.
Dougan, M, 'When Worlds Collide! Competing Visions of the Relationship between Direct Effect and Supremacy' (2007) 44 *Common Market Law Review 931.*
Leczykiewicz, D, 'Effectiveness of EU Law before National Courts: Direct Effect, Effective Judicial Protection and State Liability' in A Arnull and D Chalmers (eds), *The Oxford Handbook of European Union Law* (Oxford University Press, 2015).
Lenaerts, K and Gutiérrez-Fons, JA, 'Van Gend en Loos: A Star is Born' in Craig, P, and Schütze, R (eds), *Landmark Cases in European Law, Volume I: The Constitutional Cases* (Hart, 2025).
Prechal, S, 'Does Direct Effect Still Matter?' (2000) 37 *Common Market Law Review* 1047.
— 'Direct Effect Revisited' (2026) 51(1) *European Law Review* 17.
Robin-Oliver, S, 'The Evolution of Direct Effect in the EU: Stocktaking, Problems, Projections' (2014) 12 *International Journal of Constitutional Law* 165.
de Witte, B, 'Direct Effect, Supremacy and the Nature of the Legal Order' in P Craig and G de Búrca (eds), *The Evolution of EU Law*, 2nd edn (Oxford University Press, 2011).

The Direct Effect of General Principles of Union Law

Dashwood, A, 'From Van Duyn to Mangold via Marshall: Reducing Direct Effect to Absurdity?' (2006–2007) 8 *Cambridge Yearbook of European Legal Studies* 81.
Fontanelli, F, 'General Principles of the EU and a Glimpse of Solidarity in the Aftermath of Mangold and Kücükdeveci' (2011) 17 *European Public Law* 225.
Lenaerts, K and Gutiérrez-Fons, JA, 'The Constitutional Allocation of Powers and General Principles of EU Law' (2010) 47 *Common Market Law Review* 1629.
de Mol, M, 'The Novel Approach of the CJEU on the Horizontal Direct Effect of the Principle of Non-Discrimination' (2011) 18 *Maastricht Journal of European and Comparative Law* 109.
Muir, E, 'Of Ages in – and Edges of – EU Law' (2011) 48 *Common Market Law Review* 39.

The Direct Effect of Directives

Bobek, M, 'Why Is It Better to Treat Every Provision of a Directive as a (Horizontally) Directly Effective One' (2023) 39 *International Journal of Comparative Labour and Industrial Relations* 211.
Craig, P, 'The Legal Effect of Directives: Policy, Rules and Exceptions' (2009) 34 *European Law Review* 349.
Dougan, M, 'The "Disguised" Vertical Effect of Directives?' (2000) 59 *Cambridge Law Journal* 586.
Mastroianni, R, 'On the Distinction Between Vertical and Horizontal Direct Effect of Directives: What Role for the Principle of Equality?' (1999) 5 *European Public Law* 439.

Niglia, L, 'Form and Substance in European Constitutional Law: The "Social" Character of Indirect Effect' (2010) 16 *European Law Journal* 439.

Prechal, S, 'Individuals Challenging Directives in EU Courts' (2022) 59 *Common Market Law Review* 41.

Rasmussen, M, 'Revolutionizing European Law: A History of the Van Gend en Loos Judgment and the Making of a Transnational Constitution' (2014) 12 *International Journal of Constitutional Law* 136.

Steiert, M, 'The Landmark Case that Went Missing: Collective Redundancies, Unjustified Dismissal and the Denied Horizontality of the EU Charter of Fundamental Rights in C-196/23 Plamaro' (2025) 16 *European Labour Law Journal* 123.

Weatherill, S, 'Breach of Directives and Breach of Contract' (2001) 26 *European Law Review* 811.

The Duty of Conform Interpretation

Amstutz, M, 'In-Between Worlds: Marleasing and the Emergence of Inter-legality in Legal Reasoning' (2005) 11 *European Law Journal* 766.

Betlem, G, 'The Doctrine of Consistent Interpretation: Managing Legal Uncertainty' (2002) 22 *Oxford Journal of Legal Studies* 363.

Franklin, CNK (ed), *The Effectiveness and Application of EU and EEA Law in National Courts: Principles of Consistent Interpretation* (Intersentia, 2018).

Haket, S, *The EU Law Duty of Consistent Interpretation in German, Irish and Dutch Courts* (Intersentia, 2019).

10

Union Law in National Legal Systems (II): Primacy

I. INTRODUCTION TO THE PRIMACY OF UNION LAW

MEMBER STATES ARE under a legal obligation to comply with Union law. If a rule of national law is in contradiction with Union law, national authorities must give priority to the latter. In its simplest expression, the primacy of Union law can be described as a rule of priority that applies when two legal systems interact and come into conflict when resolving a dispute. However, the matter is more complex both in theory and in practice, and it is inaccurate to reduce it to a simple question of 'priority' between rules of Union and national law.

The characterisation of primacy as a criterion imposing the 'mere priority' of one rule over another carries strong undertones of international law, a legal system made up of rules that are negotiated, signed, and ratified by sovereign states that voluntarily commit to enforce such rules and prevent the enactment of any provisions or acts of domestic law that contradict or compromise those commitments. The principle of *pacta sunt servanda*, which involves the notion that international treaties bind the signatory states, requires them to align their domestic law with the agreed treaty. Whether an international treaty takes precedence over national laws or regulations, and whether a national judge can invalidate or only set them aside, is a matter for each state alone to decide. Only the state can determine the concrete terms and conditions in which the international rule and the conflicting national rule interact and produce effects in the national legal order. Ultimately, it is for the state to decide how to resolve conflicts between the two rules. From the standpoint of international law, a state has the duty to *fulfil the obligations set out in* an international treaty, leaving the means of achieving them to national authorities.

Union law adopts a different and more ambitious approach. Unlike international law, Union law not only declares the binding nature of its rules, but it also sets the conditions under which these rules interact with each national legal system. It establishes criteria for resolving conflicts between the rules of Union and national law. The primacy of Union law is an essential characteristic of the Union legal system that affirms the Union's ability to determine the terms governing the interaction between Union rules and national legal systems. The principle of primacy establishes the criteria to be used in the event of a contradiction between a rule of Union law and a rule of national law. In the event of such a dispute, Union law requires all national authorities to set aside the conflicting national rule and, subsequently, to extricate the national rule from the national legal system. It is not for national law to determine the outcome of such conflicts; this is a matter mainly governed by Union law and its principle of primacy.

The Court of Justice established the principle of primacy in its landmark judgment in *Costa v Enel*,[1] handed down in 1964. Flaminio Costa, a private individual who refused to pay his electricity bill supplied by the public utility Enel, argued that the national rules governing Enel's monopoly in Italy infringed several provisions of the Treaty establishing the European Economic Community (TEEC).[2] The Italian Government contended that the regulations on the internal electricity market had been adopted in 1962, four years *after* the TEEC came into force in Italy. In the view of the Italian Government, the obligations arising from Community law were no different from those created by international law. Consequently, in a case such as that between Flaminio Costa and Enel, the Italian court, following its internal system of sources, must apply the criterion *lex posterior derogat legi priori* and therefore give priority to the subsequent 1962 Italian Act over the TEEC, which had been in force since 1958. According to the Italian Government, Italy would be liable to the other Member States for its failure to comply with the provisions of the TEEC, as a result of the international responsibility it would have incurred if the breach were confirmed.

The Italian Government's argument was based on a standard approach of international law, whereby a state determines how its authorities resolve conflicts between international and domestic rules of law. This approach was rejected in *Costa v Enel* due to the autonomy of Community law and the ability of this legal system to determine its incorporation into the legal orders of the Member States. Just a year earlier, the Court of Justice had stated for the first time in its ruling in *Van Gend en Loos* that Union law is a new and autonomous legal system, resulting from a voluntary transfer of sovereign powers by its Member States. In the same way that the autonomy of Union law underpins the applicability of all its rules, it also 'makes it impossible for the States, as a corollary, to accord precedence to a unilateral and subsequent measure over a legal system accepted by them on a basis of reciprocity'.[3] Consequently, national law cannot override Union law by virtue of its *subsequent* adoption.

The Court of Justice reached this conclusion in *Costa v Enel* based on three grounds, which resonate closely with the arguments used a year before in *Van Gend en Loos*. Firstly, the effectiveness of Union law was taken into account: if the binding force of the rules of Union law were to vary from one Member State to another depending on the content of subsequent domestic legislation in each country, such an outcome would undermine the effectiveness of the Union's legal system, 'jeopardising the attainment of the objectives of the Treaty … and giving rise to the discrimination prohibited by Article [18 Treaty on the Functioning of the European Union (TFEU)]'.[4] Secondly, the Court of Justice emphasised the *unconditional nature* of the obligations contained in the Treaties. This argument is built *a contrario*, highlighting that when Member States are granted the power to derogate from the provisions of Union law, such power is explicitly provided in the Treaties, and no general power to derogate from the Treaties through subsequent national legislation is provided therein.[5] Thirdly, the Court of Justice underscored the *invocability of* Union law, a feature provided for in Article 288, second paragraph TFEU, in the case of regulations, which 'shall be binding in their entirety' and 'directly applicable in all Member States'. According to the Court of Justice, the equivalent Treaty provision at the time, 'which is subject to no reservation, would be quite

[1] Case 6/64 *Costa v Enel* EU:C:1964:66.

[2] On the historical background of the case and the circumstances surrounding Mr Costa's lawsuit, see A Arena, 'From an Unpaid Electricity Bill to the Primacy of EU Law: Gian Galeazzo Stendardi and the Making of Costa v ENEL' (2019) 30 *European Journal of International Law* 881.

[3] *Costa v Enel (n 1).*

[4] ibid.

[5] ibid.

meaningless if a State could unilaterally nullify its effects by means of a legislative measure which could prevail over [Union] law'.[6]

It should be noted that in *Costa v Enel*, the Court of Justice referred only to the *enforceability of* a national rule that is incompatible with and subsequent to a rule of Union law, remaining silent on the issue of the specific terms of validity and nullity of the national rule. However, by stating that a national rule that is incompatible with (and subsequent to) a rule of Union law cannot be applied to the detriment of Union law, the Court of Justice established that such conflicts of laws cannot be resolved in accordance with national law, but based on a criterion of Union law. The judgment in *Costa v Enel* relies on and confirms the novel approach that *Van Gend en Loos* had already introduced: it is for Union law, and for Union law alone, to determine the terms and conditions in which it is incorporated into national law, as well as how any conflicts between its rules and those of national law must be resolved.

The Court of Justice completed the theoretical construction of primacy by introducing into the equation, later in 2021, the principle of respect for the equality between Member States, a mandate enshrined in Article 4(2) TEU. In the case of *Euro Box*, the Court of Justice stated that 'the Union can respect such equality only if the Member States are unable, under the principle of the primacy of EU law, to rely on, as against the EU legal order, a unilateral measure, whatever its nature'.[7] Primacy is therefore based on the premise of the effectiveness and invocability of Union law, but also on the principle of equality between the Member States, since any limitation of the principle of primacy of Union law in one Member State would be to the detriment of the other Member States, therefore altering the balance of power on which the Treaties are founded.

As mentioned above, the judgment in *Costa v Enel* does not address the practical consequences for the national court once it has been established that the national rule is incompatible with Union law. The Court of Justice's silence in *Costa v Enel* might be linked to the fact that the Court ultimately found Italian law compatible with the Treaties. It took 14 years before the Court of Justice, in the case of *Simmenthal*,[8] ruled that a national court applying Union law

> is under a duty to give full effect to those provisions, if necessary refusing of its own motion to apply any conflicting provision of national legislation, even if adopted subsequently, and it is not necessary for the court to request or await the prior setting aside of such provision by legislative or other constitutional means.[9]

The Court of Justice later confirmed that the power to set aside national law applies in particular when the prevailing rules of Union law have direct effect.[10] Currently, this close interaction between direct effect and primacy has been clearly explained in the judgment in *NE v Bezirkshauptmannschaft Hartberg-Fürstenfeld*:

> It should also be borne in mind that the principle of primacy places the national court which is called upon within the exercise of its jurisdiction to apply provisions of EU law under a duty, where

[6] ibid.

[7] Joined Cases C-379/19, C-547/19, C-811/19 and C-840/19 *PM and Others* EU:C:2021:1034, para 249.

[8] Case C-106/77 *Simmenthal* EU:C:1978:49.

[9] ibid, para 24.

[10] Case C-409/06 *Winner Wetten* EU:C:2010:503, para 56, and more emphatically in Case C-573/17 *Daniel Adam Popławski* EU:C:2019:530, paras 61–62, where the Court of Justice stated that 'any national court, hearing a case within its jurisdiction, has, as an organ of a Member State, the obligation to disapply any provision of national law which is contrary to a provision of EU law with direct effect in the case pending before it. . . . On the other hand, *a provision of EU law which does not have direct effect may not be relied on, as such, in a dispute coming under EU law in order to disapply a provision of national law that conflicts with it*' (emphasis added). See also Joined Cases C-585/18, C-624/18 and C-625/18 *AK and others* EU:C:2019:982, paras 160–61; and Case C-924/19 PPU *FMS and others* EU:C:2020:367, para 139.

> it is unable to interpret national legislation in compliance with the requirements of EU law, to give full effect to the requirements of that law in the dispute before it, if necessary disapplying of its own motion any national legislation or practice, even if adopted subsequently, which is contrary to a provision of EU law with direct effect, and it is not necessary for that court to request or await the prior setting aside of such national legislation or practice by legislative or other constitutional means.[11]

Consequently, national law that breaches a rule of Union law with direct effect will be inapplicable in the case at hand, and all national courts are under a duty to *set aside* the relevant national provision. The Member State must subsequently ensure that the national provision is removed from the national legal system to avoid future conflicts, but, in the dispute before the national court, the contested national provision must be set aside, and the case resolved in accordance with Union law. The national court is under a duty to provide a temporary and case-by-case disapplication of the national law in the individual case, a power that Union law directly confers on the national court. Even if national law does not grant its courts the power to set aside statutes or constitutional provisions, Union law confers this prerogative on national judiciaries, and they must fulfil this duty and make it effective.

At this stage, it can be argued that the primacy of Union law has two different dimensions: the normative and the adjudicative. The *normative* dimension appears as an abstract conflict between two rules, one of Union law and the other of national law, where the former takes precedence. Section II of this chapter focuses on this dimension of primacy, which applies regardless of the rank or status of the national rule within the domestic legal system. The *adjudicative* dimension of primacy materialises when a national authority, whether administrative or judicial, must resolve an individual dispute, and the resolution depends on the choice between two conflicting provisions: one of Union law, and the other of national law. As previously explained, the national authority responsible for resolving the dispute is under a duty to set aside the conflicting national provision that violates the rule of Union law with direct effect. The Member State is then under a separate obligation, flowing from the principle of sincere cooperation (Article 4(3) TEU), to repeal or amend the conflicting national provision to avoid legal uncertainty.

The two dimensions of primacy have significant implications for the development, effectiveness, and integrity of the Union's legal system when implemented in the Member States. Adherence to both dimensions is crucial for preserving the autonomous nature of Union law and its effectiveness in all the Member States.

On one hand, the normative dimension of primacy appears in cases of abstract conflicts between the rules of Union law and national law. Such conflicts are resolved through the shared understanding that the Member States have committed to abstain from introducing rules that conflict with their Union obligations.[12] To ensure compliance, the Treaties provide for a specific remedy in proceedings before the Court of Justice, whose sole purpose is to determine whether a rule or act of a Member State conforms to Union obligations, regardless of whether the Union provision has direct effect. This is the core aim of the infringement procedure in Articles 258–259 TFEU, which empowers the Court of Justice to conduct an abstract and declarative review of a Member State's conduct in light of Union law. The judgment confirming a violation does not annul or declare the national measure invalid, as the Treaties only grant the Court of Justice a declaratory jurisdiction to assess whether the Member State has fulfilled its obligations under Union law.

On the other hand, the adjudicative dimension of primacy provides a more incisive approach towards national legal systems. Instead of simply declaring a breach of Union law,

[11] Case C-205/20 *NE v Bezirkshauptmannschaft Hartberg-Fürstenfeld* EU:C:2022:168, para 37.

[12] See the classic introduction to primacy by P Pescatore, *L'ordre juridique des Communautés Européennes* (Bruylant, 2006) 227ff.

the adjudicative dimension of primacy requires a national authority to set aside any conflicting national rule and even to annul it if the national authority has the power to do so. However, for the adjudicative dimension of primacy to deploy its consequences, the rule of Union law must be invocable against a national authority. Consequently, Union law must have direct effect, as explained in chapter nine of this book. The Court of Justice reaffirmed this link between the adjudicative dimension of primacy and direct effect in its judgments in *Popławski* and *NE*.[13]

It can be argued that primacy and direct effect are two sides of the same coin: once a rule of Union law is confirmed to have direct effect, any rule of national law incompatible with it will be required to be set aside when applied in individual disputes, and the Member State must subsequently remove the incompatibility from its legal system. If the rule of Union law does not have direct effect, the Member State will still be in breach of its obligations under Union law, but the adjudicative dimension of primacy will not be triggered, only its normative dimension. As a result, the Court of Justice has jurisdiction to hear an infringement action brought by the Commission or another Member State on the grounds of Article 258 or 259 TFEU. These proceedings will result in a declaratory judgment stating whether or not the Member State has complied with its obligations under Union law, and it will be for the defendant Member State to subsequently undertake all the necessary measures to align its legal system with Union law.

The combination of direct effect and primacy results in an unusual outcome in the practice of international law. A rule of national law, whether legislative, administrative, or even constitutional, can be set aside in a dispute as a result of its inconsistency with Union law. The authority to set aside national law is directly granted by Union law to all national authorities implementing Union law, regardless of whether such powers exist under national law. More broadly, the interplay of direct effect and primacy gives Union law a federalising role that distinguishes it from the traditional role of international law within national legal systems. This distinctive characteristic of Union law stems from the transfer of sovereign powers made by the Member States at the time of acceding to the Union, an organisation with its own institutions, its own autonomous legal system and its own rule-making powers, capable of enacting rules of law that are immediately applicable across the territory of all the Member States.[14]

The importance but also the sensitive nature of the primacy of Union law is seen in the fact that not all Member States have fully accepted it. While national courts have largely internalised the direct effect of Union law to its full extent, the same cannot be said about the primacy of Union law in either its normative or adjudicative dimension. A significant number of Member States, especially their constitutional and supreme courts, have consistently held that the primacy of Union law does not unconditionally apply to all national rules of constitutional rank. Similarly, several constitutional courts question an absolute conception of the autonomous nature of Union law, asserting instead that the ultimate source of legitimacy of Union law lies in the constitution of each Member State. The practical consequence of this sceptical approach is the introduction of limits to the primacy of Union law, limits which are grounded in the constitutions of the Member States. To summarise, there are currently *two narratives* surrounding the principle of primacy: one advocated by the Union, as reflected in the Court of Justice's case law; and another one advanced by the constitutional and supreme courts of the Member States. The tension between the two narratives will be explored in Section V of this chapter.

[13] *Daniel Adam Popławski* (n 10) paras 61–62; *NE and Bezirkshauptmannschaft Hartberg-Fürstenfeld* (n 11) para 37; Case C-582/21 *Profi Credit Polska* EU:C:2024:282, para 57; Case C-230/23 *Reprobel* EU:C:2024:951, para 51, and Case C-73/23 *Chaudfontaine Loisirs* EU:C:2024:734, para 55.

[14] E Stein, 'Lawyers, Judges and the Making of a Transnational Constitution' (1981) 75 *American Journal of International Law* 1; JHH Weiler, 'The Transformation of Europe' (1991) 100 *Yale Law Journal* 2403; and F Mancini, 'The Making of a Constitution for Europe' (1989) 26 *Common Market Law Review* 595.

Proof of the sensitive legal and political connotations that surround the principle of primacy is the fact that the Treaties remain silent and fall short of recognising it in their provisions. In 2004 the Treaty establishing a Constitution for Europe introduced in Article I-6 a 'primacy clause', stating that 'the Constitution and law adopted by the institutions of the Union in exercising competences conferred on it shall have primacy over the law of the Member States'. This provision was not incorporated into the Lisbon Treaty, as the Member States chose not to include any signs of political integration that could be interpreted as the indirect introduction of the Constitutional Treaty through the back door. The only remaining reference to Article I-6 is currently found in Declaration no 17 on primacy, annexed to the Lisbon Treaty, which states as follows:

> The Conference recalls that, in accordance with well settled case law of the Court of Justice of the European Union, the Treaties and the law adopted by the Union on the basis of the Treaties have primacy over the law of Member States, under the conditions laid down by the said case law.[15]

The outcome of the above is a cautious acknowledgement of the primacy of Union law by the Member States, as reflected in a Declaration that does not have the same legal status as the Treaty provisions themselves. However, the language of this Declaration contrasts with that of the ill-fated Article I-6, a blunt and unconditional provision that declared the primacy of Union law over all national law. Instead, Declaration No 17 refers to the primacy of Union law as accounted for by the Court of Justice in its case law, including a reference to 'the conditions laid down by the said case law', tacitly recognising that primacy is not an absolute principle, but a feature of Union law that can be subject to conditions as provided in Union law.

II. THE *NORMATIVE* DIMENSION OF PRIMACY

Primacy is not the result of a hierarchical relationship between the Union's legal system and the law of the Member States. Union law stems from a voluntary conferral of competences made by the Member States to the Union, confined to specific areas of competence. Once the Union has been granted such competence, or once it has exercised it, the Member States have agreed to comply with the obligations resulting from this transfer. In cases of conflict between the rules of national law and those of the Union acting within its competence, the Member States are committed to removing the incompatible national rules and facilitating the full effectiveness of the provisions of Union law. As a result, when such a conflict arises, the criterion for its resolution is competence, not hierarchy. Union law is not integrated into the hierarchical chain of validity of the national legal system; it is an autonomous legal system embedded within the national legal order, requiring Member States to remove any national rules incompatible with Union law. The Court of Justice has emphasised this point repeatedly, stating that:

> It cannot [be] that the incompatibility with [Union] law of a subsequently adopted rule of national law has the effect of rendering that rule of national law non-existent. Faced with such a situation, the national court is, however, obliged to disapply that rule, provided always that this obligation does not restrict the power of the competent national courts to apply, from among the various

[15] Declaration No 17 adds that the Conference decided to attach as an Annex to the Final Act the Opinion of the Council Legal Service on the primacy of EC law as set out in 11197/07 (JUR 260), which states the following: 'Opinion of the Council Legal Service of 22 June 2007 – It results from the case-law of the Court of Justice that primacy of EC law is a cornerstone principle of Community law. According to the Court, this principle is inherent to the specific nature of the European Community. At the time of the first judgment of this established case law (Costa/ENEL,15 July 1964, Case 6/64) there was no mention of primacy in the treaty. It is still the case today. The fact that the principle of primacy will not be included in the future treaty shall not in any way change the existence of the principle and the existing case law of the Court of Justice'.

> procedures available under national law, those which are appropriate for protecting the individual rights conferred by [Union] law.[16]

In practice, the conceptual foundations of primacy produce an outcome similar to that of a hierarchical legal system. The combined effect of setting aside incompatible national rules, along with the duty of the Member State to subsequently repeal and remove such rules from the national legal system, results in the effective removal of any national rule incompatible with Union law.

The normative dimension of primacy captures this unique approach towards conflicts of laws between Union and national law. There is no formal hierarchy between the two legal systems, but the duty of Member States to ensure the conformity of their domestic legal system with Union law creates a similar outcome. Therefore, before the conflicting national rule is effectively removed from the national legal system, the conflict of laws must be resolved in the abstract as an initial step in the process of determining whether a national rule complies with Union law and, if necessary, proceeding to setting it aside and ensuring its removal from the national legal order. This preliminary resolution of the conflict embodies the normative dimension of primacy, whose scope is very broad, covering rules of national constitutional and statutory law, but which is also subject to some specificities and derogations that will be described in the following sections.

1. Primacy over Constitutional Rules

Despite the legal and political sensitivity underlying a conflict between the national constitution and Union law, the Court of Justice has repeatedly stated that the rules of Union law take precedence over *all* rules of national law, including constitutional provisions. This position had already appeared in the early case law of the 1970s and remains valid to this day, with only minor qualifications that will be explained below.

In the 1970 case of *Internationale Handelsgesellschaft*,[17] the Court of Justice was confronted with an alleged conflict between the Community's export deposit scheme and the fundamental right to property enshrined in the German Basic Law. Although the national rule concerned was part of the German Constitution (*Grundgesetz*), the Court of Justice reaffirmed its stance in *Costa v Enel* and recalled that:

> [T]he validity of a [Union] measure or its effect within a Member State cannot be affected by allegations that it runs counter to either fundamental rights as formulated by the constitution of that State or the principles of a national constitutional structure.[18]

[16] Joined Cases C-10/97 to C-22/97 *IN.CO.GE.'90 and others* EU:C:1998:498, para 21. However, it is important to recall that in Case C-106/77 *Simmenthal* EU:C:1978:49, in para 17, the Court of Justice appeared to point to the opposite solution when it stated that, 'in accordance with the principle of precedence of [Union] law, the relationship between provisions of the Treaty and directly applicable measures of the institutions on the one hand and the national law of the Member States on the other is such that those provisions and measure not only by their entry into force render automatically inapplicable any conflicting provision of current national law but – in so far as they are an integral part of, and take precedence in, the legal order applicable in the territory of each of the Member States – also preclude the *valid* adoption of new national legislative measures to the extent to which they would be incompatible with [Union] provisions' (emphasis added).

[17] Case C-11/70 *Internationale Handelsgesellschaft* EU:C:1970:114.

[18] ibid, para 3. The same idea was put forward, albeit more timidly, in the Order in Case C-9/65 *San Michele* EU:C:1967:3, where the Court of Justice was faced with a request to close the proceedings on the grounds that an Italian judge had raised a question of unconstitutionality before the Italian *Corte Costituzionale*. The appellant emphasised that the *Corte Costituzionale's* decisions have the absolute effect of *res judicata*, taking precedence over decisions previously handed down by the Court of Justice. The Order of the Court of Justice reiterated some of the arguments already set out in *Costa v Enel* and confirmed that not even a ruling of a national Constitutional Court can oppose the applicability of Union law.

This formula has evolved over time and at present is articulated by the Court of Justice in the following terms:

> [B]y virtue of the principle of the primacy of EU law, a Member State's reliance on rules of national law, even of a constitutional order, cannot be allowed to undermine the unity and effectiveness of EU law. In accordance with settled case-law, the effects of the principle of the primacy of EU law are binding on all the bodies of a Member State, without, inter alia, provisions of domestic law, including constitutional provisions, being able to prevent that.[19]

The Court of Justice made use of this criterion when it reviewed the compatibility with Union law of a rule in the German Constitution that banned women from serving in armed forces posts involving the use of arms,[20] as well as a Greek constitutional provision that derogated from Union law on public procurement in the audiovisual sector.[21] This outcome also applies in cases where the Court of Justice reviews parliamentary statutes to which the national constitution accords a constitutional rank within the national legal system,[22] and to cases where a constitutional provision breaches the obligation not to seriously compromise the objectives of a directive during the transposition period.[23] The primacy of Union law also extends to conflicts with constitutional provisions as interpreted by the national Constitutional Court.[24] For instance, in *Cordero Alonso*,[25] the Court of Justice confirmed that a settled case law of the Spanish Constitutional Court on the principle of non-discrimination on the grounds of sex was incompatible with Union law,[26] and in the case of *Landtovà*,[27] where the Court of Justice held that the reiterated case law of the Czech Constitutional Court conflicted with the principle of Union law of non-discrimination on the grounds of nationality.[28] The same conflict arose in *Egenberger*, where the Court of Justice declared the German Constitutional Court's case law incompatible with Directive 2000/78 and the Charter of Fundamental Rights of the European Union ('the Charter'), which precluded judicial review of decisions relating to employment and recruitment by religious institutions in Germany.[29]

Despite the categorical approach towards constitutional rules of national law, it is also true that the primacy of Union law can be subject to some modulations in this regard. The Treaties highlight the need to respect the constitutional traditions of the Member States, a concern that is reflected in Article 4(2) TEU, which states that the Union 'shall respect the equality of Member States before the Treaties as well as their national identities, inherent in their fundamental structures, political and constitutional, inclusive of regional and local self-government'.

[19] Joined Cases C-379/19, C-547/19, C-811/19 and C-840/19 *Euro Box Promotion and Others* EU:C:2021:1034, para 25; Case C-430/21 *RS* EU:C:2022:99, para 51, and Case C-448/23 *Commission v Poland* EU:C:2025:975, para 171.

[20] Case C-285/98 *Kreil* EU:C:2000:2.

[21] Case C-57/01 *Makedoniko Metro and Michaniki* EU:C:2003:47.

[22] Case C-208/09 *Sayn-Wittgenstein* EU:C:2010:806.

[23] Joined Cases C-378/07, C-379/07, C-379/07 and C-380/07 *Angelidaki and others* EU:C:2009:250, paras 205–07.

[24] Case C-430/21 *RS* EU:C:2022:99, paras 74–75, and Case C-107/23 PPU *Lin* EU:C:2023:606, para 123.

[25] Case C-81/05 *Cordero Alonso* EU:C:2006:529.

[26] This case law finds its origin in the judgment of the *Tribunal Constitucional* in the case STC 306/1993. The conflict arose again, albeit with a different subject matter, in Case C-177/10 *Rosado Santana* EU:C:2011:557, where the Court of Justice reached exactly the opposite result to the one previously held by the *Tribunal Constitucional* (see Orders 183/2005 and 112/2008 of the Spanish court) in the case of fixed-term public employees.

[27] Case C-399/09 *Landtovà* EU:C:2011:415.

[28] Inter alia, the judgments of the *Ústavní soud* (Czech Constitutional Court) of 3 June 2003, no II ÚS 405/02 (vol 30, no 80, 245) and of 25 January 2005, no III ÚS 252/04 (vol 36, no 16, 173).

[29] Case C-414/16 *Egenberger* EU:C:2018:257. Along the same lines, but in the context of the Hungarian Constitutional Court's case law on taxation, see Joined Cases C-52/16 and C-113/16 *SEGRO* EU:C:2018:157, paras 47–48. See also the case law of the Romanian Constitutional Court in *Euro Box* and the limitations it imposed on the action of judges in anti-corruption cases, later reversed by the Court of Justice in Joined Cases C-379/19, C-547/19, C-811/19 and C-840/19 *Euro Box Promotion and Others* EU:C:2021:1034, para 257.

This provision immediately adds that the Union must also respect 'their essential State functions, including ensuring the territorial integrity of the State, maintaining law and order, and safeguarding national security. In particular, national security remains the sole responsibility of each Member State'. The national identity of each Member State, the content of which is usually reflected in the constitution, can act as a limit to the Union's actions, including the primacy of its rules. However, it should be noted that this is not a limit imposed by national law, but by Union law itself in Article 4(2) TEU, and the provision cannot be interpreted in such a way as to confer on a Member State the power to derogate unilaterally from the provisions of Union law by relying on that national identity.[30] In the event that a conflict between a rule of Union law and a rule of a national constitution is resolved in favour of the latter, it will not be the result of the national constitution superseding Union law, but because a rule of Union law, Article 4(2) TEU, facilitates an interpretation of Union law that accommodates a constitutional provision of a Member State.[31]

The same applies to the principle of legal certainty, recognised as a general principle of Union law, which allows modulations to the scope of primacy when a rule of Union law comes into conflict with a final judgment rendered by a national court.[32] As explained in section II.4 of this chapter, such a modulation of primacy is based on the premise that Union law does not as a general rule impose a reopening of final national judgments with the force of *res judicata*, except in exceptional circumstances recognised by the case law.[33] This protection of final judgments aims to preserve the stability and legal certainty produced by final rulings delivered by national courts when implementing Union law. It does not result from a national judgment superseding Union law, but from a balancing exercise between the primacy of Union law and one of its general principles: legal certainty.

2. Primacy over Parliamentary and Administrative Rules

If national constitutional rules must yield to the primacy of Union law, a fortiori the same must apply to parliamentary and administrative rules of the Member States. Parliamentary acts, regulations, delegated legislation, or internal administrative rules of public authorities, to name just a few, must adhere to the obligations derived from Union law, regardless of their rank or specific position in the national legal system. Primacy is not conditioned by or dependent on the territorial or functional peculiarities of the national rules in question: laws enacted by a municipal authority, a region, a public corporation, professional associations, or sport federations exercising public tasks must be aligned with Union law.

In the case of legislative validations, in which a national legislature intervenes to provide a legislative higher rank to an administrative or judicial decision that is alleged to breach Union law, the Court of Justice has confirmed the primacy of Union law. This issue was addressed in *Scattolon*, involving an interpretation by the Italian legislature of Directive 77/187/EEC which, in turn, differed from an interpretation of this Directive by the *Corte di Cassazione*. The Court of Justice ruled that the Italian legislature's intervention, whether to rectify or confirm the

[30] Case C-448/23 *Commission v Poland* EU:C:2025:975, para 227.

[31] On the role of Art 4(2) TEU as a rule for the resolution of constitutional conflict, see Case C-399/11 *Melloni* EU:C:2012:600, Opinion of AG Bot, pts 134–44, as well as Case C-62/14 *Gauweiler* EU:C:2015:7, Opinion of AG Cruz Villalón, pts 59–69.

[32] See, inter alia, Case C-453/00 *Kühne & Heitz* EU:C:2004:17, para 24; and Case C-234/04 *Kapferer* EU:C:2006:178, para 21.

[33] This is the case, for example, of the emergence of new facts relevant for criminal proceedings following the delivery of a conviction, or evidence of a court lacking impartiality (in this regard, see the judgment in Case C-487/19 *WŻ* EU:C:2021:798, para 160).

case law of the Italian Supreme Court, must be in conformity with Union law. Furthermore, the Court of Justice clarified that a legislative validation can amount to a breach of Article 47 of the Charter, which guarantees the fundamental right to effective judicial protection, if individuals are deprived of the right to effectively challenge the substance of the matter before national courts.

3. Primacy over Public and Private Administrative Acts

Administrative acts adopted by national administrative authorities are also subject to Union law. However, the Court of Justice has accepted that, in the case of final administrative acts, Union law can defer to considerations of legal certainty.[34] In such cases, the revocation or setting aside of a final administrative act will depend on the rules on revocation set out in national law. If such rules confer a *discretional* power on the administration to reopen final decisions, Union law requires such power to be interpreted as an *obligation*.[35] Similarly, if national law allows for the revocation of administrative acts only in cases of manifest illegality, a situation restricted to exceptional cases only, Union law imposes a less restrictive application of that criterion when the final administrative act in question breaches Union law, requiring revocation in the case of a breach of Union law.[36]

The case law of the Court of Justice has also added various cumulative requirements that must be met before a final administrative act may be reopened. First, the administrative body must, under national law, have the power to reopen that decision. Second, the administrative decision in question must have become final as a result of a judgment of a national court ruling at last instance. Third, that judgment must, in the light of a decision given by the Court of Justice subsequent to it, be based on a misinterpretation of Union law which was adopted without a question being referred to the Court of Justice for a preliminary ruling in the circumstances set out in the third paragraph of Article 267 TFEU. Fourth, the person concerned must have complained to the administrative body immediately after becoming aware of that decision of the Court of Justice.[37]

Legal acts agreed between private individuals, as well as unilateral private acts with civil effects, are also subject to the primacy of Union law. However, not all the provisions of Union law are addressed to private individuals and, as a result, they do not all produce effects between private parties, as explained in chapter nine. In any event, the fact that a private individual cannot invoke a rule of Union law against another private individual does not mean that Union law is irrelevant in those situations. As explained in chapter nine, the duty of conform interpretation of national law in light of Union law applies to any national measure, including the interpretation of private acts. Therefore, if a clause in a private contract is inconsistent with a rule of Union law that is addressed only to the Member States or to another individual, it must be interpreted in a way that complies with that rule. If such an interpretation is not possible due to the wording of the clause, the aggrieved party may be entitled to bring a claim for damages against the Member State for failure to properly transpose Union law, or, in certain

[34] See, inter alia, the judgments in Case C-453/00 *Kühne & Heitz* EU:C:2004:17, para 21; Joined Cases C-392/04 and C-422/04 *i-21 Germany and Arcor* EU:C:2006:586; Case C-2/06 *Willy Kempter* EU:C:2008:78; Case C-2/08 *Fallimento Olimpiclub* EU:C:2009:506; and Joined Cases C-924/19 PPU and C-925/19 PPU *Országos Idegenrendézeti Főigazgatóság Dél-alföldi Regionális Igazgatóság* EU:C:2020:367, para 18.

[35] *Kühne & Heitz* (n 34) para 28.

[36] *i-21 Germany and Arcor* (n 34) paras 63–64.

[37] *Kühne & Heitz* (n 34) para 28; *i-21 Germany and Arcor* (n 34) para 52; and *Országos Idegenrendézeti Főigazgatóság Dél-alföldi Regionális Igazgatóság* (n 34) para 18.

circumstances, against the other private party for the harm caused by the breach of Union law.[38]

4. Primacy over Judicial Decisions

All judgments delivered by national courts must abide by Union law and resolve disputes in accordance with the provisions of Union law. However, the Court of Justice has introduced an important qualification to the normative dimension of primacy when it comes to final judicial decisions of national courts with the force of *res judicata*. In the case of *Kapferer*, the Court of Justice held that Union law does not require a national court to set aside national procedural rules conferring the force of *res judicata* on a national judicial decision, even if that decision is based on an interpretation that is incompatible with Union law.[39] Consequently, if an individual chooses not to bring an appeal against an unfavourable ruling of a national court, or if all the national legal remedies have been exhausted, the decision of the national court will become final and its content, even if contrary to Union law, cannot be subject to further review in subsequent proceedings brought by the same parties. In such circumstances, the final decision of the national court will produce its effects, regardless of its non-conformity with Union law. The rationale of this approach is the need to safeguard the stability and legal certainty provided by final judgments resolving a dispute, an imperative subject to a general principle of Union law, legal certainty, which in this context prevails over the normative dimension of primacy.[40]

The ruling in *Kapferer* has not been entirely consistent with other strands of case law of the Court of Justice, and some tensions remain. Since 1974 and following the judgment of the Court of Justice in *Rheinmühlen I*,[41] lower national courts have the authority to refer a question for a preliminary ruling even if the higher national courts have already ruled on the matter through a final judgment with the force of *res judicata*. For example, if the Dutch Supreme Court issues a judgment and refers the case back to the lower court from which it originated, that court, regardless of the content of the Supreme Court's judgment, has the power to raise the question for a preliminary ruling and, if necessary, to set aside the previous ruling delivered on appeal by the Supreme Court. The case law established in *Rheinmühlen I* has been reaffirmed on several occasions,[42] despite its imperfect alignment with the approach taken in *Kapferer*. Advocate General Cruz Villalón highlighted this tension in *Elchinov*, where he pointed out that Union law and its principle of legal certainty sit uneasily alongside the power of lower national courts to set aside rulings issued by their higher judicial instances.[43] However, the Court of Justice has upheld both lines of reasoning, and in the case of *Elchinov* it insisted on applying the *Rheinmühlen I* test, an approach that remains in force to this day.

[38] Case C-453/99 *Courage and Crehan* EU:C:2001:465, paras 26–28.

[39] Case C-234/04 *Kapferer* EU:C:2006:178, para 21; Case C-213/13 *Impresa Pizzarotti* EU:C:2014:2067, para 60; and Case C-69/14 *Târşia* EU:C:2015:662, para 38.

[40] In the words of the Court of Justice: 'EU law does not require a national court to disapply domestic rules of procedure conferring finality on a judgment, even if to do so would make it possible to remedy a domestic situation which is incompatible with EU law. . . . Thus, in the absence of EU legislation in this area, the rules implementing the principle of *res judicata* are a matter for the national legal order, in accordance with the principle of the procedural autonomy of the Member States, but must be consistent with the principles of equivalence and effectiveness . . .' (Case C-582/21 *Profi Credit Polska* EU:C:2024:282, paras 38–39).

[41] Case C-166/73 *Rheinmühlen-Düsseldorf* EU:C:1974:3, para 4.

[42] See, inter alia, Case C-210/06 *Cartesio* EU:C:2008:723, para 88; Case C-378/08 *ERG and others* EU:C:2010:126, para 32; and Joined Cases C-188/10 and C-189/10 *Melki and Abdeli* EU:C:2010:363, para 42.

[43] Case C-173/09 *Elchinov* EU:C:2010:336, Opinion of AG Cruz Villalón, pts 20–40.

The tensions in the case law have widened over time. In *Lucchini*, the Court of Justice authorised a national court to review and set aside a final judicial decision of a Member State in the field of state aid, an area of exclusive competence of the Union.[44] Although the outcome of *Lucchini* was later subjected to further qualifications,[45] the reality remains that the principles of legal certainty and the protection of final national judgments are increasingly subject to a growing number of derogations.

For example, in the case of *Vueling Airlines*, the Court of Justice was called upon to decide whether a final judgment of a French criminal court that breached Union law could deploy its effects in other areas of national law and jurisdictions. In the case at hand, a French civil court questioned whether it was bound by the findings of fact and law previously established by the French criminal court, whose decision was clearly in breach of a regulation of Union law. In response to this query, the Court of Justice ruled that Union law does not preclude national law from protecting, for the purposes of legal certainty, the findings of a final judgment with the force of *res judicata*. However, the Court of Justice also added that such protection does not allow the Member State to extend the effects of the ruling to other judicial proceedings if the final judgment is found to be in breach of Union law.[46] Consequently, the principle of legal certainty is confined to the parties and proceedings in which the final judgment was delivered, while the principle of primacy prevents the final judgment from expanding its effects to other proceedings within the Member State. This reasoning was later reinforced, in the context of consumer protection and Directive 93/13,[47] in the cases of *Ibercaja*, *Unicaja*, *SPV Project*, *Impuls Leasing România*,[48] and *Profi Credit Polska*.[49]

The most significant exception from the principle of legal certainty is found in cases where the final judgment is issued by a national court lacking the requisite standards of independence. In such cases, the Court of Justice has stated that the final judgment does not originate from a body that constitutes a 'court' within the meaning of Union law, and as a result, it can be subject to judicial review and ultimately set aside or annulled if its content breaches Union law. As the Court of Justice has stated:

> [I]f the referring court considers that such an order was made by a body that does not constitute an independent and impartial tribunal previously established by law, within the meaning of EU law, no consideration relating to the principle of legal certainty or the alleged finality of a decision can, in the present case, be successfully relied on in order to prevent a [national court], from declaring such an order to be null and void.[50]

5. Primacy over Collective Bargaining Agreements

Social partners in the Member States may agree, through collective bargaining agreements, on the terms and conditions governing employment contracts in a given occupational sector. In most national legal systems, collective bargaining enjoys constitutional protection, and the results of negotiations, typically reflected in collective bargaining agreements, play a relevant

[44] Case C-119/05 *Lucchini* EU:C:2007:434.

[45] Case C-507/08 *Commission v Slovakia* EU:C:2010:802; and Case C-505/14 *Klausner* EU:C:2015:742.

[46] Joined Cases C-370/17 and C-37/18 *Vueling Airlines and Others* EU:C:2020:260, paras 95–96.

[47] Council Directive 93/13/EEC of 5 April 1993 on unfair terms in consumer contracts [1993] OJ L95/29.

[48] Case C-600/19 *Ibercaja Banco* EU:C:2022:394; Joined Cases C-693/19 and C-831/19 *SPV Project 1503* EU:C:2022:395; Case C-725/19 *Impuls Leasing România* EU:C:2022:396 and Case C-869/19 *Unicaja Banco* EU:C:2022:397.

[49] Case C-582/21 *Profi Credit Polska* EU:C:2024:282.

[50] Case C-487/19 *WŻ* EU:C:2021:798, para 160.

legal role in industrial relations and labour law more broadly. The case law of the Court of Justice has confirmed that collective bargaining agreements can come into conflict with Union law, in which case they must comply with Union law and, if a conflict arises, be subject to the normative dimension of primacy.[51] However, collective bargaining agreements are legal instruments agreed between employers (or employers' associations) and trade unions representing employees, and are not the result of actions taken by public authorities. Consequently, the limitations on the horizontal effect of Union law governing private acts, as described in section II.3 of this chapter, also apply to collective bargaining agreements.

6. Primacy over International Agreements Signed by the Member States with Third Countries Prior to 1958 or Prior to Accession to the Union

Article 351, first paragraph TFEU provides that:

> [T]he rights and obligations arising from agreements concluded before 1 January 1958 or, for acceding States, before the date of their accession, between one or more Member States on the one hand, and one or more third countries on the other, shall not be affected by the provisions of the Treaties.

This provision reflects the Member States' intent to balance their obligation to comply with Union law and, at the same time, to ensure compliance with their prior international obligations stemming from previous international commitments until accession. The wording of Article 351, first paragraph TFEU states that those previous international commitments 'shall not be affected' by Union law, a mandate that seeks to protect the principle of *pacta sunt servanda*, to which the Member States are bound under international law.

Nevertheless, Article 351, second paragraph TFEU qualifies the first paragraph. After having stated that Union law does not affect the prior international commitments of the Member States, it adds that 'to the extent that such agreements are not compatible with the Treaties, the Member State or States concerned shall take all appropriate steps to eliminate the incompatibilities established'. To further strengthen this obligation, the provision calls on all Member States to cooperate to ensure full compliance with Union law: 'Member States shall, where necessary, assist each other to this end and shall, where appropriate, adopt a common attitude.'

Article 351, second paragraph TFEU thus provides that, in the event of incompatibility between Union law and an international agreement pre-dating 1958 or the date of accession of a Member State, the international agreement must give way to the obligations stemming from Union law, although the necessary time and arrangements will be facilitated to ensure that the renegotiation or withdrawal from the international agreement can be done in an orderly way. This flexibility enables Member States to comply with their existing international obligations while requiring them to bring their legal systems into conformity with Union law. The practical effect of this duty is to temporarily preserve the effects of those international agreements, while also allowing individuals to claim damages from Member States that prolong the transition for an unreasonable period.[52]

[51] Case C-43/75 *Defrenne* EU:C:1976:56, para 39; Case C-165/82 *Commission v United Kingdom* EU:C:1983:311, para 11; Case C-33/89 *Kowalska* EU:C:1990:265, para 12; Case C-184/89 *Nimz* EU:C:1991:50, para 11; Case C-333/97 *Lewen* EU:C:1999:512, para 26; Case C-284/02 *Sass* EU:C:2004:722, para 25; and Case C-19/02 *Hlozek* EU:C:2004:779, para 43.

[52] Case C-812/79 *Burgoa* EU:C:1980:231, para 9; Case C-216/01 *Budějovický Budvar* EU:C:2003:618, para 172; Case C-62/98 *Commission v Portugal* EU:C:2000:358, paras 29–50; Case C-205/06 *Commission v Austria* EU:C:2009:118, para 33, and Case C-249/06 *Commission v Sweden* EU:C:2009:119, para 34.

Article 351 TFEU applies solely to international agreements concluded prior to 1958 or prior to the accession of a Member State. The flexibility provided by Article 351 TFEU does not apply in cases where a breach of Union law results from a *posterior* international agreement concluded between a Member State and a third country after those dates.[53] With regard to such agreements, Article 351 TFEU is not applicable, and Union law exerts its full effects, including the normative dimension of primacy, in full.[54]

III. THE *ADJUDICATIVE* DIMENSION OF PRIMACY

In its *normative* dimension, primacy reflects the obligation for Member States to align their national legal systems with Union law. This is a general and objective obligation that can be enforced through a judicial declarative statement explicitly recognising the incompatibility of national law with Union law. The *adjudicative* dimension of primacy concerns the next stage in the conflict between national and Union rules of law: once a national rule is confirmed to be incompatible with Union law, how is this conflict resolved in practice? If a private individual seeks to invoke a right derived from a rule of Union law but is confronted by a rule of national law that is incompatible with it, what is the appropriate mechanism to give practical effect to the primacy of Union law?

The answer to these questions is found in the Court of Justice's case law addressing the *adjudicative* dimension of primacy. This dimension focuses on the specific situation of the individual and the practicalities involved in resolving a case in which Union law must supersede national law. Therefore, the adjudicative dimension of primacy is engaged only in cases where the rule of Union law applicable to the case has direct effect. For Union law to deploy its primacy in an individual case, the relevant rule of Union law must meet the requirements of clarity, precision, and unconditionality, as outlined in chapter nine. This close connection between direct effect and primacy, especially relevant when Union law is invoked against the authorities of the Member States, is now a settled matter (after decades of hesitations) following the judgments of the Court of Justice in *Popławski* and *NE v Bezirkshauptmannschaft Hartberg-Fürstenfeld*.[55]

However, as explained above, the *normative* dimension of primacy does not require a rule of Union law to have direct effect to establish the incompatibility of a rule of national law. As a result, the normative dimension of primacy is usually resolved by means of an infringement action under Articles 258 and 260 TFEU, an adversarial procedure in which the Commission or a Member State requests the Court of Justice to make a declaratory judgment finding an infringement of Union law by a Member State.[56] In contrast, the adjudicative dimension of primacy always takes place in national courts, stemming from a claim initiated by a private party in proceedings that may involve referring questions of interpretation or validity to the Court of Justice for a preliminary ruling. For this reason, the adjudicative dimension of primacy materialises when a national court is called upon to resolve a conflict between rules of Union and national law, within the context of a specific dispute between parties.

[53] Case C-435/22 PPU *HF* EU:C:2022:852, paras 117–27.

[54] Joined Cases C-364/95 and C-365/95 *T Port and others* EU:C:1998:95, paras 59 and 65.

[55] *Daniel Adam Popławski* (n 10) paras 61–62; and *NE and Bezirkshauptmannschaft Hartberg-Fürstenfeld* (n 13) para 37.

[56] Case C-167/03 *Commission v France* EU:C:2004:35, para 15. See also Case C-422/92 *Commission v Germany* EU:C:1995:125, para 16, where the Court of Justice ruled that the Commission must show an 'interest' in an infringement procedure. It is sufficient for the Commission to establish an infringement by a Member State for a procedure under Art 258 TFEU to be brought against a Member State.

1. The Duty to Set Aside: *Simmenthal* and *Fratelli Costanzo*

Following the ruling in *Costa v Enel*, it took 14 years for the Court of Justice to address the practical implications of a conflict between Union and national law. In 1978, the Court of Justice was called to adjudicate on this matter in *Simmenthal*,[57] a reference for a preliminary ruling in which an Italian court of first instance, the *Pretore di Susa*, found a breach of Union law (Community law at the time) resulting from a national rule enacted *after* the adoption of a regulation. The Court of Justice confirmed the Italian court's suspicions as to the legality of the Italian rule with Community law, but the rule was enacted as a parliamentary legislative act, a type of rule that Italian courts are not authorised to annul. The power to annul a legislative act in Italy was, as it is now, reserved solely to the Constitutional Court. Consequently, the Italian court of first instance was obliged to refer the matter to the Constitutional Court so that the Italian legislative act could be annulled and effectively removed from the Italian legal system.

The questions raised in *Simmenthal* can be reduced to the following two issues, which were also present in *Costa v Enel*: a conflict between a subsequent rule of Italian law and a rule of Union law, and the duty (provided by the Italian Constitution) of Italian courts to refer questions of constitutionality to the Constitutional Court when the case concerns a legislative act. It is not surprising that these questions emerged in Italy, a country with dualist features in its approach to the incorporation of international law, and with a centralised system of constitutional judicial review in which the Constitutional Court holds exclusive jurisdiction over the annulment of legislation. An orthodox solution to the conflict of rules in the *Simmenthal* case would result in the international responsibility of the Italian Republic vis-a-vis the other Member States and, in the concrete case, would require referring the matter from the first-instance court to the Constitutional Court, so that the latter ruled on the constitutionality of the Italian legislative act in dispute. It is doubtful, to say the least, how effective and practical such a course of action would have been for the applicant party in the proceedings before the *Pretore di Susa*.

The Court of Justice had already addressed some of the questions raised by the *Pretore di Susa* 14 years earlier in *Costa v Enel*. Consequently, the Court of Justice reaffirmed its previous ruling, stating that the primacy of Union law 'not only ... render[s] automatically inapplicable any conflicting provision of current national law but . . . also preclude[s] the valid adoption of new national legislative measures to the extent to which they would be incompatible with [Union] provisions'.[58]

Despite the clear resonance of its earlier ruling in *Costa v Enel*, there is a notable innovation in the judgment in *Simmenthal* that appears in the reference to the effect of rendering national law 'automatically inapplicable'. In accordance with *Costa v Enel*, such an effect is deployed vis-a-vis *prior* national law as well as *posterior* national law. Based on this feature, the Court of Justice determined that any prior or subsequent incompatible national law that is in breach of Union law cannot be applied in a concrete case. Put simply, national law must be set aside to guarantee the effectiveness of Union law.

The reference to the inapplicability of national law would eventually have significant effects on the development of Union law. In practical terms, it meant that national courts assumed a new power conferred directly by Union law: the ability to set aside rules of national law, whether enacted before or after a rule of Union law, in order to ensure the effective application of Union law in resolving disputes. The Court of Justice described this duty as follows:

[57] Case C-106/77 *Simmenthal* EU:C:1978:49.
[58] *Simmenthal* (n 57) para 17.

> [E]very national court must, in a case within its jurisdiction, apply [Union] law in its entirety and protect rights which the latter confers on individuals and must accordingly set aside any provision of national law which may conflict with it, whether prior or subsequent to the [Union] rule.[59]

This statement marks the beginning of the adjudicative dimension of primacy, through which any national court ruling on a case governed by Union law is required to set aside a conflicting national law, regardless of its rank and date of enactment. Moreover, the ruling in *Simmenthal* is articulated as a duty imposed on the national court, expressed in the imperative ('*must accordingly set aside*') that leaves no discretion in the matter. It is also irrelevant that, under Italian law, the only court with the constitutional authority to annul a parliamentary statute is the Constitutional Court. In the view of the Court of Justice,

> any provision of a national legal system and any legislative, administrative or judicial practice which might impair the effectiveness of [Union] law by withholding from the national court having jurisdiction to apply such law the power to do everything necessary at the moment of its application to set aside national legislative provisions which might prevent [Union] rules from having full force and effect are incompatible with those requirements which are the very essence of [Union] law.[60]

It is difficult to overstate the importance of the judgment in *Simmenthal* and its impact on national legal systems. This ruling introduces a decentralised system of judicial review of national law, regardless of the existing model of judicial review in each Member State. This is no mere technicality, but a significant development in a continent where, after World War II, centralised systems of judicial review of legislation were established in most countries, typically reserved for constitutional courts. The rule in such systems is that, when faced with an allegedly unconstitutional parliamentary statute, national courts must refer the question to the Constitutional Court. This approach to judicial review is referred to as a 'centralised system of constitutional review', a model that can be at odds with Union law when resolving a dispute involving a conflict between a rule of Union law and a national parliamentary statute. Following the judgment in *Simmenthal*, all national courts are under a duty, on their own authority, to set aside any rule of national law and to immediately resolve the dispute before them. By requiring national courts to set aside any rule of national law, including those which are subject to the exclusive jurisdiction of constitutional courts, the Court of Justice introduced the reverse model of judicial review: a decentralised system of review of the conformity with Union law of all the rules within the national legal system, regardless of their rank and time of enactment.[61]

The scope of the *Simmenthal* doctrine is nevertheless confined to an individual case, and therefore the setting aside of a national rule will only affect the specific dispute in question. Union law does not predetermine how the national legal system must proceed to repeal and remove the incompatible national rule. The adjudicative dimension of primacy requires the national court to rule on the matter by setting aside the incompatible national rule in a concrete dispute between the parties, but the manner in which the rule will be removed from the national legal system is a matter for national law to determine.

In exceptional circumstances, the Court of Justice has imposed a duty of annulment of a national act as a result of the principle of primacy of Union law. To date, this is the case of judicial decisions rendered by courts that do not fulfil the basic standards of judicial independence, in breach of Article 19(1) TEU. This precedent was set in *W.Ż.*,[62] in which the Court of Justice specified the obligations on the part of a national court or tribunal which has referred a question

[59] ibid, para 21.
[60] ibid, para 22.
[61] V Ferreres Comella, *Constitutional Courts and Democratic Values* (Yale University Press, 2009) 125ff.
[62] Case C-487/19 *W.Ż.* EU:C:2021:798.

for a preliminary ruling, in circumstances where that national court concludes that it is apparent from all the conditions and circumstances surrounding the process of appointing a national judge that: (i) that appointment took place in clear breach of fundamental rules which form an integral part of the establishment and functioning of the judicial system concerned; and (ii) the integrity of the outcome of that procedure is undermined, giving rise to reasonable doubt in the minds of individuals as to the independence and impartiality of the judge concerned. In that case,

> it follows from the requirements laid down in the second subparagraph of Article 19(1) TEU and from the principle of primacy of Union law that that national court or tribunal must find the decision at issue delivered by that judge to be null and void, where such a consequence is essential in view of the procedural situation at issue in order to ensure the primacy of EU law, without any provision of national law being able to preclude this.[63]

The ruling in *Simmenthal* and the subsequent case law of the Court of Justice were significant developments for the effectiveness of Union law, empowering national courts to set aside any rule of national law, provided that the prevailing rule of Union law has direct effect. The next development in the case law occurred in 1989 in *Costanzo*,[64] when the Court of Justice expanded the duty to set aside to national administrative authorities. In a laconic ruling, the judgment stated that it would be

> contradictory to rule that an individual may rely upon the provisions of a directive which fulfil the conditions defined above in proceedings before the national courts seeking an order against the administrative authorities, and yet to hold that those authorities are under no obligation to apply the provisions of the directive and refrain from applying provisions of national law which conflict with them.[65]

As a result, the Court of Justice stated that in situations where an individual can rely on the direct effect of Union law, 'all organs of the administration, including decentralized authorities such as municipalities, are obliged to apply those provisions'.[66]

The *Costanzo* doctrine has gradually consolidated over time, and now represents another major feature of the adjudicative dimension of primacy.[67] Extending the duty to set aside national law to all administrative authorities marks a major development, although not without practical problems, given the notable differences between the tasks and powers of courts and those of administrative authorities.[68] Firstly, administrative authorities lack the power to refer questions for a preliminary ruling to the Court of Justice, a power that enables national courts to set aside national law with greater confidence if the Court of Justice confirms their doubts.[69] Secondly, administrative authorities are bound by the principle of legality; this mandate does not apply in the same terms to independent courts, which are not tasked with enforcing policy options following ministerial instructions, but with impartially resolving disputes

[63] ibid, paras 154, 155 and 161, and Case C-448/23 *Commission v Poland* EU:C:2025:975, para 120.

[64] Case C-103/88 *Costanzo* EU:C:1989:256.

[65] ibid, para 31.

[66] ibid.

[67] Case C-243/09 *Fuß* EU:C:2010:609, para 63; Case C-224/97 *Ciola* EU:C:1999:212, para 30; Case C-6/05 *Medipac-Kazantzidis* EU:C:2007:337, para 43; Case C-341/08 *Petersen* EU:C:2010:4, para 80; Joined Cases C-924/19 PPU and C-925/19 PPU *FMS* EU:C:2020:367, para 183; Case C-102/21 *Autonome Provinz Bozen* EU:C:2022:272, para 46; and Case C-348/22 *Autorità Garante della Concorrenza e del Mercato* EU:C:2023:301, paras 77–79.

[68] M Verhoeven, *The Obligations of National Administrative Authorities in the Case of Incompatibility between National Law and European Law* (Intersentia, 2011), as well as the critical assessments of AG Ruiz-Jarabo Colomer in Case C-205/08 *Umweltanwalt von Kärnten* EU:C:2009:397, Opinion of AG Ruiz-Jarabo Colomer, pts 51–52.

[69] The Court of Justice ruled on this feature of administrative authorities in the *Banco Santander* case, finding that the Spanish Central Economic-Administrative Tribunal, which was declared not to be a 'court or tribunal' within the meaning of Art 267 TFEU, could set aside legislative acts, despite not having jurisdiction to refer a case to the Court of Justice. See Case C-274/14 *Banco Santander* EU:C:2020:17, para 78.

between parties. With the exception of independent administrative authorities, the primary role of administrative bodies is to enact or apply rules to implement a policy programme under governmental leadership. In contrast, courts select the applicable rule and determine its correct interpretation to resolve a dispute in full independence. However, these differences have not changed the Court of Justice's view on the matter. To date, every administrative authority has the duty to set aside any rule of national law that comes into conflict with rules of Union law having direct effect.[70]

2. The Duty to Repeal: *Commission v France*

The rulings in *Simmenthal* and *Costanzo* confirmed the duty of national and administrative authorities to set aside any national rule contrary to Union law, but they remained silent on how to effectively remove such a rule from the national legal system. This self-restraint on the part of the Court of Justice reflects the need to safeguard the institutional autonomy of the Member States, leaving each country to determine how the incompatible national rule should be definitively removed from its legal system. The *Simmenthal* and *Costanzo* case law provides individuals with a sufficiently robust framework for resolving their specific disputes, enabling national courts to set aside any rule of national law. However, this power does not authorise the national court or the administrative authority to declare the unlawful national rule null and void with *erga omnes* effects. That outcome will only occur if the national legal system grants courts and the administration such power. It is for the Member State to determine, in accordance with its constitutional requirements, the authority and procedures for repealing the incompatible rule of national law.

However, Member States are not entirely free to decide how to proceed once a rule of national law has been found to be in breach of Union law. In *Commission v France*,[71] the Court of Justice held that Member States are under a duty to remove from the national legal system any national rule once a violation has been established. This ruling is of crucial importance, and brings the *Simmenthal* and *Costanzo* doctrine full circle, preventing Member States from maintaining in their legal systems a rule known to breach Union law, particularly when the rule has been set aside in the practice of national courts and/or administrative authorities. The judgment in *Commission v France* reaches this conclusion by relying on the principle of legal certainty, emphasising that the maintenance of an unlawful national rule 'gives rise to an ambiguous state of affairs by maintaining, as regards those subject to the law who are concerned, a state of uncertainty as to the possibilities available to them of relying on [Union] law'.[72]

To summarise: a finding declaring that a rule of national law breaches Union law produces two immediate effects: first, in the specific dispute that leads to the ruling, the national court or administrative authority responsible for resolving the case has a duty to set aside the incompatible national rule; second, and more generally, the Member State concerned is under a duty to repeal the incompatible national rule in accordance with the procedures provided under its constitutional arrangements. If the national court or administrative authority has the power to

[70] In some cases, depending on the internal institutional arrangements of the Member State, doubts may arise as to *which* branch of power must repeal the incompatible rule of national law: the executive or the judiciary. On this issue, see Case C-384/17 *Dooel Uvoz-Izvoz Skopje Link Logistik N&N* EU:C:2018:494, Opinion of AG Bobek, pts 104–12.

[71] Case C-167/73 *Commission v France* EU:C:1974:35, followed and reiterated later in various rulings in, inter alia, Case C-358/98 *Commission v Italy* EU:C:2000:568, paras 16–17; Case C-160/99 *Commission v France* EU:C:2000:410, para 22; and Case C-522/04 *Commission v Belgium* EU:C:2007:405, para 70.

[72] ibid, para 41.

annul as provided by national law, it is their duty not only to set aside the conflicting national rule but also to exercise such powers and proceed with the annulment. This is the case, for example, of the powers of annulment that administrative courts have in several Member States, which allow them to rule on a dispute and, if they find an unlawful provision in an administrative regulation, proceed to annul it. When the Member State has granted such powers to national courts, it is their duty to make use of them also in the case of a breach of Union law.

3. The Scope of Both Mandates

The rulings in the cases of *Simmenthal*, *Costanzo*, and *Commission v France* have developed over the years to encompass a wide range of situations where the duty to set aside rules of national law interacts with the principles of effectiveness and institutional autonomy. Member States have been very imaginative in finding ways to, voluntarily or involuntarily, limit or obstruct the implementation of Union law. These measures have also affected the duties to set aside or repeal rules of national law, thereby limiting the effectiveness of the *Simmenthal*, *Costanzo*, and *Commission v France* doctrines. It is no coincidence that the Court of Justice has repeatedly stated that:

> [A]ny provision of a national legal system and any legislative, administrative or judicial practice which might impair the effectiveness of [Union] law by withholding from the national court having jurisdiction to apply such law the power to do everything necessary at the moment of its application to set aside national legislative provisions which might prevent [Union] rules from having full force and effect are incompatible with those requirements which are the very essence of [Union] law.[73]

Despite this clear mandate, there is plenty of evidence of the inclination of Member States to restrict the powers of national courts and administrative authorities when setting aside or annulling rules and acts of national law. Evidence of these practices can be seen in the extensive case law of the Court of Justice described below.

3.1. No Duty to Create National Remedies for Reviewing of National Parliamentary Laws: Unibet

In *Unibet*,[74] the Court of Justice was invited by the Swedish Supreme Court to rule on whether Union law requires Member States to provide declaratory remedies enabling national courts to rule on the lawfulness of national legislative acts in the abstract. In this case, Unibet had entered into publicity contracts with several Swedish media outlets to promote its gambling services. The Swedish authorities ordered the media to withdraw the campaign, as required by Swedish gambling laws. No administrative or criminal proceedings were initiated against Unibet, but the company filed a lawsuit against the Swedish state, seeking a declaration that, under Union law, it had the right to promote its gaming and betting services in Sweden, which was unlawfully restricted by Swedish legislation. The national court rejected Unibet's claim on the basis that Swedish law does not provide a procedural remedy for courts to make an abstract declaration of the unlawfulness of legislative acts. Therefore, Unibet had either to appeal against an act of the public authorities implementing the legislative acts (which were never directed at Unibet), or bring an action for damages against the Swedish authorities. After several unsuccessful appeals, the Swedish Supreme Court referred the case to the Court

[73] *Simmenthal* (n 57) para 22.
[74] Case C-432/05 *Unibet* EU:C:2007:163.

of Justice, asking, among other questions, whether the absence of an independent declaratory remedy for reviewing legislative acts was compatible with Union law.

The Court of Justice concurred with the Swedish courts, ruling that Union law does not require the Member State to create specific declaratory actions to rule on the conformity of legislative acts with Union law. The judgment of the Court of Justice stated that the remedies already available to Unibet (an action against the implementing acts or a damages claim) 'would enable Unibet to obtain a judicial decision that those provisions are incompatible with [Union] law, [and thus] constitute a legal remedy securing effective judicial protection of its rights under [Union] law'.[75]

However, the judgment in *Unibet* introduces an important nuance: the national procedural framework is in conformity with Union law only as long as the available remedies do not require the individual to expose themselves to administrative or criminal penalties as the sole means of challenging national legislation. In other words, if a Member State provides for an action for damages where the validity of national legislative acts can be disputed, and, additionally, national authorities can prosecute and impose penalties on the individual, the Court of Justice considers that the Member State provides sufficient remedies to ensure effective legal protection. However, if the only available remedy is limited to the judicial review of the penalties, in the context of which the national legislative act can be indirectly reviewed, such a model does not conform with Union law. As the Court of Justice noted in paragraph 64 of the judgment in Unibet:

> If [Unibet] was forced to be subject to administrative or criminal proceedings and to any penalties that may result *as the sole form of legal remedy for disputing the compatibility of the national provision at issue with [Union] law*, that would not be sufficient to secure for it such effective judicial protection (emphasis added).[76]

3.2. *Temporal Limitation of the Annulment of an Act of National Law in Breach of Union Law: Petrotel*

As mentioned above, if the national court has jurisdiction to annul an administrative act or regulation found to be unlawful, the same powers must apply when the dispute concerns a violation of a rule of Union law. Doubts arise when the national framework imposes restrictions on the national court's powers of annulment, and also in cases where there are limitations on the retroactive effect of the annulment of an administrative act.

In *Petrotel*, a Polish court found itself unable to retroactively annul an administrative act because national law only permitted such a retroactive effect when the measure had not been suspended following an appeal. The dispute concerned the conformity of the challenged administrative act with a Union directive, so the Polish court referred the matter to the Court of Justice. In its ruling, the Court of Justice held that, in the interest of effective judicial protection,

> a national court hearing an appeal against a decision of the [national authorities] must be able to annul the decision with retroactive effect if it finds that to be necessary in order to provide effective protection for the rights of the undertaking which has brought the appeal.[77]

[75] ibid, para 61.

[76] ibid, para 64.

[77] Case C-231/15 *Petrotel* EU:C:2016:769, para 25. See also Case C-231/15 *Petrotel* EU:C:2016:440, Opinion of AG Campos Sánchez-Bordona, advocating a similar solution, but argued from a different angle. The Advocate General advocated for a principle of deference in favour of the procedural autonomy of the Member States, with the only exception, subject to very specific conditions, of retroactive annulments. Some years later, the Court of Justice further refined the scope of the ruling in *Petrotel* in Case C-764/23 *Cairo Network* EU:C:2025:691, paras 64–86, stating that the absence of a remedy of annulment can be replaced by financial compensation in damages, and still be compatible with the right to an effective legal remedy and the principle of effectiveness.

3.3. *Setting Aside National Law through Interim Relief: Factortame*

The judgment in *Simmenthal* did not address whether the adjudicative dimension of primacy also applies to interim relief in national proceedings. This issue was addressed in *Factortame*,[78] a case arising in British courts questioning whether Union law empowered national courts to set aside, on a provisional basis, a parliamentary statute through interim relief. The Court of Justice responded affirmatively, stating that:

> [T]he full effectiveness of [Union] law would be just as much impaired if a rule of national law could prevent a court seised of a dispute governed by [Union] law from granting interim relief in order to ensure the full effectiveness of the judgment to be given on the existence of the rights claimed under [Union] law. It follows that a court which in those circumstances would grant interim relief, if it were not for a rule of national law, is obliged to set aside that rule.[79]

In *Factortame*, the Court of Justice addressed a very specific situation in which national law precluded the setting aside of acts of Parliament. The Court of Justice held that Union law required the national courts to set aside such a prohibition, thereby enabling British courts to grant interim relief suspending the application of acts of Parliament. Furthermore, the same outcome should apply in cases where national law remains silent on the interim powers of the national courts. In such instances, the absence of a specific rule does not preclude national courts from setting aside, by way of interim measures, any act of national law, including acts of Parliament.

3.4. *Priority between a Preliminary Reference and a Question of Unconstitutionality: Melki/Mecanarte*

There may be situations in which a rule of national law breaches both Union law *and* the national constitution. In such cases, questions will arise as to which analysis must be carried out first: a review in light of Union law or in light of the constitution. This dilemma also has important procedural implications, as each type of review can be subject to different remedies in various Member States: the preliminary reference procedure in the case of Union law and the question of unconstitutionality in the case of domestic law. Which procedure should the national court use in the first place, and how do these remedies interact with each other?

The Court of Justice was confronted with this dilemma in 1991 in *Mecanarte*,[80] when a Portuguese court sought guidance on the use of the preliminary reference procedure in a case that also raised doubts about the constitutionality of the challenged national measure. The Court of Justice replied in categorical terms, stating that:

> [T]he effectiveness of [Union] law would be in jeopardy if the existence of an obligation to refer a matter to a constitutional court could prevent a national court hearing a case governed by [Union] law from exercising the right conferred on it by Article [267 TFEU] to refer to the Court of Justice questions concerning the interpretation or validity of [Union] law in order to enable it to decide whether or not a provision of domestic law was compatible with [Union] law.[81]

Years later, the issue arose again in a more sensitive context: in 2008, France introduced a constitutional reform that gave the Constitutional Council the authority to hear 'priority questions of constitutionality' from the French higher courts on the compatibility of legislative acts

[78] Case C-213/89 *Factortame and others* EU:C:1990:257.
[79] ibid, para 21.
[80] Case C-348/89 *Mecanarte* EU:C:1991:278.
[81] ibid, para 45.

with the fundamental rights enshrined in the constitution.[82] The reform was initially conceived to prevent the French higher courts from making a preliminary reference to the Court of Justice for a preliminary ruling before the Constitutional Council had issued its decision. The French *Cour de cassation* considered that this framework jeopardised the effectiveness of the preliminary ruling procedure and referred the matter to the Court of Justice in the case of *Melki and Abdeli*.[83]

The Court of Justice held that the French regime was compatible with Union law, provided it met several conditions. A national rule prioritising a question of unconstitutionality referred to the Constitutional Court is compatible with Union law, as long as the national courts remain free: (1) to refer to the Court of Justice for a preliminary ruling at any stage of the proceedings they deem appropriate, even at the end of the interlocutory procedure for the review of constitutionality, to raise any questions they find necessary; (2) to adopt any measures necessary to ensure provisional judicial protection of the rights conferred under the Union legal order; and (3) to disapply, at the end of such an interlocutory procedure, the national legislative provision in question if they consider it to be contrary to Union law.[84]

In addition, the Court of Justice introduced an important qualification: when the national measure under examination results from the transposition of the 'mandatory provisions' of a directive, the question of whether the directive is valid 'takes priority'.[85] In the specific case of national measures transposing directives, the Court of Justice reverses the priority, giving preference to the preliminary reference of validity, on the grounds that reviewing the national measure is essentially an indirect review of the validity of a directive, a matter that is subject to the exclusive jurisdiction of the Court of Justice. Consequently, a national rule that requires a national court to prioritise a question of unconstitutionality over a preliminary ruling in cases where the validity of a directive is at stake has the effect of undermining the exclusive jurisdiction of the Court of Justice.[86]

3.5. *The Duty to Set Aside Following a Ruling by a National Court Limiting its Effects in Time: Filipiak and Winner Wetten*

Another problem associated with the adjudicative dimension of primacy arises when a constitutional court declares a national legislative act unconstitutional and, at the same time, limits the effects of its ruling by deferring the date on which the unconstitutional provision ceases to have effect. If the breach identified by the Constitutional Court also constitutes a violation of Union law, what is the status of the contested law during the period in which the declaration of unconstitutionality is temporarily deferred? During this interval, the unconstitutional law remains in force and fully applicable, a situation that raises doubts about whether such applicability extends to cases in which a violation of Union law has also been established.

The Court of Justice clarified this issue in *Filipiak*,[87] stating that a ruling by a constitutional court that temporarily upholds the validity of a legislative act previously declared unconstitutional does not preclude a court of that Member State, by virtue of the primacy of Union law,

[82] Constitutional Law No 2008-724 of 23 July 2008 on the modernisation of the institutions of the Fifth Republic (JORF of 24 July 2008, 11890).

[83] Joined Cases C-188/10 and C-189/10 *Melki and Abdeli* EU:C:2010:363.

[84] ibid, para 57.

[85] ibid, para 56.

[86] The issue of priority in the referral of questions to the Court of Justice or to the constitutional court was raised again in Belgium (Case C-457/09 *Chartry* EU:C:2011:101), Austria (Case C-112/13 *A and B* EU:C:2014:2195), and Bulgaria (Case C-56/25 *Petlichev* EU:C:2026:87), with the same outcome as the one decided in *Melki and Abdeli*.

[87] Case C-314/08 *Filipiak* EU:C:2009:719.

from setting it aside if it also breaches Union law.[88] Shortly after, in *Winner Wetten*,[89] the Court of Justice added nuance to its position, stating that, in some instances, Union law does not preclude a national rule that breaches Union law from remaining temporarily in force in order to preserve the principle of legal certainty.[90] However, it also clarified that, as a general rule, it is solely for the Court of Justice to determine such an outcome, not for the national court to reach such a conclusion on its own.[91] Therefore, when a national court considers it necessary to maintain the effects of a provision found to be in breach of Union law for a transitional period, it must refer the matter to the Court of Justice by way of a preliminary reference.[92]

3.6. *The Preliminary Reference Procedure and the Duty to Set Aside National Law: Kücükdeveci*

National courts have expressed doubts as to whether they are required to refer a matter to the Court of Justice before setting aside a national law that breaches Union law. The judgment in *Simmenthal* only required courts to set aside a national rule when they found it incompatible with Union law, but it remained silent about the interaction between such a duty and the use of the preliminary reference procedure. This doubt arose in Member States in which national judges have a duty to refer matters of constitutionality to their Constitutional Court through a similar preliminary remedy: the question of unconstitutionality. Although the Court of Justice, in its ruling in *Simmenthal*, had already stated that these national remedies could not prevent a national court from setting aside a rule of law that breaches Union law, the question remained as to whether they should refer the matter to the Court of Justice before resolving the dispute.

In *Kücükdeveci*,[93] the Court of Justice confirmed that a national court is *not* obliged to make a reference for a preliminary ruling before setting aside a national law that is contrary to Union law. In the words of the Court of Justice:

The possibility thus given to the national court by the second paragraph of Article 267 TFEU of asking the Court for a preliminary ruling before disapplying the national provision that is contrary to European Union law cannot, however, be transformed into an obligation because national law does not allow that court to disapply a provision it considers to be contrary to the constitution unless the provision has first been declared unconstitutional by the Constitutional Court.[94]

[88] See also Case C-741/22 *Casino de Spa SA e.a.* EU:C:2024:732, paras 60–62; and Case C-73/23 *Chaudfontaine Loisirs SA* EU:C:2024:734, paras 62–64.

[89] Case C-409/06 *Winner Wetten* EU:C:2010:503.

[90] This was so in Case C-43/75 *Defrenne II* EU:C:1976:56, paras 69–75, which extends the power of the Court of Justice to limit the effects of its judgments, as provided for actions for annulment in Art 264, second para TFEU, also to the preliminary reference procedure.

[91] In the same vein, see Case C-439/19 *B v Latvijas Republikas Saeima* EU:C:2021:504, para 135.

[92] Case C-41/11 *Inter-Environnement Wallonie and Terre wallonne* EU:C:2012:103, where the Court of Justice accepted that a national supreme court could limit the temporal effects of a judgment implementing Union law, as long as the limitation is aimed at protecting an objective protected by the Treaties, as in the case of environmental protection. However, the Court of Justice takes a more stringent position when it considers, from the information available in the file, that the circumstances are not met. See, for example, Case C-407/21 *Union fédérale des consommateurs – Que choisir (UFC – Que choisir)* EU:C:2023:449, paras 78–85. See also S Verstraelen, 'The Temporal Limitation of Judicial Decisions: The Need for Flexibility Versus the Quest for Uniformity' (2013) 14 *German Law Journal* 561.

[93] Case C-555/07 *Kücükdeveci* EU:C:2010:21, para 54.

[94] However, Member States, in accordance with their internal law, can impose a duty on their courts to make references for a preliminary ruling in specific cases of constitutional relevance. The infringement of this duty will only have effects in national law and it will not always amount to a breach of Art 267 TFEU. Constitutional obligations of this kind can be found in the case law of the German Federal Constitutional Court and the Spanish Constitutional Court. This constitutional and national obligation to refer a question for a preliminary ruling will be developed in more detail in ch 12 of this book.

3.7. *Temporary Redress and the Setting Aside of National Law in the Case of Discriminatory Treatment: Nimz*

The adjudicative dimension of primacy also appears in cases of litigation in the field of equality. The Court of Justice has ruled that national courts finding a breach of the principle of equality in Union law are under a duty to extend the more favourable treatment to the disadvantaged group, as long as the Member State has not taken the appropriate measures to remedy the discrimination. Consequently, if a national court determines that the Member State has breached the principle of equality, as outlined in the Treaties or secondary legislation, the case must be resolved by granting the victim the same treatment as those who enjoyed the most favourable position.

This duty to resolve the effects of a discriminatory national rule in the most favourable terms for the victim arose in the case of *Federatie Nederlandse Vakbeweging* and was later confirmed in *Nimz*.[95] This line of case law introduces a derogation from the *Simmenthal* doctrine, which does not impose on the national court a specific solution to the case, only the setting aside of the unlawful national rule. In contrast, *Nimz* imposes not only the duty to set aside the national rule but also a specific outcome, at least until a new national rule is introduced replacing the previous discriminatory rule.[96]

IV. PRIMACY AND THE COMMON FOREIGN AND SECURITY POLICY

As previously explained, the primacy of Union law is closely connected to the applicability and direct effect of Union rules. If a rule of Union law has direct effect, it can assert its primacy over national law, particularly in its adjudicative dimension.

This combination of primacy and direct effect is severely curtailed when it comes to the Union's actions in the field of the Common Foreign and Security Policy (CFSP). As explained in chapter nine, the applicability of CFSP acts remains an open question, but based on the current state of the case law, it can be argued that CFSP measures 'providing for restrictive measures against natural or legal persons adopted by the Council on the basis of Chapter 2 of Title V TEU' (Article 275), doing so on an individualised basis, have primacy over national law, as they are subject to review before Union courts. Consequently, they are governed by a framework of judicial review equivalent to that applied to other Union rules. In principle, this also applies to CFSP acts that do not involve 'political or strategic choices' reflecting core policy decisions, if they are sufficiently clear, precise and unconditional.[97]

Regarding CFSP acts other than the measures mentioned above, the question of their primacy is less clear. Article 275, first paragraph, TFEU precludes Union courts from reviewing CFSP acts, with the only exceptions mentioned above. In the absence of a judicial route to resolve conflicts between national rules and CFSP acts, the same derogation should apply to the power of national courts to set aside national rules that are not in conformity with CFSP acts.

To summarise, CFSP acts operate at two levels of applicability and primacy: firstly, CFSP decisions that do not establish 'strategic policy options' and decisions that impose restrictive

[95] Case C-184/89 *Nimz* EU:C:1991:50, para 19.

[96] Case C-408/92 *Avdel Systems* EU:C:1994:349, paras 16–17; Case C-442/00 *Rodríguez Caballero* EU:C:2002:752, paras 42–43; Case C-81/05 *Cordero Alonso* EU:C:2006:529, paras 45–46; and Joined Cases C-128/07, C-129/07, C-130/07 and C-131/07 *Molinari* EU:C:2008:15, para 23.

[97] Joined Cases C-29/22 P and C-44/22 P *KS and KD v Council and others* EU:C:2023:901, paras 116–20.

measures against natural or legal persons in an individualised way, which are subject to judicial review in Union courts and have direct effect and primacy in the national legal systems; secondly, CFSP acts other than those concerning individualised restrictive measures or involving measures that are not 'political or strategic choices', which lack both direct effect and primacy, and are subject to the standard rules for incorporating international law in each Member State. In the latter case, CFSP acts are regarded in each national legal system as acts of international law emanating from an international organisation, with the effects that national law recognises for such measures.

V. THE RECOGNITION OF PRIMACY IN MEMBER STATES

While the principle of direct effect of Union law has been widely accepted across the Member States, the primacy of Union law has faced significant opposition, particularly from national constitutional and supreme courts. At the present time, very few Member States accept the full scope of primacy of Union law as articulated by the case law of the Court of Justice. The constitutional courts of the Member States, with varying degrees of intensity, have declined to accept both the normative and the adjudicative dimension of primacy in the terms described in the sections above. This resistance highlights the constitutional tensions inherent in Union law and questions its autonomous nature as a legal system. When the Court of Justice stated in *Van Gend en Loos* and *Costa v Enel* that Union law is an autonomous legal system stemming from its own source of authority, it asserted the independence of this legal system from national constitutional law and the constraints of national sovereignty. However, the constitutional and supreme courts of most Member States do not share this view of Union law as a fully independent and self-determined legal system embedded within the national legal order, with no connection to the ultimate source of authority of national law: the Constitution. In the eyes of constitutional courts, Union law derives its ultimate source of authority from each national constitution, which embodies the sovereign will of the people, which is none other than the nation, understood not as a European nation, but as the linguistic, historical, and cultural body politic represented by the peoples of each Member State.

According to the vision espoused by most constitutional courts, Union law is subject to limits that emerge from the constitution of each Member State. As a result, each constitutional court claims the power to review the conformity of Union law with the constitution to determine if the said limits have been complied with. Accordingly, the constitutional court of a Member State asserts jurisdiction to declare that a Union act exceeds the limits set by the constitution or violates its core provisions, with the result that the said act will not be applicable in that Member State. Several constitutional courts have explicitly made such declarations, although the practical impact of these rulings has been very limited.[98] The approach taken by each constitutional and supreme court varies, with different levels of assertiveness, as will be

[98] The most prominent example is the *PSPP* or *Weiss* judgment of the German Federal Constitutional Court, Judgment of 5 May 2020, BVerfG, 2 BvR 859/15 et al, BVerfGE 154, 17 (PSPP/Weiss). See also the similar path followed by other courts, such as the Czech Constitutional Court Pl ÚS 5/12 *Slovak Pensions XVII/Holubec*; the Danish Supreme Court Case 15/2014 *Ajos*; the Polish Constitutional Court Case K 3/21; the Romanian Constitutional Court Decision 390/2021. The courts of other Member States have established the ability to review Union law on the basis of national (constitutional) law: see the Belgian Constitutional Court in Case 62/2016; the Hungarian Constitutional Court in Case 22/16 (XII.5), the French Conseil d'État in CE Ass, 21 April 2021, Req no 393099; and the Spanish Constitutional Court in STC 26/2014. The Italian *Taricco*-Saga is a problematic development as well. See generally Ana Bobić, *The Jurisprudence of Constitutional Conflict in the European Union* (Oxford University Press, 2022).

observed in the following overview of selected case law from various national constitutional courts.

1. Germany

The German Federal Constitutional Court (GFCC) was the first national jurisdiction to openly question the primacy of Union law. The evolution of this Court over the past five decades reflects the complex role played by constitutional courts, called upon to apply and enforce the constitution, to which Union law, in the normative dimension of primacy, attributes the same legal rank and value as a ministerial decree or a local authority's ordinance. In 1974, in the case of *Internationale Handelsgesellschaft*,[99] the GFCC declared that the European integration clause in Article 24 of the German Basic Law 'aims at the transfer of sovereign rights to supranational organisations, [but it] does not open the door to a reform of the basic structures of the Constitution'. The GFCC implicitly indicated the need to reform the constitution if Union law contradicted any of its provisions. However, in the event of a conflict between the German Basic Law and Union law regarding the protection of fundamental rights, the German Constitutional Court's position was more assertive. In such instances, the GFCC affirmed that 'the guarantee of fundamental rights contained in the Constitution would prevail, as long as the institutions of the [Union] have not resolved the conflict of norms in accordance with the procedures laid down in the Treaties'.[100]

This position, clearly opposed to the normative dimension of primacy developed by the Court of Justice, had to wait until 1986 before being revisited by the GFCC. In *Wünsche*,[101] the GFCC changed the approach and shifted from the strict approach of 1974 towards a more cooperative stance, by stating that

> as long as the European Communities, and in particular the case law of the Court of Justice, generally guarantee effective protection of fundamental rights against the sovereign powers of the Communities, in terms substantially similar to the protection conferred by the Constitution, and as long as they generally safeguard the essential content of fundamental rights, the Federal Constitutional Court shall not exercise its jurisdiction in respect of the applicability of rules of [Union] law which serve as a legal basis for any acts of the German courts or authorities, nor shall it review such rules in the light of the fundamental rights provided for in the Constitution.

The GFCC's position was clear: *as long as* the Union provides a system of fundamental rights protection that is not necessarily identical but at least 'substantially similar' to the one provided in the German Basic Law, the GFCC would refrain from exercising its jurisdiction to review Union secondary law. The judgment in *Wünsche* reflects a deliberate decision by the GFCC to defer the review of Union secondary law to the Court of Justice, tacitly accepting the normative dimension of primacy established in *Costa v Enel*. This deference is made conditional on the scope and intensity of the system of fundamental rights protection embraced by the Union and the Court of Justice, which, in the GFCC's 1986 view, was substantively equivalent to Germany's constitutional framework on fundamental rights. The conditional acceptance of the primacy of Union law and the reiterated use of the expression 'as long as' (*solange* in the

[99] Judgment of 29 May 1974 (BVerfGE 37, 279).

[100] ibid, 285–286.

[101] Judgment of 22 October 1986 (BVerfG 73, 339). The full English version of the judgment is available in A Oppenheimer (ed), *The Relationship between European Community Law and National Law: The Cases* (Cambridge University Press, 1994) 461ff.

original German version) has led this line of GFCC case law to be widely known as *Solange I* and *II*, referring to the judgments of 1974 and 1986, respectively.

The tense coexistence was severely altered in 1992, as a result of the Maastricht Treaty, which introduced the status of European citizenship, expanded the use of qualified majority voting in the Council, and, most importantly, established new areas of Union competence such as monetary policy, foreign and security policy, and home affairs, all closely attached to the traditional exercise of sovereign powers by the Member States. When reviewing the constitutionality of Germany's ratification of the Maastricht Treaty,[102] the GFCC did not focus solely on the protection of fundamental rights. Instead, the analysis extended much more broadly and focused on the political and democratic implications of the Maastricht Treaty, stating from the outset that the Union lacks a European *demos* – a people – which is a crucial feature of any properly functioning democracy. The GFCC stated that the Union remained a federation of sovereign states, and these were, and will continue to be, the 'Masters of the Treaties'. Therefore, any act of the Union that exceeded the competences conferred on it by the Member States would breach the Constitution and be declared invalid (ultra vires) in Germany.

The *Maastricht* judgment was a major blow to the integration process, at least symbolically. The fact that the highest court of a founding Member State was openly questioning the idea of the Union becoming a democratic organisation, an aspiration that would only be realised by creating a 'spiritual, social and political homogeneity of the people', did not bode well for the future of European integration. The level of democratic maturity that was required of the Union in the *Maastricht* judgment appeared difficult, if not impossible, to attain even in the long term.

The fear that the *Maastricht* judgment would undermine the effectiveness of Union law in Germany did not materialise in the short term. However, further difficulties arose in 2000. In a dispute over banana imports, the GFCC was once again confronted with an alleged conflict between German and Union law regarding the protection of fundamental rights.[103] Despite the severity of the *Maastricht* judgment of 1993, the case was declared inadmissible on the grounds of the *Solange II* doctrine. It was not until 2009, when the GFCC was called to rule on the constitutionality of the Lisbon Treaty, that problems emerged again. This judgment[104] reflected a deep distrust of the integration process and the model of democracy emerging in the Union, which, in the GFCC's view, was not sufficient to justify the unconditional normative dimension of primacy in Germany.[105] It should also be noted that the democratic standard that the GFCC demanded of the Union in the *Lisbon* judgment was difficult to find within the Federal Republic of Germany itself. Furthermore, the *Lisbon* judgment enumerated the areas that are to be considered constitutionally relevant for the German polity, including social policy, citizenship, the monopoly of the use of force, taxation and fiscal policy, cultural and linguistic policy, the basic organisation of the family, and the educational system.[106] This is a very long enumeration of policy areas that reflects Germany's 'constitutional identity', highlighting the fields in which the Union must exercise particular caution, or risk having its acts declared *ultra vires* in Germany.

[102] Judgment of 12 October 1993, BVerfG 89, 155.

[103] Judgment of 7 June 2000, BVerfG 102, 147.

[104] Judgment of 30 June 2009, BVerfG 2 BvE 2/08, 2 BvE 5/08, 2 BvR 1010/08, 2 BvR 1022/08, 2 BvR 1259/08, 2 BvR 182/09 (English version available on the website of the GFCC).

[105] ibid, paras 213–25.

[106] ibid, para 249.

Only one year after the *Lisbon* judgment, the GFCC delivered an important and more pragmatic ruling in *Honeywell*,[107] where it was confronted with the case law of the Court of Justice on age discrimination in the workplace, an area that directly impacts one of the 'democratically relevant areas' mentioned in the *Lisbon* judgment. In *Honeywell*, the GFCC concluded that the Court of Justice's case law was not *ultra vires* in Germany, but reached this conclusion after having developed a detailed test based on a principle of *constitutional openness towards Union law*.[108] Furthermore, the GFCC added that the actions of the Union exceeding its competence must constitute a 'sufficiently qualified breach', that is 'of significant importance for the division of competences between the Member States and the Union'.[109] Lastly, the GFCC stated that a declaration of ultra vires would, in any case, require the matter to be referred to the Court of Justice by way of a preliminary reference.[110]

The doctrine and test laid down in *Honeywell* were applied in several cases brought by a group of German citizens and politicians who challenged the European Central Bank's (ECB) unconventional monetary policy measures during the financial crisis of 2008–2014 and its aftermath. The saga began in the case of *Gauweiler*, an action against the German Government's failure to challenge the ECB's Outright Monetary Transactions (OMT) programme, which involved the purchase of government bonds in secondary financial markets. The GFCC was sceptical about the constitutionality of the ECB's measure, but also of its conformity with Union law. Consequently, the GFCC referred the matter to the Court of Justice through a preliminary reference. The GFCC expressed serious doubts about the OMT programme's conformity with the Treaties, but also made it clear that if the Court of Justice's view did not align with that of the GFCC, it reserved the right to set aside the ruling of the Luxembourg court. The Court of Justice ruled that the OMT programme was compatible with the Treaties, while emphasising the obligation of the GFCC to comply with the ruling and Germany's obligations under Union law. Ultimately, the GFCC accepted the decision of the Court of Justice, although it reiterated its doubts about the OMT programme and the reasoning of the Court of Justice's judgment.[111]

It took only one year for the Court of Justice to receive yet another preliminary reference from the GFCC questioning the ECB's new round of unconventional monetary policy measures. In *Weiss*,[112] a referral questioning the validity of the ECB's 2015 Public Sector Purchase Programme (PSPP), the Court of Justice once again confirmed the validity of the ECB's decisions. In an unprecedented development, the GFCC responded to the *Weiss* judgment by delivering an extremely harsh ruling, declaring both the judgment of the Court of Justice and the PSPP programme ultra vires in Germany. Furthermore, the GFCC parted ways with the test previously espoused in the *Honeywell* judgment and ruled that a perceived insufficiency in the proportionality review carried out by the Court of Justice and a failure to adequately assess whether the ECB had complied with its duty to state reasons were sufficient to declare both the judgment of the Court of Justice and the ECB's actions ultra vires in Germany.

Despite the harsh tone and severe outcome of the *Weiss* ruling of the GFCC, its practical impact was quite limited. The ECB provided additional reasoning about the PSPP in the minutes of a meeting of its Governing Council. This reasoning was accepted by the GFCC as satisfying its requirements, thereby easing tensions between both courts and with financial

[107] Judgment of 6 July 2010, BVerfG 2 BvR 2661/06 (English version available on the GFCC website).

[108] ibid, para 58ff.

[109] ibid, para 61.

[110] ibid, para 66.

[111] Judgment of 21 June 2016, BVerfG 2 BvR 2728/13, 2 BvR 2729/13, 2 BvR 2730/13, 2 BvR 2731/13, 2 BvE 13/13 (English version available on the GFCC website).

[112] Case C-493/17 *Weiss and Others* EU:C:2018:1000.

markets, which had received the *Weiss* judgment with considerable composure, awaiting its real consequences, which proved to be rather insignificant. However, the precedent of an ultra vires decision coming from none other than the GFCC raised serious doubts about the constitutional foundations of the Union's legal edifice. The Court of Justice was left seriously wounded, its authority questioned by a major constitutional court, with scars that could take years to heal, and long-term consequences for the primacy of Union law.

This crisis should not overshadow other, more positive but equally important, developments in the recent case law of the GFCC, particularly in the field of fundamental rights. In two highly significant judgments delivered on 6 November 2019, the GFCC moved away from its previous approach and adopted a more constructive stance. Under the *Solange II* doctrine, the GFCC declines jurisdiction in cases where the activity of German authorities is entirely determined by Union law.[113] In the 'right to be forgotten' cases of 2019, the GFCC shifted from its position in *Solange II* and asserted jurisdiction, arguing that its review of validity would be carried out using the Charter as the constitutional benchmark, instead of the German Basic Law.[114] This development marks a significant step in integrating the Union's fundamental rights system into national legal orders, especially in one as deeply rooted in the social fabric as Germany's. By using the Charter as the benchmark of constitutional review, the GFCC decided to position itself as a domestic but strategic interpreter of Union fundamental rights law. It must be noted that, to date, no preliminary references have been submitted to the Court of Justice, despite the GFCC having ruled on numerous cases where national authorities acted in fields wholly determined by Union law. Only time will tell whether the case law emerging in 2019 is a new paradigm of constitutional cooperation between the Court of Justice and its national constitutional counterparts, or if it marks the start of a covert process of repatriation of jurisdiction in the field of fundamental rights, more focused on consolidating power for the GFCC rather than fostering an open and cooperative approach towards the integration of Union law in the national legal system.

2. France

In stark contrast to the German case, the French Republic has experienced a different evolution: what started with a robust denial of the primacy of Union law has gradually evolved into a subtle yet effective recognition of it. The first relevant decision on this matter was issued in 1968, when the administrative Supreme Court of France, the *Conseil d'État*, declared it lacked jurisdiction to rule on the compatibility between a national legislative act and Union law.[115] According to the *Conseil d'État*, only the Constitutional Council has the authority to review parliamentary acts in France; this stance remained unchanged until late 1989, when the judgment in *Nicolo* finally recognised the jurisdiction of the *Conseil d'État* to review the conformity of French legislative acts with Union law.[116] Diverging from its administrative counterpart, the civil and criminal Supreme Court, the *Cour de Cassation*, has recognised the primacy of Union law over French law, including legislative acts, since 1975.[117] It was only in 1989 that both supreme courts aligned their positions and accepted the adjudicative dimension

[113] Judgments of 6 November 2019, BVerfG 1 BvR 16/13 and 276/17 (English version available on the GFCC website).

[114] M Wendel, 'The Two-Faced Guardian: Or How One Half of the German Federal Constitutional Court Became a European Fundamental Rights Court' (2020) 57 *Common Market Law Review* 999; and P Friedl, 'A New European Fundamental Rights Court: The German Constitutional Court on the Right to Be Forgotten' (2020) 5 *European Papers* 447.

[115] Conseil d'État, Ass, 1 March 1968, Syndicat général des fabricants de semoules de France.

[116] Conseil d'État, Ass, 20 October 1989, Nicolo.

[117] Cour de cassation, Ch mixte, 24 May 1975, *Administration des Douanes v Société Cafés Jacques Vabre*.

of primacy. However, the recognition and acceptance of the normative dimension of primacy have been more complex and remain contentious to this day.

At first glance, it may seem surprising that a country with a monist tradition, such as France, would show such a degree of resistance to the effective incorporation of Union law. However, the French approach is a reaction consistent with the unique features of the legal system established by the Constitution of the Fifth Republic of 1958, which is deeply rooted in the country's constitutional history originating from the Revolution of 1789. A strict understanding of the separation of powers has shaped France into a country where laws passed by the National Assembly and the Senate, representing the will of the nation, were deemed to be unreviewable by the ordinary courts. Consequently, the only means of judicial review of parliamentary acts was through the *Conseil Constitutionnel*, founded in 1958, which was originally conceived as a body for a priori review with limited standing. The power to review acts was also limited in scope and in applicants: the *Conseil Constitutionnel* reviews parliamentary acts before they come into force, and at the request of the President of the Republic, the Prime Minister, the Presidents of the two Assemblies, or 60 Deputies or Senators. The principal exception to this system of a priori review was introduced through a constitutional amendment in 2008, when the 'priority question of constitutionality' was passed, whereby the *Conseil Constitutionnel* has the power to rule on the compatibility of legislative acts with fundamental rights upon referral from the *Conseil d'État* or the *Cour de Cassation*.

The status attributed to legislative acts and the institutional role played by the *Conseil Constitutionnel* explain the challenging process of incorporating the primacy of Union law in France. It was the structure of France's institutional framework that led the highest courts to initially deny that primacy results from the autonomous nature of Union law. According to the *Conseil d'État* and the *Cour de Cassation*, the primacy of Union law derives from Article 55 of the Constitution, a provision that states that international treaties 'shall, upon publication, prevail over Acts of Parliament'.

The difficulty in accepting the primacy of Union law over parliamentary acts also extended to the Constitution. The *Conseil Constitutionnel* clarified this point through well-established and repeated case law, which did not always align exactly with the position taken by the *Conseil d'État* or the *Cour de Cassation*.

The *Conseil Constitutionnel* also rejects the view that primacy stems from the autonomous nature of Union law. Instead of citing Article 55 of the Constitution, it bases the source of primacy on Article 88-1 of the Constitution. This is known as the 'European clause', which states that

> the Republic shall participate in the European Union constituted by States which have freely chosen to exercise some of their powers in common by virtue of the Treaty on European Union and of the Treaty on the Functioning of the European Union . . .

This provision underpins the *Conseil Constitutionnel's* interpretation of its case law regarding the conflict between, on one hand, the Constitution and primary Union law, and on the other, the Constitution and secondary Union law, which will now be examined separately.

According to the *Conseil Constitutionnel*, a conflict between the Constitution and primary Union law requires an amendment of the Constitution.[118] These conflicts should be easy to identify, since any amendment to the Treaties requires prior review by the *Conseil Constitutionnel*, which has frequently stressed the need to amend the Constitution to align it with the Union's Treaties. Constitutional amendments are not limited to cases of incompatibility with the

[118] Judgment No 92-308 DC of 9 April 1992, para 14.

Treaties, but also include situations where the Treaties may introduce 'restrictions of rights' or have an 'unfavourable effect on the conditions for the exercise of national sovereignty'.[119] In such cases, and since the *Conseil Constitutionnel's* ruling on the Maastricht Treaty, an explicit constitutional provision authorising a transfer of powers to the Union is required. This was the case for monetary policy in 1992,[120] for justice and home affairs policies in 1997[121] and 2004,[122] and again in 2007[123] concerning the participation of national parliaments in the Union's legislative procedures, as well as the *passerelle clauses* of the Treaties. Therefore, the current French Constitution contains in Title XV an extensive list of provisions explicitly granting competence to the Union in particularly sensitive policy areas where sovereign powers have been transferred to the Union.[124]

The *Conseil Constitutionnel's* case law on the compatibility between the Constitution and Union secondary law is more complex. Since 2004, the stance of the *Conseil Constitutionnel* has developed in regard to the transposition of directives, recognising that the duty to transpose is a constitutional obligation deriving from Article 88-1 of the Constitution.[125] This means that any delayed or defective transposition by the French legislature amounts to a breach of Article 88-1 of the Constitution and is therefore subject to review by the *Conseil Constitutionnel*. This approach reflects a cooperative attitude towards the enforcement of Union law in France, placing additional pressure on the French legislature to meet its obligations under Union law. The flip side of this doctrine is equally significant: parliamentary acts transposing Union directives will not be reviewed by the *Conseil Constitutionnel*; otherwise, the directive would be subject to indirect scrutiny, a task that falls exclusively to the Court of Justice.[126] A similar approach was applied in 2007 by the *Conseil d'État* in the case of *Arcelor*, but in relation to Union regulations and the implementation of Union law through administrative measures.[127]

This cooperative approach towards Union law is subject to two caveats. Firstly, the case law mentioned above does not apply to situations in which a directive is contrary to an 'explicit provision' of the Constitution that has no equivalent in Union law.[128] Therefore, in cases of clear and unequivocal incompatibility between a directive and the Constitution, it is the latter that prevails. It should be noted that the case law does not refer to the Constitution in general, but only to an 'explicit provision' of the Constitution, a situation that should only arise in exceptional circumstances, and which the *Conseil Constitutionnel* has to date avoided through constructive interpretation.[129] Secondly, another exception arises when a rule of Union law is contrary to 'a rule or principle inherent to the constitutional identity of France'.[130] In its most recent case law, the *Conseil Constitutionnel*

[119] ibid.

[120] ibid, paras 36–45.

[121] Judgment No 97-394 DC of 31 December 1997.

[122] Judgment No 2004-505 DC of 19 November 2004.

[123] Judgment No 2007-560 DC of 20 December 2007.

[124] See, inter alia, Arts 88-2, 88-6 and 88-7 of the French Constitution.

[125] Judgment No 2004-496 DC of 10 June 2004, para 7.

[126] ibid.

[127] Conseil d'État, Ass, Judgment No 287110, 8 February 2007 (Arcelor).

[128] Judgment No 2004-496 DC (n 125) para 7. The exception was confirmed a few days later in Judgment No 2004-498 DC of 29 July 2004, para 4.

[129] *Les Cahiers du Conseil constitutionnel*, Cahier no 17 (a periodical published by the Constitutional Council, including an extensive commentary on its jurisprudence), whose analysis of Judgment 2004-496 explains the exception in further detail, stating that the 'explicit provision' to which the case law refers 'must not be a jurisprudential construction, but an explicit constitutional statement, found in the *bloc de la constitutionnalité* as is the case with the definition of the electoral body contained in Article 3 of the 1958 Constitution, or the provision contained in Article 6 of the Declaration on the criteria for access to public service of Article 3 of the 1958 Constitution.

[130] The exception arose in Judgment No 2006-540 DC of 27 July 2006, para 19, followed immediately thereafter by Judgments No 2006-543 DC of 30 November 2006, and No 2008-564 DC of 19 June 2008, para 6.

has stated that it will review the conformity of Union law with France's constitutional identity only if Union law does not provide an equivalent protection to the rule or principle reflecting the constitutional identity of France. This was illustrated in the judgment in *Air France* of 2021, where the *Conseil Constitutionnel* confirmed the existence of a principle inherent to France's constitutional identity: the prohibition of the delegation of the exercise of *force publique* to private parties. In the absence of an equivalent prohibition in Union law, the *Conseil Constitutionnel* made use of the derogation in its case law and proceeded to review the constitutionality of the challenged parliamentary act (ultimately declaring its conformity with the Constitution), irrespective of the fact that it was the result of the transposition of a directive.[131]

Although the *Conseil Constitutionnel* has never fully acknowledged the normative dimension of primacy as deriving from the autonomous nature of Union law, the practical consequences of its case law have led to its tacit recognition. The interpretation of Article 88-1 of the Constitution allows the *Conseil Constitutionnel* to refrain from reviewing parliamentary laws that transpose directives, unlike many other constitutional courts in Member States, which frequently scrutinise the content of national legislative acts that implement Union law, including regulations. So far, no conflict has arisen between a rule of Union law and an 'explicit provision' of the French Constitution or 'a rule or principle inherent to the constitutional identity of France'.[132] The *Conseil Constitutionnel* has even referred questions for a preliminary ruling to the Court of Justice, as in the case of *F.*[133] This evolution confirms that, despite its unique institutional features, the *Conseil Constitutionnel* is currently well attuned to the requirements of European integration, with a rhetoric rooted in the primacy of the Constitution but a pragmatism that has broadened the normative and adjudicative dimension of the primacy of Union law into the French legal system.

3. Italy

Since 1973, following the judgment in the case of *Frontini*, the Italian *Corte Costituzionale* has been willing to recognise the primacy of Union law within the Italian legal system.[134] This and other judgments demonstrate the *Corte's* pro-European stance and its commitment to European integration, an approach that may seem surprising at first, given Italy's traditionally dualist approach.

The cooperative approach that has characterised the relations between the *Corte Costituzionale* and Union law should not obscure the existence of a subtle yet firm assertion of the national Constitution. The judgment in *Frontini* included several caveats that would align the *Corte Costituzionale* with its counterparts in other Member States. While the *Corte Costituzionale* accepted the direct applicability of Union law, it nevertheless recalled that the ultimate source of authority of Union law in the Italian legal system derives from Article 11 of the Constitution, which states that Italy 'agrees, on conditions of equality with other States, to the limitations of sovereignty that may be necessary to a world order ensuring peace and justice

[131] Judgment No 2021-940 QPC of 15 October 2021, paras 17–18.

[132] See, by way of example, the judgments of the *Conseil d'État* in the cases of 21 April 2021, *French Data Networks*, and 17 December 2021, *Gendarmerie départementale*, in which the *Conseil* threatened to undertake a full review of Union law, but failed to do so having found that an interpretation of Union law in conformity with the French Constitution was possible. See also the judgment of the *Conseil Constitutionnel* in Judgment No 2010-605 DC of 12 May 2010, delivered a few weeks before the judgment of the Court of Justice in the case of *Melki and Abdeli*, clearly aimed at avoiding a conflict between the French Constitution and Union law.

[133] Case C-168/13 PPU *Jeremy F* EU:C:2013:358.

[134] Judgment No 183, 1973.

among the Nations'.[135] Furthermore, the judgment in *Frontini* concludes with a significant statement that questions the apparent openness of Article 11 of the Constitution by asserting that, based on that provision,

> only those limitations on sovereignty which achieve the objectives set out therein can be tolerated, and it must be ruled out that the said limitations, specifically included in the Treaty of Rome . . . , do not grant the organs of [the Union] an inadmissible power enabling them to infringe the fundamental principles of our constitutional order or the inviolable rights of the individual.[136]

The judgment ends by recalling that 'if the Treaty were to receive such an aberrant interpretation, [the Constitution] guarantees that this Constitutional Court will always undertake a judicial review to ensure the compatibility of the Treaty with the aforementioned fundamental principles'.[137]

The *Frontini* judgment, despite its tone and rhetoric that sharply contrast with the approach of the German Federal Constitutional Court in *Solange I*, *Lisbon*, *and Honeywell*, introduces the possibility that the *Corte Costituzionale* might review a rule of Union law and ultimately declare it unconstitutional. The risk of such a scenario is indeed described in exceptional terms ('if the Treaty were to receive *such an aberrant interpretation*'). The exact scope of this power of review was further developed in the 1980s and 1990s, when the *Corte Costituzionale* was given the opportunity to clarify the conditions under which it would exercise review of the constitutionality of Union law.

In 1984 the *Corte Costituzionale* delivered its judgment in the seminal *Granital* case,[138] a decision that embraced the *Simmenthal* doctrine and recognised the adjudicative dimension of primacy in Italian law, while also defining the scope of the review of constitutionality of Union law. On the latter point, the *Corte Costituzionale* limited its powers of review to those Union measures that breach fundamental rights and the fundamental principles of the constitutional order. This power of review would come to be known as the *controlimiti* (counter-limits) to Union law.[139] At a later stage, in the *Fragd* case,[140] the *Corte Costituzionale* affirmed that its powers of review also extended to Union secondary legislation, although it clarified that, in cases of a breach of the Constitution, the contested measure would not be the Union law rule itself, but the national act ratifying the Treaties, on the basis that such an act authorised a transfer of sovereignty resulting in a breach of the Constitution.[141]

The *Corte Costituzionale* has considered the application of the *controlimiti* on several occasions, always concluding that Union law was compatible with the Constitution.[142] This line of reasoning confirms that the Italian legal system, like its German and French counterparts, starts from a premise that could be described as denialist and vigilant, only to gradually, subject to several caveats, accept in practice the primacy of Union law and its implications. The high point in this evolution occurred in 2008, when the *Corte Costituzionale* referred its first preliminary reference to the Court of Justice,[143] marking the beginning of many other references to follow. By requesting the interpretative assistance of the Luxembourg court, the

[135] ibid, para 9.
[136] ibid.
[137] ibid.
[138] Judgment No 170, 1984.
[139] ibid, para 7.
[140] Judgment No 232, 1989.
[141] ibid, para 6.
[142] See, inter alia, Judgments Nos 168, 1991; 117, 1994; 509, 1996; and 126, 1996.
[143] Case C-169/08 *Presidente del Consiglio dei Ministri* EU:C:2009:709, the first reference for a preliminary ruling from the Italian Corte Costituzionale, followed later by the second request in Joined Cases C-22/13, C-61/13 to C-63/13 and C-418/13 *Mascolo and Others* EU:C:2014:2401.

Corte Costituzionale tacitly recognised the autonomous nature of Union law and the role of the Court of Justice therein, and has ever since astutely used the tool to avoid constitutional conflict, even by triggering reversals of case law by the Court of Justice. This approach was confirmed in 2017 in the case of *MAS*, when the *Corte Costituzionale*, after pointing to the potential unconstitutionality of a line of case law of the Court of Justice, proposed a reconsideration of that case law, which the Luxembourg court eventually accepted.[144] This outcome confirms that conflicts between constitutional jurisdictions and the Court of Justice can be more effectively resolved when they are channelled through the preliminary ruling procedure rather than through unilateral assertions. The *Corte Costituzionale* has thus far developed the gold standard on how to handle constitutional conflicts through judicial dialogue with the Court of Justice, making a constructive and shrewd use of the preliminary reference procedure that other constitutional jurisdictions should closely follow.[145]

4. Spain

Spain is no exception within the community of European constitutional courts, and to date it has refused to recognise that Union law is based on an autonomous source or that its primacy is unlimited, especially when it comes to overriding the core provisions of the Spanish Constitution.

Regarding the foundational norm of European integration, the *Tribunal Constitucional* ruled in 1991 that its *locus* is found in Article 93 of the Constitution.[146] According to the *Tribunal Constitucional*, the authority of Union law in Spain does not stem from an autonomous source within Union law itself, in contrast to the statements made in *Van Gend en Loos* and *Costa v Enel*, but from a provision in the Spanish Constitution. This provision, Article 93, was initially regarded as an 'organic-procedural' rule that could not serve as a parameter to scrutinise the constitutionality of Union law.[147] Furthermore, because the foundations of Union law in Spain are rooted in the Constitution, the *Tribunal Constitucional* described Union law as 'infra-constitutional' law.[148]

The case law of the *Tribunal Constitucional* developed over time, and in 2004, in Declaration 1/2004,[149] it changed its interpretation of Article 93 and described it as follows:

> Article 93 CE is undoubtedly a basic constitutional support for the integration of other legislations into our own, through the transfer of the exercise of competences resulting from the Constitution, legislations that are required to coexist with internal legislation and legislations that are of a regional origin. Metaphorically, it could be said that Art 93 CE operates as a door through which the Constitution itself allows the entry of other legislations into our constitutional system through the transfer of the exercise of competences. Consequently, Art 93 CE is given a substantive or material dimension which must not be ignored.[150]

[144] Case C-42/17 *MAS* EU:C:2017:936. See D Sarmiento, 'Adults in the Deliberation Room' (2018) 38 *Quaderni costituzionali* 228.

[145] M Martins Pereira, 'Consob and the Lessons Learnt from the Taricco Saga' and D Sarmiento, 'The Consob Way – Or How the Corte Costituzionale taught Europe (Once Again) a Masterclass in Constitutional Dispute Settlement' (*EU Law Live Weekend Edition*, 16 April 2021).

[146] Judgment 29/1991 of 14 February 1991: 'This provision [Art 93 of the Spanish Constitution] certainly constitutes the ultimate basis of such a foundation [of Union Law], given that its acceptance (articulated by way of the Treaty of Accession, which is its immediate basis) is the reflection of the exercise of the State's sovereignty' (FJ 4).

[147] Judgment 29/1991 (n 146) as well as Declaration 1/1992 of 1 July 1992, para 4.

[148] See, among others, Judgments 64/1991, FJ 4; 41/2002, FJ 2; and 58/2004, FJ 10.

[149] Declaration of 13 December 2004.

[150] ibid.

In short, the *Tribunal Constitucional* declared that Article 93 has 'a substantive or material dimension which must not be ignored', serving as the genuine source of authority of Union law in Spain,[151] and also as a provision that imposes material limits on the process of European integration.

Regarding the normative dimension of primacy of Union law, the approach taken by the *Tribunal Constitucional* differs from that of its counterparts. In Declaration 1/2004, a distinction was made between *primacy* and *supremacy*. According to the *Tribunal Constitucional*:

Supremacy and primacy are categories which are developed in differentiated orders. Supremacy is sustained in the higher hierarchical character of a regulation and, therefore, is a source of validity of the lower regulations, leading to the consequent invalidity of the latter if they contravene the provisions set forth imperatively in the former. Primacy, however, is not necessarily sustained on hierarchy, but rather on the distinction between the scopes of application of different regulations, principally valid, of which, however, one or more of them have the capacity for displacing others by virtue of their preferential or prevalent application due to various reasons.[152]

As a result, while Union law enjoys *primacy*, the Constitution holds *supremacy*. Primacy is a quality that, in the event of a conflict, is resolved by the application of one rule over another; in short, it is a 'conflict rule' indicating which rule of law, among several options, applies to resolving a dispute in a particular case. The *Tribunal Constitucional* affirms this technocratic understanding of primacy by describing it as a mere 'regulatory principle or a technique aimed at ensuring the effectiveness [of Union law]'. In contrast, supremacy is a feature of the superior, hierarchical nature of the rule that possesses it (the Constitution). This rule serves as the ultimate standard for reviewing the validity of the remaining rules of the legal system.

The supremacy of the Spanish Constitution extends only to its core provisions, not to the entire constitutional document. The *Tribunal Constitucional* confirmed the existence of 'material limits' to European integration and Union law in two very specific cases: respect for the 'basic constitutional structures'; and for the system of protection of fundamental rights. The 'basic constitutional structures' are to be understood as the form of the Spanish state (a parliamentary monarchy) and the territorial distribution of power.

In the event of a conflict between a rule of Union law and the core provisions of the Constitution, it will be necessary to amend the Constitution, to amend the rule of Union law, or to proceed with the withdrawal of the Kingdom of Spain from the Union. However, the *Tribunal Constitucional* has adopted a pragmatic approach to these scenarios, arguing that in such an 'unlikely case' the *Tribunal Constitucional* would be called upon 'to approach the problems which, in such a case, would arise'.[153] In other words, should a conflict of such magnitude occur (a scenario that is recognised as 'unlikely'), the *Tribunal Constitucional* indicated its commitment to finding an interpretation that would ultimately reconcile the constitutional provisions with Union law.

An example of this pragmatic approach can be found in the case of *Melloni*, where the *Tribunal Constitucional*'s highly protective interpretation of the fundamental right to due process in criminal proceedings came into conflict with the Framework Decision on the European Arrest Warrant. When the provisions of the Framework Decision on the

[151] The Constitutional Court reacted to the criticisms from scholarly authors to the characterisation of Art 93 of the Constitution as an 'organic-procedural' rule. See the criticisms made, inter alia, by R Alonso García, *Derecho Comunitario: Sistema Constitucional y Administrativo de la Comunidad Europea* (Ramón Areces, 1994) 281 and P Pérez Tremps, *Constitución española y Comunidad Europea* (Civitas, 1993) 36–37.

[152] Declaration 1/2004 (n 149) FJ 4.

[153] ibid.

enforcement of arrest warrants in cases of convictions *in absentia* clashed with the *Tribunal Constitucional*'s case law,[154] it referred the matter to the Court of Justice through a preliminary reference. Following the judgment of the Court of Justice in *Melloni*,[155] in which the case law of the *Tribunal Constitucional* was declared incompatible with the Framework Decision, the *Tribunal Constitucional* amended its case law and thus put an end to a constitutional conflict.[156]

The *Tribunal Constitucional* has proven to be an active partner, alongside the Spanish judiciary, in its efforts to secure the effective judicial implementation of Union law. It is common for the *Tribunal Constitucional* to intervene and rule on how Spanish courts ensure the rights conferred by Union law. These cases not only involve reviewing the conformity of legislation with Union law but primarily focus on the practice and judicial decisions of Spanish courts where Union law is applied in individual cases. For instance, in a well-established line of case law, the *Tribunal Constitucional* has highlighted that the adjudicative dimension of primacy is safeguarded by the Constitution, including access to the *recurso de amparo*, an extraordinary remedy for the protection of fundamental rights. As a result, if Spanish courts ignore the interpretation of rules of Union law made by the Court of Justice, or refuse to set aside rules of Spanish law in conflict with Union law, they will incur a breach of Article 24 of the Constitution, which guarantees the fundamental right to effective judicial protection. As the *Tribunal Constitucional* has stated:

> [I]t is for this Court to ensure respect for the principle of the primacy of European Union law where . . . there is an authentic interpretation given by the Court of Justice of the European Union itself. In such cases, disregarding that rule of European Union law, as interpreted by the Court of Justice, may lead to an unreasonable and arbitrary selection of a rule applicable to the proceedings, which may give rise to a breach of the right to effective judicial protection.[157]

In sum, the *Tribunal Constitucional* has introduced substantive limits on the primacy of Union law when it comes into conflict with the core of the Spanish Constitution, but it is also willing to act as a guarantor of the correct implementation of Union law by the Spanish judiciary in the resolution of individual disputes. While the case law of the *Tribunal Constitucional* rejects a broad and unconditional understanding of the normative dimension of primacy, it fully embraces the adjudicative dimension of primacy in Spain, including a willingness to serve as its guarantor.

VI. IN SEARCH OF A THEORETICAL BASIS FOR PRIMACY: CONSTITUTIONAL PLURALISM AS A SOLUTION OR A PROBLEM

After this overview of the theoretical foundations and the practical implementation of the principle of primacy of Union law, it is clear that we face two apparently irreconcilable visions that strike at the very core of Union law. Such a stark contrast on a matter of such relevance

[154] SSTC 91/2000, FFJJ 7–8, and 177/2006, FJ 7 b).

[155] Case C-399/11 *Melloni* EU:C:2013:107.

[156] The conflict was avoided by the Constitutional Court through an autonomous interpretation of the Constitution. In other words, the Constitutional Court did not undertake to amend its previous case law as a result of the obligations stemming from Union law, but acted through an autonomous interpretation of the Spanish Constitution alone. Moreover, when referring to the judgment of the Court of Justice in *Melloni*, the Constitutional Court simply stated that it found the judgment 'very useful', but it never admitted nor implied that the ruling imposed through its binding force the final decision made by the Spanish court.

[157] STC 232/15, FJ 5.

should be of serious concern, not only from a legal and political perspective but also from a theoretical perspective. The narratives developed by the constitutional courts and supreme courts of various Member States, along with the diverging views of the Court of Justice on the matter, do not provide a consistent explanation of how Union and national legal systems interact and coexist. Consequently, this leaves the resolution of constitutional conflicts in the hands of pragmatic solutions that sometimes require political intervention rather than judicial decision-making. The willingness of some constitutional courts, namely in Germany, Poland, the Czech Republic, Denmark, and Romania, to effectively assert the primacy of their constitutions to the extent of declaring acts of Union law ultra vires, demonstrates the fragile status of Union law's primacy within Member States.

In the 1990s, following the first challenges from constitutional courts, a new academic movement emerged to provide an explanation for this apparent clash of legitimacies within a consistent theoretical framework. This movement is not monolithic, and it brings together various and diverse contributions, including the works of Miguel Poiares Maduro,[158] Mattias Kumm,[159] and Ingolf Pernice,[160] among others.[161] Put simply, constitutional pluralism is a cosmopolitan theory of law that does not posit the foundation of a legal system in a single supreme norm but in a plurality of norms that collectively confer authority on the law. From a legal-political standpoint, pluralism challenges the idea of the nation as the sole sovereign, a stance that is justified by a factual premise: the social transformation brought about by globalisation in contemporary European countries (and in the international community as a whole). To the extent that the nation of today is an open entity subject to the influx and outflow of information, capital, individuals, groups, and cultures, there are situations in which sovereignty is not solely located within the nation but is distributed across a plurality of nations, intrinsically linked to one another. The fragmentation of sovereignty implies, consequently, the fragmentation of the constitution itself, fostering a cosmopolitan understanding of the nation where sovereignty is inevitably shared within a complex legal and political structure, exemplified by the European Union.

From this perspective, constitutional pluralism appears in two dimensions: a descriptive and a normative one. In its descriptive dimension, pluralism rejects a distinction such as the one made by the Spanish Constitutional Court between sovereignty and primacy, because, from the viewpoint of a pluralist theorist, sovereignty is neither uniform nor singular, but multiple and shared. Likewise, constitutional conflicts are not to be resolved by a single guarantor, but through the participation of various guarantors, based on criteria that reflect practical rationality as the result of a discursive process. In a pluralist view of the law, the resolution of conflicts between constitutional norms requires the participation of all relevant jurisdictions, each representing its own sovereignty, with the responsibility to adjudicate on the interpretation of the rules of *its* legal system while also considering the rules of *other*

[158] M Poiares Maduro, 'Contrapunctual Law: Europe's Constitutional Pluralism in Action' in N Walker (ed), *Sovereignty in Transition* (Hart, 2003).

[159] M Kumm, 'The Jurisprudence of Constitutional Conflict: Constitutional Supremacy in Europe Before and After the Constitutional Treaty' (2005) 11 *European Law Journal* 262.

[160] I Pernice, 'Multilevel Constitutionalism and the Treaty of Amsterdam: European Constitution Making Revisited?' (1999) 26 *Common Market Law Review* 703.

[161] A Von Bogdandy, 'Pluralism, Direct Effect, and the Ultimate Say: On the Relationship between International and Domestic Constitutional Law' (2008) 6 *International Journal of Constitutional Law* 397; N Walker, 'The Idea of Constitutional Pluralism' (2002) 65 *Modern Law Review* 317; M Rosenfeld, 'Rethinking Constitutional Ordering in an Era of Legal and Ideological Pluralism' (2008) 6 *International Journal of Constitutional Law* 415; J Komárek, 'European Constitutionalism and the European Arrest Warrant: In Search of the Limits of "Contrapunctual Principles"' (2007) 44 *Common Market Law Review* 9, and N Barber, 'Legal Pluralism and the European Union' (2006) 12 *European Law Journal* 306.

legal systems. By turning constitutional conflict into a participatory process, pluralism not only describes but also prescribes how constitutional conflicts should occur and be ultimately resolved.

Constitutional pluralism is a clarifying theoretical contribution that moves Union law away from a strictly positivist conception of legal systems anchored in a traditional, monolithic view of the nation, in which the sovereign state is the only relevant actor. Pluralism also liberates Union lawyers from relying on a description of the relationship between Union and national law that is not fully reflected in the practice of national constitutional courts. In summary, pluralism offers a theoretical explanation of this reality and provides tools to resolve such conflicts using normative criteria.

However, pluralism has encountered serious limitations in accounting for the developments of recent years, particularly in the wake of multiple decisions by national courts declaring the unconstitutionality of Union law in various areas, from social policy and monetary policy to the protection of judicial independence and the fight against corruption. The phenomenon of national courts asserting constitutional supremacy over Union law, exemplified by the ruling of the GFCC in the case of *Weiss*, but also of a nationalist uprising in various Member States, has put constitutional pluralism on the ropes, with some characterising it as a nefarious theory that could ultimately lead to the disintegration of the Union's legal system.[162] This criticism may understate the efforts of pluralist theorists to provide a consistent and robust justification for the law of European integration within the Member States. However, in a paradoxical development, the pluralist toolkit has been used to legitimise certain narratives from national constitutional courts that have exploited pluralism for other purposes. This situation has prompted some scholars to seek alternative formulas that rely on a pluralist conception of the Union legal order, while overcoming some of its limitations.

A contribution that seeks to use pluralist insights while also offering a more robust institutional alternative is the proposal to establish a Mixed Chamber within the Court of Justice. This chamber would be composed of judges from both the Court of Justice and the constitutional and supreme courts of the Member States. In a rotating composition of 15 judges (following the model of the Grand Chamber of the Court of Justice), the Mixed Chamber would represent both the Union's and the Member States' voices that reflect altogether the diversity of constitutional visions and sensitivities across Europe.[163] The Mixed Chamber would hear disputes concerning competence between the Union and its Member States, and it could even broaden its jurisdiction to matters of fundamental rights. If the Union, through its existing remedial channels, resolves a dispute in a manner that continues to raise doubts among the constitutional or supreme courts of the Member States, the matter could be referred to the Mixed Chamber. The criticism that the Union asserts the *kompetenz-kompetenz* doctrine or that the Court of Justice is not an impartial arbiter in matters of competence, would be addressed by establishing a Mixed Chamber with the final say on competence issues. Since the Union is not yet a sovereign state with universal competences, but rather a composite supranational organisation where multiple constitutional orders coexist, the Mixed Chamber would offer a viable means of resolving current tensions and stabilising

[162] J Baquero Cruz, *What's Left of the Law of Integration: Decay and Resistance in European Union Law* (Oxford University Press, 2018) 27ff. See also the statement of various academics under the title 'National Courts Cannot Override CJEU Judgments: A Joint Statement in Defense of the EU Legal Order' (*Verfassungsblog*, 26 May 2020) and a more developed version of the criticisms by D Kelemen, 'On the Unsustainability of Constitutional Pluralism. European Supremacy and the Survival of the Eurozone' (2021) 28 *Maastricht Journal of European and Comparative Law* 41.

[163] JHH Weiler and D Sarmiento, 'The EU Judiciary After Weiss: Proposing A New Mixed Chamber of the Court of Justice' (*EU Law Live*, 1 June 2020).

the institutional framework to address them, certainly in clearer and more structured terms than the current arrangements.

The Mixed Chamber is only one proposal among many, aimed at providing an institutional framework to anchor constitutional pluralism within a more effective practical setting. Only time will tell if the Union and the Court of Justice can resolve the tensions ignited by the GFCC, or if they will persist, intensifying the crisis over the primacy of Union law. The resolution of this crisis depends on the Court of Justice's ability to maintain the trust of its national counterparts, as well as on institutional reforms that promote such trust and foster the development of a common European constitutional identity.

GENERAL BIBLIOGRAPHY

Alter, K, *Establishing the Supremacy of European Law: The Making of an International Rule of Law in Europe* (Oxford University Press, 2001).

Arena, A, 'From an Unpaid Electricity Bill to the Primacy of EU Law: Gian Galeazzo Stendardi and the Making of Costa v ENEL' (2019) 30 *European Journal of International Law* 1017.

De Boer, N, *Judging European Democracy: The Role and Legitimacy of National Constitutional Courts in the EU* (Oxford University Press, 2023).

Claes, M, *The National Courts' Mandate in the European Constitution* (Hart Publishing, 2006).

Cloots, E, *National Identity in EU Law* (Oxford University Press, 2015).

Walker, N (ed), *Sovereignty in Transition* (Hart, 2003).

FURTHER READING

Primacy as a Category

von Bogdandy, A and Schill, S, 'Overcoming Absolute Primacy: Respect for National Identity under the Lisbon Treaty' (2011) 48 *Common Market Law Review* 1417.

Claes, M, 'The Primacy of EU Law in European and National Law' in A Arnull and D Chalmers (eds), *The Oxford Handbook of European Union Law* (Oxford University Press, 2015).

Dougan, M, 'The primacy of Union law over incompatible national measures: Beyond disapplication and towards a remedy of nullity?' (2022) 59 *Common Market Law Review* 1301.

Maduro, MP, '"Contrapunctual Law": Europe's Constitutional Pluralism in Action' in N Walker (ed), *Sovereignty in Transition* (Hart, 2003).

Ritleng, D, 'Le principe de primauté du droit de l'Union' (2005) 41 *Revue Trimestrielle de Droit Européen* 305.

Stone Sweet, A, 'The Juridical Coup d'État and the Problem of Authority' (2007) 8 *German Law Journal* 475.

Torres Pérez, A, *Conflict of Rights in the European Union: A Theory of Supranational Adjudication* (Oxford University Press, 2009).

Turmo, A, 'National res judicata in the European Union: Revisiting the Tension Between the Temptation of Effectiveness and the Acknowledgement of Domestic Procedural Law' (2021) 58 *Common Market Law Review* 123.

Weiler, JHH, 'The Community System: The Dual Character of Supranationalism' (1981) 1 *Yearbook of European Law* 267.

de Witte, B, 'Direct Effect, Primacy, and the Nature of the Legal Order' in P Craig and G de Búrca (eds), *The Evolution of EU Law*, 2nd edn (Oxford University Press, 2011).

Primacy and the Constitutional Law of the Member States

Baquero Cruz, J, 'The Legacy of the Maastricht-Urteil and the Pluralist Movement' (2008) 14 *European Law Journal* 385.

— What's Left of the Law of Integration: Decay and Resistance in European Union Law (Oxford University Press, 2018).
Barents, R, 'The Precedence of EU Law from the Perspective of Constitutional Pluralism' (2009) 5 *European Constitutional Law Review* 323.
Bobić, A, *The Jurisprudence of Constitutional Conflict in the European Union* (Oxford University Press, 2022).
von Bogdandy, A, 'Pluralism, Direct Effect, and the Ultimate Say: On the Relationship between International and Domestic Constitutional Law' (2008) 6 *International Journal of Constitutional Law* 397.
Craig, P, 'The ECJ and Ultra Vires Action: A Conceptual Analysis' (2011) 48 *Common Market Law Review* 395.
Dani, M, 'National Constitutional Courts in Supranational Litigation: A Contextual Analysis' (2017) 23 *European Law Journal* 105.
Jaklic, K, *Constitutional Pluralism in the EU* (Oxford University Press, 2014).
Kumm, M and Ferreres Comella, V, 'The Primacy Clause of the Constitutional Treaty and the Future of Constitutional Conflict' (2005) 3 *International Journal of Constitutional Law* 159.
Mayer, F, 'Supremacy – Lost?' (2005) 6 *German Law Journal* 707.
Sarmiento, D, 'Adults in the (Deliberation) Room' (2018) 38 *Quaderni Costituzionali* 228.
Scholtes, J, The Abuse of Constitutional Identity in the European Union (Oxford University Press, 2023).
Vosskuhle, A, 'Multilevel Cooperation of the European Constitutional Courts: Der Europäische Verfassungsgerichtsverbund' (2010) 6 *European Constitutional Law Review* 175.
Weiler, JHH and Sarmiento, D, 'The EU Judiciary After Weiss – Proposing a New Mixed Chamber of the Court of Justice' (1 June 2020) EU Law Live.

The Primacy of EU law in Germany, France, Italy and Spain

Amtenbrink, F and Repasi, R, 'The German Federal Constitutional Court's Decision in Weiss: A Contextual Analysis' (2020) 45 *European Law Review* 675.
Gallo, D, 'Challenging EU Constitutional Law: The Italian Constitutional Court's New Stance on Direct Effect and the Preliminary Reference Procedure' (2019) 25 *European Law Journal* 434.
Halberstam, D and Möllers, C, 'The German Constitutional Court says "Ja zu Deutschland!"' (2009) 10 *German Law Journal* 1241.
Knecht, A, 'Breaking with Lisbon: The German Federal Constitutional Court's New Approach to EU Democracy and Responsibility for Integration' (2025) 21 *European Constitutional Law Review* 1.
Mehdi, R, 'French Supreme Courts and European Union Law: Between Historical Compromise and Accepted Loyalty' (2011) 48 *Common Market Law Review* 439.
Payandeh, M, 'Constitutional Review of EU Law after Honeywell: Contextualizing the Relationship between the German Constitutional Court and the EU Court of Justice' (2011) 48 *Common Market Law Review* 9.
Tega, D, 'The Italian Constitutional Court in its Context: A Narrative' (2021) 17 *European Constitutional Law Review* 245.
Thym, D, 'In the Name of Sovereign Statehood: A Critical Introduction to the Lisbon Judgment of the German Constitutional Court' (2009) 46 *Common Market Law Review* 179.
Torres Pérez, A, 'Melloni in Three Acts: From Dialogue to Monologue' (2014) 10 *European Constitutional Law Review* 308.
Turmo, A, 'National security as an exception to EU data protection standards: The judgment of the Conseil d'État in French Data Network and others' (2022) 59 *Common Market Law Review* 203.
Wendel, M, 'The Two-Faced Guardian: Or How One Half of the German Federal Constitutional Court Became a European Fundamental Rights Court' (2020) 57 *Common Market Law Review* 1383.

11

Judicial Protection in the European Union (I)

I. THE UNION AND ITS JUDICIARY

To GUARANTEE THE effectiveness of the Union's legal system, the Treaties establish a complete system of judicial remedies in which Union and national courts play a pivotal role. Where disputes concerning compliance with Union law require an impartial arbiter, it is for a court to interpret the relevant provisions of Union law when resolving the case. This task is carried out by the Union's judiciary, which is essential to ensuring the uniformity and effectiveness of Union law across the twenty-seven Member States.

The strategic role of courts in the development of the Union and in the implementation of its policies was aptly described by Advocate General Ruiz-Jarabo Colomer as follows:

> The European Union has been described as an integration *of law, through the law*, attesting to the crucial role of the courts at European Union constitutional level. . . . Given that it embodies an authority founded on independence, on its relationship with the law and on the resolution of disputes, the judiciary has a singular voice which is isolated from the political sphere and linked only to the will of the law. By granting special powers to . . . courts, the Treaties sought to strengthen the authority of a young legal order which was created for an unprecedented international organisation.[1]

Similar to the organisation of courts in a federal system, which operate on the basis of a division of jurisdiction between federal and state courts, the Union's judiciary operates on two levels: the Union courts and the Member States' courts. The Union's judiciary thus works as a composite system, with courts at both Union and national levels exercising the jurisdiction outlined in the Treaties.

According to Article 19(1) Treaty on European Union (TEU), Union courts are embodied by the Court of Justice of the European Union, an institution comprising two courts: the Court of Justice and the General Court.[2] Both are entrusted with the duty to 'ensure that in the interpretation and application of the Treaties the law is observed'. In the second subparagraph of Article 19(1) TEU, an indirect reference is made to national courts, stating that 'Member States shall provide remedies sufficient to ensure effective legal protection in the fields covered by Union law'.

The creation and development of a two-tier European judicial system, based on a division of functions between Union and national courts, together with the individual's right to rely on the direct effect and primacy of Union law, confirms the federal inspiration behind the Union's judicial architecture.

[1] Case C-205/08 *Umweltanwalt von Kärnten* EU:C:2009:397, Opinion of AG Ruiz-Jarabo Colomer, pt 29.

[2] It should be noted that Art 19(1) also refers to 'specialised jurisdictions'. However, following the enlargement of the General Court in 2016, the only specialised jurisdiction to have been in operation, the Civil Service Tribunal, was abolished.

1. Union Courts

The Treaties assign Union courts two fundamental tasks: first, to ensure the authoritative interpretation of Union law across all twenty-seven Member States; and second, to conduct judicial review of acts adopted by the Union's institutions, bodies, offices, and agencies.

The review of the legality of acts of the institutions, bodies, offices and agencies of the Union lies exclusively with the Union courts. If an institution of the Union, a Member State, or an individual considers a regulation, directive, or decision of the Union to be unlawful, they must challenge it before the Union courts. National courts lack the jurisdiction to declare Union acts invalid. Therefore, Union courts are granted exclusive competence to declare the invalidity of and annul Union acts, as established by the Court of Justice in the seminal case of *Foto-Frost*.[3]

However, there are two procedural qualifications to this exclusive competence of Union courts. First, when a national court has doubts over the validity of a Union act and refers the matter to the Court of Justice for a preliminary ruling on its validity, the national court, in exceptional circumstances, may grant interim relief that temporarily suspends the effects of a national measure that implements the Union act while awaiting the Court of Justice's decision, thus indirectly suspending the effects of the Union act.[4] Secondly, the Union courts' exclusive power of annulment solely concerns the declaration of invalidity of Union acts. This jurisdiction, however, does not prevent national courts from finding that a Union act is 'completely valid'.[5]

As a result of the above, Union courts have no jurisdiction to provide authoritative interpretations of national law, nor to rule on the invalidity and annulment of acts of the Member States. This limitation is important, as it highlights that the Union judiciary, while exercising significant powers, does not possess the power to provide an authoritative interpretation of national law or to rule on its invalidity. When a Member State fails to meet its legal obligations under Union law, Union courts can only declare that the Member State is in breach of those obligations. The power to repeal or amend such measures within the national legal system remains with the Member State, not with the Union or its courts.[6]

[3] Case C-314/85 *Foto-Frost* EU:C:1987:452.

[4] *Foto-Frost* (n 3) and Joined Cases C-143/88 and C-92/89 *Zuckerfabrik Süderdithmarschen and Zuckerfabrik Soest* EU:C:1991:65, para 21. This power to suspend national implementing measures in interim relief procedures is limited to the national judiciary. The case law excludes other national authorities, such as administrative authorities, from making use of these exceptional powers. See Joined Cases C-453/03, C-11/04, C-12/04 and C-194/04 *Abna* EU:C:2005:741, paras 108–11.

[5] *Foto-Frost* (n 3) para 14: '[The] courts may consider the validity of a [Union] act and, if they consider that the grounds put forward before them by the parties in support of invalidity are unfounded, they may reject them, concluding that the measure is completely valid. By taking that action they are not calling into question the existence of the [Union] measure.'

[6] Joined Cases C-10/97 to 22/97 *IN.CO.GE. '90 and Others* EU:C:1998:498, para 21: 'It cannot . . . be inferred from the judgment in Simmenthal that the incompatibility with [Union] law of a subsequently adopted rule of national law has the effect of rendering that rule of national law non-existent. Faced with such a situation, the national court is, however, obliged to disapply that rule, provided always that this obligation does not restrict the power of the competent national courts to apply, from among the various procedures available under national law, those which are appropriate for protecting the individual rights conferred by [Union] law'. The only exceptions to this well-established rule is found in the case of rulings of the Court of Justice delivered under the authority of Art 14(2) of the Statute of the European System of Central Banks and of the European Central Bank (see Joined Cases C-202/18 and C-238/18 *Rimšēvičs and ECB v Latvia* EU:C:2019:139), and in cases in which a national court faces a judicial decision delivered by a national jurisdiction in breach of basic standards of judicial independence (see Case C-487/19 *W.Ż.* EU:C:2021:798, paras 154, 155 and 161, and Case C-448/23 *Commission v Poland* EU:C:2025:975, para 120).

2. National Courts

When a private individual brings a dispute over the interpretation of Union law against a national authority or a private party, national courts have jurisdiction to adjudicate on the matter. Additionally, if the rule of Union law has direct effect, the national court has the duty to enforce the rights conferred by the Union rule and set aside any incompatible rule of national law. The combined outcome of direct effect and primacy leaves national courts in a strategic and highly relevant position, acting as pivotal players in safeguarding and effectively enforcing the rights conferred by Union law, thereby turning them into 'ordinary courts of Union law' (*juges de droit commun du droit de l'Union*). This strategic role of national courts is further reinforced by Article 19(1), second subparagraph, TEU which requires Member States to provide remedies 'sufficient to ensure effective legal protection in the fields covered by Union law'.

In resolving disputes, national courts may need to interpret provisions of Union law, especially when the wording of the applicable provision is ambiguous or subject to various interpretations. At times, national courts will have doubts about the validity of an act of Union law. In such cases, national courts do not act in isolation; they are empowered to refer the matter to the Court of Justice by requesting a preliminary ruling on questions of interpretation or validity. The preliminary ruling procedure, discussed in detail in chapter twelve of this book, serves both as a tool for judicial cooperation between national courts and the Court of Justice, and also as a mechanism to ensure the uniform interpretation and application of Union law across all Member States.

In contrast with most federal systems, the Union's judiciary lacks an appellate connection between the Union and national levels. Judgments delivered by national courts are not subject to appeal before Union courts.[7] As a result, when a final ruling by a national court is contrary to Union law, individuals have a limited range of remedies. In such cases, they can choose between several options: first, to lodge a complaint with the Commission with a view to the initiation of an infringement procedure initiated by the Commission or a Member State against another Member State;[8] and second, to file a damages claim for breach of Union law in the courts of the Member State.[9] Moreover, the case law of the Court of Justice has confirmed the authority of lower national courts to set aside rulings of higher national courts when those rulings come into conflict with Union law.[10] While these remedies address situations in which a national court's ruling is inconsistent with Union law, they are often cumbersome and not always effective for the applicant. This outcome can be avoided by referring the matter to the Court of Justice at an earlier stage of the national proceedings through a preliminary reference pursuant to Article 267 TFEU.

[7] According to the Court of Justice, the Union courts 'have jurisdiction to act only in the areas in which jurisdiction has been expressly conferred upon them by the [Treaties]. In the system of legal remedies provided for by the Treaty, an infringement of [Union] law by the national authorities, including an infringement of the third paragraph of [Article 267 TFEU], may be brought before the [Union] courts by the Commission or by another Member State, or may be brought before the competent national courts by any natural or legal person. In the latter case, it is for the national courts to ensure that rules of [Union] law are protected and thus that the effectiveness of judicial protection is not undermined in any way' (Case C-396/03 P *Killinger v Germany, Commission and Council* EU:C:2005:355, para 28).

[8] Case C-129/00 *Commission v Italy* EU:C:2003:656, para 32; and Case C-154/08 *Commission v Spain* EU:C:2009:695, para 125.

[9] Case C-224/01 *Köbler* EU:C:2003:513.

[10] Case C-166/73 *Rheinmühlen* EU:C:1974:3; Case C-379/08 *ERG and Others* EU:C:2010:126; Case C-173/09 *Elchinov* EU:C:2010:581; Case C-416/10 *Križan and Others* EU:C:2013:8; and Case C-154/15 *Gutiérrez Naranjo* EU:C:2016:980, para 74.

II. THE JURISDICTION OF UNION COURTS: DIRECT ACTIONS

The Union's judicial institution currently comprises two courts: the Court of Justice and the General Court. These courts are vested with jurisdiction to hear disputes brought against the Union and its institutions, bodies, offices and agencies by other institutions, bodies, offices and agencies, by Member States, or by individuals.

Disputes can be brought before these courts through either direct or indirect actions. Direct actions are remedies initiated in Union courts at the initiative of an applicant party. Conversely, indirect actions arise within the context of a pre-existing or parallel judicial procedure, initiated by a party or a court. The full structure of remedies, divided into direct and indirect actions, can be outlined as follows:

Direct actions

- Remedies to review the legality of Union activity:
  - (a) action for annulment;
  - (b) action for failure to act;
  - (c) action for damages;
  - (d) appeals;
  - (e) remedies with unlimited jurisdiction:
    - (i) review of sanctions;
    - (ii) staff cases;
    - (iii) review procedure;
    - (iv) other direct actions (rectification, interpretation, review, contractual disputes, etc).
- Remedies to review the legality of Member State activity: infringement proceedings

Indirect actions

- references for a preliminary ruling;
- plea of illegality;
- interim measures.

1. Remedies to Review the Legality of Union Activity

Most direct actions are legal remedies to review the legality of acts adopted by the Union through its institutions, bodies, offices, and agencies. Applicants who bring such actions before the Union courts aim to challenge an act of the Union, whether of general or individual scope, legislative or regulatory, and whether it may be adopted by an institution, body, office, or agency of the Union. Direct challenges to Union acts fall exclusively under the remit of Union courts, which have jurisdiction to rule on the invalidity and annulment of Union acts. The infringement procedure, provided for in Articles 258–60 Treaty on the Functioning of the European Union (TFEU), is the only direct action targeting the activities of the Member States and their conformity with Union law.

1.1. Action for Annulment

According to Article 263 TFEU, an action for annulment grants Union courts the power to review the legality of acts adopted by the institutions, bodies, offices, or agencies of the Union.

This review is conducted regardless of the scope of the act, whether it is legislative or non-legislative in nature, or irrespective of its capacity to produce legal effects vis-a-vis third parties. A successful action for annulment results in the annulment of the contested act, thereby removing it from the Union's legal system with retroactive effect, as if it had never existed. The legal framework of the action for annulment is inspired by the French tradition of administrative law, a model that was expanded throughout continental Europe in the early nineteenth century, mainly as a result of the Napoleonic reforms that profoundly influenced European administrative law to this day.[11]

The underlying rationale for this action is an objective, abstract review: Union courts assess the legality of the contested act itself, independent of the subjective rights of the individuals challenging it. The action for annulment embodies an approach to administrative justice that is confined to assessing whether the contested Union act complies with Union law. If the Union courts find the act to be invalid, they will declare it void without issuing orders or injunctions to restore the applicant's factual or legal situation to its previous state. This feature distinguishes the action for annulment from proceedings under Article 261 TFEU, in which Union courts exercise 'unlimited jurisdiction' and may review both the law and the facts, assess the evidence, and annul or reform the contested decision, including by altering the amount of a fine.

The action for annulment targets the acts of the Union's institutions, bodies, offices, and agencies, but not their inactivity. If such inaction amounts to a breach of Union law, the available remedy is an action for failure to act, as outlined in section II.1.2 of this chapter.

1.1.1. Jurisdiction

Article 256(1) TFEU grants the General Court jurisdiction at first instance hear actions for annulment. However, this rule is subject to several exceptions enumerated in Article 51 of the Statute of the Court of Justice. In the following cases, the jurisdiction falls exclusively on the Court of Justice:

Actions brought by a Member State against:

(a) an act of the European Parliament or of the Council, or of both institutions acting jointly, except for:

- decisions taken by the Council under the third subparagraph of Article 108(2) TFEU (State aid);
- acts of the Council adopted pursuant to a Council regulation concerning measures to protect trade within the meaning of Article 207 TFEU (common commercial policy);
- acts of the Council by which the Council exercises implementing powers in accordance with Article 291(2) TFEU;

(b) an act of the Commission under Article 331(1) TFEU (enhanced cooperation).

Actions brought by one Union institution against an act of the European Parliament, the Council, both acting jointly, the Commission, or the European Central Bank.

In these reserved cases, actions are heard directly by the Court of Justice. In all other cases, including actions brought by natural or legal persons, and actions brought by Member States against acts of the Commission (other than under Article 331(1)), the General Court has jurisdiction at first instance, with a right of appeal to the Court of Justice on points of law.

[11] On the origin and evolution of direct actions in Union courts, see D Ritleng, *Le contrôle de légalité des actes communautaires par la Cour de justice et le Tribunal de première instance des Communautés européennes* (University of Strasbourg, 1998) ch 1.

1.1.2. Reviewable Act

The value of the rule of law requires, among its various features, that all actions taken by the Union's authorities are subject to judicial review by an independent court of law. The fundamental right to an effective remedy, as enshrined in Article 47 of the Charter of Fundamental Rights of the European Union ('the Charter'), demands the availability of judicial remedies to review the actions of the Union's institutions, bodies, offices, and agencies. The relationship between the rule of law and the fundamental right to an effective remedy was aptly described by Advocate General Poiares Maduro in the following terms:

> In the context of Article [19, first para TEU], the Court sees its mission as requiring it to ensure compliance with the law in accordance with the criteria of a [Union] governed by the rule of law. . . . It is therefore incumbent on the Court to ensure, in that context, the observance of legality in accordance with the same criteria. That is the logical implication of a Union based on the rule of law. . . . In a *Union governed by the rule of law*, it is essential for measures of Union institutions and bodies to be amenable to review by a Union Court, so long as they are intended to produce legal effects vis-à-vis third parties.[12]

According to Article 263, first paragraph TFEU, for an act of a Union institution, body, office or agency to be subject to judicial review, certain conditions must be met. The act must have binding legal effects, understood in substance rather than by reference to its formal classification, a requirement that does not automatically exclude acts commonly labelled as 'soft law'. The act must also be intended to produce legal effects vis-a-vis third parties. Beyond the general requirements outlined in Article 263, first paragraph TFEU, the Court of Justice has developed additional criteria that significantly affect the reviewability of Union acts. These criteria will be examined in detail in section II.1.1.2.3 of this chapter.

1.1.2.1. Binding Act

A binding act is defined in the case law as the exercise of 'a power provided for by law which is intended to produce legal effects of such a nature as to affect adversely the interests of the applicant by modifying its legal position' by an institution, body, office or agency of the Union.[13] The determination of the binding effect of a Union act does not rely on its formal categorisation, but on its content and the ability to impact an individual's legal situation.[14] This flexible approach has enabled Union courts to review the legality of Union acts that would typically be classified as *soft law*, provided they contain provisions capable of affecting the applicant's legal position. For example, a 'code of conduct' was deemed to have a binding effect because it imposed mandatory obligations on Member States.[15]

The case law provides numerous examples of informal or *soft law* acts that are recognised as having binding effects due to their inclusion of mandatory rules.[16] This also applies to

[12] Case C-160/03 *Spain v Eurojust* EU:C:2004:817, pt 17.

[13] Case C-182/80 *Gauff* EU:C:1982:78, para 18.

[14] This pragmatic approach is already present in the earlier case law. See, for example, Case C-23/63 *Emile Henricot v High Authority* EU:C:1963:52, 454, later developed, inter alia, in Case C-101/76 *Koninklijke Scholten Honig v Commission and Council* EU:C:1977:70, para 7, where the Court of Justice stated that 'the choice of form cannot change the nature of the measure'.

[15] Case C-325/91 *France v Commission* EU:C:1992:529, paras 22–23: 'by requiring Member States annually to report to it, on a general, systematic basis, data relating to the financial relations of a particular category of undertaking achieving a specified turnover, the Commission has added new obligations not provided for in Article 5(2) of the Directive. Accordingly, it must be held that the communication constitutes an act intended to have legal effects of its own distinct from those of Article 5(2) of the Directive on transparency and that, as a result, an action for annulment will lie against it.'

[16] Joined Cases C-90/63 and C-91/63 *Commission v Belgium and Luxembourg* EU:C:1964:80, 137; Case C-9/73 *Schlüter* EU:C:1973:110, paras 17–18; Joined Cases C-69/76 and C-70/76 *Dittmeyer* EU:C:1977:25, para 4; Case C-35/93 *Develop Dr Eisbein* EU:C:1994:252, para 21; Case C-322/93 P *Peugeot v Commission* EU:C:1994:257, paras 8–11; Case T-353/94 *Postbank v Commission* EU:T:1996:119, para 35.

formal Union acts that lack binding force under the Treaty, such as recommendations, which are generally excluded from judicial review under Article 263, first paragraph TFEU. However, the case law recognises that 'in exceptional cases, the impossibility of bringing an action for annulment against a recommendation does not apply if the contested act does not constitute a genuine recommendation by virtue of its content'.[17] This pragmatic approach ensures that Union acts with significant legal consequences, regardless of their formal characterisation, can be subject to judicial review in Union courts.

1.1.2.2. An Act Intended to Produce Legal Effects

According to Article 263, first paragraph TFEU, a distinction is made between the acts of the Council, the Commission, and the ECB, and those of the European Parliament and the European Council, 'intended to produce legal effects vis-à-vis third parties'.

According to the case law, Union acts are reviewable as long as they produce legal effects. The Court of Justice has articulated this principle, stating as follows:

> Any measure the legal effects of which are binding on, and capable of affecting the interests of, the applicant by bringing about a distinct change in his legal position is an act or decision which may be the subject of an action under Article [263] for a declaration that it is void.[18]

Consequently, Union acts that do not change an individual's legal position, either because their content cannot, or because they effectively lack such an impact, are not subject to review in an action for annulment. This principle applies to confirmatory acts, which, by their very nature, do not introduce any new elements into the legal situation of individuals.[19]

Conversely, in the context of preparatory acts and other measures that form part of the process leading to the adoption of a final act, the rule is that these acts are not independently subject to judicial review in an action for annulment.[20] Any alleged illegality of a preparatory act must be challenged in an action for annulment brought against the final act.[21]

Under Article 263 TFEU, an act is challengeable if it is intended to produce binding legal effects vis-a-vis third parties and definitively determines the position of the institution, body, office or agency that adopted it. The fact that the measure forms part of a multi-stage or composite procedure does not exclude review where it produces independent legal effects and constitutes the definitive expression of the adopting body's position on the matters within its competence.[22] Conversely, considerations such as whether the act directly affects the applicant's legal position or is directly enforceable against it are relevant to standing under the fourth paragraph of Article 263 TFEU, not to the classification of the act itself.[23]

[17] Case C-16/16 *Belgium v Commission* EU:C:2018:79, para 29.

[18] Case C-60/81 *IBM v Commission* EU:C:1981:264, para 9; and Joined Cases C-68/94 and C-30/95 *France and Others v Commission* EU:C:1998:148, para 62.

[19] Case C-56/72 *Goeth-van der Schüren* EU:C:1973:18, para 15; Case C-1/76 *Wack* EU:C:1976:91, para 7; Case C-26/76 *Metro* EU:C:1977:167, para 4; Case C-9/81 *Williams* EU:C:1982:331, para 15; and Joined Cases C-166 and C-220/86 *Irish Cement* EU:C:1988:549, paras 1–16.

[20] Case C-650/18 *Hungary v Parliament* EU:C:2021:426, para 43; Case C-431/20 P *Tognoli and others* EU:C:2021:807, para 35; Case T-140/16 *Le Pen v Parliament* EU:T:2016:240 (order), paras 36–37; and Case T-482/20 *LG v Commission* (order) EU:T:2021:290, para 48.

[21] Case C-400/99 *Italy v Commission* EU:C:2001:528, para 63; Joined Cases C-463/10 P and C-475/10 P *Deutsche Post and Germany v Commission* EU:C:2011:656, para 56; Case C-650/18 *Hungary v Parliament* EU:C:2021:426, para 48; and Case C-431/20 P *Tognoli and Others* EU:C:2021:807, paras 42–43.

[22] Case C-97/23 P *Whatsapp Ireland Ltd/European Data Protection Board* EU:C:2025:210, paras 70–77.

[23] ibid, para 68.

1.1.2.3. Other Requirements of Reviewability of Union Acts

In addition to the requirements derived from Article 263 TFEU, the case law stipulates that the act must exist, a feature that refers to two different scenarios. The first scenario involves an act that has actually been adopted, as opposed to an act in respect of which the institution has not yet taken a position.[24] Similarly, a repealed act ceases to exist in law and cannot be challenged unless the applicant proves that the act continues to produce effects.[25] The second situation pertains to acts tainted by an irregularity of such gravity that it cannot be tolerated by the Union legal system. In such cases, the act must be regarded as having no legal effect, even provisional, and is considered as legally 'non-existent'.[26]

In the case of Common Foreign and Security Policy (CFSP) acts, Article 275 TFEU states that the Court of Justice 'shall not have jurisdiction with respect to the provisions relating to the common foreign and security policy, nor with respect to acts adopted on the basis of those provisions'.[27] This rule is subject to two exceptions, as explained in the second paragraph of the Article:

–judicial review of CFSP acts allegedly in breach of Article 40 TEU, a provision that draws the line between CFSP and other Union policies;[28]

–judicial review of CFSP acts adopted by the Council on the basis of Chapter 2 of Title V TEU providing for 'restrictive measures against natural or legal persons'.[29]

The Court of Justice has significantly narrowed the scope of the carve-out that excludes Union courts' jurisdiction to review CFSP acts under Article 275 TFEU. In *KS and KD*,[30] the carve-out was declared to be limited to 'strategic or political choices', thus enabling Union courts to review implementing acts under the CFSP that do not call into question such choices. For example, disputes relating to the employment conditions of staff engaged in CSDP missions in third countries under CFSP instruments are regarded as matters subject to judicial review and are not covered by the exclusion of jurisdiction in Article 275 TFEU.[31]

1.1.3. Parties

1.1.3.1. Applicants

The Treaties distinguish three categories of applicants based on their standing to bring an action.

First, Member States, the European Parliament, the Council, and the Commission are considered privileged applicants under Article 263, second paragraph TFEU. These entities have the prerogative to bring an action for annulment of a Union act without needing to demonstrate a particular interest. This broad scope allows, for instance, a Member State to challenge an act which it has approved and voted for in the Council.[32] However, it is important

[24] Case C-60/81 *IBM v Commission* EU:C:1981:264, para 20; Case C-346/87 *Bossi v Commission* EU:C:1989:59, para 23; Case C-147/96 *Netherlands v Commission* EU:C:2000:335, para 35.

[25] Case C-207/86 *Apesco v Commission* EU:C:1988:200, paras 15 and 16; and Case C-294/86 *Technointorg v Commission and Council* EU:C:1988:470.

[26] Case C-7/56 *Algera* EU:C:1957:7; Case C-15/85 *Consorzio Cooperative d'Abruzzo v Commission* EU:C:1987:111, para 10; Case C-226/87 *Commission v Greece* EU:C:1988:354, para 16; and Case C-199/92 *Hüls v Commission* EU:C:1999:358, paras 84–88.

[27] Case C-348/12 P *Council v Manufacturing Support & Procurement Kala Naft* EU:C:2013:776, para 50; Case C-176/13 P *Council v Bank Mellat* EU:C:2016:96, paras 48–52; Case C-439/13 P *Elitaliana* EU:C:2015:753, paras 41–50.

[28] On the scope of Art 40 TEU as a ground of review, see Case C-72/15 *Rosneft* EU:C:2017:236, para 64ff.

[29] On the scope of Art 275 TFEU and the definition and scope of 'restrictive measures', see Rosneft (n 28) para 94ff.

[30] Joined Cases C-29/22 P and C-44/22 P *KS and KD* EU:C:2024:725.

[31] Case C-455/14 P *H v Council* EU:C:2016:569, para 44.

[32] Case C-166/78 *Italy v Council* EU:C:1979:195, paras 5–6.

to note that this privileged standing of Member States applies only when they act as subjects of international law. Individual authorities within the state – such as a parliamentary assembly, independent regulatory bodies, or territorial authorities (eg, municipalities or regional governments) – do not enjoy privileged standing. These entities are considered to be private parties (non-privileged applicants) for the purpose of standing.[33]

Secondly, the Court of Auditors, the ECB, and the Committee of the Regions are classified as semi-privileged applicants under Article 263, third paragraph TFEU. These entities have the right to initiate legal action 'for the purpose of protecting their prerogatives.' This semi-privileged status stems from case law, notably the judgment in *Chernobyl*,[34] where the European Parliament was recognised as having standing in cases affecting its prerogatives. The Nice Treaty subsequently elevated the European Parliament's standing to that of a privileged applicant and extended semi-privileged standing to the Court of Auditors, the ECB, and the Committee of the Regions.[35]

Third, any other applicant who brings an action for annulment comes under the category of *non-privileged applicants*, *with* their standing being dependent on the type of challenged act and its effects on the applicant's legal sphere (Article 263, fourth paragraph TFEU).

As a starting point, all natural or legal persons bringing an action for annulment against Union acts must demonstrate that they have an interest in bringing proceedings. This requirement involves proving the applicant's vested and present interest in the annulment of the act.[36] The applicant's interest must be personal,[37] vested[38] and present,[39] or otherwise the action will be declared inadmissible.

The case law has provided a broad interpretation of the term 'natural and legal person' to ensure the widest range of access for applicants. The term 'legal person' includes not only private but also public entities.[40] This covers regional or local authorities within Member States, provided they have legal personality as defined by national law.[41] The case law has also recognised the standing of certain entities without legal personality. For example, an entity lacking legal personality that is subject to restrictive measures is considered a 'legal person' for the purposes of Article 263, fourth paragraph TFEU. The Union has recognised the relevance of such an entity as sufficient to justify the imposition of restrictive measures and, as a result, its standing rights to challenge the said measures.[42] More recently, the case law has

[33] Nothing impedes a Member State from making use of its privileged standing to bring an action on behalf of the public authority concerned. See, for example, Case C-222/83 *Commune de Differdange v Commission* EU:C:1984:266, para 9; Case C-298/89 *Gibraltar v Council* EU:C:1993:267, para 14; Case C-95/97 *Région Wallone v Commission* EU:C:1997:184, para 6; and Case C-310/04 *Spain v Council* EU:C:2006:521.

[34] Case C-70/88 *Parliament v Council* EU:C:1991:373, para 27.

[35] Case C-295/90 *Parliament v Council* EU:C:1992:294, paras 8–10; Case C-316/91 *Parliament v Council* EU:C:1994:76, para 16; Case C-21/94 *Parliament v Council* EU:C:1995:220, para 8; Case C-156/93 *Parliament v Council* EU:C:1995:238, para 11; Case C-187/93 *Parliament v Council* EU:C:1994:265, para 14; Case C-360/93 *Parliament v Council* EU:C:1996:84, para 18; Case C-392/95 *Parliament v Council* EU:C:1997:289, paras 14–15; Case C-189/97 *Parliament v Council* EU:C:1999:366, paras 13–17.

[36] Case C-88/76 *Exportation des Sucres v Commission* EU:C:1977:61, paras 18–19; Case C-108/86 *DM v Council and Economic and Social Committee* EU:C:1987:426, para 10; Case C-164/02 *Netherlands v Commission* EU:C:2004:54, paras 18–25.

[37] Case C-282/85 *DEFI v Commission* EU:C:1986:316, para 18.

[38] Case C-204/85 *Stroghili v Court of Auditors* EU:C:1987:21, para 11.

[39] Case C-53/85 *Azko Chemie v Commission* EU:C:1986:256, para 21; and Case C-207/86 *Apesco v Commission* EU:C:1988:200, para 12.

[40] Case C-264/16 P *Deutsche Bahn and Others v Commission* EU:C:2018:60, para 2; and Joined Cases C-515/17 P and C-561/17 P *Uniwersytet Wroclawski and Poland v REA* EU:C:2020:73, para 69.

[41] Case C-180/97 *Regione Toscana v Commission* EU:C:1997:451, paras 10–12; and Case C-452/98 *Nederlandse Antillen v Council* EU:C:2001:623, para 51.

[42] Case C-229/05 P *PKK and KNK v Council* EU:C:2007:32, para 112.

confirmed that third countries are also regarded as a 'legal person' pursuant to Article 263, fourth paragraph TFEU. In the case of *Venezuela v Council*, the Court of Justice ruled that a third country, in its capacity as a subject of international law, may be adversely affected in its rights or interests by a Union act. Consequently, the Court determined that the third country must be entitled to seek the annulment of such a measure.[43]

The standing of natural and legal persons is established under Article 263, fourth paragraph TFEU, as interpreted by the case law of the Union courts. This provision outlines four distinct scenarios:

–*Applicant as an addressee of the contested act:* A natural or legal person to whom the contested Union act is explicitly addressed has standing to bring an action for annulment. As long as the contested act identifies the applicant in clear and unconditional terms, the addressee is deemed to meet this requirement. The nature of the act and its external representation are irrelevant, provided the addressee of its provisions is clearly identified, whether it is a decision, a regulation, or an act of soft law.[44] The case of directives is unique since, according to the Treaties, they are solely addressed to the Member States.

–Applicant challenging an individual act of which the applicant is not an addressee, but which concerns the applicant directly and individually: If a Union individual act, addressed to one or a closed group of natural or legal persons, has legal effects on third parties, the Treaties recognise the standing of the latter, provided that they can demonstrate a direct and individual concern.

- *The requirement of direct concern* entails that the act has immediate legal effects on the individual's legal situation, without requiring any further implementing acts, whether by Union institutions or Member States.[45] If the Union act requires additional implementing measures of a discretional nature, the subsequent implementing acts will reduce the discretion and eventually materialise the decision made by the Union authorities. Conversely, if the Union act requires implementation but grants no discretion to the implementing authority, the applicant will have direct concern and may challenge the initial Union act.[46] According to settled case law, the requirement of 'direct concern' provided in Article 263, fourth paragraph TFEU requires the contested act 'leave no discretion to the addressees who are entrusted with the task of implementing it, such implementation being purely automatic and resulting from EU rules alone without the application of other intermediate rules'.[47]In the context of composite procedures involving both Union and national authorities, discretion is excluded where the EU act 'unconditionally binds' the authority entrusted with implementation as to the outcome of the issues decided, even if that authority retains discretion in respect of other, distinct aspects of the final decision.[48]

[43] Case C-872/19 P *Bolivarian Republic of Venezuela v Council* EU:C:2021:507, para 50.

[44] Joined Cases C-16/62 and C-17/62 *Conf des prod de fruits/Conseil CEE* EU:C:1962:47, para 3.

[45] Joined Cases C-41/70 to C-44/70 *International Fruit Company and Others v Commission* EU:C:1971:53, paras 23–28; Joined Cases C-87/77, C-130/77, C-22/83, and C-9/84 to C-10/84 *Salerno and Others v Council and Commission* EU:C:1985:318, paras 31–32; Case C-207/86 *Apesco v Commission* EU:C:1988:200, para 12; and Case C-294/83 *Les Verts v Parliament* EU:C:1986:166, para 31.

[46] Joined Cases C-445/07 P and C-455/07 P *Commission v Ente per le Ville Vesuviane*, EU:C:2009:529, para 45.

[47] Case C-404/96 P *Glencore Grain v Commission* EU:C:1998:196, para 41; Case C-486/01 P *Front National v Parliament* EU:C:2004:394, para 34; Joined Cases C-622/16 P to C-624/16 P *Scuola Elementare Maria Montessori v Commission, Commission v Scuola Elementare Maria Montessori*, and *Commission v Ferracci* EU:C:2018:873, para 42; Joined Cases C-663/17 P, C-665/17 P, and C-669/17 P *ECB and Others v Trasta Komercbanka and Others* EU:C:2019:923, para 10; Case C-414/18 *Iccrea Banca* EU:C:2019:1036, para 66; Joined Cases C-779/21 P and C-799/21 P *Commission v Front Populaire pour la liberation de la Saguia-el-Hamra et du Rio de oro (Front Polisario)* EU:C:2024:835, paras 88–99; and Joined Cases C-777/22 P and C-789/22 P *ECB and Commission v Corneli* EU:C:2025:580, para 62.

[48] *WhatsApp Ireland Ltd/European Data Protection Board* (n 22) para 96.

- The requirement of *individual concern* has become more problematic and difficult to satisfy in practice, especially as interpreted under the so-called *Plaumann* test, which stipulates that 'persons other than those to whom a decision is addressed may only claim to be individually concerned if that decision affects them by reason of certain attributes which are peculiar to them or by reason of circumstances in which they are differentiated from all other persons, and by virtue of these factors distinguishes them individually just as in the case of the person addressed'.[49] In the case of a group of individuals concerned, they must prove to belong to 'a closed class of operators whose identity could have been established by the [Union] authorities'.[50]

  - *Applicant challenging a legislative act of general scope:* In the case of Union legislative acts, an applicant must also meet the requirements of direct and individual concern. However, given the specific characteristics of legislative measures and their general scope, fulfilling both requirements can be challenging for private applicants. This is especially true with regard to establishing individual concern, as legislative measures by their very nature affect a general and indeterminate category of groups or individuals in a way that is often difficult, if not impossible, to individualise. Nonetheless, the case law has recognised that in certain exceptional circumstances, it is possible to claim an individual concern when challenging a Union legislative act:
  - Firstly, a Union legislative act can trigger individual concern when the applicant demonstrates that their individual rights have been so adversely affected that they differentiate the applicant from all other addressees. This is illustrated by legislative acts that impose measures of such severity on a closed category of individuals that they eventually affect them in a quasi-expropriatory manner. To date, the Court of Justice has recognised the legitimacy of such claims in the case of *Codorniú*, where a regulation prohibited a company, operating since 1924 under a trademark, from using its protected trademark. In this case, the Court of Justice held that the applicant 'has established the existence of a situation which, from the point of view of the contested provision, differentiates it from all other traders'.[51]
  - Secondly, an applicant will have individual concern if the Union legislature is required, by specific provisions, to take account of the consequences of the act it intends to adopt for the situation of certain individuals.[52]
  - Thirdly, a Union legislative act will individually concern a natural or legal person when the act explicitly refers to the applicant, even if the applicant is not the addressee of the measure. In such cases, the reference to the applicant is evidence that the Union legislature has taken into account the specific situation of the applicant, to the extent that it distinguishes the applicant from other individuals.[53] This criterion should be borne in

[49] Case C-25/62 *Plaumann v Commission* EU:C:1963:17, 107.

[50] Case C-62/70 *Bock v Commission* EU:C:1971:108, paras 2–5; Case C-97/85, *Deutsche Lebensmittelwerke v Commission* EU:C:1987:243, para 11; and Case C-131/92 *Arnaud and Others v Council* EU:C:1993:200, para 8. On the evolution of the *Plaumann* test and the current status of the case law, see the Opinion of Advocate General Emiliou in C-731/23 P *Nicoventures Trading and Others v Commission* EU:C:2025:435, partly followed by the Court of Justice in its judgment in the said case, at paras 64–70.

[51] Case C-309/89 *Codorníu v Council* EU:C:1994:197, para 22.

[52] Case C-11/82 *Piraiki Patraiki v Commission* EU:C:1985:18, para 31; Case C-209/94 *Buralux and Others* EU:C:1996:54, paras 30–35; Case C-152/88 *Sofrimport* EU:C:1990:259, paras 8–13; Case C-451/98 *Antillean Rice Mills* EU:C:2001:622, paras 56–68; and Case C-452/98 *Nederlandse Antillen v Council* EU:C:2001:623, paras 54–77.

[53] Case C-138/79 *Roquette v Council* EU:C:1980:249, paras 13–16; Case C-139/79 *Maizena v Council* EU:C:1980:250, paras 13–16; and Joined Cases C-239/82 and C-275/82 *Allied Corporation and Others v Commission* EU:C:1984:68, paras 4–12.

mind when comparing this case with those where a legislative act conceals an individual act applicable *de iure* and de facto only to a single operator.[54]

– *Applicant challenging a regulatory (non-legislative) act not entailing implementing measures:* The Treaty of Lisbon introduced a significant innovation to the rules governing the standing of individuals to bring actions for annulment. Article 263, fourth paragraph TFEU, now grants any natural or legal person the right to bring an action 'against a regulatory act which is of direct concern to them and does not entail implementing measures'. To fully understand the purpose of this provision, it is important to consider its history and evolution. The provision finds its roots in the Court of Justice's strict interpretation of the concept of 'individual concern', a term that had long been criticised for making it excessively burdensome for individuals to challenge general Union acts. The restrictive interpretation was the subject of criticism from commentators, Advocates General, and even the Court of First Instance (now the General Court). In 2002, in *UPA*, the Court of Justice reaffirmed its restrictive stance on the matter, declaring that it would not deviate from its established interpretation of 'individual concern'. However, the Court also indicated the possibility of reform through treaty amendment, suggesting that it was for the Member States to reform the system:

> While it is, admittedly, possible to envisage a system of judicial review of the legality of [Union] measures of general application different from that established by the founding Treaty and never amended as to its principles, it is for the Member States, if necessary, in accordance with Article 48 EU, to reform the system currently in force.[55]

This suggestion was no coincidence. At the time of delivering the ruling in *UPA*, the Convention on the Future of Europe was about to start its deliberations, and one of its working groups was convened to address this issue. The outcome of these discussions is reflected in the current wording of Article 263, fourth paragraph TFEU, which broadens the conditions of access to judicial review for individuals in specific circumstances.

As to the meaning of 'regulatory acts', Article 263, fourth paragraph TFEU refers to actions against 'regulatory acts', a puzzling reference with no equivalent definition elsewhere in the Treaties. While Article 288 TFEU refers to 'regulations' among the Union's acts, the *travaux préparatoires* of the Convention confirm that the authors of the current version of Article 263, fourth paragraph TFEU were not advocating for a more liberal approach confined to regulations only. Instead, the focus was on non-legislative acts of general application. Therefore, 'regulatory acts' should be interpreted as encompassing all non-legislative acts of general application, including delegated and implementing acts. This interpretation was confirmed by the Court of Justice in *Inuit*, following the Opinion of Advocate General Kokott.[56] Accordingly, a 'regulatory act' as defined in Article 263, fourth paragraph TFEU is an 'act of general application other than legislative acts'.[57] The term 'general application' should be assessed by analysing the content of the act rather than its formal classification. Consequently, a decision which contains provisions of general scope may, depending on its content and effects, be considered a 'regulatory act' for the purpose of an action for annulment.[58]

[54] Case C-348/20 P *Nord Stream 2 AG* EU:C:2022:548.

[55] Case C-50/00 P *Unión de Pequeños Agricultores* EU:C:2002:462, para 45.

[56] Case C-583/11 P *Inuit Tapiriit Kanatami and Others v Parliament and Council* EU:C:2013:625.

[57] Case C-244/16 P *Industrias Químicas del Vallés* EU:C:2018:177, para 40; and Case C-384/16 P *European Union Copper Task Force* EU:C:2018:176, para 33, as well as the Opinion of Advocate General Wathelet in those cases, at pts 60 and 66 respectively.

[58] This is the case of a Commission Decision approving a national scheme under State Aid rules, as confirmed in Case C-622/16 P *Scuola Elementare Maria Montessori Srl* EU:C:2018:873.

As to the standing requirements, Article 263, fourth paragraph TFEU, requires the applicant to prove both direct concern and that the act in question does not involve implementing measures. This requirement of 'direct concern' follows the same test as under the second limb: the contested act must directly affect the legal situation of the individual and it must leave no discretion to the addressees entrusted with the task of implementing it. Implementation must be purely automatic and result solely from the Union's rules, without the application of any intermediate rules, insofar as the effects on the applicant are concerned. This requirement is applied stringently, as demonstrated by the case law to date. For example, in the case of *T&L Sugars*, several importers initiated legal proceedings to annul two regulations directed at sugar producers. The Court of Justice ruled that, in such circumstances, 'the appellants do not have the status of producers of sugar and their legal situation is not directly affected by those regulations'.[59] The second requirement, that the act does not include implementing measures, must be assessed by reference to two different situations, depending on whether the implementing measures fall within the competence of the Union or those of the Member States.

If the implementing measures fall within the Union's competence, the Court of Justice has established the following two criteria:

- Firstly, reference must be made to the position of the natural or legal person pleading the right to bring proceedings under Article 263, fourth paragraph TFEU. It is irrelevant whether the act in question entails implementing measures with regard to other persons.[60]
- Secondly, the test must focus exclusively on the subject matter of the action and, where an applicant seeks only the partial annulment of an act, it is solely any implementing measures which that part of the act may entail that must, as the case may be, be taken into consideration.[61]

If the implementing measures fall within the competence of the Member States, the existence of national implementing measures will generally preclude standing under the third limb of Article 263, fourth paragraph TFEU, since the applicant can challenge those national measures before national courts and request a preliminary ruling on the validity of the underlying Union act.[62] Ultimately, individuals subject to a Union regulatory act may bring an action before the national courts against the national implementing measures and request that the national courts refer the matter to the Court of Justice for a preliminary ruling of validity, pursuant to Article 267 TFEU.[63]

1.1.3.2. Defendants

According to Article 263, first paragraph TFEU, there are two categories of potential defendants in actions for annulment. Acts of these institutions (other than recommendations and opinions) are reviewable without the additional requirement that they be 'intended to produce legal effects vis-à-vis third parties.' The second category comprises the European Parliament, the European Council, and the bodies, offices, or agencies of the Union. The acts of these entities are subject to judicial review only if they are 'intended to produce legal effects *vis-à-vis*

[59] Case C-456/13 P *T&L Sugars and Sidul Açúcares v Commission* EU:C:2015:284, para 37.

[60] Case C-274/12 P *Telefónica v Commission* EU:C:2013:852, para 30.

[61] ibid, para 31.

[62] *T&L Sugars* (n 59) paras 41–42; Case C-553/14 P *Kyocera Mita Europe v Commission* EU:C:2015:805, para 46; Case C-244/16 P *Industrias Químicas del Vallés* EU:C:2018:177, para 47; and Case T-262/10 *Microban International* EU:T:2011:623, paras 26–39.

[63] *T&L Sugars* (n 59) para 31.

third parties'. This criterion stems from the Court of Justice's judgment in *Les Verts*, which established the principle that all Union institutions must be subject to judicial review of their acts intended to produce legal effects.[64]

1.1.4. Grounds for Annulment

Article 263, second paragraph TFEU states that Union acts can be annulled on one or more of the following four grounds: lack of competence; infringement of an essential procedural requirement; infringement of the Treaties or of any rule of law relating to their application; or misuse of powers. The applicant is required to state in its submissions which of these grounds justify the annulment of the contested act. However, in exceptional circumstances, the Union courts may, on their own motion, review a Union act if it is found to be lacking in competence or to have infringed an essential procedural requirement.[65]

The ground based on lack of competence may arise in three different limbs: lack of competence *ratione personae*; lack of competence *ratione materiae*; and lack of competence *ratione loci*.

'Lack of competence *ratione personae*' usually relates to a dispute over the institution that adopted the act or the basis chosen by the defendant Union institution, body, office, or agency. These disputes are a recurring feature of litigation because the choice of legal basis depends on objective criteria subject to judicial review. The European Parliament often becomes involved in such disputes when it considers that the Council has selected a legal basis which undermines the legislative prerogatives of the European Parliament.[66] Furthermore, a lack of competence *ratione personae* can arise in the context of delegations, regardless of whether the delegation is conferred on a Union institution, body, office, or agency or on a Member State.[67]

The lack of competence *ratione materiae* can arise when a Union act regulates matters for which the Treaties do not grant the Union any powers. In this case, the applicant does not dispute the horizontal division of powers between the institutions; rather, they question the Union's competence to adopt the contested measure.[68]

The lack of competence *ratione loci* may be raised when an act of the Union has effects beyond the territorial boundaries of the Member States. However, the Union retains the power to adopt measures with extraterritorial effect, provided that the activities of the addressees of the contested act have a sufficient link to the territory of the Member States. For example, an anticompetitive agreement entered into by companies established in a third country, aimed at regulating their worldwide activities, will have effects in the Union's internal market, regardless of whether the agreement was made in a third country by foreign companies established in a third country.[69] In such cases, despite the potential indirect extraterritorial reach of Union law,

[64] Case C-294/83 *Les Verts v Parliament* EU:C:1986:166. On the requirement that the acts must produce legal effects on third parties, see also Case C-34/86 *Council v Parliament* EU:C:1986:291, para 5; and Case C-167/02 P *Rothley and Others v Parliament* EU:C:2004:193, paras 22–37.

[65] Case C-1/54 *France v High Authority* EU:C:1954:7; Case C-6/54 *Netherlands v High Authority* EU:C:1955:5; Case C-18/57 *Nold KG v High Authority* EU:C:1959:6; Case C-291/89 *Interhotel v Commission* EU:C:1991:189, para 14; Case C-304/89 *Oliveira v Commission* EU:C:1991:191, para 18; and Case C-265/97 P *VBA v Florimex and Others* EU:C:2000:170, para 114.

[66] See, inter alia, Case C-133/06 *Parliament v Council* EU:C:2008:257; and Case C-166/07 *Parliament v Council* EU:C:2009:499.

[67] Case C-23/75 *King Soda* EU:C:1975:142.

[68] Case C-376/98 *Germany v Council and Parliament* EU:C:2000:544.

[69] Case C-48/69 *ICI v Commission* EU:C:1972:70, paras 126–42; and Joined Cases C-89/85, C-104/85, C-114/85, C-116/85, C-117/85, C-125/85, C-126/85, C-127/85, C-128/85, and C-129/85 *Ahlström Osakeyhtiö and Others v Commission* EU:C:1993:120.

the case law has upheld its legality, provided that the measure in question is intended to mitigate the consequences of conduct in the internal market.[70]

An *infringement of an essential procedural requirement* constitutes a serious violation that can be divided into two different situations.[71] First, an infringement that undermines or prevents the applicant from bringing an action in court, as in the case of a failure to state reasons.[72] Second, an infringement that involves breaching a mandatory procedural rule, such as the requirement to consult other institutions, bodies, offices, or agencies, including but not limited to the ECB, the Economic and Social Committee, or the Committee of the Regions.[73]

An infringement of the Treaties or of any rule of law relating to their application is a ground for annulment, and in practice often constitutes the principal ground relied upon. This ground of annulment serves as a default mechanism, available when the contested act does not fall within the scope of any of the other grounds. It also reinforces the hierarchical structure of the Union's system of legal sources, thereby enabling a challenge against an act in breach of higher-ranking rules, such as the Treaties, general principles of law, international agreements, or legislative acts. The review conducted by Union courts in such cases includes both errors of law and errors of fact.[74] However, when the contested act is the result of complex technical or economic analyses, the case law indicates that the Union courts will exercise a limited standard of review, annuling the act only when it is clear that the defendant committed a manifest error of assessment.[75]

Finally, *misuse of powers* is a ground of review that targets a Union act adopted to achieve an objective different from the one for which the power was conferred. The earlier case law of the Court of Justice associated a misuse of powers with the subjective intention of the authority that adopted the challenged act.[76] Subsequently, the case law evolved and adopted a broader objective analysis, considering not only the intention of the author of the contested act but also other relevant factors, such as preparatory work, debates preceding the adoption of the act, and public statements made by the defendant party during the adoption process.[77] However, challenging a Union act on the grounds of an alleged misuse of powers is notoriously difficult, as the applicant must demonstrate on the basis of objective, relevant and consistent evidence that the act was adopted exclusively or at least primarily for purposes other than those stated, and successful outcomes are very rare. This difficulty explains the limited use of this ground in practice.

[70] Case C-366/10 *Air Transport Association of America and Others* EU:C:2011:864; and Case C-131/12 *Google Spain* EU:C:2014:317.

[71] Joined Cases C-209/78 to C-215/78 and C-218/78 *Van Landewyck v Commission* EU:C:1980:248, para 47; and Case C-150/84 *Bernardi v Parliament* EU:C:1986:167, para 28.

[72] Case C-137/92 P *Commission v BASF and Others* EU:C:1994:247, paras 75–76.

[73] *Roquette v Council* (n 53) para 22; and Case C-207/81 *Ditterich v Commission* EU:C:1983:123, para 19.

[74] Case C-18/62 *Barge v High Authority* EU:C:1963:56.

[75] *Roquette v Council* (n 53) para 25; Case C-42/84 *Remia v Commission* EU:C:1985:327, para 34; Case C-187/85 *Fediol v Commission* EU:C:1988:399, para 6; Case C-225/91 *Matra v Commission* EU:C:1993:239, paras 24–25; Case C-204/00 P *Aalborg Portland and Others* EU:C:2004:6, para 279; and Case C-389/21 P *ECB v Crédit Lyonnais* EU:C:2023:368, paras 55–57.

[76] Case C-6/54 *Netherlands v High Authority* EU:C:1955:5.

[77] Case C-8/55 *Fédération charbonnière de Belgique v High Authority* EU:C:1956:11; Case C-13/57 *Wirtschaftsvereinigung Eisen- und Stahlindustrie v High Authority* EU:C:1958:10; Joined Cases C-351/85 to C-360/85 *Fabrique de fer de Charleroi* EU:C:1987:392, paras 19–20; Joined Cases C-32/87, C-52/87, and C-57/87 *ISA v Commission* EU:C:1988:328, para 19; and Joined Cases C-33/86, C-44/86, C-110/86, C-226/86, and C-285/86 *Stahlwerke Peine-Salzgitter and Others v Commission* EU:C:1988:402, paras 27–28.

1.1.5. Time Limits

According to Article 263, sixth paragraph TFEU, an action for annulment 'shall be instituted within two months of the publication of the measure, or of its notification to the plaintiff, or, in the absence thereof, of the day on which it came to the knowledge of the latter, as the case may be'. However, this time limit benefits from a ten-day extension on account of distance.[78] Furthermore, when the time limit allowed for initiating proceedings against a measure adopted by an institution runs from the publication of that measure, the time limit is calculated from the end of the fourteenth day after the measure is published in the *Official Journal of the European Union*.[79]

Failure to meet the time limit is a matter of public policy that may be reviewed by the Union courts of their own motion.[80]

1.1.6. Effects of the Judgment

Once a judgment in an action for annulment becomes final, it acquires the force of *res judicata*. The specific effects of a final judgment depend on the outcome of the action, whether it is dismissed or upheld.

In the event of a *dismissal*, the judgment becomes *res judicata* only with respect to the factual and legal grounds established therein. Consequently, an act declared valid can be challenged in the future, but a new action will be declared inadmissible if the same or different parties raise the same ground or grounds that were already examined and dismissed in the first proceedings.[81]

If the action is *upheld*, Article 264, first paragraph TFEU states that 'the Court of Justice of the European Union shall declare the act concerned to be void'. The effects of a declaration of invalidity are *ex tunc* and *erga omnes*: the act is declared void from the moment it was adopted, producing its effects vis-à-vis all persons, not only the parties of the case. This rule is tempered by Article 264, second paragraph TFEU, which states that the Union court 'shall, if it considers this necessary, state which of the effects of the act which it has declared void shall be considered as definitive'. This provision empowers the court to maintain certain effects of the annulled act in the interest of legal certainty, for example, by ruling that the annulment of the challenged act will take effect from the date of the judgment or from a later date, allowing the defendant institution to adopt a new act.[82] The effects of a declaration of nullity can also be mitigated by a partial annulment, which limits the effects of the ruling to a part of the contested act rather than the entire act or provision. Partial annulment is only possible when

[78] Art 51 of the Rules of Procedure of the Court of Justice and Art 60 of the Rules of Procedure of the General Court.

[79] Art 50 of the Rules of Procedure of the Court of Justice and Art 59 of the Rules of Procedure of the General Court.

[80] Case C-4/67 *Collignon v Commission* EU:C:1967:51; Case C-108/79 *Belfiore v Commission* EU:C:1980:146, para 3; Case C-227/83 *Moussis v Commission* EU:C:1984:276, para 12; Case C-152/85 *Misset v Council* EU:C:1987:10, para 11; Case C-246/95 *Coen v Belgian State* EU:C:1997:33, para 21; and Case C-498/08 *Fornaci Laterizi*, EU:C:2009:447, para 19.

[81] Case C-62/82, *Italy v Commission*, EU:C:1983:74, paras 17–18; Joined Cases C-159/84, C-267/84, C-12/85, and C-264/85, *Ainsworth v Commission* EU:C:1987:172, para 1; and Case C-277/95 P *Lenz v Commission* EU:C:1997:7, para 50.

[82] Case C-81/72 *Commission v Council* EU:C:1973:60, para 15; Case C-92/78 *Simmenthal v Commission* EU:C:1979:53, para 107; Case C-264/82 *Timex v Council and Commission* EU:C:1985:119, para 32; Case C-34/86 *Council v Parliament* EU:C:1986:291, para 48; Case C-45/86 *Commission v Council* EU:C:1987:163, para 23; Case C-51/87 *Commission v Council* EU:C:1988:455, para 22; Case C-360/93 *Parliament v Council* EU:C:1996:84, paras 32–36; Case C-271/94 *Parliament v Council* EU:C:1996:133, para 40; and Case C-22/96 *Parliament v Council* EU:C:1998:258, para 42.

the annulled provisions are severable from the act as a whole. If the provisions are not severable, the court will declare the nullity of the whole act.[83]

Article 266, first paragraph TFEU states that the institution, body, office, or agency whose act has been declared void 'shall be required to take the necessary measures to comply with the judgment of the Court of Justice of the European Union'. Despite the removal of the annulled act from the legal order following a declaration of nullity, additional measures may be necessary to guarantee full compliance with the judgment or to provide legal certainty within the sector affected by the annulled act. In the event of the annulment of a decision imposing a pecuniary fine, the defendant must reimburse the amount of the fine and the interest accrued.[84] This obligation is binding exclusively on the defendant in relation to the party that initiated the legal action concerning the fine.[85] When the annulment results from a violation of an essential procedural requirement, the defendant may issue the act once again, following the rectification of the procedural flaw, provided that the procedural defect is capable of being remedied.[86] The defendant institution, body, office, or agency must comply with the judgment within a 'reasonable time', a period that varies depending on the specific circumstances of each case.[87]

It should be noted that actions for annulment can be brought together with an action for damages. In such cases, the court will hear both claims and decide on them in the same judgment. If the action for annulment is upheld, the action for damages will be subsequently adjudicated. However, it is important to note that an annulment does not automatically entail the upholding of the action for damages, as both actions are autonomous and subject to different legal requirements.

1.2. *Action for Failure to Act*

Judicial review of the activity of the Union is not limited to active decision-making and material conduct, it also extends to the inactivity of an institution, body, office or agency. According to Article 265 TFEU, if the European Parliament, the European Council, the Council, the Commission, the ECB, or any Union body, office, or agency 'in infringement of the Treaties, fail to act', an action can be brought before the Union courts. It must be noted that the action for failure to act does not involve the exercise of unlimited jurisdiction by the Union courts. Instead, it is limited to a declarative statement on the unlawfulness of the challenged inactivity. The defendant institution, body, office, or agency will be required to remedy the situation following the delivery of the judgment.

1.2.1. Jurisdiction

The rules on jurisdiction that apply to actions for failure to act are broadly equivalent to those that apply to actions for annulment. Article 256(1) TFEU introduces rules on jurisdiction applicable to both actions, stating that the General Court has jurisdiction to hear and determine at first instance actions referred to, inter alia, in Article 265 TFEU. However, this rule is

[83] Case C-34/86 *Council v Parliament* EU:C:1986:291, paras 40–42; Case C-68/94 *France and Société commerciale des potasses et de l'azote and Entreprise minière et chimique v Commission* EU:C:1998:148, para 257; Case C-376/98 *Germany v Council and Parliament* EU:C:2000:544, para 117; Case C-29/99 *Commission v Council* EU:C:2002:734, para 46; and Joined Cases C-239/01 and C-244/03 *Germany v Commission*, EU:C:2003:514, para 13.

[84] Case T-171/99 *Corus UK v Commission* EU:T:2001:249, paras 54–58; and Case C-221/22 P *Commission v Deutsche Telekom* EU:C:2024:488, paras 52–58.

[85] *Case C-310/97 Commission v AssiDomän Kraft Products and Others* EU:C:1999:407, paras 53–71.

[86] *Roquette v Council* (n 53).

[87] Case C-266/82 *Turner v Commission* EU:C:1984:3, para 5; and Case C-21/94 *Parliament v Council* EU:C:1995:220, para 33.

subject to the exceptions enumerated in Article 51 of the Statute of the Court of Justice. This provision specifies the cases in which jurisdiction is reserved to the Court of Justice:

- *Member State v Union institutions*: actions brought by a Member State against a failure to act by the European Parliament or the Council, or both institutions jointly. Actions against the failure to act of the Commission are within the jurisdiction of the Court of Justice only where they concern measures adopted under the first paragraph of Article 331 TFEU, relating to enhanced cooperation, as expressly provided for in Article 51(b) of the Statute of the Court of Justice.
- *Union institution v Union institution*: actions brought by a Union institution against the failure to act of the European Parliament, the Council, both those institutions failing to act jointly, or of the Commission or the ECB.

The jurisdiction of the Court of Justice is subject to an exception (thus referring the jurisdiction back to the General Court) in the case of:

- Failure to act of the Council in cases under the third subparagraph of Article 108(2) TFEU.
- Failure to act of the Council in cases pursuant to a Council regulation concerning measures to protect trade within the meaning of Article 207 TFEU.
- Failure to act of the Council in the exercise of implementing powers in accordance with the second paragraph of Article 291 TFEU.

1.2.2. Challengeable Inactivity

According to Article 265, first paragraph TFEU, an action for failure to act can be initiated when the inactivity amounts to an infringement of the Treaties. Consequently, an action will be upheld when the defendant fails to comply with a legal obligation to act.[88] Despite the specific wording of this provision, actions for failure to act are not limited to infringements of the Treaties. They may also be brought in cases of an infringement of an obligation to act established in an international agreement or in secondary Union law.[89]

When the applicant is a natural or legal person, the act that the institution, body, office, or agency of the Union has failed to adopt must be of a binding nature.[90] If the applicant is a Member State or an institution, no reference is made in the Treaty to the binding nature of the omitted act, thus being enough to prove the infringement of the duty to act.[91]

1.2.3. Parties

1.2.3.1. Applicants

Article 265 TFEU introduces two categories of applicants, each of them subject to different standing requirements. Firstly, Article 265, first paragraph TFEU stipulates that Member States, along with the institutions of the Union (excluding the Court of Justice of the European Union and the Court of Auditors) can bring an action for failure to act without the need to state a particular interest or concern.

[88] Case C-64/82 *Tradax v Commission* EU:C:1984:106, paras 22–23.

[89] Joined Cases C-10/68 and C-18/68 *Eridiana and Others v Commission* EU:C:1969:66, para 16.

[90] See Art 265, third para TFEU and the case law, inter alia, in Case C-15/70 *Chevalley v Commission* EU:C:1970:95, paras 10–11.

[91] Case C-13/83 *Parliament v Council* EU:C:1985:220, paras 54–71.

On the other hand, *natural and legal persons* can bring an action for failure to act in respect of a failure by an institution, body, office, or agency of the Union to address to that person any act other than a recommendation or an opinion. The case law has interpreted Article 265, third paragraph TFEU in accordance with the requirements on standing for private applicants in actions for annulment. According to the case law, both Articles 263 and 265 'merely prescribe one and the same method of recourse'.[92] This principle is further reinforced by the dictum that 'the possibility for individuals to assert their rights should not depend upon whether the institution concerned has acted or failed to act'.[93] Therefore, Article 265, third paragraph TFEU must be interpreted as entitling natural and legal persons to bring an action for failure to act under analogous conditions to those applicable to an action for annulment. To succeed in such an action, applicants must demonstrate that the failure to act is of direct and individual concern to them.[94]

Furthermore, when natural and legal persons bring an action for failure to act, they are required to demonstrate their interest in bringing such an action under the same requirements as those provided for actions for annulment.[95]

1.2.3.2. Defendants

Pursuant to Article 265, first paragraph TFEU, an action for failure to act may be brought against the failure to act of the European Parliament, the European Council, the Council, the Commission, or the ECB. Article 265, third paragraph TFEU extends this to bodies, offices, and agencies of the Union, in actions brought by natural and legal persons. The Court of Justice and the Court of Auditors are not listed among the potential defendants, as a consequence of the nature of their respective functions.

1.2.4. The Pre-litigation Phase and Time Limit to Bring the Action

An action for failure to act must be preceded by a prior procedure in which the relevant Union institution, body, office, or agency concerned is given the opportunity to respond to the applicant's request to act. According to Article 265, second paragraph TFEU, an action is only 'admissible' if the relevant Union institution, body, office, or agency 'has first been called upon to act'. The Treaty makes no reference to a time limit for submitting this preliminary request, but the case law requires that a 'reasonable period' must have elapsed from the time at which the authority should have taken action before the applicant submits the preliminary request.[96] Furthermore, the applicant is required to clearly identify in its request the measure that the institution, body, office or agency is required to adopt, so as to enable the latter to define its position.[97]

[92] *Chevalley v Commission* (n 90) para 6; and Case C-68/95 *T Port v Bundesanstalt für Landwirtschaft und Ernährung* EU:C:1996:452, para 59.

[93] *T Port* (n 92) para 59.

[94] Case C-15/71 *Mackprang v Commission* EU:C:1971:98, para 4; Case C-134/73 *Holz and Willemsen v Council and Commission* EU:C:1974:1, para 5; Case C-90/78 *Granaria v Council and Commission* EU:C:1979:85, paras 12–15; and Case C-60/79 *Producteurs de vins v Commission* EU:C:1979:189, 2432.

[95] Case C-33/14 P *Mory and Others v Commission* EU:C:2015:609, para 62; and Case C-596/15 P *Bionorica v Commission* EU:C:2017:886, paras 83ff.

[96] The period should not be too short (Case T-74/92 *Ladbroke Racing* EU:T:1995:10; Case T-28/95 *IECC v Commission* EU:T:1998:213, para 15; and Case T-286/97 *Goldstein v Commission* EU:T:1998:150, paras 26–29) nor too long (Case C-59/70 *Netherlands v Commission* EU:C:1971:77, paras 12–24; and Case C-170/02 P *Schlüsselverlag J S Moser and Others v Commission* and *Moser and Others v Commission* EU:C:2003:501, paras 36–38.).

[97] Case C-25/85 *Nuovo Campsider v Commission* EU:C:1986:195, para 8.

Once the request has been submitted, the Union institution, body, office or agency has two months to 'define its position'. The position can be expressed through any means that clearly reflect the 'position' of the Union institution, body, office or agency. The 'position' can take the form of a formal decision, or a letter, or email, as long as it reflects a definitive 'position' following the applicant's call to act.[98] If the Union institution, body, office or agency defines its 'position' and communicates it to the applicant, the action for failure to act will be devoid of purpose. If the applicant wishes to challenge the 'position' adopted by the authority, the available remedy is an action for annulment, provided the position constitutes a reviewable act within the meaning of Article 263 TFEU. In the absence of a 'position' within two months, the applicant must file an action for failure to act in Union courts within a further period of two months. The only exception to this rule arises in an interinstitutional context, in actions brought by one institution against another, 'where the inadmissibility of an action for failure to act would enable the institution which has been called upon to act to persist in its failure to act'.[99]

1.2.5. Effects of the Judgment

If the action for failure to act is upheld, the Union institution, body, office or agency whose failure to act has been declared contrary to the Treaties 'shall be required to take the necessary measures to comply with the judgment of the Court of Justice of the European Union'.[100] It is important to note that the Union court has no jurisdiction to adopt the omitted act on behalf of the defendant party, nor can it issue an injunction determining how the act should be adopted in the future. The ruling will declare in its operative part the existence of a failure to act, and the defendant party will be given a reasonable period to comply with the judgment.[101]

If the failure to act is remedied during the proceedings, the action will become devoid of purpose,[102] allowing the defendant to raise a plea of lack of purpose (*non-lieu à statuer*) and thereby terminate the proceedings. It should be noted that this outcome is in stark contrast with the infringement procedure, where the Court of Justice assesses compliance at the date of expiry of the period laid down in the reasoned opinion and may continue the proceedings even after the defendant Member State has subsequently remedied the alleged breach of Union law.

The applicant may bring a claim for damages alongside a claim for failure to act, seeking redress for any harm caused by the unlawful omission. The Union court will decide on the action for damages once it has previously upheld the action for failure to act.

[98] Case C-42/71 *Nordgetreide* EU:C:1972:16, para 4; Case C-125/78 *GEMA v Commission* EU:C:1979:237, paras 14–23, and Joined Cases C-596/15 P and C-597/15 P *Bionorica and Diapharm v Commission* EU:C:2017:886, paras 55–59.

[99] Case C-137/21 *European Parliament v Commission* EU:C:2023:625, paras 40–41: 'That would be the case if the communication [of the Commission] were to be classified as a position defined by an institution, for the purposes of the second paragraph of Article 265 TFEU, resulting in the inadmissibility of the present action. In such a situation, the disagreement between the parties to the present dispute as regards the scope of point (f) of the first paragraph of Article 7 of Regulation 2018/1806 and, more specifically, as to the existence of any obligation to adopt the delegated act at issue, would continue to exist. . . . Thus, a refusal to act, however explicit, on the part of an institution, after the institution in question has been called upon to act pursuant to the second paragraph of Article 265 TFEU, can be brought before the Court on the basis of that article since it does not put an end to the failure to act.'

[100] Art 266, first para TFEU.

[101] Joined Cases C-97/86, C-99/86, C-193/86 and C-215/86 *Asteris v Commission* EU:C:1988:199, paras 26–27.

[102] Case C-75/69 *Hake v Commission* EU:C:1970:65, paras 6–10; Case C-377/87 *Parliament v Council* EU:C:1988:387, para 10; Case C-383/87 *Commission v Council* EU:C:1988:388, para 10; Joined Cases C-15/91 and C-108/91 *Buckl and Others v Commission* EU:C:1992:454; and Case C-25/91 *Pesqueras Echebastar* EU:C:1993:131, paras 11–12.

1.3. *Action for Damages*

The Union can face legal action in a court of law from applicants seeking compensation for damage resulting from unlawful conduct by the Union or its servants. The Union's non-contractual liability is enshrined in the Treaties in Article 340, second paragraph TFEU, which also extends to the personal liability of its staff when acting in the performance of their duties. Furthermore, Article 41(3) of the Charter states that every person has the right 'to have the Union make good any damage caused by its institutions or by its servants in the performance of their duties, in accordance with the general principles common to the laws of the Member States'.

Damages actions in the field of non-contractual liability can be brought against the Union in respect of any unlawful act or conduct that causes damage, regardless of the policy area. This also applies to the CFSP in areas where the Union courts, despite the carve-out in Article 275 TFEU, have jurisdiction to hear the case, as confirmed in *Bank Refah*.[103]

In the case of the Union's contractual liability, national courts have jurisdiction to hear such actions (Article 274 TFEU), save where jurisdiction is conferred on the Union courts by virtue of an arbitration clause under Article 272 TFEU, a mechanism widely used in Union contracts. In the case of the Union's non-contractual liability, Article 268 TFEU states that Union courts have exclusive jurisdiction over disputes related to compensation for damage provided for in the second and third paragraphs of Article 340 TFEU. Damages actions that claim the non-contractual liability of the Union seek to establish whether an act or omission of the Union has caused damage to a Member State or to a natural or legal person. In this regard, the Union courts have unlimited jurisdiction and are responsible not only for assessing the unlawfulness of the Union's conduct, but also for establishing the amount necessary to ensure full compensation for the victim.

As an exception to the general framework described above, disputes between the Union and its staff members, including actions for damages arising from the Union's activities as an employer, fall under Article 270 TFEU and Articles 90–91 of the Staff Regulations[104].

1.3.1. Jurisdiction

According to Article 256(1) TFEU, the General Court holds jurisdiction at first instance to hear actions for damages under Articles 268 and 340 TFEU.[105]

1.3.2. Parties

1.3.2.1. Applicant

The action for damages may be brought by any natural or legal person, irrespective of nationality, who has suffered harm as a result of conduct of a Union institution, body, office or

[103] In the field of restrictive measures, where the Court of Justice has jurisdiction and there is an interaction with other legal bases in the Treaties, this was confirmed in Case C-134/19 P *Bank Refah* EU:C:2020:793, para 49. See also Case T-558/15 *Iran Insurance v Council* EU:T:2018:945, para 55; Case C-45/15 P *Safa Nicu Sepahan v Council* EU:C:2017:402; Case C-123/18 P *HTTS v Council* EU:C:2019:358; and Case T-341/07 *Sison v Council* EU:T:2011:687. See also the Order of the General Court in Case T-771/20 RENV *KS and KD v Council* EU:T:2021:798.

[104] Regulation No 31 (EEC), 11 (EAEC), laying down the Staff Regulations of Officials and the Conditions of Employment of Other Servants of the European Economic Community and the European Atomic Energy Community (consolidated), [1962] OJ P45/1385 (14 June 1962) (as amended).

[105] The Court of Justice has ruled that an action for damages brought against the Union on the basis of non-contractual liability, even if it is brought under national legislation establishing special statutory rules which differ from the ordinary rules of law governing civil liability in the Member State concerned, does not fall within the jurisdiction of the national courts. See Case C-377/09 *Françoise-Eléonor Hanssens-Ensch v European Community*, EU:C:2010:459.

agency.[106] Moreover, Member States are also entitled to bring an action for damages under Article 268 TFEU.[107]

Natural or legal persons are entitled to bring an action for damages as long as they can demonstrate a vested and present interest. Furthermore, the damage must have been suffered *personally* by the applicant. In the case of legal persons, damage must be proven to have a direct impact on the entity's own assets and not only on those of its members or shareholders.[108] When the asset affected by the unlawful harm is transferred, the right of action is transferred to the new holder of the asset,[109] unless there is evidence of fraudulent intent in the assignment.[110]

1.3.2.2. Defendant

In actions for damages, the defendant party is the Union as a legal person responsible for the acts of its institutions, bodies, offices or agencies.[111] In the case of conduct of the Union's staff members, the Union is liable for their acts only when they act in the performance of their duties.[112] In such cases, in addition to the Union's liability, the institution concerned holds the right to bring disciplinary proceedings against the staff member in accordance with the Staff Regulations. When a staff member causes harm outside the scope of their duties, they will be held personally liable. The damages will be determined by national courts in accordance with the law of the Member State where the harmful act occurred or produced its effects.

Determining the liable entity can be particularly challenging when the harm arises from actions taken by a Member State while implementing Union law. In such cases of potential shared liability, in order to distinguish between the liable conduct of the Union and that of the Member State, it is essential to assess the degree of discretion exercised by the Member State.

In cases where the Member State implements Union law with no discretion, the wrongful conduct is attributed to the Union and, as a result, the action for damages falls under the jurisdiction of the General Court. This rule is only subject to an exception when the claim brought before a national court can secure full compensation,[113] in which case the jurisdiction to hear the damages action lies with the national court.[114]

[106] Case C-9/75 *Meyer-Burckhardt v Commission* EU:C:1975:131, para 7; Case C-48/76 *Reinarz v Commission and Council* EU:C:1977:30, 411; Joined Cases C-114/79, C-115/79, C-116/79, and C-117/79 *Fournier v Commission* EU:C:1980:124, 1531; and Case C-277/95 P *Lenz v Commission* EU:C:1996:456, para 23.

[107] Case C-575/18 P *Czech Republic v Commission* EU:C:2020:530, para 82; and Case C-494/22 P *Commission v Czech Republic* EU:C:2024:684, para 83.

[108] Case C-114/83 *Société d'initiatives et de coopération agricoles v Commission* EU:C:1984:246, paras 3–5; Case C-289/83 *GAARM v Commission* EU:C:1984:398, paras 4–5. Collective damages are also excluded when claimed by the shareholders or members. See Case C-72/74 *Union Syndicale v Council* EU:C:1975:43, para 21.

[109] Case C-238/78 *Ireks-Arkady v Council and Commission* EU:C:1979:226, para 5; and Joined Cases C-256/80, C-257/80, C-265/80, and C-267/80, *Birra Wührer* EU:C:1984:341, para 12.

[110] Case C-250/78 *Contifex/EEC* EU:C:1983:49, para 15.

[111] Case C-302/87 *Parliament v Council* EU:C:1988:461, para 9; Case C-353/88 *Briantex v EEC and Commission* EU:C:1989:415, para 7; and Case C-370/89 *SGEEM and Etroy v BEI* EU:C:1993:202, para 16.

[112] Case C-5/68 *Sayag and Others* EU:C:1968:42, 585; and Case C-9/69 *Sayag and Others* EU:C:1969:37, paras 7–11.

[113] Case C-281/84 *Zuckerfabrik Bedburg* EU:C:1987:3; Joined Cases C-106/87 to C-120/87 *Asteris and Others v Greece and EEC* EU:C:1988:457, para 14; Case C-282/90 *Vreugdenhil* EU:C:1992:124, para 14; Case C-55/90 *Cato v Commission* EU:C:1992:168, para 17; and Case C-104/89 *Mulder and Others v Council and Commission* EU:C:2000:38, para 9.

[114] In Case C-281/82 *Unifrex v Commission and Council* EU:C:1984:165, para 11, the Court of Justice stated as follows: 'Where an individual considers that he has been injured by the application of a [Union] legislative measure that he considers illegal, he may, when the implementation of the measure is left to the national authorities, contest the validity of the measure, when it is implemented, before a national court in an action against the national authorities. That court may, or even must, as provided for in [Art 267 TFEU], refer the question of the validity of the [Union] measure in dispute to the Court of Justice. However, the existence of such a means of redress will be capable of ensuring the effective protection of the individuals concerned only if it may result in making good the alleged damage.' See also Case C-175/84 *Krohn v Commission* EU:C:1987:8, para 27; and Case C-81/86 *De Boer Buizen* EU:C:1987:277, para 9.

In cases where the Member State acts within a margin of discretion, national courts have jurisdiction when the applicant can secure full compensation by bringing its claim against the national authorities alone. In the remaining cases, where the claim involves damage requiring compensation from both the Union and the Member State, the case law requires that the Member State's liability be first established in national courts in accordance with national law, before the Union courts can assess the Union's non-contractual liability in respect of the same harm, in order to avoid the risk of double recovery.[115] Despite the practical disadvantages of this solution, the Court of Justice remains attached to it and justifies it as a means to prevent applicants from claiming overcompensation.[116]

In some cases, the Union legislator may determine that the shared liability between the Member State and the Union is to be addressed through joint and several liability. This option allows the applicant to bring an action for damages against the Union for the entirety of the harm caused by both the Member States and the Union. When the wording of the legislative provision is unclear, the Court of Justice provides an interpretation that best aligns with the fundamental right to an effective judicial remedy, as a means to facilitate the applicant's ability to obtain redress.[117]

These cases of shared liability must be distinguished from situations where the liability of a Member State arises from conduct in breach of Union law. In such cases, damages actions are subject to national law, but they must comply with the principles of effectiveness and equivalence as developed in the case law of the Court of Justice, outlined in chapter twelve of this book.

1.3.3. Requirements

Applicants who bring an action for damages must prove that they comply with the following three requirements: (1) the Union's act or conduct is *unlawful*; (2) the damage suffered is actual and certain; and (3) a direct *causal link* exists between the unlawful act or conduct and the damage alleged.

Until 2000, the case law was not entirely consistent as to the conditions governing a damages action. In *Bergaderm*,[118] the Court of Justice clarified that the conditions governing the Union's non-contractual liability mirror those established for the liability of Member States for breach of Union law. The test requires an assessment of both the existence of an unlawful act and the seriousness of the breach, taking into account the degree of discretion available to the Union. To achieve this outcome, the case law has developed a two-step test to determine whether the Union's act or conduct is unlawful. Firstly, the act or conduct of the Union must breach a rule of Union law 'intended to confer rights on individuals'. Secondly, the breach must be 'sufficiently serious', to the extent that the Union 'manifestly and gravely disregarded the limits on its discretion'.[119] When the Union has only limited, or even no, discretion, the mere infringement of a rule of Union law may be sufficient to establish the existence of a sufficiently serious breach.[120] In any event, the harmful act or conduct of the Union must involve a breach of a rule

[115] Joined Cases C-5/66, C-7/66 and C-13/66 to C-24/66 *Kampffmeyer and Others v Commission* EU:C:1967:31, paras 263–64.

[116] ibid 266; Case C-30/66 *Becher v Commission* EU:C:1967:44, 300; and Case T-317/12 *Holcim (Romania) v Commission* EU:T:2014:782, para 79.

[117] Case C-755/21 P *Kočner v Europol* EU:C:2024:202, paras 55–72.

[118] Case C-352/98 *Bergaderm and Goupil v Commission* EU:C:2000:361.

[119] ibid, para 43.

[120] ibid, para 44.

of Union law, thus excluding the Union's liability for the enactment of harmful measures which are lawful but nevertheless cause harm.[121]

As for the damage, it must be actual and certain[122], as reflected in a loss of assets,[123] profit,[124] or chance,[125] or in non-material damage.[126] In the case of financial loss, reparation must be 'commensurate with the loss or damage sustained',[127] including default and compensatory interest.[128] The burden of proof rests with the applicant,[129] who must provide sufficient evidence to establish the existence and extent of actual and certain damage.[130]

The causal link between the unlawful act or conduct and the alleged damage is the third and final requirement, which also falls on the applicant to prove. The case law rules out the existence of a causal link when the connection between the unlawful Union act or conduct and the damage is too remote,[131] or when the applicant has contributed through their own actions to the circumstances giving rise to the damage.[132]

1.3.4. Time Limitation

According to Article 46 of the Statute of the Court of Justice, actions for damages 'shall be barred after a period of five years from the occurrence of the event giving rise thereto'. This provision should be interpreted as referring to the time when the damage actually materialises, not to the time of the wrongful act or conduct.[133] Therefore, if the victim was unaware of the unlawful act or conduct until the harm became apparent at a later point, the limitation period begins to run from the time the harm *emerged* and became known to the victim.[134]

The five-year time limitation provided in Article 46 of the Statute of the Court of Justice can be interrupted in two situations: by bringing an action for damages in Union courts, or by filing an action for annulment or an action for failure to act against the relevant institution, body, office, or agency of the Union.[135]

[121] Joined Cases C-120/06 P and C-121/06 P *Fiamm and Others v Council and Commission* EU:C:2008:476, paras 167–79.

[122] Joined Cases C-19/69, C-20/69, and C-30/69 *Richez-Parise and Others v Commission* EU:C:1970:47, para 31; and Joined Cases C-56/74 to C-60/74 *Kampffmeyer v Council and Commission* EU:C:1976:78, para 6.

[123] *See the case law cited in n 116.*

[124] Joined Cases C-104/89 and C-37/90 *Mulder and Others v Council and Commission* EU:C:1992:217, para 26; and Case T-198/05 *Mebrom v Commission* EU:T:2007:147, para 51.

[125] Case C-281/84 *Zuckerfabrik Bedburg* EU:C:1987:3, para 14; Case C-348/06 P *Girardot v Commission* EU:C:2008:107; Case C-611/12 P *Giordano and Buono v Commission* EU:C:2014:195, Opinion of AG Cruz Villalón; Case T-271/04 *Citymo v Commission* EU:T:2007:128, para 176; and Case T-292/15 *Vakakis kai Synergates v Commission* EU:T:2018:103, paras 188–91.

[126] Case C-25/60 *De Bruyn v Assemblée* EU:C:1962:6; Case C-35/62 *Leroy v High Authority* EU:C:1963:50; Case C-84/63 *Van Steenwijk v Commission* EU:C:1964:49; Case C-87/63 *Georges v Commission* EU:C:1964:59; Case C-93/63 *Van Nuffel v Commission* EU:C:1964:60; Case C-65/63 *Prakash v Commission* EU:C:1963:11; and Case C-207/81 *Ditterich v Commission* EU:C:1983:123.

[127] Joined Cases C-46/93 and C-48/93 *Brasserie du Pêcheur v Bundesrepublik Deutschland* and *The Queen v Secretary of State for Transport, ex parte Factortame and Others* EU:C:1996:79, para 82.

[128] Case C-185/80 *Garganese v Commission* EU:C:1981:161, paras 19–20; Case T-201/17 *Printeos v Commission* EU:T:2019:81; and Case C-221/22 P *Commission v Deutsche Telekom AG* EU:C:2024:488, paras 55–58.

[129] Case C-26/74 *Roquette Frères v Commission* EU:C:1976:69, paras 22 and 24.

[130] Case C-5/71 *Zuckerfabrik Schoeppenstedt v Council* EU:C:1971:116, para 9.

[131] Case C-169/83 *Leussink-Brummelhuis v Commission* EU:C:1986:371, para 22.

[132] Case C-169/73 *Compagnie Continentale France* EU:C:1975:13, paras 22–32; and Case C-104/89 *Mulder and Others v Council and Commission* EU:C:2000:38, para 33.

[133] Joined Cases C-46/59 and C-47/59 *Meroni and Others v High Authority* EU:C:1962:44, para 806.

[134] Case C-145/83 *Adams v Commission* EU:C:1985:448, para 50.

[135] *Kampffmeyer and Others v Commission* (n 115); and Case C-11/72 *Giordano v Commission* EU:C:1973:39, para 6.

1.3.5. Effects of the Judgment

A judgment upholding an action for damages will impose a pecuniary obligation on the Union in favour of the applicant, enforceable from the date of service. Enforcement is carried out in accordance with Articles 280 and 299 TFEU, which establish the enforceability of judgments of the Court of Justice and of decisions of the Council, Commission and ECB imposing pecuniary obligations. While enforcement is carried out in accordance with the laws of the Member State in which it takes place, any seizure of Union assets must respect the Protocol on Privileges and Immunities of the European Union (Protocol No 7) and may require prior authorisation of the Court of Justice.

In the case of a dismissal of an action for damages, the judgment of the General Court, once confirmed on appeal or once the time limit for lodging an appeal has expired, has the force of *res judicata* between the parties. However, other natural or legal persons who are not parties to the proceedings are not bound by the judgment and are entitled to bring further actions for damages resulting from the same Union acts or conduct, provided that they are filed within the five-year period laid down in Article 46 of the Statute of the Court of Justice.

1.4. Appeals

Judgments and orders of the General Court can be appealed to the Court of Justice. An appeal is limited to a review on points of law only, and is subject to further restrictions following the introduction of a filtering mechanism in 2019, applicable only to specific categories of cases as defined in Article 58a of the Statute of the Court of Justice.

1.4.1. Jurisdiction

Article 256(1)(2) TFEU provides that 'decisions given by the General Court . . . may be subject to a right of appeal to the Court of Justice on points of law only, under the conditions and within the limits laid down by the Statute'.

1.4.2. Decisions Subject to Appeal

The 'decisions' subject to appeal are judgments and orders issued by the General Court, provided that they:

- are final decisions;
- dispose of the substantive issues in part only; or
- dispose of a procedural issue concerning a plea of lack of competence or inadmissibility.

The Statute and the case law have introduced additional 'decisions' subject to appeal, including those on interim measures[136] or rejections of a request for leave to intervene.[137] In contrast, decisions to stay proceedings in the General Court[138] or on costs alone[139] are not subject to an appeal.

[136] Art 57, second para of the Statute of the Court of Justice.

[137] Art 57, first para of the Statute of the Court of Justice.

[138] Order of 26 November 2003, *ABI and Others v Commission*, Joined Cases C-366/03 P to C-368/03 P, C-390/03 P, C-391/03 P and C-394/03 P, EU:C:2003:638.

[139] Art 58, second para of the Statute of the Court of Justice.

1.4.3. Parties

An appeal may be brought by 'any party which has been unsuccessful, in whole or in part, in its submissions'.[140] An appeal may also be brought by interveners who are not Member States or institutions 'only where the decision of the General Court directly affects them'.[141]

Finally, except for staff disputes, an appeal may also be brought by Member States and institutions of the Union which did not intervene in the proceedings in the General Court.[142]

1.4.4. Pleas

Article 58 of the Statute of the Court of Justice provides that an appeal to the Court of Justice 'shall be limited to points of law'. The provision goes on to specify that the appeal must be based on grounds of:

- lack of competence of the General Court;
- a breach of procedure before the General Court which adversely affects the interests of the appellant; and/or
- the infringement of Union law by the General Court.

When hearing a case on appeal, the Court of Justice cannot reassess the facts.[143] However, the case law exceptionally admits the possibility of a limited review of the General Court's assessment of the facts. For example, the appellant is entitled to challenge the terms under which the gathering of evidence took place in the General Court, or the way in which the General Court applied the rules on the burden of proof on points of law.[144] Furthermore, the case law allows for an appellate review of a 'distortion of the evidence' in exceptional cases.[145] This review applies to a finding of fact by the General Court that is manifestly inconsistent with the evidence in the file, or where the General Court has manifestly exceeded the limits of a reasonable assessment of that evidence.[146]

[140] Art 56, second para of the Statute of the Court of Justice.

[141] Art 56, second para of the Statute of the Court of Justice.

[142] In the case of a Member State that requested leave to intervene in the General Court in a staff case, but its request was not adjudicated on. See Case C-728/23 P *Spain v Robert Stockdale e.a.* EU:C:2025:710.

[143] Case C-413/06 P *Bertelsmann and Sony Corporation of America v Impala* EU:C:2008:392, para 29; Case C-194/09 P *Alcoa Transformazioni v Commission* EU:C:2011:497, paras 39–43; Joined Cases C-448/10 P to C-450/10 P *ThyssenKrupp Acciai Speciali Terni and Others v Commission* EU:C:2011:642, para 32; Case C-7/95 P *Deere v Commission* EU:C:1998:256, paras 21–22; Case C-185/95 P *Baustahlgewebe v Commission* EU:C:1998:608, para 24; and Case C-24/01 P *Glencore and Compagnie Continentale* EU:C:2002:642, para 65.

[144] Case C-53/92 P *Hilti v Commission* EU:C:1994:77, para 42; Case C-89/95 P *D v Commission* EU:C:1996:6, para 14; Case C-19/95 P *San Marco v Commission* EU:C:1996:331, para 39; Case C-390/95 P *Antillean Rice Mills* EU:C:1999:66, para 29; Case C-55/97 P *AIUFASS and AKT v Commission* EU:C:1997:465, para 25; Case C-140/96 P *Dimitriadis v Court of Auditors* EU:C:1997:493, para 27; Case C-401/96 P *Somaco v Commission* EU:C:1998:208, para 54; Joined Cases C-280/99 P to C-282/99 P *Moccia Irme and Others v Commission* EU:C:2001:348, para 78; and Case C-219/00 *Cementir v Commission* EU:C:2002:337, para 49.

[145] Case C-136/92 P *Commission v Brazzelli Lualdi and Others* EU:C:1994:211, para 49; *Antillean Rice Mills* (n 144) para 29; Case C-284/98 P *Parliament v Bieber* EU:C:2000:134, para 31; Case C-2/01 P *BAI and Commission v Bayer* EU:C:2004:2, para 47; and Joined Cases C-204/00 P, C-205/00 P, C-211/00 P, C-213/00 P, C-217/00 P, and C-219/00 P *Aalborg Portland and Others v Commission* EU:C:2004:6, para 48.

[146] Case C-132/90 P *Schwedler v Parliament* EU:C:1991:452, paras 13–25; Case C-255/90 P *Burban v Parliament* EU:C:1992:153, para 5; Case C-325/94 P *An Taisce and WWF UK* EU:C:1996:293, paras 28–30; Case C-19/95 P *San Marco v Commission* EU:C:1996:331, para 39; Case C-278/95 P *Siemens v Commission* EU:C:1997:240, para 44; Case C-154/99 P *Politi v ETF* EU:C:2000:354, para 11; and *BAI and Commission v Bayer* (n 144) para 47.

The grounds of appeal cannot merely reiterate the same arguments already brought in the proceedings at first instance.[147] The parties' arguments must be exclusively directed at identifying the errors of law committed by the General Court, not the infringements attributed to the authority that adopted the challenged act.[148] Furthermore, appellants cannot change the subject matter of the proceedings at first instance, nor can they target a different act from the one challenged at first instance, or rely on a different ground of illegality not raised before the General Court.[149]

1.4.5. Time Limits

An appeal must be brought before the Court of Justice within two months of notification of the decision of the General Court.[150]

1.4.6. Preliminary Admission

In 2019, a filtering mechanism introducing a preliminary admission procedure for appeals was introduced. This mechanism applies to appeals brought against decisions of the General Court concerning decisions of an independent board of appeal of certain Union's offices and agencies.[151] Following a reform that took effect on 1 September 2024 in which the list of offices and agencies was expanded, the current boards of appeal to which the filtering mechanism applies are the following:

- the European Union Intellectual Property Office;
- the Community Plant Variety Office;
- the European Chemicals Agency;
- the European Union Aviation Safety Agency;
- the European Union Agency for the Cooperation of Energy Regulators;
- the Single Resolution Board;
- the European Banking Authority;
- the European Securities and Markets Authority;
- the European Insurance and Occupational Pensions Authority; and
- the European Union Agency for Railways.

The filtering mechanism also applies to decisions of the General Court concerning a decision of any other independent board of appeal, set up after 1 May 2019 within any other body, office or agency of the Union, which must be seised before an action can be brought before the General Court, as well as to decisions of the General Court relating to the performance of a contract containing an arbitration clause, within the meaning of Article 272 TFEU.

[147] Case C-338/93 P *De Hoe v Commission* EU:C:1994:85, paras 17–19; Case C-26/94 P *X v Commission* EU:C:1994:346, para 13; Case C-31/95 *Del Plato v Commission* EU:C:1996:105, para 20; Case C-453/98 *Branco v Commission* EU:C:1999:554, para 96; and *Moccia Irme and Others* (n 145) para 67.

[148] Case C-30/96 P *Abello and Others v Commission* EU:C:1998:42, para 45; and Joined Cases C-238/99 P, C-244/99 P, C-245/99 P, C-247/99 P, C-250/99 P to C-252/99 P, and C-254/99 P *Limburgse Vinyl Maatschappij and Others v Commission* EU:C:2002:582, paras 416–28.

[149] Case C-244/92 P *Kupka Floridi v CES* EU:C:1993:152, paras 12–20; *Hilti v Commission* (n 144) para 49; Case C-76/93 P *Scaramuzza v Commission* EU:C:1994:371, paras 15–19; Case C-19/95 P *San Marco v Commission* EU:C:1996:331, para 49; and Case C-291/97 P *P-H v Commission* EU:C:1998:287, para 25.

[150] Art 56, first para of the Statute of the Court of Justice.

[151] ibid, Art 58a

In these cases, an appeal shall be allowed to proceed, wholly or in part, only where it raises an issue that 'is significant with respect to the unity, consistency or development of Union law'.[152]

1.4.7. Effects

The filing of an appeal does not have suspensory effect on the challenged judgment or order of the General Court, unless the Court of Justice decides otherwise.[153] An exception to this rule applies when the General Court declares a regulation null and void, in which case the effects of the ruling will take effect only from the expiry of the time limit for bringing an appeal, or, if an appeal has been brought within that period, from the date of dismissal of the appeal.[154] This rule aims to minimise the consequences that the annulment of a regulation can have for third parties and for legal certainty altogether.

The *dismissal* of an appeal confirms the decision of the General Court challenged before the Court of Justice. The Court of Justice can dismiss the appeal while substituting its own reasoning for that of the General Court, provided that the operative part of the General Court's decision is correct in its result (substitution of grounds). Conversely, it can also uphold an appeal where the operative part of the General Court's decision is vitiated by an error of law in its legal reasoning, even if the operative part might otherwise appear correct.

If the appeal is well founded, the decision of the General Court will be set aside in whole or in part. In such a case, the Court of Justice 'shall quash the decision of the General Court' and 'it may itself give final judgment in the matter . . . or refer the case back to the General Court for judgment'.[155] In practice, the case will be referred back to the General Court when it is clear that a further assessment of the facts is needed, or when the General Court did not rule on all the pleas raised by the parties.[156] In the case of a referral, the General Court 'shall be bound by the decision of the Court of Justice on points of law'.[157]

2. Direct Actions for Review of Member States' Conduct: Infringement Proceedings

Direct actions can also address the conduct of Member States and their compliance with Union law. To this end, the Treaties provide a remedy that empowers the Court of Justice to assess whether the conduct of Member States is compatible with Union law. Unlike an action for annulment, where the Union courts have the power to declare null and void the acts of a Union institution, office, agency, or body, the infringement procedure restricts the Court of Justice to issuing a declaratory ruling only, leaving the adoption of the measures necessary to comply with the judgment in the hands of the Member State concerned.

The infringement procedure plays a pivotal role in ensuring the proper enforcement of Union law. It also enables the Court of Justice to define the scope of the obligations incumbent on the Member States, providing legal certainty for both institutional actors and private stakeholders. This remedy is also an essential tool to counter the effects of recalcitrant behaviour of a Member State, thereby ensuring equality among all Member States, who are all bound to comply with the obligations that stem from Union law. In addition, infringement proceedings

[152] ibid. In this regard, see C Oró Martínez, 'Filtering of Appeals on Points of Law Before the Court of Justice' (2020) *MPIL Yearbook of Procedural Law of the CJEU*.

[153] ibid, Art 60, first para.

[154] ibid, Art 60, second para.

[155] ibid, Art 61, first para.

[156] Case C-68/91 *Moritz v Commission* EU:C:1992:531, paras 41–42.

[157] Art 61, third para of the Statute of the Court of Justice.

can play a relevant role in facilitating damages claims brought by individuals against a Member State for breach of Union law, by providing an authoritative finding of non-compliance that national courts must take into account.

The rulings of the Court of Justice in infringement procedures are of a declaratory nature, addressing only the objective compatibility of a Member State's conduct with Union law, without determining the validity or effects of the national act or conduct under review. Consequently, the Court of Justice will generally not take into account justifications based on internal difficulties, such as constitutional constraints, administrative practices or political circumstances, that could excuse the non-compliance of the Member State. The review is limited to an objective assessment of compatibility with Union law.

The Treaties set out the basic rules of the infringement procedure in Articles 258–260 TFEU, but special arrangements are available for the following cases:

- In the field of State Aid, if the Commission considers that a Member State has not complied with a decision finding aid to be incompatible with the internal market, it may bring the matter directly before the Court of Justice, bypassing the pre-litigation procedure under Article 258 TFEU.[158]
- If the Commission or a Member State considers that another Member State is making an improper use of the powers granted in Articles 114, 346, or 347 TFEU, it may bring the matter directly before the Court of Justice. This serves as an optional remedy and does not exclude the use of Articles 258–59 TFEU.
- The supervisory powers granted to the Commission in the case of public undertakings or undertakings to which Member States grant special or exclusive rights may be exercised through the issuance of 'appropriate directives or decisions to the Member States'.[159]
- The remedies provided in Article 271(a) and (d) TFEU, which authorise the Board of Governors of the European Investment Bank (subparagraph (a)) and the Governing Council of the ECB (subparagraph (d)), respectively, to initiate proceedings against a Member State for failure to fulfil obligations under the Statute of the EIB or a national central bank for failure to fulfil obligations under the Treaties and the Statute of the ESCB and ECB.

2.1. *Jurisdiction*

Article 256 TFEU states that only the Court of Justice has jurisdiction to hear infringement proceedings. Although neither the TFEU nor the Statute provide for the possibility of transferring this jurisdiction to the General Court, Article 256(3) TFEU envisages the possibility that the General Court could be given jurisdiction in certain categories of infringement proceedings, as determined by the Statute. A proposal to amend the Statute to include this option was considered in 2017, but was eventually not pursued.[160]

[158] Case C-290/83 *Commission v France* EU:C:1985:37, para 17.

[159] Joined Cases C-8/90 and C-66/90 *Netherlands and PTT Nederland v Commission* EU:C:1992:63, para 27; Case C-163/99 *Portugal v Commission* EU:C:2001:189, para 27. Not so in the case of directives, as the Court of Justice had occasion to confirm in Case C-202/88 *France v Commission* EU:C:1991:120, paras 17–18.

[160] On the amendments to Protocol no 3 on the Statute of the Court of Justice of the European Union, see doc 7586 of 28 March 2018, containing a letter from the President of the Court of Justice of the European Union, forwarding to the President of the Council of the European Union a request for the amendment of Protocol no 3 on the Statute of the Court of Justice of the European Union. See A Sikora, 'Infringement Actions Before the General Court: The Past, Present and Future of the Judicial Architecture of the Union' in D Sarmiento, H Ruiz Fabri, and B Hess (eds), *Yearbook on Procedural Law of the Court of Justice of the European Union: First edition, 2019* (MPILux Research Paper Series 2020(2)).

2.2. *Activity of the Member States Subject to Review through an Infringement Procedure*

The objective nature of the infringement procedure enables the Court of Justice to review any unlawful act or conduct of a Member State, including its failure to act.[161] The case law has consistently stated that the duration, frequency, gravity, or scope of the infringement is irrelevant in determining whether there has been a breach.[162] The challenged activity may be reflected in an individual administrative act, a public contract, or a general legislative or administrative regulation. Persistent and generalised administrative practices can also be subject to review in an infringement procedure.[163] In the case of a national rule that breaches Union law but is not applied in practice by national authorities, the case law confirms that its mere existence on the statute book constitutes an infringement reviewable through an infringement procedure.[164]

The source of the Member State's conduct is irrelevant, whether it originates from the central government, regional or local authorities,[165] or from the executive, legislature, or judiciary. However, in the case of the judiciary, the Court of Justice has stated that the existence of 'isolated or numerically insignificant judicial decisions in the context of case-law taking a different direction, or still more a construction disowned by the national supreme court, cannot be taken into account' for the purpose of an infringement procedure.[166] For the action to be upheld, it is necessary for the judicial practice to represent 'a widely-held judicial construction which has not been disowned by the supreme court, but rather confirmed by it'.[167]

2.3. *Parties*

Articles 258–59 TFEU grant standing solely to the Commission and the Member States to initiate infringement proceedings against a Member State. Private individuals or other Union institutions, bodies, offices, or agencies are not entitled to bring infringement proceedings, but may submit a complaint to the Commission requesting it to investigate a potential breach. The Commission retains full discretion as to whether to pursue the complaint. The judicial remedy available to private individuals to challenge a Member State's activity is to bring an action in national courts. In the course of national proceedings, a national court has the right, and at times the obligation, to refer the matter to the Court of Justice for a preliminary reference of interpretation pursuant to Article 267 TFEU.

The overwhelming majority of infringement proceedings are brought by the Commission, a decision that is made in the exercise of broad discretion. The case law has repeatedly held that the Commission's refusal to initiate an infringement action against a Member State, even if requested by a complainant or another Member State, does not amount to a breach of its duty

[161] Case C-31/69 *Commission v Italy* EU:C:1970:10, para 9.

[162] Case C-150/97 *Commission v Portugal* EU:C:1999:15, para 22; Case C-348/97 *Commission v Germany* EU:C:2000:317, para 62; Case C-20/01 *Commission v Germany* EU:C:2003:220, para 30; and Case C-157/03 *Commission v Spain* EU:C:2005:225, para 44.

[163] Case C-21/84 *Commission v France* EU:C:1985:184, paras 13–15; Case C-387/99 *Commission v Germany* EU:C:2004:235, para 42; and Case C-494/01 *Commission v Ireland* EU:C:2005:250, para 28.

[164] Case C-167/73 *Commission v France* EU:C:1974:35; Case C-159/78 *Commission v Italy* EU:C:1979:243, para 22; Case C-168/85 *Commission v Italy* EU:C:1986:381, para 14; Case C-104/86 *Commission v Italy* EU:C:1988:171, para 12; Case C-74/86 *Commission v Germany* EU:C:1988:198, para 10; Case C-38/87 *Commission v Greece* EU:C:1988:407, para 9; Case C-197/96 *Commission v France* EU:C:1997:155, para 14; Case C-145/99 *Commission v Italy* EU:C:2002:142, para 30; and Case C-214/04 *Commission v Italy* EU:C:2005:440, para 13.

[165] Case C-77/69 *Commission v Belgium* EU:C:1970:34, para 15; Case C-169/82 *Commission v Italy* EU:C:1984:126; and Case C-239/85 *Commission v Belgium* EU:C:1986:457, paras 13–14.

[166] Case C-129/00 *Commission v Italy* EU:C:2003:656, para 32; Case C-154/08 *Commission v Spain* EU:C:2009:695, para 125; and Case C-416/17 *Commission v France* EU:C:2018:811, para 107.

[167] *See the case law above at n 166.*

to act.[168] As a result of this broad discretion, the Commission cannot be challenged in court through an action for failure to act pursuant to Article 265 TFEU,[169] nor through an action for annulment if the Commission gives reasons to justify its decision not to proceed.[170]

Member States have standing to bring an infringement procedure against another Member State under Article 259 TFEU, a course of action rarely exercised in practice. Article 259 TFEU requires the Member State first to bring the matter before the Commission, which must deliver a reasoned opinion after each of the States concerned has had the opportunity to submit observations. If the Commission has not delivered a reasoned opinion within three months, the Member State may bring the matter directly before the Court of Justice. The few instances where a Member State has relied on Article 259 TFEU highlight the sensitive or political nature of these disputes. To date, only nine infringement proceedings have been initiated between Member States under Article 259.[171]

2.4. *The Pre-litigation Stage*

The Commission has broad discretion in deciding the appropriate time to initiate an infringement proceeding.[172] The Treaties do not prescribe a specific time limit within which the action must be filed, but the Commission should not exercise this discretion in a manner that breaches the rights of defence of the defendant Member State.[173] The fact that the Commission does not immediately commence an infringement action following the adoption of the challenged conduct by the Member State does not create a legitimate expectation that an action will not be filed. However, the defendant Member State can invoke its rights of defence if it can demonstrate that an excessive period of time between the alleged breach and the commencement of proceedings has adversely affected those rights.[174]

2.4.1. The Pre-litigation Stage under Article 258 (*Commission v Member State*)

According to Article 258 TFEU, the infringement procedure brought by the Commission consists of two stages: the pre-litigation stage; and the litigation stage before the Court of Justice. The first stage involves formalised communications between the Commission and the Member State regarding the alleged breach; the second stage takes place in adversarial proceedings before the Court of Justice.

The pre-litigation stage under Article 258 TFEU comprises two compulsory and sequential steps. In the first step, the Commission issues a *letter of formal notice* addressed to the Member State, initiating the pre-litigation process and identifying the Union rules allegedly infringed by

[168] Case C-48/65 *Lütticke v Commission* EU:C:1966:8; Case C-87/79 *Bagusat v Hauptzollamt Berlin-Packhof* EU:C:1980:88; Case C-247/87 *Star Fruit v Commission* EU:C:1989:58; and Case C-371/89 *Emrich v Commission* EU:C:1990:158.

[169] *Emrich v Commission* (n 168).

[170] *Bagusat v Hauptzollamt Berlin-Packhof* (n 168) paras 5–9.

[171] Case C-141/78 *France v United Kingdom* EU:C:1979:225; Case C-388/95 *Belgium v Spain* EU:C:2000:244; Case C-145/04 *Spain v United Kingdom* EU:C:2006:543; Case C-364/10 *Hungary v Slovakia* EU:C:2012:630; Case C-648/15 *Austria v Germany* EU:C:2017:664; Case C-591/17 *Austria v Germany* EU:C:2019:504; Case C-457/18 *Slovenia v Croatia* EU:C:2020:65; Case C-121/21 *Czech Republic v Poland*, removed from the register; and Case C-822/21 *Latvia v Sweden* EU:C:2024:373.

[172] Case C-7/68 *Commission v Italy* EU:C:1968:51; Case C-7/71 *Commission v France* EU:C:1971:121; and Case C-422/92 *Commission v Germany* EU:C:1995:125.

[173] Case C-83/99 *Commission v Spain* EU:C:2001:31, paras 22–27; and Case C-99/02 *Commission v Italy* EU:C:2004:207, paras 20–21.

[174] Case C-96/89 *Commission v Netherlands* EU:C:1991:213, paras 14–16; and Case C-475/98 *Commission v Austria* EU:C:2002:630, paras 34–39.

the Member State and the factual basis of the complaint.[175] If the Commission intends to include additional alleged infringements of Union rules or rely on additional factual grounds, it must address a supplementary letter of formal notice to the Member State. The failure to send a letter of formal notice, or to sufficiently specify in detail the relevant rules and conduct concerned, amounts to an essential procedural flaw that will lead to the inadmissibility of the action.[176]

Following the Member State's reply to the letter of formal notice, the Commission will review the situation and, if the Member State's arguments are insufficient to dispel its concerns, it will issue a *reasoned opinion* to the Member State. This document will outline the reasons and the Union rules that, in the Commission's view, the Member State continues to violate. The Commission is precluded from introducing new grounds that were not raised in the letter of formal notice.[177] The purpose of the reasoned opinion is to elaborate further on the Commission's position and to allow the Member State to take the necessary measures to comply, or to submit its observations, before the matter proceeds to the Court of Justice.

The reasoned opinion will specify a time limit for the Member State to put an end to the alleged infringement. The duration of this time limit is at the Commission's discretion, based on the circumstances of each case.[178] In any event, the Commission cannot abuse this discretion by imposing excessively short time limits that limit the Member State's options for remedying the infringement.[179] After the expiration of the time limit, the Commission may bring an infringement action before the Court of Justice; the Treaties do not prescribe a time limit for bringing the action, but it must be brought within a reasonable period.

The reasoned opinion is essential in the next phase of the procedure, as it establishes the specific moment in time by reference to which the Court of Justice assess compliance: the factual and legal situation of the Member State at the expiry of the time limit set in the reasoned opinion.[180] Therefore, any actions taken by the Member State after this date, including the repeal or amendment of the allegedly illegal acts, are irrelevant to the Court of Justice's review.[181] The expiration date of the time limit in the reasoned opinion plays the role of a 'snapshot' that captures the sole relevant moment for the purposes of ruling on the alleged infringement by the Member State.

2.4.2. The Pre-litigation Stage under Article 259 TFEU (*Member State v Member State*)

When the applicant is a Member State, Article 259 TFEU states that 'it shall bring the matter before the Commission', which will deliver a reasoned opinion after having given the opportunity to both Member States to submit observations orally and in writing. Following the issuance of the reasoned opinion, the applicant Member State may bring an infringement action before the Court of Justice. If the Commission has not issued a reasoned opinion within three months of the date on which the matter was brought before it, the applicant Member State can nevertheless initiate proceedings before the Court of Justice without the reasoned opinion.

[175] Case C-341/97 *Commission v Netherlands* EU:C:2000:434.

[176] Case C-306/91 *Commission v Italy* EU:C:1993:161, paras 22–24; and Case C-243/89 *Commission v Denmark* EU:C:1993:257, para 13.

[177] Case C-145/01 *Commission v Italy* EU:C:2003:324.

[178] Case C-74/82 *Commission v Ireland* EU:C:1984:34, para 13.

[179] Case C-293/85 *Commission v Belgium* EU:C:1988:40, para 20.

[180] Case C-166/97 *Commission v France* EU:C:1999:149, para 18; Case C-384/99 *Commission v Belgium* EU:C:2000:660, para 16; Case C-147/00 *Commission v France* EU:C:2001:175, para 26; and Case C-119/00 *Commission v Luxembourg* EU:C:2001:351, para 14.

[181] Case C-39/72 *Commission v Italy* EU:C:1973:13, para 11; Case C-309/84 *Commission v Italy* EU:C:1986:73, para 18; Case C-103/84 *Commission v Italy* EU:C:1986:229, para 8; Case C-154/85 *Commission v Italy* EU:C:1987:292, para 6; and Case C-240/86 *Commission v Greece* EU:C:1988:173, para 14.

2.5. *The Stage before the Court of Justice*

The pre-litigation stage ends once the Commission or a Member State files an application at the Court of Justice. At this point, judicial proceedings commence, which will only conclude with the delivery of the ruling by the Court of Justice, or by the withdrawal of the action by the applicant.

In infringement proceedings before the Court of Justice, the burden of proof rests on the applicant,[182] who must present the factual evidence and legal arguments supporting its claim. The use of presumptions is generally excluded in an infringement procedure.[183] Conversely, the defendant Member State has a duty of sincere cooperation with the Commission or the applicant Member State,[184] providing all necessary information at its disposal and avoiding any conduct that could obstruct the procedure.[185]

The defendant Member State is not constrained by the legal arguments put forward in the pre-litigation stage.[186] The room for manoeuvre of the defendant Member State is broader than that of the Commission, provided that any new arguments are directed at proving the conformity of its conduct with Union law. The defendant Member State may admit the infringement but seek to justify it on the grounds of the unlawfulness of the Union rule concerned. However, the Court of Justice only allows Member States to raise a plea of illegality under Article 277 TFEU when the infringement procedure concerns a breach going beyond a mere failure to transpose or implement the relevant Union act.[187]

The defence of the Member State can, in exceptional cases, rely on *force majeure*, a circumstance only available in cases where it is 'absolutely impossible' to meet the obligations arising from Union law.[188] The Court has interpreted this defence very strictly: internal political difficulties, financial constraints, or administrative problems do not constitute *force majeure*. The burden of proof to demonstrate *force majeure* rests on the defendant Member State.[189]

2.6. *Consequences of the Judgment and its Enforcement*

The judgment delivered by the Court of Justice in an infringement procedure is declaratory. If the action is upheld, the judgment will declare the Member State's failure to fulfil its obligations, remaining silent as to the validity of the challenged rules or practices of the Member

[182] Case C-96/81 *Commission v Netherlands* EU:C:1982:192, para 6; Case C-249/88 *Commission v Belgium* EU:C:1991:121, para 6; Case C-210/91 *Commission v Greece* EU:C:1992:525, para 22; Case C-375/90 *Commission v Greece* EU:C:1993:154, para 33; and Case C-68/99 *Commission v Germany* EU:C:2001:137, para 38.

[183] Case C-290/87 *Commission v Netherlands* EU:C:1989:362, para 11; Case C-61/94 *Commission v Germany* EU:C:1996:313, para 61; Case C-214/98 *Commission v Greece* EU:C:2000:624, para 42; and Case C-147/00 *Commission v France* EU:C:2001:175, para 27.

[184] Art 4(3) TEU.

[185] Case C-33/90 *Commission v Italy* EU:C:1991:476, para 18; Case C-65/91 *Commission v Greece* EU:C:1992:388, para 14; Case C-494/01 *Commission v Ireland* EU:C:2005:250, para 197; and Case C-82/03 *Commission v Italy* EU:C:2004:433, para 15.

[186] Case C-414/97 *Commission v Spain* EU:C:1999:417, paras 18–19.

[187] Case C-156/77 *Commission v Belgium* EU:C:1978:180, paras 15–25; Case C-52/83 *Commission v France* EU:C:1983:328, para 10; Case C-52/84 *Commission v Belgium* EU:C:1986:3, para 13; Case C-226/87 *Commission v Greece* EU:C:1988:354, para 14; Case C-261/99 *Commission v France* EU:C:2001:179, para 18: 'a Member State cannot, therefore, properly plead the unlawfulness of a decision addressed to it as a defence in an action for a declaration that it has failed to fulfil its obligations arising out of its failure to implement that decision . . . It is immaterial whether such unlawfulness is pleaded in the action brought against the Member State or, as in this case, in an action for annulment of the decision at issue . . .'.

[188] Case C-52/84 *Commission v Belgium* EU:C:1986:3, para 16; Case C-349/93 *Commission v Italy* EU:C:1995:53, para 13; Case C-348/93 *Commission v Italy* EU:C:1995:95, para 17; Case C-99/02 *Commission v Italy* EU:C:2004:207, paras 16–18.

[189] Case C-1/00 *Commission v France* EU:C:2001:687, para 131.

State. The obligation to repeal or amend the contested rule, or to cease the practices that led to the infringement procedures, lies solely with the Member State in accordance with its internal constitutional arrangements.

The judgment of the Court of Justice in an infringement procedure is not subject to an appeal, thus acquiring the force of *res judicata* from the date of its delivery. If the action is upheld, Article 260(1) TFEU states that 'if the Court of Justice of the European Union finds that a Member State has failed to fulfil an obligation under the Treaties, the State shall be required to take the necessary measures to comply with the judgment of the Court'. The Treaties remain silent as to the period of time in which the Member State must align its conduct with Union law as declared by the Court of Justice in its judgment, but the case law emphasises that the process of compliance 'must be initiated at once and must be completed as soon as possible'.[190]

If the Commission considers that the Member State concerned has not taken the necessary measures to comply with the judgment, it may bring the case before the Court of Justice under Article 260(2) TFEU. Article 260(3) TFEU provides a separate, accelerated mechanism for specific cases, discussed below. These remedies serve as enforcement procedures, the main difference being that the subject matter of the proceedings is not an infringement of a rule of Union law directly, but non-compliance with a judgment of the Court of Justice declaring a failure to fulfil obligations. Furthermore, a judgment under Article 260 TFEU will not be limited to a declaration of non-compliance but can also impose a lump sum and/or a penalty payment on the Member State.

The enforcement procedure under Article 260 TFEU was simplified by the Treaty of Lisbon, which removed the requirement for the Commission to deliver a reasoned opinion. The current procedure requires only that the Commission give the Member State the opportunity to submit its observations, after which the matter can be brought before the Court of Justice. The Commission is no longer required to issue a formal letter of notice followed by a reasoned opinion, as was the case under the pre-Lisbon version of the provision. Again, the burden of proof to demonstrate that the Member State has not taken the necessary measures to comply with the judgment delivered in proceedings under Articles 258–259 TFEU rests with the Commission.[191]

The operative part of a judgment establishing a failure to fulfil obligations, which describes the breach established by the Court, is of particular importance for the determination of the measures which the Member State is required to adopt to comply fully with the said judgment. The operative part of the judgment is to be understood in the light of the grounds on which the Court of Justice delivered its ruling.[192] In this regard, it should be noted that the principle of *res judicata* applies to proceedings under Article 260 TFEU.[193] Therefore, the Court of Justice has stated that these proceedings are applicable only if the complaints raised are identical in fact and in law to those put forward in the case that gave rise to the declaratory judgment ruling on the infringement of Union law.[194]

The imposition of a lump sum or penalty payment is a coercive measure designed to ensure compliance with the declaratory judgment. The Court of Justice is not entitled to prescribe the specific measures that the Member State must adopt, and it is the Member

[190] Case C-426/98 *Commission v Greece* EU:C:2002:180, para 43, and Case C-359/97 *Commission v United Kingdom* EU:C:2000:426, paras 91–96.

[191] Case C-387/97 *Commission v Greece* EU:C:2000:356, para 73.

[192] Case C-662/24 *Commission v Belgium* EU:C:2025:958, para 30.

[193] Case C-526/08 *Commission v Luxembourg* EU:C:2010:379, para 27.

[194] ibid, paras 23–26.

State's responsibility 'to take the necessary measures to comply with the judgment of the Court'. To encourage the Member State to adopt the 'necessary measures', financial coercion through lump sums and penalty payments can be an effective tool to end the infringement.

Lump sums and penalty payments serve different purposes. A lump sum is a fixed pecuniary amount determined retrospectively, intended to penalise the continuation of the infringement from the date of the original declaratory judgment (or, in the case of Article 260(3) TFEU, from the expiry of the transposition deadline) until the date on which the Member State complies or the enforcement judgment is delivered. A penalty payment is a *prospective* measure, calculated based on the duration of the infringement from the time of delivery of the enforcement judgment onwards, designed to exert continuing financial pressure on the Member State to comply. Because they pursue different objectives, the Court of Justice has ruled that both measures can be imposed cumulatively in the same proceedings.

Only the Commission can bring an action pursuant to Article 260 TFEU, bearing the burden of proof, and it must propose the lump sum and/or penalty payment applicable to the case based on its predetermined and published guidelines.[195] The Court of Justice is not bound by the Commission's guidelines on the calculation of the financial penalties, but it must rule based only on the facts and information provided by the parties in the proceedings.[196] To determine the amount of the lump sum or penalty payment, the Court of Justice takes into account several criteria, including the duration of the infringement, its gravity and the capacity of the Member State to pay.[197] In the case of penalty payments, 'regard should be had in particular to the effects of failure to comply on private and public interests and to the urgency of getting the Member State concerned to fulfil its obligations'.[198] When calculating lump sums, the Court of Justice will take into consideration the progress made by the defendant Member State in complying with the judgment.[199]

The enforcement procedure also applies, by analogy, to non-compliance with interim measures issued in an infringement procedure pursuant to Article 279 TFEU. This course of action was confirmed in *Commission v Poland*, a case in the field of environmental protection in which the Vice-President of the Court of Justice issued interim measures that were not complied with by the defendant Member State. In these circumstances, it was confirmed that the Commission is entitled to bring the case before the Court of Justice and to propose the imposition of lump sums and penalty payments.[200]

As an exception to the general enforcement procedure outlined in Article 260(2) TFEU, the Commission may also request the imposition of financial penalties in the initial infringement procedure pursuant to Article 258 TFEU. This exceptional remedy was introduced in Article 260(3) TFEU by the Lisbon Treaty, allowing the Commission to propose the imposition of financial penalties at an early stage of the dispute. It can be invoked only in specific circumstances: when the Member State concerned 'has failed to fulfil its obligation to notify measures transposing a directive adopted under a legislative procedure'.[201] This means that Article 260(3) TFEU is limited to failures to notify transposing measures, as it does not cover defective trans-

[195] Communication from the Commission – financial sanctions in infringement proceedings C/2022/9973 [2023] OJ C2/1.

[196] Case C-387/97 *Commission v Greece* EU:C:2000:356, para 89.

[197] *Commission v Greece* (n 196) para 92.

[198] ibid.

[199] Case C-278/01 *Commission v Spain* EU:C:2003:635, para 50.

[200] Case C-441/17 R *Commission v Poland* EU:C:2017:877.

[201] Case C-543/17 *Commission v Belgium* EU:C:2019:573.

position or other breaches of Union law. The financial obligation imposed under this provision 'shall not exceed the amount specified by the Commission', and takes effect on the date set by the Court in its judgment. In any event, the proportionality of the proposed financial measures, the Commission's duty to state reasons, and the methodology used to calculate the lump sum have been the subject of judicial review in the Court of Justice.[202] In line with the financial penalties provided in Article 260(2) TFEU, the remedy under Article 260(3) TFEU authorises the Commission to request both the imposition, cumulatively or separately, of lump sums and penalty payments in the same proceedings.[203]

3. Other Remedies

The Treaties outline additional direct actions that serve specific roles in the Union courts' remedial toolkit.

First, in disputes concerning staff members,[204] the imposition of fines[205] and intellectual property rights,[206] the Treaties and secondary legislation have introduced specific features or additional requirements for judicial proceedings, allowing the Union courts to exercise unlimited jurisdiction or introducing specific procedural steps prior to filing an action in Union courts.

Second, the Union courts have jurisdiction to issue judgments pursuant to any arbitration clause included in a contract concluded by or on behalf of the Union, regardless of whether that contract is governed by public or private law.[207]

Third, the Court of Justice has jurisdiction to rule on the dismissal of members of the Commission,[208] the Ombudsman,[209] the Court of Auditors,[210] as well as judges and Advocates-General of the Court of Justice and the General Court.[211]

Fourth, the Statute of the Court of Justice and the Rules of Procedure provide for the possibility for parties to request an interpretation of a judgment,[212] an action for rectification of clerical mistakes, errors in calculation and inaccuracies,[213] the revision of a judgment upon discovery of a fact which is of such a nature as to be a decisive factor and which, when the judgment was delivered, was unknown to the Court and to the party claiming revision.[214]

And finally, Article 14.2 of the Protocol on the Statute of the European System of Central Banks provides for a hybrid judicial remedy that allows a governor of a national central bank who has been relieved from office, or the Governing Council to bring an action before the Court of Justice 'on grounds of infringement of [the] Treaties or of any rule of law relating

[202] Case C-549/18 *Commission v Romania* EU:C:2020:563; Case C-550/18 *Commission v Ireland* EU:C:2020:564. See C Amalfitano, 'Commission v Romania and Commission v Ireland: A Step Forward in Clarifying the Accelerated Infringement Procedure under Article 260(3) TFEU' (*EU Law Live*, 22 July 2020).

[203] Communication from the Commission — Implementation of Article 260(3) of the Treaty [2011] OJ C12/1.

[204] Art 270 TFEU.

[205] ibid, Art 261.

[206] Art 72 of Regulation 2017/1001.

[207] Art 272 TFEU.

[208] ibid, Art 247.

[209] ibid, Art 228(2).

[210] ibid, Art 286, sixth para.

[211] Art 6 of the Statute of the Court of Justice.

[212] ibid, Art 43.

[213] Art 154 of the Rules of Procedure of the Court of Justice; Art 164(4) of the Rules of Procedure of the General Court.

[214] Art 44 of the Statute of the Court of Justice.

to their application'. The Court of Justice characterised this remedy as having the features of an action for annulment, but with very specific characteristics, most notably the power of the Court of Justice to annul the act of dismissal issued by the Member State. In *Rimsevics and ECB v Latvia*,[215] these powers of annulment of Member State acts were exercised for the first time, introducing a unique feature, unprecedented in Union and international law, that entitles the Union courts to review and annul an act of a Member State authority and remove it from the national legal system.

4. The Development of New Remedies in Union Courts

The Treaties have established a 'complete system of legal remedies and procedures' designed to enable the Union courts to review the legality or validity of the acts of the Union's institutions, bodies, offices, and agencies.[216] This vision of the Union legal system as comprising a 'complete system of legal remedies' has sparked discussions in the past, having been questioned by academic scholarship. The reality is that gaps in the Union's system of legal remedies have emerged from time to time. When such gaps appear in the remedies provided by Member States, Union law imposes specific obligations on Member States to fill the gaps and provide the necessary legal remedies. When gaps emerge in the remedies available in Union courts, the Court of Justice has addressed the matter by either interpreting the existing remedies in the Treaties broadly, creating new remedies, or employing a combination of both.

The development of new remedies in Union courts is not a frequent practice, but the case law provides several examples in which the Court of Justice has responded to remedial gaps in the Treaties. For example, Member States and individuals can rely on actions for unjust enrichment before Union courts, a course of action that can be pursued through a broad interpretation of Article 268 TFEU, which governs the jurisdiction of Union courts in respect of actions for damages against the Union.[217] Only recently, the action for unjust enrichment was made available to Member States in disputes against the Commission over the Union's own resources, where the Commission's positions were reflected in letters that did not amount to a reviewable act. To fill this gap in the system of remedies, the Court of Justice confirmed the existence of an action for unjust enrichment, which could be brought on the basis of Article 268 TFEU. Unlike a standard damages action, which requires proof of unlawfulness, damage and a causal link (as explained in section II.1.3 of this chapter), an action for unjust enrichment requires proof of enrichment on the part of the defendant for which there is no valid legal basis, and proof of impoverishment on the part of the applicant linked to that enrichment.[218] Therefore, it is not an action for damages under the conventional requirements of such actions, but a distinct and autonomous remedy with its own requirements, anchored in Article 268 TFEU.[219]

[215] Joined Cases C-202/18 and C-238/18 *Rimšēvičs and ECB v Latvia* EU:C:2019:139.

[216] *Unión de Pequeños Agricultores* (n 55) para 30.

[217] Case C-575/18 P *Czech Republic v Commission* EU:C:2020:530, paras 81–83; and Case T-147/15 *Czech Republic v Commission* EU:T:2022:281. J Nowak, 'Third Time's the Charm! Legal Protection for Member States in the Area of Traditional Own Resources (T 151/20, Czech Republic v Commission)' (*EU Law Live*, 26 May 2022).

[218] Case C-47/07 P *Masdar (UK)v Commission* EU:C:2008:726, paras 44 and 46–50.

[219] See, in more detail, J Nowak, 'On the Incompleteness of the System of Remedies Established by the EU Treaties and How to Proceed' (*EU Law Live Weekend Edition*, no 21, 2020).

GENERAL BIBLIOGRAPHY

Alemanno, A and Pech, L, 'Thinking Justice Outside the Docket: A Critical Assessment of the Reform of the EU's Court System' (2017) 54 *Common Market Law Review* 129.

Amicale des Référendaires, La Cour de justice des Communautés européennes 1952–2002: Bilan et perspectives (Bruylant, 2004).

Arnull, A, *The European Union and its Court of Justice, 2nd edn* (Oxford University Press, 2006).

— 'Judicial Review in the European Union' in A Arnull and D Chalmers (eds), *The Oxford Handbook of European Union Law* (Oxford University Press, 2015).

Barents, R, 'The Court of Justice After the Treaty of Lisbon' (2010) 47 *Common Market Law Review* 709.

— *Remedies and Procedures before the EU Courts, 2nd edn* (Kluwer Law, 2020).

Dashwood, A and Johnston, A (eds), *The Future of the Judicial System of the European Union* (Hart, 2001).

van Elsuwege, P, 'Judicial Review and the Common Foreign and Security Policy: Limits to the Gap-Filling Role of the Court of Justice' (2021) 58 *Common Market Law Review* 1731.

Iglesias Sánchez, S, 'The Jurisdiction of European Courts in the CFSP. Between Exceptionalism and Consistency of Legal Remedies in a Union Based on the Rule of Law' (2025) 229 *EU Law Live Weekend Edition* 3.

Lenaerts, K and Gutiérrez-Fons, JA, *Les méthodes d'interprétation de la Cour de justice de l'Union européenne* (Bruylant, 2020).

Lenaerts, K, Gutman, K and Novak, J, *EU Procedural Law, 2nd edn* (Oxford University Press, 2023).

Łuszcz, V (ed), *European Court Procedure. A Practical Guide* (Hart, 2020).

Mendes, J (ed), *EU Executive Discretion and the Limits of Law* (Oxford University Press, 2019).

Novak, J, 'On the Incompleteness of the System of Remedies Established by the EU Treaties and How to Proceed' (2020) 21 *EU Law Live Weekend Edition.*

Pernice, I, Kokott, J and Saunders, C (eds), *The Future of the European Judicial System in a Comparative Perspective* (Nomos, 2006).

Rasmussen, H, *On Law and Policy in the European Court of Justice* (Springer, 1986).

Sarmiento, D, 'The Reform of the General Court: An Exercise in Minimalist (but Radical) Institutional Reform' (2017) 19 *Cambridge Yearbook of European Legal Studies* 236.

Stone Sweet, A, *The Judicial Construction of Europe* (Oxford University Press, 2004).

— 'The European Court of Justice' in P Craig and G de Búrca (eds), *The Evolution of EU Law*, 2nd edn (Oxford University Press, 2011).

Turmo, A, *Res Judicata in European Union law: A Multi-Faceted Principle in a Multilevel Judicial System* (EU Law Live Press, 2022).

Türk, AH, *Judicial Review in the European Union*, 2nd edn (Edward Elgar, 2025).

Varga, Z, 'National Remedies in the Case of Violation of EU Law by Member State Courts' (2017) 54 *Common Market Law Review* 51.

SPECIALISED BIBLIOGRAPHY

Action for Annulment

Albors-Llorens, A, *Private Parties in European Community Law: Challenging Community Measures* (Clarendon Press, 1996).

Balthasar, S, 'Locus Standi Rules for Challenges to Regulatory Acts by Private Applicants: The New Article 263(4) TFEU' (2010) 35(4) *European Law Review* 542.

Cassia, P, L'accès des personnes physiques ou morales au juge de la légalité des actes communautaires (Dalloz, 2002).

Chamon, M, and De Arriba-Sellier, N, 'FBF: On the Justiciability of Soft Law and Broadening the Discretion of EU Agencies' (2022) 18 *European Constitutional Law Review* 286.

Lenaerts, K, 'Le traité de Lisbonne et la protection juridictionnelle des particuliers en droit de l'Union' (2009) 45 (5-6) *Cahiers de Droit Européen* 711.

Leonardo, L, 'Challenging EU Sanctions against Russia: The Role of the Court, Judicial Protection, and Common Foreign and Security Policy' (2023) 25 *Cambridge Yearbook of European Legal Studies* 40.

Prek, M and Lefèvre, S, 'The EU Courts as "National" Courts: National Law in the EU Judicial Process' (2017) 54(2) *Common Market Law Review* 369.

Subic, N, 'Challenging the Use of EU Funds: Locus Standi as a Roadblock for Disability Organisations' (2022) 18 *European Constitutional Law Review* 59.
Ward, A, *Judicial Review and the Rights of Private Parties in EU Law, 2nd edn* (Oxford University Press 2007).
Wildemeersch, J, *Contentieux de la légalité des actes de l'Union européenne: Le mythe du droit à un recours effectif* (Bruylant, 2019).

Action for Failure to Act

Barav, A, 'Considérations sur la spécificité du recours en carence en droit communautaire' (1975) 11 *Revue Trimestrielle de Droit Européen* 53.
Cazet, S, *Le recours en carence en droit de l'Union européenne* (Bruylant, 2012).
Daukšienė, I, and Budnikas, A, 'Has the Action for Failure to Act in the European Union Lost its Purpose?' (2014) 7 *Baltic Journal of Law & Politics* 209.

Action for Damages

Biondi, A and Farley, M, *The Right to Damages in European Law* (Kluwer Law, 2009).
Coutron, L and Picod, F, 'La responsabilité de l'Union européenne du fait de son activité administrative' in J-B Auby and J Dutheil de la Rochère (eds), *Traité de droit administratif européen*, 2nd edn (Bruylant, 2014).
Craig, P, 'The EU, the Member States and Damages Liability' in M Heidemann (ed.), *The Transformation of Private Law – Principles of Contract and Tort as European and International Law: A Liber Amicorum for Mads Andenas* (Springer, 2024).
Fink, M, 'EU Liability for Contributions to Member States' Breaches of EU Law' (2019) 56(5) Common Market Law Review 1227.
Heukels, T and McDonnell, A (eds), *The Action for Damages in Community Law* (Kluwer Law, 1997).
Hilson, C, 'The Role of Discretion in EC Law on Non-Contractual Liability' (2005) 42(3) *Common Market Law Review* 677.
Pernice, I, 'Le recours en indemnité' (1995) 31/35 *Cahiers de Droit Européen* 641.
Schermers, H G, Heukels, T and Mead, P (eds), *The Non-Contractual Liability of the European Communities* (Martinus Nijhoff, 1988).
Waelbroeck, D, 'L'exécution des arrêts d'annulation de la Cour de justice des Communautés européennes' in *Mélanges en hommage à Michel Waelbroeck* (Bruylant, 1999).
Wils, W, 'Concurrent Liability of the Community and a Member State' (1992) 17(3) *European Law Review* 191.

Appeals

Oro Martínez, C, 'Filtering of Appeals on Points of Law Before the Court of Justice' (2020) *MPIL Yearbook of Procedural Law of the CJEU.*
— 'The Filtering of Appeals by the Court of Justice: Taking Stock of the First Two Orders Allowing an Appeal to Proceed' (2022) 112 *EU Law Live Weekend Edition* 3.
Naômé, C, *Appeals Before the Court of Justice of the European Union* (Oxford University Press, 2018).

Infringement Procedures

Andersen, S, *The Enforcement of EU Law: The Role of the European Commission* (Oxford University Press, 2012).
Börzsák, L, *The Impact of Environmental Concerns on the Public Enforcement Mechanism under EU Law* (Kluwer, 2011).
Cremona, M (ed), *Compliance and the Enforcement of EU Law* (Oxford University Press, 2012).
Drake, S, and Smith, M (eds), *New Directions in the Effective Enforcement of EU Law* (Edward Elgar, 2016).
Gáspár-Szilágyi, S, 'What Constitutes "Failure to Notify" National Measures?' (2012) 19 *European Public Law* 281.

Jack, B, 'Article 260(2) TFEU: An Effective Judicial Procedure for the Enforcement of Judgments?' (2013) 19 *European Law Journal* 404.
Kelemen, D, and Pavone, T, 'Where Have the Guardians Gone? Law Enforcement and the Politics of Supranational Forbearance in the European Union' (2023) 75 *World Politics* 779.
Peers, S, 'Sanctions for an Infringement of EU Law After the Treaty of Lisbon' (2012) 18 *European Public Law* 33.
Prete, L, *Infringement Proceedings in EU Law* (Kluwer Law, 2017).
— 'The Systemic Criterion in the Use of Infringement Proceedings' (2023) 24 *German Law Journal* 1011.
Richard, A, *Procédure en manquement d'État et protection des droits fondamentaux dans l'Union européenne* (Bruylant, 2021).
Sikora, A, 'Infringement Actions Before the General Court: The Past, Present and Future of the Judicial Architecture of the Union' in Sarmiento, D, Ruiz Fabri, H and Hess, B (eds), *Yearbook on Procedural Law of the Court of Justice of the European Union: First edition*, 2019 (MPILux Research Paper Series 2020(2)).
Smulders, B and Prete, L, 'The Coming of Age of Infringement Proceedings' (2010) 47 *Common Market Law Review* 1.
Taborowski, M, 'Infringement Proceedings and Non-Compliant National Courts' (2012) 49 *Common Market Law Review* 1881.
Wendenburg, A, 'The One-Stage Infringement Procedure (Article 260(3) TFEU) and the Irrelevance of Political Crises in Member States in the Recent Case Law of the CJEU' (2021) 54 *Revista General de Derecho Europeo* 74.
Wennerås, P, 'Sanctions Against Member States Under Article 260 TFEU: Alive, But Not Kicking' (2012) 49 *Common Market Law Review* 145.

12

Judicial Protection in the European Union (II)

I. THE JURISDICTION OF UNION COURTS: INDIRECT ACTIONS

UNION COURTS CAN hear cases in ancillary proceedings that originate from other ongoing judicial proceedings. These are 'indirect actions', since they are an accessory to the development of *another* judicial procedure: the main proceedings. In the Union's judicial system, the Treaties provide several indirect actions that stem from ongoing proceedings taking place in national courts or Union courts.

The most relevant indirect action is the preliminary reference procedure, through which a national court refers a question to the Court of Justice on a point of interpretation of Union law or validity of secondary Union law. It is the only indirect action that originates in a national court. The other indirect actions are the result of the main proceedings before Union courts in direct actions: the plea of illegality, the review procedure and interim relief.

1. The Preliminary Reference Procedure

Often described as the 'jewel in the crown' or the 'keystone' (*la clé de voûte*) of the Union's judicial system, the preliminary ruling procedure is a key feature of the jurisdictional design of the Treaties. Article 267 Treaty on the Functioning of the European Union (TFEU) introduces a procedure for cooperation between the Union and national courts, through which the majority of leading rulings in the history of Union law have been delivered.

The purpose of the preliminary reference procedure is straightforward: a national court is called upon to resolve a dispute in which a rule of Union law applies. If the rule of Union law is ambiguous or its validity is called into question, the national court can refer a question to the Court of Justice for clarification of its meaning or a ruling on the validity of the rule. This procedure, inspired by the *questione di legittimità costituzionale* in the Italian Constitution, which allows Italian courts to refer such matters to the *Corte Costituzionale*,[1] has become the most prominent feature of the Union's judicial system. The strategic role played by the preliminary reference procedure is evidenced in the following developments.

First, the preliminary reference procedure is not only a tool to assist national courts in the interpretation of Union acts but also a means to *monitor the activity of Member States and their compliance with Union law*. This is the result of the preliminary reference's pragmatic role,

[1] A Boerger-De Smedt, 'Negotiating the Foundations of European Law, 1950–57: The Legal History of the Treaties of Paris and Rome' (2012) 21 *Contemporary European History* 339, 352: 'Directly inspired by the Italian constitutional system, this mechanism was first proposed and put on paper by Catalano. The jurists crafted Article 177 with great care over a period of two months. Two key elements of Catalano's initial proposal were left out of the final provision: the stipulation that the ECJ's rulings would be "binding" on national courts and the fact that the Court could also render preliminary rulings concerning the *application* of the treaty.'

which enables national courts to inquire whether Union law can be interpreted in a way that precludes the Member State from acting in a particular manner or allows it to do so. It is frequent for disputes in national courts to raise issues of compatibility between national and Union law. In such cases, the national court may rely on the preliminary reference procedure to ask the Court of Justice whether Union law precludes the application of a rule of national law in the circumstances of the case. The Court of Justice's response will clarify whether Union law must be interpreted as prohibiting or allowing a Member State to enact a provision or take a course of action. Consequently, the preliminary reference procedure acts as an additional, yet indirect, mechanism for reviewing the conformity with Union law of the conduct of the Member States.

It should be recalled that national courts have the authority under Union law to set aside national rules that breach the rules of Union law with direct effect, as confirmed in *Simmenthal* (see chapter 10 of this book). Once the Court of Justice has issued its ruling confirming whether or not the rule of national law is compatible with Union law, the national court can exercise, if necessary, the powers derived from the primacy of Union law and provide fully effective judicial protection to the successful party in the main proceedings.

Second, the preliminary reference procedure can also be used by national courts to question the validity of Union acts of secondary law, including some Common Foreign and Security Policy (CFSP) acts[2] and the acts of ratification of international agreements entered into by the Union.[3] The preliminary reference on validity allows the Court of Justice to exercise its exclusive jurisdiction to rule on the invalidity of Union acts of secondary law, removing this power from national courts. This exclusive jurisdiction is not explicitly provided for in the Treaties, but it was confirmed by the Court of Justice in the case of *Foto-Frost*, as explained in chapter 11. The exclusive jurisdiction of Union courts to rule on the invalidity of Union acts of secondary law strengthens the role played by the Court of Justice and, since 1 October 2024, the General Court in its specific areas of competence, in terms comparable to those of a constitutional court, which is generally entrusted with the exclusive jurisdiction to review the constitutionality of parliamentary acts.[4]

Taken together, these defining features of the preliminary reference procedure confirm its pivotal position within the Union's judicial system. The procedure is not only a cornerstone of judicial cooperation between Union and national courts, but also a key instrument in the federalisation of Union law and its judicial architecture.[5] In the absence of a system of appeals allowing Union courts to review decisions of national courts applying Union law, the preliminary reference procedure constitutes the principal channel of dialogue between the two levels of the Union judiciary, ensuring the coherence, consistency, and effectiveness of the Union legal order.

1.1. *Jurisdiction*

Until 1 October 2024, the preliminary reference procedure fell under the exclusive jurisdiction of the Court of Justice. Article 256(3) TFEU, introduced by the Treaty of Nice, allowed for a partial transfer of the preliminary reference jurisdiction to the General Court. This option,

[2] Case C-72/15 *Rosneft* EU:C:2017:236, para 78.

[3] The Court of Justice has ruled that it has jurisdiction to examine, in the context of a preliminary ruling on validity, whether an international agreement concluded by the Union is compatible with the Treaties and with the rules of international law which, in accordance with those Treaties, are binding on the Union. However, the review of validity does not target the agreement itself, but the acts by which the Union gave its consent, as confirmed in Case C-266/16 *Western Sahara Campaign* EU:C:2018:118, paras 43–51.

[4] It should be recalled that national courts have jurisdiction to declare the *validity* of a Union act. The judgment in Case C-314/85 *Foto-Frost* EU:C:1987:452 only precludes national courts from asserting jurisdiction to rule on the *invalidity* of Union acts.

[5] On this subject, see RM Buxbaum, 'Article 117 of the Rome Treaty as a Federalizing Device' (1969) 21 *Stanford Law Review* 49.

outlined in Article 256(3) TFEU, is limited to 'specific areas' only, aiming to reduce the Court of Justice's increasing workload, particularly in highly technical areas of the law.

Article 256(3) TFEU was put into practice on 1 October 2024 and, as of that date, the General Court has jurisdiction to hear preliminary references, although limited to cases solely within the following 'specific areas': the common system of VAT; excise duties; the Customs Code; the tariff classification of goods; compensation and assistance to passengers in cases of denied boarding or delays or cancellations of transport services; and the system for greenhouse gas emission allowance trading. In such cases, preliminary references will still be submitted to the Court of Justice, which determines whether the questions referred fall exclusively within one or several of the 'specific areas', or should instead be retained by the Court of Justice.[6]

1.2. *Notion of a 'Court or Tribunal of a Member State'*

The second and third paragraphs of Article 267 TFEU empower 'any court or tribunal of a Member State' to ask the Court of Justice for a ruling on the interpretation of the Treaties and/or the validity and interpretation of acts of the Union's institutions, bodies, offices or agencies. The definition of a 'court or tribunal' is not determined by national law, but is an autonomous concept of Union law developed through the case law of the Court of Justice. For the purpose of ensuring the widest possible access to the preliminary reference procedure, the case law has adopted a broad and flexible approach to defining a 'court or tribunal of a Member State'.

In *Vaassen-Göbbels*,[7] the Court of Justice outlined a set of criteria that a national jurisdiction must meet to qualify as a 'court or tribunal' pursuant to Article 267 TFEU. As a result, a court or tribunal of a Member State can refer a case to the Court of Justice if:

- it is established by law;[8]
- it is permanent and independent;[9]
- it follows an adversarial procedure;[10]
- it holds compulsory jurisdiction;[11] and
- it applies rules of law.[12]

The application of these requirements shows a flexible approach on the part of the Court of Justice. The aim is to maximise cooperation between national and Union courts, while ensuring the uniform interpretation of Union law across all Member States. The significant risk of divergent interpretations arising from national bodies that perform adjudicative tasks but

[6] According to the second para of Art 50b of the Protocol (No 3) on the Statute of the Court of Justice of the European Union ('the Statute of the Court of Justice'), 'Notwithstanding the first paragraph, the Court of Justice shall retain jurisdiction to hear and determine requests for a preliminary ruling that raise independent questions relating to the interpretation of primary law, public international law, general principles of Union law or the Charter of Fundamental Rights of the European Union.' On the preliminary analysis of requests for a preliminary reference undertaken by the Court of Justice, see Art 93a of the Rules of Procedure of the Court of Justice.

[7] Case C-61/65 *Vaassen-Göbbels* EU:C:1966:39.

[8] Case C-132/20 *Getin Noble Bank* EU:C:2022:235, para 72.

[9] Case C-14/86 *Pretore di Salò/X* EU:C:1987:275, paras 22–38; Case C-24/92 *Corbiau* EU:C:1993:118; Case C-403/21, *SC NV Construct SRL* EU:C:2023:47, paras 44–56; Case C-225/22 *SO v NADA* EU:C:2024:384, para 53; and Case C-326/23 CW EU:C:2024:940, para 35.

[10] Case C-33/70 *Spa Sace* EU:C:1970:118; Case 43/71 *Politi* EU:C:1971:122, para 5; Case 162/73 *Birra Dreher* EU:C:1974:17; Case 70/77 *Simmenthal* EU:C:1978:139; Case C-277/91 *Ligur Carni and Others* EU:C:1993:927; Case C-182/00 *Lutz and Others* EU:C:2002:19.

[11] Case C-54/96 *Dorsch Consult* EU:C:1997:413; Case C-195/98 *Österreichischer Gewerkschaftsbund* EU:C:2000:655.

[12] Case 138/80 *Borker* EU:C:1980:162; Case 318/85 *Greis Unterweger* EU:C:1986:106; Case C-118/97 *Pitkäranta* EU:C:1998:497; Case C-134/97 *Victoria Film* EU:C:1998:535; Case C-92/00 *HI* EU:C:2002:379, and Case C-161/03 *Cafom and Samsung* EU:C:2004:126.

are not formally part of the judiciary is mitigated by granting access to the preliminary reference procedure to as many adjudicative bodies as possible. This approach has led the Court of Justice to accept references from a diverse range of bodies, such as the board of appeal of a Dutch professional association,[13] a municipal appeals committee of the Brussels-Capital Region,[14] the British Chief Commissioner for Social Security,[15] an Italian investigative judge,[16] a regional Public Procurement Tribunal,[17] and the former Spanish Competition Authority.[18]

In recent years, the Court of Justice has adopted a stricter approach to certain requirements, possibly in response to concerns expressed within the Court itself and to developments in some national judiciaries. For example, after stating in 1995 that the Spanish Competition Authority was a 'court or tribunal' pursuant to Article 267 TFEU, the Court of Justice reached the opposite conclusion in 2003, when a reference was made from the Greek Competition Commission,[19] followed by another reference from the newly established Spanish Markets and Competition Authority.[20] A strict approach was also taken towards the non-judicial officials of national courts with adjudicative functions.[21] In the same vein, while in 2000 the Spanish Tax Tribunals were considered 'courts or tribunals' within the remit of Article 267 TFEU, the Court of Justice took a stricter approach in 2019 and ruled that they lacked independence.[22] A similar approach can be seen with regard to national administrative bodies with adjudicative tasks, such as the Czech Transport Infrastructure Access Regulatory Authority, whose powers were mostly administrative and subject to judicial review in Czech courts, where the authority participates as a defendant party.[23]

This partial tightening of the requirements, particularly regarding the independence of the 'court or tribunal', is closely connected to the growing threats to the independence of national courts in some Member States. This tendency has led the Court of Justice to develop case law interpreting Article 19(1) Treaty on European Union (TEU), in conjunction with Article 47 of the Charter of Fundamental Rights of the European Union ('the Charter'), to protect the independence of national courts from external pressures emanating from other powers within the Member State. As the protection of national courts' independence was strengthened in the case law, it became necessary to gradually align it with other provisions of the Treaties. This was the case of Article 267 TFEU and the requirement of independence for the purpose of referring a case to the Court of Justice.[24]

The pragmatic approach regarding the notion of 'court or tribunal' contrasts with the stricter interpretation provided by the Court of Justice regarding the requirement that a court

[13] Case 246/80 *Broekmeulen* EU:C:1981:218.

[14] Case C-17/00 *De Coster* EU:C:2001:651, paras 9–22.

[15] Case 150/85 *Drake* EU:C:1986:257.

[16] Case C-54/94 *Cacchiarelli and Stanghellini* EU:C:1995:56; Case C-105/03 *Pupino* EU:C:2005:386, and Case C-507/10 *Bernardi* EU:C:2011:873.

[17] Case C-203/14 *Consorci Sanitari del Maresme* EU:C:2015:664.

[18] Case C-67/91 *Asociación Española de Banca Privada* EU:C:1992:330.

[19] Case C-53/03 *Syfait and Others* EU:C:2005:333.

[20] Case C-462/19 *Anesco* EU:C:2020:715.

[21] Case C-503/15 *Panicello* EU:C:2017:126, paras 34ff.

[22] Joined Cases C-110/98 to C-147/98 *Gabalfrisa* EU:C:2000:145; and Case C-274/14 *Banco Santander* EU:C:2020:802.

[23] Case C-453/20 *CityRail* EU:C:2022:341.

[24] Proof of this realignment of the consistency of the requirement of independence in all Treaty provisions is para 55 of *Banco Santander* (n 22), where the Court of Justice openly acknowledged the need to adapt its case law on the notion of 'court or tribunal' in Art 267 TFEU as a consequence of recent developments in the case law: 'those considerations must be re-examined notably in the light of the most recent case-law of the Court concerning, in particular, the criterion of independence which any national body must meet in order to be categorised as a "court or tribunal"' for the purposes of Article 267 TFEU'. This stricter approach was put into practice in Case C-132/20 *Getin Noble Bank* EU:C:2022:235 (see also the Opinion of Advocate General Bobek in this case, at pts 44ff) and further reinforced in Case C-326/23 *CW* EU:C:2024:940.

or tribunal must be part of 'a Member State'. This requirement entails on the one hand, that a question referred for a preliminary ruling must originate from a public authority of a state rather than a private jurisdiction, and, furthermore, it must stem from a Member State and not an international body. As a result, any attempt by an international court, or a court operating outside the remit of the jurisdiction of a Member State, has been rejected by the Court of Justice. The case law provides several examples in which the Court of Justice has refused to accept references for preliminary rulings from courts of third countries,[25] international organisations,[26] or courts established directly by a treaty without institutional ties to an international organisation.[27] The exceptions to this rule involve the Benelux Court of Justice and the courts of the Unified Patent Court.[28] According to the Court of Justice, these courts are not considered conventional international jurisdictions, as they exercise national jurisdictional powers transferred to them by all or several Member States through a treaty.

1.3. *Duty or Faculty to Refer*

1.3.1. National Courts or Tribunals against whose Decisions there is no Judicial Remedy

Article 267 TFEU introduces a two-pronged scheme whereby national courts of last instance have a *duty* to refer questions to the Court of Justice, while courts whose decisions are subject to a judicial remedy have the *discretion* to do so. The language used by the provision is unambiguous: it states that any national court or tribunal 'against whose decisions there is no judicial remedy under national law . . . shall bring the matter before the Court'.[29] In contrast, any national court or tribunal whose decisions are subject to a judicial remedy 'may, if it considers that a decision on the question is necessary to enable it to give judgment', refer the matter to the Court.

The term 'judicial remedy under national law' in Article 267, third paragraph TFEU is not an autonomous concept of Union law and must be interpreted by reference to national law. The only aspect governed by a common criterion of Union law is the characterisation of extraordinary appeal procedures. If the decision of a national court or tribunal is only subject to a judicial remedy based on limited and exceptional grounds (such as an appeal for the protection of fundamental rights or a third-party action), the Court of Justice considers that the ruling is *not* subject to a 'judicial remedy under national law' pursuant to Article 267, third paragraph TFEU.[30] In contrast, limited appeals that permit review on specific grounds, including grounds for breach of Union law, are considered to be a 'judicial remedy', as in the case of appeals on

[25] However, in case of the Overseas Countries and Territories, which are territories not considered as part of the territory of the Member States, their courts are entitled to refer a question for a preliminary ruling. Joined Cases C-100/89 and C-101/89 *Kaefer and Pocacci* EU:C:1990:456, paras 8–10; and Case C-260/90 *Leplat* EU:C:1992:66.

[26] See, however, the case of the Benelux Court, which has been recognised as a court or tribunal 'of a Member State' (Case C-337/95 *Parfums Christian Dior* EU:C:1997:517, paras 19–23).

[27] Case C-196/09 *Miles and others* EU:C:2011:388.

[28] See *Parfums Christian Dior* (n 26) as well as Art 21 of the agreement establishing the Unified Patent Court. This provision is the result of the Court of Justice's objections to the first draft of the agreement in *Opinion 1/09* EU:C:2011:123, paras 81–84.

[29] Emphasis added.

[30] The Court of Justice has so held in the case of the Slovak Constitutional Court in Case C-416/10 *Križan and others* EU:C:2013:8, para 72: 'as a supreme court, the Najvyšší súd Slovenskej republiky (Supreme Court of the Slovak Republic) is even required to submit a request for a preliminary ruling to the Court of Justice when it finds that the substance of the dispute concerns a question to be resolved which comes within the scope of the first paragraph of Article 267 TFEU. The possibility of bringing, before the constitutional court of the Member State concerned, an action against the decisions of a national court, limited to an examination of a potential infringement of the rights and freedoms guaranteed by the national constitution or by an international agreement, cannot allow the view to be taken that that national court cannot be classified as a court against whose decisions there is no judicial remedy under national law within the meaning of the third paragraph of Article 267 TFEU.'

points of law. This rule also applies to proceedings where the appellate court has discretion to grant leave to appeal at a separate preliminary stage. Despite the uncertainty as to whether the appellate court will ultimately grant leave to appeal, the previous instance will be regarded as being subject to a 'judicial remedy'.[31] As a result, the court deciding on the request for leave to appeal will be under a duty to refer the matter to the Court of Justice pursuant to Article 267 TFEU, including when ruling on the leave to appeal.[32]

Another issue that has been addressed by the Court is whether Article 267 TFEU refers to courts that are structurally at the apex of the judicial hierarchy (the 'abstract' or 'organic' theory) or to any court whose decision in the particular case is not subject to further appeal (the 'concrete' theory). The provision is not entirely clear as to whether a national court of last instance refers to a jurisdiction with no hierarchical superior court or to a jurisdiction ruling in a case where there is no further appellate route. The first interpretation points towards national supreme or constitutional courts, which are at the apex of the national judicial system and have no hierarchical jurisdiction above them. The second interpretation focuses on any national court or tribunal, provided that the decision in the specific case is not subject to further appeal. The Court of Justice addressed this matter in *Lyckeskog*, where it ruled that 'supreme courts are bound by this obligation to refer . . . *as is any other national court or tribunal against whose decisions there is no judicial remedy under national law*' (emphasis added).[33] In other words, a court adjudicating in last instance, regardless of whether it sits at the apex of the national judicial system, is by definition the final judicial body before which an individual can assert the rights conferred by Union law.[34] Moreover, the notion of a court or tribunal acting as a jurisdiction 'against whose decisions there is no judicial remedy' must be determined at the time the reference is made, not at a later stage.[35]

Although the obligation to refer in Article 267(3) TFEU is drafted in seemingly unconditional terms, the case law has introduced several derogations that have moderated its impact. To alleviate the burden on national courts of last instance, especially supreme courts, of referring every case to the Court of Justice, the duty to refer can be set aside in certain situations, commonly known as the *acte clair* and *acte éclairé* doctrines.

The first derogation, encapsulated in the *acte clair* doctrine, was developed in *CILFIT*.[36] In this ruling, the Court of Justice stated that a national court ruling at last instance is exempted from its duty to refer when 'the correct application of [Union] law may be so obvious as to leave no scope for any reasonable doubt as to the manner in which the question raised is to be resolved'.[37] In such cases, 'the national court or tribunal must be convinced that the matter is equally obvious to the courts of the other Member States and to the Court of Justice'.[38] For the national court to reach this conclusion, the judgment in *CILFIT* provides several criteria, such as comparing the different linguistic versions of the provision in question, analysing the legal

[31] Case C-99/00 *Lyckeskog* EU:C:2002:329, para 16; and Case C-144/23 *Kubera* EU:C:2024:881, para 39.

[32] *Kubera* (n 31) paras 36–44.

[33] *Lyckeskog* (n 31) para 15.

[34] Case C-224/01 *Köbler* EU:C:2003:513, para 34; and Case C-173/03 *Traghetti del Mediterraneo* EU:C:2006:391, para 31.

[35] In Case C-3/16 *Aquino* EU:C:2017:209, para 38, the Court of Justice ruled that a court against whose decisions there is a judicial remedy under national law shall not be considered to be a court adjudicating at last instance, where an appeal on a point of law against a decision of that court is not examined because of discontinuance by the appellant at a later stage.

[36] Case C-283/81 *CILFIT* EU:C:1982:335.

[37] ibid, para 16.

[38] ibid.

terminology used,[39] and undertaking a contextual and teleological analysis of the provision within the broader context of Union law.[40]

The criteria developed in *CILFIT* have been subject to criticism and considered unrealistic, particularly the requirement to review all linguistic versions of a rule of Union law, a task that few national courts can realistically undertake, at least until the introduction of AI translation tools in the 2020s.[41] Other criticisms highlight the broad margin of discretion granted to national courts ruling in last instance, which contrasts with the unconditional obligation enshrined in the third paragraph of Article 267 TFEU. This critique is not unfounded and the practical implementation of the *CILFIT* doctrine seems to support the critics' concerns: in the practice of the supreme courts of the Member States, the general rule is to decide the case without a reference, whilst the exception is the referral.[42]

The development of the *CILFIT* doctrine over 40 years of application in national courts of last instance, led the Court of Justice, in 2021, to review the criteria of the *acte clair* doctrine. In *Consorzio Italian Management*, despite the Advocate General's invitation to substantially reconsider the doctrine, the *CILFIT* criteria were left mostly intact, with some clarifications. First, the Court emphasised that a national court of last instance must take into account the risk of divergent judgments within the Union on the same provision of Union law.[43] Second, national courts relying on the *acte clair* doctrine have a duty to state reasons when declining to refer.[44] And third, the Court of Justice pointed to Article 47 of the Charter and noted that the failure to give reasons when relying on the *acte clair* doctrine has consequences for the parties' right to an effective judicial remedy. This reference to the fundamental right establishes a connection between the duty to refer under Article 267 TFEU and the individual rights of the parties.[45] The preliminary reference procedure was traditionally conceived by the Court of Justice as an instrument of cooperation between courts, a dialogue between judges only. Following *Consorzio Italian Management*, it could be inferred that Article 267 TFEU is also intended to protect the procedural rights of the parties in the main proceedings.

The second derogation, the *acte éclairé* doctrine, exempts national courts of last instance from the obligation to refer in cases where the Court of Justice has previously ruled on a

[39] ibid, para 19.

[40] ibid, para 20.

[41] See Case C-461/03 *Gaston Schul Douane-expediteur* EU:C:2005:415, Opinion of AG Dámaso Ruiz-Jarabo, as well as Case C-338/95 *Wiener* EU:C:1997:352, Opinion of AG Jacobs. However, this requirement has been softened by the 2021 case law in Case C-561/19 *Consorzio Italian Management* EU:C:2021:799, para 44: 'While a national court or tribunal of last instance cannot be required to examine, in that regard, each of the language versions of the provision in question, the fact remains that it must bear in mind those divergences between the various language versions of that provision of which it is aware, in particular when those divergences are set out by the parties and are verified.'

[42] On the statistics of preliminary references originating from national courts, see the Annual Report of the Court of Justice of the European Union, available on its website.

[43] This criterion appeared in an earlier judgment, in Case C-160/14 *Ferreira da Silva e Brito and others* EU:C:2015:565, paras 50–59. The ruling in the *Consorzio Italian Management* judgment (n 41) develops the same idea in further detail at para 49 in the following terms: 'Nonetheless, where the national court or tribunal of last instance is made aware of the existence of diverging lines of case-law – among the courts of a Member State or between the courts of different Member States – concerning the interpretation of a provision of EU law applicable to the dispute in the main proceedings, that court or tribunal must be particularly vigilant in its assessment of whether or not there is any reasonable doubt as to the correct interpretation of the provision of EU law at issue and have regard, inter alia, to the objective pursued by the preliminary ruling procedure which is to secure uniform interpretation of EU law'.

[44] *Consorzio Italian Management* (n 41) para 51.

[45] ibid. The 'subjective' or rights-based approach to Art 267 TFEU has been discussed for a long time, despite the fact that the preliminary ruling procedure is intended to act only as a mechanism to articulate a 'dialogue between judges' and not a judicial remedy for a party in national proceedings. The Court of Justice has insisted on the nature of the preliminary reference as a tool of cooperation, but the ruling in *Consorzio Italian Management* appeared to have nuanced this approach. The orthodoxy was confirmed some years later in Case C-767/23 *Remling* EU:C:2026:243, when the court insisted on the importance of providing some degree of reasoning in the decision not to refer, but not on the basis of Article 47 of the Charter, nor depending on whether a party had seen its right to a fair trial undermined (see *Remling*, paras 28 and 29).

point of law whose interpretation is 'materially identical',[46] or on a similar point applicable to the case, even if the questions at issue are not strictly identical.[47] This derogation relieves the national court of last instance of the obligation to refer when the Court of Justice's case law provides sufficient guidance to decide the case. To a certain extent, the *acte éclairé* doctrine introduces a doctrine of binding precedent, but it is addressed only to national courts ruling at last instance. However, it must be noted that the acte *éclairé* doctrine applies only to questions of interpretation, not to questions of validity. In the latter case, the exclusive jurisdiction of Union courts to rule on the invalidity of Union acts means that, regardless of whether the Court of Justice has previously ruled on the validity of the same act, national courts of last instance remain under a duty to refer where they consider the act to be invalid.[48]

1.3.2. National Courts or Tribunals against whose Decisions there is a Judicial Remedy

The wording of the second paragraph of Article 267 TFEU is clear: national courts or tribunals ruling on a case that is subject to further appeal do not have a duty to refer a matter of interpretation or validity to the Court of Justice. However, this rule must be read in conjunction with the exclusive jurisdiction of Union courts to rule on the invalidity of Union acts. As a result, when a national court or tribunal, against whose decisions there is a judicial remedy, is faced with a question as to the validity of a Union act and considers that act to be invalid, it is under a duty to refer the matter to the Court of Justice. This duty applies regardless of whether there is previous case law of the Court of Justice in materially identical cases reviewing the validity of the same or similar Union acts.[49]

It is possible to derogate from this duty in three cases. First, all national courts are entitled to temporarily suspend the application of a national measure based on a Union act through interim relief while a preliminary reference on validity is pending in the Court of Justice.[50] Second, all national courts have the authority to examine the validity of Union acts and to conclude that the act is valid.[51] Third, the Union legislature can empower national courts to review certain Union acts, assigning them the role of a Union court, as in the case of EU trademarks governed by Regulation 2017/1001.[52]

1.4. *Discretion to Decide on the Need, Content and Scope of the Matter Referred to the Court of Justice for a Preliminary Ruling*

The national court is free to determine the content of the question referred for a preliminary ruling, including the number of questions, their wording, and, if it is not a court of last instance, whether to refer the question to the Court of Justice. The national court has the power to make a reference on its own motion, even when such a power is not provided for

[46] Joined Cases C-28/62 to C-30/62 *Da Costa en Schaake NV and others* EU:C:1963:6.

[47] *CILFIT* (n 36) para 14.

[48] *Gaston Schul Douane-expediteur* (n 41) contrary to the Opinion of Advocate General Ruiz-Jarabo Colomer, who proposed a recalibration of the *Foto-Frost* doctrine to prevent national courts of last instance from ending up like Sisyphus, having to perform a meaningless and endless task over and over again, particularly when the content of a rule of Union law has been previously judicially reviewed and annulled by the Union courts.

[49] *Foto-Frost* (n 4), and *Gaston Schul Douane-expediteur* (n 41).

[50] Joined Cases C-143/88 and C-92/89 *Zuckerfabrik Süderdithmarschen and Zuckerfabrik Soest* EU:C:1991:65, para 21.

[51] *Foto-Frost* (n 4) para 14.

[52] See Arts 124–28 of Regulation 2017/1001, which confers jurisdiction on national courts to review and annul EU trademarks issued by the EU Intellectual Property Office. See Case C-226/15 P *Apple & Pear Australia* EU:C:2016:250, Opinion of AG Bobek; and Case C-235/09 *DHL Express* EU:C:2010:595, Opinion of AG Cruz Villalón, pts 18–26.

under national procedural law.[53] Similarly, the position of the parties regarding the referral does not bind the court in any way. Consequently, an agreement between the parties to have the matter referred to the Court of Justice is not binding on the national court hearing the case.[54] According to settled case law:

> Article 267 TFEU establishes direct cooperation between the Court of Justice and the national courts by way of a non-contentious procedure excluding any initiative of the parties who are merely invited to be heard in the course of that procedure.[55]

The decision to refer the matter to the Court of Justice is a prerogative of the national court based solely on criteria governed by Union law. This means that national proceedings will be conducted in accordance with national procedural law, but only to the extent that the national rules do not undermine the court's decision to refer. For example, national procedural law may require national courts to hear the parties before making a reference for a preliminary ruling. However, if this requirement is designed in a way that makes it procedurally too burdensome, to the extent that it may disincentivise the national court from referring cases to the Court of Justice, the national law will breach Article 267 TFEU.[56] In the same vein, formal requirements for bringing an appeal before national courts cannot be made disproportionately restrictive, to the extent that they prevent the appellate court from referring a question to the Court of Justice.[57] According to settled case law, 'national procedural rules cannot affect the powers which a national court derives from Article 267 TFEU, nor can they release that court from its obligations under that provision'.[58]

The situation differs when one or more parties involved in the case appeal the order for reference to a higher national court. In its earliest case law, the Court of Justice held that Article 267 TFEU does not preclude a national court from reviewing an order for reference on appeal. In *Rheinmühlen II*, the Court stated that the decision of a lower court to refer a question for a preliminary ruling remains 'subject to the remedies normally available under national law'.[59] Therefore, if an appeal against the order for reference is upheld, the order would cease to have effect, and the preliminary reference proceedings would be terminated.[60] This approach was substantially reconsidered and overturned in the case of *Cartesio*,[61] delivered in 2008, where the Court highlighted the following concern:

[T]he autonomous jurisdiction which Article [267 TFEU] confers on the referring court to make a reference to the Court would be called into question, if – by varying the order for reference, by setting it aside and by ordering the referring court to resume the proceedings – the appellate court could prevent the referring court from exercising the right, conferred on it by the [TFEU], to make a reference to the Court.[62]

The ruling in *Cartesio* concludes that it is for the national court whose order for reference has been challenged on appeal

[53] Case C-166/73 *Rheinmühlen Düsseldorf* EU:C:1974:3, para 3; Case 126/80 *Salonia* EU:C:1981:136, para 7; Case 283/81 *CILFIT* (n 36) para 9, and Case C-261/95 *Palmisani* EU:C:1997:351, para 20.

[54] Case 93/78 *Mattheus* EU:C:1978:206, paras 4–6.

[55] Case C-402/98 *ATB and others* EU:C:2000:366, para 29. See also Case C-2/06 *Kempter* EU:C:2008:78, para 41; Case C-210/06 *Cartesio* EU:C:2008:723, para 90; and Case C-196/08 *Acoset* EU:C:2009:628, para 34.

[56] Case C-137/08 *VB Pénzügyi Lízing* EU:C:2010:659.

[57] Case C-3/16 *Aquino* EU:C:2017:209, paras 41ff.

[58] ibid, para 47.

[59] Case C-146/73 *Rheinmühlen II* EU:C:1974:12, para 3.

[60] Case C-31/68 *Chanel v Cepeha* EU:C:1970:52. See also Case C 205/90 *Les assurances du credit* (unpublished) and Case C-310/94 *Garage Ardon* (unpublished).

[61] Case C-210/06 *Cartesio* EU:C:2008:723.

[62] ibid, para 95.

> to draw the proper inferences from a judgment delivered on an appeal against its decision to refer and, in particular, to come to a conclusion as to whether it is appropriate to maintain the reference for a preliminary ruling, or to amend it or to withdraw it.[63]

Cartesio granted national courts a rather bizarre power, allowing them to 'draw the proper inferences' stemming from a ruling by a national higher court annulling an order for reference. This solution is anomalous, to say the least, as it attempts to combine the ability of higher courts to rule on appeals against orders for reference with the power of the referring court to freely decide whether to maintain the order for reference.

It is unsurprising that, some years later, in the case of *IS*,[64] the Court of Justice clarified the scope of the *Cartesio* doctrine in a context where clarification was very much needed. In several Member States, higher courts had quashed multiple orders to refer cases to the Court of Justice that questioned the conformity of national legislation and practices with Union standards of judicial independence. Many of these appeals quashing the orders for reference were attempts to short-circuit the dialogue between the Court of Justice and the lower courts. It is in this context, far more worrying than those surrounding the previous cases of *Rheinmühlen II* and *Cartesio*, that the Court of Justice decided to reinforce the power of national courts to refer a case pursuant to Article 267 TFEU, free from any external interference, including from higher national courts. In *IS*, the Court of Justice clarified and strengthened its position, holding in clear and categorical terms:

> [T]he principle of the primacy of EU law requires a lower court to disregard a decision of the supreme court of the Member State concerned if it considers that the latter is prejudicial to the prerogatives granted to that lower court by Article 267 TFEU and, consequently, to the effectiveness of the cooperation between the Court and the national court and tribunals established by the preliminary ruling mechanism.[65]

The case law has confirmed that the discretion to refer a case for a preliminary ruling applies not only to the court as an institution but also to the chamber assigned to rule on the case. If national law imposes a duty on a chamber to refer the case to another chamber, such an obligation cannot interfere with the ability of the first formation to refer the matter to the Court of Justice for a preliminary ruling. In the case of *PFE*, Italian national law imposed on a chamber of the Supreme Court the duty to refer the case to the full court if it was to depart from a binding precedent of the full court. The Court of Justice ruled that the chamber was entitled to raise a point of law through a preliminary reference before referring the case to the full court, even if the questions sent to the Court of Justice were aimed at challenging the conformity of the previous case law of the full court with Union law.[66] This approach was further extended in the case of *Hann-Invest*, involving a national rule that required approval of a ruling by a 'registrations judge' prior to closing the procedures, as well as allowing another chamber of the same court to compel the judicial panel responsible for the case to alter the content of its decision.[67] The Court of Justice concluded that such a mechanism is incompatible with Article 19(1) TEU, interpreted in the light of Article 47 of the Charter, as it seriously undermines the

[63] ibid, para 96.

[64] Case C-564/19 *IS* EU:C:2021:949, paras 76–82.

[65] ibid, para 81. See also the ruling in Case C-135/24 *John Cockerill SA* EU:C:2025:176, para 24: 'Even assuming that there is a rule of national law under which the legal rulings of the latter court are binding on the referring court, such a rule of law cannot take away from that court the discretion to refer to the Court of Justice questions of interpretation of the points of EU law relating to such rulings. A national court must be free, if it considers that a higher court's legal ruling could lead it to deliver a judgment contrary to EU law, to refer to the Court of Justice questions which concern it.'

[66] Case C-689/13 *PFE* EU:C:2016:199, paras 31–36.

[67] Joined Cases C-554/21, C-622/21 and C-727/21 *HANN-INVEST d.o.o. and Others* EU:C:2024:594.

independence of the judicial panel responsible for the case and the right to effective judicial protection of the parties in the proceedings.[68]

1.5. *Requirements Applicable to the National Court when Referring a Case to the Court of Justice for a Preliminary Ruling*

National courts are free to choose the subject matter of the question or questions referred to the Court of Justice, provided that they pertain to points of interpretation or validity of Union law. A question on the interpretation of national law will be deemed inadmissible, as will questions on points of fact raised in national proceedings. This does not imply that the Court of Justice disregards matters related to national law or fact, as these can be crucial to understanding the national court's doubts regarding the interpretation or validity of Union law. For instance, to determine if Union law should be interpreted as precluding a provision of national law, it is important to properly understand the scope and meaning of that specific national provision. In exceptional circumstances, it is also possible for a national court to raise doubts about the compatibility with Union law of the laws enacted by another Member State.[69]

Despite the broad discretion left to national courts, there are some requirements they must adhere to. If a national court fails to comply with the requirements set out in the Rules of Procedure and the case law of the Court of Justice, the request for a preliminary ruling will be declared manifestly inadmissible by way of a reasoned order.

Firstly, the request for a preliminary ruling must have a clear connection with the subject matter in dispute in the main proceedings.[70] In the words of the Court of Justice, Union courts will decline jurisdiction 'where it is quite obvious that the interpretation of Union law sought by [the national] court bears no relation to the actual facts of the main action or its purpose'.[71] By referring to an 'obvious' disconnect, it is confirmed that a reference will be declared inadmissible in exceptional cases only, subject to a very high standard of review. This ground of inadmissibility may apply to one, several, or all of the questions referred by the national court.[72] At times, the questions referred by a national court are reformulated by the Court of Justice on its own motion, as a means to provide a useful answer, as long as the reformulated question can be inferred from the order for reference.[73]

Secondly, a request for a preliminary ruling must concern either the interpretation of Union law or the validity of Union secondary law, or both. If this is not the case and the main proceedings stem from a purely internal situation with no connection to any rule of Union

[68] ibid, paras 61–79.

[69] Case 104/79 *Foglia/Novello* EU:C:1980:73, para 10; and Case C-318/00 *Bacardi-Martini* EU:C:2003:41. See also the Opinion of Advocate General Emiliou in Case C-440/23 *European Lotto and Betting Ltd* EU:C:2025:668, points 33–77.

[70] Case 126/80 *Salonia* EU:C:1981:136, para 6; Case C-368/89 *Roux* EU:C:1991:41, para 11; Case C-186/90 *Durighello* EU:C:1991:453, para 9; Case C-343/90 *Lourenço Dias* EU:C:1992:327, para 18; Case C-67/91 *Asociación Española de Banca Privada* EU:C:1992:330, para 26; Joined Cases C-332/92, C-333/92 and C-335/92 *Eurico Italia and Others* EU:C:1994:79, para 17; Case C-18/93 *Corsica Ferries* EU:C:1994:195, para 14; Case C-62/93 *BP Supergaz* EU:C:1995:223, para 10; Case C-143/94 *Furlanis costruzioni generali* EU:C:1995:354, para 12; Case C-415/93 *Bosman* EU:C:1995:463, para 61; Case C-508/19 *MF/Prokurator Generalny* EU:C:2022:201, para 71; and Joined Cases C-711/21 and C-712/21 *XXX* EU:C:2023:503, paras 44–49.

[71] *Bosman* (n 70) para 61.

[72] Case C-428/93 *Monin Automobiles* EU:C:1994:192, paras 13–16; Case C-421/97 *Tarantik* EU:C:1999:309, paras 33–37; and Case C-315/02 *Lenz* EU:C:2004:446, paras 52–54.

[73] Joined Cases C-297/88 and C-197/89 *Dzodzi* EU:C:1990:360, para 37; Case C-28/95 *Leur-Bloem* EU:C:1997:369, paras 27 and 32; Case C-1/99 *Kofisa Italia* EU:C:2001:10, para 32; Case C-217/05 *Confederación Española de Empresarios de Estaciones de Servicio* EU:C:2006:784, para 19; Case C-280/06 *ETI and Others* EU:C:2007:775, para 21; Case C-352/08 *Modehuis A Zwijnenburg* EU:C:2010:282, para 33; Case C-603/10 *Pelati* EU:C:2012:639, para 18; Case C-394/18 *IGI Srl* EU:C:2020:56, paras 45–48; and Case C-713/22 *LivaNova plc* EU:C:2024:642, paras 42–47.

law, the Court of Justice will decline jurisdiction.[74] There are only exceptions to this rule. The first occurs when the purpose of the referral is to remedy a reverse discrimination in national law caused by Union law.[75] The second exception arises when a case involves a purely internal situation, but national law clearly and explicitly reproduces or refers to a rule of Union law. In such cases, the Court of Justice will provide a ruling to ensure the consistent and uniform interpretation of the said rule of Union law.[76]

Thirdly, the question referred for a preliminary ruling must contain all the factual and legal information necessary for the Court of Justice to deliver a useful answer.[77] The referring court must therefore provide sufficient and coherent information; otherwise, the request for a preliminary ruling will be declared inadmissible. It is true that this is an exceptional outcome in practice, and the Court of Justice makes every effort to gather additional information from the national court or intervening parties to reconstruct the question if necessary and deliver a useful answer. However, these efforts may sometimes fail because the referring court has been unable to provide substantiated reasons for the questions, because the text of the reference contains contradictions that prevent a proper understanding of the questions, or because the questions referred are generic or ambiguous. If national procedural law prevents the national court from expressing in detail its assessment of the factual and legal arguments justifying the referral in a manner that ultimately discourages referrals to the Court of Justice, such rules must be deemed to be incompatible with Article 267 TFEU.[78]

Fourthly, the case law requires that the question referred for a preliminary ruling be raised in the context of a genuine dispute between the parties in the national proceedings.[79] The question will not be answered if the parties have artificially fabricated the dispute, a conclusion that requires a thorough factual analysis by the Court of Justice, which it will undertake only in exceptional circumstances and only when the artificial nature of the dispute can be manifestly inferred from the order for reference issued by the national court.[80]

Lastly, the national court cannot refer a preliminary reference on the validity of a Union act if the applicant in the main proceedings had undeniable standing to bring an action for annulment, pursuant to Article 263 TFEU, but failed to do so within the time limit set by the Treaties.[81] This constraint on the national court aims to prevent the circumvention of the time

[74] Case C-299/95 *Kremzow* EU:C:1997:254.

[75] Case C-448/98 *Guimont* EU:C:2000:663, para 23; and Joined Cases C-515/99, C-519/99 to C-524/99 and C-526/99 to C-540/99 *Reisch and Others* EU:C:2002:135, para 26.

[76] See *Dzodzi* (n 73).

[77] Joined Cases C-320 to C-322/90 *Telemarsicabruzzo and Others* EU:C:1993:26, para 6; Case C-157/92 *Pretore di Genova* EU:C:1993:107, para 4; Case C-167/94 *Grau Gomis and Others* EU:C:1995:113, para 8; Case C-66/97 *Banco de Fomento e Exterior* EU:C:1997:334, para 7; Case C-137/97 *Modesti* EU:C:1998:187, para 5; and Case C-422/98 *Cologne Versicherung* EU:C:1999:113, para 4.

[78] This was the situation in Bulgaria prior to Case C-614/14 *Ognyanov* EU:C:2016:514. According to the Court of Justice, at para 25, 'one effect of a national rule such as that at issue in the main proceedings is likely to be that a national court may choose to refrain from referring questions for a preliminary ruling to the Court, in order to avoid, on the one hand, being disqualified and exposed to disciplinary penalties or, on the other, lodging requests for preliminary rulings that are inadmissible. Consequently, such a rule is detrimental to the prerogatives granted to national courts and tribunals by Article 267 TFEU and, consequently, to the effectiveness of the cooperation between the Court and the national court and tribunals established by the preliminary ruling mechanism.'

[79] Case 244/80 *Foglia/Novello* EU:C:1981:302, para 18.

[80] Case 267/86 *Van Eycke* EU:C:1988:427, para 12; Case C-118/94 *Associazione italiana per il WWF and Others* EU:C:1996:86, para 15; Case C-129/94 *Ruiz Bernáldez* EU:C:1996:143, para 7; Case C-36/99 *Idéal tourisme* EU:C:2000:405, para 22; and Case C-144/04 *Mangold* EU:C:2005:709, paras 34–35. See the Opinion of Advocate General Emiliou in Case C-440/23 *European Lotto and Betting Ltd* EU:C:2025:668, pts 79–89.

[81] Case C-188/92 *TWD Textilwerke Deggendorf* EU:C:1994:90, para 23; Case C-374/12 *Valimar* EU:C:2014:2231, paras 28–29; Case C-143/14 *TMK Europe* EU:C:2015:236, para 18; Case C-72/15 *Rosneft* EU:C:2017:236, para 128; and Case C-135/16 *Georgsmarienhütte and Others* EU:C:2018:120, Opinion of AG Campos Sánchez-Bordona, at pts 29ff.

limits for actions for annulment through the preliminary reference procedure in cases where the applicant had clear standing but failed to bring an action for annulment in good time. This requirement has been subject to criticism because the standing criteria for private applicants in actions for annulment are not always simple to apply in practice, as explained in chapter eleven of this book. This is why the case law insists that the applicants have 'undeniable standing' in an action for annulment, pointing at cases in which it is beyond doubt that the applicant was entitled to bring an action for annulment in the General Court but failed to do so.[82] It should be noted that this requirement does not apply when the request for a preliminary ruling was made by the national court of its own motion.[83]

These requirements were codified in the judgment in *Ullens de Schooten*.[84] In this ruling, the Court of Justice sets out the requirements developed in the case law that all national courts must comply with when referring a case for a preliminary ruling.[85]

1.6. *Time Limits*

Article 267 TFEU grants national courts broad discretion to determine the appropriate time to refer a question for a preliminary ruling.[86] Consequently, the national court is free to refer the matter at any stage of the main proceedings, whether during the preliminary investigative phase, the written phase, the oral phase, or even during the proceedings for the enforcement of the judgment or order settling the dispute.

This broad discretion is not unlimited, and it is essential that questions are raised when the answers from the Court of Justice are relevant and useful for the resolution of the dispute. Therefore, if the reference is made too early in the proceedings, the request can be declared inadmissible for lack of sufficient factual and legal context or for a lack of an obvious connection with the relevant rules of Union law. Conversely, if the national proceedings have come to an end, in which case the Court of Justice will decline jurisdiction, not because of a lack of reasons or a connection with Union law, but because of the absence of a genuine dispute pending before the referring court.[87]

1.7. *Stay of the Main Proceedings*

Article 23 of Protocol (No 3) on the Statute of the Court of Justice of the European Union ('the Statute of the Court of Justice') refers to the preliminary reference procedure and states that 'the decision of the court or tribunal of a Member State which suspends its proceedings

[82] The implementation of the *TWD* doctrine has been ruled out in cases described by Advocate General Campos Sánchez-Bordona as 'reverse situations'. In Case C-667/13 *Banco Privado Português* EU:C:2015:151, the Court of Justice rejected the applicability of the *TWD* doctrine in a case in which the Portuguese state did not bring an action for annulment before the General Court against a decision, which was (unsuccessfully) challenged by two private banking institutions, but later questioned it before a national court. In the words of the Court of Justice, the *TWD* case law 'applies only as regards a party which invokes the unlawfulness of an EU measure before a national court, whereas it could undoubtedly have brought an action under Article 263 TFEU for the annulment of that measure, but failed to do so within the prescribed period. Consequently, the fact that Estado português, which does not contest the lawfulness of Decision 2011/346 before the national court, did not bring an action for annulment of that decision before the General Court is irrelevant for the purpose of assessing whether the questions concerning the validity of that decision are admissible' (para 30).

[83] Case C-222/04 *Ministerio dell'Economia e delle Finanze* EU:C:2006:8, paras 73–74.

[84] Case C-268/15 *Ullens de Schooten* EU:C:2016:874.

[85] ibid, paras 50–53.

[86] Case C-43/71 *Politi* EU:C:1971:122, para 5; Case C-14/86 *Pretore di Salò* EU:C:1987:275, para 11; and Case C-176/96 *Lehtonen and Castors Brain* EU:C:2000:201, paras 19–20.

[87] *Wiener* (n 41) para 11; Case C-159/90 *Grogan* EU:C:1991:378, para 12; and Case C-314/96 *Djabali* EU:C:1998:104, paras 14–23.

and refers a case to the Court of Justice shall be notified to the Court by the court or tribunal concerned'. This provision was interpreted for some time as imposing a duty on national courts to stay the main proceedings pending the outcome of the preliminary reference procedure. However, the case law has qualified that interpretation and clarified that, in certain situations, a national court may resume proceedings, provided that the purpose of the request for a preliminary ruling is not rendered redundant or unnecessary by resuming the national proceedings. According to the Court of Justice:

> The preservation of the effectiveness of that procedure is not made impossible in practice or excessively difficult by a national rule which makes it possible, between the date on which a request for a preliminary ruling is made to the Court and the date of the order or judgment by which the Court answers that request, to continue the main proceedings in order to carry out procedural steps, which the referring court considers necessary and which concern aspects unrelated to the questions referred for a preliminary ruling, namely procedural steps which are not such as to prevent the referring court from complying, in the main proceedings, with that order or that judgment.[88]

1.8. *Consequences of the Failure of a National Court to Refer a Case for a Preliminary Ruling*

A national court's decision not to refer a case to the Court of Justice can be challenged. This will take place in national courts, as it is not possible to challenge a national judicial decision directly before Union courts.

The decision not to refer can be challenged on the ground that the national court was under a duty to refer the case. Therefore, only when the court or tribunal was ruling at last instance, as required by the third paragraph of Article 267 TFEU, will it be subject to such an obligation and, consequently, to a subsequent appeal for failing to do so.

Irrespective of the fact that any challenge will take place before a national court, the grounds may derive from Union law, national law, or the European Convention on Human Rights (ECHR). These grounds of appeal can also determine the available remedy. For example, Union law requires Member States to provide damages actions for breaches of Union law by national authorities, including national courts. While national courts implement the ECHR, this instrument also provides a direct action for applicants to bring a case before the European Court of Human Rights once all domestic remedies have been exhausted.

The following sections will describe the remedies provided by Union law, national law and the ECHR, as well as the legal grounds on which those remedies can rely.

1.8.1. Remedies of Union Law

The conduct of national courts can be subject to review in the course of an infringement procedure under Articles 258 and 259 TFEU. The jurisdiction of the Court of Justice to declare a failure of the Member State to fulfil its obligations under Union law applies to the Member State as a whole, including its judiciary. For decades, the Commission was reluctant to bring infringement actions targeting national judicial decisions, having regard to the special status of courts of law, subject to strong legal protections of their independence. However, this status has not prevented national judiciaries from being subject to review in infringement proceedings before the Court of Justice, whilst recognising the specific nature of the judicial function. As a result, the case law highlights that, in the context of an infringement procedure, 'isolated

[88] Case C-176/22 *BK and ZhP* EU:C:2023:416, para 28.

or numerically insignificant judicial decisions in the context of case law taking a different direction, or still more a construction disowned by the national supreme court, cannot be taken into account'.[89]

This limitation paves the way for the scrutiny of other, more significant national judicial practices. The Court of Justice pointed in that direction when it confirmed that it will review 'a widely-held judicial construction which has not been disowned by the supreme court, but rather confirmed by it'.[90] This standard was first applied in practice to the Spanish *Tribunal Supremo*, followed later by the French *Conseil d'État* (supreme administrative court).[91] The Court of Justice also confirmed that an infringement procedure can be brought when a national court ruling at last instance fails to refer the case in circumstances where the exceptions under the *acte clair* or *acte éclairé* doctrine do not apply.[92]

In addition to an infringement action, Member States can be subject to damages claims in their national courts brought by private applicants if the Member State has breached Union law and caused damage. This principle applies to all actions of Member States, including those carried out by national courts when resolving disputes in which Union law was (wrongly) applied. The principles underlying these actions are set out in the Court of Justice's case law and apply to all Member States, which must incorporate them into their national procedural frameworks, as explained in section III.4 of this chapter.

1.8.2. Remedies of National Law

Member States are free to introduce domestic remedies for parties that request a review of the rulings of national courts. Such rulings can include the refusal to refer a question for a preliminary ruling to the Court of Justice, particularly when the national court has a duty to refer the case in the situations explained above. However, national law cannot interfere with the discretion of national courts to refer a case for a preliminary ruling pursuant to Article 267 TFEU. This discretion cannot be transformed into an obligation by national law, nor can the exercise of that discretion be reviewed and appealed, with the indirect consequence of imposing a duty on the court of first instance to refer the matter to the Court of Justice.

In the case of an appeal against the refusal to make a preliminary reference by a national court of last resort, the means to judicially review the decision will be exceptional or constrained to very specific circumstances or grounds of review.[93] In some Member States, such as Germany, Austria, Spain, the Czech Republic, Slovakia, and Slovenia, there are remedies for the protection of fundamental rights before the Constitutional Court. In these Member States, such remedies enable a party to challenge the refusal of the court of last instance to make a preliminary reference. In Germany, Austria, Slovakia, and the Czech Republic, the relevant fundamental right is the right to a lawful judge, on the basis that the Court of Justice is treated as the 'lawful judge' for questions of Union law and an unjustified refusal to refer deprives the party of access to that judge. In Spain and Slovenia, the emphasis is on the right to a fair trial, which includes procedural guarantees and rights of defence of the parties.

[89] Case C-129/00 *Commission v Italy* EU:C:2003:656, para 32.

[90] ibid.

[91] Case C-154/08 *Commission v Spain* EU:C:2009:695; and Case C-416/17 *Commission v France* EU:C:2018:626.

[92] On the infringement procedure and the duty of national courts to refer a question for a preliminary ruling, see A Turmo, 'Commission v France: Un rappel nécessaire de l'inégalité inhérente au dialogue des juges au sein de l'Union européenne' (2020) *MPIL Yearbook of Procedural Law of the CJEU*.

[93] C Lacchi, 'Review by Constitutional Courts of the Obligation of National Courts of Last Instance to Refer a Preliminary Question to the Court of Justice of the EU' (2015) 16 *German Law Review* 1317.

1.8.3. Remedies based on the ECHR

In Member States where there is no constitutional remedy for the protection of fundamental rights or other remedies that allow for the review of a decision of a court of last resort, the available course of action is to file an application before the European Court of Human Rights. When national courts of last resort fail to refer a case to the Court of Justice, this failure can be reviewed in light of Article 6 ECHR and the fundamental right to a fair trial.

The approach of the European Court of Human Rights has mostly focused on the reasoning provided by a national court of last instance for refusing to refer the case to the Court of Justice, in the specific case in which one of the parties had requested it. The case law can be summarised as follows:

> The Convention does not guarantee, as such, any right to have a case referred by a domestic court to the CJEU for a preliminary ruling. However, Article 6 § 1 requires the domestic courts to give reasons for any decision refusing to refer a request for a preliminary ruling, especially where the applicable law allows for such a refusal only on an exceptional basis. The Court has inferred from this that when it hears a complaint alleging a violation of Article 6 § 1 on this basis, its task consists in ensuring that the impugned refusal has been duly accompanied by such reasoning.
>
> . . . in the specific context of the third paragraph of Article 267 of the TFEU, this means that national courts against whose decisions there is no remedy under national law, which refuse to refer to the Court of Justice a preliminary question on the interpretation of [Union] law that has been raised before them, are obliged to give reasons for their refusal in the light of the exceptions provided for in the case-law of the Court of Justice.[94]

The case law of the European Court of Human Rights requires parties to the proceedings to raise issues of Union law with sufficient clarity, preferably at all stages of the proceedings, and to show that the points of law are relevant to the dispute.[95] In *Vergauwen and Others v Belgium*, the application was dismissed as manifestly unfounded, since the parties' request to refer the case to the Court of Justice concerned questions that were either hypothetical or irrelevant and did not fall within the obligation to refer. Consequently, the European Court of Human Rights ruled that the national court's refusal to refer the case under Article 267 TFEU was not arbitrary.[96]

1.9. Effects of the Preliminary Ruling

The purpose of the preliminary reference procedure is to assist a national court in the implementation of Union law in an individual case, but also to provide a uniform interpretation that applies to all the Member States. The preliminary reference procedure is the most powerful remedy to ensure consistency and uniformity in the interpretation of Union law. This outcome requires that the effects of the Court of Justice's rulings in preliminary reference procedures extend beyond the dispute from which the reference originates. Therefore, the judgments of the

[94] *Sanofi Pasteur v France* App no 25137/16 (ECtHR, 13 February 2020) paras 69–70. See also, in the same line of argument, *Dhahbi v Italy* App no 17120/09 (ECtHR, 8 April 2014); *Bio Farmland Betriebs SRL v Romania* App no 43639/17 (ECtHR, 13 July 2021); and *Ullens de Schooten et Rezabek v Belgique* App no 3989/07 (ECtHR, 20 September 2011). More recently, the ECtHR has applied this standard to decisions of national supreme courts at the stage of admissibility, in proceedings to decide on the leave to appeal, as was the case in *Gondert v Germany* App no 34701/21 (ECtHR, 16 December 2025).

[95] *Wallishauser v Austria (No 2)* App no 156/04 (ECtHR, 17 July 2012).

[96] See, in the same line of argument, *Ferreira Santos Pardal v Portugal* App no 30123/10 (ECtHR, 30 July 2015); *Krikorian v France* App no 6459/07 (ECtHR, 26 November 2013); *Ryon and Others v France* App no 33014/08 (ECtHR, 15 October 2013); *Sindicatul Pro Asistenta Sociala v Romania* App no 24456/13 (ECtHR, 6 March 2014); and *Baydar v Netherlands* App no 55385/14 (ECtHR, 24 April 2018).

Court of Justice delivered under Article 267 TFEU have *erga omnes* and *ex tunc* effects, subject to several exceptions that will be explained below.

1.9.1. Effects in Time

A judgment or an order resolving a preliminary reference on the interpretation or validity of a rule of Union law has an *ex tunc* effect. As a result, the judgment produces its effects from the time of the entry into force of the interpreted rule or, in the case of a declaration of invalidity, from the date of the act declared invalid. The case law is clear on this point, having stated as follows:

> [T]he interpretation which, in the exercise of the jurisdiction conferred on it by Article [267 TFEU], the Court gives to a rule of [Union] law clarifies and defines the meaning and scope of that rule as it must be or ought to have been understood and applied from the time of its entry into force. It follows that the rule as thus interpreted may, and must, be applied by the courts even to legal relationships which arose and were established before the judgment ruling on the request for interpretation . . .[97]

Union courts have the exceptional power to limit the temporal effects of a ruling in a preliminary reference procedure. In *Defrenne II*,[98] the Court of Justice applied by analogy the second paragraph of Article 264 TFEU, extending a provision originally conceived for actions for annulment to preliminary references, albeit in limited circumstances.[99] To limit the temporal effects of a ruling in a preliminary reference procedure, the Court of Justice requires evidence (a) of a risk of serious economic repercussions owing in particular to the large number of legal relationships entered into in good faith on the basis of rules considered to be validly in force, and (b) of conduct by individuals and national authorities who were led to adopt practices that proved to be incompatible with Union law because of objective, significant uncertainty regarding the implications of the relevant Union provisions, to which the conduct of other Member States or the Commission may even have contributed. This power to limit temporal effects lies exclusively with the Court of Justice, and it is for it alone to determine whether the conditions are satisfied.[100]

Member States have the power to introduce time limitations on claims by parties seeking to enforce the rights that flow from the interpretation provided by the Court of Justice in the preliminary reference. For instance, if a preliminary ruling finds that a national tax is in breach

[97] Case C-61/79 *Italian Denkavit* EU:C:1980:100, para 16; Joined Cases C-66/79, C-127/79 and C-128/79 *Salumi and Others* EU:C:1980:101, para 9; Case C-811/79 *Ariete* EU:C:1980:195, para 6; Case C-826/79 *Mireco* EU:C:1980:198, para 7; Case C-309/85 *Barra and Others* EU:C:1988:42, para 11; Case C-24/86 *Blaizot and Others* EU:C:1988:43, para 27; Case C-62/93 *BP Supergaz* EU:C:1995:223, para 39; Joined Cases C-367/93 to C-377/93 *Roders and Others* EU:C:1995:261, para 42; Case C-137/94 *Richardson* EU:C:1995:342, para 31; *Bosman* (n 70) para 141; Joined Cases C-197/94 and C-252/94 *Bautiaa and Société française maritime* EU:C:1996:47, para 47; Case C-188/95 *Fantask and Others* EU:C:1997:580, para 36; Case C-231/96 *Edis* EU:C:1998:401, para 15; Case C-262/96 *Sürül* EU:C:1999:228, para 107; Case C-184/99 *Grzelczyk* EU:C:2001:458, para 50; and Case C-347/00 *Barreira Pérez* EU:C:2002:560, para 44.

[98] Case C-43/75 *Defrenne* EU:C:1976:56, paras 70–74.

[99] Case C-423/04 *Richards* EU:C:2006:256, para 42; Case C-2/09 *Kalinchev* EU:C:2010:312, para 51; Case C-338/11 *Santander Asset Management SGIIC and Others* EU:C:2012:286, para 60; and Case C-82/12 *Transportes Jordi Besora* EU:C:2014:108, para 42. On the limitation of temporal effects in preliminary reference rulings, see D Düsterhaus, 'Eppur Si Muove! The Past, Present, and (possible) Future of Temporal Limitations in the Preliminary Ruling Procedure' (2017) 36 *Yearbook of European Law* 237.

[100] Case C-409/06 *Winner Wetten* EU:C:2010:503, para 67; and Case C-439/19 *Latvijas Republikas Saeima* EU:C:2021:504, para 135. However, it appears that in national litigation before administrative courts, in which national administrative courts also have the power to limit the temporal effects of their judgments, the case law has opened the possibility for these jurisdictions to limit the effects of their judgments in cases concerning the interpretation of Union law. In this regard, see Case C-41/11 *Inter-Environnement Wallonie and Terre wallonne* EU:C:2012:103; Case C-379/15 *Association France Nature Environnement* EU:C:2016:603; Case C-24/19 *A and Others* EU:C:2020:503; and Case C-64/20 *UH* EU:C:2021:207, para 36.

of Union law, taxpayers who paid the unlawful tax are entitled to recover the overpaid sums, but national law may set a time-limit for making such claims. Member States can apply limitation periods and other procedural conditions to such claims to guarantee a certain degree of legal certainty. These national procedural rules must comply with the principles of effectiveness and equivalence to avoid undermining the full of effect of Union law. A careful balance between the effectiveness of Union law and the protection of legal certainty will be needed on the part of the Member State, as discussed in section III.2 of this chapter.[101]

1.9.2. Effects on Parties and Third Parties

The ruling of the Court of Justice in preliminary reference procedures produces its effects *erga omnes*, thus binding the referring court and the parties in the main proceedings, as well as any other court, authority and private party in the Union subject to the same rules that were subject to interpretation in the preliminary reference procedure.[102] The fact that a Member State constrains the effects of national judgments to the parties of the dispute only, does not limit in any way the *erga omnes* effects of the ruling of the Court of Justice.[103]

1.9.2.1. Effects on the Referring Court and the Parties

The obligation to comply with a preliminary ruling delivered by the Court of Justice lies primarily with the referring court and the parties involved in the main proceedings. A judgment of the Court of Justice in a preliminary reference procedure is not an advisory opinion; it is binding on the referring court as regards the interpretation or validity of the Union law provisions at issue, and failure to comply can result in an appeal in accordance with domestic remedies. If the referring court encounters difficulties in interpreting the judgment of the Court of Justice or the General Court, or if it considers that the judgment contains legal or factual errors, it can refer the case again for another preliminary ruling, but it is not empowered to depart from the judgment delivered by the Union courts.

1.9.2.2. Effects on other Bodies and Powers of the Member State

The interpretation or review of the validity of a rule of Union law carried out by the Court of Justice or the General Court is also binding on all of the Member State's bodies and powers, including the legislature and the executive. As stated in the judgment in *Kühne & Heitz*,[104] a judgment delivered in a preliminary reference procedure extends its effects to the Member State in its entirety, requiring all authorities to undertake the necessary measures of review and ensure compliance with Union law. This may require the review and revocation of national administrative acts adopted during the period when a different interpretation was employed, or when the act declared invalid was applied. This obligation also applies to situations in which the administrative acts have become final, either because of the expiry of time limits for challenge, or because a judicial ruling with the force of *res judicata* has confirmed the administrative act. However, the duty to review and withdraw such acts will only arise when four cumulative conditions are met, as laid down in Kühne & Heitz: the administrative body

[101] See, inter alia, *Edis* (n 97) para 39; Case C-260/96 *Spac* EU:C:1998:402, para 23; and Joined Cases C-216/99 and C-222/99 *Prisco and CASER* EU:C:2002:472, para 70.

[102] Case C-68/74 *Alaimo* EU:C:1975:11, para 7; Case C-216/22 *A.A.* EU:C:2024:122, para 43 and Case C-448/23 *Commission v Poland* EU:C:2025:975, para 216.

[103] See, for example, the shift that took place in French administrative courts, in which the case of 11 December 2006, *De Groot en Slot Allium BV et Bejo Zaden BV* stands out, particularly the conclusions of the *Rapporteur Public* Mattias Guyomar, on the material scope of judgments of the Court of Justice in preliminary references, and their impact in national procedures.

[104] Case C-453/00 *Kühne and Heitz* EU:C:2004:17, para 22.

has the power under national law to reopen the decision; the decision has become final as a result of a judgment of a national court ruling at last instance; that judgment is, in the light of a subsequent preliminary ruling, based on a misinterpretation of Union law adopted without a question being referred to the Court of Justice; and the person concerned complained to the administrative body immediately after becoming aware of the preliminary ruling.[105]

1.9.2.3. Effects on other Member States and Institutions

The effects of a ruling in a preliminary reference procedure are not confined exclusively to the bodies of the Member State from which the reference originates. As mentioned above, a preliminary ruling from the Union courts has *erga omnes* effects, applying to all Member States and to all institutions, bodies, offices, and agencies of the Union.[106] As a result, the interpretation provided by the Court of Justice in a preliminary ruling referred by a Danish court is also binding on the Austrian, Spanish and Irish courts and administrations, as well as those of all the remaining Member States.

1.9.3. Material Scope of the Effects

The effects mentioned above apply to the entirety of the content of the preliminary ruling, including both the reasoning and the operative part. The same applies to a judgment in a preliminary ruling going beyond the scope of the questions asked by the referring court.[107] This is not frequently the case, but it is not unusual for the Court of Justice to address ancillary points of law in order to provide a useful answer to the referring court.

1.9.4. The Case of Rulings in Preliminary References of Validity: Declarations of Invalidity

Unlike a ruling upholding an action for annulment, a preliminary ruling of validity finding that a Union act is unlawful will not lead to an annulment, but to a declaration of invalidity. The terminological difference between an 'annulment' and a declaration of 'invalidity' is relevant: while an annulment involves the immediate and retroactive removal of the unlawful Union act, a declaration of invalidity has a similar effect, but relies on the action of the courts and administrative bodies of the Member States, which must draw the necessary consequences from the ruling of the Court of Justice.[108] In other words, whereas an annulment results in the immediate disappearance of the contested Union act, a declaration of invalidity imposes a duty on all public authorities to set aside the act and draw the necessary consequences from the judgment of the Court of Justice:

> When the Court is moved under Article [267 TFEU] to declare an act of one of the institutions to be [invalid] there are particularly imperative requirements concerning legal certainty in addition to those concerning the uniform application of [Union] law. It follows from the very nature of such a declaration that a national court *may not apply the act declared to be void* without once more creating serious uncertainty as to the [Union] law applicable (emphasis added).[109]

[105] ibid, paras 24 and 28.

[106] Joined Cases C-117/76 and C-16/77 *Ruckdeschel and Others* EU:C:1977:160, para 13.

[107] See the judgment of the French *Conseil d'État* in case CE Ass, 11 December 2006, *Société De Groot en Slot Allium BV et Société Bejo Zaden BV*, req n° 234560.

[108] See, by way of example, the judgments declaring Union acts to be 'invalid' in Case C-66/80 *International Chemical Corporation* EU:C:1981:102; Joined Cases C-522/07 and C-65/08 *Dinter* EU:C:2009:663; Joined Cases C-92/09 and C-93/09 *Volker und Markus Schecke and Eifert* EU:C:2010:662.

[109] *International Chemical Corporation* (n 108) para 12.

This difference in treatment is explained by the cooperative and bilateral nature of the preliminary ruling procedure, in which two levels of jurisdictions are involved and where the national court retains the responsibility to apply the ruling to the facts of the case. However, this justification does not seem sufficient if, ultimately, the practical effect of an annulment and a declaration of invalidity is the same. In practice, the referring national court will have to decide the case in the same terms as if the contested act had been annulled.[110] The same applies to any court or administrative body faced with cases involving the contested act.[111] Therefore, the distinction between 'annulment' and a declaration of 'invalidity', however deep-rooted it may be in the case law, appears somewhat artificial, and it may even contribute to create a certain degree of legal uncertainty.[112]

2. The Plea of Illegality

Article 277 TFEU provides a remedy that allows any party involved in proceedings before Union courts, where an act of general application is at issue, to invoke the inapplicability of that act. This remedy is available regardless of the two-month time limit provided in Article 263 TFEU to bring an action for annulment. The plea of illegality is an indirect remedy, as it is triggered in the context of another judicial procedure before the Union courts. Its purpose is to ensure that an unlawful act of general application is not imposed, whether directly or indirectly, on anyone, regardless of the time at which the plea is raised. This remedy addresses the gap produced by the restrictive rules of standing in actions for annulment, which are particularly demanding for private applicants seeking to directly challenge a Union act of a general scope. As a result, when a private applicant lacks standing to challenge a general Union act, they will still be entitled to raise a plea of illegality against that act if it is ever to be enforced through subsequent Union implementing measures.

2.1. *Jurisdiction*

The plea of illegality can only be raised in proceedings before Union courts, most commonly in an action for annulment, but also in an action for failure to act, a damages action or in proceedings on staff cases. Jurisdiction to hear the plea of illegality is assigned to the court that is hearing the proceedings in which the plea is invoked.

The plea of illegality may be raised by a Member State in infringement proceedings in exceptional circumstances only. Unlike other proceedings, the case law allows Member States to rely on the plea only when the infringement goes beyond a mere failure to fulfil

[110] ibid.

[111] ibid, pt (1) of the judgment: 'When the Court is moved under Article [267 TFEU] to declare an act of one of the institutions to be void there are particularly imperative requirements concerning legal certainty in addition to those concerning the uniform application of [Union] law. It follows from the very nature of such a declaration that a national court may not apply the act declared to be void without once more creating serious uncertainty as to the [Union] law applicable.'

[112] The General Court itself does not seem to find much sense in the distinction between 'annulment' and 'invalidity', equating the two in practical terms and in terms of their consequences for third parties. See, by way of example, the order in Case T-305/08 *Italy v Commission* EU:T:2012:70, para 23: 'In such circumstances, it must be held that the invalidity of the contested regulation produces, in the present case, effects equivalent to those of a judgment of annulment, those effects having, in principle and unless expressly limited by the judgment of annulment, retroactive effect from the date of entry into force of the rule interpreted, as in the case of a judgment of annulment. Accordingly, a judgment annulling that regulation, which is now invalid, would not entail any additional legal consequences . . . as compared with the consequences of the invalidity pronounced.'

obligations arising from a failure to transpose or implement the relevant Union act.[113] According to settled case law:

> [A] Member State cannot, therefore, properly plead the unlawfulness of a decision addressed to it as a defence in an action for a declaration that it has failed to fulfil its obligations arising out of its failure to implement that decision . . . It is immaterial whether such unlawfulness is pleaded in the action brought against the Member State or, as in this case, in an action for annulment of the decision at issue . . .[114]

The Court of Justice has ruled that a plea of illegality is not available in preliminary reference proceedings, arguing that only the referring national court, not the parties in the national proceedings, has the authority to make a reference and determine the scope of the questions submitted to the Court of Justice.[115]

2.2. *Acts of General Application*

The challenged act in a plea of illegality must be of 'general application', having been the legal basis of the challenged act in the main proceedings. For example, if a regulation of the Council and the European Parliament is the legal basis of a Commission decision, the addressee of this decision can challenge it through an action for annulment, and may simultaneously raise a plea of illegality against the provision of the regulation being implemented by the Commission decision.

Prior to the Lisbon Treaty, the plea of illegality was limited only to 'regulations', although the case law had extended the use of the plea to any other act of general application, regardless of its formal characterisation.[116] The Lisbon Treaty introduced an amendment to align the wording of the current Article 277 TFEU with the case law, replacing the reference to 'regulations' with the term 'act of general application'.

The contested act must have served as the legal basis for the challenged act in the main proceedings. This requirement means that the plea will only be available in cases where there is a 'close relationship' between the act of general application (the contested act in the plea of illegality) and the implementing act (the contested act in the direct action).[117] In exceptional cases, a plea of illegality may be allowed even if the contested provision of the general act is not the legal basis for the implementing act, provided that a 'close relationship' between both provisions is established.[118]

2.3. *Standing*

Article 277 TFEU refers to 'any party' involved in proceedings before Union courts in which an act of general application is at issue. Member States, private parties, as well as institutions,

[113] Case C-156/77 *Commission v Belgium* EU:C:1978:180, paras 15–25; Case C-52/83 *Commission v France* EU:C:1983:328, para 10; Case C-52/84 *Commission v Belgium* EU:C:1986:3, para 13; Case C-226/87 *Commission v Greece* EU:C:1988:354, para 14; Case C-261/99 *Commission v France* EU:C:2001:179, para 18; and Case C-620/16 *Commission v Germany* EU:C:2019:256, para 89.

[114] *Commission v France* (n 113) para 18.

[115] Case C-44/65 *Hessische Knappschaft* EU:C:1965:122; and Case C-216/82 *Universität Hamburg* EU:C:1983:248, para 10.

[116] Case C-92/78 *Simmenthal v Commission* EU:C:1979:53, paras 39–43.

[117] Case C-21/64 *Macchiorati Dalmas e figli* EU:C:1965:30; and Case C-275/80 *Krupp v Commission* EU:C:1981:247, para 32.

[118] Case C-32/65 *Italy v Council and Commission* EU:C:1966:42; Case C-18/62 *Barge v High Authority* EU:C:1963:56; and Joined Cases C-140/82, C-146/82, C-221/82 and C-226/82 *Walzstahl-Vereinigung and Thyssen v Commission* EU:C:1984:66, para 20.

bodies, offices, and agencies of the Union can raise a plea of illegality, provided they do so in their capacity as parties in such proceedings.

In the case of private applicants, it should be noted that a plea of illegality is limited to those private parties lacking standing to challenge a Union act of general application within the prescribed time limit.[119] The plea of illegality is conceived as a way to offset the strictures of the standing rules, particularly those in the fourth paragraph of Article 263 TFEU, but not as a means to circumvent the time limits for annulment actions. This limitation is analogous to the restrictions placed on parties before national courts when they seek to rely on the preliminary reference on validity, having previously failed to use the action for annulment despite having undeniable standing to bring such an action. It should be noted that this restriction applies only to private parties, not to privileged or semi-privileged parties.[120]

In exceptional circumstances, the Union courts may, of their own motion, review the invalidity of the general act on which the contested act is based. This will arise only in cases involving grounds of public policy, whether due to a lack of jurisdiction or the infringement of an essential procedural requirement.[121]

2.4. *Time Limits*

The plea of illegality may be raised at any time during the proceedings in which it is invoked, 'notwithstanding the expiry of the period laid down in Article 263 TFEU'.

2.5. *Effects of the Judgment*

A ruling upholding a plea of illegality has inter partes effects and will not result in the annulment of the act of general application. As stated in Article 277 TFEU, a plea of illegality aims at a declaration of the 'inapplicability' of the general act in the particular case only. Consequently, the act declared inapplicable will remain part of the Union legal system.[122] However, the institution, body, office, or agency that enacted the act is under an obligation, immediately from the date of delivery of the ruling, to draw the necessary consequences from the judgment and take appropriate measures to remedy the illegality identified.[123]

3. The Review Procedure

The Court of Justice has jurisdiction to review, on a proposal from the First Advocate General, the decisions of the General Court delivered in preliminary ruling proceedings. Article 256(3) TFEU states that decisions of the General Court in preliminary ruling proceedings may exceptionally be reviewed by the Court of Justice, 'where there is a serious risk of the unity or consistency of Union law being affected'.

The review procedure is also available when the General Court acts as an appellate jurisdiction over decisions of specialised courts, pursuant to Article 256(2) TFEU. From 2005

[119] Case C-156/77 *Commission v Belgium* EU:C:1978:180, para 20.

[120] Case C-11/00 *Commission v ECB* EU:C:2003:395; and Case C-442/04 *Spain v Council* EU:C:2008:276.

[121] Case C-14/59 *Société des fonderies de Pont-à-Mousson v High Authority* EU:C:1959:31; and Case T-134/03 *Common Market Fertilizers v Commission* EU:T:2005:339, paras 51–52.

[122] Joined Cases C-15/73 to C-33/73, C-52/73, C-53/73, C-57/73 to C-109/73, C-116/73, C-117/73, C-123/73, C-132/73 and C-135/73 to C-137/73 *Kortner v Council* EU:C:1974:16, para 36.

[123] Joined Cases C-14/60, C-16/60, C-17/60, C-20/60, C-24/60, C-26/60, C-27/60 and C-1/61 *Meroni and Others v High Authority* EU:C:1961:16; and Joined Cases C-75/82 and C-117/82 *Razzouk and Others v Commission* EU:C:1984:116, para 19.

to 2016, the General Court held this appellate jurisdiction over the European Union Civil Service Tribunal. Following the entry into force of the reform of the General Court doubling its members, that specialised court was dissolved and the review procedure in appellate staff cases ceased to be applicable.

For the Court of Justice to initiate the review of a preliminary ruling decision of the General Court, it acts on a proposal made by the First Advocate General. According to Article 62 of the Statute of the Court of Justice, the proposal must be submitted within one month of delivery of the decision by the General Court, and within the following month the Court of Justice determines whether the decision should be reviewed. During this initial two-month period, the decision of the General Court is suspended. If the Court of Justice decides to review the decision, the suspension continues for the duration of the review procedure.

The judgment of the Court of Justice finding that the reviewed decision of the General Court affects the unity or consistency of Union law will 'replace' the decision.[124] Therefore, the Court of Justice resolves the matter definitively and does not refer it back to the General Court.

4. Interim Measures

Articles 278–279 TFEU introduce a framework for the adoption of interim measures by Union courts. Article 278 TFEU gives parties the right to request the suspension of the application of the contested Union acts in judicial proceedings. Article 279 TFEU introduces a power for Union courts to 'prescribe any necessary interim measures'. Together, these provisions provide the basis for a broad scheme of interim measures that can be addressed to Union acts, as well as to acts of the Member States and private parties, which can be invoked in the course of any direct action, but subject to the following requirements.

First, the adoption of an interim measure is an ancillary remedy dependent on other proceedings lodged in Union courts. An interim measure can only be requested within the context of *another* pending judicial proceeding. Therefore, an application to suspend a Union act can only be brought if the act has been previously or simultaneously challenged in an action for annulment.[125] As a result, the interim measure will only produce its effects during the time in which the proceedings in Union courts are ongoing, ceasing to have effect upon the delivery of the judgment in the main proceedings.[126]

Second, interim measures can target any type of Union act, including regulations, directives, decisions or soft law acts, whether legislative or regulatory in nature. The standard of review is more stringent in the case of acts of general application due to their broader effects and impact in the case of suspension.[127] In infringement proceedings, interim measures can be addressed to Member States, regardless of the scope of the national measure at issue. Therefore, Union courts can order Member States to suspend the application of general measures, such as a legislative act, or individual decisions aimed at a specific addressee. The use of interim relief against a Member State is rare, but recent years have seen a significant increase

[124] Art 62b of the Statute of the Court of Justice.

[125] See Art 160(1)–(2) of the Rules of Procedure of the Court of Justice and Art 156(1) of the Rules of Procedure of the General Court.

[126] See Art 162(3) of the Rules of Procedure of the Court of Justice and Art 158(3) of the Rules of Procedure of the General Court. The measures ordered by the President of the General Court therefore come to an end once the General Court has delivered its judgment, even if an appeal is brought before the Court of Justice. See Case T-191/98 R-II *Cho Yang Shipping* EU:T:2000:171, para 41.

[127] Case C-44/75 R *Könecke v Commission* EU:C:1975:72, para 2.

in requests by the Commission against Member States' actions, even in the context of Article 260 TFEU proceedings.[128]

Third, the content of an interim measure will vary depending on the type of action used in the main proceedings and the impact of the challenged act on the parties. The standard case of interim relief is a suspension of a Union act challenged in an action for annulment. However, Union courts can issue positive interim orders requiring the defendant to act in a specific manner[129] or order a suspension subject to other accessory obligations on the part of the defendant during the main proceedings.[130]

Fourth, despite the broad scope of Articles 278–279 TFEU, Union courts are not entitled to grant interim relief in preliminary reference procedures. The case law has confirmed this exception on the grounds that the most suitable jurisdiction to provide interim measures is the national referring court. In some cases, national courts may be under a duty to adopt suspensive interim measures, especially when, reviewing the validity of a Union act, they decide to refer the matter to the Union courts through a preliminary reference of validity.[131] In such cases, the national court is entitled to temporarily suspend the application of a national measure implementing the contested Union act as between the parties to the main proceedings, subject to the conditions laid down in *Zuckerfabrik* and *Atlanta*: the court must entertain serious doubts as to the validity of the Union act, the matter must be referred to the Court of Justice, there must be urgency and a threat of serious and irreparable harm, and the court must take due account of the Union's interest.[132]

4.1. *Jurisdiction, Standing and Time Limits*

The Vice-President of the Court of Justice[133] and the President of the General Court[134] have jurisdiction to decide on applications for interim relief brought by the parties. In the Court of Justice, the Vice-President has the power to refer the case to a collegiate formation. This option is not available in the Rules of Procedure of the General Court, where the President may delegate this authority to the Vice-President.

Only the parties to the main proceedings can apply for interim measures,[135] a right that can be exercised at any time during the proceedings, but not after the close of the oral phase of the main proceedings. Following this stage, the application will be declared inadmissible.[136]

4.2. *Requirements*

The case law requires three conditions to be met: the first two are laid down in the Rules of Procedure and refer to the establishment of a prima facie case (*fumus boni iuris*) and its urgency

[128] See, by way of example, the Orders in Case C-441/17 R *Commission v Poland* EU:C:2017:877, Case C-238/18 R *ECB v Latvia* EU:C:2018:581; and Case C-619/18 R *Commission v Poland* EU:C:2018:1021.

[129] Joined Cases C-160/73, C-161/73, and C-170/73 R *Miles Druce & Co* EU:C:1973:106; Case C-3/75 R *Johnson & Firth Brown* EU:C:1975:3; and Case C-393/96 P (R) *Antonissen v Council and Commission* EU:C:1997:42.

[130] Case T-94/00 R *Roquette Frères* (unpublished).

[131] *Zuckerfabrik* (n 50); Case C-213/89 *The Queen v Secretary of State for Transport, ex parte Factortame* EU:C:1990:257; Case C-465/93 *Atlanta Fruchthandelsgesellschaft* EU:C:1995:369, and Case C-432/05 *Unibet* EU:C:2007:163.

[132] *Zuckerfabrik* (n 50) paras 16–17.

[133] See Art 1 of Decision 2012/671/EU of the Court of Justice of 23 October 2012 on the judicial role of the Vice-President of the Court of Justice.

[134] Art 158(1) of the Rules of Procedure of the General Court.

[135] Art 160(2) of the Rules of Procedure of the Court of Justice and Art 156(2) of the Rules of Procedure of the General Court.

[136] Cases 25/58 and 26/58 R *Hüttenwerk Salzgitter v High Authority* (unpublished).

(*periculum in mora*).[137] The third requirement is the creation of case law and it consists of a balancing test, whereby the court must weigh the interests at stake.[138] Overall, the purpose of interim relief is to avoid serious and irreparable harm to the applicant's interests, while ensuring that the main proceedings are not deprived of their purpose.

The requirement of *fumus boni iuris* implies that the application for interim measures must demonstrate that the arguments raised in the main proceedings are not *prima facie* without merit. Therefore, the application must include enough arguments to support the plausibility of the case. This condition is met if, during the proceedings for interim relief, there is a serious legal or factual question whose resolution is not immediately clear, leading to the conclusion that the action is not prima facie without reasonable merit.[139]

The requirement of *periculum in mora* aims to establish the urgency of the request by demonstrating that irreparable harm would occur if the interim measure were not granted.[140] Urgency must be assessed in light of the need to avoid serious and irreparable damage to the party requesting interim relief.[141] It is the responsibility of the party claiming such damage to establish its likelihood. While it is not necessary that the applicant demonstrate with absolute certainty that the damage will occur, the applicant is nonetheless required to prove the facts supporting the prospect of such damage.[142] Moreover, the damage must be actual and imminent, not hypothetical,[143] the burden of proof falling on the party seeking the interim measure.

The requirement for a balancing *test* applies only when the two previous conditions are fulfilled, requiring that the adverse effects of the interim relief on the defendant and third parties do not outweigh the benefits for the applicant.[144] Although the burden of proof rests with the applicant, Union courts take into consideration all interests invoked by both parties and conduct the balancing test having regard to all the circumstances of the case.[145] As a result of the balancing test, the interim measure can be adapted to the circumstances of all the parties to the case, departing from the measures requested by the applicant if necessary.[146]

4.3. *Effects*

As a rule, the Vice-President/President decides on the application for interim measures by way of a reasoned order. If the application is upheld, the Vice-President/President will specify the conditions under which the interim measure is to be implemented, including the possibility

[137] Art 160(3) of the Rules of Procedure of the Court of Justice and Art 156(3) of the Rules of Procedure of the General Court.

[138] Case C-76/08 R *Commission v Malta* (unpublished) EU:C:2008:252, para 21; Case C-573/08 R *Commission v Italy* (unpublished) EU:C:2009:775, para 11; and Case C-431/14 P-R *Greece v Commission* EU:C:2014:2418, para 19.

[139] Case 43/59 R *Von Lachmüller and Others* EU:C:1959:24; Joined Cases 44/59 and 45/59 R *Fiddelaar v Commission* EU:C:1960:38; Case C-232/81 R *Agricola Commerciale Olio* EU:C:1981:191, para 5; Case 42/82 R *Commission v France* EU:C:1982:83, para 14; Case C-272/91 R *Commission v Italy* EU:C:1992:49, paras 19–24; and Case C-431/14 P-R *Greece v Commission* EU:C:2014:2418, para 20.

[140] Case 4/78 R *Salerno and Others v Commission* EU:C:1978:3, para 11; and Case 120/83 R *Raznoimport v Commission* EU:C:1983:224, para 15.

[141] Case C-76/08 R *Commission v Malta* (unpublished) EU:C:2008:252, para 31; and Case C-573/08 R *Commission v Italy* (unpublished) EU:C:2009:775, para 17.

[142] Case C-76/08 R *Commission v Malta* (unpublished) EU:C:2008:252, para 32; and Case C-573/08 R *Commission v Italy* (unpublished) EU:C:2009:775, para 18.

[143] Case 142/87 R *Commission v Belgium* EU:C:1987:281, para 25; and Case C-296/93 R *France and Ireland v Commission* EU:C:1993:327, para 26.

[144] *Johnson & Firth Brown* (n 129); Case 92/78 R *Simmenthal* EU:C:1978:106, para 18; Case 176/88 R *Hanning v Parliament* EU:C:1988:381, para 14; and Case 56/89 R *Publishers Association v Commission* EU:C:1989:238, para 35.

[145] Case 45/87 R *Commission v Ireland* EU:C:1987:132, para 33; Case 194/88 R *Commission v Italy* EU:C:1988:462, para 16; and Case C-87/94 R *Commission v Belgium* EU:C:1994:166, paras 39–42.

[146] *Johnson & Firth Brown* (n 129) para 7; and Case T-29/92 R *Asia Motor France* EU:T:1992:92.

of requiring financial guarantees where appropriate.[147] The interim measure remains in effect until the judgment in the main proceedings is delivered, unless ordered otherwise.[148] The Vice-President/President has the power to amend or revoke the terms of the interim measures at the request of a party, in light of the circumstances of the case.[149]

The dismissal of a request for interim measures does not preclude the parties from making a new application at a later stage of the main proceedings, provided the new application is based on new facts.[150]

Only the orders of the President and Vice-President of the General Court ruling on an application for interim measures are subject to appeal to the Court of Justice.[151] In contrast, no appeal is available against orders rendered by the Vice-President of the Court of Justice in interim measures proceedings.

In the case of interim measures pursuant to Article 279 TFEU brought against a Member State in the context of infringement proceedings, the Commission can rely on Article 260(2) TFEU to ensure compliance with the order of the Vice-President of the Court of Justice.[152]

II. PROCEDURE BEFORE THE UNION COURTS

Direct and indirect actions before Union courts are governed by a set of common procedural rules, to which specific provisions are added for each remedy. These common rules serve as a 'basic procedural code' applicable to both courts. The key features of these rules are set out in the Statute of the Court of Justice, and elaborated in the Rules of Procedure of each court. The common rules concern the representation of parties in court, the language regime, the division of the procedure into a written and an oral stage, and the requirements for the participation of the parties.

Article 19 of the Statute of the Court of Justice establishes the basic rules governing the representation of parties in Union courts. Representatives are categorised into two groups: first, Member States and Union institutions are represented by 'an agent appointed for each case';[153] second, other parties (such as undertakings, natural persons, public bodies of the Member States, third countries, etc) are represented by 'a lawyer', provided that they are 'authorised to practise before a court of a Member State or of another State which is a party to the [EEA]'.[154] In the case of lawyers linked to an employer by an employment relationship (in-house lawyers), the Court of Justice has held that they lack the necessary independence to represent their

[147] Art 162(2) of the Rules of Procedure of the Court of Justice and Art 158(2) of the Rules of Procedure of the General Court.

[148] Art 162(3) of the Rules of Procedure of the Court of Justice and Art 158(3) of the Rules of Procedure of the General Court.

[149] Art 163 of the Rules of Procedure of the Court of Justice and Art 159 of the Rules of Procedure of the General Court. See Case T-74/00 R *Artegodan and Others v Commission* EU:T:2000:173, paras 77–99; and Case T-198/01 R *Technische Glaswerke Ilmenau v Commission* EU:T:2004:222, paras 77–99 and 123.

[150] Art 164 of the Rules of Procedure of the Court of Justice and Art 160 of the Rules of Procedure of the General Court. See Case 51/79 *Buttner v Commission* EU:C:1979:183, para 1; and Case T-235/95 *Goldstein v Commission* EU:T:1998:56, para 27.

[151] Art 57(2)–(3) of the Statute of the Court of Justice.

[152] Case C-441/17 R *Commission v Poland* EU:C:2017:877.

[153] Art 19(1) of the Statute of the Court of Justice.

[154] Art 19(3) of the Statute of the Court of Justice. Furthermore, Art 19(4) entitles teachers who are nationals of Member States to act in legal proceedings, provided that the law of their Member State recognises this right for them on the same terms as for lawyers.

employers and are therefore not authorised to represent them in direct actions.[155] However, in preliminary ruling proceedings, if in-house lawyers are permitted to represent their employers in the main national proceedings, they will be entitled to participate in the preliminary ruling proceedings before Union courts.[156]

The linguistic regime is premised on the principle that all official languages of the Union can be used as the language of the procedure, but only one will be assigned to each individual case. The rules on the language of the procedure distinguish between direct actions and references for a preliminary ruling. In direct actions, the language of the procedure is chosen by the applicant, unless the defendant is a Member State, in which case the official language will be that of the Member State.[157] In preliminary ruling proceedings, the language of the procedure is that of the referring court or tribunal, although the use of other official languages may exceptionally be authorised at the oral stage of the proceedings in specific circumstances.[158]

All procedures before Union courts consist of two separate stages: the written part and the oral part.[159] In the written part, the parties are notified of the contested acts, pleadings, and any supporting documents or exhibits, including the collection of evidence in writing. The oral part of the procedure involves hearing the agents and lawyers, as well as, if necessary, witnesses and independent experts. The oral part concludes with the delivery of the Advocate General's Opinion, if there is one, or at the end of the hearing if the case is heard without an Opinion. At the end of the oral part of the procedure, the Court deliberates, renders its decision, and makes it public by serving it on the parties and publishing it, thereby bringing the proceedings to a close.

The Statute of the Court of Justice allows third parties to intervene in proceedings before Union courts. In the case of the Member States and institutions of the Union, the Statute of the Court of Justice grants the right to intervene regardless of their interest in the outcome of the dispute (a logical extension, consistent with their status as privileged applicants under the first paragraph of Article 263 TFEU).[160] For bodies, offices, and agencies of the Union, as well as 'any other person', intervention is only allowed if they can 'establish an interest in the result of a case submitted to the Court'.[161] Furthermore, natural and legal persons are barred from intervening in inter-institutional disputes, in which only institutions and/or Member States are involved.[162] In preliminary ruling proceedings, the rule is qualified in that only the parties to the main proceedings before the national court, the Member States, the Commission, and the institution, body, office, or agency of the Union that adopted the act whose validity or interpretation is contested may intervene in the proceedings.[163] The European Parliament, the

[155] Joined Cases C-515/17 P and C-561/17 P *Uniwersytet Wrocławski* EU:C:2020:73, paras 61–64. However, the employment relationship must be closely linked to the legal advisory functions, which was not the case in *Uniwersytet Wrocławski*, where the representation of a university was undertaken by a professor of law, whose employment relationship with the party was strictly attached to teaching activities (*Uniwersytet Wrocławski*, paras 66–68). The Court of Justice has clarified that 'the condition of independence provided for in EU law must be interpreted as limiting findings of inadmissibility to only those situations where it is quite obvious that the representative concerned is unable to carry out the task of defending his or her client while acting in that client's interests to the greatest possible extent, with the result that that representative must be removed in the interests of the client'. See Case C-110/21 P *Universität Bremen v REA* EU:C:2022:555, para 67. A full rectification of the application is now allowed by the case law, following the ruling in Case C-776/22 P *Studio Legale Ughi e Nunziante* EU:C:2025:644.

[156] Art 47(2) of the Rules of Procedure of the Court of Justice. In this regard, see Case C-293/93 *Houtwipper* EU:C:1994:330; and Case C-359/09 *Ebert* EU:C:2011:44.

[157] Art 37(1) of the Rules of Procedure of the Court of Justice and Art 45(1) of the Rules of Procedure of the General Court.

[158] Art 37(3) of the Rules of Procedure of the Court of Justice.

[159] Art 20 of the Statute of the Court of Justice.

[160] ibid, Art 40(1).

[161] ibid, Art 40(2).

[162] ibid, final indent.

[163] ibid, Art 23(1).

Council, and the European Central Bank are also authorised to submit observations when the case concerns the validity or interpretation of an act adopted jointly by the European Parliament and the Council, or of an act of the Council, the ECB, or in other cases where they consider that the case is relevant to them.[164]

III. NATIONAL COURTS IN THE UNION'S JUDICIAL SYSTEM

1. The National Judge as a Union Judge

Chapter eleven of this book portrayed the division of tasks between Union and national courts, emphasising the role of national courts as 'ordinary courts of Union law' (*juges de droit commun du droit de l'Union*). It falls upon national courts to perform the fundamental task of resolving all disputes in which Union law is applied in litigation between private parties, between a private party and a Member State, or between the authorities of a Member State. These categories of cases comprise the overwhelming majority of disputes that take place across the Union every day. In quantitative terms, national courts are those that most closely interact with parties in litigation on a daily basis.

National courts play a crucial role in guaranteeing the effectiveness of Union law. In disputes in national proceedings that require the interpretation of a rule of Union law, it is up to national courts to refer the matter to the Court of Justice for a preliminary ruling, as a means to provide coherence and a uniform interpretation of Union law in all the Member States. When the Court of Justice rules that Union law must be interpreted as precluding a national measure, it is for national courts to apply Union law and, if necessary, to set aside the incompatible national rule. The principles of direct effect and primacy are tools at the service of national courts, enabling them to provide the most effective judicial protection to the parties to the case. National courts also serve as the conduit for private enforcement of Union law, transforming the claims of private litigants into an indirect mechanism to ensure proper enforcement of Union law throughout all Member States.

Despite the strategic importance of national courts in the Union's legal system, their actions as ordinary courts of Union law are subject to some limitations. The main constraint is that Union law does not generally provide common procedural rules for national proceedings; instead, it relies on national procedural law when national courts resolve disputes involving Union law. Therefore, if a case before, for example, a Dutch court, concerns the interpretation of a Union regulation, the rules on jurisdiction, admissibility, evidence, oral hearings, and enforcement of the final decision will in principle be subject to the rules of procedure provided in Dutch law. At most, certain aspects of the national procedure may be governed by specific provisions of Union law governing a specific feature of the procedure (for example, the protection of victims in criminal proceedings, harmonised by Directive 2012/29). Nevertheless, the general procedural framework governing the case will remain subject to national law.

The decisions of national courts are not subject to an appeal before Union courts, irrespective of their content or the national jurisdiction ruling on the case. However, Union law provides several mechanisms to address errors of national courts. The Commission can decide to bring an infringement procedure against the Member State of a court or tribunal that delivered a judgment incompatible with Union law, or the aggrieved party may bring an action for

[164] ibid, Art 23(2).

damages against the Member State. These actions are not always entirely effective and can sometimes be a lengthy and costly alternative to a proper appellate remedy.

Member States have a wide margin of manoeuvre in establishing the procedural framework under which national courts implement Union law. This power is recognised in Union law by the principle of 'procedural autonomy'. However, this principle is not absolute, and the case law requires Member States to act in conformity with a number of other principles that delineate the scope of national procedural autonomy. This is the role played by the principles of effectiveness, equivalence and effective judicial protection, which will now be discussed.

2. The Principles of Effectiveness and Equivalence

2.1. *The Principle of Effectiveness*

The principle of effectiveness requires Member States, when laying down or implementing domestic procedural rules applicable to national courts, to avoid rendering 'impossible in practice or excessively difficult the exercise of rights conferred by Union law'.[165] This principle aims to counter national procedural rules that *hinder* the practical exercise of the rights conferred by Union law. Its scope is very broad, covering many areas of national procedural practice. In the following sections, some examples of the impact of the principle of effectiveness in national courts will be described, focusing on interim measures, procedural time limits, review by national courts of their own motion, and rules on the burden of proof.

2.1.1. Interim Measures

One of the hallmarks of the principle of effectiveness is the obligation it places on all Member States to provide effective interim relief for the parties that request it, even in the absence of a domestic framework governing such measures. Member States are under the duty of Union law, as derived from the principle of effectiveness, to ensure that their courts uphold the rights conferred by Union law, including through provisional measures aimed at safeguarding the effectiveness of national judicial proceedings. Without effective interim relief, exercising rights in court can be rendered futile. Therefore, national courts are required under Union law to grant interim relief in accordance with the requirements set out in the Court of Justice's case law.

The obligations arising from the principle of effectiveness in the area of interim relief serve as a minimum standard of protection applicable across all Member States. Nothing prevents national law from introducing more protective rules governing interim measures in national courts. This means that it is perfectly possible for national law to add requirements that enhance standards of procedural fairness among the parties, such as an appeal against the decisions of a national court on interim measures.[166]

National courts have the authority to grant interim measures in cases involving the interpretation of Union law, where acts of both Union and national law are under review. Once the minimum requirements set out in the case law are met, the national court is empowered to suspend the contested act and take any other measures necessary to ensure the effectiveness of the proceedings.[167] In the case of the suspension of a national implementing measure of a

[165] Case 33/76 *Rewe* EU:C:1976:188, para 5; Case 45/76 *Comet* BV EU:C:1976:191, para 13; Case C-128/93 *Fisscher* EU:C:1994:353, para 39; Case C-410/92 *Johnson* EU:C:1994:401, para 21; Case C-246/96 *Magorrian and Cunningham* EU:C:1997:605, para 37; and Case C-670/22 *MN (EncroChat)* EU:C:2024:372, para 129.

[166] Case C-334/95 *Krüger* EU:C:1997:378, para 52.

[167] *Zuckerfabrik* (n 50).

Union act, the national court is under the duty to immediately refer the question of validity to the Court of Justice for a preliminary ruling, ensuring that Union courts confirm the invalidity of the suspended act.[168]

The requirements for granting interim relief where a national measure implementing a Union act is at issue are the same as those outlined above for interim measures before Union courts (see section I.4 in this chapter). This is a reasonable parallelism, inasmuch as national courts are empowered to suspend acts of both national and Union law. It would be inconsistent to allow interim relief to suspend Union acts in national courts under one set of requirements, and a different type of interim relief to suspend the same act in Union courts. Consequently, the case law of the Court of Justice requires national courts, when deciding on a point of Union law, to grant interim relief if the following three conditions are met: the establishment of a prima facie case (*fumus boni iuris*); the establishment of its urgency (*periculum in mora*);[169] and the weighing of the conflicting interests at stake.[170] It should be noted that these conditions are specific to the suspension of national measures implementing Union acts. The general conditions for interim relief in cases in which Union law is implemented, but its validity is not at issue, are governed by national procedural law, subject to the principles of equivalence and effectiveness.

2.1.2. Time Limits

In all the legal systems of the Member States, the enforcement of a right or the use of remedies may be subject to a time limit to provide legal certainty in the legal sphere. Time limits are not intended to restrict the rights of parties but to prevent abusive or careless conduct. Therefore, Member States enjoy a broad discretion in introducing and delimiting the scope of time limits in national proceedings, including in cases where a national court rules on points of Union law. This discretion is subject to the requirements introduced by the principle of effectiveness.[171]

The Court of Justice has reviewed multiple national rules on time limitations, particularly when their duration has been considered to be excessively short. For instance, if a national tax is found to breach Union law, taxpayers are entitled to make a claim to recover an undue payment made to the tax authorities. The principle of effectiveness does not preclude the Member State from introducing a time limit to reclaim the unduly paid tax,[172] but it can be tempting for the Member State to reduce its duration to the shortest possible extent to prevent a large number of claims. If the time limit is excessively short, the principle of effectiveness applies, and it can result in the incompatibility of the time limit with Union law.[173] For example, time limits of five years[174] and three years[175] for the recovery of unduly paid tax have been deemed compatible with the principle of effectiveness. However, when a Member State retroactively reduces the duration of a time limit to claim an unduly paid amount, a reasonable

[168] ibid, para 19.

[169] Art 160(3) of the Rules of Procedure of the Court of Justice and Art 156(3) of the Rules of Procedure of the General Court.

[170] ibid, paras 31–32.

[171] *Rewe* (n 165) para 5; *Comet BV* (n 165) paras 17–18; and Case 61/79 *Denkavit* EU:C:1980:100, para 23.

[172] Case C-78/98 *Preston and Others* EU:C:2000:247, para 43.

[173] Case C-473/00 *Cofidis* EU:C:2002:705, para 37.

[174] Case C-90/94 *Haahr Petroleum* EU:C:1997:368, paras 48–52.

[175] Case C-231/96 *Edis* EU:C:1998:401, para 35; *Spac* (n 101) para 19; Joined Cases C-279/96, C-280/96, and C-281/96 *Ansaldo Energia* EU:C:1998:403, paras 17–18; Case C-343/96 *Dilexport* EU:C:1999:59, para 70; and *Prisco and CASER* (n 101) para 70.

transitional period must be provided, or otherwise, the reduction of the time limit will breach the principle of effectiveness.[176]

Recovery of undue payments has been fertile ground to test the principle of effectiveness, but it is not the only one. In *Emmott*, the Court of Justice ruled that the principle of effectiveness precludes the introduction of time limits to claims invoking the rights in a non-transposed Directive on social security allocations in the field of equality on the grounds of sex.[177] In subsequent case law, the Court of Justice moderated its position and ruled that Member States may impose time limits, even for rights stemming from a non-transposed Directive, provided that the time limit does not effectively deprive the applicant of the possibility of bringing a case in a national court within a reasonable time.[178]

2.1.3. The Burden of Proof

In the absence of Union rules on the gathering of evidence in national proceedings, Member States are free to regulate the means of evidence, the rules on its examination, and the consequences in the resolution of the dispute.[179] However, national rules on the gathering of evidence or the determination of the burden of proof among the parties must comply with the principle of effectiveness.[180] The Court of Justice has ruled on the conformity of national rules governing presumptions in national court proceedings,[181] as well as presumptions that make their rebuttal excessively difficult for one of the parties.[182] Furthermore, national courts are under a duty to use all procedural means available under national law to facilitate the gathering and production of evidence, including the issuance of measures of inquiry or the ordering of disclosure of information from third parties.[183]

2.1.4. *Ex Officio* Application of Union Law

National procedural law can introduce limitations to the powers of national courts, such as rules in civil proceedings that constrain the role of the court to the arguments and facts presented by the parties (principle of party autonomy, or *ne ultra petita*). In such cases, if a defendant party fails to respond to the applicant's allegations with convincing legal grounds, the national court cannot introduce new arguments *ex officio*, regardless of how well founded

[176] See also Case C-255/00 *Grundig Italiana* EU:C:2002:525, paras 36–42, where the Court declared a transitional period of 90 days to be insufficient and imposed a minimum of six months. See the criticism of this judgment made by Advocate General Ruiz-Jarabo Colomer in Case C-30/02 *Recheio-Cash & Carry* EU:C:2003:666, Opinion of AG Ruiz-Jarabo.

[177] Case C-208/90 *Emmott* EU:C:1991:333.

[178] Case C-338/91 *Steenhorst-Neerings* EU:C:1993:857; Case C-188/95 *Fantask and Others* EU:C:1997:580, paras 50–52; Case C-327/00 *Santex* EU:C:2003:109, paras 57–61; Case C-445/06 *Danske Slagterier* EU:C:2009:178, paras 53–56; Case C-542/08 *Barth* EU:C:2010:193, paras 33–36; Case C-452/09 *Iaia and Others* EU:C:2011:323, paras 16–23; Case C-470/99 *Universale-Bau and Others* EU:C:2002:746, paras 74–78; Case C-241/06 *Lämmerzahl* EU:C:2007:597, paras 50–51; Case C-406/08 *Uniplex (UK)* EU:C:2010:45, para 38; and Case C-314/09 *Strabag and Others* EU:C:2010:567, para 37.

[179] Joined Cases C-310/98 and C-406/98 *Met-Trans and Sagpol* EU:C:2000:154, paras 29–30.

[180] Case 199/82 *San Giorgio* EU:C:1983:318, para 14; Case C-242/95 *GT-Link* EU:C:1997:376, para 26; and Case C-161/08 *Internationaal Verhuis- en Transportbedrijf Jan de Lely* EU:C:2009:308, paras 66–67.

[181] See the case law rejecting the presumption of passing on an indirect tax for the purpose of imputing unjust enrichment to an entrepreneur, as in *San Giorgio* (n 180) para 14; *Dilexport* (n 175) paras 48–54; Case C-441/98 *Michailidis* EU:C:2000:479, paras 36–37; and Case C-147/01 *Weber's Wine World and Others* EU:C:2003:533, paras 110–11.

[182] In which case the Court of Justice may itself define the minimum conditions to be laid down by national law, as in the case of the abuse of rights arising in Case C-110/99 *Emsland Stärke* EU:C:2000:695, para 54; Case C-255/02 *Halifax and Others* EU:C:2006:121, paras 69ff; and Case C-196/04 *Cadbury Schweppes* EU:C:2006:544, para 64.

[183] Case C-526/04 *Laboratoires Boiron* EU:C:2006:528, para 55; Case C-55/06 *Arcor* EU:C:2008:244, para 191; and Case C-264/08 *Direct Parcel Distribution* EU:C:2010:43, para 35.

they may be. This is a standard feature of civil proceedings in many Member States, whereas in others it is possible for national courts to introduce new arguments or grounds of review of their own motion (*ex officio* review).

The principle of effectiveness requires that the rules of national law limiting the ability of national courts to act on their own motion do not make it excessively difficult for parties to exercise their rights under Union law. This involves a complex and individual assessment that the Court of Justice has developed in its case law with considerable caution, at the risk of altering the delicate balances that national law struggles to maintain when defining the powers of national courts acting on their own motion.

First, the Court of Justice conducts a detailed analysis of the national rules on *ex officio* reviews.[184] When the power of a national court to act on its own motion is discretional, there is a duty to interpret national law in conformity with Union law. This duty can result in turning the national court's discretion to act on its own motion into an *obligation* if such action is necessary to ensure that the interpretation conforms with Union law.

Second, if the national rules on *ex officio* review preclude the national court from implementing Union law in a way that would make it impossible for the applicant to rely on them in court, the national court is under a duty to apply Union law of its own motion.[185] For example, if the limitation on *ex officio* review applies to proceedings at first instance and there is no available appeal to challenge the ruling, the national court of first instance must apply Union law of its own motion.

Third, account must be taken of the principles underlying national procedural law to avoid introducing obligations that could disrupt the normal course of judicial proceedings in the Member State where the dispute is being heard.[186] On this ground, the Court of Justice has held that Union law does not impose a general obligation on national courts to raise points of Union law of their own motion in civil proceedings governed by the principle of party autonomy.[187] In contrast, in administrative or criminal litigation, other constraints limit the ability of national courts to apply Union law on their own motion, such as the prohibition of *reformatio in pejus,* which restricts courts from aggravating on appeal the situation of the appellant. The case law confirms that Union law does not impose on national courts a duty to apply Union law in a manner that would result in a *reformatio in pejus* prohibited under national law. Otherwise

> such an obligation would be contrary not only to the principles of respect for the rights of the defence, legal certainty and protection of legitimate expectations, which underlie the prohibition, but would expose an individual who brought an action against an act adversely affecting him to the risk that such an action would place him in a less favourable position than he would have been in, had he not brought that action.[188]

An exception to this rule applies when Union law introduces in an act of secondary law an obligation for national courts to implement rules of Union law of their own motion. In such cases, the obligation does not stem from the principle of effectiveness but directly from the act of secondary law that introduces the obligation. It is not necessary for the obligation to be explicitly laid down; it is sufficient for it to be inferable from the spirit and purpose of the rule

[184] Case C-431/93 *Van Schijndel* EU:C:1995:441, paras 13–14.
[185] ibid, para 18; and Case C-312/93 *Peterbroeck* EU:C:1995:437, para 16.
[186] *Van Schijndel* (n 184) para 22.
[187] ibid.
[188] Case C-455/06 *Heemskerk and Schaap* EU:C:2008:650, para 47.

of secondary law. This has been confirmed by the Court of Justice in cases concerning the rules on unfair terms in Directive 93/13/EEC[189] as well as in the case of the Union's Customs Code.[190]

2.2. *The Principle of Equivalence*

Following the judgment in *Rewe*,[191] the Court of Justice requires Member States, when establishing the procedural rules applicable in national courts, to provide them on conditions equivalent to those governing similar domestic situations.[192] The principle of equivalence is an embodiment, in the field of procedural law, of the principle of non-discrimination. Member States enjoy discretion to establish the appropriate procedural rules to safeguard the rights of individuals in accordance with the principle of procedural autonomy, but this power does not justify discriminatory treatment based on whether the right exercised by the individual derives from national or Union law.

The principle of equivalence requires Member States to treat comparable situations in similar terms. This requirement of comparability is not absolute; it is sufficient for the applicant relying on Union law to prove that its position is *similar*, but not necessarily *identical*, to that of an applicant invoking national law only.[193] When implementing this principle, the case law highlights the importance of the purpose, cause of action, and the 'essential characteristics of the two actions under comparison'.[194] If the analysis of comparability results in an affirmative answer, a proportionality review follows, in which the Member State bears the burden of proof to justify the aims that underpin the difference of treatment. To date, the case law shows that the standard of review is very strict, and once a comparable situation is established, it is highly likely that the ruling will confirm a breach of the principle of equivalence.[195]

A different situation arises when the difference of treatment stems from the Member State's compliance with its international obligations, particularly regarding the enforcement of judgments from international courts, such as the European Court of Human Rights. If national law has introduced a judicial remedy to review final domestic judicial decisions that are found to be in breach of the ECHR, as confirmed by the European Court of Human Rights, but has not introduced an equivalent remedy for breaches of Union law, the question arises as to whether the absence of such a remedy breaches the principle of equivalence. In *XC*, the Court of Justice replied to this question in the negative, highlighting the differences between the system of remedies for the protection of fundamental rights provided by Union law and those of the Convention.[196] To the extent that Union law confers on individuals the right to invoke the direct effect and primacy of Union law before any national authority, the Court of Justice

[189] Case C-126/97 *Eco Swiss* EU:C:1999:269; *Cofidis* (n 173); Case C-168/05 *Mostaza Claro* EU:C:2006:675; Case C-429/05 *Rampion and Godard* EU:C:2007:575; Case C-368/09 *Pannon* EU:C:2010:441; and Case C-40/08 *Asturcom Telecommunications* EU:C:2009:615.

[190] Case C-1/06 *Bonn Fleisch* EU:C:2007:396, para 42.

[191] *Rewe* (n 165) para 5.

[192] *Edis* (n 97) para 36; Case C-326/96 *Levez* EU:C:1998:577, para 41; Case C-78/98 *Preston and Others* EU:C:2000:247, para 55; Joined Cases C-392/04 and C-422/04 *i-21 Germany and Arcor* EU:C:2006:586, para 62; Case C-300/21 *Österreichische Post* EU:C:2023:370, para 53; and Joined Cases C-182/22 and C-189/22 *Scalable Capital* EU:C:2024:531, para 32.

[193] Case C-118/08 *Transportes Urbanos* EU:C:2010:39, para 35.

[194] See Case C-118/08 *Transportes Urbanos* EU:C:2009:437, Opinion of AG Poiares Maduro, pts 28–40.

[195] *Edis* (n 97); *Ansaldo Energia* (n 175); *Dilexport* (n 175); Case C-122/96 *Saldanha* EU:C:1997:458, para 19; Case C-323/95 *Hayes* EU:C:1997:169, para 17; Case C-43/95 *Data Delecta* EU:C:1996:357, para 15; and Case C-180/95 *Draehmpaehl* EU:C:1997:208, para 29.

[196] Case C-234/17 *XC* EU:C:2018:853.

ruled that there is no comparability between the two legal systems and their respective judicial remedies, and therefore no violation of the principle of equivalence.[197]

3. The Principle of Effective Legal Protection in Article 19 TEU and the Right to an Effective Remedy in Article 47 of the Charter

In addition to the principles of equivalence and effectiveness, Union law enshrines in Article 47 of the Charter the fundamental right to an effective remedy and to a fair trial in both Union and national courts. This fundamental right guarantees that everyone, irrespective of nationality or residence, will have their case heard by an independent and impartial tribunal. When this right of the Charter is invoked in national courts, the case can fall within the scope of application of Union law. Effective judicial protection under the Charter is only available when the underlying dispute involves a situation governed by Union law.[198] The case law has confirmed that Article 47 of the Charter has direct effect and does not require further implementing rules of Union or national law to be directly invoked in court.[199]

Despite this fundamental right being enshrined in Article 47 of the Charter, its presence in Union law as a general principle has been recognised since 1986, following the ruling in *Johnston*.[200] As previously mentioned, this fundamental right applies to both Union and national courts, but in the case of the latter, its practical implementation is closely connected to the principles of equivalence and effectiveness. At times, the fundamental right to an effective remedy and the aforementioned principles appear in the case law invoked together, while at other times they are addressed separately. Since the entry into force of the Charter in 2009, the fundamental right to an effective remedy has increasingly assumed an autonomous role, not necessarily connected to the principles of equivalence and effectiveness.[201]

The Court of Justice has repeatedly stated that the principles of equivalence and effectiveness 'embody the general obligation on the Member States to ensure judicial protection of an individual's rights under [Union] law'.[202] Therefore, it appears that both principles serve as a specific expression of the fundamental right to an effective remedy. However, recent case law suggests a more nuanced picture: the fundamental right to an effective remedy has assumed autonomous significance in primary law, in Article 47 of the Charter and Article 19 TEU, while the principles of equivalence and effectiveness continue to operate in the areas where they have traditionally played a role.[203] For example, although the fundamental right to an effective remedy includes aspects of the organisational nature of courts (such as the appointment of judges or measures to guarantee their independence), the principles of equivalence and

[197] ibid, paras 36–47.

[198] Case C-265/13 *Torralbo Marcos* EU:C:2014:187, paras 32–43.

[199] Case C-414/16 *Egenberger* EU:C:2018:257, para 78; Case C-556/17 *Torubarov* EU:C:2019:626, para 56; Joined Cases C-585/18, C-624/18, and C-625/18 *AK and Others* EU:C:2019:982, para 162; and Joined Cases C-924/19 PPU and C-925/19 PPU *FMS and Others* EU:C:2020:367, para 140.

[200] Case C-222/84 *Johnston* EU:C:1986:206.

[201] S Prechal and R Widdershoven, 'Effectiveness or Effective Judicial Protection: A Poorly Articulated Relationship' in T Baumé and others (eds), *Today's Multi-Layered Legal Order: Current Issues and Perspectives: Liber Amicorum in Honour of Arjen W H Meij* (Zutphen, 2011).

[202] Case C-268/06 *Impact* EU:C:2008:223, para 47; Case C-378/07 *Angelidaki and Others* EU:C:2009:250, para 176; Case C-12/08 *Mono Car Styling* EU:C:2009:466, para 49; Case C-63/08 *Pontin* EU:C:2009:666, para 43; Joined Cases C-317/08, C-318/08, C-319/08, and C-320/08 *Alassini and Others* EU:C:2010:146, para 49; and Case C-166/13 *Mukarubega* EU:C:2014:2336, para 52.

[203] See, inter alia, *Unibet* (n 131); Case C-275/06 *Promusicae* EU:C:2008:54; Case C-279/09 *DEB* EU:C:2010:811, and Case C-69/10 *Samba Diouf* EU:C:2011:524.

effectiveness are constrained to the review of national procedural rules governing the courses of remedial action under national procedural law.

4. Damages Actions in National Courts for Breach of Union Law by the Member States

Actions or failures to act by the Member States that breach Union law can cause harm to individuals. The failure to transpose a Directive on time can prevent a company from claiming rights from another company or from a national authority to which it is entitled by Union law; a national tax in breach of the free movement of capital can preclude or restrict an individual from enjoying his or her right to perform an economic activity in another Member State. In both examples, the right holder will not only see its rights breached, but it may also suffer quantifiable financial harm. For Union law to be genuinely effective, individuals should have the right, in the case of a breach of Union law, to claim compensation for damages caused by the unlawful conduct of a Member State. This is the underlying rationale of the case law that emerged in the early 1990s in the cases of *Francovich* and *Brasserie du Pêcheur*.

The case law has developed this remedy in considerable detail, locating its legal basis in the general principle of sincere cooperation enshrined in Article 4(3) TEU. Moreover, the Court of Justice has stated that the right to seek damages from the Member States is 'inherent in the system of the Treaty'.[204]

The action for damages against Member States for a breach of Union law is a strategic tool in the Union's system of judicial remedies, acting as a means to guarantee full judicial protection for individuals. When a Directive is invoked between private parties and the applicant cannot rely on the direct effect of the relevant provision of the Directive, a damages claim offers the judicial protection that other remedies do not. Therefore, damages actions act as a complementary remedy when there is no other judicial route available to pursue the enforcement of Union law in national courts.

The basic rules that govern the substantive requirements of a damages action against a Member State are provided by Union law and, more specifically, by the case law of the Court of Justice. Union law acts as a minimum standard that must be complied with by all the Member States, and nothing precludes them from introducing more favourable liability regimes for individuals.[205] Furthermore, in the absence of rules of Union law on the procedural requirements that apply to this course of action, the Member States are entitled, in accordance with the principle of procedural autonomy, to determine appropriate terms for the exercise of the claim in national courts. As a result, the rules on the jurisdiction of national courts, time limits, the production of evidence, the burden of proof, etc, will be governed by national law, provided that it aligns with the principles of equivalence and effectiveness.[206]

The action for damages against Member States for breach of Union law can be brought against any type of conduct by any authority of the Member State, including the legislature, the executive, the judiciary, or other independent national institutions. The same applies to the different levels of government: central/federal, regional, or municipal. In the case of actions

[204] Joined Cases C-6/90 and C-9/90 *Francovich* EU:C:1991:428, para 35.

[205] The case law seems to have qualified this point by recognising the power of Member States to introduce more protective standards for situations not covered by Union law, thus allowing for a differentiation of regimes depending on whether the claim is based on Union law or national law. In this respect, compare the solution envisaged in Case C-118/08 *Transportes Urbanos* EU:C:2010:39, paras 33ff, and Case C-278/20 *Commission v Spain* EU:C:2022:503, paras 181–85.

[206] For a detailed explanation of the role played by the principles of effectiveness and equivalence in the context of actions on Member State liability for breach of Union law, see *Commission v Spain* (n 205).

by an official or civil servant of the Member State, the harm will be attributed to the Member State if the actions or positions taken by the official result from the exercise of their official authority.[207] For Union law, when the harm is the result of an action or omission stemming from any manifestation of the Member State's public authority, the ensuing harm can be subject to liability and financial compensation.

Rules on liability for breach of Union law can also apply to relations between private parties. In *Courage and Crehan*, the Court of Justice held that Union law provides a right of action for private parties who have suffered harm due to the anti-competitive conduct of other private parties.[208] In 2014, the Union legislature introduced Directive 2014/104, harmonising these remedies across the Member States in the field of competition.[209]

There are no compelling reasons to exclude private party liability resulting from other breaches of Union law in other fields of practice. The judgment in *Courage and Crehan* is not necessarily confined to competition, and the Court of Justice made no indication in that regard. Whether the infringing party is a Member State or a private individual should be irrelevant, in the same way that the subject matter of the infringed rule should make no difference either. This is the logic behind the Court of Justice's ruling in *Courage and Crehan*, which has recently been reinforced by the introduction of explicit legislative provisions on private enforcement, such as Article 82 of the General Regulation on Data Protection or Article 54 of the Digital Services Act.[210]

Focusing now on the case of Member State liability, the case law requires three conditions to be satisfied: 1) the rule of Union law infringed must be intended to confer rights on individuals; 2) the breach must be sufficiently serious; and 3) there must be a direct causal link between the breach of the obligation resting on the state and the damage sustained by the injured parties.[211] These requirements mirror those governing damages actions brought against the Union, as described in chapter eleven. The Court of Justice acknowledged this parallelism between both remedies when it stated in *Bergaderm* as follows:

> [T]he conditions under which the State may incur liability for damage caused to individuals by a breach of [Union] law cannot, in the absence of particular justification, differ from those governing the liability of the [Union] in like circumstances. The protection of the rights which individuals derive from [Union] law cannot vary depending on whether a national authority or a [Union] authority is responsible for the damage.[212]

The first requirement demands that the breached rule of Union law must confer rights on individuals with a sufficiently clear basis in the provision. However, this requirement does not imply that the rule must have direct effect.[213] If the direct effect of the rule were a precondition to bring a damages action against a Member State, this remedy could not serve as a

[207] Case C-470/03 *AGM-COS.MET* EU:C:2007:213, para 57: 'The decisive factor for attributing the statements of an official to the State is whether the persons to whom the statements are addressed can reasonably suppose, in the given context, that they are positions taken by the official with the authority of his office.'

[208] Case C-453/99 *Courage and Crehan* EU:C:2001:465; Case C-435/18 *Otis Gesellschaft and Others* EU:C:2019:1069, para 21; Case C-882/19 *Sumal* EU:C:2021:800, para 32; and Case C-819/19 *Stichting Cartel Compensation* EU:C:2021:904, para 48.

[209] Directive 2014/104/EU of the European Parliament and of the Council of 26 November 2014 on certain rules governing actions for damages under national law for infringements of competition law of the Member States and of the European Union [2014] OJ L349/1.

[210] In this respect, see W Wurmnest and M Gömann, 'Comparing Private Enforcement of EU Competition and Data Protection Law' (2022) 13 *Journal of European Tort Law* 154.

[211] Joined Cases C-46/93 and C-48/93 *Brasserie du Pêcheur and Factortame* EU:C:1996:79, para 51.

[212] Case C-352/98 P *Bergaderm and Goupil v Commission* EU:C:2000:361, para 41.

[213] *Brasserie du Pêcheur* (n 211) paras 18–23; Case C-571/16 *Kantarev* EU:C:2018:807, paras 97 and 104; Case C-735/19 *Euromin Holdings (Cyprus) Limited* EU:C:2020:1014, para 81; and Case C-278/20 *Commission v Spain* EU:C:2022:503, paras 142–43.

complementary means of protection to compensate for the shortfalls of other remedial routes, including those where a rule of Union law lacks direct effect. Therefore, for damages claims against Member States to serve their strategic purpose within the Union's judicial system, the term 'rights', as it currently appears in the case law on Member State liability, should be interpreted in broader terms than the notion of direct effect.

The second requirement refers to a 'sufficiently serious breach' of a rule of Union law. A mere violation of a rule is not enough, as the Member State must have 'manifestly and gravely disregarded the limits on its discretion'.[214] Several factors are enumerated in the case law to assist in the determination of a sufficiently serious breach:[215]

- the clarity and precision of the Union rule breached;
- the measure of discretion left by that rule to national or Union authorities;
- whether the infringement and the damage caused was intentional or involuntary;
- whether any error of law was excusable or inexcusable;
- the fact that the position taken by the Union may have contributed towards the adoption or maintenance of national measures or practices contrary to Union law; and
- the adoption or retention of national measures or practices contrary to Union law.

Irrespective of the factors just mentioned, the Court of Justice identifies two cases in which a sufficiently serious breach is more readily established: first, when a breach has been declared by a judgment of the Court of Justice and the Member State concerned has failed to take all appropriate measures to end the infringement;[216] and second, when a national court of last resort manifestly breaches a rule of Union law, having refused to refer the matter to the Court of Justice through a request for a preliminary ruling.[217]

The third and final requirement demands the existence of a direct causal link between the breach of the Union rule and the harm suffered by the claimant. It is for the national court to establish the existence of this causal link, in accordance with the rules on evidence provided in national law.

The case law on Member State liability for a breach of Union law has faced significant criticism. Some authors contend that the requirements outlined above are excessively burdensome for claimants, imposing a substantial strain that requires considerable time and financial resources, with little prospects of a favourable outcome. Moreover, assigning an important means of judicial protection to such an onerous remedy would seem to raise questions about the Union judicial system's capacity to provide a genuinely comprehensive system of remedies. It has been suggested that, rather than relying on particularly burdensome damages claims, Union law should focus on expanding protections under the principles of direct effect and primacy. This strategy would minimise the use of damages actions as a final, uphill remedy with uncertain results. Writing extrajudicially, Advocate General Ruiz-Jarabo Colomer captured this critique with characteristic style, dismissing the prevailing conception of Member State liability as little more than 'a beautiful fairytale' and recalling, with deliberate irony, the remark attributed to Oscar Wilde that 'really beautiful things always make me cry'.[218]

[214] *Brasserie du Pêcheur* (n 211) para 55.

[215] ibid, para 56.

[216] ibid, para 57.

[217] Case C-224/01 *Köbler* EU:C:2003:513, para 55; and Case C-140/09 *Fallimento Traghetti del Mediterraneo* EU:C:2010:335, paras 32 and 43.

[218] D Ruiz-Jarabo Colomer, 'Once Upon a Time – Francovich: From Fairy Tale to Cruel Reality?' in MP Maduro and L Azoulai (eds), *The Past and Future of EU Law: The Classics of EU Law Revisited on the 50th Anniversary of the Rome Treaty* (Hart Publishing, 2010).

GENERAL BIBLIOGRAPHY

See the general bibliography in chapter eleven.

FURTHER READING

The Preliminary Reference Procedure

Amalfitano, C, 'The Future of the Preliminary Rulings in the EU Judicial System' (2023) 133 EU Law Live Weekend Edition 3.

Andenas, M, *Article 177 References to the European Court: Policy and Practice* (Butterworths, 1994).

Anderson, D and Demetriou, M, *References to the European Court*, 2nd edn (Sweet & Maxwell, 2002).

Barbier de la Serre, E, 'Accelerated and Expedited Procedures before the EC Courts: A Review of the Practice' (2006) 43 *Common Market Law Review* 783.

Bobek, M, 'Learning to Talk: Preliminary Rulings, the Courts of the New Member States and the Court of Justice' (2008) 45 *Common Market Law Review* 1611.

— 'Preliminary Rulings before the General Court: What Judicial Architecture for the European Union?' (2023) 60 Common Market Law Review 1515.

Broberg, M and Fenger, N, *Preliminary References to the European Court of Justice*, 3rd edn (Oxford University Press, 2021).

— 'If You Love Somebody Set Them Free: On the Court of Justice's Revision of the Acte Clair Doctrine' (2022) 59 Common Market Law Review 711.

Fenger, N and Broberg, M, 'Finding Light in the Darkness: On the Actual Application of the Acte Clair Doctrine' (2011) 30 *Yearbook of European Law* 190.

Grossio, L and Petric, D (eds), 'Perspectives on the Reformed EU Judicial Architecture' (2025) 10 *European Papers* 327.

Kornezov, A, 'The New Format of the Acte Clair Doctrine and its Consequences' (2016) 53 *Common Market Law Review* 1317.

Krommendijk, J, *National Courts and Preliminary References to the Court of Justice* (Edward Elgar, 2021).

de la Mare, T and Donnelly, C, 'Preliminary Rulings and EU Legal Integration: Evolution and Stasis' in P Craig and G de Búrca (eds), *The Evolution of EU Law*, 2nd edn (Oxford University Press, 2011).

Pertek, J, *La pratique du renvoi préjudiciel en droit communautaire: coopération entre CJCE et juges nationaux* (Litec, 2001).

Šadl, U and Wallerman, A, '"The Referring Court Asks, in Essence": Is Reformulation of Preliminary Questions by the Court of Justice a Decision-Writing Fixture or a Decision-Making Approach?' (2019) 25 *European Law Journal* 369.

Sarmiento, D, 'Amending the Preliminary Reference Procedure for the Administrative Judge' (2009) 2 *Review of European Administrative Law* 55.

Sharpston, L and Barnard, C, 'The Changing Face of Article 177 References' (1997) 34 *Common Market Law Review* 1113.

Tridimas, T, 'Knocking on Heaven's Door: Fragmentation, Efficiency and Defiance in the Preliminary Ruling Procedure' (2003) 40 *Common Market Law Review* 9.

— 'The ECJ and the National Courts: Dialogue, Cooperation and Instability' in A Arnull and D Chalmers (eds), *The Oxford Handbook of European Union Law* (Oxford University Press, 2015).

Wahl, N and Prete, L, 'The Gatekeepers of Article 267 TFEU: On Jurisdiction and Admissibility of References for Preliminary Rulings' (2018) 55 *Common Market Law Review* 401.

Wallerman, A, 'Can Two Walk Together, Except They Be Agreed? Preliminary Reflections and (the Erosion of) National Procedural Autonomy' (2019) 44 *European Law Review* 207.

The Plea of Illegality

Coutron, L, La contestation incidente des actes de l'Union européenne (Bruylant, 2008).

Eliantonio, M, and van Wolferen, M, 'The plea of illegality in European Union law: the missing piece in the puzzle of a "complete system of remedies"?' in Eliantonio, M, and Dragos, D, *Indirect Judicial Review in Administrative Law* (Routledge 2022).

Karayigit, MT 'The Plea of Illegality as a Pillar of the Incidental Review' (2019) 25 *European Public Law* 689.
Sinaniotis, D, 'The Plea of Illegality in EC Law' (2001) 7 *European Public Law* 103.
Türk, AH, 'Incidental review' in Türk, AH, Judicial Review in the European Union, 2nd edn (Edward Elgar, 2025).

Interim Measures

Barbier de la Serre, E, and Lavin, C, 'Le droit du référé européen depuis 2007: entre prudence et coups d'audace' (2019) *Cahiers de Droit Européen* 613.
Korogiannakis, N, 'Recent Case Law of the CJEU on Interim Measures and Award of Damages in EU Public Procurement Law' (2017) 18 *ERA Forum* 95.
Lenaerts, K, and Radley, M, 'Recent Case- Law of the European Court of Justice in Interim Measures Cases' (2016) 1 *European Law Reporter* 2.
Orzan, MF, 'The Procedural Features of Interim Relief Before the Court of Justice of the European Union' in Palombino, FM, Virzo, R, and Zara, G (eds), *Provisional Measures Issued by International Courts and Tribunals* (TMC Asser Press, 2021) 199.
Sinaniotis, D, *The Interim Protection of Individuals before the European and National Courts* (Kluwer Law International, 2006).

The Principles of Effectiveness and Equivalence

Arnaldos, E, and Eliantonio, M, 'The Duty of National Courts of Applying EU Law Ex Officio' (2023) 149 *EU Law Live Weekend Edition* 3.
Dougan, M, *National Remedies before the Court of Justice: Issues of Harmonisation and Differentiation* (Hart, 2004).
Gentile, G, 'Effective judicial protection: enforcement, judicial federalism and the politics of EU law' (2023) 2 *European Law Open* 128.
van Gerven, W, 'Of Rights, Remedies and Procedures' (2000) 37(2) *Common Market Law Review* 501.
Kilpatrick, C and Novitz, T (eds), *The Future of Remedies in Europe* (Hart, 2000).

State Liability for Infringement of EU Law

Biondi, A, and Farley, M, *The Right to Damages in European Law* (Kluwer Law International, 2009).
Craig, P, 'Once More Unto the Breach: The Community, the State and Damages Liability' (1997) 113 *Law Quarterly Review* 67.
Harlow, C, *State Liability: Tort Law and Beyond* (Oxford University Press, 2004).
Prechal, S, 'Member State Liability and Direct Effect: What's the Difference After All?' (2006) 17 *European Business Law Review* 299.
Tridimas, T, 'Liability for Breach of Community Law: Growing Up and Mellowing Down?' (2001) 38 *Common Market Law Review* 301.
Wathelet, M and van Raepenbusch, S, 'La responsabilité des États membres en cas de violation du droit communautaire: vers un alignement de la responsabilité de l'État sur celle de la Communauté ou l'inverse' (1997) 33 *Cahiers de Droit Européen* 53.

13

The Internal Market: The Fundamental Freedoms (I)

I. INTRODUCTION TO THE INTERNAL MARKET

THE EUROPEAN PROJECT was conceived with the long-term objective of securing peace in Europe and the more immediate aim of creating a common economic area in which the factors of production could move freely. The establishment of such an economic area was intended to foster de facto solidarity among the participating states, thereby making armed conflict between them highly unlikely. The origins of this project date back to 1952, when it was initially designed to create a single market for coal and steel. This was followed in 1958 by the establishment of a broader common market encompassing a wide range of goods, services, labour, and capital. The success of the common market led the Member States, in 1986, to take a further step by setting the objective of completing and transforming it into an *internal market*, later complemented by the introduction of a single currency, the euro. The objective of completing the internal market by 1992 was set out in the Single European Act, while the Maastricht Treaty consolidated this development and laid the foundations for Economic and Monetary Union.

The idea of a single market is neither novel nor uniquely European. Its intellectual foundations lie in the principles of free trade, inspired by the works of Adam Smith and David Ricardo. The emergence of modern economic liberalism and free-trading states in the eighteenth and nineteenth centuries was strongly influenced by these thinkers. The economic liberalism they advocated promotes the dismantling of barriers to trade in order to encourage specialisation, which in turn is expected to increase productivity, reduce costs, and improve consumer welfare through better and cheaper goods and services. Both the benefits and the externalities of free trade among states were well understood by the late nineteenth century and continued to shape economic policy throughout the twentieth century. The creation of the General Agreement on Tariffs and Trade (GATT) in 1948 represented a coordinated global effort to embed free-trade principles within a multilateral framework. The European Communities constitute another, more advanced, example of the implementation of free-trade principles among a group of states.

The European Union represents a particularly advanced model of economic integration, in which 27 Member States have chosen to exercise jointly certain sovereign powers in order to establish an internal market based on free-trade principles. That model is not unique, nor can it be defined as a widespread form of economic integration in international practice. The Union's internal market is unique as it operates according to its own economic, political, and legal logic. It reflects a deliberate choice by the Member States among a range of possible integration models, each with its own advantages and drawbacks, but one that has proved particularly well suited to the long-term objectives of the European project. The following three chapters examine the core features of the internal market, together with the principal instruments and institutional actors through which it is realised.

As a preliminary step, it is useful to consider the different models of economic integration available to sovereign states, of which the Union's internal market is only one example. The historical development of the internal market will also be outlined, with particular emphasis on its gradual evolution over more than 70 years and the political and economic challenges it has overcome. Finally, the economic and political externalities generated by the internal market will be examined.

1. Economic Integration: Options and Evolution

Sovereign nations can engage in trade and establish economic ties with varying degrees of intensity. At the most basic level, two states may create a limited trade regime facilitating the exchange of one or more categories of goods, such as agricultural or industrial products. Through international treaties, the parties agree to reduce or remove tariffs on those goods, thereby promoting trade between firms that produce and market them in each country. This form of international cooperation through bilateral trade agreements is often regarded as the historical starting point of modern global trade.

A more advanced form of integration is the establishment of a free trade area, within which most or even all goods may circulate freely across the borders of the participating states. Such agreements eliminate tariffs and customs duties on goods originating in the territories of the parties. The scope of a free trade area depends on the level of ambition pursued and may extend beyond goods to include services, workers (both employed and self-employed), capital, and direct investment. Free trade areas may be bilateral, involving two states, or multilateral, involving more than two states. They may also be regional in nature, as illustrated by the European Free Trade Association (EFTA), comprising Switzerland, Liechtenstein, Norway, and Iceland, or by comprehensive trade arrangements such as the Comprehensive and Progressive Agreement for Trans-Pacific Partnership. Alternatively, trade liberalisation may pursue a multilateral scope, as exemplified by the framework established under the General Agreement on Tariffs and Trade (GATT) and its successor, the World Trade Organization (WTO).

In practice, free trade areas often overlap. For example, States A, B, and C may form a free trade area, while State B simultaneously participates in another free trade arrangement with States X and Z. Such overlapping regimes, which are common in international practice, introduce significant legal and administrative complexity. One key mechanism developed to address this complexity is the system of rules of origin, which ensures that only goods genuinely produced within the participating states benefit from preferential treatment, thereby preventing trade deflection through third countries. Moreover, modern free trade agreements increasingly go beyond the reduction or elimination of tariffs and customs duties, the traditional instruments of economic protectionism, to address non-tariff barriers such as regulatory standards and technical requirements imposed on economic operators. As a result, free trade areas often coincide with a gradual process of regulatory alignment or mutual recognition.

Once a free trade area has been established, the participating states may decide to adopt a common external tariff applicable to trade with third countries. The adoption of such a tariff by States A, B, and C implies that imports from States X, Y, or Z are subject to identical customs duties, regardless of the state through which the goods enter the free trade area. The creation of a customs union therefore requires the development of uniform rules and a coordinated approach to external trade relations. For instance, if State B wishes to facilitate the import of specific goods from State Y, this decision must be agreed by all members of the customs union, since those goods would subsequently circulate freely throughout the territories of States A, B, and C. Over time, this process may lead to the emergence of a common commercial policy governing relations with third countries.

Following the removal of internal barriers to goods, services, labour, and capital within a free trade area, a further step towards deeper economic integration is the establishment of a common economic and monetary policy. This stage involves the adoption of coordinated fiscal and budgetary policies and, eventually, a shared currency. The principal objectives of such integration are to reduce exchange-rate risks, simplify cross-border payments within the internal market, and lower transaction costs for economic operators. Firms operating across States A, B, and C benefit from the free movement of goods and services under uniform or comparable tax rules and from conducting transactions in a single currency. This level of integration represents the highest degree of economic integration, but it also requires a significant pooling of sovereignty and the creation of common political institutions. For democratic states, this process is particularly demanding, as it requires the development of shared parliamentary structures and safeguards to ensure respect for the rule of law and fundamental rights. Economic integration may evolve gradually, but at advanced stages it inevitably entails significant degrees of political integration.

The European Union has followed this trajectory and today combines an internal market, a customs union, a common commercial policy, a coordinated economic policy, and a single currency. While monetary policy is fully centralised for the euro area Member States, economic and fiscal policy remains subject to coordination rather than centralisation. These achievements are supported by political institutions endowed with legislative powers and democratic legitimacy, exercised directly through the European Parliament and indirectly through the Council. They are complemented by legal mechanisms designed to safeguard the rule of law and fundamental rights. European economic integration is therefore an established reality, making the Union one of the most advanced and integrated economic areas in the world. With a population approaching half a billion, the Union's internal market constitutes a major economic force, enabling the Union and its Member States to exert their influence and leverage on the global stage – an influence that individual states would be unable to achieve on their own.

Such a high level of economic integration inevitably entails costs and externalities. Each step forward in the integration process involves a transfer of sovereign powers, a development that may encounter resistance within Member States. Nationalist sentiment often reflects a paradoxical combination of support for enhanced international influence and mistrust of external constraints on domestic decision-making. Economic integration, while strengthening national economies and increasing international leverage, necessarily requires states to accept limits on unilateral action. Moreover, the creation and operation of an internal market within a democratic framework produces distributive effects, generating both winners and losers. These outcomes may fuel social discontent or encourage political movements opposed to European integration. The United Kingdom's withdrawal from the Union provides a salient illustration. Proponents of Brexit initially promised renewed prosperity, reduced immigration, and restored sovereignty following the withdrawal of the United Kingdom from the Union. In practice, the post-withdrawal period has been marked by marginal economic growth, continued migration pressures, and diminished international influence. These developments call into question traditional conceptions of sovereignty as the capacity to act independently, suggesting instead that, in an increasingly interconnected world, middle-sized states (as is the case of the European states) may exercise their sovereignty more effectively through cooperation with other states than in isolation.

2. The Creation and Development of the European Internal Market

The European Economic Community (EEC), established in 1958, was designed to create a common market subject to a 12-year transitional period ending on 31 December 1969. Following the completion of that transitional period, the EEC made significant progress in adopting and implementing the legislative measures necessary to give effect to the common market. However, the enlargement of the Communities to include new Member States (Denmark, Ireland and the United Kingdom in 1973), combined with the prolonged economic crisis of the 1970s, resulted in a slowdown of integration and, by the end of the decade, a clear impasse.[1]

In 1982, the European Council meeting in Copenhagen invited the European Commission to propose a strategy to deepen the common market and move towards the creation of a single market without internal frontiers. This initiative formed part of a broader political effort to relaunch European integration following the period of so-called 'Eurosclerosis' of the 1970s. This request led to the publication of the Commission's White Paper, which set out an ambitious programme for completing the internal market by removing all remaining barriers to trade. Published in 1985, the White Paper identified and classified 279 legislative measures required to achieve this objective by 1992. In order to realise this programme within a relatively short timeframe, the Member States agreed on the Single European Act, signed in 1986, which amended the Treaties and introduced major changes to the legal and institutional framework of the common market. Following the fall of the Berlin Wall in November 1989, the end of the Cold War, and the signing of the Maastricht Treaty in February 1992, the process of integration accelerated considerably. This period of transformation resulted in the attribution of broad legislative competences to the Union, exemplified by what is now Article 114 Treaty on the Functioning of the European Union (TFEU), originally introduced by the Single European Act and later consolidated within the post-Maastricht Treaty framework, and in Treaty provisions confirming the transition from a common market characterised by internal borders to an internal market in which such borders have largely been eliminated. Within this 'area', Member States mutually recognise one another's legislation, enabling the free movement of all factors of production, as well as of citizens.

These developments are now reflected in Article 26 TFEU, which formally identifies the establishment of the internal market as a core objective of the Union. The internal market is defined as 'an area without internal frontiers in which the free movement of goods, persons, services and capital is ensured in accordance with the provisions of the Treaties'. The emphasis on the absence of internal frontiers is deliberate and echoes the objectives of the 1985 White Paper and the broader programme aimed at dismantling barriers to trade between Member States. The transformation of the market into an 'area without internal frontiers' has implications not only for economic activity but also for individuals, whose movement across Member States must be facilitated. It is this evolution of the internal market that underpins the creation of the Area of Freedom, Security and Justice, which seeks to accompany economic integration with measures ensuring the free movement of persons in a Union without internal borders, as will be discussed in chapter eighteen of this book.

3. The Structure of the Union's Internal Market

The Union's internal market is a distinctive project with few equivalents in international practice. Its uniqueness lies, inter alia, in the close interaction between internal market rules and

[1] M Egan, *Constructing a European Market: Standards, Regulation and Governance* (Oxford University Press, 2001) chs 6–7.

other Union policies, as well as in the specific institutional framework developed within the European project. In order to understand the structure of the internal market, it is necessary to analyse its constituent elements, taking into account both its internal and external dimensions. Two complementary forms of integration employed by the Union are of particular relevance. The first is *negative integration*, which relies on the freedoms of movement to prohibit certain restrictive measures adopted mainly by Member States. The second is *positive integration*, which involves the approximation or unification of rules governing economic activity within the internal market.

3.1. Freedom of Movement, Competition and State Aid

The first dimension primarily concerns the obligations of the Member States and is grounded in Titles II, III and IV of Part Three TFEU. These provisions impose both negative obligations, requiring Member States to refrain from adopting measures that hinder free movement, and positive obligations, requiring them to take steps to facilitate it. The achievement of free movement relies on a combination of negative and positive integration measures, which will be examined in greater detail in section I.3.3 of this chapter. These measures are embodied in two fundamental mechanisms of the internal market: the freedoms of movement; and the harmonisation or standardisation of national legislation. The legal bases for the freedoms of movement are found in Titles II, III and IV of Part Three TFEU, while legislative harmonisation is supported by a range of Treaty provisions reflecting the cross-cutting nature of Union competences. In this respect, Articles 114, 115 and 352 TFEU play a particularly significant role due to their horizontal scope, as explained further in section I.3.3 of this chapter and in chapter four of this book.

The second dimension of the internal market framework concerns the conduct of economic operators. For the internal market to function effectively, it is essential that undertakings refrain from practices that distort or restrict competition. Certain forms of market behaviour are capable of undermining the internal market by preventing consumers from benefiting from competition. For example, market-sharing or price-fixing agreements between undertakings may shield inefficient producers from competitive pressure, depriving consumers of better products at lower prices. Likewise, undertakings holding a dominant position may engage in exclusionary or exploitative conduct in order to preserve or strengthen their market power. To address such risks, Article 101 TFEU prohibits agreements and concerted practices between undertakings that have as their object or effect the restriction of competition, while Article 102 TFEU prohibits the abuse of a dominant position. These provisions are directed not at Member States, but at undertakings themselves. Responsibility for enforcing competition rules lies with both the European Commission and national competition authorities, which may impose sanctions or authorise concentrations subject to conditions, as discussed in greater detail in chapter fifteen of this book.

State aid control occupies an intermediate position between the obligations imposed on Member States and those imposed on undertakings. Articles 107–09 TFEU establish a general prohibition on state aid that distorts or threatens to distort competition and affects trade between Member States. For instance, if a regional authority seeks to support a local footwear industry, it must do so in a manner that does not disadvantage competing producers in other Member States. To prevent public interventions that undermine the internal market, such as selective subsidies favouring individual undertakings or sectors, State aid rules establish criteria for identifying unlawful aid and for determining the conditions under which aid may be considered compatible with the internal market. State aid policy therefore occupies a hybrid space within Union law, as it regulates the conduct of both Member States, which grant the aid, and undertakings, which receive it.

3.2. The External Dimension of the Internal Market: the Customs Union and the Common Commercial Policy

The internal market is achieved through the removal of internal barriers to trade and the adoption of Union-wide regulatory standards governing the production, marketing, and provision of goods and services, as well as commercial practices. In addition to its internal dimension, the Union must also take account of the importance of international markets and the extensive volume of transactions involving goods and services between European economic operators and third countries with stable economies and/or significant export capacity, such as China, the United States or India. In an increasingly globalised economy, the external dimension of the internal market has therefore become ever more significant. To structure the relationship between the internal market and global trade, the Union relies on two core instruments: the Customs Union and the Common Commercial Policy.

The Customs Union constitutes a single trading area for goods encompassing the entire territory of the Member States. Within this framework, customs duties and charges having equivalent effect on internal trade in goods between Member States are eliminated, resulting in the establishment of a common external customs tariff applicable to trade with third countries. The Customs Union is governed by Articles 28-32 TFEU. As provided in Article 30 TFEU, 'Customs duties on imports and exports and charges having equivalent effect shall be prohibited between Member States. This prohibition shall also apply to customs duties of a fiscal nature.' Consequently, the entry and exit of goods to and from the Union are subject to a common set of rules and customs duties, irrespective of the Member State through which they enter or leave the Union. This common framework is laid down in Regulation (EU) No 952/2013 establishing the Union Customs Code, together with its implementing and delegated acts. Once goods originating in third countries have complied with the applicable customs formalities and, where required, customs duties have been paid, they are released for free circulation and may move freely throughout the territory of the 27 Member States. Compliance with Union customs rules is therefore a prerequisite for the free movement of goods from third countries within the internal market.

The Common Commercial Policy (CCP) of the Union comprises a body of rules and uniform principles governing trade relations between the Union and third countries. Articles 206–207 TFEU define both the objectives of the CCP and the means available to the Union to achieve them. These objectives include the contribution to the harmonious development of world trade, the progressive abolition of restrictions on international trade and on foreign direct investment, and the reduction of customs and other barriers. To pursue these aims, the Union is empowered, under Article 207 TFEU, to adopt the instruments necessary for the conduct of a common commercial policy, including:

> [T]he conclusion of tariff and trade agreements relating to trade in goods and services, and the commercial aspects of intellectual property, foreign direct investment, the achievement of uniformity in measures of liberalisation, export policy and measures to protect trade such as those to be taken in the event of dumping or subsidies.

The Customs Union and the CCP fall within the Union's exclusive competence.[2] As a result, the Union alone is empowered to legislate and adopt legally binding acts in these fields, while Member States may do so only where specifically authorised by the Union or for the purpose of implementing Union acts.[3] In practice, Member States have transferred their competence in

[2] Art 3(1)(a) and (e) TFEU.

[3] ibid, Art 2(1).

international trade to the Union, particularly as regards trade in goods, tariffs, the common external customs regime, and the commercial aspects of intellectual property and foreign direct investment, notwithstanding the existence of limited areas of mixed competence in certain service sectors. If, for example, the Italian Republic wished to negotiate a bilateral trade agreement with Mexico, granting preferential treatment for agricultural products, such negotiations could take place only within the framework of Union action. Any agreement concluded would apply uniformly across all 27 Member States, not solely to Italy. Once Mexican goods enter the Union through Italy, they may circulate freely throughout the internal market. Accordingly, decisions concerning the entry of goods from third countries are not matters of purely national concern, but issues of Union-wide significance that require collective decision-making in order to safeguard the interests of all participants in the internal market.

3.3. Negative and Positive Integration in the Union's Internal Market: the Four Freedoms versus Market Regulation

The Union's internal market aims to remove all obstacles to the free movement of all factors of production, for which the Treaties introduce two complementary techniques: *negative* and *positive integration*. The former is a prohibition addressed mostly to Member States, precluding them from maintaining or erecting trade barriers. The latter empowers the Union to adopt rules for the harmonisation or unification of national laws, with the aim of eliminating regulatory divergences that hinder free movement. The two techniques complement each other, as they both pursue a common objective: the establishment and proper functioning of the internal market. However, when applied to specific situations, these two techniques interact in a specific way: when a Union harmonising measure fully regulates a given matter, it becomes the governing provision for resolving disputes. This harmonising rule, acting as a lex specialis, determines the applicable legal framework, and the Treaty freedoms play an interpretative role, but give way to the direct applicability of the legal framework.

The techniques of negative integration are reflected in the fundamental freedoms of movement affecting goods, establishment, the provision of services, workers, and capital. An additional freedom that has emerged more recently is the free movement of persons, which guarantees the right to move of non-economic natural persons. These freedoms operate as prohibitions addressed to the Member States and, to a lesser extent, the Union, imposing standstill obligations that impede the introduction of national barriers to trade within the internal market.

Positive integration, on the other hand, is reflected in an extensive body of Union legislation, notably directives and regulations. Such legislation is adopted on the basis of the various competences attributed to the Union in specific policy areas and legal bases, as discussed in chapter four of this book. The Union employs a wide range of legislative and non-legislative instruments to establish uniform or harmonised standards, whether in particular sectors or activities, such as tobacco regulation or transport, or across the economy as a whole through horizontal and cross-cutting measures, including rules on unfair commercial practices or electronic commerce. Certain legal bases are tailored to specific policy fields, such as agriculture, environmental protection, social policy, or energy. In parallel, the Treaties also provide for general legal bases enabling the Union to legislate across the internal market. A prominent example is Article 114 TFEU, which authorises the adoption of measures for the approximation of the laws, regulations, and administrative provisions of the Member States with the aim of facilitating the establishment and proper functioning of the internal market.

There is a close and dynamic relationship between negative and positive integration. In the early stages of European integration, when the Community's legislative output was limited, legislation was either narrow in scope or confined to specific products or activities. In that context, negative integration played a central role: in the absence of comprehensive harmonisation, the freedoms of movement operated as powerful tools to prevent national regulatory diversity from obstructing trade. Economic operators could engage in cross-border activity despite divergent national rules, relying on the Treaty freedoms whenever those differences constituted barriers to market access.

As the Union progressively acquired broader legislative powers and its decision-making procedures became more effective, most notably through the transition from unanimity to qualified majority voting in the Council, the role of positive integration expanded. The adoption of Union legislation increasingly provided economic operators with a common regulatory framework, reducing reliance on litigation based on the freedoms of movement. In policy areas where Union rules have established a fully harmonised framework, negative integration has consequently assumed a subsidiary role, remaining relevant primarily where harmonisation is absent or incomplete.

II. BASIC FEATURES OF THE FUNDAMENTAL FREEDOMS

1. Legal Framework

The fundamental freedoms are outlined in Titles III–IV of Part Three TFEU, which refer to the Union's policies and internal actions. Despite the distinction between the free movement of goods (Title III) and the free movement of persons, services, and capital (Title IV), this separation is largely artificial and has minimal practical impact. Additionally, the enumerated freedoms under Titles III–IV do not fully capture the subtleties and nuances of the fundamental freedoms. For example, the freedom of establishment operates differently from the other freedoms, despite the omission of any reference to it in Title IV. Likewise, the free movement of persons is characterised by distinct features, encompassing economically active persons (such as workers and the self-employed) on one hand, and economically inactive persons on the other. Each group is governed by particular provisions laid out in the Treaties, which are further elaborated in chapters six and fourteen of this book.

2. Addressees and Beneficiaries

The fundamental freedoms are prohibitions, articulated as stand-still obligations addressed to the Member States and, to a lesser extent, the Union. The term 'Member State' should be interpreted broadly to encompass all territorial levels, including federal, central, regional, and municipal authorities,[4] all branches of government (legislative, executive, and judicial), and any public body or office (ministers, directors-general, mayors, public entities, undertakings in which a public authority holds a controlling interest, etc).[5]

[4] Joined Cases C-1/90 and C-176/90 *Aragonesa de Publicidad Exterior y Publivia v Departamento de Sanidad y Seguridad Social de Cataluña* EU:C:1991:327, para 8: 'Article [34 TFEU] may apply to measures adopted by all the authorities of the Member States, be they the central authorities, the authorities of a federal State, or other territorial authorities'.

[5] Case C-434/85 *Allen & Hanburys/Generics (UK)* EU:C:1988:109, para 25; and Case C-227/06 *Commission v Belgium* EU:C:2008:160, para 37.

The fundamental freedoms are also addressed to the Union, which is precluded from introducing barriers to trade that would undermine the functioning of the internal market.[6] This is an exceptional scenario, as the Union's objectives include establishing and maintaining the proper functioning of the internal market, not the opposite. Therefore, the Union is presumed to act in accordance with the fundamental freedoms. The Court of Justice is responsible for assessing whether Union legislation and other policy actions are compatible with the fundamental freedoms. In doing so, the Court acknowledges that the Union legislature has a considerable margin of discretion, particularly where it is required to take 'political, economic and social choices' and perform 'complex assessments'.[7] Union action will only be deemed incompatible with the fundamental freedoms if it is shown to be 'manifestly inappropriate', having regard to the objective which the competent institution is seeking to pursue, a standard that affords the Union legislature considerably greater latitude than the standard applied to Member State measures.

Natural and legal persons are not the intended addressees of the fundamental freedoms. This is because private entities, especially companies, have other means to hinder free movement, mainly through anti-competitive practices. In such cases, the Treaty includes specific provisions to address these practices, which will be further detailed in chapter fifteen of this book. In any event, the case law has recognised the ability of certain private entities, particularly legal persons, to exercise powers analogous to those of the state, which may restrict free movement.[8] This is the case of private entities that are endowed with regulatory public powers conferred by law, or that exercise de facto regulatory authority over access to a profession or an economic activity. Such entities may include, for example, professional associations or sports federations.[9] A similar principle applies to private entities that, through their activities, perform a role in the market akin to that of a public authority or possess equivalent capacity to regulate the market. Examples of this category include private associations that wield considerable influence over specific economic activities, such as the Union of European Football Associations (UEFA)[10] or trade unions.[11]

3. Scope of Application

3.1. Cross-border Link

Reliance on fundamental freedoms is predicated on the presence of a cross-border element connecting at least two Member States. For example, Article 34 TFEU prohibits quantitative restrictions on imports and measures of equivalent effect 'between Member States'. Conversely, an internal quantitative restriction that exclusively affects local products (for example, a regulation enacted by Lower Saxony in Germany prohibiting the entry of a specific food product

[6] Case C-15/83 *Denkavit Nederland* EU:C:1984:183, para 15; Case C-51/93 *Meyhui v Schott Zwiesel Glaswerke* EU:C:1994:312, para 11; Case C-114/96 *Kieffer and Thill* EU:C:1997:316, para 27; and Case C-434/02 *Arnold André* EU:C:2004:800, para 57.

[7] Joined Cases C-154/04 and C-155/04 *Alliance for Natural Health and Others* EU:C:2005:449, para 52.

[8] J Baquero Cruz, *Between Competition and Free Movement: The Economic Constitutional Law of the European Community* (Hart Publishing, 2002).

[9] Joined Cases C-266/87 and C-267/87 *The Queen v Royal Pharmaceutical Society of Great Britain, ex parte Association of Pharmaceutical Importers* EU:C:1989:205, paras 13–16; and Case C-292/92 *Hünermund and Others v Landesapothekerkammer Baden-Württemberg* EU:C:1993:932, paras 15–18.

[10] Case C-415/93 *Union royale belge des sociétés de football association and Others v Bosman and Others* EU:C:1995:463, paras 83–84.

[11] Case C-341/05 *Laval and Partneri* EU:C:2007:809, paras 98–99.

originating from Schleswig-Holstein) lacks a cross-border link and falls outside the scope of Article 34 TFEU. The existence of a cross-border link is a prerequisite for the application of all free movement rules.

Although the cross-border link may appear to limit the effectiveness of free movement rules, the Court of Justice has interpreted the Treaties so that any restriction, whether actual or potential, is sufficient to trigger the application of the Treaty freedoms. In the case of *potential* restrictions, it is sufficient to demonstrate that the Member State measure in question is liable to impede trade within the internal market, not having to prove that it has actually produced such an effect in practice.

The case law accepts the existence of a cross-border link in cases where an individual invokes the freedoms of movement against the Member State of his or her nationality, provided there has been prior movement.[12] For example, a student who relocates to another Member State and then returns to her country of nationality to continue her studies, only to face administrative restrictions on the recognition of her qualifications obtained abroad, can be considered to be in a cross-border situation. Similarly, the cross-border link may be established through legal connections, as opposed to physical movement. This is exemplified by individuals who hold dual nationality and maintain a connection with two Member States through legal obligations and nationality, not necessarily through physical movement.[13]

3.2. *Direct Effect*

The Treaty provisions on free movement have direct effect.[14] This feature has significant practical implications, as it allows any natural or legal person subject to a restrictive measure of a Member State to challenge that measure before any competent court or authority within that Member State and rely on its primacy over national law. The direct effect of a free movement provision entails the obligation to set aside any national measure that is confirmed to breach the free movement provision. As explained in chapter ten, the adjudicative dimension of primacy empowers national courts and administrative authorities to annul national rules that contravene Union law. As a result, a company that successfully invokes a free movement provision is entitled to request the setting aside of the national law, decree, or administrative practice that has restricted its right to free movement.

3.3. *Reverse Discrimination*

The requirement of a cross-border link thus excludes purely internal situations from the scope of application of the free movement rules. If national measures affecting trade between Member States are the only relevant acts subject to the free movement rules, situations that are purely internal, characterised by the absence of a cross-border link, are left outside the scope of the fundamental freedoms.

The fundamental freedoms can trigger the setting aside and subsequent repeal of national rules or practices that hinder the cross-border movement of goods, services, workers, and capital. A Danish regulation on food labelling that is contrary to Article 34 TFEU will be set aside and eventually repealed, but this does not prevent the measure from being applied in purely

[12] Case C-19/92 *Kraus v Land Baden-Württemberg* EU:C:1993:125, paras 15–16.

[13] Case C-148/02 *García Avello* EU:C:2003:539, para 27.

[14] The case law has confirmed that the Treaty provisions on free movement have direct effect on several occasions, including, inter alia, in Case C-83/78 *Pigs Marketing Board* EU:C:1978:214, para 67; in the case of the freedom of establishment and the freedom to provide services, see Case 2/74 *Reyners* EU:C:1974:68, para 25; on the free movement of persons, see Case C-413/99 *Baumbast* EU:C:2002:493, para 84; on the free movement of capital, see Joined Cases C-163/94, C-165/94 and C-250/94 *Sanz de Lera* EU:C:1995:451, paras 41–47.

internal situations for local goods only. If the Danish authorities choose to enforce the national rule solely for local goods, Article 34 TFEU will not be applicable in that case. This situation has been described as a 'reverse discrimination', and, in line with a well-established case law of the Court of Justice, it falls outside the scope of Union law.[15] It is the responsibility of the Member State to mitigate, eliminate, or maintain any reverse discrimination that may arise from the implementation of free movement rules.[16]

Despite repeated attempts to broaden the scope of the freedoms to provide a coherent solution to the problems caused by reverse discrimination, the Court has been reluctant to interfere with the regulatory autonomy of the Member States. This reluctance has not prevented the Court from responding to requests from national courts seeking guidance on how to deal with cases of reverse discrimination arising in connection with Union law within the context of national law.[17] Moreover, if a rule of free movement results in a reverse discrimination in a Member State, it is always possible for the latter to promote in the Union's legislative institutions a measure that harmonises or unifies the legal framework, thus putting an end to divergences between the Member States (and to any internal discrimination).

3.4. *Relationship between Free Movement Rules and Union Secondary Legislation*

The complementary relationship between negative and positive integration is reflected in how free movement rules and Union secondary legislation interact. According to case law, 'where a matter is regulated in a harmonised manner at [Union] level, any national measures must be assessed in the light of the provisions of that harmonising measure and not of Articles 30, 34 and 36 of the Treaty'.[18]

Directives or regulations that harmonise or unify the legal framework for a specific sector constitute a *lex specialis* and supersede the free movement rule in a particular dispute. Therefore, reliance on free movement rules remains relevant in two circumstances: firstly, when the Union has not yet established a comprehensive legal framework through secondary law; and secondly, when the existing Union framework does not fully regulate the matter at issue, rendering the Treaty freedoms directly applicable to the specific case. In any event, the interpretation of Union secondary legislation must be consistent with primary law, including the Treaty rules on free movement.[19] Any interpretation of Union secondary legislation that leads to a conclusion inconsistent with the Treaty's rules on free movement must be rejected.

III. FREE MOVEMENT OF GOODS

1. Definition of 'Goods'

The Court of Justice has interpreted the term 'goods' in Articles 34–35 TFEU broadly, to capture as many protectionist national measures as possible. Goods are defined as 'products

[15] Case C-286/81 *Oosthoek's Uitgeversmaatschappij* EU:C:1982:438, para 9; Case C-448/98 *Guimont* EU:C:2000:663, para 21; and Case C-293/02 *Jersey Produce Marketing Organisation* EU:C:2005:664, para 26.

[16] MP Maduro, 'The Scope of European Remedies: The Case of Purely Internal Situations and Reverse Discrimination' in C Kilpatrick, T Novitz and P Skidmore (eds), *The Future of Remedies in Europe* (Hart Publishing, 2000) 117.

[17] Case C-448/98 *Guimont* (n 15) paras 21–22; Case C-393/08 *Sbarigia* EU:C:2010:388, para 23; and Case C-84/11 *Susisalo and Others* EU:C:2012:374, para 20.

[18] Case C-324/99 *DaimlerChrysler* EU:C:2001:682, para 32; Case C-37/92 *Vanacker and Lesage* EU:C:1993:836, para 9; Case C-322/01 *Deutscher Apothekerverband* EU:C:2003:664, para 36; Case C-540/22 *SN and Others* EU:C:2024:530, para 59; and Case C-115/24 *UJ* EU:C:2025:694, paras 120–22.

[19] Case C-367/21 *Hewlett Packard Development Company LP* EU:C:2024:61, para 48.

which can be valued in money and which are capable, as such, of forming the subject of commercial transactions'.[20] This broad definition has allowed goods as diverse as bees (or animals in general),[21] works of art,[22] coins that are not legal tender,[23] waste,[24] electricity,[25] and gas to be classified as 'goods'.[26]

If it is doubtful whether a particular item or transaction qualifies as a 'good', other free movement rules may be applicable, depending on the particularities of each case. For example, purchasing a tailor-made suit involves both acquiring a good and receiving a service provided by the tailor. In such cases, the determination of the applicable free movement rule is based on the integrated nature of the service and, in particular, on the identification of the predominant element of the transaction:

> [I]n addition to the legal sales transaction, [retail trade] consists, *inter alia*, in selecting an assortment of goods offered for sale and in offering a variety of services aimed at inducing the consumer to conclude the abovementioned transaction with the trader in question rather than with a competitor.[27]

In other cases, the distinction between the integrated nature of the service and the transaction of goods is not entirely clear. In such instances, both freedoms may be applicable to the facts.[28] This was the case of digital television decoders, which were goods on the market but necessary to facilitate access to audiovisual services. In this case, the Court of Justice reviewed the contested national measures in light of both the rules on the free movement of goods (ie, the decoders) and the freedom to provide services (ie, the audiovisual service).[29]

2. Restrictions of a Fiscal Nature

Fiscal power is the traditional tool of economic protectionism used by states. The adoption of tariffs and customs duties on foreign products serves as a primary instrument through which states can protect their domestic markets from the entry of more competitively priced goods from abroad. Imposing such fiscal measures on imported goods increases their cost and raises prices for consumers in the domestic market. This, in turn, reduces the competitiveness of these imported goods, to the point that there is no longer an incentive to import them into the market. In a free trade area, the imposition of such barriers is prohibited, as otherwise each Member State could prioritise the protection of its domestic products, thereby impeding competition with more efficient or cost-effective products from other Member States. Consequently, other Member States would be incentivised to implement similar measures and retaliate against the protectionist policies of the first state, thereby triggering a spiral that would ultimately undermine the fundamental purpose of the internal market.

[20] Case C-7/68 *Commission v Italy* EU:C:1968:51, 237.

[21] Case C-67/97 *Bluhme* EU:C:1998:584, para 19.

[22] Joined Cases C-60/84 and C-61/84 *Cinéthèque* EU:C:1985:329, para 9.

[23] Case C-7/78 *Thompson* EU:C:1979:209, para 19.

[24] Case C-2/90 *Commission v Belgium* EU:C:1992:310, para 28; and Case C-221/06 *Stadtgemeinde Frohnleiten and Gemeindebetriebe Frohnleiten* EU:C:2007:657, paras 36–38.

[25] Case C-393/92 *Gemeente Almelo and Others v Energiebedrijf IJsselmij* EU:C:1994:171, para 28; and Case C-158/94 *Commission v Italy* EU:C:1997:500, para 17.

[26] Case C-159/94 *Commission v France* EU:C:1997:501, paras 44ff.

[27] Case C-418/02 *Praktiker Bau- und Heimwerkermärkte* EU:C:2005:425, para 34.

[28] Joined Cases C-34/95, C-35/95 and C-36/95 *De Agostini and TV-Shop* EU:C:1997:344, paras 48–49; Case C-405/98 *Gourmet International Products* EU:C:2001:135, paras 34 and 42; Case C-452/04 *Fidium Finanz* EU:C:2006:631, para 34, and Case C-366/24 *Amazon EU Sàrl* EU:C:2025:990, paras 49–50.

[29] Case C-390/99 *Canal Satélite Digital* EU:C:2002:34, paras 32–33.

The Treaties set out specific provisions to prevent the use of national fiscal mechanisms for protectionist purposes. To address all potential scenarios, the Treaties distinguish between fiscal measures that are applied to goods by reason of their crossing of a border (Article 30 TFEU) and internal taxation that directly or indirectly discriminates against goods from other Member States (Article 110 TFEU). The former concerns customs duties and charges having equivalent effect of a Member State applied to goods *solely by reason of their crossing a border*, while the latter concerns national fiscal measures applied to goods from other Member States *that are already within the territory of the Member State*.

2.1. *Article 30 TFEU*

Article 30 TFEU provides as follows:

> Customs duties on imports and exports and charges having equivalent effect shall be prohibited between Member States. This prohibition shall also apply to customs duties of a fiscal nature.

This provision prohibits two types of fiscal measures: first, it bans customs duties on imports and exports between Member States; second, it prevents the imposition of charges that have an equivalent effect to customs duties on imports and exports. The former is of negligible practical significance today, given the high degree of development of the internal market over the past seven decades. Member States are no longer allowed to levy customs duties on goods from other Member States, a practice that was only permissible during the transitional period in the early years of the European Communities. The prohibition on customs duties became unconditional upon the expiry of the transitional period on 1 January 1970. Subsequent Treaty amendments, including the consolidation effected by the Treaty of Amsterdam (1997), removed the obsolete references to the transitional arrangements and gave the provision its current wording,[30] turning the original stand-still clause into a categorical prohibition applicable to all the Member States.

The second category of measures prohibited by Article 30 TFEU includes measures that have an effect equivalent to a customs duty on imports and exports. While these measures do not formally constitute a customs duty, their economic consequences are analogous, given their effect on the final price of goods imported from other Member States. Even if the measure is not formally a customs duty, it can be considered as a 'charge having equivalent effect' due to the equivalence of its economic impact to that of a customs duty.

The Court of Justice defined such measures in *Commission v Italy* (statistical levy)[31] in the following terms:

> Any pecuniary charge, however small and whatever its designation and mode of application, which is imposed unilaterally on domestic or foreign goods by reason of the fact that they cross a frontier, and which is not a customs duty in the strict sense, constitutes a charge having equivalent effect . . . even if it is not imposed for the benefit of the State, is not discriminatory or protective in effect and if the product on which the charge is imposed is not in competition with any domestic product.[32]

The reference to 'any pecuniary charge' in the case law on Article 30 TFEU indicates that the provision applies to fiscal measures enacted by Member States. Non-fiscal measures, such as quantitative restrictions or measures having equivalent effect that restrict goods crossing a

[30] The judgment in *Van Gend en Loos*, one of the leading rulings of the Court of Justice, was delivered in a case concerning the interpretation of the provision that preceded Art 30 TFEU.

[31] Case C-24/68 *Commission v Italy* EU:C:1969:29.

[32] ibid, para 14. See also Case C-39/17 *Lubrizol France* EU:C:2018:438, para 24; Case C-305/17 *FENS* EU:C:2018:986, para 29; and Case C-558/22 *Autorità di Regolazione per Energia Reti e Ambiente (ARERA)* EU:C:2024:209, para 98.

border, are governed by Articles 34–35 TFEU, not Article 30 TFEU. Furthermore, the economic value of the national measure is irrelevant, as the prohibition does not take into account any *de minimis* thresholds and will apply 'however small' the charge may be. In *Commission v Italy*, cited above, the charge amounted to 10 Italian lira as a fee for collecting statistical information at the border. The Court of Justice ruled that such an amount was a discriminatory restriction that importers were not obliged to bear.[33]

As previously mentioned, the particular form or designation of the financial charge is irrelevant. In this regard, the Court of Justice has classified a variety of charges as equivalent to customs duties, including those related to the collection of statistical data at border crossings, health inspections,[34] and postal charges for the dispatch of goods from another Member State.[35]

The prohibition in Article 30 TFEU applies solely to charges imposed on goods by reason of their crossing a border between two Member States. If the measure is applied as part of a general system of internal taxation to all goods, including goods from other Member States that have already crossed the border, Article 110 TFEU applies, which will be examined in more detail in the following section. The Court of Justice has interpreted the concept of 'border' broadly, including not only borders between Member States but also 'internal borders', that is, demarcation lines within the territory of a Member State. The latter arose in *Legros*,[36] where the Court of Justice addressed whether goods taxed due to being brought into the territory of the island of Réunion, an outermost region forming part of the French Republic, constituted a 'crossing of a border' within the meaning of Article 30 TFEU. The Court of Justice answered that question in the affirmative, stating that:

> A charge levied at a regional frontier by reason of the introduction of products into a region of a Member State constitutes an obstacle to the free movement of goods which is at least as serious as a charge levied at the national frontier by reason of the introduction of the products into the whole territory of a Member State.[37]

This approach has made it possible to apply Article 30 TFEU to cases where, for example, a municipal tax introduced by the Comune di Carrara taxed the extraction and movement of marble from its municipal territory in the interior of Italy.[38] This broad scope of application has drawn criticism from legal scholars. For example, Enchelmaier and Oliver argue that the original objective of Article 30 TFEU has been excessively stretched, since the provision aims to prevent protectionist measures against goods from other Member States. This objective is difficult to discern when the border crossing involves two municipalities or two regions that have no direct link to the borders of other Member States and are outside the conventional channels of trade flows within the internal market.[39]

The aim of the fiscal measure is irrelevant in determining the applicability of Article 30 TFEU, even if the beneficiary is not the state treasury but rather a private third party. In *Diamantarbeiders*, the Court of Justice ruled that a levy applied to the value of imported diamonds, designed to finance a social fund to support workers in the sector, was a 'charge

[33] ibid, para 14.

[34] Case C-39/73 *Rewe Zentralfinanz v Landwirtschaftskammer Westfalen-Lippe* EU:C:1973:105, 1039; and Case C-314/82 *Commission v Belgium* EU:C:1984:118, para 16.

[35] Case C-39/82 *Donner* EU:C:1983:3, para 13.

[36] Case C-163/90 *Legros and Others* EU:C:1992:326.

[37] ibid, para 16.

[38] Case C-72/03 *Carbonati Apuani* EU:C:2004:506; and Case C-402/14 *Viamar* EU:C:2015:830.

[39] S Enchelmaier and P Oliver, 'Free Movement of Goods: Recent Developments in the Case Law' (2007) 44 *Common Market Law Review* 652.

having equivalent effect' as prohibited by Article 30 TFEU.[40] The Court of Justice reached a similar conclusion in the case of an Italian scheme that taxed exports of goods and allocated the revenue to the protection of the country's historical, artistic, and cultural heritage. The Italian Government regarded the amounts paid to the treasury as negligible, but they were sufficient for the Court of Justice to confirm the applicability of Article 30 TFEU.[41]

The case law provides various examples of measures to which Article 30 TFEU does not apply. This is the case where the charge constitutes consideration for a service actually rendered to the importer or exporter, provided that such a service confers a specific advantage on the importer or exporter, that the charge is proportionate to the service rendered, and that it does not exceed the actual cost of the service.[42] For example, charging a fee for using public warehouses in border areas does not qualify as a 'charge having equivalent effect.'[43] However, charges for the provision of services during night hours by customs staff,[44] or a fee for the collection of information for statistical purposes, are considered to constitute charges having equivalent effect pursuant to Article 30 TFEU.[45] Similarly, where an inspection is required by Union law, the charge imposed for carrying out that inspection does not constitute a charge having equivalent effect, provided that the amount charged does not exceed the actual cost of the inspection and that the obligation genuinely derives from Union law.[46]

2.2. *Article 110 TFEU*

While charges levied by reason of the fact that a good crosses a border between two Member States are subject to Article 30 TFEU, internal taxes that apply within a Member State are governed by Article 110 TFEU. This provision targets two types of tax measures, described in the two situations outlined below:

> No Member State shall impose, directly or indirectly, on the products of other Member States any internal taxation of any kind in excess of that imposed directly or indirectly on similar domestic products.

Furthermore, no Member State shall impose on the products of other Member States any internal taxation of such a nature as to afford indirect protection to other products.

The first paragraph focuses on fiscal measures that discriminate, either directly or indirectly, between *similar* products. The second paragraph refers to fiscal measures that afford indirect protection to domestic products in competition with products from other Member States, even where the products are not 'similar' but are in a relationship of competition. An example of the first type is a measure that discriminates between two types of beer products: lager and stout. An example of the second type is a measure discriminating between beer and wine, two distinct but competing products.

[40] Joined Cases C-2/69 and C-3/69 *Sociaal Fonds voor de Diamantarbeiders v Brachfeld and Others* EU:C:1969:30, para 18.

[41] Case C-7/68 *Commission v Italy* EU:C:1968:51, para 2.

[42] Case C-132/82 *Commission v Belgium* EU:C:1983:135, paras 10–14; and Case C-39/82 *Donner* EU:C:1983:3, para 12.

[43] Case C-132/82 *Commission v Belgium* EU:C:1983:135, but see AG Mancini's Conclusions to the contrary, in particular pt 6.

[44] Case C-340/87 *Commission v Italy* EU:C:1989:219, para 17; and Case C-209/89 *Commission v Italy* EU:C:1991:139, para 9.

[45] Case C-24/68 *Commission v Italy* EU:C:1969:29, paras 16–17.

[46] Case C-46/76 *Bauhuis* EU:C:1977:6, paras 34–36; and Case C-389/00 *Commission v Germany* EU:C:2003:111, para 39. This is also the case where the activity is imposed by international law (Case C-89/76 *Commission v Netherlands* EU:C:1977:123, para 16). However, where the service is merely permitted, but not mandated by Union law or an international rule, the measure falls within the scope of Art 30 TFEU (Case C-314/82 *Commission v Belgium* EU:C:1984:118, para 8).

Article 110 TFEU applies to fiscal measures that tax a good itself, but not its producer, importer, or distributor. Fiscal measures that tax the activity of the latter will fall within the scope of other free movement rules, such as the freedom of establishment or the freedom to provide services. According to the case law, Article 110 TFEU is only applicable to

> pecuniary charges resulting from a general system of internal taxation applied systematically, in accordance with the same objective criteria, to categories of products irrespective of their origin or destination fall within Article [110 TFEU].[47]

A fiscal measure that is not imposed 'specifically on exported or imported products or in such a way as to differentiate them' is not subject to Article 110 TFEU, 'given that it applies to economic activities carried out by industrial, commercial, financial or agricultural undertakings and not to products as such'.[48] For example, a tax levied by a Member State on the registration of motor vehicles for the purpose of being put into circulation in its territory is neither a customs duty nor a charge having equivalent effect to a customs duty within the meaning of Articles 28 and 30 TFEU. According to settled case law, such a tax is an internal charge and must therefore be examined in the light of Article 110 TFEU.[49]

2.2.1. Taxation of Similar Goods

The first paragraph of Article 110 TFEU prohibits internal tax measures that are directly or indirectly levied on products from other Member States, regardless of their nature, 'in excess of that imposed directly or indirectly on similar domestic products'. The wording of the provision highlights two main features: first, the products must be 'similar'; second, the test for applying the first paragraph of Article 110 TFEU is based on the existence of discrimination, using the treatment of domestic products as a comparator.

The case law has evolved over time in defining the notion of 'similarity' between products. Initially, the case law adopted a formalistic approach, relying on the customs nomenclature as a point of reference,[50] only to depart from it in the 1980s and adopt an economic analysis that focused on the objective characteristics of the two categories of products.[51] The current approach is outlined in *Commission v Denmark*, a case involving two categories of alcoholic beverages, where the criterion was described as follows:

> In order to determine whether products are similar within the terms of the prohibition laid down in the first paragraph of [Article 110 TFEU], it is necessary to consider . . . whether they have similar characteristics and meet the same needs from the point of view of consumers. The court endorsed a broad interpretation of the concept of similarity . . . and assessed the similarity of the products not according to whether they were strictly identical, but according to whether their use was similar and comparable. Consequently, in order to determine whether products are similar it is necessary first to consider certain objective characteristics of both categories of beverages, such as their origin, the method of manufacture and their organoleptic properties, in particular taste and alcohol content,

[47] Case C-393/04 *Air Liquide Industries Belgium* EU:C:2006:403, para 56.

[48] ibid, para 57. See also Case C-558/22 *Autorità di Regolazione per Energia Reti e Ambiente (ARERA)* EU:C:2024:209, para 101.

[49] Case C-101/00 *Tulliasiamies and Siilin* EU:C:2002:505 para 57; Case C-402/09 *Tatu* EU:C:2011:219, paras 32–33; Case C-402/14 *Viamar* EU:C:2015:830, para 33; and Case C-676/21 *A and Veronsaajien oikeudenvalvontayksikkö* EU:C:2023:63, para 26.

[50] Case C-27/67 *Fink-Frucht GmbH v Hauptzollamt München-Landsbergerstraße* EU:C:1968:22, 232–33; and Case C-45/75 *Rewe-Zentrale v Hauptzollamt Landau-Pfalz* EU:C:1976:22, para 12.

[51] Case C-168/78 *Commission v France* EU:C:1980:51, para 13; Case C-216/81 *Cogis* EU:C:1982:275, para 7; and Case C-106/84 *Commission v Denmark* EU:C:1986:99, para 12.

> and secondly to consider whether or not both categories of beverages are capable of meeting the same need from the point of view of consumers.[52]

This approach led the Court of Justice to conclude that table wine and liqueur wine are 'similar' products within the meaning of the first paragraph of Article 110 TFEU.[53] The same conclusion was reached when it held that dark tobacco and light tobacco are 'similar' products.[54] However, in the case of Scotch whisky and fruit wines, the Court of Justice ruled that they are not 'similar' products, as the two beverages have clearly different characteristics.[55]

The first paragraph of Article 110 TFEU relies on a discrimination test, covering both direct and indirect discrimination. The provision prohibits *explicit* differences of treatment between imported and domestic products, such as an imported product being subject to a tax that is not levied on similar domestic products,[56] or a tax that applies to all products but has more unfavourable effects on imported products than on similar domestic products.[57]

The analysis becomes more complex when it focuses on indirect and apparently neutral differences in treatment, with no a priori discriminatory treatment between imported and domestic goods. If the analysis of the national tax measure reveals that it has the effect of providing an advantage to the domestic product, it will amount to indirect discrimination in breach of the first paragraph of Article 110 TFEU. The *intention* of the Member State is irrelevant, since it is the discriminatory *effect* in favour of the domestic product that matters. For example, a tax that only applies to dark tobacco but not to light tobacco will breach the first paragraph of Article 110 TFEU if it is established that dark tobacco is mostly an imported product, whereas light tobacco is produced and sold locally.[58] Similarly, a tax that applies a higher rate to vehicles with large engine capacity will breach the first paragraph of Article 110 TFEU if it is established that vehicles with smaller engines are taxed more favourably and, moreover, if they are a type of vehicle predominantly produced domestically.[59]

2.2.2. Taxation of Different but Competing Goods

It is common for two categories of products not to be considered 'similar', yet they still compete in the market. In such cases, the second paragraph of Article 110 TFEU states that 'no Member State shall impose on the products of other Member States any internal taxation of such a nature as to afford indirect protection to other products'.

In assessing whether two different products are in competition with each other, the case law relies on an economic criterion, set out in the following terms:

> In order to determine the existence of a competitive relationship within the meaning of the second paragraph of Article [110 TFEU], it [is] necessary to consider not only the present state of the market but also possible development regarding the free movement of goods within the [Union] and the further potential for the substitution of products for one another which might be revealed by

[52] *Commission v Denmark* (n 51) para 12.

[53] ibid.

[54] Case C-302/00 *Commission v France* EU:C:2002:123, paras 24–28.

[55] Case C-243/84 *Walker v Ministeriet for Skatter og Afgifter* EU:C:1986:100, para 12.

[56] Case 57/65 *Lütticke v Hauptzollamt Saarlouis* EU:C:1966:34.

[57] This was so in Case C-127/75 *Bobie Getränkevertrieb v Hauptzollamt Aachen Nord* EU:C:1976:95; Case C-90/94 *Haahr Petroleum v Abenrå Havn and Others* EU:C:1997:368; Case C-114/95 *Texaco v Middelfart Havn and Others and Olieselskabet Danmark v Trafikministeriet and Others* EU:C:1997:371; Case C-242/95 *GT-Link v De Danske Statsbaner* EU:C:1997:376; and Case C-221/06 *Stadtgemeinde Frohnleiten and Gemeindebetriebe Frohnleiten* EU:C:2007:657.

[58] Case C-302/00 *Commission v France* EU:C:2002:123, para 30.

[59] Case C-132/88 *Commission v Greece* EU:C:1990:165, para 17.

> intensification of trade, so as fully to develop the complementary features of the economies of the Member States in accordance with the objectives laid down by Article 2 of the Treaty.[60]

This approach has led the Court of Justice to rule that wine and beer are different products, but in competition with each other. In this case, the criterion of substitutability plays a relevant role, as the average consumer can adapt their preferences towards either of the two products, substituting one for the other. When demand is elastic, it suggests that the products are in competition. In *Commission v United Kingdom*, the Court of Justice elaborated the substitutability test as follows:

> [F]or the purpose of measuring the possible degree of substitution, attention should not be confined to consumer habits in a Member State or a given region. Those habits, which were essentially variable in time and space, could not be considered to be immutable; the tax policy of a Member State must not therefore crystallize given consumer habits so as to consolidate an advantage acquired by national industries concerned to respond to them.[61]

The criterion is not solely based on the elasticity of demand and it can be nuanced by other factors, such as production processes, product characteristics, or consumer preferences and behaviour patterns. In *Commission v United Kingdom*, the Court of Justice concluded that wine and beer were in competition only for a specific category of wine, namely the lightest and least expensive varieties of wine.[62] In *Commission v Sweden*,[63] the Court of Justice held that there was competition only between beer and wine of a certain alcohol content and price,[64] but found that there was no violation of the second paragraph of Article 110 TFEU because the Commission did not establish that the tax differential caused a shift in the purchasing preferences of an average consumer.[65]

3. Quantitative Restrictions and Measures having Equivalent Effect

Measures of a fiscal nature are not the only obstacles to the free movement of goods across Member States. In fact, the most restrictive measures with a significant impact on the movement of goods are often not fiscal but are those that quantitatively limit their entry or exit. These measures have traditionally been called 'quotas', and the Treaty refers to them as 'quantitative restrictions' and 'measures having an effect equivalent to a quantitative restriction'. The latter category encompasses a far broader range of national measures than traditional quotas, including national rules governing the characteristics, manufacture, or sale of a product. As the internal market has evolved and become more sophisticated, Member States have moved away from protecting local producers through fiscal measures or quotas, focusing more closely on measures that may disguise their protectionist intent or effects. A rule that prohibits all products containing a certain component may appear to be a neutral measure, but if imported products are the only ones using that component in the production of goods, the measure conceals a protectionist effect and therefore constitutes a restriction on the free movement of goods.

[60] Case C-170/78 *Commission v United Kingdom* EU:C:1983:202, para 7.
[61] ibid, para 8.
[62] ibid.
[63] Case C-167/05 *Commission v Sweden* EU:C:2008:202.
[64] ibid, para 56.
[65] ibid, para 58.

The Court of Justice has developed in considerable detail the concept of 'measures having an effect equivalent to a quantitative restriction'. Over time, the case law has evolved, not always providing an entirely consistent approach. There is a reason for this troubled evolution: as the Member States adapt their strategies to protect and/or promote local products, so the interpretation of the Treaty must adjust to new scenarios. On some occasions, the Court of Justice has reversed its own case law; in others, it has added nuances or refined its approach in response to new legislative measures introduced by the Union legislator for certain categories of goods. All these developments will be examined in the following section of this chapter.

Articles 34–36 TFEU contain the relevant provisions on quantitative restrictions and measures having equivalent effect. Article 34 TFEU deals with quantitative restrictions and measures having equivalent effect to a quantitative restriction *on imports*. Article 35 TFEU, with similar wording, targets quantitative restrictions and measures having equivalent effect to a quantitative restriction *on exports*. Both provisions introduce a prohibition in the following terms:

Article 34

Quantitative restrictions on imports and all measures having equivalent effect shall be prohibited between Member States.

Article 35

Quantitative restrictions on exports, and all measures having equivalent effect, shall be prohibited between Member States.

The Court of Justice has interpreted these two provisions differently, despite their textual similarity. Article 34 TFEU has been given a broad interpretation, with the aim of addressing the measures most commonly used by Member States to protect local products. The main threat to local products comes from imports of competing goods; therefore, protectionist measures primarily target the *entry* of products from other Member States. When focusing on exporting local products, Member States often adopt the opposite approach: they encourage the export of local products to maximise exports and boost the local economy. While it is rare for a country to restrict the outflow of its local products, in certain situations – such as in the case of essential or strategic products, for reasons of public health or security of supply – Member States can be inclined to adopt such measures (a scenario observed during the most critical times of the COVID-19 pandemic in 2020). For this reason, the interpretation of Article 34 TFEU has traditionally been expansive, whereas Article 35 TFEU has been interpreted more restrictively.[66] This asymmetry appears to have diminished in recent times,[67] but the case law is not yet entirely conclusive. Given its practical relevance, this section will focus primarily on the interpretation of Article 34 TFEU, and will refer to Article 35 TFEU only in cases of divergence in interpretation between the two provisions.

Quantitative restrictions and measures having an equivalent effect to a quantitative restriction can be derogated from or justified under certain conditions. A Member State is entitled to maintain or adopt a restrictive measure that impedes the import of goods from another Member State, as long as it falls within one of the derogations and/or justifications provided in the Treaties and in the case law. This is the purpose of Article 36 TFEU and the case law on overriding reasons in the public interest developed by the Court of Justice, to which section III.6.4 of this chapter is devoted.

[66] Case C-15/79 *Groenveld* EU:C:1979:253; Case C-155/80 *Oebel* EU:C:1981:177; and Joined Cases C-141/81, C-142/81 and C-143/81 *Holdijk* EU:C:1982:122.

[67] Case C-205/07 *Gysbrechts and Santurel Inter* EU:C:2008:730.

4. Quantitative Restrictions

Quantitative restrictions (QRs) are 'measures which amount to a total or partial restraint of, according to the circumstances, imports, exports or goods in transit'.[68] A measure that prohibits the entry of a product or sets quantitative limits on its entry (eg, a maximum number of tonnes of cotton imported annually) is a QR. Such measures are exceptional in contemporary trading practices, but there are several examples in the case law that confirm the continued relevance of the prohibition in Article 34 TFEU. For instance, in *Henn and Darby*, the Court of Justice ruled on whether a ban on importing pornographic material into the United Kingdom was a QR contrary to Article 34 TFEU.[69] In *Hedley Lomas*, it was confirmed that the refusal of a Member State to issue licences for the export of live sheep to another Member State amounts to a QR.[70] Similarly, a rule that imposes quantitative limits on the export of a particular product, such as in the case of Spanish bulk wine, also constitutes a QR, but subject to the prohibition in Article 35 TFEU.[71] In contrast, a measure that imposes quantitative limits on the release for consumption of cigarettes in the territory of a Member State does not constitute a 'quantitative restriction on imports', within the meaning of Article 34 TFEU, because it does not restrict the quantity of cigarettes which can be imported into that Member State.[72]

5. Measures Having an Equivalent Effect to a Quantitative Restriction: *Dassonville*

As noted above, Member States do not usually resort to quantitative restrictions to protect local goods but instead develop more sophisticated strategies in the form of regulatory requirements, which the Treaty refers to as 'measures having an equivalent effect to a quantitative restriction' (MEE). The definition of an MEE is not provided in the Treaties, but in the case law of the Court of Justice, beginning with the seminal case of *Dassonville*[73] and the extensive case law that has developed thereafter.

The *Dassonville* formula defines MEEs in the following terms:

> [A]ll trading rules enacted by Member States which are capable of hindering, directly or indirectly, actually or potentially, intra-Community trade are to be considered as measures having an effect equivalent to quantitative restriction.[74]

It should be noted that this definition also applies to the prohibition of MEEs on exports under Article 35 TFEU.[75]

The scope of the *Dassonville* formula is very broad and covers any national measure, including administrative practices, that may actually or potentially hinder trade in goods in the internal market. The formula is not limited to directly discriminatory MEEs, but also covers indirect discrimination disguised as neutral measures applicable to all products. The extensive scope of the *Dassonville* formula can be explained by the context in which the ruling was

[68] Case C-2/73 *Geddo v Ente Nazionale Risi* EU:C:1973:89, para 7.

[69] Case C-34/79 *Henn and Darby* EU:C:1979:295.

[70] Case C-5/94 *The Queen v Ministry of Agriculture, Fisheries and Food, ex parte Hedley Lomas* EU:C:1996:205.

[71] Case C-47/90 *Delhaize Frères v Promalvin and Others* EU:C:1992:250; Case C-388/95 *Belgium v Spain* EU:C:2000:244.

[72] Case C-96/22 *CDIL - Companhia de Distribuição Integral Logística Portugal SA* EU:C:2023:1024, para 32.

[73] Case C-8/74 *Dassonville* EU:C:1974:82.

[74] ibid, para 5.

[75] Case C-53/76 *Bouhelier* EU:C:1977:17, para 16; Case C-68/76 *Commission v France* EU:C:1977:48, para 16; and Case C-412/97 *ED Srl* EU:C:1999:324, para 10.

delivered. In the 1970s, the common market had stalled, and there were only modest signs of its development, amid broader economic stagnation across Europe. The Community institutions of that period struggled to reach political agreements to advance the common market agenda, leaving many protectionist measures in force in the Member States. In this context, it is unsurprising that the Court of Justice opted for a broad interpretation of Article 34 TFEU. The decision paid off, and the *Dassonville* formula was followed by a significant increase in litigation brought against the Member States, resulting in numerous rulings striking down domestic protectionist measures. A gradual retreat from protectionist practices culminated in the 1990s with the transition from the common market to the internal market, together with a round of broad liberalising reforms in strategic markets, such as telecommunications, energy, and transport. This evolution in the regulatory and economic landscape explains why the Court of Justice refined and adapted its interpretation of *Dassonville* until it reached its current formulation.

Although the *Dassonville* formula refers to 'trading rules', MEEs apply not only to national regulatory measures but also to administrative practices with a restrictive effect. For example, an advertising campaign promoted by the public authorities of a Member State can constitute an MEE, as was the case of a 'Buy Irish' campaign promoted by the Irish authorities to encourage the purchase of local products.[76] Similarly, individual acts of the authorities, provided they have a certain degree of consistency and generality, can also amount to an MEE.[77]

An MEE can reflect an activity undertaken by a Member State, but also a failure to act if the result of the omission amounts to a restriction on free movement. This was the case in *Commission v France*,[78] where the Commission questioned the conduct of the French authorities, whose passivity in the face of organised and continuous sabotage of truck drivers transporting Spanish strawberries across French territory led to a successful infringement action against France. The Court of Justice upheld the Commission's action and ruled that the passive conduct of a Member State can be as damaging as an active measure and could therefore constitute a breach of Article 34 TFEU read in conjunction with Article 4(3) TEU:

> The fact that a Member State abstains from taking action or, as the case may be, fails to adopt adequate measures to prevent obstacles to the free movement of goods that are created, in particular, by actions by private individuals on its territory aimed at products originating in other Member States is just as likely to obstruct intra-Community trade as is a positive act.

Article [34] therefore requires the Member States not merely themselves to abstain from adopting measures or engaging in conduct liable to constitute an obstacle to trade but also, when read with Article 4(3) TEU, to take all necessary and appropriate measures to ensure that that fundamental freedom is respected on their territory.[79]

The ruling in *Commission v France* had direct consequences and resulted in the adoption of Regulation 2679/98,[80] a coordination instrument that allows the Commission, Member States, and economic operators to respond to obstacles to the free movement of goods caused by the inaction or conduct of a Member State, which will be discussed in section III.6.4.2 of this chapter.

[76] Case C-249/81 *Commission v Ireland* EU:C:1982:402; and Case C-45/87 *Commission v Ireland* EU:C:1988:435.

[77] Case C-21/84 *Commission v France* EU:C:1985:184, para 13; Case C-192/01 *Commission v Denmark* EU:C:2003:492, para 40; Case C-212/03 *Commission v France* EU:C:2005:313, para 17; Case C-88/07 *Commission v Spain* EU:C:2009:123, para 54.

[78] Case C-265/95 *Commission v France* EU:C:1997:595.

[79] ibid, paras 31–32. See also the judgment in Case C-112/00 *Schmidberger* EU:C:2003:333, paras 58–59.

[80] Council Regulation (EC) No 2679/98 of 7 December 1998 on the functioning of the internal market in relation to the free movement of goods among the Member States [1998] OJ L337/8.

The *Dassonville* formula refers to MEEs having an 'actual or potential' effect on free movement. This reference is consistent with the broad interpretation of Article 34 TFEU, as it facilitates actions against measures whose restrictive effect is merely potential, even if not yet materialised, without requiring proof that the restriction is real, certain and present. For example, French legislation regulating the composition of *foie gras* may qualify as an MEE, even if the production of this product is largely confined to France. The fact that the regulation could potentially hinder producers in other Member States is sufficient to trigger the prohibition under Article 34 TFEU.[81] Similarly, a Spanish regulation governing the use of the term 'Ibérico' in relation to pork products is also capable of constituting an MEE with potentially restrictive effects, despite the fact that Iberian pig products are predominantly produced in Spain.[82]

6. Types of Restrictions

The *Dassonville* formula prohibits Member State measures that discriminate between domestic and imported products (distinctly applicable measures) and those that, although neutral and applicable to both categories, may affect imported products more than local products (indistinctly applicable measures). This distinction is relevant, as it not only broadens the scope of application of Article 34 TFEU but also determines the grounds of justification applicable to each type of restriction. In the case of distinctly applicable measures, Member States can only invoke the grounds enumerated in Article 36 TFEU as a defence. In contrast, in the case of indistinctly applicable measures, the range of justifications that Member States can invoke is considerably wider and includes various 'overriding reasons in the public interest' (also known as 'mandatory requirements'), which will be discussed in section 3.5.2 of this chapter.

In recent years, Member States have become more sophisticated in their regulatory strategies, well aware of the constraints of Article 34 TFEU. At the same time, the broadening of the *Dassonville* formula ultimately caught measures that had no protectionist effect whatsoever, resulting in legal uncertainty and unnecessary litigation. For these reasons, the Court of Justice refined the *Dassonville* formula in the 1990s to exclude from the scope of Article 34 TFEU a category of national measures: 'certain selling arrangements' applicable to the sale of goods. The definition of a 'selling arrangement' was later subject to a strict interpretation in the case law. At the same time, additional refinements appeared in the case law, such as the distinction between restrictions on use and product requirements, or the introduction of the 'market access test'. These developments will be analysed in the following sections.

6.1. *Distinctly Applicable Measures*

The clearest illustration of an MEE is provided by national measures that directly discriminate between imported and local products, creating an additional burden on the former that makes it difficult for them to compete with local products in the local market. Thus, the imported product faces artificially created national barriers that make importing it burdensome or costly,

[81] Case C-184/96 *Commission v France* EU:C:1998:495, para 17; Case C-325/00 *Commission v Germany* EU:C:2002:633, para 25; Case C-126/91 *Schutzverband gegen Unwesen i.d. Wirtschaft v Rocher* EU:C:1993:191, para 21; Case C-67/97 *Bluhme* EU:C:1998:584, para 22; and Case C-110/05 *Commission v Italy* EU:C:2009:66, para 56. However, the Court has also found cases where the potential effect was remote and in conformity with Art 34 TFEU. See Case C-69/88 *Krantz v Ontvanger der Directe Belastingen* EU:C:1990:97, para 11; Case C-93/92 *CMC Motorradcenter v Baskiciogullari* EU:C:1993:838, para 12; and Case C-44/98 *BASF* EU:C:1999:440, paras 16 and 21.

[82] Case C-169/17 *Asociación Nacional de Productores de Ganado Porcino* EU:C:2018:440, para 22.

compared to the conditions for selling local products. There are numerous examples of these practices: a national measure that imposes compulsory inspections on imported products but not on local ones;[83] requirements that imported products have a licence or equivalent certificate as a prerequisite for marketing;[84] or mandatory obligations that impose product requirements or advertising measures solely on imported products.[85]

According to the case law, an obligation to indicate the country of a product can amount to a distinctly applicable MEE. Information about goods is a consumer right, but not when the sole purpose of the information is to encourage consumers to purchase local goods at the expense of imported goods. The obligation to provide information on the origin of the product can be justified when the product has particular characteristics or qualities stemming from the place where the good is produced. This approach has led the Court of Justice to reject, for instance, an Irish measure requiring sellers of souvenirs bearing traditional Irish designs to indicate the country of origin if they were not made in Ireland.[86] The same outcome applied to a German regulation reserving the names *Sekt* and *Weinbrand* to sparkling wines produced in Germany from a fixed minimum proportion of home-grown grapes.[87] By demanding that producers from other Member States use names different from those already established in the German market, an unnecessary barrier to imports was created, contrary to Article 34 TFEU.[88]

Rules on minimum or maximum prices may also fall under the category of a distinctly applicable MEE in breach of Article 34 TFEU. If a maximum price is set at an abnormally low level, the effect of the measure may be to hinder the sale of imported products, which already bear the burden of transport costs from the exporting Member State, in contrast to local products.[89] The same rationale applies to minimum prices, which can deprive imported products of the opportunity to compete with local products at more attractive prices.[90] In any event, a national rule that prohibits sales below cost does not necessarily breach Article 34 TFEU, as it may affect all products indistinctly, both imported and local.[91]

6.2. *Indistinctly Applicable Measures*

Nowadays, it is rare for Member States to protect local products through directly discriminatory measures. To protect local products, national authorities may employ more refined methods, such as rules on product requirements. Member States also rely on other indirect

[83] Case C-4/75 *Rewe Zentralfinanz v Landwirtschaftskammer Bonn* EU:C:1975:98, para 4; Case C-251/78 *Denkavit Futtermittel* EU:C:1979:252, para 10; Case C-132/80 *United Foods* EU:C:1981:87, para 28; and Case C-50/85 *Schloh v Auto contrôle technique* EU:C:1986:244.

[84] Joined Cases C-51/71 to C-54/71 *International Fruit Company and Others v Produktschap voor Groenten en Fruit* EU:C:1971:128, para 9; Case C-251/78 *Denkavit Futtermittel* EU:C:1979:252, para 11; Case C-40/82 *Commission v United Kingdom* EU:C:1984:33, para 24; Case C-124/81 *Commission v United Kingdom* EU:C:1983:30, para 9; Case C-21/84 *Commission v France* EU:C:1985:184, paras 11–12; and Case C-434/04 *Ahokainen and Leppik* EU:C:2006:609, para 22.

[85] Case C-59/82 *Weinvertriebs-GmbH* EU:C:1983:101, paras 7–8; Case C-152/78 *Commission v France* EU:C:1980:187, para 13; and Case C-320/93 *Ortscheit v Eurim-Pharm* EU:C:1994:379, para 9.

[86] Case C-113/80 *Commission v Ireland* EU:C:1981:139, paras 15–17.

[87] Indications of origin of products are permitted under Union law, but under strict conditions, as confirmed by the case law. See, inter alia, Case C-3/91 *Exportur v Lor and Confiserie du Tech* EU:C:1992:420, para 11; Case C-47/90 *Delhaize Frères v Promalvin and Others* EU:C:1992:250; and Joined Cases C-465/02 and C-466/02 *Germany v Commission* EU:C:2005:636.

[88] Case C-12/74 *Commission v Germany* EU:C:1975:23, paras 7–8; and Case C-286/86 *Ministère public v Déserbais* EU:C:1988:434, para 9.

[89] Case C-65/75 *Tasca* EU:C:1976:30, para 13; and Case C-531/07 *Fachverband der Buch- und Medienwirtschaft* EU:C:2009:276, paras 20–22.

[90] Case C-82/77 *Van Tiggele* EU:C:1978:10, para 18; and Case C-333/14 *The Scotch Whisky Association* EU:C:2015:845, paras 31–32.

[91] Case C-63/94 *Belgapom/ITM and Vocarex* EU:C:1995:270.

measures which can be equally harmful to imported goods, such as rules on use or those governing a commercial activity. The way the Court of Justice has addressed these national practices will be examined in the sections that follow.

6.2.1. Product Requirements: *Cassis de Dijon*

The most common MEEs applied indistinctly to all goods are product requirements: national rules that apply, inter alia, to the product's physical characteristics. The Court of Justice described and listed several examples of product requirements in the following terms:

> [O]bstacles to free movement of goods which are the consequence of applying, to goods coming from other Member States where they are lawfully manufactured and marketed, rules that lay down requirements to be met by such goods (such as those relating to designation, form, size, weight, composition, presentation, labelling, packaging) constitute measures of equivalent effect prohibited by Article 30 [34 TFEU].[92]

Product requirements have the effect of imposing a double regulatory burden on the imported good. A Dutch producer of lawnmowers must comply with the product requirements under Dutch law, but if he chooses to export the product to Denmark, he must also meet the Danish requirements governing the same products on Danish territory. This double regulatory burden adds extra costs to the Dutch producer that the Danish lawnmower producer does not face. In an internal market where all Member States share certain quality standards and are governed by a principle of mutual recognition, an economic operator should not be subjected to a double regulatory burden.

To alleviate the harmful effects of the double regulatory burden, the Court of Justice issued a landmark ruling in 1979 that introduced the principle of mutual recognition. In *Cassis de Dijon*,[93] the Court of Justice reviewed a German rule requiring all liqueur wines to have a minimum alcohol content of 25 per cent to be marketed in Germany. Cassis, a blackcurrant liqueur produced in France, has an alcohol content of 15–20 per cent, which prevented it from being legally marketed in Germany.

According to the Court of Justice,

> obstacles to movement within the [Union] resulting from disparities between the national laws relating to the marketing of the products in question must be accepted in so far as those provisions may be recognized as being necessary in order to satisfy mandatory requirements relating in particular to the effectiveness of fiscal supervision, the protection of public health, the fairness of commercial transactions and the defence of the consumer.[94]

This dictum confirms that the double regulatory burden is a harsh reality that must be borne in the absence of a common regulatory Union framework, provided the local regulation is aimed at the fulfilment of an objective of general interest. However, the Court of Justice takes a further step and focuses on the specific case of goods produced in accordance with the rules applicable in the Member State of production. In that specific situation, as long as the good has been produced in compliance with the said rules, the Court of Justice argues as follows (as applied to the case of alcoholic beverages):

> [T]here is therefore no valid reason why, provided that they have been lawfully produced and marketed in one of the Member States, alcoholic beverages should not be introduced into any other Member State; the sale of such products may not be subject to a legal prohibition on the marketing of beverages with an alcohol content lower than the limit set by the national rules.[95]

[92] Joined Cases C-267/91 and C-268/91 *Keck and Mithouard* EU:C:1993:905, para 15.
[93] Case C-120/78 *Rewe/Bundesmonopolverwaltung für Branntwein* EU:C:1979:42.
[94] ibid, para 8.
[95] ibid, para 14.

The seminal judgment in *Cassis de Dijon* introduced the principle of mutual recognition, a fundamental tool not only for the internal market but also for other policy fields such as the Area of Freedom, Security and Justice. This principle is predicated on the existence of mutual trust between Member States and on the existence of common or equivalent standards that foster such trust. In 1979, the Court of Justice considered that the Member States had achieved a sufficient level of regulatory equivalence, allowing it to introduce and develop a principle of the internal market that plays a key role to this day.

The practical implications of *Cassis de Dijon* are significant. A product lawfully manufactured and marketed in the Member State of origin enjoys, as a general rule, freedom of movement, even if it does not meet the product requirements of other Member States. Imposing a dual regulatory burden is only permitted when a Member State, through local regulations, finds it necessary to enforce certain standards in the pursuit of an overriding public interest. These justifications, known in earlier case law as 'mandatory requirements' and now more broadly as 'overriding reasons in the public interest' must be interpreted strictly and must conform with the principle of proportionality. In sum, the ruling in *Cassis de Dijon* offers a balanced outcome that reconciles the need to combat the harmful effects of the double regulatory burden with the legitimate interest of a Member State to address objectives of general interest, such as environmental protection, road safety, financial stability, or combating tax fraud.

The principle of mutual recognition applies to product requirements, ie national provisions regulating the characteristics, composition, or presentation of a product. In the wake of *Cassis de Dijon*, many examples of product requirements that breach Article 34 TFEU have emerged in the case law. For instance, Belgian legislation requiring margarine to be marketed in cubic form, to differentiate it from and avoid confusion with butter, was declared contrary to Article 34 TFEU, as it imposed a double packaging requirement on the margarine producer, which was disproportionately burdensome and mainly affected imported margarine.[96] German legislation reserving the bottling of certain wines in Bocksbeutel-shaped bottles to quality wines from specific regions was deemed to prevent the sale in Germany of wines from other Member States bottled in the same type of bottle. The Court of Justice concluded that Italian wines complied with the legislation of their country of origin, and compliance with German law would require the Italian producer to undertake a new and onerous bottling process, contrary to Article 34 TFEU.[97] Another German regulation prohibited the marketing of Mars brand confectionery with a '+10%' marking on the packaging, as the marking exceeded the limits permitted under German unfair competition law. The Court held that packaging complying with the law of the country of origin was sufficient to market the product in Germany, otherwise the producer would be required to repackage the product or develop specific packaging lines for the sale of the product in Germany only.[98]

The principle of mutual recognition and the judgment in *Cassis de Dijon* have been subject to some criticism. A broad understanding of the principle can have adverse effects, as it might encourage a race to the bottom in regulatory standards, leading to a potential decline in safety, health, or consumer protection standards. If the only standard considered is that of the country of origin, other Member States may be tempted to lower their own standards to make local products more competitive. This reaction could cause a generalised lowering of standards with harmful consequences. However, this risk has not generally materialised in practice, as the principal effects of the application of the principle of mutual recognition have been not a lowering of national standards but rather the introduction of common rules at Union level

[96] Case C-261/81 *Rau v De Smedt* EU:C:1982:382, para 13.
[97] Case C-16/83 *Prantl* EU:C:1984:101, para 21.
[98] Case C-470/93 *Verein gegen Unwesen in Handel und Gewerbe Köln/Mars* EU:C:1995:224, para 13.

through secondary Union legislation. *Cassis de Dijon* has thus proved to be a major catalyst in the development of Union legislation that introduces common European standards to prevent regulatory arbitrage and aggressive local deregulation.

6.2.2. Measures on the Use of a Product: *Commission v Italy*

The principle of mutual recognition has proven to be an effective tool for challenging indistinctly applicable MEEs in the Member States, as it significantly reduces the capacity of such measures to survive scrutiny under Article 34 TFEU unless they are objectively justified and proportionate. The combination of the *Dassonville* formula and the principle of mutual recognition has widened the scope of Article 34 TFEU, bringing a broad range of potentially restrictive national measures within the scope of this provision. It is no longer necessary to prove that a national measure is directly discriminatory; rather, it suffices to show that a product, once lawfully manufactured and marketed in a Member State, encounters obstacles when accessing the market of another Member State. In the 1960s and 1970s, the prototype of an MEE was a directly or indirectly discriminatory measure targeting a product's characteristics. In the 1980s, and more notably in the 1990s, a new trend emerged in which national rules targeted the use of products, the performance of an activity, or the selling arrangements of a product.

Some commentators raised concerns about the expansive scope of MEEs that resulted from *Dassonville* and *Cassis de Dijon*. These criticisms were heard and started to be reflected in the Opinions of several Advocates General of the Court of Justice, who proposed a return to the original terms of Article 34 TFEU while maintaining the benefits that the case law had provided thus far. In this context, a new approach began to emerge in the case law, eventually culminating in the 'market access test' applicable to national measures on the *use* of a product, an approach that gradually complemented, rather than replaced, earlier discrimination-based analyses.

The leading case introducing the new test is *Commission v Italy* (Italian trailers),[99] an infringement procedure in which the Commission challenged Italy's rules banning the towing of trailers by motorbikes on Italian roads. The case did not involve a measure related to product characteristics (trailers), but rather a ban on a specific use (towing a trailer with a motorbike). In such a case, the principle of mutual recognition is less effective, as rules on use are not necessarily linked to a product's characteristics. Although compliance with the regulations of the Member State of production confers a presumption in favour of the importer, extending the principle of mutual recognition to national rules on use could unduly restrict the regulatory autonomy of Member States. As a result, the Court of Justice applied a different standard to the scrutiny of national rules on use: the market access test.

The market access test does not focus on whether a national measure is directly or indirectly discriminatory, but on its capacity to hinder the access of goods into a Member State. While the language of market access first appeared in the case law on freedom of establishment and services, it has acquired specific contours within the field of the free movement of goods. In *Commission v Italy*, after referring to the judgments in *Dassonville* and *Cassis de Dijon* and confining them to measures on product requirements, the Court of Justice added that Article 34 TFEU also applies to 'Any other measure which hinders access of products originating in other Member States to the market of a Member State.'[100]

This is the concise yet effective criterion used by the Court of Justice to determine that the Italian rule on trailers amounts to an MEE within the scope of Article 34 TFEU. The

[99] Case C-110/05 *Commission v Italy* EU:C:2009:66.

[100] ibid, para 37.

judgment's reasoning clearly illustrates how the market access test works, making no reference to the measure's discriminatory nature or to the principle of mutual recognition. The market access test focuses exclusively on how a prohibition on *use* impacts the conditions of access of the product to a Member State:

> [A] prohibition on the use of a product in the territory of a Member State has a considerable influence on the behaviour of consumers, which, in its turn, affects the access of that product to the market of that Member State.
>
> Consumers, knowing that they are not permitted to use their motorcycle with a trailer specially designed for it, have practically no interest in buying such a trailer . . . Thus, Article 56 of the Highway Code prevents a demand from existing in the market at issue for such trailers and therefore hinders their importation.
>
> It follows that the prohibition laid down in Article 56 of the Highway Code, to the extent that its effect is to hinder access to the Italian market for trailers which are specially designed for motorcycles and are lawfully produced and marketed in Member States other than the Italian Republic, constitutes a measure having equivalent effect to quantitative restrictions on imports within the meaning of Article [34 TFEU], unless it can be justified objectively.[101]

In *Commission v Italy*, the Court of Justice confirmed a development that began in the 1990s: the expansive approach initiated in *Dassonville* and *Cassis de Dijon* entered a more nuanced cycle, at least as regards national rules on product requirements. As regards other types of Member States' measures with the potential to hinder free movement, the case law has shifted towards a market access test. *Commission v Italy* marks the culmination of this evolution, as it applies this test to restrictions on use. Shortly after, in *Mickelsson*,[102] the Court of Justice applied the market access test to a Swedish restriction on the use of jet skis, which were prohibited from being used outside designated waterways. The Court of Justice clarified that *partial* restrictions on use also fell under the market access test, since:

> Even if the national regulations at issue do not have the aim or effect of treating goods coming from other Member States less favourably, which is for the national court to ascertain, the restriction which they impose on the use of a product in the territory of a Member State may, depending on its scope, have a considerable influence on the behaviour of consumers, which may, in turn, affect the access of that product to the market of that Member State.[103]

The market access *test* is not limited to total or partial prohibitions on rules of use. It also applies to any national measure that may affect the conditions of access of the good to the market of a Member State, except for certain selling arrangements, which will be discussed in the following section of this chapter. Therefore, it can be argued that *Commission v Italy* applies to measures that affect a commercial activity involving the sale of goods, such as the requirement for a licence or restrictions on certain activities of an economic operator. For instance, in *Humanplasma*[104] the Court of Justice ruled on an Austrian measure restricting the marketing of blood products derived from plasma to cases where donors had not been financially remunerated. The measure was indistinctly applicable, as it applied regardless of whether the plasma originated from Austrian donors or donors from other Member States, but it was neither a product-related requirement nor a measure concerning the use of the product. In this case, the Court of Justice applied the market access test as follows:

[101] ibid, paras 56–58.
[102] Case C-142/05 *Mickelsson and Roos* EU:C:2009:336.
[103] ibid, para 26.
[104] Case C-421/09 *Humanplasma* EU:C:2010:760.

> [N]ational legislation such as that at issue in the main proceedings is capable of hindering intra-Community trade and therefore constitutes a measure of equivalent effect to a quantitative restriction on imports within the meaning of Article [34 TFEU].[105]

To conclude, the market access test acts as a safety net, and in some strands of the case law as a primary analytical tool, for those cases where it is doubtful whether the national contested measure is directly or indirectly discriminatory and has the potential to hinder free movement. At the same time, the test is designed to scrutinise national measures beyond the scope of product requirements. Following the judgment in *Commission v Italy*, the test found fertile ground in the review of national measures on the use of products, but subsequent developments confirm that the test applies to all types of measures, provided they do not constitute product requirements subject to the *Cassis de Dijon* test.[106] The only category excluded from the scope of the market access test is that of certain selling arrangements, insofar as they are indistinctly applicable and affect imported and domestic goods in the same manner in law and in fact, as will now be explained.

6.2.3. Certain Selling Arrangements: *Keck and Mithouard*

Following the rulings in *Dassonville* and *Cassis de Dijon*, there were doubts as to whether the conditions of sale of a product fell within the scope of Article 34 TFEU as interpreted in that case law. As discussed above, rules governing product requirements can have the (intended or unintended) effect of adversely affecting products imported from other Member States. The same is true for certain requirements on the use of a product or certain activities of market operators. However, the selling arrangements that apply to a product – the conditions under which a retailer makes a product available to the consumer – are not necessarily protectionist in nature, nor are they likely to have the effect of restricting the access of imported products to the local market, provided that they do not in practice impede market access for goods from other Member States, as they tend to affect, de facto and *de jure*, all products equally. In other words, rules specifically addressed to the retailer of the product, and not to the producer or importers, do not per se create a risk for the free movement of goods from other Member States. Accordingly, throughout the 1980s, commentators called for restricting the scope of the *Dassonville* formula and excluding certain categories of MEEs, in particular those that affected the conditions of sale of goods.

This concern was eventually acknowledged, and the Court of Justice addressed it in its judgment in *Keck and Mithouard*, following a series of cases in which it became clear that the *Dassonville* formula required further refinement. The issue was raised during the British Sunday trading saga, a series of preliminary rulings concerning the British ban on the opening of retail shops on Sundays.[107] A straightforward interpretation of the *Dassonville* formula led to the conclusion that the prohibition on opening on Sundays was an indistinctly applicable MEE. The Court of Justice hesitated and issued several rulings on the matter,[108] leaving a trail of litigation across the United Kingdom that showed how difficult it was to reconcile the *Dassonville* formula with national rules on selling arrangements.

In *Keck and Mithouard*, the Court of Justice introduced an exception to its previous case law and confirmed the exclusion of non-discriminatory selling arrangements from the scope of

[105] ibid, para 30.

[106] Case C-456/10 *ANETT* EU:C:2012:241, paras 36–38; Case C-443/10 *Bonnarde* EU:C:2011:641, para 22; and Case C-333/14 *The Scotch Whisky Association* EU:C:2015:845, para 32.

[107] Case C-145/88 *Torfaen Borough Council v B & Q Plc* EU:C:1989:593.

[108] Case C-306/88 *Rochdale Borough Council v Anders* EU:C:1992:510; Case C-304/90 *Reading Borough Council v Payless DIY and Others* EU:C:1992:512; and Case C-69/93 *Council of the City of Stoke-on-Trent and Norwich City Council v B & Q Plc* EU:C:1994:226.

Article 34 TFEU. Before reaching this conclusion, the Court of Justice acknowledged the excessively broad scope of the *Dassonville* formula and the negative impact it had on legal certainty:

> In view of the increasing tendency of traders to invoke Article [34] of the Treaty as a means of challenging any rules whose effect is to limit their commercial freedom even where such rules are not aimed at products from other Member States, the Court considers it necessary to re-examine and clarify its case-law on this matter.[109]

The Court of Justice then introduced an exclusion of selling arrangements, provided they are indistinctly applicable, from the scope of application of Article 34 TFEU:

> [C]ontrary to what has previously been decided, the application to products from other Member States of national provisions restricting or prohibiting certain selling arrangements is not such as to hinder directly or indirectly, actually or potentially, trade between Member States within the meaning of the *Dassonville* judgment . . . , so long as those provisions apply to all relevant traders operating within the national territory and so long as they affect in the same manner, in law and in fact, the marketing of domestic products and of those from other Member States.[110]

In subsequent rulings, the Court of Justice clarified the concept of a selling arrangement in further detail. This category of measures includes, inter alia, the obligation to close petrol stations at night,[111] the prohibition on opening on Sundays,[112] the obligation for retailers to hold a municipal licence,[113] and the requirement for retailers to have a presence in a given territory.[114] National rules requiring the sale of products in certain types of retail outlets, such as the obligation to sell processed infant formulae only in pharmacies,[115] or tobacco only in licensed premises, are also considered selling arrangements.[116] Rules on discounts, price reductions, rebates and the gift of free units relating to biocidal products are considered to be a selling arrangement.[117] A ban on doorstep selling of certain products also counts as a selling arrangement,[118] as does a ban on resale at a loss, as was the case in *Keck and Mithouard*. Restrictions on advertising may also be regarded as a selling arrangement, provided that the advertising restriction primarily affects retail trade and does not prevent access to the market for imported products more than for domestic products.[119]

It should be noted that the exception introduced in *Keck and Mithouard* does not imply a complete exclusion of selling arrangements from the scope of application of Article 34 TFEU. On the contrary, the exclusion only relates to selling arrangements that are indistinctly applicable to both imported and local goods. If the selling arrangement directly discriminates against imported products, Article 34 TFEU applies in full, and once the restriction has been

[109] Joined Cases C-267/91 and C-268/91 *Keck and Mithouard* EU:C:1993:905, para 14.

[110] ibid, para 16.

[111] Joined Cases C-401/92 and C-402/92 *Tankstation 't Heukske and Boermans* EU:C:1994:220.

[112] Joined Cases C-69/93 and C-258/93 *Punto Casa and PPV* EU:C:1994:226; Case C-418/93 *Semeraro Casa Uno and Others v Sindaco del Comune di Erbusco and Others* EU:C:1996:242; and Case C-483/12 *Pelckmans Turnhout* EU:C:2014:304.

[113] Case C-20/03 *Burmanjer and Others* EU:C:2005:307.

[114] Case C-254/98 *TK-Heimdienst* EU:C:2000:12; Case C-323/93 *Centre d'insémination de la Crespelle v Coopérative de la Mayenne* EU:C:1994:368; Case C-322/01 *Deutscher Apothekerverband* EU:C:2003:664; and Case C-141/07 *Commission v Germany* EU:C:2008:492.

[115] Case C-391/92 *Commission v Greece* EU:C:1995:199.

[116] Case C-387/93 *Banchero* EU:C:1995:439, para 35; and Case C-189/95 *Baustahlgewebe v Commission* EU:C:1998:608, para 57.

[117] Case C-147/21 *Comité interprofessionnel des huiles essentielles françaises (CIHEF)* EU:C:2023:31, paras 38–39.

[118] Case C-441/04 *A-Punkt Schmuckhandel* EU:C:2006:141, para 17.

[119] Case C-292/92 *Hünermund and Others v Landesapothekerkammer Baden-Württemberg* EU:C:1993:932; Case C-412/93 *Leclerc-Siplec v TF1 and M6* EU:C:1995:26; Case C-6/98 *ARD* EU:C:1999:532; and Case C-71/02 *Karner* EU:C:2004:181.

established, the Member State may invoke grounds of justification provided in Article 36 TFEU. The selling arrangements excluded from the scope of Article 34 TFEU are those measures that are indistinctly applicable and affect, *de jure* and de facto, both local and imported products. Where a formally neutral selling arrangement has a greater impact in practice on access to the market for goods from other Member States, it will fall within the scope of Article 34 TFEU.[120] It is only within this defined scope, as outlined in paragraph 16 of *Keck and Mithouard*, that the Member State can successfully argue the inapplicability of Article 34 TFEU.

In any event, the impact of *Keck and Mithouard* is currently mitigated by Directive 2005/29 on unfair commercial practices, within its material scope, namely business-to-consumer commercial practices directly connected with the promotion, sale or supply of products to consumers.[121] This Directive introduces a full harmonisation of national measures that cover a wide range of commercial practices. This type of harmonisation prevents Member States from introducing higher standards of protection in the form of selling arrangements, including standards on consumer protection, but does not extend to all forms of selling arrangements governed by national law. Article 2(d) of the Directive defines 'business-to-consumer commercial practice' as 'any act, omission, course of conduct or representation, commercial communication including advertising and marketing, by a trader, directly connected with the promotion, sale or supply of a product to consumers'. Furthermore, the Directive details the categories of commercial practices covered and classifies them into three categories (Article 5). The Annex to the Directive provides a 'blacklist' of 31 prohibited commercial practices that are considered unfair in all circumstances, including multiple examples of conduct that can be defined as selling arrangements.[122] As a result, although Article 34 TFEU has a limited ability

[120] A revealing example of how the *Keck* doctrine applies to measures that are more likely to have an effect in economic operators of other Member States is found in Case C-366/24 *Amazon EU Sàrl* EU:C:2025:990, at para 58, in which the Court of Justice analysed whether a minimum charge for the delivery of books not collected from a retailer was a selling arrangement. According to the Court of Justice, 'although [such measure] applies to all book retailers, the imposition by a national measure of minimum charges for the delivery of books that are not collected from a book retailer has a particular impact on distance selling, since it entails an increase in the overall price of the book paid by the purchaser in order to take possession of that book outside of those shops. Thus, such imposition of charges as provided for by the legislation of a Member State is more likely to affect traders from other Member States, who are less able to deliver books ordered by distance selling to those shops, than traders in the first Member State. Such imposition of charges is thus liable to further impede access to the market for books from other Member States and therefore constitutes a measure having an effect equivalent to a quantitative restriction within the meaning of Article 34 TFEU.' See also Case C-148/15 *Deutsche Parkinson Vereinigung* EU:C:2016:776, para 23.

[121] Directive 2005/29/EC of the European Parliament and of the Council of 11 May 2005 concerning unfair business-to-consumer commercial practices in the internal market and amending Council Directive 84/450/EEC, Directives 97/7/EC, 98/27/EC and 2002/65/EC of the European Parliament and of the Council and Regulation (EC) No 2006/2004 of the European Parliament and of the Council [2005] OJ L149/22.

[122] Annex I mentions, inter alia, practices such as: claiming to be a signatory to a code of conduct when the trader is not; displaying a trust mark, quality mark or equivalent without having obtained the necessary authorisation; claiming that a code of conduct has an endorsement from a public or other body which it does not have; claiming that a trader (including the trader's commercial practices) or a product has been approved, endorsed or authorised by a public or private body when the trader has not or making such a claim without complying with the terms of the approval, endorsement or authorisation; making an invitation to purchase products at a specified price without disclosing the existence of any reasonable grounds the trader may have for believing that he or she will not be able to offer for supply or to procure another trader to supply, those products or equivalent products at that price for a period that is, and in quantities that are, reasonable having regard to the product, the scale of advertising of the product and the price offered (bait advertising); falsely stating that a product will only be available for a very limited time, or that it will only be available on particular terms for a very limited time, in order to elicit an immediate decision and deprive consumers of sufficient opportunity or time to make an informed choice; undertaking to provide after-sales service to consumers with whom the trader has communicated prior to a transaction in a language which is not an official language of the Member State where the trader is located and then making such service available only in another language without clearly disclosing this to the consumer before the consumer is committed to the transaction; stating or otherwise creating the impression that a product can legally be sold when it cannot, or presenting rights given to consumers in law as a distinctive feature of the trader's offer.

to address potentially restrictive selling arrangements, this constraint is counterbalanced by Directive 2005/29 and the introduction of Union-wide standards regulating such practices.

6.3. *MEEs on Exports (Article 35 TFEU)*

So far, this chapter has focused on quantitative restrictions and MEEs that apply to imported goods. It is time to turn to the rules governing exports, which fall under the rules of Article 35 TFEU. The most significant threats to trade in goods come from protectionist measures that restrict the entry of foreign products into a Member State. Therefore, it is not surprising that most attention is given to the Treaty rules that target restrictions on imports rather than on exports. This also explains why the Court of Justice has traditionally interpreted Articles 34 and 35 TFEU differently – expanding the scope of Article 34 TFEU while applying a narrower standard under Article 35 TFEU.

Until 2008, the prevailing interpretation confined Article 35 TFEU to quantitative restrictions and distinctly applicable MEEs only.[123] As a result, indistinctly applicable MEEs affecting the export of goods were not prohibited under Article 35 TFEU. This approach changed in *Gysbrechts*,[124] a ruling in which the Court of Justice reviewed a Belgian law that prohibited sellers, in the context of distance selling contracts, from requiring a consumer to provide payment card details before the end of the withdrawal period. This had the practical effect of depriving online sellers of their only effective means of securing payment in cross-border transactions. By making it more burdensome to sell online in cross-border transactions, the measure disproportionately affected exports. However, as the measure applied indistinctly to the sale of both domestic and imported goods, it fell outside the scope of Article 35 TFEU under the Court's earlier, more restrictive interpretation.

The Court of Justice resolved the case by reconsidering its previous case law and confirming the applicability of Article 35 TFEU to an indistinctly applicable MEE affecting exports, as was the case of the Belgian legislation under scrutiny:

> [E]ven if a prohibition such as that at issue in the main proceedings is applicable to all traders active in the national territory, its actual effect is none the less greater on goods leaving the market of the exporting Member State than on the marketing of goods in the domestic market of that Member State.[125]

Having recognised the restrictive impact of indistinctly applicable measures in the context of the exports, the Court of Justice confirmed the applicability of Article 35 TFEU:

> It must therefore be held that a national measure, such as that at issue in the main proceedings, prohibiting a supplier in a distance sale from requiring an advance or any payment before expiry of the period for withdrawal constitutes a measure having equivalent effect to a quantitative restriction on exports.[126]

The judgment in *Gysbrechts* marks a significant step in aligning the protections offered by Articles 34–35 TFEU. However, it remains uncertain whether the latest developments in the notion of MEEs applied to imports – particularly following the rulings in *Commission v Italy*, *Mickelsson*, and others, as described in the previous section – also apply to the recently broadened scope of application of Article 35 TFEU. In her Opinion in *Gysbrechts*, Advocate General

[123] Case C-15/79 *Groenveld* EU:C:1979:253, para 7; Case C-155/80 *Oebel* EU:C:1981:177, para 8; Joined Cases C-141/81 to C-143/81 *Holdijk* EU:C:1982:122, para 11; Case C-237/82 *Jongeneel Kaas* EU:C:1984:44, para 22; and Case C-80/92 *Commission v Belgium* EU:C:1994:118, para 25.

[124] Case C-205/07 *Gysbrechts and Santurel Inter* EU:C:2008:730.

[125] ibid, para 43.

[126] ibid, para 44.

Trstenjak called for a complete alignment of both provisions, but some commentators, having examined the relevant wording of the judgment in *Gysbrechts*, are more cautious. Recent developments suggest that the interpretation of Article 35 TFEU still contains some nuances absent from Article 34 TFEU. In recent rulings, the Court of Justice has focused closely on the indirectly disproportionate effects of the contested measure on exports, as compared with the effects on domestic trade, even when product requirements are not involved.[127] This may indicate that, while Article 35 TFEU now applies to indistinctly applicable MEEs, the Court of Justice might be hesitant to use the market access test (or a market *exit* test in the case of exports) to Article 35 TFEU, at least for the time being.[128]

6.4. *Justifications*

Restrictions on the free movement of goods can be justified under certain conditions. Member States may invoke non-economic reasons to justify a restrictive measure if it serves an objective of general interest. This is the role played by Article 36 TFEU and the overriding reasons in the public interest (also known as 'mandatory requirements') developed by the case law of the Court of Justice.

Article 36 TFEU sets out a comprehensive list of grounds of justification that Member States can invoke when national measures restrict the free movement of goods. These grounds are in principle applicable to all restrictions falling under Articles 34–35 TFEU, subject to the conditions laid down therein. The traditional position in the case law was that the Article 36 grounds were available for both distinctly and indistinctly applicable measures, whereas the judge-made 'mandatory requirements' were available only for indistinctly applicable measures. In *Cassis de Dijon*, the Court of Justice did not expand the list of grounds in Article 36 TFEU, but instead developed an additional category of judge-made justifications, initially known as 'mandatory requirements', applicable to indistinctly applicable measures in order to enable the Member States to invoke a broader range of public interest objectives beyond those listed in Article 36 TFEU. This has created a framework in which distinctly applicable MEEs may only be justified under Article 36 TFEU, while indistinctly applicable measures may benefit from both the Article 36 TFEU grounds *and* the 'overriding reasons in the public interest' recognised in the case law. This development is the result of the evolution of markets: when Article 36 TFEU was introduced, it reflected the realities of the 1950s. Seven decades later, policies and markets have evolved into new areas, such as environmental protection, which have emerged as relevant fields of public policy. The case law of the Court of Justice has adapted the Treaties to these new realities, enabling Member States to justify certain restrictive measures by reference to objectives of general interest.

Justifications alone do not suffice to confirm the compatibility of a Member State's restrictive measure with Union law. In addition, national authorities must prove that the restrictive measure complies with the principle of proportionality. This means that the assessment of a national measure under the free movement of goods provisions is conducted in a three-step analysis. First, it must be determined if the national measure amounts to a 'restriction'. If the answer is positive, the second step requires the Member State to prove that the measure is justified by reference to a ground under Article 36 TFEU or an overriding reason in the public interest. And third, if the measure is capable of being justified, a further analysis requires

[127] Case C-15/15 *New Valmar* EU:C:2016:464, para 37; Case C-518/16 *ZPT AD* EU:C:2018:126, para 43; and Case C-648/18 *Hidroelectrica* EU:C:2020:723, para 33.

[128] In some cases, the Court of Justice appears to introduce a market access test in cases concerning Art 35 TFEU. See, for example, Case C-161/09 *Kakavetsos-Fragkopoulos* EU:C:2011:110, para 29.

confirmation that the measure conforms with the principle of proportionality. A restrictive national measure can be justified on grounds of environmental protection, but if there are less restrictive measures available that achieve the same goals just as effectively, the measure will breach the principle of proportionality. This framework is now well established and consistently applied in every case concerning the free movement of goods. While the first two steps are met in most cases, recent evidence suggests that most disputes reach a critical juncture in the third step, in which the principle of proportionality determines the outcome of the dispute. This principle will be explained in more detail in section III.6.4.3 of this chapter.

The grounds of justification provided in Article 36 TFEU and the overriding reasons in the public interest must be interpreted strictly. The case law rejects any expansive interpretation, following the principle that any exception to a general rule must be narrowly construed. The case law also rejects any justification based solely on economic grounds. Grounds of justification serve a wide range of public policy objectives, but they cannot be invoked to regulate the market with economic purposes: public security, public health, or consumer protection are objectives unrelated to the economic interests of local businesses or industries.

When invoking a ground of justification, the burden of proof falls on the Member State. The party alleging a restriction or the Commission must prove that the challenged national measure constitutes a 'restriction', whilst the Member State must provide the legal and factual evidence demonstrating that the measure is justified. This allocation of the burden of proof is particularly important in infringement proceedings (generally brought by the Commission acting as the applicant), but also in national court proceedings, where cases will be frequently brought by private parties against national authorities.

6.4.1. Article 36 TFEU

Article 36 TFEU introduces an exhaustive list of grounds of justification in the following terms:

> The provisions of Articles 34 and 35 shall not preclude prohibitions or restrictions on imports, exports or goods in transit justified on grounds of public morality, public policy or public security; the protection of health and life of humans, animals or plants; the protection of national treasures possessing artistic, historic or archaeological value; or the protection of industrial and commercial property. Such prohibitions or restrictions shall not, however, constitute a means of arbitrary discrimination or a disguised restriction on trade between Member States.

Public morality has become less frequently invoked in recent years, as national policies have shifted towards more liberal positions on a wide range of policy issues. As a result of this evolution, the rulings of the 1960s and 1970s of the Court of Justice interpreting this justification reflect national policy options which are hard to find in the current practice of the Member States. In the limited number of cases where this justification was invoked, the Court of Justice emphasised that Member States have a broad margin of discretion in defining what amounts to 'morality' within their jurisdictions.[129] For example, in 1979, the Court ruled in *Henn and Darby* on a British measure prohibiting the import of pornographic publications from the

[129] Case C-34/79 *Henn and Darby* EU:C:1979:295, paras 15–16: 'In principle, it is for each Member State to determine in accordance with its own scale of values and in the form selected by it the requirements of public morality in its territory. . . . Each Member State is entitled to impose prohibitions on imports justified on grounds of public morality for the whole of its territory, as defined in [the] Treaty, whatever the structure of its constitution may be and however the powers of legislating in regard to the subject in question may be distributed. The fact that certain differences exist between the laws enforced in the different constituent parts of a Member State does not thereby prevent that State from applying a unitary concept in regard to prohibitions on imports imposed, on grounds of public morality, on trade with other Member States.'

Netherlands.[130] The Court stated that the measure was capable of being justified under the ground of public morality and, therefore, did not violate Article 34 TFEU.[131] The outcome was very different several years later, in *Conegate*,[132] when the Court of Justice reviewed a British ban on the import of certain erotic objects from Germany. In this case, the British authorities failed to successfully invoke the ground of public morality, as it was proven that equivalent objects were already being lawfully marketed in the United Kingdom.[133]

The ground based on public policy focuses on the powers of Member States to address genuine threats to internal public order. According to well-established case law, public policy pursuant to Article 36 TFEU is defined in the following terms:

> [R]eliance by a national authority on the concept of public policy presupposes, in any event, the existence, in addition to the perturbation of the social order which any infringement of the law involves, of a genuine and sufficiently serious threat to the requirements of public policy affecting one of the fundamental interests of society.[134]

Member States have faced significant challenges in invoking this ground likely due to its broad and potentially indeterminate nature. This has prompted the Court of Justice to adopt a particularly strict interpretation of the derogation, although it has, in certain instances, accepted with the Member States' arguments. This was evident in the case of *Thompson*, where a prohibition on the export of coins no longer constituting legal tender was under scrutiny. The Court of Justice found that the measure could rely on the ground of public policy, as 'it stems from the need to protect the right to mint coinage which is traditionally regarded as involving the fundamental interests of the State'.[135] More recently, in *Van Gennip*,[136] the Court of Justice upheld a Belgian measure prohibiting the sale of pyrotechnic articles in quantities exceeding one kilogram of pyrotechnic composition unless the consumer held an administrative authorisation. In that case, the Court emphasised

> that pyrotechnic articles are inherently dangerous products since, in particular articles of which the pyrotechnic composition exceeds 1 kg, they can prejudice the safety of persons. [Furthermore] due to their very nature and depending on the circumstances in which they are used, [they] can affect public order.[137]

The measure was therefore justified under the ground of public policy. In contrast, the Court of Justice has been more hesitant to accept this ground when confronted with restrictive measures designed to prevent public disorder or disturbances.[138]

Despite their apparent similarities, the ground of public security has a different scope from public policy. While public policy aims to maintain public order, public security refers to the protection of the State's strategic and vital interests. In *Campus Oil*, referring to the supply of petroleum products as a matter of public security, the Court of Justice emphasised that

[130] ibid.

[131] ibid, para 16.

[132] Case C-121/85 *Conegate* EU:C:1986:114.

[133] ibid, para 16: 'a Member State may not rely on grounds of public morality in order to prohibit the importation of goods from other Member States when its legislation contains no prohibition on the manufacture or marketing of the same goods on its territory'.

[134] Case C-503/03 *Commission v Spain* EU:C:2006:74, para 46; Case C-319/06 *Commission v Luxembourg* EU:C:2008:350, para 50; and Case C-137/17 *Van Gennip and Others* EU:C:2018:771, para 58.

[135] Case C-7/78 *Thompson* EU:C:1979:209, para 34.

[136] Case C-137/17 *Van Gennip and Others* EU:C:2018:771.

[137] ibid, para 59.

[138] Case C-231/83 *Cullet v Leclerc* EU:C:1985:29; and Case C-265/95 *Commission v France* EU:C:1997:595.

> because of their exceptional importance as an energy source in the modern economy, [petroleum products] are of fundamental importance for a country's existence since not only its economy but above all its institutions, its essential public services and even the survival of its inhabitants depend upon them.[139]

The reference to the 'survival of its inhabitants' is a relevant indicator of the interests pursued by a measure based on public security grounds.[140] It is also important to note other provisions in the Treaties that aim to protect the essential security interests of Member States, such as Article 346(1)(b) TFEU, which authorises Member States to 'take such measures as it considers necessary for the protection of the essential interests of its security which are connected with the production of or trade in arms, munitions and war material'.[141]

The protection of the health and life of humans, as well as that of animals and plants, is the most frequently invoked justification. Consistent with the approach to the previous justifications, the case law recognises that Member States have broad discretion when defining the level of protection they wish to ensure for health within their territory. Moreover, there are significant differences among Member States that can lead to varied approaches to the protection of public health, such as climate, demographics, disease patterns or dietary habits.[142] Similarly, in the absence of scientific evidence regarding the potential risks of a product, Member States are entitled, on the basis of the precautionary principle, to introduce restrictive measures on health grounds without waiting for the risks to be fully established.[143] In return, the case law sets a high standard of proof for the Member States, requiring them to provide evidence of genuine public health concerns.[144] For example, in *DocMorris*, the Court of Justice rejected a German measure prohibiting the online sale of medicinal products for human use, both prescription-only and over-the-counter.[145] While the Court of Justice accepted the German Government's arguments with regard to prescription medicines, it did not accept the arguments with regard to other medicinal products. In the case of prescription medicines, Germany successfully justified the ban on public health grounds, such as ensuring the accuracy of the prescription, verifying the purchaser's identity, and addressing the risk of abuse. In addition, the Court accepted that the need for personalised advice by a pharmacist and the problems of comprehension that might arise from selling the product in a language different from that of the patient justified the restriction. These considerations did not apply to other medicinal

[139] Case C-72/83 *Campus Oil* EU:C:1984:256, para 7.

[140] Case C-398/98 *Commission v Greece* EU:C:2001:565; Case C-367/89 *Richardt* EU:C:1991:376; and Case C-70/94 *Werner v Bundesrepublik Deutschland* EU:C:1995:328.

[141] On this provision, see Commission, Interpretive Communication on the application of Article 296 of the Treaty in the field of defence procurement COM (2006) 779 and the case law interpreting the provision, notably the rulings in Case C-414/97 *Commission v Spain* EU:C:1999:417; Case C-273/97 *Sirdar* EU:C:1999:523; Case C-285/98 *Kreil* EU:C:2000:2; Case C-186/01 *Dory* EU:C:2003:146; Case C-239/06 *Commission v Italy* EU:C:2009:784; and Case C-615/10 *Insinööritoimisto InsTiimi* EU:C:2012:324, para 39.

[142] Case C-94/83 *Heijn* EU:C:1984:285, para 16; Case C-54/85 *Ministère public v Mirepoix* EU:C:1986:123, para 15; and Case C-170/04 *Rosengren and Others* EU:C:2007:313, para 48.

[143] Case C-157/96 *The Queen v Ministry of Agriculture, Fisheries and Food and Commissioners of Customs & Excise, ex parte National Farmers' Union and Others* EU:C:1998:191, para 63; Case C-192/01 *Commission v Denmark* EU:C:2003:492, para 47; Case C-236/01 *Monsanto Agricoltura Italia and Others* EU:C:2003:431, para 106; and Case C-319/05 *Commission v Germany* EU:C:2007:678, paras 91–95.

[144] Case C-40/82 *Commission v United Kingdom* EU:C:1984:33, para 38; Case C-90/86 *Zoni* EU:C:1988:403, para 14; Case C-274/87 *Commission v Germany* EU:C:1989:51, paras 7–10; Case C-97/83 *Melkunie BV* EU:C:1984:212, para 14; Case C-473/98 *Kemikalieinspektionen* EU:C:2000:379, para 40; and Case C-333/14 *The Scotch Whisky Association* EU:C:2015:845, paras 34–35.

[145] Case C-322/01 *Deutscher Apothekerverband eV v DocMorris NV* EU:C:2003:664.

products that do not require a prescription,[146] leading the Court of Justice to find the ban disproportionate in respect of the latter category.[147]

Finally, the protection of industrial and commercial property, as a ground invoked by the Member States, raises specific problems. Patents, trademarks, designs, designations of origin, and copyrights are protected under this heading, but it should be noted that their scope is generally limited to the territory of one or several Member States. A patent granted by the German authorities is valid only in the territory of the Federal Republic of Germany or in another Member State that grants an equivalent right within its territory. The territorial scope of these rights sits uncomfortably with the rationale of the free movement of goods, which promotes the free circulation of products even when the host country protects certain goods that enjoy exclusive territorial rights. An approach to balance these two imperatives was adopted in *Deutsche Grammophon*, where the Court of Justice introduced the following criterion:

> Although [the Treaty] permits prohibitions or restrictions on the free movement of products, which are justified for the purpose of protecting industrial and commercial property, Article 36 TFEU only admits derogations from that freedom to the extent to which they are justified for the purpose of safeguarding rights which constitute the specific subject-matter of such property.[148]

According to the case law, the 'specific subject-matter of the property' varies depending on the type of intellectual property right concerned. In the case of patents, it consists of the exclusive right to use an invention with a view to manufacturing industrial products and putting them into circulation for the first time. In the case of trademarks, it is the right to put a product into circulation for the first time bearing the protected mark. In the case of copyright, it is the right to exploit commercially the marketing of the protected work.[149] Exclusivity allows the proprietor to enjoy an exclusive right in the territory where the proprietor enjoys protection and to take legal action in case of infringement. However, this broad protection ends once the proprietor has placed the product on the market of another Member State, thus causing the *exhaustion* of the right. In such a case, the exclusive right loses its effectiveness vis-a-vis the right to free movement. As a result, Article 36 TFEU prevents Member States from banning parallel imports, as once the protection of the title is exhausted, the product can be re-imported into its country of origin.[150] This practice is common in the pharmaceutical sector, where medicines enjoy patent rights, but can also be subject to parallel imports once the protection provided by the patent is exhausted. The same approach also applies in the field of trademarks. [151]

6.4.2. Overriding Reasons in the Public Interest ('Mandatory Requirements')

Cassis de Dijon introduced the principle of mutual recognition, but it also led to the emergence of an additional category of justifications, which do not expand the exhaustive list of grounds in Article 36 TFEU, but instead constitute a distinct, judge-made category of justifications operating alongside Article 36 TFEU. Overriding reasons in the public interest

[146] ibid, paras 106–07.

[147] ibid, paras 117–24.

[148] Case C-78/70 *Deutsche Grammophon v Metro SB* EU:C:1971:59, para 11.

[149] Case C-187/80 *Merck/Stephar and Exler* EU:C:1981:180, para 11.

[150] Case C-104/75 *De Peijper* EU:C:1976:67, paras 24–28; and Case C-10/89 *CNL-SUCAL v HAG* EU:C:1990:359, para 12.

[151] Case C-16/74 *Centrafarm BV and Others v Winthorp BV* EU:C:1974:115, para 8; and Joined Cases C-427/93, C-429/93, and C-436/93 *Bristol-Myers Squibb and Others v Paranova* EU:C:1996:282, para 27.

('mandatory requirements' in the original terminology of the earlier case law) cover a broad range of objectives in support of an overriding general interest. In line with the grounds of justification under of Article 36 TFEU, overriding reasons in the public interest must be interpreted strictly, are subject to the principle of proportionality, and exclude economic motivations. As previously mentioned, these justifications were introduced to allow Member States to justify restrictive, indistinctly applicable measures to free movement. However, the case law has evolved over time, and while some later judgments contain nuanced reasoning, the traditional position is that overriding reasons in the public interest are applicable only to indistinctly applicable MEEs, whereas distinctly applicable measures may only be justified under Article 36 TFEU.

Following the distinction developed by Barnard, overriding reasons in the public interest can be categorised into three groups: those aimed at protecting public goods; those protecting individual interests; and those safeguarding public order.[152]

The first category includes environmental protection,[153] public health,[154] forms of cultural expression,[155] protection of national or regional socio-cultural characteristics,[156] media pluralism,[157] animal welfare,[158] fairness in commercial transactions,[159] and the promotion and protection of the official languages of a Member State.[160]

The second category refers to the protection of individual interests, as long as it is not aimed at safeguarding economic or commercial interests. It includes, inter alia, consumer protection,[161] protection of working conditions,[162] protection of the interests of minors,[163] and road safety.[164]

Third, the maintenance of public order includes the prevention of risks to the financial balance of the social security system,[165] the combating of tax evasion and avoidance,[166] the protection of fundamental rights,[167] and the fight against crime.[168]

[152] C Barnard, *The Substantive Law of the EU. The Four Freedoms*, 8th edn (Oxford University Press, 2025) 174–79.

[153] Case C-302/86 *Commission v Denmark* EU:C:1988:421, para 8; Case C-389/96 *Aher-Waggon GmbH* EU:C:1998:357, para 19; Case C-320/03 *Commission v Austria* EU:C:2005:684, para 35; Case C-242/17 *L.E.G.O.* EU:C:2018:804, paras 64–65; Case C-558/22 *Autorità di Regolazione per Energia Reti e Ambiente (ARERA)* EU:C:2024:209, para 108; and Case C-624/22 *BP France SAS* EU:C:2024:640, para 68.

[154] Case C-178/84 *Commission v Germany* EU:C:1987:126, paras 44–46; Case C-358/95 *Morellato v USL No 11 di Pordenone* EU:C:1997:149, paras 14–15; and Joined Cases C-1/90 and C-176/90 *Aragonesa de Publicidad Exterior y Publivia v Departamento de Sanidad y Seguridad Social de Cataluña* EU:C:1991:327, para 13.

[155] Joined Cases C-60/84 and C-61/84 *Cinéthèque v Fédération nationale des cinémas français* EU:C:1985:329, paras 20–24.

[156] Case C-145/88 *Torfaen Borough Council v B & Q Plc* EU:C:1989:593, para 14.

[157] Case C-368/95 *Vereinigte Familiapress Zeitungsverlags- und Vertriebs GmbH v Bauer Verlag* EU:C:1997:325, para 18.

[158] Case C-219/07 *Nationale Raad van Dierenkwekers in Liefhebbers and Andibel* EU:C:2008:353, para 27; and Case C-142/05 *Mickelsson and Roos* EU:C:2009:336, para 30.

[159] Case C-58/80 *Dansk Supermarked* EU:C:1981:17, para 11.

[160] Case C-15/15 *New Valmar* EU:C:2016:464, para 50.

[161] Case C-120/78 *Rewe v Bundesmonopolverwaltung für Branntwein* EU:C:1979:42, paras 8–12; and Case C-448/98 *Guimont* EU:C:2000:663, para 30.

[162] Case C-155/80 *Oebel* EU:C:1981:177, para 12.

[163] Case C-244/06 *Dynamic Medien* EU:C:2008:85, para 42; and Case C-662/21 *Booky.fi Oy* EU:C:2023:239, para 39.

[164] Case C-54/05 *Commission v Finland* EU:C:2007:168, para 40; Case C-265/06 *Commission v Portugal* EU:C:2008:210, para 36; and Case C-110/05 *Commission v Italy* EU:C:2009:66, para 60.

[165] Case C-120/95 *Decker v Caisse de maladie des employés privés* EU:C:1998:167, paras 39–40.

[166] Case C-823/79 *Carciato* EU:C:1980:230, para 9; Case C-161/09 *Kakavetsos-Fragkopoulos* EU:C:2011:110, para 59; and Case C-456/10 *ANETT* EU:C:2012:241, para 50.

[167] Case C-112/00 *Schmidberger* EU:C:2003:333, para 82; and Case C-36/02 *Omega* EU:C:2004:614, para 37.

[168] Case C-256/06 *Jäger* EU:C:2008:20, para 38.

6.4.3. Proportionality

Once the Member State has successfully invoked a ground of justification under Article 36 TFEU or an overriding reason in the public interest, the next step involves reviewing the national measure in light of the principle of proportionality. This analysis examines the balance between the objectives of general interest pursued by the Member State's measure and the means employed. If the measure is justified on the grounds of public policy, but operates as a total ban, with no exceptions, on an economic activity, it may be contrary to the principle of proportionality. The purpose of the proportionality review is to ensure that any justified restriction is limited to its essential components, avoiding any expansive use of restrictive practices in the Member States.

The principle of proportionality is applied in two steps, known as the suitability and necessity tests. The suitability test requires a logical and consistent link between the objectives of general interest pursued and the contested measure.[169] The necessity test examines whether less restrictive alternative measures are available that would achieve the same objective equally effectively. If such alternatives are equally or more effective than the contested measure in achieving the aims, the restriction will be considered disproportionate.[170] Both tests are carried out separately and sequentially, so that the necessity test will only be conducted once the contested national measure passes the suitability test.

When implementing the principle of proportionality, the burden of proof falls on the Member State,[171] which must provide the appropriate factual and legal evidence to demonstrate the suitability and necessity of the measure.[172] The judicial review of the measure will focus not only on the facts at the time of adoption of the measure (parliamentary debates, explanatory memoranda, and ministerial declarations, etc), but also on relevant elements that shed light on the effects of the measure after its adoption.[173] The context of the measure is particularly important when reviewing its proportionality.[174] However, '[the] burden of proof cannot be so extensive as to require the Member State to prove, positively, that no other conceivable measure could enable that objective to be attained under the same conditions'.[175]

6.4.4. Fundamental Rights

Fundamental rights play a crucial role in free movement rules, particularly at the time of implementing the derogations and justifications outlined above. The Court of Justice confirmed the relevance of fundamental rights in two different situations, both linked to the review of derogations and justifications to restrictive national measures. Firstly, the protection of a fundamental right can serve as a mandatory requirement itself, which the Member State may rely on to justify a restriction. Secondly, the use of derogations and justifications by the Member State must be in conformity with fundamental rights. Each scenario will be examined separately in this section.

A Member State can rely on the protection of a fundamental right to justify a restriction to the free movement of goods. This was confirmed in *Schmidberger*,[176] a case involving the closure

[169] Case C-132/80 *United Foods* EU:C:1981:87, para 28.

[170] Case C-170/04 *Rosengren and Others* EU:C:2007:313, para 50.

[171] Case C-42/02 *Lindman* EU:C:2003:613, para 25; Case C-227/06 *Commission v Belgium* EU:C:2008:160, para 63; Case C-456/10 *ANETT* EU:C:2012:241, para 50; and Case C-110/05 *Commission v Italy* EU:C:2009:66, para 62.

[172] Case C-333/14 *The Scotch Whisky Association* EU:C:2015:845, para 65.

[173] ibid.

[174] ibid, paras 57–58.

[175] Case C-110/05 *Commission v Italy* EU:C:2009:66, para 66.

[176] Case C-112/00 *Schmidberger* EU:C:2003:333.

of the Brenner motorway between Austria and Italy, which significantly affected the flow of goods by road between both countries. The Austrian authorities argued that the closure resulted from a demonstration organised by protesters concerned about the environmental impact of road traffic in the area, authorised under Austrian law. The fundamental right of expression and assembly are enshrined and protected by the Austrian Constitution, and the authorities were compelled to guarantee these rights under national law. When reviewing the restrictive national measure, the Court of Justice clarified what role fundamental rights play as a justification for restricting free movement. The response to this question was articulated as follows:

> [S]ince both the [Union] and its Member States are required to respect fundamental rights, the protection of those rights is a legitimate interest which, in principle, justifies a restriction of the obligations imposed by [Union] law, even under a fundamental freedom guaranteed by the Treaty such as the free movement of goods.[177]

The Court of Justice clarified that the protection of fundamental rights can act as a justification for a restriction of the free movement of goods. For this justification to succeed, the Member State must prove that the fundamental right is recognised and protected within its legal order and forms part of the fundamental rights recognised as general principles of Union law.[178] In some cases, it may be necessary to take into account the unique cultural and historical features that comprise the public policy of a Member State.[179]

The second scenario arises when a Member State invokes a justification other than the protection of a fundamental right. In such cases, the justification must be in conformity with fundamental rights. While in the first scenario the fundamental right serves as the justification itself, in this second scenario the fundamental right acts as a filter for the Member State's alleged justification. This scenario has been referred to as 'the derogation situation', as it requires a review in light of Union fundamental rights whenever a Member State claims that its measures amount to a derogation or a justification for the prohibition to restrict free movement. This situation first arose in *ERT*,[180] a preliminary reference concerning the Greek audiovisual monopoly that granted exclusive rights to the Greek public broadcaster. In this context, the Court of Justice relied on the fundamental right to freedom of expression and information, as recognised in both the European Convention on Human Rights and in Union law, in the following terms:

> [W]here a Member State relies on [freedom of movement] in order to justify rules which are likely to obstruct the exercise of the freedom to provide services, such justification, provided for by [Union] law, must be interpreted in the light of the general principles of law and in particular of fundamental rights. Thus the national rules in question can fall under the exceptions provided for by the [Treaties] only if they are compatible with the fundamental rights the observance of which is ensured by the Court.[181]

In this situation, the fundamental right in question is not the one provided in national law, but the fundamental right enshrined in Union law, specifically in the Charter of Fundamental Rights of the European Union.[182] This distinction is highly relevant, as otherwise fundamental

[177] ibid, para 74.
[178] ibid, paras 71 and 76.
[179] Case C-36/02 *Omega* EU:C:2004:614, paras 37–38.
[180] Case C-260/89 *ERT* EU:C:1991:254.
[181] ibid, para 43.
[182] Case C-441/02 *Commission v Germany* EU:C:2006:253, para 108; Case C-390/12 *Pfleger* EU:C:2014:281, para 57; Case C-98/14 *Berlington Hungary Tanácsadó és Szolgáltatók ft* EU:C:2015:386, para 74; and Case C-201/15 *AGET Iraklis* EU:C:2016:972, para 63.

rights could be used to undermine the primacy of Union law, entitling a Member State to derogate from free movement rules relying on national law. Moreover, *ERT* introduces an additional means of enforcement of Union fundamental rights by introducing a means of review in cases where the only connection with Union law is the Member State's invocation of a ground of justification for a restriction on a Treaty freedom.[183]

7. Legislative Instruments on the Free Movement of Goods

Free movement rules play a relevant role in the absence of Union harmonisation, serving as tools of negative integration that target national measures that undermine the proper functioning of the internal market. Even in the absence of harmonised Union rules governing specific sectors, there are horizontal legislative instruments that underpin the enforcement of the free movement rules provided in the Treaties. These instruments introduce cooperation mechanisms designed to mitigate or prevent the harmful consequences of restrictive national practices. The three main legislative acts that assume such a role are Directive 2015/1535 on technical regulations,[184] Regulation 2019/515 on mutual recognition,[185] and Regulation 2679/98 on the functioning of the internal market.[186] These instruments act as complementary tools to the provisions in Articles 34–36 TFEU, aiming to coordinate actions between the Union (primarily through the actions of the European Commission) and the Member States, thereby avoiding lengthy and costly ex post litigation in both national and Union courts.

7.1. *Directive 2015/1535 on Technical Regulations*

Directive 2015/1535 lays down a framework for administrative cooperation between Member States, coordinated by the Commission, whereby Member States are required to notify 'technical regulations' affecting the 'technical specifications' of products and rules on Information Society services. The notification of the draft technical regulation triggers a procedure whereby the Commission informs the other Member States, and a stand-still period begins in which the Member State proposing the draft is prevented from adopting the measure during a period of three or six months, depending on whether other Member States deliver an opinion stating that the measure may create obstacles to the free movement of goods or to the free provision of Information Society services.[187] The stand-still period can be extended by an additional 12 months 'if, within three months of that date, the Commission announces its intention to propose or adopt a directive, regulation or decision on the matter in accordance with Article 288 TFEU'.[188]

[183] Case C-390/12 *Pfleger* EU:C:2014:281, para 57.

[184] Directive (EU) 2015/1535 of the European Parliament and of the Council of 9 September 2015 laying down a procedure for the provision of information in the field of technical regulations and rules on information society services [2015] OJ L241/1.

[185] Regulation (EU) 2019/515 of the European Parliament and of the Council of 19 March 2019 on the mutual recognition of goods lawfully placed on the market in another Member State and repealing Regulation (EC) No 764/2008 [2019] OJ L91/1.

[186] Council Regulation (EC) No 2679/98 of 7 December 1998 on the functioning of the internal market in relation to the free movement of goods among the Member States [1998] OJ L337/8.

[187] Directive 2015/1535, Art 6(2).

[188] ibid, Art 6(3).

The Directive covers national measures affecting both product requirements and requirements on use. The definitions in Article 1(1)(c)–(d) of the Directive provide several examples of both types of measures. In the case of product requirements, the Directive lists, by way of example,

> levels of quality, performance, safety or dimensions, including the requirements applicable to the product as regards the name under which the product is sold, terminology, symbols, testing and test methods, packaging, marking or labelling and conformity assessment procedures.

In the case of requirements on use, the Directive defines them as follows:

> [A] requirement, other than a technical specification, imposed on a product for the purpose of protecting, in particular, consumers or the environment, and which affects its life cycle after it has been placed on the market, such as conditions of use, recycling, reuse or disposal, where such conditions can significantly influence the composition or nature of the product or its marketing.

The Directive provides both the Commission and the Member States with a valuable source of information on the requirements being developed at the Member State level with a potential to restrict the free movement of goods and services. Although following the stand-still period the Member State can proceed with the enactment of the rule, the Commission will have all the relevant information if it decides to initiate an infringement procedure and bring the case to court. Moreover, undertakings will have access to the observations from other Member States, as a means to prove the existence of doubts over the legality of the national measure.

The Court of Justice has interpreted the Directive in terms that recognise its direct effect if a Member State fails to notify the technical regulation. Following some initial hesitations, the case law confirmed the direct effect of the Directive in *CIA Security*,[189] a ruling with significant practical consequences: if a Member State fails to comply with its duty to notify a draft technical regulation, the national rules, once in force, are unenforceable against private parties. This outcome implies that the technical regulation cannot be relied upon in national courts, as categorically confirmed by the Court of Justice:

> Directive [2015/1535] is to be interpreted as meaning that breach of the obligation to notify renders the technical regulations concerned inapplicable, so that they are unenforceable against individuals.[190]

This outcome results from the existence of a serious procedural defect: the failure to notify a technical regulation. According to the Court of Justice, the breach of this duty to notify affects an 'essential' obligation intended to protect the free movement of goods. As a result:

> The effectiveness of [Union] control will be that much greater if the directive is interpreted as meaning that breach of the obligation to notify constitutes a substantial procedural defect such as to render the technical regulations in question inapplicable to individuals.[191]

The ruling in *CIA Security* is an important contribution to enhancing the effectiveness of Directive 2015/1535, as it encourages Member States to notify draft technical regulations, as failure to do so renders the national rules unenforceable. Despite some initial doubts as to the precise scope of *CIA Security*,[192] recent case law confirms the approach of this ruling and it is currently a settled matter that exerts significant pressure on Member States to ensure

[189] Case C-194/94 *CIA Security International v Signalson and Securitel* EU:C:1996:172.

[190] ibid, para 54.

[191] ibid, para 48.

[192] See Case C-443/98 *Unilever* EU:C:2000:57, Opinion of AG Jacobs, as well as the judgment in Case C-514/19 *Union des industries de la protection des plantes* EU:C:2020:803.

compliance with the Directive.[193] Furthermore, the Court of Justice has stated that the breach of the obligation to notify draft technical regulations constitutes a violation of a 'sufficiently precise provision' for the purposes of claiming damages against the Member State.[194]

7.2. *Regulation 2019/515 on Mutual Recognition*

In addition to the *ex ante* mechanisms in Directive 2015/1535, ex post procedures are made available in Regulation 2019/515, which aims to facilitate the mutual recognition of goods lawfully marketed in another Member State. Unlike Directive 2015/1535, which focuses on the *prevention* of national technical rules in breach of the freedom of movement of goods, Regulation 2019/515 applies where national authorities intend to deny or restrict market access to goods that are lawfully marketed in another Member State on the basis of national product requirements.

Regulation 2019/515 is the result of a lengthy evolution that began with Decision 3052/95/EC,[195] a cooperation mechanism that achieved only modest success. Regulation 764/2008 was introduced subsequently,[196] improving the previous framework until its reform by Regulation 2019/515, which has been applicable since 19 April 2020. This Regulation lays down an obligation on national authorities to contact the economic operator concerned when the authority 'intends to assess goods . . . to establish whether the goods or goods of that type are lawfully marketed in another Member State'.[197] The economic operator has 20 working days to supply a 'voluntary recognition declaration'.[198] The national authority will decide on the matter and, in any event, notify its decision to both the Member States and the Commission. While the procedure outlined in Article 5 is ongoing, the economic operator has the right to continue to market the product in the Member State unless the national authority orders its provisional suspension on grounds of serious risk to public safety or health, or a general ban on the product.

In addition to this system of cooperation, Regulation 2019/515 introduces a dispute settlement mechanism, whereby the Commission is empowered, through the 'SOLVIT procedure', to issue opinions on the conformity of the Member State's decision with Regulation 2019/515 and free movement rules.[199] The Commission's opinion is not legally binding, but it is notified to all the Member States and made public. If the opinion is critical of the Member State's decision, it will have a significant influence if the economic operator chooses to challenge the restrictive measure in a national court. In the same terms as Directive 2015/1535, the provisions of Regulation 2019/515 do not impose substantive prohibitions on the Member States; instead, they provide a cooperation mechanism with tools for both the Commission and economic operators to support them in the proper enforcement of free movement rules.

[193] Case C-443/98 *Unilever* EU:C:2000:496, para 45; Case C-226/97 *Lemmens* EU:C:1998:296, para 33; and Case C-613/14 *James Elliott Construction Limited* EU:C:2016:821, para 64; Case C-604/21 *Vapo Atlantic SA* EU:C:2023:175, para 42; and Case C-120/24 *Unigames* EU:C:2025:174, para 62.

[194] Case C-86/22 *Papier Mettler Italia Srl* EU:C:2023:1023, para 89.

[195] Decision No 3052/95/EC of the European Parliament and of the Council of 13 December 1995 establishing a procedure for the exchange of information on national measures derogating from the principle of the free movement of goods within the Community [1995] OJ L321/1.

[196] Regulation (EC) No 764/2008 of the European Parliament and of the Council of 9 July 2008 laying down procedures relating to the application of certain national technical rules to products lawfully marketed in another Member State and repealing Decision No 3052/95/EC [2008] OJ L218/21.

[197] Regulation 2019/515, Art 5.

[198] ibid, Art 4.

[199] Regulation 2019/515, Art 8.

7.3. *Regulation 2679/98 on the Functioning of the Internal Market*

Following the ruling in *Commission v France* (Spanish strawberries), which expanded the scope of free movement rules to the *failure to act* of a Member State, the Council introduced a legal instrument to promote cooperation and accelerate preventive actions in situations like the one encountered at the French border by the Spanish companies exporting strawberries in the internal market. Regulation 2679/98, also known as the Monti Regulation (after the Commissioner responsible for the internal market at the time), introduces a cooperation procedure between the Commission and the alleged infringing Member State, targeting the actions or inactions of a national authority liable to cause serious disruption to the free movement of goods.

Regulation 2679/98 defines the concept of an 'obstacle' (a stricter and more aggravated concept than a 'restriction' under Articles 34–35 TFEU), as well as of 'inaction'. Article 1(2) closely follows the wording in *Commission v France* and defines 'inaction' in the following terms:

> [T]he term 'inaction' shall cover the case when the competent authorities of a Member State, in the presence of an obstacle caused by actions taken by private individuals, fail to take all necessary and proportionate measures within their powers with a view to removing the obstacle and ensuring the free movement of goods in their territory.

A cooperation procedure is outlined in Articles 4–5, introducing a notification mechanism to the Member State concerned, which is required to take 'all necessary and proportionate measures so that the free movement of goods is assured in the territory of the Member State in accordance with the Treaty', and to inform the Commission of any actions its authorities have taken or intend to take.

In contrast with the Technical Regulations Directive and the Mutual Recognition Regulation, the procedures in Regulation 2679/98 have not been as successful as expected. This may be because the threshold for triggering the Regulation is higher than that of Articles 34-35 TFEU, requiring 'serious disruption' rather than a mere restriction. Member States are also empowered to adopt measures restricting freedom of movement to protect fundamental rights, as recognised in national law.[200] As a result, Member States can justify their conduct relying only on the protection of fundamental rights, which contrasts with the requirements of Articles 34–36 TFEU which also require a proportionality test subject to strict interpretation. Overall, it is more effective for the Commission to make use of the infringement procedure under Article 258 TFEU than to rely on the tools provided by Regulation 2679/98. In fact, the Court of Justice has confirmed that engaging the mechanisms of Regulation 2679/98 is not a precondition which the Commission must satisfy before commencing the pre-litigation procedure under Article 258 TFEU, and that this regulation does not in any way restrict the Commission's powers under Article 258 TFEU.[201] This may have contributed to the modest success of the Regulation, especially when compared with the Commission's frequent use of the infringement procedure under Article 258 TFEU when Member States are involved in unlawful inaction.

GENERAL BIBLIOGRAPHY

Baquero Cruz, J, *Between Competition and Free Movement: The Economic Constitutional Law of the European Community* (Hart, 2002).

[200] Regulation 2679/98, Art 2.

[201] Case C-320/03 *Commission v Austria* EU:C:2005:684, para 35.

Barnard, C, *The Substantive Law of the EU*, 8th edn (Oxford University Press, 2025).
Barnard, C and Scott, J (eds), *The Law of the Single European Market: Unpacking the Premises* (Hart, 2002).
Butler, G, Research Handbook on EEA *Internal Market Law* (Edward Elgar Publishing, 2026).
Caro de Sousa, P, *The European Fundamental Freedoms. A Contextual Approach* (Oxford University Press, 2015).
Egan, M, *Constructing a European Market* (Oxford University Press, 2001).
Garben, S, and Govaere, I (eds), *The Internal Market 2.0* (Hart, 2021).
Lyons, T, *EU Customs Law*, 4th edn (Oxford University Press, 2025).
Maduro, M, *We the Court: The European Court of Justice and the European Economic Constitution* (Hart, 1998).
Majone, G, *Regulating Europe* (Routledge, 1996).
Molle, W, *The Economics of European Integration*, 5th edn (Routledge, 2006).
Ni Chaoimh, E, *The Legislative Priority Rule and the EU Internal Market for Goods: A Constitutional Approach* (Oxford University Press, 2022).
Nic Shuibhne, N, *Regulating the Internal Market* (Edward Elgar, 2006).
Weatherill, S, *The Internal Market as a Legal Concept* (Oxford University Press, 2017).
— 'The Several Internal Markets' (2017) 36 *Yearbook of European Law* 125.
Weimer, M, *Risk Regulation in the Internal Market. Lessons from Agricultural Biotechnology* (Oxford University Press, 2019).
Weiss, F, and Kaupa, C, *European Union Internal Market Law* (Cambridge University Press, 2014).
Zglinski, J, *Europe's Passive Virtues: Deference to National Authorities in EU Free Movement Law* (Oxford University Press, 2020).

FURTHER READING

Basic Features of Free Movement Rules

Dougan, M, 'Minimum Harmonization and the Internal Market' (2000) 37 *Common Market Law Review* 853.
Enchelmaier, S, 'Free Movement of Goods: Evolution and Intelligent Design in the Foundations of the European Union' in P Craig and G de Búrca (eds), *The Evolution of EU Law, 3rd edn* (Oxford University Press, 2021).
Gormley, L, 'Silver Threads among the Gold… 50 Years of the Free Movement of Goods' (2007) 31 *Fordham International Law Journal* 1637.
Gormley, L, *EU Law of Free Movement of Goods and Customs Union* (Oxford University Press, 2009).
Hilson, C, 'Discrimination in Community Free Movement Law' (1999) 24 *European Law Review* 445.
Janssens, C, *The Principle of Mutual Recognition in EU Law* (Oxford University Press, 2013).
Oliver, P and Roth, W-H, 'The Internal Market and the Four Freedoms' (2004) 41 *Common Market Law Review* 407.
Oliver, P (ed), *Free Movement of Goods in the European Union, 5th edn* (Oxford University Press, 2010).
Van den Bogaert, S, 'Horizontality' in C Barnard and J Scott (eds), *The Law of the Single European Market: Unpacking the Premises* (Hart, 2002).
Zglinski, J, 'The End of Negative Market Integration: 60 Years of Free Movement of Goods Litigation (1961–2020)' (2023) 30 *Journal of European Public Policy* 407.

Free Movement of Goods and Fiscal Measures

Banks, K, 'The Application of the Fundamental Freedoms to Member State Tax Measures: Guarding against Protectionism or Second-Guessing National Policy Choices?' (2008) 33 *European Law Review* 482.
Easson, A, 'Fiscal Discrimination: New Perspectives on Article 95 of the EEC Treaty' (1981) 18 *Common Market Law Review* 521.
Snell, J, 'Non-Discriminatory Tax Obstacles in Community Law' (2007) 56 *International and Comparative Law Quarterly* 339.
White, E, 'In Search of the Limits to Article 30 of the EEC Treaty' (1989) 26 *Common Market Law Review* 235.

Quantitative Restrictions and Measures Having an Equivalent Effect

Albors-Llorens, A (ed), *Cassis de Dijon: 40 Years On* (Hart, 2021).

Chalmers, D, 'Repackaging the Internal Market – The Ramifications of the Keck Judgment' (1994) 19 *European Law Review* 385.

Gormley, L, 'Reasoning Renounced? The Remarkable Judgment in Keck and Mithouard' (1994) 5 *European Business Law Review* 63.

Oliver, P, 'Of Trailers and Jet Skis: Is the Case Law on Article 34 TFEU Hurtling in a New Direction?' (2010) 33 *Fordham International Law Journal* 1423.

Sokol, T, 'Public Health Emergencies and Export Restrictions: Solidarity and a Common Approach or Disintegration of the Internal Market' (2020) 57 *Common Market Law Review* 1819.

Spaventa, E, 'Leaving Keck Behind? The Free Movement of Goods after the Rulings in Commission v Italy and Mickelsson and Roos' (2009) 34 *European Law Review* 914.

Stuyck, J, 'The Court of Justice and the Unfair Commercial Practices Directive' (2015) 52 *Common Market Law Review* 721.

Weatherill, S, 'The Principle of Mutual Recognition: It Doesn't Work, Because It Doesn't Exist' (2018) 43 *European Law Review* 224.

Derogations and Justifications

Barnard, C, 'Derogations, Justifications and the Four Freedoms: Is State Interest Really Protected?' in C Barnard and O Odudu (eds), *The Outer Limits of European Union Law* (Hart, 2009).

Huhta, K, 'The Evolution of the Public Security Defence in EU Free Movement Law: Lessons from the Energy Sector' (2023) 25 *Cambridge Yearbook of European Legal Studies* 225.

Nic Shuibhne, N and Masi, M, 'Proving Public Interest: The Growing Impact of Evidence in Free Movement Case Law' (2013) 50 *Common Market Law Review* 965.

Nic Shuibhne, N, Koutrakos, P and Syrpis, P (eds), *Exceptions from EU Free Movement Law: Derogation, Justification and Proportionality* (Hart, 2016).

Spaventa, E, 'On Discrimination and the Theory of Mandatory Requirements' (2001) 3 *Cambridge Yearbook of European Legal Studies* 123.

14

The Internal Market: The Fundamental Freedoms (II)

I. FREEDOM OF ESTABLISHMENT

In an open and competitive internal market, natural and legal persons are free to move, change their place of residence or their registered office subject to the conditions laid down by Union law, or establish secondary establishments. Within the Union's internal market, the freedom of establishment allows self-employed individuals and companies to operate in any Member State on a permanent basis, thus facilitating the provision of services or the sale of goods across one or several Member States. The key factor for the freedom of establishment is the performance of a stable and continuous activity in another Member State. If the self-employed person or company carries out only a temporary activity in another Member State, the case will fall under the provisions on the freedom to provide services.

Besides the freedom of establishment, which has direct effect and is enshrined in Article 49(1) Treaty on the Functioning of the European Union (TFEU), the Treaties lay down legal bases that empower the European Parliament and the Council to adopt directives and regulations through the ordinary legislative procedure, to facilitate the establishment of economic operators in other Member States.[1] Article 50(2) TFEU outlines the objectives of this legislation, which include promoting cooperation between public administrations of the Member States, removing administrative practices that hinder freedom of establishment, and facilitating the establishment of subsidiaries or branches in other Member States.[2] This legal basis does not constitute a general legal basis for the regulation of the financial sector or for intellectual property rights as such, which typically rely on other Treaty provisions, notably Article 114 TFEU or specific sectoral bases.[3]

More specifically, Article 53(1) TFEU introduces an additional legal basis, conferring on the Parliament and the Council the power to adopt directives, under the ordinary legislative procedure, on

[1] Case C-348/22 *Autorità Garante della Concorrenza e del Mercato* EU:C:2023:301, paras 51–58.

[2] Art 50(2)(a)–(h) TFEU.

[3] See, inter alia, Directive 2006/123/EC of the European Parliament and of the Council of 12 December 2006 on services in the internal market [2006] OJ L376/36; Directive (EU) 2017/1132 of the European Parliament and of the Council of 14 June 2017 on certain aspects of company law [2017] OJ L169/46; Directive (EU) 2019/2121 of the European Parliament and of the Council of 27 November 2019 amending Directive (EU) 2017/1132 as regards cross-border conversions, mergers and divisions [2019] OJ L321/1; Directive (EU) 2019/1151 of the European Parliament and of the Council of 20 June 2019 amending Directive (EU) 2017/1132 relating to certain aspects of company law [2019] OJ L186/80; and Directive 2007/36/EC of the European Parliament and of the Council of 11 July 2007 on the exercise of certain rights of shareholders in listed companies [2007] OJ L184/17.

> the mutual recognition of diplomas, certificates and other evidence of formal qualifications and for the coordination of the provisions laid down by law, regulation or administrative action in Member States concerning the taking-up and pursuit of activities as self-employed persons.

This legal basis underpins several legal instruments aimed at facilitating specific professional activities and mobility within the internal market, including directives harmonising the recognition of professional qualifications[4] and directives regulating the financial sector or intellectual property rights.[5]

1. Definition of 'Establishment'

Article 49(1) TFEU enshrines the freedom of establishment for natural and legal persons and specifies the activities protected by the Treaties in the following terms:

> Within the framework of the provisions set out below, restrictions on the freedom of establishment of nationals of a Member State in the territory of another Member State shall be prohibited. Such prohibition shall also apply to restrictions on the setting-up of agencies, branches or subsidiaries by nationals of any Member State established in the territory of any Member State.

The freedom of establishment guarantees that any national of a Member State, whether a natural or legal person, has the right to carry out an economic activity on a *stable and permanent basis* in another Member State. The key defining feature of this freedom is the duration of the activity and the stable, regular presence of the right holder in another Member State. Otherwise, the activity should be regarded as temporary or sporadic, in which case the applicable provision is the freedom to provide services (Article 56 TFEU).

The permanent nature of the activity in another Member State is assessed by focusing on the presence and the connections established within the host Member State, and it is not governed by a minimum fixed period of time. The case law does not provide a single criterion to define a specific degree of permanence, thus requiring a case-by-case evaluation of the activity and the operator's presence in the host Member State. The case law provides criteria in the field of services that define the 'temporary' nature of an economic activity, which, *a contrario senso*, clarifies the definition of a permanent activity in another Member State:

> [T]he temporary nature of the activities in question has to be determined in the light, not only of the duration of the provision of the service, but also of its regularity, periodicity or continuity. The fact that the provision of services is temporary does not mean that the provider of services within the meaning of the Treaty may not equip himself with some form of infrastructure in the host Member State (including an office, chambers or consulting rooms) in so far as such infrastructure is necessary for the purposes of performing the services in question.[6]

In the case of natural persons (the self-employed), permanent presence is primarily determined by the individual's physical presence, for which the place of permanent residence can be

[4] See Directive 2005/36/EC of the European Parliament and of the Council of 7 September 2005 on the recognition of professional qualifications [2005] OJ L255/22.

[5] See, inter alia, Directive (EU) 2019/790 of the European Parliament and of the Council of 17 April 2019 on copyright and related rights in the Digital Single Market [2019] OJ L130/92; Directive (EU) 2016/97 of the European Parliament and of the Council of 20 January 2016 on insurance distribution [2016] OJ L26/19; Directive 2014/65/EU of the European Parliament and of the Council of 15 May 2014 on markets in financial instruments [2014] OJ L173/349.

[6] Case C-55/94 *Gebhard v Consiglio dell'Ordine degli Avvocati e Procuratori di Milano* EU:C:1995:411, para 27. In the same vein, see the judgments in Case C-63/86 *Commission v Italy* EU:C:1988:9, para 29; Case C-298/99 *Commission v Italy* EU:C:2002:194, para 56; Case C-215/01 *Schnitzer* EU:C:2003:662, paras 31–32; Case C-456/02 *Trojani* EU:C:2004:488, para 28; Case C-134/05 *Commission v Italy* EU:C:2007:435, para 43; and Case C-404/05 *Commission v Germany* EU:C:2007:723, para 34.

decisive. In the case of legal persons, it is possible, as will be explained below, for permanent presence to materialise through a transfer of the registered office, central administration or principal place of business to another Member State, or through presence in another Member State by way of a secondary establishment, such as an agency, branch or subsidiary. Once this permanent presence in the host Member State occurs, Article 49 TFEU prohibits the host Member State from introducing discriminatory measures or non-discriminatory restrictions that hinder or render less attractive the exercise of the freedom of establishment.

2. Right Holders

Article 49(2) TFEU distinguishes between two types of beneficiaries of the freedom of establishment: self-employed natural persons; and legal persons. In the case of self-employed natural persons, they must hold the nationality of a Member State and intend to conduct an economic activity in another Member State on a stable and continuous basis. In the case of legal persons, the means of incorporation is irrelevant, as the decisive criterion is that the legal person be constituted in accordance with the law of a Member State and engaged in an economic activity.

The case law of the Court of Justice defines a self-employed person as any natural person who carries out an economic activity outside any relationship of subordination to another natural or legal person.[7] Economic activity is not constrained to the categories of professions legally recognised in each Member State. In *Jany*, the Court of Justice ruled that prostitution constituted an economic activity within the scope of Article 49 TFEU, despite the activity being prohibited in several Member States, as long as it is exercised on a self-employed basis, voluntarily and outside any relationship of subordination.[8]

Legal persons engaged in economic activities are also entitled to freedom of establishment, regardless of their corporate form. Article 54, second paragraph, TFEU defines 'companies or firms' as 'companies or firms constituted under civil or commercial law, including cooperative societies, and other legal persons governed by public or private law, save for those which are non-profit-making'. Therefore, a foundation, an association, or bodies representative of economic activities (such as a Bar association), to the extent that they are involved in the sale of goods or services in the market in return for remuneration, enjoy the protections of Article 49 TFEU.[9] Consequently, entities that are genuinely non-profit making are excluded from the scope of Article 54 TFEU and thus from the assimilation with nationals of Member States for the purposes of the freedom of establishment, although such entities may, depending on the circumstances, still fall within the scope of other Treaty freedoms where they engage in

[7] Case C-107/94 *Asscher* EU:C:1996:251, paras 25–26; Case C-268/99 *Jany and Others* EU:C:2001:616, para 34; and Joined Cases C-151/04 and C-152/04 *Nadin and Nadin-Lux* EU:C:2005:775, para 31.

[8] *Jany* (n 7) para 70: 'prostitution is being carried on by the person concerned in a self-employed capacity [when the following conditions] are satisfied . . .: outside any relationship of subordination concerning the choice of that activity, working conditions and conditions of remuneration; under that person's own responsibility; and in return for remuneration paid to that person directly and in full'.

[9] Case C-113/13 *Azienda sanitaria locale n 5 'Spezzino' and Others (ANPAS)* EU:C:2014:2440, paras 62–65. If the entity carries out economic activities on an incidental and residual basis, it will be considered to be non-profit-making and excluded from the scope of Art 49 TFEU. However, when the economic activity acquires autonomous relevance, Art 49 TFEU is applicable to the case. This requires a case-by-case analysis, as reflected in *ANPAS*, where the Court of Justice reviewed an entity's cost reimbursement scheme to verify whether the activity was profit-driven or not: 'As regards the reimbursement of costs, it must be ensured that profit making, even indirect, cannot be pursued under the cover of a voluntary activity and that volunteers may be reimbursed only for expenditure actually incurred for the activity performed, within the limits laid down in advance by the associations themselves' (para 62). See also Case C-50/14 *CASTA and Others* EU:C:2016:56, paras 74–78.

economic activities. This provision must be interpreted restrictively, and the mere fact that an entity is formally constituted as non-profit-making does not automatically trigger the exclusion in Article 54(2) TFEU, so that each situation requires a careful assessment of the nature of the entity and the activity concerned.[10]

3. Cross-border Link

The freedom of establishment applies solely to natural and legal persons conducting an economic activity 'in the territory of another Member State'. The reference to another Member State introduces the requirement of a cross-border link, as an essential prerequisite to rely on Article 49 TFEU. The Court of Justice has interpreted this requirement broadly, aiming to expand the scope of the provision to cover the widest possible range of national restrictive measures that obstruct the freedom of establishment.

Article 49 TFEU is addressed to both the host Member State and the Member State of origin. In the case of the latter, Article 49 TFEU targets situations in which domestic authorities make it difficult for an economic operator to *exit* the Member State of origin in order to establish itself in another Member State within the internal market. Article 49 TFEU also applies to situations of *return*, where a self-employed natural person or a legal person (more often the former), having exercised the freedom of establishment in another Member State, returns to their Member State of nationality and faces restrictions that hinder or make less attractive the return. The ruling in *Knoors*[11] provides relevant guidance in this regard:

> Although it is true that the provisions of the Treaty relating to establishment and the provision of services cannot be applied to situations which are purely internal to a Member State, the position nevertheless remains that the reference in Article [49] to 'nationals of a Member State' who wish to establish themselves 'in the territory of another Member State' cannot be interpreted in such a way as to exclude from the benefit of [Union] law a given Member State's own national when the latter, owing to the fact that they have lawfully resided on the territory of another Member State and have there acquired a trade qualification which is recognized by the provisions of [Union] law, are, with regard to their State of origin, in a situation which may be assimilated to that of any other persons enjoying the rights and liberties guaranteed by the Treaty.[12]

Despite the broad scope given to this freedom, there are some limitations to the expansive interpretation of the cross-border link. There is no such link in cases where a natural self-employed person or a legal person establishes itself in another territory within the same Member State. For instance, the obstacles faced by self-employed persons in Belgium when relocating their place of establishment from one region to another within Belgium did not satisfy the requirement of a cross-border link as defined by Article 49 TFEU.[13] The Court of Justice has clarified that the fact that Article 26(2) TFEU provides that the internal market is 'an area without internal frontiers' cannot be interpreted as meaning that such frontiers include 'frontiers' or territorial demarcations *within* a Member State.[14]

[10] In this respect, see Case C-70/95 *Sodemare and Others v Regione Lombardia* EU:C:1997:301, para 33, on the powers of Member States to limit certain services to the requirement that the provider be a non-profit.

[11] Case C-115/78 *Knoors v Staatssecretaris van Economische Zaken* EU:C:1979:31.

[12] ibid, para 24. In the same vein, see Case C-19/92 *Kraus v Land Baden-Württemberg* EU:C:1993:125, para 15; and Case C-234/97 *Fernández de Bobadilla* EU:C:1999:367, para 30.

[13] However, the Advocate General was of the opposite opinion and considered that the case came within the scope of free movement rules. See the Opinion of Advocate General Sharpston in Case C-212/06 *Gouvernement de la Communauté française and Gouvernement wallon* EU:C:2008:398, pts 128–29.

[14] Case C-212/06 *Gouvernement de la Communauté française and Gouvernement wallon* EU:C:2008:178, paras 39–40.

4. Legal Persons

4.1. *Legal Framework*

The Treaties lay down the conditions under which the freedom of establishment applies to legal persons. Firstly, Article 49(1) TFEU states that the freedom of establishment in another Member State 'shall also apply to restrictions on the setting-up of agencies, branches or subsidiaries by nationals of any Member State established in the territory of any Member State'. Secondly, the provision introduces, in its second paragraph, the scope of the right of establishment:

> Freedom of establishment shall include the right to take up and pursue activities as self-employed persons and to set up and manage undertakings, in particular companies or firms within the meaning of the second paragraph of Article 54, under the conditions laid down for its own nationals by the law of the country where such establishment is effected, subject to the provisions of the Chapter relating to capital.

Article 54 TFEU elaborates on the definition of a 'company or firm' for the purposes of freedom of establishment, as applied to legal persons:

> Companies or firms formed in accordance with the law of a Member State and having their registered office, central administration or principal place of business within the Union shall, for the purposes of this Chapter, be treated in the same way as natural persons who are nationals of Member States.
>
> 'Companies or firms' means companies or firms constituted under civil or commercial law, including cooperative societies, and other legal persons governed by public or private law, save for those which are non-profit-making.

To facilitate the mobility of companies incorporated in a Member State, the Union legislator adopted several acts of secondary legislation, including Directive 2019/2121, which introduces a harmonised framework for cross-border conversions, mergers, and divisions.[15] This Directive reflects and builds upon key developments in the case law of the Court of Justice, while also introducing new harmonised rules aimed at balancing corporate mobility with the protection of stakeholders, which will be discussed below.

4.2. *Content of the Right*

Company mobility is an essential aspect of the internal market. Without the possibility for companies to move between Member States, whether by setting up secondary establishments or transferring their registered office, the freedom of establishment of companies would be meaningless. In addition, the mobility of legal persons must be reconciled with the interests of third parties, in particular creditors, workers and minority shareholders. It is this balance between guaranteeing and promoting mobility while safeguarding third parties' interests that is reflected in the case law of the Court of Justice, to which reference is made below.

To clarify the scope of the rights conferred by the freedom of establishment on legal persons, it is important to distinguish among the three stages in which a company can exercise this freedom: the moment of departure from the Member State of origin (section 4.2.1); the moment of entry into the host Member State (section 4.2.2); and the development of the activity once the establishment has taken place (section 4.2..3).

[15] Directive (EU) 2019/2121 of the European Parliament and of the Council of 27 November 2019 amending Directive (EU) 2017/1132 as regards cross-border conversions, mergers and divisions [2019] OJ L321/1.

4.2.1. Right of Departure

Article 49 TFEU guarantees the right of companies or firms to leave their Member State of origin and transfer their registered office to another Member State, subject to the conditions laid down by Union law and, in the absence of harmonisation, to the connecting factors defined by the law of the Member State of origin. Obstacles created by a Member State to discourage the mobility of a legal person amount to a restriction on the freedom of establishment, a principle that has progressively emerged in the case law, although it was not yet fully recognised at the time of the judgment in *Daily Mail*:

> Even though [the provisions of the Treaty] are directed mainly to ensuring that foreign nationals and companies are treated in the host Member State in the same way as nationals of that State, they also prohibit the Member State of origin from hindering the establishment in another Member State of one of its nationals or of a company incorporated under its legislation which comes within the definition contained in Article [54 TFEU]. As the Commission rightly observed, the rights guaranteed by Articles [49 TFEU] et seq would be rendered meaningless if the Member State of origin could prohibit undertakings from leaving in order to establish themselves in another Member State.[16]

The laws of the Member States differ significantly in defining the link between a company and its Member State of incorporation. In some Member States, for a company to be governed by the law of that state requires both the registered office and the central administration of the company to be located in the territory of the Member State (the *real seat* theory). In other Member States, it is sufficient for a company to have its registered office within their territory (and not its central administration) for it to hold nationality (the *incorporation* theory). In Member States operating under the real seat theory, if a company chooses to transfer its central administration to another Member State, it may lose its legal personality under the law of the Member State of origin, effectively requiring dissolution and re-incorporation in the host Member State. This requirement may discourage company mobility within the internal market and may constitute a restriction on the company's freedom of establishment, even though, at least at the time of *Daily Mail*, the Court of Justice accepted that, in the absence of Union harmonisation, the Member State of origin could determine the conditions under which a company retains its legal personality when it seeks to transfer its seat to another Member State.

The Court of Justice was initially reluctant to question real seat regimes that required companies to be dissolved and re-incorporated upon the transfer of their central administration to another Member State. This stance is clearly seen in the first significant ruling on the matter, delivered in *Daily Mail*. An investment company established in the UK, Daily Mail, sought to transfer its central management and control to the Netherlands before a significant asset sale to avoid UK capital gains tax on the transaction, which was more onerous than the Dutch tax regime. Daily Mail intended to keep its registered office in the United Kingdom, a choice that, in principle, was permitted under UK law but required prior consent of the Treasury under UK tax legislation. The Court of Justice examined whether a legal person has the right to transfer its central management and control to another Member State while retaining its legal personality under the law of its Member State of incorporation, pointing first to the diversity of company law across Member States[17] and second to the need for Union legislation or agreements to address the limitations of company mobility that that diversity gave rise to.[18] Taking these features into account, the Court of Justice concluded as follows:

[16] Case C-81/87 *The Queen v Treasury and Commissioners of Inland Revenue, ex parte Daily Mail and General Trust PLC* EU:C:1988:456, para 16.

[17] ibid, para 20.

[18] ibid, paras 21–22.

> Articles [49 and 54 TFEU] of the Treaty cannot be interpreted as conferring on companies incorporated under the law of a Member State a right to transfer their central management and control and their central administration to another Member State while retaining their status as companies incorporated under the legislation of the first Member State.[19]

This approach has evolved significantly over the years. In 2017, in *Polbud*,[20] the Court of Justice summarised its case law to date, illustrating how much it had developed since *Daily Mail*. The facts of *Polbud* involved a cross-border conversion of a Polish company that aimed to transfer its registered office to Luxembourg, while maintaining its principal place of business in Poland. In order to be able to cancel the company's registration in the Polish commercial register, Polish law required the prior liquidation of the company. This step involved liquidating the company as a preliminary step to its conversion into a Luxembourg company. Using a more expansive approach than in *Daily Mail*, the Court observed that Polbud sought to establish itself in Luxembourg under Luxembourg company law, which allowed a company to have its registered office in Luxembourg and its principal place of business in another Member State.[21] The Court further emphasised that Member States may not introduce general presumptions of fraud or abuse in a way that, as an unsubstantiated precaution, results in the adoption of highly restrictive measures, such as the liquidation of the company prior to the exercise of its right to freedom of establishment.[22] While nothing prevents Polish authorities from examining, in individual cases, whether the cross-border conversion constitutes an abuse of law, such analysis must be conducted on a case-by-case basis, not by means of general presumptions that discourage freedom of movement.[23] In the case at hand, the Court of Justice ruled that the Polish legislation was contrary to the freedom of establishment, as it introduced a disproportionate measure in light of the objectives pursued.

The same approach applies when the Member State of origin restricts a company's right to establish a subsidiary or branch in another Member State. In contrast with cases of conversion, the creation of secondary establishments, a widespread practice in corporate life, has met with less resistance in the Member States.[24] However, where the secondary establishment is used to circumvent the legislation of the Member State of origin, legitimate doubts may arise regarding its protection under the Treaty. This was the case in *Centros*,[25] where two Danish nationals incorporated a company in the UK with a branch in Denmark for the sole purpose of benefiting from the UK's rules on incorporation, which were more favourable (and less costly) than the Danish rules.

In *Centros*, the Court of Justice introduced an important distinction between national company law rules on incorporation and measures for the protection of a company's creditors. It ruled that a Member State may not refuse to register a branch of a company lawfully formed in another Member State on the ground that the company was formed there solely in order to circumvent the more restrictive rules of the Member State in which the branch is to be established. Therefore, insofar as the United Kingdom allowed the incorporation of companies whose operations are conducted entirely through branches in other Member States, the Danish authorities were not entitled to restrict the freedom of establishment by refusing to register the branch. Consequently, nationals of a Member State who form a

[19] ibid, para 24.
[20] Case C-106/16 *Polbud – Wykonawstwo sp z oo*. EU:C:2017:804.
[21] ibid, para 35.
[22] ibid, para 63.
[23] ibid, para 64.
[24] Case C-200/98 *X and Y* EU:C:1999:566, and Case C-276/22 *Edil Work 2* EU:C:2024:348, paras 30–34.
[25] Case C-212/97 *Centros* EU:C:1999:126.

company in another Member State and then establish a branch in their Member State of origin do not abuse Article 49 TFEU, as they are simply exercising the rights conferred by the Treaty. However, the Court of Justice added an important nuance, noting that, to ensure compliance with (in this case, Danish) rules on the protection of shareholders and creditors, Danish authorities are entitled to adopt

> any appropriate measure for preventing or penalising fraud, either in relation to the company itself, if need be in cooperation with the Member State in which it was formed, or in relation to its members, where it has been established that they are in fact attempting, by means of the formation of a company, to evade their obligations towards private or public creditors established in the territory of the Member State concerned.[26]

The judgment in *Centros* illustrates what has been described as a case of regulatory arbitrage in company law, whereby Member States may compete to attract investment and business activity by adopting more favourable corporate legal frameworks. The Court of Justice does not oppose this outcome, provided it does not lead to a deregulatory race to the bottom that compromises the protection of third parties or creditors through fraudulent practices.[27] When there is a risk of harm, Member States are entitled to introduce measures to ensure compliance with the rules on the protection of third-party interests.[28] Therefore, while rules on the incorporation of legal persons may be subject to regulatory competition, this does not extend to rules that safeguard third-party interests. The outcome is a framework in which regulatory competition coexists with the obligation to protect third-party interests and other operators in the internal market.

4.2.2. The Right of Entry: Subsidiaries, Branches and Agencies

Article 49, first paragraph TFEU precludes Member States from introducing restrictions on the setting up of agencies, branches, or subsidiaries by nationals of any Member State established in the territory of any Member State. The aim of this provision is to promote the exchange of goods and services between Member States through the creation of secondary establishments in several Member States. The extent to which the Member States of origin can restrict this right was discussed above. This section examines the measures taken by the *host* Member State that effectively restrict the expansion of a company from another Member State.

The reference to agencies, branches or subsidiaries is a non-exhaustive enumeration of the forms that an undertaking wishing to operate in another Member State may adopt.[29] This flexible approach is reflected in the case law as follows:

> [T]he concept of branch, agency or other establishment implies a place of business which has the appearance of permanency, such as the extension of a parent body, has a management and is materially equipped to negotiate business with third parties so that the latter, although knowing that there will if necessary be a legal link with the parent body, the head office of which is abroad, do not have to deal directly with such parent body but may transact business at the place of business constituting the extension.[30]

Since the 1970s, the Court of Justice has repeatedly held that Member States may not require an undertaking to transfer its principal place of business into their territory as a condition for conducting an economic activity. Such a requirement would amount to 'the very negation' of

[26] ibid, paras 24 and 39.
[27] Case C-276/22 *Edil Work 2* EU:C:2024:348, paras 45–49.
[28] See also, to this effect, the judgment in Case C-594/14 *Kornhaas* EU:C:2015:806.
[29] Case C-205/84 *Commission v Germany* EU:C:1986:463, para 21.
[30] Case C-33/78 *Somafer SA v Saar-Ferngas AG* EU:C:1978:205, para 12.

freedom of establishment.[31] Therefore, a Member State cannot prevent, save where justified by overriding reasons of public interest and subject to proportionality, access to its territory through a branch rather than a subsidiary.[32] While Member States may require the company to maintain a 'permanent' presence within their territory, the particular form of this presence cannot be limited to a specific type of corporate form.[33] For instance, a Member State may not make an employee's right to join a national social security system conditional upon the employer, which enjoys freedom of establishment, operating through a specific legal form imposed by the host Member State.[34]

4.2.3. The Right to Pursue an Activity in the Host Member State

Once the company or firm is established in the host Member State, it must receive treatment equal to that afforded to other local companies or firms engaged in the same economic activity. Freedom of establishment grants rights not only during the entry, exit, and return of the company or firm, but also *during the pursuit of an economic activity* in another Member State.

There are numerous examples of protectionism of local economic activity in a host Member State, but a field in which multiple restrictions have been found is taxation, especially direct taxation. The Court of Justice has developed an extensive body of case law in this domain in an attempt to reconcile the fiscal sovereignty of Member States to tax economic activities within their territory with the rights of natural and legal persons to move freely within the internal market.

As a matter of principle, it is clear that taxation, insofar as it involves a forceful transfer of private wealth to the state as a result of carrying out an economic activity, has the potential to restrict freedom of establishment. For this reason, the Court of Justice has carefully recognised and confirmed the power of Member States to tax the profits generated by an economic activity carried out in their territory, provided that the tax regime is non-discriminatory and applies on equal terms to local natural and legal persons.[35] This approach has led the case law to focus particularly on the comparability between local operators and those from other Member States exercising freedom of establishment, having regard to the objective pursued by the national tax measure at issue. Such cases often arise in the taxation of multinational groups, comprising several companies domiciled in several Member States, but with a single centre of operations where the group's main establishment is located.

For example, a group of companies ('Z') has its parent company and subsidiaries in Member State A. Another group of companies ('Y') has its parent company in Member State A and a subsidiary in Member State B. National tax legislation allows groups of companies to

[31] Case C-39/75 *Coenen v Sociaal Economische Raad* EU:C:1975:162, para 6; Case C-76/81 *Transporoute v Ministère des Travaux Publics* EU:C:1982:49; and Case C-205/84 *Commission v Germany* EU:C:1986:463, para 52.

[32] Case C-101/94 *Commission v Italy* EU:C:1996:221, para 21; Case C-338/09 *Yellow Cab Verkehrsbetrieb* EU:C:2010:814, para 34; and Case C-563/17 *Associação Peço a Palavra and Others* EU:C:2019:144, paras 59–61.

[33] *Yellow Cab* (n 32) para 34.

[34] Case C-79/85 *Segers v Bedrijfsvereniging voor Bank- en Verzekeringswezen, Groothandel en Vrije Beroepen* EU:C:1986:308, para 15: 'It is established that entitlement to reimbursement of sickness costs pertains to a person and not to a company. However, the requirement that a company formed in accordance with the law of another Member State must be accorded the same treatment as national companies means that the employees of that company must have the right to be affiliated to a specific social security scheme. Discrimination against employees in connection with social security protection indirectly restricts the freedom of companies of another Member State to establish themselves through an agency, branch or subsidiary in the Member state concerned.'

[35] Case C-250/95 *Futura Participations and Singer v Administration des contributions* EU:C:1997:239, para 22; Case C-446/03 *Marks & Spencer* EU:C:2005:763, paras 31–35; Case C-446/04 *Test Claimants in the FII Group Litigation* EU:C:2006:774, para 167; Case C-337/08 X *Holding* EU:C:2010:89, para 20; Joined Cases C-398/16 and C-399/16 *X and X* EU:C:2018:110, para 20; Case C-484/19 *Lexel* EU:C:2021:34, para 34; and C-340/22 *Cofidis* EU:C:2023:1019, paras 40–46.

be taxed on a consolidated basis in the Member State where the parent is resident, in this case Member State A. However, under Article 49 TFEU, subject to an assessment of comparability in light of the aim of the national tax measures, both groups may be in a comparable situation and their only difference – the fact that the subsidiaries operate in different Member States – may not suffice to change the comparability of their situation vis-à-vis the tax authorities. Therefore, Member State A cannot introduce a more favourable tax regime to group Z solely because its subsidiaries are domiciled in the same Member State. If Member State A were to apply discriminatory tax treatment between the two groups, its tax rules would amount to a restriction on group Y's freedom of establishment. Otherwise, Member States would create tax incentives for companies *not* to exercise freedom of establishment and retain their entire activity in Member State A, an outcome that is incompatible with the aims of the internal market.

The case law on direct taxation has met with considerable resistance from the Member States. However, the Court of Justice, with some hesitations over time, has taken a strict approach towards discriminatory tax treatment in the Member States. The problem posed by this approach is that tax law, by its very nature, frequently distinguishes between resident and non-resident taxpayers, as all tax systems have specific provisions on the tax treatment of non-resident natural and legal persons. Taking the argument to its extreme, it could be argued that all tax regimes applicable only to non-resident natural or legal persons breach the freedom of establishment, a conclusion that is obviously absurd. It is for this reason that, in addition to introducing a criterion based on the comparability between resident and non-resident taxpayers, the case law has developed specific justifications for cases of direct taxation, particularly when Member States introduce measures aimed at combating tax avoidance or aggressive tax planning. Member States may adopt more restrictive measures when it is confirmed that an economic operator has entered into a 'wholly artificial arrangement which does not reflect economic reality, aimed at circumventing the application of the legislation of the Member State concerned', the sole purpose of which is to obtain more favourable tax treatment.[36] According to settled case law:

> Whilst the pursuit by a taxpayer of the tax regime most favourable for him cannot, as such, set up a general presumption of fraud or abuse . . . the fact remains that such a taxpayer cannot enjoy a right or advantage arising from EU law where the transaction at issue is purely artificial, lacks economic substance and is designed to circumvent the application of the legislation of the Member State concerned.[37]

The burden of proof of a fraudulent or abusive practice falls upon the Member State, and to date the case law requires a high standard of proof. As previously explained, a general presumption of fraud or abuse is a disproportionate measure and cannot justify a restriction on the freedom of establishment.

5. Discrimination and the Market Access Test: *CaixaBank*

The wording of Article 49, first paragraph TFEU, explicitly prohibits any discrimination against an operator seeking access to another Member State or already present in that Member

[36] Case C-196/04 *Cadbury Schweppes and Cadbury Schweppes Overseas* EU:C:2006:544, para 51; Case C-255/02 *Halifax and Others* EU:C:2006:121, paras 74–75; and Case C-524/04 *Test Claimants in the Thin Cap Group Litigation* EU:C:2007:161, para 83.

[37] Case C-116/16 *T Danmark* EU:C:2019:135, para 81; and Case C-115/16 *N Luxembourg 1* EU:C:2019:134, para 109. See also Case C-196/04 *Cadbury Schweppes and Cadbury Schweppes Overseas* EU:C:2006:544, paras 50–51; Case C-371/10 *National Grid Indus* EU:C:2011:785, para 84; Case C-464/14 *SECIL* EU:C:2016:896, para 60; and Case C-322/11 *K* EU:C:2013:716, para 61.

State. It is therefore unsurprising that the case law employs a test of both direct and indirect discrimination to identify measures that restrict the freedom of establishment. There are numerous examples of Member States discriminating against economic operators from other Member States who have entered the local market. For instance, legislation that makes the issuance of a licence conditional on a minimum percentage of shareholders being nationals of the host Member State is a discriminatory measure restrictive of the freedom of establishment.[38]

By its very nature, the freedom of establishment also involves a test based on the terms of access to the market rather than solely on discriminatory practices. This applies clearly to national measures that target the exit from the Member State, where it is difficult to find a comparable domestic situation. In such cases, the discrimination test is not a sufficiently effective tool, thereby opening the door to other means of review based on market access criteria. It is not a coincidence that it was precisely in the context of Article 49 TFEU and the freedom of establishment that the Court of Justice applied and developed the 'market access test', which was discussed in chapter thirteen in the area of freedom of movement of goods.

The market access test was articulated in general terms in *Gebhard*,[39] a case concerning the freedom of establishment of self-employed natural persons, which will be discussed in more detail in section I.6.3 of this chapter. The market access test has also been extended to the activity of legal persons, as confirmed in *CaixaBank*.[40] In this case, a Spanish bank established a subsidiary in France to enter the French retail banking market. At the time, French legislation applicable to all credit institutions prohibited the payment of remuneration of sight accounts. This measure prevented *CaixaBank* from offering an attractive product to potential new customers in the French market, even though it applied to all banks on an equal footing. In its reasoning, the Court of Justice noted the following:

> That prohibition hinders credit institutions which are subsidiaries of foreign companies in raising capital from the public, by depriving them of the possibility of competing more effectively, by paying remuneration on sight accounts, with the credit institutions traditionally established in the Member State of establishment, which have an extensive network of branches and therefore greater opportunities than those subsidiaries for raising capital from the public.

Where credit institutions which are subsidiaries of foreign companies seek to enter the market of a Member State, competing by means of the rate of remuneration paid on sight accounts constitutes one of the most effective methods to that end. Access to the market by those establishments is thus made more difficult by such a prohibition.[41]

This line of reasoning contributed to the development of a market access test that assesses the restrictive potential of a national measure based on its effect on the ability of economic operators from other Member States to access the local market. Consequently, restrictions on the freedom of establishment also encompass any measures that 'prohibit, impede or render less attractive the exercise of that freedom'.[42]

At present, the market access test is the main standard of review for Member State actions under Article 49 TFEU. An important exception exists in the realm of direct taxation, as noted in section I.4.2.3 of this chapter. When reviewing the restrictive impact of national direct tax

[38] Case C-270/83 *Commission v France* EU:C:1986:37, para 18, and Case C-3/88 *The Queen v Ministry of Agriculture, Fisheries and Food, ex parte Agegate* EU:C:1989:650.

[39] Case C-55/94 *Gebhard v Consiglio dell'Ordine degli Avvocati e Procuratori di Milano* EU:C:1995:411.

[40] Case C-442/02 *CaixaBank France* EU:C:2004:586.

[41] ibid, paras 13–14.

[42] *CaixaBank France* (n 40) para 11; Case C-298/05 *Columbus Container Services* EU:C:2007:754, para 34; Case C-157/07 *Krankenheim Ruhesitz am Wannsee-Seniorenheimstatt GmbH* EU:C:2008:588, para 30; and Case C-96/08 *CIBA* EU:C:2010:185, para 19.

measures, the Court of Justice uses a criterion of comparability between the situation of the resident undertaking and that of the undertaking exercising its freedom of establishment in another Member State. In the absence of comparability, the national tax measure is not considered to constitute a restriction, and Article 49 TFEU does not apply, and the direct tax measure is not subject to the freedom of establishment. This approach has faced criticism, most notably from Advocate General Bobek in the case of *Hornbach*,[43] but it remains a well-established position in the case law, and it is revealing of the way in which the Court of Justice maintains a certain degree of deference towards the Member States in a highly sensitive policy area.

6. Self-employed Natural Persons

6.1. *Legal Framework*

Economically active natural persons who pursue an activity on a self-employed basis, outside any relationship of subordination, are also protected by the freedom of establishment. This includes self-employed individuals, who are beneficiaries of Article 49 TFEU and other secondary legislation that regulate the conditions under which self-employed persons acquire legal residence in the host Member State, as well as legislation on the recognition of their professional qualifications.

The requirements imposed on the self-employed to access legal residence in another Member State are outlined in Directive 2004/38,[44] which sets out the rights and obligations of the self-employed and their families insofar as they are Union citizens exercising free movement, for the duration of their economic activity. Directive 2004/38, further elaborated in chapter six of this book, addresses the situation of all natural persons exercising free movement and provides a common framework applicable to self-employed persons, service providers, workers, and economically inactive persons.

Self-employed natural persons can conduct professional activities subject to certain qualifications and experience. This applies, among others, to doctors, lawyers or pharmacists – professionals who have completed higher education studies and are admitted to a professional body in a Member State – subject to compulsory requirements of access that pave the way to that profession. To support and facilitate the movement of these professionals within the internal market, several directives were initially adopted for specific professions (nurses, doctors, dentists, veterinarians, and lawyers, although the latter initially only for services, not establishment). In the 1990s, a directive was introduced to simplify the recognition of professional titles for the remaining regulated professions. These instruments of secondary Union law are described in further detail in section I.8.2 of this chapter.

6.2. *Content of the Right*

Article 49 TFEU grants self-employed natural persons the right to exit their Member State of origin and to access and carry out their professional activities in another Member State. Unlike legal persons, whose existence is a creation of law, natural persons are physical individuals, not a legal fiction (as in the case of a company or a firm). Consequently, Article 49 TFEU applies

[43] Case C-382/16 *Hornbach-Baumarkt* EU:C:2018:974, Opinion of AG Bobek, pts 20ff.

[44] Directive 2004/38/EC of the European Parliament and of the Council of 29 April 2004 on the right of citizens of the Union and their family members to move and reside freely within the territory of the Member States amending Regulation (EEC) No 1612/68 and repealing Directives 64/221/EEC, 68/360/EEC, 72/194/EEC, 73/148/EEC, 75/34/EEC, 75/35/EEC, 90/364/EEC, 90/365/EEC and 93/96/EEC [2004] OJ L158/77.

not only to the economic activities of the natural person but also to their living conditions and those of their family members. This distinction explains why the freedom of establishment, when applied to natural persons, can trigger not only the application of Article 49 TFEU but also of fundamental rights, in particular the right to respect for privacy and family life, as enshrined in Article 7 of the Charter.

6.2.1. Right of Departure

The home Member State has a duty to facilitate the exercise of the self-employed person's freedom of establishment by not adopting any measure that makes it more difficult or less attractive to transfer their economic activity to another Member State. According to the Court of Justice:

> Even though Article [49] of the Treaty, like the other provisions concerning freedom of establishment, is, according to its terms, aimed particularly at ensuring that foreign nationals are treated in the host Member State in the same way as nationals of that State, it also prohibits the Member State of origin from hindering the establishment in another Member State of one of its own nationals.[45]

These restrictions may occur, for example, in the field of taxation when changing residence to another Member State, or by imposing obligations on professionals in regulated sectors who cease their activity in the Member State of origin.[46] Similarly, immigration rules of the Member State of origin, insofar as they interfere with the effective exercise of free movement rights under Union law and have a restrictive effect on family life when moving to another Member State, can also hinder the right to exercise freedom of movement and consequently breach Article 49 TFEU.[47]

6.2.2. Right of Entry

Following the same approach that applies to legal persons, self-employed natural persons also have the right to set up a secondary establishment in another Member State. Self-employed persons may conduct their main activity in their Member State of origin while simultaneously maintaining one or more secondary establishments in another Member State. Article 49 TFEU protects this practice, which has been developed through the case law of the Court of Justice. In *Klopp*, a German lawyer established in Düsseldorf sought to open an office in Paris to provide a service closer to his clients in France. The Paris Bar refused Mr Klopp authorisation to practise in Paris through a secondary establishment. The French authorities did not deny Mr Klopp's right to move his main establishment to Paris but refused to allow him to continue his practice in Düsseldorf while operating a secondary establishment in France. The Court of Justice dismissed this approach, stating:

> That freedom of establishment is not confined to the right to create a single establishment within the [Union] is confirmed by the very words of Article [49] of the Treaty, according to which the progressive abolition of the restrictions on freedom of establishment applies to restrictions on the setting up of agencies, branches or subsidiaries by nationals of any Member State established in the territory of another Member State. That rule must be regarded as a specific statement of a general principle, applicable equally to the liberal professions, according to which the right of establishment includes

[45] Case C-251/98 *Baars* EU:C:2000:205, para 28.
[46] Case C-162/99 *Commission v Italy* EU:C:2001:35.
[47] Case C-60/00 *Carpenter* EU:C:2002:434; and Case C-202/13 *McCarthy and Others* EU:C:2014:2450.

> freedom to set up and maintain, subject to observance of the professional rules of conduct, more than one place of work within the [Union].[48]

Member States cannot reserve access to a self-employed professional activity for their own nationals, except in the case of activities connected with the exercise of official authority. Historically, until recent years, professionals such as lawyers or notaries, among others, were considered to be directly connected to the exercise of official authority, thus reserving the activity to nationals of the Member State. In the course of an abundant case law, the Court of Justice confirmed that the activities of notaries were not as a whole directly linked to the exercise of official authority and must therefore be open and accessible to nationals of other Member States.[49]

6.2.3. Right to Pursue an Activity in the Host Member State

The pursuit of a professional activity in the host Member State must be carried out without having to face any obstacles that may hinder or make the exercise of the activity less attractive to the self-employed natural person. For example, rules requiring periods of prior residence in the host Member State to access certain rights or services amount to a restriction of the freedom of establishment.[50] Obligations for individuals carrying out an economic activity to purchase specific goods also amount to a restriction that discourages access to the Member State's market.[51] In the field of direct taxation, self-employed persons from other Member States, provided they are in a comparable situation to local self-employed persons, are often subjected to more burdensome substantive or procedural tax provisions. This discriminatory treatment, whether direct or indirect, is incompatible with Article 49 TFEU.[52] Furthermore, the host Member State must provide the self-employed person with the same rights to social benefits as those available to local self-employed persons on an equal footing, subject to the material scope and conditions laid down in Union law. This is particularly significant when a social benefit is closely linked to a professional activity, as in the case of aid for the performance of a trade (social renting of business premises, financial support to SMEs or start-ups, among others),[53] but also in cases of social assistance for family support or social integration, as its denial may hinder or make less attractive the exercise of the freedom of establishment.[54]

6.3. Discrimination and the Market Access Test: Gebhard

In its first decades of existence, the case law on free movement primarily focused on restrictions of a discriminatory nature, particularly when a host Member State introduced requirements applicable only to foreign self-employed natural persons. In the course of time, the case law evolved and adopted a more effects-based approach that shifted its focus from outright

[48] Case C-107/83 *Ordre des avocats au barreau de Paris v Klopp* EU:C:1984:270, para 19. Similarly, see Case C-143/87 *Stanton v Inasti* EU:C:1988:378, para 11; and Case C-171/02 *Commission v Portugal* EU:C:2004:270, para 42.

[49] See section 1.7 of this chapter.

[50] Case C-203/98 *Commission v Belgium* EU:C:1999:380, para 13. By analogy, see also Case C-302/97 *Konle* EU:C:1999:271, para 23.

[51] Case C-182/83 *Fearon v Irish Land Commission* EU:C:1984:335, paras 10–11.

[52] Case C-80/94 *Wielockx v Inspecteur der directe belastingen* EU:C:1995:271; Case C-107/94 *Asscher v Staatssecretaris van Financiën* EU:C:1996:251; Case C-346/04 *Conijn* EU:C:2006:445; Case C-9/02 *de Lasteyrie du Saillant* EU:C:2004:138; Case C-314/08 *Filipiak* EU:C:2009:719; Case C-302/12 *X* EU:C:2013:756; and Case C-464/05 *Geurts and Vogten* EU:C:2007:631.

[53] Case C-197/84 *Steinhauser v Ville de Biarritz* EU:C:1985:260, para 16.

[54] Case C-63/86 *Commission v Italy* EU:C:1988:9, para 14; and Case C-305/87 *Commission v Greece* EU:C:1989:218, para 23.

discrimination to the restrictive effects of the contested measure. This shift was necessary to address restrictions on the departure of a self-employed natural person from their Member State of origin, which are not comparable to those faced by a local self-employed natural person. As a result, the Court of Justice expanded its analysis to include both the deterrent effect of national measures on the exercise of free movement and the barriers encountered by self-employed individuals exercising the freedom of establishment. This approach was crystallised in *Gebhard*,[55] a case where the Milan Bar Council imposed a disciplinary sanction on a German lawyer, registered in Germany, for using the title *avvocato* in Italy without having been admitted to the Milan Bar. The Court of Justice did not focus on the comparability between lawyers and possible discrimination, but instead targeted the economic obstacle created by the Milan Bar Council. After examining Mr Gebhard's situation, the Court concluded:

> [N]ational measures liable to hinder or make less attractive the exercise of fundamental freedoms guaranteed by the Treaty must fulfil four conditions: they must be applied in a non-discriminatory manner; they must be justified by imperative requirements in the general interest; they must be suitable for securing the attainment of the objective which they pursue; and they must not go beyond what is necessary in order to attain it.[56]

Although the market access test, as defined in *Gebhard*, originally referred to the requirement of non-discriminatory application as one of its four conditions, its focus has gradually shifted away from discrimination over time, without excluding it, to the point that the current case law focuses primarily on the restrictive effect of the contested measure.[57] The formula currently employed by the Court of Justice assesses the impact that the measure can have on the ability of the self-employed natural person to exercise or continue to exercise their freedom of establishment. The current formulation is expressed as follows:

> [A]ll measures which prohibit, impede or render less attractive the exercise of the freedom guaranteed by Article 49 TFEU, even if they apply without discrimination as to nationality, must be regarded as restrictions on that freedom of establishment.[58]

This approach allows the Court of Justice to examine a large number of national measures, regardless of whether they have a direct or indirect discriminatory effect, thereby broadening the scope of review to nearly all aspects of national law. In return for this expanded scope, the case law has also broadened the range of overriding reasons in the public interest that may justify restrictions by Member States. Additionally, as the number of potentially restrictive measures expands, the Court of Justice is increasingly required to conduct a proportionality analysis of the contested national measures, and it is frequently drawn to analyse complex areas where it does not always possess the appropriate expertise. Academic scholarship has criticised the high price paid by the Court of Justice for introducing the market access test, which has extended its oversight into many fields of national policy. It remains uncertain what alternatives exist: a standard of review solely focused on discriminatory practices would leave outside the scope of Article 49 TFEU a vast range of potentially restrictive measures, creating dubious incentives for Member States to introduce further barriers to the freedom of establishment. The question of an appropriate market access test remains unresolved, and so far no satisfactory alternative has emerged.

[55] Case C-55/94 *Gebhard v Consiglio dell'Ordine degli Avvocati e Procuratori di Milano* EU:C:1995:411.
[56] ibid, para 37.
[57] Case C-325/20 *BEMH and Conseil national des centres commerciaux* EU:C:2021:611, para 24.
[58] Case C-598/22 *Società Italiana Imprese Balneari* EU:C:2024:597, para 48.

7. Derogations and Exclusions

Article 52(1) TFEU sets out a list of grounds of justification that allow Member States to adopt restrictive measures with an impact on the freedom of establishment. Although the provision refers only to 'foreign nationals', it is applicable to both natural and legal persons:

> The provisions of this Chapter and measures taken in pursuance thereof shall not prejudice the applicability of provisions laid down by law, regulation or administrative action providing for special treatment for foreign nationals on grounds of public policy, public security or public health.

The grounds of justification in Article 52(1) TFEU must be interpreted strictly and cannot be based on economic criteria. The case law interprets this provision following the same criteria applied to the interpretation of Article 36 TFEU on free movement of goods, as explained in chapter thirteen of this book.

In cases of indirectly discriminatory measures and measures that fail a market access test, Member States can also rely on justifications not explicitly listed in the Treaties, known as 'overriding reasons in the public interest' (also known as 'mandatory requirements'). An enumeration of the relevant justifications was established in 1991 in *Gouda*,[59] but this list has grown considerably over time. The ruling in *Gouda* refers to professional rules aimed at protecting recipients of services, the protection of intellectual property, the protection of workers, consumer protection, and the conservation of national historical, artistic, or cultural heritage. At present, in addition to these overriding reasons in the public interest, other justifications are added to the list, including those related to the protection of creditors, minority shareholders, and workers,[60] the protection of the environment,[61] the promotion of tourism,[62] road safety,[63] the prevention of unfair competition,[64] the combating of tax avoidance,[65] the need to preserve the balanced allocation of the power to impose taxes between Member States,[66] the sound administration of justice,[67] and the financial balance of the social security system.[68]

Apart from the justifications mentioned above, the Treaties provide for the possibility of excluding certain activities in their entirety from the scope of application of freedom of establishment. This is the case of activities connected with the exercise of official authority, as provided in Article 51(1) TFEU:

> The provisions of this Chapter shall not apply, so far as any given Member State is concerned, to activities which in that State are connected, even occasionally, with the exercise of official authority.

The Court of Justice has interpreted this provision very strictly, excluding from its scope only those activities that directly and specifically involve the exercise of public authority. It has also excluded activities that, although involving close contact with the exercise of official authority,

[59] Case C-288/89 *Stichting Collectieve Antennevoorziening Gouda and Others* EU:C:1991:157.

[60] Case C-208/00 *Überseering* EU:C:2002:632, para 92.

[61] Case C-17/00 *De Coster* EU:C:2001:651, paras 36–37; Joined Cases C-151/04 and C-152/04 *Nadin and Nadin-Lux* EU:C:2005:775, para 52; and Case C-338/09 *Yellow Cab Verkehrsbetrieb* EU:C:2010:814, para 50.

[62] *Yellow Cab* (n 61) para 50.

[63] Case C-55/93 *Van Schaik* EU:C:1994:363, para 19; Joined Cases C-128/10 and C-129/10 *Naftiliaki Etaireia Thasou and Amaltheia I Naftiki Etaireia* EU:C:2011:163, para 45; and Case C-509/12 *Navileme and Nautizende* EU:C:2014:54, para 23.

[64] Case C-60/03 *Wolff & Müller* EU:C:2004:610, para 41.

[65] Case C-290/04 *FKP Scorpio Konzertproduktionen* EU:C:2006:630, para 35; and Case C-196/04 *Cadbury Schweppes and Cadbury Schweppes Overseas* EU:C:2006:544, para 51.

[66] Case C-446/03 *Marks & Spencer* EU:C:2005:763, para 51.

[67] Case C-295/23 *Halmer Rechtsanwaltsgesellschaft UG* EU:C:2024:1037, para 65.

[68] Case C-158/96 *Kohll v Union des caisses de maladie* EU:C:1998:171, para 41.

require the exercise of discretionary powers or economic activities in the market. The Court of Justice has ruled on a wide range of professions, confirming that they are not covered by the exclusion in Article 51(1) TFEU, when assessed with regard to the specific activities concerned rather than the profession as a whole. To date, these professions include, among others, lawyers,[69] traffic experts,[70] public sector computer programmers,[71] vehicle inspectors,[72] court-appointed translators,[73] notaries,[74] industrial certification services,[75] security officers[76] and insurance supervisors.[77]

8. Secondary Legislation

Union secondary legislation harmonises or approximates the rules applicable to various sectors of economic activity. For instance, the insurance industry, commercial and investment banking, transport, telecommunications, and energy are areas where companies and professionals can establish themselves in other Member States under the provisions of Union secondary legislation. In such cases, the conditions for access, the rights of businesses and self-employed persons, and the limits to Member State action are outlined in directives or regulations. As explained in chapter thirteen, if an activity is regulated by secondary legislation, the applicable framework for the mobility of operators applies as a *lex specialis*, insofar as it governs the specific aspects of market access and activity concerned, and the national measure must be assessed in the light of the harmonising measure rather than directly under the Treaty provisions on freedom of establishment.

In addition to the directives and regulations applicable to specific sectors, the freedom of establishment has led to two legislative texts of major practical importance, with a broad scope and applicable to a wide range of economic activities. These are Directive 2006/123 on services in the internal market, which, despite its title, also regulates certain aspects of the freedom of establishment, and Directive 2005/36 on professional qualifications.

8.1. Chapter III of Directive 2006/123 on Services in the Internal Market

Directive 2006/123 on services in the internal market ('the Services Directive')[78] is a major piece of legislation aimed at regulating economic services within the internal market, whether provided on an occasional or permanent basis. Therefore, in the latter dimension, the Services Directive lays down rules governing the conditions of *establishment* of natural and legal persons within the internal market.

[69] Case C-2/74 *Reyners v Belgian State* EU:C:1974:68, para 46.

[70] Case C-306/89 *Commission v Greece* EU:C:1991:463, para 7.

[71] Case C-3/88 *Commission v Italy* EU:C:1989:606, para 13.

[72] Case C-438/08 *Commission v Portugal* EU:C:2009:651, para 41.

[73] Case C-372/09 *Peñarroja Fa* EU:C:2011:156, para 44; and Case C-79/09 *Commission v Netherlands* EU:C:2010:171, para 45.

[74] Case C-47/08 *Commission v Belgium* EU:C:2011:334, paras 88ff; Case C-151/14 *Commission v Latvia* EU:C:2015:577, para 74; and Case C-342/15 *Piringer* EU:C:2017:196, para 54.

[75] Case C-593/13 *Rina Services and Others* EU:C:2015:399, para 22.

[76] Case C-355/98 *Commission v Belgium* EU:C:2000:113, para 26; Case C-283/99 *Commission v Italy* EU:C:2001:307, para 20; Case C-465/05 *Commission v Italy* EU:C:2007:781, para 40; and Case C-114/97 *Commission v Spain* EU:C:1998:519, para 37.

[77] Case C-42/92 *Thijssen v Controledienst voor de verzekeringen* EU:C:1993:304, para 11.

[78] Directive 2006/123/EC of the European Parliament and of the Council of 12 December 2006 on services in the internal market [2006] OJ L376/36.

Despite its horizontal and cross-sectoral scope, the Services Directive excludes a significant number of economic activities from its scope of application. Article 2(2) of the Directive enumerates, among other things, activities as relevant as financial services, electronic communications, transport, healthcare, audiovisual services, gambling, and insurance services. Most of these sectors are governed by specific Union legislation which acts as a *lex specialis* in relation to both the Services Directive and the Treaty rules on freedom of establishment.[79]

The definition of 'establishment' is directly inspired by Article 49 TFEU and the case law of the Court of Justice. Article 4(5) defines establishment as 'the actual pursuit of an economic activity, as referred to in Article 49 of the Treaty, by the provider for an indefinite period and through a stable infrastructure from which the business of providing services is actually carried out'. Therefore, there is a strict parallelism between the cases in which Article 49 TFEU applies and those governed by the Services Directive, with an important exception that affects the cross-border link.

Unlike the protections provided by the Treaties, the Services Directive, and specifically its provisions on freedom of establishment in Chapter III, also applies to purely internal situations within a Member State, in certain circumstances, as recognised by the Court of Justice on the basis of the wording, objectives, and scheme of the Directive. As previously explained, the requirement of a cross-border link is an essential prerequisite for the application of Article 49 TFEU. However, in the case of the Services Directive, the scope of application of Chapter III extends to all situations where a natural or legal person is restricted in their aim to establish themselves in a place other than that of their main establishment, whether in another Member State or within their home Member State. This extension to purely domestic situations was confirmed by the Court of Justice in *College van Burgemeester*,[80] inferring this outcome from the wording, objectives, and preparatory work of the Services Directive:

> [T]o ensure that the *effet utile* of the specific legal framework that the EU legislature intended to establish in adopting Directive 2006/123 is not undermined, it must be accepted, contrary to what was argued by the German government at the hearing, that the scope of that directive is capable of extending, in certain cases, beyond what is strictly laid down in the provisions of the FEU Treaty relating to freedom of establishment and the free movement of services, without prejudice to the obligation on the Member States, under Article 3(3) of that directive, to apply the provisions of that directive in compliance with the rules of the FEU Treaty.[81]

National laws anticipated this interpretation of the Services Directive by transposing it in a way that included both cross-border and purely domestic situations. In practice this meant that various national provisions transposing the Directive did not distinguish between an establishment with cross-border connections and those in purely internal contexts. For example, Article 14 of the Belgian Loi of 26 March 2010 prohibits nationality/residence tests, principal establishment requirements, and economic needs tests, among others. These provisions apply to *prestataires* as defined in the law, without distinguishing between domestic and foreign service providers. The same can be seen in the Spanish legislation, where Article 4(1) of Law 17/2009 states that 'providers of services may freely establish themselves in Spanish territory in order to exercise a service activity, without any limitations other than those established in accordance with the provisions of this Law', without distinguishing between service providers established

[79] Case C-278/22 *AUTOTECHNICA FLEET SERVICES* EU:C:2023:1026, paras 38–54.
[80] Joined Cases C-360/15 and C-31/16 *X* EU:C:2018:44.
[81] ibid, para 107.

in Spain or in another Member State. Similar provisions are also available in the Netherlands, Italy and Poland, to name a few examples.[82]

The Services Directive outlines the prohibitions derived from Article 49 TFEU and defines them in detail, using terms consistent with the Court of Justice's case law. Articles 9–13 of the Services Directive set out the conditions under which a Member State can make the pursuit of an economic activity subject to prior authorisation, as well as the conditions to which the authorisation regime is subject. The provisions of the Services Directive require Member States to ensure non-discriminatory treatment of all economic operators, as well as duties to state reasons for refusals of authorisations, rules on the duration of authorisations, and procedural fairness.

Article 14 introduces several requirements that are absolutely prohibited, considered to be *per se* disproportionate restrictions on the freedom of establishment. These prohibitions reflect the rulings of the Court of Justice to date. By way of example, Article 14(2) of the Services Directive prohibits making access to, or the exercise of, a service activity conditional on the provider being registered in the professional bodies or associations of the host Member State where the provider is already registered in another Member State. This prohibition reflects a settled line of case law on the registration of professional activities as discussed earlier (see, inter alia, the cases of *Gebhard* and *Klopp*).

Finally, Article 15 of the Services Directive introduces a list of requirements that are not prohibited outright but are suspected of being incompatible with the freedom of establishment, also derived from case law, which are subject to a proportionality review carried out on a case-by-case basis.[83] By way of example, Article 15 refers, inter alia, to the requirement for a service provider to take a specific legal form, restrictions related to the territory of performance of the activity,[84] as well as requirements related to the shareholding of a company, the minimum number of employees, or fixed minimum and/or maximum tariffs that the provider must comply with. If the reviewed national measures do not fall under either Article 14 or Article 15 of the Services Directive, their assessment must be undertaken in light of Article 49 TFEU.[85]

Professional activities falling within the scope of the Services Directive are subject to its provisions rather than directly to Article 49 TFEU, without prejudice to the interpretative role of Article 49 TFEU as a norm of primary law and to its application where the Directive does not fully regulate the matter. The scope left uncovered by the Services Directive and specific-sector Union legislation is somewhat limited, but the Treaties still exert considerable influence, as certain areas of economic activity remain subject to exclusions or lack specific Union legislation. Similarly, the emergence of new economic activities in the digital sector can create gaps that may need to be addressed by relying on Article 49 TFEU. For instance, the regulation of digital platforms in industries such as transport or tourism raised questions that were initially assessed under the Treaty freedoms before the adoption of sector-specific Union legislation. In addition, Article 49 TFEU is a rule of Union primary law and, consequently, it plays an interpretative role in the implementation of Union secondary law. The case law of the Court of Justice on Article 49 TFEU to date is a highly relevant source of inspiration for interpreting

[82] See Art 2/3 of the Dutch Dienstenwet (12 November 2009); Art 1(1) of the Italian Decreto Legislativo no 59 (26 March 2010); and Art 2 of the Polish Prawo przedsiębiorców (6 March 2018).

[83] Case C-503/23 *Centro di Assistenza Doganale (Cad) Mellano Srl* EU:C:2024:933, paras 73–94; Case C-295/23 *Halmer Rechtsanwaltsgesellschaft UG* EU:C:2024:1037, paras 61–74; and Case C-674/23 *AEON NEPREMIČNINE d.o.o. and Others* EU:C:2025:113, paras 58–80.

[84] Case C-16/23 *FA.RO di YK & C Sas* EU:C:2024:886, paras 87–90; and *Centro di Assistenza Doganale (Cad) Mellano* (n 83) paras 86–94.

[85] Case C-254/23 *INTERZERO* EU:C:2025:569, para 96.

the Services Directive. The fact that this Directive has codified much of the case law on freedom of establishment only confirms the interpretative role that the case law on Article 49 TFEU continues to play today.

8.2. Professional Qualifications: Directive 2005/36

Regulated professions are activities that require a specific level of qualifications as a condition of access or pursuit, and are governed by national law. Due to the barriers to access they can create for incoming foreign professionals from other Member States, regulated professions are subject to a specific regime governed by secondary Union law and the case law of the Court of Justice. Initially, the Union legislator recognised the right of host Member States to recognise or refuse to recognise previous studies carried out by a professional in their country of origin. This approach focused on a sectoral analysis of each activity individually, but it was soon superseded by case law. In *Vlassopoulou*,[86] a Greek lawyer practising law in Germany and advising on Greek and Union law applied to the German Ministry of Justice for admission as a *Rechtsanwältin* (lawyer) to the Amtsgericht (Local Court) of Mannheim and the Landgerichte (Regional Courts) of Mannheim and Heidelberg. The Ministry rejected the application on the grounds that Ms Vlassopoulou had not obtained a German law degree and had not passed the two German State examinations. According to the German authorities, this conclusion was not discriminatory, since Ms Vlassopoulou was subject to the same conditions for access to the profession as German nationals.

Faced with this response, which illustrates the limitations of the principle of non-discrimination in certain areas of free movement, the Court of Justice found that the German requirement, while non-discriminatory in form, was liable to hinder the exercise of the freedom of establishment and amounted to a breach of Article 49 TFEU for the following reasons:

> It must be stated in this regard that, even if applied without any discrimination on the basis of nationality, national requirements concerning qualifications may have the effect of hindering nationals of the other Member States in the exercise of their right of establishment guaranteed to them by Article [49 TFEU]. That could be the case if the national rules in question took no account of the knowledge and qualifications already acquired by the person concerned in another Member State.

It follows that the Member State in which authorisation is sought to pursue a profession, access to which is subject, under national rules, to possession of a diploma or professional qualification, must take into account the diplomas, certificates and other evidence of formal qualifications which the person concerned has acquired for the purpose of pursuing the same profession in another Member State, by comparing the ability attested by those diplomas with the knowledge and aptitude required by the national provisions.[87]

Vlassopoulou marked an important step forward that contributed to the subsequent evolution of the Union's secondary legislation on the matter and ultimately resulted in the adoption of Directive 2005/36 on the recognition of professional qualifications. This Directive introduces a general legal framework for the recognition of professional qualifications applicable to all regulated professions, combining elements of the *Vlassopoulou* approach with the earlier sectoral system, which was retained for certain professions.

Title III of Directive 2005/36 sets out the conditions under which qualified professionals can enjoy freedom of establishment. To achieve this, the Directive divides qualified professionals

[86] Case C-340/89 *Vlassopoulou v Ministerium für Justiz, Bundes- und Europaangelegenheiten Baden-Württemberg* EU:C:1991:193.

[87] ibid, paras 15–16.

into three groups: professionals subject to the general regime; professionals whose qualifications are recognised on the basis of professional experience listed in Annex IV (professional activities in specific industrial sectors, manufacturing, and retail trade); and professionals benefiting from automatic recognition on the basis of harmonised minimum training requirements listed in Chapter III (doctors, nurses responsible for general care, veterinary surgeons, dentists, midwives, pharmacists, and architects).

The general regime, which applies to all regulated professions not covered by Chapters II and III, is based on the principle of mutual recognition of professional qualifications where they are based on equivalent requirements for access in both the home and host Member States. In the case of substantial differences between the two Member States, Directive 2005/36 allows the host Member State to require a traineeship of no more than three years or an aptitude test. Furthermore, Articles 16–19 introduce a system of recognition of professional experience acquired in another Member State for the professions listed in Annex IV, provided that such experience meets the conditions of duration and form specified in the Directive.

Directive 2005/36 consolidated and rationalised the rules on the recognition of qualifications, reducing the room for manoeuvre of Member States wishing to protect their regulated professionals from competition from other Member States. Although the system still depends on a national decision on recognition made by the host Member State, there is a significant difference between the sectoral and highly discretional system of the 1980s and the current framework, which is based on a general principle of mutual recognition and only allows restrictions in strictly justified cases provided by the host Member State.

II. FREEDOM TO PROVIDE SERVICES

The services sector accounts for around 70 per cent of the Union's gross domestic product. If the internal market is to achieve its full potential, services and service providers must be able to move freely across the Union, fostering competition, boosting productivity, and reducing prices for consumers. Services were not the primary focus of the Union's objectives in its early decades. Initially, the European project focused mostly on creating a common market for goods, while services were still subject to numerous restrictions in most Member States. The sensitive nature of certain sectors, such as energy, telecommunications, transport or health, along with regulatory and cultural divergences between Member States, contributed to the slow process of liberalising the services sector in Europe.

Services experienced a significant boost in the 1990s and the first decade of the twenty-first century. From 1992 onwards, a gradual liberalisation process took place through Union legislation (mainly in the form of directives) in highly strategic sectors such as energy, telecommunications, the postal sector, and transport. At the same time, the Court of Justice expanded its case law on services, broadening the scope of application of free movement rules to include recipients of services, while the focus of scrutiny shifted from a discrimination-based review to a market access test. This mix of positive and negative integration was vital for the opening of multiple markets, allowing services to be provided on an equal footing with other free movement rules.

The culmination of this process occurred in 2004, when the European Commission proposed an ambitious directive aimed at harmonising the conditions of access to all services markets within the Union. The draft directive adopted a well-established technique in the field of goods: the principles of mutual recognition and the 'country of origin' principle, by analogy with the landmark ruling of the Court of Justice in *Cassis de Dijon*. The proposal faced significant opposition and criticism, with opponents describing it as a strategy to impose an unfettered liberalisation of services and a decline of quality standards across sectors, including public health, education, and social services. After extensive negotiations, the Commission revised its proposal, and ultimately the Council and the European Parliament adopted Directive 2006/123, establishing a framework for a wide range of services within the internal market. Following a tumultuous legislative process, the freedom to provide services is now primarily governed by two sources: generally, the relevant provisions of the TFEU, and more specifically, the provisions of Directive 2006/123.

The rules on the freedom to provide services share many features with those governing the freedom of establishment, as both freedoms concern economic operators providing services. The operator providing services under the freedom of establishment does so by relocating on a stable and continuous basis in another Member State, while the operator enjoying the freedom to provide services does so on a temporary basis, without the need for permanent establishment in another Member State. Both situations involve a cross-border element, but the key difference lies in the temporary or permanent nature of the activity in the host Member State. Since both freedoms relate to service activities, the interpretation of the Treaties and Union secondary legislation shares many common features that apply to both freedoms.

Besides the freedom to provide services provided in Article 56 TFEU, as a right that natural and legal persons can rely on and invoke with direct effect, the Treaty lays down various legal bases empowering the Union legislator to adopt general or sector-specific measures to facilitate the provision of services within the internal market. Article 59(1) TFEU grants the European Parliament and the Council, acting through the ordinary legislative procedure, the power to adopt directives 'in order to achieve the liberalisation of a specific service'. Furthermore, the reference in Article 62 TFEU to the rules on freedom of establishment, including Article 53(1) TFEU, allows the Union legislator to introduce measures facilitating the provision of services, and not only for a specific service.[88]

Article 56, second paragraph TFEU provides an additional legal basis, authorising the European Parliament and the Council, acting in accordance with the ordinary legislative procedure, with the power to extend the right to provide services 'to nationals of a third country who provide services and who are established within the Union'.

1. Definition of 'Service'

Article 56(1) TFEU introduces the freedom to provide services in the following terms:

> Within the framework of the provisions set out below, restrictions on freedom to provide services within the Union shall be prohibited in respect of nationals of Member States who are established in a Member State other than that of the person for whom the services are intended.

The definition of a 'service' is developed in Article 57 TFEU. This provision lays down a description of the activities covered by this freedom:

> Services shall be considered to be 'services' within the meaning of the Treaties where they are normally provided for remuneration, in so far as they are not governed by the provisions relating to freedom of movement for goods, capital and persons.

[88] Case C-348/22 *Autorità Garante della Concorrenza e del Mercato* EU:C:2023:301, paras 51–58.

'Services' shall in particular include:

(a) activities of an industrial character;

(b) activities of a commercial character;

(c) activities of craftsmen;

(d) activities of the professions.

Without prejudice to the provisions of the Chapter relating to the right of establishment, the person providing a service may, in order to do so, temporarily pursue his activity in the Member State where the service is provided, under the same conditions as are imposed by that State on its own nationals.

Despite the broad definition in Article 57 TFEU, the case law of the Court of Justice provides additional criteria to identify when an economic activity must be characterised as a 'service'.

First, a 'service' as defined by Article 57 TFEU must be of a temporary nature, meaning that the provider or recipient of the service moves temporarily to provide/receive the service, and not with a view to developing a stable and continuous presence in another Member State.[89] If the service is provided by means of a stable and continuous presence in another Member State, it will be subject to the rules of the freedom of establishment and the provisions of Article 49 TFEU. It is also important to note that the temporary or occasional nature of the service does not exclude the existence of some degree of infrastructure (such as an office, chambers, or a studio) in the host Member State, provided that this infrastructure is necessary for the purposes of performing the service.[90]

Second, services protected by the Treaties and Union secondary legislation must have an economic nature. Article 57, first paragraph, TFEU defines services as those 'normally provided for remuneration.' Regardless of the type of services, if there is remuneration as consideration for the activity, the activity will be regarded as a 'service' pursuant to Article 57 TFEU. According to the Court of Justice, 'the essential characteristic of remuneration lies in the fact that it constitutes consideration for the service in question, and is normally agreed upon between the provider and the recipient of the service'.[91] The amount of remuneration is irrelevant in this context, and the definition of a 'service' applies even to non-profit activities where, nevertheless, a non-negligible economic consideration is involved.[92]

This definition of a 'service' includes activities of a social nature but carried out in exchange for financial remuneration. Consequently, public education, predominantly funded through public funds, does not qualify as a 'service',[93] but private education, where an undertaking provides educational services in return for payment that constitutes genuine remuneration for those services, falls under the definition of a 'service'.[94] The same applies to the health sector, although with some caveats. The case law has applied the concept of 'service' to public health systems, where services are provided on an ad hoc basis at the patient's request, with payments for these services ultimately constituting remuneration, even where channelled through social security mechanisms rather than paid directly by the patient.

[89] Case C-63/86 *Commission v Italy* EU:C:1988:9, para 19; Case C-298/99 *Commission v Italy* EU:C:2002:194, para 56; Case C-55/94 *Gebhard v Consiglio dell'Ordine degli Avvocati e Procuratori di Milano* EU:C:1995:411, para 27; and Case C-215/01 *Schnitzer* EU:C:2003:662, paras 30–32.

[90] See also the judgment in Case C-502/20 *Institut des Experts en Automobiles* EU:C:2021:678, para 36.

[91] Case C-355/00 *Freskot* EU:C:2003:298, paras 54–55; Case C-169/08 *Presidente del Consiglio dei Ministri* EU:C:2009:709, para 23; and Case C-372/09 *Peñarroja Fa* EU:C:2011:156, para 37.

[92] Case C-281/06 *Jundt* EU:C:2007:816, para 49.

[93] Case C-263/86 *Belgian State v Humbel and Edel* EU:C:1988:451, paras 17–19.

[94] Case C-109/92 *Wirth v Landeshauptstadt Hannover* EU:C:1993:916, para 17.

The legal or illegal status of the activity in the Member State where the recipient is established is irrelevant for the purpose of characterising an activity as a 'service'. In *Grogan*, the Court of Justice ruled that the termination of pregnancy, as lawfully carried out in clinics in the United Kingdom, was an economic activity and therefore a 'service' within the meaning of Article 57 TFEU.[95] Prostitution is also an economic activity, provided it is carried out voluntarily and outside any relationship of subordination.[96] Gambling and lotteries are heavily regulated, and in some Member States, certain games of chance are either illegal or controlled by a State monopoly. However, when provided on a cross-border basis they qualify as a 'service'.[97]

2. Right Holder

Holders of the right to the freedom to provide services are, in the first place, economic operators actively offering cross-border services to third parties. The case law of the Court of Justice also extended the range of right holders to include *recipients* of services, as persons who receive a service in exchange for payment. This is the 'passive' dimension of the freedom to provide services, as established in *Luisi and Carbone*.[98] In this case, the question was whether a penalty imposed by the Italian authorities on two Italian nationals for leaving the territory of Italy for leisure and in possession of 500,000 Italian lire in cash was in breach of Article 56 TFEU. Essentially, the question raised by the Italian court asked whether a person travelling to another Member State to *receive* a service (in this case, touristic services) should benefit from the protection of the freedom to provide services. The Court of Justice responded affirmatively, stating as follows:

> [T]he freedom to provide services includes the freedom, for the recipients of services, to go to another Member State in order to receive a service there, without being obstructed by restrictions, even in relation to payments and that tourists, persons receiving medical treatment and persons travelling for the purpose of education or business are to be regarded as recipients of services.[99]

The case of *Luisi and Carbone* concerned a restriction imposed by the Member State of origin on the recipient of the services. The Court of Justice then held that the same protection should be afforded in the host Member State. In *Cowan*,[100] a British tourist who had been assaulted in the Paris métro was excluded from a compensation scheme provided under French law and reserved exclusively for French nationals and holders of a French residence permit. The Court of Justice confirmed that the principle of non-discrimination also applies to nationals of other Member States receiving services in another Member State, ensuring that Union law guarantees a natural person the freedom to move to another Member State to receive services and the protection of that person's rights in the Member State concerned, on an equal footing with nationals of that State.[101]

Holders of the right to the freedom to provide services include both legal and natural persons. Unlike the freedom of establishment, where residence requirements raise specific questions about the legal form of a company in the host Member State or the conditions of

[95] Case C-159/90 *Society for the Protection of Unborn Children Ireland v Grogan and Others* EU:C:1991:378, para 21.

[96] Case C-268/99 *Jany and Others* EU:C:2001:616, para 48.

[97] Case C-347/09 *Dickinger and Ömer* EU:C:2011:582, paras 60-63, and C-390/12 *Pfleger e.a.* EU:C:2014:281, paras 39-49.

[98] Joined Cases C-286/82 and C-26/83 *Luisi and Carbone v Ministero dello Tesoro* EU:C:1984:35.

[99] ibid, para 16.

[100] Case C-186/87 *Cowan v Trésor public* EU:C:1989:47.

[101] See also Case C-274/96 *Bickel and Franz* EU:C:1998:563, para 15; Case C-224/97 *Ciola* EU:C:1999:212, paras 11–13; and Case C-211/08 *Commission v Spain* EU:C:2010:340, paras 51–52.

residence of the natural person and his/her family, the freedom to provide services does not raise these questions as frequently due to the temporary nature of the activity. In any case, natural persons who move to provide or receive a service will enjoy the right to residence for a maximum period of three months in another Member State, in accordance with Article 6 of Directive 2004/38. A different issue arises in cases where the provider or the recipient of the service does not move, a situation that will be discussed in the following section.

3. Cross-border Link

Article 56 TFEU refers to services 'in respect of nationals of Member States who are established in a Member State other than that of the person for whom the services are intended'. The existence of a cross-border link is therefore an essential requirement to trigger the freedom to provide services, requiring that the provision of the service involve a transnational element.

However, the cross-border element does not necessarily require the physical displacement of either the provider or the recipient, or of both, as it is sufficient for the service alone to make the movement - that is, that the provider and recipient are established in different Member States. Therefore, when a service provider or a recipient of a service provides and/or receives the service without physically moving to another Member State, a cross-border link still exists as long as both parties are established in two different Member States. Digital markets have facilitated and driven a significant increase in dematerialised services, where neither party travels to another Member State. The Court of Justice's case law confirms that, in such cases, a cross-border link exists and the service is subject to Article 56 TFEU.[102]

4. Content of the Right

Similarly to the freedom of establishment, the freedom to provide services can be invoked against restrictive measures stemming from the Member State of origin of the service provider, as well as in the host Member State of destination of the service. In both cases, the right holder may be either the service provider or the recipient of the service, activating the protection of Article 56 TFEU in both situations.

4.1. *Provision/Reception of Services in the Member State of Origin*

Restrictive measures imposed by the Member State of origin of the service are frequent, particularly when an economic activity is reserved for local operators only, or the rules are designed to benefit local operators. For example, a national decision that allocates a certain percentage of moorings in a marina exclusively for vessels registered in the Member State constitutes a restriction on the freedom to provide services.[103] Similarly, a measure prohibiting or limiting the purchase of advertising space restricts the ability of an advertising space provider to offer its services to a client from another Member State.[104] A similar outcome can be found in the

[102] Case C-352/85 *Bond van Adverteerders v Netherlands State* EU:C:1988:196, paras 14–16; Case C-384/93 *Alpine Investments v Minister van Financiën* EU:C:1995:126, para 42; and Case C-405/98 *Gourmet International Products* EU:C:2001:145, para 39.

[103] Case C-224/97 *Ciola* EU:C:1999:212, paras 11–12.

[104] Case C-352/85 *Bond van Adverteerders v Netherlands State* EU:C:1988:196; Case C-288/89 *Stichting Collectieve Antennevoorziening Gouda v Commissariaat voor de Media* EU:C:1991:323; and *Alpine Investments* (n 102), para 19.

field of direct taxation, when a national fiscal measure imposes a higher tax burden on services provided to recipients in other Member States.

4.2. *Provision/Reception of Services in the Member State of Destination*

Services may also encounter obstacles contrary to Article 56 TFEU in the Member State of destination. Although the principle of mutual recognition applies in the field of services, the case law of the Court of Justice has used a more nuanced approach in this context in contrast with other freedoms.[105] In principle, in the absence of legislative harmonisation at Union level, the Member State of destination of the service cannot impose additional requirements on the provider of a cross-border service to those already in force in the Member State of origin. This reflects a principle of mutual recognition within the scope of Article 56 TFEU, but subject to certain requirements developed in the case law. Such requirements must be based on rules that are justified in the general interest, 'in so far as that interest is not safeguarded by the rules to which the provider of such a service is subject in the Member State where he is established'.[106]

The judgment in *Guiot* exemplifies how these principles apply to a specific case. The facts of the case involve a company established in Luxembourg that was required to pay social security contributions in Belgium in respect of the construction workers it posted to Belgium to carry out construction work. The company already paid its workers' social security contributions in Luxembourg, but Belgian legislation required payment of an equivalent contribution on the grounds that the work was carried out on Belgian territory. The Court of Justice examined the aims and activities covered by both the Belgian and Luxembourg contribution systems and found that, with minor exceptions, they provided equivalent protection.[107] Therefore, from the point of view of the worker's protection, the Belgian contribution did not enhance the protections already provided by the Luxembourg scheme.[108] Instead, it was an additional and redundant requirement imposed by the Member State of destination, which only increased the costs for a company from another Member State seeking to operate within the Belgian construction market, placing it at a disadvantage compared with local operators. As a result, the Court of Justice held that the measure was a restriction on the freedom to provide services.

The Member State of destination of a service may introduce other measures, apparently neutral and applicable to all operators but which have a restrictive effect on free movement. For example, imposing on an economic activity an obligation to obtain a licence with a limited territorial scope can amount to a restriction on the freedom to provide services.[109] Excessive formal requirements prior to the performance of the activity, such as demanding certified translations, specific language requirements, or an oath of allegiance to the Republic or the head of state, can also potentially constitute a restriction on the provision of services.[110] Taxation can also constitute a restriction if services from other Member States are taxed more heavily than those offered by local operators in comparable situations.

The Court of Justice has recently clarified the scope of its review, stating that national legislation which does not specifically regulate the conditions concerning the provision of services

[105] Case C-272/94 *Guiot* EU:C:1996:147, paras 11 and 20; and Case C-496/01 *Commission v France* EU:C:2004:137, para 71.

[106] Case C-180/89 *Commission v Italy* EU:C:1991:78, para 17; Case C-198/89 *Commission v Greece* EU:C:1991:79, para 18; Case C-43/93 *Vander Elst v Office des migrations internationales* EU:C:1994:310, para 16; Case C-272/94 *Guiot* EU:C:1996:147, para 11; and Case C-212/11 *Jyske Bank Gibraltar* EU:C:2013:270, para 60.

[107] *Guiot* (n 105) paras 19–20.

[108] ibid, para 21.

[109] Case C-134/05 *Commission v Italy* EU:C:2007:435, para 64; and Case C-465/05 *Commission v Italy* EU:C:2007:781, para 58.

[110] Case C-465/05 *Commission v Italy* EU:C:2007:781, paras 45–46.

by the relevant undertakings, and whose restrictive effects on the freedom to provide services are too uncertain and indirect to be regarded as capable of hindering that freedom, does not contravene the prohibition laid down in Article 56 TFEU.[111]

5. Discrimination and Market Access

Article 57, third paragraph TFEU states that a provider of a cross-border service has the right to temporarily carry out his activity 'under the same conditions as are imposed by that State on its own nationals'. This reference might appear to limit the types of restrictive measures covered by the Treaties to those of a discriminatory nature. However, as seen earlier in the context of freedom of establishment, the provision of services in cross-border situations does not always lend itself well to a discrimination analysis, as there is often no suitable comparator against which to assess the treatment of the cross-border service provider relative to the domestic service provider. For this reason, the Court of Justice's case law began to develop the use of the market access test in the 1990s, especially in cases where there was no useful comparator. The *Säger* judgment of 1991[112] clearly showed the limitations of the discrimination test, a reality that contributed to a shift towards a market access test expressed as follows:

> Article [56] of the Treaty requires not only the elimination of all discrimination against a person providing services on the ground of his nationality but also the abolition of any restriction, even if it applies without distinction to national providers of services and to those of other Member States, when it is liable to prohibit or otherwise impede the activities of a provider of services established in another Member State where he lawfully provides similar services.[113]

Therefore, restrictions covered by Article 56 TFEU include directly discriminatory measures, indirectly discriminatory measures, as well as measures that hinder market access. The formula used by more recent case law has added to the formulation of the market access test the reference that measures may 'render less attractive' the activities of the service provider. In this way, the market access test under Article 56 TFEU is now fully aligned with the formulation used in the case law on freedom of establishment.

It should be recalled that there is a significant exception to the use of the market access test, namely in the field of direct taxation. As previously highlighted in the case of freedom of establishment, the Court of Justice has adopted a distinct approach in its interpretation of Article 56 TFEU when national measures are fiscal in nature and apply to cross-border situations. The territorial nature of the Member States' taxing power, together with the use of jurisdictional criteria based on territoriality, and the existence of bilateral international mechanisms to prevent double taxation, have led the Court of Justice to restrict the scope of Article 56 TFEU to national tax measures where there are comparable legal and factual situations between the taxable person with cross-border links and the local taxable person.[114] This, as explained above, results in the exclusion of a significant number of cases that, in other areas of policy, would be assessed under the freedom to provide services through the market access test, but are instead subject to the comparability test in the field of direct taxation.

[111] Case C-674/20 *Airbnb Ireland* EU:C:2022:303, para 42; and Case C-411/21 *Instituto do Cinema e do Audiovisual IP* EU:C:2022:836, para 29.

[112] Case C-76/90 *Säger v Dennemeyer* EU:C:1991:331.

[113] ibid, para 12.

[114] Case C-134/03 *Viacom Outdoor* EU:C:2005:94; Case C-544/03 *Mobistar and Belgacom Mobile* EU:C:2005:518; and Case C-625/17 *Vorarlberger Landes- und Hypothekenbank* EU:C:2018:939.

6. Justifications and Exclusions

A restrictive measure on the freedom to provide services can be justified, provided that it pursues an overriding reason relating to the public interest and complies with the principle of proportionality. To this end, Article 62 TFEU refers to the grounds of justification listed in Article 52(1) TFEU ('public policy, public security and public health'). The case law of the Court of Justice recognises a broad range of overriding reasons in the public interest available to the Member States, applicable to both the freedom of establishment and the freedom to provide services. Reference is made to section I.7 of this chapter, where some of the overriding reasons in the public interest recognised so far are discussed.

As with other fundamental freedoms, the traditional position is that directly discriminatory restrictions can only rely on the grounds provided in Article 52(1) TFEU. In contrast, indirectly discriminatory restrictions and restrictions contrary to the market access test can rely on both the explicit justifications of the Treaty and the overriding reasons in the public interest established by case law. However, this distinction has become less rigid in practice. While it was strictly applied during the 1970s and 1980s, it has become less clear in recent times. It is now not uncommon for the case law to consider justifications based on overriding reasons in the public interest even where the measure at issue has discriminatory features, particularly where the public interest at stake is of particular importance. This evolution is due to the emergence of new legitimate interests of growing relevance for Member States, such as environmental protection, which has risen in the list of priorities of the national authorities in recent years.

In addition to pursuing an objective of general interest, justifications must be in conformity with the principle of proportionality. As explained above, this principle is of fundamental importance. In the recent case law of the Court of Justice, it is at this stage, where the principle of proportionality is involved, that most cases on free movement raise the most complex issues.

Besides the justifications mentioned above, the Treaties introduce exclusions that keep certain activities outside the scope of Article 56 TFEU. Following the same pattern as the freedom of establishment, activities related to the exercise of public authority are also excluded from the rules on the freedom to provide services by virtue of Article 62 TFEU, which applies Article 51 TFEU to the freedom to provide services. On this point, see section I.7 of this chapter.

The case of transport services raises a specific issue. Article 58(1) TFEU states that 'freedom to provide services in the field of transport shall be governed by the provisions of the Title relating to transport'. This provision means that the liberalisation of transport services is to be achieved through the adoption of secondary legislation under the transport Title (Title VI of Part Three TFEU, Articles 90–100), rather than through the direct application of Article 56 TFEU. As a result, Union law safeguards operators in this sector only to the extent that the Union legislature has adopted legislation on the matter. This has resulted in problematic situations, such as the case of hot-air balloons, which were not covered by the Union's legislative measures on the liberalisation of air transport, but also fell outside the scope of Article 56 TFEU. This outcome led the Court of Justice to rule that, in such cases, when no specific Treaty provision on transport applies, operators can invoke the principle of non-discrimination on grounds of nationality, as provided in Article 18 TFEU.[115]

[115] Case C-382/08 *Neukirchinger* EU:C:2011:27, paras 28–29; and Case C-628/11 *International Jet Management* EU:C:2014:171, paras 53–54. It should be noted that in both cases there were acts of secondary legislation which, although not directly applicable to the facts of the case, contained clear and precise provisions laying down the objectives that the transport legislation was intended to achieve. Insofar as the national challenged measures at issue were not, a priori, compatible with those objectives, the Court of Justice ruled that Art 18 TFEU was applicable to the case.

7. Secondary Legislation

Directive 2006/123 on services in the internal market introduces a broad harmonisation effort that covers a wide range of the services provided within the internal market. At the same time, there is an abundance of Union legislative measures aimed at regulating the provision of services across the internal market on a sectoral basis, in areas such as financial services, energy, and healthcare, among others. Therefore, Article 56 TFEU operates as a subsidiary rule for activities not covered by general or sector-specific Union legislation, while also serving as a benchmark for interpreting the said legislation and remaining applicable to issues falling outside the scope of the Directive.

This section will focus on the main legislative instrument for services: Directive 2006/123 on services in the internal market. It will also pay careful attention to a case of sectoral harmonisation: cross-border healthcare, as an example of an economic activity initially governed by Article 56 TFEU and later harmonised by the Union legislator.

7.1. *Directive 2006/123 on Services in the Internal Market*

As explained above, Directive 2006/123 introduces a general regime applicable to a large number of economic sectors, aiming to create a common legal framework for services provided within the internal market. In section I.8.1 of this chapter, reference was made to the provisions of the Directive governing the permanent establishment of companies and self-employed persons in a Member State (including purely internal situations, as Chapter III applies to situations both with and without a cross-border link). In the following section, the focus shifts to Chapter IV and its rules regarding the provision of services.

Directive 2006/123 defines services in Article 4(1) as 'any self-employed economic activity, normally provided for remuneration, as referred to in Article [57] of the Treaty'. The reference to Article 57 TFEU confirms that, in case of doubt, the case law on the concept of 'service' outlined above applies.

Article 16 of Directive 2006/123 is the key provision of Chapter IV, which sets out the conditions under which Member States may impose requirements on cross-border service providers. This provision resulted from a haphazard legislative process, which began with a more ambitious proposal aimed at establishing a general 'country of origin' rule under which the service provider would be subject exclusively to the law of the Member State of establishment. Although the principle of mutual recognition could be inferred from the case law and had been successfully applied in certain sectors through sector-specific legislation (see, for example, the audiovisual and e-commerce sectors), concerns were raised about its impact in certain economic areas, such as health, education, or other services associated with social services or welfare. These concerns prompted a significant revision of the text, leading to the current wording in Article 16.

Firstly, Article 16 establishes the obligation for Member States to respect the right of operators to provide services in a Member State other than the one in which they are established, as well as the freedom of access to and exercise of services within their territory. A general principle of the freedom to provide services in both the Member State of origin and the Member State of destination/host is therefore introduced, subject to the limitations and derogations expressly provided in the Directive, and in line with the case law set out above.

Secondly, Article 16 introduces a rule similar to that in the judgment in *Säger*, by prohibiting the application of new (local) requirements to services from other Member States. However, the wording is somewhat unclear, as it is framed in negative terms, listing the requirements that

Member States may *not* adopt if they do not adhere to the principles of non-discrimination, necessity, and proportionality. Moreover, when defining these principles, Directive 2006/123 uses terms that do not match some of the definitions established in the case law of the Court of Justice, leading to some conceptual confusion. Next, a list of requirements that are prohibited under Article 16 is introduced, including the obligation to be established in the host Member State, the obligation to acquire a particular form or type of infrastructure, or requirements regarding the use of equipment and material that are an integral part of the provision of services, among others.

While the Directive already introduces several exclusions of economic activities in Article 2(2), additional sectors are included in the list in Article 17. Therefore, fields such as the legal profession, certain aspects of copyright, and services governed by other instruments of secondary legislation (gas, postal services, electricity, etc), and social security services are excluded from the scope of Chapter IV.

As can be seen, the substantive framework generally aligns with that established by the Court of Justice's case law in interpreting the Treaties. Directive 2006/123 codifies the developments made to date in the interpretation of Article 56 TFEU, without introducing significant novelties, and even causes some confusion in the use of various categories. The main contribution of the Directive is the development of a structured, codified, and common framework for all economic operators to understand the standards they can demand from local authorities. Similarly, the Directive has been transposed into law across all Member States, resulting in a shared and consistent framework for services. This development facilitates common practices and the protection of services across all Member States – particularly important in an area where cultural differences can create substantial barriers to the development of an integrated services market in Europe.

7.2. *Directive 2011/24 on Patients' Rights in Cross-border Healthcare*

Healthcare is a service with limited permeability to cross-border activity, mainly due to the presence of well-established public health systems in the Member States with closely monitored capacities to meet the demand of citizens. Furthermore, the existence of divergences between the public health systems of the Member States hinders cross-border cooperation. This is compounded by the reluctance in parts of European society towards liberalising a service that, in most Member States, holds the status of a public service. As a result, it is not surprising that healthcare remained largely politically and administratively insulated and outside the scope of the freedom to provide services for several decades, at least until the 1990s.

Following a series of judgments on services in the field of healthcare, the Court of Justice confirmed the applicability of Article 56 TFEU to this sector, particularly in relation to the requirements of prior authorisation for receiving a health service in another Member State. In *Kohll*[116] and *Vanbraekel*,[117] the Court of Justice held that the obligation to seek prior authorisation before receiving a healthcare service not requiring hospitalisation in another Member State amounted to a restriction on the freedom to provide services. Therefore, patients covered by a social security scheme in one Member State are entitled to receive health services in another Member State under the coverage of their social security system. This general principle applies to healthcare services that do not require hospitalisation, allowing the patient to travel to another Member State, receive the service, and, upon returning to

[116] Case C-158/96 *Kohll v Union des caisses de maladie* EU:C:1998:171.

[117] Case C-368/98 *Vanbraekel* EU:C:2001:400.

their Member State of affiliation, claim reimbursement of the costs up to the level of reimbursement that would have been provided for the same treatment in the Member State of affiliation. The principle was developed further in *Geraets-Smits and Peerbooms*,[118] as well as in *Müller-Fauré and van Riet*,[119] where the Court of Justice acknowledged that healthcare services requiring hospitalisation can require prior authorisation from the health authorities or the patient's insurer.

This case law resulted in a notable rise in the movement of patients between Member States, particularly for those residing in areas with high cross-border mobility. Furthermore, patients within public health systems facing long waiting lists viewed this case law as a solution to their problems, a perception that was put to the test in *Watts*.[120] In that case, the Court of Justice upheld the legality of requiring prior authorisation when waiting lists exist, but only if the Member State takes into consideration the patient's individual circumstances. Consequently, patients on a waiting list needing an operation in a hospital may be authorised to receive care in another Member State if the waiting time in the Member State of affiliation would exceed the medically acceptable period, having regard to the patient's individual medical situation.

As in other fields of policy, the momentum of the case law paved the way for legislative harmonisation. The Union legislature responded to the developments in the Court of Justice's case law by adopting Directive 2011/24 on the application of patients' rights in cross-border healthcare.[121] Chapter III of this Directive, concerning the reimbursement of cross-border healthcare costs, codifies the Court of Justice's case law and establishes the right of patients to access healthcare services in other Member States, subject to certain conditions aligned with the case law outlined above. In more recent developments following the enactment of Directive 2011/24, the Court of Justice confirmed the applicability of the Directive to the provision of telemedicine services between two Member States, where the healthcare service is provided exclusively via information and communication technologies, to a patient by a healthcare provider established in a Member State other than the patient's Member State of affiliation, at a distance and therefore without the patient and the provider being simultaneously physically present in the same location.[122]

Directive 2011/24 confirms, as a general rule, the applicability of Regulation 883/2004 on the coordination of social security systems where public health services are provided within social security frameworks. For situations not covered by the Regulation, or where the patient chooses to seek treatment under the Directive rather than the Regulation, Article 8 of the Directive introduces the right of free movement, with certain qualifications for services that require the patient to stay overnight in hospital or to use highly specialised and cost-intensive medical infrastructure or equipment, for which a system of prior authorisation may apply.

III. FREE MOVEMENT OF WORKERS

The mobility of workers is an essential feature of the internal market. There is little point in enabling the movement of companies if they cannot move their employees. From the early stages of the integration process, workers were recognised as one of the main beneficiaries of free movement rules, unlike other freedoms such as the free movement of capital, which was

[118] Case C-157/99 *Smits and Peerbooms* EU:C:2001:404.

[119] Case C-385/99 *Müller-Fauré and van Riet* EU:C:2003:270.

[120] Case C-372/04 *Watts* EU:C:2006:325.

[121] Directive 2011/24/EU of the European Parliament and of the Council of 9 March 2011 on the application of patients' rights in cross-border healthcare [2011] OJ L88/45.

[122] Case C-115/24 *UJ v Österreichische Zahnärztekammer* EU:C:2025:694, paras 90–92.

not fully liberalised until 1 July 1990. It was in the area of free movement of workers that the first cases of mobility of natural persons emerged in the Court of Justice's case law. Unlike goods, capital, or companies, natural persons present specific challenges when exercising free movement, ranging from the integration of their families to the application of labour legislation, or the coordination of social security systems, among others. These matters have been addressed in the case law and the legislation from a very early date, as will now be explained.

Articles 45–48 TFEU introduce and develop the right to free movement of workers in the internal market. Among these provisions, Article 46 TFEU establishes the legal basis for the European Parliament and the Council to 'issue directives or make regulations setting out the measures required to bring about freedom of movement for workers as defined in Article 45.' Article 48 TFEU provides an additional legal basis, focusing on the adoption of measures for migrant workers and self-employed workers to 'aggregate' social benefits subject to social security schemes. Both legal bases rely on the ordinary legislative procedure and require a qualified majority in the Council, although Article 48 TFEU provides that where a member of the Council declares that a draft legislative act under that Article would affect important aspects of its social security system, it may request that the matter be referred to the European Council.

1. Definition of 'Worker'

The Treaties do not provide a definition of 'worker', but the case law has consistently stated that the concept must be interpreted autonomously, in accordance with criteria based solely on Union law.[123] Therefore, the notion of 'worker' is defined according to objective criteria that characterise an employment relationship, taking into account the rights and obligations of the person concerned. The standard formulation used in the case law is as follows:

> [T]he essential feature of an employment relationship . . . is that for a certain period of time a person performs services for and under the direction of another person in return for which he receives remuneration.[124]

This definition requires a factual and legal analysis based on the relationship between the employer and the worker. The outcome of this criterion results in a broad notion of what constitutes a worker. It makes no difference whether the employer is a private or a public entity,[125] the form of participation in the company,[126] or the fact that the worker resides in one Member State and works in another (the case of 'frontier workers').[127]

To benefit from the rights under Article 45 TFEU, the worker must be a national of a Member State. When defining the content of the right to free movement of workers, Article 45(2) TFEU states that the prohibition of discrimination applies only to workers 'of the Member States'. Consequently, a third-country national who is legally residing in a Member State does not have the right to free movement directly on the basis of Article 45 TFEU. A

[123] Already in 1964, the Court of Justice stated that 'nothing in Article [45 to 48] of the Treaty leads to the conclusion that these provisions have left the definition of the term 'worker' to national legislation. [Articles 45 to 48] would therefore be deprived of all effect and the above-mentioned objectives of the Treaty would be frustrated if the meaning of such a term could be unilaterally fixed and modified by national law' (Case 75/63 *Unger v Bedrijfsvereniging voor Detailhandel en Ambachten* EU:C:1964:19).

[124] Case C-66/85 *Lawrie-Blum* EU:C:1986:284, para 17.

[125] Case C-152/73 *Sotgiu v Deutsche Bundespost* EU:C:1974:13, para 5; and Case C-270/13 *Haralambidis* EU:C:2014:2185, para 38.

[126] Case C-232/09 *Danosa* EU:C:2010:674, para 51.

[127] Case C-379/11 *Caves Krier Frères* EU:C:2012:798, para 27; and Case C-20/16 *Bechter* EU:C:2017:488, para 32.

Union legislative instrument can grant such a right to third-country nationals subject to certain conditions, but the right of free movement does not arise directly from the Treaty.

The economic dimension of the worker's activity is another key requirement. It is essential that some form of remuneration exists, however small, in return for performing a genuine and effective activity. As repeatedly stated in the case law, the limited amount of remuneration has no bearing on whether a person is considered a worker for the purposes of Union law.[128] Therefore, the activity of an apprentice within a training programme or traineeship, whether in the public or private sector, may constitute an employment relationship within the meaning of Article 45 TFEU.[129] The same applies to semi-professional sportspersons, particularly when they are subject to rules adopted by sporting associations governing their work.[130]

The economic activity cannot be so residual that it ends up being of a 'purely marginal and ancillary' nature.[131] In such cases, it is considered that there is no significant economic activity to categorise the relationship as an employment relationship. The Court of Justice's case law has interpreted this exclusion strictly, so that individuals performing even short-term activities will be considered a 'worker'.[132] Moreover, the fact that remuneration is supplemented by income from third parties, whether private (family) or public (social security), does not alter the fact that there is such remuneration, and therefore that an economic activity is deemed to exist.[133] This pragmatic approach is well encapsulated in *Kurz*, where the Court of Justice ruled that:

> [N]either the *sui generis* nature of the employment relationship under national law, nor the level of productivity of the person concerned, the origin of the funds from which the remuneration is paid or the limited amount of the remuneration can have any consequence in regard to whether or not the person is a worker for the purposes of [Union] law.[134]

The worker must have a close territorial connection with the Union. A worker who is a national of a Member State and is employed by an undertaking from another Member State is regarded as a 'worker' when they carry out an activity in a third country.[135] Similarly, a worker who is a national of a Member State employed by the embassy of another Member State in a third country also falls within the scope of Article 45 TFEU, provided that the employment relationship has a sufficiently close link with the law of a Member State.[136]

Article 45 TFEU applies to individuals actively seeking employment in another Member State.[137] In this way, free movement provides protection not only to those who have received a job offer before relocating to the host Member State, but also to jobseekers who move with the

[128] Case 53/81 *Levin v Staatssecretaris van Justitie* EU:C:1982:105, para 16; Case 344/87 *Bettray v Staatssecretaris van Justitie* EU:C:1989:226, para 16; and Case C-456/02 *Trojani* EU:C:2004:488, para 16.

[129] Case C-188/00 *Kurz* EU:C:2002:694, para 34; Case C-109/04 *Kranemann* EU:C:2005:187, para 17; and Case C-807/23 *Katharina Plavec* EU:C:2025:234, para 33.

[130] Case C-333/21 *European Superleague Company* EU:C:2023:1011, paras 85–86; and Case C-650/22 *Fédération internationale de football association (FIFA)* EU:C:2024:824, para 77.

[131] Case C-357/89 *Raulin v Minister van Onderwijs en Wetenschappen* EU:C:1992:87, para 10.

[132] Joined Cases C-22/08 and C-23/08 *Vatsouras and Koupatantze* EU:C:2009:344, paras 25–30.

[133] Case 53/81 *Levin v Staatssecretaris van Justitie* EU:C:1982:105, para 14; and Case 139/85 *Kempf v Staatssecretaris van Justitie* EU:C:1986:223, para 14.

[134] Case C-188/00 *Kurz* EU:C:2002:694, para 32. Similarly, see Case 66/85 *Lawrie-Blum v Land Baden-Württemberg* EU:C:1986:284, paras 16–17; Case 197/86 *Brown v Secretary of State for Scotland* EU:C:1988:323, para 21; Case 344/87 *Bettray v Staatssecretaris van Justitie* EU:C:1989:226, paras 15–16; Case C-357/89 *Raulin v Minister van Onderwijs en Wetenschappen* EU:C:1992:87, para 10; and Case C-3/90 *Bernini v Minister van Onderwijs en Wetenschappen* EU:C:1992:89, paras 14–17.

[135] Case C-248/96 *Grahame and Hollanders v Bestuur van de Nieuwe Algemene Bedrijfsvereniging* EU:C:1997:543, para 36; Case 237/83 *Prodest v Caisse primaire d'assurance maladie de Paris* EU:C:1984:277, para 7; Case C-60/93 *Aldewereld v Staatssecretaris van Financiën* EU:C:1994:271, paras 24–25; and Case C-544/11 *Petersen* EU:C:2013:124, paras 34–43.

[136] Case C-214/94 *Boukhalfa v Bundesrepublik Deutschland* EU:C:1996:174, paras 15–17.

[137] Case C-138/02 *Collins* EU:C:2004:172, para 29; and *Vatsouras and Koupatantze* (n 132), para 36.

aim of finding a position in the host Member State's labour market without a prior job offer. The case of jobseekers is subject to specific requirements established by legislative acts and the Treaties, as outlined in the case law of the Court of Justice. Article 14(4)(b) of Directive 2004/38 provides that Union citizens who have entered the territory of the host Member State in order to seek employment may not be expelled for as long as they can provide evidence that they are continuing to seek employment and that they have a genuine chance of being engaged. In addition, Article 24 of Directive 2004/38 authorises Member States to restrict access to social benefits for jobseekers, except for benefits specifically aimed at improving the employability of jobseekers.[138] If the jobseeker has been granted a residence right for the purposes of allowing the exercise of parental authority, the host Member State cannot limit access to parental benefits for the parents of children holding the nationality of that Member State.[139] When it comes to the right of residence, Member States may impose limitations on jobseekers' right of residence, making it contingent on their active pursuit of employment. This requirement is fulfilled if the person is registered with the employment office of the host Member State and can demonstrate that they are continuing to seek employment and have a genuine chance of being engaged.

2. Cross-border Link

Article 45 TFEU requires a cross-border link in the employment relationship. This means that the provision will apply only to workers who relocate to another Member State or whose employment relationship has a relevant connection with the law of another Member State. Conversely, when all elements of an employment relationship remain within the territory of a single Member State, the situation is considered to be purely internal and Article 45 TFEU does not apply.[140] The mere expectation that a decision of a Member State will hinder a worker from being employed in another Member State does not establish a sufficient cross-border connection to trigger Article 45 TFEU.[141]

3. Content of the Right

Article 45(2) TFEU outlines the rights entailed by the freedom of movement for workers. The list is not exhaustive, but it captures the main rights linked to any worker exercising free movement within the internal market. The provision refers to the worker's right to:

- accept offers of employment actually made;
- move freely within the territory of Member States for the purpose of employment;
- stay in a Member State for the purpose of employment, in accordance with the laws, regulations and administrative provisions applicable to the employment of nationals of that State;

[138] *Vatsouras and Koupatantze* (n 132) para 45.
[139] Case C-397/23 *Jobcenter Arbeitplus Bielefeld* EU:C:2025:602, para 44.
[140] Case C-175/78 *The Queen v Saunders* EU:C:1979:88, paras 10–12; Case C-134/94 *Esso Española v Comunidad Autónoma de Canarias* EU:C:1995:414, paras 13–16; Joined Cases C-225/95, C-226/95 and C-227/95 *Kapasakalis and Others v Elliniko Dimosio* EU:C:1998:332, para 22; Case C-18/95 *Terhoeve* EU:C:1999:22, para 26; Case C-95/99 *Khalil and Others* EU:C:2001:532, para 69; Case C-208/05 *ITC* EU:C:2007:16, para 29; Case C-212/06 *Gouvernement de la Communauté française and Gouvernement wallon* EU:C:2008:178, para 33; Case C-139/12 *Caixa d'Estalvis i Pensions de Barcelona* EU:C:2014:174, para 42; and Case C-268/15 *Ullens de Schooten* EU:C:2016:874, para 47.
[141] Case C-180/83 *Moser v Land Baden-Württemberg* EU:C:1984:233, para 18.

- remain in the territory of a Member State after having been employed in that Member State.

These rights are complemented by those granted in Regulation 492/2011 on freedom of movement for workers[142] and Directive 2004/38 on the residence rights of citizens and their family members. Regulation 492/2011 establishes the right of access to the labour market of another Member State, as well as equal treatment in employment conditions during the period of stay in that Member State. Directive 2004/38 sets out the conditions for the legal residence of workers and their family members. Furthermore, the Court of Justice's case law has interpreted Article 45 TFEU across a broad range of cases and now provides comprehensive guidance for interpreting Regulation 492/11 and Directive 2004/38.[143]

The rights enjoyed by free-moving workers are set out in the following sections, in which a distinction is made based on the time of entry into the host Member State, the duration of employment in the host Member State, and the specificities of the social security and residence conditions of the worker and their family members.

3.1. *Right of Access to the Labour Market*

Article 1 of Regulation 492/2011 implements Article 45 TFEU. It establishes the right of any national of a Member State, regardless of their place of residence,

> to take up an activity as an employed person, and to pursue such activity, within the territory of another Member State in accordance with the provisions laid down by law, regulation or administrative action governing the employment of nationals of that State.

This is a non-discrimination rule imposing on the host Member States an obligation to treat workers from other Member States under the same conditions as local workers. The obligation covers both direct and indirect discriminatory measures.

In practice, direct discrimination is rarely found. The explicit wording of Article 45 TFEU and Regulation 492/2011 clearly prohibits such practices. Apart from the general prohibition of discriminatory measures between local workers and workers from other Member States, Articles 3–6 of Regulation 492/2011 establish the right of every worker from another Member State to:

- be excluded from any special recruitment procedures or conditions applicable only to foreign nationals, and from any recruitment quotas limiting the hiring of foreign nationals;[144]
- seek employment in the territory of another Member State, and receive the same assistance there as that which the employment offices of that Member State grant to their own nationals seeking employment;[145]

[142] Regulation (EU) No 492/2011 of the European Parliament and of the Council of 5 April 2011 on freedom of movement for workers within the Union [2011] OJ L141/1.

[143] In some cases, the Court of Justice has referred to secondary legislation to interpret Art 45 TFEU, which is certainly an unusual approach towards constitutional interpretation. This practice is used when a case does not fall within the scope of secondary law, but specific criteria are needed to resolve the case. By way of example, a three-month period of residence provided for in secondary law may be a useful criterion for interpreting the Treaty and requiring a minimum period of stay in a host Member State. In such a case, the Court of Justice can use the three-month period introduced in the legislation as a benchmark to interpret the Treaties and provide an answer to the case.

[144] Art 3(2). Taking into account prior work experience in the public sector in the host Member State falls under the scope of Art 3 of Regulation 492/2011, as confirmed in Case C-132/22 *BM and NP* EU:C:2023:489, para 40.

[145] Art 5.

- not make their access to employment dependent on medical, professional or other criteria that discriminate on the basis of nationality.[146]

Neutral but indirectly discriminatory measures restricting access to employment are more frequent in practice, but are equally unlawful. Article 3(1)(b) of Regulation 492/2011 prohibits any measures 'where, though applicable irrespective of nationality, their exclusive or principal aim or effect is to keep nationals of other Member States away from the employment offered'. There are numerous examples of such measures, including requirements for a minimum period of residence or employment in the Member State,[147] language requirements,[148] or the obligation to have obtained qualifications in an establishment within the Member State to qualify for certain positions.[149]

3.2. *Right to Work*

Once access to the labour market of the host Member State has been obtained, the exercise of an employment activity must also be carried out without any discrimination against free-moving workers. Article 7(1) of Regulation 492/2011 states in categorical terms that:

> A worker who is a national of a Member State may not, in the territory of another Member State, be treated differently from national workers by reason of his nationality in respect of any conditions of employment and work, in particular as regards remuneration, dismissal, and, should he become unemployed, reinstatement or re-employment.

Regulation 492/2011 further specifies this prohibition and lists specific cases in which the worker must be treated in the same way as local workers:

- access to tax advantages;[150]
- access to social advantages, in terms of housing, including access to home ownership as needed;[151]
- access to vocational schools and retraining centres;[152]

[146] Art 6.

[147] Case C-419/92 *Scholz v Opera Universitaria di Cagliari and Cinzia Porcedda* EU:C:1994:62, para 11; Case C-138/02 *Collins* EU:C:2004:172, para 37; and Case C-346/05 *Chateignier* EU:C:2006:711, para 36.

[148] Case C-379/87 *Groener v Minister for Education and City of Dublin Vocational Education Committee* EU:C:1989:599, paras 18–23; Case C-281/98 Angonese EU:C:2000:296, para 41; and Case C-202/11 *Las* EU:C:2013:239, para 31.

[149] Case C-40/05 *Lyyski* EU:C:2007:10, paras 37–40.

[150] Art 7(2) of Regulation 492/2011. See also the judgments in Case C-279/93 *Finanzamt Köln-Altstadt v Schumacker* EU:C:1995:31, para 23; Case C-391/97 *Gschwind* EU:C:1999:409, para 32; Case C-376/03 *D* EU:C:2005:424, para 37; Case C-336/96 *Commission v Belgium* EU:C:1994:67, para 49; Case C-383/05 *Talotta* EU:C:2007:181, para 19; Case C-527/06 *Renneberg* EU:C:2008:566, paras 35–36; and Case C-9/14 *Kieback* EU:C:2015:406, para 20.

[151] Arts 7(2) and 9(1) of Regulation 492/2011. See also the judgments in Case 207/78 *Ministère public v Even* EU:C:1979:144, para 21; Case 65/81 *Reina v Landeskreditbank Baden-Württemberg* EU:C:1982:6, para 17; Case C-111/91 *Commission v Luxembourg* EU:C:1993:92, para 17; Case C-57/96 *Meints v Minister van Landbouw, Natuurbeheer en Visserij* EU:C:1997:564, para 36; Case C-85/96 *Martinez Sala v Freistaat Bayern* EU:C:1998:217, para 25; Case C-35/97 *Commission v France* EU:C:1998:431, paras 37–39; Case C-3/99 *Leclere and Deaconescu* EU:C:2001:303, para 37; Case C-258/04 *Ioannidis* EU:C:2005:559, para 34; and Case C-206/10 *Commission v Germany* EU:C:2011:283, para 34.

[152] Art 7(3) of Regulation 492/2011. See also the rulings in Case 293/83 *Gravier v Ville de Liège* EU:C:1985:69, para 30; Case 24/86 *Blaizot v Université de Liège and Others* EU:C:1988:43, para 11; Case 39/86 *Lair v Universität Hannover* EU:C:1988:322, para 12; Case 197/86 *Brown v Secretary of State for Scotland* EU:C:1988:323, para 10; Case C-147/03 *Commission v Austria* EU:C:2005:427, paras 50 and 61–66; and Case C-40/05 *Lyyski* EU:C:2007:10, para 28.

- access to a family allowance[153] or integration assistance in the form of school assistance benefits for disabled children;[154]
- equal treatment in relation to membership of trade union organisations and the exercise of trade union rights, including the right to vote and have access to administrative or management positions in a trade union organisation.[155]

These prohibitions also apply to working conditions laid down in collective or individual agreements. As a result, Regulation 492/2011 declares null and void:

> [Any] clause of a collective or individual agreement or of any other collective regulation concerning eligibility for employment, remuneration and other conditions of work or dismissal . . . in so far as it lays down or authorises discriminatory conditions in respect of workers who are nationals of the other Member States.[156]

3.3. *Right of Residence*

According to Article 45(3)(c) TFEU, workers exercising free movement have the right to stay in the host Member State for the purpose of employment. This right also covers those actively seeking employment in another Member State on the basis of Article 45 TFEU as interpreted by the case law of the Court of Justice, during the period in which they actively search for work and can demonstrate a genuine chance of being engaged.

The worker's right of residence in the host Member State also extends to family members, as laid down in Articles 6–7, read in conjunction with Articles 23–24 of Directive 2004/38. The conditions of residence, the types of residence, and the rights attached to each of them, as well as the grounds for expulsion, are prescribed in Directive 2004/38 and discussed in more detail in chapter six of this book. In addition, the right to remain in the territory of a Member State after having been employed there, as provided in Article 45(3)(d) TFEU, is governed by Regulation (EU) No 635/2006 (which codified Regulation No 1251/70), supplemented by Article 17 of Directive 2004/38 on the right of permanent residence for persons who have ceased their occupational activity.

4. Discrimination and Market Access

Article 45 TFEU and secondary Union legislation prohibit discriminatory measures in the field of employment. Since the 1990s, a criterion based on a market access test has also emerged in the free movement of workers, in line with developments in other fundamental freedoms.

In *Kraus*,[157] the Court of Justice stated that the Treaties prohibit measures of the Member States, even if they are applied without discrimination on grounds of nationality, which '[are] liable to hamper or to render less attractive the exercise by [Union] nationals, including those of the Member State which enacted the measure, of fundamental freedoms guaranteed by the Treaty'.[158] This analysis, based in subsequent case law on the comparison of the treatment of foreign workers with that of local workers, but on the actual obstacle posed by the measure to

[153] Case C-27/23 *FV* EU:C:2024:404, paras 32–35.
[154] Case C-257/24 *PE vs Städteregion Aachen* EU:C:2025:567, para 41.
[155] Art 8 of Regulation 492/2011.
[156] ibid, Art 7(4).
[157] Case C-19/92 *Kraus v Land Baden-Württemberg* EU:C:1993:125.
[158] ibid, para 32.

those exercising freedom of movement, has become the most common standard of review in the Court of Justice's current case law.

For example, the market access test in the field of employment is used to highlight the restrictive nature of a measure that requires studies at a university in a host Member State to access an employment programme.[159] A measure requiring proof of language proficiency through a single type of certificate issued by a single official body also acts as an obstacle to the free movement of workers.[160] An obligation to register a worker's vehicle in the worker's Member State of residence, when the vehicle is used for work activities in another Member State, is a non-discriminatory measure but it amounts to an obstacle to the exercise of free movement.[161] Even a clearly discriminatory measure, such as one that restricts the pension rights of civil servants from a Member State who move to join an EU institution or an international organisation, as opposed to civil servants who transfer within the same Member State, is also reviewed in light of the market access test.[162]

5. Justifications and Exclusions

Article 45(3) TFEU states that the rights attached to the free movement of workers are 'subject to limitations justified on grounds of public policy, public security or public health'. Member States may therefore invoke these grounds when adopting measures that discriminate against or hinder access to the labour market for workers from other Member States.

Together with the Treaty derogations in Article 45(3) TFEU, the case law has recognised the right of Member States to justify restrictive measures by overriding reasons in the public interest, which have been developed on a case-by-case basis in the Court of Justice's case law. See section I.6 of this chapter, where a description of the main overriding reasons in the public interest recognised to date is available.

The traditional position is that directly discriminatory measures can only be justified on the grounds explicitly listed in Article 45(3) TFEU. In contrast, indirect discriminatory measures and those falling under the market access test can be justified on the basis of both Article 45(3) TFEU and the overriding reasons of general interest recognised in the case law. In recent years the case law has blurred this distinction and, at present, Member States have been allowed to invoke overriding reasons in the public interest to justify both direct and indirect discrimination, as well as restrictions falling under the market access test. This development must be understood with caution and is largely explained by the evolving classification of measures as directly or indirectly discriminatory rather than by a general acceptance of overriding reasons in the public interest as justifications for direct nationality discrimination.

Article 45(4) TFEU excludes from the scope of the freedom of movement of workers the case of 'employment in the public service'. Although the wording of this provision differs from that of the equivalent provision applicable to the freedom of establishment and the freedom to provide services, it is an exclusion with elements common to those of other freedoms. In fact, the case law frequently cross-references precedents in which both Article 45(4) and Article 51(1) TFEU are subject to interpretation.[163]

[159] Case C-40/05 *Lyyski* EU:C:2007:10, para 37.
[160] Case C-317/14 *Commission v Belgium* EU:C:2015:63, para 23.
[161] Case C-420/15 *U* EU:C:2017:408, para 20.
[162] Case C-515/14 *Commission v Cyprus* EU:C:2016:30, para 45.
[163] See, by way of example, Case C-47/08 *Commission v Belgium* EU:C:2011:334, paras 83–86.

Article 45(4) TFEU allows the Member States to reserve access to certain posts in the public service exclusively for their own nationals. This exclusion does not entitle Member States to restrict the free movement of public employees once they have taken up the post. This outcome is in line with the principle according to which an exception to a general rule must be interpreted strictly. Therefore, once a worker has taken up a position in the administration, the Member State may not take measures that discriminate against the worker, or that hinder or make less attractive their freedom of movement.[164]

To date, the Court of Justice has confirmed the strict interpretation of the exclusion in Article 45(4) TFEU, applying it only to positions in the public service that involve direct or indirect participation in the exercise of powers conferred by public law and in the discharge of functions whose purpose is to safeguard the general interests of the State. Teachers in public schools,[165] nurses in public health centres,[166] employees of the public railway service,[167] municipal civil servants performing administrative or technical functions,[168] or researchers in public research centres linked to sensitive projects for the security or interest of the Member State have not been considered to be posts involving the exercise of public authority.[169] In contrast, the case law suggests that positions in the police, the judiciary, the armed forces, or the tax administration may involve the exercise of public authority and, consequently, may be reserved for nationals of the Member State.

6. Secondary Legislation

6.1. *Regulation 883/2004 on the Coordination of Social Security Systems*

Labour mobility can pose challenges in coordinating the different social security schemes to which the free-moving worker contributes. For example, if an individual works in Italy for five years, Belgium for eight years, Luxembourg for two years, and then returns to Italy to work until retirement, questions may arise about the applicable social security scheme during the periods spent in other Member States or the method used to calculate total benefit entitlements, including retirement benefits. To ensure that coordination issues between social security schemes do not hinder the free movement of workers, Regulation 883/2004 sets out the principle of aggregation of periods and rules on the determination of the applicable legislation, providing legal certainty and clear rules when multiple social security schemes are involved during an employee's career.[170] Regulation 883/2004 applies to both employed and self-employed persons, and it also extends to all Union citizens, as well as to stateless persons and refugees who are or have been subject to the legislation of one or more Member States, and to their family members and survivors.[171]

Firstly, Regulation 883/2004 states that a person must be subject to the legislation of only one social security scheme at any given time, in conjunction with the rule that the applicable

[164] Case C-152/73 *Sotgiu v Deutsche Bundespost* EU:C:1974:13, paras 4–5; Case C-392/05 *Alevizos* EU:C:2007:251, para 69; and Case C-20/16 *Bechter* EU:C:2017:488, para 34.

[165] Case C-66/85 *Lawrie-Blum v Land Baden-Württemberg* EU:C:1986:284, paras 20–21; and Case C-4/91 *Bleis v Ministère de l'Éducation nationale* EU:C:1991:448, paras 6–7.

[166] Case C-307/84 *Commission v France* EU:C:1986:222, para 13.

[167] Case C-149/79 *Commission v Belgium* EU:C:1982:195, paras 8–9.

[168] ibid.

[169] Case C-225/85 *Commission v Italy* EU:C:1987:284, para 12.

[170] Regulation (EC) No 883/2004 of the European Parliament and of the Council of 29 April 2004 on the coordination of social security systems [2004] OJ L166/1.

[171] Arts 2 and 11 of Regulation 883/2004.

legislation is that of the Member State where the person pursues an activity as an employed or self-employed person (*lex loci laboris*).[172] The determination of the applicable legislation depends on the specific cross-border situation provided for in the Regulation, and in cases where the worker habitually carries out their activity in one Member State but spends part of their working time in one or more Member States at the employer's initiative, the applicable social security scheme may, depending on the circumstances (such as whether the worker is posted or pursues activities in two or more Member States), be that of the Member State of residence.[173]

The material scope of Regulation 883/2004 is very broad and aims to encompass all benefits normally included in social security schemes. To tailor the provisions to the features of each benefit, Title III regulates benefits individually and provides for the applicable specificities. This list includes benefits for sickness,[174] maternity/paternity,[175] invalidity,[176] old age,[177] survivors,[178] accidents at work and occupational diseases,[179] death,[180] unemployment,[181] early retirement,[182] and family[183] as well as special non-contributory cash benefits (limited to those listed in Article 70 of the Regulation).

Regulation 883/2004 introduces an aggregation principle, according to which institutions applying legislation under which the acquisition, retention, duration or recovery of the right to benefits, or the coverage of a legislation, is subject to the fulfilment of periods of insurance, employment, self-employment or residence, will take into account periods completed under the legislation of other Member States as though they were periods completed under the legislation which it applies. For retirement benefits, Article 52 of the Regulation sets out the system for calculating the amount due to the person concerned based on two amounts: the independent benefit (calculated solely under the legislation of the Member State concerned, where applicable) and the pro rata benefit. The pro rata amount is calculated by applying to the theoretical amount the ratio between the duration of the periods completed before the materialisation of the risk under the legislation of the Member State concerned, and the total duration of the periods completed before the materialisation of the risk under the legislation of all the Member States concerned. The competent institution then compares the independent benefit and the pro rata benefit and awards the higher of the two.

6.2. *The Posted Workers Directives*

When a company established in one Member State sends its workers temporarily to another Member State to provide a service, the specific issue of 'posted workers' arises. The company exercises its freedom to provide services under Article 56 TFEU and, since it is not permanently establishing itself in another Member State, it remains subject to the law of its Member State of establishment for most purposes. However, the host Member State is entitled to apply a core set of mandatory employment terms and conditions to the posted workers. When the posting originates from a Member State with lower labour costs or more competitive working conditions

[172] ibid, Art 11.
[173] ibid, Art 12(1).
[174] ibid, Arts 17–35.
[175] ibid.
[176] ibid, Arts 44–49.
[177] ibid, Arts 50–60.
[178] ibid.
[179] ibid, Arts 36–41.
[180] ibid, Arts 42–49.
[181] ibid, Arts 61–65.
[182] ibid, Art 66.
[183] ibid, Arts 67–69.

than those in the Member State where the service is to be provided, tensions may arise with local workers and trade unions in the host Member State, or even with the posted workers themselves. These issues were first addressed by the Court of Justice, notably in *Rush Portuguesa*,[184] where the Court held that Union law does not preclude Member States from extending their legislation, or collective labour agreements entered into by both sides of industry, to any person who is employed, even temporarily, within their territory, no matter in which country the employer is established. Although the ruling qualified this outcome and permitted the host Member State to adopt measures to prevent fraud and abusive practices,[185] the ruling's ambiguity led to the adoption of a directive aimed at clarifying the conditions under which a company may post its workers to another Member State.

Directive 96/71,[186] followed by Directive 2014/67,[187] introduced a substantive and procedural framework aimed at balancing, on one hand, the right to provide services in another Member State with its workers, and, on the other hand, the application of minimum standards of social protection for posted workers to prevent unfair competition and social dumping. When a company posts its workers for a period of less than one year, now understood, following the amendments introduced by Directive 2018/957, as a period of up to 12 months (extendable to 18 months upon notification), it is under a duty to respect the terms and conditions of employment of the host Member State in a number of matters listed in Article 3 of Directive 96/71, provided these are laid down in law, regulation or administrative provisions, and/or in universally applicable collective agreements or arbitration awards. Among others, Article 3 includes remuneration, minimum paid annual leave, and health, safety and hygiene standards at work.[188] If the posting exceeds one year, or the extended period referred to above, Article 3(1a) provides that the undertaking is under a duty to guarantee posted workers all the applicable terms and conditions of employment laid down by law, regulation or administrative provision, or by universally applicable collective agreements in the Member State where the work is carried out, with the exception of procedures, formalities and conditions governing the conclusion and termination of the employment contract, including non-compete clauses, and supplementary occupational retirement pension schemes.[189]

[184] Case C-113/89 *Rush Portuguesa v Office national d'immigration* EU:C:1990:142.

[185] ibid, para 17.

[186] Directive 96/71/EC of the European Parliament and of the Council of 16 December 1996 concerning the posting of workers in the framework of the provision of services [1997] OJ L18/1.

[187] Directive 2014/67/EU of the European Parliament and of the Council of 15 May 2014 on ensuring compliance with Directive 96/71/EC concerning the posting of workers in the framework of the provision of services and amending Regulation (EU) No 1024/2012 on administrative cooperation through the Internal Market Information System ('IMI Regulation') [2014] OJ L159/11.

[188] Art 3 of Directive 96/71, as amended in 2018, includes: maximum work periods and minimum rest periods; minimum paid annual leave; remuneration, including overtime rates (this point does not apply to supplementary occupational retirement pension schemes); the conditions of hiring-out of workers, in particular the supply of workers by temporary employment undertakings; health, safety and hygiene at work; protective measures with regard to the terms and conditions of employment of pregnant women or women who have recently given birth, of children and of young people; equality of treatment between men and women and other provisions on non-discrimination; the conditions of workers' accommodation where provided by the employer to workers away from their regular place of work, and allowances or reimbursement of expenditure to cover travel, board and lodging expenses for workers away from home for professional reasons.

[189] It must be noted that when the posted workers are nationals of a third country, the host Member State is entitled to introduce measures on the entry, residence and access to employment of third-country workers. In such cases, the national measures will be scrutinised in light of Art 56 TFEU and not of Directive 96/71. See Case C-540/22 *SN and Others* EU:C:2024:530, paras 61 and 66. The same applies to national rules on the taxation of posted workers, as confirmed in Case C-387/22 *Nord Vest Pro Sani Pro* EU:C:2024:786, paras 38–40.

IV. FREE MOVEMENT OF CAPITAL

Capital is another factor of production whose mobility is crucial for the functioning of the internal market. Firms and individuals with the ability to invest should be able to move their capital between Member States, promoting a better allocation of savings and investment and the necessary means to finance economic activity. Before the introduction of the euro, within a fragmented internal market characterised by fluctuating inflation rates, different currencies, and a variety of tax systems, Member States predominantly regarded the free movement of capital as a potential risk rather than an opportunity. For this reason, the liberalisation of capital movements did not take effect until 1 July 1990, following the adoption of Directive 88/361, and was subsequently enshrined in the Treaties with the entry into force of the Maastricht Treaty.

Although the liberalisation of capital movements did not take full effect until 1990, significant steps were taken in previous years to facilitate the gradual opening of national economies to free capital flows from other Member States. In 1988, Directive 88/361 was adopted,[190] aiming to achieve the complete lifting of restrictions on capital movements between Member States by 1 July 1990. This Directive contains provisions of significant relevance, in particular the nomenclature of activities considered 'capital movements' set out in Annex I, which the Court of Justice still uses as its main point of reference for interpreting Article 63 TFEU.

The Treaties introduce several legal bases that allow the European Parliament and the Council to adopt measures on capital movements within the internal market. In addition to the general legal bases for the freedom of establishment and services,[191] Article 133 TFEU also provides a legal basis for the European Parliament and the Council, acting in accordance with the ordinary legislative procedure and after consulting the European Central Bank (ECB), to adopt 'the measures necessary for the use of the euro as the single currency'.

The free movement of capital is the only freedom with an extraterritorial scope (see section IV.2 of this chapter), a feature that results in the introduction of specific legal bases to facilitate the movement of capital to or from a third country. Consequently, Article 64(2) TFEU empowers the European Parliament and the Council, acting in accordance with the ordinary legislative procedure, to adopt 'measures on the movement of capital to or from third countries involving direct investment – including investment in real estate – establishment, the provision of financial services or the admission of securities to capital markets'.

The Treaties also provide legal bases for the Union to enact legislation restricting the free movement of capital. In particular, Article 64(3) TFEU grants the Council, acting in accordance with a special legislative procedure and acting unanimously after consulting the European Parliament, the authority to lay down 'measures which constitute a step backwards in Union law as regards the liberalisation of the movement of capital to or from third countries'. Furthermore, Article 66 TFEU includes an additional safeguard measure, allowing the Council to adopt 'strictly necessary … safeguard measures' when capital movements with third countries 'threaten to cause serious difficulties for the operation of economic and monetary union'. These measures cannot exceed six months and must be adopted following consultation with the ECB.

[190] Council Directive 88/361/EEC of 24 June 1988 for the implementation of Article 67 of the Treaty [1988] OJ L178/5.

[191] Arts 50, 53(1), 59 and 62 TFEU.

1. Definition of 'Capital'

The Treaties do not define 'capital', but they provide for the content of the right to free movement in Article 63(1) TFEU in clear terms: 'all restrictions on the movement of capital between Member States and between Member States and third countries shall be prohibited'. The definition of capital has largely been developed through case law, but also in Directive 88/361, which provides a list of activities classified as 'capital movements'.

Direct investments are the first group of activities regarded as capital movements. The nomenclature in Annex I to Directive 88/361 defines direct investments as any types of investment

> which serve to establish or to maintain lasting and direct links between the person providing the capital and the entrepreneur to whom or the undertaking to which the capital is made available in order to carry on an economic activity.[192]

Directive 88/361 adds that the concept of direct investment 'must therefore be understood in its widest sense'.[193] It is thus an investment where an economic operator makes a lasting investment in an economic activity (generally a shareholding in a company) with the aim of participating in the management or control of that company, or at least of exercising a definite influence on it.

Secondly, capital movements of a personal nature, such as loans, gifts, dowries, inheritances, debt repayments, or transfers during a stay abroad, are also covered by Article 63(1) TFEU. This includes securities transactions on the stock and money markets,[194] participation in collective investment undertakings,[195] and credits linked to commercial transactions or the provision of services within the internal market.[196]

The Court of Justice confirmed the interpretative role of Annex I of Directive 88/361 in *Trummer and Mayer*,[197] but the nomenclature is not exhaustive and nothing prevents activities not listed from qualifying as 'capital movements' for the purpose of Article 63(1) TFEU. For instance, in *Verkooijen*, the Court of Justice confirmed that the receipt of dividends from a company established in another Member State constitutes a transaction falling within the scope of the free movement of capital, even though it is not explicitly listed in Annex I.[198]

The definition of 'capital' is also relevant in distinguishing the free movement of capital from other freedoms of movement, particularly the freedom of establishment and the freedom to provide services. In the case of freedom of establishment, the case law emphasises that the object of the national measure in question will determine whether it falls under the scope of Article 49 or Article 63 TFEU. If the national measure is intended to apply only to shareholdings that enable an individual to exercise a definite influence on a company's decisions and to determine its activities, its applicable standard of review will be the freedom of establishment.[199] If national measures apply to holdings acquired solely with the intention of

[192] Annex I, Explanatory Notes.
[193] ibid.
[194] ibid, paras III and V.
[195] ibid, Section IV.
[196] ibid, Section VIII.
[197] Case C-222/97 *Trummer and Mayer* EU:C:1999:143, paras 21–22.
[198] Case C-35/98 *Verkooijen* EU:C:2000:294, paras 27–29.
[199] Case C-446/04 *Test Claimants in the FII Group Litigation* EU:C:2006:774, para 37; Case C-81/09 *Idryma Typou* EU:C:2010:622, para 47; Case C-310/09 *Accor* EU:C:2011:581, para 32; Case C-31/11 *Scheunemann* EU:C:2012:481, para 23; Case C-35/11 *Test Claimants in the FII Group Litigation* EU:C:2012:707, para 91; and Case C-47/12 *Kronos International* EU:C:2014:2200, para 31.

making a financial investment, with no intention to influence the management and control of the company, they must be examined exclusively in the light of the free movement of capital.[200] It is also possible that the national measure does not clearly fall within the scope of either Article 49 or Article 63 TFEU; in such cases, it is necessary to take account of the facts of the particular case to determine whether the situation in the main proceedings falls within the scope of one or the other free movement rules.[201]

There may also be an overlap between the free movement of capital and the freedom to provide services, particularly in cases involving financial services. However, the Court of Justice has also emphasised the need to determine which freedom applies to the case, denying that there is a subordinate relationship between the freedom to provide services and the free movement of capital.[202] To determine the applicable freedom, it is necessary to examine the national measure in question and to clarify how it affects the exercise of those fundamental freedoms, as well as whether, in the circumstances of the main proceedings, one of the freedoms takes precedence over the other.[203] The case will be resolved by applying a single freedom if it is shown that one of them is entirely accessory to the other in the circumstances of the concrete case.[204]

It should be noted that the free movement of capital is the only fundamental freedom with an extraterritorial scope of application. As will now be explained, capital from third countries enjoys the right to enter and exit the internal market, which is not the case for goods, services, or workers. Therefore, when the direct investment or financial transaction originates from or has its destination in a third country, the rules on the free movement of capital are in principle applicable.[205]

The Court of Justice has also confirmed the existence of situations involving capital movements that do not overlap with any other freedoms, in which case only Article 63 TFEU applies. These include cases such as the acquisition of and investment in real estate,[206] currency transactions,[207] loans,[208] and the purchase of shares in capital companies where the national rule does not specifically target shareholders with controlling shareholdings but applies to all investors regardless of the size of their holding,[209] as well as special rights retained by the State in privatised undertakings in liberalised sectors (so-called 'golden shares').[210]

[200] Case C-436/08 *Haribo Lakritzen Hans Riegel and Österreichische Salinen* EU:C:2011:61, para 35; Case C-310/09 *Accor* EU:C:2011:581, para 32; Case C-31/11 *Scheunemann* EU:C:2012:481, para 23; Case C-35/11 *Test Claimants in the FII Group Litigation* EU:C:2012:707, para 92; and Case C-47/12 *Kronos International* EU:C:2014:2200, para 32.

[201] Case C-35/11 *Test Claimants in the FII Group Litigation* EU:C:2012:707, paras 93–94; Case C-168/11 *Beker* EU:C:2013:117, paras 27–28; Case C-375/12 *Bouanich* EU:C:2014:138, para 30; Case C-47/12 *Kronos International* EU:C:2014:2200, para 37; and C-295/23 *Halmer Rechtsanwaltsgesellschaft UG* EU:C:2024:1037, paras 52–53.

[202] Case C-452/04 *Fidium Finanz* EU:C:2006:631, para 32.

[203] Case C-71/02 *Karner* EU:C:2004:181, para 47; and *Fidium Finanz* (n 202) para 34.

[204] *Fidium Finanz* (n 202) para 34, referring to similar precedents in Case C-275/92 *HM Customs and Excise v Schindler* EU:C:1994:119, para 22; Case C-390/99 *Canal Satélite Digital* EU:C:2002:34, para 31; and Case C-20/03 *Burmanjer and Others* EU:C:2005:307, para 35.

[205] Case C-101/05 *Skatteverket v A* EU:C:2007:804, paras 28–35.

[206] Case C-302/97 *Konle* EU:C:1999:271, para 39; Joined Cases C-515/99, C-519/99, C-524/99 and C-526/99 to C-540/99 *Reisch and Others* EU:C:2002:135, para 32; Case C-483/99 *Commission v France* EU:C:2002:327, para 38; and Case C-364/01 *Barbier* EU:C:2003:665, para 63.

[207] Joined Cases C-358/93 and C-416/93 *Bordessa and Others* EU:C:1995:54, para 14.

[208] Case C-478/98 *Commission v Belgium* EU:C:2000:497, para 18.

[209] Case C-531/06 *Commission v Italy* EU:C:2009:315, paras 47–48.

[210] Case C-367/98 *Commission v Portugal* EU:C:2002:326, para 39; and Case C-483/99 *Commission v France* EU:C:2002:327, para 41.

2. Cross-border Link and the Extraterritorial Nature of Free Movement of Capital

The free movement of capital requires a cross-border link between at least two Member States or between a Member State and a third country. Therefore, Article 63 TFEU cannot be invoked if the contested national measure relates to a capital movement limited to the territory of a single Member State.[211] To the extent that the capital movement, regardless of the residence of the parties to the transaction, has links to another Member State or a third country, Article 63 TFEU is applicable to the case. For instance, a cross-border link sufficient to trigger the free movement of capital exists where both the deceased and the heir are resident in the same Member State (eg, Germany), provided the inheritance includes assets situated in another Member State, such as capital claims against a financial institution in Austria.

The requirement of a cross-border link is a feature common to the other freedoms of movement. However, Article 63 TFEU includes a differentiating element in terms of its territorial scope of application, insofar as it extends to capital movements between Member States and third countries. The extraterritorial nature of the free movement of capital is linked to the liberalisation efforts of the 1980s, aimed at reinforcing the internal market by establishing a genuine European capital market. This objective could only be realised by opening European capital markets to investment from third countries.

Although Article 63 TFEU enshrines the applicability of free movement of capital rules to third countries without qualification, the fact remains that specific provisions, particularly Articles 64(2) and 65(4) TFEU, contain rules that empower the Union and the Member States to introduce restrictions and safeguards with respect to third-country capital movements. Furthermore, the case law has tightened the standard of review under Article 63 TFEU in cases of capital movements linked to third countries, depending on whether effective mechanisms of administrative cooperation in tax matters exist between the Member State concerned and the third country.[212]

3. Discrimination and Market Access

Although Article 63 TFEU does not in itself refer to the material scope of the right to the free movement of capital, Article 65 TFEU, when regulating the permitted restrictions on that right, sets out various examples that provide useful guidance for identifying the content of the freedom. After enumerating the grounds on which Member States may restrict the free movement of capital, Article 65(3) TFEU states that such measures 'shall not constitute a means of arbitrary discrimination or a disguised restriction on the free movement of capital and payments as defined in Article 63 [TFEU]'.

Article 65(3) TFEU provides that the free movement of capital prohibits discriminatory measures that arbitrarily differentiate between capital flows. Indeed, the pre-Maastricht Treaty provisions on capital prohibited the use of certain criteria, such as nationality, the place of residence of the parties involved in the transaction, or the location of the investment, to justify a

[211] Case C-364/01 *Barbier* EU:C:2003:665, para 58; Case C-43/07 *Arens-Sikken* EU:C:2008:490, para 30; Case C-11/07 *Eckelkamp* EU:C:2008:489, para 39; Case C-318/07 *Persche* EU:C:2009:33, paras 30–31; and Case C-67/08 *Block* EU:C:2009:92, para 20.

[212] Case C-451/05 *ELISA* EU:C:2007:594, paras 94–95; and Case C-101/05 *Skatteverket v A* EU:C:2007:804, para 63: '[W]here the legislation of a Member State makes the grant of a tax advantage dependent on satisfying requirements, compliance with which can be verified only by obtaining information from the competent authorities of a third country, it is, in principle, legitimate for that Member State to refuse to grant that advantage if, in particular, because that third country is not under any contractual obligation to provide information, it proves impossible to obtain such information from that country.'

difference of treatment. These criteria remain in force today, as confirmed by the case law of the Court of Justice, which continues to scrutinise restrictive measures taken by Member States.

There are various examples of national measures that are directly discriminatory and restrict the free movement of capital. The case of *golden shares* in privatised undertakings within liberalised sectors is paradigmatic of this approach: national provisions that grant special rights to the Member State or to shareholders resident in that Member State, as opposed to shareholders from other Member States.[213] Administrative authorisation requirements imposed on foreign investors also constitute discriminatory measures that restrict the free movement of capital, as they impose onerous (and sometimes discretionary) burdens on foreign investors that local investors are not required to bear.[214]

The discrimination analysis also includes national measures that are indirectly discriminatory and neutral in appearance, but detrimental to foreign operators. Several *golden shares* cases concerned national rules applicable irrespective of the shareholder's nationality, but having the effect of preventing foreign shareholders from exercising their rights.[215] More recent developments in the case law have increasingly incorporated a market access analysis, based on the obstacle posed by the measure and the investor's ability to access the market of the Member State in question. This development is consistent with the approach taken in the case law regarding other freedoms of movement, where the analysis of restrictions has shifted towards an assessment of the obstacles to the exercise of the freedom, rather than focusing exclusively on discrimination between operators.[216]

Despite the importance of the market access test in the application of Article 63 TFEU, it is important to note that in the context of direct taxation, the case law has qualified this approach, focusing primarily on a comparability-based analysis rather than on whether the national measure constitutes an obstacle to market access.[217] This nuance suggests that fiscal national measures will only be considered restrictive if it is established that the non-resident taxpayer is in a situation objectively comparable to that of the resident taxpayer having regard to the objective pursued by the national tax provision at issue. If there is no such comparability, the national measure is not regarded as constituting a restriction, and Article 63 TFEU does not apply.[218]

4. Justifications

Article 65(1) TFEU introduces several justifications to the free movement of capital, with wording that differs from that used in the context of other freedoms of movement. This provision enshrines the applicability of Article 63 TFEU and then confirms the right of Member States:

[213] Case C-367/98 *Commission v Portugal* EU:C:2002:326.

[214] Case C-302/97 *Konle* EU:C:1999:271, para 23; and Case C-423/98 *Albore* EU:C:2000:401, para 16.

[215] Case C-463/00 *Commission v Spain* EU:C:2003:272, para 61; and Case C-98/01 *Commission v United Kingdom* EU:C:2003:273, para 47.

[216] Case C-302/97 *Konle* EU:C:1999:271, para 39; Case C-478/98 *Commission v Belgium* EU:C:2000:497, para 19; Joined Cases C-515/99, C-519/99 to C-524/99 and C-526 to C-540/99 *Reisch and Others* EU:C:2002:135, para 32; Case C-112/05 *Commission v Germany* EU:C:2007:623, paras 56 and 68; Case C-567/07 *Woningstichting Sint Servatius* EU:C:2009:593, para 21; and Joined Cases C-105/12 and C-107/12 *Essent* EU:C:2013:677, para 47.

[217] Case C-446/04 *Test Claimants in the FII Group Litigation* EU:C:2006:774; and Case C-374/04 *Test Claimants in Class IV of the ACT Group Litigation* EU:C:2006:773.

[218] Case C-157/10 *Banco Bilbao Vizcaya Argentaria* EU:C:2011:813, para 29; Case C-256/06 *Jäger* EU:C:2008:20, para 32; Case C-132/10 *Halley* EU:C:2011:586, para 22; Case C-679/17 *Huijbrechts* EU:C:2018:940, para 21; Case C-512/03 *Blanckaert* EU:C:2005:516, para 39; and Case C-318/07 *Persche* EU:C:2009:33, para 38.

(a) to apply the relevant provisions of their tax law which distinguish between taxpayers who are not in the same situation with regard to their place of residence or with regard to the place where their capital is invested; and

(b) to take all requisite measures to prevent infringements of national law and regulations, in particular in the field of taxation and the prudential supervision of financial institutions, or to lay down procedures for the declaration of capital movements for purposes of administrative or statistical information, or to take measures which are justified on grounds of public policy or public security.

Although this wording suggests greater discretion on the part of the Member States, the interpretation of these provisions to date has not differed significantly from that of other freedoms.[219] At most, the case law has additionally limited the ability of Member States to invoke the exceptions in Article 65(1) TFEU by requiring that any justification must also satisfy the principle of legal certainty, in the sense that the national legislation must be sufficiently precise and foreseeable to enable persons concerned to ascertain the extent of their rights and obligations.[220]

In addition to the grounds listed in Article 65(1) TFEU, the case law has recognised the right of Member States to invoke overriding reasons in the public interest.[221] The grounds recognised to date are common to all the freedoms of movement, and reference is made here to section I.7 of this chapter.

Grounds of justification must be interpreted strictly and cannot be based on economic grounds. In the case of free movement of capital, this requirement can be particularly challenging for Member States, as restrictions are frequently justified on grounds such as the protection of certain economic activity or the prevention of loss of tax revenue.[222] This reasoning is not covered by Article 65 TFEU or the case law on overriding reasons in the public interest, so Member States may not rely on it, even if it may be the genuine basis for the measure in question.

5. Secondary Legislation: the Foreign Direct Investment Regulation

The growing complexity of geopolitics and the rise of third-country investors acquiring stakes in strategic sectors in the European internal market have raised concerns about the security and public order implications of such investments. As a result, the Union enacted Regulation 2019/452, also known as the FDI Screening Regulation, which came into force on 10 April 2019 and became fully applicable on 11 October 2020.[223] As of 2026, the Regulation is in the process of being amended following a political agreement between the European Parliament

[219] Case 203/80 *Casati* EU:C:1981:261, para 27; Case C-54/99 *Église de scientologie* EU:C:2000:124, paras 17–18; Case C-367/98 *Commission v Portugal* EU:C:2002:326, para 52; Case C-78/21 *AS 'PrivatBank'* EU:C:2023:137, paras 73–82; Case C-39/23 *Keva* EU:C:2024:648, paras 65–70; Case C-419/23 *CN and Nemzeti Földügyi Központ* EU:C:2024:1016, paras 59–66; and Case C-420/23 *Faurécia – Assentos de Automóvel Lda* EU:C:2024:534, paras 28–34.

[220] *Église de scientologie* (n 219) para 22.

[221] Case C-367/98 *Commission v Portugal* EU:C:2002:326, para 49; Joined Cases C-515/99, C-519/99 to C-524/99, and C-526 to C-540/99 *Reisch and Others* EU:C:2002:135, para 33; and Case C-601/23 *Credit Suisse Securities (Europe) Ltd v Diputación Foral de Bizkaia* EU:C:2024:1048, paras 70–74.

[222] See, inter alia, Case C-319/02 *Manninen* EU:C:2004:484, para 49; Case C-367/98 *Commission v Portugal* EU:C:2002:326, para 52; Case C-35/98 *Verkooijen* EU:C:2000:294, paras 47–48; and Case C-194/06 *Orange European Smallcap Fund* EU:C:2008:289, para 93.

[223] Regulation (EU) 2019/452 of the European Parliament and of the Council of 19 March 2019 establishing a framework for the screening of foreign direct investments into the Union [2019] OJ L79 I/1. It should be noted that the Union adopted, shortly after, Regulation (EU) 2022/2560 of the European Parliament and of the Council of 14 December 2022 on foreign subsidies distorting the internal market [2022] OJ L330/1. This instrument is conceived to address distortions in the internal market caused by subsidies granted by non-EU countries to companies operating within the Union.

and the Council on 11 December 2025, aimed at strengthening certain features of the current framework.[224]

The FDI Screening Regulation established, for the first time, a common European framework for screening foreign direct investments into the Union. Before its adoption, the authority to evaluate and regulate foreign investments was held solely by Member States, which operated highly divergent national screening regimes or, in many cases, lacked any screening system. Regulation 2019/452 was therefore introduced as a response to growing concerns about the acquisition of strategic European assets by foreign investors, especially from third countries with significant state involvement, in sectors such as energy, technology, transport, and defence.

Regulation 2019/452 does not establish a Union-level mechanism to prohibit or approve investments; rather, it creates a cooperation mechanism facilitating coordination and information sharing between Member States and the Commission. It enables national authorities to exchange views and assess whether a foreign investment could compromise security or public order within one or more Member States, or could affect projects or programmes of Union interest. Its scope of application is limited to foreign direct investments that may affect security or public order, made by natural persons or undertakings of a third country—that is, those intending to establish or maintain lasting and direct links with the undertaking in which capital is made available in order to carry on an economic activity in a Member State. Situations involving third-country investors exercising special rights or control in undertakings established in a Member State may also fall within the scope of the Regulation, depending on the definition of 'foreign direct investment' and the national screening mechanism concerned.[225]

Under Regulation 2019/452, each Member State retains the right to screen such investments on grounds of security or public order, but subject to common procedural requirements to ensure that national screening mechanisms are transparent, predictable, and non-discriminatory. Investors must have access to legal remedies, and confidential information must be protected throughout the process. The criteria that may be used to determine whether an investment affects security or public order are broadly defined and non-exhaustive, including, inter alia, the impact of an investment on critical infrastructure such as energy, transport, water, health or data processing or storage; on critical technologies such as artificial intelligence or cybersecurity; on the supply of critical inputs like raw materials; or on the freedom and pluralism of the media.

The main innovation of the Regulation is the establishment of a Union-wide cooperation mechanism. When a Member State screens a foreign investment, it must notify the Commission and the other Member States, providing basic information about the investor, the target undertaking, and the nature of the investment. This notification triggers a consultation period during which other Member States may submit comments if they believe the investment could affect their own security or public order. The Commission may also issue a non-binding opinion, particularly when the investment is likely to affect projects or programmes of Union interest (eg, Horizon Europe, Galileo, Copernicus, and the Trans-European Networks). The Regulation sets precise time limits for this procedure, ensuring that comments or opinions are submitted within a defined timeframe, generally within 35 calendar days of receiving the complete information. Although the screening Member State retains the responsibility for the final decision, it

[224] The revised framework extends its scope to certain intra-EU investments controlled by third-country entities, it establishes a common minimum substantive scope, covering strategic sectors such as dual-use and military goods, advanced technologies, critical infrastructure, raw materials, and certain financial services, while introducing harmonised procedural standards, including a two-phase review, retroactive powers, and a 45-day initial screening deadline.

[225] See Art 2 of Regulation 2019/452 and the judgment of the Court of Justice in Case C-106/22 *Xella Magyarország* EU:C:2023:568.

must give 'due consideration' to the observations and opinions received. This means that while there is no formal obligation to follow the observations, the Member State must justify its position if it chooses to disregard serious concerns raised by others, and the decision is subject to strict judicial review, as confirmed by the Court of Justice in *Xella Magyarország*.[226]

To enhance the overall coherence of the system, the Regulation requires Member States to designate screening contact points, report annually on their screening activities, and share relevant information with the Commission. The Commission, in turn, presents an annual report summarising the main trends in foreign investment and the functioning of the framework, which it presents to the European Parliament and the Council.[227]

GENERAL BIBLIOGRAPHY

Andenas, M, and Roth, WH, *Services and Free Movement in EU Law* (Oxford University Press, 2003).
Barnard, C, *The Substantive Law of the EU. The Four Freedoms*, 8th edn (Oxford University Press, 2025).
Barnard, C, and Scott, J (eds), The Law of the Single European Market: Unpacking the Premises (Hart, 2002).
Edwards, V, *EC Company Law* (Oxford University Press, 1999).
Ghosh, J, *Principles of the Internal Market and Direct Taxation* (Key Haven Publications, 2007).
Hatzopoulos, V, *Regulating Services in the European Union* (Oxford University Press, 2012).
Van der Mei, AP, *Cross-Border Access to Public Benefits* (Hart, 2002).
Snell, J, *Goods and Services in EC Law. A Study of the Relationship Between the Freedoms* (Oxford University Press, 2002).
Usher, J, *The Law of Money and Financial Services in the European Community* (Clarendon Press, 2000).
White, R, *Workers, Establishment and Services in the European Union* (Oxford University Press, 2004).

FURTHER READING

Freedom of Establishment

Edwards, V, 'The Secondary Establishment of Companies: The Case Law of the Court of Justice' (1998) 18 *Yearbook of European Law 1*.
Hatzopoulos, V, 'Killing national health and insurance systems but healing patients? The EU's freedom of establishment case law concerning healthcare' (2010) 47 *Common Market Law Review* 117.
Paschalidis, P, *Freedom of Establishment and Private International Law for Corporations* (Oxford University Press, 2012).
Schön, W, 'Playing Different Games? Regulatory Competition in Tax and Company Law Compared' (2005) 42 *Common Market Law Review 331*.
Siems, M, 'Convergence, Competition, Centros and Conflicts of Law: European Company Law in the 21st Century' (2002) 27 *European Law Review 47*.
Wymeersch, E, 'The transfer of the company's seat in European company law' (2003) 40 *Common Market Law Review* 661.

Freedom to Provide Services

Barnard, C, 'Unravelling the Services Directive' (2008) 45 *Common Market Law Review 323*.
Cremona, M (ed), Market Integration and Public Services in the European Union (Oxford University Press, 2011).
Freedland, M, and Prassl, J (eds), Viking, Laval and Beyond (Hart, 2015).

[226] ibid.
[227] European Commission, Report from the Commission to the European Parliament and the Council: Fifth Annual Report on the Screening of Foreign Direct Investments into the Union (COM(2024) 23 final, 17 January 2024).

Klamert, M, *Services Liberalization in the EU and the WTO: Concepts, Standards and Regulatory Approaches* (Cambridge University Press, 2014).

Van Leeuwen, B, 'Repositioning free movement of services: A substantive perspective on the structure and dynamics of the internal market' (2025) 62 Common Market Law Review 705.

Vriesendorp, K, 'Article 16 of the Services Directive: The potential and future of a dormant provision' (2023) 48 *European Law Review* 62.

Wiberg, M, *The EU Services Directive: Law or Simply Policy?* (Asser Press, 2014).

Free Movement of Workers

Dougan, M, 'Cross-border educational mobility and the exportation of student financial assistance' (2008) 33 European Law Review 723.

Dougan, M, 'Expanding the Frontiers of Union Citizenship by Dismantling the Territorial Boundaries of the National Welfare States?' in C Barnard and O Odudu (eds), *The Outer Limits of European Union Law* (Hart Publishing, 2009).

Ellis, E, 'Social Advantages: A New Lease of Life' (2003) 40 *Common Market Law Review 639*.

Nic Shuibhne, N, 'Reconnecting Free Movement of Workers and Equal Treatment in an Unequal Europe' (2018) 43 *European Law Review 447*.

Niesten, H, 'Personal and family tax benefits in the EU Internal Market: From Schumacker to fractional tax treatment' (2018) 55 Common Market Law Review 819.

Paju, J, *The European Union and Social Security Law* (Hart Publishing, 2017).

Rogers, N and Scannell, R, *Free Movement of Persons in the Enlarged European Union*, 2nd edn (Sweet & Maxwell, 2012).

Vanistendael, F, 'The Consequences of Schumacker and Wielockx: Two Steps Forward in the Tax Procession of Echternach' (1996) 33 *Common Market Law Review 345*.

Free Movement of Capital

Flynn, L, 'Coming of Age: The Free Movement of Capital Case Law 1993–2002' (2002) 39 *Common Market Law Review 773*.

Gerner-Beuerle, C, 'Shareholders Between the Market and the State: The VW Law and Other Interventions in the Market Economy' (2012) 49 *Common Market Law Review 367*.

Lopez Martins, M, and Beltrán de Lubiano, J, 'The First Steps of the Foreign Subsidies Regulation' (2025) 247 EU Law Live Weekend Edition 3.

Peers, S, 'Free movement of capital: Learning lessons or slipping on spilt milk' in C Barnard and J Scott (eds), The Law of the Single European Market: Unpacking the Premises (Hart, 2002).

Snell, J, 'The varieties of capitalism and the limits of European integration' (2012) 13 Cambridge Yearbook of European Legal Studies 415.

Stegink RGJ, *Comparing complements: The concept of foreign subsidy under the EU Foreign Subsidies Regulation in light of EU State aid law and WTO subsidy law* (2025) 62 Common Market Law Review 1089.

15

The Internal Market: Competition and State Aid

I. FOUNDATIONS AND OBJECTIVES OF COMPETITION POLICY

THE RULES ON freedom of movement are the first pillar of the internal market, aimed at preventing barriers to trade between the Member States. However, the Member States are not the only entities capable of creating trade barriers and distorting the market. Companies with individual or collective market power, or colluding to reduce competition, can create artificial advantages from their position, eradicating competition, harming consumers, and undermining economic growth. This business conduct, where one or more undertakings leverage their market power or act in concert with the direct or indirect effect of harming the proper functioning of the market, is prohibited, both preventively and actively, by the Treaty rules on competition.

Competition policy and its regulatory framework are relatively recent developments, emerging in the early twentieth century in the United States as large corporate groups emerged in industrial sectors. The Sherman Antitrust Act of 1890, along with the Clayton Antitrust Act of 1914, provided US courts with effective legislative instruments to prohibit market conduct that fosters the formation of cartels, price fixing, or abuses by a single operator with a dominant position. This legal and practical framework guided the introduction of various provisions on market conduct by undertakings within sectors covered by the Coal and Steel Community Treaty. The framework was further refined in 1957, with the drafting of the Treaty's provisions establishing the European Economic Community. The basic features of this design have endured to the present day.

The economic theory underpinning competition policy suggests that competitive markets can generate numerous benefits. First, competition among companies drives efficiency, leading to the removal of unprofitable or overpriced services. Second, consumer preferences drive a continuous process of market adjustment, in which the production of goods and services aligns with consumer demand. Price is a key factor in purchasing decisions, motivating companies to aim to reduce prices. Third, these effects ripple through the entire production chain, increasing efficiency. This, in turn, helps develop a market in which supply and demand reach equilibrium at each stage. Competition policy seeks to promote this efficiency by intervening when a market failure might otherwise cause an inefficient outcome.[1] The task of competition authorities is to ensure that undertakings operate within an open and efficient market. They

[1] S Bishop and M Walker, *The Economics of EC Competition Law: Concepts, Application and Measurement* (3rd edn, Sweet & Maxwell 2010) 190–98.

also aim to prevent economic operators from undermining the balance that should exist in a genuinely competitive market.

1. The Evolution of Competition Policy in the Union

The Union's competition policy has evolved into a highly sophisticated framework. Given the practical importance of competition rules in the daily activities of businesses, the Union has provided a comprehensive legal and institutional framework. However, it is worth noting that this framework has evolved and changed over the decades.

The first major step in implementing a European competition policy was the introduction of Regulation 17/62 in 1962,[2] which gave the Commission powers to investigate and sanction anti-competitive conduct. It also empowered the institution to approve agreements between companies, both vertical and horizontal. In the initial years of the Commission's operations, particularly through the Directorate General for Competition, the focus was primarily on analysing vertical agreements involving undertakings from different Member States. *Grundig*,[3] a leading case decided in 1966, involved the broad territorial protection of a distributor, which risked fragmenting the internal market. This case, occurring shortly after Regulation 17/62 came into force, enabled both the Commission and the Court of Justice to establish the foundations of the EEC's earliest competition policy and to develop a consistent interpretation of the Commission's powers in competition investigations. Shortly after, in 1967, the first block exemption regulation was introduced,[4] providing a framework that allowed the Commission to operate more efficiently and focus its attention solely on the most harmful conduct.

Competition policy evolved alongside changes in markets. The liberalisation of regulated sectors in the 1980s and 1990s led to increased involvement of the Commission in areas where the state acted as arbiter of competitive markets, but with a limited number of operators. The functioning of traditionally closed markets, such as postal, telecommunications, or energy markets, required adapting competition law tools to apply them to strategic sectors where competition had been largely absent until then. Similarly, the technological revolution and the development of the digital economy gave rise to new business models and players with unprecedented market power and the ability to provide significant consumer benefits. The influence of major technological players, such as Apple, Google and Amazon, has once again prompted a shift in the Commission's priorities. From the early 2000s, it became necessary to adjust the tools used to align competition policy with the realities of an increasingly digitalised economy and markets.

The institutional framework for competition policy established in the 1950s and 1960s centralised most of the powers within the Commission. Over time, Member States established their own competition authorities, whose practices were largely inspired by the Commission's actions and policies at the Union level. The growth of expertise in competition law among national authorities and national courts, combined with the increasing workload faced by the Commission in a rapidly expanding market following the accession of an ever-increasing number of Member States, prompted significant organisational changes in the late 1990s. Under the leadership of Commissioner Mario Monti, the legal and institutional framework

[2] Council Regulation (EEC) No 17 on the application of Articles 85 and 86 of the Treaty (now Articles 101 and 102 TFEU) [1962] OJ 13/204.

[3] Joined Cases C-56/64 and C-58/64 *Consten and Grundig v Commission of the EEC* EU:C:1966:41.

[4] Commission Regulation No 67/67/EEC of 22 March 1967 on the application of Article 85(3) of the Treaty (now Article 101 TFEU) to categories of exclusive agreements [1967] OJ 57/849.

of competition policy underwent a decentralisation process, culminating in the adoption of Regulation 1/2003.[5] This reform introduced a system of shared powers between the Commission and national competition authorities, which remains in place today. Its goal was to prioritise the role of national authorities while maintaining the Commission's authority and leadership as the guardian of strategic decisions with a Union dimension.

2. Legal and Institutional Framework

Competition policy is one of the few exclusive competences of the Union listed in Article 3(1) Treaty on the Functioning of the European Union (TFEU), which refers to 'the establishing of the competition rules necessary for the functioning of the internal market'. The practical consequence of including competition policy among the Union's exclusive competences is the Union's leading role in defining and combating anti-competitive practices within the internal market. The involvement of the Member States is subject to explicit authorisation granted by the Union to intervene in this policy area. It should be noted that the internal market policy is a shared competence (Article 4(2)(a) TFEU), an area in which Member States must legislate and act together with the Union when regulating specific markets or establishing the general framework on the functioning of markets. However, regarding market conduct by undertakings in the European market and its alleged anti-competitive character, the Union remains the sole authority authorised to act and combat such conduct.

The Treaties establish a legal basis empowering the institutions to adopt the measures necessary to implement the Union's competition policy. Article 103 TFEU grants the Council powers to adopt 'the appropriate regulations or directives to give effect to the principles set out in Articles 101 and 102'. These two provisions set out the basic rules of conduct for businesses in the internal market: the prohibition of anti-competitive agreements and of abuses of dominance. To ensure compliance with these rules, Article 103 TFEU enumerates the measures that may be adopted under this legal basis: establishment of fines and periodic penalty payments, administrative control systems over companies, sector-specific regimes, and specific powers granted to the Commission and the Court of Justice. The legal basis provided by Article 103 TFEU has allowed for the adoption of the Union's normative instruments in the field of competition.

The basic legal framework of the Union's competition policy is contained in Chapter I of Title VII of Part III TFEU. Chapter I is divided into two sections, the first focusing on 'rules applying to undertakings' and the second on 'aids granted by states'. Competition policy *stricto sensu* refers to the conduct of undertakings outlined in Chapter I, with the relevant framework provided by Articles 101–06 TFEU. Furthermore, through the legal basis set out in Article 103 TFEU, the Union legislator has adopted various acts of significant importance for developing competition policy, including Regulation 1/2003 and the various block exemption regulations.[6] These legislative acts are complemented by multiple *soft law* instruments where

[5] Council Regulation (EC) No 1/2003 of 16 December 2002 on the implementation of the rules on competition laid down in Articles 81 and 82 of the Treaty (now Articles 101 and 102 TFEU) [2003] OJ L1/1. Public consultation on the revision of this regulation was opened in July 2025.

[6] See, inter alia, Commission Regulation (EU) No 330/2010 of 20 April 2010 on the application of Article 101(3) of the Treaty on the Functioning of the European Union to categories of vertical agreements and concerted practices, replaced as of 1 June 2022 by Commission Regulation (EU) No 2022/720 of 10 May 2022 on the application of Article 101(3) of the Treaty on the Functioning of the European Union to categories of vertical agreements and concerted practices, [2022] OJ L134/4].

the Commission sets out interpretative criteria applied to its powers, in the interest of transparency and legal certainty.[7]

The institutional framework of competition policy is heavily influenced by the powers granted to the Commission by the Treaty and the Union legislator. This institution is responsible for implementing competition policy, although it has been exercising this role in coordination with national competition authorities since 2004. The Commission's relevance, both at the regulatory and executive levels, is unquestionable, given the resources and the scope of powers at its disposal (compared to those of its national counterparts) and the significance of the cases it handles. When national authorities decide autonomously, they adhere to criteria previously established by the Commission in similar cases and, when applying Union rules, inform the Commission of the steps they are taking before issuing a decision.

This framework is characterised by the intervention of independent institutions that are not subject to political control or direction. The Commission enjoys independence vis-à-vis the Member States by virtue of a direct mandate in the Treaties (Article 17(3) Treaty on European Union (TEU)). In the case of Member States, national competition authorities must comply with the minimum independence standards mandated by Union law, particularly as outlined in Directive 2019/1.[8] Ensuring independence in the daily operations of national competition authorities is crucial, as the importance and impact of their decisions often create strong incentives from political or economic spheres to influence or steer their decisions.

II. ARTICLE 101 TFEU AND 'AGREEMENTS' BETWEEN UNDERTAKINGS

Anti-competitive conduct can be divided into two categories: collective and individual. In the first case, two or more undertakings voluntarily agree, either explicitly or tacitly, to engage in practices that have as their object or effect the distortion of the market to their advantage. Article 101 TFEU is the relevant provision prohibiting this business conduct, defined in paragraph 1 as follows:

> The following shall be prohibited as incompatible with the internal market: all agreements between undertakings, decisions by associations of undertakings and concerted practices which may affect trade between Member States and which have as their object or effect the prevention, restriction or distortion of competition within the internal market, and in particular those which:
>
> (a) directly or indirectly fix purchase or selling prices or any other trading conditions;
>
> (b) limit or control production, markets, technical development, or investment;
>
> (c) share markets or sources of supply;
>
> (d) apply dissimilar conditions to equivalent transactions with other trading parties, thereby placing them at a competitive disadvantage;

[7] See, inter alia, Commission – Guidelines on the application of Article 81(3) of the Treaty [2004] OJ C101/97; Commission Notice on the definition of the relevant market for the purposes of Community competition law [1997] OJ C372/5; and Commission – Guidance on the Commission's enforcement priorities in its application of Article 82 of the EC Treaty to abusive exclusionary conduct by dominant undertakings [2009] OJ C45/7. On the legal effects of these instruments, see Case C-360/09 *Pfleiderer* EU:C:2011:389, paras 21–22; Case C-428/14 *DHL* EU:C:2016:27, paras 29–44; Case C-23/14 *Post Danmark v Konkurrencerådet* EU:C:2015:651, para 52; and Case C-226/11 *Expedia Inc v Autorité de la concurrence* ECLI:EU:C:2012:795, paras 14–38.

[8] Directive (EU) No 2019/1 of the European Parliament and of the Council of 11 December 2018 to empower the competition authorities of the Member States to be more effective and to ensure the proper functioning of the internal market [2019] OJ L11/3.

(e) make the conclusion of contracts subject to acceptance by the other parties of supplementary obligations which, by their nature or according to commercial usage, have no connection with the subject of such contracts.

Such conduct will automatically be void and subject to investigations by the Commission or national competition authorities, which possess significant powers to carry out this task, including the authority to impose sanctions on the undertakings concerned. Furthermore, when such conduct causes economic harm to third parties, those third parties can launch private enforcement actions in national courts, primarily through damages claims of substantial economic scale brought by natural or legal persons harmed by the anti-competitive behaviour.[9]

1. The Prohibition of Article 101 TFEU

1.1. *Concept of 'Undertaking'*

The addressees of the conduct referred to in Article 101 TFEU are 'undertakings', the definition of which has been developed in the case law. In *Höfner*, the Court of Justice referred to the term as follows:

> [I]n the context of competition law . . . the concept of an undertaking encompasses every entity engaged in an economic activity, regardless of the legal status of the entity and the way in which it is financed.[10]

This definition reflects a *functional* conception of 'undertaking' that is unrelated to the formal structure it may assume, and focuses solely on the activity it performs in the market. Similarly, the concept of 'undertaking' in Article 101 TFEU is autonomous and specific to competition law. Consequently, some entities may fall under this category and be subject to competition rules, but not to other provisions of the Treaty in other fields of policy areas that address a different type of 'undertaking'.[11]

The key criterion for defining an 'undertaking' is the performance of an economic activity. If an activity involves offering goods or services in the market in exchange for remuneration, it will be regarded as an economic activity under Articles 101–02 TFEU, as explained below. The public nature of the undertaking or the source of the payment is irrelevant for this purpose. Therefore, services provided to national authorities by a public body, such as Eurocontrol, during public procurement procedures, qualify as an economic activity insofar as they are equivalent to services offered by other economic operators in the market of consultancy services.[12] The fact that Eurocontrol is a non-profit organisation does not prevent its activities from being classified as economic and falling within the scope of Article 101 TFEU. Similarly, a sports club involved in the organisation of economic activities, or a public body entrusted with the provision of services of general interest that are of an economic nature, will also be considered an 'undertaking'.[13]

[9] It should be noted that in the Union and in the Member States' legal systems, the nature of claims for damages arising from antitrust offences is purely compensatory and it excludes punitive damages, in contrast with the case of other countries, such as the United States.

[10] Case C-41/90 *Höfner and Elser v Macrotron* EU:C:1991:161, para 21.

[11] Case T-155/04 *SELEX Sistemi Integrati v Commission* EU:T:2006:387, para 54.

[12] Case C-113/07 P *SELEX Sistemi Integrati v Commission* EU:C:2009:191, para 76.

[13] Case C-49/07 *MOTOE* EU:C:2008:376, para 27; Case C-244/94 *FFSA and Others v Ministère de l'Agriculture et de la Pêche* EU:C:1995:392, para 22.

Although the concept of 'undertaking' is interpreted broadly, the case law recognises three areas where an activity is not considered 'economic'. Firstly, entities performing an activity under the supervision of the state and within an organisational framework based on the principle of solidarity are not 'undertakings'. Solidarity is considered to exist in an 'inherently uncommercial act of involuntary subsidisation of one social group by another'.[14] Secondly, an activity, however economic it may be, will not fall under the scope of Article 101 TFEU if it involves the exercise of public powers. Not all exercise of such powers is excluded; only that which forms part of the 'essential functions of the State'.[15] Thirdly, public authorities' purchase of goods and services related to the pursuit of non-economic objectives of general interest do not constitute an economic activity within the meaning of Article 101 TFEU.[16]

Article 101 TFEU refers to 'undertakings' in the plural but excludes two or more companies that are part of the same group. Therefore, agreements between a subsidiary and its parent company do not fall under the prohibition of Article 101 TFEU as they constitute an individual economic unit. The functional concept of 'undertaking' is delimited by the notion of 'economic unit', which refers to a set of entities ultimately controlled by one single entity; this assessment must be made on a case-by-case basis.[17] Control is understood as the ability to exercise decisive influence over another entity.[18] For instance, an economic unit between a parent company and its subsidiaries is presumed when the parent holds a significant shareholding in the subsidiaries, based on the control it exerts. However, this presumption can be rebutted if it is proven that the subsidiary enjoys genuine autonomy in setting its market strategy.[19] When multiple firms own a subsidiary and none has control over it, the doctrine of economic unity does not apply, and the conduct of these firms falls outside the scope of Article 101 TFEU.[20]

1.2. *Types of Conduct*

Article 101 TFEU refers to three types of prohibited conduct that undertakings might engage in collectively: agreements, concerted practices and decisions by associations of undertakings. Despite this enumeration, practice shows some overlaps between the three types of conduct.[21] The key feature is a 'meeting of minds' between two or more undertakings, which has been interpreted quite broadly, even to include unilateral conduct tacitly accepted by another undertaking.[22] This collusive activity is deliberately concerted among them to impact the market. The classification clarifies the category of unlawful conduct. However, its application is flexible. Ultimately, the determining factor is that each participating undertaking freely and voluntarily accepts the risk of engaging in collusion, even if they may be unaware of its anticompetitive object or effect.[23]

[14] Case C-70/95 *Sodemare and Others v Regione Lombardia* EU:C:1997:55, Opinion of AG Fennelly, para 29.

[15] Case C-343/95 *Calì & Figli v Servizi Ecologici Porto di Genova* EU:C:1997:160, para 22.

[16] Case C-205/03 P *FENIN v Commission* EU:C:2006:453, para 26.

[17] Case C-882/19 *Sumal, SL and Mercedes Benz Trucks España, SL* EU:C:2021:800, paras 46–47.

[18] Case C-633/16 *Ernst & Young P/S v Konkurrencerådet* EU:C:2018:371, para 45.

[19] Case C-15/74 *Centrafarm BV and Others v Sterling Drug* EU:C:1974:114, 1147; and Case C-30/87 *Bodson v Pompes funèbres des régions libérées* EU:C:1988:225, para 19.

[20] Case C-22/71 *Béguelin Import v G.L. Import Export* EU:C:1971:113; Case T-145/89 *Baustahlgewebe v Commission* EU:T:1995:66; Case C-73/95 P *Viho v Commission* EU:C:1996:405; Case C-217/05 *Confederación Española de Empresarios de Estaciones de Servicio* EU:C:2006:784; and Case C-97/08 P *Akzo Nobel and Others v Commission* EU:C:2009:536.

[21] Case T-305/94 *LVM v Commission* EU:T:1999:80; and Case C-49/92 P *Commission v Anic Partecipazioni* EU:C:1999:356.

[22] Case C-74/04 P *Commission v Volkswagen AG* EU:C:2006:460, para 37.

[23] Case C-49/92 P *Commission v Anic Partecipazioni* EU:C:1999:356, paras 86–87; and Case C-234/89 *Stergios Delimitis v Henninger Bräu AG* EU:C:1991:91, para 24.

1.2.1. Agreements

'Agreements' are binding accords resulting from a 'concurrence of will' between two or more undertakings, regardless of their qualification or form. A contract is undoubtedly an 'agreement' for these purposes, but so is any accord, whatever its form, provided it reflects the parties' intent.[24]

This broad definition of 'agreement' covers a wide range, including agreements subject to a time limit that has expired but are still effective,[25] the internal rules of an association representing the interests of a group of companies,[26] a *gentlemen's agreement* without binding effects for the parties,[27] a unilateral document of one company accepted by another (for example, the payment of an invoice that includes anti-competitive conditions),[28] or a collective agreement.[29] Ultimately, the decisive criterion is the existence of an intention by two or more undertakings, evidenced by expressions of intent, to engage in a practice with anti-competitive effects in the market where they operate.[30]

1.2.2. Concerted Practices

Undertakings can avoid adopting agreements that reveal their strategies through more subtle practices where there is no formal conjunction of wills but which 'knowingly substitutes practical cooperation between them for the risks of competition'.[31] This is the case of concerted practices, defined in the case law as:

> [A]ny direct or indirect contact between such operators, the object or effect whereof is either to influence the conduct on the market of an actual or potential competitor or to disclose to such a competitor the course of conduct which they themselves have decided to adopt or contemplate adopting on the market.[32]

This definition highlights the need for two or more undertakings to have reached a tacit accord to cooperate. This is an unwritten accord, but there must be a concurrence of wills that can be inferred from the conduct of all the undertakings involved. According to the case law, each of them must seek to:

> [C]ontribute by its own conduct to the common objectives pursued by all the participants and that it was aware of the actual conduct planned or put into effect by other undertakings in pursuit of the same objectives or that it could reasonably have foreseen it and that it was prepared to take the risk.[33]

Consensus must be reflected in the existence of 'direct or indirect contact',[34] but there must have been (even quiet) participation in a succession of meetings, discussions, or soundings between

[24] Case T-41/96 *Bayer AG v Commission* EU:T:2000:242, para 69: 'the concept of an agreement within the meaning of Article 85(1) of the Treaty, as interpreted by the case-law, centres around the existence of a concurrence of wills between at least two parties, the form in which it is manifested being unimportant so long as it constitutes the faithful expression of the parties' intention'.

[25] Case C-51/75 *EMI Records/CBS United Kingdom* EU:T:1976:85, para 30.

[26] Case T-61/89 *Dansk Pelsdyravlerforening v Commission* EU:T:1992:79, paras 4–5.

[27] Case T-41/96 *VAG-Händlerbeirat eV v SYD-Consult* EU:T:2000:242, para 68.

[28] Case C-277/87 *Sandoz Prodotti Farmaceutici v Commission* EU:C:1989:363.

[29] Case C-67/96 *Albany* EU:C:1999:430, para 59.

[30] Case T-9/89 *Hüls v Commission* EU:T:1992:31, paras 290–294; Case T-11/89 *Shell v Commission* EU:T:1992:33, para 107; Case T-18/03 *CD-Contact Data v Commission* EU:T:2009:132, para 47; and Case C-338/00 P *Volkswagen v Commission* EU:C:2003:473, paras 63–65.

[31] Case C-48/69 *Imperial Chemical Industries Ltd v Commission* EU:C:1972:70, para 64.

[32] Joined Cases C-40/73 to C-48/73, 50/73, 54/73 to 56/73, 111/73, 113/73 and 114/73 *Suiker Unie and Others v Commission* EU:C:1975:174, paras 174–75.

[33] Case C-194/14 P *AC-Treuhand AG v Commission* EU:C:2015:717, para 30.

[34] Case C-8/08 *T-Mobile Netherlands and Others* EU:C:2009:343, paras 32–33.

representatives of the undertakings,[35] or at least some form of tacit or passive acceptance, as in the case of not explicitly opposing the application of automated commercial conditions via an electronic tool.[36] Contacts do not have to be consistent or regular; a single meeting may be sufficient to establish the existence of a concerted practice. The Court of Justice has repeatedly stated that the key issue is determining whether the contacts allowed the participating undertakings to consider the information exchanged with their competitors. This enables them to assess their behaviour in the relevant market and consciously replace competition risks with practical cooperation between them.[37]

Contrary to ordinary commercial practices in a competitive market, there must also be anomalous cooperation between undertakings, which will likely reduce the normal competitive uncertainty that should govern independent market behaviour. For example, the exchange of confidential commercial information, such as information relating to pricing or discounting strategies, or any other information that, when shared with a competitor, helps create a predictable environment for their conduct,[38] is anomalous behaviour that does not normally occur between competitors under conventional market conditions. This might even be the case of public announcements, which, depending on the circumstances, invite competitors to collude.[39]

Finally, coordination between undertakings must materialise in some conduct in the market, or otherwise there will be no concerted practice within the meaning of Article 101 TFEU. The Commission bears the burden of proving the existence of cooperative conduct in the sense described above. However, undertakings may demonstrate that such cooperation was not subsequently reflected in the market.[40] The Court of Justice has emphasised that concerted practice requires, in addition to concertation between the undertakings, 'subsequent conduct on the market, and a relationship of cause and effect between [the concerted practice and the conduct on the market]',[41] although 'there does not need to be a direct link between that practice and consumer prices'.[42]

1.2.3. Decisions by Associations of Undertakings

Thirdly, Article 101 TFEU refers to decisions of associations of undertakings, a reference to collusive practices stemming from the institutional will of an organisation representing business interests. By not specifying the type of organisation, the provision has been interpreted broadly to encompass the conduct of professional associations,[43] non-profit associations,[44] federations of associations,[45] sports organisations,[46] or commercial organisations, among others.[47]

[35] Case C-49/92 P *Commission v Anic Partecipazioni* EU:C:1999:356, para 94.
[36] Case C-74/14 *'Eturas' UAB v Lietuvos Respublikos konkurencijos taryba* EU:C:2016:42, para 28.
[37] Case C-8/08 *T-Mobile Netherlands and Others* EU:C:2009:343, para 61.
[38] Case T-202/98 *Tate & Lyle and Others v Commission* EU:T:2001:185, para 60.
[39] D Bailey and R Whish, *Competition Law*, 10th edn (Oxford University Press, 2021) 597–99; Joined Cases C-89/85, C-104/85, C-114/85, C-116/85, C-117/85 and C-125/85 to C-129/85 *A Ahlström Osakeyhtiö and others v Commission* EU:C:1993:120, paras 126–127.
[40] Joined Cases C-29/83 and C-30/83 *CRAM v Commission* EU:C:1984:130, para 17.
[41] Case C-199/92 P *Hüls v Commission* EU:C:1999:358, para 161.
[42] Case C-8/08 *T-Mobile Netherlands and Others* EU:C:2009:343, para 39.
[43] Case C-71/74 *Fruit-in Groentenimporthandel and Frubo v Commission* EU:C:1975:61, paras 28–31.
[44] Case C-35/96 *Commission v Italy* EU:C:1998:303, paras 39ff.
[45] Case T-193/02 *Piau v Commission* EU:T:2005:22, para 72.
[46] ibid, para 69.
[47] Case C-123/83 *BNIC v Clair* EU:C:1985:33, para 16.

Nor do the 'decisions' of these organisations need to be in any particular legal form or have any specific legal effects. It is sufficient that the act reflects the association's intention to coordinate the actions of some or all of its members. Therefore, the association's statutes, by-laws, or other internal rules can amount to a 'decision' for these purposes. Similarly, codes of conduct[48] or non-binding recommendations addressed to members can also fall into this category.[49]

1.2.4. Horizontal and Vertical Cooperation Agreements

Collusive behaviour can vary widely in form and function, exhibiting high variability and adaptability. Markets change, and so do companies' practices as they adjust their strategies to consumer preferences or other external factors that influence how goods and services are sold. To capture the reality of the market, both the Commission and the case law classify collusion into two categories of cooperation agreements: horizontal and vertical.

Horizontal cooperation encompasses all types of agreements and concerted practices between undertakings operating at the same level of the commercial chain, competing actually or potentially with each other. Two undertakings are considered competitors if they are active in the same relevant market. An undertaking is a *potential* competitor of another undertaking if, in the absence of an agreement, in the case of a minor but permanent relative price increase, the first undertaking is likely to undertake within a short time the necessary additional investments or necessary switching costs to enable it to enter the relevant market on which the second undertaking is active.[50] Two undertakings active in the same product market, but in different geographic markets, are more likely to be potential competitors.[51]

There are numerous examples of horizontal cooperation. The Commission's Guidelines on Horizontal Cooperation provide several examples, but these are far from a closed enumeration.[52] The most common examples of horizontal cooperation between companies are information exchanges, research and development agreements, specialisation, production or purchasing agreements, or marketing agreements.[53]

Vertical agreements take place between undertakings that do not compete in the same market, but between undertakings that cooperate in the same production or distribution chain. Regulation 2022/720 defines this type of cooperation as:

> [A]n agreement or concerted practice between two or more undertakings, each of which operates, for the purposes of the agreement or the concerted practice, at a different level of the production or distribution chain, and relating to the conditions under which the parties may purchase, sell or resell certain goods or services.[54]

A manufacturer and a distributor do not compete in the same market, yet their ability to distort it is very high.[55]

[48] Case T-144/99 *Institut des mandataires agréés v Commission* EU:T:2001:105, paras 72–80.

[49] Case C-45/85 *Verband der Sachversicherer v Commission* EU:C:1987:34, para 30.

[50] Commission – Guidelines on the applicability of Article 101 of the Treaty on the Functioning of the European Union to horizontal co-operation agreements [2023] OJ C259/1, para 16.

[51] ibid, paras 10 and 16.

[52] ibid.

[53] ibid, paras 5–7.

[54] Art 1(a) of Commission Regulation (EU) No 330/2010 of 20 April 2010 on the application of Article 101(3) of the Treaty on the Functioning of the European Union to categories of vertical agreements and concerted practices [2010] OJ L102/1, replaced by Art 1(a) of Commission Regulation (EU) No 2022/720 of 10 May 2022 on the application of Article 101(3) of the Treaty on the Functioning of the European Union to categories of vertical agreements and concerted practices [2022] OJ L134/4.

[55] See Commission Notice — Guidelines on Vertical Restraints [2022] OJ C248/1.

Vertical agreements can differ significantly across markets. However, several standardised categories appear in various markets, such as exclusive or selective distribution agreements, agency agreements, franchise agreements, or intellectual property licensing. Due to the specificities of each market, vertical agreements might be subject to individual or general block exemptions, either based on the type of agreement or on the specific market in which they are concluded, an assessment usually carried out in accordance with the Commission's Guidelines on Vertical Restraints.[56]

1.3. *Restrictions by Object or by Effect*

Article 101(1) TFEU focuses on business conduct 'which may affect trade between Member States and which has as its object or effect the prevention, restriction or distortion of competition within the internal market'. This provision contains three distinct elements that will be analysed below: the restriction; the object; and the effect. The restriction results directly from the agreement, concerted practice, or associative decision. Conversely, the object and the effect relate to the anti-competitive content of the agreement, concerted practice, or associative decision. Article 101(1) TFEU applies only to conduct that is restrictive and whose object or effect is to directly or indirectly restrict competition in a market. These three elements will be examined separately in the following sections.

1.4. *Restriction of Competition*

The Treaty introduces an economic criterion for defining unlawful conduct that affects competition. Article 101(1) TFEU employs the expression 'prevention, restriction or distortion of competition'. The three terms used in the provision are not implemented separately. The case law considers them to reflect the same reality: a restriction of competition.

First, the restriction must impact a specific market. Therefore, it is essential to analyse the factual situation covered by the agreement, practice, or decision and clearly identify the market affected by the conduct. This analysis will determine the 'relevant market'.

Second, the restriction has an economic effect on the competitive process. For these purposes, 'competition' in the market has been defined by the case law as 'effective' competition, ie:

> [T]he degree of competition necessary to ensure the attainment of the objectives of the Treaty. Its intensity may vary to an extent dictated by the nature of the product concerned and the structure of the relevant market. Furthermore, its parameters may assume unequal importance, as price competition does not constitute the only effective form of competition or that to which absolute priority must in all circumstances be given.[57]

This broad definition of 'competition', characterised by its economic features, includes various restrictions. The case law has emphasised that restrictions are not limited to price competition but also encompass any consequences on the market, such as the loss of autonomy for an undertaking to set its commercial policy independently in the market[58] or the geographic isolation of a territory from the rest of the market.[59]

[56] Communication from the Commission on Guidelines on vertical restraints [2022] OJ C248/1.

[57] Case C-26/76 *Metro v Commission* ('Metro I') EU:C:1977:167, paras 20–21; Case C-198/01 *CIF* EU:C:2003:430, para 68; and Case T-168/01 *GlaxoSmithKline Services v Commission* EU:T:2006:265, para 109.

[58] Case C-40/73 *Suiker Unie and Others v Commission* EU:C:1975:174, paras 174–75.

[59] Joined Cases C-56/64 and C-58/64 *Consten and Grundig v Commission of the EEC* EU:C:1966:41, 428.

1.4.1. Object

Not all restrictions on competition are unlawful. For conduct to breach Article 101 TFEU, there must be a causal link with an agreement, practice, or associative decision, the object or effect of which is specifically to restrict competition. The Treaty refers to two distinct aspects of a business conduct: the 'object' of the agreement, practice, or decision; and its resulting 'effect'. Both aspects apply separately and sequentially.[60] First, it is necessary to establish whether the agreement, practice, or decision has the restriction of competition *as its object*. If not, then it is appropriate to assess whether the *effect* of the agreement, practice, or decision is a restriction of competition.

A restriction by object is a restriction that potentially prevents trade between Member States and may, by its very nature, be regarded as harmful to the proper functioning of normal competition.[61] These are, therefore, agreements or practices whose 'degree of harm' to competition is such that it is unnecessary to perform an economic analysis of their effects on the market.[62] This analysis of the agreed or concerted conduct involves determining whether, from the content of the provisions or clauses and the economic and legal context in which they are adopted, it is inferred that its 'objective aims' are to restrict competition beyond any alternative explanation.[63] Moreover, although the parties' intention is not an essential element in establishing the restrictive nature of an agreement, there is nothing to prevent the Commission or the courts from taking it into account. [64]

Article 101(1) TFEU enumerates five types of agreements whose object is restrictive of competition, including price fixing, output limitation, and market sharing. This list is not exhaustive, but it reveals a category of agreements whose object is so serious and harmful to competition that they cannot be economically justified.[65]

The traditional categories of restrictions by object have been replaced in recent case law by introducing open criteria allowing a wider range of agreements to be qualified under this category.[66] As a result, the spectrum of agreements that are restrictive by object alone, without the need to consider their individual effects on the market, has increased considerably, as has the legal uncertainty introduced by the new approach. The shift from a fixed 'closed list' where agreements restrictive by object are enumerated and categorically prohibited, to an open system subject to individual case-by-case analysis, enhances the Commission's powers but also raises uncertainty for companies when assessing the legality of their agreements. This open-ended trend is being rationalised in recent decisions of the Court of Justice. It first raised the relevant standard for a restriction to be considered harmful by object, thus excluding cases where there may be an alternative explanation.[67] It further clarified that only pro-competitive effects that are demonstrated, sufficiently significant, and specifically related to the agreement

[60] Case C-56/65 *Société Technique Minière v Maschinenbau Ulm* EU:C:1966:38, 371.

[61] Case C-209/07 *Beef Industry Development Society and Barry Brothers* EU:C:2008:643, para 17.

[62] Case C-172/14 *ING Pensii* EU:C:2015:484, para 31.

[63] Case C-307/18 *Generics (UK) Ltd and Others v CMA* EU:C:2020:52, paras 87–90; Case C-298/22 *Banco BNP/BIC Português SA and Others v Autoridades da Concorrência* EU:C:2024:638, para 56.

[64] Case C-96/82 *IAZ and Others v Commission* EU:C:1983:310, paras 23–25.

[65] Joined Cases C-239/11 P, C-489/11 P and C-498/11 P *Siemens and Others v Commission* EU:C:2013:866, para 218.

[66] Case C-32/11 *Allianz Hungária Biztosító and Others* EU:C:2013:160; Case C-67/13 P *Groupement des cartes bancaires (CB) v Commission* EU:C:2014:2204; Case C-298/22 *Banco BNP/BIC Português SA and Others v Autoridades da Concorrência* EU:C:2024:638, paras 52–56; C-176/19 P *Commission v Servier and Others* EU:C:2024:549, paras 107–08; and Case C-151/19 P *Commission v KRKA, tovarna zdravil, d.d.*, EU:C:2024:546, paras 74–75.

[67] Case C-307/18 *Generics (UK) Ltd v Competition and Markets Authority* EU:C:2020:52, para 84; and Case C-228/18 *Gazdasági Versenyhivatal v Budapest Bank Nyrt* EU:C:2020:265, para 82.

concerned qualify as ambivalent effects capable of casting doubt on the existence of an anti-competitive object.[68]

1.4.2. Effect

If an agreement, practice, or decision is not restrictive by object, it is necessary to analyse its *effects* on competition. To determine the effects of such an agreement, it is essential to consider the economic and legal context in which it was adopted and how, together with other acts, it may have a cumulative effect on competition.[69] The case law requires a prior delimitation of the relevant market and an analysis of the counterfactual scenario (what effect the *absence* of the conduct in question would have on the market).[70] The analysis of the agreement must also take into account the nature and the limited or unlimited quantity of the products covered by the contract, the position and importance of the operators on the market for the products in question, the isolated nature of the agreement at issue or, on one hand, the place it occupies in a set of agreements, the strictness of the clauses designed to protect exclusivity or, on the other hand, the possibilities left to other trade flows in the same products using re-exports and parallel imports.[71] It is sufficient to demonstrate that the existence of anticompetitive effects is only *potential*.[72]

As can be seen, the restriction-by-effect analysis focuses solely on the conduct's harmful impact, disregarding other potentially beneficial economic effects on competition. In contrast to US antitrust law, where the restriction analysis involves weighing all factors within an overall economic assessment (the so-called *rule of reason*), Union law defers the analysis of the restriction's positive effects to the exemptions enumerated in Article 101(3) TFEU.

As the case law has repeatedly held:

> Article [101] of the Treaty expressly provides, in its third paragraph, for the exemption of agreements that restrict competition where they satisfy a number of conditions, in particular where they are indispensable to the attainment of certain objectives and do not afford undertakings the possibility of eliminating competition in respect of a substantial part of the products in question. It is only within the specific framework of that provision that the pro and anti-competitive aspects of a restriction may be weighed.[73]

1.5. *Affecting Trade between Member States*

Article 101 TFEU only applies to conduct that affects trade between Member States. Actions that are limited to a single Member State will, as a general rule, be relevant to national competition law, but not to Union law. In any event, the Court of Justice's interpretation of this

[68] Case C-331/21 *EDP – Energias de Portugal SA and Others v Autoridade da Concorrência* EU:C:2023:812, para 104; and Case C-211/22 *Super Bock Bebidas SA and Others v Autoridade da Concorrência* EU:C:2023:529, para 36.

[69] Case C-23/67 *Brasserie de Haecht* EU:C:1967:54, p 117.

[70] 'The competition in question must be understood within the actual context in which it would occur in the absence of the agreement in dispute. In particular, it may be doubted whether there is an interference with competition if the said agreement seems really necessary for the penetration of a new area by an undertaking'. Case C-56/65 *Société Technique Minière v Maschinenbau Ulm* EU:C:1966:38, 359; and Case T-328/03 *O2 (Germany) v Commission* EU:T:2006:116, para 68.

[71] Case C-56/65 *Société Technique Minière v Maschinenbau Ulm*, EU:C:1966:38, paras 371–72.

[72] Case C-606/23 *AS 'Tallinna Kaubamaja Grupp' and AS 'KIA Auto' v Konkurences padome* EU:C:2024:1004, para 36.

[73] Case T-65/98 *Van den Bergh Foods v Commission* EU:T:2003:281, para 107; Case T-112/99 *M6 and Others v Commission* EU:T:2001:215, para 109; and Case T-328/03 *O2 (Germany) v Commission* EU:T:2006:116, para 65.

criterion is broad, and there are cases where conduct may be subject to the Treaties even if its direct scope of application is limited to a single Member State.[74]

Affecting trade between Member States is a requirement expressly provided for in Article 101(1) TFEU, but its definition has been elaborated in the case law and various interpretative acts issued by the Commission.[75] The most well-established criterion describes this effect as the foreseeability

> with a sufficient degree of probability, based on a set of objective factors of law or of fact that the agreement in question may have an influence, direct or indirect, actual or potential, on the pattern of trade between Member States.[76]

The fact that the criterion includes potential effects (that the agreement *may* have a direct or *indirect*, actual or *potential* influence) makes it possible to justify the impact on trade between Member States in almost all cases. Therefore, if the effects of an agreement are confined to a single Member State, an effect may arise insofar as the compartmentalisation of the internal market affects trade between Member States.[77] Similarly, an agreement whose effects are projected onto third states may also affect trade between Member States, provided there is a risk that the agreement will affect the conduct of undertakings in the internal market.[78]

The Commission has published interpretative criteria that determine the thresholds for the 'appreciability' of an effect on trade. Therefore, an agreement does not appreciably affect trade between Member States if the parties' combined market share in any relevant market in the Union affected by the agreement does not exceed five per cent, and the aggregate annual Union turnover of the undertakings concerned in the products covered by the agreement does not exceed EUR 40 million.[79]

1.6. *The De Minimis Threshold*

Certain conduct between undertakings may qualify as restrictive of competition, but the impact may be so limited that it does not exceed a minimum level of seriousness, meaning the 'appreciability' requirement for applying Article 101 TFEU is not met.[80] In these cases, the Commission considers that the conduct does not breach the prohibition of Article 101 TFEU, as outlined in the *de minimis* Notice.[81]

The *de minimis* doctrine has its origin in the case law of the Court of Justice, which recognises that an agreement does not fall under the prohibition of Article 101 TFEU 'when it has only an insignificant effect on the markets, taking into account the weak position which the persons concerned have on the market of the product in question',[82] so that the requirement of

[74] D Bailey and R Whish, *Competition Law*, 10th edn (Oxford University Press, 2021) 154.

[75] Commission – *Guidelines on the application of Article 81(3) of the Treaty* [2004] OJ C101/07.

[76] Case C-56/65 *Société Technique Minière v Maschinenbau Ulm* EU:C:1966:38, 370.

[77] Case C-8/72 *Vereeniging van Cementhandelaren v Commission* EU:C:1972:84; Case C-246/86 *Belasco and Others v Commission* EU:C:1989:301; and Case T-66/89 *Publishers Association v Commission* EU:T:1992:84.

[78] *Commission Notice, Guidelines on the effect on trade concept contained in Articles 81 and 82 of the Treaty* [2004] OJ C101/81, paras 108–09; Case C-306/96 *Javico v Yves Saint Laurent* EU:C:1998:173, para 28.

[79] *Commission Notice, Guidelines on the effect on trade concept contained in Articles 81 and 82 of the Treaty* [2004] OJ C101/81, para 52.

[80] Case C-226/11 *Expedia Inc v Autorité de la concurrence* EU:C:2012:795, para 25.

[81] Commission – *Notice on agreements of minor importance which do not appreciably restrict competition under Article 101(1) of the Treaty on the Functioning of the European Union* [2014] OJ C291/1.

[82] Case C-5/69 *Voelk v Vervaecke* EU:C:1969:35, para 7; Case C-180/98 *Pavlov and Others* EU:C:2000:428; Case T-199/08 *Ziegler v Commission* EU:T:2011:285, para 44; Case T-208/08 *Gosselin Group and Stichting Administratiekantoor Portielje v Commission* EU:T:2011:287; and Case C-226/11 *Expedia* EU:C:2012:795, paras 16–17.

'appreciability' of the restriction of competition to which the application of that provision is conditional is not satisfied.[83]

This criterion has been further clarified in the *de minimis* Notice, which specifies that agreements will not exceed the *de minimis* threshold if the combined market share of the parties to the agreement does not exceed 10 per cent in any relevant market affected by the agreement, in the case of agreements between undertakings that are actual or potential competitors in those markets, or where the market share of each of the parties to the agreement does not exceed 15 per cent on any of the relevant markets affected by the agreement, in the case of agreements between undertakings which are not actual or potential competitors on any of those markets. In cases where it is difficult to determine whether the agreement is between competitors or between non-competitors, the 10 per cent threshold applies.[84] In line with the case law, the Notice clarifies that the requirement to establish the 'appreciability' of the restriction, that is, that the potential effect be significant, does not apply to restrictions by object, which do not require proof of any potential effect.[85]

1.7. *Ancillary Restraints*

Another example of the inapplicability of Article 101 TFEU is an agreement that is ancillary to a legitimate aim of an activity or transaction that is not covered by that provision. The conditions set out by the Court of Justice to consider an agreement as ancillary are that the restriction of the commercial autonomy of the parties is objectively necessary and proportionate to that activity or transaction or to its implementation.[86] The legitimate aim can be 'purely commercial', meaning that a commercial transaction would not have been objectively carried out absent the restriction.[87] It can also be 'regulatory' when, for instance, the restriction refers to the rules of professional conduct for regulated professions,[88] or to the rules of certain sports.[89]

2. Exemptions

A restrictive agreement may, despite its harmful effects, have positive impacts on the market. It may be an agreement that promotes research in strategic areas of general interest or helps facilitate the entry of a new product on the market, thereby leading to increased competition in the medium to long term. Agreements, practices, and decisions that restrict competition must be analysed considering multiple factors, including their positive effects on the market. To enable the Commission to conduct this overall analysis, Article 101(3) TFEU provides that paragraph 1 of the provision may be declared inapplicable to conduct

> which contributes to improving the production or distribution of goods or to promoting technical or economic progress, while allowing consumers a fair share of the resulting benefit, and which does not:
>
> (a) impose on the undertakings concerned restrictions which are not indispensable to the attainment of these objectives;

[83] *Expedia (n 82)* para 25.
[84] Commission – *Notice on agreements of minor importance which do not appreciably restrict competition under Article 101(1) of the Treaty on the Functioning of the European Union* [2014] OJ C291/1, paras 8–9.
[85] ibid, *paras 2 and 13, referring to Case C-226/11 Expedia Inc v Autorité de la concurrence EU:C:2012:795, paras 35–37.*
[86] Case C-382/12 P *MasterCard Inc and Others v Commission* EU:C:2014:2201, para 89.
[87] Case C-230/16 *Coty Germany GmbH v Parfümerie Akzente GmbH* EU:C:2017:941, para 35.
[88] Case C309/99, *Wouters and Others* EU:C:2002:98, paras 86–94 and 97–110.
[89] Case C-519/04 P *Meca-Medina and Majcen v Commission* EU:C:2006:492.

(b) afford such undertakings the possibility of eliminating competition in respect of a substantial part of the products in question.

Once these conditions are met, the conduct will be 'exempt' from scrutiny, as paragraph 3 refers to the inapplicability of Article 101 TFEU to this type of action. Therefore, these are not justifications, but exemptions that allow the application of Article 101 TFEU to be circumvented. Moreover, the exemptions cover all restrictive conduct, including the conduct listed in Article 101(1)(a)–(e) TFEU. These exemptions may be of an individual scope, in which case they will be examined on a case-by-case basis, depending on the overall circumstances of each case. Alternatively, they may be general and apply to a broader category of conduct.

2.1. *Individual Exemptions: Article 101(3) TFEU*

Regulation 1/2003 introduced a major reform of the legal framework for competition policy. Among other innovations, it abolished the former system of notification and individual exemption under Regulation 17 and replaced it with a directly applicable exception system. Under this system, Article 101(3) TFEU is applied directly: agreements that satisfy its four cumulative conditions are not prohibited, without any prior decision to that effect. Undertakings must therefore self-assess whether their conduct satisfies Article 101(3), while the Commission, national competition authorities and national courts may apply Article 101 TFEU in full, including Article 101(3), in individual cases. To provide legal certainty, the Commission has adopted Guidelines on the application of Article 101(3) TFEU, which codify the Court of Justice's case law and the Commission's interpretation of this provision.[90]

The first condition for Article 101(3) TFEU to apply requires that the conduct 'contributes to improving the production or distribution of goods or promoting technical or economic progress'. Although Article 101(3) TFEU only refers to goods, the Commission applies it equally to services.[91] According to the Guidelines, to meet this requirement it is necessary for the pro-competitive effects resulting from the agreement to outweigh the anti-competitive effects, for which the nature of the efficiencies, their relationship to the conduct, the likelihood and importance of each efficiency, and the material moment in time at which the alleged efficiency will be obtained must be verified.[92]

The second requirement is to prove that consumers are given their fair share of the benefits resulting from the conduct. The term 'fair share' suggests that the pass-on of benefits must at least offset any actual or likely negative impact caused by the restriction of competition under Article 101(1) TFEU. Therefore, the positive effects must be balanced against the negative effects and compensated for in each relevant market.[93]

The third condition concerns the indispensability of the conduct to achieve the efficiencies created. To establish that this condition is met, the Commission requires a two-part test: first, analysing whether the restrictive agreement is reasonably necessary to achieve the efficiencies; and second, whether the individual restrictions on competition resulting from the agreement are also reasonably necessary to attain the efficiencies. The first step requires that the efficiencies be specific to the agreement, so that there is no other economically feasible, less restrictive way to achieve them.[94] The second step must determine whether the absence of the restriction

[90] Commission Notice, Guidelines on the application of Article 81(3) of the Treaty [2004] OJ C101/97.

[91] ibid, para 48.

[92] ibid, para 51.

[93] ibid, para 85; and Joined Cases C-56/64 and C-58/64 *Consten and Grundig v Commission of the EEC* EU:C:1966:41, 429.

[94] Commission Notice, Guidelines on the application of Article 81(3) of the Treaty [2004] OJ C101/97, para 75.

would eliminate or substantially reduce the efficiencies, or make their attainment significantly less likely.[95]

Finally, the agreement must not afford the undertakings 'the possibility of eliminating competition in respect of a substantial part of the products in question'. This requirement is interpreted in an autonomous and specific way, although Article 102 TFEU must be taken into account when an undertaking with a dominant position participates in the agreement.[96] The elimination of competition depends on the degree of competition that existed before the agreement and the effects of the agreement on competition. Therefore, the weaker the competition in the market prior to the conduct, the smaller the further reduction necessary to eliminate competition within the meaning of Article 101(3) TFEU.[97]

2.2. *Block Exemptions*

Undertakings bear the burden of proving that an individual exemption applies to their conduct. However, once the Commission has declared a category of act to be exempt, the undertaking only needs to demonstrate that its conduct falls within that category. To achieve this, and in line with the legal basis of Article 103(2)(b) TFEU, the Commission has introduced various regulations containing 'block exemptions', which simplify decision-making for companies by providing pre-established standards that legally confirm the legality of the conduct.

The Commission has adopted block exemption regulations on a general basis, applicable to both horizontal[98] and vertical agreements.[99] There are also sector-specific block exemption regulations and notices, particularly for technology transfer agreements,[100] agriculture and food, postal services, professional services, telecommunications, and transport.[101]

3. Consequences of the Infringement of Article 101 TFEU

3.1. *Nullity*

Article 101(2) TFEU states that 'agreements or decisions prohibited by this Article shall be automatically void'. Without the need for a prior declaration, this provision renders private acts that restrict competition null and void, immediately and *ex tunc*. The purpose of this rule

[95] ibid, para 79.

[96] ibid, para 106.

[97] ibid, para 107.

[98] Commission Regulation (EU) 2023/1066 of 1 June 2023 on the application of Article 101(3) of the Treaty on the Functioning of the European Union to certain categories of research and development agreements [2023] OJ L143/9; and Commission Regulation (EU) 2023/1067 of 1 June 2023 on the application of Article 101(3) of the Treaty on the Functioning of the European Union to certain categories of specialisation agreements [2023] OJ L143/20. These regulations replaced, respectively, Regulations (EU) 1217/2010 and 1218/2010, which expired on 30 June 2023.

[99] Commission Regulation (EU) 2022/720 of 10 May 2022 on the application of Article 101(3) of the Treaty on the Functioning of the European Union to categories of vertical agreements and concerted practices [2022] OJ L134/4; Commission Regulation (EU) 461/2010 of 27 May 2010 on the application of Article 101(3) of the Treaty on the Functioning of the European Union to categories of vertical agreements and concerted practices in the motor vehicle sector [2010] OJ L129/52.

[100] Commission Regulation (EU) No 316/2014 of 21 March 2014 on the application of Article 101(3) of the Treaty on the Functioning of the European Union to certain categories of technology transfer agreements [2014] OJ L93/17.

[101] Among them, *Commission Notice on the application of the competition rules to the postal service and on the assessment of certain State measures relating to postal services* [1998] OJ C39/2; Council Regulation (EC) 246/2009 of 26 February 2009 on the application of Article 81(3) of the Treaty to certain categories of agreements, decisions and concerted practices between liner shipping companies (consortia) [2009] OJ L79/1; and Council Regulation (EC) 487/2009 of 25 May 2009 on the application of Article 81(3) of the Treaty to certain categories of agreements, decisions and concerted practices in the air transport sector [2009] OJ L148/1.

is to reinforce the competition system and maximise its practical effectiveness. Unsurprisingly, the Court of Justice has described this provision as 'a fundamental provision which is essential for the accomplishment of the tasks entrusted to the [Union] and, in particular, for the functioning of the internal market'.[102]

The nullity of the agreement arises *ex lege*, by operation of the Treaty, without the need for any intermediation of other rules, whether national or Union rules.[103] It is not necessary for a competition authority or a national court to declare the conduct in question null and void. As soon as anti-competitive conduct is established, the effects of the agreement or act adopted between the undertakings are deprived of legal effect, ceasing to have effect between the parties and vis-a-vis third parties. The Court of Justice has held that 'an agreement which is null and void by virtue of this provision has no effect as between the contracting parties and cannot be set up against third parties'.[104] However, the practical terms in which the nullity deploys its effects in private law will be governed by the provisions of national law.[105]

The nullity resulting from Article 101(2) TFEU applies only to those parts of the agreement affected by the prohibition, or to the entire agreement if it is not possible to separate those elements from the agreement itself.[106] The agreement may therefore be void only in part, provided that the agreement as a whole can survive without the anti-competitive clause(s).[107] The severability of the illegal clause from the rest of the agreement is a matter for national law. This referral to national law may lead to a degree of fragmentation, as an agreement may be severable under conditions that vary across the Member States in which it has produced its effects.

3.2. *Sanctions*

Infringement of Article 101 TFEU may result in the Commission adopting measures, including sanctions. The sanctioning regime is particularly important as it aims both to ensure that the infringing conduct ceases and to have a punitive effect, deterring companies from repeating such behaviour in the future.

Article 23 of Regulation 1/2003 sets out the basic sanctioning framework applicable to infringements of Article 101 TFEU, as well as infringements of Commission decisions implementing that provision and other actions hindering the Commission's investigative tasks. Fines can amount to up to 10 per cent of the total turnover in the preceding business year of each undertaking whose conduct constitutes the breach of Article 101 TFEU,[108] and are calculated following the Commission's guidelines.[109] The penalty system provides a limitation period of five years from the day the infringement is committed. In cases of ongoing or continuing breaches, the limitation period only starts to run on the day the infringement ceases.[110]

[102] Case C-126/97 *Eco Swiss* EU:C:1999:269, para 36.

[103] Art 1(1) of Regulation 1/2003 clearly states that 'agreements, decisions and concerted practices referred to in Article [101(1)] of the Treaty which do not satisfy the conditions of Article [101(3)] of the Treaty shall be prohibited, without any prior decision to that effect being required'.

[104] Case C-22/71 *Béguelin Import v GL Import Export* EU:C:1971:113, para 29.

[105] P Van Cleynenbreugel, 'Embedding Procedural Autonomy: The Directive and National Procedural Rules' in M Bergström, M Iacovides and M Strand (eds), *Harmonising EU Competition Litigation: The New Directive and Beyond* (Hart, 2016) 99–120.

[106] Case C-25/21 *ZA and Others v Repsol Comercial de Productos Petrolíferos SA* EU:C:2023:298, para 74.

[107] Case C-56/65 *Société Technique Minière v Maschinenbau Ulm* EU:C:1966:38, p 372; and Case C-319/82 *Société de vente de ciments v Kerpen & Kerpen* EU:C:1983:374, para 11.

[108] Regulation 1/2003, Art 23(2).

[109] *Guidelines on the method of setting fines imposed pursuant to Article 23(2)(a) of Regulation (EC) No 1/2003* [2006] OJ C210/2.

[110] Art 25(2) of Regulation 1/2003.

Sanctions imposed by the Commission can be challenged before the General Court under Article 263 TFEU. Moreover, Article 31 of Regulation 1/2003 confers on Union courts full jurisdiction to rule on these actions. As a result, Union courts have the power to amend the Commission's decision and, consequently, repeal, reduce, or increase the fine initially imposed.

3.3. *Damages Actions*

Article 101 TFEU has direct horizontal effect between private individuals. Any company or natural person who has suffered harm as a result of conduct contrary to this provision may invoke it before national courts. This right also includes the right to claim financial damages caused by the companies responsible for the anti-competitive conduct.[111] In *Courage*, the Court of Justice defined the basic features of this type of action for damages within the framework of the procedural autonomy that allows Member States to determine, in accordance with their national legal systems, how rights derived from the Union legal system can be enforced. The ruling in *Courage* confirms that Article 101 TFEU has direct effect, as well as the illegality of any national rule that prevents an individual from claiming damages as compensation for harm caused by the performance of a contract contrary to the Treaty, even when the individual has been a party to the contract (provided that it is established that this party does not bear significant responsibility for the distortion of competition).[112]

Directive 2014/104 on damages actions for breaches of competition law[113] harmonised the basic rules for these actions in national courts, respecting the Member States' procedural autonomy. The result of this scheme is a common, harmonised procedural framework applicable to all Member States, which provides any victim of conduct contrary to Article 101 TFEU, regardless of their place of residence, with a uniform substantive and procedural framework for claiming damages in national courts. The Directive enshrines the right of a victim who has suffered harm due to an infringement of competition law to claim 'full compensation', understood as restitution of the situation the victim would have been in had the infringement of competition law not been committed.[114] Furthermore, the Directive specifies that compensation must cover actual loss, loss of profit, and payment of interest.[115] Any amounts exceeding these items are considered to go beyond compensation or restitution and thus amount to overcompensation, such as punitive, multiple or other types of damages.

III. ARTICLE 102 TFEU AND ABUSE OF A DOMINANT POSITION

The Treaties not only prohibit coordinated or agreed conduct between two or more undertakings, but they also aim to prevent the harmful effects on competition caused by the unilateral behaviour of a single operator holding a dominant position in the market, or a group of operators having a collective dominant position. This is the purpose of the first paragraph of Article 102 TFEU, which establishes the foundations for prohibiting abuse of a dominant position:

[111] Case C-453/99 *Courage and Crehan* EU:C:2001:465, para 31.
[112] ibid, para 36.
[113] Directive 2014/104/EU of the European Parliament and of the Council of 26 November 2014 on certain rules governing actions for damages under national law for infringements of competition law of the Member States and of the European Union [2014] OJ L349/1.
[114] Directive 2014/104, Art 3(2).
[115] ibid, Art 3(3).

> Any abuse by one or more undertakings of a dominant position within the internal market or in a substantial part of it shall be prohibited as incompatible with the internal market in so far as it may affect trade between Member States.

Dominance in a market is not illegal. A company may hold a dominant position because of its ability to produce superior products or provide better services. Such dominance can be a fair and deserved outcome for operators who, through their effort and talent, win the favour of consumers. Article 102 TFEU prohibits situations in which a company, having attained a position of dominance, engages in abusive practices that hinder other companies from operating in the same market, thereby preventing the emergence or development of activities by competitors. In other words, dominance implies a qualified legal status, which the case law describes as 'a special responsibility not to allow [an undertaking's] conduct to impair genuine undistorted competition on the common market'.[116] The second paragraph of Article 102 TFEU provides examples of this type of abusive conduct and lists, without being exhaustive, the following:

> (a) directly or indirectly imposing unfair purchase or selling prices or other unfair trading conditions;
> (b) limiting production, markets or technical development to the prejudice of consumers;
> (c) applying dissimilar conditions to equivalent transactions with other trading parties, thereby placing them at a competitive disadvantage;
> (d) making the conclusion of contracts subject to acceptance by the other parties of supplementary obligations which, by their nature or according to commercial usage, have no connection with the subject of such contracts.

Determining abusive conduct requires an analysis of several features. Firstly, it is important to consider certain specificities applicable to undertakings in the context of Article 102 TFEU. Secondly, the relevant market, both product and geographic, must be clearly delineated, since dominance occurs in a specific market whose perimeter must be defined in advance. Thirdly, the existence of dominance on the part of the operator must be assessed, for which various criteria objectively determine this feature. Finally, the classification of the conduct as abusive must be examined in accordance with the criteria set out in the Court of Justice's case law. For this analysis, the Guidelines on the Commission's enforcement priorities in applying Article 102 TFEU to abusive exclusionary conduct by dominant undertakings play an important role.[117]

In line with the trend of the case law on restrictions by object under Article 101 TFEU, the Court of Justice has recently confirmed that the general framework applicable to all exclusionary abuses involves proving two cumulative elements: whether the conduct deviates from competition on the merits because it is apt to foreclose competitors at least as efficient as the dominant undertaking or competitors that could become so in the absence of the conduct, and whether it has such potential effect.[118] Although the case law links both elements to the foreclosure of equally efficient competitors,[119] the Commission favours an interpretation that dilutes the concept of deviation from competition on the merits by disconnecting it from the

[116] Case C-322/81 NV *Nederlandsche Banden-Industrie-Michelin v Commission* EU:C:1983:313, para 57.

[117] Guidelines on the application of Article 102 of the Treaty on the Functioning of the European Union to abusive exclusionary conduct by dominant undertakings [2025].

[118] Case C-333/21 *European Superleague Company SL v FIFA and UEFA* EU:C:2023:1011, paras 129 and 131; Case C-48/22 P *Google LLC and Alphabet Inc v Commission* EU:C:2024:726, para 167.

[119] Case C-377/20 *Servizio Elettrico Nazionale and Others v AGCM* EU:C:2022:379, para 79; Case C-333/21 *European Superleague Company SL v FIFA and UEFA* EU:C:2023:1011, paras 126–27; Case C-48/22 P *Google LLC and Alphabet Inc v Commission* EU:C:2024:726, paras 164–65.

foreclosure of equally efficient competitors. This confers on enforcers broad discretion to deem certain conducts per se anticompetitive and with little proof of a potential effect.[120]

In contrast with Article 101 TFEU, the wording of Article 102 TFEU does not include exemptions or justifications of abuses of a dominant position, but the case law has stated that the provision does not apply to conduct that is subject to an 'objective justification', ie that the conduct is objectively necessary to achieve a legitimate aim.[121] Moreover, the Court of Justice has acknowledged the possibility, which has not yet materialised in practice, for the dominant undertaking to be able to 'demonstrate that the exclusionary effect arising from its conduct may be counterbalanced, or outweighed, by advantages in terms of efficiency which also benefit the consumer'.[122] Therefore, Article 102 TFEU enshrines an approach focused on identifying abusive conduct that will rarely be tolerated once detected. This does not prevent the Commission or the Court of Justice from conducting an economic analysis in which the advantages and disadvantages of the conduct are weighed. However, in general terms, this type of assessment is considerably more limited in the context of Article 102 TFEU.

1. Definition of 'Undertaking'

The definition of 'undertaking' provided by Article 102 TFEU broadly coincides with the one adopted in Article 101 TFEU, but with two important qualifications. Firstly, the 'single economic entity' doctrine does not apply in cases of abuse. While agreements between a parent company and a subsidiary are considered to be adopted by a single company, this is not the case when the parent company is dominant and favours its group companies. Secondly, situations of dominance and potential abuse also extend to public undertakings providing economic services of general interest. In these cases, there is a joint application of Article 102 and 106 TFEU, and the case law provides for a specific interpretative criterion that will be discussed in section V.1 of this chapter.

2. Definition of the Relevant Market

The first step in analysing a situation of abuse of dominance is to determine the relevant market, which involves examining two features: the product market; and the geographic market. For this purpose, the Commission has issued guidance in its Notice on the definition of the relevant market for the purposes of Union competition law.[123]

2.1. The Product Market

An undertaking operates in a market by providing a particular good or service in competition with other interchangeable goods or services. The key criterion for determining in which market a dominant undertaking operates is the substitutability of the product or service. The 2024 Commission Notice describes the product market in the following terms:

[120] Commission – Guidelines on the application of Article 102 of the Treaty on the Functioning of the European Union to abusive exclusionary conduct by dominant undertakings [2025] paras 52–59.

[121] Joined Cases C-468/06 to C-478/06 *Sot Lélos kai Sia v GlaxoSmithKline* EU:C:2008:504, para 34.

[122] Case C-23/14 *Post Danmark A/S v Konkurrencerådet* EU:C:2015:651, para 48.

[123] Commission – Notice on the definition of the relevant market for the purposes of Union competition law [2024] OJ C/2024/1645.

> The relevant product market comprises all those products that customers regard as interchangeable or substitutable to the product(s) of the undertaking(s) involved, based on the products' characteristics, their prices and their intended use, taking into consideration the conditions of competition and the structure of supply and demand on the market.

Substitutability must be assessed from the perspective of both demand and supply. On the *demand* side, it is necessary to verify cross-product elasticity. This is determined when an increase in the price of one product causes consumers to switch easily to alternative available products. For example, if a rise in the price of table wine results in greater demand for beer, this is evidence of demand substitutability.[124] By contrast, *supply* substitutability, a secondary criterion used only when its effects are equivalent to those of demand substitutability in terms of efficiency and immediate response, takes into account the adaptability of firms, in particular when a firm can produce and market the relevant products in the short term without significant additional costs or risks, in response to small permanent price changes.[125]

2.2. *The Geographic Market*

According to the Commission, the relevant geographic market includes the area where the undertakings concerned are involved in the supply of the relevant products and services, in which the conditions of competition are sufficiently homogeneous and which can be distinguished from neighbouring geographic areas, in particular because the conditions of competition are notably different in those areas.[126] In conducting this analysis, the Commission takes into account, on the one hand, the distribution of the parties' and their competitors' market shares, and, on the other hand, pricing and price differentials at both the national and Union levels.[127] Based on these elements of assessment, the Commission will define the geographic market, which may have a local or a global dimension.

3. Dominant Position

An undertaking holds a dominant position when, based on various characteristics, it exerts *market power*. This power falls within the scope of Article 102 TFEU when the undertaking acquires

> a position of economic strength . . . which enables it to prevent effective competition from being maintained on the relevant market by giving it the power to behave to an appreciable extent independently of its competitors, customers and ultimately of its consumers.[128]

A dominant position is not the result of a single factor, but a combination of facts assessed individually or in combination. The Commission's approach follows the Court of Justice's ruling in *Hoffmann-La Roche*, which stated the following:

> Such a position does not preclude some competition, which it does where there is a monopoly or a quasi-monopoly, but enables the undertaking which profits by it, if not to determine, at least to have an appreciable influence on the conditions under which that competition will develop, and in any case to act largely in disregard of it so long as such conduct does not operate to its detriment.

[124] Notice on the definition of the relevant market, paras 25–30.
[125] ibid, paras 32–37.
[126] ibid, para 38.
[127] ibid, para 39.
[128] Case C-27/76 *United Brands v Commission* EU:C:1978:22, para 65.

> A dominant position must also be distinguished from parallel courses of conduct which are peculiar to oligopolies in that in an oligopoly the courses of conduct interact, while in the case of an undertaking occupying a dominant position the conduct of the undertaking which derives profits from that position is to a great extent determined unilaterally.
>
> The existence of a dominant position may derive from several factors which, taken separately, are not necessarily determinative but among these factors a highly important one is the existence of very large market shares.[129]

The Commission has systematised this finding in its Guidance,[130] focusing on the following three criteria.

3.1. *Market Share*

A firm's market share is the most relevant factor in determining dominance, but it is not always conclusive. Practice shows that a market share of more than 70 per cent is indicative of dominance, in which case it is not necessary to resort to other factors to confirm this conclusion.[131] On the other hand, a market share of 50–70 per cent, while giving rise to a presumption of dominance, must be considered in conjunction with other economic factors.[132] A 40–50 per cent market share does not automatically lead to dominance either. It requires an analysis that also considers changes in market share over time, the market share of the closest competitors, and the number and strength of other competitors.[133] Finally, a market share of less than 40 per cent presupposes the absence of dominance. However, this does not preclude the possibility that a single undertaking may be found to exercise market power in light of exceptional circumstances.[134]

Therefore, the higher the market share and the longer the period over which it is held, the more likely it is that the market share is a decisive indication of dominance.[135]

3.2. *Entry Barriers*

The difficulties a competitor faces when entering a market are also relevant indicators for determining the existence of dominance. The definition of a barrier to entry is not unambiguous and depends on various factors, which require an economic analysis of the relevant market.

The Commission has categorised the factual situations constituting a barrier to entry by analysing them from a counterfactual perspective: situations where a competitor is in a position to enter the market. A competitor does not face barriers to entry and will be able to expand into the new market if the entry is likely, timely, and sufficient. Entry is *likely* when it is sufficiently profitable for the competitor, considering factors such as barriers to expansion or entry, the potential reactions of the allegedly dominant firm and other competitors, and the risks and costs of failure. Entry will be *timely* if it can be achieved quickly enough to deter or

[129] Case C-85/76 *Hoffmann-La Roche* EU:C:1979:36, para 39.

[130] *Commission – Guidance on the Commission's enforcement priorities in applying Article 102 of the Treaty on the Functioning of the European Union to abusive exclusionary conduct by dominant undertakings* [2009] OJ C45/7.

[131] Case T-30/89 *Hilti v Commission* EU:T:1991:70, para 92; and Case T-65/98 *Van den Bergh Foods v Commission* EU:T:2003:281, para 154.

[132] Case C-62/86 *AKZO v Commission* EU:C:1991:286, para 60.

[133] Case C-27/76 *United Brands v Commission* EU:C:1978:22, paras 108–10.

[134] Case C-250/92 *Gøttrup-Klim and Others Grovvareforeninger v Dansk Landbrugs Grovvareselskab* EU:C:1994:413, para 48; and Case T-219/99 *British Airways v Commission* EU:T:2003:343, paras 211–24. The Commission's Guidance on Art 102 TFEU (n 130) states that 'there may be specific cases below that threshold where competitors are not in a position to constrain effectively the conduct of a dominant undertaking, for example where they face serious capacity limitations. Such cases may also deserve attention on the part of the Commission' (para 14).

[135] Guidance on Art 102 TFEU (n 130) para 15.

prevent the exercise of substantial market power. Lastly, entry will be *sufficient* if it can deter any attempts by the allegedly dominant undertaking to increase prices in the relevant market.[136]

The Commission's Guidance provides various examples of barriers to entry as defined in Article 102 TFEU. By way of example, the Guidance highlights, first and foremost, barriers of a legal nature, such as tariffs or quotas. Secondly, barriers can include advantages specifically enjoyed by the dominant undertaking, such as economies of scale and scope, privileged access to essential inputs or natural resources, important technologies, or an established distribution and sales network. Third, the conduct of the allegedly dominant undertaking may also create barriers if, for instance, it has made significant investments that would have to be matched by new entrants or competitors, or if it has entered into long-term contracts with its customers that produce appreciable foreclosure effects.[137]

In any case, it is necessary to consider the existence of countervailing buyer power, ie, the competitive pressures exerted by the customers of the allegedly dominant firm.[138] It may be that the size or importance of a customer to the alleged dominant firm is sufficient to deter or prevent the firm from attempting to profitably raise prices. If a firm's market power is offset by the power of its customers, the firm's position cannot be said to be sufficiently robust to be deemed dominant.[139]

3.3. *Collective Dominance*

Article 102 TFEU does not preclude the possibility that abusive conduct may be the work of 'one or more undertakings'. Therefore, undertakings operating in a duopoly or oligopoly may engage in abuse of a dominant position. These cases are qualified as 'collective dominance' and require careful analysis of the links between the dominant undertakings.

Initially, the case law had not developed the notion that the actions of undertakings in an oligopolistic market could give rise to collective dominance.[140] This approach evolved in the late 1980s in the early case law of the newly established Court of First Instance.[141] Some years later, the judgment in *Almelo* introduced the notion of collective dominance as applicable to a group of undertakings.[142] Over time, a three-pronged *test* has been developed for the determination of collective dominance: (1)All members of the dominant oligopoly must be able to observe the behaviour of the other members and check whether they are adopting the same course of action. (2)Tacit coordination must be sustainable over time, ie there must be an incentive not to deviate from the common line of conduct in the market.(3)To establish the requisite legal standard, the existence of a collective dominant position, it must be shown that the foreseeable reaction of actual and potential competitors and consumers would not call into question the expected results of the ordinary course of action.

The triple *test* should not be applied automatically, and it is necessary to consider the overall economic situation of coordination. Although the three steps of the triple test facilitate the determination of a situation of collective dominance, the final result will depend on a holistic analysis in which the economic analysis will be decisive.[143]

[136] ibid, para 16.
[137] ibid, para 17.
[138] Case T-228/97 *Irish Sugar v Commission* EU:T:1999:246, paras 97–104.
[139] Guidance on Art 102 TFEU (n 130) para 18.
[140] Case C-322/81 *Michelin v Commission* EU:C:1983:313.
[141] Case T-68/89 *SIV and Others v Commission* EU:T:1992:38, paras 358–60.
[142] Case C-393/92 *Gemeente Almelo and Others v Energiebedrijf IJsselmij* EU:C:1994:171, paras 41–42.
[143] On the triple test, see Case T-342/99 *Airtours v Commission* EU:T:2002:146, para 62. The holistic approach which qualifies the mechanical nature of the triple test and requires an overall economic analysis is found in Case C-413/06 P *Bertelsmann and Sony Corporation of America v Impala* EU:C:2008:392, para 125.

As an alternative to the scenario of oligopolistic collective dominance, it is also possible to establish dominance based on cross-company agreements that may even fall under Article 101 TFEU.[144] However, establishing abuse requires the existence of conduct capable of producing exclusionary effects that go beyond the anti-competitive effects inherent in each of the underlying potentially anti-competitive agreements.[145]

4. Abuse

An undertaking does not infringe Article 102 TFEU simply because it is dominant. However, the conduct of one or more dominant undertakings becomes unlawful when it is abusive vis-à-vis other operators, whether they are competitors or customers. As will be explained below, the definition of abuse is broad and flexible, giving rise to a variety of potentially abusive situations. Likewise, companies engaging in such conduct may justify their actions, although in terms significantly more restrictive than those provided for in Article 101 TFEU.

4.1. Definition and Types of Abuse

Article 102 TFEU does not define 'abuse', but it includes an enumeration of abusive conducts. The Court of Justice has provided some interpretative guidelines on the concept, primarily based on the definition developed in the *Hoffmann-La Roche* case, which describes 'abuse' as

> an objective concept relating to the behaviour of an undertaking in a dominant position which is such as to influence the structure of a market where, as a result of the very presence of the undertaking in question, the degree of competition is weakened and which, through recourse to methods different from those which condition normal competition in products or services on the basis of the transactions of commercial operators, has the effect of hindering the maintenance of the degree of competition still existing in the market or the growth of that competition.[146]

This seminal case law has recently been revisited by the Court of Justice to establish, as mentioned above, a general legal test applicable at least to exclusionary abuses. This general test ensures that abusive conduct is conduct made possible by dominance, thereby entailing the leveraging of that position that causes the dominant undertaking to breach its special responsibility. It requires demonstration that the conduct is apt to foreclose hypothetical competitors at least as efficient as the dominant undertaking but that are non-dominant. This also requires showing that the conduct is capable of having that potential effect, as stated in *Google Shopping*:

> In addition, conduct may be categorised as 'abuse of a dominant position' not only where it has the actual or potential effect of restricting competition on the merits by excluding equally efficient competing undertakings from the market or markets concerned, but also where it has been proven to have the actual or potential effect – or even the object – of impeding potentially competing undertakings at an earlier stage, through the placing of obstacles to entry or the use of other blocking measures or other means different from those which govern competition on the merits, from even entering that or those market(s) and, in so doing, preventing the growth of competition therein to the detriment of consumers, by limiting production, product or alternative service development or innovation.[147]

[144] Joined Cases T-68/89, T-77/89 and T-78/89 *Società Italiana Vetro SpA, Fabbrica Pisana SpA and PPG Vernante Pennitalia SpA v Commission* EU:T:1992:38, para 354.
[145] Case C-307/18 *Generics (UK) Ltd v Competition and Markets Authority* EU:C:2020:52, para 172.
[146] *Hoffmann-La Roche* (n 129) para 91.
[147] Case C-48/22 P *Google LLC and Alphabet Inc v Commission* EU:C:2024:726, para 167.

In practice, the Commission carries out an economic analysis of the allegedly abusive conduct, focusing on the harm caused by the conduct vis-à-vis competitors and consumers on a case-by-case basis. Although the Treaties include a list of cases of abusive conduct, the mere subsuming of the facts under these categories does not automatically trigger the applicability of Article 102 TFEU.

4.1.1. Price Discrimination and Discounts

Article 102(c) TFEU explicitly bans the abusive practice of applying dissimilar conditions to equivalent transactions with other third parties, thereby placing the third parties at a competitive disadvantage. Such discriminatory conduct occurs when a dominant undertaking sets different prices based on criteria unrelated to the cost structure of the product or service. For instance, a firm might lower its prices in a specific geographic territory to isolate that market segment and prevent competitors from entering it. For customer discrimination to be considered abusive, the case law requires not only differentiated treatment but also that it results in a competitive disadvantage, based on

> an analysis of all the relevant circumstances of the case leading to the conclusion that that behaviour affects the costs, profits or any other relevant interest of one or more of those partners, so that that conduct is such as to affect that situation.[148]

Apart from discrimination, a rebate policy can also cause customer dependence on the dominant undertaking, making it impossible for other firms to compete. Sometimes rebates may be conditional, which can lead to actual or potential foreclosure effects similar to exclusive purchasing obligations, without necessarily requiring a sacrifice from the dominant undertaking.[149]

The Court of Justice has ruled on several occasions on rebate policies pursued by undertakings in a dominant position. In the case of fidelity rebates (also known as loyalty discounts), which are linked exclusively to whether customers obtain their supplies exclusively or predominantly from the dominant undertaking, the aim is to prevent customers from purchasing from competing manufacturers. The case law has held that the effect of such fidelity rebates

> is to apply dissimilar conditions to equivalent transactions with other trading parties in that two purchasers pay a different price for the same quantity of the same product depending on whether they obtain their supplies exclusively from the undertaking in a dominant position or have several sources of supply.
>
> . . . these practices by an undertaking in a dominant position and especially on an expanding market tend to consolidate this position by means of a form of competition which is not based on the transactions effected and is therefore distorted.[150]

The analysis of such rebates requires an overall assessment, taking into account all the circumstances of the case, in particular the criteria and arrangements for granting the rebate. It also involves examining whether, by using an advantage not based on any economic benefit justifying it, the rebate tends to foreclose or reduce the buyer's ability to choose sources of supply, to deny competitors access to the market, to apply dissimilar conditions to equivalent transactions with third parties, or to strengthen a dominant position by distorting competition.[151] In particular, to determine the capability to foreclose through the rebates, consideration

[148] Case C-525/16 *MEO v Autoridade da Concorrência* EU:C:2018:270, para 37.

[149] Guidance on Article 102 TFEU (n 130) para 37.

[150] *Hoffmann-La Roche* (n 129) para 90.

[151] *Michelin v Commission* (n 140), para 71; Case T-65/89 *BPB Industries and British Gypsum v Commission* EU:T:1993:31, para 120; and Case T-228/97 *Irish Sugar v Commission* EU:T:1999:246, para 197.

must be given to the size of the dominant undertaking's position on the relevant market, the proportion of the market affected by the rebates, the conditions and arrangements for granting them, their duration and amount, and whether there is a strategy aimed at driving out competitors at least as efficient as the dominant undertaking.[152]

4.1.2. Predatory Pricing

When a dominant undertaking deliberately incurs losses or foregoes short-term profits to exclude one or more actual or potential competitors, such behaviour is considered abusive. Predatory pricing suppresses competition and harms consumers in the medium-to-long term, as the price reduction is only temporary and will be followed by an increase once competition in the market has disappeared. The dominant firm will have greater resources available and can afford to artificially and substantially lower prices for a period, until its competitors are driven out of the market.

The case law considers two scenarios in which predatory pricing contrary to Article 102 TFEU may arise:

- In the first scenario, a firm sets prices below average variable costs, without any interest in charging such prices other than to eliminate competitors and raise prices by exploiting its monopolistic situation.[153]
- A second scenario involves a firm that sets prices below the average total cost, which comprises both fixed and variable costs, but above the average variable cost. In this case, the prices may eliminate from the market firms that may be as efficient as the dominant firm but, due to their lower economic capacity, cannot withstand competition.[154]

Establishing and proving predatory practice contrary to Article 102 TFEU is difficult. Displaying a company's cost structure requires complex economic and accounting analyses, the proof of which will rest with the Commission. Likewise, the obligation to prove the intent to exclude a competitor depends on evidence that is not always easy to establish. Economists disagree on the real harm of predatory practices, which some consider irrational or non-existent. However, the Commission follows the indications of the Court of Justice and conducts a cost analysis based on the two assumptions mentioned above, focusing on the average long-term cost structure.[155] The Court of Justice itself appeared to relax its initial stance in subsequent case law, using as a reference the variable costs of the entire sector rather than those of the undertaking in a single customer relationship.[156] However, in more recent cases, the General Court has relied on the cost benchmark based on the long-run average incremental costs of the affected products.[157]

4.1.3. Refusal to Supply and the *Essential Facilities* Doctrine

Companies enjoy freedom of contract, which allows them to choose with whom they do business. This freedom can become an abusive practice when a company refuses to contract with an operator dependent on its supply, thereby reducing competition. Initially, the case law used

[152] Case C-413/14 P *Intel Corp v Commission* EU:C:2017:632, para 139.
[153] Case C-62/86 *AKZO v Commission* EU:C:1991:286, para 71.
[154] ibid, para 72.
[155] Guidance on Article 102 TFEU (n 130), para 26.
[156] Case C-209/10 *Post Danmark* EU:C:2012:172, para 37.
[157] Case T-671/19 *Qualcomm, Inc v Commission* EU:T:2024:626, paras 408–43.

strict criteria, limited to situations where the supplying company refused to contract because it aimed to enter the same market as its customer:

> [A]n undertaking being in a dominant position as regards the production of raw material and therefore able to control the supply to manufacturers of derivatives, cannot, just because it decides to start manufacturing these derivatives (in competition with its former customers) act in such a way as to eliminate their competition which in the case in question, would amount to eliminating one of the principal manufacturers . . . in the Common Market.[158]

This strict approach must be qualified when the dominant undertaking has exclusive access to an essential facility, such as infrastructure, whether owned or exclusively licensed. Advocate General Jacobs defined these *essential facilities* in the following terms:

> An essential facility can be a product such as a raw material or a service, including provision of access to a place such as a harbour or airport or to a distribution system such as a telecommunications network. In many cases the relationship is vertical in the sense that the dominant undertaking reserves the product or service to, or discriminates in favour of, its own downstream operation at the expense of competitors on the downstream market. It may however also be horizontal in the sense of tying sales of related but distinct products or services.[159]

The case law has adopted this definition of essential facilities and applies the doctrine to vertical supply relationships, considering several criteria that will arise in 'exceptional circumstances':[160] firstly, the refusal must concern a product or service that is objectively necessary, ie indispensable to be able to compete effectively in a downstream market; secondly, it must be proven that the refusal will lead to the elimination of effective competition in the downstream market; and thirdly, it must be established that the refusal will harm consumers.

For a refusal to share essential facilities to be considered abusive, the case law requires proof that the service itself is indispensable to the competitor's business.[161] The indispensability of the service must be reflected in a *refusal of access* to the resource. In contrast, the more recent case law suggests that conditional access, for example by subjecting access to unfair conditions of sale, allows for the application of a more flexible general test. Under the more recent test, it is not necessary to prove indispensability but only the existence of objectively unlawful or 'non-merit-based' conduct and a potential exclusionary effect resulting from such conduct.[162] This adapted and more lenient test depends on the content, as well as the legal and economic context of the refusal, and may stem from regulatory obligations, particularly in sectors where Union legislation has already defined the obligations imposed on an operator owning or holding exclusive rights over essential facilities.[163] It may also be the result of the

[158] Joined Cases C-6/73 and C-7/73 *Istituto Chemioterapico Italiano and Commercial Solvents v Commission* EU:C:1974:18, para 25. See, to that effect, the judgments in Case C-311/84 *CBEM v CLT and IPB* EU:C:1985:394, para 26; and Joined Cases C-468/06 to C-478/06 *Sot Lélos kai Sia* EU:C:2008:504, para 70.

[159] Case C-7/97 *Bronner* EU:C:1998:569, pt 50.

[160] Joined Cases C-241/91 P and C-242/91 P *RTE and ITP v Commission* EU:C:1995:98.

[161] Case C-7/97 *Bronner* EU:C:1998:569, para 41.

[162] Case C-165/19 P *Slovak Telekom v Commission* EU:C:2021:239, para 50: 'where a dominant undertaking gives access to its infrastructure but makes that access, provision of services or sale of products subject to unfair conditions, the conditions laid down by the Court of Justice in paragraph 41 of the judgment in Bronner do not apply. It is true that where access to such an infrastructure – or service or input – is indispensable in order to allow competitors of the dominant undertaking to operate profitably in a downstream market, this increases the likelihood that unfair practices on that market will have at least potentially anticompetitive effects and will constitute abuse within the meaning of Article 102 TFEU . . . . Nevertheless, as regards practices other than a refusal of access, the absence of such an indispensability is not in itself decisive for the purposes of the examination of potentially abusive practices on the part of a dominant undertaking . . .'.

[163] Case C-42/21 *Lithuanian Railways* EU:C:2023:12, and Case C-48/22 *Google and Alphabet* EU:C:2024:726.

dominant undertaking's not having developed the assets for its own use, or having decided to grant access and then refusing, degrading, or limiting access in specific cases that deviate from its general access policy.[164]

4.2. *Justifications*

Unlike Article 101 TFEU, the wording of Article 102 TFEU omits any reference to cases justifying the conduct of a dominant undertaking. This silence emphasises the seriousness of abuse cases, the existence of which, once established, warrants a strong response from competition authorities. However, economic realities are complex and varied, and sometimes a dominant undertaking can legitimately justify the economic rationale behind apparently abusive behaviour, or its lack of harm to the market. For these reasons, the Commission and the case law of the Union courts have developed several justifications that companies accused of abusing their dominant position in the market can invoke. These justifications are based on the principles of objective necessity and proportionality.[165]

At a theoretical level, the Court of Justice has recognised that a dominant undertaking may justify conduct that would otherwise constitute abuse by asserting efficiencies sufficient to ensure that consumers are unlikely to suffer any net harm. In such cases, the dominant undertaking must meet the following cumulative conditions, which draw inspiration from those of Article 101(3) TFEU:[166]

- Behavioural efficiencies have been or are likely to be realised. For example, they may be technical improvements in the quality of goods or a reduction in the cost of production or distribution.
- The conduct is indispensable to obtain these efficiencies: there must be no alternatives to the conduct that are less competitively harmful and also capable of producing the same efficiencies.
- The likely efficiencies gained as a result of the conduct outweigh any potential adverse effects on competition and consumer welfare in the affected markets.
- The conduct does not eliminate effective competition by eliminating all or most of the existing or potential sources of competition. Where there is no residual competition and no foreseeable threat of entry, the protection of rivalry and competitive play outweighs possible efficiency gains.

The principle of proportionality demands an assessment of whether the dominant undertaking's behaviour is objectively necessary.[167] The factors that support objective necessity must be external to the dominant undertaking. For example, exclusionary conduct might be considered objectively necessary for health or safety reasons linked to the nature of the product in question.[168] In proving that such conduct is objectively necessary, it should be borne in mind that public health and safety standards are generally established and enforced by public authorities. Therefore, it is not for the undertaking in a dominant position to take measures on its own

[164] Case C-233/23 *Alphabet Inc and Others v AGCM* EU:C:2025:110, paras 46, 51 and 54.

[165] Joined Cases C-468/06 to C-478/06 *Sot Lélos kai Sia v GlaxoSmithKline* EU:C:2008:504, paras 34 and 76.

[166] See Guidance on Article 102 TFEU (n 130) para 30. In the case law, see Case C-250/92 *Gøttrup-Klim and Others Grovvareforeninger v Dansk Landbrugs Grovvareselskab* EU:C:1994:413, para 52.

[167] See A Albors-Llorens, 'The Role of Objective Justification and Efficiencies in the Application of Article 82 EC' (2007) 44 *Common Market Law Review* 1727.

[168] Case C-27/76 *United Brands v Commission* EU:C:1978:22; Case T-65/89 *BPB Industries and British Gypsum v Commission* EU:T:1993:31; Case T-30/89 *Hilti AG v Commission* EU:T:1991:70; and Case C-209/10 *Post Danmark* EU:C:2012:172.

initiative to remove products which, rightly or wrongly, it regards as dangerous or of inferior quality compared to its own.[169]

5. Digital Markets

The complexity of digital markets and the role of certain operators with significant market power have revealed weaknesses in the Union's framework regarding abuse in competition law. Legislative measures were enacted to address these shortcomings, leading to the introduction of the Digital Markets Act (DMA)[170] alongside the Digital Services Act.[171] While the former is a market-oriented instrument aimed at promoting fair practices in core platform services, the latter addresses content moderation and the prevention of illegal content on online platforms. For competition law purposes, this section will focus exclusively on the DMA.

The DMA imposes numerous obligations on cross-border providers of core platform services ('gatekeepers'), which act as essential gateways for business users to access end users. Most of these obligations involve *ex ante* prohibitions on practices that would otherwise breach Article 101 or 102 TFEU, or were under investigation by the Commission at the time of the DMA's adoption.

This new framework marks a major policy shift with significant institutional implications. Implementation, supervision, and enforcement are handled by the Commission, which acts as the main regulatory authority, while national competition authorities have a limited role in investigations. The legislator has chosen a centralised approach with the DMA, diverging from the methods used in other areas of Union economic regulation, such as electronic communications, data protection, or consumer law, where enforcement is delegated to national authorities. The DMA highlights that the pan-European reach of the targeted gatekeepers requires centralised enforcement, as a decentralised model could lead to regulatory fragmentation, which the DMA aims to prevent. This centralised model has drawn inspiration from the EU Merger Regulation and other areas of Union policy, such as the Single Supervisory Mechanism for banking supervision.

The DMA operates based on a predetermined list of 'core platform services' provided by 'gatekeepers', which must be explicitly designated by the Commission. While core platform services include digital offerings such as online intermediation services, online search engines, online social networking services, and video-sharing platform services, the definition of a 'gatekeeper' has led the Commission to designate seven gatekeepers that provide twenty-three core platform services.[172] Gatekeepers are subject to various obligations and prohibitions, including, inter alia, ensuring that third parties can inter-operate with the gatekeeper's own services in specific situations, allowing their business users to access the data they generate, preventing gatekeepers from restricting the ability of business users or consumers to link up to or promote offers to end users outside their platforms, or preventing users from uninstalling any pre-installed software or app should they wish to do so.

[169] Guidance on Article 102 TFEU (n 130), para 29.

[170] Regulation (EU) 2022/1925 of the European Parliament and of the Council of 14 September 2022 on contestable and fair markets in the digital sector and amending Directives (EU) 2019/1937 and (EU) 2020/1828 [2022] OJ L265/1.

[171] Regulation (EU) 2022/2065 of the European Parliament and of the Council of 19 October 2022 on a Single Market For Digital Services and amending Directive 2000/31/EC [2022] OJ L277/1.

[172] The designated gatekeepers and the core services concerned are those of Alphabet (Search, Maps, Play, Shopping, YouTube, Android, Chrome, Ads), Amazon (Marketplace, Ads), Apple (AppStore, iOS, Safari, iPadOS), Booking.com (Online Intermediation), ByteDance (TikTok), Meta (Facebook, Instagram, WhatsApp, Messenger, Ads), and Microsoft (Windows, LinkedIn).

The DMA mainly serves as a preventive tool, operating on an *ex ante* basis to redirect abusive behaviour by gatekeepers. In this regard, the Commission can launch procedures against gatekeepers alongside reporting obligations designed to foster a continuous dialogue with the Commission aimed at preventing breaches of the legal framework.[173] This preventive approach coexists with a stringent system of fines, used by the Commission as a last resort once the preventive mechanisms have failed to work effectively.

The DMA can also be seen as a response to the legal hurdles in creating a 'level playing field' through competition rules, particularly Article 102 TFEU, to ensure contestability and fairness in digital markets, regardless of efficiency concerns. This concept is based on the principle, which during the liberalisation process led to the combined application of Articles 102 and 106 TFEU, where the state's granting of exclusive or special rights to dominant undertakings creates a conflict of interest that automatically results in their maintaining, strengthening, or expanding their dominance unless they ensure equal opportunity.[174] This reasoning was applied to exclusive and special rights without state origin in cases involving sports federations.[175] However, more recently, the Court of Justice has confirmed that the principle of equality of opportunity cannot be imposed on dominant companies regardless of efficiency considerations to maintain fairness and contestability in digital markets.[176]

IV. MERGERS IN THE INTERNAL MARKET: REGULATION 139/2004

Merger control is the third pillar of the Union's competition policy. Unlike the prohibitions in Articles 101–02 TFEU, merger control involves *preventive* and *ex ante* supervision of business conduct. The aim of merger control law is to prevent commercial or other business decisions that involve a change in the control structure of one or more undertakings from directly or indirectly causing a harmful alteration in the market, by modifying the position, ownership, or nature of the economic operators involved. Furthermore, commercial or other business operations between undertakings may lead to the creation of a dominant position, or further strengthen the existing dominance of one operator, reduce the constraints on other operators, or increase the likelihood of undertakings coordinating their behaviour, making pre-existing coordination easier, more stable, or more effective.

Union law on mergers requires administrative scrutiny by the Commission or national competition authorities. In the case of mergers subject to the jurisdiction of the Commission, the legal framework is outlined in Regulation 139/2004 on the control of concentrations between undertakings,[177] along with a set of soft law instruments adopted by the Commission.[178] Authorisation by the competition authority can be either unconditional or conditional on the acceptance of commitments by the undertakings concerned. The rules on mergers also include

[173] Commission Implementing Regulation (EU) 2023/814 of 14 April 2023 on detailed arrangements for the conduct of certain proceedings by the Commission pursuant to Regulation (EU) 2022/1925 of the European Parliament and of the Council [2023] OJ L102/6.

[174] Case C-553/12 P *Commission v Dimosia Epicheirisi Ilektrismou AE (DEI)* EU:C:2014:2083

[175] Case C-333/21 *European Superleague Company SL v FIFA and UEFA* EU:C:2023:1011; and Case C-124/21 P International Skating Union *v Commission* EU:C:2023:1012

[176] Case C-48/22 P *Google LLC and Alphabet Inc v Commission* EU:C:2024:726.

[177] Council Regulation (EC) 139/2004 of 20 January 2004 on the control of concentrations between undertakings (EC Merger Regulation) [2004] OJ L24/1.

[178] Guidelines on the assessment of horizontal mergers (5 February 2004); Guidelines on the assessment of non-horizontal mergers (2004); Notice on the definition of the relevant market (2024); Notice on a procedure (2023); Notice on restrictions directly related and necessary to concentrations (2005); Notice on case referrals (2005); and Best Practices on the conduct of EC merger control proceedings, prepared by DG Competition.

a sanctioning regime and the attribution of investigative powers to the authorities, enabling them to gather all necessary information from the companies involved in the transaction.

1. Definition of 'Concentration'

Not every business transaction is a 'concentration'. Article 3 of Regulation 139/2004 provides a definition of 'concentration' that restricts its scope of application to only three cases defined as follows:

- the merger of two or more formerly independent undertakings or parts of undertakings;
- the acquisition, by one or more natural or legal persons already controlling at least one undertaking, of direct or indirect control of the whole or parts of one or more other undertakings;
- the creation of a fully functioning joint venture in the market on a lasting basis.

While a 'merger' can be defined objectively, the definition of 'control' is more complex and requires a case-by-case analysis. Article 3(2)–(3) of Regulation 139/2004 stipulates that the notion of 'control' must be applied considering the factual and legal circumstances to determine whether rights, contracts, or other means confer the possibility of exercising 'decisive influence' over an undertaking. Thus, Article 3(3) states that control exists where a legal or natural person has acquired rights over all or part of the assets of an undertaking or has rights that enable it to exercise decisive influence over decision-making in the organs of an undertaking. Furthermore, Article 3(4) specifies that the creation of a joint venture also constitutes a case of concentration.

2. Union Dimension

The Commission exercises its powers over mergers only in relation to operations with a 'Community dimension' (now referred to as 'Union dimension'), as defined in Article 1 of Regulation 139/2004. To this end, an exhaustive criterion based on the turnover thresholds of the involved undertakings is provided for, followed by a residual criterion for cases where these thresholds are not met.

The threshold criterion enables the automatic determination of the Union dimension of an operation where the worldwide turnover of the participating undertakings exceeds EUR 5 billion, and where, at the Union level, the turnover of at least two of the participating undertakings each exceeds EUR 250 million.[179]

Article 1(3) then adds four cumulative cases that together define an alternative test for 'Union dimension', applicable to concentrations that do not meet primary thresholds. Concentrations meeting all of the following conditions have a 'Union dimension':

- where the aggregate worldwide turnover of all the undertakings concerned is more than EUR 2.5 billion;
- where in at least three Member States the aggregate turnover of all the undertakings concerned is more than EUR 100 million in each of those Member States;

[179] The rule goes on to clarify that the operation will not have a Union dimension where each of the undertakings concerned achieves more than two thirds of its aggregate Union-wide turnover within one and the same Member State.

- where in each of the at least three Member States referred to in the previous case, the aggregate turnover of each of at least two of the undertakings concerned is more than EUR 25 million; and
- where the aggregate Union-wide turnover of each of at least two of the undertakings concerned exceeds EUR 100 million.

The thresholds may be subject to revision by the Council, although, to date, they have remained in their original amounts. The revision of the thresholds must be approved by a qualified majority of the Council on a proposal from the Commission.[180]

3. Distribution of Tasks between European and National Authorities

Regulation 139/2004 establishes a system of exclusive competence for the Commission, granting this institution the power to decide on concentrations with a Union dimension. This rule aims to prevent the same concentration from being subject to different legal regimes in various Member States. However, there are exceptions to this rule, whereby a concentration with a Union dimension may require authorisation from a national competition authority.

First, Member States may take appropriate measures to protect 'legitimate interests', provided that these measures are compatible with the general principles and other provisions of Union law. Article 21(4) of Regulation 139/2004 does not specify the interests legitimately invoked by the Member States, but it follows that these are general interests linked to strategic objectives of the Member State concerned, such as public security, ensuring the provision of essential services or goods, or defence, among others.

Second, the Commission may refer a concentration with a Union dimension to a national authority if the undertakings have requested it, and have indicated that the concentration could significantly affect competition in a market within a Member State that presents all the characteristics of a distinct market. In such cases, the Commission can refer the case to the national authority, provided that the impact of the concentration on a specific market in a Member State is established. A consultation procedure with the Member States will precede the decision to refer the case.

Third, the Commission may refer a concentration with a Union dimension to a national authority at the request of that national authority. This scenario is intended for cases where a concentration either threatens to significantly affect competition in a market within a Member State that presents all the characteristics of a distinct market, or affects (not necessarily significantly) competition in that national market, which does not constitute a substantial part of the internal market. Article 9(3) of Regulation 139/2004 sets out this mechanism, allowing the Commission to conduct the procedure or, alternatively, to refer the case wholly or partly to the national competition authorities of the concerned Member State. These authorities will then apply national competition law to the case.

Fourthly, Regulation 139/2004 provides for the reverse scenario, where companies subject to the notification obligation request the Commission to exercise jurisdiction over a concentration that, in principle, does not have a Union dimension. Article 4(5) of Regulation 139/2004 empowers the undertakings concerned by the operation to send the Commission a reasoned submission explaining why the concentration should be examined, provided that the concentration is capable of being reviewed under the national competition law of at least three Member States.

[180] Art 1(4)–(5) of Regulation 139/2004.

Fifth and finally, one or several national competition authorities may request that the Commission assume jurisdiction over a concentration that, a priori, lacks a Union dimension. Article 22 of Regulation 139/2004 provides for this option, provided that the requesting Member State(s) can prove that the concentration affects trade between Member States and threatens to significantly affect competition within the territory of the Member State(s) making the request.[181] However, if the threshold for merger control is not met at the Union level, and the referring Member State itself lacks jurisdiction under its national merger control rules, the Commission cannot acquire competence to review the merger by referral. Article 22 is applicable only if one of the national competition authorities has jurisdiction, thereby preventing a situation in which the absence of jurisdiction by both the Commission and the national competition authorities would result in the Commission acquiring jurisdiction under Article 22.[182] Therefore, Article 22 allows Member States that do not have national merger control rules (ie, Luxembourg) to request that the Commission scrutinise concentrations that might have adverse effects within their territory and affect trade between Member States.[183]

4. Procedure

Merger control procedures are governed by a specific legal framework. Implementing Regulation 2023/914[184] implements the procedural provisions of Regulation 139/2004, along with the Notice on simplified procedures.[185]

Article 4 of Regulation 139/2004 sets out a general obligation to notify the Commission of a concentration with a Union dimension before its implementation. This obligation applies immediately after the agreement is concluded, a public bid is announced, or a controlling interest is acquired. Once the Commission determines that the notified concentration meets the criteria of Articles 1–2 of Regulation 139/2004, it proceeds with its publication, which includes the names of the undertakings involved, their country of origin, the nature of the concentration, and the economic sectors affected. Failing to comply with the notification requirement results in the imposition of fines under Article 14(2)(a) of Regulation 139/2004.[186]

While the procedure remains pending before the Commission, the transaction is suspended. Article 7(1) of Regulation 139/2004 establishes the suspension obligation in strict terms and is subject to a penalty regime in the event of non-compliance.[187] However, it also allows the Commission to grant a waiver from the suspension obligation, taking into account the effects

[181] In this respect, see *Commission – Guidance on the application of the referral mechanism set out in Article 22 of the Merger Regulation to certain categories of cases* [2021] OJ C113/1, as well as the guidelines in the *Commission Notice on Case Referral in respect of concentrations (Text with EEA relevance)* [2005] OJ C56/2.

[182] Joined Cases C-611/22 P and C-625/22 P *Illumina v Commission* EU:C:2024:677.

[183] Case T-289/24 *Brasserie Nationale and Munhowen v Commission* EU:T:2025:655.

[184] Commission Implementing Regulation (EU) 2023/914 of 20 April 2023 implementing Council Regulation (EC) 139/2004 on the control of concentrations between undertakings and repealing Commission Regulation (EC) 802/2004 [2023] OJ L119/22.

[185] *Commission Notice on a simplified treatment for certain concentrations under Council Regulation (EC) No 139/2004 on the control of concentrations between undertakings* [2023] OJ C160/1.

[186] Case T-332/09 *Electrabel v Commission* EU:T:2012:672; Case T-704/14 *Marine Harvest ASA v Commission* EU:T:2017:753; Case C-10/18 P *Marine Harvest ASA v Commission* EU:C:2020:149; Case T-425/18 *Altice Europe v Commission* EU:T:2021:607. The case law has confirmed that the Commission can impose fines for the breach of both the notification and standstill obligations, as they are two separate infringements that can lead to different fines. See Case C-746/21 P *Altice v Commission* EU:C:2023:836.

[187] Any 'operations which contribute to lasting change of control over one of the target undertakings' give rise to a breach of the standstill obligation if they are carried out prior to the authorisation. See Case C-633/16 *Ernst & Young v Konkurrencerådet* EU:C:2018:371.

of the suspension on one or more undertakings involved in the concentration or on a third party, as well as the potential threat to competition posed by the concentration. Article 7(3) of Regulation 139/2004 adds that the waiver, which may be requested at any time, may be granted subject to conditions and obligations aimed at ensuring effective competition.

The merger process is split into two stages. The first involves a preliminary investigation under Article 6(1) of Regulation 139/2004, from which the Commission may conclude that the concentration with a Union dimension is compatible with the internal market; if so, the concentration will proceed. However, the Commission may reach a different conclusion and decide that the concentration raises doubts about its compatibility with the internal market, in which case the transaction moves to the second phase of the procedure. The first phase must be concluded within 25 working days.[188]

During the second phase of the procedure, when the Commission conducts a detailed examination of the transaction, Article 8 of Regulation 139/2004 sets out the scenarios in which the procedure can be concluded. Firstly, the Commission may consider the transaction compatible with the internal market, subject to conditions. Secondly, the Commission may conclude that the transaction is incompatible with the internal market, in which case the transaction cannot proceed. If the companies fail to comply with the Commission's decision, either by failing to adhere to the commitments made or by disregarding the prohibition on implementing the concentration, Regulation 139/2004 grants the Commission extensive enforcement powers over the companies concerned, including the authority to impose interim measures, coercive measures, and sanctions.[189]

5. Substantive Conditions

Article 2 of Regulation 139/2004 outlines the substantive requirements that a concentration must satisfy to be compatible with the internal market. These requirements aim to achieve two main objectives: firstly, to prevent the creation or reinforcement of dominance that could disrupt the functioning of the market; and secondly, to prevent situations that reduce competition, even where they do not necessarily involve consolidating an operator's position of dominance. This dual aim is reflected in the factors listed in Article 2(2), which the Commission must take into account, namely:

(a) the need to preserve and develop effective competition in the internal market in view, *inter alia*, of the structure of all the markets concerned and actual or potential competition from undertakings located inside or outside the Union;

(b) the market position of the undertakings concerned, their economic and financial strength, the choice of suppliers and users, their access to sources of supply or markets, the existence of legal or other barriers to entry to those markets, changes in supply and demand for the products and services in question, the interests of intermediate and final consumers, and the development of technical or economic progress, insofar as this is to the benefit of consumers and does not constitute an obstacle to competition.

Given these circumstances, if the concentration is likely to significantly hinder effective competition in the internal market or a substantial part of it, especially due to the creation or strengthening of a dominant position, the Commission will declare it incompatible with

[188] Art 10(1) of Regulation 139/2004.
[189] ibid, Art 8(4)–(7).

the functioning of the internal market.[190] In practice, such situations can arise through three channels: the creation or strengthening of a dominant position (unilateral non-coordinated effects), the reduction of competitive pressure on other market participants by eliminating key competitive forces (other non-coordinated effects),[191] or by increasing the likelihood of collusion or increasing the likelihood that firms will coordinate their behaviour, or by facilitating or increasing the stability or effectiveness of pre-existing coordination (coordinated effects).

Regulation 139/2004 and the Commission's practice differentiate between horizontal and vertical mergers. Horizontal mergers involve the merger or control of two or more undertakings competing in the same market. Vertical mergers refer to a transaction between two or more undertakings operating within the production chain of a good or service.

5.1. *Horizontal Mergers*

The Commission's Guidelines on the assessment of horizontal mergers define them as transactions between undertakings that 'are actual or potential competitors in the same relevant market'.[192] The assessment of a horizontal merger involves, first, defining the relevant product and geographic market, and second, conducting a competitive assessment of the merger.

When assessing the impact of a merger on competition, it is essential to distinguish between two types of effects resulting from a horizontal merger. According to the Commission, a horizontal merger can significantly hinder effective competition in two ways, depending on the effects:

- The elimination of a large part of the competitive constraint on one or more firms, which will consequently have increased market power without having to resort to coordinated behaviour, either because the merged firm accumulates significant market power or because an important competitive force is eliminated, which leads to a reduction of competitive pressure on the other market participants. This type of transaction is referred to as a 'merger with non-coordinated effects'.[193]
- The modification of the nature of competition in such a way as to make it much more likely that undertakings that previously did not coordinate their behaviour will now coordinate and raise their prices or otherwise harm effective competition. This type of transaction is referred to as a 'merger with coordinated effects'.[194]

5.2. *Vertical Mergers*

Besides horizontal mergers, a transaction can lead to the merger or acquisition of control over several firms in different markets or within the same production chain. These transactions are known as 'non-horizontal mergers' and encompass a broad range of scenarios. For example, transactions involving firms at different levels of the supply chain are described as 'vertical mergers'. Conversely, transactions between companies whose relationship is neither horizontal nor vertical but operate in closely related markets are referred to as 'conglomerate mergers'.

[190] ibid, Art 2(3).

[191] Case T-399/16 *CK Telecoms v Commission* EU:T:2020:217, paras 97–105.

[192] *Guidelines on the assessment of horizontal mergers under the Council Regulation on the control of concentrations between undertakings* [2004] OJ C31/5. The Commission has launched a review of the EU Merger Guidelines and DG COMP published draft new Merger Guidelines for consultation on 30 April 2026. At the time of publication of this book, the draft states that it has not been adopted and the 2004 Horizontal Merger Guidelines had not yet been replaced.

[193] See the criteria used by the Commission to assess this type of horizontal merger, in the Guidelines (n 192) paras 24–38.

[194] ibid, paras 39–60.

Mergers of this type raise very different competition concerns compared to horizontal mergers. To start with, vertical or conglomerate mergers do not lead to a loss of direct competition between the merging firms within the same relevant market. Therefore, unlike a horizontal merger, such a merger is not the main source of anti-competitive effects. Furthermore, vertical and conglomerate mergers can lead to efficiencies by integrating complementary activities or products, creating beneficial effects for competition.[195] However, it should be noted that in digital environments, conglomerate competition problems arising from the accumulation of market power across a set of related markets or ecosystems, even if there is no horizontal overlap per se, become more serious given the existence of strong network effects and economies of scale.

Non-horizontal mergers can also have both non-coordinated and coordinated effects, which should be analysed separately. In the case of non-coordinated effects, these may arise when the transaction leads to anticompetitive foreclosure. This happens when the access of actual or potential rivals to sources of supply or markets is hindered or eliminated due to the merger.[196] Coordinated effects emerge when the merger changes the nature of competition, increasing the likelihood that firms which previously did not coordinate their behaviour are much more likely to coordinate and raise their prices or otherwise harm effective competition.[197]

The Commission's analysis of a non-horizontal merger is mainly counterfactual, comparing the competitive conditions that would result from the merger against those that would prevail in its absence.[198] The time benchmark refers to the competitive conditions prevailing at the moment of the merger; however, in exceptional cases, reasonably foreseeable future market changes may be taken into account. The Commission also considers potential market entry or exit in the absence of the merger, as well as future market developments in the event of imminent regulatory changes.[199] In addition to potential entry, other factors that could outweigh a significant obstacle to effective competition include high countervailing buyer power or verifiable efficiencies inherent in the merger that benefit consumers.[200]

V. STATE PARTICIPATION IN THE ECONOMY AND SERVICES OF GENERAL ECONOMIC INTEREST

The role of the state in the modern economy is undeniable. In addition to managing its economic policy (and monetary policy in countries with their own currency), the state influences the decisions of economic operators through its industrial, fiscal, and social policies. In the second half of the twentieth century, with the growth of the welfare state and an extensive administrative structure aimed at benefiting citizens, public authorities became designers and conductors of economic policy, as well as active participants in market activity. The emergence of large public companies in strategic sectors such as energy, telecommunications, and the audiovisual industry led to a profound transformation of the state's role in the economy, turning it into an active player in the market.

[195] *Guidelines on the assessment of non-horizontal mergers under the Council Regulation on the control of concentrations between undertakings* [2008] OJ C265/6, paras 12–14.
[196] ibid, para 18.
[197] ibid, para 19.
[198] ibid, para 20.
[199] By way of example, see Case *E.ON/MOL* (COMP/M.3696, 2005) paras 457–63.
[200] Guidelines on the assessment of horizontal mergers (n 192) paras 64–88.

The Union has had to reconcile the state's active role in the economy with the creation and development of an internal market at the Union level, operating according to the rules of an open market. Direct state intervention in the economy, through the establishment of public companies or the granting of special rights to private companies, is subject to certain conditions defined in the Treaties, as will now be explained.

To begin with, the Treaties affirm the importance of the state's role in the economy, particularly in providing strategic services to support the development of public policies. These services are recognised and defined in the Treaties and Union legislation as services of general economic interest. They are essential for the common good, highly strategic for the state and its citizens, and of an economic nature, as their introduction and provision notably influence markets. For example, a social security system based on monetary contributions from beneficiaries is an economic service with a significant impact on the labour sector, since it relies on contributions from workers and employers, but it is also a service of general interest due to its close links with the social policy and welfare objectives pursued by the state.

Article 14 TFEU makes an explicit reference to services of general economic interest, balancing the need to preserve their existence and viability with the requirement that they remain consistent with the basic rules of a free market economy:

> Without prejudice to Article 4 of the Treaty on European Union or to Articles 93, 106 and 107 of this Treaty, and given the place occupied by services of general economic interest in the shared values of the Union as well as their role in promoting social and territorial cohesion, the Union and the Member States, each within their respective powers and within the scope of application of the Treaties, shall take care that such services operate on the basis of principles and conditions, particularly economic and financial conditions, which enable them to fulfil their missions.

Furthermore, Protocol No 26, on services of general interest, elaborates on the wording of Article 14 TFEU and highlights certain features of this type of service, including the need for such services to be provided as closely as possible to users' needs and to meet certain standards of quality, safety, equality, and affordability.

While Article 14 TFEU and Protocol No 26 highlight the role of services of general economic interest and their contribution to social welfare, Article 106 TFEU establishes the market standards they must adhere to. This provision is of particular importance, as it adjusts the rules on free movement and competition to the actions of the state when it chooses to act directly or indirectly as a market operator. Article 106(1)–(2) TFEU defines the scope within which public undertakings or private undertakings exercising special rights granted by the state must operate:

(1) In the case of public undertakings and undertakings to which Member States grant special or exclusive rights, Member States shall neither enact nor maintain in force any measure contrary to the rules contained in the Treaties, in particular to those rules provided for in Article 18 and Articles 101 to 109.

(2) Undertakings entrusted with the operation of services of general economic interest or having the character of a revenue-producing monopoly shall be subject to the rules contained in the Treaties, in particular to the rules on competition, in so far as the application of such rules does not obstruct the performance, in law or in fact, of the particular tasks assigned to them. The development of trade must not be affected to such an extent as would be contrary to the interests of the Union.

As shown above, Article 106 TFEU consists of two parts. First, it defines the limits of state action through public undertakings or the granting of special or exclusive rights to private undertakings. Second, it provides for a specific regime that balances competition rules with the activity of services of general economic interest.

Article 106(1) TFEU refers to 'undertakings', including those in public ownership and those receiving special or exclusive rights from the state. The definition of 'public undertaking' in this provision has been interpreted broadly by the Court of Justice. A public undertaking is understood to be 'any undertaking over which the public authorities may exercise, directly or indirectly, a dominant influence', and a dominant influence is presumed to exist 'when the public authorities directly or indirectly hold the major part of the undertaking's subscribed capital, control the majority of the votes, or can appoint more than half of the members of its administrative, managerial or supervisory body'.[201] Conversely, the notion of special or exclusive rights refers to private companies, without state control but benefiting from special conditions allowing them to operate in the market, either as a monopoly or under advantageous economic conditions. In such cases, Article 106(1) TFEU imposes on these private undertakings, as well as on public undertakings, obligations to comply with the competition and internal market rules of the Treaties.[202]

Article 106(1) TFEU sets out a general obligation to comply with the competition standards set out in the Treaties, including those in Articles 101–02 TFEU. Although the reference to competition rules is broad and general, it remains true that public undertakings or undertakings holding special or exclusive rights are likely to conflict with Article 102 TFEU and the provisions on abuse of a dominant position. Moreover, the Court of Justice has stated on several occasions that Member States may be held liable for a breach of Article 101 TFEU in combination with the principle of sincere cooperation enshrined in Article 4(3) TEU, for example, by attributing to a group of undertakings the power to fix prices.[203] For instance, if a public undertaking operates as the sole operator in a market, a monopolistic position will have been created, increasing the likelihood of abusive conduct by the dominant operator. This situation was acknowledged by the Court of Justice when it stated

> that an undertaking vested with a legal monopoly may be regarded as occupying a dominant position within the meaning of Article [102] of the Treaty [. . .] and that the territory of a Member State to which that monopoly extends, may constitute a substantial part of the common market.[204]

The existence of a legally recognised monopoly is not, in itself, contrary to Article 106 TFEU, a provision that is only breached in conjunction with Articles 101–02 TFEU. However, the Member State that creates the monopoly must justify the reasons for adopting that measure. These justifications must be interpreted in light of Article 102 TFEU, as the legally recognised monopoly creates a situation of dominance that is liable to abuse. In some cases, the Court of Justice has acknowledged that it is not always necessary to infer a potential abuse amounting to an autonomous infringement of Article 102 TFEU, but instead that

> a Member State infringes the prohibitions laid down by Articles [102 TFEU] and [106(1) TFEU] where the undertaking in question is led, by the mere exercise of the exclusive or special rights conferred upon it, to exploit its dominant position in an abusive manner or where those rights are capable of creating a situation in which that undertaking is led to commit such abuses.[205]

[201] Cases C-188-190/80 *France, Italy and United Kingdom v Commission* EU:C:1982:257, para 25.

[202] Case C-155/73 *Sacchi*, EU:C:1974:40; and Case C-10/71 *Muller* EU:C:1971:85.

[203] Case C-229/83 *Association des Centres distributeurs Édouard Leclerc v SARL 'Au blé vert'* EU:C:1985:1; and Joined Cases C-184/13 to C-187/13, C-194/13, C-195/13 and C-208/13 *API v Ministero delle Infrastrutture e dei Trasporti* EU:C:2014:2147.

[204] Case C-41/90 *Höfner and Elser v Macrotron* EU:C:1991:161, paras 29–31. See also Case C-311/84 *CBEM v CLT and IPB* EU:C:1985:394, para 16; and Case C-322/81 *Michelin* EU:C:1983:313, para 28.

[205] Case C-553/12 P *Commission v DEI* EU:C:2014:2083, para 23.

Therefore, the case law requires Member States to provide a high degree of justification for the decision to introduce a framework in which one operator dominates a market, which requires clear and transparent objectives of general interest and compliance with the principle of proportionality.[206] The case law does not go as far as to require that a market failure act as a prerequisite for the conferral of exclusive or special rights, but a considerable degree of justification is required on the part of the Member State.[207]

VI. STATE AID POLICY

1. State Aid Policy Objectives

The power of Member States to inject financial resources into the economy can distort competition and create imbalances in the internal market. If a Member State chooses to promote investment in a specific activity and provides financial support to one or more local companies to boost that activity, it may harm other companies operating in the same sector within the internal market. On the one hand, it may be difficult, if not impossible, for competing foreign companies to access that Member State if they do not receive financial support from the state, unlike the local company that does. On the other hand, the creation or promotion of local undertakings supported by the state makes it easier for these firms to expand into other Member States, competing with other companies throughout the internal market but under privileged conditions unavailable to other operators.

The previous example illustrates the risks involved when a Member State commits to developing policies that involve the financial support of companies operating within the internal market. This does not mean Member States distort competition every time they provide financial support to a company. On the contrary, such aid may be justified and necessary to achieve specific objectives of general interest (during the COVID-19 pandemic, Member States provided financial support to companies to counter the effects of massive lockdowns and other restrictions on movement). The risk arises when a Member State's intervention artificially distorts the market, leading to harmful and unjustified distortion for other operators in the internal market.

To mitigate the risks posed by subsidies, grants, or economically advantageous schemes provided by Member States to certain companies, the Treaties introduce several prohibitions and procedures to combat aid harmful to the internal market. Such measures fall under the category of 'state aid'. They are governed by Articles 107–09 TFEU and by two legislative acts: Regulation 2015/1588 on horizontal block exemptions;[208] and Regulation 2015/1589 on procedural rules.[209] The Commission has also regulatory powers directly conferred by Article

[206] Case C-41/90 *Höfner and Elser v Macrotron* EU:C:1991:161, paras 29–31; Case C-179/90 *Merci Convenzionali Porto di Genova v Siderurgica Gabrielli* EU:C:1991:464, paras 16–22; Case C-67/96 *Albany* EU:C:1999:430, paras 93–120; Case C-148/97 *Deutsche Post* EU:C:2000:74, paras 38–44; Case C-340/99 *TNT Traco* EU:C:2001:281, paras 52–60; Case C-475/99 *Ambulanz Glöckner* EU:C:2001:577, paras 55–65; and Case C-351/12 *OSA* EU:C:2014:110, paras 82–90.

[207] Case C-254/23 *INTERZERO* EU:C:2025:569, paras 65–69.

[208] Council Regulation (EU) 2015/1588 of 13 July 2015 on the application of Articles 107 and 108 of the Treaty on the Functioning of the European Union to certain categories of horizontal State aid [2015] OJ L248/1. The public consultation on the revision of this regulation was opened in July 2025.

[209] Council Regulation (EU) 2015/1589 of 13 July 2015 laying down detailed rules for the implementation of Article 108 of the Treaty on the Functioning of the European Union [2015] OJ L248/9.

108(4) TFEU, under which it may adopt block exemption regulations relating to the categories of State aid provided for in Regulation 2015/1588.[210]

State aid policy is an exclusive competence of the Union (Article 3(1)(b) TFEU). Therefore, the determination of whether a national measure constitutes 'state aid' and its compatibility with the internal market is an assessment that only the Union and its institutions can make. Member States may participate in this analysis if they have been granted competence from the Union through an explicit legislative act. As a result, State aid policy is centralised within the Union, particularly in the Commission, whose Directorate-General for Competition is responsible for handling this portfolio. Union and national courts also play a key role in interpreting and implementing State aid rules. However, certain aspects of State aid policy, such as determining the compatibility of aid with the internal market, fall within the exclusive competence of the Commission, and even national courts cannot replace the Commission's assessment on this matter.[211]

The rules on State aid are closely connected to the performance of economic analyses in each case. To assess the degree of harm caused by aid to competitors or the market, it is necessary to conduct complex macroeconomic and microeconomic analyses. However, the core features of the State aid rulebook are legal, and their compliance relies on a legal analysis. Whether aid is 'selective' or 'affects trade between Member States' depends on a legal analysis based on the interpretation of the Treaties. For this reason, courts have shown their willingness to engage in intensive judicial review in the field of State aid, compared to their more nuanced approach in competition policy, where the prominent role of economic analyses and complex technical assessments constrains the margin of manoeuvre of courts.

2. Concept of 'Aid'

The Treaties define 'state aid' in Article 107(1) TFEU in the following terms:

> [A]id granted by a Member State or through State resources in any form whatsoever which distorts or threatens to distort competition by favouring certain undertakings or the production of certain goods.

Member State measures falling under this definition will be regarded as 'state aid'. In such cases, they are prohibited and may be granted only if the Commission declares them compatible with the internal market. Member States must bear the burden of proof whenever they decide to grant economically advantageous measures to certain undertakings or categories of undertakings, until the Commission confirms the compatibility of the aid subject to review. However, if the Member State considers that the proposed measure does not fall within the

[210] For example, it has adopted Commission Regulation (EU) 2023/2831 of 13 December 2023 on the application of Articles 107 and 108 of the Treaty on the Functioning of the European Union to de minimis aid [2023] OJ L2831/1.

[211] Case C-354/90 *Fédération Nationale du Commerce Extérieur des Produits Alimentaires v France* EU:C:1991:440, para 14: 'the principal and exclusive role conferred on the Commission by Articles [107] and [108] of the Treaty, which is to hold aid to be incompatible with the common market where this is appropriate, is fundamentally different from the role of national courts in safeguarding rights which individuals enjoy as a result of the direct effect of the prohibition laid down in the last sentence of Article [108] of the Treaty. Whilst the Commission must examine the compatibility of the proposed aid with the common market, even where the Member State has acted in breach of the prohibition on giving effect to aid, national courts do no more than preserve, until the final decision of the Commission, the rights of individuals faced with a possible breach by State authorities of the prohibition laid down by the last sentence of Article 93(3) of the Treaty. When those courts make a ruling in such a matter, they do not thereby decide on the compatibility of the aid with the common market, the final determination on that matter being the exclusive responsibility of the Commission, subject to the supervision of the Court of Justice.'

definition of 'state aid' in Article 107(1) TFEU, it is not under an obligation to request the intervention of the Commission.

For a measure to qualify as 'aid', it must be directed at an 'undertaking'. Support measures aimed at non-economic entities or public bodies that do not carry out economic activities are not covered by Article 107(1) TFEU. Consequently, activities involving the exercise of public authority, such as law enforcement, maritime, or air traffic control,[212] do not constitute economic activities subject to State aid rules. Other activities closely linked to policies of general interest may be exempt from State aid rules if the activity is not economic and no services are provided on the market in exchange for payment. This criterion applies to activities such as health, education, or cultural and environmental conservation, where it is essential to determine whether the measure is intended to support a particular economic activity.

For example, measures to finance the public education system are not subject to State aid rules. However, if the state decides to support private education services that are predominantly financed by students, their parents, or commercial revenue, State aid rules will apply, as this constitutes an economic activity in a market (private education).[213] As a rule, social objectives do not necessarily deprive an activity of its economic nature. The presence of redistributive features, such as compulsory affiliation to a system or a guarantee of universal benefits, along with a broad regulatory framework governing the activity under state supervision, may confirm the non-economic nature of the activity. In contrast, the existence of private operators competing on the basis of price, variety, or accessibility indicates the activity's economic nature.[214]

Four requirements must be met to characterise a national measure as 'state aid'. To this end, both the case law and the Commission's Communication on the notion of State aid[215] provide useful criteria for unpacking the four requirements drawn from an interpretation of Article 107(1) TFEU.

2.1. *State Origin*

The first requirement is that the measure must be attributable to the state and involve a transfer of state resources to one or more undertakings. This requirement raises two separate questions: firstly, the criteria for imputability to the state and secondly, the determination of whether public or private resources are used.

The criteria for *imputability* to the state have been interpreted broadly to prevent Member States from circumventing the aid regime through formalistic subterfuge. To the extent that the decision to grant an advantage can be attributed, directly or indirectly, to an authority of the Member State, it can be imputed to the Member State and considered a 'state' measure. This will be the case even where a public authority appoints a private or public body to administer a measure granting an advantage.[216] However, where the grant of an advantage to certain undertakings is the inherent consequence of a general scheme which does not aim, either by its purpose or its general scheme, to create a benefit that constitutes an additional burden on the

[212] Case C-364/92 *SAT v Eurocontrol* EU:C:1994:7, para 27; Case C-113/07 P SELEX *Sistemi Integrati v Commission* EU:C:2009:191, para 71; and Commission Decision of 16 October 2002 on State aid N 438/02 – Belgium – Aid to the port authorities [2002] OJ C284/2.

[213] See *Commission Notice on the notion of State aid as referred to in Article 107(1) of the Treaty on the Functioning of the European Union* [2016] OJ C262/1, paras 28–32.

[214] G Van de Casteele, 'Notion of Undertaking' in L Flynn (ed), *EU Competition Law, Volume 4: State Aid* (Claeys & Casteels Law Publishers, 2016) 204–205.

[215] Commission Notice (n. 213).

[216] Case T-358/94 *Air France v Commission* EU:T:1996:194, para 62.

state and the advantage does not depend on the control exercised by public authorities over the operators concerned, it is understood that there is no imputability to the state.[217]

When the measure is granted through public undertakings, it is necessary to determine whether it is appropriate to consider that the public authorities were involved in its adoption.[218] The case law has confirmed that the mere fact that a public undertaking has adopted a measure is insufficient to regard it as imputable to the state.[219] However, the imputability to the state of a measure taken by a public undertaking may be inferred from various indicators based on the circumstances of the case and the context in which the measure was taken.[220] Both the case law and the Communication on the notion of State aid provide some criteria for identifying these indicators. These include the requirement that the entity adopting the measure take into account the prior requirements or guidelines issued by the public authority, the existence of organic links between the entity and the Member State, the nature of the entity's activities, or its legal status.[221] The rule that can be inferred from the case law is that a measure is imputable to the state where the involvement of public authorities in the adoption of the measure can reasonably be inferred from the circumstances of the case as a whole.

A second determining factor is the *public nature of the resources,* which must be state resources and not private resources. The Commission considers that all public sector resources fall under the category of 'state resources',[222] including funds from public territorial entities (such as regional, provincial, local, or other territorial public bodies)[223] and, in certain cases, funds from private entities closely linked to a public activity or origin.

Transfers within a group of state-controlled companies can amount to State aid if, for example, resources are transferred from the parent company to its subsidiary.[224] Likewise, the fact that the measure is not financed directly by the state, but by public or private bodies created or designated by the state to manage the aid, does not necessarily mean the measure is not financed through state resources.[225] Subsidies financed through parafiscal charges or compulsory contributions imposed by the state and managed and apportioned in accordance with public rules will also qualify as a transfer of state resources, even if public authorities do not administer them.[226]

However, the simple fact that a state measure indirectly has a negative impact on state revenues does not make the transaction a transfer of state resources.[227] For instance, a national regulation setting a minimum price for certain goods does not involve a transfer of state resources.[228] Similarly, a state regulation that results in financial redistribution from one private entity to another without additional state intervention does not, in principle, involve a

[217] Joined Cases C-72/91 and C-73/91 *Sloman Neptun v Seebetriebsrat Bodo Ziesemer der Sloman Neptun* EU:C:1993:97, para 21; Case C-222/07 *UTECA v Administración General del Estado* EU:C:2009:124, para 46.

[218] Case C-482/99 *France v Commission (Stardust)* EU:C:2002:294, para 52.

[219] *France v Commission (Stardust)* (n 218); and Case T-442/03 *SIC v Commission* EU:T:2008:228, paras 93–100.

[220] *France v Commission (Stardust)* (n 218) para 55.

[221] ibid, paras 55–56 and the Opinion of AG Jacobs in the same case, points 65–68; Case C-242/13 *Commerz Nederland* EU:C:2014:2224, para 35; Case T-387/11 *Nitrogénművek Vegyipari Zrt v Commission* EU:T:2013:98, para 63; and Case T-507/12 *Slovenia v Commission* EU:T:2016:35, para 86.

[222] Case T-358/94 *Air France v Commission* EU:T:1996:194, para 56.

[223] Case C-248/84 *Germany v Commission* EU:C:1987:437, para 17; and Joined Cases T-92/00 and T-103/00 *Territorio Histórico de Álava and Others v Commission* EU:T:2002:61, para 57.

[224] Case C-39/94 *SFEI and Others* EU:C:1996:285, para 62.

[225] Case C-78/76 *Steinike & Weinlig* EU:C:1977:52, para 21.

[226] Case C-173/73 *Italy v Commission* EU:C:1974:71, para 16; Joined Cases C-78/90 to C-83/90 *Compagnie Commerciale de l'Ouest* EU:C:1992:118, para 35; and Case C-206/06 *Essent Netwerk Noord* EU:C:2008:413, paras 58–74.

[227] Case C-379/98 *PreussenElektra* EU:C:2001:160, para 62.

[228] Case C-82/77 *Van Tiggele* EU:C:1978:10, paras 25–26.

transfer of state resources either, as long as the funds pass directly from one private entity to another without passing through a public or private body designated by the state to manage the transfer.[229]

2.2. *Selective Advantage*

The second requirement aims to determine whether the state measure creates a selective advantage in favour of one or more undertakings at the expense of other operators. When the measure affects all operators in the market equally, it is not considered a selective measure and therefore does not fall under the concept of 'state aid'.

An 'advantage' refers to any economic benefit that an undertaking would not have obtained under normal market conditions, that is, in the absence of state intervention.[230] The assessment of whether there is an advantage is based on the measure's *effects* and not on the cause and purpose of the state intervention.[231] Furthermore, the specific form of the measure is irrelevant to determining whether it confers an economic advantage.[232] For example, the relief of an economic burden may constitute an advantage, such as in the case of a tax exemption granted to a single undertaking or a limited group of undertakings, rather than to all competitors alike.[233]

The compensation for costs incurred in providing a service of general economic interest is subject to specific criteria arising from the interaction between Articles 106–07 TFEU. In *Altmark*, the Court of Justice stated that such measures can be excluded from the notion of an 'advantage' if four cumulative conditions are met.[234] First, the recipient undertaking must have public service obligations to discharge, which must be clearly defined. Second, the parameters used to calculate the compensation must be established in advance in an objective and transparent manner. Third, the compensation must not exceed what is necessary to cover all or part of the costs incurred in the discharge of public service obligations, taking into account the relevant receipts and a reasonable profit. Fourth, if the undertaking that is to discharge public service obligations is not chosen following a public procurement procedure to select a tenderer capable of providing these services at the lowest cost to the community, the level of compensation must be determined based on an analysis of the costs which a typical undertaking, well-run and adequately provided with means to meet the public service requirements, would have incurred in fulfilling these obligations, taking into account the relevant receipts and a reasonable profit for discharging the obligations. To facilitate the interpretation of the *Altmark* criteria, the Commission has published a Communication explaining the terms in which it applies them.[235]

Economic transactions carried out by public bodies (including public undertakings) do not confer an advantage on their counterpart and therefore do not constitute aid, provided they are conducted under normal market conditions.[236] This principle has been developed in

[229] ibid, paras 25–26; Case C-379/98 *PreussenElektra* EU:C:2001:160, paras 59–62; and Case C-222/07 *UTECA* EU:C:2009:124, paras 43–47.

[230] Case C-39/94 *SFEI and Others* EU:C:1996:285, para 60; and Case C-342/96 *Spain v Commission* EU:C:1999:210, para 41.

[231] Case C-173/73 *Italy v Commission* EU:C:1974:71, para 13.

[232] Case C-280/00 *Altmark Trans* EU:C:2003:415, para 84.

[233] Case C-387/92 *Banco Exterior de España* EU:C:1994:100, para 13; Case C-156/98 *Germany v Commission* EU:C:2000:467, para 25; Case C-6/97 *Italy v Commission* EU:C:1999:251, para 15; Case C-172/03 *Heiser* EU:C:2005:130, para 36; Case C-241/94 *France v Commission* EU:C:1996:353, para 40; Case C-5/01 *Belgium v Commission* EU:C:2002:754, paras 38–39; Case T-565/08 *Corsica Ferries France SAS v Commission* EU:T:2012:415, paras 137–138; and Joined Cases C-533/12 P and C-536/12 P *SNCM and France v Commission* EU:C:2014:2142.

[234] Case C-280/00 *Altmark Trans* EU:C:2003:415, paras 87–95.

[235] *Commission Communication on the application of EU State aid rules to compensation granted for the provision of services of general economic interest* [2012] OJ C8/4.

[236] Case C-39/94 *SFEI and Others* EU:C:1996:285, paras 60–61.

relation to various economic transactions, to the extent that the case law has over time developed 'market economy operator' principles for determining whether the investment of a public body amounts to State aid. In such cases, it must be assessed whether, in similar circumstances, a private investor of comparable size operating under normal market economy conditions would have been encouraged to make the investment in question, irrespective of whether the means employed formally constitute instruments only available to public authorities (such as tax exemptions), provided that the effects sought are those of a private investor (long-term profitability).[237] In the same vein, the case law has developed a 'private creditor test' and a 'private vendor test' to assess whether the state's behaviour resembles that of a creditor or a vendor, respectively, acting under normal market conditions.[238]

Finally, the 'advantage' must favour 'certain undertakings or the production of certain goods', so that only measures that grant a *selective* advantage to certain undertakings, categories of undertakings, or certain economic sectors fall within the scope of Article 107(1) TFEU. This means that measures of purely general scope that do not favour certain undertakings or the production of certain goods do not fall within the notion of State aid. However, both the Commission and the Union courts remain vigilant regarding such general measures. Neither the large number of beneficiary undertakings nor the diversity and importance of the sectors to which they belong is sufficient on its own to establish that we are dealing with a general economic policy measure.[239] In the specific case of tax measures, the Commission must conduct a threefold analysis, which involves:

> [F]irst of all, the identification of the common or 'normal' tax regime applicable in the Member State concerned, next, the assessment of whether the tax measure at issue derogates from that common regime, in so far as it differentiates between operators which are, in the light of the objective pursued by the common regime, in a comparable factual and legal situation and, lastly, the assessment of whether such a derogation is justified by the nature and general scheme of that regime.[240]

The case law and the Commission distinguish between material and regional selectivity to determine whether a measure is 'selective'. The *material* selectivity of a measure means that it applies only to certain undertakings (or groups of undertakings) or certain sectors of the economy in a given Member State. Material selectivity can be established *de jure* or de facto.[241] *Regional* selectivity refers to measures that only apply to certain parts of the territory of a Member State, which, because they do not use the whole of the Member State as a reference, are not necessarily selective[242] as long as one of the following scenarios is met: (a) the central government of a Member State unilaterally decides to adopt a lower tax rate in a certain

[237] L Puglisi and N Robins, 'The Market Economy Operator Principle: An Economic Role Model for Assessing Economic Advantage' in L Hancher and JJ Piernas (eds), *Research Handbook on European State Aid Law* (Edward Elgar, 2021) 15, 29–32.

[238] Case C-525/04 P *Spain v Commission* EU:C:2007:698; Case C-73/11 P *Frucona v Commission* EU:C:2013:32; Case C-256/97 *DMTransport* EU:C:1999:332; and Joined Cases T-268/08 and T-281/08 *Land Burgenland and Austria v Commission* EU:T:2012:90.

[239] Case C-75/97 *Belgium v Commission* EU:C:1999:311, para 32; and Case C-143/99 *Adria-Wien Pipeline* EU:C:2001:598, para 48.

[240] Joined Cases C-51/19 P and C-64/19 P *World Duty Free Group SA v Commission* EU:C:2021:793, para 19. The relevant reference framework may be constituted by various objectives taken together. See Case C-453/23 *E sp z oo v Prezydent Miasta Mielca* EU:C:2025:285, para 72.

[241] Joined Cases C-182/03 and C-217/03 *Belgium and Forum 187 v Commission* EU:C:2006:416, para 122; Case T-211/05 *Italy v Commission* EU:T:2009:304, para 120; Joined Cases C-78/08 to C-80/08 *Paint Graphos and Others* EU:C:2011:550, para 52; Case C-458/09 P *Italy v Commission* EU:C:2011:769, paras 59–60; and Case T-287/11 *Heitkamp Bauholding v Commission* EU:T:2016:60, para 129ff.

[242] Case C-88/03 *Portugal v Commission* EU:C:2006:511, para 57; and Joined Cases C-428/06 to C-434/06 *Unión General de Trabajadores de La Rioja* EU:C:2008:488, para 47.

geographical area;[243] (b) the measure results from a symmetrical tax distribution model where all regions or municipalities have the same powers; or (c) only certain regional or municipal entities within a Member State can adopt tax measures in their territory (asymmetrical devolution of powers), in which case an analysis should be conducted on whether the entity has institutional, procedural, and economic and financial autonomy.[244]

2.3. *Distortion of Competition*

Third, the state measure must result in an act that 'distorts or threatens to distort competition'. This occurs when the measure is likely to improve the beneficiary's competitive position vis-à-vis other undertakings with which it competes. Therefore, the measure must have an impact in a competitive market where two or more undertakings compete to offer a product or service to their customers.[245] It follows from the above that there is no distortion of competition where a service is subject to a statutory monopoly in which there is no competition with other services.[246]

2.4. *Effect on Trade between Member States*

Fourth and finally, State aid must 'affect trade between Member States', it being sufficient that the measure reinforces the position of an undertaking compared to other undertakings competing in intra-Union trade.[247] It is therefore not necessary for the beneficiary to be engaged in cross-border trade; what matters is whether the advantageous measure has an effect that makes it more difficult or less attractive for operators from other Member States to enter the market of the Member State where the beneficiary undertaking operates.[248] Similarly, the amount of aid is not in itself determinative, as even a relatively modest advantage may affect trade between Member States.[249] It is also irrelevant whether or not the beneficiary exports all or most of its production outside the Union.[250]

3. Compatible Aid

Measures that meet the conditions outlined above are regarded as 'state aid' and are consequently prohibited unless the Commission declares them compatible with the internal market. The term 'compatibility' refers to State aid that satisfies the requirements of Article 107(1) TFEU, but nevertheless, as it falls within one of the cases provided for in the Treaties or secondary legislation, it is considered to be compatible. For this reason, when referring to State aid 'compatible with the internal market', reference is made to 'state aid', the implementation and use of which by the beneficiary is lawful.

[243] Case C-88/03 *Portugal v Commission* EU:C:2006:511, paras 63–66.

[244] *Portugal v Commission* (n 243) para 58; Case C-428/06 *Unión General de Trabajadores de La Rioja* EU:C:2008:488, paras 95ff; and Joined Cases C-106/09 P and C-107/09 P *Commission and Spain v Government of Gibraltar and United Kingdom* EU:C:2011:732, paras 75ff.

[245] Case C-730/79 *Philip Morris* EU:C:1980:209, para 11; Case C-280/00 *Altmark Trans* EU:C:2003:415; and Joined Cases T-298/97 to T-312/97 *Alzetta* EU:T:2000:151, para 80.

[246] Case T-295/12 *Germany v Commission* EU:T:2014:675, para 158.

[247] Case C-518/13 *Eventech v The Parking Adjudicator* EU:C:2015:9, para 66; Joined Cases C-197/11 and C-203/11 *Libert and Others* EU:C:2013:288, para 77; and Case T-288/97 *Friuli Venezia Giulia* EU:T:2001:115, para 41.

[248] *Libert and Others* (n 247) para 78; and Case C-280/00 *Altmark Trans* EU:C:2003:415, para 78.

[249] *Altmark Trans* (n 248), paras 77–78.

[250] Case C-142/87 *Belgium v Commission ('Tubemeuse')* EU:C:1990:125, para 35; and Case C-494/06 P *Commission v Italian Republic and Wam SpA* EU:C:2009:272, para 62.

The Treaty provides for two types of compatibility: automatic and discretional. The Council and the Commission can also approve categories of aid exempt from prior declaration of compatibility, known as 'block exemptions', generally provided for in a Regulation.

3.1. *Automatically Compatible Aid*

Article 107(2) TFEU specifies three cases of aid whose compatibility is automatic and does not rely on a discretionary assessment by the Commission. In these cases, it is sufficient for the requirements of each case to be met for a Member State to be certain that the aid is compatible with the internal market.

Firstly, Article 107(2)(a) refers to 'aid having a social character, granted to individual consumers, provided that such aid is granted without discrimination related to the origin of the products concerned'. This type of compatibility concerns social measures intended to benefit specific groups, such as travel aid for residents in remote or peripheral areas,[251] aid for workers exposed to serious health risks,[252] or aid to support the purchase of certain products by economically disadvantaged groups.[253]

Secondly, Article 107(2)(b) refers to 'aid to make good the damage caused by natural disasters or exceptional occurrences'. This type of aid is also developed in Article 50 of Regulation 651/2014 (the General Block Exemption Regulation). This provision makes explicit reference to damage caused by earthquakes, avalanches, landslides, floods, tornadoes, hurricanes, volcanic eruptions, and natural fires, which are exempted, provided that the Member State authorities have formally recognised the event as a natural disaster and established a direct causal link between the disaster and the damage suffered. Article 107(2)(b) was one of the legal bases used to adopt specific measures under the temporary framework for State aid during the COVID-19 pandemic.[254]

Thirdly and finally, Article 107(2)(c) refers to a very specific case applicable to one Member State, Germany, concerning aid 'in order to compensate for the economic disadvantages caused by [the] division' of Germany during the Cold War.[255]

3.2. *Allegedly Compatible Aid*

In addition to the cases of automatic compatibility, Article 107(3) TFEU enumerates five cases of aid whose compatibility depends on a discretional decision by the European Commission. These are five instances where the Commission has broad discretion. Therefore, unlike in cases of automatic compatibility, the Commission is not obliged to declare compatibility once the conditions of the rule have been met, but may assess, according to discretional criteria, whether or not the aid is compatible following a complex technical analysis. There is no right to have aid declared compatible based on any of the cases outlined in Article 107(3) TFEU.

In practice, Article 107(3) TFEU applies once it is established that the aid does not fall within any of the categories of aid provided for in the block exemption regulations. This is

[251] See Commission Decisions in: Case NN 25/2005 *Mobility Passport* (20 April 2005); Case N 656/2006 *Réunion social aid scheme* (4 December 2006); Case SA.32888 *Air Transport Tax* (29 June 2011); and Case SA.33966 *Guadeloupean Residents* (20 April 2012).

[252] Commission Decision N 011/2006 (30 May 2007).

[253] Cases T-445/05 *Associazione italiana del risparmio gestito and Fineco Asset Management* EU:T:2009:50, para 182; Case T-177/07 *Mediaset* EU:T:2010:233; and Case C-403/10 P *Mediaset* EU:C:2011:533.

[254] *Commission – Temporary Framework for State aid measures to support the economy in the current COVID-19 outbreak* [2020] OJ C91I/1, as subsequently amended, para 15.

[255] Case T-445/05 *Associazione italiana del risparmio gestito and Fineco Asset Management v Commission* EU:T:2009:50, para 70; Case C-156/98 *Germany v Commission* EU:C:2000:467, para 52; Case C-334/99 *Germany v Commission* EU:C:2003:55, para 120; and Case C-277/00 *Germany v Commission* EU:C:2004:238, para 49.

an important point, as several cases outlined in paragraphs (a)–(e) are developed in the block exemption regulations, which serve as a *lex specialis* regarding Article 107(3) TFEU. If none of the scenarios set out in secondary legislation apply, the Commission will rely directly on Article 107(3) TFEU and will do so on a case-by-case basis, conducting a detailed assessment of the specific characteristics of the aid involved.[256]

To this end, the Commission has published several documents, in the form of guidelines, designed to facilitate the application of the provision to each individual case of aid, based on a common set of principles for assessing the individual compatibility of measures developed in the 2012 State aid modernisation package.[257] These principles include: (i) a contribution to a well-defined objective of common interest; (ii) the necessity of state intervention; (iii) the appropriateness of the aid to meet that objective and satisfy that necessity; (iv) the incentive effect of the aid for the beneficiaries; (v) proportionality; (vi) the avoidance of undue negative effects on competition and trade between Member States; and (vii) transparency.[258] These principles are reflected in various guidelines for analysing categories of aid, briefly described in the following sections.

3.2.1. Article 107(3)(a) TFEU

Aid to promote the economic development of areas where the standard of living is abnormally low or where there is serious underemployment and of the regions referred to in Article 349, given their structural, economic and social situation.

Article 107(3)(a) provides for the compatibility of so-called 'regional aid', which aims to reduce economic imbalances in certain territories within the Member States. The condition for applicability is that the region receiving the aid has a GDP per capita of less than 75 per cent of the Union's average gross domestic product.[259] This scenario is outlined in Articles 13–16 of Regulation 651/2014, which distinguishes between regional investment and regional operating aid on the one hand, and regional urban development aid on the other. If an aid measure does not fall within one of the cases specified in Regulation 651/2014, the 2021 Guidelines on national regional aid apply.[260]

3.2.2. Article 107(3)(b) TFEU

Aid to promote the execution of an important project of common European interest or to remedy a serious disturbance in the economy of a Member State.

This case of discretional compatibility covers two different situations: on the one hand, the implementation of important projects of common European interest; and on the other hand, the adoption of measures to remedy a serious disturbance in the economy of a Member State. Important Projects of Common European Interest (IPCEIs) are cross-border, cutting-edge innovation and infrastructure initiatives led by Member States that can significantly

[256] Case C-730/79 *Philip Morris v Commission* EU:C:1980:209, paras 24–26; Case C-301/87 *France v Commission* EU:C:1990:67, para 49; Case C-261/89 *Italy v Commission* EU:C:1991:367, para 20; and Joined Cases T-102/07 and T-120/07 *Freistaat Sachsen and Others v Commission* EU:T:2010:62, para 134.

[257] *Communication from the Commission to the European Parliament, the Council, the European Economic and Social Committee and the Committee of the Regions — State Aid Modernisation (SAM)* COM(2012) 209 final.

[258] P Nicolaides, 'In Search of Economically Rational Environmental State Aid: The Case of Exemption from Environmental Taxes' (2014) 10 *European Competition Journal* 155.

[259] The reference to regions with a GDP per capita of less than 75% of the EU-27 average was foreseen in the Commission Communication on the method for the application of Article 92(3)(a) and (c) to regional aid [1988] OJ C212/2 and now in the Guidelines on national regional aid [2021] OJ C153/1, paras 157–60.

[260] *Guidelines on national regional aid* [2021] OJ C153/1.

contribute to the achievement of Union strategies (for instance, projects on batteries, hydrogen, or cloud infrastructure), while generating positive spill-over effects for the benefit of the Union's economy and its citizens in general beyond the participating Member States. IPCEIs are primarily funded from national budgets, so Member States are decisive in determining the project's scope, selecting the participating companies, and agreeing on the project's governance.

In 2014, the European Commission adopted a Communication on IPCEIs, revised in 2021,[261] which outlines the criteria under which Member States can support this type of project in accordance with State aid rules and, in particular, Article 107(3)(b) TFEU. The basic principles that Member States must comply with are set out in the Communication, including: (a) the aid must relate to a clearly defined project with clearly defined objectives; (b) the project must align with one of the Union's objectives and significantly enhance the competitiveness of Union enterprises; (c) more than one Member State must be involved; (d) the benefits of the project should not be limited solely to the enterprises within the sector concerned but must affect the European economy as a whole; (e) the project must rely on both public and private sources of co-financing; and (f) the size of the project must be significant in both quantitative and qualitative terms.

The case of 'serious disturbances in the economy of a Member State' has become particularly relevant in recent years, especially following the financial crisis that began in 2008 and during the COVID-19 pandemic. Prior to these events, both the Commission and the Court of Justice interpreted this ground of compatibility restrictively, in such a way that only in exceptional cases was it found to be fulfilled, requiring a measurable impact on the overall economy of the Member State and on a sector, but not necessarily on a specific region or individual company. From 2008 onwards, this approach became more nuanced, with the Commission recognising the potential to invoke this ground of compatibility to support individual financial institutions.[262] The financial crisis also prompted greater flexibility in the interpretation of State aid rules, as evidenced by the adoption of the Temporary Framework for State aid measures aimed at supporting access to finance during the economic and financial crisis.[263] This approach was applied again in 2020 in the context of the COVID-19 pandemic, resulting in a new Temporary Framework to support the economic measures adopted by Member States.[264] In 2022, another temporary framework was introduced to support Member States' economies in the wake of the Russian invasion of Ukraine.[265]

3.2.3. Article 107(3)(c) TFEU

Aid to facilitate the development of certain economic activities or areas, where such aid does not adversely affect trading conditions to an extent contrary to the common interest.

The case provided for in Article 107(3)(c) TFEU is the most frequent in the Commission's practice and allows for the approval of projects to support sectoral activities or regions of the Member States. Currently, most initiatives in this category are subject to the block exemption

[261] *Commission – Criteria for the analysis of the compatibility with the internal market of State aid to promote the execution of important projects of common European interest* [2021] C/2021/8481 final.

[262] Commission Communication on the application from 1 August 2013 of State aid rules to support measures in favour of banks in the context of the financial crisis [2013] OJ C216/1.

[263] *Commission – Temporary framework for State aid measures to support access to finance in the current financial and economic crisis* [2009] OJ C83/1, as subsequently amended.

[264] *Commission – Temporary Framework for State aid measures to support the economy in the context of the current COVID-19 outbreak* [2020] OJ C91I/1, as subsequently amended.

[265] *Commission – Temporary Framework for State aid measures to support the economy following the aggression against Ukraine by Russia* [2022] OJ C131/1.

regulations, either in Regulation 651/2014, the agriculture and fisheries exemption regulations, or the infrastructure exemption regulations (GBERs). This paragraph also includes the case of State aid for rescuing and restructuring non-financial undertakings in difficulty.[266] If the measure does not fall under one of the relevant Regulations, the Commission adopts sectoral Guidelines outlining the applicable criteria. In the absence of an applicable Regulation or Guidelines, Article 107(3)(c) TFEU will be directly applicable.

3.2.4. Article 107(3)(d) TFEU

Aid to promote culture and heritage conservation where such aid does not affect trading conditions and competition in the Union to an extent contrary to the common interest.

Finally, the Treaty provides a case of discretional compatibility for aid aimed at promoting culture and heritage conservation, currently outlined in Articles 53–54 of Regulation 651/2014. These provisions set out the basic framework under which this type of aid will be exempt, notably including aid for museums, archives, libraries, monuments and historic buildings, artistic education, and music and literary publishing. Article 54 provides for a specific regime applicable to audiovisual works, particularly aid supporting the production of works, pre-production and distribution.

3.3. *The Block Exemption Scheme*

In practice, most state measures that fall within the category of State aid are not subject to a case-by-case analysis under Articles 107–08 TFEU but instead fall within the block exemption regulations. These tools assist Member States and their authorities by providing a list of criteria and scenarios that enable the adoption of financial support measures for companies without requiring individual notification to the Commission. The basic framework for block exemptions is set out in Regulation 651/2014, which declares certain categories of aid compatible with the internal market.[267]

Regulation 651/2014 establishes a general and sector-specific exemption framework that covers various cases of measures that qualify as State aid but, due to their characteristics, are deemed compatible with the internal market without requiring notification to the Commission. According to data provided by the Commission, approximately 90 per cent of State aid measures fall within the scope of Regulation 651/2014.[268]

Regulation 651/2014 contains an enumeration of general categories of aid that are covered by the exemptions, including regional aid, aid to small and medium enterprises, aid for environmental protection, aid for research, development and innovation, aid for training, aid for the employment of disadvantaged or disabled workers, aid for culture and heritage conservation, aid for local infrastructure, aid for regional airports, and aid for ports.[269] In addition, Regulation 651/2014 also specifies the categories of aid to which the exemption regime does not apply, making them subject to the general notification regime. These include export-related aid, aid related to the primary agriculture and fisheries sector, aid granted on an ad hoc basis

[266] Commission – Guidelines on State aid for rescuing and restructuring non-financial undertakings in difficulty [2014] OJ C249/1.

[267] Commission Regulation (EU) 651/2014 of 17 June 2014 declaring certain categories of aid compatible with the internal market in application of Articles 107 and 108 of the Treaty [2014] OJ L187/1, as amended by Commission Regulation (EU) 2021/1237 of 23 July 2021 [2021] OJ L270/39, following the 2020 review and the adoption of the recovery plan *NextGenerationEU*.

[268] Commission, 'State Aid: Commission Adopts New GBER Rules to Further Facilitate Public Support for Jobs and Growth' (Press Release IP/16/3398, 13 October 2016).

[269] Art 1(1) of Regulation 651/2014.

in favour of individual companies, or aid granted to support companies in difficulty, among others.[270]

Regulation 651/2014 also contains several notification thresholds, above which the notification regime does not apply. For example, investment aid for SMEs exceeding EUR 8.25 million per undertaking and per investment project must be notified. In the case of operating aid for heritage conservation, the maximum threshold is set at EUR 82.5 million per undertaking per year.

The Commission has also adopted a *de minimis* threshold regime, which sets amounts below which a Member State's financial support measure does not constitute State aid. Unlike the block exemption scheme, the *de minimis* aid scheme directly targets the concept of aid, ensuring that the measure in question will be deemed not to meet the requirements of Article 107(1) TFEU and therefore does not require notification to the Commission. The general de minimis aid scheme is provided for in Regulation 2023/2831,[271] establishing, as a general rule, thresholds of up to EUR 300,000 per undertaking over three years.[272] A higher threshold of EUR 750,000 applies under Regulation 2023/2832 to undertakings providing services of general economic interest. The *de minimis* rules apply only to aid for which it is possible to calculate precisely the gross grant equivalent of the aid *ex ante* without any need to undertake a risk assessment.[273]

4. State Aid Procedure

Member States have, with the exceptions described above, the obligation to notify a measure falling under the category of State aid. In contrast, the Commission has a mandate, directly derived from Article 108 TFEU, to continually review existing aid schemes in the Member States. The procedure to be followed is outlined in Regulation 2015/1589, which sets down detailed rules for applying Article 108 TFEU.[274]

Regulation 2015/1589 distinguishes between 'existing aid' and 'new aid'. Existing aid is a measure that fulfils the requirements of Article 107(1) TFEU but receives preferential treatment owing to the timing of its approval. It benefits from a specific approval procedure, which will be explained below.

Regulation 2015/1589 distinguishes between 'aid schemes' and 'individual aid'. The former refers to a national regulatory framework that sets the conditions applicable to an aid. Regulation 2015/1589 defines them as:

> [A]ny act on the basis of which, without further implementing measures being required, individual aid awards may be made to undertakings defined within the act in a general and abstract manner and any act on the basis of which aid which is not linked to a specific project may be awarded to one or several undertakings for an indefinite period of time and/or for an indefinite amount'.[275]

[270] Art 1(2)–(5) of Regulation 651/2014.

[271] Commission Regulation (EU) 2023/2831 of 13 December 2023 on the application of Articles 107 and 108 of the Treaty on the Functioning of the European Union to de minimis aid [2023] OJ L, 15.12.2023. A higher threshold applies to undertakings providing services of general economic interest: see Commission Regulation (EU) 2023/2832 of 13 December 2023 on the application of Articles 107 and 108 of the Treaty on the Functioning of the European Union to de minimis aid granted to undertakings providing services of general economic interest [2023] OJ L, 15.12.2023.

[272] ibid, Art 3(2) of Regulation 2023/2831.

[273] ibid, Art 4(1) of Regulation 2023/2831.

[274] Council Regulation (EU) 2015/1589 of 13 July 2015 laying down detailed rules for the application of Article 108 of the Treaty on the Functioning of the European Union [2015] OJ L248/9.

[275] Article 1, section (d). On the concept of 'act' within the meaning of Regulation 2015/1589, see the judgment in Case C-337/19 P *Commission v Belgium and Magnetrol International* EU:C:2021:741, paras 72ff.

By contrast, individual aid is not granted through an aid scheme, or it is aid granted under an aid scheme that must be notified. This distinction has important procedural consequences, which will be explained below.

Lastly, it should be noted that where the modalities of an aid measure are so indissolubly linked to its object that it is impossible to evaluate them separately, their effect on the compatibility or incompatibility of that aid viewed as a whole must therefore of necessity be determined in the framework of the procedure prescribed in Article 108 TFEU.[276] Such modalities are therefore among the factors which the Commission is required to examine and, as the case may be, to approve, with the result that, if they lead to an infringement of provisions or general principles of EU law, a decision adopted by the Commission authorising that aid would necessarily be rendered unlawful.[277] For example, if the aid has been granted and is inextricably linked to a procurement procedure, the Commission must also review the Member State's compliance with Union procurement law as part of its assessment on the compatibility of the aid.[278]

4.1. *Existing Aid*

Article 1(b) of Regulation 2015/1589 enumerates the types of aid that fall under the category of 'existing' aid:

- aid schemes and individual aid which existed before the entry into force of the Treaty in the respective Member State and which continue to apply after the entry into force of the TFEU;[279]
- aid schemes and individual aid authorised by the Commission or the Council;[280]
- aid deemed to have been authorised by tacit approval of the Commission under Article 4(6) of Regulation 659/1999 or Regulation 2015/1589;[281]

[276] Case C-284/21 P *Commission v Braesch and Others* EU:C:2023:58, para 97, and Case C-59/23 P *Austria v Commission* EU:C:2025:686, para 54.

[277] *Braesch* (n 276), para 99, and *Austria v Commission* (n 276) para 54.

[278] This was the case in *Austria v Commission* (n 276) where the Court of Justice found that a potential infringement, by an indissociable aspect of the aid measure at issue, of provisions or general principles of EU law, such as the EU public procurement rules, precludes that measure from being declared compatible with the internal market in a procedure under Art 108 TFEU. That case concerned the conformity of the direct award of a contract for the construction of the two new nuclear reactors with Union public procurement rules, necessary for the organisation of an open, impartial and unconditional tender procedure for the award of a contract for the construction of infrastructure. In the view of the Court of Justice, the proper implementation of those rules is 'likely to have an impact, inter alia, on the cost of the investment required for that construction and on the properties of that infrastructure and, accordingly, on the extent of any advantage granted to an undertaking or group of undertakings by that means'. *Austria v Commission* (n 276), paras 75–76. See also, and by analogy, Cases C-214/12 P, C-215/12 P and C-223/12 P *Land Burgenland and Others v Commission* EU:C:2013:682, para 94; Case C-127/16 P *SNCF Mobilités v Commission* EU:C:2018:165, para 140, and Cases C-331/20 P and C-343/20 P *Volotea and easyJet v Commission* EU:C:2022:886, para 126.

[279] Case C-346/03 *Atzeni and Others* EU:C:2006:130, para 52; Case T-11/07 *Frucona Košice v Commission* EU:T:2010:498; Case C-73/11 P *Frucona Košice v Commission*, EU:C:2013:32; Case C-262/11 *Kremikovtzi*, EU:C:2012:760; Case C-672/13 *OTP Bank* EU:C:2015:185; and Case C-357/14 P *Electrabel and Dunamenti Erőmű v Commission* EU:C:2015:642.

[280] Case C-313/90 *CIRFS and Others v Commission* EU:C:1993:111, para 35; Case C-47/91 *Italy v Commission* EU:C:1994:358, para 21; and Case T-20/03 *Kahla/Thüringen Porzellan v Commission* EU:T:2008:395, paras 92–93.

[281] Art 1(b)(iii) of Regulation 2015/1589 refers to aid 'which is deemed to have been authorised pursuant to Article 4(6) of Regulation (EC) No 659/1999 or to Article 4(6), or prior to Regulation (EC) No 659/1999 but in accordance with this procedure'.

- aid deemed to be existing aid after ten years from the date the aid was granted, under Article 17 of Regulation 2015/1589;[282]
- aid considered as existing aid because it can be established that at the time it was put into effect it did not constitute aid, and that it subsequently became an aid due to the evolution of the internal market or the liberalisation of an activity by Union law.[283]

Articles 21–23 of Regulation 2015/1589 set out the procedural rules applicable to existing aid, also known as the 'cooperation procedure'. The Commission conducts an ongoing review of existing aid granted by Member States and, in particular, monitors cases where an aid scheme is not, or is no longer, compatible with the internal market. When such a case arises, the Commission must inform the Member State concerned of this preliminary conclusion. It grants it one month to submit its observations. If the Commission concludes that the existing aid scheme is not or is no longer compatible with the internal market, it will issue a recommendation proposing to the Member State the adoption of appropriate measures, which may include one of the following three options: (a) a substantive amendment of the aid scheme; (b) the introduction of procedural requirements; or (c) the abolition of the aid scheme.

The Member State may accept the measures proposed by the Commission, in which case it must formally notify the Commission and be bound by its acceptance.[284] If the Member State does not accept the proposed measures, the Commission will initiate a formal investigation procedure under Article 4(4) of Regulation 2015/1589.[285]

4.2. *Notification of New Aid*

All 'new aid' must be notified to the Commission before it is formally implemented, unless one of the exemptions under the block exemption framework applies. The notification procedure allows the Commission to analyse the aid and assess its compatibility with the internal market before it is implemented. A 'pre-notification' phase may precede the notification, but once formal notification is made, the Commission proceeds in two stages. The first is a preliminary assessment. If the outcome of this assessment confirms indications of incompatibility with the internal market, the Commission will proceed to the second phase, referred to in Regulation 2015/1589 as a 'formal investigation'.

4.2.1. Pre-Notification

In cases that present novel features or which, due to their size or complexity, warrant prior informal discussions with the Commission services, Member States may use the pre-notification procedure. This procedure is not included in Regulation 2015/1589, but its existence is well established in practice, and the Commission has reflected it in its Code of Best

[282] See Art 17 of Regulation 2015/1589, according to which 'the powers of the Commission to recover aid shall be subject to a limitation period of 10 years'.

[283] Article 1(b)(v) of Regulation 2015/1589. See also the judgments in Case T-298/97 *Alzetta and Others v Commission* EU:T:2000:151, paras 143–44; Case T-227/01 *Diputación Foral de Álava and Gobierno Vasco v Commission* EU:T:2009:315, para 250; Joined Cases C-182/03 and C-217/03 *Belgium and Forum 187 ASBL v Commission* EU:C:2006:416, para 71; and Joined Cases T-443/08 and T-455/08 *Freistaat Sachsen and Land Sachsen-Anhalt and Mitteldeutsche Flughafen AG and Flughafen Leipzig-Halle GmbH v Commission* EU:T:2011:117, para 188.

[284] Art 23(1) of Regulation 2015/1589. See also the judgments in Case T-354/05 *TF1 v Commission* EU:T:2009:66, para 46; Case C-311/94 *IJssel-Vliet Combinatie v Minister van Economische Zaken* EU:C:1996:383, paras 42–43; and the Opinion of Advocate General Mengozzi in Case C-117/10 *Commission v Council*, EU:C:2013:786, pts 62–72.

[285] Art 23(2) of Regulation 2015/1589. See Case T-20/03 *Kahla/Thüringen Porzellan v Commission* EU:T:2008:395, para 148; and Case T-527/13 *Italy v Commission* EU:T:2015:429, para 89.

Practices for the conduct of State aid control procedures.[286] Although pre-notification does not result in a formal decision by the Commission, it facilitates the Commission's work and allows the processing of the case to be expedited.

Within the framework of a pre-notification procedure, the Member State and the Commission may agree on the information to be provided at the time of formal notification. Both parties may also discuss legal and economic matters informally and confidentially, enabling the Member State to amend the proposal before proceeding to formal notification. Overall, a pre-notification process should not exceed six months, although the duration may be extended in particularly complex aid cases.[287]

4.2.2. Preliminary Assessment

The formal notification of new aid starts with a preliminary assessment that allows the Commission to evaluate the compatibility concerns regarding the national measure. Therefore, if, after this initial review, the Commission determines that the notified measure does not constitute aid or, if it does constitute aid, it does not raise doubts about its compatibility with the internal market, it will declare this through a formal Decision. Otherwise, if the proposed measure raises doubts about its compatibility with the internal market, the Commission will open the formal investigation phase.

The preliminary assessment should be completed within two months, but Regulation 2015/1589 states that this period can be extended with the consent of the Commission and the Member State concerned.[288] Similarly, the preliminary assessment can be processed through an expedited procedure in simple cases and concluded within a maximum of 25 days.[289] The speed with which the case is handled is crucial, as the aid will be suspended during the procedure, and the Member State cannot approve or disburse it to the beneficiaries.[290]

4.2.3. Formal Investigation

The formal investigation procedure is initiated by a Decision of the Commission, which will summarise the main issues of fact and law, lay down an initial assessment of the proposed measure, and outline the Commission's doubts as to its compatibility with the internal market.[291] The opening of the procedure gives the Member State concerned and any interested parties the right to submit comments within a period not exceeding one month.[292]

After the procedure has been completed and the parties have been heard, the Commission may conclude that the notified measure does not constitute aid or, if it does, that it is compatible with the internal market, in which case a Decision reflecting this outcome will be adopted

[286] Commission Notice — Code of Best Practices for the conduct of State aid control procedures [2025] OJ C/2025/2810, which replaced the 2018 Code [2018] OJ C253/14.

[287] ibid, paras 15–17.

[288] Art 4(5) of Regulation 2015/1589.

[289] See Code of Best Practices (n 286) paras 37–40.

[290] On the *stand-still* effect of the notification procedure, see Case C-367/95 P *Commission v Sytraval and Brink's France* EU:C:1998:154, para 37; and Case T-239/04 *Italy v Commission* EU:T:2007:260, paras 86–89.

[291] On the appealability of decisions to initiate a formal investigation procedure, see Case C-400/99 *Italy v Commission* EU:C:2005:275, paras 45–65; Joined Cases T-195/01 and T-207/01 *Government of Gibraltar v Commission* EU:T:2002:111, paras 68–88; and Case T-394/08 *Regione autonoma della Sardegna and Others v Commission* EU:T:2011:493, para 77.

[292] Art 6 of Regulation 2015/1589.

(a 'positive decision').[293] In such cases, conditions may be added to ensure the aid is compatible with the internal market.[294]

Alternatively, the Commission may conclude that the notified aid is incompatible with the internal market, in which case it will instruct the Member State not to implement the measure. This is a 'negative decision'[295] and must clearly state the reasons behind the Commission's conclusion.[296] The negative decision is addressed to the Member State that notified the aid, and it is notified as soon as possible, followed by publication in the *Official Journal of the European Union* in a non-confidential version.[297]

4.2.4. The Simplified Procedure

In addition to the notification procedure outlined above, the Commission has introduced a simplified procedure for certain categories of new aid. This procedure, as set out in the Notice on a simplified procedure and now integrated into the Code of Best Practices,[298] applies to aid falling under the 'standard assessment' sections of existing frameworks or guidelines, to aid falling within the Commission's 'well-established decision-making practice', and to prolongations or extensions of existing schemes.[299] If the requirements for processing the application through a simplified procedure are satisfied, the Commission will decide within 25 working days.[300]

4.3. *Unlawful Aid*

Non-notified aid is 'unlawful aid'. Aid is unlawful when it is put into effect in breach of Article 108(3) TFEU, that is, without awaiting the Commission's decision.[301] To this end, Article 12 of Regulation 2015/1589 authorises the Commission to examine, on its own initiative, any information from any source regarding alleged unlawful aid.[302] In practice, such information often comes from complaints lodged by competitors of the companies benefiting from the allegedly unlawful aid, or by other Member States. In such cases, the Commission can open a formal investigation procedure.[303]

One of the main features of the unlawful aid procedure is the Commission's power to suspend the aid. The legal basis for this power is reflected in the *standstill* clause of Article 108(3) TFEU, although it has been further elaborated in Regulation 2015/1589. On the one hand, the Commission can issue a 'suspension injunction', the effect of which is to suspend the granting of the unlawful aid until a decision on its compatibility is made.[304] On the other hand, if the unlawful aid has already been granted, the Commission may issue a 'recovery

[293] Art 9(2)–(3) of Regulation 2015/1589.

[294] Art 9(4) of Regulation 2015/1589. On conditional decisions, see Case T-349/03 *Corsica Ferries France v Commission* EU:T:2005:221, paras 229–33; and Case C-352/14 *Iglesias Gutiérrez* EU:C:2015:691, para 28. Of particular relevance is the TWD doctrine, established in Joined Cases T-244/93 and T-486/93 *TWD v Commission* EU:T:1995:160, paras 53–60, according to which the Commission may adopt a measure conditional upon recovery from the Member State of aid previously declared unlawful.

[295] Art 9(5) of Regulation 2015/1589.

[296] Case C-70/72 *Commission v Germany* EU:C:1973:87, paras 20–21.

[297] Art 32(2) of Regulation 2015/1589. Also, on the disclosure of information in a negative decision, see Joined Cases T-109/05 and T-444/05 *NLG v Commission* EU:T:2011:235; and Case T-511/09 *Niki Luftfahrt v Commission* EU:T:2015:284, paras 45–57 and 62.

[298] Code of Best Practices (n 286), Section 6.

[299] ibid, Section 6.

[300] ibid, para 79.

[301] Case C-301/87 *France v Commission* EU:C:1990:67.

[302] Art 12(1) of Regulation 2015/1589.

[303] ibid, Art 12(2).

[304] ibid, Art 13(1).

injunction', which consists of provisionally recovering any unlawful aid pending its final decision on compatibility.[305] In this second scenario, Regulation 2015/1589 stipulates three conditions that must be met: a) there are no doubts about the aid character of the measure concerned; b) the urgency to act; and c) the existence of a serious risk of causing substantial and irreparable damage to a competitor.[306] Failure by the Member State to comply with an injunction entitles the Commission to refer the case directly to the Court of Justice.[307]

Unlawful aid, once found to be incompatible with the internal market, must be repealed, and its economic effects neutralised through recovery.[308] This consequence triggers a recovery procedure of the unlawful aid, the starting point of which is a 'recovery decision' issued by the Commission.[309] Unless the Commission, for reasons of legal certainty, decides that the unlawful aid is not recoverable,[310] the Member State is required to make all necessary efforts to recover the amounts granted so far, together with interest from the date on which the unlawful aid became available to the beneficiary until its recovery.[311] Recovery must be carried out 'without delay' and in accordance with the applicable procedures under national law.[312]

The Court of Justice has held that Article 108(3) TFEU has direct effect and may be relied upon by any interested party before national courts.[313] Therefore, while the power to declare the incompatibility of aid is exclusive to the Commission, national courts may support it by taking other measures to safeguard the effectiveness of Article 108(3) TFEU. Among other measures, national courts may order: the prevention of the payment of unlawful aid; the recovery of unlawful aid (irrespective of its compatibility);[314] recovery of interest covering the unlawful period;[315] damages in favour of competitors and other third parties;[316] or interim measures targeting unlawful aid.[317] Any Commission decision confirming the compatibility of the aid, which is nevertheless unlawful because it was granted in breach of the standstill obligation, does not have the effect of regularising *a posteriori* the implementing acts in violation of the standstill obligation.[318]

[305] ibid, Art 13(2).

[306] ibid.

[307] ibid, Art 14.

[308] Case C-52/84 *Commission v Belgium* EU:C:1986:3, paras 14–16; Case C-277/00 *Germany v Commission* EU:C:2004:238, paras 74–76; and Case C-667/13 *Banco Privado Português and Massa Insolvente do Banco Privado Português* EU:C:2015:151, paras 59–60. In general, see the codification of case law and practice in *Commission – Towards an effective implementation of Commission decisions ordering Member States to recover unlawful and incompatible State aid* [2007] OJ C272/4.

[309] Art 16(1) of Regulation 2015/1589.

[310] See, among many others, Case C-52/84 *Commission v Belgium* EU:C:1986:3, paras 14–16; Case C-142/87 *Belgium v Commission* EU:C:1990:125; Case C-78/98 *Commission v Belgium* EU:C:2001:370; Case C-261/99 *Commission v France* EU:C:2001:179; Case C-527/12 *Commission v Germany* EU:C:2014:2193; and Case C-214/07 *Commission v France* EU:C:2008:619.

[311] Art 16(2) of Regulation 2015/1589.

[312] ibid, Art 16(3).

[313] Case C-120/73 *Lorenz GmbH v Bundesrepublik Deutschland and Others* EU:C:1973:152; Joined Cases C-91/83 and C-127/83 *Heineken* EU:C:1984:307; Case C-143/99 *Adria-Wien Pipeline and Wietersdorfer & Peggauer Zementwerke* EU:C:2001:598, paras 26–27; Case C-295/97 *Piaggio* EU:C:1999:313; and Case C-345/02 *Pearle and Others* EU:C:2004:448, paras 30–32.

[314] Case C-39/94 *SFEI and Others* EU:C:1996:285, para 40; Case C-368/04 *Ölleitung in Österreich* EU:C:2006:644, para 47; and Case C-199/06 *CELF and Ministre de la Culture et de la Communication* EU:C:2008:79, para 41.

[315] *CELF* (n 314) paras 50–52 and 55; and Case T-459/93 *Siemens v Commission*, EU:T:1995:100, para 83.

[316] *CELF* (n 314) paras 53 and 55; Case C-334/07 P *Commission v Freistaat Sachsen* EU:C:2008:709, para 54; Case C-278/05 *Robins and Others* EU:C:2007:56, para 71; Case C-424/97 *Haim* EU:C:2000:357, para 38; and Case C-5/94 *Hedley Lomas* EU:C:1996:205, para 28.

[317] The case law and practice of national courts and the European Commission are codified in the Commission notice on the enforcement of State aid law by national courts [2021] OJ C305/1.

[318] Case C-354/90 *Fédération Nationale du Commerce Extérieur des Produits Alimentaires v France* EU:C:1991:440, para 16.

GENERAL BIBLIOGRAPHY

Bacon, K, *European Union Law of State Aid*, 3rd edn (Oxford University Press, 2017).

Bailey, D and John, LE, (eds), *Bellamy & Child: European Union Law of Competition*, 8th edn (Oxford University Press, 2018).

Bailey, D and Whish, R, *Competition Law*, 11th edn (Oxford University Press, 2024).

Bernatt, M, *Populism and Antitrust: The Illiberal Influence of Populist Government on the Competition Law System* (Cambridge University Press, 2022).

Biondi, A, Eeckhout, P and Flynn, J (eds), *The Law of State Aid in the European Union* (Oxford University Press, 2004).

Bishop, S and Walker, M, *The Economics of EC Competition Law: Concepts, Application and Measurement*, 3rd edn (Sweet & Maxwell, 2010).

Buendía Sierra, JL, *Exclusive Rights and State Monopolies under EC Law* (Oxford University Press, 1999).

Ezrachi, A, *EU Competition Law: An Analytical Guide to the Leading Cases*, 8th edn (Hart 2024).

Fumagalli, C, Motta, M and Calcagno, C, *Exclusionary Practices: The Economics of Monopolisation and Abuse of a Dominant Position* (Cambridge University Press, 2018).

Ibáñez Colomo, P, *The Shaping of EU Competition Law* (Cambridge University Press, 2018).

— *The New EU Competition Law* (Hart, 2023).

— *The New Law of State Aid and Subsidies* (Hart, 2026).

Iñiguez, G, 'Competition in Times of Democratic Crisis: Domestic Judicial Reforms and the Effectiveness of EU Competition Law' (2025) 26 *Cambridge Yearbook of European Legal Studies* 30.

Kerse, C and Khan, N, *EU Antitrust Procedure*, 6th edn (Sweet & Maxwell, 2012).

Kilian, W, *EU Digital Markets Law. A Concise Guide to the Regulations and Directives on IT and Media Law* (Edward Elgar, 2025).

Kokkoris, I and Lemus, C (eds), *Research Handbook on the Law and Economics of Competition Law Enforcement* (Edward Elgar, 2022).

Lindsay, A and Berridge, A, *The EU Merger Regulation: Substantive Issues* (Sweet & Maxwell, 2017).

Lovdahl Gormsen, L, *A Principled Approach to Abuse of Dominance in European Competition Law* (Cambridge University Press, 2010).

Piernas López, J, *The Concept of State Aid under EU Law: From Internal Market to Competition and Beyond* (Oxford University Press, 2015).

Quigley, C, *European State Aid Law and Policy*, 4th edn (Hart, 2022).

Sauter, W, *Coherence in EU Competition Law* (Oxford University Press, 2016).

Tuytschaever, F and Wijckmans, F, *Vertical Agreements in EU Competition Law*, 4th edn (Oxford University Press, 2025).

Veljanovski, C, *Cartel Damages: Principles, Measurement and Economics* (Oxford University Press, 2020).

FURTHER READING

The Internal Market and Competition Law

Akman, P, Brook, O and Stylianou, K (eds), *Research Handbook on Abuse of Dominance and Monopolization* (Edward Elgar, 2023).

Albors-Llorens, A, 'The Role of Objective Justification and Efficiencies in the Application of Article 82 EC' (2007) 44 *Common Market Law Review* 1727.

Bergström, M, Iacovides, M and Strand, M, *Harmonising EU Competition Litigation: The New Directive and Beyond* (Hart, 2016).

Bostoen, F and Vanwamel, D, 'The Digital Markets Act: A partial solution to antitrust's remedy problem' (2024) 61 *Common Market Law Review* 1575.

Bouzoraa, Y, and Lindeboom, J, 'How the Court of Justice Facilitates Competition Law Enforcement Against Open Digital Platforms' (2025) 225 *EU Law Live Weekend Edition* 3.

Broberg, M, *The European Commission's Jurisdiction to Scrutinise Mergers* (Kluwer Law, 2013).

Di Porto, F and Podszun, P (eds), *Abusive Practices in Competition Law* (Edward Elgar, 2018).

Doherty, B, 'Just What are Essential Facilities?' (2001) 38 *Common Market Law Review* 397.

Eifert, M, Metzger, A, Schweitzer, H, and Wagner, G, 'Taming the giants: the DMA/DSA package' (2021) 58 *Common Market Law Review* 987.
Franck, J-U, and Peitz, M, 'The Digital Markets Act and the Whack-A-Mole Challenge' (2024) 61 *Common Market Law Review* 299.
Ibáñez Colomo, P, 'Competition on the Merits' (2024) 61 *Common Market Law Review* 387.
Monti, G, 'The Scope of Collective Dominance under Article 82' (2001) 38 *Common Market Law Review* 131.
Moreno Belloso, N and Petit, N, 'The EU Digital Markets Act (DMA): A Competition Hand in a Regulatory Glove' (2023) 48 *European Law Review* 391.
Parcu, P, Monti, G and Botta, M (eds), *The Interaction of Competition Law and Sector Regulation: Emerging Trends at the National and EU Level* (Edward Elgar, 2022).
Witt, A, 'The Digital Markets Act – Regulating the Wild West' (2023) 60 *Common Market Law Review* 625.
Wollenschläger, F, Wurmnest, W and Möllers, T (eds), *Private Enforcement of European Competition and State Aid Law: Current Challenges and the Way Forward* (Wolters Kluwer, 2020).

Services of General Economic Interest

Burke, JM, *A Critical Account of Article 106(2) TFEU: Government Failure in Public Service Provision* (Hart, 2018).
Maziarz, A, 'Services of General Economic Interest: Towards Common Values?' (2016) 15 *European State Aid Law Quarterly* 16.
Prosser, T, *The Limits of Competition Law: Markets and Public Services* (Oxford University Press, 2005).

State Aid

Barents, R, *Directory of EU Case Law on State Aids*, 4th edn (Kluwer Law, 2022).
Biondi, A, 'State Aid Is Falling Down, Falling Down: An Analysis of the Case Law on the Notion of Aid' (2013) 50 *Common Market Law Review* 1719.
Cremona, M (ed), *Market Integration and Public Services in the European Union* (Oxford University Press, 2011).
Flynn, L (ed), *EU Competition Law: Volume 4: State Aid* (Claeys & Casteels Law, 2016).
Hancher, L, Ottervanger, T and Slot, PJ, *EU State Aids*, 6th edn (Sweet & Maxwell, 2021).
Hancher, L and Piernas López, J (eds), *Research Handbook on European State Aid Law*, 2nd edn (Edward Elgar, 2021).
— *The Future of EU State Aid Law: Consolidation and Expansion* (EU Law Live Press, 2023).
Kyriazis, D, *Fiscal State Aid Law and Harmful Tax Competition in the European Union* (Oxford University Press, 2023).
McMahon, C, 'Selectivity as discrimination: lessons from the case law on fiscal measures for identifying State aid' (2024) *Yearbook of European Law* 261.
Parcu, P, Monti, G and Botta, M (eds), *EU State Aid Law: Emerging Trends at the National and EU Level* (Edward Elgar, 2020).
Pastor Merchante, F, *The Role of Competitors in the Enforcement of State Aid Law* (Hart, 2019).
Rubini, L, *The Definition of Subsidy and State Aid. WTO and EC Law in Comparative Perspective* (Oxford University Press, 2009).

16

The Union's External Action

I. THE UNION AS AN INTERNATIONAL ACTOR AND ITS EXTERNAL ACTION: OBJECTIVES AND LEGAL FRAMEWORK

POLICYMAKING WITHIN THE Union is characterised by two distinct yet closely interconnected dimensions. The first is the internal dimension, which concerns the formulation and implementation of policies within the Union's 27 Member States. The second is the external dimension, which seeks to shape and develop the Union's relations with the wider international community. This external dimension is a core component of the Union's mission, as it enables the Member States, acting collectively, to promote their shared principles and values beyond the Union's borders. It also affords them a degree of international influence and visibility that they could scarcely achieve when acting individually.

The articulation of a common, coherent and effective external action has long been among the most formidable challenges of the European project. Despite the self-evident importance of this objective, Member States continue to pursue and safeguard their own international interests, shaped by distinct historical trajectories, economic ties and security considerations. For example, Spain has traditionally regarded Latin America as a particularly proximate and strategically significant region, while France has cultivated enduring relationships in Africa and parts of Asia, drawing on its historical colonial connections. Similarly, the foreign policy outlook of the Baltic States and Finland is profoundly influenced by their geographical proximity to Russia, leading them to view external relations as an integral component of their broader security strategy. Taken together, these divergent perspectives help to explain why the establishment of a genuinely common foreign policy has proven difficult for the Union, and why it is likely to remain so in the foreseeable future.

In the early stages of the European project, external action functioned primarily as an extension of the common market. It centred on the development of a common commercial policy and a customs union, aimed at strengthening the Communities' trade relations with the rest of the world and ensuring coherence in a market that necessarily depended on stable and strategic external links. As the Communities evolved, this relatively narrow conception of external action became increasingly inadequate. The expansion of Union policies into more sensitive and politically salient areas, combined with the growing awareness among Member States of the need to enhance their international presence in an increasingly polarised global environment, contributed to a gradual broadening of the scope of external action.

This transformation was reflected in the creation of the European Union in 1992, which prompted a re-examination of the foundations of the European project and led to the establishment of the Common Foreign and Security Policy (CFSP) as a framework autonomous from traditional Community policies. Although initially embryonic, this development marked the emergence of a distinct foreign policy dimension at Union level. Subsequent Treaty reforms progressively strengthened the coherence and autonomy of the Union's external action, a process that culminated with the entry into force of the Lisbon Treaty in 2009. Since then, the Union's external action has evolved into a strategic and cross-sectoral policy, encompassing economic, political and security-related dimensions.

Today, the Union's external action constitutes an overarching framework that brings together the common commercial policy, policies of economic cooperation and partnership with third countries and regions, and the CFSP. It also extends to the international dimension of the internal Union policies, ranging from the internal market and social policy to environmental, climate and energy policy. In sum, the Union's external action is a multi-sectoral endeavour that spans a wide range of fields and relies on a combination of legal, economic and institutional instruments to achieve its objectives.

The importance of the Union's external action can scarcely be overstated, particularly at a time when a renewed emphasis on spheres of influence threatens the autonomy of states situated outside such power blocs. In this context, the ability of the Union and its Member States to speak with a single voice on the international stage is of fundamental importance. As the world's largest integrated market, encompassing a vast area of prosperity, innovation and liberal values, the Union derives much of its global influence from the coherence and unity of its external action. The consequences of failing to maintain such unity could be profound, not only for the European project as a whole but also for the individual Member States. Recent developments, including the invasion of Ukraine, the strains in transatlantic relations, growing tensions with China and a deepening of instability in the Middle East, have underscored the strategic necessity for the Union to articulate a coherent and credible external position. In the absence of a united external voice, the Union risks amplifying its own strategic vulnerabilities and emboldening external actors seeking to undermine both the European project and the values upon which it is founded.

1. Common Principles and Objectives of the Union's External Action

Following the reforms introduced in 2009 by the Lisbon Treaty, the founding Treaties were amended and now include new rules on the Union's external action, including a detailed outline of the common principles and objectives guiding the Union's actions in the international sphere. This development stems from the codifying role played by the Lisbon Treaty, enshrined in Article 21 Treaty on European Union (TEU), which distinguishes between principles and objectives. Principles are to be 'respected' by the Union, whereas objectives are to be 'pursued' by the Union (Article 21(3) TEU).

The principles and objectives are common and apply to the development and implementation of the various areas of the Union's external action covered by Title V TEU and by Part Five of the Treaty on the Functioning of the European Union (TFEU), as well as to the external aspects of its other policies. In other words, the principles and objectives encompass the three main areas where external action takes place, and reflect the evolution of this policy over time: firstly, the external action related to the Union's economic policies (the common commercial policy, cooperation with third countries, humanitarian aid, and restrictive measures); secondly, the CFSP; and thirdly, the external action that complements the Union's internal policies. The same principles and objectives are applicable across these three main areas of the Union's external action.

By addressing the principles and objectives of external action in a unified way, the Treaties aim to provide coherence to the Union's international policies. This coherence is explicitly reflected in the second subparagraph of Article 21(3) TEU, which states that 'the Union shall ensure consistency between the different areas of its external action and between these and its other policies'. To achieve this, coherence also has an institutional dimension, as the same provision immediately enumerates the institutions responsible for implementing external action, which must ensure 'consistency' and 'cooperation' at the external level. The second subparagraph of Article 21(3) TEU explicitly refers to the Council, the Commission, and the High Representative of the Union for Foreign Affairs and Security Policy as guarantors of such coherence and cooperation. The provision also emphasises the crucial role of these three institutional actors in shaping the Union's external action, which will be examined in section I.5 of this chapter.

The principles guiding the Union's actions on the international stage run in parallel to the values that underpin its policies, as outlined in the Treaties in Articles 1–2 TEU. The Union is guided in its international activities by the principles set out in Article 21(1) TEU, which have inspired its formation, development, and enlargement, and which it must strive to promote globally:

- democracy;
- the rule of law;
- the universality and indivisibility of human rights and fundamental freedoms;
- respect for human dignity;
- the principles of equality and solidarity;
- respect for the principles of the United Nations Charter and international law.

Regarding the objectives, Article 21(2) TEU outlines the aims to be pursued by the Union in defining and implementing all its policies and actions at the international level, in order to:

- safeguard its values, fundamental interests, security, independence and integrity;
- consolidate and support democracy, the rule of law, human rights and the principles of international law;
- preserve peace, prevent conflicts and strengthen international security, in accordance with the purposes and principles of the Charter of the United Nations, with the principles of the Helsinki Final Act and with the aims of the Charter of Paris, including those relating to external borders;
- foster the sustainable economic, social and environmental development of developing countries, with the primary aim of eradicating poverty;
- encourage the integration of all countries into the world economy, including through the progressive abolition of restrictions on international trade;
- help develop international measures to preserve and improve the quality of the environment and the sustainable management of global natural resources, in order to ensure sustainable development;
- assist populations, countries and regions confronting natural or man-made disasters; and
- promote an international system based on stronger multilateral cooperation and good global governance.

2. The Scope of the Union's External Action

As previously explained, the Union's external action covers a broad spectrum of policies, guided by shared principles and objectives, and organised into three main areas. This division into three areas has relevant implications for competences and the institutional distribution of powers and tasks, but it cannot be equated with the previous division of European policies into 'pillars', as outlined by the Maastricht Treaty.[1] One of the objectives of the Lisbon Treaty in 2009 was to establish a more uniform and coherent external action, as specified in Article 21(3) TEU. Thus, the Union's actions in each area reflect their particular characteristics, but there is no strict institutional and competence-based partition between them.

The three main areas of the Union's external action are outlined in Article 21(3) TEU, which refers to: (1) the areas covered by Part Five TFEU, mainly related to the Union's external action in the commercial and economic sectors; (2) the CFSP; and (3) the external dimension of the Union's internal policies.

2.1. *External Action Linked to the Union's Commercial and Economic Policies*

Part Five TFEU focuses on 'the Union's External Action', with a twofold aim: to set out the legal bases for the Union's policies most closely linked to international economic policy and to develop the principles that govern the horizontal and vertical balance of power in the Union's external actions. As part of the first aim, the TFEU addresses three policies with an economic dimension: the common commercial policy, international cooperation, and restrictive measures.

2.1.1. The Common Commercial Policy

The external dimension of the internal market is reflected in the Union's common commercial policy, through which the Union develops trade relations with third countries in ways that are consistent with and support the Union's internal market. Title II of Part Five TFEU defines the objectives, content, and legal bases of the Union's common commercial policy. Article 207 TFEU describes the basic contents of this policy, including:

> [C]hanges in tariff rates, the conclusion of tariff and trade agreements relating to trade in goods and services, and the commercial aspects of intellectual property, foreign direct investment, the achievement of uniformity in measures of liberalisation, export policy and measures to protect trade such as those to be taken in the event of dumping or subsidies.

In sum, the common commercial policy covers a vast range of features of what is conventionally called 'international trade', a competence which is exclusive in nature, thus placing it solely in the hands of the Union.

2.1.2. International Cooperation with Third Countries and Humanitarian Aid

Title III of Part Five TFEU brings together under the heading 'Cooperation with third countries and humanitarian aid' all bilateral or multilateral actions aimed at fostering economic cooperation with developing countries and providing humanitarian aid to countries affected by natural or man-made disasters. These legal bases result from the successive reforms introduced by the Maastricht, Nice, and Lisbon Treaties and reflect the evolution of these policy

[1] On the 'pillars' of the Union in the Maastricht Treaty, see RA Wessel, *The European Union's Foreign and Security Policy: A Legal Institutional Perspective* (Kluwer Law, 1999).

areas towards the 'community method'. The Union's competence in these policies is shared, and the Treaties explicitly state that they are 'without prejudice to the Member States' competence to negotiate in international bodies and to conclude agreements' (Articles 209(2), 212(3), and 214(4) TFEU).[2]

Despite the evident overlap of actions that can arise under the heading of 'cooperation with third countries', the Court of Justice has highlighted the importance of selecting the correct legal basis, particularly when distinguishing between development cooperation and economic, financial, and technical cooperation. In *Parliament v Council* (guarantees to the European Investment Bank), the Court of Justice emphasised the importance of defining the scope of Chapter 2 on economic, financial, and technical cooperation restrictively, as this policy mainly targets countries other than developing nations. To maintain the autonomy of Chapter 1 (development cooperation), the Court of Justice allowed a certain degree of expansion of the scope of Chapter 2, but only under the condition that this approach did not lead to the undermining of Chapter 1:

> It is true that . . . in its literal sense the term 'third countries' used in Article [212 TFEU] is sufficiently wide to encompass both developing countries and other third countries. It cannot, however, be implied from this, without restricting the scope of Article [209 TFEU], that all economic, financial and technical cooperation measures with developing countries within the meaning of Article [208 TFEU] may be undertaken on the sole basis of Article [212 TFEU].[3]

2.1.3. Restrictive Measures

'International sanctions' hold a specific place in the Union's external action. Under the heading of 'restrictive measures', the Treaties provide the legal basis for the Union to impose measures aimed at the total or partial interruption of economic and financial relations with third countries, as well as the imposition of measures restricting the rights of natural or legal persons. These measures have a specific and dual status, as they are adopted within the CFSP (as part of the Union's general foreign policy), but are implemented through the instruments of the 'community method' to maximise their effectiveness. This arrangement leads to what Wessel has defined as a 'twin relationship', since the implementation of restrictive measures requires the prior enactment of a CFSP act, leading to two autonomous but inextricably connected Union acts.[4]

Article 29 TEU states that the Council 'shall adopt decisions which shall define the approach of the Union to a particular matter of a geographical or thematic nature'. This legal basis requires unanimity in the Council (Article 31(1) TEU) to adopt restrictive measures. If the restrictive measures require the use of other Union competences to reinforce their effectiveness, Article 215 TFEU empowers the Union, in accordance with the 'community method' (with limited involvement of the European Parliament), to adopt the necessary measures. Using the 'community method' enables the Union to implement its restrictive measures with a range of legal instruments provided in Article 288 TFEU, thereby ensuring uniform application across all Member States.

[2] On shared competence in these areas, see Opinion *1/78* EU:C:1979:224 (international agreement on natural rubber); and the judgments in Joined Cases C-181/91 and C-248/91 *Parliament v Council and Commission* (Bangladesh) EU:C:1993:271, paras 14–16; and Case C-316/91 *Parliament v Council* EU:C:1994:76, para 41.

[3] Case C-155/07 *Parliament v Council* EU:C:2008:605, para 39.

[4] RA Wessel, 'Legality in EU Common Foreign and Security Policy: The Choice of the Appropriate Legal Basis' in C Kilpatrick and J Scott (eds), *Contemporary Challenges to EU Legality* (Oxford University Press, 2021) 71.

The Union's restrictive measures have a significant international dimension, a feature that requires the use of Article 215 TFEU rather than other legal bases in the Treaties. This was made evident in *Parliament v Council* (restrictive measures against Al-Qaida),[5] a case in which the European Parliament supported the use of the legal basis in Article 75 TFEU on the prevention and fight against terrorism, where the European Parliament holds broader powers. The Court of Justice rejected the European Parliament's interpretation, stating that Union implementing acts of restrictive measures adopted under Article 29 TEU must rely on Article 215 TFEU, regardless of whether the matter has connections to other sectoral legal bases. The fact that the measures adopted directly impacted fundamental rights does not alter this outcome. In reaching this conclusion, the Court of Justice emphasised the guarantees provided by Union law as a whole:

> [I]t is to be noted that the duty to respect fundamental rights is imposed, in accordance with Article 51(1) of the Charter of Fundamental Rights of the European Union, on all the institutions and bodies of the Union. In addition, under both Article 75 TFEU and Article 215(3) TFEU, the acts referred to in those articles are to include necessary provisions on legal safeguards.[6]

2.1.4. Association, Partnership and other Means of Cooperation

The Union can establish particularly close connections with one or more third countries, either for strategic reasons or because these countries have a specific connection with the Union, such as being neighbouring countries. To this end, Article 217 TFEU states that the Union may conclude with one or more third countries, or with international organisations, 'agreements establishing an association involving reciprocal rights and obligations, common action and special procedure'. These agreements, known as 'association agreements', extend beyond standard cooperation relations with third countries, to the extent of creating, in the words of the Court of Justice, 'special, privileged links with a non-member country' which must be allowed, at least to a certain extent, to take part in the Union's policies.[7] As a result, association agreements enable third countries to participate in certain Union policies, such as the free movement of goods or workers. This participation will require the creation of joint bodies responsible for managing and implementing the agreement.

Association agreements are a frequent tool for preparing the accession of a new Member State. The first association agreements were signed in 1961 and 1963 with Greece and Turkey, respectively, to facilitate their accession to the European Communities.[8] These pre-accession association agreements were followed by two others, Malta (1970) and Cyprus (1972),[9] which were an early template for the adoption of association agreements with accession candidate countries, later known as 'Europe agreements'. The validity of these agreements has been superseded by the accession of the signatory third countries to the Union; however, they paved the way for other association agreements with third countries seeking accession, specifically the Stabilisation and Association Agreements concluded with Albania, Bosnia and Herzegovina, Kosovo, Montenegro, Serbia, and North Macedonia.[10]

[5] Case C-130/10 *Parliament v Council* EU:C:2012:472.

[6] ibid, para 83.

[7] Case C-12/86 *Demirel* EU:C:1987:400, para 9.

[8] Agreement of 12 September 1963 establishing an Association between the European Economic Community and Turkey [1964] OJ 3687, and its Additional Protocol of 23 November 1970 [1972] OJ L293/3.

[9] Agreement of 5 December 1970, establishing an Association between the European Economic Community and Malta [1970] OJ L61/1 and Agreement of 19 December 1972, establishing an Association between the European Economic Community and the Republic of Cyprus [1973] OJ L133/3.

[10] Stabilisation and Association Agreements concluded with North Macedonia (2001), Albania (2006), Montenegro (2010), Serbia (2008), Bosnia and Herzegovina (2008, entered into force in 2015), and Kosovo (2015).

Association agreements may include provisions not only on access to the internal market but also on non-economic policies, as seen in the association agreement with Ukraine, which contains provisions on foreign and security policy.[11] An association agreement can also serve as the basis for a bilateral or multilateral system that creates a territorial area of integration, primarily economic, without establishing a new international organisation, but with equivalent levels of cooperation. This is illustrated by the European Economic Area, a mixed agreement concluded by the Union and the Member States on the one hand, and the Member States of the European Free Trade Association (EFTA), excluding Switzerland, on the other.[12]

Article 8 TEU refers to the 'preferential relations' that the Union may establish with 'neighbouring countries', 'aiming to create an area of prosperity and good neighbourliness, founded on the values of the Union and characterised by close and peaceful relations based on cooperation'. Article 8(2) TEU introduces a legal basis for the Union to conclude 'specific agreements' with neighbouring countries, in terms that echo those of Article 217 TFEU. In practice, relations with neighbouring countries have been structured through a variety of legal instruments, including association agreements concluded on the basis of Article 217 TFEU (notably with Ukraine), as well as cooperation agreements and other external action instruments relying, inter alia, on Article 212 TFEU. These instruments collectively underpin the European Neighbourhood Policy, launched in 2004 to provide a coherent framework for the Union's relations with its Eastern neighbours (Armenia, Azerbaijan, Georgia, Moldova and Ukraine, with cooperation with Belarus largely suspended)[13] and with the countries of the Southern Mediterranean (Algeria, Egypt, Israel, Jordan, Lebanon, Morocco and Tunisia, with cooperation with Libya and Syria remaining limited or suspended, and Palestine enjoying a specific status).

2.2. *Common Foreign and Security Policy*

The CFSP encompasses the Union's international policy in broad geostrategic terms, including global security and defence matters. This policy area does not include the Union's economic interests or the objectives of specific Union policies. Operating under the umbrella of the CFSP, the Union acts as a geopolitical player in the broadest sense of the term.

This policy is guided by the common principles and objectives applicable to the Union's actions, but its institutional design displays significant differences. As is well known, the CFSP was established in 1992 as the Second Pillar of the Union, functioning as an intergovernmental decision-making forum until the Lisbon Treaty entered into force in 2009. At present, the CFSP is one of the Union's policies that comprise its external action. However, it possesses so many institutional specificities that it is still regarded as an intergovernmental Union policy, a Second Pillar in disguise.

No matter how the CFSP is categorised, the reality is that the differences between this policy area and the rest reveal significant contrasts: the heightened role of national governments, mainly through the powers assumed by the European Council and the Council; the exclusion of legislative acts and the limitations on primacy and direct effect; the introduction of a specific institutional player, the High Representative, responsible for the

[11] Association Agreement between the European Union and its Member States, of the one part, and Ukraine, of the other part [2014] OJ L161/3.

[12] Agreement on the European Economic Area [1994] OJ L1/3.

[13] As of December 2025, Ukraine, Moldova, and Georgia are formally candidate countries engaged in accession negotiations, moving them primarily into the sphere of Enlargement Policy rather than Neighbourhood Policy, while Belarus has suspended its participation in the Eastern Partnership.

implementation of the CFSP; and the jurisdictional limitations of the Court of Justice, whose role is limited to monitoring compliance with Article 40 TEU and to the review of the legality of restrictive measures against natural or legal persons under Article 275, second paragraph TFEU.

The scope of the CFSP is broad, a feature that creates a substantial risk of overlap with other Union policies. For this reason, the Treaties introduce several criteria to clearly define the precise scope of the CFSP, a matter that has been the subject of interpretation in recent case law of the Court of Justice. Before the entry into force of the Lisbon Treaty, Union policies subject to the 'community method' held a certain pre-eminence vis-à-vis the CFSP. The Lisbon Treaty introduced Article 40 TEU, according to which the implementation of the CFSP 'shall not affect the application of the procedures and the extent of powers of the institutions laid down by the Treaties for the exercise of the Union competences' in Articles 3–6 TFEU. Immediately afterwards, the provision adds that the implementation of the policies referred to in Articles 3–6 TFEU shall not affect the application of the Union's powers under the CFSP. Article 40 TEU thus balances the scope of the CFSP with that of the policies subject to the 'community method', replacing the pre-Lisbon preeminence of Community policies with a mutual non-affectation clause and thereby preserving the autonomy of each area of Union action.[14]

As proof of the CFSP's autonomy, the Treaties establish a specific institutional framework that includes its own system of acts (Article 25 TEU), distinct decision-making procedures (Article 31 TEU), and its own institutional actors, such as the High Representative of the Union for Foreign Affairs and Security Policy and the Political and Security Committee (Articles 27 and 38 TEU). To a certain extent, the CFSP's institutional arrangement represents the opposite end of the traditional 'community method': unanimity voting is the norm and qualified majority voting is the exception; the Council and the European Council hold the upper hand in the decision-making process; and Union acts adopted under the CFSP are excluded from the legislative nature enjoyed by acts adopted under the ordinary procedures, with consequent limitations on their primacy and direct effect, as well as more limited judicial review. This 'thin' constitutional design is offset by the ambitious aims and commitments that the Member States have agreed upon within the CFSP, such as the explicit commitment to mutual support and solidarity among the Member States. Article 24(3) TEU states that Member States 'shall support the Union's external and security policy actively and unreservedly in a spirit of loyalty and mutual solidarity and shall comply with the Union's action in this area'. The provision further states that Member States 'shall work together to enhance and develop their mutual political solidarity [and shall] refrain from any action which is contrary to the interests of the Union or likely to impair its effectiveness as a cohesive force in international relations'. This provision reflects mainly a political commitment, as its enforcement cannot be monitored by either the Commission or the Court of Justice.

The Common Security and Defence Policy is an integral part of the CFSP, as outlined in Article 42(1) TEU. It is governed by the general rules of the CFSP and specific rules in the chapter on security and defence (Articles 42–46 TEU). The Common Security and Defence Policy

[14] Former Art 47 TEU, prior to its amendment by the Lisbon Treaty, stated as follows: 'Subject to the provisions amending the Treaty establishing the European Economic Community with a view to establishing the European Community, the Treaty establishing the European Coal and Steel Community and the Treaty establishing the European Atomic Energy Community, and to these final provisions, nothing in this Treaty shall affect the Treaties establishing the European Communities or the subsequent Treaties and Acts modifying or supplementing them.' This provision was interpreted by the Court of Justice, which confirmed the pre-eminence of 'Community' policies over the CFSP (Case C-91/05 *Commission v Council (ECOWAS)* EU:C:2008:288, paras 59–62). The post-Lisbon case law confirms the more balanced content of Art 40 TEU, which reflects the 'balancing test' traditionally used by the case law in matters of the selection of a legal basis, as confirmed in Case C-403/05 *Parliament v Commission* EU:C:2007:624.

articulates the civilian and military operational assets that enable the Union to participate in international missions, provided these missions are aimed at peacekeeping, conflict prevention and strengthening international security in accordance with the principles of the United Nations Charter.[15] Given the strategic role played by the armed forces of the Member States, the Common Security and Defence Policy establishes cooperative mechanisms to conduct international missions launched under this policy. To this end, a specific type of enhanced cooperation is introduced to facilitate the closer involvement of a limited number of Member States in the field of security and defence matters, known as 'permanent structured cooperation' (Article 46 TEU).[16]

2.3. *External Action Linked to the Union's Internal Policies*

As discussed in chapter four, the Union's internal policies also have an external dimension. The Union's ability to conduct a policy internally encompasses an implicit power to advance that competence in the international sphere. Articles 3(2) and 216 TFEU enshrine this external dimension of the Union's policies.

The external dimension of the Union's policies can be expressly provided for in the legal basis of the policy, or it may be deduced from the wording of the competences granted or exercised by the Union. In the first case, Article 79(3) TFEU provides an example, as it states that the Union may conclude agreements with third countries for the readmission of third-country nationals. Similarly, Article 219(4) TFEU affirms the power of the Union to conclude agreements in the field of economic and monetary policy. In the second case, which is more common in practice, there are numerous examples of Union actions in fields such as environmental policy, social policy, energy, or the Area of Freedom, Security and Justice, followed by external action in those fields.

3. Coherence of the Union's External Action: Multiple Competences, Unity of Action and Mutual Solidarity

The diversity of areas in the Union's external action poses a risk of dispersion and of lack of internal coherence. To prevent this outcome, Article 21(3) TEU states that the Union 'shall ensure consistency between the different areas of its external action and between these and its other policies'. This obligation mainly rests on the Council and the Commission, assisted by the High Representative of the Union for Foreign Affairs and Security Policy, who are tasked with ensuring such coherence and cooperate to this end. Despite the clarity of this provision, maintaining coherence in the Union's external action remains a challenge and will likely continue to be one as long as the CFSP keeps its institutional specificities. Despite the progress made since the creation of the Second Pillar in the Maastricht Treaty, Member States continue to prioritise the development of a European foreign policy through inter-governmental channels, such as those provided by the institutional framework of the CFSP.

[15] Examples of civilian missions are EUAM Ukraine (Advisory Mission), EULEX Kosovo, and EUMA Armenia. Examples of military operations are EUNAVFOR ASPIDES (Red Sea), Operation ALTHEA (Bosnia and Herzegovina), EUNAVFOR Atalanta, EUNAVFOR MED IRINI, and EUMAM Ukraine (Military Assistance Mission).

[16] A variety of Member States participate in permanent structured cooperation (PESCO) projects such as Military Mobility, the European Medical Command, the Integrated Unmanned Ground Systems 2 (iUGS 2), Cyber Rapid Response Teams (CRRT), and the European Patrol Corvette (EPC).

The horizontal nature and the emphasis on achieving unity of action are reflected in Article 22 TEU, which grants the European Council the authority to adopt decisions regarding the strategic interests and objectives of the Union, both in the CFSP and in other areas of the Union's external action. Consequently, it is the European Council's responsibility to ensure a comprehensive vision of the Union's foreign policy, covering all the areas outlined in section I.2 of this chapter. Paradoxically, this holistic vision of the Union's external action rests upon the institution that most clearly embodies the paradigm of intergovernmental integration, the European Council. Furthermore, decisions on strategic interests and objectives must be made by unanimity, the voting rule that the Community method seeks to avoid.

4. The Union's International Legal Personality

According to Article 47 TEU, the Union has legal personality. This provision is one of the novelties introduced by the Lisbon Treaty, which attributes legal personality to the Union as a whole. Prior to the adoption of Article 47 TEU, legal personality was vested in each of the three European Communities, while the Union enjoyed a functional legal personality recognised for the exercise of its tasks, but not formally conferred in any Treaty provision.[17] The Treaty of Amsterdam reinforced this perception by granting the Union the power to conclude international agreements with third countries and international organisations.[18] In these agreements, the Union appeared as a signatory party, recognising the functional dimension of legal personality not explicitly recognised in the Treaties. Article 47 TEU finally settles this matter by explicitly conferring legal personality on the Union as a whole.[19]

Article 47 TEU does not refer to the 'international' legal personality of the Union.[20] Following the reform introduced by the Lisbon Treaty, the Union's legal personality, apart from being attributed exclusively to the Union (with the exception of Euratom, which remains operational today), is granted to confer on the organisation the necessary capacity to act under both international and national law, and to be recognised as a legal subject within those legal systems. At the national level, Article 335 TFEU states that 'in each of the Member States, the Union shall enjoy the most extensive legal capacity accorded to legal persons under their laws'. Legal capacity enables the Union to enter into contracts with third parties to acquire or dispose of movable and immovable property, or to be a party or intervener in legal proceedings. This internal dimension, referred to in Article 335 TFEU, is also reflected in the Union's external dimension, granting the Union the legal capacity to conclude agreements with third countries and international organisations, as will be explained in section III.2 of this chapter. Furthermore, legal personality confers on the Union powers of representation on the international level, as explained in section III.1 of this chapter.

[17] See N Blokker, 'The Macro Level: The Structural Impact of General International Law on EU Law: International Legal Personality of the European Communities and the European Union: Inspirations from Public International Law' (2016) 35 *Yearbook of European Law* 494, and I Österdahl, 'The EU and the Member States, Other States and International Organisations: The Common European Security and Defence Policy After Nice' (2001) 70 *Nordic Journal of International Law* 395.

[18] Art 24 TEU, as introduced by the Treaty of Amsterdam.

[19] It should be noted that Euratom, still operational and with its Treaty in force, keeps its own legal personality under Art 184 EAEC, separate from the legal personality of the Union.

[20] Some of the landmark judgments of the Court of Justice relied on the '*international* legal personality' of the Communities of the time to support the primacy of Union law (*Costa/Enel*) or competence at the international level (*AETR*). The absence in the Treaty of the adjective 'international' does not seem to have altered this understanding of Union law.

5. The Institutional Framework for the Union's External Action

The Union's external action, as a general and horizontal policy covering various policy areas, is based on a common institutional framework and relies heavily on the actions of the European Council, the Council, and the Commission. The European Parliament and the Court of Justice have limited powers at different stages of the Union's external action. Additionally, specific actors are established to support the Union's external action, in particular the High Representative of the Union for Foreign Affairs and Security Policy ('the High Representative') and the European External Action Service (EEAS).

The High Representative is a creation of the Lisbon Treaty, entrusted with the mission of strengthening the coherence of the Union's external action and providing the organisation with a common voice in various policy areas with international connections. To ensure that the High Representative has an institutional anchorage that guarantees continuous presence and active participation in all relevant decision-making procedures, the High Representative's status is hybrid, simultaneously holding the roles of Vice-President of the European Commission and Chair of the Foreign Affairs Council. By wearing these 'two hats', the High Representative is in a privileged position to bring effectiveness, coherence, and unity of action to the Union's foreign policy. This role is outlined in Article 27 TEU, which enumerates the tasks of the High Representative in the CFSP, including powers to propose, implement decisions adopted by the European Council and the Council, represent the Union for matters relating to the CFSP, and conduct political dialogue with third parties on behalf of the Union.

The High Representative is assisted by the European External Action Service (EEAS), a functionally autonomous body of the Union composed of officials from the General Secretariat of the Council and the Commission, together with staff seconded from the diplomatic services of the Member States, serving either as EU officials or as temporary agents. Prior to the entry into force of the Lisbon Treaty, the Union's external representation was exercised primarily by the Commission through its network of delegations abroad, alongside more fragmented arrangements in the field of the CFSP. Following the establishment of the EEAS, external representation is now carried out through Union delegations operating under the authority of the High Representative, without prejudice to the Commission's continuing role in representing the Union in areas falling within its competences.[21]

It is important to emphasise that a significant part of the tasks of the High Representative and the EEAS is carried out within the framework of the CFSP, a Union policy that is separate from other policies that also form part of the Union's external action. Therefore, the common commercial policy, international economic cooperation, humanitarian aid, and the external dimension of the Union's internal policies are implemented in accordance with the institutional arrangements applicable to those policies, where the tasks of the High Representative coexist with those of the Commission and the Council. In this context, the High Representative and the EEAS are entrusted with ensuring the consistency and coherence of the Union's external action as a whole and are therefore closely associated, where appropriate, with the conception and coordination of policies with an international dimension outside the CFSP, without prejudice to the competences of the other Union institutions.

[21] On the evolution and development of the EEAS, see L Erkelens and S Blockmans, 'Setting up the European External Action Service: An Act of Institutional Balance' (2012) 8 *European Constitutional Law Review* 246.

II. THE UNION'S EXTERNAL COMPETENCES

1. The Principle of Conferral and the Existence of External Competence

European external action is organised through various competences expressly or implicitly conferred on the Union. Competence is the measure of the Union's power in each policy area, defining the scope of its sphere of action and, consequently, that of the Member States. As with internal policies, the Union's external action is subject to the principle of conferral enshrined in Articles 4(1) and 5 TEU, so that 'competences not conferred upon the Union in the Treaties remain with the Member States'.

The *existence* of competence in external matters is the premise upon which the Union's external actions are based. Before defining the scope of competence, it is essential to establish the existence of such competence of the Union, either *explicitly* or *implicitly*. Article 216(1) TFEU addresses this question by stating:

> The Union may conclude an agreement with one or more third countries or international organisations where the Treaties so provide or where the conclusion of an agreement is necessary in order to achieve, within the framework of the Union's policies, one of the objectives referred to in the Treaties, or is provided for in a legally binding Union act or is likely to affect common rules or alter their scope.

Explicit external competence must be recognised in the Treaties, as referred to in Article 216(1) TFEU when referring to the Union's powers to conclude agreements 'where the Treaties so provide'. Such express powers are conferred, inter alia, by Article 37 TEU (CFSP), Article 79(3) TFEU (agreements on the readmission of third-country nationals), Article 186 TFEU (cooperation in research and technological development), Article 207 TFEU (trade agreements within the framework of the common commercial policy), Article 212(3) TFEU (agreements on economic, financial and technical cooperation with third countries), and Article 219 TFEU (agreements on monetary policy).

By contrast, implied external competence is not expressly conferred by the Treaties but arises where the conclusion of an international agreement is necessary to achieve one of the objectives of the Union within the framework of its policies, where it is provided for in a legally binding Union act, or where it is likely to affect common rules or alter their scope (Articles 3(2) and 216(1) TFEU). This enumeration of cases in which the Union acts through implied competence stems from an evolution in case law, beginning with the *AETR* case,[22] which states that the Union must possess the necessary competence externally to ensure the proper functioning of the internal market and the effective implementation of its internal rules. Where these conditions are satisfied, the Union enjoys implied competence to conclude agreements with third countries and international organisations.

2. The Nature of External Competence: Exclusive, Shared, and CFSP Competence

For conceptual and practical reasons, it is important to distinguish between the *existence* and the *nature* of external competence. The former refers to the attribution of competence to the Union, which is the first logical step in determining the powers available to the Union. The latter is established once the existence of the competence has been confirmed, indicating the precise scope of that competence. While the existence of competence informs us whether the Union *can* act, the nature of the competence clarifies *how far* it can act.

[22] Case C-22/70 *Commission v Council* EU:C:1971:32.

The determination of the nature of external competence was systematised in the Lisbon Treaty, which introduced a typology of the Union's competences in Articles 2–6 TFEU, encompassing the competences that constitute the Union's external action. The Treaties distinguish between exclusive competences (Article 3 TFEU), shared competences (Article 4 TFEU), and supporting, coordinating, and complementary competences (Article 6 TFEU), while acknowledging the distinctiveness of the Union's competence in the areas of economic policy (Article 2(3) TFEU and Article 5 TFEU) and the CFSP (Article 2(4) TFEU). Further details and a description of the legal consequences of this typology can be found in chapter four of this book.

The Union's competences in the field of external action are primarily classified into three categories: exclusive competences (which include the common commercial policy and those derived from the Union's internal policies); shared competences (such as development cooperation, environment, and social policy); and competences within the CFSP.

2.1. *Exclusive Competences*

The Treaties confer on the Union two types of exclusive competences with an external dimension. First, Article 3(1)(e) TFEU establishes that the Union holds exclusive competence in the common commercial policy. Second, Article 3(2) TFEU codifies the Court of Justice's case law on implied external competences of the Union and enumerates the situations where the exercise of Union's internal competences gives rise to external exclusive competence.

2.1.1. Exclusivity in the Common Commercial Policy: Article 3(1)(e) TFEU

Reference has already been made to the Union's common commercial policy in section I.2.1.1 of this chapter. This policy falls under exclusive competence, as explicitly stated in Article 3(1)(e) TFEU. The Treaties did not expressly address the nature of the competence of the common commercial policy until the Lisbon Treaty; however, the case law of the Court of Justice had confirmed its exclusive character several decades earlier in Opinion 1/75 (OECD agreement) concerning international trade in goods.[23]

The Lisbon Treaty also introduced Article 207(1) TFEU, which defines the material scope of this exclusive competence, encompassing tariff rates, the conclusion of tariff and trade agreements related to trade in goods and services, and the commercial aspects of intellectual property, foreign direct investment, the achievement of uniformity in liberalisation measures, export policy, and measures to protect trade, such as those taken in the event of dumping or subsidies. This enumeration was updated in the Lisbon Treaty, now incorporating significant innovations, including services and 'the commercial aspects of intellectual property' (areas that were the subject of shared competence until the Lisbon Treaty).[24]

[23] Opinion *1/75* EU:C:1975:145 (OECD agreement) 1363–1365; Case C-41/76 *Donckerwolke and Others* EU:C:1976:182, para 32; Opinion *1/78* EU:C:1979:224 (international natural rubber agreement) paras 52–60; Opinion *2/91* EU:C:1993:106 (ILO Convention 170) para 8; and Case C-347/03 *Regione Autonoma Friuli-Venezia Giulia and ERSA* EU:C:2005:285, paras 71–83.

[24] On services, see Opinion 2/15 EU:C:2017:376 (Singapore) paras 33–37; and Case C-137/12 *Commission v Council* EU:C:2013:675, paras 51–77. On the commercial aspects of intellectual and industrial property, see Case C-389/15 *Commission v Council* (revised Lisbon settlement) EU:C:2017:798, paras 45–77; Opinion 2/15, cited above in this footnote, para 112; and Case C-414/11 *Daiichi Sankyo* EU:C:2013:520, paras 49–55. Note, however, that intellectual and industrial property only covers its 'commercial aspects'. In Opinion 3/15 EU:C:2016:657 (Marrakesh Treaty) paras 60–101, the Court of Justice held that the rules of an agreement concerning exceptions or limitations to the rights of reproduction, distribution and making available to the public to facilitate access to works for blind persons did not constitute 'commercial aspects' and therefore did not fall under the Union's exclusive competence.

The fact that the common commercial policy is an exclusive competence of the Union does not deprive the Member States of all powers to act in this area. The Court of Justice has been careful to define the scope of Article 3(1)(e) TFEU and to preserve a degree of action for the Member States. For instance, agreements in the common commercial policy whose financing is an essential component fall under the responsibility of the Member States, allowing them to participate in the negotiation and conclusion of such agreements.[25] Similarly, when a trade agreement provides for the creation of a dispute settlement mechanism whose decisions may remove disputes from the jurisdiction of the courts of the Member States, the competence for its conclusion is shared.[26] In transitional situations, Member States that began negotiating a trade agreement prior to the conferral of exclusive competence on the Union retain the authority to continue negotiations,[27] or their participation may be necessary to ensure the Union's own participation in the agreement.[28]

2.1.2. Exclusivity in the External Dimension of the Union's Internal Policies: Article 3(2) TFEU

Article 3(2) TFEU outlines the situations in which the exercise of a Union internal competence leads to exclusive external competence, reflecting the current state of the case law from the Court of Justice. The TFEU also addresses the existence of external competence in Article 216(1) TFEU, but with different terminology, which creates some confusion when interpreting these provisions. Thus far, these differences do not appear to have altered the traditional interpretation of the Union's external competence. On the contrary, by codifying in the Lisbon Treaty the types of situations recognised in the case law, the Treaties now provide considerably more clarity on the matter, and the Court of Justice has not yet drawn any inference from the differing terminology used in both provisions.

2.1.2.1. Conclusion of an International Agreement Provided for in a Legislative Act of the Union

The first sentence of Article 3(2) TFEU refers to situations where the Union has exclusive competence to conclude an international agreement, provided that its conclusion is preceded by a legislative act of the Union. Article 216(1) TFEU expands the scope of this competence by mentioning a 'legally binding Union act', omitting any reference to the act's 'legislative' nature.

This situation finds its roots in Opinion 1/94 (GATS and TRIPS), where the Court of Justice stated:

> Whenever the Community has included in its internal legislative acts provisions relating to the treatment of nationals of non-member countries or expressly conferred on its institutions powers to negotiate with non-member countries, it acquires exclusive external competence in the spheres covered by those acts.[29]

The proviso introduced in Article 3(2) TFEU, which limits this situation to the provisions contained in a Union 'legislative act', exists *due* to the concurrent competences of the Union, where Member States retain areas of regulatory competence even after the Union has exercised

[25] Opinion 1/78 EU:C:1979:224 (international agreement on natural rubber) para 60.

[26] Opinion 2/15 EU:C:2017:376 (Singapore) paras 290–92.

[27] Opinion 1/78 EU:C:1979:224 (international agreement on natural rubber) para 60.

[28] Joined Cases C-3/76, C-4/76 and C-6/76 *Cornelis Kramer and Others* EU:C:1977:114, paras 34–45.

[29] Opinion 1/94 EU:C:1994:384 (GATS and TRIPS agreements), para 95. See also Case C-468/98 *Commission v Sweden* EU:C:2002:626, para 83.

its competences. This applies to shared competences of the Union that do not preclude Member States from exercising their own, such as research, technological development, space, development cooperation, and humanitarian aid. It should be noted that Article 4(3)–(4) TFEU emphasises that the exercise of these competences by the Union does not prevent Member States from exercising theirs.

The same applies to the supporting, coordinating, or complementary competences provided for in Article 6 TFEU, the implementation of which by the Union excludes any harmonisation of the laws and regulations of the Member States (second subparagraph of Article 2(5) TFEU). It is therefore reasonable to conclude that the Union's exclusive external competence cannot, as a rule, cover those policies subject to the Union's supporting, coordinating, or complementary competences, which include, inter alia, the protection and improvement of human health, culture, education, tourism, or industry.

2.1.2.2. Competence Necessary to Enable the Union to Exercise its Internal Competence

The second situation provided for in Article 3(2) TFEU establishes the exclusive competence of the Union where 'the conclusion of an international agreement . . . is necessary to enable the Union to exercise its internal competence'. This scenario reflects a principle of complementarity between internal and external Union competence, as external action is necessary and complementary to the Union's internal policy. This exclusive competence is complementary to, but may exist in parallel with, internal competence, allowing the Union to conclude international agreements even in the absence of fully exercised internal competence. To the extent that the agreement is necessary to attain the objectives of the internal competence, the Union is entitled to conclude the agreement.

The notion of complementarity was introduced in Opinion 1/76, where the Court of Justice emphasised the following:

> Although the internal [Union] measures are only adopted when the international agreement is concluded and made enforceable . . . , the power to bind the [Union] vis-à-vis third countries nevertheless flows by implication from the provisions of the Treaty creating the internal power and in so far as the participation of the [Union] in the international agreement is, as here, necessary for the attainment of one of the objectives of the [Union].[30]

In this case, external competence was essential, as the Community at the time aimed to rationalise the economic situation in inland waterway transport in the Rhine and Moselle basins. There was a significant presence of vessels flying the Swiss flag, a third country, on these waterways. To introduce measures to rationalise transport on these waterways, it was necessary to conclude agreements with the Swiss Confederation so that the resulting regulation would encompass all economic operators in the market. In this case, the Court of Justice considered that, although there was no explicit legal basis in a specific Treaty provision conferring express external competence, the conclusion of an agreement with Switzerland was crucial for achieving the objectives of the Community's common transport policy.

The Lisbon Treaty added nuance to the terms related to this situation as developed in case law, broadening them and introducing vaguer language. The original approach in case law linked the Union's exclusive external competence to an existing and specific internal competence that was inextricably connected to the envisaged external measure. In other words,

[30] Opinion *1/76* (EU:C:1977:63) (draft agreement establishing a European laying-up fund for inland waterway vessels) para 4.

the principle of complementarity was to be interpreted strictly, ensuring that the connection between the internal and external dimensions of competence was clear and unequivocal.[31] However, Article 216(1) TFEU has arguably broadened the scope of the principle by referring to the competence to conclude an agreement necessary to achieve, 'within the framework of the Union's policies, one of the objectives referred to in the Treaties'. This reference to the 'framework' of the policy, rather than the policy itself, may imply that complementarity also encompasses implied internal competences, paralleling those outlined in Article 352 TFEU.[32]

2.1.2.3. Competence Likely to Affect Common Rules or Alter their Scope

The third situation referred to in Article 3(2) TFEU provides for the exclusive competence of the Union to conclude agreements when they are 'likely to affect common rules or alter their scope'. This provision closely follows the wording of Article 216(1) TFEU and reproduces the *AETR* case law from 1971, which affirms the Union's implicit competence in external matters when it exercises its competences internally through the adoption of 'common rules'. The wording of the *AETR* ruling as follows:

> In particular, each time the [Union], with a view to implementing a common policy envisaged by the Treaty, adopts provisions laying down common rules, whatever form these may take, the Member States no longer have the right, acting individually or even collectively, to undertake obligations with third countries which affect those rules.
>
> As and when such common rules come into being, the [Union] alone is in a position to assume and carry out contractual obligations towards third countries affecting the whole sphere of application of the [Union] legal system.
>
> With regard to the implementation of the provisions of the Treaty the system of internal [Union] measures may not therefore be separated from that of external relations.[33]

As pointed out by De Baere, the *AETR* doctrine is a consequence of the principle of primacy applied to the Union's external action.[34] This formulation enables the adoption of 'common rules' at the internal level to display their pre-emptive effect not only over national law but also concerning the external actions of the Member States. If a Member State chooses to enter into an international agreement with a third country on a matter previously regulated by a 'common rule' of the Union, such conduct will breach Union law, since it encroaches on the exclusive competence of the Union as set out in Article 3(2) TFEU.

However, different nuances have been added to the *AETR* doctrine over time, to the point of circumscribing much of its potential. Firstly, the Court of Justice has refined the definition of 'common rules' by anchoring it in acts of Union secondary legislation. In Opinion 2/15 (Singapore), the Court of Justice clarified the *AETR* doctrine with regard to 'common rules', finding that

> provisions of secondary law which the Community, now the European Union, has progressively laid down are 'common rules' and that, when the European Union has thus exercised its internal competence, it must, in parallel, have exclusive external competence in order to prevent the Member States from entering into international commitments that could affect those common rules or alter their scope.[35]

[31] Opinion 1/94 EU:C:1994:384 (GATS and TRIPS Agreements) paras 86 and 100; and Opinion 2/92 EU:C:1995:83 (Third Revised OECD Decision) para 32. On the strict interpretation of the principle of complementarity, see G De Baere, *Constitutional Principles of EU External Relations* (Oxford University Press, 2008) 55–58.

[32] See M Cremona, 'External Relations of the European Union: The Constitutional Framework for International Action' in P Craig and G De Búrca (eds), *The Evolution of EU Law*, 3rd edn (Oxford University Press, 2021).

[33] Case C-22/70 *Commission v Council (AETR)* EU:C:1971:32, paras 17–19.

[34] De Baere (n 31).

[35] Opinion 2/15 EU:C:2017:376 (Singapore) para 233.

Therefore, the *AETR* doctrine mainly applies in situations where the Union has exercised its competence through secondary legislation. The mere existence of competence does not pre-empt the actions of the Member States, as confirmed by Article 2(2) TFEU when it refers to the shared competences of the Union: 'The Member States shall exercise their competence to the extent that the Union has not exercised its competence'. Consequently, in areas of shared competence of the Union, the *AETR* doctrine will in principle apply once the Union has exercised its competence through the adoption of secondary legislation.

Likewise, the *AETR* doctrine does not produce absolute pre-emption of an entire policy area solely because the Union has exercised its competence. On the contrary, total field pre-emption occurs only when the Union 'has achieved complete harmonisation' in a given area.[36] In cases of partial or fragmented harmonisation, where only certain aspects of an area of policy are covered, the *AETR* doctrine will only apply to those aspects included in the Union's secondary legislation. Member States will retain the power to negotiate international agreements with third countries in areas not covered by the Union. This dimension of the *AETR* doctrine is illustrated in the *Open Skies* case law,[37] in which the Commission brought multiple infringement actions against Member States that had concluded bilateral air transport agreements with the United States. While Union secondary legislation regulated access to air traffic routes and licensing conditions within the internal market, it did not govern the allocation of traffic rights on intra-EU routes to non-EU carriers, nor did it regulate the operating licences of such carriers within the Union. In the absence of complete harmonisation in these areas, the Court of Justice held that the Union's internal competence in the field of air transport had not been fully exercised. Accordingly, the Court upheld the Commission's actions only to the extent that the bilateral agreements encroached on matters that had been fully harmonised by Union common rules, while allowing Member States to retain external competence in respect of aspects falling outside the scope of Union regulation.

2.2. *Shared Competences*

Articles 2(2) and 4 TFEU define the Union's shared competences. In the policy areas listed in Article 4 TFEU, the Union is empowered to legislate and to adopt legally binding acts; however, Member States may exercise their competence only to the extent that the Union has not exercised its own. As discussed above, the exercise by the Union of an internal shared competence may give rise to exclusive external competence, in accordance with Article 3(2) TFEU. The Treaties nevertheless identify specific situations in which, despite the exercise of internal competence by the Union, external competence must continue to be exercised concurrently by the Union and the Member States within the same policy field. This is the case where Union legislation establishes only minimum harmonisation, where the Treaties expressly provide for parallel competences, or where the Union has exercised its competence only partially or has been conferred competence with respect to only certain aspects of a given policy area.

First, in certain policy areas the Treaties confer upon the Union the power to establish only minimum standards, thereby allowing Member States to maintain or introduce higher levels of

[36] See Opinion *1/94* EU:C:1994:384 (GATS and TRIPS Agreements) para 96; Opinion *2/92* EU:C:1995:83 (Third Revised OECD Decision) para 33; and the judgments in Case C-467/98 *Commission v Denmark* EU:C:2002:625, para 84; and Case C-476/98 *Commission v Germany* EU:C:2002:631, para 110.

[37] Case C-466/98 *Commission v United Kingdom* EU:C:2002:624; Case C-467/98 *Commission v Denmark* EU:C:2002:625; Case C-468/98 *Commission v Sweden* EU:C:2002:626; Case C-469/98 *Commission v Finland* EU:C:2002:627; Case C-471/98 *Commission v Belgium* EU:C:2002:628; Case C-472/98 *Commission v Luxembourg* EU:C:2002:629; Case C-475/98 *Commission v Austria* EU:C:2002:630; and Case C-476/98 *Commission v Germany* EU:C:2002:631.

protection in their domestic legal orders. This approach is illustrated by Article 193 TFEU, which provides that environmental protection measures adopted pursuant to Article 192 TFEU 'shall not prevent any Member State from maintaining or introducing more stringent protective measures'. In such circumstances, the Union's external action is characterised by shared competence, in which Union regulation at the internal level and Member State action at the international level coexist and operate concurrently within the limits of their respective competences.[38]

Secondly, the Treaties also provide for situations of parallel competence between the Union and the Member States. Unlike cases of minimum harmonisation, parallel competence does not entail the establishment of a minimum threshold above which Member States may raise their domestic levels of protection. Rather, in areas of parallel competence the Union acts without prejudice to the continued capacity of the Member States to engage externally, including by negotiating in international fora and concluding international agreements. This approach is reflected in Articles 209(2) TFEU and 212(3) TFEU, which govern development cooperation and economic, financial and technical cooperation with third countries respectively, and which expressly provide that the Union's competence in these fields is 'without prejudice to the Member States' competence to negotiate in international bodies and to conclude international agreements'. Similarly, Article 211 TFEU implicitly recognises the coexistence of Union and Member State competences by providing that, within their respective spheres of competence, both may cooperate with third countries and international organisations. This parallel nature of competence is further confirmed by Article 4(4) TFEU in the fields of development cooperation and humanitarian aid, which states that while the Union has competence to carry out activities and conduct a common policy, the exercise of that competence 'shall not result in Member States being prevented from exercising theirs'. A further illustration of parallel competence is found in Article 219(3) TFEU on agreements concerning monetary or foreign exchange regime matters, which provides that, without prejudice to Union competence and Union agreements concerning economic and monetary union, Member States may negotiate in international bodies and conclude international agreements.

Thirdly, the Union may have exercised its competence only partially, or the Treaties may confer competence on the Union with respect to only certain aspects of a broader policy field. In such circumstances, where an international agreement contains provisions falling both within the Union's competence and within the competences retained by the Member States, the Union will exercise its competence in parallel with that of the Member States,[39] resulting in the conclusion of a mixed agreement, as explained in chapter seven of this book.

Where the Union acts externally in areas of shared competence, both the Union and the Member States play a central role in the negotiation of international agreements. The outcome of such negotiations must ensure that the agreements concluded are compatible with Union law. Even in situations of shared competence, the Union and the Member States remain bound by the principle of sincere cooperation. In this respect, the Court of Justice has consistently held that Article 4(3) TEU, which enshrines the principle of sincere cooperation, applies across all fields of Union activity, including those involving shared competence, both internally and externally:

[38] Opinion *2/91* EU:C:1993:106 (ILO Convention 170), paras 12 and 18; and Case C-246/07 *Commission v Sweden* EU:C:2010:203, paras 72–73.

[39] Opinion *1/78* EU:C:1979:224 (international natural rubber agreement) para 60; and Opinion *1/08* EU:C:2009:739 (GATS amendment) para 150.

> [The] duty of sincere cooperation is of general application and does not depend either on whether the [Union] competence concerned is exclusive or on any right of the Member States to enter into obligations towards non-member countries.[40]

The principle of sincere cooperation plays a central role in ensuring that Member States act in a coordinated and consistent manner when engaging internationally in areas of shared competence. Although the allocation of competences does not, as such, preclude Member States from concluding international agreements in fields where the Union lacks competence or where Member State participation is permitted, they remain subject to a duty of coordination and restraint. In particular, Member States must refrain from actions that could undermine the effectiveness or uniform application of Union common rules. Accordingly, even where Member States act within their own sphere of competence in policy areas also exercised by the Union, their international action is circumscribed by the obligations flowing from Article 4(3) TEU.

2.3. *CFSP Competences*

A distinction must be drawn between the Union's conventional external competences, discussed in the preceding sections, and its external competences in the field of the CFSP. This distinction is warranted for two principal reasons. First, the historical development of the CFSP reveals structural and functional differences when compared with policies governed by the so-called 'Community method'. The CFSP originated as an expressly intergovernmental domain and has evolved into a distinct policy area governed by its own rules and procedures, as laid down in the Treaties, under a separate Title devoted to the Union's external action in the TEU. Secondly, by establishing a separate legal framework for the CFSP, the Treaties have effectively removed it from the general system for the attribution and classification of competences set out in Articles 2–6 TFEU. As a result, the typology of competences applicable to other areas of Union action (namely exclusive, shared, and supporting, coordinating or complementary competences) does not readily apply to the CFSP. It may therefore be argued that CFSP competences constitute a *sui generis* category, governed by a distinct constitutional regime laid down in Title V TEU.

The *sui generis* character of the common foreign and security policy reflects the fundamentally intergovernmental logic that continues to govern its operation. Any residual doubt in this regard is dispelled by Declarations Nos 13 and 14 annexed to the Treaties, which expressly reaffirm the intergovernmental nature of the CFSP by emphasising, inter alia, the continued application of its 'specific rules and procedures'. Significantly, these Declarations make no reference to the allocation or nature of CFSP competences as such, focusing instead on the distinct procedural and institutional framework governing this policy area.

It is true that Article 4(1) TFEU provides that 'the Union shall share competence with the Member States where the Treaties confer on it a competence which does not relate to the areas referred to in Articles 3 and 6 [TFEU]'. Since the CFSP is not expressly mentioned in that provision, it might be argued that it falls within the residual category of shared competences under Article 4(1) TFEU. Such an interpretation, however, does not reflect the intention of the Member States as expressed in the current Treaties. As evidenced by Declarations Nos 13 and 14

[40] Case C-266/03 *Commission v Luxembourg* EU:C:2005:341, para 58; Case C-433/03 *Commission v Germany* EU:C:2005:462, para 64; Case C-246/07 *Commission v Sweden* EU:C:2010:203, para 71, and Case C-271/23 *Commission v Hungary* EU:C:2026:45, paras 155–59.

annexed thereto, and by the deliberate placement of the CFSP outside the TFEU, the Member States chose to subject this policy area to a distinct constitutional regime. The inclusion of the CFSP in Title V TEU, with its own objectives, rules and procedures, and characterised by pronounced intergovernmental features, confirms that the CFSP cannot be classified as a shared competence within the meaning of Article 2(2) TFEU. Rather, it constitutes a *sui generis* competence, governed autonomously by the specific provisions of Title V TEU.[41]

III. IMPLEMENTATION OF THE UNION'S EXTERNAL ACTION

1. International Representation

The Union has legal personality and legal capacity, both within its Member States and internationally.[42] These features imply that the Union decides who assumes its external representation, a task that the Treaties have allocated to various institutional players.

Firstly, the Treaties assign to the Council, particularly to the Foreign Affairs Council, the responsibility of elaborating the Union's external action in accordance with the strategic guidelines set by the European Council. The Council also ensures the unity, consistency and effectiveness of the Union's actions.[43] This mandate includes the authority to define the general direction of the Union's policy in the international arena, in a way that aligns with the power of the European Council and the Council to set the political direction.

Secondly, the Commission is entrusted with the Union's external representation, 'with the exception of the common foreign and security policy, and other cases provided for in the Treaties'.[44] These derogations indicate that the Commission has been tasked with the Union's external representation only in the fields of policy subject to the 'community method', while representation in the area of the CFSP is a task for the High Representative and the President of the European Council. The Treaties provide that the High Representative 'shall conduct the Union's common foreign and security policy' and contribute with proposals to the development of that policy, which he or she carries out as mandated by the Council.[45] Likewise, the President of the European Council

> shall, at his level and in that capacity, ensure the external representation of the Union on issues concerning its common foreign and security policy, without prejudice to the powers of the High Representative of the Union for Foreign Affairs and Security Policy.[46]

Another institutional player worth mentioning is the Union's delegations in third countries and international organisations, as outlined in Article 221 TFEU, which states that 'Union delegations shall be placed under the authority of the High Representative of the Union for Foreign Affairs and Security Policy. They shall act in close cooperation with Member States' diplomatic and consular missions'.

This complex institutional framework confirms that the Union's international representation is a shared task among various actors. While the design and conception of the Union's external action, understood in its broadest sense, lie with the European Council and the

[41] See P Craig, *The Lisbon Treaty: Law, Politics and Treaty Reform* (Oxford University Press, 2010) 182.

[42] Art 47 TEU and Art 335 TFEU.

[43] Art 16(6) TEU, third para.

[44] Art 17(1) TEU. This exclusion has been interpreted restrictively in the case law, as evidenced in Case C-551/21 *Commission v High Representative and Council* EU:C:2024:281, para 73.

[45] Art 18(2) TEU.

[46] ibid, Art 15(6).

Council, its implementation is the task of the High Representative with the support of the Union's delegations in third countries and international organisations. However, the Union's external representation, as a manifestation of the power to act internationally on behalf of the Union, is twofold: in the CFSP, representation is vested in the High Representative (and, in some cases, in the President of the European Council), whereas in other areas, it is entrusted to the Commission. The two-tier nature of the Union's international representation is reflected in Decision 2010/427, which establishes the organisation and functioning of the European External Action Service (EEAS). Article 5 of Decision 2010/427 states that the Head of each Delegation 'shall receive instructions from the High Representative and the EEAS', but in 'areas where the Commission exercises the powers conferred upon it by the Treaties, the Commission may, in accordance with Article 221(2) TFEU, also issue instructions to delegations'.

In areas of shared competence, the external representation of the Union must be closely coordinated with that of the Member States, and vice versa. To this end, Article 34(1) TEU provides that Member States 'shall coordinate their action in international organisations and at international conferences . . . , shall uphold the Union's positions in such forums [and the] High Representative of the Union for Foreign Affairs and Security Policy shall organise this coordination'. This mandate also extends to the diplomatic and consular missions of the Member States under Article 35 first paragraph TEU, reflecting the principle of sincere cooperation between the Union and its Member States.

In the case of the Union's representation in international court proceedings, the Court of Justice has confirmed the applicability of Article 335 TFEU. Therefore, this provision, which enshrines the Commission's power to appear in national courts on behalf of the Union, also applies to its participation in international court proceedings, where the Union is represented by the Commission.[47] In such cases, the Commission is not required to submit its pleadings to the Council for prior approval, as the Court of Justice has confirmed that the Commission does not express a position 'in' a body set up by an international agreement, but 'before' an international court.[48] Therefore, even though Article 218(9) TFEU is not applicable to representation in international court proceedings, it cannot be ruled out that, if the Commission defines a policy position on a new issue in its written or oral pleadings, that position must receive prior approval from the Council.

2. Treaty-making Power

Article 218 TFEU establishes a common procedure for concluding international agreements of the Union, including CFSP agreements. By referring to 'agreements', Article 218 TFEU applies to 'any undertaking entered into by entities subject to international law which has binding force, whatever its formal designation'.[49] The procedure for concluding agreements reflects international practice and the specific competences of the Union's external action. Consequently, unlike the Union's legislative procedures, the Commission does not hold a monopoly on initiative, since the power to conclude international agreements is assigned to the Council. Similarly, the stages involved in concluding an international agreement, which will be elaborated upon, include specificities applicable solely to CFSP agreements, even though Article 218 TFEU, as a general rule, applies to all agreements.

[47] See Case C-73/14 *Council v Commission* EU:C:2015:663, para 58.
[48] ibid, para 63.
[49] Opinion *1/75* EU:C:1975:145 (rules on local expenditure) 1360–61.

2.1. *Negotiation*

According to Article 218(3) TFEU, the negotiation of an agreement is preceded by a recommendation from the Commission submitted to the Council. This recommendation usually results from prior informal discussions with the third country or countries concerned, as well as with the Council. When the envisaged agreement relates exclusively or principally to the CFSP, the recommendation will be submitted to the Council by the High Representative. This power of recommendation by the Commission or the High Representative should not be confused with the Commission's right of legislative initiative provided for in Articles 293–294 TFEU.

Once the recommendation has been submitted, the Council adopts a decision authorising the opening of negotiations and, depending on the subject of the proposed agreement, nominates either the Union negotiator or the head of the Union's negotiating team.[50] The Council may also address directives to the negotiator and designate a special committee, which must be consulted during the negotiations. Therefore, the Council has considerable discretion, both in choosing whether the Commission or the High Representative will lead the negotiations[51] and in establishing the substantive limits and red lines that will guide the Union's negotiating team. This decision does not constitute a delegated act within the meaning of Article 290 TFEU but rather specific instructions subject only to Article 218 TFEU. Moreover, the Court of Justice has ruled that the Council decision produces legal effects in the relations between the Union and its Member States and among the Union's institutions.

2.2. *Signature and Conclusion of the Agreement*

The Council, based on a proposal from the negotiator, adopts a decision authorising the signing of the agreement. This decision is made by qualified majority or unanimously, depending on the situation outlined in Article 218(8) TFEU. In such a decision, the Council may determine the provisional application of the agreement prior to its entry into force. Provisional application is governed by international rules on the law of treaties, particularly Article 25 of the 1969 Vienna Convention. Furthermore, the European Parliament is 'immediately and fully informed at all stages of the procedure'.[52]

Once the agreement's signature has been authorised, the Council, acting on a proposal from the negotiator, may adopt a decision concluding the agreement through which the Union signifies its consent to be bound by the international agreement. As this is the primary act expressing the Union's consent, its adoption by decision is subject to specific voting rules within the Council and the participation of the European Parliament. However, the act of signature and the designation of the signatory fall, as a general rule, on the Commission pursuant to the sixth sentence of Article 17(1) TEU. On this point, the Court of Justice has stated that:

> [T]he steps necessary for the purpose of the signing of an international agreement after that signing has been authorised by the Council, including the step of designating the signatory, outside the CFSP, fall within the scope of the Commission's power to 'ensure the Union's external representation', unless the EU Treaty or the FEU Treaty allocate the power to organise that signing to another institution of the European Union. The latter reservation, reflected in the phrase 'other cases provided for in the Treaties', constitutes, as the Advocate General observes in point 72 of her Opinion and as follows

[50] Art 218(3) TFEU.

[51] This discretion does not exist when the Treaties specifically provide for the Commission's power to conduct negotiations, as in the case of the common commercial policy (Art 207(3) TFEU) or agreements on monetary or foreign exchange rate matters with one or more third States or international organisations (Art 219(3) TFEU), in which case the Commission plays a specific role, as it must be 'fully associated with the negotiations'.

[52] Art 218(10) TFEU.

from the wording of the sixth sentence of Article 17(1) TEU, an exception to the Commission's powers provided for in that provision.[53]

Article 218(8) TFEU stipulates that the Council acts by qualified majority throughout the procedure. However, the decision is made by unanimity in the following cases:

- agreements covering an area where unanimity is required for the adoption of a Union act;[54]
- association agreements;[55]
- agreements referred to in Article 212 TFEU with the states which are candidates for accession;[56]
- the agreement on accession of the Union to the European Convention for the Protection of Human Rights and Fundamental Freedoms (which enters into force after it has been 'approved' by the Member States in accordance with their respective constitutional requirements);[57] and
- common commercial policy agreements in the following fields:
  - trade in services and the commercial aspects of intellectual property, as well as foreign direct investment, where the Council acts unanimously when such agreements include provisions for which unanimity is required for the adoption of internal rules; [58]
  - trade in cultural and audiovisual services, where these agreements risk prejudicing the Union's cultural and linguistic diversity;[59] and
  - trade in social, education and health services, where these agreements risk seriously disturbing the national organisation of such services and prejudicing the responsibility of Member States to deliver them.[60]

Article 218(6) TFEU categorises the areas in which the European Parliament participates in the adoption of decisions to conclude international agreements into three types. First, the European Parliament is excluded from the procedure for concluding agreements that relate 'exclusively' to the CFSP.[61] Second, the European Parliament must give its consent in the following cases:

- association agreements;[62]
- the agreement on accession of the Union to the European Convention for the Protection of Human Rights and Fundamental Freedoms;[63]
- agreements establishing a specific institutional framework by organising cooperation procedures;[64]
- agreements with important budgetary implications for the Union;[65]

[53] Case C-551/21 *Commission v High Representative and Council* EU:C:2024:281, para 77.
[54] Art 218(8) TFEU.
[55] ibid.
[56] ibid.
[57] ibid.
[58] ibid, Art 207(4).
[59] ibid.
[60] ibid, Art 207(4)(a).
[61] ibid, Art 218(6).
[62] ibid, Art 218(6)(a)(i).
[63] ibid, Art 218(6)(a)(ii).
[64] ibid, Art 218(6)(a)(iii).
[65] ibid, Art 218(6)(a)(iv).

- agreements covering fields to which either the ordinary legislative procedure applies, or the special legislative procedure where consent by the European Parliament is required.[66]

In all other cases, the European Parliament is to be consulted.[67]

Overall, the European Parliament has gained substantial powers in the Union's external action, especially after the entry into force of the Lisbon Treaty, as most international agreements fall within the areas subject to either an ordinary or a special legislative procedure.

2.3. *Prior Judicial Review of International Agreements and the Jurisdiction of the Court of Justice to Deliver Opinions*

An international agreement can be subject to indirect judicial review by challenging the Council decision through which the Union grants its consent. Litigation concerning the content of an international agreement can lead to legal uncertainty at the international level and may undermine trust among the signatory states. To avoid this scenario, Article 218(11) TFEU establishes a preliminary consultative mechanism whereby the Court of Justice is empowered to deliver an Opinion on the compatibility with the Treaties of any envisaged international agreement that has not yet been concluded.[68] This procedure results in a binding Opinion that prevents the Council from proceeding with conclusion if the Court of Justice declares the agreement to be incompatible with the Treaties.[69]

The opinion procedure can only be initiated by the Member States, the European Parliament, the Council, or the Commission. The subject matter of the Opinion is an 'agreement envisaged' (a draft, not a final agreement), allowing the Court of Justice to deliver its position on a text that has been drafted but not yet concluded, or on a draft that has not yet been finalised and whose terms remain unprepared for negotiations. However, the Union has several alternatives available to it, the legality of which it must be aware of before participating in the negotiations.[70] The approach adopted by the case law is pragmatic, enabling the Court to examine 'agreements envisaged' at very different stages of maturity:

> [A] request for an Opinion can be submitted to the Court before the commencement of international negotiations, where the subject-matter of the envisaged agreement is known, even though there are a number of alternatives still open and differences of opinion on the drafting of the texts concerned, if the documents submitted to the Court make it possible for the Court to form a sufficiently certain judgment on the question raised by the Council . . . and that the admissibility of a request for an

[66] ibid, Art 218(6)(a)(v).

[67] ibid, Art 218(6)(b).

[68] The Court of Justice has emphasised that Art 218(11) TFEU 'has the aim of forestalling complications which would result from legal disputes concerning the compatibility with the Treaties of international agreements binding upon the European Union. . . . A possible decision of the Court, after the conclusion of an international agreement binding upon the European Union, to the effect that such an agreement is, by reason either of its content, or of the procedure adopted for its conclusion, incompatible with the provisions of the Treaties could not fail to provoke, not only in the internal European Union context, but also in that of international relations, serious difficulties and might give rise to adverse consequences for all interested parties, including third countries' (Opinion 1/09 EU:C:2011:123 (unified patent dispute settlement system), paras 47–48; see also Opinion 3/94 EU:C:1995:436 (framework agreement on bananas), para 17; Opinion 2/94, EU:C:1996:140 (accession of the Community to the ECHR) para 3; Opinion 1/08 EU:C:2009:739 (amendment of the GATS) para 107).

[69] Although CFSP agreements are subject to the procedure provided for in Art 218 TFEU, it should be noted that Art 275 TFEU provides that the Court of Justice 'shall not have jurisdiction with respect to the provisions relating to the common foreign and security policy nor with respect to acts adopted on the basis of those provisions'. Therefore, although a CFSP agreement can be subject to indirect review by means of an opinion procedure, in principle the Court of Justice will not be able to rule on its compatibility with the provisions of Ch 2 of Title V TEU, curtailing the effectiveness of the procedure provided for in Art 218(11) TFEU.

[70] Opinion *1/94* EU:C:1994:384 (GATS and TRIPS Agreements) para 12; Opinion *2/94* EU:C:1996:140 (accession of the Community to the ECHR) paras 16–18; and Opinion *1/09* (n 68), para 53.

> Opinion cannot be challenged on the ground that the Council has not yet adopted the decision to open the international negotiations . . .[71]

The case law distinguishes between requests for an Opinion aimed at determining the Union's competence and those intended to clarify the compatibility between the proposed agreement and a substantive provision of the Treaties. In the latter scenario, the request for an Opinion must provide sufficient information about the content of the agreement itself; otherwise, the Court will declare the request inadmissible.[72]

Article 218(11) TFEU does not specify a time limit for requesting an Opinion, although there is an implicit time constraint: the conclusion of the agreement by the Union. Once the Council has given its consent, the Court of Justice no longer has jurisdiction to deliver an Opinion, as the agreement will no longer be an agreement 'envisaged', but rather an existing and consented agreement. From that point onwards, the procedural course of action to judicially review the agreement will be through an action for annulment or a preliminary reference of validity, though in proceedings that concern not the agreement itself, but rather the Council's decision to conclude it.[73]

2.4. *Specific Cases*

2.4.1. Mixed Agreements

When competence in a policy area is shared between the Union and the Member States, the responsibility for concluding an agreement may rest with both, resulting in a mixed agreement. The need to present a consistent international position requires the Member States and the Union to collaborate closely during the negotiation and conclusion processes, as well as when implementing the obligations undertaken.[74]

Although there are no specific Treaty provisions concerning the conclusion of mixed agreements, and even though the general rules of Article 218 TFEU also apply to them, their negotiation and ratification are governed by specific practices. In particular, the negotiation process involves a more intense participation from the representatives of the Member States, coupled with closer coordination by the Commission in its role as the Union's negotiator. The most significant challenge arises during conclusion, which requires consent of all 27 Member States in accordance with their respective constitutional requirements. The delays caused by the multiple national approval processes often justify the provisional application of the mixed agreement pending its formal signature and entry into force. Consequently, the Court of Justice has emphasised the obligation of sincere cooperation among the Member States when concluding a mixed agreement.[75] These duties emerge once the Council authorises the Commission to negotiate a mixed agreement, marking the start of concerted action between the Union and the Member States at the international level. The case law has emphasised that, from that moment onwards, the Member States have:

[71] Opinion *1/09* (n 68) para 53; Opinion *1/78* EU:C:1979:224 (international agreement on natural rubber) para 34; and Opinion *2/94* (n 68) para 13.

[72] Opinion *2/94* EU:C:1996:140, para 19; Opinion *2/13* EU:C:2014:2454, para 147; and Opinion *1/20* (Modernised Energy Charter Treaty), EU:C:2022:485, paras 39–40.

[73] See, inter alia, Case C-122/95 *Germany v Council* EU:C:1998:94, para 42; and Case C-266/16 *Western Sahara Campaign UK* EU:C:2018:118, paras 50–51, where the Court held as follows: 'it must be held that, in a situation where, as in this case, the Court has received a request for a preliminary ruling concerning the validity of an international agreement concluded by the European Union, that request must be understood as relating to the EU act approving the conclusion of that international agreement'.

[74] *Ruling 1/78* EU:C:1978:202 (IAEA Convention on the Protection of Nuclear Material, Facilities and Transport) paras 34–36 (by analogy with the Euratom Treaty); Opinion *2/91* EU:C:1993:106 (ILO Convention 170) para 36; Opinion *1/94* EU:C:1994:384 (GATS and TRIPS agreements) para 108; and Case C-25/94 *Commission v Council* EU:C:1996:114, para 48.

[75] Case C-804/79 *Commission v United Kingdom* EU:C:1981:93, para 28.

> [I]f not a duty of abstention on the part of the Member States, at the very least a duty of close cooperation between the latter and the [Union] institutions in order to facilitate the achievement of the [Union] tasks and to ensure the coherence and consistency of the action and its international representation.[76]

2.4.2. CFSP Agreements

Article 37 TEU confers on the Union the power to conclude agreements with one or more States or international organisations 'in areas covered by [Chapter 2 of Title V TEU on CFSP]'. Despite this reference, CFSP agreements are governed by the rules on conclusion provided in Article 218 TFEU.

Having said that, it should be noted that Article 218 TFEU contains several specificities applicable only to CFSP agreements. First, the power to submit recommendations to the Council does not lie with the Commission but with the High Representative, both in cases of decisions to open negotiations and in instances of suspending the application of an agreement or establishing positions to be adopted on the Union's behalf in a body set up by an agreement. Likewise, Article 218(6) TFEU excludes the active participation of the European Parliament in CFSP agreements, as long as they are agreements that 'exclusively' concern the CFSP (although the right of the European Parliament to be immediately and fully informed at all stages of the procedure is preserved). Furthermore, in the case of CFSP agreements, the Council will act unanimously and not by qualified majority, as mandated by Article 218(8) TFEU.

These procedural specificities of CFSP agreements can lead to institutional tensions, particularly with the European Parliament. The fact that Article 218(6) TFEU excludes this institution when the agreement 'exclusively' concerns the CFSP has raised several questions regarding the scope of agreements adopted under Article 37 TEU and those covered by other policies. The Court of Justice has confirmed that, in such cases, the standard criteria for selecting legal bases apply. Therefore, to ensure symmetry between the institutional balance for the Union's internal and external actions, the legal basis applicable to the relevant policy field will determine the procedures to follow, establishing a correspondence between the procedures for the adoption of an internal act and those applicable to the conclusion of international agreements.[77]

The Court of Justice has summarised its doctrine on the determination of legal bases in areas connected to the CFSP in the following terms:

> [A] decision by which the Council establishes the position to be adopted on behalf of the European Union . . . which concerns exclusively the CFSP must, in principle, be adopted unanimously, in accordance with the second subparagraph of Article 218(8) TFEU. On the other hand, if such a decision comprises several components or pursues a number of objectives, some of which fall within the CFSP, the voting rule applicable for its adoption must be determined in the light of its main or predominant purpose or component. Thus, if the main or predominant purpose or component of the decision falls within a field in respect of which unanimity is not required for the adoption of an EU measure, that decision must, in accordance with the first subparagraph of Article 218(8) TFEU, be adopted by qualified majority.[78]

[76] Case C-266/03 *Commission v Luxembourg* EU:C:2005:341, para 60; Case C-433/03 *Commission v Germany* EU:C:2005:462, para 66; and Case C-246/07 *Commission v Sweden* EU:C:2010:203, para 75.

[77] Case C-658/11 *Parliament v Council* EU:C:2014:2025, para 57.

[78] Case C-244/17 *Commission v Council* (partnership agreement with Kazakhstan) EU:C:2018:662, para 38; and Case C-180/20 *Commission v Council* (agreement with Armenia) EU:C:2021:658, para 35.

2.4.3. Administrative Arrangements

The proliferation of legal instruments has led to the emergence of new types of 'agreements' that can display legal effects and bind the Union in the international sphere. The Union's institutions often sign memoranda of understanding, *modi vivendi*, or administrative arrangements with various international organisations or third countries. As long as these instruments do not produce legal effects, they are not considered 'international agreements' under the meaning of Article 216 TFEU and can be concluded by the Union's institutions, bodies, offices, or agencies. However, when these instruments, regardless of their formal title, have the potential to produce legal effects and bind the Union at the international level, they are regarded as 'international agreements' subject to the procedural rules for concluding agreements set out in Article 218 TFEU. To ascertain whether the instrument in question produces legal effects, the decisive criterion is the intention of the parties.[79]

The Court of Justice ruled on this matter in *France v Commission*,[80] an action for annulment where France challenged an agreement concluded between the Commission and the United States Government concerning the implementation of competition policy. In this case, the Court of Justice found that the agreement produced legal effects, and it was therefore considered an 'international agreement'.[81] Only the Union has legal personality and the legal capacity to bind itself through international agreements. As a result, the Commission lacked the power to bind the Union by entering into an international agreement without following the procedure laid down in Article 218 TFEU.[82]

2.4.4. Decisions Taken in the Framework of Bodies Set up by an International Agreement

The Union participates in the activities of international organisations. It may be bound, as a subject of international law, by decisions adopted within a body that is part of an international organisation. In such cases, the Union's position within an international body is determined in accordance with Article 218(9) TFEU, which specifies the Council's power to adopt a decision establishing 'the positions to be adopted on the Union's behalf in a body set up by an agreement, when that body is called upon to adopt acts having legal effects'. This provision states that the power rests with the Commission when the decision pertains to a policy other than the CFSP. When the decision pertains to the CFSP, the recommendation is submitted by the High Representative; in all other cases, the recommendations stem from the Commission.[83]

IV. THE COMMON SECURITY AND DEFENCE POLICY

According to Article 24(1) TEU, the Union's competence in the CFSP covers 'all areas of foreign policy and all questions relating to the Union's security, including the progressive framing of a common defence policy that might lead to a common defence'. Section 2 of Chapter 2, Title V TEU, includes provisions on the Common Security and Defence Policy (CSDP).

The CSDP is described in Article 42(1) TEU as an 'integral part' of the CFSP. It is conceived to provide the Union with an operational capacity drawing on civilian and military assets to be

[79] Case C-233/02 *France v Commission* EU:C:2004:173, para 42.

[80] Case C-327/91 *France v Commission* EU:C:1994:305.

[81] ibid, para 23.

[82] ibid, paras 36–42.

[83] Although Art 218(9) TFEU does not explicitly refer to an 'exclusive or principal' involvement in the CFSP, paragraph 3 of this provision refers to those terms when settling the division of tasks between the Commission and the High Representative at the time of submitting recommendations to the Council.

used on missions outside the Union for peace-keeping, conflict prevention and strengthening international security in accordance with the principles of the United Nations Charter.

The CSDP is conceived as an evolving policy, currently at a nascent stage, but with the possibility of developing into a common defence policy in the future. For the time being, the CSDP acts as a framework in which a common Union defence policy is 'progressively framed', but the aim is to promote and eventually create a genuinely common Union defence. The decision to move to a common defence is left to a unanimous decision of the European Council, which shall then recommend to the Member States the adoption of such a decision in accordance with their respective constitutional requirements.

Article 42(1) TEU refers to the 'tasks' that the Council may entrust to a group of Member States which are willing and have the necessary capability to undertake them, by the use of civilian and military means. This list is further detailed in Article 43(1) TEU, which includes:

- joint disarmament operations;
- humanitarian and rescue tasks;
- military advice and assistance tasks;
- conflict prevention and peace-keeping tasks;
- tasks of combat forces in crisis management, including peace-making and post-conflict stabilisation.

A special reference is made to the fight against terrorism in Article 43(1) TEU, as all the tasks listed above can be employed to contribute to this fight and to support third countries in combating terrorism in their territories.

The CSDP relies on the civilian and military capabilities of the Member States to undertake its tasks. However, Member States are under an obligation to 'undertake progressively to improve their military capabilities'. To this end, the Treaties refer to various means intended to support the Member States in that endeavour, as well as to strengthen the CSDP:

- *Military structures*: to implement the CFSP decisions and measures with an impact in the CSDP, the Political and Security Committee exercises, under the responsibility of the Council and of the High Representative, the political control and strategic direction of the crisis management operations referred to in Article 43 TFEU,[84] assisted by the Military Committee[85] and the Military Staff.[86] The Military Committee is composed of the Chiefs of Defence of the Member States. The Military Staff's mission is to perform 'early warning, situation assessment and strategic planning for the tasks referred to in Article 43 TEU, including identification of European national and multinational forces and to implement policies and decisions as directed by the European Union Military Committee'.
- *Multinational forces*: Since 2003, the Union has launched multinational military operations in North Macedonia, Bosnia and Herzegovina, the Democratic Republic of the Congo, Chad and the Central African Republic, Somalia and the Horn of Africa, the Gulf of Aden, Mali, Mozambique, the Central and Southern Mediterranean (Libya), the Red Sea, and missions related to Ukraine.
- *CFSP bodies and specialised entities*:

[84] Art 38 TEU.

[85] Council Decision 2001/79/CFSP of 22 January 2001 setting up the Military Committee of the European Union [2001] OJ L27/4.

[86] Council Decision 2001/80/CFSP of 22 January 2001 on the establishment of the Military Staff of the European Union [2001] OJ L27/7.

- *The European Defence Agency*: a *sui generis* CFSP/CSDP body of the Union now expressly anchored in Article 45 TEU and governed by Council Decision (CFSP) 2015/1835.[87] It has legal personality and operates on an intergovernmental basis, acting under the Council's authority and political supervision, with the High Representative having a leading role within the Agency's structure and serving as the essential link with the Council; participation reflects differentiated engagement by Member States. Its tasks focus on supporting Member States and the Council in improving defence capabilities for crisis management, promoting and enhancing European armaments cooperation (including collaborative programmes), strengthening defence research and technology and the European defence technological and industrial base, and contributing to the identification of capability shortfalls and priorities (including through capability planning instruments and support to cooperative frameworks such as permanent structured cooperation).
- *The Satellites Centre*: a specialised CFSP body with legal personality, originating from a WEU satellite centre and established as an EU body by Council Joint Action 2001/555/CFSP, operational from 1 January 2002 and now governed by Council Decision 2014/401/CFSP.[88] It is a *sui generis* operational support entity (rather than an 'agency' in the classic TFEU administrative sense) subject to political supervision within the CFSP framework and operational direction by the High Representative. Its core task is to support CFSP/CSDP decision-making and action, including crisis-management missions and operations, by providing, at the request of the Council or the High Representative, geospatial intelligence products and services derived from the exploitation of relevant space assets and collateral data, including satellite and aerial imagery, and related services.
- *The Institute for Security Studies*: a specialised CFSP body with legal personality, originally established by Joint Action 2001/554/CFSP and continued under Council Decision 2014/75/CFSP,[89] functioning as the Union's in-house analytical and research centre for CFSP/CSDP and related external action. Under the Decision, the Political and Security Committee exercises political supervision (under the responsibility of the Council) while the High Representative gives operational direction, without prejudice to the Institute's intellectual independence and operational autonomy. Its core task is to contribute to the development of EU strategic thinking and to provide strategic analysis, policy research and forward-looking studies in support of EU decision-making, while fostering informed debate and a shared European strategic culture.

The Treaties introduce various coordinating measures between the CSDP and other policy areas and other international obligations of the Member States. In the case of the North Atlantic Treaty Organization (NATO), the second subparagraph of Article 42(7) TEU states that commitments and cooperation in the CSDP 'shall be consistent with commitments under the North Atlantic Treaty Organisation, which, for those States which are members of it, remains the foundation of their collective defence and the forum for its implementation.' The Union has developed a close strategic partnership with NATO, reflected in a set of permanent political, operational and institutional arrangements between the two organisations.[90] Taken together, these instruments

[87] Council Decision (CFSP) 2015/1835 of 12 October 2015 defining the statute, seat and operational rules of the European Defence Agency (recast) [2015] OJ L266/55.

[88] Council Decision 2014/401/CFSP of 20 June 2014 on the EU Satellite Centre [2014] OJ L221/42.

[89] Council Decision 2014/75/CFSP of 10 February 2014 on the European Union Institute for Security Studies [2014] OJ L41/13.

[90] The foundational permanent arrangement is the EU–NATO Declaration on ESDP of 16 December 2002, followed by the 'Berlin Plus' agreements of 2003, as well as the agreement between the European Union and the North Atlantic Treaty Organisation on the Security of Information [2003] OJ L80/35.

ensure that Union action under the CSDP is structurally consistent with NATO commitments, while preserving the Union's capacity for autonomous crisis-management operations.

Article 42(7) TEU also introduces a mutual defence clause. This provision is the successor to Article V of the modified 1948 Brussels Treaty of 1954, which governed the Western European Union (WEU), and established a collective defence obligation among its members. When the WEU was progressively wound down and its functions absorbed into the Union framework, the Lisbon Treaty codified this legacy in Article 42(7) TEU, introducing for the first time a legally binding mutual assistance obligation under Union primary law, while preserving the intergovernmental character of defence policy and respecting the specific security and defence policies of certain Member States, including those with neutrality traditions, as well as the primacy of NATO for its members. In contrast with other provisions on mutual support, such as Article 222 TFEU, the mutual defence clause of Article 42(7) TEU does not establish an EU-level operational response. Its implementation is decentralised, typically through bilateral or ad hoc measures outside CSDP missions, with EU institutions playing only a limited coordinating role.[91]

In practice, the mutual defence clause has been formally invoked only once, by France in November 2015 following the terrorist attacks in Paris. France chose to activate Article 42(7) TEU rather than NATO's Article 5 collective defence clause, framing the request as one for flexible, tailor-made assistance. The response took the form of bilateral and ad hoc contributions by other Member States, including military support in external theatres, intelligence cooperation, and relief of French forces engaged in ongoing operations, rather than the deployment of a CSDP operation under the institutional framework of the Union.

A group of Member States can undertake closer cooperation in the field of security and defence. To this end, Articles 42(6) and 46 TEU provide for the participation of Member States in 'permanent structured cooperation' (PESCO). This format for closer cooperation is a specific form of enhanced cooperation applied to the CSDP and is based on the experience of previous military cooperation initiatives among groups of Member States prior to the Lisbon Treaty.[92] It is a voluntary initiative of each Member State and requires the fulfilment of 'criteria' and the making of necessary 'binding commitments' on military capabilities, as set out in Protocol No 10, on permanent structured cooperation established by Article 42 TEU. Member States wishing to participate in PESCO shall notify their intention to the Council and to the High Representative of the Union for Foreign Affairs and Security Policy. Within three months following the notification, the Council shall adopt a decision by qualified majority establishing permanent structured cooperation and determining the list of participating Member States.[93] All Member States that do not participate in PESCO have a right, if they wish to join the initiative at a later stage, to notify their intention to the Council and to the High Representative.[94] The reverse situation is provided for in Article 46(4) TEU: if a participating Member State no longer fulfils the criteria or is no longer able to meet the commitments under permanent

[91] F Fazio, 'The EU's Mutual Defence Clause: Legal and Strategic Considerations on Article 42(7) TEU in Light of the War in Ukraine' (2025) 8 *Nordic Journal of European Law* 1.

[92] See, for example, the case of the Franco-German brigade, set up on 12 January 1989, later developed into the 'Eurocorps', currently in place and available to both the Union and NATO with its deployable land forces headquarters and ability to plan and command large-scale military operations. Eurocorps has its headquarters in Strasbourg and it is governed by the Treaty on the European Corps and the Status of its Headquarters, signed in Brussels on 22 November 2004, which entered into force on 26 February 2009. On Eurocorps and its interactions with the CSDP, see A Miglio and G Perotto, 'EU Law and Inter Se Agreements in Defence Matters: Mapping the Interplay' (2022) 14 *Perspectives on Federalism* 1.

[93] Art 46(2) TEU.

[94] ibid, Art 46(3).

structured cooperation, the Council may, by qualified majority, adopt a decision suspending the participation of the Member State concerned. For the purposes of this Article, the qualified majority is defined in accordance with Article 238(3)(a) TFEU, which requires the vote of the participating Member States only.

PESCO was activated in December 2017 by the adoption of Council Decision 2017/2315.[95] In Annex I, the Decision enumerates the principles of PESCO, described as

> an ambitious, binding and inclusive European legal framework for investments in the security and defence of the EU's territory and its citizens [that] also provides a crucial political framework for all Member States to improve their respective military assets and defence capabilities through well-coordinated initiatives and concrete projects based on more binding commitments.

Annex II enumerates the binding common commitments in the five areas set out in Article 2 of Protocol No 10, including, inter alia, the regular increase of defence budgets in real terms, increasing joint and 'collaborative' strategic defence capabilities projects, developing the interoperability of national military forces, and increasing efforts in the cooperation on cyber defence.[96]

PESCO operates through individual projects, in which Member States voluntarily decide to participate. Participating Member States that intend to propose an individual project shall inform the other participating Member States in due time before presenting their proposal, to gather support and give them the opportunity to join in collectively submitting the proposal.[97] By early 2026, PESCO encompassed a total of 68 projects in areas such as training, land systems, air systems, maritime, cyber and space. The decisions and recommendations of the Council within the framework of PESCO, other than those provided for in Article 46(2)–(5) TEU on participation in and withdrawal from the initiative, shall be adopted unanimously, the unanimity being constituted only by the votes of the representatives of the participating Member States.

GENERAL BIBLIOGRAPHY

Blockmans, S, and Koutrakos, P (eds), Research Handbook on the EU's Common Foreign and Security Policy (Edward Elgar, 2018).

Butler, G, *Constitutional Law of the EU's Common Foreign and Security Policy: Competence and Institutions in External Relations* (Hart, 2019).

Butler, G, and Wessel, R (eds), *EU External Relations Law: The Cases in Context* (Hart, 2022).

Cardwell, P, *EU External Relations Law and Policy in the Post-Lisbon Era* (TMC Asser Press, 2012).

Chamon, M and Govaere, I (eds), *EU External Relations Post-Lisbon: The Law and Practice of Facultative Mixity* (Brill Nijhoff, 2020).

De Baere, G, *Constitutional Principles of EU External Relations* (Oxford University Press, 2008).

— *EU International Relations Law*, 2nd edn (Hart, 2015).

Eeckhout, P, *EU External Relations Law*, 2nd edn (Oxford University Press, 2011).

Koutrakos, P, *The EU Common Security and Defence Policy* (Oxford University Press, 2013).

Van Vooren, B, *EU External Relations Law and the European Neighbourhood Policy* (Routledge, 2012).

Van Vooren, B, and Wessel, R, *EU External Relations Law* (Cambridge University Press, 2014).

Wouters, J, Hoffmeister, F, De Baere, G, and Ramopoulos, T, *The Law of EU External Relations: Cases, Materials, and Commentary on the EU as an International Legal Actor*, 3rd edn (Oxford University Press, 2021).

[95] Council Decision (CFSP) 2017/2315 of 11 December 2017 establishing Permanent Structured Cooperation (PESCO) and determining the list of participating Member States [2017] OJ L331/57.

[96] The full list of PESCO projects is available online at www.pesco.europa.eu.

[97] Art 5 Decision (CFSP) 2017/2315.

FURTHER READING

The Union's External Policies

Cremona, M, *Structural Principles in EU External Relations Law* (Hart 2018).
Eckes, C, *EU Powers Under External Pressure. How the EU's External Actions Alter its Internal Structures* (Oxford University Press, 2019).
Hoffmeister, F, 'Strategic autonomy in the European Union's external relations law' (2023) 60 *Common Market Law Review* 667.
Kübek, G, and Mancini, I, 'EU Trade Policy between Constitutional Openness and Strategic Autonomy' (2023) 19 *European Constitutional Law Review* 518.
Larik, J, *Foreign Policy Objectives in European Constitutional Law* (Oxford University Press, 2016).
Lonardo, L, 'Common Foreign and Security Policy and the EU's External Action Objectives: An Analysis of Article 21 of the Treaty on the European Union' (2018) 14 *European Constitutional Law Review* 584.
Moser, C, *Accountability in EU Security and Defence. The Law and Practice of Peacebuilding* (Oxford University Press, 2020).
Wessel, R, *The European Union's Foreign and Security Policy: A Legal Institutional Perspective* (Kluwer Law, 1999).

The Union's External Competences and Legal Bases

Cardwell, PJ, 'On "Ring-Fencing" the Common Foreign and Security Policy in the Legal Order of the European Union' (2015) 64 *Northern Ireland Legal Quarterly* 443.
Eckes, C, 'Common Foreign and Security Policy: The Consequences of the Court's Extended Jurisdiction' (2016) 22 *European Law Journal* 492.
van Elsuwege, P, 'EU External Action after the Collapse of the Pillar Structure: In Search of a New Balance between Delimitation and Consistency' (2010) 47 *Common Market Law Review* 987.
Sánchez-Taberno, SR, 'The Choice of Legal Basis and the Principle of Consistency in the Procedure for Conclusion of International Agreements in CFSP Contexts: Parliament v Council (Pirate-Transfer Agreement with Tanzania)' (2017) 54 *Common Market Law Review* 899.
Wessel, RA, 'Integration and Constitutionalisation in EU Foreign and Security Policy' in R Schütze (ed), *Governance and Globalization: International and European Perspectives* (Cambridge University Press, 2018) 339.

Implementation of the Union's External Action

de Baere, G and Wessel, RA, 'EU Law and the EEAS: Of Complex Competences and Constitutional Consequences' in J Bátora and D Spence (eds), *The European External Action Service: European Diplomacy Post-Westphalia* (Palgrave Macmillan, 2015) 175.
Delgado Casteleiro, A, *The International Responsibility of the European Union* (Cambridge University Press, 2016).
Driessen, B, 'Provisional Application of International Agreements by the EU' (2020) 57 *Common Market Law Review* 1693.
Gatti, M, *European External Action Service: Promoting Coherence through Autonomy and Coordination* (Brill Nijhoff, 2016).
Helwig, N, 'The High Representative of the Union: The Quest for Leadership in EU Foreign Policy' in J Bátora and Spence, D (eds), *The European External Action Service: European Diplomacy Post-Westphalia* (Palgrave Macmillan, 2015) 87.
Mendez, M, *The Legal Effects of EU Agreements* (Oxford University Press, 2013).
Neframi, E, *Les accords mixtes de la Communauté européenne: aspects communautaires et internationaux* (Bruylant, 2007).

The Common Security and Defence Policy

Duke, S and Ojanen, H, 'Bridging Internal and External Security: Lessons from the European Security and Defence Policy' (2006) 28 *Journal of European Integration* 477.

Fazio, F, 'The EU's Mutual Defence Clause: Legal and Strategic Considerations on Article 42(7) TEU in Light of the War in Ukraine' (2025) 8 *Nordic Journal of European Law* 1.

Graf von Kielmansegg, S, 'The Meaning of Petersberg: Some Considerations on the Legal Scope of ESDP Operations' (2007) 44 *Common Market Law Review* 629.

Kurowska, X (ed), *Explaining the EU's Common Security and Defence Policy* (Palgrave Macmillan, 2023).

Lonardo, L, *EU Common Foreign and Security Policy. Between Law and Geopolitics* (Springer, 2023).

Miglio, A and Perotto, G, 'EU Law and Inter Se Agreements in Defence Matters: Mapping the Interplay' 14(3) *Perspectives on Federalism* (2022) 1.

Naert, F, *International Law Aspects of the EU's Security and Defence Policy* (Intersentia, 2010).

Pagani, F, 'A New Gear in the CFSP Machinery: Integration of the Petersberg Tasks in the Treaty on European Union' (1998) 9 *European Journal of International Law* 737.

17

Economic and Monetary Union

I. BACKGROUND AND CREATION OF THE ECONOMIC AND MONETARY UNION

THE ECONOMIC AND Monetary Union (EMU) is one of the most significant achievements of European integration. While the establishment of the internal market was the primary objective of the European Communities, a subsequent stage of integration consisted in the creation of a genuinely European economic and monetary policy, designed to complement the internal market and supported by its own institutional and legal framework. This transition has posed considerable challenges for the Member States, as it entails a substantial transfer of sovereign powers and a corresponding loss of fiscal and monetary autonomy, both of which are central to national governance. In exchange, participation in the EMU enables Member States to strengthen the Union's overall economic and political capacity, enhance the functioning of the internal market, and stimulate economic activity. Undertakings benefit from a more integrated and stable economic environment, which provides stronger incentives to operate and invest within the Union. Ultimately, the Union can achieve its objectives only insofar as it promotes the prosperity and well-being of its citizens. In this respect, the EMU plays a pivotal role in realising those objectives and in unlocking the Union's full economic and political potential for the benefit of Member States, citizens, and businesses alike.

The creation of the EMU has required an intensive and sustained collective effort spanning several decades and continuing to the present day.[1] The origins of the EMU can be traced back to 1969, when the heads of state or government, meeting in The Hague, identified the establishment of a European economic and monetary union as a new objective of the integration process. That objective was further developed in the Werner Report, published on 8 October 1970, which proposed the gradual establishment of the EMU within a 10-year timeframe, through a multi-stage process. The report envisaged, inter alia, the liberalisation of capital movements, the progressive fixing of exchange rates, and the creation of a system of full convertibility of national currencies. However, this ambitious project was effectively brought to a halt by the early 1970s currency crises, following the United States' decision in August 1971 to abandon the gold-dollar convertibility that underpinned the Bretton Woods system. This development triggered a prolonged period of instability in international currency markets and interrupted the momentum towards monetary integration in Europe.[2]

[1] H James, *Making the European Monetary Union: The Role of the Committee of Central Bank Governors and the Origins of the European Central Bank* (Harvard University Press, 2012) 36ff; H Ungerer, *A Concise History of European Monetary Integration: From EPU to EMU* (Quorum, 1997).

[2] E Mourlon-Druol, 'History of an Incomplete EMU' in F Amtenbrink and C Herrmann (eds), *The EU Law of Economic and Monetary Union* (Oxford University Press, 2020) 25.

After several unsuccessful attempts to stabilise national currencies against the US dollar, the Member States took a decisive step in 1979 with the establishment of the European Monetary System (EMS). The EMS was based on a system of fixed but adjustable exchange rate parities, operating through central rates expressed against the newly created European Currency Unit (ECU), which itself was calculated on the basis of a weighted average of the participating currencies. Despite repeated speculative attacks, the EMS maintained a significant degree of monetary stability within the internal market over an extended period. Its relative success reinforced the perception that the creation of an economic and monetary union was essential to ensure monetary stability and to safeguard the achievements of European integration. As the integration process moved beyond the common market, particularly following the adoption of the Single European Act and the internal market programme in 1985-1986, it became increasingly apparent that currency conversion costs and exchange rate volatility posed a serious threat to deeper economic integration. These challenges were further intensified by the progressive liberalisation of capital movements, which underscored the need for a predictable and stable monetary framework in the long term. It was against this background that the Hanover European Council of June 1988 decided to establish a committee, chaired by Jacques Delors, tasked with examining the concrete steps leading towards economic and monetary union.[3]

The Delors Report set out a detailed roadmap for the establishment of the EMU, structured around three successive stages, each pursuing three core objectives: the coordination of Member States' economic policies; the introduction of common budgetary rules to impose limits on national deficits; and the creation of an independent institution responsible for conducting European monetary policy. The report envisaged the implementation of the EMU over a period of approximately 10 years. The first stage focused on the liberalisation of capital movements between Member States and ran from 1 July 1990 to 31 December 1993. The second stage, spanning from 1 January 1994 to 31 December 1998, aimed to strengthen the convergence of national economic policies and enhance cooperation among national central banks, including their progressive reform towards institutional independence. The third stage involved the adoption of a common monetary policy within a newly established Eurosystem, as well as the introduction of euro banknotes and coins.

The Delors Report was implemented broadly in accordance with its original timetable and structure. During the first stage, which began on 1 July 1990, significant measures were adopted to advance the completion of the internal market and to develop accompanying policies, with particular emphasis on reducing economic disparities between Member States. This phase also introduced the initial steps towards economic policy coordination and the liberalisation of capital movements.[4] The second stage commenced on 1 January 1994 and was marked by the adoption of binding rules on economic policy coordination. During this period, the currency composition of the ECU was frozen, and the European Monetary Institute was established with the task of preparing the transition to Stage Three of the EMU. At this stage, the Madrid European Council of December 1995 also decided that the future common currency would be called the 'euro', a designation that became effective in December 1995.[5]

The third and final stage of the implementation of the EMU constituted the most decisive phase of the EMU. This stage applied only to those Member States that had satisfied

[3] On the Delors Report, see K Dyson and K Featherstone, *The Road to Maastricht: Negotiating Economic and Monetary Union* (Oxford University Press, 1999); and Mourlon-Druol (n 2) 30–33.

[4] Council Decision 90/141/EEC of 12 March 1990 on the achievement of progressive convergence of economic policies and performance during the first stage of economic and monetary union [1990] OJ L078/23; and Council Directive 88/361/EEC of 24 June 1988 for the implementation of Article 67 of the Treaty [1988] OJ L178/5.

[5] Presidency Conclusions, European Council, Madrid, 15–16 December 1995.

the convergence criteria and whose domestic legislation had been brought into conformity with the requirements of the Treaties, namely Belgium, Germany, Spain, France, Ireland, Italy, Luxembourg, the Netherlands, Austria, Portugal, and Finland. Accordingly, on 1 January 1999, the national currencies of those Member States were irrevocably fixed and replaced by the euro as the official currency, although its practical use was initially confined to non-cash transactions and payment transfers. On 1 January 2001, Greece joined the group of Member States participating in the common currency, following the Council's determination that it fulfilled the necessary conditions. The physical circulation of euro banknotes and coins began on 1 January 2002. From that point onwards, the European Central Bank (ECB) was fully entrusted with the conduct of the Union's monetary policy in the euro area, as additional Member States progressively adopted the euro: Slovenia on 1 January 2007; Cyprus and Malta on 1 January 2008; Slovakia on 1 January 2009; Estonia on 1 January 2011; Latvia on 1 January 2014; Lithuania on 1 January 2015; Croatia on 1 January 2023; and Bulgaria on 1 January 2026. All remaining Member States are legally obliged to adopt the euro once they fulfil the convergence criteria, with the sole exception of Denmark, which benefits from a formal opt-out pursuant to Protocol No 16 on certain provisions concerning Denmark.

II. THE CONSTITUTIONAL FRAMEWORK OF THE ECONOMIC AND MONETARY UNION

1. The Union's Competences in Economic and Monetary Matters

The competences that define the EMU reflect the delicate institutional and political balances forged during the negotiations of the 1980s and 1990s, which ultimately culminated in the Maastricht Treaty and the creation of the common currency. Although the EMU is rooted in economic integration, the decision to adopt the euro was inherently political, shaped by the fall of the Berlin Wall and the collapse of the post-war bloc system that had dominated European politics in the second half of the twentieth century. The strength of the German Deutsche Mark exerted significant pressure on the national currencies of the European Communities, while simultaneously conferring a degree of economic influence on a single Member State that others did not possess. The reunification of East and West Germany, and its acceptance by the other Member States – particularly France and the United Kingdom – was accompanied by Germany's decision to relinquish its powerful national currency, thereby paving the way for the establishment of a common European currency.

The historical context facilitated the emergence of a European currency that was strongly inspired by the institutional and economic design of the German Deutsche Mark, which placed primary emphasis on price stability and relied on a highly independent central bank.[6] Achieving this objective required conferring exclusive competence in monetary policy on the Union; absent such exclusivity, the institution created for this purpose would have faced significant difficulty operating in a policy area as sensitive and politically exposed as monetary policy. This approach ultimately prevailed, leading to the establishment of an independent monetary authority, modelled on the Bundesbank's tradition of independence: the ECB, together with the European System of Central Banks (ESCB).

[6] On the German imprint on the institutional design of European monetary policy, see M Sandbu, *Europe's Orphan. The Future of the Euro and the Politics of Debt* (Princeton University Press, 2015) 12ff; and M Brunnermeier, H James and J-P Landau, *The Euro and the Battle of Ideas* (Princeton University Press, 2015) 40ff.

A monetary policy without an accompanying economic policy is like an aeroplane without any wings. If economic conditions across the Member States do not converge and are not guided by a framework of common policy coordination, there is a serious risk that monetary policy will prove ineffective and ultimately fail to achieve its objectives. Economic policy has a pronounced fiscal dimension, encompassing both revenue (taxation) and expenditure (budgetary decisions). Fiscal matters are closely intertwined with national sovereignty, as well as with the capacity of national political systems to propose and implement distinct policy choices. This dimension is particularly significant in representative democracies, where political parties make commitments to voters that are subsequently reflected in the implementation of electoral programmes or manifestos. The creation of the Economic Union sought to strike a balance between these competing considerations. Its purpose is to coordinate the economic policies of the Member States while preserving a substantial degree of political autonomy and decision-making authority at national level. To that end, the Economic Union is equipped with instruments designed to ensure common standards of public debt and budgetary discipline across the Union, without depriving national institutions of their capacity to design and implement their own economic policies.

The outcome was the creation of a *sui generis* competence specifically tailored to the Economic Union, now reflected in Article 5 Treaty on the Functioning of the European Union (TFEU). That provision states that 'Member States shall coordinate their economic policies within the Union', and empowers the Council to adopt appropriate measures, 'in particular broad guidelines for these policies'. Article 5(2) and (3) TFEU also extend coordination to the employment and social policies of the Member States. The use of the term 'coordination' is legally significant. It makes clear that economic union does not constitute either an exclusive or a shared competence, as the Member States deliberately chose not to confer on the Union the power to conduct economic policy autonomously. Instead, coordination presupposes the existence of autonomous national economic policies, which are guided at Union level in order to promote consistency and convergence, but without giving rise to a common European economic policy that would be binding in substance on the Member States. Because this competence is neither exclusive nor shared, nor a supporting, coordinating or supplementary competence within the meaning of Articles 3, 4 or 6 TFEU, it follows that economic policy under Union law constitutes a *sui generis* competence.

2. The Development of the EMU and the Balance between Inter-governmental and Functional Integration

One of the defining features of the evolution of the EMU has been its hybrid character, combining elements of the 'community method' with other modes of action, including mechanisms that operate outside the Union's legal and institutional framework, where the Member States act at the international level. This hybrid development accelerated markedly during the financial crisis of 2008–13, a period in which significant steps were taken to deepen economic integration among the Member States. Those developments led to the conclusion of several international treaties between the Member States (*inter se* agreements), designed to complement and reinforce Union policies, while being agreed upon outside the Union's formal decision-making procedures and involving only a discrete or ancillary role for Union institutions.[7] A prominent example is the Treaty on Stability, Coordination and Governance in

[7] On inter se agreements, B de Witte, 'Old-Fashioned Flexibility: International Agreements between Member States of the European Union' in G de Búrca and J Scott (eds), *Constitutional Change in the EU: From Uniformity to Flexibility?* (Hart, 2000) 31–58.

the Economic and Monetary Union, signed in 2012, which supplements the budgetary discipline rules laid down in the Treaties.[8] Similarly, the Treaty establishing the European Stability Mechanism created an international organisation entrusted with providing financial assistance to Member States whose currency is the euro. That mechanism was established by an international treaty outside the Union's institutional framework, reflecting the hybrid nature of EMU governance.[9]

This hybrid approach reflects the strong resistance of the Member States to allowing the Union to assume further fiscal powers. As explained in section III.2.3 and III.4.3 of this chapter, the Treaties impose several substantive limits on the Union's economic and monetary policies, including the 'no-bailout' clause prohibiting the Union and the Member States from assuming the commitments of other Member States, and the prohibition of monetary financing by the ECB. These constraints are constitutional in nature, as they are enshrined directly in the Treaties. During the financial crisis, however, it became necessary to provide large-scale financial assistance to several Member States. In order to do so without formally breaching the Treaties' constitutional limits, the Union facilitated the adoption of international assistance mechanisms agreed upon *inter se* by the Member States, generally those participating in the euro area. This process unfolded with the active involvement and institutional support of the Union, as the Commission, the European Council, the ECB, and the Eurogroup all played a central role in the design and implementation of those financial assistance programmes.

The result is an EMU constrained by constitutional limits enshrined in the Treaties, particularly in the field of economic policy, which may nevertheless be complemented through international cooperation among the Member States.[10] This distinctive mode of development has led to a certain pre-eminence of the Member States, often at the expense of the Union's institutions, especially in matters relating to economic governance. Within this framework, a particularly important role is played by the Eurogroup, a specific formation composed of the ministers responsible for economic and financial affairs of the Member States whose currency is the euro. At the same time, several measures initially adopted at the international level have gradually been incorporated into the Union's policy framework. This evolution mirrors developments in other areas, such as the Area of Freedom, Security and Justice, where an originally intergovernmental design has progressively evolved into a model more fully integrated within the Union's institutional structures.

The establishment of structured mechanisms for coordination and cooperation among the Member States in economic matters, particularly within the euro area, thus lays the groundwork for their possible integration into the Union's institutional framework. For the time being, however, such integration remains a prospective development, rather than an achieved or fully realised outcome.

3. External Control: Parliamentary and Judicial Control of the EMU

The contrast between the *sui generis* nature of the Union's economic policy competence and its exclusive competence in monetary policy gives rise to distinct models of external control. A *sui generis* competence, marked by the predominant role of the Member States, entails weaker external oversight by the Union's institutions and a corresponding increase in control exercised

[8] Treaty on Stability, Coordination and Governance in the Economic and Monetary Union, done at Brussels on 2 March 2012.

[9] Treaty establishing the European Stability Mechanism (ESM), done at Brussels on 2 February 2012.

[10] A Estella de Noriega, *Legal Foundations of EU Economic Governance* (Cambridge University Press, 2018) 36ff.

by national institutions within each Member State. By contrast, the exercise of an exclusive Union competence presupposes strong and centralised institutional oversight at Union level. This structural divergence has led to the development of predominantly political forms of external control in the field of economic policy, whereas monetary policy is subject to a combination of political oversight and judicial review within the Union's institutional framework.

In the field of economic policy, the primary source of external control lies with the European Parliament,[11] whose role is reflected in several instances. For example, the *inter se* agreements referred to above include reporting obligations vis-à-vis the European Parliament. Likewise, within the framework of the European Semester, the European Parliament 'shall be involved in a regular and transparent manner',[12] and it is empowered to require the Commission to appear before it in order to report on its assessment of the national medium-term fiscal-structural plans.[13] The European Parliament also plays an active role in the appointment of the Commissioner responsible for Economic and Monetary Affairs, as well as in the appointment and removal of the heads of the European Supervisory Authorities. Finally, legislative acts adopted within the Union's economic policy framework involve the European Parliament as a co-legislator, thereby reinforcing its function of democratic oversight in this area.[14]

Alongside the European Parliament, national parliaments provide an additional layer of external scrutiny, directed primarily at the governments of the Member States. This involvement is readily explained by the central role played by Member States in both the design and implementation of economic policy. In addition to the ordinary channels of political accountability available at national level, the Treaties establish specific participation mechanisms for national parliaments, notably those set out in Protocols No 1 and No 2, as well as in various acts of secondary legislation.[15] By way of example, the European Semester explicitly involves national parliaments and imposes reporting obligations on the Union's institutions, thereby ensuring that national parliaments are adequately informed and able to exercise their functions of political oversight over their respective governments.[16]

In the field of monetary policy, the independence of the ECB makes the exercise of comprehensive political control inherently limited. As a consequence, the ECB is subject to reporting obligations vis-à-vis the European Parliament, while the design and implementation of monetary policy remain within the exclusive competence of the Eurosystem. In response to this constrained framework of political oversight, recent years have witnessed an increased reliance on judicial review as a counterbalancing mechanism. Such judicial oversight is exercised by the Court of Justice of the European Union, which recognises the technical and discretionary nature of the ECB's actions, while at the same time ensuring effective judicial protection for all parties entitled to bring proceedings before the Union's courts.[17]

[11] R Repasi, 'European Parliament and National Parliaments' in F Amtenbrink and C Herrmann (eds), *The EU Law of Economic and Monetary Union* (Oxford University Press, 2020).

[12] Art 2a(4) of Council Regulation No 1466/97 of 7 July 1997 on the strengthening of the surveillance of budgetary positions and the surveillance and coordination of economic policies [1997] OJ L209/1, repealed and replaced by Regulation (EU) 2024/1263 of the European Parliament and of the Council of 29 April 2024 on the effective coordination of economic policies and on multilateral budgetary surveillance and repealing Council Regulation (EC) No 1466/97 [2024] OJ L 2024/1263.

[13] Art 27 of Regulation 2024/1263.

[14] Arts 121(6), 125(2) and 126(14) TFEU.

[15] See Protocol (No 1) on the role of national parliaments in the European Union [2016] C202/203; and Protocol (No 2) on the application of the principles of subsidiarity and proportionality [2008] C202/206.

[16] Art 3(4) of Council Regulation (EC) No 1466/97, as amended by Regulation (EU) No 1175/2011 [2011] OJ L306/12.

[17] D Sarmiento and M Hartmann, 'European Monetary Union and the Courts' in F Amtenbrink and C Herrmann (eds), *The EU Law of Economic and Monetary Union* (Oxford University Press, 2020).

4. Economic and Monetary Union at Multiple Speeds

The exclusive nature of the Union's competence in monetary policy led several Member States to decline participation in the euro. The United Kingdom chose not to join the project, while Denmark expressed significant reservations and secured an opt-out under Protocol No 16, which ultimately culminated in a negative referendum in 2000.[18] This reluctance resulted in the establishment of special legal regimes applicable to those Member States, while others have continued their convergence towards the common currency at different speeds. As a consequence, although the Union's monetary policy is institutionally strong by virtue of its exclusive competence, it remains territorially fragmented due to the political and economic sensitivities it entails. This has given rise to a system of monetary integration at different speeds, as discussed in chapter five of this book.

The Union's economic policy exhibits a different form of fragmentation. This fragmentation stems less from political resistance among Member States and more from the asymmetric pace of integration between countries participating in the common currency and those that have not yet adopted the euro. The gravity of the international financial crisis between 2008 and 2013 posed an existential threat to the euro, compelling the euro area Member States to undertake far-reaching reforms that other Member States were not prepared to embrace. This dynamic led to an enhanced role for the Eurogroup and the adoption of key legislative measures that nevertheless differentiated between euro-area countries and non-euro-area Member States. By way of example, the Single Supervisory Mechanism (SSM) became operational in November 2014, but its practical operation differs significantly depending on whether the supervised credit institutions are established within the euro area. A similar pattern can be observed with respect to bank resolution, which is governed by a Directive applicable to all 27 Member States, alongside a Regulation and the Single Resolution Mechanism (SRM), which applies exclusively to euro-area countries and those in close cooperation.

This fragmentation is not ideal, as the proper functioning of the EMU requires a high degree of coherence and unity of action, particularly in periods of economic stress. Nevertheless, experience has shown that the risks traditionally associated with fragmentation and internal divisions in economic and monetary policy were often overstated. This is evidenced by the Union's response to the COVID-19 pandemic and to the Russian invasion of Ukraine. When confronted with major external shocks, the Member States have demonstrated their capacity to deliver a coordinated and uniform economic response, while the actions of the ECB have been closely aligned with those of central banks outside the euro area. In this sense, fragmentation has functioned less as a precursor to disintegration and more as a transitional phase, facilitating the progression towards higher levels of integration in European economic and monetary policy.

III. THE ECONOMIC UNION

1. The Union's Economic Policy as a *Sui Generis* Competence

Article 119(1) TFEU provides that the Union's economic policy 'is based on the close coordination of Member States' economic policies, on the internal market and on the definition of common objectives'. That policy is to be conducted in accordance with the guiding principles of stable prices, sound public finances and monetary conditions and a sustainable balance

[18] The Danish referendum of 28 September 2000 resulted in a 53.2% vote against adopting the euro, with 87.5% of the eligible voting population participating.

of payments. However, Title VIII TFEU does not establish a legal basis empowering the Union to legislate autonomously in the field of economic policy. Instead, it sets out a framework for the coordination of Member States' economic policies, the objective of which is to preserve overall coherence rather than to develop an independent European economic policy.

This design explains why the Union's economic policy falls within the specific competence provided for in Article 5(1) TFEU, rather than within the general categories of competences defined in Articles 3, 4, and 6 TFEU. It is also significant that, unlike other Treaty provisions on Union competences, Article 5(1) TFEU opens by referring to 'the Member States' rather than to the Union. This wording underscores that the primary responsibility for economic policy remains with the Member States, rather than with the Union's institutions. As a result, a policy framework whose sole operational mechanism is the coordination of national policies necessarily lacks the instruments required to pursue a fully fledged Union policy. This structural feature explains the absence of general legislative powers for the Union in the field of economic policy, save for those explicitly conferred by the Treaties with the aim of reinforcing the coordination of Member States' economic policies.

Among the limited legislative powers set out in Title VIII TFEU, Article 121(6) TFEU confers on the European Parliament and the Council the authority to adopt, by means of regulations and in accordance with the ordinary legislative procedure, 'detailed rules for the multilateral surveillance procedure' referred to in Article 121(3) and (4) TFEU of the economic policies of the Member States. The Treaties thus provide a competence to regulate coordination mechanisms, but not to legislate on economic policies as such, with the exception of Article 122 TFEU in situations of severe difficulties. A further exception is found in Article 125(2) TFEU, which empowers the Council, on a proposal from the Commission and after consulting the European Parliament, to adopt measures to specify definitions necessary for applying the prohibitions in Articles 123, 124 and 125 TFEU. Apart from these circumscribed exceptions, the Union's economic policy framework is not accompanied by any further general legislative powers.

Notwithstanding this scarcity of competences, economic policy coordination has reached its most advanced stage in practice, particularly in the aftermath of the financial crisis of 2008–13. The legal basis of Article 121(6) TFEU was used to establish preventive and corrective coordination mechanisms, which significantly intensified the supervision of Member States' economic policies, especially following the introduction of the European Semester, discussed below. In parallel, the Member States concluded several international *inter se* agreements aimed at reinforcing the Stability and Growth Pact, in areas covered by Articles 121 and 126 TFEU. The Court of Justice has further clarified that the establishment by the Member States of a financial assistance mechanism, subject to strict macroeconomic conditionality, does not infringe the provisions of Title VIII TFEU. This interpretation has enabled the Member States to rely on international agreements to complement the Union's coordination powers – an approach that has already been implemented in practice.[19]

2. Member States' Economic Policy Coordination Mechanisms

The Union's economic policy is based on three pillars: coordination of national economic policies; budgetary stability; and the individual responsibility of each Member State. These

[19] For example, see the Treaty on Stability, Coordination and Governance in the Economic and Monetary Union, the Treaty establishing the European Stability Mechanism (ESM), the Agreement on the transfer and mutualisation of contributions to the Single Resolution Fund or the Euro Plus Pact.

pillars are interconnected, as the coordination of economic policies aims, among other things, to facilitate the achievement of budgetary stability by the Member States. Since economic policies remain fundamentally national, each Member State bears the consequences of its choices. Therefore, it is not for the Union to assist the Member States in the event of economic mismanagement. At the same time, pursuing sound budgetary policies contributes to balanced public finances and ensures that Member States are not forced to seek financial assistance. All three pillars are reflected in the Treaties and various acts of secondary legislation, as described below.

2.1. *The Broad Guidelines of Article 121 TFEU and the European Semester*

Article 121 TFEU establishes a mechanism for the coordination of Member States' economic policies, centred on the adoption of 'broad guidelines' to be taken into account by the Member States when designing and implementing their national economic policies. Those broad guidelines are adopted in the form of a Council Recommendation, based on a Conclusion of the European Council and acting on a Recommendation from the Commission. Where a Member State fails to comply with the broad guidelines or its economic policies risk jeopardising the proper functioning of economic and monetary union, Article 121(4) TFEU provides for the addressing of 'warnings' to the Member State concerned, as well as 'recommendations', but without attaching any sanctioning powers.

The broad guidelines thus serve as the principal strategic framework guiding Member States' economic policies. However, their general nature, combined with the absence of coercive enforcement mechanisms in cases of non-compliance, reveals the limited effectiveness of this coordination tool. In response, a comprehensive reform of multilateral economic surveillance was introduced in 2011 and further reformed in 2024. Relying on Article 121(6) TFEU, the Union adopted a series of legislative measures (commonly referred to as the 'six-pack' and the 'two-pack'),[20] which significantly strengthened economic policy coordination. These instruments established a system of closer and more structured surveillance, facilitating in recent years a more substantive coordination of economic strategies among the Member States, particularly within the euro area.

The outcome of these reforms is the European Semester, an annual cycle through which the Commission analyses the economic situation of each Member State and proposes measures aimed at strengthening national budgetary planning. The European Semester constitutes a system of budgetary and economic surveillance that supplements, rather than replaces, the more limited coordination mechanisms established under Article 121 TFEU. Moreover,

[20] The so-called six-pack consists of five regulations and one directive: Regulation No 1173/2011 of the European Parliament and of the Council of 16 November 2011 on the effective enforcement of budgetary surveillance in the euro area [2011] OJ L306/1; Regulation (EU) No 1174/2011 of the European Parliament and of the Council of 16 November 2011 on enforcement measures to correct excessive macroeconomic imbalances in the euro area [2011] OJ L306/8; Regulation 1466/97 was repealed and replaced by Regulation (EU) 2024/1263 of the European Parliament and of the Council of 29 April 2024 on the effective coordination of economic policies and on multilateral budgetary surveillance [2024] OJ L 2024/1263; Regulation No 1176/2011 of the European Parliament and of the Council of 16 November 2011 on the prevention and correction of macroeconomic imbalances [2011] OJ L306/25; Council Regulation No 1177/2011 of 8 November 2011 amending Regulation No 1467/97 on speeding up and clarifying the implementation of the excessive deficit procedure [2011] OJ L306/33 (as further amended by Council Regulation (EU) 2024/1264 of 29 April 2024 [2024] OJ L 2024/1264); and Council Directive 2011/85/EU of 8 November 2011 on requirements for budgetary frameworks of the Member States [2011] OJ L306/41 (as amended by Council Directive (EU) 2024/1265 of 29 April 2024 [2024] OJ L2024/1265). The two-pack consists of the following two regulations: Regulation No 472/2013 of the European Parliament and of the Council of 21 May 2013 on the strengthening of economic and budgetary surveillance of euro area Member States experiencing or threatened with severe difficulties with respect to their financial stability [2013] OJ L140/1; and Regulation No 473/2013 of the European Parliament and of the Council of 21 May 2013 on common provisions for monitoring and assessing draft budgetary plans and for the correction of excessive deficits of the euro area Member States [2013] OJ L140/11.

Member States whose currency is the euro are subject to an even more stringent framework, which includes a sanctioning regime in cases of non-compliance with budgetary stability requirements. Those Member States are also required to submit their draft budgetary plans to the Commission for assessment and to establish independent fiscal institutions, among other obligations, thereby reinforcing fiscal discipline within the euro area.

2.2. *The Stability and Growth Pact and the Treaty on Stability, Coordination and Governance*

The Union's principal instrument of economic policy is preventive in nature and focuses primarily on the budgetary policies of the Member States. The Stability and Growth Pact constitutes the legal framework through which Member States are required to pursue sound and sustainable public finances, by maintaining limited annual deficits and sustainable levels of public debt. Although the Stability and Growth Pact is rooted in the Treaties, it has been further reinforced in recent years through an international *inter se* agreement, namely the Treaty on Stability, Coordination and Governance,[21] which introduced additional mechanisms to strengthen compliance with the budgetary discipline laid down in the founding Treaties. In addition, parts of the 'six-pack' and 'two-pack' legislative reforms contain provisions that apply specifically to Member States whose currency is the euro, imposing more stringent obligations with regard to budgetary management.

The Stability and Growth Pact is based on Article 126 TFEU and is further elaborated in Protocol No 12 on the excessive deficit procedure, which sets out the quantitative reference values applicable to the Member States. Article 126(2) TFEU establishes the obligation for Member States to avoid excessive government deficits, with the Commission monitoring compliance by reference to both the ratio of government deficit to gross domestic product (GDP) and the ratio of government debt to GDP. Protocol No 12 specifies those reference values, fixing the deficit threshold at 3 per cent of GDP and the debt threshold at 60 per cent of GDP.[22]

The Stability and Growth Pact establishes a specific enforcement procedure, initiated by the Commission, where a Member State fails to comply with the requirements of Article 126(2) TFEU and there is a risk of an excessive deficit. In such circumstances, the Council is empowered to determine the existence of an excessive deficit and to address 'recommendations' to the Member State concerned, requiring it to take action to bring that situation to an end. Where the Member State fails to act upon the Council's 'recommendations', the Council may subsequently give notice to the Member State requiring it to take, within a specified time limit, the measures to achieve deficit reduction. If the excessive deficit persists, the Council may, in accordance with Article 126(11) TFEU, decide to apply or intensify sanctions. These may include the publication of additional information, a requirement to lodge a non-interest-bearing deposit with the Union, an invitation to the European Investment Bank to reconsider its lending policy towards the Member State concerned, or the imposition of fines of appropriate size. Decisions adopted by the Council under this procedure are taken by qualified majority and without the participation of the Member State concerned.[23]

Compliance with the Stability and Growth Pact has been uneven. In November 2003, both France and Germany incurred excessive deficits which the Council chose not to sanction, notwithstanding the Commission's recommendation that corrective action be taken. This situation was aggravated by the Council's decision to adopt a legal instrument other than that prescribed by

[21] Treaty on Stability, Coordination and Governance in the Economic and Monetary Union, done at Brussels on 2 March 2012 (TSCG).

[22] Art 1 of Protocol (No 12) on the excessive deficit procedure.

[23] Art 126(13) TFEU.

Article 104 EC (now Article 126 TFEU). As a result, the Commission brought an action against the Council, which the Court of Justice partially upheld.[24] The fact that the Member States concerned were the two largest economies in the euro area – France and Germany – created the perception that the rules of the Pact were not applied uniformly to all Member States, thereby undermining its credibility. The financial crisis that began in 2008 further compounded these weaknesses, particularly when the budgetary forecasts of the most severely affected Member States collapsed under the impact of the economic shock. These developments ultimately prompted a strengthening of the Pact through the adoption of an instrument that, following vetoes by the United Kingdom and the Czech Republic, had to be concluded as an international *inter se* agreement: the Treaty on Stability, Coordination and Governance. That Treaty reinforces the obligations laid down in Article 126 TFEU and requires the introduction of budgetary stability rules, as defined in Article 3(1)(b) of the Treaty, into national law through provisions of binding and permanent character, preferably constitutional or provisions of equivalent legal effect.[25] The Treaty also establishes a system of judicial remedies before the Court of Justice to ensure compliance with the obligation to incorporate the so-called 'golden rule' into national law. This includes a dispute settlement mechanism based on Article 273 TFEU,[26] as well as lump sums and penalty payments under Article 260(2) TFEU in cases of non-compliance.[27]

The Stability and Growth Pact came under intense pressure during the euro area crisis and was widely criticised for its rigidity, complexity, and pro-cyclical effects. Although it sought to enforce fiscal discipline through common numerical thresholds, namely a 3 per cent deficit and a 60 per cent debt-to-GDP ratio, it allowed limited scope for growth-enhancing investment and insufficiently accommodated the differing fiscal realities of the Member States. The COVID-19 pandemic further exposed these shortcomings. In response, the Union activated the general escape clause in March 2020, temporarily suspending the application of the preventive and corrective arms of the Stability and Growth Pact and enabling unprecedented levels of public borrowing, alongside significant Union-level spending under the NextGenerationEU programme. As the expiry of the clause approached, a broad consensus emerged that a simple return to the pre-existing framework of the Stability and Growth Pact would be both politically untenable and economically counterproductive. Rising inflation, divergent debt trajectories, and the substantial investment requirements associated with the green and digital transitions underscored the need for a more flexible and credible system.

From a political perspective, the reform reflected a compromise between Member States emphasising fiscal discipline and debt sustainability and those seeking greater policy space for investment and counter-cyclical fiscal action. The European Commission's proposals of April 2023, building on earlier Council conclusions, aimed to reconcile these positions by replacing uniform adjustment requirements with country-specific, multi-annual fiscal-structural plans. These plans are designed to ensure gradual debt reduction while safeguarding public investment. Adopted in April 2024,[28] the reform modernises the legal architecture of

[24] Case C-27/04 *Commission v Council* EU:C:2004:436.

[25] Art 3(2) of the TSCG on Stability sets out the obligation in the following terms: 'The rules set out in paragraph 1 shall be implemented in the national law of the Contracting Parties at the latest one year after the date of entry into force of this Treaty by provisions which have binding force and are of a permanent nature, preferably of constitutional rank, or compliance with which is otherwise fully ensured throughout the national budgetary procedures'.

[26] Art 8(1) TSCG.

[27] ibid, Art 8(2).

[28] Regulation (EU) 2024/1263 of the European Parliament and of the Council of 29 April 2024 on the effective coordination of economic policies and on multilateral budgetary surveillance and repealing Council Regulation (EC) No 1466/97 [2024] OJ L2024/1263 (preventive arm) and Council Regulation (EU) 2024/1264 of 29 April 2024 amending Regulation (EC) No 1467/97 on speeding up and clarifying the implementation of the excessive deficit procedure [2024] OJ L2024/1264 (corrective arm).

fiscal surveillance and marks a shift away from punitive uniformity towards enhanced national ownership, balancing economic realism with fiscal responsibility across the Union.

Each Member State is required to prepare a four-year national medium-term fiscal-structural plan, which may be extended to up to seven years where the Member State commits to a set of reform and investment commitments that enhance debt sustainability and long-term sustainable and inclusive growth.[29] These plans are intended to reflect the diversity of Member States' fiscal positions and economic challenges, thereby enabling a differentiated approach that accommodates national specificities while preserving multilateral oversight and equal treatment across the Union.[30] The plans are to specify national fiscal targets, measures to address macroeconomic imbalances, and priority investments and reforms aimed at supporting sustainable and inclusive growth. The overarching objective is to strike an appropriate balance between fiscal consolidation and economic resilience, while avoiding pro-cyclical fiscal policies that could jeopardise economic recovery or long-term growth.

Debt sustainability is the central focus of the revised framework. Member States are required to ensure that government debt follows a credible downward trajectory or remains at a prudent level below 60 per cent of GDP, while government deficits must remain below 3 per cent of GDP in the medium term.[31]

To give effect to these objectives, the European Commission will issue a risk-based and differentiated 'reference' trajectory for each Member State whose debt or deficit exceeds the Treaty reference values. This trajectory, expressed in terms of multi-annual net expenditure, will set out the fiscal adjustments required over a four-year period to achieve the prescribed debt and deficit targets.

Where a Member State undertakes substantial reforms and investments that enhance fiscal sustainability or long-term growth potential, such as those relating to the green and digital transitions, social and economic resilience, energy security, or defence, the fiscal adjustment period may be extended from four years to a maximum of seven years.

Two safeguards ensure consistency and fairness:

- a debt sustainability safeguard, requiring an average annual decline in the debt ratio; and
- a deficit resilience safeguard, ensuring a sufficient margin below the three per cent deficit threshold.

The net expenditure path serves as the sole operational indicator for fiscal surveillance. Once a Member State has submitted medium-term fiscal-structural plan, the Council, acting on a recommendation from the Commission, endorses that path, together with the associated reform and investment commitments.[32]

To strengthen transparency and accountability, a control account is established to record deviations from the agreed net expenditure trajectory. Persistent or significant deviations will trigger corrective action under the excessive deficit procedure.[33]

Under the revised corrective arm, the Commission may prepare a report under Article 126(3) TFEU to initiate a debt-based excessive deficit procedure when:

- the government debt ratio exceeds 60 per cent of GDP;[34]

[29] Arts 2(6) and 17 of Regulation (EU) 2024/1263.

[30] Regulation (EU) 2024/1263, recital 39; Arts 20–22.

[31] Arts 2(5)–(6) of Regulation (EU) 2024/1263; Protocol (No 12) on the excessive deficit procedure; Regulation (EU) 2024/1264, recital (15).

[32] Art 17(1)–(3) of Regulation (EU) 2024/1263.

[33] Regulation (EU) 2024/1264, recital (15); Art 3(3).

[34] ibid, recital (15); Art 3(3)(a).

- the deficit is not close to balance or in surplus;[35] and
- deviations recorded in the control account exceed 0.3 per cent of GDP in a single year or 0.6 per cent cumulatively.[36]

In assessing compliance, the Commission and the Council will take into account a range of relevant factors, including the scale of any deviations, the Member State's debt-related challenges, progress in implementing agreed reforms and investments, and the impact of extraordinary expenditure, such as increased defence spending.

The framework retains the deficit-based rules of the excessive deficit procedure, including the requirement for a minimum annual structural adjustment of 0.5 per cent of GDP. Persistent non-compliance may result in financial sanctions of up to 0.05 per cent of GDP of the preceding year, applied every six months until the necessary corrective measures are adopted.[37]

2.3. Stabilisation Mechanisms and their Limits: Financial Assistance and the 'No bail-out' Principle

The Stability and Growth Pact and the Treaty on Stability, Coordination and Governance are primarily preventive instruments, designed to avert excessive deficits and the emergence of economic imbalances within the Member States. Where these mechanisms prove insufficient and an imbalance arises in a Member State's public finances, Union law provides a range of instruments to support the Member State concerned, particularly those whose currency is the euro. At the same time, such stabilisation mechanisms are subject to constitutional constraints that limit the Union's ability to conduct financial assistance operations using its own resources. This limitation reflects the principle that economic policy remains, in the first instance, the responsibility of the Member States, which must therefore bear the consequences of their own economic policy choices. This constitutional framework is embodied in the 'no bail-out' rule, which operates as a strict guiding principle subject to limited exceptions, notably where an imbalance is not attributable to the Member State itself but results from an unforeseen external shock. In such circumstances, the Union may intervene through appropriate solidarity measures.

The prohibition on the Union or the Member States assuming the commitments of another Member State is laid down in Article 125 TFEU. The first part of that provision establishes the non-assumption of liability by the Union for the commitments of the Member States, while the second part does the same with respect to the Member States *inter se*:

> The Union shall not be liable for or assume the commitments of central governments, regional, local or other public authorities, other bodies governed by public law, or public undertakings of any Member State, without prejudice to mutual financial guarantees for the joint execution of a specific project. A Member State shall not be liable for or assume the commitments of central governments, regional, local or other public authorities, other bodies governed by public law, or public undertakings of another Member State, without prejudice to mutual financial guarantees for the joint execution of a specific project.

The Court of Justice interpreted this provision in *Pringle*,[38] a case where the compatibility of the European Stability Mechanism (ESM) with Article 125 TFEU was questioned. The Court of Justice provided a pragmatic response by emphasising that the objective of Article 125 TFEU, as reflected in the *travaux préparatoires* of the Maastricht Treaty, is to ensure that the Member

[35] ibid, recital (15); Art 3(3)(b).
[36] ibid, Art 3(3)(c).
[37] ibid, recital (20).
[38] Case C-370/12 *Pringle* EU:C:2012:756.

States pursue a sound budgetary policy.[39] The rule precluding the assumption of liability for another Member State's commitments operates as a strong incentive for Member States to pursue policies aimed at budgetary stability, on the understanding that they bear the risk of incurring fiscal imbalances independently, without financial assistance from the Union or from other Member States. However, Article 125 TFEU cannot be interpreted as meaning that the absence of liability for the commitments of another Member State may give rise to a threat to the financial stability of the Union as a whole, and in particular of the euro area. Accordingly, where the Union or the Member States establish a system of financial assistance designed to safeguard financial stability and provided that such assistance is subject to strict conditions and that the beneficiary Member State remains responsible for its own commitments towards its creditors, such arrangements do not infringe Article 125 TFEU.[40] As the Court of Justice has held:

> [T]he activation of financial assistance by means of a stability mechanism such as the ESM is not compatible with Article 125 TFEU unless it is indispensable for the safeguarding of the financial stability of the euro area as a whole and subject to strict conditions.

Article 125 TFEU does not prohibit the granting of financial assistance by one or more Member States to a Member State which remains responsible for its commitments to its creditors provided that the conditions attached to such assistance are such as to prompt that Member State to implement a sound budgetary policy.[41]

The 'no bail-out' principle also allows for exceptions where a budgetary imbalance originates from external factors beyond the control of the Member State or Member States concerned. Article 122(2) TFEU refers to situations of 'severe difficulties caused by natural disasters or exceptional occurrences beyond [the Member State's] control'. In such circumstances, the Council may, on a proposal from the Commission, grant Union financial assistance to the Member State concerned under conditions. Article 122(2) TFEU was relied upon during the initial phase of the financial crisis that began in 2008, until it became apparent that the systemic nature of the crisis required structural macroeconomic measures not encompassed by that provision. The severe economic disruption caused by the COVID-19 pandemic in 2020 once again led to recourse to this legal basis, as the circumstances fell within the notion of an 'exceptional occurrence' beyond the control of the Member States.[42]

As noted above, the Union has established a number of mechanisms to provide financial assistance to Member States, including in situations that might otherwise appear to conflict with the 'no bail-out' principle set out in Article 125 TFEU. In its judgment in *Pringle*, the Court of Justice confirmed that, provided the objective is to safeguard financial stability and to preserve sound budgetary policy, the Union and/or the Member States may establish mechanisms to grant financial assistance to a Member State. On that basis, the ESM was established in 2012 by the Treaty establishing the European Stability Mechanism.[43] All Member States whose currency is the euro participate in the ESM as parties to the Treaty and are represented in its governing bodies. Notwithstanding the Commission's attempts to transform the ESM into a Union body (referred to in 2017 as a 'European Monetary Fund'),[44] it remains an international

[39] ibid, para 135.

[40] ibid, para 137.

[41] ibid, paras 136–37.

[42] See Council Regulation 2020/672 of 19 May 2020 establishing a European instrument for temporary support to mitigate unemployment risks in an emergency (SURE) following the COVID-19 outbreak [2020] OJ L159/1; and Council Regulation 2020/2094 of 14 December 2020 establishing a European Union Recovery Instrument to support the recovery in the aftermath of the COVID-19 crisis [2020] OJ L433/23.

[43] Treaty establishing the European Stability Mechanism (ESM), done at Brussels on 2 February 2012.

[44] Proposal for a Council Regulation on the establishment of the European Monetary Fund COM(2017) 827 final.

organisation composed of the Member States whose currency is the euro.[45] The mission of the ESM is to enable euro-area Member States to prevent and resolve financial crises, while safeguarding long-term financial stability.

In the specific case of Member States whose currency is the euro, Regulation 472/2013 introduces a general framework applicable to financial assistance programmes, irrespective of the source of the support.[46] It thus creates a common framework aimed at preventing situations similar to those that led to the financial assistance programmes for Greece, Portugal, and Ireland in 2010 and 2011, when strict conditionality was imposed in exchange for financial assistance. These programmes significantly affected the economies of the Member States involved, which faced limited democratic scrutiny and a fragmented institutional framework. Consequently, Regulation 472/2013 introduces clarity and a transparent structure for these programmes, providing three assistance scenarios with corresponding monitoring mechanisms: enhanced surveillance;[47] a macroeconomic adjustment programme;[48] and post-programme surveillance.[49] Besides streamlining the surveillance and conditionality mechanisms, Regulation 472/2013 ensures that the implementation of these programmes falls within the Union's remit. Prior to the adoption of Regulation 472/2013, there were serious concerns about the accountability of decisions made under the programmes in an intergovernmental context. The initial rulings of the Court of Justice confirmed the absence of appropriate external scrutiny.[50] Regulation 472/2013 addresses the shortcomings of the earlier programmes, confirming the Union's role in the adoption and implementation of these programmes. It assigns tasks and responsibilities to each participating institution and facilitates the judicial review of decisions taken in the course of financial assistance.

3. The Institutional Framework of the Union's Economic Policy

Although the Union's economic policy is framed within the common institutional architecture designed by the Treaties, recent years have seen the emergence of new specialised agencies and *sui generis* entities, such as the Eurogroup. This section highlights some of the main entities that support the activities of the Union's institutions in this policy area.

3.1. The Eurogroup

Article 137 TFEU establishes that the arrangements for meetings between ministers of those Member States whose currency is the euro are laid down by the Protocol on the Eurogroup. Protocol No 14, annexed to the Treaties, defines the tasks of the Eurogroup in Article 1 as follows:

[45] The reform proposals have materialised in a reform of the ESM Treaty in 2021, through an international reform agreement, signed on 27 January and 8 February 2021, which confirms the international nature of the ESM and the failure of the Commission's attempts to incorporate it into the institutional structure of the Union.

[46] Regulation No 472/2013 of the European Parliament and of the Council of 21 May 2013 on strengthening economic and budgetary surveillance in euro area Member States experiencing or threatened with severe difficulties with respect to their financial stability [2013] OJ L140/1.

[47] Art 2 of Regulation 472/2013.

[48] ibid, Art 7.

[49] ibid, Art 14.

[50] The first approach taken by the Court of Justice is seen in Case C-128/12 *Sindicato dos Bancários do Norte* EU:C:2013:149, an order declaring that the Court lacked jurisdiction to assess the compatibility with the Charter of Fundamental Rights of national measures adopted to implement the first financial assistance programmes. This approach, partly due to the adoption of Regulation 472/2013, evolved into a complete reversal in Case C-8/15 P *Ledra Advertising v Commission and ECB* EU:C:2016:701 and Case C-258/14 *Florescu* EU:C:2017:448. See M Markakis and D Dermine, 'Bailouts, the Legal Status of Memoranda of Understanding and the Scope of Application of the Charter: Florescu' (2018) 55 *Common Market Law Review* 643.

> The Ministers of the Member States whose currency is the euro shall meet informally. Such meetings shall take place, when necessary, to discuss questions related to the specific responsibilities they share with regard to the single currency.

The Eurogroup is not a formation of the Council, but rather an informal body intended to provide the EMU with an intergovernmental forum for coordination. It does not affect the role of the Council, which remains central to Union-level decision-making in economic matters, nor does it encroach upon the independence of the ECB. The Eurogroup was established by a Resolution of the European Council of 13 December 1997[51] in order to enable the ministers of the Member States whose currency is the euro to exchange views and coordinate their positions on matters relating to the single currency. As the Court of Justice held in *Chrysostomides*,[52] the Eurogroup 'provides a bridge between the national level and the EU level for the purpose of coordinating the economic policies of the [Member States whose currency is the euro]'.[53] Furthermore, the Eurogroup does not have any competences under Union law, as Article 1 of Protocol No 14 states that its meetings are held solely 'to discuss questions related to the specific responsibilities [the Member States] share with regard to the single currency'.

The Eurogroup is composed of the Ministers of the Member States whose currency is the euro and the Commission. The ECB is also invited to participate in such meetings. The representatives of the Ministers of the Member States and the Commission prepare the Eurogroup meetings.[54] The presidency of the Eurogroup is held by one of the Eurogroup's members for a term of two and a half years, elected by a majority of the Ministers of the Member States whose currency is the euro.[55]

Owing to its informal nature, the Eurogroup does not adopt decisions capable of producing legal effects. Any agreements reached within the Eurogroup must therefore be implemented either by the Union institutions or by the Member States themselves. This characteristic precludes the Eurogroup from being held liable for damages arising from its actions and prevents its agreements from being subject to judicial review before the Union courts. The Court of Justice confirmed this position in *Chrysostomides*, after the General Court had previously reached a different conclusion. According to the Court of Justice, since the Eurogroup's agreements are informal and it lacks autonomous powers, legal remedies must be directed against the implementing measures adopted by the Union institutions, rather than against the acts of the Eurogroup itself:

Individuals may thus bring before the EU judicature an action to establish non-contractual liability of the European Union against the Council, the Commission and the ECB in respect of the acts or conduct that those EU institutions adopt following such political agreements, as is shown here by the actions brought at first instance by the applicants at first instance.[56]

3.2. *The European Stability Mechanism (ESM)*

The ESM is an international financial organisation established by the Member States whose currency is the euro to address situations of severe macroeconomic imbalance. Its creation in 2012 provided a more robust institutional and legal foundation for earlier mechanisms,

[51] The Resolution stated that the 'Ministers of the States participating in the euro-area may meet informally among themselves to discuss issues connected with their shared specific responsibilities for the single currency. The Commission, and the European Central Bank (ECB) when appropriate, will be invited to take part in the meetings.'

[52] Case C-597/18 P *Chrysostomides & Co and Others v Council* EU:C:2020:1028.

[53] ibid, para 84.

[54] Art 1 of the Protocol (No 14) on the Eurogroup.

[55] ibid, Art 2.

[56] *Chrysostomides* (n 52) para 93. In the same vein, see Joined Cases C-105/15 P to C-109/15 P *Mallis and Malli v Commission and ECB* EU:C:2016:702, paras 57–60.

most notably the European Financial Stability Facility, a special purpose vehicle set up in 2010 to grant financial assistance to Ireland, Portugal, and Greece. The ESM is an international economic organisation created by the euro-area Member States through an international treaty and is headquartered in Luxembourg.[57]

With the objective of preventing and resolving financial crises, as well as safeguarding long-term financial stability, the ESM mobilises financial resources to provide assistance to euro-area Member States facing, or at risk of, severe financing difficulties. Such assistance may take the form of loans granted under a macroeconomic adjustment programme, as in the cases of Cyprus and Greece, or may be provided to address other emergency situations, including the Pandemic Crisis Support instrument, a credit line made available to ESM members to support domestic financing of healthcare, treatment, and prevention-related costs during the COVID-19 pandemic. ESM assistance may be preventive in nature (precautionary financial assistance),[58] or may be aimed at the recapitalisation of financial institutions in participating Member States.[59] In 2021, a reform of the Treaty establishing the ESM was agreed, expanding the ESM's mandate to include a common backstop to the Single Resolution Fund (SRF), closer cooperation between the Commission and the ESM in the financial assistance process, and enhanced preventive instruments.[60]

The creation of the ESM led to the first application of the simplified revision procedure of the TFEU under Article 48(6) TEU. In 2011, the European Council adopted Decision 2011/199/EU,[61] amending Article 136 TFEU by adding a third paragraph as follows:

> The Member States whose currency is the euro may establish a stability mechanism to be activated if indispensable to safeguard the stability of the euro area as a whole. The granting of any required financial assistance under the mechanism will be made subject to strict conditionality.

This new provision serves a confirmatory, rather than constitutive, function, since it was not strictly necessary to introduce such a rule in order to establish the ESM. This was confirmed by the Court of Justice in *Pringle*, where it expressly held that 'the amendment of Article 136 TFEU by Article 1 of Decision 2011/199 confirms the existence of a power possessed by the Member States [and consequently] that decision does not confer any new power on the Member States'.[62]

Furthermore, in *Pringle*, the Court of Justice confirmed that the ESM Treaty is compatible with Union law, in particular with the 'no bail-out' clause. The Court held that an organisation such as the ESM, whose primary objective is to safeguard financial stability and whose financial assistance is subject to strict macroeconomic conditionality aimed at promoting a sound budgetary policy in the Member State concerned, does not infringe Article 125 TFEU.[63] In the same judgment, the Court of Justice examined the ESM Treaty from a range of additional perspectives, including the involvement of Union institutions in the implementation of ESM assistance programmes, and ultimately concluded that the Treaty is compatible with Union law.[64]

[57] Treaty establishing the European Stability Mechanism (ESM), done at Brussels on 2 February 2012, as amended by the Agreement amending the Treaty establishing the European Stability Mechanism, signed on 27 January and 8 February 2021.

[58] ibid, Art 14.

[59] ibid, Art 15.

[60] On the reform of the ESM Treaty, see A Peychev, 'Reforming the European Stability Mechanism: Too Much but Never Enough' (2021) 20 *European View*.

[61] European Council Decision 2011/199/EU of 25 March 2011 amending Article 136 of the Treaty on the Functioning of the European Union in relation to a stability mechanism for Member States whose currency is the euro [2011] OJ L91/1.

[62] *Pringle* (n 38) para 184. Paragraph 185 of the judgment is even more categorical, stating that 'the right of a Member State to conclude and ratify the ESM Treaty is not conditional upon the entry into force of Decision 2011/199'.

[63] ibid, paras 129–47.

[64] ibid, paras 155ff.

3.3. *The European System of Financial Supervision*

Following the financial crisis that began in 2008, the European System of Financial Supervision (ESFS) was established as a network of multilevel macroprudential and microprudential authorities to ensure uniform and consistent financial supervision across the internal market. The current framework is based on recommendations contained in the report of the High Level Group on Financial Supervision in the EU, chaired by Jacques de Larosière,[65] most of which were implemented in 2010 and 2011 with the creation of the European Systemic Risk Board,[66] the three European Supervisory Authorities (the European Banking Authority,[67] the European Securities and Markets Authority,[68] and the European Insurance and Occupational Pensions Authority),[69] the Joint Committee of the European Supervisory Authorities, and national supervisors.

Within the European System of Financial Supervision, a prominent role is played by the three European Supervisory Authorities, each of which has its own legal personality and is represented by its respective Chairperson. Their activities are governed by the principle of independence, and they are accountable to the European Parliament and the Council, as well as subject to judicial review before the Union courts. Their tasks include contributing to the development of regulatory and implementing technical standards, which are subsequently adopted by the Commission, and exercising oversight over national competent authorities, for which they have been granted specific coordination and, in some cases, direct supervisory powers.

3.4. *The Institutional Set-up of the Banking Union*

Reference should be made to the institutional framework established for the Banking Union, which will be examined in greater detail in section 4 of this chapter. Two of the three pillars of the Banking Union are the SSM and the SRM. The former performs a preventive function, aimed at ensuring the sound functioning and regulatory compliance of credit institutions, whereas the latter fulfils a corrective, or palliative, role once a credit institution encounters difficulties at the point of non-viability or is likely to fail. The SSM is primarily organised around the supervisory authority of the ECB, to which Regulation (EU) No 1024/2013 confers specific prudential supervisory tasks pursuant to Article 127(6) TFEU.[70] The SRM operates under the coordination of the Single Resolution Board (SRB), an EU agency acting in close cooperation with the national resolution authorities. While the ECB is a Union institution recognised by the Treaties, the SRB is an agency established by regulation and endowed with its own legal personality.[71]

[65] Report of the High Level Group on Financial Supervision in the EU, 25 February 2009, ec.europa.eu/economy_finance/publications/pages/publication14527_en.pdf.

[66] Regulation No 1092/2010 of the European Parliament and of the Council of 24 November 2010 on macro-prudential oversight of the financial system in the European Union and establishing a European Systemic Risk Board [2010] OJ L331/1.

[67] Regulation No 1093/2010 of the European Parliament and of the Council of 24 November 2010 establishing a European Supervisory Authority (European Banking Authority), amending Decision No 716/2009/EC and repealing Commission Decision 2009/78/EC [2010] OJ L331/12.

[68] Regulation No 1095/2010 of the European Parliament and of the Council of 24 November 2010 establishing a European Supervisory Authority (European Securities and Markets Authority), amending Decision No 716/2009/EC and repealing Commission Decision 2009/77/EC [2010] OJ L331/84.

[69] Regulation No 1094/2010 of the European Parliament and of the Council of 24 November 2010 establishing a European Supervisory Authority (European Insurance and Occupational Pensions Authority), amending Decision No 716/2009/EC and repealing Commission Decision 2009/79/EC [2010] OJ L331/48.

[70] Council Regulation No 1024/2013 of 15 October 2013 entrusting the European Central Bank with specific tasks concerning policies relating to the prudential supervision of credit institutions [2013] OJ L287/63.

[71] Arts 42ff of Regulation No 806/2014 of the European Parliament and of the Council of 15 July 2014 establishing uniform rules and a uniform procedure for the resolution of credit institutions and certain investment firms in the framework of a Single Resolution Mechanism and a Single Resolution Fund and amending Regulation No 1093/2010 [2014] OJ L225/1.

IV. MONETARY UNION

Alongside the Union's economic policy, the Treaties establish an independent monetary policy for the Union, conducted by a central bank that may act as lender of last resort to the banking sector, with the primary objective of maintaining price stability and, without prejudice to that objective, supporting the Union's general economic policies. For historical reasons, the development of a European monetary policy gained significant momentum in the late 1980s, culminating in its formal establishment by the Maastricht Treaty, shortly after the fall of the Berlin Wall, German reunification, and a broader geostrategic reassessment of Europe's role. The introduction of the euro represented a major step forward in the process of integration. However, this achievement occurred at a time when the Union's economic policy remained at an early stage of development, largely confined to mechanisms for the coordination of national economic policies. This asymmetry between the Union's monetary and economic policy frameworks had tangible consequences during the financial crisis that began in 2008. While the Union possessed strong and effective monetary policy instruments to respond to the crisis, it lacked comparably robust tools in the field of economic policy. Although certain structural deficiencies in the Union's economic policy framework have since been addressed in light of the lessons drawn from that crisis, the asymmetry remains evident in the Treaties. They continue to enshrine a strong, independent, and exclusive monetary policy at Union level, in contrast to the more limited and less robust coordination mechanisms available in the field of economic policy.

1. Monetary Policy as an Exclusive Competence of the Union

The Union's monetary policy is an exclusive competence, as provided for in Article 3(1)(c) TFEU, which refers to 'monetary policy for the Member States whose currency is the euro' when enumerating the areas of exclusive Union competence. Accordingly, pursuant to Article 2(1) TFEU, only the Union is empowered to legislate and to adopt legally binding acts in the field of monetary policy for those Member States whose currency is the euro.

As noted above, this exclusive competence is territorially limited in scope, as it applies only to the Member States whose currency is the euro, numbering 21 since 1 January 2026. Moreover, although monetary policy is conducted independently of other Union policies, it may interact with, or overlap with, policy areas falling within other Union competences. By way of example, the development of a digital euro has highlighted that, while the project is intrinsically linked to monetary policy, it also raises important issues relating to the internal market, consumer protection, and data protection, which fall within the scope of other Union competences.

The scope of the Union's competence in the field of monetary policy is determined by reference to the objectives and instruments laid down in the Treaties, in the absence of a specific provision defining the concept of 'monetary policy' in detail. Accordingly, on the basis of a grammatical, systematic, and teleological interpretation of the relevant Treaty provisions, Advocate General Pitruzzella defined 'monetary policy' as follows:

> [I]t follows from a textual, systematic and teleological analysis of the relevant provisions of the Treaties that the concept of monetary policy (*Währungspolitik*, in German), which, under Article 3(1)(c) TFEU, falls within the exclusive competence of the Union for the Member States whose currency is the euro, must be understood to mean that it is not limited to the definition and conduct of monetary policy in operational terms (monetary policy in the strict sense; *Geldpolitik*, in German), within the meaning of the first indent of Article 127(2) TFEU. Rather, it must be understood in the broad sense, in that it also includes a regulatory dimension relating to the single currency, which includes provisions of monetary law.[72]

[72] Joined Cases C-422/19 and C-423/19 *Hessischer Rundfunk* EU:C:2020:756, Opinion of AG Pitruzzella, pt 57.

The Court of Justice has endorsed this broad interpretation of 'monetary policy'. It has emphasised that the Union's exclusive competence in this field encompasses three core elements: the existence of a single currency (the euro), the definition and implementation of a single monetary policy, and the definition and implementation of a single exchange-rate policy.[73]

With this broad definition, the risk of overlap or tension with economic policy inevitably increases. However, the Court of Justice has emphasised that 'an economic policy measure cannot be treated as equivalent to a monetary policy measure for the sole reason that it may have indirect effects on the stability of the euro'.[74] For this reason, monetary policy is characterised by its 'singleness',[75] and by its comprehensive and coherent nature, framed by clearly defined objectives and supported by specific instruments. Provided that the Union pursues the monetary policy objectives laid down in the Treaties and employs the instruments conferred upon it, its actions do not cease to fall within the scope of monetary policy merely because they produce indirect effects on the economic stability of the euro area.

2. Monetary Policy Objectives and Instruments

The scope of the Union's exclusive competence in the field of monetary policy is defined primarily by the objectives set out in the Treaties. Indeed, the objectives of monetary policy constitute its most clearly delineated feature, to the extent that they represent one of the defining characteristics of the common currency. These objectives draw inspiration from the post-war German Bundesbank model, the institutional design and policy orientation of which were profoundly shaped by Germany's experience of hyperinflation during the inter-war period. By taking the Bundesbank as the principal reference point in the construction of the Union's monetary policy framework, the Treaties enshrined objectives that are strongly influenced by the German monetary tradition. Accordingly, Articles 119(2) TFEU and 127(1) TFEU confine the primary objective of the Union's monetary policy to the maintenance of price stability and, without prejudice to price stability, the support of the general economic policies of the Union with a view to contributing to the achievement of the objectives set out in Article 3 TEU.[76]

These two objectives do not enjoy equal status. Price stability constitutes the 'primary objective' of Union monetary policy and must therefore take precedence. By contrast, support for the general economic policies of the Union does not have primary status, as reflected both in the absence of any qualifying adjective in Articles 119(2) and 127(1) TFEU and in the express stipulation that such support must be provided 'without prejudice to the objective of price stability'. While the Treaties do not define the concept of price stability, the ECB has developed its own monetary policy strategy to give concrete expression to that objective. Following a comprehensive review completed in July 2021, the ECB stated that price stability is best maintained 'by aiming for 2% inflation over the medium term'.[77] This revision represents a modification of the approach adopted in 2003, which defined price stability as an inflation rate below, but close to, 2%.

[73] Joined Cases C-422/19 and C-423/19 *Hessischer Rundfunk* EU:C:2021:63, following the conclusions of Advocate General Pitruzzella, at para 37: 'action by the Member States and the Union will involve three elements: a single currency (the euro), the definition and implementation of a single monetary policy and the definition and implementation of a single exchange rate policy'.

[74] *Pringle* (n 38) para 56; and Case C-62/14 *Gauweiler* EU:C:2015:400, para 52.

[75] Case law repeatedly refers to the 'singleness' of monetary policy as a characteristic criterion in this area. See *Gauweiler* (n 74) paras 47–48.

[76] On the objectives and their jurisprudential interpretation, see M Ioannidis, SJ Hlásková Murphy and C Zilioli, 'The Mandate of the ECB: Legal Considerations in the ECB's Monetary Policy Strategy Review' (2021) ECB Occasional Paper Series, No 276.

[77] The monetary policy strategy was agreed by the Governing Council on 8 July 2021.

In order to achieve these objectives, the Union (acting in particular through the Eurosystem) relies on a monetary policy transmission mechanism. In other words, monetary policy operates through instruments that must have effects at both the macroeconomic and microeconomic levels within the euro area. The effective and smooth functioning of the transmission mechanism is essential to ensure that monetary policy decisions are properly reflected in the real economy. The need to safeguard the proper functioning of the transmission mechanism may justify the adoption of specific monetary policy measures aimed at correcting distortions or imbalances that affect its operation. This was particularly evident during the euro area sovereign debt crisis that reached its peak in 2012, when the ECB's monetary policy was impaired by substantial divergences in sovereign bond interest rates across the euro area. Where artificial and excessive imbalances in financing conditions affected only certain Member States, the transmission of monetary policy was disrupted. This situation ultimately led to the adoption of the Outright Monetary Transactions (OMT) programme, a government bond purchase programme on the secondary market.

In *Gauweiler*, the Court of Justice endorsed the ECB's actions in the following terms:

> The ability of the ESCB to influence price developments by means of its monetary policy decisions in fact depends, to a great extent, on the transmission of the 'impulses' which the ESCB sends out across the money market to the various sectors of the economy. Consequently, if the monetary policy transmission mechanism is disrupted, that is likely to render the ESCB's decisions ineffective in a part of the euro area and, accordingly, to undermine the singleness of monetary policy. Moreover, since disruption of the transmission mechanism undermines the effectiveness of the measures adopted by the ESCB, that necessarily affects the ESCB's ability to guarantee price stability. Accordingly, measures that are intended to preserve that transmission mechanism may be regarded as pertaining to the primary objective laid down in Article 127(1) TFEU.[78]

The instruments available to the ECB are set out in the Statute of the ESCB and of the ECB annexed to the Treaties, in particular in Chapter IV. Broadly speaking, these instruments may be grouped into five categories: (1) minimum reserve requirements imposed on credit institutions in respect of their accounts with the ECB and the national central banks; (2) open market and credit operations, including the purchase and sale of securities and other negotiable instruments; (3) the determination of collateral requirements applicable to financial institutions and the establishment of lists of eligible assets; (4) the oversight of payment and clearing systems; and (5) monetary policy communication.[79] Through these instruments, the ECB, acting within the framework of the Eurosystem, develops and implements its monetary policy strategy by transmitting its decisions through the monetary policy transmission mechanism.

In recent years, developments in the financial system, together with broader policy challenges such as climate change, have prompted the ECB and the Eurosystem to reassess the relevance of their objectives and methods. In the environmental context, the emergence of 'green finance' and increasing regulatory pressure on the financial sector to channel investment towards environmentally sustainable activities have raised questions concerning the legality of a monetary policy that takes environmental considerations into account. The precise enumeration of objectives in the Treaties limits the scope for pursuing goals other than price stability and, without prejudice thereto, support for the Union's general economic policies. Nevertheless, the scale of the current environmental crisis and the potential role of central banks in addressing it have led to an evolution in the ECB's approach, which has gradually

[78] *Gauweiler* (n 74) para 50.

[79] On the objectives and means of the Eurosystem's monetary policy, see K Tuori, 'Monetary Policy (Objectives and Instruments)' in F Amtenbrink and C Herrmann (eds), *The EU Law of Economic and Monetary Union* (Oxford University Press, 2020) 629ff.

incorporated environmental considerations as a relevant factor within the framework of Union monetary policy.[80] Comparable challenges arise from the proliferation of cryptocurrencies and the development of new digital payment infrastructures operating outside traditional payment systems. In this context, the prospective introduction of a digital euro will require a re-evaluation of established central banking practices, in order to ensure that monetary policy transmission mechanisms continue to function effectively.

3. Constitutional Limits to Monetary Policy

In order to ensure the effective pursuit of monetary policy objectives, the Treaties lay down a number of constitutional constraints on the actions of the ECB and the Eurosystem. These constraints are designed to promote price stability and to safeguard the independence of the ECB and the national central banks, thereby ensuring that the Union's monetary policy remains insulated from financing pressures exerted by the Member States. Such pressures may distort inflation targeting, undermine the effectiveness of monetary policy, and generate imbalances within the internal market.

3.1. Prohibition of Monetary Financing

The main constitutional limitation is set out in Article 123 TFEU, which prohibits the ECB and the national central banks from engaging in any monetary financing in favour of the Union institutions, bodies, offices or agencies, central governments or other public authorities of the Member States. The provision reads as follows:

> Overdraft facilities or any other type of credit facility with the European Central Bank or with the central banks of the Member States (hereinafter referred to as 'national central banks') in favour of Union institutions, bodies, offices or agencies, central governments, regional, local or other public authorities, other bodies governed by public law, or public undertakings of Member States shall be prohibited, as shall the purchase directly from them by the European Central Bank or national central banks of debt instruments.

The prohibition of monetary financing pursues two principal objectives. First, it is intended to encourage Member States to maintain sound and sustainable budgetary policies. Where a central bank directly finances the state budget, the risk of inflation increases significantly. Once inflation reaches elevated levels, the ECB's capacity to respond effectively is considerably constrained, particularly where inflationary pressures stem from a policy of budgetary financing by the central bank itself.[81] Second, monetary financing may give rise, indirectly, to a redistribution of wealth among Member States. If the ECB were to support one or more Member States through monetary financing, it would, in effect, deploy resources drawn from all Member States to finance another, thereby creating a mechanism of fiscal redistribution that runs counter to the principle laid down in Article 125 TFEU, that the Union and the Member States shall not assume the commitments of another Member State. Although fiscal redistribution exists within the Union, it operates through specific mechanisms subject to legislative approval and democratic control, rather than through the conduct of monetary policy by the ECB, whose primary objective is the maintenance of price stability in the euro area.

[80] C Zilioli and M Ioannidis, 'Climate Change and the Mandate of the ECB: Potential and Limits of Monetary Contribution to European Green Policies' (2022) 59 *Common Market Law Review*.

[81] *Gauweiler* (n 74) para 100.

The Court of Justice has interpreted Article 123 TFEU on several occasions, principally in the context of the ECB's adoption of unconventional monetary policy programmes involving the purchase of bonds issued by Member States. The *Gauweiler* case concerned the OMT government bond purchase programme intended to restore the transmission mechanism of Union monetary policy, which had been impaired during the euro area sovereign debt crisis as a result of the loss of market confidence in several Member States.[82] In *Weiss*, the ECB was confronted with a different set of circumstances, namely the risk of prolonged below-target inflation and the need to stimulate economic activity in an environment of persistently low interest rates. This situation prompted renewed reliance on unconventional monetary policy measures, in particular the Public Sector Purchase Programme (PSPP), including the purchase of securities issued by central governments of Member States and by private sector entities.[83] In both cases, the Court of Justice upheld the ECB's actions and found the programmes at issue to be compatible with Article 123 TFEU.

The Court's interpretation of Article 123 TFEU in *Gauweiler* and *Weiss* is consistent with its interpretation of Article 125 TFEU in *Pringle*. Provided that the ECB's actions pursue the objectives laid down in the Treaties and that appropriate safeguards are in place to ensure compliance with those objectives, such actions are compatible with Article 123 TFEU. In *Gauweiler* and *Weiss*, the Court examined the objectives of the ECB's programmes, namely the restoration of the monetary policy transmission mechanism (*Gauweiler*) and counteracting the risks of prolonged below-target inflation (*Weiss*), and held them to be consistent with the objectives of price stability and, without prejudice thereto, support for the Union's general economic policies, as set out in Articles 119(2) and 127(1) TFEU. The Court of Justice then determined that the non-conventional measures under consideration – primarily the purchase of Member State bonds – included sufficient safeguards to prevent monetary financing: *inter alia*, purchases were made exclusively on the secondary market, subject to purchase ceilings, issuer limits, and a 'blackout period' between the issuance of the bond and the purchase date by the ESCB in order to avoid affecting the bond's market price, etc.[84]

3.2. *Lender of Last Resort*

One of the core functions traditionally associated with a central bank in a market economy is that of lender of last resort. Although this function is not usually expressly enumerated among a central bank's formal statutory tasks, market participants must be able to rely on the existence of a solvent backstop with effectively unlimited financial capacity standing behind the banking system. Such a backstop may intervene, where necessary, to support one or more credit institutions, thereby contributing to the stability of the financial system. At the same time, the lender of last resort function must be balanced against the need to ensure that credit institutions remain accountable for mismanagement, just as Member States that fail to pursue

[82] ibid.

[83] Case C-493/17 *Weiss and Others* EU:C:2018:1000.

[84] In the *Gauweiler* case, Advocate General Cruz Villalón distanced himself from the position finally adopted by the Court of Justice by suggesting that the ECB should refrain from participating in the monitoring processes of financial assistance programmes in which the OMT programme was implemented. In the words of the Advocate General: 'However, should the exceptional circumstances motivating the implementation of the OMT programme arise, in order for the OMT programme to maintain its role as a monetary policy measure, it is essential that the ECB disassociates itself from any direct involvement in the monitoring of the financial assistance programme implemented by the State concerned. There would be nothing to prevent the ECB from being informed and even being heard, but under no circumstances could the ECB be allowed, in the event that a programme such as the OMT is under way, to continue to be involved in the monitoring of the financial assistance programme to which the Member State concerned is subject and which, at the same time, is the subject of significant ECB intervention in the secondary market for government bonds. In short, in order for the OMT programme to maintain its character as a monetary policy measure, aimed exclusively at restoring the monetary policy transmission channels, I consider it necessary to maintain this functional distance between the two programmes' (pt 150 of the conclusions).

sound budgetary policies must bear the consequences of poor fiscal governance. Nevertheless, the role of the central bank as lender of last resort remains essential for maintaining confidence in a highly complex and interconnected financial system, which is increasingly exposed to external shocks in a globalised and unstable economic environment,[85] even though this role remains a contingent function that, in an ideal scenario, should never materialise.[86]

Neither the Treaties nor the Statute of the ESCB and of the ECB expressly assign the lender of last resort function to the Eurosystem. However, Article 14.4 of the Statute of the ESCB and of the ECB permits national central banks to perform functions 'other than those specified in this Statute', provided that such functions do not interfere with the objectives and tasks of the Eurosystem as a whole. Within the scope of these non-Eurosystem tasks, which fall within the responsibility of the national central banks rather than the Eurosystem as a whole, guidelines have been developed for situations in which support to credit institutions is required. This form of financial assistance is the sole responsibility of the national central banks of the Eurosystem, although it is subject to non-objection by the Governing Council of the ECB. Known as *emergency liquidity assistance* (ELA), it is available only to solvent credit institutions experiencing temporary liquidity shortages. Consequently, an insolvent credit institution with no realistic prospect of overcoming its difficulties in the short term cannot rely on ELA, since such support would risk encouraging or rewarding mismanagement within the internal market.

The ECB's role in the operation of ELA is therefore indirect and mostly concerned with oversight. On the one hand, ELA operations remain the exclusive responsibility of the national central banks, which alone bear any financial losses arising from such assistance. On the other hand, the Governing Council of the ECB exercises oversight by monitoring ELA operations and may object to them where they would interfere with the objectives and tasks of the Eurosystem, in particular under Article 14.4 of the Statute of the ESCB and of the ECB. A procedural framework has existed since the early years of EMU and was later updated. That framework was subsequently updated and, for the first time, publicly disclosed by an agreement of the Governing Council dated 9 November 2020.[87]

During the financial crisis that began in 2008, national central banks made frequent use of ELA to mitigate the impact of the crisis on a range of financial institutions. The operational details governing such assistance are subject to strict confidentiality, as the Governing Council of the ECB determines the thresholds within which national central banks may grant ELA. Disclosure of this information to the market could undermine the effectiveness of the assistance by triggering speculative behaviour. As a result, the provision of ELA has long been characterised by a high degree of opacity, which has, in turn, given rise to criticism and questions about the ECB's role in the support or resolution of certain banks. The Court of Justice has upheld the confidentiality of Governing Council deliberations in that context in *Banco Espírito Santo*.[88] At the same time, the ECB itself, recognising the need to enhance transparency and prevent the emergence of competing or misleading narratives, has more recently introduced a number of measures aimed at improving transparency and communication in relation to ELA operations.[89]

[85] On the inherently unstable nature of the modern market economy, see M Wolf, *The Shifts and the Shocks: What We've Learned – and Still Have to Learn – From the Financial Crisis* (Penguin Books, 2015).

[86] A Steinbach, 'The Lender of Last Resort in the Eurozone' (2016) 53 *Common Market Law Review* 361–83.

[87] Agreement on Emergency Liquidity Assistance, 9 November 2020.

[88] Case C-442/18 P *ECB v Espírito Santo Financial (Portugal)* EU:C:2019:1117, para 43.

[89] See Section 8.3 of the above-mentioned Agreement of 9 November 2020, which expressly sets out the different communication options available to the national central banks, as well as the ECB's powers in the event that it decides to object to the publication of certain information on ELA.

4. The euro

The euro has replaced the national currencies of the Member States of the euro area. The establishment of a single currency constitutes one of the principal consequences of the implementation of the Union's monetary policy. This is reflected in Article 3(4) TEU, and Articles 119(2) and 133 TFEU, which refer to the euro as the Union's 'single currency'.

Although Union law does not contain an explicit definition of the concept of a 'single currency', the euro is conceived in accordance with the modern understanding of money, grounded in the notion of 'fiat money', that is, a currency issued by public authority and not backed by precious metals such as gold or silver, or by any other tangible asset. Such a currency may be represented in scriptural (accounting) form or in physical form, namely banknotes and/or coins. The latter dimension is of particular historical significance, given that money has traditionally circulated through physical media. In practice, the Union's single currency, the euro, currently materialises in two forms: scriptural and physical.

The principal legal consequence of the creation of a currency such as the euro is its recognition as 'legal tender'. This status is enshrined in Article 128(1) TFEU, which provides that 'banknotes issued by the ECB and the national central banks shall be the only such notes to have the status of legal tender within the Union'. Although this provision refers expressly only to banknotes, nothing precludes, as explained by Advocate General Pitruzzella, the extension of legal tender status to other forms of representation of the euro, whether coins or a future digital euro.[90] The Court of Justice has further confirmed that the concept of 'legal tender' constitutes an autonomous concept of Union law, which must be interpreted not only in light of the wording of Article 128(1) TFEU, but also by reference to its context and the objectives it pursues. In that regard, the case law has defined the concept of 'legal tender' as follows:

> [T]he concept of 'legal tender' of a means of payment denominated in a currency unit signifies, in its ordinary sense, that that means of payment cannot generally be refused in settlement of a debt denominated in the same currency unit, at its full face value, with the effect of discharging the debt.[91]

This definition is consistent with the provisions of Regulation 974/98 on the introduction of the euro[92] and Recommendation 2010/191 on the scope and effects of legal tender of euro banknotes and coins.[93] In summary, the status of legal tender for euro banknotes and coins entails their mandatory acceptance, acceptance at face value, and the power to settle payment obligations. These characteristics must be ensured by the authorities of the Member States, without prejudice to their competence to regulate the conditions for the settlement of cash payment obligations under both public and private law.[94]

The legal framework governing the single currency further encompasses rules relating to the production and issuance of euro banknotes and coins, as well as provisions concerning authenticity checks and recirculation procedures.[95]

With regard to euro banknotes, ECB Decision 2013/211 outlines seven denominations, ranging from EUR 5 to EUR 500 banknotes, and lays down rules on reproductions that use all

[90] Conclusions in *Hessischer Rundfunk* (n 73) pt 97.

[91] ibid, para 46.

[92] Council Regulation No 974/98 of 3 May 1998 on the introduction of the euro [1998] OJ L139/1.

[93] Commission Recommendation 2010/191/EU of 22 March 2010 on the scope and effects of legal tender of euro banknotes and coins [2010] OJ L83/70.

[94] See *Hessischer Rundfunk* (n 73) para 56; and Art 1 of Recommendation 2010/191 (n 93).

[95] Case C-772/21 *Brink's Lithuania* EU:C:2023:305.

or part of a euro banknote.[96] Reproductions must meet several criteria set out in Article 2(3) of the Decision to avoid the risk of the general public mistaking them for genuine euro banknotes. The withdrawal of a banknote type or series is also regulated by the Decision and falls under the responsibility of the Governing Council.[97]

Euro banknotes are 'authorised' exclusively by the ECB, and they are 'issued' by both the ECB and the national central banks. Regulation 974/98 on the introduction of the euro[98] states that only the ECB and the national central banks may put into circulation banknotes denominated in euro in the participating Member States, 'with effect from the respective cash changeover dates'.[99] For national central banks, ECB Decision 2010/29 introduces the banknote allocation key,[100] which is defined as the percentage derived by combining the ECB's share in the total euro banknote issue with the application of the subscribed capital key (rounded to the nearest multiple of 0.0005 of a percentage point) to the national central banks' share in that total.[101] It is the responsibility of the national central banks to put into circulation, monitor, and withdraw euro banknotes within their territory, while also assuming a number of obligations vis-à-vis euro banknote holders, such as accepting banknotes for exchange.[102]

In the case of euro coins, the regime differs from that of euro banknotes, as Article 128 TFEU clarifies that, while the 'authorisation' of the issue of banknotes is an exclusive right of the ECB, the issuance of euro coins is a competence that belongs to the Member States, subject to the prior approval of the ECB on the volume of the issue. This competence is governed by various provisions of Union law, primarily Regulation 974/98 on the introduction of the euro and Regulation 651/2012 on the issuance of euro coins.[103] Euro coins are issued and put into circulation at face value, although a 'minor proportion, not exceeding 5 per cent of the cumulated total net value and volume of circulation coins issued by a Member State' may be released onto the market above face value.[104] The rules also establish a specific framework for the issuance of commemorative coins, in principle limited to two issues per year in each Member State,[105] and rules concerning the issuance of collector coins, whose legal tender status is confined strictly to the territory of the issuing Member State.[106]

The production of banknote components and security features follows a specific regime, including the accreditation of manufacturers. ECB Decision 2020/637 sets out the conditions applicable to manufacturers of euro banknote components and euro secure items, which are subject to an accreditation procedure that restricts their ability to operate in other commercial activities.[107] Accredited manufacturers are subject to a regime of registration, inspections, and penalties, with violations potentially leading to fines and even immediate cessation of activity.[108] Regulation 1338/2001 also introduces rules on the protection of the euro against counterfeiting, including a regime for checking the authenticity of euro banknotes by 'cash

[96] Decision 2013/211/EU of the European Central Bank of 19 April 2013 on the denominations, specifications, reproduction, exchange and withdrawal of euro banknotes [2013] OJ L118/37, Art 1.

[97] ibid, Art 6.

[98] Council Regulation No 974/98 of 3 May 1998 on the introduction of the euro [1998] OJ L139/1.

[99] ibid, Art 10(1).

[100] Decision 2011/67/EU of the European Central Bank of 13 December 2010 on the issue of euro banknotes [2011] OJ L35/26.

[101] Art 1(d) of Decision 2011/67/EU.

[102] ibid, Art 8.

[103] Regulation No 651/2012 of the European Parliament and of the Council of 4 July 2012 on the issuance of euro coins [2012] OJ L201/135.

[104] ibid, Art 3.

[105] ibid.

[106] ibid, Art 4.

[107] Decision 2020/637 of the European Central Bank of 27 April 2020 on accreditation procedures for manufacturers of euro components and euro secure items [2020] OJ L149/12.

[108] ibid, Art 14.

handlers'.[109] These include entities involved in exchanging banknotes or coins of different currencies (*bureaux de change*), transporters of funds, and other economic agents with high cash circulation, such as casinos or traders engaged in secondary activities involving processing and distributing euro banknotes to the public via automated teller machines. The obligations incumbent on cash handlers are further developed by ECB Decision 2010/597, which governs the conditions for checking the authenticity and fitness of euro banknotes for circulation, as well as the checks to be carried out on cash handlers.[110]

4.1. *The Digital Euro*

In recent years, the emergence of 'cryptoassets' – software-based instruments protected by cryptographic techniques and not always backed by underlying assets – has presented an alternative to traditional state-issued currencies. This development has coincided with a profound transformation in e-commerce, which accelerated markedly during the COVID-19 pandemic, and with unprecedented growth in digital payment systems. The increasing sophistication of cryptoassets, particularly those issued in the form of tokens traded on blockchain-based networks, has prompted public authorities to respond at the regulatory level. Within the Union, the Commission launched a comprehensive initiative in 2020 to regulate digital finance, notably through the Retail Payments Strategy and the Digital Finance Strategy and the proposal that resulted in the Regulation on Markets in Crypto-assets (MiCA).[111]

Cryptoassets are not directly comparable to traditional state-issued currencies, yet they may function as alternative means of payment. Confronted with the risk that fragmentation of financial and payment systems could undermine the effectiveness of monetary policy, several central banks have embarked on the development of 'central bank digital currencies' (CBDCs), understood as electronic representations of value issued and backed by a central bank. Such instruments do not constitute cryptoassets in the strict sense, as their value is anchored to the sovereign currency and supported by sovereign authority, and they are not necessarily based on blockchain technology. The objective of CBDCs is to adapt the traditional functions of money to the realities of digital commerce and to prevent the fragmentation of payment systems. In addition, CBDCs offer certain advantages over physical cash, particularly in relation to the prevention of tax evasion, money laundering, and other forms of economic crime.[112]

In this context, the ECB launched its 'digital euro' project in October 2021, following earlier experiences in jurisdictions such as China and Sweden, which were at an advanced stage of implementing hybrid digital currency models. In such models, the monetary authority is responsible for issuing the digital currency, while distribution and user interaction are mediated by intermediaries, including commercial banks. Some uncertainty has arisen as to the appropriate legal bases for this initiative, given that it encompasses elements of monetary policy as well as other areas of Union action, including consumer protection, the internal market, and the protection of personal data.

[109] Council Regulation No 1338/2001 of 28 June 2001 laying down measures necessary for the protection of the euro against counterfeiting [2001] OJ L181/6.

[110] Decision 2010/597/EU of the European Central Bank of 16 September 2010 on the authenticity and fitness checking and recirculation of euro banknotes [2010] OJ L267/1.

[111] Communication from the Commission on a Retail Payments Strategy for the EU (Communication) COM(2020) 592 final; Communication from the Commission on a Digital Finance Strategy for the EU, COM(2020) 591 final; and 'Proposal for a Regulation on crypto-asset markets' COM(2020) 593 final.

[112] AAM Mooij, 'European Central Bank Digital Currency: The Digital Euro. What Design of the Digital Euro Is Possible within the European Central Bank's Legal Framework?' (2021) BRIDGE Networking Paper Series No 14.

In its Report on a Digital Euro,[113] the ECB explored different design options and highlighted the hybrid and token-based model, involving both the ECB and intermediaries, operated on proprietary technical infrastructure and inspired by existing systems such as TARGET2, the Eurosystem's real-time gross settlement system. Should the digital euro be introduced, the euro would exist in three forms of representation: scriptural; physical; and digital. The digital euro would not replace the existing forms, but would function as an additional means of payment. Despite the rapid decline in its use, cash is expected to continue to play a significant role for as long as physical and digital transactions coexist, which is likely to be the case for a considerable period of time.

As of early 2026, the digital euro initiative continues to advance: after the preparation phase (November 2023–October 2025) concluded as scheduled, the Eurosystem, led by the ECB, moved to the next technical readiness phase aimed at ensuring that basic systems, standards and operational frameworks are in place for a potential future issuance, including development of a draft rulebook and selection of platform providers, while supporting the Union legislative process on the proposed Regulation on the establishment of the digital euro, which lawmakers are expected to adopt in 2026. Policymakers indicated that if that legislation is agreed as planned, a pilot exercise could begin as early as 2027 and the digital euro could be ready for a first issuance around 2029, with ongoing debates in the European Parliament and Council over design features such as privacy, offline functionality and financial sector impacts, and the ECB stressing the project's role in strengthening European payment sovereignty and resilience alongside existing cash and account-based instruments.[114]

4.2. *Regulatory Powers over the Single Currency*

The issuance, circulation and verification of the single currency, in both banknotes and coins, entail significant regulatory intervention at both Union and national level. The Treaties lay down the foundations of the regulatory framework within which the institutions must act when adopting rules relating to the single currency, seeking to strike a balance between the democratic principle, the independence of the ECB and the national central banks, and the residual powers of the Member States. As a general rule, Article 133 TFEU provides that 'the European Parliament and the Council, acting in accordance with the ordinary legislative procedure, shall lay down the measures necessary for the use of the euro as the single currency'. Accordingly, the competence to adopt rules governing the use of the euro rests with the Union legislature, acting on a proposal from the Commission. That competence is, however, expressly exercised 'without prejudice to the powers of the European Central Bank', and Article 133 TFEU further requires that legislative measures adopted on that basis be preceded by consultation of the ECB. In that regard, Article 128(1) TFEU confers on the ECB 'the exclusive right to authorise the issue of euro banknotes within the Union', with the result that legislative action may not encroach upon that exclusive competence or undermine the ECB's institutional autonomy in the exercise of its tasks. In addition, Article 132 TFEU empowers the ECB to adopt regulations and 'take decisions necessary for carrying out the tasks entrusted to the ESCB under the Treaties and the Statute of the ESCB and of the ECB'.

[113] European Central Bank, Report on a Digital Euro, October 2020, www.ecb.europa.eu/pub/pdf/other/Report_on_a_digital_euro~4d7268b458.en.pdf.

[114] 'The future of money: a central bank perspective', contribution by Piero Cipollone, Member of the Executive Board of the ECB, to a roundtable at Aspen Institute Italia, Rome, 19 December 2025, available at www.ecb.europa.eu/press/key/date/2025/html/ecb.sp251219~fd2fee081a.en.html

Member States whose currency is the euro do not retain competence in the field of monetary policy, which is an exclusive competence of the Union. Nevertheless, Article 128(2) TFEU confers on the Member States the power to issue euro coins, subject to the approval of the volume of the issue by the ECB and to the other conditions and limits laid down by Union law. Moreover, as noted above, Member States may continue to exercise certain regulatory powers, in particular to regulate the procedures for the settlement of pecuniary obligations under public or private law.[115]

5. Institutional Organisation

The Union's monetary policy is structured around a distinctive institutional framework designed to reconcile the establishment of a strong single currency with the preservation of national institutional traditions, some of which are deeply embedded in the economic history of the Member States, such as the *Bundesbank*, the *Banque de France* or the *Banca d'Italia*. At the same time, that framework must accommodate the differentiated modalities of participation in the Union's monetary policy, given that only some Member States form part of the euro area, while others do not. The original design of the euro envisaged a short transitional period after which all Member States, with the exception of the United Kingdom and Denmark, would ultimately adopt the single currency. That design, however, did not fully materialise, and more than two decades after the introduction of the euro, six Member States have yet to adopt it, with no clear indication that most of them will do so in the near future. The institutional framework of monetary policy therefore seeks to balance these two dimensions by establishing a Union institution, the ECB, and its governing bodies, alongside governance structures in which national central banks are integrated to differing degrees depending on their participation in the Union's monetary policy, namely the ESCB and the Eurosystem.

5.1 The European System of Central Banks and the Eurosystem

The ESCB is the principal governance structure for monetary policy in the Union. As stated in Article 282(1) TFEU, the ESCB comprises 'the European Central Bank, together with the national central banks'.[116] Pursuant to Article 8 of the Statute of the ESCB and of the ECB, the ESCB 'shall be governed by the decision-making bodies of the ECB'. During the transitional period in which certain Member States have not adopted the euro, one forum within the ESCB is the General Council, which is constituted as a third decision-making body of the ECB, alongside the Governing Council and the Executive Board.[117] This transitional arrangement reflects the original, and ultimately unrealised, conception of a fully integrated monetary policy encompassing all Member States, in which the ESCB, bringing together the ECB and all national central banks, would operate as the central decision-making forum. That initial design has resulted in the ESCB, which includes all Member States, being endowed today with limited functions and governed by a body exercising only modest decision-making powers.

The ESCB has no legal personality and functions solely as a governance structure.[118] Legal personality, together with the guarantee of institutional independence, is conferred exclusively

[115] *Hessischer Rundfunk* (n 73) para 56; and Art 1 of Recommendation 2010/191.

[116] In the same vein, see Art 1 of the Statute of the ESCB and of the ECB.

[117] ibid, Art 44.

[118] J Langer, 'ESCB/Eurosystem/National Central Banks' in F Amtenbrink and C Herrmann (eds), *The EU Law of Economic and Monetary Union* (Oxford University Press, 2020).

on the ECB and on the national central banks. Given that national central banks retain their own legal personality and independence, the ECB does not possess the power to adopt binding decisions addressed to them outside the framework of the Governing Council, in which the governors of the national central banks are represented. Accordingly, monetary policy is implemented by the national central banks on the basis of decisions adopted collectively within the Governing Council of the ECB, while ensuring their participation in the formulation of that policy through the Union's institutional decision-making structures.

The delays of the transitional period have led to the emergence and consolidation of a second governance structure comprising only the ECB and the national central banks of the Member States whose currency is the euro. This second structure is the Eurosystem, which was expressly recognised in the Treaties with the entry into force of the Lisbon Treaty on 1 December 2009. The current wording of Article 282(1) TFEU clarifies that the ECB and the national central banks of the Member States whose currency is the euro together form the Eurosystem. In this way, the Treaties establish a distinct framework in which, following the model of the ESCB, both the ECB and the participating national central banks operate while retaining their own legal personality and full institutional independence. In practice, the core functions of monetary policy are now exercised within the framework of the Eurosystem, rather than that of the ESCB as a whole.

5.2. *The ECB and the Hybrid Status of National Central Banks*

The Statute of the ESCB and of the ECB and the functioning of its decision-making bodies are examined in chapter three of this book. More broadly, however, the Union's system of monetary governance encompasses both the ECB and the national central banks, which retain their own legal personality and full institutional independence. In the case of the national central banks, their integration into the ESCB and the Eurosystem entails a complex balance between their subjection to the ECB's monetary policy instructions and guidelines and the preservation of their status as independent institutions. The Court of Justice has characterised the position of the ECB and the national central banks as one of a 'hybrid status', in which the governors of the national central banks perform a 'dual professional role' (*dédoublement fonctionnel*). Accordingly, the governor of a national central bank participates in the ECB's principal decision-making body, the Governing Council, while simultaneously representing the interests and responsibilities of the central bank of which he or she is governor. That hybrid status extends throughout the Eurosystem and also underpins the possibility for Union authorities to adopt enforcement measures against Member States that interfere with the independence of a national central bank.[119]

This balance is achieved through the active participation of national central banks in the ECB's main decision-making body, the Governing Council, combined with the imposition by the Treaties and by the ECB of specific standards of conduct on those banks. Thus, Article 131 TFEU and Article 14.1 of the Statute of the ESCB and of the ECB require Member States to ensure that their national legislation, including the statutes of their national central banks, is compatible with the Treaties and with the Statute of the ESCB and of the ECB. In addition, the ECB is vested with powers that shape the status and development of national central banks. First, the ECB's convergence reports set out in detail the requirements of independence and compliance with the Treaties that must be met by Member States whose currency is not the euro, and over time the ECB has developed a body of doctrine applied to each

[119] In the case of the Court of Justice, the functional split of the ECB and national central banks enables it, on the basis of the second subparagraph of Art 14(2) of the Statute of the ESCB and of the ECB, to annul an act of the national authorities which is contrary to the independence of the national central bank (Joined Cases C-202/18 and C-238/18 *Ilmārs Rimšēvičs and ECB v Republic of Latvia* EU:C:2019:139, para 76).

Member State subject to convergence obligations, including standards governing the conduct of national central banks. Secondly, under Article 127(4) TFEU, the ECB enjoys a mandatory right of consultation in respect of 'any proposed Union act in its fields of competence' and 'any draft legislative provision' adopted by national authorities. The opinions delivered by the ECB pursuant to that provision have enabled it to articulate principles applicable not only to Member States subject to the convergence rules, but also to those whose currency is the euro.

5.3. *The External Dimension of Monetary Policy*

Globalisation requires monetary policy to take close account of developments in the international economy and to engage actively in international economic fora. At the same time, as discussed in chapter sixteen, the Union's external action is, as a matter of principle, attributed to the Union as a whole, and in particular to the institutions responsible for its external representation, namely the Commission and the High Representative. In the specific field of monetary policy, Article 138 TFEU establishes a tailored framework governing the international dimension of the euro, notably within the international monetary system. To that end, Article 138(1) TFEU provides, as a general rule, that common positions 'on matters of particular interest for economic and monetary union within the competent international financial institutions and conferences' are to be adopted by the Council on a proposal from the Commission, after consultation of the ECB. Article 138(2) TFEU adopts the same procedural approach for the adoption of 'appropriate measures to ensure unified representation within the international financial institutions and conferences'. In both cases, the Council acts with the participation limited to representatives of the Member States whose currency is the euro.[120]

The negotiation and conclusion of international agreements in monetary matters are also subject to specific rules laid down in Article 219 TFEU. In a manner comparable to Article 138 TFEU, that provision centralises the Union's external action in the field of economic and monetary policy within the Council, which is entrusted with the task of reaching consensus and deciding on the arrangements for negotiating and concluding such agreements. Article 219 TFEU requires, however, that those decisions ensure that the Union expresses a single position and that the ECB is consulted in advance. In addition, Article 219(4) TFEU provides that Member States 'may negotiate in international bodies and conclude international agreements'. That authorisation reflects the *sui generis* nature of the Union's competences in economic policy, which continue, to a significant extent, to remain within the remit of the Member States.

V. BANKING UNION

The financial crisis that unfolded between 2008 and 2013 exposed significant weaknesses in the Union's economic governance model, which combines a centralised monetary policy with largely decentralised economic and fiscal policies. Those weaknesses were further exacerbated by the absence, at the time, of a European banking sector governed by uniform rules and subject to common supervision, with no Union authority vested with comprehensive powers to oversee the banking industry within the internal market. From 2010 onwards, a rapid process of legislative reform was initiated in order to address, at least in part, those structural deficiencies. As noted above, the fiscal dimension of economic policy was substantially reinforced through the introduction of a new framework for fiscal surveillance and discipline applicable to the Member States. In parallel, the establishment of the ESM provided the euro area Member

[120] Art 138(3) TFEU.

States, through an intergovernmental structure outside the Union's institutional framework, with a financial backstop designed to manage future macroeconomic imbalances.

Alongside those measures, the Union laid the foundations for a Banking Union, intended to establish a common legal and institutional framework governing the three pillars of the supervision of the Union's financial system: prudential supervision of financial institutions, a bank resolution regime applicable to credit institutions in difficulty, and a European framework for the protection of bank deposits. Those pillars are underpinned by a network of European financial authorities created to ensure uniform application and enforcement of the common legal framework. In the field of prudential supervision, competences were allocated among the ECB, the national competent authorities and the European Banking Authority. Bank resolution was entrusted to a Union agency, the Single Resolution Board (SRB), operating in close cooperation with national resolution authorities. Although a fully fledged European Deposit Insurance Scheme (EDIS) remains under negotiation, the basic elements of deposit protection are already reflected in several Union legal instruments.[121]

The Banking Union was further complemented by the establishment of specialised Union authorities in the fields of securities markets and occupational pensions, namely ESMA and EIOPA, as well as by the creation of a macroprudential oversight body responsible for monitoring and analysing systemic risks within the Union, namely the European Systemic Risk Board (ESRB).

The defining feature of the Banking Union lies in its high degree of supranational integration and the distinctive nature of its institutional design. Two of its pillars (prudential banking supervision and bank resolution) were established as 'single mechanisms', namely the SSM and the SRM. Within those mechanisms, Union and national authorities operate as a single administrative system: while each mechanism is headed by a Union institution or agency, decision-making and implementation depend on the close and structured involvement of national authorities. To date, the system has functioned effectively, demonstrating that integrated governance arrangements combining European and national levels can deliver coherent and efficient outcomes. In that sense, the Banking Union has also served as a laboratory for other policy areas that may, in the future, draw inspiration from the 'single mechanism' model in their institutional design.

1. Prudential Banking Supervision

1.1. *The Single Supervisory Mechanism*

The first pillar of the Banking Union is the SSM, which establishes a common legal and institutional framework for the prudential supervision of credit institutions in the Member States whose currency is the euro, while allowing other Member States to participate through specific arrangements. The SSM creates an integrated system of administrative governance through which Union institutions, together with the participating Member States, exercise prudential supervision over credit institutions established in their territories. That supervision is conducted under a uniform legal framework and implemented jointly by common institutions, ensuring a high degree of consistency across participating jurisdictions.

The SSM framework has both a substantive and an institutional dimension. The substantive dimension is formed by two core legislative instruments applicable to the banking sector throughout the Union: Directive 2013/36 on access to the activities of credit institutions and the prudential supervision of credit institutions (the Capital Requirements Directive,

[121] In this regard, see D Sarmiento, 'The European Banking Governance. The Single Supervisory Mechanism and the Union's Constitutional Challenge' (2016) 28 *Revue Européenne de Droit Public* 109.

'CRD IV'),[122] and Regulation 575/2013 on prudential requirements for credit institutions and investment firms (the Capital Requirements Regulation, 'CRR').[123] Both instruments have since been substantially amended and supplemented by a package of reforms, most recently CRD VI and CRR III. The CRD harmonises key aspects of banking activity, including authorisation and supervisory powers, while the CRR lays down detailed and highly technical rules governing capital requirements and other prudential standards. Both instruments apply to all credit institutions operating within the internal market, irrespective of whether they are established in euro area or non-euro area Member States.

From an institutional perspective, the operation of the SSM varies depending on whether a Member State has adopted the euro. For euro area Member States, Regulation 1024/2013 establishes a specific supervisory framework by conferring on the ECB defined tasks relating to the prudential supervision of credit institutions.[124] Accordingly, all credit institutions established in the euro area fall within the ECB's supervisory remit under that Regulation, although the direct exercise of day-to-day supervisory tasks is differentiated between the ECB and the national competent authorities. Member States whose currency is not the euro may nevertheless participate in the SSM through a close cooperation arrangement provided for in Regulation 1024/2013. This possibility was used, for example, by Bulgaria during the period preceding its adoption of the euro, which took place on 1 January 2026.[125] In non-euro area Member States that do not participate in the SSM, prudential supervision continues to be exercised by national competent authorities, albeit within the substantive legal framework laid down by the CRD and the CRR. [126]

Regulation 1024/2013 introduces the basic rules governing the SSM's institutional framework, with the ECB at the helm. However, the SSM comprises an institutional structure composed of two levels: one European and one national, meaning that national competent authorities continue to play a significant role. As stated in Article 6 of Regulation 1024/2013, the ECB 'shall carry out its tasks within a single supervisory mechanism composed of the ECB and the national competent authorities', while also providing that the ECB 'shall be responsible for the effective and consistent functioning of the SSM'.

Regulation 1024/2013 sets out a closed list of supervisory tasks conferred on the ECB. These include, inter alia, the tasks to:

- to grant and withdraw authorisations of credit institutions;[127]
- assess notifications of the acquisition and disposal of qualifying holdings in credit institutions;[128]
- carry out supervisory reviews of the structures, strategies, processes and mechanisms put in place by credit institutions and of the adequacy of their own funds;[129]

[122] Directive 2013/36/EU of the European Parliament and of the Council of 26 June 2013 relating to the taking up and pursuit of the business of credit institutions and the prudential supervision of credit institutions and investment firms, amending Directive 2002/87/EC and repealing Directives 2006/48/EC and 2006/49/EC [2013] OJ L176/338.

[123] Regulation (EU) No 575/2013 of the European Parliament and of the Council of 26 June 2013 on prudential requirements for credit institutions and investment firms and amending Regulation No 648/2012 [2013] OJ L176/1.

[124] Council Regulation No 1024/2013 of 15 October 2013 entrusting the European Central Bank with specific tasks concerning policies relating to the prudential supervision of credit institutions [2013] OJ L287/63, further developed by the so-called 'SSM Framework Regulation' provided for in Regulation No 468/2014 of the European Central Bank of 16 April 2014 laying down the framework for cooperation within the Single Supervisory Mechanism between the European Central Bank and national competent authorities and with designated national authorities [2014] OJ L141/1.

[125] Decision (EU) 2020/1015 of the European Central Bank of 24 June 2020 on the establishment of close cooperation between the ECB and Българска народна банка (Bulgarian National Bank) (ECB/2020/30) [2020] OJ L 224I/1.

[126] On the institutional framework of the SSM, see B Wolfers and T Voland, 'Level the Playing Field: The New Supervision of Credit Institutions by the European Central Bank' (2014) 51 *Common Market Law Review* 1463.

[127] Art 4(1)(a) of Regulation 1024/2013.

[128] ibid, Art 4(1)(c).

[129] ibid, Art 4(1)(f).

- ensure compliance with prudential requirements (own funds, large exposures, liquidity, leverage, etc).[130]

This list of tasks is accompanied by an individualised allocation of powers for the exercise of these tasks. Therefore, the ECB may make use of powers to request information,[131] conduct general investigations,[132] on-site inspections,[133] and to impose administrative pecuniary penalties (sanctions).[134]

Due to the integrated nature of the SSM, the ECB performs its tasks by applying both Union law and the law of the Member States. This is a rare and institutionally significant feature within the Union legal order, as it expressly requires a Union institution to apply national law in the exercise of its Union-law competences. This obligation is introduced in Article 4(3) of Regulation 1024/2013 and is limited to two cases.

- where the applicable Union law is composed of Directives, the ECB applies 'the national legislation transposing those Directives';
- where the applicable Union law is composed of Regulations and where those Regulations explicitly grant options to Member States, the ECB 'shall apply also the national legislation exercising those options'.

This obligation to apply national law is an unusual feature in an institutional system where Union institutions apply Union law and their decisions are judicially reviewed only by Union courts.[135] When the duty is imposed on the ECB to apply the rules of a Member State to resolve a case, the legality of the ECB's decision can only be reviewed by Union courts, but such review must be undertaken in light of national law. In such cases, can Union courts examine the entirety of national law, or only the prudential supervisory rule relevant to the specific case? If the national rule violates Union law, is the ECB required to set it aside? Regarding national rules that transpose directives, does the doctrine of direct effect apply to the ECB? Some of these questions appear to have been answered in the judgment of the Court of Justice in *ECB and Commission v Corneli*,[136] where it confirmed that Union institutions have a duty to interpret national law in conformity with Union law, to the extent of ensuring the effectiveness of Union law when a Member State transposes a directive. In that case, involving ECB decisions placing Banca Carige under temporary administration, the Italian legislature had made a contested transposition of the Bank Recovery and Resolution Directive (BRRD), and the General Court had annulled the ECB's decisions on the ground that it was not possible to undertake an interpretation of the Italian legislative rule in conformity with the BRRD. The Court of Justice disagreed, emphasising that Union institutions have the same duties as national courts when confronted with the enforcement of a rule of national law that transposes a Directive.[137]

1.2. *Significant and Less Significant Entities*

The ECB does not assume responsibility for all supervisory tasks within the SSM, nor does it act as the direct supervisor of all credit institutions. In order to ensure the sustainability of the

[130] ibid, Art 4(1)(e).
[131] ibid, Art 10.
[132] ibid, Art 11.
[133] ibid, Art 12.
[134] ibid, Art 18.
[135] On the application of national law by the EU institutions, see M Prek and S Lefèvre, 'The EU Courts as "National" Courts: National Law in the EU Judicial Process' (2017) 54 *Common Market Law Review* 369.
[136] Joined Cases C-777/22 P and C-789/22 P *ECB and Commission v Corneli* EU:C:2025:580.
[137] ibid, paras 134–41. See also Cases T-647/21 and T-99/22 *Sber Vermögensverwaltungs AG* EU:T:2024:127, paras 59–64; and Case T-667/21 *BAWAG PSK Bank für Arbeit und Wirtschaft und Österreichische Postsparkasse AG* EU:T:2024:131, paras 58–62.

system and to avoid overburdening the ECB with the supervision of an excessive number of institutions, Regulation (EU) No 1024/2013 establishes a division of supervisory powers and functions between the ECB and the national competent authorities. Under that framework, the ECB exercises the supervisory powers conferred by the SSM Regulation in respect of 'significant' credit institutions, while national competent authorities remain responsible for the direct supervision of 'less significant' institutions. Article 6(4) of Regulation (EU) No 1024/2013 provides that a credit institution is to be classified as 'significant' where it satisfies one or more of a set of criteria, including in particular the following:

- the total value of its assets exceeds EUR 30 billion;
- the ratio of its total assets to GDP of the participating Member State of establishment exceeds 20 per cent, unless the total value of its assets is below five billion euros;
- the ECB takes a decision confirming such significance after having conducted a comprehensive assessment of the credit institution.[138]

That allocation of supervisory responsibilities does not imply that the ECB is deprived of decision-making powers in relation to 'less significant' credit institutions. On the contrary, Regulation (EU) No 1024/2013 entrusts the ECB with certain tasks that apply to all credit institutions, irrespective of their classification. First, the ECB enjoys exclusive competence to grant and withdraw authorisations for credit institutions, as well as to assess notifications concerning the acquisition and disposal of qualifying holdings in such institutions. Secondly, the ECB is empowered to issue regulations, guidelines or general instructions addressed to national supervisory authorities.[139] In addition, it retains the authority to assume direct supervisory competence at any time over one or more individual credit institutions where this is necessary to ensure the consistent application of high supervisory standards.[140]

1.3. *Investigations and On-site Inspections*

In the exercise of its supervisory powers, the ECB may conduct investigations into individual credit institutions in order to verify compliance with applicable prudential requirements. Such investigations may give rise to obligations for the institutions concerned to produce documents, permit the examination of books and records, provide written or oral explanations, and submit to interviews.[141] Credit institutions have the duty to cooperate with the ECB, and if they obstruct an investigation they may face administrative pecuniary penalties, as outlined below.

The most notable example of investigatory tasks is on-site inspections, where the ECB, together with the staff of the national competent authority, conducts an in-person verification at the premises of the credit institution under investigation, with or without prior notice.[142] Due to the potential intrusiveness of this measure, Regulation 1024/2013 provides that the inspection may require, in accordance with national law, prior judicial authorisation.[143] In such cases, the national court reviews the ECB's decision to order the inspection within the limits laid down by national law, in particular to ensure that the measure is not arbitrary or disproportionate.[144]

[138] Art 6 of Regulation 1024/2013 and Arts 43–44, as well as Arts 50–72 of the SSM Framework Regulation. On the ECB's competence to take over supervision of less significant institutions, see Case C-450/17 P *Landeskreditbank Baden-Württemberg - Förderbank* EU:C:2019:372.

[139] Art 6(5)(a) of Regulation 1024/2013.

[140] ibid, Art 6(5)(b).

[141] ibid, Art 11(1).

[142] ibid, Art 12.

[143] ibid.

[144] ibid, Art 13(2).

Investigations conducted by the ECB typically culminate in the adoption of recommendations addressed to the credit institution concerned. Depending on the seriousness of the practices or conduct identified, those recommendations may include requirements to take specific action and, where appropriate, the imposition of administrative pecuniary penalties.[145] Throughout the investigative process, the credit institution enjoys the right to be heard, which entails an obligation on the ECB to state reasons for its decisions, thereby enabling the institution to submit observations and, where appropriate, to put forward relevant arguments. Failure to respect the right to be heard may result in the annulment of both the investigation and the measures adopted on its basis.

1.4. *Administrative Penalties*

Regulation 1024/2013 grants the ECB authority to impose administrative pecuniary penalties (sanctions) on supervised credit institutions. This authority is limited to cases where institutions 'intentionally or negligently breach a requirement under relevant directly applicable acts of Union law in relation to which administrative pecuniary penalties shall be made available to competent authorities under the relevant Union law'.[146] In other words, when the ECB identifies a breach of a Union rule in one of the areas where it exercises supervisory competence, it may exercise its discretionary power to impose administrative pecuniary penalties. This authority includes the power to impose pecuniary penalties and applies only to the credit institution, and not to natural persons (such as managers and staff of the institution).

Pecuniary penalties can reach up to twice the amount of profits gained or losses avoided as a result of the breach. When this amount cannot be determined, the penalty may reach up to 10% of the total annual turnover in the preceding business year.[147] Within these thresholds, Regulation 1024/2013 requires penalties to be 'effective, proportionate and dissuasive'.[148] Additionally, as a general rule, administrative pecuniary penalties are subject to publication, subject to the safeguards and exceptions laid down in Regulation 1024/2013 in order to avoid disproportionate harm or risks to financial stability.[149] The publication of penalties can significantly impact the market, and in some particularly sensitive cases, the ECB may decide not to publish the measure.[150]

In line with national traditions, the ECB's sanctioning procedures are divided into an investigation phase and a resolution phase.[151] The investigation is conducted by the 'Investigating Unit', an independent body within the ECB's supervisory infrastructure, whose task is to investigate the matter, gather information, and, where appropriate, propose the imposition of an administrative pecuniary penalty on a credit institution.[152] Once the proposal is made, the decision rests with the Supervisory Board and the Governing Council, acting on a draft decision from the Supervisory Board under the 'non-objection procedure' laid down in Article 26(8) of Regulation 1024/2013. Administrative pecuniary penalties can be challenged before the ECB's Administrative Board of Review[153] and, by way of an action for annulment, before the General Court.

In cases where the ECB determines that a credit institution is in breach of national law, yet within an area harmonised by Union law, it is the responsibility of the national competent

[145] See the Guide to on-site inspections and internal model investigations, www.bankingsupervision.europa.eu/ecb/pub/pdf/ssm.osi_guide201809.en.pdf

[146] Art 18(1) of Regulation 1024/2013.

[147] ibid, Art 18(1); and Art 128 of the SSM Framework Regulation.

[148] ibid, Art 18(3). See also the Guidance on the method for setting financial penalties, www.bankingsupervision.europa.eu/ecb/pub/pdf/ssm.guidetothemethodofsettingadministrativepecuniarypenalties_202103~400cbafa55.en.pdf.

[149] ibid, Art 18(6); and Art 132 of the SSM Framework Regulation.

[150] Art 132(1) of the SSM Framework Regulation. On the determination of the publication criteria, see Case T-203/18 *VQ v ECB* EU:T:2020:313, paras 77–99.

[151] Arts 123–27 of the SSM Framework Regulation.

[152] ibid, Art 125.

[153] Art 24 of Regulation 1024/2013.

authorities to exercise the power to impose administrative pecuniary penalties. Article 18(5) of Regulation 1024/2013 empowers the ECB in such cases to 'require national competent authorities to open proceedings with a view to taking action' to ensure that appropriate penalties are imposed.

2. Banking Resolution

The financial and sovereign debt crises that unfolded between 2008 and 2013 exposed weaknesses not only in the financial system itself, but also in the divergent legal responses adopted by the Member States when confronted with stress situations in the financial sector. While certain Member States had developed advanced crisis-management frameworks, others relied almost exclusively on traditional insolvency law. In the context of financial institutions, and banks in particular, ordinary bankruptcy rules are manifestly inadequate, as they fail to take account of the systemic importance of certain credit institutions for the financial system as a whole and of the need to protect specific categories of stakeholders, such as depositors. In a crisis scenario, it is therefore essential that both the Union and the Member States possess instruments enabling financial institutions to withstand severe stress or, where insolvency is unavoidable, to be wound down in an orderly manner, so as to prevent the amplification of stress or the emergence of contagion effects across the financial system.

The second pillar of the Banking Union consists of the institutional and legal framework designed to harmonise and streamline preventive and corrective bank resolution procedures. The objective of the bank resolution regime is to equip the competent authorities with a set of tools allowing for early and decisive intervention in failing institutions, with a view to ensuring the continuity of their critical functions and, where necessary, limiting the adverse consequences of a liquidation scenario. Central to that framework is a foundational principle underpinning the entire system: in the context of a failing institution, losses shall be borne first by shareholders and, subsequently, by creditors in accordance with the hierarchy of claims in insolvency. This principle, commonly referred to as the 'bail-in' principle, ensures that the costs of failure are allocated to shareholders and creditors rather than to taxpayers.

The European resolution framework is organised in a manner comparable to prudential supervision, in the form of a 'mechanism' known as the SRM. Like the SSM, the SRM operates on two interconnected levels: European and national. At Union level, the resolution framework operates through the SRB, which exercises the core technical and operational resolution functions, with the involvement of the European Commission and, in certain cases, the Council in the endorsement and oversight of resolution schemes in accordance with Union law. At national level, the national resolution authorities are responsible for implementing the resolution powers conferred on them under both Union and national law.

Following the model established by the SSM, the SRM is underpinned by both a substantive and an institutional legal framework. From a substantive perspective, the resolution regime is set out in two core legislative instruments that define the foundations of the system and the principal resolution tools: Directive 2014/59[154] and Regulation 806/2014.[155] The former constitutes an internal market harmonisation measure and applies to all 27 Member States. The latter, by contrast, is a uniform instrument establishing the SRM and is, as a general rule,

[154] Directive 2014/59/EU of the European Parliament and of the Council of 15 May 2014 establishing a framework for the restructuring and resolution of credit institutions and investment firms, and amending Council Directive 82/891/EEC, and Directives 2001/24/EC, 2002/47/EC, 2004/25/EC, 2005/56/EC, 2007/36/EC, 2011/35/EU, 2012/30/EU and 2013/36/EU, and Regulations No 1093/2010 and No 648/2012 of the European Parliament and of the Council [2014] OJ L173/190.

[155] Regulation No 806/2014 of the European Parliament and of the Council of 15 July 2014 on uniform rules and a uniform procedure for the resolution of credit institutions and certain investment firms in the framework of a Single Resolution Mechanism and a Single Resolution Fund and amending Regulation No 1093/2010 [2014] OJ L225/1.

applicable only to the Member States whose currency is the euro, without prejudice to the possibility for other Member States to opt into the mechanism through close cooperation. Union law thus establishes a layered resolution framework, comprising a general harmonisation regime applicable throughout the Union and a uniform regime creating the SRM for participating Member States. Regulation (EU) No 806/2014 does not introduce substantive departures from the provisions of Directive 2014/59; rather, it develops and, in functional terms, 'transposes' the Directive's rules for the Member States participating in the SRM. The substantive resolution framework therefore operates through a form of two-level harmonisation, consisting of a general harmonising layer applicable to all Member States under Directive 2014/59 and a more specific and uniform layer, aligned with that Directive, but applicable only to a subset of Member States.

2.1. *Preventive and Corrective Resolution*

The Union's resolution framework is built around two complementary modes of action that operate sequentially over time. First, preventive resolution is concerned with preparing for potential resolution scenarios through advance planning for each credit institution and group, including the establishment of minimum requirements for own funds and eligible liabilities (MREL). Secondly, corrective resolution constitutes the subsequent phase in which the risk materialises, triggering the need for swift intervention measures, either to preserve the continuity of the institution's critical functions or, where necessary, to ensure its orderly winding-up.

Resolution planning is implemented through the adoption of resolution plans for individual institutions and groups. A resolution plan sets out the strategies and options to be applied once the conditions for resolution are met. It includes an analysis of relevant scenarios and assets that may be used as collateral, specifies the resolution actions to be taken, contains a resolvability assessment, and identifies the forms of financial support that may be available during the resolution process.[156] Once the resolution plan has been approved, the institution must take all necessary steps to ensure its implementation, although simplified obligations may apply to certain institutions depending on their size.[157] Additionally, there is a MREL requirement, for own funds and eligible liabilities, along with an obligation for institutions to ensure their resolvability under the resolution tools established within the European framework.[158] It should be recalled that the Union's resolution model is founded on the principle that losses be borne first by shareholders and, subsequently, by creditors. In order to avoid recourse to public funds, credit institutions must be resolvable through the bail-in tool established by the relevant legislation, for which compliance with MREL is essential.

The 'bail-in' stage of resolution occurs when an institution is failing or likely to fail, provided that resolution is deemed necessary in the public interest. In such cases, the ECB must issue a determination stating that the institution is 'failing or likely to fail' and promptly notify the SRB and the Commission.[159] The rules provide examples of circumstances in which an institution is deemed to be failing or likely to fail, including the following: the institution has infringed, or there are objective elements to support a determination that it will infringe in the near future, the requirements for continuing authorisation; its assets are less than its liabilities; the institution is, or will in the near future be, unable to pay its debts as they fall due; or extraordinary public financial support is required.[160]

[156] Art 10 of Directive 2014/59.
[157] ibid, Art 4.
[158] ibid, Art 45.
[159] ibid, Art 32(1). This ECB decision is not subject to appeal, as confirmed by the Court of Justice in Joined Cases C-551/19 and C-552/19 P *ABLV Bank AS v ECB* EU:C:2021:369.
[160] Art 32(4) of Directive 2014/59.

The SRB, with the Commission's endorsement, adopts a resolution scheme using one of the various resolution tools outlined in the rules. The choice of resolution tool is tailored to the specific needs of each case, offering options such as the sale of business tool, the bridge institution tool, the asset separation tool, and the bail-in tool.[161] The SRB is also required to conduct a resolution valuation of the institution, a process essential for selecting the most suitable resolution tool and for making decisions regarding the write-down and conversion of capital instruments necessary for the specific case. An impartial third party will perform the valuation; however, in urgent situations, it may also be carried out by the SRB itself. This valuation is a vital part of the resolution mechanism.

The resolution scheme is adopted by the SRB and endorsed by the Commission, in cooperation with the national resolution authorities of the Member State where the credit institution under resolution is located. The Commission's involvement reflects the requirements of the Meroni doctrine and the principle of institutional balance, ensuring that the exercise of discretionary powers within the resolution framework remains subject to appropriate political and legal oversight. The legality of the decision-making system under the SRM was confirmed by the General Court in 2022 and later confirmed and further developed by the Court of Justice in *Commission v SRB*.[162] Resolution measures are therefore adopted with the involvement of several actors, both at Union and national levels, providing evidence that the SRM is a joint legal and institutional framework in two tiers. Cooperation within the SRM is crucial for the effective functioning of the resolution system. For this reason, Articles 30–31 of the Regulation establish various obligations for close cooperation among the SRB, the Commission, and national resolution authorities.

2.2. *The Single Resolution Fund*

The European resolution framework is founded on the 'bail-in' principle, pursuant to which losses are to be borne first by shareholders and creditors. The corollary of that principle is the prohibition, as a general rule, on rescuing failing financial institutions through recourse to taxpayers' funds. Although Union legislation does not exclude all forms of public intervention in absolute terms, it provides for the possibility of using the SRF where bail-in measures prove insufficient to ensure the effective implementation of a resolution action. The SRF is not financed by contributions from Member States, but through mandatory contributions levied on credit institutions subject to the resolution regime. In this manner, the underlying principle is preserved whereby neither national budgets nor the Union budget are called upon to support failing institutions; instead, the financial sector itself provides a collective financial buffer where additional resources are required.

The SRF is established by Regulation (EU) No 806/2014 and by an intergovernmental agreement of 21 May 2014, on the transfer and mutualisation of contributions to the Single Resolution Fund. While Directive 2014/59 and Regulation (EU) No 806/2014 lay down the conditions governing both *ex ante* and ex post extraordinary contributions to be borne by credit institutions, the intergovernmental agreement regulates the rules on the transfer and mutualisation of those contributions within the SRF. The Fund has been progressively capitalised over an eight-year period starting in 2016 and has achieved its target level of at least 1% of the total amount of covered deposits of all credit institutions established in the participating Member States. The SRB is the administrator of the SRF and is responsible for its

[161] ibid, Arts 37–44.

[162] See, inter alia, Case T-510/17 *Del Valle and Others v SRB and Commission* EU:T:2022:312, paras 221ff; and Case C-551/22 *Commission v SRB* EU:2024:520.

management, although recourse to the Fund in the context of a resolution action is subject to specific procedural requirements.

The system of contributions to the SRF is established by Delegated Regulation 2015/63[163] and Implementing Regulation 2015/81.[164] Those provisions set out the criteria for calculating contributions, which are largely calibrated by reference to each institution's individual risk profile. Accordingly, the level of the contribution varies depending on the degree of risk assumed by the institution, with riskier institutions required to contribute more than those pursuing more conservative strategies. That approach was upheld by the Court of Justice in *Iccrea*, in which the Court confirmed that the Commission enjoys a broad margin of discretion when defining and applying the individual risk profile criteria used to calculate contributions for each institution.[165]

2.3. *Creditor Rights: 'No Creditor Worse Off'*

The European resolution model has far-reaching implications for the protection of property rights. The 'bail-in' principle entails that the parties primarily exposed in a resolution scenario are the shareholders and creditors of the credit institution concerned, who may be subject to measures of write-down or conversion of capital instruments. Such measures may have effects analogous to expropriation and entail limitations on the fundamental right to property, particularly where the outcome of resolution is less favourable for shareholders or creditors than that which would have resulted from ordinary insolvency proceedings. In order to prevent such outcomes and to ensure that write-down or conversion measures do not amount to disproportionate interferences with property rights, the resolution framework requires that, after the adoption of a resolution scheme, an independent person assesses whether shareholders and creditors would have received more favourable treatment under normal insolvency proceedings than under the resolution action.[166]

This safeguard, commonly referred to as the 'no creditor worse off' principle, constitutes a core guarantee for the protection of shareholders and creditors. The Court of Justice has repeatedly affirmed the central role of that principle in safeguarding the fundamental right to property of persons affected by resolution measures.[167] To preserve the effectiveness of the mechanism, the case law further establishes that, in the context of the sale of business tool, shareholders and creditors may not circumvent the resolution framework by bringing ordinary civil actions against the acquirer, but must instead rely on the compensation mechanisms provided for under the 'no creditor worse off' principle.[168]

3. **Protection of Bank Deposits**

The third pillar of the Banking Union remains under negotiation, with no agreement currently in sight. Its objective is the establishment of a European Deposit Insurance Scheme (EDIS),

[163] Commission Delegated Regulation 2015/63 of 21 October 2014 supplementing Directive 2014/59/EU of the European Parliament and of the Council as regards ex ante contributions to resolution financing mechanisms [2015] OJ L11/44.

[164] Council Implementing Regulation 2015/81 of 19 December 2014 specifying uniform conditions for implementing Regulation No 806/2014 of the European Parliament and of the Council as regards ex ante contributions to the Single Resolution Fund [2015] OJ L15/1.

[165] Case C-414/18 *Iccrea Banca SpA* EU:C:2019:1036, paras 32ff.

[166] Arts 73ff of Directive 2014/59.

[167] Case C-526/14 *Kotnik and Others* EU:C:2016:570, para 91; Case C-41/15 *Dowling and Others* EU:C:2016:836, para 54; and Case C-410/20 *Banco Santander* EU:C:2022:351, para 36.

[168] *Banco Santander* (n 167) paras 48–49, Joined Cases C-775/22, C-779/22 and C-794/22 *Banco Santander (II)* EU:C:2024:679, paras 82–84.

intended to function as a safety net in order to enhance stability and confidence in the internal market and among depositors. Prudential supervision contributes to the stability of the banking sector through common oversight standards. At the same time, the resolution framework enables timely intervention, support and, where appropriate, the orderly winding-up of failing institutions. Deposit guarantee schemes, in turn, are designed to provide certainty and confidence to users of the banking system. It is this third pillar that continues to lack consensus among the Member States.

However, Union law has harmonised national deposit guarantee schemes, so that bank deposit guarantees are now governed by common rules, mainly outlined in Directive 2014/49 on deposit guarantee schemes.[169] The Directive sets a common protection level, under which aggregate deposits of each depositor are covered up to a maximum amount of EUR 100,000. The Directive also introduces criteria for calculating the repayable amount,[170] the repayment time limits,[171] and the financing and operational regimes of the Member States' deposit guarantee schemes.[172] Additionally, it provides for the possibility of cooperation between deposit guarantee schemes across different Member States, including voluntary cross-border arrangements to support the progressive integration of the banking sector within the internal market.

Despite this harmonised framework, it remains the case that lasting financial stability and an effective severing of the link between bank risk and sovereign risk can only be achieved through a deeper integration of deposit guarantee schemes. The creation of a single, fully mutualised European deposit insurance fund has, however, proved politically sensitive and difficult for some Member States to accept. As a result, ongoing discussions have focused on intermediate solutions in which national guarantee funds would coexist with a supranational European guarantee. In that regard, the Commission's 2015 EDIS proposal envisaged a phased approach, moving from a reinsurance mechanism for national schemes to a co-insurance system and ultimately to a fully fledged insurance scheme for participating deposit guarantee schemes. Under that proposal, oversight would be entrusted to the SRB, which would be responsible for authorising the disbursement of funds when clearly defined conditions are met. The onset of the COVID-19 pandemic in early 2020, together with the severe economic consequences of the Russian invasion of Ukraine, has effectively stalled this initiative, pending further assessment of the state of the banking system and of the potential implications of such a scheme for individual Member States.

BIBLIOGRAPHY

Constitutional Framework of EMU

Adamski, D, 'Economic Constitution of the Euro Area after Gauweiler' (2015) 52 *Common Market Law Review* 1451.

Adamski, D, Amtenbrink, F and de Haan, J (eds), *The Cambridge Handbook of European Monetary, Economic and Financial Integration* (Cambridge University Press, 2023).

Amtenbrink, F Herrmann, C and Repasi, R (eds), *The EU Law of Economic and Monetary Union* (Oxford University Press, 2020).

Estella de Noriega, A, *Legal Foundations of EU Economic Governance* (Cambridge University Press, 2018).

Hinarejos, A, *The Euro Area Crisis in Constitutional Perspective* (Oxford University Press, 2015).

[169] Directive 2014/49/EU of the European Parliament and of the Council of 16 April 2014 on deposit guarantee schemes [2014] OJ L173/149.

[170] Art 7 of Directive 2014/49.

[171] ibid, Art 8.

[172] ibid, Arts 10–11.

Ioannidis, M, 'Europe's New Transformations: How the EU Economic Constitution Changed During the Eurozone Crisis' (2016) 53 *Common Market Law Review.*
Lenaerts, K, 'EMU and the EU's Constitutional Framework' (2014) 39 *European Law Review.*
Markakis, M, *Accountability in the Economic and Monetary Union: Foundations, Policy and Governance* (Oxford University Press, 2020).
Menéndez, AJ, 'The Existential Crisis of the European Union' (2013) 14 *German Law Journal.*
Tuori, K, 'The European Financial Crisis: Constitutional Aspects and Implications' *EUI Working Papers* LAW 2012/28.
Tuori, K and Tuori, K, *The Eurozone Crisis: A Constitutional Analysis* (Cambridge University Press, 2014).
de Witte, B, 'Old-Fashioned Flexibility: International Agreements between Member States of the European Union' in G de Búrca and J Scott (eds), *Constitutional Change in the EU: From Uniformity to Flexibility?* (Hart, 2000) 31–58.

The Union's Economic Policy

De Gregorio Merino, A, 'Legal Developments in the Economic and Monetary Union During the Debt Crisis: The Mechanisms of Financial Assistance' (2012) 49 *Common Market Law Review* 1613.
Dermine, P, *The New Economic Governance of the Eurozone* (Oxford University Press, 2022).
Fabbrini, F, *Economic Governance in Europe: Comparative Paradoxes and Constitutional Challenges* (Oxford University Press, 2016).
Markakis, M and Dermine, P, 'Bailouts, the Legal Status of Memoranda of Understanding and the Scope of Application of the Charter: Florescu' (2018) 55 *Common Market Law Review* 643.

The Monetary Policy of the Union

Amtenbrink, F, *The Democratic Accountability of Central Banks* (Hart, 1999).
Fromage, D, Dermine, P, Nicolaides, P and Tuori, K, 'ECB Independence and Accountability Today: Towards a (Necessary) Redefinition' (2019) 26 *Maastricht Journal of European and Comparative Law* 3.
Steinbach, A, 'The Lender of Last Resort in the Eurozone' (2016) 53 *Common Market Law Review* 361.
Zilioli, C and Ioannidis, M, 'Climate Change and the Mandate of the ECB: Potential and Limits of Monetary Contribution to European Green Policies' (2022) 59 *Common Market Law Review* 1027.
Zilioli, C and Selmayr, M, *The Law of the European Central Bank* (Hart, 2001).
— 'The Constitutional Status of the European Central Bank' (2007) 44 *Common Market Law Review* 355.

The Banking Union

Bovenschen, W, ter Kuile, G and Wissink, L, 'Tailor-Made Accountability Within the Single Supervisory Mechanism' (2015) 52 *Common Market Law Review* 943.
Hinojosa Martínez, L and Beneyto Pérez, JM (eds), *European Banking Union: The New Regime* (Kluwer Law International, 2015).
Moloney, N, 'European Banking Union: Assessing Its Risks and Resilience' (2014) 51 *Common Market Law Review* 1609.
Prek, M and Lefèvre, S, 'The EU Courts as "National" Courts: National Law in the EU Judicial Process' (2017) 54 *Common Market Law Review* 369.
Sarmiento, D, 'The European Banking Governance: The Single Supervisory Mechanism and the Union's Constitutional Challenge' (2016) 28 *Revue Européenne de Droit Public*, 109.
Schammo, P, 'Institutional Change in the Banking Union: The Case of the Single Supervisory Mechanism' (2021) 40 *Yearbook of European Law.*
Wojcik, K-P, 'Bail-in in the Banking Union' (2016) 53 *Common Market Law Review* 91.
Wolfers, B and Voland, T, 'Level the Playing Field: The New Supervision of Credit Institutions by the European Central Bank' (2014) 51 *Common Market Law Review* 1463.
Zilioli, C and Wojcik, K-P, *Judicial Review in the European Banking Union* (Edward Elgar, 2021).

18

The Area of Freedom, Security and Justice

I. ORIGINS AND DEVELOPMENT OF THE AREA OF FREEDOM, SECURITY AND JUSTICE

THE CREATION OF the Area of Freedom, Security and Justice is the product of several decades of collective effort, during which Member States have gradually integrated their competences in immigration, justice, and home affairs. Initially, this policy aimed to manage the spillover effects of the internal market. The establishment of a borderless trading area where goods, services, persons, and capital move freely has also increased the risk of criminal activities exploiting these freedoms. The free movement of goods makes it difficult for police authorities to combat the trafficking of illegal goods; the free movement of persons can enable individuals with criminal backgrounds to evade justice; the free movement of capital can facilitate money laundering, etc.

To address these challenges, the Union has progressively developed policies aimed at strengthening internal and external border controls, enhancing police and judicial cooperation, and promoting the harmonisation of both procedural and substantive criminal law across the Member States.

Migration and asylum policies warrant particular attention in this context. Immigration is a complex and multifaceted phenomenon that has acquired new dimensions as a result of globalisation. Moreover, economic inequalities, political instability, armed conflicts, and climate-related disasters can trigger large-scale population movements. These developments have prompted the Union and its Member States, constituting one of the world's wealthiest regions, to pursue a common immigration, border and asylum policy. The objective is to regulate border crossings and to design migration and asylum systems that are coherent, effective, and consistent with international law and fundamental rights.

The political sensitivity of these matters, together with the practical difficulties inherent in their regulation and implementation, is reflected in the lengthy process that led to the establishment of the Area of Freedom, Security and Justice. That process reached completion only with the entry into force of the Lisbon Treaty on 1 December 2009.

Since 1975, when intergovernmental cooperation in justice and home affairs began to take shape through the TREVI framework, with ministers meeting regularly (typically twice a year) to discuss issues of common interest linked to the development of the common market, a significant process of Europeanisation has taken place in the fields of immigration and judicial and police cooperation. On 1 January 1993, checks on goods at the internal borders of the then European Economic Community, one of the key measures for completing the internal market, as set out in the Commission's 1985 White Paper, were abolished. Border controls on persons, however, remained in place, and Member States continued to coordinate their actions primarily through international cooperation mechanisms.

At the Rhodes European Council of 2 and 3 December 1988, a coordination group was established to enhance joint action in areas related to the free movement of persons. An ad hoc working group on immigration subsequently drafted a number of agreements, later ratified by the Member States, which contributed to the adoption of the Dublin Convention of 15 June 1990 on the determination of the state responsible for examining asylum applications lodged in one of the Member States of the European Communities. In parallel, intergovernmental cooperation in justice and home affairs was strengthened and formally incorporated into Title VI of the Treaty on European Union (TEU) by the Maastricht Treaty of 1992. The creation of a dedicated 'pillar' for Justice and Home Affairs preserved the intergovernmental character of Member State action in this policy field, while embedding it within the institutional framework of the Union and allowing only limited involvement of the Commission, the European Parliament, and the Court of Justice.

The so-called Schengen *acquis* and the gradual development of a common framework for internal and external border controls played a central role in this evolution. As early as the 1950s, the Benelux countries had established a common travel area, operational through the Benelux Treaty signed on 3 February 1958. Building on this initiative, and as part of efforts to develop a common European immigration policy, five Member States (France, Germany, Belgium, the Netherlands, and Luxembourg) signed the Schengen Agreement on 14 June 1985, followed by the Convention implementing the Schengen Agreement of 19 June 1990. Its objective was to abolish internal border controls and to introduce common controls at the external borders of the participating states. The Schengen framework also included common visa rules for third-country nationals, as well as an innovative and sophisticated system for the exchange of information accessible to police and judicial authorities (the Schengen Information System).

The Treaty of Amsterdam introduced major reforms that entered into force on 1 May 1999. Most notably, it transferred immigration and asylum policy, together with judicial cooperation in civil matters, from the intergovernmental pillar to the 'Community method'. At the same time, all Member States except the United Kingdom and Ireland adopted the Schengen Convention, and the Schengen *acquis* was fully incorporated into Union law through a Protocol annexed to the Treaty of Amsterdam. This reallocation of competences, however, was not completed in 1999. Police and judicial cooperation in criminal matters remained within the intergovernmental framework of Title VI TEU until its full integration into the 'Community method' with the entry into force of the Lisbon Treaty in 2009.

The period between 1993 and 2009 was therefore characterised by both significant policy development in immigration, justice, and home affairs, and by pronounced institutional asymmetries. Member States remained reluctant to relinquish control over policy areas closely linked to national sovereignty. At the same time, the deepening of the internal market made further integration unavoidable, as the effective functioning of the free movement of goods, persons, and capital (essential to the economic and social development of the Member States) depended increasingly on common rules in these fields. As a result, integration proceeded at varying speeds and through different methods, oscillating between intergovernmental cooperation and the traditional Community method, in an attempt to balance effective Union action with the protection of national interests.

The most significant asymmetries were ultimately resolved with the entry into force of the Lisbon Treaty, which consolidated the relevant Treaty provisions into a single policy framework covering immigration, border control, and judicial and police cooperation in both civil and criminal matters. This framework is now referred to as the Area of Freedom, Security and Justice. It should be recalled that the negotiations leading to the adoption of the Lisbon Treaty took place against the backdrop of a sharp increase in international terrorist activity, notably associated with Al-Qaeda under the leadership of Osama bin Laden. The terrorist attacks of 11 September 2001 in the United States, followed by attacks in several European capitals, underscored the need to enhance the effectiveness of counter-terrorism efforts. This context provided a strong political impetus for closer integration of Member States' security policies and helps to explain the determination to establish a more unified and effective Area of Freedom, Security and Justice.

Following the entry into force of the Lisbon Treaty on 1 December 2009, the Area of Freedom, Security and Justice was incorporated into Title V of the Treaty on the Functioning of the European Union (TFEU) and structured into five chapters, including general provisions (Chapter 1) and four substantive policy areas: policies on border checks, asylum and immigration (Chapter 2); judicial cooperation in civil matters (Chapter 3); judicial cooperation in criminal matters (Chapter 4); and police cooperation (Chapter 5). Protocol No 19 annexed to the Treaties governs the integration of the Schengen *acquis* into Union law, while Protocol No 21 establishes the special arrangements applicable to the United Kingdom and Ireland (the latter having been superseded as regards the United Kingdom upon its withdrawal from the Union). Lastly, Protocol No 22 provides for the Danish position on the Area of Freedom, Security and Justice.

The result is an Area of Freedom, Security and Justice that is largely integrated into the 'Community method'. Its policies are generally subject to the Commission's right of legislative initiative, qualified majority voting in the Council, the effective participation of the European Parliament, and comprehensive judicial review by the Court of Justice of the European Union. Nevertheless, certain intergovernmental features persist, particularly in the fields of police cooperation and judicial cooperation in criminal matters. Articles 82(3) and 83(3) TFEU establish safeguard mechanisms allowing a Member State to refer a draft directive to the European Council where it considers that the initiative would affect fundamental aspects of its criminal justice system. In addition, several areas remain subject to unanimity in the Council, including aspects of operational police cooperation and the adoption of minimum rules harmonising criminal offences in areas not otherwise covered by Union policy.

Similarly, Article 89 TFEU provides for the establishment of a framework enabling competent authorities of one Member State to operate on the territory of another, subject to conditions and limitations laid down through a special legislative procedure requiring unanimity in the Council. Taken together, these arrangements illustrate that the Area of Freedom, Security and Justice has been fully embedded within the Union's legal order as a distinct policy area, while retaining certain intergovernmental characteristics that reflect its historical development and the particular sensitivity of the matters it regulates.

II. BORDER CHECKS, ASYLUM AND IMMIGRATION

Article 77 TFEU sets out the basic framework of the Union's policy on border checks, encompassing both internal and external borders. The regime governing internal borders is closely linked to the development of the Schengen *acquis*, which, since its inception in 1985, has pursued the progressive abolition of controls on the movement of persons at borders between participating states. External borders raise distinct issues, as they are intrinsically connected to the establishment of a common immigration policy and to the development of standardised systems for border management and administrative coordination. This section examines the framework laid down by the Treaties and its subsequent evolution through secondary legislation and international agreements.

1. Border Control and Management

The determination of the Union's internal and external borders is primarily governed by the 'Schengen *acquis*'. At present, the Schengen framework applies to 29 states: 25 Member States (all except Ireland and Cyprus, the latter being formally part of the Schengen area but still awaiting a Council decision on the full abolition of internal border controls); and four associated third countries, namely Iceland, Norway, Switzerland, and Liechtenstein. Bulgaria and Romania acceded to the Schengen area through a Council decision of December 2024, with controls on internal land borders lifted on 1 January 2025.

Within this framework, internal borders are defined by reference to external borders. Internal borders are those separating Schengen states from one another, whereas external borders are those separating Schengen states from non-Schengen states. By way of example, the border between Sweden and Norway qualifies as an internal border, while the border between Hungary and Ukraine constitutes an external border.[1] The Convention implementing the Schengen Agreement remains in force and continues to apply to those matters that have not been replaced or codified by subsequent Union legislation. In addition, the Member States are expressly authorised to conclude international agreements with third countries in order to enhance the management of the Union's common borders.

The 'Schengen *acquis*' may broadly be understood as pursuing four principal objectives: the abolition of controls on persons crossing internal borders (by land, sea, and air); the strengthening of controls at external borders; the facilitation of the internal movement of persons within the Schengen area; and the establishment of a common policy on visas and other short-stay residence permits. In support of these objectives, the 'Schengen acquis' is complemented by an institutional framework designed to reinforce border management. This framework includes the creation of specialised agencies, such as the European Border and Coast Guard Agency (Frontex), as well as a range of cooperation mechanisms involving other Union agencies and the Member States.

1.1. *Internal Borders*

Article 77(1)(a) TFEU provides that the Union is to develop a policy 'ensuring the absence of any controls on persons, whatever their nationality, when crossing internal borders'. To give effect to that objective, Article 77(2)(e) TFEU confers a legal basis on the European Parliament and the Council, acting in accordance with the ordinary legislative procedure, to adopt measures concerning 'the absence of any controls on persons, whatever their nationality, when crossing internal borders'. On that basis, the Union adopted Regulation (EU) 2016/399

[1] The 'Schengen *acquis*' and its progeny is mainly composed of Regulation (EU) 2016/399 of the European Parliament and of the Council of 9 March 2016 establishing a Union Code on the rules governing the movement of persons across borders [2016] OJ L77/1; Regulation (EU) 2018/1861 of the European Parliament and of the Council of 28 November 2018 on the establishment, operation and use of the Schengen Information System (SIS) in the field of border checks, amending the Convention implementing the Schengen Agreement and amending and repealing Regulation (EC) No 1987/2006 [2018] OJ L312/1; Regulation (EU) 2018/1860 of the European Parliament and of the Council of 28 November 2018 on the use of the Schengen Information System for returning illegally staying third-country nationals [2018] OJ L312/1; Regulation (EU) 2017/2226 of the European Parliament and of the Council of 30 November 2017 establishing an Entry-Exit System (EES) for recording entry and exit data and refusal of entry data on third-country nationals crossing the external borders of the Member States, determines the conditions for access to the EES for law enforcement purposes and amends the Convention implementing the Schengen Agreement and Regulations (EC) 767/2008 and (EU) 1077/2011 [2017] OJ L327/20; and Regulation (EU) 2018/1240 of the European Parliament and of the Council of 12 September 2018 establishing a European Travel Information and Authorisation System (ETIAS) and amending Regulations (EU) 1077/2011, (EU) 515/2014, (EU) 2016/399, (EU) 2016/1624 and (EU) 2017/2226 [2018] OJ L236/1.

establishing a Union Code on the rules governing the movement of persons across borders (the Schengen Borders Code, hereinafter 'the Code'), which lays down the core regulatory framework governing internal border controls within the Schengen area.

The Code classifies internal borders into three categories: (a) the common land borders of the Member States, including river and lake borders; (b) the airports of the Member States for internal flights; and (c) the sea, river, and lake ports of the Member States used for regular internal ferry connections.[2] As a general rule, Article 22 of the Code states that internal borders may be crossed 'at any point without a border check on persons, irrespective of their nationality, being carried out'.[3] Accordingly, the principle of free movement without internal border checks applies within the Schengen area both to Union citizens and to third-country nationals lawfully staying in a Member State participating in the Schengen area.

At the same time, the Code sets out a number of situations in which national authorities may carry out checks and, where necessary, temporarily reintroduce controls at internal borders. The legal framework governing the reintroduction of internal border controls has undergone several modifications in recent years, largely in response to serious threats to public policy and internal security, including large-scale secondary movements of third-country nationals following the Arab Spring and armed conflicts in the Middle East.

First, the Code establishes a system of checks within the territory of the Member States, which empowers national authorities to exercise police or other public authority powers in areas close to internal borders. Such checks are permitted provided that they are not equivalent to border controls, are based on general police information or experience, and are designed and implemented in a manner clearly distinct from systematic checks on persons at the external borders.[4] Similarly, Member States retain their power to carry out security checks on persons at ports and airports, as well as to establish the obligation to hold or carry documents.[5]

The legal framework governing the reintroduction of internal border controls was substantially amended by Regulation (EU) 2024/1717.[6] This reform was a response to the persistence of 'temporary' controls by several Member States since 2015. Under the amended Code, the time limits for reintroducing controls have been extended to better reflect actual practice, while introducing stricter procedural safeguards.

For unforeseeable threats requiring immediate action, a Member State may reintroduce controls for up to one month, renewable for a maximum duration of three months. For foreseeable threats, controls may be introduced for up to six months and renewed for a total maximum duration of two years. In exceptional circumstances where the threat persists, the Council may, on a proposal from the Commission, recommend a further extension of up to six months, renewable up to three times (meaning the overall duration, including extensions, may not exceed approximately three years).

Additionally, the 2024 reform introduced a new 'transfer procedure'. This allows Member States to apprehend third-country nationals present without authorisation in the Schengen area in the vicinity of an internal border and, instead of initiating a standard return procedure under Directive 2008/115/EC (the Return Directive), they may be transferred to the Member State from which they directly entered, subject to safeguards and cooperation arrangements.

[2] Art 2 of the Code.
[3] ibid, Art 22.
[4] ibid, Art 23(a).
[5] ibid, Art 23(b)–(c).
[6] Regulation (EU) 2024/1717 of the European Parliament and of the Council of 13 June 2024 amending Regulation (EU) 2016/399 on a Union Code on the rules governing the movement of persons across borders [2024] OJ L 2024/1717.

1.2. External Borders

External borders are defined as the states' 'land borders, including river and lake borders, sea borders and their airports, river ports, sea ports and lake ports, provided that they are not internal borders'.[7] Therefore, to the extent that a border of a Schengen state is not considered to be an 'internal border', it is regarded as an 'external border' to which the rules of Title II of the Code apply, as explained below. In any case, the concept of 'external border' as set out in Union law does not affect the competence of the Member States concerning the geographical demarcation of their borders, in accordance with international law.[8]

'External borders' are the geographical borders of the Member States at which border checks on persons are carried out by border guards in accordance with Union law. This involves border checks on persons performed by border guards, which may also extend to means of transport and objects in the possession of those crossing the border. The Code sets out the entry conditions for third-country nationals whose intended stay on the territory of the Member States does not exceed 90 days within any 180-day period.[9] In such cases, a third-country national must hold a valid travel document – issued within the previous 10 years and valid for at least three months after the intended date of departure – a valid visa, if required, and documents justifying the purpose and conditions of the intended stay, as well as sufficient means of subsistence. In addition, the third-country national must not be the subject of an alert in the Schengen Information System (SIS) for the purpose of refusing entry, must not be considered a threat to public policy, internal security, public health, or the international relations of any Member State, and must provide biometric data where the creation of an individual file in the Entry/Exit System (EES) is required.

One of the central elements of the framework governing checks at external borders, particularly with regard to third-country nationals, concerns visa requirements. The concept of a 'visa' is defined in Article 2 of Regulation No 810/2009 establishing a Community Code on Visas (the 'Visa Code')[10] and refers to an authorisation issued by a Member State for two specific situations: firstly, an intended stay on the territory of the Member States not exceeding 90 days within any 180-day period; and secondly, transit through the international transit areas of airports within the Member States. For this second case, the Visa Code sets out a specific regime for so-called 'airport transit visas'.[11] In the first case, the Visa Code specifies rules regarding the procedures and conditions for issuing a visa, including the allocation of responsibility among the Member State for examining and deciding on the application. In principle, this is the Member State of the main destination of the visit, or, where several Member States are visited during a single journey and no main destination can be identified, the Member State whose external border the applicant intends to cross to enter the territory of the Member States.[12]

The visa regime allows nationals of certain third countries to be exempt from visa requirements for political, economic, and security reasons. Regulation 2018/1806[13] sets out the list of third countries whose nationals are required to hold a visa when crossing the external borders

[7] Art 2(2) of the Code.

[8] Art 77(4) TFEU.

[9] Art 6(1) of the Code.

[10] Regulation (EC) 810/2009 of the European Parliament and of the Council of 13 July 2009 establishing a Community Code on Visas [2009] OJ L243/1.

[11] Art 3 of the Visa Code.

[12] ibid, Art 5.

[13] Regulation (EU) 2018/1806 of the European Parliament and of the Council of 14 November 2018 listing the third countries whose nationals must be in possession of visas when crossing the external borders and those whose nationals are exempt from that requirement [2018] OJ L303/39.

of the Member States, as well as those whose nationals are exempt from that requirement. Such exemptions are subject to specific conditions, and failure to comply with those conditions may lead to the temporary suspension of the exemption regime. In particular, Article 8 of Regulation 2018/1806 identifies, by way of example, circumstances that may justify a temporary suspension. These include a substantial increase in the number of third-country nationals refused entry, a significant rise in asylum applications lodged by nationals of the country concerned, a lack of cooperation on readmission, or an increased risk or imminent threat to public policy or internal security within the Member States.

The list of third countries whose nationals are exempt from the visa requirement is set out in Annex II to Regulation 2018/1806. That list is divided into four categories: states (currently 61); special administrative regions of the People's Republic of China, namely Hong Kong and Macao; British nationals who are not British citizens; and entities or territorial authorities not recognised as states by at least one Member State, such as Taiwan and the authorities of Kosovo.

1.3. Integrated Border Management of the Union

The Union's external borders require significant coordinated effort among Member States, along with the deployment of technical tools for integrated border management. With the development of the Schengen area, a system covering information on the movement of people was introduced, resulting in the creation of the Schengen Information System (SIS) [14] and the Schengen Entry/Exit System (EES).[15] The Union has also established the European Border and Coast Guard Agency (Frontex), tasked with supporting Member States in their surveillance and control activities at external borders,[16] and has established the Instrument for Financial Support for Border Management and Visa Policy (BMVI), which replaced the border component of the previous Internal Security Fund. The BMVI provides financial assistance to Member States to ensure strong and effective European integrated border management at the Union's external borders.[17]

2. Immigration

Article 79 TFEU confers upon the Union the competence to develop a common immigration policy aimed at ensuring the efficient management of migration flows, the fair treatment of third-country nationals residing legally in the Member States, and the prevention of illegal immigration and trafficking in human beings. These objectives are reflected in Article 79(2)

[14] Regulation (EU) 2018/1860 of the European Parliament and of the Council of 28 November 2018 on the use of the Schengen Information System for the return of illegally staying third-country nationals [2018] OJ L312/1; Regulation (EU) 2018/1861 of the European Parliament and of the Council of 28 November 2018 on the establishment, operation and use of the Schengen Information System (SIS) in the field of border checks, and amending the Convention Implementing the Schengen Agreement and amending and repealing Regulation (EC) No 1987/2006 [2018] OJ L312/14; and Regulation (EU) 2018/1862 of the European Parliament and of the Council of 28 November 2018 on the establishment, operation and use of the Schengen Information System (SIS) in the field of police cooperation and judicial cooperation in criminal matters [2018] OJ L312/56.

[15] Regulation (EU) 2017/2226 of the European Parliament and of the Council of 30 November 2017 establishing an Entry-Exit System (EES) to register entry and exit data and refusal of entry data of third-country nationals crossing the external borders of the Member States, and determining the conditions of access to the EES for law enforcement purposes, and amending the Convention implementing the Schengen Agreement and Regulations (EC) No 767/2008 and (EU) No 1077/2011 [2017] OJ L327/20.

[16] See section II.4.1 in this chapter.

[17] Regulation (EU) 2021/1148 of the European Parliament and of the Council of 7 July 2021 establishing, as part of the Integrated Border Management Fund, the Instrument for Financial Support for Border Management and Visa Policy [2021] OJ L251/94.

(a)–(d) TFEU, which identifies the specific areas in which the Union is empowered, in principle in accordance with the ordinary legislative procedure and by qualified majority voting in the Council, to adopt legislative measures.

At the same time, Article 79(5) TFEU expressly limits the scope of that competence by providing that neither the legal basis itself nor the legislative acts adopted under it 'shall affect the right of Member States to determine volumes of admission of third-country nationals coming from third countries to their territory in order to seek work, whether employed or self-employed'.

On that basis, the Union has adopted a range of legislative instruments regulating the conditions of entry and residence of specific categories of third-country nationals, such as family members, students, and highly qualified workers, as well as measures aimed at combating illegal immigration. Particular emphasis has been placed on the fight against trafficking in human beings, which was initially addressed through a Framework Decision adopted in 2002 and subsequently reinforced and replaced by Directive 2011/36/EU on preventing and combating trafficking in human beings and protecting its victims.[18]

The legal framework described above has been significantly reshaped by the Pact on Migration and Asylum adopted in 2024. The Pact introduces a new governance architecture for migration and asylum, aimed at ensuring greater responsibility-sharing, more efficient border procedures, and faster, more coordinated decision-making across the Union. While most of the legislative instruments forming part of the Pact entered into force in June 2024, their core operational provisions are subject to a transitional period and will become fully applicable from mid-2026.

The Pact establishes an integrated approach covering pre-entry screening, asylum and border procedures, solidarity mechanisms, and return, thereby recalibrating the balance between control at the external borders and protection obligations under Union and international law. These reforms constitute the most far-reaching overhaul of the Union's asylum and migration system since the adoption of the 2008–13 legislative package.

2.1. *Legal Immigration*

The Commission initially proposed a comprehensive approach to regulating legal immigration, which was rejected by a majority of Member States. More specifically, the Commission's 2001 proposal for a Council Directive on the conditions of entry and residence of third-country nationals for the purpose of paid employment and self-employed economic activities failed to secure sufficient political support in the Council. This first failed attempt led to a change of approach from 2005 onwards, focusing on sectoral strategies aimed at regulating specific categories of third-country nationals.

Currently, the Union has a framework for the immigration of highly qualified third-country workers provided in Directive 2021/1883,[19] for seasonal workers in Directive 2014/36,[20] for workers within the framework of intra-corporate transfers,[21] and for persons

[18] Directive 2011/36/EU of the European Parliament and of the Council of 5 April 2011 on preventing and combating trafficking in human beings and protecting victims, and replacing Council Framework Decision 2002/629/JHA [2011] OJ L101/1.

[19] Directive (EU) 2021/1883 of the European Parliament and of the Council of 20 October 2021 on the conditions of entry and residence of third-country nationals for the purposes of highly qualified employment and repealing Council Directive 2009/50/EC [2021] OJ L382/1.

[20] Directive 2014/36/EU of the European Parliament and of the Council of 26 February 2014 on the conditions of entry and stay of third-country nationals for the purpose of employment as seasonal workers [2014] OJ L94/375-390.

[21] Directive 2014/66/EU of the European Parliament and of the Council of 15 May 2014 on the conditions of entry and residence of third-country nationals in the framework of an intra-corporate transfer [2014] OJ L157/1.

admitted for purposes of research, studies, training, voluntary service, pupil exchange, educational projects, or au pairing.[22] This sectoral regulation based on specific categories has not prevented the adoption of broader and more general regulations, such as Directive 2024/1233 (recast) on the single permit,[23] Directive 2003/109 on the status of long-term residents,[24] and the Directive on family reunification.[25]

The Union may also conclude international agreements whose association regimes include equal treatment clauses for third-country workers legally resident, particularly in relation to working conditions, remuneration, and certain aspects of social security, without conferring free-movement rights comparable to those enjoyed by Union citizens. For instance, association agreements with various North African countries and Turkey confer non-discrimination rights to their nationals in regular situations.[26] This non-discrimination right covers employment conditions, remuneration, and social security in employment-related areas, making these rights strictly socio-economic and distinct from the general free movement rights enjoyed by Union citizens.[27]

2.2. *Illegal Immigration and Return Policies*

Illegal immigration is a highly complex phenomenon that requires a differentiated response to a wide range of situations. While the Union has established a general regulatory framework, it has also adopted targeted measures addressing specific categories of irregular migration, an approach that has proved challenging in practice. Union rules on illegal immigration may be grouped into three main categories: measures aimed at preventing illegal immigration; provisions governing the treatment and management of third-country nationals in an irregular situation within the Member States; and rules laying down the conditions and procedures for return and removal.

Within the framework of the Pact on Migration and Asylum, new instruments have been introduced to strengthen the link between border control, asylum procedures, and return. In particular, the Screening Regulation establishes a uniform framework for the initial screening of irregular arrivals at the external borders, with the aim of swiftly identifying the appropriate follow-up procedure, whether asylum, return, or refusal of entry.[28]

2.2.1. Prevention

With regard to the prevention of illegal immigration, the Union has developed a range of instruments for the control and management of external borders, as outlined above. In addition, specific measures have been adopted that target private actors, with the aim of creating incentives within the private sector to reduce illegal immigration.

[22] Directive (EU) 2016/801 of the European Parliament and of the Council of 11 May 2016 on the conditions of entry and residence of third-country nationals for the purposes of research, studies, training, voluntary service, pupil exchange schemes or educational projects and au pairing [2016] OJ L132/21.

[23] Directive (EU) 2024/1233 of the European Parliament and of the Council of 24 April 2024 on a single application procedure for a single permit for third-country nationals to reside and work in the territory of a Member State and on a common set of rights for third-country workers legally residing in a Member State (recast) [2024] OJ L, 2024/1233.

[24] Council Directive 2003/109/EC of 25 November 2003 concerning the status of third-country nationals who are long-term residents [2004] OJ L16/44.

[25] Council Directive 2003/86/EC of 22 September 2003 on the right to family reunification [2003] OJ L251/12.

[26] See the Euro-Mediterranean Association Agreements concluded with Morocco, Israel, Jordan, Egypt, Algeria, Lebanon and Tunisia, as well as the Interim Agreement with the Palestinian Authority, and the Association Agreement with Turkey.

[27] Case C-179/98 *Mesbah* EU:C:1999:249; and Case C-275/02 *Ayaz* EU:C:2004:570.

[28] Regulation (EU) 2024/1356 of the European Parliament and of the Council of 14 May 2024 establishing a screening of third-country nationals at the external borders and amending Regulation (EU) 2021/1148 [2024] OJ L1356.

By way of example, Article 26 of the Convention implementing the Schengen Agreement imposes obligations on carriers conveying third-country nationals by air, sea, or land. Such carriers are required to return a third-country national whose entry into the Schengen area has been refused either to the third state that issued the travel document or to another third state where the person's admission is guaranteed. Carriers are also legally obliged to take the measures required to ensure that third-country nationals carried by them are in possession of the required travel documents for entry into the Schengen area, and may be subject to penalties for breach of that obligation.[29]

Article 27 of the Schengen Implementing Convention also commits the Schengen states to establish appropriate penalties for any person who, for financial gain, assists a third-country national enter or remain in the Schengen area in breach of the applicable law. This obligation has also been incorporated into Union secondary legislation, namely Directive 2002/90 on the definition of the facilitation of unauthorised entry, transit, and residence[30] and Framework Decision 2002/946/JHA on strengthening the penal framework to prevent the facilitation of unauthorised entry, transit, and residence.[31] Both instruments complement other measures to combat illegal employment, trafficking in human beings, and the sexual exploitation of children, and define the facilitation of illegal immigration in terms of criminal law and penalties.[32]

At the operational level, Regulation 2019/1240 establishes a European network of immigration liaison officers to enhance coordination and optimise the use of liaison officers deployed in third countries by the Member States.[33] This network includes law enforcement authorities, as well as the Commission and Union agencies responsible for preventing and combating irregular immigration and related cross-border crime, smuggling of migrants, and trafficking in human beings. Regulation 2019/1240 provides for the creation of local or regional networks of immigration liaison officers in third countries, as well as bilateral or multilateral cooperation mechanisms for the joint deployment of liaison officers.[34] These mechanisms are supplemented by rules governing the secure exchange of information, with content stored on a common platform subject to specific conditions, including rules on the processing of personal data.[35] Exchanges of information can also occur bilaterally and in sectoral areas, such as air carriers' obligation to communicate passenger data under the API Regulation.[36]

2.2.2. Treatment of Vulnerable Persons in an Irregular Situation

Preventive measures are designed to prevent third-country nationals from entering the Union illegally. Where such entry nevertheless occurs, Union legislation provides for measures intended to mitigate the adverse consequences of an irregular situation. Although the primary response is generally the return of the individual to the country of origin (as discussed in the

[29] Regulation (EU) 2025/12 of the European Parliament and of the Council of 19 December 2024 on the collection and transfer of advance passenger information for enhancing and facilitating external border checks [2025] OJ L, 2025/12.

[30] Council Directive 2002/90/EC of 28 November 2002 defining the facilitation of unauthorised entry, transit and residence [2002] OJ L328/17.

[31] Council Framework Decision 2002/946/JHA of 28 November 2002 on the strengthening of the penal framework to prevent the facilitation of unauthorised entry, transit and residence [2002] OJ L328/1.

[32] Directive 2011/36 (n 18).

[33] Regulation (EU) 2019/1240 of the European Parliament and of the Council of 20 June 2019 on the creation of a European network of immigration liaison officers [2019] OJ L198/88.

[34] Art 6 of Regulation 2019/1240.

[35] ibid, Arts 9–10.

[36] Regulation (EU) 2025/12, on the collection and transfer of advance passenger information for enhancing and facilitating external border checks, (n 29).

following section), the Union has also adopted specific rules for persons requiring particular protection.

In particular, measures have been enacted for third-country nationals who are victims of trafficking in human beings or who have been subjected to actions facilitating illegal immigration. Directive 2004/81/EC establishes a harmonised framework for issuing residence permits to third-country nationals who are victims of trafficking in human beings and, where a Member State so decides, to third-country nationals who have been the subjects of an action to facilitate illegal immigration, where they cooperate with the competent authorities, while laying down specific safeguards applicable to minors.[37]

In cases involving victims of human trafficking who are in an irregular situation in a Member State, or who have entered the territory of a Member State illegally, Directive 2004/81 provides safeguards to ensure that the individual has a reflection period before being granted a residence permit. If such a permit is granted, it will be valid for a minimum of six months and may be renewed provided certain conditions relating to cooperation with the authorities are met.[38] In the case of persons subject to actions facilitating illegal immigration and minors, the application of Directive 2004/81 is optional for Member States. In particular, the Directive's application to persons who have been the subject of an action to facilitate illegal immigration is optional for Member States, without prejudice to their ability to adopt more favourable national provisions.[39]

2.2.3. Return

Third-country nationals staying illegally are, as a general rule, subject to a return procedure to their country of origin. In 2008, the Union adopted Directive 2008/115[40] to harmonise common standards and procedures for returning illegally staying third-country nationals. This Directive, known as the Return Directive, coexists with several additional instruments aimed at facilitating return procedures, a practice that faces multiple legal, logistical, and humanitarian challenges. These include Directive 2001/40 on mutual recognition concerning the expulsion of third-country nationals,[41] Directive 2003/110 on assistance in cases of transit for removal by air,[42] Decision 2004/573 on joint flights for the removal of third-country nationals who are subjects of individual removal orders,[43] Regulation 2016/1953 on the European travel document,[44] as well as various readmission agreements with third countries, concluded on the legal basis of Article 79(3) TFEU.[45]

[37] Council Directive 2004/81/EC of 29 April 2004 on the residence permit issued to third-country nationals who are victims of trafficking in human beings or who have been the subject of an action to facilitate illegal immigration, who cooperate with the competent authorities [2004] OJ L261/19.

[38] ibid, Art 8.

[39] ibid, Art 4.

[40] Directive 2008/115/EC of the European Parliament and of the Council of 16 December 2008 on common standards and procedures in Member States for returning illegally staying third-country nationals [2008] OJ L348/98.

[41] Council Directive 2001/40/EC of 28 May 2001 on the mutual recognition of decisions on the expulsion of third-country nationals [2001] OJ L149/34.

[42] Council Directive 2003/110/EC of 25 November 2003 on assistance in cases of transit for the purposes of removal by air [2003] OJ L321/26.

[43] Council Decision 2004/573/EC of 29 April 2004 on the organisation of joint flights for removals from the territory of two or more Member States of third-country nationals who are the subject of removal orders [2004] OJ L261/28.

[44] Regulation (EU) 2016/1953 of the European Parliament and of the Council of 26 October 2016 on the establishment of a European travel document for the return of illegally staying third-country nationals, and repealing Council Recommendation of 30 November 1994 [2016] OJ L311/13.

[45] As of the date of the publication of this book, the Union has concluded international readmission agreements with Albania, Armenia, Azerbaijan, Bosnia and Herzegovina, Cape Verde, Georgia, Hong Kong, Macao, Moldova, Montenegro, North Macedonia, Pakistan, Serbia, Sri Lanka, Turkey, and Ukraine.

The Return Directive states that Member States may detain third-country nationals subject to return procedures, but only under specific conditions. The Return Directive enumerates two grounds – namely, the risk of absconding and the situation where the third-country national avoids or hampers the preparation of return or the removal process[46] – and the Court of Justice's case law has confirmed that these grounds are exhaustive, requiring Member States to undertake an individualised assessment based on one of them.[47] The Return Directive specifies that detention should be 'for as short a period as possible and only maintained as long as removal arrangements are in progress and carried out with due diligence'. The Court of Justice has clarified that, as a general rule, detainees subject to return procedures cannot be detained in the same facilities as ordinary prisoners. Detention must be accompanied by rights of access to justice and judicial review,[48] and these rights cannot be waived by the detainee.[49]

In parallel, the Union institutions have continued to pursue further reforms aimed at increasing the effectiveness of return procedures, including proposals to replace or substantially revise elements of the Return Directive. As of the date of publication of this book, several aspects of this reform agenda remain politically contested and subject to ongoing negotiations.

3. Asylum

Asylum is a fundamental right recognised in international law and a core obligation of states insofar as it entails respect for the principle of *non-refoulement*, most prominently enshrined in the 1951 Geneva Convention relating to the Status of Refugees and its 1967 Protocol.[50] According to the Convention, a refugee is a person who

> owing to well-founded fear of being persecuted for reasons of race, religion, nationality, membership of a particular social group or political opinion, is outside the country of his nationality and is unable or, owing to such fear, is unwilling to avail himself of the protection of that country; or who, not having a nationality and being outside the country of his former habitual residence as a result of such events, is unable or, owing to such fear, is unwilling to return to it.[51]

The Convention establishes the principle that a refugee may not be returned to a country where he or she fears persecution and recognises a range of fundamental rights, including freedom of religion, freedom of movement, the right to education, and access to work.

The Treaty of Amsterdam conferred upon the European Community the competence to adopt minimum standards in certain areas of asylum policy. That competence was subsequently transferred to the Union by the Treaty of Lisbon through the introduction of Article 78 TFEU, which provides that the Union 'shall develop a common policy on asylum, subsidiary protection and temporary protection with a view to offering appropriate status to any third-country national requiring international protection and ensuring compliance with the principle of non-refoulement'. The same provision further specifies that such policy 'must be

[46] Art 15(1) of Directive 2008/115.

[47] Case C-61/11 *El Dridi* EU:C:2011:268.

[48] Case C-146/14 PPU *Mahdi* EU:C:2014:1936.

[49] Joined Cases C-473/13 and C-514/13 *Bero and Bouzalmate* EU:C:2014:2095; and Case C-474/13 *Pham* EU:C:2014:2096.

[50] The Convention relating to the Status of Refugees, done at Geneva on 28 July 1951 (United Nations Treaty Series, vol 189, p 150, No 2545 (1954)), entered into force on 22 April 1954. It was supplemented and amended by the Protocol relating to the Status of Refugees, done at New York on 31 January 1967, which in turn entered into force on 4 October 1967.

[51] Art 1 of the Geneva Convention.

in accordance with the Geneva Convention of 28 July 1951 and the Protocol of 31 January 1967 relating to the status of refugees, and other relevant treaties'.

In parallel, Article 18 of the Charter of Fundamental Rights of the European Union guarantees that the right to asylum shall be guaranteed

> with due respect for the rules of the Geneva Convention of 28 July 1951 and the Protocol of 31 January 1967 relating to the status of refugees and in accordance with the Treaty on European Union and the Treaty on the Functioning of the European Union.

Article 19 of the Charter complements this protection by prohibiting collective expulsions and by prohibiting removal, expulsion, or extradition 'to a State where there is a serious risk that he or she would be subjected to the death penalty, torture or other inhuman or degrading treatment or punishment'.

Article 78(2) TFEU further delineates the main components of the Union's asylum policy, which the Union legislator has developed through the ordinary legislative procedure. This legislative framework has given rise to the Common European Asylum System (CEAS), encompassing rules on the content of refugee and subsidiary protection status, complementary mechanisms applicable in situations of mass influx, common procedures for the granting and withdrawal of protection, criteria for determining the Member State responsible for examining an application, and standards governing the reception conditions of applicants for international protection within the Member States.

The European asylum framework has evolved incrementally and is currently undergoing another phase of reform. Political instability and armed conflicts in the Middle East and parts of the Maghreb have generated large-scale displacement, placing sustained pressure on the CEAS and exacerbating tensions among the Member States. More recently, the Russian invasion of Ukraine (which commenced in February 2022) triggered a further wave of mass displacement towards the Union, accompanied by the instrumentalisation of migrants and refugees at the Union's external borders by Russia and Belarus. Combined with growing dissatisfaction regarding the effectiveness of existing solidarity mechanisms for managing large-scale arrivals, these developments culminated in the adoption of the Pact on Migration and Asylum in May 2024, which is scheduled to become fully applicable from June 2026.

The legal framework of the CEAS consists of three parts, focusing on: (a) the recognition and content of refugee status and the status of persons eligible for subsidiary protection; (b) procedures for status determination and mechanisms for determining the responsible Member State; and (c) rules on the reception of applicants for international protection.

3.1. *Recognition and Content of Refugee Status and the Status of Persons Eligible for Subsidiary Protection*

Directive 2011/95 establishes the uniform standards to be applied by Member States for the qualification of third-country nationals or stateless persons as beneficiaries of international protection, or for persons eligible for subsidiary protection.[52] Therefore, the CEAS not only covers persons who qualify as refugees but also includes individuals who do not qualify as refugees but nevertheless face a real risk of suffering serious harm, such as the death penalty, torture, inhuman or degrading treatment or punishment, or serious and individual threats to

[52] Directive 2011/95/EU of the European Parliament and of the Council of 13 December 2011 on standards for the qualification of third country nationals or stateless persons as beneficiaries of international protection, for a uniform status for refugees or for persons eligible for subsidiary protection and for the content of the protection granted [2011] OJ L337/9.

their life or person by reason of indiscriminate violence in situations of international or internal armed conflict, if returned to their country of origin. This category is known as 'subsidiary protection'.[53]

Directive 2011/95 requires all Member States to carry out an individual assessment of each application for international protection, in accordance with the criteria for the assessment of facts and circumstances specified in Article 4. Refugee status is granted only to those who face 'persecution' or a risk of persecution in their country of origin, and is denied if the competent authority establishes that there is no well-founded fear of persecution or that effective protection against persecution is available.[54] The definition of acts of persecution is set out in Article 9 of Directive 2011/95 and aligns with the criteria of the Geneva Convention, listing acts such as physical or mental violence, including sexual violence, legal, administrative, police or judicial measures which are in themselves discriminatory or which are implemented in a discriminatory manner, prosecution or punishment which is disproportionate or discriminatory, denial of judicial redress resulting in a disproportionate or discriminatory punishment, prosecution or punishment for refusal to perform military service in a conflict, or acts of a gender-specific or child-specific nature. Article 10 of Directive 2011/95 further clarifies the definition by listing the grounds for persecution, which include race, religion, nationality, membership of a particular social group, or political opinion. It should be noted that Directive 2011/95 will be repealed and replaced by Regulation 2024/1347, with effect from 12 June 2026.

The granting of international protection involves applying the principle of *non-refoulement*, as established in Article 19(2) of the Charter and Article 21 of Directive 2011/95, which refers to the 'international obligations' of the Member States. Once international protection is granted, Directive 2011/95 guarantees the right to a residence permit, preservation of family unity, access to employment, access to education, social welfare, and healthcare.

3.2. Status Determination Procedures and Mechanisms for Determining the Responsible Member State

The CEAS provides a uniform framework for procedures related to applications for international protection, including rules for determining the responsible Member State. These procedural rules are currently set out in Directive 2013/32 on common procedures for granting and withdrawing international protection,[55] and Regulation 604/2013, which establishes the criteria and mechanisms for determining the Member State responsible for examining an application for international protection.[56]

Directive 2013/32 defines the territorial scope of the CEAS. It limits it to applications for international protection made within the territory, including at the border, in territorial waters, or transit zones of Member States, and to the withdrawal of international protection.[57] This excludes applications for diplomatic or territorial asylum submitted to the diplomatic representations of Member States.[58]

[53] Art 2(f)–(g) of Directive 2011/95.

[54] Art 8 of Directive 2011/95.

[55] Directive 2013/32/EU of the European Parliament and of the Council of 26 June 2013 on common procedures for granting and withdrawing international protection [2013] OJ L180/60.

[56] Regulation (EU) 604/2013 of the European Parliament and of the Council of 26 June 2013 establishing the criteria and mechanisms for determining the Member State responsible for examining an application for international protection lodged in one of the Member States by a third-country national or a stateless person [2013] OJ L180/31.

[57] Art 3 of Directive 2013/32.

[58] See Case C-638/16 PPU *X and X* EU:C:2017:173.

Applicants for international protection have the right to access the procedure under conditions that allow the application to be made 'as soon as possible'.[59] An application for international protection is considered to have been made the moment the applicant submits the required form or, if provided for by national law, when an official report is received by the competent authorities of the Member State concerned. Applicants may be accompanied by their dependents in the application.[60] Applicants are permitted to remain in the Member State until the competent authority has reached a decision, although this right does not include the right to obtain a residence permit.[61]

Applicants have the right to be informed in a language they understand or are reasonably supposed to understand, about the procedure to follow, as well as their rights and obligations during the process. They must not be prevented from contacting the United Nations High Commissioner for Refugees (UNHCR) or any other organisation providing legal advice or counselling, and must be notified of the decision on their application within a reasonable time. Articles 14–17 of Directive 2013/32 emphasise the relevance of the personal interview, which is a right of the applicant before the determining authority decides on the application.[62] Article 18 outlines the conditions under which a medical examination of the applicant is necessary, particularly where there are indicia of past persecution or serious harm. The case law of the Court of Justice has addressed the conditions governing the collection of statements and evidence by the national authorities, particularly with regard to certain grounds of persecution, such as those related to sexual orientation.[63]

Directive 2013/32 introduces the concept of 'safe third country' and 'safe country of origin' as criteria determining the admissibility of an application for international protection. If the country of origin is included in the list of countries designated as 'safe' under Article 37 of the Directive, the Member State may reject the application for international protection as manifestly unfounded. While the Directive does not establish uniform Union-wide criteria as regards the national designation of safe countries of origin,[64] it restricts the rejection of an application on this basis solely to cases where the applicant is a national of the 'safe' country, is stateless, or has previously had his or her habitual residence in that country. Additionally, Annex I of the Directive lists several criteria that must be satisfied before a third country can be classified as 'safe'.[65]

As a result of increasing pressure from some Member States, the Union is in the process of facilitating the processing of asylum applications in safe third countries as a way of speeding up procedures and easing the burden on national asylum systems. This trend was initially codified in the Asylum Procedures Regulation (EU) 2024/1348, but was significantly expanded in May 2025, when the Commission proposed further amendments to remove the requirement for a connection between the applicant and the safe third country.[66] According to the proposal, transit through a safe third country before reaching the Union could be considered a sufficient link for the application of the safe third country concept. Additionally, when there is no connection or transit, the concept can still be applied where there is an agreement or

[59] Art 6(2) of Directive 2013/32.

[60] ibid, Art 7(2).

[61] ibid, Art 9.

[62] See Case C-348/15 *Moussa Sacko* EU:C:2017:591; and Case C-517/17 *Addis* EU:C:2020:579.

[63] Joined Cases C-148/13 and C-150/13 *A, B and C* EU:C:2014:2406; and Case C-473/16 *F* EU:C:2018:36.

[64] See Art 37 of Directive 2013/32.

[65] On the definition of 'safe' third country, see Case C-406/22 *Ministerstvo vnitra České republiky, Odbor azylové a migrační politiky* EU:C:2024:841; and Joined Cases C-758/23 and C-759/23 *Alace* EU:C:2025:260.

[66] Commission Proposal for a Regulation of the European Parliament and of the Council establishing a list of safe countries of origin at Union level, COM(2025) 259 final.

arrangement with a safe third country (with the exclusion of unaccompanied minors). This policy introduces a form of 'externalisation' of asylum procedures to third countries outside the Union, a highly debated approach that raises significant concerns about its compliance with fundamental rights, especially in cases where applicants are transferred to a third country for detention and placed in locations with no links or connections that could improve their living conditions or facilitate their return to the country of origin from which they are fleeing.

The CEAS also encompasses criteria for determining the Member State responsible for examining an application for international protection. These criteria originated in the 1990 Dublin Convention, later converted into a regulation, now Regulation 604/2013, commonly referred to as 'Dublin II'. This system is founded on two principles: the exclusive competence of a single Member State;[67] and the criterion of the allocation of competence to the Member State where the applicant first crossed the external border. If this location cannot be determined, the first Member State in which the application for international protection was lodged will be responsible for examining it.[68] These rules of responsibility are subject to several exceptions, such as those applying to unaccompanied minors and family members who are applicants for international protection.[69] It should be noted that Regulation 604/2013 will be repealed and replaced by the Asylum and Migration Management Regulation (Regulation 2024/1351), applicable from 12 June 2026, which introduces a new solidarity mechanism between the Member States, explained in section 3.5.2 of this chapter.

Recent experience has shown that the implementation of the Dublin system can be ineffective in some Member States. In 2011, the European Court of Human Rights ruled against the transfer of an asylum seeker from Belgium to Greece, where Greece was responsible for examining the application under the Dublin Regulation, on the grounds that serious systemic deficiencies had been established with regard to the treatment of applicants for international protection.[70] Shortly after, the Court of Justice reached a similar conclusion in the case of *NS* and established that, in such cases, responsibility should lie with the Member State conducting the determination procedure and not the first Member State of entry.[71]

3.3. *Rules on the Reception of Applicants for International Protection*

Applicants for international protection hold a specific legal status during the processing of their application. Directive 2013/33, which sets standards for the reception of applicants for international protection, codifies several rights derived from international law and the practice of Member States.[72] As a general rule, Directive 2013/33 requires Member States to issue, within three days of the application being lodged, a document certifying that the applicant is authorised to remain in the territory of the Member State where the application is being processed. This document helps the applicant exercise their rights to reside and move freely within the host Member State and within the area designated to them by that Member State.[73] Directive 2013/33 also specifies the circumstances under which an applicant may be subject to detention, limiting these cases to justified situations but never on the basis that the person is

[67] Art 3(1) of Regulation 604/2013.

[68] ibid, Art 3.

[69] ibid, Arts 8–11.

[70] *MSS v Belgium and Greece* App no 30696/09 (ECtHR, 21 January 2011).

[71] See Joined Cases C-411/10 and C-493/10 *NS and ME* EU:C:2011:865, whose case law was subsequently codified in Art 3(2) of Regulation (EU) 604/2013.

[72] Directive 2013/33/EU of the European Parliament and of the Council of 26 June 2013 laying down standards for the reception of applicants for international protection [2013] OJ L180/96.

[73] Art 6(1) of Directive 2013/33.

merely an applicant for international protection.[74] Detention should, as a rule, take place in specialised centres, and, when held in prisons, applicants for international protection should be kept separately from ordinary prisoners. Applicants in detention must have access to family members, legal advisers, and representatives of non-governmental organisations.[75]

3.4. *Exceptional Situations of Mass Inflows*

Article 78(2)(c) TFEU grants the Union the power to adopt measures establishing 'a common system for the temporary protection of displaced persons in the event of a massive inflow'. This has materialised through the adoption of Directive 2001/55 on temporary protection,[76] an instrument that sets out minimum standards for granting temporary protection during a mass influx of displaced persons from third countries who are unable to return to their country of origin.

'Temporary protection' is an exceptional procedure whereby, in the event of a mass influx or imminent mass influx of displaced persons from third countries who are unable to return to their country of origin, immediate and temporary protection is granted to such persons, in particular if there is also a risk that the asylum system will be unable to process this influx without adverse effects for its efficient operation, in the interests of the persons concerned and other persons requesting protection.[77] This was the mechanism used by the Union and its Member States to support persons displaced from Ukraine due to the Russian aggression that began in 2022.[78]

Temporary protection lasts, as a general rule, for one year, and is automatically extended by six-month periods for a maximum of one further year. Where the reasons for temporary protection persist, the Council may, by qualified majority on a proposal from the Commission, extend that protection by up to one further year, bringing the maximum total duration to three years.[79] The existence of a mass influx is confirmed by a Council decision adopted by qualified majority on a proposal from the Commission, which must detail the facts justifying the measure and specify the date when temporary protection will start. Once temporary protection is granted, Member States must take the necessary steps to ensure that beneficiaries hold residence permits for the entire duration, and that all facilities are provided for obtaining visas, including transit visas.[80] Persons enjoying temporary protection are authorised to engage in paid employment or self-employment for the period of protection and are guaranteed access to suitable accommodation or the means to obtain it.[81]

Article 78(3) TFEU states that if

> one or more Member States being confronted by an emergency situation characterised by a sudden inflow of nationals of third countries, the Council, on a proposal from the Commission, may adopt provisional measures for the benefit of the Member State(s) concerned.

[74] ibid, Art 8.

[75] ibid, Art 10.

[76] Council Directive 2001/55/EC of 20 July 2001 on minimum standards for giving temporary protection in the event of a mass influx of displaced persons and on measures promoting a balance of efforts between Member States in receiving such persons and bearing the consequences thereof [2001] OJ L212/12.

[77] Art 2(a) of Directive 2001/55.

[78] Council Implementing Decision (EU) 2022/382 of 4 March 2022 establishing the existence of a mass influx of displaced persons from Ukraine within the meaning of Article 5 of Directive 2001/55/EC, and having the effect of introducing temporary protection [2022] OJ L71/1, as successively extended by the Council.

[79] Art 4 of Directive 2001/55.

[80] ibid, Art 8.

[81] ibid, Arts 12–13.

This enables the Union to take ad hoc measures outside the mechanisms set out in the Temporary Protection Directive. This provision was invoked in 2015, following a large influx of applicants seeking international protection, mainly from Syria, where a prolonged and violent armed conflict was taking place, forcing a substantial part of the population to flee the country. The Council adopted two successive decisions establishing a mechanism for the relocation of applicants to alleviate migratory pressure on the frontline Member States, namely Greece and Italy.[82] Several Member States challenged the second of those decisions before the Court of Justice.[83] Although the legality of the measure was upheld, a significant number of Member States did not comply with their obligations, and the Commission was even compelled to take legal action against several of them, successfully bringing infringement proceedings pursuant to Article 258 TFEU against Poland, Hungary and the Czech Republic.[84]

3.5. *The 2024 Pact on Migration and Asylum*

The Pact on Migration and Asylum represents the most comprehensive reform of the Common European Asylum System (CEAS) since its creation. Formally adopted in May 2024 and entering into force on 11 July 2024, the new framework will apply from June 2026, following a two-year transition phase. The Pact replaces or recasts most CEAS legislation through a coherent package consisting of the Asylum and Migration Management Regulation (AMMR),[85] the Asylum Procedures Regulation (APR)[86] and the Return Border Procedure Regulation,[87] the Screening Regulation,[88] the Eurodac Regulation (recast),[89] the Qualification Regulation,[90] and the recast Reception Conditions Directive.[91] It is complemented by a Crisis and Force Majeure Regulation,[92] which establishes exceptional measures in cases of migratory pressure or instrumentalisation of migration.

3.5.1. Screening, Eurodac and Border Procedures

At the external borders, the Screening Regulation introduces a uniform *pre-entry screening* applicable to all irregular arrivals and persons requesting protection without fulfilling

[82] Council Decision (EU) 2015/1523 of 14 September 2015 and Council Decision (EU) 2015/1601 of 22 September 2015, both establishing provisional measures in the area of international protection for the benefit of Italy and Greece [2015] OJ L239/146 and [2015] OJ L248/80 respectively.

[83] Joined Cases C-643/15 and C-647/15 *Slovakia and Hungary v Council* EU:C:2017:631.

[84] Joined Cases C-715/17, C-718/17 and C-719/17 *Commission v Poland, Hungary and Czech Republic* EU:C:2020:257.

[85] Regulation (EU) 2024/1351 of the European Parliament and of the Council of 14 May 2024 on asylum and migration management, amending Regulations (EU) 2021/1147 and (EU) 2021/1060 and repealing Regulation (EU) No 604/2013 [2024] OJ L1351.

[86] Regulation (EU) 2024/1348 of the European Parliament and of the Council of 14 May 2024 establishing a common procedure for international protection in the Union and repealing Directive 2013/32/EU [2024] OJ L1348.

[87] Regulation (EU) 2024/1349 of the European Parliament and of the Council of 14 May 2024 establishing a return border procedure, and amending Regulation (EU) 2021/1148 [2024] OJ L1349.

[88] Regulation (EU) 2024/1356 of the European Parliament and of the Council of 14 May 2024 introducing the screening of third-country nationals at the external borders and amending Regulations (EC) No 767/2008, (EU) 2017/2226, (EU) 2018/1240 and (EU) 2019/817 [2024] OJ L1356.

[89] Regulation (EU) 2024/1358 of the European Parliament and of the Council of 14 May 2024 on the establishment of Eurodac for the comparison of biometric data [2024] OJ L, 2024/1358, 22.5.2024.

[90] Regulation (EU) 2024/1347 of the European Parliament and of the Council of 14 May 2024 on standards for the qualification of third-country nationals or stateless persons as beneficiaries of international protection [2024] OJ L1347.

[91] Directive (EU) 2024/1346 of the European Parliament and of the Council of 14 May 2024 laying down standards for the reception of applicants for international protection [2024] OJ L1346.

[92] Regulation (EU) 2024/1359 of the European Parliament and of the Council of 14 May 2024 addressing situations of crisis and force majeure in the field of migration and asylum and amending Regulation (EU) 2021/1147 [2024] OJ L, 2024/1359.

entry conditions.[93] The procedure includes identity, health, and security checks and must be completed within seven days at the border (or three days inland).[94] It determines whether the person should enter the asylum procedure, a return procedure, or another status-determination process, while also ensuring the collection of biometric data.[95]

The Eurodac recast Regulation expands Eurodac's scope beyond asylum applications to include irregular migrants and beneficiaries of international protection.[96] It transforms Eurodac into a centralised asylum and migration database, recording individuals (not applications) and storing facial images in addition to fingerprints, ensuring interoperability with other Union information systems.[97]

The APR establishes a mandatory border procedure for specific categories of applicants (including those from countries with low recognition rates or posing security risks).[98] It also introduces strict time limits (12 weeks for the asylum phase, 12 weeks for the return phase).[99] These procedures are linked, forming a single chain that ensures rapid determination and return when applicable. Member States must maintain a *reference capacity* of 30,000 places for border procedures, with proportional distribution across the Union. Safeguards remain for minors and vulnerable applicants, who may not be detained except under exceptional circumstances.[100]

3.5.2. The Asylum and Migration Management Regulation and the Flexible Solidarity Mechanism

The AMMR replaces the Dublin III Regulation and redefines both *responsibility* and *solidarity* in EU asylum law. Responsibility continues to lie primarily with the Member State of first irregular entry or visa issuance, but transfer procedures have been simplified and deadlines shortened to reduce secondary movements.[101] The AMMR introduces a permanent, flexible solidarity mechanism designed to ensure a fairer distribution of asylum responsibilities among Member States while preserving their freedom to choose the form of contribution.[102]

Each year, the Commission shall present a Migration Management Report assessing pressures on national asylum systems and triggering a Solidarity Pool in which Member States declare their contributions.[103] The contributions are quantified using a reference formula that combines GDP (50 per cent) and population size (50 per cent), thereby reflecting both economic and demographic capacity.[104] Where Member States fall short of meeting the Commission's solidarity target collectively, a proportional redistribution mechanism applies, ensuring the burden is shared. A Member State may offset its relocation obligations by providing equivalent financial or operational support, a feature that gives the system its 'flexible' character. However, in situations of severe migratory pressure or crisis, the Council, acting on

[93] Regulation (EU) 2024/1356, Art 1(1).
[94] ibid, Art 6.
[95] ibid, Arts 9 and 14–16.
[96] Regulation (EU) 2024/1358 of the European Parliament and of the Council of 14 May 2024 establishing Eurodac for the comparison of biometric data [2024] OJ L 1358, Art 1(1).
[97] ibid, Art 3(2).
[98] Regulation (EU) 2024/1348 (n 86), Arts 41–44.
[99] ibid, Arts 41(11) and 55.
[100] ibid, Arts 44(3) and 57.
[101] Regulation (EU) 2024/1351, Arts 3 and 26.
[102] ibid, Arts 44–53.
[103] ibid, Art 61.
[104] ibid, Annex I.

a Commission proposal, may adjust the balance between relocation and financial support to guarantee sufficient relief for the frontline states.[105]

The AMMR also establishes a Solidarity Pool, managed by the Commission, that records voluntary pledges and implements them in accordance with operational needs.[106] A principle of mandatory solidarity with voluntary choice of means replaces earlier ad hoc arrangements and aims to prevent the systemic imbalances and non-compliance that characterised the 2015 relocation mechanism.[107] More importantly, the Regulation also guarantees procedural rights, clarifies take-charge and take-back obligations, and introduces corrective measures against secondary movements. As a result, an applicant who moves irregularly to another Member State may have reduced reception rights until returned to the responsible state.[108]

The Crisis and Force Majeure Regulation supplements the AMMR by establishing derogations during mass influxes or 'instrumentalisation' of migrants.[109] In such cases, registration and border-procedure deadlines can be temporarily extended (up to four and 18 weeks, respectively), accompanied by enhanced solidarity measures, including compulsory relocation and targeted Union funding. Vulnerable groups, particularly minors under 12, remain exempt from extended border detention.[110]

4. Institutional Framework

The complexity of migration and asylum policy has prompted the Union to develop innovative management structures in which national authorities cooperate closely with one another and with newly established Union bodies. The global scale of migratory movements, together with the need to strengthen external border control and asylum procedures, has driven the creation of Union agencies endowed with dedicated resources, specialised personnel, and coordination and operational powers exercised alongside those of the Member States.

4.1. *The European Border and Coast Guard and its Agency (Frontex)*

Regulation 2019/1896 establishes the European Border and Coast Guard, aiming to ensure the European integrated management of external borders.[111] The European Border and Coast Guard consists of the national authorities of the Member States responsible for border management, including coast guards to the extent that they carry out border control tasks, the national authorities responsible for return, and the European Border and Coast Guard Agency (Frontex).[112]

Frontex is the permanent agency of the European Border and Coast Guard and is designed to have a standing corps of up to 10,000 operational staff by 2027. Its headquarters are located in Warsaw, and its activities are grounded in the principle of shared responsibility with the Member States. Accordingly, while Frontex provides technical and operational assistance in the management of external borders and in the implementation of return-related measures

[105] ibid, Art 50.

[106] ibid, Art 52.

[107] ibid, Art 44(1) and Recitals 25–27.

[108] ibid, Art 34(3).

[109] Regulation (EU) 2024/1351 of the European Parliament and of the Council of 14 May 2024 addressing situations of crisis and force majeure in the field of migration and asylum [2024] OJ L, 2024/1359 Arts 2–4.

[110] ibid, Art 10(2).

[111] Regulation (EU) 2019/1896 of the European Parliament and of the Council of 13 November 2019 on the European Border and Coast Guard and repealing Regulations (EU) No 1052/2013 and (EU) 2016/1624 [2019] OJ L295/1.

[112] Art 4 of Regulation 2019/1896.

(either at the request of, or with the consent of, a Member State or, in exceptional circumstances, following a Council decision adopted on a proposal from the Commission), the primary responsibility for controlling external borders and enforcing return decisions remains with the Member States.

Regulation (EU) 2019/1896 has significantly strengthened Frontex's obligations with regard to the protection of fundamental rights, particularly in the context of return operations. Article 80(1), read in conjunction with the Charter of Fundamental Rights of the European Union and the Union's international human rights and refugee law obligations, requires Frontex to guarantee the protection of fundamental rights in the performance of its tasks, in particular compliance with the principle of *non-refoulement*. Article 80(2) prohibits the European Border and Coast Guard from disembarking, forcing to enter, conducting to, or otherwise handing over or returning persons to the authorities of a country in breach of the principle of non-refoulement, or from which there is a risk of such expulsion, return, extradition or transfer to another country in breach of that principle. This includes protection against removal to a country where there is a serious risk of being sentenced to the death penalty, subjected to torture, persecution, or other inhuman or degrading treatment or punishment, or where life or freedom would be threatened on grounds of race, religion, nationality, sexual orientation, membership of a particular social group, or political opinion.

In situations involving damage caused by members of the teams during their operations, Article 84 of Regulation 2019/1896 establishes a civil liability regime under which the host Member State is liable under its national law; where the damage is caused by gross negligence or wilful misconduct, the host Member State may seek reimbursement from the home Member State (for seconded staff) or from the Agency (for its statutory staff).[113]

4.2. *European Union Asylum Agency*

In 2022, the Union legislator replaced the European Asylum Support Office with the European Union Agency for Asylum (EUAA) to provide operational, technical support and training to the authorities of Member States. Regulation 2021/2303 establishing the EUAA[114] gives the Agency authority to provide immediate operational assistance to Member States facing disproportionate pressure on their asylum and reception systems. Its seat is in Valletta, Malta.

The Agency also maintains a mandatory Asylum Reserve Pool of around 500 experts provided by the Member States, deployable within seven working days. Its operations rely on close cooperation with the authorities of Member States through the deployment of information-sharing mechanisms, networks, and best practices.

III. JUDICIAL COOPERATION IN CIVIL AND CRIMINAL MATTERS

Judicial cooperation is a core component of the Area of Freedom, Security and Justice. National courts play a central role in the implementation of Union policies, both by resolving disputes between individuals in which Union law applies and by addressing criminal conduct and contributing to crime prevention. The Union, for its part, does not possess a judiciary of its own beyond the jurisdictions of the Court of Justice of the European Union, which ensures

[113] See Case C-136/24 P *Hamoudi v Frontex* EU:C:2025:257; and Case C-679/23 P *WS and Others v Frontex* EU:C:2025:427.

[114] Regulation (EU) 2021/2303 of the European Parliament and of the Council of 15 December 2021 on the European Union Agency for Asylum and repealing Regulation (EU) No 439/2010 [2021] OJ L468/1.

the legality of Union acts and the uniform interpretation of law through the preliminary ruling procedure. As a result, national courts remain the primary fora for the resolution of the vast majority of disputes, whether of a public or private nature. In this context, Union policy seeks not only to strengthen the functioning of national judicial systems, but also to enhance judicial cooperation between them in civil and criminal matters.

The cornerstone of judicial cooperation within the Area of Freedom, Security and Justice is to promote the mutual recognition of judicial decisions and of decisions in extrajudicial matters. To attain this objective, the Union has focused on adopting legislative measures in the field of procedural law, particularly in situations involving cross-border elements. At the same time, in order to ensure the effective functioning of the internal market and to reinforce police and judicial cooperation among the Member States, the Union may also adopt measures that indirectly affect substantive law, in particular through the harmonisation of procedural rules or conflict of laws rules, but only in matters with cross-border implications. While the Treaties do not confer upon the Union the power to establish a comprehensive civil or criminal law system replacing those of the Member States, Union action has nevertheless contributed to the approximation of national laws in these fields, thereby facilitating judicial cooperation between the Member States. It should be noted, however, that the application of these measures is subject to specific 'opt-out' regimes for certain Member States, in particular Denmark and Ireland.

1. Civil Matters

Article 81 TFEU provides the legal basis for Union action to strengthen judicial cooperation in civil matters with cross-border implications. This policy area is founded on the principle of mutual recognition of judicial and extrajudicial decisions, and the relevant measures are generally adopted under the ordinary legislative procedure, by qualified majority voting in the Council. An exception to this rule is laid down in Article 81(3) TFEU, which concerns measures relating to family law with cross-border implications; such measures are adopted by the Council in accordance with a special legislative procedure requiring unanimity after consulting the European Parliament.

The legal basis set out in Article 81 TFEU imposes two general constraints on the Union legislature. First, measures adopted in the field of judicial cooperation in civil matters are guided by the principle of mutual recognition, ensuring that this legal basis is not used to undermine, fragment, or restrict the effects of judgments in cross-border situations. Second, although it is not a mandatory condition for Union action, the legislature may justify the adoption of measures in this field where they are considered to be 'particularly necessary for the proper functioning of the internal market'. The original wording of this provision, as introduced by the Treaty of Amsterdam, confined Union action under what was then the 'third pillar' to measures 'in so far as necessary' for the proper functioning of the internal market. The Lisbon Treaty amended this approach by introducing the current wording, which allows for the adoption of measures even where the connection with the internal market is less direct, provided the cross-border element is satisfied.

Union legislative activity in the field of judicial cooperation in civil matters is very broad. For the purposes of clarity, it may be grouped into three categories: first, measures concerning judicial cooperation in civil matters with cross-border implications and of a procedural nature; second, measures aimed at the harmonisation and unification of the rules of private international law; and third, measures designed to approximate specific aspects of the procedural law of the Member States.

1.1. *Judicial Cooperation in Civil Matters*

Article 81 TFEU explicitly refers to various areas of action aimed at regulating judicial cooperation in civil matters with cross-border implications, where it is essential to adopt instruments that facilitate such cooperation and the free movement of judgments and of decisions in extrajudicial cases throughout the territory of the Member States. Paragraph 2 refers to these measures in points (a), (b), and (d), among others, to ensure 'the mutual recognition and enforcement between Member States of judgments and of decisions in extrajudicial cases', 'the cross-border service of judicial and extrajudicial documents', and 'cooperation in the taking of evidence'.

The cross-border service of judicial and extrajudicial documents in civil and commercial matters is extensively developed in Regulation 2020/1784,[115] while cooperation in the taking of evidence in those fields is currently reflected in Regulation 2020/1783.[116] The recognition and enforcement of judgments is generally covered by Regulation 1215/2012 (Brussels I Recast),[117] a similar regime being applicable in relations with Iceland, Norway and Switzerland through the 2007 Lugano Convention, which mirrors the predecessor Regulation 44/2001 rather than the Recast.[118] Additionally, the Union has adopted specific provisions on recognition and enforcement in sectoral areas. This is the case for matrimonial matters and parental responsibility (Regulation 2019/1111, or 'Brussels II ter' or 'Brussels II Recast'),[119] maintenance obligations,[120] insolvency proceedings,[121] succession,[122] and protective measures in civil matters.[123] Additional measures have been introduced, including a European Enforcement Order for uncontested claims, to facilitate the recognition of judgments, court settlements, and authentic instruments, abolishing the need for an intermediate 'exequatur' procedure in many instances.[124]

Measures on judicial cooperation in civil matters have not always achieved the necessary consensus among the Member States, resulting in the use of enhanced cooperation on several occasions. This has been the case for the recognition and enforcement of measures on matrimonial property regimes[125] and on the property consequences of registered partnerships, as well as for the law applicable to divorce and legal separation ('Rome III').[126]

[115] Regulation (EU) 2020/1784 of the European Parliament and of the Council of 25 November 2020 on the service in the Member States of judicial and extrajudicial documents in civil or commercial matters [2020] OJ L405/40.

[116] Regulation (EU) 2020/1783 of the European Parliament and of the Council of 25 November 2020 on cooperation between the courts of the Member States in the taking of evidence in civil or commercial matters [2020] OJ L405/1.

[117] Regulation (EU) 1215/2012 of the European Parliament and of the Council of 12 December 2012 on jurisdiction and the recognition and enforcement of judgments in civil and commercial matters [2012] OJ L351/1.

[118] Convention on jurisdiction and the recognition and enforcement of judgments in civil and commercial matters (Lugano Convention) [2007] OJ L 339/3.

[119] Council Regulation (EU) 2019/1111 of 25 June 2019 on jurisdiction, the recognition and enforcement of judgments in matrimonial matters and the matters of parental responsibility and international child abduction [2019] OJ L178/1.

[120] Council Regulation (EC) 4/2009 of 18 December 2008 on jurisdiction, applicable law, recognition and enforcement of decisions and cooperation in matters relating to maintenance obligations [2009] OJ L7/1.

[121] Regulation (EU) 2015/848 of the European Parliament and of the Council of 20 May 2015 on insolvency proceedings [2015] OJ L141/19.

[122] Regulation (EU) 650/2012 of the European Parliament and of the Council of 4 July 2012 on jurisdiction, applicable law, recognition and enforcement of decisions and acceptance and enforcement of authentic instruments in matters of succession and on the creation of a European Certificate of Succession [2012] OJ L201/107.

[123] Regulation (EU) 606/2013 of the European Parliament and of the Council of 12 June 2013 on mutual recognition of protection measures in civil matters [2013] OJ L181/4.

[124] Regulation (EC) 805/2004 of the European Parliament and of the Council of 21 April 2004 creating a European Enforcement Order for uncontested claims [2004] OJ L143/15.

[125] Council Regulation (EU) 2016/1103 of 24 June 2016 implementing enhanced cooperation in the area of jurisdiction, applicable law and the recognition and enforcement of decisions in matters of matrimonial property regimes [2016] OJ L183/1.

[126] Council Regulation (EU) No 1259/2010 of 20 December 2010 implementing enhanced cooperation in the area of the law applicable to divorce and legal separation ('Rome III') [2010] OJ L343/10.

1.2. *Private International Law*

Article 81(2)(c) TFEU refers to the adoption of measures to ensure 'the compatibility of the rules applicable in the Member States concerning the conflict of laws and of jurisdiction'. This legal basis has enabled the Union to develop a comprehensive body of rules that largely unifies the rules of private international law across the Member States, both regarding the conflict rules on applicable law and the rules on international jurisdiction. The Union has now adopted several regulations that in some instances have transformed pre-existing international agreements into uniform Union acts, thereby increasing legal certainty for citizens and businesses.

The Union's rules on international jurisdiction in civil and commercial matters are mainly contained in Regulation 1215/2012, also referred to as 'Brussels I Recast', which recast Regulation 44/2001, itself the successor instrument that transposed the 1968 Brussels Convention into secondary Union legislation.[127] The Union legislator has also adopted rules on international jurisdiction in the aforementioned sectoral areas, such as matrimonial matters, parental responsibility, maintenance, succession, and insolvency proceedings.

The conflict of laws referred to in Article 81(2)(c) TFEU are the rules on applicable law that determine the application of national civil law to contractual and non-contractual obligations, as well as to divorce and legal separation, the latter introduced through enhanced cooperation.[128] As regards contractual obligations, Regulation 593/2008 transposes and updates the content of the Rome Convention of 1980 into secondary Union law, thereby accounting for its current name ('Rome I').[129] The rules on the law applicable to non-contractual obligations are currently governed by Regulation 864/2007, commonly referred to as 'Rome II', which provides specific rules for *inter alia* environmental damage, product liability, and acts of unfair competition.[130]

1.3. *Civil Procedural Harmonisation*

Article 81(2) TFEU outlines several situations in which the Union may adopt measures to harmonise civil procedure, where necessary for the proper functioning of judicial cooperation. These legal bases allow for the harmonisation of specific procedural rules of the Member States, including effective access to justice; the elimination of obstacles to the proper functioning of civil proceedings; and the development of alternative methods of dispute settlement. Based on this premise, Directive 2002/8 on legal aid in cross-border disputes was adopted,[131] as was Directive 2008/52 on certain aspects of mediation in civil and commercial matters.[132] Furthermore, Regulation (EU) 2023/2844 on the digitalisation of judicial cooperation and access to justice now seeks to modernise these processes by establishing the 'digital by default'

[127] Convention of 27 September 1968 on jurisdiction and the enforcement of judgments in civil and commercial matters, [1998] OJ C27/1.

[128] Council Regulation (EU) 1259/2010 of 20 December 2010 implementing enhanced cooperation in the area of the law applicable to divorce and legal separation [2010] OJ L343/10.

[129] Regulation (EC) 593/2008 of the European Parliament and of the Council of 17 June 2008 on the law applicable to contractual obligations (Rome I) [2008] OJ L177/6.

[130] Regulation (EC) No 864/2007 of the European Parliament and of the Council of 11 July 2007 on the law applicable to non-contractual obligations (Rome II) [2007] OJ L199/40.

[131] Council Directive 2003/8/EC of 27 January 2003 to improve access to justice in cross-border disputes by establishing minimum common rules relating to legal aid for such disputes [2003] OJ L26/41.

[132] Directive 2008/52/EC of the European Parliament and of the Council of 21 May 2008 on certain aspects of mediation in civil and commercial matters [2008] OJ L136/3.

principle for the transmission of communications between competent authorities in cross-border civil, commercial and criminal cases.[133]

2. Criminal Matters

Judicial cooperation in criminal matters is founded on Article 82 TFEU, which establishes a framework for mutual recognition of judgments and judicial decisions in criminal matters and for the approximation of certain aspects of criminal procedure. In parallel, Article 83 TFEU authorises the Union to lay down 'minimum rules' concerning the definition of criminal offences and sanctions in areas of particularly serious crime with a cross-border dimension. By this means, the Union is empowered to adopt measures designed to facilitate the recognition of judgments and judicial decisions in criminal matters between the Member States, thereby ensuring the effective operation of the principle of mutual recognition throughout the Union.

The harmonisation of national criminal policies raises specific and sensitive challenges. The legal traditions of the Member States differ significantly in their approaches to defining criminal offences and sanctions. In addition, criminal policy often reflects cultural and social preferences particular to each Member State, or responds to distinct historical experiences. By way of illustration, the criminalisation of Holocaust denial is treated differently across Member States: it is criminalised under §130 of the Strafgesetzbuch in Germany, while in Spain the Constitutional Court struck down the offence of mere denial as incompatible with freedom of expression, retaining only 'justification' as a criminal offence. At the same time, Union action in this field must ensure the effective protection of the rights of both defendants and victims. This task becomes especially complex in cases involving cross-border elements. Overall, the achievement of mutual recognition of judicial decisions in criminal matters requires a high degree of legislative and judicial coordination, and the Union is equipped with the competences conferred by Articles 82–83 TFEU to support and facilitate this process. It is important to note that under Articles 82(3) and 83(3) TFEU, an 'emergency brake' mechanism exists, allowing a Member State to refer a draft directive to the European Council where it considers that the draft affects fundamental aspects of its criminal justice system.

2.1. *Instruments of Judicial Cooperation in Criminal Matters*

The first category of legislative measures in the field of criminal law relates to cross-border judicial cooperation, in particular measures aimed at strengthening cooperation between the judicial authorities of the Member States. The relevant legal bases are set out in Article 82(1)(a)–(d) TFEU, as well as Article 82(2)(a) TFEU. These provisions respectively refer to the adoption of rules to ensure the recognition of judgments and judicial decisions in criminal matters throughout the Union, to the prevention and settlement of conflicts of jurisdiction between Member States, to the facilitation of cooperation between judicial authorities, and to the mutual admissibility of evidence between Member States.

[133] Regulation (EU) 2023/2844 of the European Parliament and of the Council of 13 December 2023 on the digitalisation of judicial cooperation and access to justice in cross-border civil, commercial and criminal matters, and amending certain acts in the field of judicial cooperation [2023] OJ L2844.

Through these legal bases, the Union has created the European Protection Order in Directive 2011/99,[134] the European Investigation Order in criminal matters in Directive 2014/41,[135] rules on the execution of freezing and confiscation orders now primarily governed, for participating Member States, by Regulation (EU) 2018/1805,[136] which replaced Framework Decision 2003/577/JHA and Framework Decision 2006/783/JHA in that respect, as well as rules on the mutual recognition of financial penalties, custodial sentences and other measures involving deprivation of liberty, supervision measures as an alternative to provisional detention, and decisions rendered in the absence of the person concerned at the trial.

The legislator has also introduced harmonisation measures aimed at facilitating cooperation in the organisation and functioning of criminal courts, as in the case of Framework Decision 2009/315 on the organisation and content of the exchange of information extracted from the criminal record between Member States.[137] Framework Decision 2008/675 provides for mechanisms for criminal courts to take into account convictions in the course of new criminal proceedings in other Member States.[138] In order to avoid situations of conflict between two or more Member States, Framework Decision 2009/948 provides for mechanisms on prevention and settlement of conflicts of exercise of jurisdiction in criminal proceedings.[139]

Among all the instruments for judicial cooperation in criminal matters, the most significant is provided for in Framework Decision 2002/584 on the European arrest warrant. This judicial cooperation mechanism aims to facilitate the recognition of judicial decisions issued by one Member State with a view to the arrest and surrender by another Member State of a requested person, for the purposes of criminal prosecution or executing a custodial sentence or detention order. The European arrest warrant is a crucial mechanism for the proper functioning of the Area of Freedom, Security and Justice, although its implementation has faced challenges, as demonstrated by the extensive case law of the Court of Justice rendered to date.[140] Framework Decision 2002/584 limits the use of the European arrest warrant to acts for which the law of the issuing Member State provides for a custodial sentence or detention order with a maximum of at least 12 months, or for the execution of a sentence, a custodial sentence or detention order of at least four months. It also introduces a system of automatic mutual recognition, 'without verification of the double criminality of the act', for 32 categories of offences listed in Article 2(2), which include the most frequent forms of serious crime such as participation in a criminal organisation, terrorism, trafficking in human beings, corruption, and computer-related crime, among others.

[134] Directive 2011/99/EU of the European Parliament and of the Council of 13 December 2011 on the European Protection Order [2011] OJ L338/2.

[135] Directive 2014/41/EU of the European Parliament and of the Council of 3 April 2014 regarding the European Investigation Order in criminal matters [2014] OJ L130/1.

[136] Regulation (EU) 2018/1805 of the European Parliament and of the Council of 14 November 2018 on the mutual recognition of freezing orders and confiscation orders [2018] OJ L303/1.

[137] Council Framework Decision 2009/315/JHA of 26 February 2009 on the organisation and content of the exchange of information extracted from the criminal record between Member States [2009] OJ L93/23.

[138] Council Framework Decision 2008/675/JHA of 24 July 2008 on taking account of convictions in the Member States of the European Union in the course of new criminal proceedings [2008] OJ L220/32.

[139] Council Framework Decision 2009/948/JHA of 30 November 2009 on prevention and settlement of conflicts of exercise of jurisdiction in criminal proceedings [2009] OJ L328/42.

[140] See, among many others, Case C-303/05 *Advocaten voor de Wereld* EU:C:2007:261; Case C-66/08 *Kozłowski* EU:C:2008:437; Case C-42/11 *Lopes da Silva Jorge* EU:C:2012:517; Case C-396/11 *Radu* EU:C:2013:39; Case C-573/17 *Popławski* EU:C:2019:530; and Joined Cases C-404/15 and C-659/15 PPU *Aranyosi and Căldăraru* EU:C:2016:198.

2.2. *Harmonisation of Criminal Procedural Law*

Besides the rules aimed at enhancing judicial cooperation in criminal matters in cross-border situations, Article 82 TFEU empowers the Union to adopt measures to harmonise national criminal procedures, to the extent necessary to facilitate mutual recognition and judicial cooperation in criminal matters with a cross-border dimension. This authority has led to the creation of several harmonisation instruments, notably Directive 2012/29 on the rights, support and protection of victims of crime,[141] and Directive 2016/343 on certain aspects of the presumption of innocence and of the right to be present at the trial in criminal proceedings.[142] Additionally, rules have been introduced to address specific aspects of criminal proceedings, such as the right to interpretation and translation,[143] the right to information,[144] the right of access to a lawyer, legal aid in criminal proceedings and European arrest warrant proceedings, procedural safeguards for children who are suspects or accused persons in criminal proceedings.[145]

2.3. *Harmonisation of Criminal Law*

Article 83 TFEU grants the Union the authority to harmonise by means of directives the substantive rules of criminal law of the Member States that establish criminal offences and impose penalties. Since this legislation directly affects the core of the Member States' *ius puniendi*, the Treaties place several limits on the Union's powers. First, measures can only harmonise national criminal laws, although minimum rules on the definition of criminal offences and sanctions may have a directly creative effect in Member States where the conduct is not already criminalised. As Article 83(1) TFEU states, the Union may adopt 'minimum rules concerning the definition of criminal offences and sanctions in the areas of particularly serious crime'. Second, harmonisation can only target criminal behaviour that is 'particularly serious' and has 'a cross-border dimension'. Third, the second subparagraph of Article 83(1) TFEU lists the 'areas of crime' where harmonisation measures may be adopted: terrorism; trafficking in human beings and sexual exploitation of women and children; illicit drug trafficking; illicit arms trafficking; money laundering; corruption; counterfeiting of means of payment; computer crime; and organised crime.[146] All other 'areas of crime' are therefore excluded; however, the Council, acting unanimously and having obtained the consent of the European

[141] Directive 2012/29/EU of the European Parliament and of the Council of 25 October 2012 establishing minimum standards on the rights, support and protection of victims of crime and replacing Council Framework Decision 2001/220/JHA [2012] OJ L315/57.

[142] Directive (EU) 2016/343 of the European Parliament and of the Council of 9 March 2016 on the strengthening of certain aspects of the presumption of innocence and of the right to be present at trial in criminal proceedings [2016] OJ L65/1.

[143] Directive 2010/64/EU of the European Parliament and of the Council of 20 October 2010 on the right to interpretation and translation in criminal proceedings [2010] OJ L280/1.

[144] Directive 2012/13/EU of the European Parliament and of the Council of 22 May 2012 on the right to information in criminal proceedings [2012] OJ L142/1.

[145] Directive (EU) 2016/800 of the European Parliament and of the Council of 11 May 2016 on procedural safeguards for children who are suspects or accused persons in criminal proceedings [2016] OJ L132/1.

[146] Directive (EU) 2017/541 of the European Parliament and of the Council of 15 March 2017 on combating terrorism and replacing Council Framework Decision 2002/475/JHA and amending Council Decision 2005/671/JHA [2017] OJ L88/6; Directive 2011/36/EU of the European Parliament and of the Council of 5 April 2011 on preventing and combating trafficking in human beings and protecting victims, and replacing Council Framework Decision 2002/629/JHA [2011] OJ L101/1; Directive (EU) 2024/1385 of the European Parliament and of the Council of 14 May 2024 on combating violence against women and domestic violence [2024] OJ L 2024/1385; Directive 2013/40/EU of the European Parliament and of the Council of 12 August 2013 on attacks against information systems and replacing Council Framework Decision 2005/222/JHA [2013] OJ L218/8; Directive 2014/62/EU of the European Parliament and of the Council of 15 May 2014 on the protection of the euro and other currencies against counterfeiting by criminal law, and replacing Council Framework Decision 2000/383/JHA [2014] OJ L151/1; Directive (EU) 2018/1673 of the European Parliament and of the Council of 23 October 2018 on combating money laundering by criminal law [2018] OJ L284/22.

Parliament, may decide to identify additional areas of crime and thereby extend the list. By Decision 2022/2332 of 28 November 2022, the Council identified the violation of EU restrictive measures as an 'area of crime' to be added to the list of Article 83(1).[147]

Apart from the harmonisation linked to the above enumeration of 'areas of crime', Article 83(2) TFEU provides for another case that empowers the Union to adopt 'minimum rules', in this case 'in an area which has been subject to harmonisation measures'. Such is the case, for example, with the approximation of criminal laws and regulations of the Member States in environmental matters, a field with a significant Union legislative agenda that requires at times the support of criminal law at Union level.[148] The procedure for adopting minimum rules will be 'the same ordinary or special legislative procedure as was followed for the adoption of the harmonisation measures in question'. This is the legal basis on which minimum standards for criminal harmonisation have been adopted in the areas of the financial sector,[149] environmental protection,[150] and the Union's financial interests.[151]

The approximation of criminal laws and regulations of the Member States is subject to an emergency brake procedure, allowing any Member State to refer the matter to the European Council and suspend the legislative process for four months, as outlined in Article 83(3) TFEU. To activate this mechanism, the draft directive proposing 'minimum rules' must affect 'fundamental aspects' of the criminal justice system of the concerned Member State. Once invoked, the European Council has four months to reach a consensus and refer the draft back to the Council. If no consensus is reached, and if at least nine Member States wish to establish enhanced cooperation on the basis of the draft directive concerned, they must notify the European Parliament, the Council, and the Commission accordingly, and enhanced cooperation shall be deemed to be granted under Article 20(2) TEU and Article 329(1) TFEU, without the usual authorisation procedure.

3. Institutional Framework

3.1. *Eurojust*

To improve coordination between investigating and prosecuting authorities, Article 85 TFEU establishes the Agency for Criminal Judicial Cooperation (Eurojust). This agency is governed by Regulation 2018/1727,[152] and has its own legal personality, with its seat in The Hague.

[147] The result of the Council Decision is the adoption of Directive (EU) 2024/1226 of the European Parliament and of the Council of 24 April 2024 on the definition of criminal offences and penalties for the violation of Union restrictive measures, and amending Directive (EU) 2018/1673 [2024] OJ L1226.

[148] Before the entry into force of the Lisbon Treaty and Art 83 TFEU, the Court of Justice had occasion to confirm the competence of the Union to adopt criminal harmonisation measures in areas where the Union had adopted prior harmonisation measures. See Case C-176/03 *Commission v Council* EU:C:2005:542; and Case C-440/05 *Commission v Council* EU:C:2007:625.

[149] Directive 2014/57/EU of the European Parliament and of the Council of 16 April 2014 on criminal sanctions for market abuse [2014] OJ L173/179.

[150] Directive 2008/99/EC of the European Parliament and of the Council of 19 November 2008 on the protection of the environment through criminal law [2008] OJ L328/28; and Directive 2009/123/EC of the European Parliament and of the Council of 21 October 2009 amending Directive 2005/35/EC on ship-source pollution and on the introduction of penalties for infringements [2009] OJ L280/52, both having been repealed by Directive (EU) 2024/1203 of 11 April 2024 (OJ L, 2024/1203, 30.4.2024) with effect from 21 May 2026.

[151] Directive (EU) 2017/1371 of the European Parliament and of the Council of 5 July 2017 on the fight against fraud to the Union's financial interests by means of criminal law [2017] OJ L198/29.

[152] Regulation (EU) 2018/1727 of the European Parliament and of the Council of 14 November 2018 on the European Union Agency for Criminal Judicial Cooperation (Eurojust) and replacing and repealing Council Decision 2002/187/JHA [2018] OJ L295/138.

As outlined in Article 2 of Regulation 2018/1727, Eurojust supports and enhances coordination and cooperation among the national authorities responsible for investigating and prosecuting serious crimes within its competence, especially when such crimes affect two or more Member States or are to be prosecuted on common bases. Following the invasion of Ukraine, Eurojust's mandate was expanded by Regulation 2022/838 to allow the agency to preserve, analyse, and store evidence relating to genocide, crimes against humanity, war crimes, and related criminal offences (which led to the establishment of the Core International Crimes Evidence Database (CICED)). This support is based on operations conducted and information supplied by the European authorities of the Member States, Europol, the European Public Prosecutor's Office, and the Anti-Fraud Office (OLAF). Additionally, Eurojust may, at the request of a Member State, assist with investigations and prosecutions involving that Member State and a third country, subject to the conditions laid down in Regulation 2018/1727 governing cooperation with third countries and international organisations, including the existence of an appropriate cooperation framework or an objectively justified need in the specific case.

Eurojust handles serious forms of crime largely aligned with those addressed by the European Union Agency for Law Enforcement Cooperation (Europol): terrorism; drug trafficking; trafficking in human beings; counterfeiting; money laundering; cybercrime; offences against property or public property (including fraud and corruption); offences affecting the financial interests of the Union; offences against the environment; and participation in a criminal organisation.[153] At the request of a Member State, Eurojust can also assist in the investigation and prosecution of other types of crime.

3.2. *OLAF*

OLAF is an operationally independent investigation service of the Commission. It formulates anti-fraud policies for the Commission and is authorised to investigate fraud against the Union budget, corruption, and serious misconduct within European institutions. Its legal framework is currently outlined in Regulation 883/2013,[154] which was significantly amended by Regulation 2020/2223 to ensure a close relationship and avoid duplication with the European Public Prosecutor's Office.[155]

In 1999, the Parliament, the Council, and the Commission signed an Interinstitutional Agreement of 25 May 1999 on internal investigations to ensure that OLAF's investigations are properly conducted. Some of these rules, now incorporated into the Staff Regulations of Officials of the European Union, require staff to cooperate with OLAF and provide a certain degree of protection for officials who report possible cases of fraud or corruption. To this end, OLAF is empowered to conduct administrative investigations, understood as 'checks, controls, and other measures taken by the Office to establish, where necessary, the irregular nature of the activities under investigation'.[156] OLAF's investigations are concluded by the drafting of a report under the authority of the Director General, which details the established facts, the preliminary legal qualification, the estimated financial impact of the established facts, and the conclusions of the investigation.[157]

[153] See Annex I of Regulation 2018/1727.

[154] Regulation (EU, Euratom) 883/2013 of the European Parliament and of the Council of 11 September 2013 concerning investigations conducted by the European Anti-Fraud Office (OLAF) and repealing Regulation (EC) 1073/1999 of the European Parliament and of the Council and Council Regulation (Euratom) 1074/1999 [2013] OJ L248/1.

[155] Regulation (EU, Euratom) 2020/2223 of the European Parliament and of the Council of 23 December 2020 amending Regulation (EU, Euratom) No 883/2013, as regards cooperation with the European Public Prosecutor's Office and the effectiveness of the European Anti-Fraud Office investigations [2020] OJ L437/49.

[156] Art 2(4) of Regulation 883/2013.

[157] ibid, Art 11.

OLAF is headed by a Director-General appointed by the Commission for a seven-year non-renewable term of office.[158] The Director-General's actions are regularly reviewed by the Supervisory Committee, which consists of five independent members with substantial investigative or judicial experience, appointed by common accord of the European Parliament, the Council, and the Commission.[159]

3.3. *The European Public Prosecutor's Office*

Article 86 TFEU authorises the Council to establish, by means of regulations, a European Public Prosecutor's Office, whose mandate is primarily devoted to combating offences prejudicial to the Union's financial interests. This authority has been realised through enhanced cooperation, currently materialised in Regulation 2017/1939 on the establishment of the European Public Prosecutor's Office, which has been operational since 1 June 2021.[160]

The European Public Prosecutor's Office is an independent body responsible for investigating, prosecuting, and bringing to judgment the perpetrators of, and accomplices to, criminal offences affecting the financial interests of the Union, including fraud, corruption, misappropriation, money laundering and cross-border VAT fraud involving total damage of at least EUR 10 million. As outlined in Article 86(4) TFEU, the list of offences may be extended in the future to include serious crime having a cross-border dimension, for example terrorism. To extend the list of offences, the European Council must act unanimously after obtaining the consent of the European Parliament and after consulting the Commission.

To date, 24 Member States participate in the European Public Prosecutor's Office through enhanced cooperation, with Poland officially joining on 29 February 2024 and Sweden on 16 July 2024. It operates under a dual structure with two tiers: central and decentralised (national). The central level, based in Luxembourg, comprises the College, the Permanent Chambers, the European Chief Prosecutor, the Deputy European Chief Prosecutors, the European Prosecutors, and the Administrative Director.[161] At the decentralised level, the European Delegated Prosecutors are responsible for investigating offences and prosecuting before national courts, acting independently of national authorities.

Article 22 of Regulation 2017/1939 defines the material competence within which the European Public Prosecutor's Office operates, circumscribing it to offences affecting the financial interests of the Union, as provided for in Directive 2017/1371, and offences regarding participation in a criminal organisation as defined in Framework Decision 2008/841/JHA, provided the criminal activity focuses on committing any offence affecting the financial interests of the Union. Furthermore, the jurisdiction of the European Public Prosecutor's Office includes any other offence if it is 'inextricably linked to criminal conduct' connected to an offence affecting the financial interests of the Union.

Regarding territorial jurisdiction, the European Public Prosecutor's Office is authorised to act in respect of offences affecting the financial interests of the Union that are committed totally or partly within one or more Member States, or by a national of a Member State, provided that the Member State has jurisdiction over such offences when committed outside its territory.[162] An additional extension of territorial jurisdiction applies to cases where the offence is committed outside one or more Member States by a person subject to the Staff Regulations

[158] ibid, Art 17.

[159] ibid, Art 15.

[160] Council Regulation (EU) 2017/1939 of 12 October 2017 implementing enhanced cooperation on the establishment of the European Public Prosecutor's Office [2017] OJ L283/1.

[161] ibid, Art 8.

[162] ibid, Art 23.

or the Conditions of Employment at the time of the offence, provided that the Member State has jurisdiction for such offences when committed outside its territory.

IV. VALUES AND PRINCIPLES IN THE AREA OF FREEDOM, SECURITY AND JUSTICE

1. Values, Principles and Fundamental Rights

Within the Area of Freedom, Security and Justice, the Union is empowered to adopt measures in domains inextricably linked to human dignity, individual liberty, and other fundamental rights. These measures encompass diverse policy areas, such as immigration and asylum, which profoundly impact the lives of millions of individuals and their families. They further extend to criminal policy, which governs measures that may result in the deprivation of liberty, and judicial cooperation in civil matters, which is essential for the operation of businesses and the resolution of private disputes in areas such as family law or succession.

Given the sensitive nature of these fields, there is an inherent risk of undermining the values of the Union enshrined in Article 2 TEU, as well as the general principles of Union law derived from the Treaties and the case law of the Court of Justice. These values and principles serve as the mandatory framework guiding all actions of the Union and the Member States when implementing policies within the Area of Freedom, Security and Justice.

Article 2 TEU states that the Union is founded on the values of respect for human dignity, freedom, democracy, equality, the rule of law, and respect for human rights, including the rights of persons belonging to minorities. These values represent the 'very identity' of the Union and influence the interpretation of primary and secondary Union law.[163] The Area of Freedom, Security and Justice, including Union policies on immigration, asylum, and judicial cooperation in civil and criminal matters, has a direct impact on the values on which the Union is founded. It encompasses measures that affect individuals and their families in fundamental ways, shaping their living conditions, their freedom of movement, and the exercise of other fundamental rights. In order to ensure that such measures are adopted and applied under fair and equitable conditions, Union law establishes a range of procedural mechanisms designed to guarantee due process before independent courts operating under the rule of law. As a result, the development of the Area of Freedom, Security and Justice has been closely intertwined with the protection of these values. Striking an appropriate balance between the effective functioning of the Area of Freedom, Security and Justice and the safeguarding of those values has emerged as one of the most contentious issues addressed by the Court of Justice in recent years, as will be examined in the following sections.

Beyond the values enshrined in Article 2 TEU, Union law has developed a broad set of general principles that are applicable to the Area of Freedom, Security and Justice. In the context of immigration and asylum, Article 80 TFEU provides that these policies 'shall be governed by the principle of solidarity and fair sharing of responsibility, including its financial implications, between the Member States'. Articles 81(1) and 82(1) TFEU stipulate that judicial cooperation in civil and criminal matters 'shall be based on the principle of mutual recognition of judgments and judicial decisions'. In addition, the Charter of Fundamental

[163] Case C-808/21 *Commission v Czech Republic* EU:C:2024:962, para 160; and Case C-814/21 *Commission v Poland* EU:C:2024:963, para 157: 'Article 2 TEU is not merely a statement of policy guidelines or intentions, but contains values which are an integral part of the very identity of the European Union as a common legal order, values which are given concrete expression in principles containing legally binding obligations for the Member States.'

Rights of the European Union enshrines rights of particular relevance to immigration and asylum policies, such as Article 19, which prohibits collective expulsions and decisions involving return, expulsion, or extradition to a state where there is a serious risk of exposure to the death penalty, torture, or other inhuman or degrading treatment or punishment. The Charter further guarantees, in Article 48, the presumption of innocence and the rights of the defence, while Article 49 enshrines the principles of legality and proportionality of criminal offences and penalties.

This framework of values and principles decisively shapes the practical operation of the Area of Freedom, Security and Justice. The Union legislature, whose activity in this field has been extensive, is bound by the values and principles outlined above; failure to comply with them may result in the annulment of legislative acts by the Union's courts. Union external action is likewise constrained by these values and principles, which preclude the conclusion of international agreements that would conflict with them. At the level of individual cases, these values and principles exert a strong influence both in the field of immigration and asylum and in judicial cooperation in civil and criminal matters, thereby limiting the scope of police and judicial action by the Member States. They also interact with the values and principles of the Member States, which are typically embedded in constitutional provisions and safeguarded by national courts, ultimately by constitutional courts. Union law must therefore strike a delicate balance between the effectiveness of Union policies, the protection of Union values and principles, and respect for the constitutional traditions and national identities of the Member States. The manner in which the principles of mutual recognition and solidarity interact with fundamental rights, other values and principles, and the constitutional traditions of the Member States is examined in the sections that follow.

2. Mutual Recognition

The principle of mutual recognition has its roots in the internal market and the case law of the Court of Justice on free movement of goods. This principle requires national authorities in one Member State to recognise compliance with the rules applicable to a product in its country of origin, thereby easing the product's movement across the internal market. It is not an absolute mandate, but rather a general rule of recognition of other Member States' decisions, which can only be overridden where objectives of general interest and the principle of proportionality are successfully invoked (see chapter thirteen of this book). Mutual recognition has now been extended to the enforcement of judicial decisions, following the Tampere European Council in 1999, where it was endorsed and described as 'the cornerstone of judicial cooperation in both civil and criminal matters within the Union', applicable 'both to judgments and to other decisions of judicial authorities'.[164] The Union's legislative activity following the Tampere European Council reflected the importance of the principle of mutual recognition, as applied to civil and criminal judgments, through various instruments such as the Framework Decision 2002/584 on the European arrest warrant, Directive 2014/41 on the European Investigation Order in criminal matters, and other instruments on the recognition and enforcement of judgments in civil matters.

The principle of mutual recognition, as applied to civil and criminal judgments, is enshrined in primary law, in particular in Articles 81 and 82 TFEU, within the broader framework of the Area of Freedom, Security and Justice laid down in Article 67 TFEU. The Court of Justice has

[164] Presidency Conclusions of the European Council meeting in Tampere on 15 and 16 October 1999, para 33.

repeatedly stated that this principle finds its basis in the mutual trust between Member States. According to the Court of Justice:

> The principle of mutual trust requires, particularly as regards the area of freedom, security and justice, each of those States, save in exceptional circumstances, to consider all the other Member States to be complying with EU law and particularly with the fundamental rights recognised by EU law . . .
>
> Thus, when Member States implement EU law, they may, under EU law, be required to presume that fundamental rights have been observed by the other Member States, so that not only may they not demand a higher level of national protection of fundamental rights from another Member State than that provided by EU law, but also, save in exceptional cases, they may not check whether that other Member State has actually, in a specific case, observed the fundamental rights guaranteed by the European Union . . .[165]

The premise underpinning the principle of mutual recognition in the Area of Freedom, Security and Justice is based on the obligation of all Member States to accept the terms and conclusions reached by a national court when delivering a civil or criminal judgment, assuming that the court has correctly applied Union law and fundamental rights. This approach supports the effective and expedient recognition of judicial decisions across the Union, contributing to the development of a genuine and effective Area of Freedom, Security and Justice.

However, mutual trust is not synonymous with 'blind trust'. Over time, the case law of the Court of Justice has recognised several features that may justify deviating from the principle of mutual recognition. These situations remain exceptional and have so far been recognised most prominently in cases involving breaches of absolute fundamental rights and cases of systemic deficiencies affecting the rule of law in the issuing Member State.

In *Aranyosi and Căldăraru*,[166] the Court of Justice ruled on the powers of the judge of the executing Member State in cases where a real risk exists in the issuing Member State of a breach of the prohibition of torture and inhuman or degrading treatment or punishment provided for in Article 4 of the Charter. It should be noted that the European Court of Human Rights has characterised this fundamental right as 'absolute' and therefore it cannot be restricted by measures justified by objectives of general interest. As an absolute fundamental right, the Court of Justice emphasises, adopting the approach of its Strasbourg counterpart, that 'in any circumstances, including those of the fight against terrorism and organised crime, the [European Convention of Human Rights] prohibits in absolute terms torture and inhuman or degrading treatment or punishment, irrespective of the conduct of the person concerned'. The absolute nature of the fundamental right in question confirms the limited margin of appreciation available to Member States when confronted with potential violations of Article 4 of the Charter. On this basis, the judgment in *Aranyosi and Căldăraru* empowers the executing judicial authority to postpone the execution of a recognition of a European arrest warrant and, where the risk cannot be discounted within a reasonable time, to bring the surrender procedure to an end where there are sufficient elements to support the existence of a real risk of inhuman or degrading treatment in the Member State of issue.

This power of review, also known as the 'two-step test', involves a twofold analysis, the verification of which falls on the executing judicial authority. Firstly, if that authority in the executing Member State has evidence of a 'real risk' of violating Article 4 of the Charter, the judge must evaluate whether the assessment of that risk relies

[165] Case C-158/21 *Puig Gordi and Others* EU:C:2023:57, para 94; see also Joined Cases C-562/21 PPU and C-563/21 PPU *Openbaar Ministerie* EU:C:2022:100, para 41.

[166] Joined Cases C-404/15 and C-659/15 PPU *Aranyosi and Căldăraru* EU:C:2016:198.

> on information that is objective, reliable, specific, and properly updated on the detention conditions prevailing in the issuing Member State and that demonstrates that there are deficiencies, which may be systemic or generalised, or which may affect certain groups of people, or which may affect certain places of detention.[167]

Secondly, the authority must 'make a further assessment, specific and precise, of whether there are substantial grounds to believe that the individual concerned will be exposed to that risk because of the conditions for his detention envisaged in the issuing Member State'.[168] The mere existence of evidence of deficiencies – whether systemic or generalised, or affecting particular groups, or specific detention facilities – does not necessarily imply that, in a specific case, the person concerned will be subject to inhuman or degrading treatment if surrendered to the authorities of that Member State.[169]

The 'two-step test' is followed by a number of procedural safeguards to avoid an instrumentalisation of the case law that would compromise the effectiveness of cross-border judicial cooperation. First, the Court of Justice stresses the importance of the executing judicial authority, when carrying out the 'two-step test', requesting from the judicial authority of the issuing Member State to ensure as a matter of urgency the provision of all the necessary supplementary information on the conditions in which it is envisaged that the individual concerned will be detained in that Member State.[170] The executing judicial authority may fix a time limit for the receipt of the supplementary information requested from the issuing judicial authority.[171] Secondly, if the executing judicial authority concludes that there is a real risk that the person who is the subject of the warrant will be subject to a violation of Article 4 of the Charter, the execution of the warrant 'must be postponed but it cannot be abandoned'.[172] In that event, the executing judicial authority must inform Eurojust, giving the reasons for the delay. In addition, pursuant to that provision, a Member State which has experienced repeated delays on the part of another Member State in the execution of European arrest warrants for the reasons referred to in the preceding paragraph is to inform the Council with a view to an evaluation, at Member State level, of the implementation of the Framework Decision.[173] In any event, if at the end of the 'two-step test' the executing authority concludes that it is required to bring the requested person's detention to an end, it is then required, pursuant to Articles 12 and 17(5) of the Framework Decision, to attach to the provisional release of that person any measures it deems necessary to prevent them from absconding and to ensure that the material conditions necessary for their effective surrender remain fulfilled until a final decision on the execution of the European arrest warrant has been taken.[174]

The 'two-step test' has been expanded to cover other 'exceptional' situations where there is no breach of an absolute fundamental right, but a risk of breach of the essence of a fundamental right in the context of systemic or generalised deficiencies in the issuing State. In *LM*,[175] the Irish High Court expressed several concerns regarding the independence of Polish courts, especially after the enactment of various judicial reforms that cast doubt on judicial independence in Poland. These concerns materialised when Irish courts were required to recognise arrest warrants issued by Polish courts. The Court of Justice agreed to broaden the application of the

[167] ibid, para 89.
[168] ibid, para 92.
[169] ibid, para 93.
[170] ibid, para 95.
[171] ibid, para 97.
[172] ibid, para 98.
[173] ibid, para 99.
[174] ibid, para 102.
[175] Case C-216/18 PPU *LM v Minister for Justice and Equality* EU:C:2018:586.

'two-step test' to this context, recognising that judicial independence is crucial for the proper functioning of mutual recognition principles. The Court of Justice stated:

> The high level of trust between Member States on which the European arrest warrant mechanism is based is thus founded on the premiss that the criminal courts of the other Member States — which, following execution of a European arrest warrant, will have to conduct the criminal procedure for the purpose of prosecution, or of enforcement of a custodial sentence or detention order, and the substantive criminal proceedings — meet the requirements of effective judicial protection, which include, in particular, the independence and impartiality of those courts.[176]

Despite multiple attempts by national courts to ease the 'two-step test', the Court of Justice has consistently adhered to its doctrine and, to date, it remains essential that the executing judicial authority consistently fulfil the two criteria: assessing the real risk of a breach in a general and systemic manner, followed by an examination *in concreto* of the breach and its impact on the individual whose arrest is sought in the case of surrender to the issuing State.[177] While the initial assessment can be highly abstract, the second demands an individualised yet prospective analysis, as the evaluation by the executing authority is merely indicative and forward-looking, making the practical application of the test particularly challenging. Criticism has centred on the lack of practical value of this case law and its excessive caution, but the Court of Justice appears unwilling to reconsider the foundations of mutual recognition, as outlined in both the legislative instruments of judicial cooperation and the Treaty itself.

3. Solidarity

Solidarity is a principle of Union law as well as a value expressly reflected in Article 2 TEU as a defining characteristic of the society on which the Union is founded and which is common to the Member States.[178] The Treaties have given the principle of solidarity special significance in various Union policies, including immigration and asylum. Likewise, in the context of combating fraud against the Union's financial interests, the principle of solidarity has gained particular importance, as reflected in recent case law of the Court of Justice.

3.1. *Immigration and Asylum*

Article 67 TFEU states that the Union should ensure the absence of internal border controls for persons and develop a common policy on asylum, immigration, and external border control, 'based on solidarity between Member States, which is fair towards third-country nationals'. Likewise, Article 80 TFEU concludes the chapter on policies regarding border controls, asylum, and immigration by affirming the principle of solidarity in the following terms:

> The policies of the Union set out in this Chapter and their implementation shall be governed by the principle of solidarity and fair sharing of responsibility, including its financial implications, between the Member States. Whenever necessary, the Union acts adopted pursuant to this Chapter shall contain appropriate measures to give effect to this principle.

[176] ibid, para 58.

[177] See also Joined Cases C-354/20 PPU and C-412/20 PPU *Openbaar Ministerie* EU:C:2020:1033; Joined Cases C-562/21 PPU and C-563/21 PPU *X and Y* EU:C:2022:100; and Case C-158/21 *Puig Gordi and Others* EU:C:2023:57.

[178] Case C-156/21 *Hungary v Parliament and Council* EU:C:2022:97, para 129; Case C-157/21 *Poland v Parliament and Council* EU:C:2022:98, para 147.

The significance of the principle of solidarity is reflected in the emergency mechanisms outlined in the Treaties for addressing situations of a sudden inflow of third-country nationals. These mechanisms enable the Council, under Article 78(3) TFEU, to enact 'provisional measures for the benefit of the Member State(s) concerned'. This legal basis was put into practice in 2015 following an unprecedented influx of people displaced mainly by the instability and armed conflict in Syria arriving on the Mediterranean shores. In September 2015 the Council adopted two successive decisions: Decision (EU) 2015/1523 of 14 September 2015 (relocation of 40,000 applicants) and Decision (EU) 2015/1601 of 22 September 2015 (relocation of a further 120,000 applicants in clear need of international protection from Italy and Greece to other Member States over two years). Decision 2015/1601 was rejected outright by several Member States, chiefly Hungary and Slovakia, which brought actions to annul it, supported by Poland. Moreover, Hungary, Poland and the Czech Republic refused to accept the relocation of individuals under the mechanism established by those Decisions, prompting the Commission to bring infringement proceedings against the three states for failure to meet their obligations.

The Court of Justice dismissed the actions against Decision 2015/1601[179] and upheld the infringement procedures brought by the Commission against Hungary, Poland, and the Czech Republic,[180] using this opportunity to develop a case law emphasising the relevance of the principle of solidarity and Article 80 TFEU, as a principle that 'governs the Union's asylum policy'.[181] On the basis of this principle, the Court rejected Hungary and Poland's arguments regarding the practical effectiveness of the relocation decisions, as well as concerns about security and public order that might arise from their implementation. The principle of solidarity requires all Member States to make an effort and share the burdens, however challenging, in recognition of the unsustainable situation faced by the most exposed Member States due to migratory pressure. In the words of the Court of Justice:

> [T]he burdens entailed by the provisional measures provided for in Decisions 2015/1523 and 2015/1601, since they were adopted under Article 78(3) TFEU for the purpose of helping the Hellenic Republic and the Italian Republic to better cope with an emergency situation characterised by a sudden influx of third-country nationals on their territory, must, in principle, be divided between all the other Member States, in accordance with the principle of solidarity and fair sharing of responsibility between the Member States, which, in accordance with Article 80 TFEU, governs the Union's asylum policy.[182]

Furthermore, Member States' failure to fulfil their obligations under the Treaties takes on particular significance when the infringement also affects the principle of solidarity. When enforcing a judgment in a case of non-compliance, in its case law, the Court of Justice has shown that it pays special attention to whether the infringement involves a transfer of the fair distribution of responsibility for asylum decisions to other Member States, enabling it to conclude whether the conduct of the accused Member State is contrary to the principle of solidarity. This approach has serious implications for the defendant Member States, as the lump sum and periodic penalty payment imposed by the Court of Justice in the enforcement proceedings of Article 260 TFEU can be substantially increased.[183] When a Member State unilaterally breaches the balance between the benefits and obligations of Union membership, it undermines the principle of equality among Member States under Union law. According to the

[179] Joined Cases C-643/15 and C-647/15 *Slovak Republic and Hungary v Council* EU:C:2017:631.
[180] Joined Cases C-715/17, C-718/17 and C-719/17 *Commission v Poland, Hungary and Czech Republic* EU:C:2020:257.
[181] ibid, para 181.
[182] ibid.
[183] As confirmed by the Court of Justice in Case C-123/22 *Commission v Hungary* EU:C:2024:493.

Court of Justice, 'that failure in the duty of solidarity accepted by the Member States by the fact of their accession to the European Union strikes at the very root of the EU legal order'.[184]

It should be noted that the Union has recently moved from an ad hoc emergency approach to a permanent structural framework designed to address the inherent limitations of the previous Dublin system. Under the 2024 Asylum and Migration Management Regulation,[185] which entered into force on 11 June 2024 and is set for full operational application from 1 July 2026, a new 'mandatory but flexible' solidarity mechanism has been established. This mechanism ensures that all Member States contribute to supporting 'Member States under migratory pressure' or those facing significant migratory situations; in its first annual cycle based on the 2025 European Annual Asylum and Migration Report, the Commission identified Cyprus, Greece, Italy, and Spain as eligible for solidarity support once the Pact becomes applicable, thereby operationalising the principle of fair sharing of responsibility enshrined in Article 80 TFEU.

3.2. *Solidarity and Regulation 2020/2092 on Financial Conditionality*

The principle of solidarity also has a particular dimension in the area of budgetary cooperation, as a principle whose practical application relies on mutual trust between Member States. Mutual trust is particularly reflected in the proper use of the common financial resources allocated to the Union's budget. If Member States fail to meet their obligations and promote misuse of the Union's own resources, trust between the Member States is undermined and, consequently, the principle of solidarity is compromised. As the Court of Justice states,

> the Union budget is one of the principal instruments for giving practical effect, in the Union's policies and activities, to the principle of solidarity, mentioned in Article 2 TEU, which is itself one of the fundamental principles of EU law . . . , and, secondly, that the implementation of that principle, through the Union budget, is based on mutual trust between the Member States in the responsible use of the common resources included in that budget. That mutual trust is itself based . . . on the commitment of each Member State to comply with its obligations under EU law and to continue to comply, as is moreover stated in recital 5 of the contested regulation, with the values contained in Article 2 TEU, which include the value of the rule of law.[186]

The financial dimension of the principle of solidarity, particularly in the actions of Member States and the management of the Union's budget, has led to the development of mechanisms aimed at safeguarding the Union's financial interests, such as Regulation 2020/2092 on a general regime of conditionality for protecting the Union budget. The application of this Regulation against Hungary in 2022 and 2023 marked the first time the Union's budget was protected through a suspension of funding in response to systemic rule of law deficiencies.

Judicial and police cooperation in criminal matters is particularly important for the protection of the Union's financial resources, especially when budgetary management falls directly upon the Member States. To ensure financial solidarity among Member States, it is crucial that there be no doubt about the diligence and integrity with which the Member States implement the Union's budget. Accordingly, the tools adopted by the Union under Articles 82–86 TFEU are designed to combat conduct that harms the Union's financial interests, thereby preserving mutual trust between Member States and upholding financial solidarity within the Union.

[184] ibid, para 117.

[185] Regulation (EU) 2024/1351 of the European Parliament and of the Council of 14 May 2024 on asylum and migration management, amending Regulations (EU) 2021/1147 and (EU) 2021/1060 and repealing Regulation (EU) No 604/2013 [2024] OJ L1351.

[186] Case C-156/21 *Hungary v European Parliament and Council* EU:C:2022:97, para 129; and Case C-157/21 *Poland v European Parliament and Council* EU:C:2022:98, para 147.

GENERAL BIBLIOGRAPHY

Acosta, D and Murphy, C (eds), *EU Security and Justice Law* (Hart 2014).
Battjes, H, *European Asylum Law and International Law* (Martinus Nijhoff, 2006).
Colson, R and Field, S (eds), *EU Criminal Justice and the Challenges of Diversity: Legal Cultures in the Area of Freedom, Security and Justice* (Cambridge University Press, 2016).
De Coninck, J, 'Pens Poised. The New EU Pact on Migration and Asylum' (2024) 204 *EU Law Live Weekend Edition* 3.
Fletcher, M, Herlin-Karnell, E and Matera, C (eds), *The European Union as an Area of Freedom, Security and Justice* (Routledge, 2017).
Hailbronner, K and Thym, D (eds), *EU Immigration and Asylum Law: Commentary*, 2nd edn (Beck–Hart–Nomos, 2016).
Iglesias Sánchez, S and González Pascual, M (eds), *Fundamental Rights in the EU Area of Freedom, Security and Justice* (Cambridge University Press, 2021).
Mitsilegas, V, *EU Criminal Law*, 2nd edn (Hart 2022).
Peers, S, 'Mission Accomplished? EU Justice and Home Affairs Law after the Treaty of Lisbon' (2011) 48 *Common Market Law Review* 661.
— *EU Justice and Home Affairs Law*, 5th edn, 2 vols (Oxford University Press, 2023).
Pradel, J, Corstens, G and Vermeulen, G, *Droit pénal européen*, 3rd edn (Dalloz, 2009).

FURTHER READING

Immigration and Asylum

Coleman, N, *European Readmission Policy: Third Country Interests and Refugee Rights* (Martinus Nijhoff, 2009).
Majcher, I, *The European Union Returns Directive and Its Compatibility with International Human Rights Law* (Brill Nijhoff, 2019).
Mancano, L, *The Law of EU Border Controls: Constitutional Compliance and Conditions for an Area without Internal Frontiers* (Oxford University Press, 2025).
Montaldo, S, 'Not in my backyard! Outsourcing EU asylum procedures to third countries: A challenge for the Common European Asylum System' (2025) 62 *Common Market Law Review* 327.
Moreno-Lax, V, *Accessing Asylum in Europe. Extraterritorial Border Controls and Refugee Rights under EU Law* (Oxford University Press, 2017).
O'Keeffe, D, 'The Schengen Convention: A Suitable Model for European Integration?' (1991) 11 *Yearbook of European Law* 77.
Peers, S, 'The new EU asylum laws: taking rights half-seriously' (2023) 43 *Yearbook of European Law* 113.
Thym, D, *European Migration Law* (Oxford University Press, 2023).

Judicial Cooperation in Civil and Commercial Matters

Dickinson, A, *The Rome II Regulation. The Law Applicable to Non-Contractual Obligations* (Oxford University Press, 2008).
Dickinson, A and Lein, E (eds), *The Brussels I Regulation Recast* (Oxford University Press, 2015).
Hartley, TC, 'Recent Developments under the Brussels I Regulation' (2020) 69 *International and Comparative Law Quarterly* 979.
Guez, P and Lahlou, Y, 'The Brussels I bis Regulation: Has Shown Some Progress but Can Do Better' (2016) *International Business Law Journal* 195.
Lazić, V and Mankowski, P, *The Brussels I-bis Regulation: Interpretation and Implementation* (Edward Elgar, 2023).
Kramer, XE, 'Cross-Border Enforcement and the Brussels I-bis Regulation: Towards a New Balance Between Mutual Trust and National Control over Fundamental Rights' (2013) 60 *Netherlands International Law Review* 343.
Requejo Isidro, M (ed), *Brussels I bis: A Commentary on Regulation (EU) No 1215/2012* (Edward Elgar, 2022).
Rizcallah, C, 'Mutual Trust under the European Arrest Warrant and Ongoing Challenges for Fundamental Rights' (2024) 174 *EU Law Live Weekend Edition* 3.

Storskrubb, E, *Civil Procedure and EU Law. A Policy Area Uncovered* (Oxford University Press, 2008).
Wilderspin, M, 'Judicial Cooperation in Civil Matters' in Kellerbauer, M, Klamert, M, and Tomkin, J (eds), *The EU Treaties and the Charter of Fundamental Rights: A Commentary* (Oxford University Press, 2019).
— *European Private International Family Law. The Brussels IIb Regulation* (Oxford University Press, 2023).

Judicial Cooperation in Criminal Matters

Ambos, K, *European Criminal Law* (Cambridge University Press, 2018).
Groussot, X and Popov, Z, 'What's Wrong with OLAF? Accountability, Due Process and Criminal Justice in European Anti-Fraud Policy' (2010) 47 *Common Market Law Review* 605.
Herrnfeld, H-H, Brodowski, D and Burchard, C, (eds), *The European Public Prosecutor's Office: Article-by-Article Commentary* (Nomos, 2020).
Kostoris, R (ed), *Handbook of European Criminal Procedure* (Springer, 2018).
Mitsilegas, V, *EU Criminal Law after Lisbon: Rights, Trust and the Transformation of Criminal Justice in Europe* (Hart, 2016).
Peers, S, 'EU Justice and Home Affairs Law (Non-Civil)' in Craig, P and de Búrca, G (eds), *The Evolution of EU Law*, 2nd edn (Oxford University Press, 2011).
Spencer, JR, 'The European Arrest Warrant (2003–2004)' (2004) 6 *Cambridge Yearbook of European Legal Studies* 201.

Mutual Recognition and the Area of Freedom, Security and Justice

Anagnostaras, G, 'Mutual Confidence Is Not Blind Trust! Fundamental Rights Protection and the Execution of the European Arrest Warrant: Aranyosi and Căldăraru' (2016) 53 *Common Market Law Review* 1675.
Bonelli, M and Correia de Carvalho, M, 'No need to look, trust me! Mutual trust and distrust in the European arrest warrant system' (2024) 3 *European Law Open* 281.
Herlin-Karnell, E, 'From Mutual Trust to the Full Effectiveness of EU Law: 10 Years of the European Arrest Warrant' (2013) 38 *European Law Review* 79.
Janssens, C, *The Principle of Mutual Recognition in EU Law* (Oxford University Press, 2013).
Lenaerts, K, 'La Vie après L'Avis: Exploring the Principle of Mutual (Yet Not Blind) Trust' (2017) 54 *Common Market Law Review* 805.
Maiani, F and Migliorini, S, 'One Principle to Rule Them All? Anatomy of Mutual Trust in the Law of the Area of Freedom, Security and Justice' (2020) 57 *Common Market Law Review* 359.
Martufi, A, 'Effective judicial protection and the European arrest warrant: Navigating between procedural autonomy and mutual trust' (2022) 59 *Common Market Law Review* 1371.
Mitsilegas, V, 'The Constitutional Implications of Mutual Recognition in Criminal Matters in the European Union' (2006) 43 *Common Market Law Review* 1277.

Index